Everyday Theory

A Contemporary Reader

Everyday Theory

A Contemporary Reader

Becky McLaughlin
University of South Alabama

Bob Coleman
University of South Alabama

PEARSON

Longman

New York San Francisco Boston
London Toronto Sydney Tokyo Singapore Madrid
Mexico City Munich Paris Cape Town Hong Kong Montreal

Vice President and Editor-in-Chief: *Joseph Terry*
Managing Editor: *Erika Berg*
Executive Marketing Manager: *Ann Stypuloski*
Production Manager: *Douglas Bell*
Project Coordination, Text Design, and Electronic Page Makeup: *WestWords, Inc.*
Cover Design Manager/Cover Designer: *John Callahan*
Cover Illustration: Photothèque R. Magritte-ADAGP/Art Resource, NY.
   Magritte, Rene (1898–1967) Copyright © ARS, NY. Les Valeurs personnelles,
   1952. Oil on canvas. Private Collection.
Senior Manufacturing Buyer: *Alfred C. Dorsey*
Printer and Binder: *R. R. Donnelley and Sons Company, Crawfordsville*
Cover Printer: *Phoenix Color Corporation*

Library of Congress Cataloging-in-Publication Data

Everyday theory : a contemporary reader / Becky McLaughlin, Bob Coleman.
      p. cm.
   Includes bibliographical references and index.
   ISBN 0-321-19540-X (paper)
      1. Theory (Philosophy) I. McLaughlin, Becky Renee. II. Coleman, Bob

  B842.E94 2005
  142—dc22

                                                      2004044561

Please visit our website at http://www.ablongman.com

ISBN 0-321-19540-X

1 2 3 4 5 6 7 8 9 10—DOC—07 06 05 04

CONTENTS

PREFACE

Every semester, students use anthologies in critical-theory and literary-criticism courses. Teachers of these courses know that the texts they assign are typically hard for students to read, not just because of a seeming disconnect between what students are reading in theory courses and what they are doing in other literature and humanities courses, but also because of an apparent disconnect between the texts and the students' own lives. While this feeling of disconnection no doubt has many causes, we suspect that a key part of the problem results from the way anthologies typically organize and present the readings: either in chronological order—for example, from Plato to Homi Bhabha, or from T. S. Eliot to Judith Butler—or in groups of theoretical schools or methodologies—for example, feminist, formalist, poststructural, and postcolonial. Both of these organizational schemes reflect the increasingly unrealistic "coverage model."

As teachers of critical theory who have used unsatisfying coverage models, we recognize the need for an alternative pedagogy. Indeed, in our experience, students come into theory classes with little, if any, knowledge of theorists, schools of theory, or theoretical issues up for debate. Our alternative pedagogy, *Everyday Theory,* targets the students' sense of disconnect by asking them to approach theory through their life experiences. While students may not come and go talking of Jacques Lacan and Arthur Danto, they all possess significant practical wisdom, what the ancient Greeks called *phronesis,* which is not mutually exclusive to the abstract wisdom and preoccupations of theoretical probing. Some or all of their experience may be un- or undertheorized; that circumstance, however, is precisely the point of their taking theory classes. As they reflect on the intersecting trajectories of theory and their everyday concerns, one possible effect is the defamiliarization of some aspects of their lives. We think of such reflection as a key point of education.

With such goals in mind, we have abandoned the coverage models in favor of a thematic organization that greets students with topics that speak to their interests. Clearly, we believe that theory and the everyday are not incompatible, although we recognize that it is frequently tempting to think otherwise. Because reading theoretical texts can be daunting, students need to be encouraged to look at and reflect upon their daily experiences in order to see how theories already structure their lives and to realize how many types of theories they themselves have internalized and thus draw upon to solve problems, make decisions, do their jobs, and examine their own beliefs and the beliefs of others.

Organization

Our nine thematic sections underscore how students' daily lives are shaped by the issues that also are of profound concern to theorists: "Reading and Writing," "Education and Institutions," "Money and Power," "Culture and Ethnicity," "Politics and Rhetoric," "Art and Entertainment," "Desire and Sexuality," "Identity and Spirituality," and "Technology and Progress." These nine groupings meet students where they are when they first enter our theory classes rather than requiring them to catch up before leaving the starting gate. The thematic approach does not magically make theory transparent, but it does pitch theory to students through categories and issues that speak to them. We have selected these nine headings for precisely this reason. Reading and writing are integral activities of every student's experience of education and institutions. Likewise, the issues of desire and sexuality concern many students no less than the issues of money and power. Culture and ethnicity, like identity and spirituality, are paramount matters. Finally, politics and rhetoric, technology and progress, and art and entertainment also inspire and shape students' lives.

We have selected 45 readings of varying lengths—five readings per section heading—by theorists who are, by and large, representative of contemporary theory (from the 1960s to the present). Although we have eschewed the coverage model, we do not view theory as synchronic or ahistorical; we believe that contemporary theory framed through students' own experience can, and does, connect with them better than beginning at the "beginning" and moving forward to cover all of the bases. We offer the nine thematic sections in order to show both the dialogic and the dialectical aspects of theory: Michel Foucault and Paul Fussell rub shoulders in the "Money and Power" section; unanticipated delights like Jean-Pierre Vernant appear in the "Identity and Spirituality" section, along with Jacques Lacan, Monique Wittig, Caroline Walker Bynum, and Robert Bellah; and, hardly arbitrary, but certainly wonderfully unexpected, Kenneth Burke and Donna Haraway share the "Technology and Progress" section with Thomas Kuhn, Stephen Greenblatt, and relative newcomer Arlie Russell Hochschild. We believe that when students learn to recognize that their interests are not incompatible with the concerns of these theorists, they will begin to have a better sense of the contexts of their own critical orientation—its neighborliness to what probably previously seemed foreign, or at least ivory towerish.

Our approach offers students a pragmatic immediacy many times lacking or opaque in the chronological or methodological pedagogies. Indeed, our "Education and Institutions" section introduction orients what is probably for many students a first encounter with Clifford Geertz, Jacques Derrida, and Pierre Bourdieu. Students use their own experiences—what they already know about education and institutions—to grasp or get a handle on the texts. With this approach in mind, we have written the nine section introductions in accessible language, using examples from the students' everyday experience to help them make connections to examples and issues the theorists raise and examine in their texts. Our approach aids in student comprehension and engagement. Moreover, once engaged, students can use the theorists' ideas as frameworks for self-reflection, for examining other texts in the particular section or other sections in *Everyday Theory,* or for analyzing ideas both within and outside of their other classes.

Our nine thematic sections allow for reading and assignment sequences that highlight the dialogic interface between students and the intellectual activity of "doing theory." This organization also helps students to see that an argument like Geertz's—"Something is happening to the way we think about the way we think"—reflects back to them a semblance of their own situation. Indeed, "something is happening to the way *they* think about the way *they* think." We believe that the substance and vitality of *Everyday Theory* manifests Geertz's claim. *Everyday Theory* is just such a rethinking of what an introductory critical-theory textbook should look like and what it should enable students and teachers to do.

Framework and Pedagogy

To complement *Everyday Theory*'s novel thematic arrangement, we have written an overall introduction for students as well as nine accessible section introductions that introduce the general topics and specific readings included in each one of the thematic sections. Within these nine essays, we embed helpful questions: some ask students to use their own experience to make sense of key terms and ideas the theorists use; other questions ask students to think about and compare the trajectories of the theorists' arguments, looking particularly for points of intersection and divergence vis-à-vis the section themes. In addition to helping students converse with individual theorists, these questions also assist students in assembling larger conversations among the theorists within the section and between thematic sections. Likewise, a series of questions appears at the end of each thematic section. These questions are presented in order of increasing complexity: some target basic, "nuts and bolts" reading comprehension; some ask students to make connections between theorists' arguments; and the most abstract questions ask students to make metaobservations about the readings. All of our questions are clearly written to foster lively classroom discussions and promote fruitful paper topics.

We also provide biographical introductions for each of the 45 theorists. These introductions do more than simply explain where the theorist is from, what critical schools or methodologies he or she represents or is often associated with, and what other works he or she has written. Indeed, the biographical introductions reflect our *everyday* orientation. Neither "just the facts" nor an exhaustively detailed and potentially overwhelming account of the theorists, the bios aim to provide information that helps humanize the theorists rather than underscoring their identities as "author functions." We also provide a glossary in order to help further student learning. While not exhaustive, our glossary helpfully targets important critical terminology that students will frequently encounter in their theory reading.

While we are committed to our approach, we recognize that there is no one best way to teach theory. Indeed, one size does not fit all, so we include in Appendix A of *Everyday Theory* alternative tables of contents to suit different pedagogical approaches. People who prefer a chronological approach will find a table of contents organized by the theorists' biographical dates. Similarly, people who focus their courses on major twentieth-century methodologies such as poststructuralism, cultural studies, or feminist theory will find a table of contents to suit their needs. Likewise, professors who structure their courses around scholarly themes such as aesthetics, authorship, or the body will also find an alternative table of contents constructed with them in mind.

In constructing *Everyday Theory*, we have also kept in mind the importance of providing students with full texts wherever possible. Almost all of the 45 reading selections in the nine sections of *Everyday Theory* are unabridged. In addition, Appendix B provides excerpts from eight significant foundational texts: Book 10 of Plato's *Republic*, Wordsworth's preface to *Lyrical Ballads*, Nietzsche's "On Truth and Lies in a Nonmoral Sense," Freud's *Interpretation of Dreams*, de Saussure's *Course in General Linguistics*, Du Bois's "Criteria for Negro Art," Woolf's *A Room of One's Own*, and John Crowe Ransom's "Criticism, Inc." We chose these texts either because of their influence on theorists and issues in the nine sections or because of their capacity to supplement and thereby enrich the mosaic of theory our 45 readings offer.

Literature and Theory

The texts in *Everyday Theory* come from diverse disciplines—anthropology, psychology, history, sociology, linguistics, philosophy, and literature—and thus display differences in style and argument. Without a framework like the everyday in place to help make sense of the aims, purposes, and debates in contemporary critical theory, the theoretical texts students encounter can truly appear alienating. Although many selections in *Everyday Theory* were not written for the purpose of explaining or interpreting a literary text, this does not mean that those texts will prove unhelpful when students are thinking about literature—quite the contrary. If students read Geertz's "Blurred Genres," for example, they will quickly see how Geertz's anthropological theory reflects the influences of literature and literary theorists as well as the influence of philosophers, linguists, and sociologists. Similarly, James Clifford, another anthropologist whose writing appears in *Everyday Theory*, uses a poem by William Carlos Williams to introduce his ethnographic theories. In Williams's poetry, Clifford finds language, ideas, images, and contradictions that provide valuable ways of thinking about seemingly intuitive, commonsense, and objective notions about culture.

But while there is certainly an important link between literature and theory, much of what falls under the rubric of contemporary critical theory does not make literature its primary focus. Instead, critical theorists write not only about the arts and sciences, but also about politics and economics, local communities and world cultures, spiritual and secular concerns, technologies and jobs, immigrants and native peoples, dreams and desires, and health and happiness. The disparate terms in this list may not be ones we usually associate with English classes. Some may appear to relate more directly to work in other disciplines, while others will resonate with everyday experiences or interests outside the university. We believe, however, that if students are asked to think about how the terms in the list relate to their everyday lives—to decisions they make, to their work and paycheck, to their family, to their favorite movies and television shows, to the music they like and don't like, to their goals and daydreams, to their past and future, and to their education—they will find that the terms also ring true to their understanding of many of the ideas they encounter in *Everyday Theory*.

Approaching Theory

It has been our experience, and perhaps yours, that many students want us to hand them a key to unlock the metaphorical door that they believe stands between them and the meaning of the text. Well, as we already know, there is no key. Theories exist because the meaning of a theory, a text, or a word is frequently in question. Not everyone agrees about the purposes of theory, nor does everyone agree on what students should learn about theory. Indeed, the lack of consensus is well illustrated by the debates that occur not only among theorists themselves, but also among teachers of theory. While many of us may share certain educational goals, our means of achieving those goals are, at times, significantly different. In particular, our individual theoretical orientations are often quite opposed.

We think this book is strong in large part because its construction mirrors our (the authors') differences—indeed, at times it seems we are the dialectic—as much as it reflects our consensus. We had no debate about our book's title and about its rubric, the *everyday* experience of students, but we did debate section titles. Similarly, we argued about which reading selections to include and how to write this preface; we had more than a couple of mild disagreements about how to write the book's introduction and about how to write the nine section introductions. The process has underscored how very differently we understand some fundamental issues. One of us views theory very much like a religion and claims to inhabit theory. The other understands theory less reverently as ideas about ideas. One of us is at home in abstraction, idealism, and Lacanian psychoanalysis. The other is more at home in concrete textuality, rhetoric, and neopragmatism. Isaiah Berlin would identify one of us as an intellectual hedgehog and the other as an intellectual fox. Indeed, in *The Hedgehog and the Fox*, Berlin states, "There is a line among the fragments of the Greek poet Archilochus which says: 'The fox knows many things, but the hedgehog knows one big thing'" (3). What Berlin sees in this contrast is "one of the deepest differences which divide writers and thinkers, and, it may be, human beings in general" (3).

Theory helps us all look at and think about difference and consensus in the various spaces we find ourselves occupying daily. In the classroom, for example, it introduces us not only to academic and professional discourses that shape research and teaching in the arts and sciences, but also to attitudes toward innovation, social justice, and power that affect our civic lives. We can take theory out of the classroom as well, because it introduces us to paradigm shifts that are not simply of academic or elitist concern, but are important to anyone who thinks democratically and globally. Hence, theory shows us ways to consider the benefits and costs of forces that suffuse everyone's daily life. It can help us read and examine a host of texts: literary texts in and out of classes; visual texts in our increasingly visual culture; and social texts as wide ranging as clothing, public events, election campaigns, public spectacles, and geographic spaces. And theory can help us reflect on our place(s) in the world and how different forces can operate to situate us in and out of particular identities.

We hope that *Everyday Theory* excites and challenges both you and your students. We have designed the section groupings and selected the readings with the utmost respect for the artistic, intellectual, and social processes inherent in higher education and everyday life. We believe that *Everyday Theory* will offer your students wonderful opportunities to develop confidence in their own theoretical abilities, abilities that can help them achieve their goals, whatever those goals may be.

Acknowledgments

We are grateful to the following readers, whose comments have helped us in significant ways during the development of the manuscript for *Everyday Theory*: Paul Almonte, Salt Lake Community College; Megan Becker-Leckrone, University of Nevada, Las Vegas; Barbara Ching, University of Memphis; Ngwarsungu Chiwengo, Creighton University; Gregory Dobbins, California State University, Davis; Paul Doherty, Boston College; David Downing, Indiana University of Pennsylvania; Fidel Fajardo-Acosta, Creighton University; Laurie Finke, Kenyon College (Ohio); Ronald Fortune, Illinois State University; Marc Geisler, Western Washington University; Lori Howard, Georgia State University; Dan Lochman, Southwest Texas State University; Brian Locke, University of Utah; Renee Major, Louisiana State University; Christian Moraru, University of North Carolina, Greensboro; Sally Parry, Illinois State University; Deirdre Pettipiece, Arizona State University; Paulus Pimomo, Central Washington University; Matt Potolsky, University of Utah; Natashe Saje, Westminster College; Karen Schiff, Clemson University; Paul Schmidt, Georgia State University; and Christopher Shinn, Florida State University.

Becky and Bob would like to thank Erika Berg, Michele Cronin, Elissa Adams, Rebecca Gilpin, Michael Greer, Pat McCutcheon, Jenny Bevington, and

---

Note: Complete bibliographical information for all outside references mentioned in *Everyday Theory* can be found in the Works Cited section on pp. 809–810.

the staff at Longman for making this book possible. We owe a great debt of gratitude to our colleagues at the University of South Alabama for their enthusiastic support, particularly Sue Walker, Jean McIver, David Johnson, John Coker, Linda Payne, Ellen Harrington, Adam Cohen, Karen Burns, and Mavis Seal. Bob would like to thank Stephanie Girard at Spring Hill College, Ronald Christ, Michael McKeon, Claire Berardini, Joe Thomas, Scott Campbell, Dawn Skorczewski, Michael Gilmore, Derek Attridge, Kelly Brown, Andy Baker, Lauren Murphey, Bob Clark, and especially his fall 2003 students at the University of South Alabama who helped test *Everyday Theory:* Melinda Akridge, Vivian Battiste, Roger Blackwelder, Suzanne Bullock, Joseph Campbell, Dominique De Sanctis, Deidre Dowling, Marjorie Hall, Michael Herndon, Libby Jones, Anne Morris, Debra Morrow, Suraj Shankar, and Heather Stephenson. Becky would like to thank Emily Bingham, Paige Buffington, Mike Cartmell, Dan Collins, Michelle Comstock, Eric Daffron, Lynn Fisher, Suella Gerber, Jane Huber, Jazzbo, Susan Jordan, Dave McLaughlin, Joe McLaughlin, Marilyn McLaughlin, Moira Amado Miller, Jerry Phillips, Pilgrim, Carolina Randolph, Matthias Steup, Bonny Stitt, Ron Walker, and especially her fall 2002 students at the University of South Alabama who allowed her to experiment with *Everyday Theory* in its very early stages: Andy Baker, Bob Bartholomew, Lisa Bernard, Bill Jordan, Pete Lee, Maura McKenna, Chrissy Morrison, Amanda Odom, William Turnage, Stasia Weston, and Angie Yawn.

Becky McLaughlin
Bob Coleman

INTRODUCTION

Why *Everyday Theory?*

The title *Everyday Theory* may sound like a contradiction in terms, an oxymoron, or, at best, a conceit not unlike the one used by seventeenth-century poet John Donne in "The Flea," a poem in which a bloodsucking flea becomes a marriage bed or temple. If you've never read the poem, you might wonder how Donne can place something as ordinary and insignificant as a flea in a meaningful metaphorical relationship with something as sacred and profound as the marriage bed or temple. You might wonder the same thing of a book that couples the everyday, which is usually taken to mean the mundane, the obvious, or the taken for granted, with theory, which is often taken to be abstract, esoteric, or opaque. Perhaps you are already skeptical, saying to yourself, "The editors' notion of the everyday must be very different from mine if they're connecting it to something as disconnected from real life as theory." As the editors of *Everyday Theory*, we found something rather appealing in the title's oxymoronic quality. More importantly, we felt that the title launched us into a fruitful way of both selecting and presenting the material you will find in this anthology, for in settling upon *Everyday Theory* as our title, we took upon ourselves the task of showing theory's relevance, that is, the important role it can and does play in our everyday lives.

Although we believe that the concept of everyday theory is a sound one, that each of us brushes up against theoretical questions and issues every day, we also recognize that it may not be readily apparent to everyone just how this is the case. Therefore, we will begin with examples of the everyday, but before we do so, we would like to let you know what to expect as you read this introduction. You will find yourself occasionally bumping into the names of writers and texts that do not appear in this anthology. These outside references are not meant to frustrate or derail you. They are meant to supplement your understanding of

1

certain ideas and concepts that are under discussion. We hope the effect of these vectors pointing to textual materials that lie outside this anthology will be similar to the effect of a friend's recommendation that you see a movie you haven't yet seen or buy a CD containing the music of a recording artist you haven't yet heard.

What Is the Everyday?

What we are calling the everyday could be as ordinary an event as filling your car with gas when the needle sits on empty. It could be eating a supersized hamburger and french fries at a fast-food chain. It could be showering and dressing for work. Or it could be doing an assignment for class. On the other hand, the everyday need not be limited to the ordinary, banal, or mundane, for our everyday existence also includes profoundly powerful experiences of love, desire, ambition, illness, and alienation, to name only a few. "Okay," you say, "these examples of the everyday sound familiar enough. But what do they have to do with theory?"

To locate the intersection between the everyday and the theoretical, let's now attempt a definition of theory. In fact, it might be very fruitful, on your first day of theory class, to ask yourself, "What precisely is theory?" If, in answering this question, you were to do some brainstorming or survey your classmates and teachers, you might find yourself provided with a variety of answers, all of which would be instructive. Here, for example, is a possible list: Theory is (1) a lens; (2) an apparatus; (3) a practice; (4) a theorem; (5) a hypothesis; (6) a perspective; (7) a philosophy; (8) a formula; (9) a system; (10) a method; (11) a doctrine; (12) a dogma; (13) a discourse; (14) a leap or jump; (15) a concept; (16) a construct; (17) an explanation; (18) an interpretation; (19) textual analysis; (20) intellectual masturbation; (21) basic understanding or reasoning; (22) conclusions, suppositions, or propositions; (23) a position or stance.

What Is Theory?

One rather broad and simple way to think of theory is as a lens or camera angle. For example, we see filmmaker and film critic Laura Mulvey investigating through the lens of psychoanalysis the ways in which painter and sculptor Allen Jones has manipulated the female body to either fetishize or castrate it. In other words, she uses a lens to interrogate an artist's lens, the result of which is a feminist critique of the artist's work. Theory can also be an exploration and explanation of a particular phenomenon such as Georges Poulet's articulation of what happens when we read a book, an "explanation" sometimes referred to as phenomenology or reader response. Another way to think of theory is in terms of ideological or ethical concerns (e.g., political stances or positions), that is, notions about how we ought to exist in the world or how we ought to respond to the people, events, and institutions that make up the world around us. As an example, we have Frantz Fanon's arguments for how the native intellectual should respond to colonialism or its residual effects. Although we may think of theory as a discourse, we can also use it to examine, analyze, and critique a discourse such as that permeating the prison system, a task taken on by Michel Foucault in *Discipline and Punish,* a chapter of which appears in this anthology. We can even see theory as a leap or jump when it suddenly derails our usual way of thinking about something and sends us off in a completely new direction: Darwin's hypothesis concerning human evolution, Freud's theories about the polymorphous perversity of children, and Einstein's theory of relativity, for example.

Clearly, most of the definitions in the foregoing list suggest positive, creative uses of theory, while a couple suggest negative, limiting ones. For example, we would want to argue that although each definition may have some validity given a particular context, when theory becomes nothing more than intellectual masturbation, it loses its relevance for the community; when it becomes formulaic, doctrinal, or dogmatic, it ceases to be theory, for theory is precisely a restless questioning, a space in which unresolved issues can be identified and pursued. The term "theory" may suggest a type of specialized discourse or a collection of "-isms," but it is a diverse field that is not simple pluralism. As David Carroll argues in the introduction to *The States of 'Theory',* "even if it is a manifestation of a certain form of plurality or multiplicity, . . . it does not assume or defend the peaceful coexistence of positions that are supposedly noncontradictory, self-sufficient or autonomous, each unto itself" (7). In other words, theory is not a cafeteria where formalism and postcolonialism sit pleasantly and silently cheek by jowl like Jell-o and meatloaf, waiting to be selected by the critic hungry for this one day and that the next. It may more closely resemble a battlefield on which one theory attacks another, on which theory occasionally attacks itself like a dog nipping at its own tail, and on which theories join together to create hybrids or coalitions in order to strengthen their position vis-à-vis the perceived opposition.

A less violent and more fruitful analog, however, is provided by contemporary poet Gary Snyder, whose interest in Buddhism, Asian poetry, and the culture of the native Americans helped strengthen the beatific (as opposed to beaten-down) elements in the work of Jack Kerouac and Allen Ginsberg. Snyder says that poetry is "a tool, a net or trap to catch and present; a sharp edge; a medicine, or that little awl that unties knots" (quoted in Berry: 28). The same, we think, can be said of theory. It can be the sharp-edged focus we need when our vision has become blurred, our sensibility glib or complacent, or our intellect lazy and vain. In a book of essays called *Standing by Words,* Wendell Berry argues that "one of the great practical uses of literary disciplines, of course, is to resist glibness—to slow language down and make it thoughtful" (28). He is speaking specifically of poetry when he says that "verse checks the merely impulsive flow of speech, subjects it to another pulse, to measure, to extra-linguistic considerations; by inducing the hesitations of difficulty, it admits into language the influence of the Muse and of musing" (28), but he could just as well be speaking of theory, because theory, too, resists glibness, slows language down and makes it thoughtful, subjects it to another pulse, induces the hesitations of difficulty, and admits into language the influence of musing and the reciprocal need to muse.

How Do the Two Intersect?

In order to locate the intersection between theory and the everyday, perhaps it will help to think about something all of us do every day, something that we generally think of as a natural phenomenon: the act of looking. Let's say you and your class-mates are asked to view a still life made up of random objects such as a pair of mir-rored sunglasses, a postcard, a paper plate, a plastic bottle of mouthwash taken from a hotel toilette kit, a wool sweater, a Coke can, and a spool of thread. And let's say that you are each asked to occupy a particular spot in the classroom with respect to the still life. Obviously, you cannot all occupy the same spot, and thus some of you will be seated at close range and others at a distance. In addition, some of you may have your view slightly obscured by other students, while others may not. Out of necessity, then, you will each possess a spatial relation to the still life that is different from that of those seated around you. Next, let's say that you are asked to describe only what you see and not what you assume to be there. Nothing is said about the relative importance of each object, only that each object must be described in relation to the objects around it. Your assumption going in to the exer-cise might be that everyone will see pretty much the same thing. After all, everyone occupies the same general space, everyone has been given the same instructions, and everyone is equally familiar with the objects that make up the still life.

If, however, each of you were asked to read your description aloud, what do you suppose the result of this exercise would be? You would find each description slightly different from the one that preceded it. Some might see the mirrored sun-glasses as central, while others might describe in loving detail the picture on the front of the postcard. Some might give more attention to the large objects and less to the small, while others might attempt to be democratic in the amount of atten-tion they give to each object. Whatever the case, differences in what each of you sees would soon become apparent. It would also soon become apparent that describing only what you see and not what you assume or "know" to be there (the back of the Coke can, for example) would be a difficult task indeed. Try describing a wool sweater without talking about its neck, sleeves, or waist—none of which you might be able to see from where you sit—and look how far you get. No doubt, once these problems and differences of vision began emerging, caused in part by the inequities of vantage point, there would arise the need to justify what you see. And so a paradigm shift would occur, a movement from the assumption that everyone sees the same thing (the assumption of pure objectivity) to the equally faulty assumption that everyone has complete personal agency when seeing—"I'm entitled to my own opinion"—and that everyone's vision is absolutely indepen-dent of outside influences (the assumption of pure subjectivity).

Perhaps what you might question after this exercise is the notion that seeing is a natural phenomenon, one that we do not learn or need to learn, and that all you have to do is train your eyes on something and vision will automatically occur. Even though the eye is easily tricked, it continues to play a powerful role in Western culture as proof of veracity. "I saw it with my own eyes," we say, as if that statement alone is enough to signify truth. But as the still-life exercise sug-gests, an entire classroom of people can view the same material objects and yet speak of them quite differently. We may believe that we look with innocent eyes at the world around us—innocent not in a moral sense, but in the physical sense of optical organs objectively processing raw data—and yet when we enter a scene, we enter with eyes carrying cultural, psychological, and social baggage that never gets left behind. Because looking is a highly selective, highly mediated act, it is, in some sense, an act involving choice. In other words, we generally see what we believe to be there or what we want to see. Although we may like to believe that we see with clear eyes, we are not omniscient creatures able to remove ourselves from a particular time and place in history, and thus our view is always already necessarily partial, skewed, blinkered, myopic, or cockeyed. Understood in this way, the visual becomes a heavily politicized field ripe for critique (an important arm of theory), and because seeing has always been intimately connected to understanding (in fact, we use the phrase "I see" to mean "I understand"), it has been and continues to be an ongoing topic of discussion among theorists.

Illustrating the Intersection

On April 4, 1874, an article titled "Learning to See" appeared in the magazine *Every Saturday*. The article was first published anonymously, but it was written by Samuel Scudder, who was considered the most productive biologist of his time. In this brief essay, Scudder recounts his first meeting with the celebrated zoologist and geologist Louis Agassiz. Scudder had enrolled at Harvard as a student of natural history in the hope of devoting himself to the study of insects, but the first task Agassiz set before him was to look at a specimen of a fish and be prepared to say what he had seen. Within ten minutes of observing the specimen, Scudder was sure that he had seen all there was to see, but, unable to locate his professor, he returned "to a steadfast gaze at [his] mute companion" (662). After several hours, some of which were filled with despair at the absurdity of the task, he was finally given an opportunity to recite what he had discovered. Although Scudder's list of detailed observations was extensive, to his dismay Agassiz replied that he had not looked very carefully, for he had overlooked one of the fish's most conspicuous features. Scudder was then asked to continue looking at the fish.

In this second bout with the specimen, he discovered "one new thing after another" until he recognized "how just the Professor's criticism had been" (663). Unfortunately, when he was next examined by Agassiz, he was still unable to identify the feature overlooked in the first viewing. But he admitted that he now saw just how little he had seen before. "That is next best," said Agassiz, who sent him home to ponder what he had seen. After a restless night spent thinking about the fish, Scudder was finally able to produce the answer, but when he asked what he was to do next, Agassiz told him to continue looking at the fish. As Scudder points out, just when he thought he had exhausted all possibility of further discovery, new features emerged. This early lesson in the methods of observation was one of the most valuable of his education, for what Scudder seems to credit Agassiz with was teaching him the "trick" of real seeing, of pushing beyond the readily apparent.

If Scudder's essay suggests that one has only to look long enough and hard enough in order to see, Walker Percy's "The Loss of the Creature" argues otherwise. In this essay, Percy claims that all sight is mediated by the "symbolic complex" and that, because of this, a "true" encounter with an object (or the "creature," as Percy calls it) is almost an impossibility. In other words, to use an example drawn from the everyday existence of shopping malls, fast-food restaurants, billboards, and television, we cannot view a Coke, a Pepsi, or a Mountain Dew simply and plainly as a thing in itself because we have been too infected by the slogans of the soft-drink industry (always Coca-Cola; the Pepsi Generation; do the Dew). Only someone who has never heard of a soft drink, of industry, or of the soft-drink industry, that is, someone living completely divorced from the machinations of the symbolic complex—our sign system, our cultural matrix—could drink a Coke, for example, and taste its essential "Cokeness" rather than the packaging, profiteering, and propagandizing in which the Coke is embedded.

For Percy, then, the classroom is the last place where an encounter with the creature might take place, for he argues that the very way in which education is packaged operates "to remove the thing [in this case, one's education] from the sovereignty of the knower" (62). Needless to say, he is somewhat pessimistic about reclaiming the creature in the "preformed complex" of the traditional classroom, but he does make some suggestions as to how this task might be accomplished, one of which is to make strange the object of study. He suggests, for example, that the English teacher splay a dogfish out for her students and that the biology teacher place a Shakespearean sonnet on the dissecting boards of his pupils. What Percy seems to be talking about is the metaphoric principle, in which disparate experiences or objects are placed together to create new meaning, a principle that many poets have put to good use in their poetry. e.e. cummings readily comes to mind, for he strained the bounds of syntax, indulged in grammatical shifts and the splitting and interweaving of words, and developed the nonlogical structure of poems through fragmentation, juxtaposition, and montage, thereby creating such lines as "my father moved through dooms of love / through same of am through haves of give, / singing each morning out of each night / my father moved through depths of height" (2115).

We may not want to equate poetry with theory, but new innovations in poetry give rise to new ways of thinking about poetry and how it operates, a project undertaken by theorists as diverse as William Wordsworth, T.S. Eliot, Martin Heidegger, Hélène Cixous, and Lyn Hejinian. The poem, then, functions as a kind of uncanny object, at times appearing *unheimlich* (unhomey or unfamiliar) because of its elliptical, fragmented, and highly condensed language, and at other times appearing *heimlich* (homey or familiar) because of its connection to the rhythms of music, song, and dance—an uncanny object that straddles whatever gap exists between literature and theory, thus partaking of both. And it is around a poem that Stanley Fish builds his counterintuitive argument about the relationship between interpretation and sight or recognition. As Fish tells us in "How to Recognize a Poem When You See One," when students are told they are dealing with a poem, they immediately see whatever is placed before them with poem-seeing eyes, and thus "interpretation is not the art of construing [or decoding] but the art of constructing. Interpreters do not decode poems; they make them" (327). While Percy views the symbolic complex as an obstacle to sight, a theorist such as Fish views it as a necessity. According to Fish, without the symbolic complex, you would be unable to see anything at all. In other words, the fish Scudder was asked to look at by his professor could be seen only if Scudder already understood the concepts of "fish," "specimen," and "seeing" itself. Without these concepts or categories of understanding, which are provided by the symbolic complex, there would be no fish to examine.

How Do We Read Theory?

Theory is anti-fast. It takes time. Like anything of real and lasting value, theory is not something to be immediately consumed and digested. As a little aside that may be useful, we offer the following anecdote: One of our theory classes had been reading a string of difficult essays, and during a class meeting, a general cry of outrage erupted. This cry was aptly articulated by one very frustrated student who said, "Either I'm stupid and I need to get a lot smarter, or those theorists just don't know how to write. *Somebody's* to blame for the difficulties I'm having!" What we would like to offer as an answer to this cry of frustration is that nobody is to blame, or, perhaps more accurately, there is no real need to assign blame to either reader or writer. Yes, reading theory may tie you up in knots, but it is also, as Gary Snyder insists of poetry, that little awl which can be used for untying knots. Note the little awl with which psychoanalytic theorist Jacques Lacan comforted his audience after a particularly arduous seminar on Sophocles' *Antigone*:

> It may have seemed demanding to some of you. . . . I might almost say that on this occasion I have put you to the test of eating raw rabbits. You can relax now. Take a lesson from the boa constrictor. Have a little nap and the whole thing will pass through. You will even notice on waking that you have digested something after all. (284)

What was it that Lacan had demanded of his audience? What was it that he compared to the eating of raw rabbits? It was the same thing many of us ask of you: that we, teachers and students, accompany one another "in breaking the stones along the road of the text" (Lacan 284). Reading is not easy—it can be as hard as breaking stones with your head or bare hands—but you are always gaining more as you read than you are consciously aware of, for the work of reading continues even while you sleep, eat a hamburger and french fries, or shower and dress for work. Why not, then, take Lacan's suggestion to heart? As you read, think of yourself as a boa constrictor swallowing something three times the size of your head that may take days, weeks, or even months to digest.

It may also be helpful to recognize, as nineteenth-century theologian Friedrich Schleiermacher did, that the "normal" situation for a reader is rarely one of immediate and unimpeded understanding of a text's subject matter:

> The more lax practice of the art of understanding . . . proceeds on the assumption
> that understanding arises naturally. . . . The more rigorous practice proceeds on
> the assumption that misunderstanding arises naturally, and that understanding
> must be intended and sought at each point. (quoted in Gadamer: xiii)

Harold Bloom seems to echo Schleiermacher when he speaks of reading as an agon, a struggle or fight. For Bloom, a good poem (like good theory) is combative, and thus meaning is taken only by combat, which "consists in *a reading encounter,* and in an interpretive moment within that encounter. Poetic warfare is conducted by a kind of strong reading. . . . There is relaxed reading and alert reading, and the latter, I will suggest, is always an agon" (5–6). Part of the fight, then, involves not only alert reading but also alert rereading.

In explicating remarks made by Roland Barthes about rereading, Barbara Johnson argues that what Barthes implies is that "a single reading is composed of the already-read" and "that what we can see in a text the first time is already in us, not in it." In other words, she continues, "when we read a text once . . . , we can see in it only what we have already learned to see before." Perhaps this explains why certain texts seem utterly opaque on a first reading but begin to open up after successive readings. Take phenomenologist Martin Heidegger, for instance, who makes statements such as "Thinging, things are things" (200) or "The calling, gathered together with itself, which gathers to itself in the calling, is the pealing as the peal" (207). These statements represent moments when his essay "Language" seems more akin to poetry than theory, and, in fact, Heidegger's later work shows a shift from analytical discourse to a poetic prose style that attempts to break down the traditional boundaries between poetry and philosophy. Poetry and philosophy may have been at odds since the days of Plato, but in Heidegger's works and in the works of many other theorists, the two finally meet and merge in the most profound of marriages. Following in the footsteps of Heidegger is postmodern writer Edmond Jabès, who writes the following lines in an essay called "The Book":

> Without body we would be a breath in the wind, silence within silence. Without
> body there would be no book. As if the absence of books were a suppression of
> the body. But could we, without body even distinguish presence from absence,
> waking from sleep, dawn from dusk? And what is a breath for the wind, a
> silence for silence when it is the body which speaks or is quiet, breathes or
> expires? When it is the body which names and comes to terms with names? And
> what is the book except the body's long preparation for the hidden words of its
> absence? (135)

If this snippet from Jabès's essay were to appear as lines of verse in a book of poetry, the task of understanding it would, no doubt, immediately become less daunting, since most of you have already learned strategies for navigating your way through a poem. In fact, conceptualizing theory as poetry, and actually rearranging the lines of prose into lines of verse, might not be a bad way to begin grappling with a theoretical text. After all, there are no rules for creative reading, except, perhaps, that you allow yourself to be innovative and patient with both yourself and the text at hand.

How Do We Understand Theory's Purpose?

Let us return to the ordinary event of filling your car with gas, for now that we have clarified the terms, perhaps the connection between theory and the everyday will come into view. As you pump gas into your car, you may believe that you are doing the most natural thing in the world, nothing worth really noticing or examining (except, perhaps, with respect to fluctuating fuel prices), but the car is not a natural object any more than is something as unnatural and obviously artificial as a fashion accoutrement like the bustle or the whalebone corset. And it is theory that allows us to suspend our naturalizing impulses with respect to the car, to obtain critical distance from it so that we can interrogate its effects, and to make strange the object of study (in this case, the car) in order to avoid the hasty conclusions and easy assumptions that attend the familiar.

One of the reasons that theory can sometimes seem impenetrable, then, is that language itself has been or is being intentionally denaturalized to assist in the denaturalizing of whatever is under investigation. As Bruce Fink says of Lacan, for example, he is "adamant about refusing to understand, about striving to defer understanding, because in the process of understanding, everything is brought back to the level of the status quo, to the level of what is already known," and thus, says Fink, Lacan practices a kind of writing that "overflows with extravagant, preposterous, and mixed metaphors, precisely to jolt one out of the easy reductionism inherent in the very process of understanding" (71). Hence we have, in the space of two brief paragraphs, mention made of eating raw rabbits, learning lessons from the boa constrictor, breaking stones, and traveling the road of a text.

Because theory slows us down and makes us thoughtful, it allows us to view the car as a piece of technology, created by human ingenuity, which has had a profound impact on how we understand and utilize space and time. "It is the speed of our auto and our airplane which organizes the great masses of the earth," says Jean-Paul Sartre. What he means by this is that before the car existed, certain connections could not be made because the distance between connectives was so great as to be inconceivable. Because of its speedy transportation capabilities, the car has enabled us to create object relations or connections where none existed before. For example, we might describe the distance from one place to another by saying, "It's 60 miles." But we might just as intelligibly say, "It's an hour from here to there." What does it mean to use time to measure space? It means that the car has now become a measuring rod. A car can travel 60 miles in approximately one hour's time; thus, the distance between two places can be measured temporally as well as spatially.

But what if we were walking or riding a horse or a bike? In these instances, the car would cease to be an appropriate measuring rod to determine distance. For many of us in wealthy western countries, however, our feet, a horse, or a bike is used only for recreational purposes. It is hard to imagine actually having to get around without a car. In fact, many cities and towns are constructed in such a way as to make any transportation that is not motorized nearly impossible. Here, technology has imposed forced choices, a point C.S. Lewis makes in *The Aboli-tion of Man* and that Wendell Barry nicely summarizes:

> . . . the person who makes a technological choice does not choose for himself alone, but for others; past a certain scale, he chooses for *all* others. Past a certain scale, if the break with the past is great enough, he chooses for the past, and if the effects are lasting enough he chooses for the future. He makes, then, a choice that can neither be chosen against nor unchosen. Past a certain scale, there is no dissent from technological choice. (60)

For Lewis, making a technological choice may be an everyday event, but it is also one that entails a weighty responsibility indeed, a responsibility that requires the checking of impulse, a resistance to glibness, the influence of musing, and the intro-duction of thoughtful hesitation. In Lewis's view, the slogan "Quality Without Question," which appears in bold, red letters on the side of a popular freight line, would be the worst sort of contradiction in terms, a clever but glib use of allitera-tion that glosses over the impossible desire to have one's cake and eat it, too.

Watching a Theorist at Work

We may think that driving cars and eating hamburgers have done nothing except enhance our lives (we can now move and eat with speed and efficiency), but, as political historian Clive Ponting theorizes, along with the notion of progress comes the notion of barbarism, for the twentieth century's massive achievements in agricultural and industrial output have been catastrophic for the world's envi-ronment. What we like to call progress has as its dark underbelly a barbarism involving the destruction of animals and natural habitats and a concomitant increase in pollution: "Although there were some localized environmental improvements, by the 1990s pollution had become a major global problem. The output of carbon dioxide from the burning of fossil fuels, in particular from vehi-cles, threatened irreversible damage to the world's climatic systems" (534). For Ponting, the car is hardly an innocent bystander in this world drama. It is neither silent nor neutral. The car speaks volumes about who we are and what we value. Advertisers know this—they know that we think of the car as an extension of our identity—and they capitalize (quite literally) on this knowledge every day in magazine ads and television commercials touting the benefits of owning the latest metal merchandise. As for the french fry, while this introduction was being writ-ten, the United States was at war with Iraq, a war during which the famous side-kick to the hamburger was suddenly being called the "freedom fry" in an attempt to censure our recalcitrant French allies, and thus we see how something as ordi-nary as a sliver of fried potato can become an instrument of war propaganda. It is either very funny or very frightening that an everyday french fry can suggest the power of language, the potential for its rhetorical manipulation, and the need always to be aware of who is saying what, and how and when it is being said.

Ponting is a Senior Lecturer in politics at the University of Wales, and he writes history books, but he is also a theorist. In 1999, for instance, he published what some postmodernist writers might call a "grand narrative," with all the problems of subjectivity, bias, and artificiality that narrative entails, but Ponting's *The 20th Century: A World History* is instructive in its self-reflexive approach. The *Irish Times* claims on the back cover of the book that the book is "a judicious mixture of narrative and analysis, where theory and actuality are in correct balance." And in Ponting's introduction, we see this judicious mixture at work, for he begins by discussing the questions raised when one attempts to write a historical narrative of the twentieth century: (1) "How should it be structured?" and (2) "Is a century a coherent period to study?" Before blithely setting out to write his narrative, he interrogates himself as to how to proceed (and shares this interrogation with his reading audience), finally stating that his aim "has been to try and develop a different angle of vision through a comparative approach" (11) and that "the same material in the hands of a different historian would produce different conclusions" (12). No doubt, the latter observation is why he humbly chose to subtitle his book *A World History* rather than *The World History*.

For Ponting, "the book's major theme is the struggle between progress and barbarism" (8), and in the last chapter, he makes use of an unfinished Gustav Flaubert work to articulate this theme. As Ponting tells us, when Flaubert died in 1880, he left behind part of a novel, *Bouvard et Pecuchet*, in which two Parisian clerks make predictions about the future of humanity. According to Flaubert's rough sketch, "Bouvard takes a rosy view of future of mankind. Modern man is progressing. . . . Future inventions; means of travel. . . . Evil will disappear as want disappears. . . . Communion of all peoples." Pecuchet, however, "takes a gloomy view of the future of mankind. Modern man has been diminished and become a machine. . . . Impossibility of peace. Barbarity caused by excessive individualism and ravings of science. . . . America will have conquered the world" (quoted in Ponting: 531–532). As it turns out, both men are right. Progress and barbarism are not mutually exclusive. But does this recognition leave Ponting unable to draw conclusions? No, in his final paragraph, he argues thus:

> Given the way the world evolved in the twentieth century and the distribution
> of economic and political power at the end of the century, it seems likely that,
> as in the past, the world will, over the next few decades, continue to be charac-
> terized by progress for a minority and barbarism for the overwhelming major-
> ity. (546)

Theory allows one to see the possibility of alternative conclusions, but it also allows one to choose and argue for a particular conclusion. We would argue that in our everyday lives, we are continually forced to make choices, some seemingly easy and others incredibly difficult. If nothing else, theory offers the possibility of making informed choices rather than impulsive ones; it offers the possibility of acting ethically rather than arbitrarily.

Like Bouvard and Pecuchet, we co-editors are very good friends and committed colleagues, and yet we disagree—not on what the future holds for humankind, necessarily, but on what constitutes the everyday, what theory is, and how to articulate the link between the two. If we were to be egregiously simplistic and provocative to boot, we might say that one of us prefers American theorists and the other, French theorists. Or we might say that one of us prefers language articulated in "plain style," while the other prefers "écriture féminine." If we were to be more accurate about our differences, however, we might simply say that one of us prefers the application of theory, while the other prefers the inhabitation of it, that is, living in and through a theoretical perspective. In putting this book together, then, we have had numerous discussions that sometimes escalated into heated argument, but we continue to believe that this kind of earnest engagement and collaboration is what allows us to learn and to grow into more thoughtful people. As a result of these discussions (many of them pleasurable, a few distressing, but all fruitful), we have identified many of our differences, but we have also discovered a great deal of common ground. We see this dialogic model as analogous to the field of theory, and we hope that it will prove useful as you read the texts in this anthology, discuss them with your classmates, and "do" the work of theory.

I

READING AND WRITING

Two of the most everyday activities you engage in as a student are reading and writing. In just about any class you take, especially in the humanities, you will find a schedule of required reading, paper assignments, and essay tests on the syllabus. For most of you, then, the relationship between reading and writing is fairly obvious: you read, and then you are called upon to produce in writing some indication that you've grasped what you've read. Given the way classrooms and teachers presently operate, there is very little chance of making your way through college without having to read and write. No doubt, this inevitability gives rise to certain feelings such as excitement, anxiety, dread, frustration, or some combination thereof. In other words, when asked to read or write, you will have what some theorists refer to as an affective response.

For some of you, the acts of reading and writing are pleasurable, but for others of you, they are not. Or perhaps for some of you, reading is pleasurable, but writing is a pain in the neck, or vice versa. Why is this the case? What happens to us when we read? What happens to us when we write? Is the act of reading a radically different process from the act of writing? If so, why are the two acts so frequently coupled? These are some of the questions that the theorists in this section attempt to answer as they discuss aspects of reading and writing.

The first class in which you were asked to focus on the relationship between reading and writing in a very explicit way was probably a composition class. As we introduce the theorists in this section, let's take that early classroom experience as a starting point. What if you were asked to write, as your first assignment, a paper on the writing process? Would you be puzzled? Would you say to yourself that you have no writing process and therefore nothing to write about? Perhaps. But if you were given Roland Barthes's "An Almost Obsessive Relation to Writing Instruments," you would suddenly find that you do indeed bring some method to the madness of writing, for what Barthes is talking about in this brief interview is precisely the ordinariness, the everyday of his writing process or work habits. In fact, in his response to the initial question asked by the interviewer, "Do you have a method of working?" Barthes is careful to make a distinction between the words "method" and "methodology." As he makes clear, he wishes to talk about his work habits in concrete, material terms rather than in an abstract, disembodied way. Ironically, he does not wish to theorize, and so he tells us of his contempt for Bic pens; his love of fine fountain pens; the arrangement of objects such as typewriter and note cards in his work space; his need for a table made of wood ("I might say that I'm on good terms with wood," he states parenthetically); his placement of "pleasure" books by the bed, or what he calls "the locus of irresponsibility"; and his "work" books at his desk, or what he calls "the locus of responsibility." "It's not for nothing that I'm called a structuralist!" he quips, suggesting a rather humorous, but nevertheless useful, way of conceptualizing in everyday terms something as complicated as structuralism. He even tells us of his struggle to learn to type once he had made the recognition that to ask someone else to type his manuscripts for him was akin to a form of enslavement.

It is clear that the everyday of ink, tables, and typists takes center stage for Barthes just as it might for you if you began to think about what conditions help you write and what conditions do not. Something as apparently insignificant as the color of ink on the page, the chair you sit on, or the type of music you listen to while writing might suddenly take on new significance. "Insignificance is the true locus of significance," says Barthes, a statement that might initially strike you as counterintuitive but one that gives our everyday experience its due. By the time you have finished reading Barthes's interview, perhaps applauding him for demystifying writing but taking him to task for his snobbery toward Bic pens, a pen everyone can afford, unlike the expensive fountain pen, you may already have become conscious of the fact that you, too, have work habits and that you, too, have preferences regarding writing instruments and organization of work space but that your work habits and preferences have simply remained unnoticed or unremarked upon until now. In practical terms, what Barthes can offer you is the opportunity to think about the act of writing so that you can locate moments of pleasure or pain connected to it and notice practices that either aid or hinder your writing process. And once you begin to take yourself seriously as a writer, you will begin to take your readers seriously, too. Suddenly, it becomes impossible to think about writing without thinking about its correlative, reading, or vice versa.

As the theorists in this section suggest, writing does not occur in a vacuum. It is neither an empty nor a solitary act. One must have something to write about, and one must have readers. This, then, is where Jean-Paul Sartre enters the scene. Whereas Barthes speaks of his relation to writing instruments, Sartre speaks of the writer's relation to his or her creation, taking as his project the attempt to answer a question that always hovers over the classroom in loud silence: "Why write?" After reading Sartre's essay, we may not have learned whether Sartre shares Barthes's contempt for Bic pens, but we will have gotten an earnest and provocative answer to a very relevant question. In moving from Barthes to Sartre, then, we shift from a concern with one sort of relationship—that between a writer and his or her tools (and although Barthes can be said to use a writing instrument such as a fountain pen, he cannot be said to view writing as an instrumental process or as a mere translation of thought into language)—to a concern with another sort of relationship—that between a writer and reader. As it turns out, however, this apparently dual relationship is really triangular; in other words, Sartre begins his discussion by articulating the connection between a writer and his or her world, a connection that leads to the forging of an intimate link between writer and reader, and ends his discussion by articulating the connection between a reader and his or her world.

In answer to the question posed in his title, Sartre asserts that everyone has his or her own reasons for writing. For some, writing is seen as a form of escape, while for others it is seen as a means of conquering. But, as Sartre argues, there are other avenues by which one can escape or conquer. Why does it have to be writing? In asking this, he calls into question the validity of these reasons and proposes a more fundamental reason that one is compelled to write: one writes in order to make oneself feel essential in relation to the world. Although Sartre does not go as far as to say that we construct the world, he does argue that through our perceptions, the world is manifested or revealed. We may not be the world's producers, but we are its directors, for it is we who set up relationships between one thing and another.

For example, a shiny, red apple huddled beside a pockmarked orange can make us more aware of the apple's smoothness and the orange's roughness than if each remains in isolation. In addition, the choice of the word "huddled" rather than "nestled" can suggest a particular type of contact between apple and orange. In other words, we create meaningful connections among the objects that exist in the world "by introducing order where there was none, by imposing the unity of mind on the diversity of things." And this imposition is, as Sartre points out, no small responsibility, for if we create in our art what might be called bad object relations, that is, relations showing one person or group oppressing another, we must do so only for the purpose of relieving the oppression. What he is suggesting here is the dialectical or reciprocal relationship between literature and life. In the simpler, but no less profound, terms of Nigerian writer Chinua Achebe, "*People create stories create people; or rather, stories create people create stories.*" Not only do people shape stories, but stories shape people. This is why Sartre is led to argue that if as a reader I am given a picture of a world full of injustices, "it is not so that I may contemplate them coldly, but that I may animate them with my indignation, that I may disclose them and create them with their nature as injustices, that is, as abuses to be suppressed."

The problem for the artist, however, is that if one paints or writes about the apple and orange, one loses sight of them as objects, or so Sartre argues. What he means is that in representing something on a canvas or on paper, we become so closely identified with our representation that any possibility of objectivity is lost. Because we are too close to our creation, we cannot view it as someone who has more distance could. No doubt, we have all had the experience of myopia, of having something shoved so close to our faces that it is impossible to see it without distortion occurring. The point Sartre is driving at is this: writers cannot exist for themselves alone. In order for their creations to be seen, they need readers. One does not write for oneself, says Sartre. "That would be the worst blow." He goes even further, in fact, arguing that one *cannot* write for oneself because when one reads one's own work, all one finds there is oneself. The reader, then, is an integral part of the creative process. When a person reads, he or she is engaging in what Sartre calls "directed creation." Comparing the literary object to a "peculiar top which exists only in movement," Sartre argues that the literary object exists only as long as the act of reading is taking place. Once the reader ceases to read, the words on the page become nothing more than meaningless black marks; the peculiar top stops spinning. It takes a reader to complete the creative act of writing. But because writer and reader are equally important agents in the creative act, each must behave with generosity toward the other. What is always at stake for Sartre is the freedom of writer and reader to enter a relationship of shared responsibility. One does not write for slaves.

Although Sartre and Georges Poulet are often lumped together under the same category of phenomenology, they articulate the relationship between writer and reader in radically different ways. In fact, for Poulet, the crucial relationship is that of the reader to a book. Unlike Barthes's reference to an ordinary writing instrument in his title or Sartre's simple question, Poulet's title "Phenomenology of Reading" may be a bit off-putting until you understand what is meant by phenomenology. In very simple terms, phenomenology is a branch of philosophy that focuses on human consciousness and perception, and it takes as its aim an exploration and articulation of the relationship between perceiving subject (the reader) and perceived object (the book). If we were to rewrite Poulet's title along Barthesian lines, it might read, "A Highly Pleasurable, but Almost Paranoid, Relation to Reading Books." A rewrite along Sartrean lines, on the other hand, might produce the following questions as appropriate titles: "What Happens When We Read?" "Where Does the Book Go?" "Who Am I When I Read: You or Me?"

The odd thing about reading Poulet, the odd thing about the *phenomenon* of reading Poulet, is that despite his rather dry title, his introductory paragraph is anything but dry. For just as he is seduced by books, we are seduced by the charm of his opening paragraph, a paragraph in which he compares books on display to animals in a pet store. Like a cute puppy wagging its tail and looking at a potential buyer with sad, brown eyes, a book waits for a reader to come along and release it from its status as material object. The book waits, and hopes, for the transformation that will occur once a reader has opened the book and begun to read the lines on the page. For Poulet, the book is an object, but it is a special kind of object, unlike a vase, a statue, a sewing machine, or a plate, for example. What makes the book different from other objects is its openness. The book allows a reader to get inside it, but the book also gets inside the reader. According to Poulet, all notions of "outside" and "inside" collapse when you read a book. And while a vase may suggest the possibility of interiority (you could, if you found a vase large enough, climb inside), the relationship between perceiving subject and perceived object is not reciprocal (you cannot get the vase inside yourself). While Sartre continually refers to the freedom of the reader, Poulet refers instead to the reader's willing enslavement. Once you have suc- cumbed to the siren call of the book, there is no turning back, no escaping what Poulet refers to as a "take-over" or a usurpation. As a reader, you become the "prey of language"; you are "bound hand and foot to the omnipotence of fiction."

You may not be accustomed to thinking of yourself as the "prey of lan- guage," a prisoner to "the omnipotence of fiction," but if you think carefully about your own reading experiences, it may be easier to see where Poulet is com- ing from. Even if movies and television have replaced books as a form of enter- tainment or escape, all of us have probably had at least one really engrossing encounter with a book (the kind you cannot put down; the kind that makes you want to ignore your "outside" responsibilities; the kind that allows you to forget where you are and what time it is), and that is precisely the kind of reading expe- rience Poulet is talking about. In fact, he uses as a prime example the reading of a cheap thriller, saying, "It gripped me." How is it possible that something so flimsy, something made of everyday materials such as cardboard, paper, and glue—something so easily destroyed by water damage or fire—can grip us? Why is it that some books are able to make us laugh so hard that our first impulse is to find someone with whom to share the funny passage? Why is it that some books make us care so deeply about the characters that if one dies, we feel the same grief that we would feel if we had lost a loved one? Why is it that when we finish reading a really good book, we find ourselves at a loss, sad, missing the charac- ters who had temporarily become a part of our landscape? These may not be pre- cisely the questions Poulet asks, but his essay certainly gives rise to them. The central question for Poulet, and for us, is this: What happens when we read?

How Poulet responds to this central question differs dramatically from how Jonathan Culler responds to the question in his essay "Literary Competence." Whereas Poulet subjectively describes reading as a welcome transformation, that is, his consciousness becomes host for the consciousness of the author, Culler seeks to describe objective aspects of an ideal reader's reading process. Mirroring in some key ways a scientific approach, Culler's method of structural poetics seeks to account for the knowledge readers need to make sense of literary texts. According to Culler, readers who demonstrate literary competence understand expectations of genre as well as rhetorical nuances. In contrast, someone with lit- tle familiarity with reading poetry, for example, will have trouble reading texts by John Milton, Robert Browning, Emily Dickinson, and Wallace Stevens. While the novice reader of poetry can comprehend literally the words of Milton's *Paradise Lost,* simply understanding the words does not mean understanding lit- erary aspects of the poem per se. As Culler notes, "understanding depends on mastery of a system," and ideal readers of literature have mastered the system of grammatical rules, rhetorical gestures, and inflections, and, similarly, they well understand generic conventions and literary history. Is such mastery necessary in order to be swept away in the manner Poulet describes? In other words, if one is not a practiced, competent reader, will one eagerly choose, as Poulet does, to crack open a novel, a play, or a book of poems rather than to turn on one's television, computer, or radio?

As we have already noted, you often write in college to demonstrate that you have grasped what you have read. In effect, you are demonstrating your competence, your skill as a reader, thinker, and writer. To better account for competence, Culler looks to structuralist poetics in order to develop a theory about how an ideal reader would account for the effects that literary texts produce. His approach is not hermeneutical, that is, he is not proposing a theory of interpretation; the aim of poetics is not to help one decide what a particular text means. Instead, poetics involves the reader's careful attention to "the underlying system which makes literary effects possible." The focus on the "underlying system," what Culler also calls a competent reader's "internalized grammar," helps one to "construct a theory of literary discourse, which would account for the possibilities of interpretation."

Culler's structuralist poetics may strike you as counterintuitive. After all, the everyday practices in many literature classes seem to involve the development of one's own interpretation of the texts one reads. And yet, in standing on its head such a seemingly appropriate goal, Culler offers you a way to think systematically not only about writing and reading but also about yourself. Barthes's discussion of ink, tables, and typists gets you to think about the conditions that enable you to write; similarly, Culler asks you to reflect on your assumptions and methods of making sense of what you read. Culler focuses neither on Sartre's freedom of the reader nor on Poulet's pleasurable surrender to a book; rather, Culler wants you to distinguish facts about reading processes and to theorize "a model to account for them." Some readers, no doubt, will find Culler's systematic approach bloodless, but other readers will find intellectual stimulation in the reflective process of developing theories to account not only for how we make sense of texts but also for deepening self-awareness. Indeed, as Culler asks, "How better to facilitate a reading of oneself than by trying to make explicit one's sense of the comprehensible and the incomprehensible, the significant and the insignificant, the ordered and the inchoate?" By deepening our understanding of how language in literary texts invites and frustrates our attempts at arriving at intelligibility, Culler believes we also are better prepared to account for ourselves.

The sciencelike aspects of Culler's structuralist theory may appear more reliable than Poulet's phenomenological approach, but both Poulet's and Culler's emphases on literature may seem anachronistic given our high-tech environments. In "The Condition of Virtuality," N. Katherine Hayles assesses how contemporary theories of, and advances in, information technologies are reshaping not only our awareness of our bodies and environments but also, in the process, our relationship to reading and writing. The condition of "virtuality" that Hayles examines results from our daily interaction with a host of information technologies: computers, e-mail, digital imaging, CD-ROM video games, and electronic books. Our interface with technologies of information gives many people the sense that information is disembodied or antithetical to the material, according to Hayles. This book you are reading is something concrete, something material. You experience the words on the page differently than the words on a computer screen. Like Poulet, perhaps, when you read a book you experience the text as the pleasurable merging of the author's consciousness with your own. Is your experience of reading a novel that you hold in your two hands the same as your experience of reading the same text from your computer screen? How would a hypertext version of the same novel affect your experience of it? Will folks who have grown up using computers from an early age experience the same kind of pleasure from reading an electronic book as folks like Poulet experience from reading a novel?

According to Hayles, "the impact of virtuality on literary theory and practice will be far-reaching and profound. At present, virtuality is largely terra incognita for the literary establishment." It already seems as if, eons ago, contemporary information technologies made Barthes's once innovative electric typewriter obsolete. Information technologies such as fiber optic cable, bandwidth, the latest computer software, and satellite systems reshape our everyday conceptions of cities, power, knowledge, life, and even our own bodies. These transformations no doubt affect our everyday theories of reading and writing. Not surprisingly, Hayles says that "the changing material conditions under which it [literature] is written and read in an information age" profoundly impact it. Try to imagine what Barthes's relation would be to laptops and the Internet. One can imagine that Barthes would be more than "almost obsessive" about e-mail. What kind of consciousnesses would Poulet find in a virtual book? Does hypertext technology rewrite Culler's theory of literary competence and poetics? If Hayles's analysis of virtuality's pervasiveness is accurate, then you are reading this book in what she terms "the late age of print." "Should we respond with optimism to the products of virtual writing," Hayles asks, "or regard them (as an elderly gentleman informed me when he heard some of these arguments) as abominations that are rotting the minds of American youth? Whatever we make of them, one thing is certain. Literature will not remain unchanged." From reading Hayles, one presumes that reading and writing similarly will not remain unchanged. Like Barthes, Sartre, Poulet, and Culler, Hayles asks us to reflect on basic questions: What happens to us when we read? What happens to us when we write? The discernable difference, however, is that Hayles—if she is correct—gives us a turn of the screw: what happens when we read and write in the condition of virtuality?

Jean-Paul Sartre (1905–1980)

French born, Sartre is the most celebrated of the post–World War II existentialist philosophers. When he was named the recipient of the 1964 Nobel Prize for literature, Sartre refused the honor for political reasons, equating the prize with the values of bourgeois society. Before the Second World War, Sartre taught philosophy and had started to write innovative texts such as *Nausea* (1938), which mingled literary and philosophical styles. During the war, from 1940 and 1941, Sartre was a prisoner in Germany. After his release, he joined the French Resistance. His reputation as a patriot and as an uncompromising intellectual added to his prestige after the war. With Simone de Beauvoir and Maurice Merleau-Ponty, Sartre founded an important literary journal, *Les Temps Modernes*. A major feminist and existential philosopher, Beauvoir was also Sartre's lover. In addition to *Nausea* and *Les Temps Modernes,* Sartre's other major literary endeavors are the plays *The Flies* (1943) and *No Exit* (1945). His major philosophical works include *Being and Nothingness* (1943) and *Existentialism* (1946). In the latter text, Sartre defends existentialism from several charges, including "inviting people to remain in a kind of desperate quietism" and "dwelling on human degradation." This selection, "Why Write?" comes from the collection *"What is Literature" and Other Essays* (1988), translated by Bernard Frechtman in 1949.

Why Write?

Each one has his reasons: for one, art is a flight; for another, a means of conquering. But one can flee into a hermitage, into madness, into death. One can conquer by arms. Why does it have to be *writing,* why does one have to manage his escapes and conquests by *writing*? Because, behind the various aims of authors, there is a deeper and more immediate choice which is common to all of us. We shall try to elucidate this choice, and we shall see whether it is not in the name of this very choice of writing that the engagement of writers must be required.

Each of our perceptions is accompanied by the consciousness that human reality is a "revealer," that is, it is through human reality that "there is" being, or, to put it differently, that man is the means by which things are manifested. It is our presence in the worlds which multiplies relations. It is we who set up a relationship between this tree and that bit of sky. Thanks to us, that star which has been dead for millennia, that quarter moon, and that dark river are disclosed in the unity of a landscape. It is the speed of our auto and our airplane which organizes the great masses of the earth. With each of our acts, the world reveals to us a new face. But, if we know that we are directors of being, we also know that we are not its producers. If we turn away from this landscape, it will sink back into its dark permanence. At least, it will sink back; there is no one mad enough to think that it is going to be annihilated. It is we who shall be annihilated, and the earth will remain in its lethargy until another consciousness comes along to awaken it. Thus, to our inner certainty of being "revealers" is added that of being inessential in relation to the thing revealed.

One of the chief motives of artistic creation is certainly the need of feeling that we are essential in relationship to the world. If I fix on canvas or in writing a certain aspect of the fields or the sea or a look on someone's face which I have disclosed, I am conscious of having produced them by condensing relationships, by introducing order where there was none, by imposing the unity of mind on the diversity of things. That is, I feel myself essential in relation to my creation. But this time it is the created object which escapes me; I can not reveal and produce at the same time. The creation becomes inessential in relation to the creative activity. First of all, even if it appears to others as definitive, the created object always seems to us in a state of suspension; we can always change this line, that shade, that word. Thus, it never *forces itself*. A novice painter asked his teacher, "When should I consider my painting finished?" And the teacher answered, "When you can look at it in amazement and say to yourself '*I'm* the one who did *that!*'"

Which amounts to saying "never." For it is virtually considering one's work with someone else's eyes and revealing what one has created. But it is self-evident that we are proportionally less conscious of the thing produced and more conscious of our productive activity. When it is a matter of pottery or carpentry, we work according to traditional norms, with tools whose usage is codified; it is Heidegger's famous "they" who are working with our hands. In this case, the result can seem to us sufficiently strange to preserve its objectivity in our eyes. But if we ourselves produce the rules of production, the measures, the criteria, and if our creative drive comes from the very depths of our heart, then we never find anything but ourselves in our work. It is we who have invented the laws by which we judge it. It is our history, our love, our gaiety, that we recognize in it. Even if we should regard it without touching it any further, we never *receive* from it that gaiety or love. We put them into it. The results which we have obtained on canvas or paper never seem to us *objective*. We are too familiar with the processes of which they are the effects. These processes remain a subjective discovery; they are ourselves, our inspiration, our ruse, and when we seek to *perceive* our work, we create it again, we repeat mentally the operations which produced it; each of its aspects appears as a result. Thus, in the perception, the object is given as the essential thing and the subject as the inessential. The latter seeks essentiality in the creation and obtains it, but then it is the object which becomes the inessential.

This dialectic is nowhere more apparent than in the art of writing, for the literary object is a peculiar top which exists only in movement. To make it come into view a concrete act called reading is necessary, and it lasts only as long as this act can last. Beyond that, there are only black marks on paper. Now, the writer can not read what he writes, whereas the shoemaker can put on the shoes he has just made if they are his size, and the architect can live in the house he has built. In reading, one foresees; one waits. He foresees the end of the sentence, the following sentence, the next page. He waits for them to confirm or disappoint his foresights. The reading is composed of a host of hypotheses, of dreams followed by awakenings, of hopes and deceptions. Readers are always ahead of the sentence they are reading in a merely probable future which partly collapses and partly comes together in proportion as they progress, which withdraws from one page to the next and forms the moving horizon of the literary object. Without waiting, without a future, without ignorance, there is no objectivity.

Now the operation of writing involves an implicit quasi-reading which makes real reading impossible. When the words form under his pen, the author doubtless sees them, but he does not see them as the reader does, since he knows them before writing them down. The function of his gaze is not to reveal, by stroking them, the sleeping words which are waiting to be read, but to control the sketching of the signs. In short, it is a purely regulating mission, and the view before him reveals nothing except for slight slips of the pen. The writer neither foresees nor conjectures; he *projects*. It often happens that he awaits, as they say, the inspiration. But one does not wait for himself the way he waits for others. If he hesitates, he knows that the future is not made, that he himself is going to make it, and if he still does not know what is going to happen to his hero, that simply means that he has not thought about it, that he has not decided upon anything. The future is then a blank page, whereas the future of the reader is two hundred pages filled with words which separate him from the end. Thus, the writer meets everywhere only *his* knowledge, *his* will, *his* plans, in short, himself. He touches only his own subjectivity; the object he creates is out of reach; he does not create it *for himself*. If he rereads himself, it is already too late. The sentence will never quite be a thing in his eyes. He goes to the very limits of the subjective but without crossing it. He appreciates the effect of a touch, of an epigram, of a well-placed adjective, but it is the effect they will have on others. He can judge it, not feel it. Proust never discovered the homosexuality of Charlus, since he had decided upon it even before starting on his book. And if a day comes when the book takes on for its author a semblance of objectivity, it is that years have passed, that he has forgotten it, that its spirit is quite foreign to him, and doubtless he is no longer capable of writing it. This was the case with Rousseau when he reread the *Social Contract* at the end of his life.

Thus, it is not true that one writes for himself. That would be the worst blow. In projecting his emotions on paper, one barely manages to give them a languishing extension. The creative act is only an incomplete and abstract moment in the production of a work. If the author existed alone he would be able to write as much as he liked; the work as *object* would never see the light of day and he would either have to put down his pen or despair. But the operation of writing implies that of reading as its dialectical correlative and these two connected acts necessitate two distinct agents. It is the conjoint effort of author and reader which brings upon the scene that concrete and imaginary object which is the work of the mind. There is no art except for and by others.

Reading seems, in fact, to be the synthesis of perception and creation.[1] It supposes the essentiality of both the subject and the object. The object is essential because it is strictly transcendent, because it imposes its own structures, and because one must wait for it and observe it; but the subject is also essential because it is required not only to disclose the object (that is, to make *there be* an object) but also so that this object might *be* (that is, to produce it). In a word, the reader is conscious of disclosing in creating, of creating by disclosing. In reality, it is not necessary to believe that reading is a mechanical operation and that signs make an impression upon him as light does on a photographic plate. If he is inattentive, tired, stupid, or thoughtless, most of the relations will escape him. He will never manage to "catch on" to the object (in the sense in which we see that fire "catches" or "doesn't catch"). He will draw some phrases out of the shadow, but they will seem to appear as random strokes. If he is at his best, he will project beyond the words a synthetic form, each phrase of which will be no more than a partial function: the "theme," the "subject," or the "meaning." Thus, from the very beginning, the meaning is no longer contained in the words, since it is he, on the contrary, who allows the signification of each of them to be understood; and the literary object, though realized *through* language, is never given *in* language. On the contrary, it is by nature a silence and an opponent of the word. In addition, the hundred thousand words aligned in a book can be read one by one so that the meaning of the work does not emerge. Nothing is accomplished if the reader does not put himself from the very beginning and almost without a guide at the height of this silence; if, in short, he does not invent it and does not then place there, and hold on to, the words and sentences which he awakens. And if I am told that it would be more fitting to call this operation a re-invention or a discovery, I shall answer that, first, such a re-invention would be as new and as original an act as the first invention. And, especially, when an object has never existed before, there can be no question of re-inventing it or discovering it. For if the silence about which I am speaking is really the goal at which the author is aiming, he has, at least, never been familiar with it; his silence is subjective and anterior to language. It is the absence of words, the undifferentiated and lived silence of inspiration, which the word will then particularize, whereas the silence produced by the reader is an object. And at the very interior of this object there are more silences—which the author does not tell. It is a question of silences which are so particular that they could not retain any meaning outside of the object which the reading causes to appear. However, it is these which give it its density and its particular face.

To say that they are unexpressed is hardly the word; for they are precisely the inexpressible. And that is why one does not come upon them at any definite moment in the reading; they are everywhere and nowhere. The quality of the marvelous in *The Wanderer (Le Grand Meaulnes),* the grandiosity of *Armance,* the degree of realism and truth of Kafka's mythology, these are never given. The reader must invent them all in a continual exceeding of the written thing. To be sure, the author guides him, but all he does is guide him. The landmarks he sets up are separated by the void. The reader must unite them; he must go beyond them. In short, reading is directed creation.

On the one hand, the literary object has no other substance than the reader's subjectivity; Raskolnikov's waiting is *my* waiting which I lend him. Without this impatience of the reader he would remain only a collection of signs. His hatred of the police magistrate who questions him is my hatred which has been solicited and wheedled out of me by signs, and the police magistrate himself would not exist without the hatred I have for him via Raskolnikov. That is what animates him, it is his very flesh.

But on the other hand, the words are there like traps to arouse our feelings and to reflect them toward us. Each word is a path of transcendence; it shapes our feelings, names them, and attributes them to an imaginary personage who takes it upon himself to live them for us and who has no other substance than these borrowed passions; he confers objects, perspectives, and a horizon upon them.

Thus, for the reader, all is to do and all is already done; the work exists only at the exact level of his capacities; while he reads and creates, he knows that he can always go further in his reading, can always create more profoundly, and thus the work seems to him as inexhaustible and opaque as things. We would readily reconcile that "rational intuition" which Kant reserved to divine Reason with this absolute production of qualities, which, to the extent that they emanate from our subjectivity, congeal before our eyes into impermeable objectivities.

Since the creation can find its fulfillment only in reading, since the artist must entrust to another the job of carrying out what he has begun, since it is only through the consciousness of the reader that he can regard himself as essential to his work, all literary work is an appeal. To write is to make an appeal to the reader that he lead into objective existence the revelation which I have undertaken by means of language. And if it should be asked *to what* the writer is appealing, the answer is simple. As the sufficient reason for the appearance of the aesthetic object is never found either in the book (where we find merely solicitations to produce the object) or in the author's mind, and as his subjectivity, which he cannot get away from, cannot give a reason for the act of leading into objectivity, the appearance of the work of art is a new event which cannot *be explained* by anterior data. And since this directed creation is an absolute beginning, it is therefore brought about by the freedom of the reader, and by what is purest in that freedom. Thus, the writer appeals to the reader's freedom to collaborate in the production of his work.

It will doubtless be said that all tools address themselves to our freedom since they are the instruments of a possible action, and that the work of art is not unique in that. And it is true that the tool is the congealed outline of an operation. But it remains on the level of the hypothetical imperative. I may use a hammer to nail up a case or to hit my neighbor over the head. Insofar as I consider it in itself, it is not an appeal to my freedom; it does not put me face to face with it; rather, it aims at using it by substituting a set succession of traditional procedures for the free invention of means. The book does not serve my freedom; it requires it. Indeed, one cannot address himself to freedom as such by means of constraint, fascination, or entreaties. There is only one way of attaining it; first, by recognizing it, then, having confidence in it, and finally, requiring of it an act, an act in its own name, that is, in the name of the confidence that one brings to it.

Thus, the book is not, like the tool, a means for any end whatever; the end to which it offers itself is the reader's freedom. And the Kantian expression "finality without end" seems to me quite inappropriate for designating the work of art. In fact, it implies that the aesthetic object presents only the appearance of a finality and is limited to soliciting the free and ordered play of the imagination. It forgets that the imagination of the spectator has not only a regulating function, but a constitutive one. It does not play; it is called upon to recompose the beautiful object beyond the traces left by the artist. The imagination can not revel in itself any more than can the other functions of the mind; it is always on the outside, always engaged in an enterprise. There would be finality without end if some object offered such a set ordering that it would lead us to suppose that it has one even though we cannot ascribe one to it. By defining the beautiful in this way one can—and this is Kant's aim—liken the beauty of art to natural beauty, since a flower, for example, presents so much symmetry, such harmonious colors, and such regular curves, that one is immediately tempted to seek a finalist explanation for all these properties and to see them as just so many means at the disposal of an unknown end. But that is exactly the error. The beauty of nature is in no way comparable to that of art. The work of art *does not have* an end; there we agree with Kant. But the reason is that it is an end. The Kantian formula does not account for the appeal which resounds at the basis of each painting, each statue, each book. Kant believes that the work of art first exists as fact and that it is then seen. Whereas, it exists only if one *looks* at it and if it is first pure appeal, pure exigence to exist. It is not an instrument whose existence is manifest and whose end is undetermined. It presents itself as a task to be discharged; from the very beginning it places itself on the level of the categorical imperative. You are perfectly free to leave that book on the table. But if you open it, you assume responsibility for it. For freedom is not experienced by its enjoying its free subjective functioning, but in a creative act required by an imperative. This absolute end, this imperative which is transcendent yet acquiesced in, which freedom itself adopts as its own, is what we call a value. The work of art is a value because it is an appeal.

If I appeal to my readers so that we may carry the enterprise which I have begun to a successful conclusion, it is self-evident that I consider him as a pure freedom, as an unconditioned activity; thus, in no case can I address myself to his passivity, that is, try to *affect* him, to communicate to him, from the very first, emotions of fear, desire, or anger. There are, doubtless, authors who concern themselves solely with arousing these emotions because they are foreseeable, manageable, and because they have at their disposal sure-fire means for provoking them. But it is also true that they are reproached for this kind of thing, as Euripides has been since antiquity because he had children appear on the stage. Freedom is alienated in the state of passion; it is abruptly engaged in partial enterprises; it loses sight of its task which is to produce an absolute end. And the book is no longer anything but a means for feeding hate or desire. The writer should not seek to *overwhelm;* otherwise he is in contradiction with himself; if he wishes to *make demands* he must propose only the task to be fulfilled. Hence, the character of pure presentation which appears essential to the work of art. The reader must be able to make a certain aesthetic withdrawal. This is what Gautier foolishly confused with "art for art's sake" and the Parnassians with the imperturbability of the artist. It is simply a matter of precaution, and Genet more justly calls it the author's politeness toward the reader. But that does not mean that the writer makes an appeal to some sort of abstract and conceptual freedom. One certainly creates the aesthetic object with feelings; if it is touching, it appears through our tears; if it is comic, it will be recognized by laughter. However, these feelings are of a particular kind. They have their origin in freedom; they are loaned. The belief which I accord the tale is freely assented to. It is a Passion, in the Christian sense of the word, that is, a freedom which resolutely puts itself into a state of passivity to obtain a certain transcendent affect by this sacrifice. The reader renders himself credulous; he descends into credulity which, though it ends by enclosing him like a dream, is at every moment conscious of being free. An effort is sometimes made to force the writer into this dilemma: "Either one believes in your story, and it is intolerable, or one does not believe in it, and it is ridiculous." But the argument is absurd because the characteristic of aesthetic consciousness is to be a belief by means of engagement, by oath, a belief sustained by fidelity to one's self and to the author, a perpetually renewed choice to believe. I can awaken at every moment, and I know it; but I do not want to; reading is a free dream. So that all feelings which are exacted on the basis of this imaginary belief are like particular modulations of my freedom. Far from absorbing or masking it, they are so many different ways it has chosen to reveal itself to itself. Raskolnikov, as I have said, would only be a shadow, without the mixture of repulsion and friendship which I feel for him and which makes him live. But, by a reversal which is the characteristic of the imaginary object, it is not his behavior which excites my indignation or esteem, but my indignation and esteem which give consistency and objectivity to his behavior. Thus, the reader's feelings are never dominated by the object, and as no external reality can condition them, they have their permanent source in freedom; that is, they are all generous—for I call a feeling generous which has its origin and its end in freedom. Thus, reading is an exercise in generosity, and what the writer requires of the reader is not the application of an abstract freedom but the gift of his whole person, with his passions, his prepossessions, his sympathies, his sexual temperament, and his scale of values. Only this person will give himself generously; freedom goes through and through him and comes to transform the darkest masses of his sensibility. And as activity has rendered itself passive in order for it better to create the object, vice-versa, passivity becomes an act; the man who is reading has raised himself to the highest degree. That is why we see people who are known for their toughness shed tears at the recital of imaginary misfortunes; for the moment they have become what they would have been if they had not spent their lives hiding their freedom from themselves.

Thus, the author writes in order to address himself to the freedom of readers, and he requires it in order to make his work exist. But he does not stop there; he also requires that they return this confidence which he has given them, that they recognize his creative freedom, and that they in turn solicit it by a symmetrical and inverse appeal. Here there appears the other dialectical paradox of reading; the more we experience our freedom, the more we recognize that of the other; the more he demands of us, the more we demand of him.

When I am enchanted with a landscape, I know very well that it is not I who create it, but I also know that without me the relations which are established before my eyes among the trees, the foliage, the earth, and the grass would not exist at all. I know that I can give no reason for the appearance of finality which I discover in the assortment of hues and in the harmony of the forms and movements created by the wind. Yet, it exists; there it is before my eyes, and I can make *there be* being only if being already *is*. But even if I believe in God, I can not establish any passage, unless it be purely verbal, between the divine, universal solicitude and the particular spectacle which I am considering. To say that He made the landscape in order to charm me or that He made me the kind of person who is pleased by it is to take a question for an answer. Is the marriage of this blue and that green deliberate? How can I know? The idea of a universal providence is no guarantee of any particular intention, especially in the case under consideration, since the green of the grass is explained by biological laws, specific constants, and geographical determinism, while the reason for the blue of the water is accounted for by the depth of the river, the nature of the soil and the swiftness of the current. The assorting of the shades, if it is willed, can only be something *thrown into the bargain;* it is the meeting of two causal series, that is to say, at first sight, a fact of chance. At best, the finality remains problematic. All the relations we establish remain hypotheses; no end is proposed to us in the manner of an imperative, since none is expressly revealed as having been willed by a creator. Thus, our freedom is never *called forth* by natural beauty. Or rather, there is an appearance of order in the ensemble of the foliage, the forms, and the movements, hence, the illusion of a calling forth which seems to solicit this freedom and which disappears immediately when one regards it. Hardly have we begun to run our eyes over this arrangement, than the call disappears; we remain alone, free to tie up one color with another or with a third, to set up a relationship between the tree and the water or the tree and the sky, or the tree, the water and the sky. My freedom becomes caprice. To the extent that I establish new relationships, I remove myself further from the illusory objectivity which solicits me. I *muse* about certain motifs which are vaguely outlined by the things; the natural reality is no longer anything but a pretext for musing. Or, in that case, because I have deeply regretted that this arrangement which was momentarily perceived was not offered to me by somebody and consequently is not *real,* the result is that I fix my dream, that I transpose it to canvas or in writing. Thus, I interpose myself between the finality without end which appears in the natural spectacles and the gaze of other men. I transmit it to them. It becomes human by this transmission. Art here is a ceremony of the *gift* and the gift alone brings about the metamorphosis. It is something like the transmission of titles and powers in the matriarchate where the mother does not possess the names, but is the indispensable intermediary between uncle and nephew. Since I have captured this illusion in flight, since I lay it out for other men and have disengaged it and rethought it for them, they can consider it with confidence. It has become intentional. As for me, I remain, to be sure, at the border of the subjective and the objective without ever being able to contemplate the objective ordonnance which I transmit.

The reader, on the contrary, progresses in security. However far he may go, the author has gone farther. Whatever connections he may establish among the different parts of the book—among the chapters or the words—he has a guarantee, namely, that they have been expressly willed. As Descartes says, he can even pretend that there is a secret order among parts which seem to have no connection. The creator has preceded him along the way, and the most beautiful disorders are effects of art, that is, again order. Reading is induction, interpolation, extrapolation, and the basis of these activities rests on the reader's will, as for a long time it was believed that that of scientific induction rested on the divine will. A gentle force accompanies us and supports us from the first page to the last. That does not mean that we fathom the artist's intentions easily. They constitute, as we have said, the object of conjectures, and there is an *experience* of the reader; but these conjectures are supported by the great certainty we have that the beauties which appear in the book are never accidental. In nature, the tree and the sky harmonize only by chance; if, on the contrary, in the novel, the protagonists find themselves in a *certain* tower, in a *certain* prison, if they stroll in a *certain* garden, it is a matter both of the restitution of independent causal series (the character had a certain state of mind which was due to a succession of psychological and social events; on the other hand, he betook himself to a determined place and the layout of the city required him to cross a certain park) and of the expression of a deeper finality, for the park came into existence only *in order to* harmonize with a certain state of mind, to express it by means of things or to put it into relief by a vivid contrast, and the state of mind itself was conceived in connection with the landscape. Here it is causality which is appearance and which might be called "causality without cause," and it is the finality which is the profound reality. But if I can thus in all confidence put the order of ends under the order of causes, it is because by opening the book I am asserting that the object has its source in human freedom.

If I were to suspect the artist of having written out of passion and in passion, my confidence would immediately vanish, for it would serve no purpose to have supported the order of causes by the order of ends. The latter would be supported in its turn by a psychic causality and the work of art would end by re-entering the chain of determinism. Certainly I do not deny when I am reading that the author may be impassioned, nor even that he might have conceived the first plan of his work under the sway of passion. But his decision to write supposes that he withdraws somewhat from his feelings, in short, that he has transformed his emotions into free emotions as I do mine while reading him; that is, that he is in an attitude of generosity.

Thus, reading is a pact of generosity between author and reader. Each one trusts the other; each one counts on the other, demands of the other as much as he demands of himself. For this confidence is itself generosity. Nothing can force the author to believe that his reader will use his freedom; nothing can force the reader to believe that the author has used his. Both of them make a free decision. There is then established a dialectical going-and-coming; when I read, I make demands; if my demands are met, what I am then reading provokes me to demand more of the author, which means to demand of the author that he demand more of me. And, vice-versa, the author's demand is that I carry my demands to the highest pitch. Thus, my freedom, by revealing itself, reveals the freedom of the other.

It matters little whether the aesthetic object is the product of "realistic" art (or supposedly such) or "formal" art. At any rate, the natural relations are inverted; that tree on the first plane of the Cézanne painting first appears as the product of a causal chain. But the causality is an illusion; it will doubtless remain as a proposition as long as we look at the painting, but it will be supported by a deep finality; if the tree is placed in such a way, it is because the rest of the painting *requires* that this form and those colors be placed on the first plane. Thus, through the phenomenal causality, our gaze attains finality as the deep structure of the object, and, beyond finality, it attains human freedom as its source and original basis. Vermeer's realism is carried so far that at first it might be thought to be photographic. But if one considers the splendor of his texture, the pink and velvety glory of his little brick walls, the blue thickness of a branch of woodbine, the glazed darkness of his vestibules, the orange-colored flesh of his faces which are as polished as the stone of holy-water basins, one suddenly feels, in the pleasure that he experiences, that the finality is not so much in the forms or colors as in his material imagination. It is the very substance and temper of the things which here give the forms their reason for being. With this realist we are perhaps closest to absolute creation, since it is in the very passivity of the matter that we meet the unfathomable freedom of man.

The work is never limited to the painted, sculpted, or narrated object. Just as one perceives things only against the background of the world, so the objects represented by art appear against the background of the universe. On the background of the adventures of Fabrice are the Italy of 1820, Austria, France, the sky and stars which the Abbé Blanis consults, and finally the whole earth. If the painter presents us with a field or a vase of flowers, his paintings are windows which are open on the whole world. We follow the red path which is buried among the wheat much farther than Van Gogh has painted it, among other wheat fields, under other clouds, to the river which empties into the sea, and we extend to infinity, to the other end of the world, the deep finality which supports the existence of the field and the earth. So that, through the various objects which it produces or reproduces, the creative act aims at a total renewal of the world. Each painting, each book, is a recovery of the totality of being. Each of them presents this totality to the freedom of the spectator. For this is quite the final goal of art: to recover this world by giving it to be seen as it is, but as if it had its source in human freedom. But, since what the author creates takes on objective reality only in the eyes of the spectator, this recovery is consecrated by the ceremony of the spectacle—and particularly of reading. We are already in a better position to answer the question we raised a while ago: the writer chooses to appeal to the freedom of other men so that, by the reciprocal implications of their demands, they may re-adapt the totality of being to man and may again enclose the universe within man.

If we wish to go still further, we must bear in mind that the writer, like all other artists, aims at giving his reader a certain feeling that is customarily called aesthetic pleasure, and which I would very much rather call aesthetic joy, and that this feeling, when it appears, is a sign that the work is achieved. It is therefore fitting to examine it in the light of the preceding considerations. In effect, this joy, which is denied to the creator, insofar as he creates, becomes one with the aesthetic consciousness of the spectator, that is, in the case under consideration, of the reader. It is a complex feeling but one whose structures and condition are inseparable from one another. It is identical, at first, with the recognition of a transcendent and absolute end which, for a moment, suspends the utilitarian round of ends-means and means-ends,[2] that is, of an appeal or, what amounts to the same thing, of a value. And the positional consciousness which I take of this value is necessarily accompanied by the non-positional consciousness of my freedom, since my freedom is manifested to itself by a transcendent exigency. The recognition of freedom by itself is joy, but this structure of non-thetical consciousness implies another: since, in effect, reading is creation, my freedom does not only appear to itself as pure autonomy but as creative activity, that is, it is not limited to giving itself its own law but perceives itself as being constitutive of the object. It is on this level that the phenomenon specifically is manifested, that is, a creation wherein the created object is given *as object* to its creator. It is the sole case in which the creator gets any enjoyment out of the object he creates. And the word enjoyment which is applied to the positional consciousness of the work read indicates sufficiently that we are in the presence of an essential structure of aesthetic joy. This positional enjoyment is accompanied by the non-positional consciousness of being essential in relation to an object perceived as essential. I shall call this aspect of aesthetic consciousness the feeling of security; it is this which stamps the strongest aesthetic emotions with a sovereign calm. It has its origin in the authentication of a strict harmony between subjectivity and objectivity. As, on the other hand, the aesthetic object is properly the world insofar as it is aimed at through the imaginary, aesthetic joy accompanies the positional consciousness that the world is a value, that is, a task proposed to human freedom. I shall call this the aesthetic modification of the human project, for, as usual, the world appears as the horizon of our situation, as the infinite distance which separates us from ourselves, as the synthetic totality of the given, as the undifferentiated ensemble of obstacles and implements—but never as a demand addressed to our freedom. Thus, aesthetic joy proceeds to this level of the consciousness which I take of recovering and internalizing that which is non-ego par excellence, since I transform the given into an imperative and the fact into a value. The world is *my task,* that is, the essential and freely accepted function of my freedom is to make that unique and absolute object which is the universe come into being in an unconditioned movement. And, thirdly, the preceding structures imply a pact between human freedoms, for, on the one hand, reading is a confident and exacting recognition of the freedom of the writer, and, on the other hand, aesthetic pleasure, as it is itself experienced in the form of a value, involves an absolute exigence in regard to others; every man, insofar as he is a freedom, feels the same pleasure in reading the same work. Thus, all mankind is present in its highest freedom; it sustains the being of a world which is both *its* world and the "external" world. In aesthetic joy the positional consciousness is an *image-making* consciousness of the world in its totality both as being and having to be, both as totally ours and totally foreign, and the more ours as it is the more foreign. The non-positional consciousness *really* envelops the harmonious totality of human freedoms insofar as it makes the object of a universal confidence and exigency.

To write is thus both to disclose the world and to offer it as a task to the generosity of the reader. It is to have recourse to the consciousness of others in order to make one's self to be recognized as *essential* to the totality of being; it is to wish to live this essentiality by means of interposed persons; but, on the other hand, as the real world is revealed only by action, as one can feel himself in it only by exceeding it in order to change it, the novelist's universe would lack thickness if it were not discovered in a movement to transcend it. It has often been observed that an object in a story does not derive its density of existence from the number and length of the descriptions devoted to it, but from the complexity of its connections with the different characters. The more often the characters handle it, take it up, and put it down, in short, go beyond it toward their own ends, the more real will it appear. Thus, of the world of the novel, that is, the totality of men and things, we may say that in order for it to offer its maximum density the disclosure-creation by which the reader discovers it must also be an imaginary engagement in the action; in other words, the more disposed one is to change it, the more alive it will be. The error of realism has been to believe that the real reveals itself to contemplation, and that consequently one could draw an impartial picture of it. How could that be possible, since the very perception is partial, since by itself the naming is already a modification of the object? And how could the writer, who wants himself to be essential to this universe, want to be essential to the injustice which this universe comprehends? Yet, he must be; but if he accepts being the creator of injustices, it is in a movement which goes beyond them toward their abolition. As for me who read, if I create and keep alive an unjust world, I can not help making myself responsible for it. And the author's whole art is bent on obliging me to *create* what he *discloses,* therefore to compromise myself. So both of us bear the responsibility for the universe. And precisely because this universe is supported by the joint effort of our two freedoms, and because the author, with me as medium, has attempted to integrate it into the human, it must appear truly *in itself,* in its very marrow, as being shot through and through with a freedom which has taken human freedom as its end, and if it is not really the city of ends that it ought to be, it must at least be a stage along the way; in a word, it must be a becoming and it must always be considered and presented not as a crushing mass which weighs us down, but from the point of view of its going beyond toward that city of ends. However bad and hopeless the humanity which it paints may be, the work must have an air of generosity. Not, of course, that this generosity is to be expressed by means of edifying discourses and virtuous characters; it must not even be premeditated, and it is quite true that fine sentiments do not make fine books. But it must be the very warp and woof of the book, the stuff out of which the people and things are cut; whatever the subject, a sort of essential lightness must appear everywhere and remind us that the work is never a natural datum, but an *exigence* and a *gift.* And if I am given this world with its injustices, it is not so that I might contemplate them coldly, but that I might animate them with my indignation, that I might disclose them and create them with their nature as injustices, that is, as abuses to be suppressed. Thus, the writer's universe will only reveal itself in all its depth to the examination, the admiration, and the indignation of the reader; and the generous love is a promise to maintain, and the generous indignation is a promise to change, and the admiration a promise to imitate; although literature is one thing and morality a quite different one, at the heart of the aesthetic imperative we discern the moral imperative. For, since the one who writes recognizes, by the very fact that he takes the trouble to write, the freedom of his readers, and since the one who reads, by the mere fact of his opening the book, recognizes the freedom of the writer, the work of art, from whichever side you approach it, is an act of confidence in the freedom of men. And since readers, like the author, recognize this freedom only to demand that it manifest itself, the work can be defined as an imaginary presentation of the world insofar as it demands human freedom. The result of which is that there is no "gloomy literature", since, however dark may be the colors in which one paints the world, he paints it only so that free men may feel their freedom as they face it. Thus, there are only good and bad novels. The bad novel aims to please by flattering, whereas the good one is an exigence and an act of faith. But above all, the unique point of view from which the author can present the world to those freedoms whose concurrence he wishes to bring about is that of a world to be impregnated always with more freedom. It would be inconceivable that this unleashing of generosity provoked by the writer could be used to authorize an injustice, and that the reader could enjoy his freedom while reading a work which approves or accepts or simply abstains from condemning the subjection of man by man. One can imagine a good novel being written by an American Negro even if hatred of the whites were spread all over it, because it is the freedom of his race that he demands through this hatred. And, as he invites me to assume the attitude of generosity, the moment I feel myself a pure freedom I can not bear to identify myself with a race of oppressors. Thus, I require of all freedoms that they demand the liberation of colored people against the white race and against myself insofar as I am a part of it, but nobody can suppose for a moment that it is possible to write a good novel in praise of anti-Semitism.[3] For, the moment I feel that my freedom is indissolubly linked with that of all other men, it can not be demanded of me that I use it to approve the enslavement of a part of these men. Thus, whether he is an essayist, a pamphleteer, a satirist, or a novelist, whether he speaks only of individual passions or whether he attacks the social order, the writer, a free man addressing free men, has only one subject—freedom.

Hence, any attempt to enslave his readers threatens him in his very art. A blacksmith can be affected by fascism in his life as a man, but not necessarily in his craft; a writer will be affected in both, and even more in his craft than in his life. I have seen writers, who before the war, called for fascism with all their hearts, smitten with sterility at the very moment when the Nazis were loading them with honors. I am thinking of Drieu la Rochelle in particular; he was mistaken, but he was sincere. He proved it. He had agreed to direct a Nazi-inspired review. The first few months he reprimanded, rebuked, and lectured his countrymen. No one answered him because no one was free to do so. He became irritated; he no longer *felt* his readers. He became more insistent, but no sign appeared to prove that he had been understood. No sign of hatred, nor of anger either; nothing. He seemed disoriented, the victim of a growing distress. He complained bitterly to the Germans. His articles had been superb; they became shrill. The moment arrived when he struck his breast; no echo, except among the bought journalists whom he despised. He handed in his resignation, withdrew it, again spoke, still in the desert. Finally, he kept still, gagged by the silence of others. He had demanded the enslavement of others, but in his crazy mind he must have imagined that it was voluntary, that it was still free. It came; the man in him congratulated himself mightily, but the writer could not bear it. While this was going on, others, who, happily, were in the majority, understood that the freedom of writing implies the freedom of the citizen. One does not write for slaves.

The art of prose is bound up with the only regime in which prose has meaning, democracy. When one is threatened, the other is too. And it is not enough to defend them with the pen. A day comes when the pen is forced to stop, and the writer must then take up arms. Thus, however you might have come to it, whatever the opinions you might have professed, literature throws you into battle. Writing is a certain way of wanting freedom; once you have begun, you are engaged, willy-nilly.

Engaged in what? Defending freedom? That's easy to say. Is it a matter of acting as guardian of ideal values like Benda's clerk before the betrayal,[4] or is it concrete, everyday freedom which must be protected by our taking sides in political and social struggles? The question is tied up with another one, one very simple in appearance but which nobody ever asks himself: "For whom does one write?"

Notes

1. The same is true in different degrees regarding the spectator's attitude before other works of art (paintings, symphonies, statues, etc.).
2. In *practical life* a means may be taken for an end as soon as one searches for it, and each end is revealed as a means of attaining another end.
3. This last remark may arouse some readers. If so, I'd like to know a single good novel whose express purpose was to serve oppression, a single good novel which has been written against Jews, negroes, workers, or colonial people. "But if there isn't any, that's no reason why someone may not write one some day." But you then admit that you are an abstract theoretician. You, not I. For it is in the name of your abstract conception of art that you assert the possibility of a fact which has never come into being, whereas I limit myself to proposing an explanation for a recognized fact.
4. The reference here is to Benda's *La Trahison dés clercs,* translated into English as *The Treason of the Intellectuals.*—Translator's note.

Roland Barthes (1915–1980)

Born in Cherbourg, France, Barthes was one of the most influential literary critics and theorists of the twentieth century. Indeed, in 1976, Barthes was recognized for his immense accomplishments by being elected to a prestigious academic chair position in literary semiology in Paris. His pioneering work in structuralism helped to redefine ways of reading for a generation of critics in the 1960s and 1970s. Barthes's critical focus shifted effortlessly from classic writers of French literature, such as Balzac, to experimental contemporaries such as Robbe-Grillet. Barthes was equally adept at applying his structural and semiotic approaches to fashion, commodities, and popular entertainment such as wrestling. Like other major structuralists, Barthes's thinking was particularly influenced by the linguistic theories of Ferdinand de Saussure, but Barthes was also influenced by classical rhetoric and by political upheavals in France in the late 1960s. Barthes's 1968 essay "The Death of the Author" signals the transition of his theoretical orientation from structuralism to attitudes toward textuality that are more akin to poststructuralist concerns with open-endedness and ruptures in intelligibility.

The list of Barthes's influential books is long; some of the most celebrated include *Writing Degree Zero* (1953), which explores, among many things, the density and opacity of language; *Mythologies* (1957), which examines not the sign systems of literary texts, but the sign systems of bourgeois popular culture; *S/Z* (1970), which presents a groundbreaking analysis of *Sarrasine,* a novella by Balzac; and *The Pleasure of the Text* (1973), which examines readerly bliss and desire. While his earlier books develop theories of the sign as it relates to structuralism, Barthes's later books tend toward linguistic attitudes closer to those of poststructuralism. Scholars and theorists recognize that much of his work has anticipated major intellectual and artistic trends from the 1980s onward. This reading selection, "An Almost Obsessive Relation to Writing Instruments," is a September 27, 1973, interview collected in *The Grain of the Voice: Interviews, 1962–1980.*

An Almost Obsessive Relation to Writing Instruments

Do you have a method of working?

It all depends on what you mean by method. As far as methodology is concerned, I have no opinion. But if you're talking about work habits, obviously I have a method of working. And on that basis your question interests me, because there is a kind of censorship which considers this topic taboo, under the pretext that it would be futile for a writer or an intellectual to talk about his writing, his daily schedule, or his desk.

When a great many people agree that a problem is insignificant, that usually means it is not. Insignificance is the locus of true significance. This should never be forgotten. That is why it seems so important to me to ask a writer about his writing habits, putting things on the most material level, I would even say the most minimal level possible. This is an anti-mythological action: it contributes to the overturning of that old myth which continues to present language as the instrument of thought, inwardness, passion, or whatever, and consequently presents writing as a simple instrumental practice.

As always, history clearly shows us the way to understand that actions which are secularized and trivialized in our society, such as writing, are actually heavily charged with meaning. When writing is placed in its historical or even anthropological context, it can be seen that for a long time writing was attended by great ceremony. In ancient Chinese society, one prepared oneself for writing, for handling the ink brush, through an almost religious asceticism. In certain Christian monasteries of the Middle Ages, the copyists began their work only after a day of meditation.

Personally, I call the set of those "rules" (in the monastic sense of the word) which predetermine the work—and it is important to distinguish the different coordinates: working time, working space, and the action of writing itself—the "protocols" of work. The etymology is clear: it means the first page glued to a manuscript in preparation for writing.

Do you mean that your own work is inscribed in a ceremonial?

In a certain manner, yes. Take the gesture, the action of writing. I would say, for example, that I have an almost obsessive relation to writing instruments. I often switch from one pen to another just for the pleasure of it. I try out new ones. I have far too many pens—I don't know what to do with all of them! And yet, as soon as I see a new one, I start craving it. I cannot keep myself from buying them.

When felt-tipped pens first appeared in the stores, I bought a lot of them. (The fact that they were originally from Japan was not, I admit, displeasing to me.) Since then I've gotten tired of them, because the point flattens out too quickly. I've also used pen nibs—not the "Sergeant-Major," which is too dry, but softer nibs, like the "J." In short, I've tried everything . . . except Bics, with which I feel absolutely no affinity. I would even say, a bit nastily, that there is a "Bic style," which is really just for churning out copy, writing that merely transcribes thought.

In the end, I always return to fine fountain pens. The essential thing is that they can produce that soft, smooth writing I absolutely require.

Because you write all your work by hand?

It's not that simple. In my case, there are two stages in the creative process. First comes the moment when desire is invested in a graphic impulse, producing a calligraphical object. Then there is the critical moment when this object is prepared for the anonymous and collective consumption of others through transformation into a typographical object (at that moment, the object is already beginning its commercialization). In other words—first I write the text with a pen, then I type the whole thing on a typewriter (with two fingers, because I don't know how to type).

Up until now, these two states—handwriting, typewriting—were, in a way, sacred for me. But I should note that I am trying to change my ritual.

I have just bought myself a present: an electric typewriter. Every day I practice typing for a half an hour, in the fond hope of acquiring a more "typewriterly" writing.

I was led to this decision by personal experience. Since I'm often very busy, I have sometimes been obliged to have things typed for me by others (I don't like to do this, but it has happened). When I thought about this, it bothered me. Without going into a big demagogical speech, I'll just say that to me this represented an alienated social relationship: a person, the typist, is confined by the master in an activity I would almost call an enslavement, when writing is precisely a field of liberty and desire! In short, I said to myself: "There's only one solution. I really must learn to type." Philippe Sollers, to whom I mentioned this resolution, reassured me, moreover, that once you learn to type well enough, writing directly at the typewriter creates a kind of unique spontaneity which has its own beauty.

My conversion, I admit, is far from accomplished. I doubt that I'll ever completely stop writing things out by hand, outmoded and eccentric though that may be. In any case, that's my situation. I'm making an honest effort to change with the times. And I've gotten a little bit used to my new regime.

Do you attach equal importance to your workplace?

I simply cannot work in a hotel room. It's not the hotel itself that bothers me. It's not a question of ambiance or decor, but of spatial organization (it's not for nothing that I'm called a structuralist!).

To be able to function, I need to be able structurally to reproduce my usual work space. In Paris, the place where I work (every day from 9:30 a.m. to 1 p.m.; this regular workaday schedule for writing suits me better than an aleatory schedule, which supposes a state of continual excitement) is in my bedroom. This space is completed by a music area (I play the piano every day, at about the same time: 2:30 in the afternoon) and by a "painting" area—I say "painting" with lots of quotation marks (about once a week I perform as a Sunday painter, so I need a place to splatter paint around).

In my country house, I have faithfully reproduced those three areas. It's not important that they're not in the same room. It isn't the walls but the structures that count.

But that's not all. The working space itself must also be divided into a certain number of functional microplaces. First there should be a table. (I like it to be of wood. I might say that I'm on good terms with wood.) There has to be a place on the side, another table where I can spread out the different things I'm working on. And there has to be a place for the typewriter, and a desk for my different memos, notes, "microplannings" for the next few days, "macroplannings" for the trimester, etc. (I never look at them, mind you. Their simple presence is enough.) Finally, I have my index-card system, and the slips have an equally strict format: one quarter the size of my usual sheet of paper. At least that's how they were until the day standards were readjusted within the framework of European unification (in my opinion, one of the cruelest blows of the Common Market). Luckily, I'm not *completely* obsessive. Otherwise, I would have had to redo all my cards from the time I first started writing, twenty-five years ago.

Since you're an essayist rather than a novelist, what part does documentation play in the preparation of your books?

What I enjoy is not the scholarly work. I don't like libraries. I even find it very difficult to read there. What I do enjoy is the excitement provoked by immediate and phenomenological contact with the tutor text. So I don't try to set up a preliminary library for myself, I'm content to read the text in question, in a rather fetishistic way: writing down certain passages, moments, even words which have the power to move me. As I go along, I use my cards to write down quotations, or ideas which come to me, and they do so, curiously, already in the rhythm of a sentence, so that from that moment on, things are already taking on an existence as writing.

After that, a second reading isn't indispensable. On the other hand, from then on, I'm plunged into a kind of frenzied state. I know that everything I read will somehow find its inevitable way into my work. The only problem is to keep what I read for amusement from interfering with reading directed toward my writing. The solution is very simple: the books I read for pleasure, for example a classic, or one of Jakobson's books on linguistics, which I particularly enjoy, those I read in bed at night before going to sleep. I read the others (as well as avant-garde texts) at my worktable in the morning. There is nothing arbitrary about this. The bed is the locus of irresponsibility. The table, that of responsibility.

> *And these unexpected comparisons that are your specialty, how do you arrive at them? Do you make an outline before you begin writing?*

Correspondences are not a question of writing but of textual analysis. Some people have the structural reflex and see things in oppositive terms. Others don't have it. Period.

As for the sacred outline, I admit having sacrificed at its altars during a certain period in the beginnings of semiology. Since then there has been that whole movement challenging the dissertation and its format. My university experience has also shown me the very oppressive, not to say repressive, constraints brought to bear upon students by the myth of the outline and syllogistic, Aristotelian development (this was even one of the problems we attempted to examine this year in my seminar). In short, I opted for an aleatory cutting-up, a *découpage* (into what I call "miniatures"). My aim is to deconstruct the dissertation, to deflate the reader's anxiety, and to reinforce the critical part of writing by fracturing the very notion of the "subject" of a book. But don't make the mistake of thinking that because I tend more and more to produce my texts in fragments I have renounced all constraint. When one replaces logic with chance, it must be closely watched lest it become, in its turn, mechanical. Personally, I proceed according to a method I would call, inspired by certain Zen definitions, "controlled accident." In the second part devoted to Sade in *Sade, Fourier, Loyola,* for example, chance intervenes only in the initial constructive action of giving a title to each fragment. In *The Pleasure of the Text,* these fragments are chosen according to letters of the alphabet. In the end, each book requires a search for its own appropriate form.

> *Have you never thought about writing a novel?*

A novel is not defined by its object, but by forsaking the serious temper, *l'esprit de sérieux*. To cross out or correct a word, to watch over euphony or a figure of speech, to discover a neologism, all this has for me a gourmand savor of language, a truly novelistic pleasure.

But the two aspects of writing that give me the keenest pleasure are, first, to begin, and second, to complete. Frankly, it's so that I can multiply my pleasure many times over that I've decided (provisionally) in favor of discontinuous writing.

Georges Poulet (1902–1991)

Born in Belgium, Poulet was an influential critic and theorist who taught at the prestigious Johns Hopkins University in the 1950s before returning to Europe to teach. Poulet is, perhaps, most associated with the Geneva school of criticism. Members of the Geneva school practiced phenomenology, a branch of philosophy that emphasizes how our consciousness experiences the world. In this approach, we understand the hard facts of reality through our experience of them. Poulet believed that, during the act of reading, the author's consciousness merges with the reader's. In "Phenomenology of Reading," Poulet writes of his experience when reading: "I am aware of a rational being, of a consciousness; the consciousness of another, no different from the one I automatically assume in every human being I encounter, except that in this case the consciousness is open to me, welcomes me, lets me look deep inside itself, and even allows me, with unheard-of license, to think what it thinks and feel what it feels." Stylistically, Poulet's philosophic criticism is artistic, as evidenced by the following eloquent passage from "Phenomenology of Reading": "As soon as I replace my direct perception of reality by the words of a book, I deliver myself, bound hand and foot to the omnipotence of fiction. I say farewell to what is, in order to feign belief in what is not. I surround myself with fictitious beings; I become the prey of language. There is no escaping this takeover. Language surrounds me with its unreality." In passages such as the foregoing, we see that Poulet's identification of consciousness contrasts with that of methodologies which emphasize sciencelike objectivity and analytic attention to structure. By emphasizing the role of the reader and her or his reading experience, Poulet's writing models one version of the critical approach known as reader-response criticism.

Phenomenology of Reading

At the beginning of Mallarmé's unfinished story, *Igitur*, there is the description of an empty room, in the middle of which, on a table there is an open book. This seems to me the situation of every book, until someone comes and begins to read it. Books are objects. On a table, on bookshelves, in store windows, they wait for someone to come and deliver them from their materiality, from their immobility. When I see them on display, I look at them as I would at animals for sale, kept in little cages, and so obviously hoping for a buyer. For—there is no doubting is—animals do know that their fate depends on a human intervention, thanks to which they will be delivered from the shame of being treated as objects. Isn't the same true of books? Made of paper and ink, they lie where they are put, until the moment someone shows an interest in them. They wait. Are they aware that an act of man might suddenly transform their existence? They appear to be lit up with that hope. Read me, they seem to say. I find it hard to resist their appeal. No, books are not just objects among others.

This feeling they give me—I sometimes have it with other objects. I have it, for example, with vases and statues. It would never occur to me to walk around a sewing machine or to look at the underside of a plate. I am quite satisfied with the face they present to me. But statues make me want to circle around them, vases make me want to turn them in my hands. I wonder why. Isn't is because they give me the illusion that there is something in them which, from a different angle, I might be able to see? Neither vase nor statue seems fully revealed by the unbroken perimeter of its surfaces. In addition to its surfaces it must have an interior. What this interior might be, that is what intrigues me and makes me circle around them, as though looking for the entrance to a secret chamber. But there is no such entrance (save for the mouth of the vase, which is not a true entrance since it gives only access to a little space to put flowers in). So the vase and the statue are closed. They oblige me to remain outside. We can have no true rapport—whence my sense of uneasiness.

So much for statues and vases. I hope books are not like them. Buy a vase, take it home, put it on your table or your mantel, and, after a while, it will allow itself to be made a part of your household. But it will be no less a vase, for that. On the other hand, take a book, and you will find it offering, opening itself. It is this openness of the book which I find so moving. A book is not shut in by its contours, is not walled-up as in a fortress. It asks nothing better than to exist outside itself, or to let you exist in it. In short, the extraordinary fact in the case of a book is the falling away of the barriers between you and it. You are inside it; it is inside you; there is no longer either outside or inside.

Such is the initial phenomenon produced whenever I take up a book, and begin to read it. At the precise moment that I see, surging out of the object I hold open before me, a quantity of significations which my mind grasps, I *realize* that what I hold in my hands is no longer just an object, or even simply a living thing. I am aware of a rational being, of a consciousness; the consciousness of another, no different from the one I automatically assume in every human being I encounter, except that in this case the consciousness is open to me, welcomes me, lets me look deep inside itself, and even allows me, with unheard-of license, to think what it thinks and feel what it feels.

Unheard-of, I say. Unheard-of, first, is the disappearance of the "object." Where is the book I held in my hands? It is still there, and at the same time it is there no longer, it is nowhere. That object wholly object, that thing made of paper, as there are things made of metal or porcelain, that object is no more, or at least it is as if it no longer existed, as long as I read the book. For the book is no longer a material reality. It has become a series of words, of images, of ideas which in their turn begin to exist. And where is this new existence? Surely not in the paper object. Nor, surely, in external space. There is only one place left for this new existence: my innermost self.

How has this come about? By what means, through whose intercession? How can I have opened my own mind so completely to what is usually shut out of it? I do not know. I know only that, while reading, I perceive in my mind a number of significations which have made themselves at home here. Doubtless they are still objects: images, ideas, words, objects of my thought. And yet, from this point of view, there is an enormous difference. For the book, like the vase, or like the statue, was an object among others, residing in the external world: the world which objects ordinarily inhabit exclusively in their own society or each on its own, in no need of being thought by my thought; whereas in this interior world where, like fish in an aquarium, words, images and ideas disport themselves, these mental entities, in order to exist, need the shelter which I provide; they are dependent on my consciousness.

This dependence is at once a disadvantage and an advantage. As I have just observed, it is the privilege of exterior objects to dispense with any interference from the mind. All they ask is to be let alone. They manage by themselves. But the same is surely not true of interior objects. By definition they are condemned to change their very nature, condemned to lose their materiality. They become images, ideas, words, that is to say purely mental entities. In sum, in order to exist as mental objects, they must relinquish their existence as real objects.

On the one hand, this is cause for regret. As soon as I replace my direct perception of reality by the words of a book, I deliver myself, bound hand and foot to the omnipotence of fiction. I say farewell to what is, in order to feign belief in what is not. I surround myself with fictitious beings; I become the prey of language. There is no escaping this takeover. Language surrounds me with its unreality.

On the other hand, the transmutation through language of reality into a fictional equivalent has undeniable advantages. The universe of fiction is infinitely more elastic than the world of objective reality. It lends itself to any use; it yields with little resistance to the importunities of the mind. Moreover—and of all its benefits I find this the most appealing—this interior universe constituted by language does not seem radically opposed to the *me* who thinks it. Doubtless what I glimpse through the words are mental forms not divested of an appearance of objectivity. But they do not seem to be of a nature other than my mind which thinks them. They are objects, but subjectified objects. In short, since everything has become part of my mind, thanks to the intervention of language, the opposition between the subject and its objects has been considerably attenuated. And thus the greatest advantage of literature is that I am persuaded by it that I am freed from my usual sense of incompatibility between my consciousness and its objects.

This is the remarkable transformation wrought in me through the act of reading. Not only does it cause the physical objects around me to disappear, including the very book I am reading, but it replaces those external objects with a congeries of mental objects in close *rapport* with my own consciousness. And yet the very intimacy in which I now live with my objects is going to present me with new problems. The most curious of these is the following: I am someone who happens to have as objects of his own thought, thoughts which are part of a book I am reading, and which are therefore the cogitations of another. They are the thoughts of another, and yet it is I who am their subject. The situation is even more astonishing than the one noted above. I am thinking the thoughts of another. Of course, there would be no cause for astonishment if I were thinking it as the thought of another. But I think it as my very own. Ordinarily there is the *I* which thinks, which recognizes itself (when it takes its bearings) in thoughts which may have come from elsewhere but which it takes upon itself as its own in the moment it thinks them. This is how we must take Diderot's declaration "Mes pensées sont *mes* catins" ("My thoughts are *my* whores"). That is, they sleep with everybody without ceasing to belong to their author. Now, in the present case things are quite different. Because of the strange invasion of my person by the thoughts of another, I am a self who is granted the experience of thinking thoughts foreign to him. I am the subject of thoughts other than my own. My consciousness behaves as though it were the consciousness of another.

This merits reflection. In a certain sense I must recognize that no idea really belongs to me. Ideas belong to no one. They pass from one mind to another as coins pass from hand to hand. Consequently, nothing could be more misleading than the attempt to define a consciousness by the ideas which it utters or enter-tains. But whatever these ideas may be, however strong the tie which binds them to their source, however transitory may be their sojourn in my own mind, so long as I entertain them I assert myself as subject of these ideas: I am the subjec-tive principle for whom the ideas serve for the time being as the predications. Furthermore, this subjective principle can in no wise be conceived as a predica-tion, as something which is discussed, referred to. It is I who think, who contem-plate, who am engaged in speaking. In short, it is never a *HE* but an *I*.

Now what happens when I read a book? Am I then the subject of a series of predications which are not *my* predications? That is impossible, perhaps even a contradiction in terms. I feel sure that as soon as I think something, that some-thing becomes in some indefinable way my own. Whatever I think is a part of *my* mental world. And yet here I am thinking a thought which manifestly belongs to another mental world, which is being thought in me just as though I did not exist. Already the notion is inconceivable and seems even more so if I reflect that, since every thought must have a subject to think it, this *thought* which is alien to me and yet in me, must also have in me a *subject* which is alien to me. It all hap-pens, then, as though reading were the act by which a thought managed to bestow itself within me with a subject not myself. Whenever I read, I mentally pronounce an *I,* and yet the *I* which I pronounce is not myself. This is true even when the hero of a novel is presented in the third person, and even when there is no hero and nothing but reflections or propositions: for as soon as something is presented as *thought,* there has to be a thinking subject with whom, at least for the time being, I identify, forgetting myself, alienated from myself, "JE est un autre," said Rimbaud. Another *I,* who has replaced my own, and who will con-tinue to do so as long as I read. Reading is just that: a way of giving way not only to a host of alien words, images, ideas, but also to the very alien principle which utters them and shelters them.

The phenomenon is indeed hard to explain, even to conceive, and yet, once admitted, it explains to me what might otherwise seem even more inexplicable. For how could I explain, without such takeover of my innermost subjective being, the astonishing facility with which I not only understand but even *feel* what I read. When I read as I ought, i.e., without mental reservation, without any desire to preserve my independence of judgment, and with the total commitment required of any reader, my comprehension becomes intuitive and any feeling pro-posed to me is immediately assumed by me. In other words, the kind of comprehension in question here is not a movement from the unknown to the known, from the strange to the familiar, from outside to inside. It might rather be called a phenomenon by which mental objects rise up from the depths of consciousness into the light of recognition. On the other hand—and without contradiction—reading implies something resembling the apperception I have of myself, the action by which I grasp straightaway what I think as being thought by a subject (who, in this case, is not I). Whatever sort of alienation I may endure, reading does not interpret my activity as subject.

Reading, then, is the act in which the subjective principle which I call *I,* is modified in such a way that I no longer have the right, strictly speaking, to consider it as my *I.* I am on loan to another, and this other thinks, feels, suffers, and acts within me. The phenomenon appears in its most obvious and even naivest form in the sort of spell brought about by certain cheap kinds of reading, such as thrillers, of which I say "It gripped me." Now it is important to note that this possession of myself by another takes place not only on the level of objective thought, that is with regard to images, sensations, ideas which reading affords me, but also on the level of my very subjectivity. When I am absorbed in reading, a second self takes over, a self which thinks and feels for me. Withdrawn in some recess of myself, do I then silently witness this dispossession? Do I derive from it some comfort or, on the contrary, a kind of anguish? However that may be, someone else holds the center of the stage, and the question which imposes itself, which I am absolutely obliged to ask myself, is this: "Who is the usurper who occupies the forefront? What is this mind who all alone by himself fills my consciousness and who, when I say *I,* is indeed that *I?*"

There is an immediate answer to this question, perhaps too easy an answer. This *I* who thinks in me when I read a book, is the *I* of the one who writes the book. When I read Baudelaire or Racine, it is really Baudelaire or Racine who thinks, feels, allows himself to be read within me. Thus a book is not only a book, it is the means by which an author actually preserves his ideas, his feelings, his modes of dreaming and living. It is his means of saving his identity from death. Such an interpretation of reading is not false. It seems to justify what is commonly called the biographical explication of literary texts. Indeed every word of literature is impregnated with the mind of the one who wrote it. As he makes us read it, he awakens in us the analogue of what he thought or felt. To understand a literary work, then, is to let the individual who wrote it reveal himself to us *in* us. It is not the biography which explicates the work, but rather the work which sometimes enables us to understand the biography.

But biographical interpretation is in part false and misleading. It is true that there is an analogy between the works of an author and the experiences of his life. The works may be seen as an incomplete translation of the life. And further, there is an even more significant analogy among all the works of a single author. Each of the works, however, while I am reading it, lives in me its own life. The subject who is revealed to me through my reading of it is not the author, either in the disordered totality of his outer experiences, or in the aggregate, better organized and concentrated totality, which is the one of his writings. Yet the subject which presides over the work can exist only in the work. To be sure, nothing is unimportant for understanding the work, and a mass of biographical, bibliographical, textual, and general critical information is indispensable to me. And yet this knowledge does not coincide with the internal knowledge of the work. Whatever may be the sum of the information I acquire on Baudelaire or Racine, in whatever degree of intimacy I may live with their genius. I am aware that this contribution (*apport*) does not suffice to illuminate for me in its own inner meaning, in its formal perfection, and in the subjective principle which animates it, the particular work of Baudelaire or Racine the reading of which now absorbs me. At this moment what matters to me is to live, from the inside, in a certain identity with the work and the work alone. It could hardly be otherwise. Nothing external to the work could possibly share the extraordinary claim which the work now exerts on me. It is there within me, not to send me back, outside itself, to its author, nor to his other writings, but on the contrary to keep my attention riveted on itself. It is the work which traces in me the very boundaries within which this consciousness will define itself. It is the work which forces on me a series of mental objects and creates in me a network of words, beyond which, for the time being, there will be no room for other mental objects or for other words. And it is the work, finally, which, not satisfied thus with defining the content of my consciousness, takes hold of it, appropriates it, and makes of it that *I* which, from one end of my reading to the other, presides over the unfolding of the work, of the single work which I am reading.

And so the work forms the temporary mental substance which fills my consciousness; and it is moreover that consciousness, the *I*-subject, the continued consciousness of what is, revealing itself within the interior of the work. Such is the characteristic condition of every work which I summon back into existence by placing my consciousness at its disposal. I give it not only existence, but awareness of existence. And so I ought not to hesitate to recognize that so long as it is animated by this vital inbreathing inspired by the act of reading, a work of literature becomes (at the expense of the reader whose own life it suspends) a sort of human being, that it is a mind conscious of itself and constituting itself in me as the subject of its own objects.

II

The work lives its own life within me; in a certain sense, it thinks itself, and it even gives itself a meaning within me.

This strange displacement of myself by the work deserves to be examined even more closely.

If the work thinks itself in me, does this mean that, during a complete loss of consciousness on my part, another thinking entity invades me, taking advantage of my unconsciousness in order to think itself without my being able to think it? Obviously not. The annexation of my consciousness by another (the other which is the work) in no way implies that I am the victim of any deprivation of consciousness. Everything happens, on the contrary, as though, from the moment I become a prey to what I read, I begin to share the use of my consciousness with this being who I have tried to define and who is the conscious subject ensconced at the heart of the work. He and I, we start having a common consciousness. Doubtless, within this community of feeling, the parts played by each of us are not of equal importance. The consciousness inherent in the work is active and potent; it occupies the foreground; it is clearly related to its own world, to objects which are *its* objects. In opposition, I myself, although conscious of whatever it may be conscious of, I play a much more humble role, content to record passively all that is going on in me. A lag takes place, a sort of schizoid distinction between what I feel and what the other feels; a confused awareness of delay, so that the work seems first to think by itself, and then to inform me what it has thought. Thus I often have the impression, while reading, of simply witnessing an action which at the same time concerns and yet does not concern me. This provokes a certain feeling of surprise within me. I am a consciousness astonished by an existence which is not mine, but which I experience as though it were mine.

This astonished consciousness is in fact the consciousness of the critic: the consciousness of a being who is allowed to apprehend as its own what is happening in the consciousness of another being. Aware of a certain gap, disclosing a feeling of identity, but of identity within difference, critical consciousness does not necessarily imply the total disappearance of the critic's mind in the mind to be criticized. From the partial and hesitant approximation of Jacques Rivière to the exalted, digressive and triumphant approximation of Charles Du Bos, criticism can pass through a whole series of nuances which we would be well advised to study. That is what I now propose to do. By discovering the various forms of identification and non-identification to be found in recent critical writing in French literature, I shall be able perhaps to give a better account of the variations of which this relationship—between criticizing subject and criticized object—is capable.

Let me take a first example. In the case of the first critic I shall speak of, this fusion of two consciousnesses is barely suggested. It is an uncertain movement of the mind toward an object which remains hidden. Whereas in the perfect identification of two consciousnesses, each sees itself reflected in the other, in this instance the critical consciousness can, at best, attempt but to draw closer to a reality which must remain forever veiled. In this attempt it uses the only mediators available to it in this quest, that is the senses. And since sight, the most intellectual of the five senses, seems in this particular case to come up against a basic opacity, the critical mind must approach its goal blindly, through the tactile exploration of surfaces, through a groping exploration of the material world which separates the critical mind from its object. Thus, despite the immense effort on the part of the sympathetic intelligence to lower itself to a level where it can, however lamely, make some progress in its quest toward the consciousness of the other, this enterprise is destined to failure. One senses that the unfortunate critic is condemned never to fulfill adequately his role as reader. He stumbles, he puzzles, he questions awkwardly a language which he is condemned never to read with ease; or rather, in trying to read the language, he uses a key which enables him to translate but a fraction of the text.

This critic is Jacques Rivière.

And yet it is from this failure that a much later critic will derive a more successful method of approaching a text. With this later critic, as with Rivière, the whole project begins with an attempt at identification on the most basic level. But this most primitive level is the one in which there flows, from mind to mind, a current which has only to be followed. To identify with the work means here, for the critic, to undergo the same experiences, beginning with the most elementary. On the level of indistinct thought, of sensations, emotions, images, and obsessions of preconscious life, it is possible for the critic to repeat, within himself, that life of which the work affords a first version, inexhaustibly revealing and suggestive. And yet such an imitation could not take place, in a domain so hard to define, without the aid of a powerful auxiliary. This auxiliary is language. There is no critical identification which is not prepared, realized, and incarnated through the agency of language. The deepest sentient life, hidden in the recesses of another's thoughts, could never be truly transposed, save for the mediation of words which allow a whole series of equivalences to arise. To describe this phenomenon as it takes place in the criticism I am speaking of now, I can no longer be content with the usual distinctions between the signifier (*signifiant*) and the signified (*signifié*) for what would it mean here to say that the language of the critic *signifies* the language of the literary work? There is not just equation, similitude. Words have attained a veritable power of recreation; they are a sort of material entity, solid and three-dimensional, thanks to which a certain life of the senses is reborn, finding in a network of verbal connotations the very conditions necessary for its replication. In other words, the language of criticism here dedicates itself to the business of mimicking physically the apperceptual world of the author. Strangely enough, the language of this sort of mimetic criticism becomes even more tangible, more tactile than the author's own; the poetry of the critic becomes more "poetic" than the poet's. This verbal *mimesis*, consciously exaggerated, is in no way servile, nor does it tend at all toward the pastiche. And yet it can reach its object only insofar as that object is deeply enmeshed in, almost confounded with, physical matter. This form of criticism is thus able to provide an admirable equivalent of the vital substratum which underlies all thought, and yet it seems incapable of attaining and expressing thought itself. This criticism is both helped and hindered by the language which it employs; helped, insofar as this language allows it to express the sensuous life in its original state, where it is still almost impossible to distinguish between subject and object; and yet hindered, too. because this language, too congealed and opaque, does not lend itself to analysis, and because the subjectivity which it evokes and describes is as though forever mired in its objects. And so the activity of criticism in this case is somehow incomplete, in spite of its remarkable successes. Identification relative to objects is accomplished almost too well; relative to subjectivity it is barely sketched.

This, then, is the criticism of Jean-Pierre Richard.

In its extreme form, in the abolition of any subject whatsoever, this criticism seems to extract from a literary work a certain condensed matter, a material essence.

But what, then, would be a criticism which would be the reverse, which would abolish the object and extract from the texts their must *subjective* elements?

To conceive such a criticism, I must leap to the opposite extreme. I imagine a critical language which would attempt deliberately to strip the literary language of anything concrete. In such a criticism it would be the artful aim of every line, of every sentence, of every metaphor, of every word, to reduce to the near nothingness of abstraction the images of the real world reflected by literature. If literature, by definition, is already a transportation of the real into the unreality of verbal conception, then the critical act in this case will constitute a transposition of this transposition, thus raising to the second power the "derealization" of being through language. In this way, the mind puts the maximum distance between its thought and what *is*. Thanks to this withdrawal, and to the consequent dematerialization of every object thus pushed to the vanishing point, the universe represented in this criticism seems not so much the equivalent of the perceivable world, or of its literary representation, as rather its image crystallized through a process of rigorous intellectualization. Here criticism is no longer mimesis; it is the reduction of all literary form to the same level of insignificance. In short, what survives this attempted annihilation of literature by the critical act? Nothing perhaps save a consciousness ceaselessly confronting the hollowness of mental objects, which yield without resistance, and an absolutely transparent language, which, by coating all objects with the same clear glaze, makes them ("like leaves seen far beneath the ice") appear to be infinitely far away. Thus, the language of this criticism plays a role exactly opposite to the function it has in Jean-Pierre Richard's criticism. It does indeed bring about the unification of critical thought with the mental world revealed by the literary work; but it brings it about at the expense of the work. Everything is finally annexed by the dominion of a consciousness detached from any object, a *hyper*-critical consciousness, functioning all alone, somewhere in the void.

Is there any need to say that this hyper-criticism is the critical thought of Maurice Blanchot?

I have found it useful to compare the criticism of Richard to the criticism of Blanchot. I learn from this confrontation that the critic's linguistic apparatus can, just as he chooses, bring him closer to the work under consideration, or can remove him from it indefinitely. If he so wishes, he can approximate very closely the work in question, thanks to a verbal mimesis which transposes into the critic's language the sensuous themes of the work. Or else he can make language a pure crystallizing agent, an absolute translucence, which, suffering no opacity to exist between subject and object, promotes the exercise of the cognitive power on the part of the subject, while at the same time accentuating in the object those characteristics which emphasize its infinite distance from the subject. In the first of the two cases, criticism achieves a remarkable *complicity,* but at the risk of losing its minimum lucidity; in the second case, it results in the most complete dissociation; the maximum lucidity thereby achieved only confirms a separation instead of a union.

Thus criticism seems to oscillate between two possibilities: a union without comprehension, and a comprehension without union. I may identify so completely with what I am reading that I lose consciousness not only of myself, but also of that other consciousness which lives within the work. Its proximity blinds me by blocking my prospect. But I may, on the other hand, separate myself so completely from what I am contemplating that the thought thus removed to a distance assumes the aspect of a being with whom I may never establish any relationship whatsoever. In either case, the act of reading has delivered me from egocentricity: another's thought inhabits me or haunts me, but in the first case I lose myself in that alien world, and in the other we keep our distance and refuse to identify. Extreme closeness and extreme detachment have then the same regrettable effect of making me fall short of the total critical act: that is to say, the exploration of that mysterious interrelationship which, through the mediation of reading and of language, is established to our mutual satisfaction between the work read and myself.

Thus extreme proximity and extreme separation each have grave disadvantages. And yet they have their privileges as well. Sensuous thought is privileged to move at once to the heart of the work and to share its own life; clear thought is privileged to confer on its objects the highest degree of intelligibility. Two sorts of insight are here distinguishable and mutually exclusive: there is penetration by the senses and penetration by the reflective consciousness. Now rather than contrasting these two forms of critical activity, would there not be some way, I wonder, not of practicing them simultaneously, which would be impossible, but at least of combining them through a kind of reciprocation and alternation?

Is not this perhaps the method used today by Jean Starobinski? For instance, it would not be difficult to find in his work a number of texts which relate him to Maurice Blanchot. Like Blanchot he displays exceptional lucidity and an acute awareness of distance. And yet he does not quite abandon himself to Blanchot's habitual pessimism. On the contrary, he seems inclined to optimism, even at times to a pleasant utopianism. Starobinski's intellect in this respect is analogous to that of Rousseau, yearning for an immediate transparence of all beings to each other which would enable them to understand each other in an ecstatic happiness. From this point of view, is not the ideal of criticism precisely represented by the *fête citadine* (street celebration) or *fête champêtre* (rustic feast)? There is a milieu or a moment in the feast in which everyone communicates with everyone else, in which hearts are open like books. On a more modest scale, doesn't the same phenomenon occur in reading? Does not one being open its innermost self? Is not the other being enchanted by this opening? In the criticism of Starobinski we often find that crystalline temp of music, that pure delight in understanding, that perfect sympathy between an intelligence which enters and that intelligence which welcomes it.

In such moments of harmony, there is no longer any exclusion, no inside or outside. Contrary to Blanchot's belief, perfect translucence does not result in separation. On the contrary, with Starobinski, all is perfect agreement, joy shared, the pleasure of understanding and of being understood. Moreover, such pleasure, however intellectual it may be, is not here exclusively a pleasure of the mind. For the relationship established on this level between author and critic is not a relationship between pure minds. It is rather between incarnate beings, and the particularities of their physical existence constitute not obstacles to understanding, but rather a complex of supplementary signs, a veritable language which must be deciphered and which enhances mutual comprehension. Thus for Starobinski, as much physician as critic, there is a reading of *bodies* which is likened to the reading of *minds*. It is not of the same nature, nor does it bring the intelligence to bear on the same area of human knowledge. But for the critic who practices it, this criticism provides the opportunity for a reciprocating exchange between dif-ferent types of learning which have, perhaps, different degrees of transparency.

Starobinski's criticism, then, displays great flexibility. Rising at times to the heights of metaphysics, it does not disdain the farthest reaches of the subcon-scious. It is sometimes intimate, sometimes detached; it assumes all the degrees of identification and non-identification. But its final movement seems to consist in a sort of withdrawal, contradistinction with its earlier accord. After an initial inti-macy with the object under study, this criticism has finally to detach itself, to move on, but this time in solitude. Let us not see this withdrawal as a failure of sympathy but rather as a way of avoiding the encumbrances of too prolonged a life in common. Above all we discern an acute need to establish bearings, to adopt the judicious perspective, to assess the fruits of proximity by examining them at a distance. Thus, Starobinski's criticism always ends with a view from afar, or rather from above, for while moving away it has also moved imperceptibly toward a dominating (*surplombante*) position. Does this mean that Starobinski's criticism like Blanchot's is doomed to end in a philosophy of separation? This, in a way, must be conceded, and it is no coincidence that Starobinski treats with spe-cial care the themes of melancholy and nostalgia. His criticism always concludes with a double farewell. But this farewell is exchanged by two beings who have begun by living together; and the one left behind continues to be illuminated by that critical intellect which moves on.

The sole fault with which I might reproach such criticism is the excessive ease with which it penetrates what it illuminates.

By dint of seeing in literary works only the thoughts which inhabit them, Starobinski's criticism somehow passes through their forms, not neglecting them, it is true, but without pausing on the way. Under its action literary works lose their opacity, their solidity, their objective dimension; like those palace walls which become transparent in certain fairy tales. And if it is true that the ideal act of criticism must seize (and reproduce) that certain relationship between an object and a mind which is the work itself, how could the act of criticism succeed when it suppresses one of the (polar) terms of this relationship?

My search must continue, then, for a criticism in which this relationship sub-sists. Could it perhaps be the criticism of Marcel Raymond and Jean Rousset? Raymond's criticism always recognizes the presence of a double reality, both mental and formal. It strives to comprehend almost simultaneously in inner expe-rience and a perfected form. On the one hand, no one allows himself to be absorbed with such complete self-forgetfulness into the thought of another. But the other's thought is grasped not at its highest, but at its most obscure, at its cloudiest point, at the point at which it is reduced to being a mere self-awareness scarcely perceived by the being which entertains it, and which yet to the eyes of the critic seems the sole means of access by which he can penetrate within the precincts of the alien mind.

But Raymond's criticism presents another aspect which is precisely the reverse of this confused identification of the critic's thought with the thought crit-icized. It is then the reflective contemplation of a formal reality which is the work itself. The work stands *before* the critical intelligence as a perfected object, which is in fact an enigma, an external thing existing in itself and with which there is no possibility of identification nor of inner knowledge.

Thus Raymond perceives sometimes a subject, sometimes an object. The subject is pure mind; it is a sheer indefinable presence, an almost inchoate entity, into which, by very virtue of its absence of form, it becomes possible for the critic's mind to penetrate. The work, on the contrary, exists only within a definite form, but this definition limits it, encloses it within its own contours, at the same time constraining the mind which studies it to remain on the outside. So that, if on the one hand the critical thought of Raymond tends to lose itself within an undefined subjectivity, on the other it tends to come to a stop before an impenetrable objectivity.

Admirably gifted to submit his own subjectivity to that of another, and thus to immerse itself in the obscurest depths of every mental entity, the mind of Raymond is less well equipped to penetrate the obstacle presented by the objective surface of the works. He then finds himself marking time, or moving in circles around the work, as around the vase or the statue mentioned before. Does Raymond then establish an insurmountable partition between the two realities—subjective, objective—unified though they may be in the work? No, indeed, at least not in his best essays, since in them, by careful intuitive apprehension of the text and participation by the critic in the powers active in the poet's use of language, there appears some kind of link between the objective aspects of the work and the undefined subjectivity which sustains it. A link not to be confused with a pure relation of identity. The perception of the formal aspects of the work becomes somehow an analogical language by means of which it becomes possible for the critic to go, within the work, beyond the formal aspects it presents. Nevertheless this association is never presented by Raymond as a dialectical process. The usual state described by his method of criticism is one of plentitude, and even of a double plenitude. A certain fullness of experience detected in the poet and relived in the mind of the critic, is connected by the latter with a certain perfection of form: but why this is so, and how it does become so, is never clearly explained.

Now is it then possible to go one step further? This is what is attempted by Jean Rousset, a former student of Raymond and perhaps his closest friend. He also dedicates himself to the task of discerning the structure of a work as well as the depth of an experience. Only what essentially matters to him is to establish a connection between the objective reality of the work and the organizing power which gives it shape. A work is not explained for him, as for the structuralists, by the exclusive interdependence of the objective elements which compose it. He does not see in it a fortuitous combination, interpreted *a posteriori* as if it were an *a priori* organization. There is not in his eyes any system of the work without a principle of systematization which operates in correlation with that work and which is even included in it. In short, there is no spider-web without a center which is the spider. On the other hand, it is not a question of going from the work to the psychology of the author, but of going back, within the sphere of the work, from the objective elements systematically arranged, to a certain power of organization, inherent in the work itself, as if the latter showed itself to be an intentional consciousness determining its arrangements and solving its problems. So that it would scarcely be an abuse of terms to say that is speaks, by means of its structural elements, an authentic language, thanks to which it discloses itself and means nothing but itself. Such then is the critical enterprise of Jean Rousset. It sets itself to use the objective elements of the work in order to attain, beyond them, a reality not formal, nor objective, written down however in forms and expressing itself by means of them. Thus the understanding of forms must not limit itself merely to the recording of their objective aspects. As Focillion demonstrated from the point of view of art history, there is a "life of forms" perceptible not only in the historic development which they display from epoch to epoch, but within each single work, in the movement by which forms tend therein sometimes to stabilize and become static, and sometimes to change into one another. Thus the two contradictory forces which are always at work in any literary writing, the will to stability and the protean impulse, help us to perceive by their interplay how much forms are dependent on what Coleridge called a shaping power which determines them, replaces them and transcends them. The teaching of Raymond finds then its most satisfying success in the critical method of Jean Roussett, a method which leads the seeker from the continuously changing frontiers of form to what is beyond form.

It is fitting then to conclude this inquiry here, since it has achieved its goal, namely to describe, relying on a series of more or less adequate examples, a critical method having as guiding principle the relation between subject and object. Yet there remains one last difficulty. In order to establish the interrelationship between subject and object, which is the principle of all creative work and of the understanding of it, two ways, at least theoretically, are opened, one leading from the objects to the subject, the other from the subject to the objects. Thus we have seen Raymond and Rousset, through perception of the objective structures of a literary work, strive to attain the subjective principle which upholds it. But, in so doing, they seem to recognize the precedence of the subject over its objects. What Raymond and Rousset are searching for in the objective and formal aspects of the work, is something which is previous to the work and on which the work depends for its very existence. So that the method which leads from the object to the subject does not differ radically at bottom from the one which leads from subject to object, since it does really consist in going from subject to subject through the object. Yet there is the risk of overlooking an important point. The aim of criticism is not achieved merely by the understanding of the part played by the subject in its interrelation with objects. When reading a literary work, there is a moment when it seems to me that the subject present in this work disengages itself from all that surrounds it, and stands alone. Had I not once the intuition of this, when visiting the Scuola di San Rocco in Venice, one of the highest summits of art, where there are assembled so many paintings of the same painter, Tintoretto? When looking at all these masterpieces brought there together and revealing so manifestly their unity of inspiration. I had suddenly the impression of having reached the common essence present in all the works of a great master, an essence which I was not able to perceive, except when emptying my mind of all the particular images created by the artist. I became aware of a subjective power at work in all these pictures, and yet never so clearly understood by my mind as when I had forgotten all their particular figurations.

One may ask oneself: What is this subject left standing in isolation after all examination of a literary work? Is it the individual genius of the artist, visibly present in his work, yet having an invisible life independent of the work? Or is it, as Valéry thinks, an anonymous and abstract consciousness presiding, in its aloofness, over the operations of all more concrete consciousness? Whatever it may be, I am constrained to acknowledge that all subjective activity present in a literary work is not entirely explained by its relationship with forms and objects within the work. There is in the work a mental activity profoundly engaged in objective forms; and there is, at another level, forsaking all forms, a subject which reveals itself to itself (and to me) in its transcendence over all which is reflected in it. At this point, no object can any longer express it, no structure can any longer define it; it is exposed in its ineffability and in its fundamental indeterminacy. Such is perhaps the reason why the critic, in his elucidation of works, is haunted by this transcendence of mind. It seems then that criticism, in order to accompany the mind in this effort of detachment from itself, needs to annihilate, or at least momentarily to forget, the objective elements of the work, and to elevate itself to the apprehension of a subjectivity without objectivity.

Jonathan Culler (1944–)

Culler has written widely on literary theory from the 1970s to the present. One of his longstanding objectives is to promote poetics rather than hermeneutics as a critical approach in literary studies. Hermeneutics is a methodological approach that seeks to provide new meanings, through interpretation, to literary texts. The aim of poetics, as Culler defines it in the preface to one of his early books, *Structuralist Poetics* (1975), is different: poetics "strives to define the conditions of meaning. Granting new attention to the activity of reading, it would attempt to specify how we go about making sense of texts, what are the interpretive operations on which literature itself, as an institution, is based." In books like *Structuralist Poetics* and *Ferdinand de Saussure* (1986), Culler also helps American critics and students of literature better understand the positive influences of linguistics for literary study. In *On Deconstruction: Theory and Criticism after Structuralism* (1982), Culler analyzes the rise of deconstruction and helps American critics assess the impact of certain theories and practices of Jacques Derrida and Paul De Man on English studies.

Culler received an A.B. in history and literature from Harvard (1966) and went to St. John's College at Oxford on a Rhodes Scholarship (1966–1969). At St. John's, he earned a Ph.D. in modern languages (1972). Since 1977, Culler has taught literature and theory at Cornell University. He has continued to write about theory in books such as *Literary Theory: A Very Short Introduction* (1997) and *Framing the Sign: Criticism and Its Institutions* (1987). He has also written about undergraduate curriculum issues, such as in his essay "Imagining the Coherence of the English Major," which appeared in the Winter 2003 *ADE*

Bulletin. The essay included here, "Literary Competence," is a chapter from *Structuralist Poetics* and builds on some of Roland Barthes's theories of textual analysis that strive, in Culler's words, to "make explicit the underlying system which makes literary effects possible."

Literary Competence

> *To understand a sentence means*
> *to understand a language. To*
> *understand a language means to*
> *be master of a technique.*
>
> Wittgenstein

When a speaker of a language hears a phonetic sequence, he is able to give it meaning because he brings to the act of communication an amazing repertoire of conscious and unconscious knowledge. Mastery of the phonological, syntactic and semantic systems of his language enables him to convert the sounds into discrete units, to recognize words, and to assign a structural description and interpretation to the resulting sentence, even though it be quite new to him. Without this implicit knowledge, this internalized grammar, the sequence of sounds does not speak to him. We are nevertheless inclined to say that the phonological and grammatical structure and the meaning are *properties* of the utterance, and there is no harm in that way of speaking so long as we remember that they are properties of the utterance only with respect to a particular grammar. Another grammar would assign different properties to the sequence (according to the grammar of a different language, for example, it would be nonsense). To speak of the structure of a sentence is necessarily to imply an internalized grammar that gives it that structure.

We also tend to think of meaning and structure as properties of literary works, and from one point of view this is perfectly correct: when the sequence of words is treated *as a literary work* it has these properties. But that qualification suggests the relevance and importance of the linguistic analogy. The work has structure and meaning because it is read in a particular way, because these potential properties, latent in the object itself, are actualized by the theory of discourse applied in the act of reading. "How can one discover structure without the help of a methodological model?" asks Barthes (*Critique et vérité,* p. 19). To read a text as literature is not to make one's mind a *tabula rasa* and approach it without preconceptions; one must bring to it an implicit understanding of the operations of literary discourse which tells one what to look for.

Anyone lacking this knowledge, anyone wholly unacquainted with literature and unfamiliar with the conventions by which fictions are read, would, for example, be quite baffled if presented with a poem. His knowledge of the language would enable him to understand phrases and sentences, but he would not know, quite literally, what to *make* of this strange concatenation of phrases. He would be unable to read it *as* literature—as we say with emphasis to those who would use literary works for other purpose—because he lacks the complex "literary competence" which enables others to proceed. He has not internalized the "grammar" of literature which would permit him to convert linguistic sequences into literary structures and meanings.

If the analogy seems less than exact it is because in the case of language it is much more obvious that understanding depends on mastery of a system. But the time and energy devoted to literary training in schools and universities indicate that the understanding of literature also depends on experience and mastery. Since literature is a second-order semiotic system which has language as its basis, a knowledge of language will take one a certain distance in one's encounter with literary texts, and it may be difficult to specify precisely where understanding comes to depend on one's supplementary knowledge of literature. But the difficulty of drawing a line does not obscure the palpable difference between understanding the language of a poem, in the sense that one could provide a rough translation into another language, and understanding the poem. If one knows French, one can translate Mallarmé's "Salut", but that translation is not a thematic synthesis—it is not what we would ordinarily call "understanding the poem"—and in order to identify various levels of coherence and set them in relation to one another under the synoptic heading or theme of the "literary quest" one must have considerable experience of the conventions for reading poetry.

The easiest way to grasp the importance of these conventions is to take a piece of journalistic prose or a sentence from a novel and set it down on the page as a poem. The properties assigned to the sentence by a grammar of English remain unchanged, and the different meanings which the text acquires cannot therefore be attributed to one's knowledge of the language but must be ascribed to the special conventions for reading poetry which lead one to look at the language in new ways, to make relevant properties of the language which were previously unexploited, to subject the text to a different series of interpretive operations. But one can also show the importance of these conventions by measuring the distance between the language of a poem and its critical interpretation—a distance bridged by the conventions of reading which comprise the institution of poetry.

Anyone who knows English understands the language of Blake's "Ah! Sun-flower":

> Ah, Sun-flower, weary of time,
> Who countest the steps of the Sun,
> Seeking after that sweet golden clime
> Where the traveller's journey is done:
>
> Where the Youth pined away with desire,
> And the pale Virgin shrouded in snow
> Arise from their graves, and aspire
> Where my Sun-flower wishes to go.

But there is some distance between an understanding of the language and the thematic statement with which a critic concludes his discussion of the poem: "Blake's dialectical thrust at asceticism is more than adroit. You do not surmount Nature by denying its prime claim of sexuality. Instead you fall utterly into the dull round of its cyclic aspirations."[1] How does one reach this reading? What are the operations which lead from the text to this representation of understanding? The primary convention is what might be called the rule of significance: read the poem as expressing a significant attitude to some problem concerning man and/or his relation to the universe. The sunflower is therefore given the value of an emblem and the metaphors of "counting" and "seeking" are taken not just as figurative indications of the flower's tendency to turn towards the sun but as metaphorical operators which make the sunflower an instance of the human aspirations compassed by these two lines. The conventions of metaphorical coherence—that one should attempt through semantic transformations to produce coherence on the levels of both tenor and vehicle—lead one to oppose time to eternity and to make "that sweet golden clime" both the sunset which marks the closure of the daily temporal cycle and the eternity of death when "the traveller's journey is done". The identification of sunset and death is further justified by the convention which allows one to inscribe the poem in a poetic tradition. More important, however, is the convention of thematic unity, which forces one to give the youth and virgin of the second stanza a role which justifies choosing them as examples of aspiration; and since the semantic feature they share is a repression of sexuality, one must find a way of integrating that with the rest of the poem. The curious syntactic structure, with three clauses each depending on a "where," provides a way of doing this:

> The Youth and the Virgin have denied their sexuality to win the allegorical abode of the conventionally visualized heaven. Arriving there, they arise from their graves to be trapped in the same cruel cycle of longings; they are merely at the sunset and aspire to go where the Sun-flower seeks his rest, which is precisely where they already are.[2]

Such interpretations are not the result of subjective associations. They are public and can be discussed and justified with respect to the conventions of reading poetry—or, as English allows us to say, of *making* sense. Such conventions are the constituents of the institution of literature, and in this perspective one can see that is may well be misleading to speak of poems as harmonious totalities, autonomous natural organisms, complete in themselves and bearing a rich immanent meaning. The semiological approach suggests, rather, that the poem be thought of as an utterance that has meaning only with respect to a system of conventions which the reader has assimilated. If other conventions were operative its range of potential meanings would be different.

Literature, as Genette says, "like any other activity of the mind, is based on conventions of which, with some exceptions, it is not aware" (*Figures*, p. 258). One can think of these conventions not simply as the implicit knowledge of the reader but also as the implicit knowledge of authors. To write a poem or a novel is immediately to engage with a literary tradition or at the very least with a certain idea of the poem or the novel. The activity is made possible by the existence of the genre, which the author can write against, certainly, whose conventions he may attempt to subvert, but which is nonetheless the context within which his activity takes place, as surely as the failure to keep a promise is made possible by the institution of promising. Choices between words, between sentences, between different modes of presentation, will be made on the basis of their effects; and the notion of effect presupposes modes of reading which are not random or haphazard. Even if the author does not think of readers, he is himself a reader of his own work and will not be satisfied with it unless he can read it as producing effects. One would find very strange the notion of a poet saying, "when I reflect on the sunflower I have a particular feeling, which I shall call 'p' and which I think can be connected with another feeling which I shall call 'q'," and then writing "if p then q" as a poem on the sunflower. This would not be a poem because even the poet himself cannot read the meanings in that series of signs. He can take them as referring to the feelings in question, but that is very much another matter. His text does not explore, evoke or even make use of the feelings, and he will be unable to read it as if it did. To experience any of the satisfactions of having written a poem he must create an order of words which he can read according to the conventions of poetry: he cannot simply assign meaning but must make possible, for himself and for others, the production of meaning.

"Every work," wrote Valéry, "is the work of many things besides an author;" and he proposed that literary history be replaced by a poetics which would study "the conditions of the existence and development of literature." Among all the arts, it is "the one in which convention plays the greatest role," and even those authors who may have thought their works due only to personal inspiration and the application of genius

> had developed, without suspecting it, a whole system of habits and notions which were the fruit of their experience and indispensable to the process of production. However little they might have suspected all the definitions, all the conventions, the logic and the system of combinations that composition presupposes, however much they believed that they owed nothing but to the instant itself, their work necessarily called into play all these procedures and these inevitable operations of the mind.[3]

The conventions of poetry, the logic of symbols, the operations for the production of poetic effects, are not simply the property of readers but the basis of literary forms. However, for a variety of reasons it is easier to study them as the operations performed by readers than as the institutional context taken for granted by authors. The statements authors make about the process of composition are notoriously problematic, and there are few ways of determining what they are taking for granted. Whereas the meanings readers give to literary works and the effects they experience are much more open to observation. Hypotheses about the conventions and operations which produce these effects can therefore be tested not only by their ability to account for the effects in question but by their ability, when applied to other poems, to account for the effects experienced in those cases. Moreover, when one is investigating the process of reading one can make alterations in the language of a text so as to see how this changes literary effects, whereas that kind of experimentation is not possible if one is investigating the conventions assumed by authors, who are not available to give their reactions to the effects of proposed alterations in their texts. As the example of transformational grammar suggests, the best way of producing a formal representation of the implicit knowledge of both speakers and hearers is to present sentences to oneself or to colleagues and then to formulate rules which account for the hearers' judgments about meaning, well-formedness, deviance, constituent structure, and ambiguity.

To speak, therefore, as I shall do, of literary competence as a set of conventions for reading literary texts is in no way to imply that authors are congenital idiots who simply produce strings of sentences, while all the truly creative work is done by readers who have artful ways of processing these sentences. Structuralist discussions may seem to promote such a view by their failure to isolate and praise an author's "conscious art", but the reason is simply that here, as in most other human activities of any complexity, the line between the conscious and the unconscious is highly variable, impossible to identify, and supremely uninteresting. "*When* do you know how to play chess? All the time? or just while you are making a move? And the *whole* of chess during each move?"[4] When driving a car is it consciously or unconsciously that you keep to the correct side of the road, change gears, apply the brakes, dip the headlights? To ask of what an author is conscious and of what unconscious is as fruitless as to ask which rules of English are consciously employed by speakers and which are followed unconsciously. Mastery may be largely unconscious or it may have reached a stage of highly self-conscious theoretical elaboration, but it is mastery in both cases. Nor does one in any way impugn the author's talent in speaking of his mastery as an ability to construct artefacts which prove extremely rich when subjected to the operations of reading.

The task of a structuralist poetics, as Barthes defines it, would be to make explicit the underlying system which makes literary effects possible. It would not be a "science of contents" which, in hermeneutic fashion, proposed interpretations for works,

> but a science of the conditions of content, that is to say of forms. What interests it will be the variations of meaning generated and, as it were, capable of being generated by works; it will not interpret symbols but describe their polyvalency. In short, its object will not be the full meanings of the work but on the contrary the empty meaning which supports them all. (*Critique et vérité*, p. 57)

In this sense structuralism effects an important reversal of perspective, granting precedence to the task of formulating a comprehensive theory of literary discourse and assigning a secondary place to the interpretation of individual texts. Whatever the benefits of interpretation to those who engage in it, within the context of poetics it becomes an ancillary activity—a way of using literary works—as opposed to the study of literature itself as an institution. To say that is in no way to condemn interpretation, as the linguistic analogy should make perfectly evident. Most people are more interested in using language to communicate than in studying the complex linguistic system which underlies communication, and they need not feel that their interests are threatened by those who make the study of linguistic competence a coherent and autonomous discipline. Similarly, a structuralist poetics would claim that the study of literature involves only indirectly the critical act of placing a work in situation, reading it as a gesture of a particular kind, and thus giving it a meaning. The task is rather to construct a theory of literary discourse which would account for the possibilities of interpretation, the "empty meanings" which support a variety of full meanings but which do not permit the work to be given just any meaning.

This would not need to be said if interpretive criticism had not tried to persuade us that the study of literature means the elucidation of individual works. But in this cultural context it is important to reflect on what has been lost or obscured in the practice of an interpretive criticism which treats each work as an autonomous artefact, an organic whole whose parts all contribute to a complex thematic statement. The notion that the task of criticism is to reveal thematic unity is a post-Romantic concept, whose roots in the theory of organic form are, at the very least, ambiguous. The organic unity of a plant is not easily translated into thematic unity, and we are willing to admit that the botanical gaze be allowed to compare one plant with another, isolating similarities and differences, or to dwell on formal organization without immediately invoking some teleological purpose or thematic unity. Nor has discourse on literature always been so imperiously committed to interpretation. It used to be possible, in the days before the poem became pre-eminently the act of an individual and emotion recollected in tranquillity, to study its interaction with norms of rhetoric and genre, the relation of its formal features to those of the tradition, without feeling immediately compelled to produce an interpretation which would demonstrate their thematic relevance. One did not need to move from poem to world but could explore it within the institution of literature, relating it to a tradition and identifying formal continuities and discontinuities. That this should have been possible may tell us something important about literature or at least lead us to reflect on the possibility of loosening interpretation's hold on critical discourse.

Such loosening is important because if the analyst aims at understanding how literature works he must, as Northrop Frye says, set about "formulating the broad laws of literary experience, and in short writing as though he believed that there is a totally intelligible structure of knowledge attainable about poetry, which is not poetry itself, or the experience of it, but poetics" (*Anatomy of Criticism*, p. 14). Few have put the case for poetics more forcefully than Frye, but in his perspective, as this quotation shows, the relationship between poetry, the experience of poetry and poetics remains somewhat obscure, and that obscurity affects his later formulations. His discussions of modes, symbols, myths and genres lead to the production of taxonomies which capture something of the richness of literature, but the status of his taxonomic categories is curiously indeterminate. What is their relation to literary discourse and to the activity of reading? Are the four mythic categories of Spring, Summer, Autumn and Winter devices for classifying literary works or categories on which the experience of literature is based? As soon as one asks why these categories are to be preferred to those of other possible taxonomies it becomes evident that there must be something implicit in Frye's theoretical framework which needs to be made explicit.

The linguistic model provides a slight reorientation which makes apparent what is needed. Study of the linguistic system becomes theoretically coherent when we cease thinking that our goal is to specify the properties of objects in a corpus and concentrate instead on the task of formulating the internalized competence which enables objects to have the properties they do for those who have mastered the system. To discover and characterize structures one must analyse the system which assigns structural descriptions to the objects in question, and thus a literary taxonomy should be grounded on a theory of reading. The relevant categories are those which are required to account for the range of acceptable meanings which works can have for readers of literature.

The notion of literary competence or of a literary system is, of course, anathema to some critics, who see in it an attack on the spontaneous, creative and affective qualities of literature. Moreover, they might argue, the very concept of literary competence, which carries the presumption that we can distinguish between competent and incompetent readers, is objectionable for precisely those reasons which lead one to propose it: the postulation of a norm for "correct" reading. In other human activities where there are clear criteria for success and failure, such as playing chess or climbing mountains, we can speak of competence and incompetence, but the richness and power of literature depend, precisely, on the fact that it is not an activity of this kind and that appreciation is varied, personal, and not subject to the normative legislation of self-styled experts.

Such arguments, however, would seem to miss the point. None would deny that literary works, like most other objects of human attention, can be enjoyed for reasons that have little do with understanding and mastery—that texts can be quite blatantly misunderstood and still be appreciated for a variety of personal reasons. But to reject the notion of misunderstanding as a legislative imposition is to leave unexplained the common experience of being shown where one went wrong, of grasping a mistake and seeing why it was a mistake. Though acquiescence may occasionally be disgruntled yielding to a higher authority, none would maintain that it was always thus; more often one feels that one has indeed been shown the way to a fuller understanding of literature and a better grasp of the procedures of reading. If the distinction between understanding and misunderstanding were irrelevant, if neither party to a discussion believed in the distinction, there would be little point to discussing and arguing about literary works and still less to writing about them.

Moreover, the claims of schools and universities to offer literary training cannot be lightly dismissed. To believe that the whole institution of literary education is but a gigantic confidence trick, would strain even a determined credulity, for it is, alas, only too clear that knowledge of a language and a certain experience of the world do not suffice to make someone a perceptive and competent reader. That achievement requires acquaintance with a range of literature and in many cases some form of guidance. The time and effort devoted to literary education by generations of students and teachers create a strong presumption that there is something to be learned, and teachers do not hesitate to judge their pupil's progress towards a general literary competence. Most would claim, no doubt with good reason, that their examinations are designed not simply to determine whether their students have read various set works but to test their acquisition of an ability.

"Everyone who has seriously studied literature," Northrop Frye maintains, "knows that the mental process involved is as coherent and progressive as the study of science. A precisely similar training of the mind takes place, and a similar sense of the unity of the subject is built up" (*ibid.*, pp. 10–11). If that seems overstated it is no doubt because what is explicit in the teaching of science usually remains implicit in the teaching of literature. But it is clear that study of one poem or novel facilitates the study of the next: one gains not only points of comparison but a sense of how to read. One develops a set of questions which experience shows to be appropriate and productive and criteria for determining whether they are, in a given case, productive; one acquires a sense of the possibilities of literature and how these possibilities may be distinguished. We may speak, if we like, of extrapolating from one work to another, so long as we do not thereby obscure the fact that the process of extrapolation is precisely what requires explanation. To account for extrapolation, to explain what are the formal questions and distinctions whose relevance the student learns, would be to formulate a theory of literary competence. If we are to make any sense at all of the process of literary education and of criticism itself we must, as Frye argues, assume the possibility of "a coherent and comprehensive theory of literature, logically and scientifically organized, some of which the student unconsciously learns as he goes on, but the main principles of which are as yet unknown to us" (p. 11).

It is easy to see why, from this perspective, linguistics offers an attractive methodological analogy: a grammar, as Chomsky says, "can be regarded as a theory of a language", and the theory of literature of which Frye speaks can be regarded as the "grammar" or literary competence which readers have assimilated but of which they may not be consciously aware. To make the implicit explicit is the task of both linguistics and poetics, and generative grammar has placed renewed emphasis on two fundamental requirements for theories of this kind: that they state their rules as formal operations (since what they are investigating is a kind of intelligence they cannot take for granted intelligence used in applying rules but must make them as explicit as possible) and that they be testable (they must reproduce, as it were, attested facts about semiotic competence).

Can this step be taken in literary criticism? The major obstacle would seem to be that of determining what will count as evidence about literary competence. In linguistics it is not difficult to identify facts that an adequate grammar must account for: though one may need to speak of "degrees of grammaticalness" one can produce lists of sentences which are incontestably well formed and sentences which are unquestionably deviant. Moreover, we have a sufficiently strong intuitive sense of paraphrase relations to be able to say roughly what a sentence means for speakers of a language. In the study of literature, however, the situation is considerably more complex. Notions of "well-formed" or "intelligible" literary works are notoriously problematic, and it may be difficult to secure agreement about what should count as a proper "understanding" of a text. That critics should differ so widely in their interpretations might seem to undermine any notion of a general literary competence.

But in order to overcome this apparent obstacle we have only to ask what we want a theory of literature to account for. We cannot ask it to account for the "correct" meaning of a work since we manifestly do not believe that for each work there is a single correct reading. We cannot ask it to draw a clear line between the well-formed and the deviant work if we believe that no such line exists. Indeed, the striking facts that do require explanation are how it is that a work can have a variety of meanings but not just any meaning whatsoever or how it is that some works give an impression of strangeness, incoherence, incomprehensibility. The model does not imply that there must be unanimity on any particular count. It suggests only that we must designate a set of facts, of whatever kind, which seem to require explanation and then try to construct a model of literary competence which would account for them.

The facts can be of many kinds: that a given prose sentence has different meanings if set down as a poem, that readers are able to recognize the plot of a novel, that some symbolic interpretations of a poem are more plausible than others, that two characters in a novel contrast with one another, that *The Waste Land* or *Ulysses* once seemed strange and now seems intelligible. Poetics bears, as Barthes says, not so much on the work itself as on its intelligibility (*Critique et vérité*, p. 62) and therefore problematic cases—the work which some find intelligible and others incoherent, or the work which is read differently in two different periods—furnish the most decisive evidence about the system of operative conventions. Any work can be made intelligible if one invents appropriate conventions: the most obscure poem could be interpreted if there were a convention which permitted us to replace every lexical item by a word beginning with the same letter of the alphabet and chosen according to the ordinary demands of coherence. There are numerous other bizarre conventions which might be operative if the institution of literature were different, and hence the difficulty of interpreting some works provides evidence of the restricted nature of the conventions actually in force in a culture. Moreover, if a difficult work later becomes intelligible it is because new ways of reading have been developed in order to meet what is the fundamental demand of the system: the demand for sense. A comparison of old and new readings will shed light on the change in the institution of literature.

As in linguistics, there is no automatic procedure for obtaining information about competence, but there is no dearth of facts to be explained.[5] To take surveys of the behaviour of readers would serve little purpose, since one is interested not in performance itself but in the tacit knowledge or competence which underlies it. Performance may not be a direct reflection of competence, for behaviour can be influenced by a host of irrelevant factors: I may not have been paying attention at a given moment, may have been led astray by purely personal associations, may have forgotten something important from an earlier part of the text, may have made what I would recognize as a mistake if it were pointed out to me. One's concern is with the tacit knowledge that recognition of a mistake would show rather than with the mistake itself, and so even if one were to take surveys one would still have to judge whether particular reactions were in fact a direct reflection of competence. The question is not what actual readers happen to do but what an ideal reader must know implicitly in order to read and interpret works in ways which we consider acceptable, in accordance with the institution of literature.

The ideal reader is, of course, a theoretical construct, perhaps best thought of as a representation of the central notion of acceptability. Poetics, Barthes writes, "will describe the logic according to which meanings are engendered in ways that can be *accepted* by man's logic of symbols, just as the sentences of French are *accepted* by the linguistic intuitions of Frenchmen" (*Critique et vérité*, p. 63). Though there is no automatic procedure for determining what is acceptable, that does not matter, for one's proposals will be sufficiently tested by one's readers' acceptance or rejection of them. If readers do not accept the facts one sets out to explain as bearing any relation to their knowledge and experience of literature, then one's theory will be of little interest; and therefore the analyst must convince his readers that meanings or effects which he is attempting to account for are indeed appropriate ones. The meaning of a poem within the institution of literature is not, one might say, the immediate and spontaneous reaction of individual readers but the meanings which they are willing to accept as both plausible and justifiable when they are explained. "Ask yourself: How does one *lead* anyone to comprehension of a poem or of a theme? The answer to this tells us how meaning is to be explained here."[6] The paths by which the reader is led to comprehension are precisely those of the logic of literature: the effects must be related to the poem in such a way that the reader sees the connection to be just in terms of his own knowledge of literature.

One cannot therefore emphasize too strongly that every critic, whatever his persuasion, encounters the problems of literary competence as soon as he begins to speak or write about literary works, and that he takes for granted notions of acceptability and common ways of reading. The critic would not write unless he thought he had something new to say about a text, yet he assumes that his reading is not a random and idiosyncratic phenomenon. Unless he thinks that he is merely recounting to others the adventures of his own subjectivity, he claims that his interpretation is related to the text in ways which he presumes his readers will accept once those relations are pointed out: either they will accept his interpretation as an explicit version of what they intuitively felt or they will recognize from their own knowledge of literature the justice of the operations that lead the critic from text to interpretation. Indeed, the possibility of critical argument depends on shared notions of the acceptable and the unacceptable, a common ground which is nothing other than the procedures of reading. The critic must invariably make decisions about what can in fact be taken for granted, what must be explicitly defended, and what constitutes an acceptable defence. He must show his readers that the effects he notices fall within the compass of an implicit logic which they are presumed to accept; and thus he deals in his own practice with the problems which a poetics would hope to make explicit.

William Empson's *Seven Types of Ambiguity* is a work from a non-structuralist tradition which shows considerable awareness of the problems of literary competence and illustrates just how close one comes to a structuralist formulation if one begins to reflect on them. Even if Empson were content to present his work as a display of ingenuity in discovering ambiguities, his enterprise would still be governed by conceptions of plausibility. But of course he wants to make broader claims for his analysis and finds that to do so entails a position very like that recommended above:

> I have continually employed a method of analysis which jumps the gap between two ways of thinking; which produces a possible set of alternative meanings with some ingenuity, and then says it is grasped in the preconsciousness of the reader by a native effort of the mind. This must seem very dubious; but then the facts about the apprehension of poetry are in any case very extraordinary. Such an assumption is best judged by the way it works in detail. (p. 239)

Poetry has complex effects which are extremely difficult to explain, and the analyst finds that his best strategy is to assume that the effects he sets out to account

for have been conveyed to the reader and then to postulate certain general operations which might explain these effects and analogous effects in other poems. To
those who protest against such assumptions one might reply, with Empson, that
the test is whether one succeeds in accounting for effects which the reader accepts
when they are pointed out to him. The assumption is in no way dangerous, for
the analyst "must convince the reader that he knows what he is talking about"—
make him see the appropriateness of the effects in question—and "must coax the
reader into seeing that the cause he names does, in fact, produce the effect which
is experienced; otherwise they will not seem to have anything to do with each
other" (p. 249). If the reader is brought to accept both the effects in question and
the explanation he will have helped to validate what is, in essence, a theory of
reading. "I have claimed to show how a properly-qualified mind works when it
reads the verse, how those properly-qualified minds have worked which have not
at all understood their own working" (p. 248). Such claims about literary competence are not to be verified by surveys of readers' reactions to poems but by
readers' assent to the effects which the analyst attempts to explain and the efficacy of his explanatory hypotheses in other cases.

   It is Empson's self-awareness and outspokenness as much as his brilliance
which make his work invaluable to students of poetics; he has little respect for
the critical piety that meanings are always implicitly and objectively present in
the language of the poem, and thus he can attend to the operations which produce meanings. Discussing the translation of a Chinese fragment,

>   Swiftly the years, beyond recall.
>   Solemn the stillness of this spring morning.

he notes that

> these lines are what we should normally call poetry only by virtue of their
> compactness; two statements are made as if they were connected, and the reader
> is forced to consider their relations for himself. The reason why these facts
> should have been selected for a poem is left for him to invent; he will invent a
> variety of reasons and order them in his own mind. This, I think, is the essential
> fact about the poetical use of language. (p. 25)

This is indeed an essential fact, and one should hasten to point out what it
implies: reading poetry is a rule-governed process of producing meanings; the
poem offers a structure which must be filled up and one therefore attempts to
invent something, guided by a series of formal rules derived from one's experience
of reading poetry, which both make possible invention and impose limits on it. In
this case the most obvious feature of literary competence is the intent at totality
of the interpretive process: poems are supposed to cohere, and one must therefore
discover a semantic level at which the two lines can be related to one another. An
obvious point of contact is the contrast between "swiftly" and "stillness", and
there is thus a primary condition on "invention': any interpretation should succeed in making thematic capital out of this opposition. Moreover, "years" in the
first sentence and "this morning" in the second, both located in the dimension of
time, provide another opposition and point of contact. The reader might hope to

find an interpretation which relates these two pairs of contrasts. If this is indeed what happens it is no doubt because the experience of reading poetry leads to implicit recognition of the importance of binary oppositions as thematic devices: in interpreting a poem one looks for terms which can be placed on a semantic or thematic axis and opposed to one another.

The resulting structure or "empty meaning" suggests that the reader try to relate the opposition between "swiftly" and "stillness" to two ways of thinking about time and draw some kind of thematic conclusion from the tension between the two sentences. It seems eminently possible to produce in this way a reading which is "acceptable" in terms of poetic logic. On the one hand, taking a large panoramic view, we can think of the human life-span as a unit of time and of the years as passing swiftly; on the other, taking the moment of consciousness as the unit, we can think of the difficulty of experiencing time except discontinuously, of the stillness of a clock's hand when one looks at it. "Swiftly the years" implies a vantage point from which one can consider the passage of time, and the swiftness of passage is compensated for by what Empson calls "the answering stability of self-knowledge" implicit in this view of life (p. 24). "This morning" implies other mornings—a discontinuity of experience reflected in the ability to separate and name—and hence an instability which makes "stillness" the more valued. This process of binary structuring, then, can lead one to find tension within each of the lines as well as between the two lines. And since thematic contrasts should be related to opposed values we are led to think about the advantages and disadvantages of these two ways of conceiving of time. A variety of conclusions are of course possible. The claim is not that competent readers would agree on an interpretation but only that certain expectations about poetry and ways of reading guide the interpretive process and impose severe limitations on the set of acceptable or plausible readings.

Empson's example indicates that as soon as one reflects seriously on the status of critical argument and the relation of interpretation to text one approaches the problems which confront poetics, in that one must justify one's reading by locating it within the conventions of plausibility defined by a generalized knowledge of literature. From the point of view of poetics, what requires explanation is not the text itself so much as the possibility of reading and interpreting the text, the possibility of literary effects and literary communication. To account for the notions of acceptability and plausibility on which criticism relies is, as J.-C. Gardin emphasizes, the primary task of the systematic study of literature.

> This is in any case the only sort of objective that a "science" may set for itself, even if it be a science of literature: the regularities unveiled by natural phenomena correspond, in the literary field, to certain convergences of perception for members of a given culture. ("Semantic analysis procedures in the sciences of man", p. 33)

But one should stress that even if the analyst showed little explicit interest in notions of acceptability and merely set out to explain in a systematic way his own reading of literature, the results would be of considerable moment for poetics. If he began by noting his own interpretations and reactions to literary works and succeeded in formulating a set of explicit rules which accounted for the fact that he produced these interpretations and not others, one would then possess the basis of an account of literary competence. Adjustments could be made to include other readings which seemed acceptable and to exclude any readings which seemed wholly personal and idiosyncratic, but there is every reason to expect that other readers would be able to recognize substantial portions of their own tacit knowledge in his account. To be an experienced reader of literature is, after all, to have gained a sense of what can be done with literary works and thus to have assimilated a system which is largely interpersonal. There is little reason to worry initially about the validity of the facts which one sets out to explain; the only risk one runs is that of wasting one's time. The important thing is to start by isolating a set of facts and then to construct a model to account for them, and though structuralists have often failed to do this in their own practice, it is at least implicit in the linguistic model: "Linguistics can give literature the generative model which is the principle of all science, since it is a matter of making use of certain rules to explain particular results" (Barthes, *Critique et vérité*, p. 58).

Since poetics is essentially a theory of reading, critics of every persuasion who have tried to be explicit about what they are doing have made some contribution to it and indeed in many cases have more to offer than structuralists themselves. What structuralism does provide is a reversal of critical perspective and a theoretical framework within which the work of other critics can be organized and exploited. Granting precedence to the task of formulating a theory of literary competence and relegating critical interpretation to a secondary role, it leads one to reformulate as conventions of literature and operations of reading what others might think of as facts about various literary texts. Rather than say, for example, that literary texts are fictional, we might cite this as a convention of literary interpretation and say that to read a text as literature is to read it as fiction. Such a reversal may, at first sight, seem trivial, but to restate propositions about poetic or novelistic discourse as procedures of reading is a crucial reorientation for a number of reasons, wherein lie the revitalizing powers of a structuralist poetics.

First of all, to stress literature's dependence on particular modes of reading is a firmer and more honest starting point than is customary in criticism. One need not struggle, as other theorists must, to find some objective property of language which distinguishes the literary from the non-literary but may simply start from the fact that we can read texts as literature and then inquire what operations that involves. The operations will, of course, be different for different genres, and here by the same model we can say that genres are not special varieties of language but sets of expectations which allow sentences of a language to become signs of different kinds in a second-order literary system. The same sentence can have a different meaning depending on the genre in which it appears. Nor is one upset, as a theorist working on the distinctive properties of literary language must be, by the fact that the boundaries between the literary and the non-literary or between one genre and another change from age to age. On the contrary, change in modes of reading offers some of the best evidence about the conventions operative in different periods.

Second, in attempting to make explicit what one does when reading or interpreting a poem one gains considerably in self-awareness and awareness of the nature of literature as an institution. As long as one assumes that what one does is natural it is difficult to gain any understanding of it and thus to define the differences between oneself and one's predecessors or successors. Reading is not an innocent activity. It is charged with artifice, and to refuse to study one's modes of reading is to neglect a principal source of information about literary activity. By seeing literature as something animated by special sets of conventions one can attain more easily a sense of its specificity, its peculiarity, its difference, shall we say, from other modes of discourse about the world. Those differences lie in the work of the literary sign: in the ways in which meaning is produced.

Third, a willingness to think of literature as an institution composed of a variety of interpretive operations makes one more open to the most challenging and innovatory texts, which are precisely those that are difficult to process according to received modes of understanding. An awareness of the assumptions on which one proceeds, an ability to make explicit what one is attempting to do, makes it easier to see where and how the text resists one's attempts to make sense of it and how, by its refusal to comply with one's expectations, it leads to that questioning of the self and of ordinary social modes of understanding which has always been the result of the greatest literature. My readers, says the narrator at the end of *A la recherche du temps perdu,* will become "les propres lecteurs d'eux-mêmes": in my book they will read themselves and their own limits. How better to facilitate a reading of oneself than by trying to make explicit one's sense of the comprehensible and the incomprehensible, the significant and the insignificant, the ordered and the inchoate. By offering sequences and combinations which escape our accustomed grasp, by subjecting language to a dislocation which fragments the ordinary signs of our world, literature challenges the limits we set to the self as a device or order and allows us, painfully or joyfully, to accede to an expansion of self. But that requires, if it is to be fully accomplished, a measure of awareness of the interpretive models which inform one's culture. Structuralism, because of its interest in the adventures of the sign, has been exceedingly open to the revolutionary work, finding in its resistance to the operations of reading confirmation of the fact that literary effects depend on these conventions and that literary evolution proceeds by displacement of old conventions of reading and the development of new.

And so, finally, structuralism's reversal of perspective can lead to a mode of interpretation based on poetics itself, where the work is read against the conventions of discourse and where one's interpretation is an account of the ways in which the work complies with or undermines our procedures for making sense of things. Though it does not, of course, replace ordinary thematic interpretations, it does avoid premature foreclosure—the unseemly rush from word to world— and stays within the literary system for as long as possible. Insisting that literature is something other than a statement about the world, it establishes, finally, an analogy between the production or reading of signs in literature and in other areas of experience and studies the ways in which the former explores and dramatizes the limitations of the latter. In this kind of interpretation the meaning of the work is what it shows the reader, by the acrobatics in which it involves him, about the problems of his condition as *homo significans,* maker and reader of signs. The notion of literary competence thus comes to serve as the basis of a reflexive interpretation.

The pages that follow have the dual function of indicating and evaluating the work which structuralists themselves have done on various aspects of the literary system and of proposing areas where investigation might well be fruitful. The theoretical programme has attracted more attention and effort than what one might call the axioms of the middle range, and so what is offered is best considered as a framework into which the investigations of many critics—not structuralists alone—might fit, rather than as a presumptuous account of "literary competence" itself.

———

Notes

1. Harold Bloom, *The Visionary Company* (New York, 1961), p. 42.
2. *ibid.*
3. P. Valéry, *Œuvres,* II, pp. 629 and I, pp. 1439–41.
4. Ludwig Wittgenstein, *Philosophical Investigations,* p. 59.
5. See N. Chomsky, *Aspects of the Theory of Syntax,* p. 19.
6. L. Wittgenstein, *op. cit.,* p. 144.

N. Katherine Hayles (1943–)

N. Katherine Hayles is a professor of English and design and media arts at the University of California at Los Angeles, specializing in literature and science of the twentieth century, electronic textuality, modern and postmodern American and British fiction, and critical theory and science fiction. Her impressive range of expertise calls attention to some of the ways in which the boundaries of English studies are being redrawn. Hayles earned her Ph.D. in English literature from the University of Rochester in 1977 and taught English at the University of Iowa before joining the UCLA faculty in 1992. Before earning a master's degree in English in 1970, Hayles worked as a research chemist and as a chemical research consultant. Her background in science makes her one of the nation's leading scholars of relations between science and literature. Her scholarly work examines a host of topics, including the impact of the transition from typewriters to computers, cybernetics, hypertext, avant-garde fiction, and the rhetoric of chaos. Her academic honors and fellowships are many, including the prestigious Rene Wellek prize for best book in literary theory, which she won in 1998-1999 for *How We Became Posthuman: Virtual Bodies in Cybernetics, Literature, and Informatics.* In *How We Became Posthuman,* Hayles examines how the technologies and discoveries of the Information Age affect our understanding of the human body, and in the essay included here, "The Condition of Virtuality," Hayles examines some of these same concerns. Hayles's other books include

Coding the Signifier: Rethinking Semiosis from the Telegraph to the Computer (2002), *Chaos and Order: Complex Dynamics in Literature and Science* (1991), *Chaos Bound: Orderly Disorder in Contemporary Literature and Science* (1990), and *The Cosmic Web: Scientific Field Models and Literary Strategies in the Twentieth Century* (1984).

The Condition of Virtuality

Virtuality is the condition millions of people now inhabit. What it means to be in a condition of virtuality was whimsically demonstrated with a device developed at Xerox PARC and exhibited at SIGGRAPH '95, the huge computer graphics convention where developers come to hawk their latest wares, hard, and soft. From the twenty-foot ceilings of the Art Show exhibit thin red cords dangle like monstrous strings of spaghetti left behind by naughty giants who got in a food fight. Sometimes the strings hang quiescent; at other times they writhe like lively plastic snakes. Connected by transducers to data lines, the cords are sensing devices that measure the flow of information moving through the room. The more bits being sent over the wires, the more the cords gyrate. They are information weather vanes. Inside the walls of the gigantic Los Angeles Convention Center, a sprawling complex larger than many small towns, which way the wind blows has ceased to be a concern of the ordinary citizen. But how currents of information flow—who has access, at what baud rate, to which data banks— occupies on a daily basis nearly every one of the fifty thousand people who have come to this show.

Let me offer a strategic definition. *Virtuality is the cultural perception that material objects are interpenetrated by information patterns.* Note that the definition plays off a duality—materiality on the one hand, information on the other. The bifurcation between them is a historically specific construction that emerged in the wake of World War II. When I say virtuality is a cultural perception, I do not mean it is merely a psychological phenomenon. It is also a mindset that finds instantiation in an array of powerful technologies. The perception facilitates the development of the technologies, and the technologies reinforce the perception.[1] The analyses that constructed information and materiality as separable and discrete concepts developed in a number of scientific and technical fields during the 1940s and 1950s. The construction of these categories was far from arbitrary. The negotiations that produced them took into account existing technologies and accepted explanatory frameworks and the needs of emerging techno-scientific industries for reliable quantification. If the categories are not arbitrary, however, neither are they "natural." Whatever "nature" may be, it is a holistic interactive environment, not a reenactment of the constructed bifurcations that humans impose to understand it better.

One of the important sites for the construction of the information/materiality duality was molecular biology. In the contemporary view, the body is said to "express" information encoded in the genes. The content is provided by the genetic pattern; the body's materiality articulates a preexisting semantic structure. Control resides in the pattern, which is regarded as bringing the material object into being. The idea that reproduction might be governed by an informational code was suggested by Erwin Schrodinger in his influential 1945 book, *What Is Life? The Physical Aspect of the Living Cell*.[2] In his analysis of the discourse of molecular biology as "rhetorical software," Richard Doyle has shown how, in the decades following Schrodinger's book, the gene was conceived as the originary informational pattern that produces the body, even though logically the gene is contained within the body, not the other way around.[3] This "impossible inversion," as Doyle calls it, is aptly illustrated by a popular science book of the 1960s that Doyle discusses, George Gamow's *Mr. Tompkins Inside Himself*.[4] On a visit to his doctor, Mr. Tompkins is sitting in the waiting room when he hears a sucking sound and feels a strange sensation of constriction. Somehow he is drawn into a hypodermic needle and then injected inside his own body. This mind-bending scenario reenacts the same maneuver that is carried out in more stolid fashion in the scientific discourse, when DNA is conceptualized as the genotypic pattern that produces the body as its phenotypic expression. Doyle's point is that this conceptual inversion is a rhetorical rather than an experimental accomplishment. It is in this sense that the discourse functions as rhetorical software, for it operates as if it were running a program on the hardware of the laboratory apparatus to produce results that the research alone could not accomplish.

By the 1970s, this vision reaches rhetorical apotheosis in Richard Dawkins's *The Selfish Gene*.[5] Although Doyle does not discuss Dawkins's text in detail, it provides a perfect illustration of his argument. In Dawkins's rhetoric, the genes are constructed as informational agents who control the "lumbering robots" that we call human beings. Virtually every human behavior, from mate choice to altruism, is treated by Dawkins as if it were controlled by the genes for their own ends, independent of what humans might think. Although he frequently issues disclaimers that this is merely a colorful way of talking, the metaphors do more than spice up the argument. As I have argued elsewhere, they function like discursive agents who *perform* the actions they describe.[6] Through this discursive performativity, informational pattern triumphs over the body's materiality—a triumph achieved by first distinguishing between pattern and materiality and then privileging pattern over materiality. The effect of this "impossible inversion" is the same, whether it occurs in Gamow's cartoons, Dawkins's metaphors, or the lavishly funded Human Genome Project. *It constructs information as the site of mastery and control over the material world.*

It is no accident that molecular biology and other sciences of information flourished during the immediate post–World War II period. The case can be made that World War II, more than previous global events, made the value of information real. The urgency of war highlights the fact that information is time-dependent. It matters little what information one has if a message can move only as fast as a horse can run, for by the time it arrives at its destination, its usefulness has often passed. Shakespeare's history plays are full of messages that arrive too late. Only when technological infrastructures have developed sufficiently to make rapid message transmission possible does information come into its own as a commodity as important to military success as guns and infantry. From this we can draw an obvious but nonetheless important conclusion. *The efficacy of information depends on a highly articulated material base.* Without such a base, from rapid transportation systems to fiber-optic cables, information becomes much more marginal in its ability to affect outcomes in the material world. Ironically, once this base is in place, the perceived primacy of information over materiality obscures the importance of the very infrastructures that make information valuable.

Nowhere is the privileging of information over materiality more apparent than in Hans Moravec's *Mind Children.*[7] Moravec argues that human beings are essentially informational patterns rather than bodily presences. If a technology can replicate the pattern, it has captured all that really matters in a human being. To illustrate, he offers a fantastic scenario in which "you" have your consciousness downloaded into a computer. Although the technology could be envisioned in any number of ways (since it is imaginary in any case), he significantly has the robot surgeon conducting the operation physically destroy your brain in the process. As "you" are transferred into a computer, the trashed body is left behind, an empty husk. Once "you" are comfortably inside your shiny new body, "you" effectively become immortal. For when that body wears out or becomes obsolete, "you" can simply transfer your consciousness to a new model.

I will not bother to lay out all the reasons why this vision, in addition to being wildly implausible, is wrong-headed and dangerous. Let me instead point out a correlation that helps to explain the appeal of this fantasy (for those who find it appealing). In Moravec's text, and at many other sites in the culture, *the information/matter dichotomy maps onto the older and more traditional dichotomy of spirit/matter.* The underlying premise informing Moravec's scenario is the belief that an immaterial essence, which alone comprises the individual's true nature, can be extracted from its material instantiation and live free from the body. As this wording makes clear, the contemporary privileging of information is reinforced by religious yearnings and belief that have been around for a long time and that are resonant with meaning for many people. There are, of course, also significant differences between a mindset that identifies human being with the soul and one that identifies it with information. Spirituality is usually associated with mental and physical discipline, whereas the imagined escape of the soul-as-information from the body depends only on having access to the appropriate high technology. For Moravec, the difference means the problem of mortality has been rationalized so that it is possible to make steady progress toward achieving a solution rather than flailing around in mystical nonsense. This construction of the situation obscures the fact that his text is driven by a fear of death so intense it mystifies the power of the very technologies that are supposed to solve the problem.

To probe further the implications of constructing information and materiality as discrete categories, let us return to the period immediately following World War II. In addition to molecular biology, another important site for articulating the distinction was information theory. In 1948 Claude Shannon, a brilliant theorist who worked at Bell Laboratories, defined a mathematical quantity he called information and proved several important theorems concerning it.[8] Lacan to the contrary, a message does not always arrive at its destination. In information theoretic terms, no message is ever sent. What is sent is a signal. The distinction information theory posits between signal and message is crucial. A message has an information content specified by a probability function that has no dimensions, no materiality, and no necessary connection with meaning. It is a pattern, not a presence. Only when the message is encoded in a signal for transmission through a medium—for example, when ink is printed on paper or electrical pulses are sent racing along telegraph wires—does it assume material form. The very definition of information, then, encodes the distinction between materiality and information that was also becoming central in molecular biology during this period.

Why did Shannon define information as a pattern rather than a presence? The transcripts of the Macy Conferences, a series of annual meetings where the basic principles of cybernetics were hammered out, indicate that the choice was driven by the twin engines of reliable quantification and theoretical generality.[9] Shannon's approach had other advantages that turned out to incur large (and mounting) costs when his premise interacted with certain predispositions already at work within the culture. Abstracting information from a material base meant that information could become free-floating, unaffected by changes in context. The technical leverage this move gained was considerable, for by formalizing information into a mathematical function, Shannon was able to develop theorems, powerful in their generality, that held true regardless of the medium in which the information was instantiated. Not everyone agreed that this move was a good idea, despite its theoretical power. Malcontents grumbled that divorcing information from context and thus from meaning had made the theory so narrowly formalized that it was not useful as a general theory of communication. Shannon himself frequently cautioned that the theory was meant to apply only to certain technical situations, not to communication in general. In other circumstances, the theory may have become a dead end, a victim of its own excessive formalization and decontextualization. But not in the post–World War II era. As we have seen, the time was ripe for theories that reified information into a free-floating, decontextualized, quantifiable entity that could serve as the master key unlocking the secrets of life and death.

How quickly the theory moved from the meticulously careful technical applications urged by Shannon to cultural fantasy can be seen in Norbert Wiener's suggestion in 1950 that it would be possible to telegraph a human being.[10] We can see here the prototype for Moravec's scenario of downloading consciousness into a computer. The proposal implies that a human being is a message instantiated within a biological substrate but not intrinsic to it.[11] Extract the information from the medium, and you have a pattern you can encode into a signal and reconstitute in another medium at the end of the channel. The fantasy has not lost its appeal as the century races toward the millennium; indeed, it now circulates so widely as to be virtually ubiquitous. Telegraphing a person to a remote location may have been a startling idea in the 1950s, but by the 1990s it has achieved the status of a cultural icon. What is "Beam me up, Scotty," but the same operation carried out with a different (imaginary) technology? Moravec's vision is extreme only in that it imagines "you" rematerialize inside a computer. If you had simply reoccupied your same body, nobody would have raised an eyebrow. Whether the enabling assumptions occur in molecular biology, information theory, or mass media, their appeal is clear. Information conceived as pattern and divorced from a material medium is information free to travel across time and space. Hackers are not the only ones who believe that information wants to be free. The great dream and promise of information is that it can be free from the material constraints that govern the mortal world. If we can become the information we have constructed, we too can soar free, immortal like the gods.

In the face of such a powerful dream, it can be a shock to remember that for information to exist, it must *always* be instantiated in a medium, whether that medium is the page from the *Bell Laboratories Journal* on which Shannon's equations are printed, the computer-generated topological maps used by the Human Genome Project, or the television tube that images the body disappearing into a golden haze when the Star Trek transporter locks onto it. The point is not only that abstracting information from a material base is an imaginary act. More fundamentally, conceiving of information as a thing separate from the medium that instantiates it is a prior imaginary act that constructs a holistic phenomenon as a matter/information duality.[12]

As I write these words, I can feel the language exerting an inertial pull on my argument, for I can gesture toward the unity that the world is only through the dichotomies constructed to describe it. Even as I point to the historical contingency of the terms, the very history that exposes this contingency reinscribes the information/materiality dichotomy I want to contest. This reinscription is complicated and exacerbated by the fact that the matter/information duality is enmeshed in a network of related dichotomies that help to support, distinguish, and define it. In order of increasing generality, these include signal/not-signal, information/noise, and pattern/randomness. Although I cannot avoid using these constructions, I want to show that they function as dialectics rather than dichotomies. In Derrida's phrase, they are engaged in an economy of supplementarity. Each of the privileged terms—signal, information, pattern—relies for its construction on a supplement—not-signal noise, randomness. As an electrical engineer employed by AT&T, Shannon had a vested interest in eliminating noise. One of his most important theorems proves that there is always a way to encode a message so as to reduce the noise to an arbitrarily small quantity. But since noise is the supplement that allows information to be constructed as the privileged term, it cannot be eliminated from the communication situation, only compensated for in the final result.[13] We can arrive at the same conclusion through a different route by thinking more deeply about what it means to define information as a probability function. The definition implies that randomness always already interpenetrates pattern, for probability as a concept posits a situation in which there is no *a priori* way to distinguish between effects extrapolated from known causes and those generated by chance conjunctions. Like information and noise, pattern and randomness are not opposites bifurcated into a dichotomy but interpenetrating terms joined in a dialectic.

I am now in a position to restate my major theme in a different key. As I have shown, the concept of information is generated from the interplay between pattern and randomness. Similarly, materiality can be understood as being generated by a dialectic of presence and absence. In each dialectic, one term has historically been privileged over the other. When the terms are inverted, assumptions become visible that otherwise would remain transparent. Deconstruction gained theoretical leverage by placing absence rather than presence at the origin of language; the Maximum Entropy Formalism gained theoretical leverage by regarding randomness rather than pattern as the generator of information.[14] When information is privileged over materiality, the pattern/randomness dialectic associated with information is perceived as dominant over the presence/absence dialectic associated with materiality. The condition of virtuality implies, then, a widespread perception that presence/absence is being displaced and preempted by pattern/randomness.

As this displacement suggests, the impact of virtuality on literary theory and practice will be far-reaching and profound. At present, virtuality is largely *terra incognita* for the literary establishment. In *City of Bits,* William Mitchell has written insightfully about how technologies of information are forcing a reconceptualization of the city on many levels, from architecture to traffic flow and urban planning.[15] My interests lies in how these same technologies are facing a reconceptualization of literary theory and practice. In the next section, I explore the effects on literature of the changing material conditions under which it is written and read in an information age. Part of what is at stake for me in this analysis is to show that materiality, far from being left behind, interacts at every point with the new forms that literature is becoming as it moves into virtuality.

The Virtual Book

We have seen it dozens of times—that moment in a film when a book is opened and the camera's eye zooms through the pages into the imagined world beyond. Once we are in the world, the page is left behind. It no longer appears on the screen, no longer frames the world we witness. The filmic convention captures a reader's sense that the imagined world of the text lives less on the page than in the scene generated out of the words by the mind's eye. Virtual books, that is, books imaged on and through computer screens, operate according to a different convention. As with film, the user is sometimes given the illusion that she is moving through the screen into an imagined world beyond. But unlike film, this imagined world contains texts that the user is invited to open, read, and manipulate. Text is not left behind but remains in complex interplay with the perceived space into which the screen opens. Technically speaking, of course, the interplay is possible because the computer is an interactive medium. My focus here is on how this interactivity is rendered through visual conventions. *Visually* it is possible because textual space is rendered as having depth—if not a full three dimensions, at least the "two and a half" dimensions of text windows stacked behind each other. Texts can play a part in the three-dimensional world of the screen image because in this interactive medium, they have similarly rich dimensionality. The correlation suggests that in electronic textuality, spatiality is of primary concern.

The changed conventions that operate with virtual texts are apparent in *Myst,* the game that ranks second on the U.S. best-seller list for CD-ROMs. As the game opens, three-dimensional Roman letters spelling "MYST" appear. Then a book tumbles out of space and comes to rest in the foreground. Imagine that you are sitting here at the keyboard with me so we can work together on solving the problems that *Myst* presents to us (a favorite way to interact with this challenging and complex game). As we peer at the screen, we notice that the same letters appear on the book. It comes closer, inviting us to enter. We plunge into it and find ourselves spinning through the air. Finally we come to rest on the island, the first of many worlds that *Myst* offers for exploration. We find that we have not left the book behind, for scattered about are pages giving important clues about the island's previous occupants. When we pick a page up (by clicking on it), it comes close enough for us to read. The significance of the pages becomes clearer when we enter the library, perhaps the island's most important structure. In addition to the books lining the walls, the library features two podiums on which rest, respectively, two books. When we open one of them (by clicking on it), we are greeted by a black rectangle inset on a white page. Inserting a nearby page into the book causes the rectangle to buzz into flickering life, and we realize it is a screen. Amid noise and static the image of a man appears on the screen. He tries to ask who we are, tries to communicate a message so broken up by static that we can catch only a few words asking us to find more blue (or red) pages and insert them into the book. When we do, the image gets progressively clearer and the messages become more intelligible.

To recapitulate: a book appears on the screen; we go through the book to the island, where we find fragments of more books. Reassembling the book in the library activates the screen inside the book; from the screen comes a message directing us back to the task of finding and reassembling the book. What are we to make of this extraordinarily complex interplay between screen and book? Here I want to point out something that is visually apparent to anyone who plays *Myst*. While the screens appear in a variety of high-tech settings, the books look archaic, with heavy leather bindings, watermarked covers, and ornate typefaces.

Moreover, the screens are usually activated by solving various numerical or coding problems, whereas the books require physical reassembly. The visual richness of the books compared to the screens, their fragmentation and archaic appearance, hint that books have become fetishized. When we open the book in the library, we do not find the information we seek imprinted on its pages. Instead we interact with a screen emphasizing that the book has become fragmented and urging us to put it back together. Books are associated with the object of desire—finding out information—but metonymically, by a glancing connection based on proximity rather than a direct gaze.

The fetishistic quality of the books in *Myst* is consistent with their representation as anachronisms. Everything about their presentation identifies them as artifacts from the late age of print. Books still exist in this virtual world, but they have ceased to be ordinary, matter-of-fact media for transmitting information.

Instead they become fragmented objects of vicarious desire, visually sensuous in a way that implies they are heavy with physicality, teasing us with the promise of a revelation that will come when we restore them to a fabled originary unity. The same kind of transformations are evident at many sites where virtuality reigns. Let me give two more examples, this time from the Art Show at SIGGRAPH '95.

Roman Verostoko's "Illuminated Universal Turing Machine" illustrates how the function of the book changes when its materiality is conceived as interpenetrated by informational patterns. The title alludes to a conceptual computer proposed by Alan Turing in the 1950s.[16] The Universal Turing Machine is simply a string of binary code that includes instructions on how to read the code, including the code that describes itself. Verostko appropriated the code describing the Universal Turing Machine (which visually appears as a string of ones and zeros) and used a computer to print it out on thick parchment, formatted as if it were the text of a medieval illuminated manuscript. Then he fed the same string of code into a program for a line plotter and used it to generate the four illustrations surrounding the text, which look like not-quite-random nests of snaky red lines. In the center of the side margins are two gorgeous gold decals that repeat, in simplified form, one of the motifs of the line drawings; Verostko noted that he intended the decals to suggest control points for the computer. Like *Myst*, this work shows a keen interest in the physical and visual properties of the codex book, including its arrangement of space, tradition of combining text and image, and use of colored inks and gold leaf. But the book's traditional function of conveying verbal information has been given over to computer code. Just as illuminated manuscripts were used for sacred or canonical works, so Verostko uses his visually splendid work to enshrine the universal computer code that is universal precisely because it both explains and enacts its own origin. As with *Myst*, the materiality of the book is celebrated for its archaic and physical qualities, but it is a materiality interpenetrated by the information patterns that generated it and that are rendered visually incarnate in the drawings. In this work commenting upon and exemplifying the late age of print, the book supplies image and visual form, while the computer supplies text and signifying code.

The materiality of the codex book is also celebrated in Andre Kopra's "The Ornament of Grammar," although the properties selected for celebration are very different than in Verostko's work. Kopra intended his title to allude to Owen Jones's nineteenth-century text *The Grammar of Ornament*, a collection of decorative patterns from different cultures. Kopra's work consists of a collection of ten different texts bound in cheap black generic paper covers, printed on inexpensive paper, and displayed in an unpainted pine bookcase holding multiple copies of each of the ten texts. The pages of the books are filled with line drawings generated by computer programs. The drawings are laid out on a grid of thirty-six by thirty-six squares, yielding a total of forty-one different patterns. As one flips through a book, the drawings grow progressively more complex, an effect achieved by varying the parameters of the computer program generating them. Some of the books use rectilinear patterns; others feature curved lines. The patterns tease the eye, challenging the reader to discern in their visual form the algorithm that created them. Commenting on the tension between the underlying code and visual surface, Kopra wrote that the "possibility of rationalizing visual imagery is called into question by an apparent encyclopedia of the arbitrary."[17]

The material qualities celebrated in this piece include the print book's sturdiness, its relative cheapness and portability, its technological robustness and ease of use, and its potential for mass production. (When I talked with him about the work, Kopra mentioned that several of the books had been stolen by the time SIGGRAPH ended, a fact which delighted him. He said the perfect ending of the display, from his point of view, would have been to have the bookcase emptied by bibliophilic thieves). Although he focuses on different material qualities, Kopra echoes Verostko in having the book's verbal content displaced by visual forms generated from a computer. The computer's role in producing the book is highlighted by the interplay between pattern and randomness in the visual forms. This interplay at once instantiates the dialectic of pattern/randomness and draws into question the ability of computer codes to produce significance, as if recollecting for the reader Shannon's move of divorcing information from meaning. Kopra's work has an ironic undertone that reflects, he says, his growing concern that we are drowning in an ocean of information that is produced not because it is meaningful but because it can be used to generate a profit. For him the SIGGRAPH context in which the work was exhibited was significant, for over the years he has seen SIGGRAPH itself change from a coterie gathering of people who shared mutual interests to a huge commercial enterprise where millions of dollars are at stake.[18]

In an art show devoted to computer graphics, the focus on the book was remarkable. In addition to Verostko and Kopra, at least a dozen other artists produced works that were concerned with the interplay between print and algorithm. For them, the codex book functions as a crossroads in which one can see displayed the traffic between visual objects and computer programs, words and codes, images and language, fragmentation and wholeness, handwork and machine production, pattern and randomness, and rationality and numerical permutations of the arbitrary. The overarching message is that the interpenetration of materiality by informational patterns is everywhere around us, even—or especially—in the books, at once virtual and physical, that are being produced in this late age of print.

Spatiality and Virtual Writing

Not all virtual books, of course, have their verbal content displaced by codes. Usually the codes work to introduce into the text's visual form a spatial dimensionality that operates in complex syncopation with language. The interplay between spatiality and text is central to electronic hypertexts. As most readers will know, hypertexts are electronic documents that are structured as networks of discrete units, or lexias, rather than as a linear sequence of bound pages. Hypertexts have encoded within them certain "hot spots" or interactive links. When a reader clicks on them, the link is activated and a new block of text comes up on the screen. As George Landow has pointed out, hypertexts are now becoming the standard way to convey information in many technical and engineering areas because they are easily updated, richly associational, and reader-directed. They can be found in everything from manuals for aircraft mechanics to electronic directories for museums. The World Wide Web is a vast hypertext, and most of the documents within it are also hypertexts. Hypertext also provides a rapidly expanding arena for literary writing, both creative and critical.

In literary hypertexts, spatial form and visual image become richly significant. For hypertexts written in Storyspace (a hypertext authoring program developed by Mark Bernstein, Michael Joyce, and Jay Bolter), the map view shows how different lexias are linked to one another. The way they are arranged in space is used to indicate logical or narrative relationships. Some lexias may nest inside others; others may have multiple connections; still others may function as autonomous units or dead ends. Color coding also indicates various kinds of relationships, from highlighted text within lexias to different-colored links and boxes. In Toolbook (another authoring program), sound can be added to enhance textual or visual effects. As a result, space in hypertexts operates as much more than an empty container into which virtual objects are placed. Rather it becomes a topography that the reader navigates using multiple functionalities, including cognitive, tactile, auditory, visual, kinesthetic, and proprioceptive faculties.

Since I am focusing here on spatiality, let us dwell for a moment on proprioception. Proprioception is the sense that tells us where the boundaries of our bodies are. Associated with inner ear mechanisms and internal nerve endings, it makes us feel that we inhabit our bodies from the inside. Proprioceptive coherence, a term used by phenomenologists, refers to how these boundaries formed through a combination of physiological feedback loops and habitual usage. An experienced tennis player, for example, frequently feels proprioceptive coherence with the racquet, experiencing it as if it were an extension of her arm. In much the same way, an experienced computer user feels proprioceptive coherence with the keyboard, experiencing the screen surface as a space into which her subjectivity can flow. This effect marks an important difference between screen and print. Although a reader can imaginatively project herself into a world represented within a print text, she is not likely to feel that she is becoming physically attached to the page itself. On the contrary, because the tactile and kinesthetic feedback loops are less frequent, less sensually complicated, and much less interactive, she normally feels that she is moving *through* the page into some other kind of space. The impression has a physiological basis. The physical stimuli the reader receives with print are simply not adequate to account for the congnitive richness of the represented world; the more the imagination soars, the more the page is left behind. This difference in the way that proprioceptive coherence works with the computer screen compared to the printed page is an important reason why spatiality becomes such a highly charged dimensionality in electronic hypertexts.

It makes sense, then, to insist as Michael Joyce does that virtual writing is also topographical writing.[19] He points to a number of assumptions that we absorb through our everyday work with electronic texts; together, they make our experience of electronic texts distinctively different from print texts. They include the following items, which I have adapted from Joyce's list and altered to suit my purposes here.

1. *Writing is inwardly elastic.* It expands and contracts; it allows the writer to work backward and forward; and it instantly adjusts the screen image to reflect these changes.

2. *The topology of the text is constructed rather than given.* Mechanisms that construct this topology include such humble devices as file names, as well as the more explicitly spatial commands used in hypertexts. As Joyce points out, file names are more powerful than they may appear. They imply that writing done at different times is the same writing if it has the same file name, and that writing stored under different file names is different, even if it was done at the same time and contains the same text. File names also imply that writing is recognized as identical with itself through labeling rather than through spatial proximity within the computer. Unlike in printed books, where the physical location of the pages coincides with labeling conventions, in electronic texts memory address and physical proximity have no necessary relation to one another. Topology is constructed by naming, not by physical assembly.

3. *Changes in a text can be superficial, corresponding to surface adjustments, or structural, corresponding to changes in topography.* Superficial changes are carried out through such formatting tools as spell-checkers and font alterations, while structural changes involve such editorial functions as cut, copy, and paste. The different way these tools are organized within the authoring program, and the different coding operations to which they correspond, embody the assumption that the text possesses both surface and depth. Alterations in the surface are of a different kind than alterations in the topography.

The power of these assumptions lies in the fact that we do not need to be consciously aware of them to be affected by them. Like posture and table manners, they implant and reinforce cognitive presuppositions through physical actions and habitual motions, whether or not we recognize that they do so. As with any ritual, to perform them is on some level to accept and believe them.[20] The materiality of these interactions is one way in which our assumptions about virtual writing are being formed. Through mechanisms and procedures whose full impact we are only beginning to understand, virtual writing is being constituted as distinctively different from print. Even when its output is printed and bound into codex books, we know from the inside that it operates according to spatial principles and a topographical logic of its own.

The Physics of Virtual Writing and the Formation of the Virtual Subject

With all of this emphasis on spatiality, the reader may wonder how time enters into virtual writing. To understand the interaction between time and space in this medium, it is important to know something about the way the medium works.

When computers speak their native languages—assembly code, and beneath that machine language—they operate within a profoundly non-Cartesian space. Distance at this level is measured by clock cycles. The computer's CPU (central processing unit) has a characteristic clock rate. When you buy a faster computer, you are essentially buying a faster clock rate. Imagine a drummer on a Viking sailing ship, pounding out the beat for the rowers' strokes.[21] Every two beats, a rowing cycle is completed. The drummer's pace controls the rate at which the oars move, and consequently the speed at which the boat slices through the water. Similarly, inside the computer the CPU reads a byte of code every two clock cycles. The clock rate thus controls the rate at which computations occur. It follows that addresses at memory locations 1, 50, 1000, and 1001 are all equidistant. Each is exactly two cycles away if it is in local memory, and eight cycles away if it is in remote memory.

How does this non-Cartesian relation between time and space express itself at the level of the user's experience? It is relatively easy for a computer program to generate a two-dimensional array, for it simply assigns each pixel on the screen an address. But to build a three-dimensional representation, the program must layer a series of two-dimensional planes on top of one another, as if a mountain had been cut horizontally into very thin slices and was being reassembled by the computer. This means that three-dimensional representations take many more cycles to build than two-dimensional maps. Hence the user experiences the sensory richness of a three-dimensional topography as a lag in the flow of the computer's response. In *Myst*, for example, the user experiences movement through the represented three-dimensional space as a series of jumps interspersed by pauses. You click, and the computer pauses and then jumps to a point perhaps ten feet away where a flight of steps begins; you click again, and the computer pauses and jumps halfway up the steps. Distance within the screen is experienced as an inertial pull on your time as you navigate the topology. The result is an artifactual physics that emerges from the interaction of the computer clock cycle with the user's experience. In this physics born of interactivity, the more complex the screen topography, the more inertial pull is exerted on the user's flow. The exact relation between the two is determined by the structure and programming of the underlying codes. Thus these codes, which normally remain invisible to the nonspecialist, are nevertheless felt and intuitively grasped by the user, in much the same way that the earth's gravity is felt and intuitively understood by someone who never heard of Newton's laws. Apples fall down; it takes effort to climb mountains. As inhabitants of cyberspace, we similarly understand in our muscles and bones that space belongs to the computer, and flow belongs to the user.

The physics of virtual writing illustrates how our perceptions change when we work with computers on a daily basis. We do not need to have software sockets inserted into our heads (as William Gibson envisions in *Neuromancer*) to become cyborgs. We already are cyborgs in the sense that we experience, through the integration of our bodily perceptions and motions with computer architectures and topologies, a changed sense of subjectivity.

Much has been written about how the transition from orality to writing affected subjectivity. In *Preface to Plato,* Eric Havelock initiates a fascinating line of inquiry when he asks why Plato is so adamant about banishing poets from the republic.[22] Havelock suggests that poetry is associated with oral culture and consequently with a fluid, changing, situational, and dispersed subjectivity. Plato wants to establish a fixed, stable, unchanging reality, and to do this, he needs a fixed, coherent, stable subject to perceive it. So the poets have to go, for they produce through their linguistic interventions exactly the kind of subject that Plato does not want and cannot tolerate. Similarly influential has been the work of Walter Ong on the differences between oral and written culture, Elizabeth Eisenstein on the effects of printing in early modern Europe, and Marshall McLuhan on the effects of electronic technologies.[23]

We are only beginning to understand the effect of computers on culture and on subjectivity. Marsha Kinder has documented the importance of "shifting," the perception young children have watching such programs as the Power Rangers that they can morph and shapeshift into various forms;[24] Brenda Laurel and Rachel Strickland have embodied similar perceptions in their virtual reality simulation "Placeholder";[25] and Allucquère Roseanne Stone, in *The War of Desire and Technology at the Close of the Mechanical Age,* has written about the virtual subject as a "multiple" (analogous to someone who experiences multiple personalities) warranted by the body rather than contained within it.[26] Catherine Richards and Don Idhe have focused on proprioceptive coherence, looking at the way perception of body boundaries changes through technological interactions and interventions.[27] Michael Joyce, Jay Bolter, George Landow, and David Kolb, among others, have pointed out how navigating the topologies of electronic hypertexts creates new conditions for writing and reading and thus for both producing and expressing new kinds of subjectivities.[28] Operating without any illusions about comprehensiveness or rigor, I venture below to sum up a few salient comparisons between the oral subject, the written subject, and the virtual subject.

In the transition from the written to the virtual subject, deconstruction played a significant theoretical role, for in reinterpreting writing (emphasizing its instabilities, lack of originary foundations, intertextualities, and indeterminancies), in effect it made the written subject move much closer to the virtual subject than had traditionally been the case. This process is typical of what I have called elsewhere seriation (a term appropriated from archeological anthropology), an uneven process of change in which new artifacts or ideas emerge by partially replicating and partially innovating upon what came before. Although the shape of virtual subjectivity is only beginning to emerge and is therefore difficult to envision clearly, certain features are coming into focus. Proprioceptive coherence in interplay with electronic prostheses plays an important role in reconfiguring perceived body boundaries, especially when it gives the user the impression that her subjectivity is flowing into the space of the screen. When the interface is configured as keyboard and screen, the user will perceive that space belongs to the computer, flow to the user. The symbiotic relation between humans and intelligent machines

The Oral Subject	The Written Subject	The Virtual Subject
Fluid	Fixed	• Formed through dynamic interfaces with computers
changing	coherent	• When interface is keyboard and screen, space belongs to the computer, flow to the user
situational	stable	
	self-identical	• Body boundaries extended or disrupted through proprioceptive coherence formed in conjunction with computer interfaces
dispersed	normalized	
conflicting	decontextualized	• A cyborg

has complex effects that do not necessarily all point in the same direction. For example, it can evoke resistance and a privileging of human qualities that machines do not share, such as emotion, or it can lead to the opposite view that humans should leave to machines the things they do best, such as memory recall, and concentrate on the things humans do best, like language and complex pattern recognition. Whatever the symbiosis is taken to mean, it seems clear that the virtual subject will in some sense be a cyborg.

What Is to Be Done?

Should we respond with optimism to the products of virtual writing, or regard them (as an elderly gentlemen informed me when he heard some of these arguments) as abominations that are rotting the minds of American youth? Whatever we make of them, one thing is certain. Literature will not remain unchanged. It is sometimes difficult to convey adequately to an academic audience the very rapid pace with which computer technologies are penetrating virtually every aspect of our culture. In this respect, academia in general and literature departments in particular tend to lag far behind other sectors of the society. With some noteworthy exceptions, academia is not where it is happening as far as computer culture is concerned.

Yet academics can make, I believe, vitally important contributions to the development of these technologies. Perhaps the most crucial are interventions that provide historical contexts showing how and why the technologies developed as they did. Although certain paths of development may be overdetermined, they are never inevitable. Other paths and other interpretations are always possible. The point I want to underscore is that it is a *historical construction* to believe that computer media are disembodying technologies, not an obvious truth. In fact, this belief requires systematic erasure of many significant aspects of our interactions with computers. It is almost never used as a working hypothesis by the people who are engaged in developing the technologies, for they cannot afford to ignore the materiality of the interfaces they create or the effects of these interfaces on their customers. If we articulate interpretations that contest the illusion of disembodiment, and if these interpretations begin to circulate through the culture, they can affect how the technologies are understood and consequently how they will be developed and used. Technologies do not develop on their own. People develop them, and people are sensitive to cultural beliefs about what the technologies can and should mean.

Brenda Laurel has called recognizing the importance of embodied interaction an "endangered sensibility" that she believes the arts and humanities should fight to retain and restore. For me, this means being attentive to the materialities of the media and their implications. The illusion that information is separate from materiality leads not only to a dangerous split between information and meaning but also to a flattening of the space of theoretical inquiry. If we accept that the materiality of the world is immaterial to our concerns, we are likely to miss the very complexities that theory at its best tries to excavate and understand.

The implications of my strategic choice of definition now stand, I hope, fully revealed. Virtuality is not about living in an immaterial realm of information, but about the cultural perception that material objects are interpenetrated with informational patterns. What this interpenetration means and how it is to be understood will be our collective invention. The choices we make are consequential, for it is in the complex, doubly figured, and intensely ambiguous condition of virtuality that our futures lie.

Notes

1. For an important collection of essays arguing convincingly that how people understand and use technology is crucial to directing technological change, see *Does Technology Drive History? The Dilemma of Technological Determinism,* eds. Merritt Roe Smith and Leo Marx (Cambridge: MIT Press, 1994).
2. Erwin Schrödinger; *What Is Life: The Physical Aspect of the Living Cell* (Cambridge: Cambridge University Press and New York: Macmillan, 1945).
3. Richard Doyle, *On Beyond Living: Rhetorical Transformations in the Life Sciences* (Stanford: Stanford University Press, 1997).
4. George Gamow, *Mr. Tompkins Inside Himself: Adventures in the New Biology* (New York: Viking Press, 1967).
5. Richard Dawkins, *The Selfish Gene* (New York: Oxford University Press, 1976).
6. N. Katherine Hayles, "Narratives of Evolution and the Evolution of Narratives" in *Cooperation and Conflict in General Evolutionary Processes,* eds. John L. Casti and Anders Karlqvist (New York: John Wiley and Sons, 1994), pp. 113–32.
7. Hans Moravec, *Mind Children: The Future of Robot and Human Intelligence* (Cambridge: Harvard University Press, 1988).
8. Claude Shannon, *The Mathematical Theory of Communication* (Urbana: University of Illinois Press, 1949).

9. *Cybernetics: Circular Causal and Feedback Mechanisms in Biological and Social Systems,* 5 vols., ed. Heinz von Foerster, [transcripts for the 6th–10th Conferences on Cybernetics sponsored by the Josiah Macy Foundation] (New York: Josiah Macy, Jr. Foundation, 1950–55). For a definition of information that, *contra* Shannon, argued it should be connected with meaning, see Donald M. MacKay, *Information, Mechanism, and Meaning* (Cambridge: MIT Press, 1969).

10. Norbert Wiener, *Cybernetics: Or Control and Communication in the Animal and the Machine* (Cambridge: MIT Press, 1948) and *The Human Use of Human Beings: Cybernetics and Society* (Boston: Houghton Mifflin, 1950).

11. Jay Clayton in "The Voice in the Machine," presented at the English Institute at Cambridge, MA in August 1995 and included in this volume, argued that the telegraph could have been interpreted in the 1880s as a disembodying technology. Significantly, however, his research indicates that during the late nineteenth century it was perceived as an odd or different kind of embodiment but not as a disembodiment. Wiener's proposal, coming seventy years later, occurred in a different cultural context that was much more inclined to construct the telegraph, along with many other technologies, as disembodying media. The comparison is further evidence for Clayton's (and my) point that perceptions of how the body related to technologies are historical constructions, not biological inevitabilities.

12. The tendency to ignore the material realities of communication technologies has been forcefully rebutted in two important works, Friedrich A. Kittler's *Discourse Networks 1800/1900,* trans. Michael Metteer (Stanford: Stanford University Press, 1990), and *Materialities of Communication,* eds. Hans Ulrich Gumbrecht and K. Ludwig Pfeiffer, trans. William Whobrey (Stanford: Stanford University Press, 1994).

13. Michel Serres plays multiple riffs upon the interconversion of noise and information in *The Parasite,* trans. Lawrence R. Schehr (Baltimore: Johns Hopkins University Press, 1982).

14. More information on this inversion can be found in *The Maximum Entropy Formalism: A Conference Held at the Massachusetts Institute of Technology on May 2–4, 1978,* eds. Raphael D. Levine and Myron Tribus (Cambridge: MIT press, 1979).

15. William J. Mitchell, *City of Bits: Space, Place, and the Infobahn* (Cambridge: MIT Press, 1995).

16. The Universal Turing Machine is conveniently described by Roger Penrose in *The Emperor's New Mind: Concerning Computers, Minds, and the Laws of Physics* (New York: Oxford University Press, 1989). Verostko drew on this description specifically in creating his work (artist's note at the Art Show, SIGGRAPH '95).

17. Artist's Note, Art Show, SIGGRAPH '95.

18. Andre Kopra, private communication.

19. Michael Joyce, *Of Two Minds: Hypertext Pedagogy and Poetics* (Ann Arbor: University of Michigan Press, 1995).

20. Paul Connerton makes this point about ritual in *How Societies Remember* (Cambridge and New York: Cambridge University Press, 1989).

21. I am indebted to Nicholas Gessler for suggesting this metaphor to me and for pointing out the significance of the CPU's non-Cartesian operation.

22. Eric Havelock, *Preface to Plato* (Cambridge: Harvard University Press, 1963).

23. Walter Ong, *Orality and Literacy: The Technologizing of the Word* (New York: Routledge, 1988); Elizabeth Eisenstein, *The Printing Press as an Agent of Change: Communications and Cultural Transformations in Early Modern Europe* (Cambridge: Cambridge University Press, 1979); and Marshall McLuhan, *Understanding Media: The Extensions of Man* (New York: McGraw-Hill, 1964).

24. Marsha Kinder, "Screen Wars: Transmedia Appropriations from Eisenstein to *A TV Dante* and *Carmen Sandiego*" presented at the English Institute, Cambridge, MA, August 1995.

25. The simulation is documented in a video of the same name. A discussion of how the simulation was produced and what its goals are can be found in Brenda Laurel and Rachel Strickland's essay "Placeholder" in *Immersed in Technology*, ed. Mary Anne Moser (Cambridge: MIT Press, forthcoming 1995).

26. Allucquère Roseanne Stone, *The War of Desire and Technology at the Close of the Mechanical Age* (Cambridge: MIT Press, 1995).

27. Catherine Richards's virtual reality video, "Spectral Bodies," illustrates how proprioceptive coherence can be disrupted by even such low-tech methods as massaging a blindfolded subject's arms at certain key points with an electrical vibrator. Don Idhe also discusses proprioceptive coherence in *Technology and the Lifeworld*.

28. Michael Joyce, *Of Two Minds*; Jay David Bolter, *Writing Space: The Computer, Hypertext, and the History of Writing* (Hillsdale, N.J.: E. Erlbaum Associates, 1991); George P. Landow, *Hypertext: The Convergence of Contemporary Critical Theory and Technology* (Baltimore: Johns Hopkins University Press, 1994); David Kolb, *Socrates in the Labyrinth* [hypertext diskette] (Cambridge: Eastgate Systems, 1995); and Kolb's essay by the same title in Landow (1994).

Questions to Consider

1. How does reading Barthes change your view of your own writing processes and habits? Do you share any of Barthes's obsessions with the materials of writing? of reading?

2. How is technology changing our relationships to texts and to writing? Has storytelling moved from a textual to a visual or virtual medium today? How is watching a film like reading a novel? How is it different?

3. Each of the essays in this section is in some way concerned with the ethical and social responsibilities of the writer. Choose two readings and explore the way each understands and describes the ethics of writing (or reading). In what way are reading, writing, and literacy connected to social issues? How is your own writing connected to social issues? Distinguish between the different kinds of writing you do and the different kinds of social responsibilities associated with each.

4. For Poulet, reading would seem to be a private, interior experience; for Culler, Hayles, or Sartre, it may be more social. How is reading a social act? How is meaning made in the process of reading? Who is in control of this process, and where does meaning happen or get created? Is it created by the writer? the reader? both? the language? What has to take place in order for meaning to be created? How would you characterize your own reading experience?

5. Reading and writing are everyday activities that readers (at least literate, fluent readers) may take for granted. The readings in this section show that both of these processes or activities can be understood and described in

very different terms. How do these readings, taken together, contribute to your understanding of either reading or writing now? If you were asked to define reading, how would you respond? Do you read different kinds of material differently? If so, can you describe those differences?

6. A key word that is often implicit in these essays is "interpretation." What does it mean to interpret a text or an event in the eyes of these critics? How might one define interpretation differently depending on which of the critics one is influenced by? Is "reading" really a kind of metaphor for interpretation? Can you read without interpreting? or vice versa?

II

EDUCATION AND INSTITUTIONS

Generally, we understand education to mean systematic instruction in schools, colleges, and universities, and institutions to mean entities or objects of established law, custom, and practice such as universities, judicial courts, or churches. In addition to schools and colleges, we receive educations from our families, our jobs, our environments, and mass media such as television and the Internet. Within universities, we find institutions of literature and of taste just as within capitalism we find institutions of commerce and of inequality. The interrelationships between education and institutions may sometimes seem abstract, but they affect you daily. For example, in addition to directing your pursuit of knowledge, your education trains you to work within the logic of institutions.

Critical theory has much to say about how knowledge and institutional logic shape or direct our thinking. Theorists examine how knowledge and specialized vocabularies are transmitted across disciplines to help construct new understanding for people both within and outside of universities. They also examine relationships between the pursuit of knowledge in the university and the demands of outside institutions such as businesses, industry, the military, and governments. Also, not surprisingly, theorists examine and debate what institutions of higher education should teach you. Should learning center on acquiring facts—knowing names and dates, or memorizing nations and their capitals or the elements of the periodic table—or on sharpening critical thinking—making connections between two things, ideas, or texts that seemingly don't have much in common? Or should education mingle the memorization and critical-thinking teaching methods, which we call pedagogies? As you read the texts in this section, look for intersections between your own educational experiences and the theorists' arguments. How are decisions made about which methods and curriculum are most appropriate? What is the university's mission? Is it to prepare you for a fulfilling, productive, and civic life? How do we know what counts as fulfilling, productive, and civic?

In "Blurred Genres: The Refiguration of Social Thought," Clifford Geertz examines a significant methodological change in much university research. According to Geertz, "Something is happening to the way we think about the way we think." He observes that researchers in the social sciences are turning away from theories and analogies in the hard sciences and turning toward theories and analogies in the humanities to help frame their research arguments. The effect is a reshaping of where we think the boundaries of these disciplines lie. Geertz calls this reshaping interdisciplinarity "refiguration," and it affects not only researchers, but also students, as well as institutions outside the university. Generally, it affects "what it is we want to know," according to Geertz. If social scientists no longer generally agree that their aim is "to find out the dynamics of collective life and alter them in desired directions," then what has happened intellectually to disrupt the consensus?

Geertz's title reflects the lack of consensus. While some people are anxious about blurring distinctions between disciplines, many others find the interdisciplinarity and methodological improvisation intellectually liberating. It has now become a commonplace observation that work in literary studies today often has the look of psychology, anthropology or history; such hybrid scholarship has been influential in reshaping and reenergizing the field of English studies. Similarly, exciting research in the social sciences that draws on theories of drama or linguistics rather than on physics or mathematics seeks to tackle societal as well as intellectual problems from fresh perspectives. According to Geertz, "there has come into our view of what we read and what we write a distinctly democratical temper. The properties connecting texts with one another, that put them, ontologically anyway, on the same level, are coming to seem as important in characterizing them as those dividing them." We might consider the "distinctly democratical temper" and the disciplinary mingling or blurring as evidence of thinking "outside the box"—thinking that seeks novel ways to make sense, right wrongs, and enhance our quality of life.

Like Geertz, Jacques Derrida is also thinking about the way we think, as demonstrated in "The Principle of Reason: The University in the Eyes of Its Pupils," an address he delivered at Cornell University in 1983. However, Derrida's focus is more abstract—he sees the university as an institution—and his writing style is more philosophical than Geertz's. If you are unfamiliar with European philosophical traditions, you may wonder about the form of Derrida's argument. In his typical fashion, Derrida meticulously unpacks the idea of "reason" and demonstrates contradictions in aims and goals for research. As you examine his analysis of reason and its binary opposite, unreason, pay attention to his analogies and metaphors. Consider the practice or application for theory and research Derrida advocates. Does he provide a vision of the university's reason for being that prepares students for a fulfilling, productive, and civic life?

Also like Geertz, Derrida makes an argument about blurred genres. He says that we mistakenly distinguish between "oriented" and "basic" research, where the former is directed toward "its utilization" and the latter toward "knowledge, truth, the disinterested exercise of reason, under the sole authority of the principle of reason." It is a mistake, however, he argues, to understand basic research as noble and unsullied by utilitarian and belligerent ends. Derrida says that all research now has military and national security applications: "Never before has so-called basic scientific research been so deeply committed to aims that are at the same time military aims. The very essence of the military, the limits of military technology and even the limits of its accountability are no longer definable." Geertz recognizes a "distinctly democratic temper" in blurred genres, whereas Derrida, at a higher level of abstraction, warns of a dystopic co-optation of knowledge production; he does not see much in the way of progressive refigurations of institutional power. The lack of distinction between basic and oriented research greatly affects the university's reason for being. How does the institutional mission blur if the organization subordinates its cherished reason for being to other institutions like the military, big business, or high-tech industries? What type of solution does Derrida propose?

Where Geertz and Derrida examine the blurring of research in universities, Pierre Bourdieu focuses on how taste and consumption patterns perpetuate social distinctions inside and outside of educational institutions. In the introduction to his 1984 book *Distinction: A Social Critique of the Judgment of Taste,* Bourdieu says that our consumption of "cultural goods" marks and legitimates "social differences." We are well aware of how economic hierarchies legitimate social distinctions such as power and prestige: the rich "naturally" deserve their lavish homes and property, expensive cars, and the latest consumer goods and electronics. Bourdieu researches how hierarchies are also legitimized by what he calls cultural capital, defined as educationally acquired knowledge and sensibilities such as taste. For example, knowing that Shakespeare wrote the plays *Julius Caesar* and *Hamlet* illustrates cultural capital, as does knowing that the Nigerian playwright Wole Soyinka wrote *Kongi's Harvest* and that Soyinka won the 1986 Nobel prize for literature. Enjoyment of Shakespeare and Soyinka signals discriminating taste that can also register one's social standing.

Similarly, taste is signaled by our choices of food, drink, and pastimes. For instance, in certain social circles, a taste for sushi can confer more prestige than a taste for McNuggets; likewise, drinking Heineken beer out of a glass as opposed to drinking Old Milwaukee out of a can might signal a higher status. But drinking a chic microbrew or, better yet, a glass of French wine presumably signals even greater cultural capital just as there is typically more social cachet in golf and tennis than in bowling and professional wrestling. As Bourdieu argues, however, such distinctions are not natural; they are arbitrary. How do they arise, and what is their relationship to education and institutions?

According to Bourdieu, "taste classifies, and it classifies the classifier. Social subjects, classified by their classifications, distinguish themselves by the distinctions they make, between the beautiful and the ugly, the distinguished and the vulgar, in which their position in the objective classification is expressed or betrayed." The more cultural capital you possess, the greater are your chances for higher social standing. Cultural elites, according to Bourdieu, understand that their privileges are linked to taste or aesthetic disposition, which they acquire particularly through education. Folks planning for college know that a degree from Harvard, Princeton, or Brown opens more doors than a degree from a community college. In addition to universities, what other institutions or forces legitimize hierarchies of social standing as "natural"? Conversely, what forces or institutions might challenge or call into question the distinction and merit generated by taste?

For quite a long time, scholars and theorists characterized the distinctions of taste—for example, the preference for poetry as opposed to soap operas or for fine wine as opposed to beer—in terms of "high" versus "low," with low being ascribed to tastes that are associated with popular or mass culture. Are these distinctions still applicable and meaningful? Scholars continue to write books and articles about Shakespeare, Leonardo da Vinci, Virginia Woolf, and Herman Melville, but their methodologies are often quite different from those of a generation ago. The change in perspective reflects, perhaps, Geertz's discussion of the refiguration of social thought: there no longer seems to be a shared norm or mainstream view of "what it is we want to know." Knowledge awaits us at every turn. Not too long ago, researchers in universities shunned popular or mass culture such as film, television, and celebrities; the clear message was that popular culture was unworthy of scholarly attention. Today, however, research in popular culture is active, vibrant, and increasingly well respected, and courses on popular icons like Madonna and on once-marginalized genres like the Western and detective fiction now rub shoulders in course schedules with traditional fare such as art history, Shakespeare, biology, and political science.

Why were issues of mass culture previously deemed unworthy of scholarly attention? Perhaps Geertz's focus on blurred genres can help us. Some would argue that the blurring of genres, such as the pastiche or medley of "high" and "low," characterizes our contemporary, postmodern culture. Might the blurring signal, among other things, a "distinctly democratical temper," a politics attempting to delegitimate the "naturalness" of boundaries and hierarchies? Or should we be more skeptical or suspicious? Might we better understand this blurring as a sophisticated means for established institutions to maintain the status quo, to continue to legitimate "social differences"? These are the kinds of questions critical theorists examine; they are questions that relate to you.

Just as many folks have found Bourdieu's analysis of aesthetic judgment and prestige helpful in examining authority and power, you might use Bourdieu's theories of taste to discuss the idealization of "basic" as opposed to "oriented" research in Derrida's essay. Or you might compare Bourdieu's theory of cultural consumption with canon debates such as the one Mary Louise Pratt analyzes in her 1990 essay "Humanities for the Future: Reflections on the Western Culture Debate at Stanford." To frame her analysis, Pratt turns to Bourdieu's theory of cultural capital and asks, "What is to count as 'cultural capital' in a culturally plural nation and a globalized human world? How will that capital be constructed and deployed, how will people be asked to identify with it? How might the United States project itself into the future as a cultural and political entity?" Implicit in Pratt's questions is an awareness of change along the lines of Geertz's declaration that "something is happening to the way we think about the way we think."

Just as many social scientists used to agree on a general disciplinary aim, folks in literature departments and the humanities used to take it for granted that their educational mission was to further students' systematic instruction in *the* Western tradition. Assigned reading in literature departments, for instance, typically focused on either British or American writers: Chaucer and Shakespeare, Coleridge and Keats, and Hardy and Lawrence in British literature classes; Emerson and Thoreau, Hawthorne and Melville, and Whitman and Frost in American literature classes. The few canonical female writers covered might have male pseudonyms. Mary Ann Evans, for instance, used the pen name George Eliot. Typically, African-American writers were completely off the canonical radar screen. Why were female and minority writers rarely granted the status of high culture? The answer is related to the reason why Stanford's required Western civilization course created so much controversy, not only at the university, but across the nation as well.

As Pratt points out, courses in Western civilization are not hallowed tradition. They are a product of the twentieth century and not a part of American education at the country's founding in the eighteenth century. That their genesis had much to do with military aims suggestively links the readings in such courses to Derrida's discussion of the blurring of basic and oriented research. Also, Pratt and many others question the institutional sense of requiring a course with a narrowly focused, Eurocentric reading list in a "culturally plural nation." Who makes the decisions about which texts to include and which texts to exclude, and on what basis? Are the decisions based on "taste"? on a text's "intrinsic" merit? on its politics—its "democratical temper," its elitism, or its endorsement of the status quo? Which side you take in canononical debates like the one at Stanford can have a lot to do with your reaction to Pratt's rhetorical question, "Does the United States not badly need to revitalize its image and understanding of itself?" Implicit in Pratt's question are two others: one is about the role that authorized reading lists or canons play both nationally and internationally, and the other is about the social value of distinctions, that is, of labeling some works, but not others, great. It may seem logical or natural to grant the superlative of greatness to some books. What books do you consider great, and why? What makes a book great? Is it the style or form of the writing? the content or message? the quality of effect the book has on readers?

It may come as a surprise to you that many people object to the category of great literature. Why, you might ask, would anyone object? In his 1998 text, "The Inspirational Value of Great Works of Literature," Richard Rorty analyzes some antagonisms toward literature. According to Rorty, the scholarship of many leading critics demonstrates "knowingness," a highly theorized, antiromantic detachment that is suspicious of literature's charm, eloquence, and cultural privilege. Rorty says that knowingness is "a state of soul which prevents shudders of awe. It makes one immune to romantic enthusiasm." Why would scholars in English studies distrust or dislike literature? Might it have something to do with criticisms of taste such as Bourdieu's or with criticisms similar to Pratt's of narrowly focused canons whose relevance to globalization and our multicultural society is questionable? Like Pratt, Rorty says that he would "cheerfully admit that canons are temporary, and touchstones replaceable." Nevertheless, he adds, "this should not lead us to discard the idea of greatness. We should see great works of literature as great because they have inspired many readers, not as having inspired many readers because they are great." How do you think the other theorists in this section would respond to Rorty's argument? Might Rorty characterize one or more of the other essays in this section as illustrating "knowingness"?

Rorty sees a parallel between "knowingness" in English departments and the changes in philosophy departments that refigured the discipline earlier in the twentieth century: "Philosophy in the English-speaking world became 'analytic,' antimetaphysical, unromantic, and highly professional"; "its desire to be dryly scientific, and thereby to differentiate itself from the sloppy thinking it believes to be prevalent in literature departments, has made it stiff, awkward, and isolated." What is wrong with being "highly professional" and "scientific"? Are the changes Rorty criticizes in English departments related to methodological refigurations like the ones Geertz analyzes? Are they similar to the larger institutional changes Derrida describes? Is "great literature" implicated in the maintenance of social hierarchies, which Bourdieu criticizes in his analysis of taste, or in the Eurocentric narrowness, which Pratt attacks in her arguments about canons?

Despite Rorty's cautionary tale about the ascendancy of analytic philosophy, might we interpret differently that attitude that Rorty calls "knowingness"? Might its antagonism to literature be part of revisionary efforts to dismantle institutional inequalities promoted by taste and the "aesthetic disposition"? Does "knowingness" reflect the "distinctly democratical temper," or is Rorty's disenchantment well founded because knowingness is, indeed, dismally disabling or, perhaps, authoritarian? Thinking about the connection Rorty makes between "knowingness" and the "School of Resentment" may prove helpful. The "School of Resentment" is theorist Harold Bloom's label for critics who he believes "substitute knowing theorization for awe, and resentment over the failures of the past for visions of a better future." What are the politics of such a characterization?

Some might want to argue that Rorty is seeking a middle ground between reactionary or backward-looking approaches to literature that support teaching a restricted canon of mostly "dead white male" writers and radical approaches that are too quick to throw out the baby with the bathwater, to destroy something irreplaceable—the notion of "great works"—in the name of scientific, political, and professional progress. Someone else, however, might argue instead that pleas about "inspirational value" and "great works" are conservative and that they perpetuate the aesthetic ideology that privileges taste and cultural capital, which in turn legitimate social differences based on class, gender, race, and sexuality. What is your take on Rorty's argument? Do great works give us hope? Do they contribute to a fulfilling, productive, and civic life? If so, how? What is the role of inspiration in education and other institutions?

Clifford Geertz (1923–)

A renowned cultural anthropologist with an inimitable writing style, Geertz is the recipient of 14 honorary degrees from universities including Harvard, the University of Chicago, Bates College, Brandeis, Yale, Williams College, Princeton, and the University of Cambridge. In a recent book, *Available Light: Anthropological Reflections on Philosophical Topics* (2000), Geertz offers the following reflection on his vocation: "Everyone knows what cultural anthropology is about: it's about culture. The trouble is that no one is quite sure what culture is. Not only is it an essentially contested concept, like democracy, religion, simplicity, or social justice; it is a multiply defined one, multiply employed, ineradicably imprecise" (11). Geertz came to the study of cultural anthropology with a background in the humanities and not in the sciences. Indeed, he graduated from Antioch College, in Ohio, in 1950 with a degree in philosophy and then earned his Ph.D. in anthropology from Harvard University in 1956. Since 1970, Geertz has taught at the Institute for Advanced Study in Princeton, New Jersey. Geertz's prestige as an innovative thinker extends beyond anthropology into English studies, history, and philosophy. In particular, his emphasis on "blurred genres" and "thick description" has proved enormously helpful for thinking about interdisciplinary studies such as the application of ethnographic analysis to literary and historical texts.

In the reading selection presented next, "Blurred Genres: The Refiguration of Social Thought," from his 1983 book *Local Knowledge: Further Essays in Interpretive Anthropology*, Geertz explores a paradigm shift in the production of knowledge in the social sciences. Once-distinct disciplinary boundaries separating the social sciences from the humanities are blurring, Geertz argues, because many significant scholars are often turning away from the hard sciences' models of understanding and turning toward the humanities' metaphors and linguistic theories in order to account for social and cultural phenomena in novel ways. Geertz reads this intellectual shift as signifying a significant revaluation of what counts as knowledge. Revaluation is evident as well in his 1973 book *The Interpretations of Cultures*, where Geertz likens "thick description" to the acts of literary critics: identifying and sorting "structures of signification" and "determining their social ground and import" (9). Geertz's interdisciplinary reading of the "contested concept" of culture has influenced many critics and theorists, including the New Historicist scholar Stephen Greenblatt.

Blurred Genres: The Refiguration of Social Thought

I

A number of things, I think are true. One is that there has been an enormous amount of genre mixing in intellectual life in recent years, and it is, such blurring of kinds, continuing apace. Another is that many social scientists have turned away from a laws and instances ideal of explanation toward a cases and interpretations one, looking less for the sort of thing that connects planets and pendulums and more for the sort that connects chrysanthemums and swords. Yet another is that analogies drawn from the humanities are coming to play the kind of role in sociological understanding that analogies drawn from the crafts and technology have long played in physical understanding. Further, I not only think these things are true, I think they are true together; and it is the culture shift that makes them so that is my subject: the refiguration of social thought.

This genre blurring is more than just a matter of Harry Houdini or Richard Nixon turning up as characters in novels or of midwestern murder sprees described as though a gothic romancer had imagined them. It is philosophical inquiries looking like literary criticism (think of Stanley Cavell on Beckett or Thoreau, Sartre on Flaubert), scientific discussions looking like belles lettres *morceaux* (Lewis Thomas, Loren Eiseley), baroque fantasies presented as deadpan empirical observations (Borges, Barthelme), histories that consist of equations and tables or law court testimony (Fogel and Engerman, Le Roi Ladurie), documentaries that read like true confessions (Mailer), parables posing as ethnographies (Castenada), theoretical treatises set out as travelogues (Lévi-Strauss), ideological arguments cast as historiographical inquiries (Edward Said), epistemological studies constructed like political tracts (Paul Feyerabend), methodological polemics got up as personal memoirs (James Watson). Nabokov's *Pale Fire,* that impossible object made of poetry and fiction, footnotes and images from the clinic, seems very much of the time; one waits only for quantum theory in verse or biography in algebra.

Of course to a certain extent this sort of thing has always gone on—Lucretius, Mandeville, and Erasmus Darwin all made their theories rhyme. But the present jumbling of varieties of discourse has grown to the point where it is becoming difficult either to label authors (What *is* Foucault—historian, philosopher, political theorist? What Thomas Kuhn—historian, philosopher, sociologist of knowledge?) or to classify works (What is George Steiner's *After Babel*—linguistics, criticism, culture history? What William Gass's *On Being Blue*—treatise, causerie, apologetic?). And thus it is more than a matter of odd sports and occasional curiosities, or of the admitted fact that the innovative is, by definition, hard to categorize. It is a phenomenon general enough and distinctive enough to suggest that what we are seeing is not just another redrawing of the cultural map—the moving of a few disputed borders, the marking of some more picturesque mountain lakes—but an alteration of the principles of mapping. Something is happening to the way we think about the way we think.

We need not accept hermetic views of *écriture* as so many signs signing signs, or give ourselves so wholly to the pleasure of the text that its meaning disappears into our responses, to see that there has come into our view of what we read and what we write a distinctly democratical temper. The properties connecting texts with one another, that put them, ontologically anyway, on the same level, are coming to seem as important in characterizing them as those dividing them; and rather than face an array of natural kinds, fixed types divided by sharp qualitative differences, we more and more see ourselves surrounded by a vast, almost continuous field of variously intended and diversely constructed works we can order only practically, relationally, and as our purposes prompt us. It is not that we no longer have conventions of interpretation; we have more than ever, built—

often enough jerry-built—to accommodate a situation at once fluid, plural, uncentered, and ineradicably untidy.

So far as the social sciences are concerned, all this means that their oft-lamented lack of character no longer sets them apart. It is even more difficult than it always has been to regard them as underdeveloped natural sciences, awaiting only time and aid from more advanced quarters to harden them or as ignorant and pretentious usurpers of the mission of the humanities, promising certainties where none can be, or as comprising a clearly distinctive enterprise, a third culture between Snow's canonical two. But that is all to the good: freed from having to become taxonomically upstanding, because nobody else is, individuals thinking of themselves as social (or behavioral or human or cultural) scientists have become free to shape their work in terms of its necessities rather than according to received ideas as to what they ought or ought not to be doing. What Clyde Kluckhohn once said about anthropology—that it's an intellectual poaching license—not only seems more true now than when he said it, but true of a lot more than anthropology. Born omniform, the social sciences prosper as the condition I have been describing becomes general.

It has thus dawned on social scientists that they did not need to be mimic physicists or closet humanists or to invent some new realm of being to serve as the object of their investigations. Instead they could proceed with their vocation, trying to discover order in collective life, and decide how what they were doing was connected to related enterprises when they managed to get some of it done; and many of them have taken an essentially hermeneutic—or, if that word frightens, conjuring up images of biblical zealots, literary humbugs, and Teutonic professors, an "interpretive"—approach to their task. Given the new genre dispersion, many have taken other approaches: structuralism, neo-positivism, neo-Marxism, micro-micro descriptivism, macro-macro system building, and that curious combination of common sense and common nonsense, sociobiology. But the move toward conceiving of social life as organized in terms of symbols (signs, representations, *significiants, Darstellungen* . . . the terminology varies), whose meaning (sense, import, *signification, Bedeutung* . . .) we must grasp if we are to understand that organization and formulate its principles, has grown by now to formidable proportions. The woods are full of eager interpreters.

Interpretive explanation—and it is a form of explanation, not just exalted glossography—trains its attention on what institutions, actions, images, utterances, events, customs, all the usual objects of social-scientific interest, mean to those whose institutions, actions, customs, and so on they are. As a result, it issues not in laws like Boyle's, or forces like Volta's, or mechanisms like Darwin's, but in constructions like Burckhardt's, Weber's, or Freud's: systematic unpackings of the conceptual world in which *condottiere,* Calvinists, or paranoids live.

The manner of these constructions itself varies: Burckhardt portrays, Weber models, Freud diagnoses. But they all represent attempts to formulate how this people or that, this period or that, this person or that makes sense to itself and, understanding that, what we understand about social order, historical change, or psychic functioning in general. Inquiry is directed toward cases or sets of cases, and toward the particular features that mark them off; but its aims are as far-reaching as those of mechanics or physiology: to distinguish the materials of human experience.

With such aims and such a manner of pursuing them come as well some novelties in analytical rhetoric, the tropes and imageries of explanation. Because theory, scientific or otherwise, moves mainly by analogy, a "seeing-as" comprehension of the less intelligible by the more (the earth is a magnet, the heart is a pump, light is a wave, the brain is a computer, and space is a balloon), when its course shifts, the conceits in which it expresses itself shift with it. In the earlier stages of the natural sciences, before the analogies became so heavily intramural—and in those (cybernetics, neurology) in which they still have not—it has been the world of the crafts and, later, of industry that have for the most part provided the well-understood realities (well-understood because, *certum quod factum,* as Vico said, man had made them) with which the ill-understood ones (ill-understood because he had not) could be brought into the circle of the known. Science owes more to the steam engine than the steam engine owes to science; without the dyer's art there would be no chemistry; metallurgy is mining theorized. In the social sciences, or at least in those that have abandoned a reductionist conception of what they are about, the analogies are coming more and more from the contrivances of cultural performance than from those of physical manipulation—from theater, painting, grammar, literature, law, play. What the lever did for physics, the chess move promises to do for sociology.

Promises are not always kept, of course, and when they are, they often turn out to have been threats; but the casting of social theory in terms more familiar to gamesters and aestheticians than to plumbers and engineers is clearly well under way. The recourse to the humanities for explanatory analogies in the social sciences is at once evidence of the destabilization of genres and the rise of "the interpretive turn," and their most visible outcome is a revised style of discourse in social studies. The instruments of reasoning are changing and society is less and less represented as an elaborate machine or a quasi-organism and more as a serious game, a sidewalk drama, or a behavioral text.

II

All this fiddling around with the proprieties of composition, inquiry, and explanation represents, of course, a radical alteration in the sociological imagination, propelling it in directions both difficult and unfamiliar. And like all such changes in fashions of the mind, it is about as likely to lead to obscurity and illusion as it is to precision and truth. If the result is not to be elaborate chatter or the higher nonsense, a critical consciousness will have to be developed; and as so much more of the imagery, method, theory, and style is to be drawn from the humanities than previously, it will mostly have to come from humanists and their apologists rather than from natural scientists and theirs. That humanists, after years of regarding social scientists as technologists or interlopers, are ill equipped to do this is something of an understatement.

Social scientists, having just freed themselves, and then only partially, from dreams of social physics—covering laws, unified science, operationalism, and all that—are hardly any better equipped. For them, the general muddling of vocational identities could not have come at a better time. If they are going to develop systems of analysis in which such conceptions as following a rule, constructing a representation, expressing an attitude, or forming an intention are going to play central roles—rather than such conceptions as isolating a cause, determining a variable, measuring a force, or defining a function—they are going to need all the help they can get from people who are more at home among such notions than they are. It is not interdisciplinary brotherhood that is needed, nor even less highbrow eclecticism. It is recognition on all sides that the lines grouping scholars together into intellectual communities, or (what is the same thing) sorting them out into different ones, are these days running at some highly eccentric angles.

The point at which the reflections of humanists on the practices of social scientists seem most urgent is with respect to the deployment in social analysis of models drawn from humanist domains—that "wary reasoning from analogy," as Locke called it, that "leads us often into the discovery of truths and useful productions, which would otherwise lie concealed." (Locke was talking about rubbing two sticks together to produce fire and the atomic-friction theory of heat, though business partnership and the social contract would have served him as well.) Keeping the reasoning wary, thus useful, thus true, is, as we say, the name of the game.

The game analogy is both increasingly popular in contemporary social theory and increasingly in need of critical examination. The impetus for seeing one or another sort of social behavior as one or another sort of game has come from a number of sources (not excluding, perhaps, the prominence of spectator sports in mass society). But the most important are Wittgenstein's conception of forms of life as language games, Huizinga's ludic view of culture, and the new stratagics of von Neumann's and Morgenstern's *Theory of Games and Economic Behavior.* From Wittgenstein has come the notion of intentional action as "following a rule"; from Huiziniga, of play as the paradigm form of collective life; from von Neumann and Morgenstern, of social behavior as a reciprocative maneuvering toward distributive payoffs. Taken together they conduce to a nervous and nervous-making style of interpretation in the social sciences that mixes a strong sense of the formal orderliness of things with an equally strong sense of the radical arbitrariness of what order: chessboard inevitability that could as well have been otherwise.

The writings of Erving Goffman—perhaps the most celebrated American sociologist right now, and certainly the most ingenious—rest, for example, almost entirely on the game analogy. (Goffman also employs the language of the stage quite extensively, but as his view of the theater is that it is an oddly mannered kind of interaction game—ping-pong in masks—his work is not, as base, really dramaturgical.) Goffman applies game imagery to just about everything he can lay his hands on, which, as he is no respecter of property rights, is a very great deal. The to-and-fro of lies, meta-lies, unbelievable truths, threats, tortures, bribes, and blackmail that comprises the world of espionage is construed as an "expression game"; a carnival of deceptions rather like life in general, because, in a phrase that could have come from Conrad or Le Carré, "agents [are] a little like us all and all of us [are] a little like agents." Etiquette, diplomacy, crime, finance, advertising, law, seduction, and the everyday "realm of bantering decorum" are seen as "information games"—mazy structure of players, teams, moves, positions, signals, information states, gambles, and outcomes, in which only the "gameworthy"—those willing and able "to dissemble about anything"—prosper.

What goes on in a psychiatric hospital, or any hospital or prison or even a boarding school in Goffman's work, is a "ritual game of having a self," where the staff holds most of the face cards and all of the trumps. A tête-à-tête, a jury deliberation, "a task jointly pursued by persons physically close to one another," a couple dancing, lovemaking, or boxing—indeed, all face-to-face encounters— are games in which, "as every psychotic and comic ought to know, any accurately improper move can poke through the thin sleeve of immediate reality." Social conflict, deviance, entrepreneurship, sex roles, religious rites, status ranking, and the simple need for human acceptance get the same treatment. Life is just a bowl of strategies.

Or, perhaps better, as Damon Runyon once remarked, it is three-to-two against. For the image of society that emerges from Goffman's work, and from that of the swarm of scholars who in one way or another follow or depend on him, is of an unbroken stream of gambits, ploys, artifices, bluffs, disguises, conspiracies, and outright impostures as individuals and coalitions of individuals struggle—sometimes cleverly, more often comically—to play enigmatical games whose structure is clear but whose point is not. Goffman's is a radically unromantic vision of things, acrid and bleakly knowing, and one that sits rather poorly with traditional humanistic pieties. But it is no less powerful for that. Nor, with its uncomplaining play-it-as-it-lays ethic, is it all that inhumane.

However that may be, not all gamelike conceptions of social life are quite so grim, and some are positively frolicsome. What connects them all is the view that human beings are less driven by forces than submissive to rules, that the rules are such as to suggest strategies, the strategies are such as to inspire actions, and the actions are such as to be self-rewarding—*pour le sport*. As literal games—baseball or poker or Parcheesi—create little universes of meaning, in which some things can be done and some cannot (you can't castle in dominoes), so too do the analogical ones of worship, government, or sexual courtship (you can't mutiny in a bank). Seeing society as a collection of games means seeing it as a grand plurality of accepted conventions and appropriate procedures—tight, airless worlds of move and countermove, life *en règle*. "I wonder," Prince Metternich is supposed to have said when an aide whispered into his ear at a royal ball that the czar of all the Russians was dead, "I wonder what his motive could have been."

The game analogy is not a view of things that is likely to commend itself to humanists, who like to think of people not as obeying the rules and angling for advantage but as acting freely and realizing their finer capacities. But that it seems to explain a great deal about a great many aspects of modern life, and in many ways to catch its tone, is hardly deniable. ("If you can't stand the Machiavellianism," as a recent *New Yorker* cartoon said, "get out of the cabal.") Thus if the game analogy is to be countered it cannot be by mere disdain, refusing to look through the telescope, or by passioned restatements of hallowed truths, quoting scripture against the sun. It is necessary to get down to the details of the matter, to examine the studies and to critique the interpretations—whether Goffman's of crime as character gambling, Harold Garfinkel's of sex change as identity play, Gregory Bateson's of schizophrenia as rule confusion, or my own of the complicated goings-on in a mideastern bazaar as an information contest. As social theory turns from propulsive metaphors (the language of pistons) toward ludic ones (the language of pastimes), the humanities are connected to its arguments not in the fashion of skeptical bystanders but, as the source of its imagery, chargeable accomplices.

III

The drama analogy for social life has of course been around in a casual sort of way—all the world's a stage and we but poor players who strut and so on—for a very long time. And terms from the stage, most notably "role," have been staples of sociological discourse since at least the 1930s. What is relatively new—new, not unprecedented—are two things. First, the full weight of the analogy is coming to be applied extensively and systematically, rather than being deployed piecemeal fashion—a few allusions here, a few tropes there. And second, it is coming to be applied less in the depreciatory "mere show," masks and mummery mode that has tended to characterize its general use, and more in a constructional, genuinely dramaturgical one—making, not faking, as the anthropologist Victor Turner has put it.

The two developments are linked, of course. A constructionalist view of what theater is—that is, poicsis—implies that a dramatistic perspective in the social sciences needs to involve more than pointing out that we all have our entrances and exits, we all play parts, miss cues, and love pretense. It may or may not be a Barnum and Bailey world and we may or may not be walking shadows, but to take the drama analogy seriously is to probe behind such familiar ironies to the expressive devices that make collective life seem anything at all. The trouble with analogies—it is also their glory—is that they connect what they compare in both directions. Having trifled with theater's idiom, some social scientists find themselves drawn into the rather tangled coils of its aesthetic.

Such a more thoroughgoing exploitation of the drama analogy in social theory—as an analogy, not an incidental metaphor—has grown out of sources in the humanities not altogether commensurable. On the one hand, there has been the so-called ritual theory of drama associated with such diverse figures as Jane Harrison, Francis Fergusson, T. S. Eliot, and Antonin Artaud. On the other, there is the symbolic action—"dramatism," as he calls it—of the American literary theorist and philosopher Kenneth Burke, whose influence is, in the United States anyway, at once enormous and—because almost no one actually uses his baroque vocabulary, with its reductions, ratios, and so on—elusive. The trouble is, these approaches pull in rather opposite directions: the ritual theory toward the affinities of theater and religion—drama as communion, the temple as stage; the symbolic action theory toward those of theater and rhetoric—drama as persuasion, the platform as stage. And this leaves the basis of the analogy—just what in the theatron is like what in the agora—hard to focus. That liturgy and ideology are histrionic is obvious enough, as it is that etiquette and advertising are. But just what that means is a good deal less so.

Probably the foremost proponent of the ritual theory approach in the social sciences right now is Victor Turner. A British formed, American re-formed anthropologist, Turner, in a remarkable series of works trained on the ceremonial life of a Central African tribe, has developed a conception of "social drama" as a regenerative process that, rather like Goffman's of "social gaming" as strategic interaction, has drawn to it such a large number of able researchers as to produce a distinct and powerful interpretive school.

For Turner, social dramas occur "on all levels of social organization from state to family." They arise out of conflict situations—a village falls into factions, a husband beats a wife, a region rises against the state—and proceed to their denouements through publicly performed conventionalized behavior. As the conflict swells to crisis and the excited fluidity of heightened emotion, where people feel at once more enclosed in a common mood and loosened from their social moorings, ritualized forms of authority—litigation, feud, sacrifice, prayer—are invoked to contain it and render it orderly. If they succeed, the breach is healed and the status quo, or something resembling it, is restored; if they do not, it is accepted as incapable of remedy and things fall apart into various sorts of unhappy endings: migrations, divorces, or murders in the cathedral. With differing degrees of strictness and detail, Turner and his followers have applied this schema to tribal passage rites, curing ceremonies, and judicial processes; to Mexican insurrections, Icelandic sagas, and Thomas Becket's difficulties with Henry II; to picaresque narrative, millenarian movements, Caribbean carnivals, and Indian peyote hunts; and to the political upheaval of the sixties. A form for all seasons.

This hospitableness in the face of cases is at once the major strength of the ritual theory version of the drama analogy and its most prominent weakness. It can expose some of the profoundest features of social process, but at the expense of making vividly disparate matters look drably homogeneous.

Rooted as it is in the repetitive performance dimensions of social action—the reenactment and thus the reexperiencing of known form—the ritual theory not only brings out the temporal and collective dimensions of such action and its inherently public nature with particular sharpness; it brings out also its power to transmute not just opinions but, as the British critic Charles Morgan has said with respect to drama proper, the people who hold them. "The great impact [of the theater]," Morgan writes, "is neither a persuasion of the intellect nor a beguiling of the senses. . . . It is the enveloping movement of the whole drama on the soul of man. We surrender and are changed." Or at least we are when the magic works. What Morgan, in another fine phrase, calls "the suspense of form . . . the incompleteness of a known completion," is the source of the power of this "enveloping movement," a power, as the ritual theorists have shown, that is hardly less forceful (and hardly less likely to be seen as otherworldly) when the movement appears in a female initiation rite, a peasant revolution, a national epic, or a star chamber.

Yet these formally similar processes have different content. They say, as we might put it, rather different things, and thus have rather different implications for social life. And though ritual theorists are hardly incognizant of that fact, they are, precisely because they are so concerned with the general movement of things, ill-equipped to deal with it. The great dramatic rhythms, the commanding forms of theater, are perceived in social processes of all sorts, shapes, and significances (though ritual theorists in fact do much better with the cyclical, restorative periodicities of comedy than the linear, consuming progressions of tragedy, whose ends tend to be seen as misfires rather than fulfillments). Yet the individuating details, the sort of thing that makes *A Winter's Tale* different from *Measure for Measure*, *Macbeth* from *Hamlet*, are left to encyclopedic empiricism: massive documentation of a single proposition—*plus ça change, plus c'est le même changement*. If dramas are, to adapt a phrase of Susanne Langer's, poems in the mode of action, something is being missed: what exactly, socially, the poems say.

This unpacking of performed meaning is what the symbolic action approaches are designed to accomplish. Here there is no single name to cite, just a growing catalogue of particular studies, some dependent on Kenneth Burke, some on Ernst Cassirer, Northrop Frye, Michel Foucault, or Emile Durkheim, concerned to say what some bit of acted saying—a coronation, a sermon, a riot, an execution—says. If ritual theorists, their eye on experience, tend to be hedgehogs, symbolic action theorists, their eye on expression, tend to be foxes.

Given the dialectical nature of things, we all need our opponents, and both sorts of approach are essential. What we are most in want of right now is some way of synthesizing them. In my own analysis of the traditional Indic polity in Bali as a "theater state"—cited here not because it is exemplary, but because it is mine—I have tried to address this problem. In this analysis I am concerned, on the one hand (the Burkean one), to show how everything from kin group organization, trade, customary law, and water control to mythology, architecture, iconography, and cremation combines to a dramatized statement of a distinct form of political theory, a particular conception of what status, power, authority, and government are and should be: namely, a replication of the world of the gods that is at the same time a template for that of men. The state enacts an image of order that—a model for its beholders, in and of itself—orders society. On the other hand (the Turner one), as the populace at large does not merely view the state's expressions as so many gaping spectators but is caught up bodily in them, and especially in the great, mass ceremonies—political operas of Burgundian dimensions—that form their heart, the sort of "we surrender and are changed" power of drama to shape experience is the strong force that holds the polity together. Reiterated form, staged and acted by its own audience, makes (to a degree, for no theater ever wholly works) theory fact.

But my point is that some of those fit to judge work of this kind ought to be humanists who reputedly know something about what theater and mimesis and rhetoric are, and not just with respect to my work but to that of the whole steadily broadening stream of social analyses in which the drama analogy is, in one form or another, governing. At a time when social scientists are chattering about actors, scenes, plots, performances, and personae, and humanists are mumbling about motives, authority, persuasion, exchange, and hierarchy, the line between the two, however comforting to the puritan on the one side and the cavalier on the other, seems uncertain indeed.

IV

The text analogy now taken up by social scientists is, in some ways, the broadest of the recent refigurations of social theory, the most venturesome, and the least well developed. Even more than "game" or "drama," "text" is a dangerously unfocused term, and its application to social action, to people's behavior toward other people, involves a thoroughgoing conceptual wrench, a particularly outlandish bit of "seeing-as." Describing human conduct in the analogy of player and counterplayer, or of actor and audience, seems, whatever the pitfalls, rather more natural than describing it in that of writer and reader. Prima facie, the suggestion that the activities of spies, lovers, witch doctors, kings, or mental patients are moves or performances is surely a good deal more plausible than the notion that they are sentences.

But prima facie is a dubious guide when it comes to analogizing; were it not, we should still be thinking of the heart as a furnace and the lungs as bellows. The text analogy has some unapparent advantages still insufficiently exploited, and the surface dissimilarity of the here-we-are-and-there-we-are of social interaction to the solid composure of lines on a page is what gives it—or can when the disaccordance is rightly aligned—its interpretive force.

The key to the transition from text to text analogue, from writing as discourse to action as discourse, is, as Paul Ricoeur has pointed out, the concept of "inscription": the fixation of meaning. When we speak, our utterances fly by as events like any other behavior; unless what we say is inscribed in writing (or some other established recording process), it is as evanescent as what we do. If it is so inscribed, it of course passes, like Dorian Gray's youth, anyway; but at least its meaning—the *said,* not the *saying*—to a degree and for a while remains. This too is not different for action in general: its meaning can persist in a way its actuality cannot.

The great virtue of the extension of the notion of text beyond things written on paper or carved into stone is that it trains attention on precisely this phenomenon: on how the inscription of action is brought about, what its vehicles are and how they work, and on what the fixation of meaning from the flow of events—history from what happened, thought from thinking, culture from behavior—implies for sociological interpretation. To see social institutions, social customs, social changes as in some sense "readable" is to alter our whole sense of what such interpretation is and shift it toward modes of thought rather more familiar to the translator, the exegete, or the iconographer than to the test giver, the factor analyst, or the pollster.

All this comes out with exemplary vividness in the work of Alton Becker, a comparative linguist, on Javanese shadow puppetry, or the *wayang* as it is called. Wayang-ing (there is no other suitable verb) is, Becker says, a mode of text building, a way of putting symbols together to construct an expression. To construe it, to understand not just what it means but how it does so, one needs, he says, a new philology.

Philology, the text-centered study of language, as contrasted to linguistics, which is speech-centered, has of course traditionally been concerned with making ancient or foreign or esoteric documents accessible to those for whom they are ancient or foreign or esoteric. Terms are glossed, notes appended, commentaries written, and, where necessary, transcriptions made and translations effected—all toward the end of producing an annotated edition as readable as the philologist can make it. Meaning is fixed at a meta-level; essentially what a philologist, a kind of secondary author, does is reinscribe: interpret a text with a text.

Left at this, matters are straightforward enough, however difficult they may turn out to be in practice. But when philological concern goes beyond routinized craft procedures (authentication, reconstruction, annotation) to address itself to conceptual questions concerning the nature of texts as such—that is, to questions about their principles of construction—simplicity flees. The result, Becker notes, has been the shattering of philology, itself by now a near obsolescent term, into disjunct and rivalrous specialties, and most particularly the growth of a division between those who study individual texts (historians, editors, critics—who like to call themselves humanists), and those who study the activity of creating texts in general (linguists, psychologists, ethnographers—who like to call themselves scientists). The study of inscriptions is severed from the study of inscribing, the study of fixed meaning is severed from the study of the social processes that fix it. The result is a double narrowness. Not only is the extension of text analysis to nonwritten materials blocked, but so is the application of sociological analysis to written ones.

The repair of this split and the integration of the study of how texts are built, how the said is rescued from its saying, into the study of social phenomena—Apache jokes, English meals, African cult sermons, American high schools, Indian caste, or Balinese widow burning, to mention some recent attempts aside from Becker's—are what the "new philology," or whatever else it eventually comes to be called, is all about. "In a multicultured world," Becker writes, "a world of multiple epistemologies, there is need for a new philologist—a specialist in contextual relations—in all areas of knowledge in which text-building . . . is a central activity: literature, history, law, music, politics, psychology, trade, even war and peace."

Becker sees four main orders of semiotic connection in a social text for his new philologist to investigate: the relation of its parts to one another; the relation of it to others culturally or historically associated with it; the relation of it to those who in some sense construct it; and the relation of it to realities conceived as lying outside of it. Certainly there are others—its relation to its *materia*, for one; and, more certainly yet, even these raise profound methodological issues so far only hesitantly addressed. "Coherence," "inter-textuality," "intention," and "reference"—which are what Becker's four relations more or less come down to—all become most elusive notions when one leaves the paragraph or page for the act or institution. Indeed, as Nelson Goodman has shown, they are not all that well defined for the paragraph or page, to say nothing of the picture, the melody, the statue, or the dance. Insofar as the theory of meaning implied by this multiple contextualization of cultural phenomena (some sort of symbolic constructivism) exist at all, it does so as a catalogue of wavering intimations and half-joined ideas.

How far this sort of analysis can go beyond such specifically expressive matters as puppetry, and what adjustments it will have to make in doing so, is, of course, quite unclear. As "life is a game" proponents tend to gravitate toward face-to-face interaction, courtship and cocktail parties, as the most fertile ground for their sort of analysis, and "life is a stage" proponents are attracted toward collective intensities, carnivals and insurrections, for the same reason, so "life is a text" proponents incline toward the examination of imaginative forms: jokes, proverbs, popular arts. There is nothing either surprising or reprehensible in this; one naturally tries one's analogies out where they seem most likely to work. But their long-run fates surely rest on their capacity to move beyond their easier initial successes to harder and less predictable ones—of the game idea to make sense of worship, the drama idea to explicate humor, or the text idea to clarify war. Most of these triumphs, if they are to occur at all, are, in the text case even more than the others, still to come. For the moment, all the apologist can do is what I have done here: offer up some instances of application, some symptoms of trouble, and some pleas for help.

V

So much, anyway, for examples. Not only do these particular three analogies obviously spill over into one another as individual writers tack back and forth between ludic, dramatistic, and textualist idioms, but there are other humanistic analogies on the social science scene at least as prominent as they: speech act analyses following Austin and Searle; discourse models as different as those of Habermas's "communicative competence" and Foucault's "archaeology of knowledge"; representationalist approaches taking their lead from the cognitive aesthetics of Cassirer, Langer, Gombrich, or Goodman; and of course Lévi-Strauss's higher cryptology. Nor are they as yet internally settled and homogeneous: the divisions between the play-minded and the strategy-minded to which I alluded in connection with the game approach, and between the ritualists and the rhetoricians in connection with the drama approach, are more than matched in the text approach by the collisions between the against-interpretation mandarins of deconstructionism and the symbolic-domination tribunes of neo-Marxism. Matters are neither stable nor consensual, and they are not likely soon to become so. The interesting question is not how all this muddle is going to come magnificently together, but what does all this ferment mean.

One thing it means is that, however, raggedly, a challenge is being mounted to some of the central assumptions of mainstream social science. The strict separation of theory and data, the "brute fact" idea; the effort to create a formal vocabulary of analysis purged of all subjective reference, the "ideal language" idea; and the claim to moral neutrality and the Olympian view, the "God's truth" idea—none of these can prosper when explanation comes to be regarded as a matter of connecting action to its sense rather than behavior to its determinants. The refiguration of social theory represents, or will if it continues, a sea change in our notion not so much of what knowledge is but of what it is we want to know. Social events do have causes and social institutions effects; but it just may be that the road to discovering what we assert in asserting this lies less through postulating forces and measuring them than through noting expressions and inspecting them.

The turn taken by an important segment of social scientists, from physical process analogies to symbolic form ones, has introduced a fundamental debate into the social science community concerning not just its methods but its aims. It is a debate that grows daily in intensity. The golden age (or perhaps it was only the brass) of the social sciences when, whatever the differences in theoretical positions and empirical claims, the basic goal of the enterprise was universally agreed upon—to find out the dynamics of collective life and alter them in desired directions—has clearly passed. There are too many social scientists at work today for whom the anatomization of thought is wanted, not the manipulation of behavior.

But it is not only for the social sciences that this alteration in how we think about how we think has disequilibrating implications. The rising interest of sociologists, anthropologists, psychologists, political scientists, and even now and then a rogue economist in the analysis of symbol systems poses—implicitly anyway, explicitly sometimes—the question of the relationship of such systems to what goes on in the world; and it does so in a way both rather different from what humanists are used to and rather less evadable—with homilies about spiritual values and the examined life—than many of them, so it seems, would at all like.

If the social technologist notion of what a social scientist is is brought into question by all this concern with sense and signification, even more so is the cultural watchdog notion of what a humanist is. The specialist without spirit dispensing policy nostrums goes, but the lectern sage dispensing approved judgments does as well. The relation between thought and action in social life can no more be conceived of in terms of wisdom than it can in terms of expertise. How it is to be conceived, how the games, dramas, or texts that we do not just invent or witness but live have the consequence they do remains very far from clear. It will take the wariest of wary reasonings, on all sides of all divides, to get it clearer.

Jacques Derrida (1930–)

In English studies in particular and in the humanities in general, the influence of the Algerian-born Derrida has been enormous. It would be hard to overstate his influence on efforts to revolutionize critical practices in English studies over the last thirty years through deconstruction, his methodological approach. In opposition to the then-dominant theory of New Criticism, which tended to view literary art as an "organic whole," the theory of deconstruction holds that texts—literary or otherwise—are fissured or open and not seamless and systematically perfect. A critic practicing deconstruction would show how a text's language masks contradictory impulses; in other words, rather than demonstrating how the text logically fits together as an integrated unity, the deconstructionist unpacks the various implications of the text's language to show how its rhetoric actually breaks down or short-circuits the text's ostensible meaning. In the 1970s and 1980s, deconstruction was simultaneously hailed by many as revivifying English studies and denigrated by many others as seemingly destroying the discipline. In key texts like "Structure, Sign, and Play in the Discourse of the Human Sciences," Derrida attacks theories of semiotics and structuralism. In "Plato's Pharmacy," from his 1972 book *Dissemination,* Derrida dissects theories of speech, writing, rhetoric, and undecidability. In such texts, Derrida's challenging writing style is evident; reading Derrida's abstract writing requires patience, because he carefully unpacks the connotations of key words and often coins new words and phrases. When reading a text by Derrida, it often helps to think of yourself as a translator: do not try to be absolutely literal in making sense of his metaphors and his propositions. Derrida's inventive writing invites readers to be creative in making sense of it; for patient and imaginative readers, the intellectual rewards can be many.

Derrida has taught both in France and in the United States. Some of his most influential books include *Speech and Phenomena* (trans. 1973), *Of Grammatology* (trans. 1978), *Writing and Difference* (trans. 1978), *Dissemination* (trans. 1981), *Glas* (trans. 1986), *The Post Card* (trans. 1987), and *Specters of Mark: The State of the Debt, the Work of Mourning, and the New International* (trans. 1994).

The Principle of Reason:
The University in the Eyes of Its Pupils

Today, how can we not speak of the university?

I put my question in the negative, for two reasons. On the one hand, as we all know, it is impossible, now more than ever, to dissociate the work we do, within one discipline or several, from a reflection on the political and institutional conditions of that work. Such a reflection is unavoidable. It is no longer an external complement to teaching and research; it must make its way through the very objects we work with, shaping them as it goes, along with our norms, procedures, and aims. We cannot not speak of such things. On the other hand, the question "how can we not" gives notice of the *negative,* or perhaps we should say *preventive,* complexion of the preliminary reflections I should like to put to you. Indeed, since I am seeking to initiate discussion, I shall content myself with saying how one should not speak of the university. Some of the typical risks to be avoided, it seems to me, take the form of a bottomless pit, while others take the form of a protectionist barrier.

Does the university, today, have what is called a *raison d'être?* I have chosen to put my question in a phrase—*raison d'être,* literally, "reason to be"—which is quite idiomatically French. In two or three words, that phrase names everything I shall be talking about: reason and being, of course, and the essence of the University in its connections to reason and being; but also the cause, purpose, direction, necessity, justification, meaning and mission of the University; in a word, its destination. To have a *raison d'être,* a reason for being, is to have a justification for existence, to have a meaning, an intended purpose, a destination; but also, to have a cause, to be explainable according to the "principle of reason" or the "law of sufficient reason," as it is sometimes called—in terms of a reason which is also a cause (a ground, *ein Grund*), that is to say also a footing and a foundation, ground to stand on. In the phrase *raison d'être,* that idea of causality takes on above all the sense of final cause, in the wake of Leibniz, the author of the formulation— and it was much more than a formulation—"the Principle of Reason." To ask whether the University has a reason for being is to wonder why there is a University, but the question "why" verges on "with a view to what?" The University with a view to what? What is the University's view? What are its views? Or again: what do we see from the University, whether for instance, we are simply in it, on board; or whether, puzzling over destinations, we look out from it while in port or, as French has it, *"au large,"* on the open sea, "at large"? As you may have noticed, in asking "what is the view from the University?" I was echoing the title of the impeccable parable James Siegel published in *Diacritics* two years ago: "Academic Work: The View from Cornell" [Spring, 1981]. Today, indeed, I shall do no more than decipher that parable in my own way. More precisely, I shall be transcribing in a different code what I read in that article—the dramatic, exemplary nature of the topology and politics of this university, in terms of its views and its site: the topolitics of the Cornellian point of view.

Starting with its first words, Metaphysics associates sight with knowledge, and knowledge with knowing how to learn and knowing how to teach. I am referring of course to Aristotle's *Metaphysics.* I shall return presently to the political import of its opening lines; for the moment, let us look at the very first sentence: "All men, by nature, have the desire to know." Aristotle thinks he sees a sign of this in the fact that sensations give pleasure, "even apart from their usefulness." The pleasure of useless sensations explains the desire to know for the sake of knowing, the desire for knowledge with no practical purpose. And this is more true of sight than of the other senses. We give preference to sensing "through the eyes" not only for taking action, but even when we have no praxis in view. This one sense, naturally theoretical and contemplative, goes beyond practical usefulness and provides us with more to know than any other; indeed, it unveils countless differences. We give preference to sight just as we give preference to the uncovering of difference.

But is sight enough? For learning and teaching, does it suffice to know how to unveil differences? In certain animals, sensation engenders memory, and that makes them more intelligent and more capable of learning. But for knowing how to learn, and learning how to know, sight, intelligence and memory are not enough. We must also know how to hear, and to listen. I might suggest somewhat playfully that we have to know how to shut our eyes in order to be better listeners. Bees know many things, since they can see; but they cannot learn, since they are among the animals that lack the faculty of hearing. Thus, despite appearances to the contrary, the University, the place where people know how to learn and learn how to know, can never be a kind of hive. Aristotle, let us note in passing, has ushered in a long tradition of frivolous remarks on the philosophical commonplace of the bee, the sense and senses of the bee, and the bee's reason for being. Marx was doubtless not the last to have overworked that topos, when he insisted on distinguishing human industry from animal industry, as exemplified in bee society. Seeking such nectar as may be gathered from the vast anthology of philosophical bees, I find a remark of Schelling's, in his *Lessons on the Method of Academic Studies*,[1] more to my taste. An allusion to the sex of bees often comes to the aid of the rhetoric of naturalism, organicism, or vitalism as it plays upon the theme of the complete and interdisciplinary unity of knowledge, the theme of the university as an organic social system. This is in the most classic tradition of interdisciplinary studies. I quote Schelling:

> The aptitude for doing thoughtful work in the specialized sciences, the capacity to work in conformity with that higher inspiration which is called scientific genius, depends upon the ability to see each thing, including specialized knowledge, in its cohesion with what is originary and unified. Any thought which has not been formed in this spirit of unity and totality [*der Ein- und Allheit*] is empty in itself, and must be challenged; whatever is incapable of fitting harmoniously within that budding, living totality is a dead shoot which sooner or later will be eliminated by organic laws; doubtless there also exist, within the realm of science, numerous sexless bees [*geschlechtlose Bienen*] who, since they have not been granted the capacity to create, multiply in inorganic shoots the outward signs of their own witlessness [*ihre eigne Geistlosigkeit*]. [*Philosophies de l'université*, p. 49]

(I don't know what bees, not only deaf but sexless, Schelling had in mind at the time. But I am sure that even today such rhetorical weapons would find many an eager buyer. One professor has recently written that a certain theoretical movement was mostly supported, within the university, by homosexuals and feminists—a fact which seemed very significant to him, and doubtless a sign of asexuality.)

Opening the eyes to know, closing them—or at least listening—in order to know how to learn and to learn how to know: here we have a first sketch of the rational animal. If the University is an institution for science and teaching, does it have to go beyond memory and sight? In what rhythm? To hear better and learn better, must it close its eyes or narrow its outlook? In cadence? What cadence? Shutting off sight in order to learn is of course only a figurative manner of speaking. No one will take it literally, and I am not proposing to cultivate an art of blinking. And I am resolutely in favor of a new university Enlightenment [*Aufklärung*]. Still, I shall run the risk of extending my figuration a little farther, in Aristotle's company. In his *De anima* (421b) he distinguishes between man and those animals that have hard, dry eyes [*tôn skelophtalmôn*], the animals lacking eyelids, that sort of sheath or tegumental membrane [*phragma*] which serve to protect the eye and permits it, at regular intervals, to close itself off in the darkness of inward thought or sleep. What is terrifying about an animal with hard eyes and a dry glance is that it always sees. Man can lower the sheath, adjust the diaphragm, narrow his sight, the better to listen, remember, and learn. What might the University's diaphragm be? The University must not be a scleroph-thalmic animal, a hard-eyed animal; when I asked, a moment ago, how it should set its sights and adjust its views, that was another way of asking about its reasons for being and its essence. What American English calls "the faculty," those who teach, is in French *le corps enseignant,* the teaching corps (just as we say "the diplomatic corps") or teaching body. What can the University's body see or not see of its own destination, of that in view of which it stands its ground? Is the University the master of its own diaphragm?

Now that I have opened up this perspective, allow me to close it off quick as a wink and, in the twinkling of an eye, let me confide in you, to make what in French I could call a *confidence* but in English must call a confession.

Before preparing the text of a lecture, I find I must prepare myself for the scene I shall encounter as I speak. That is always a painful experience, an occasion for silent, paralytic deliberation. I feel like a hunted animal, looking in darkness for a way out where none is to be found. Every exit is blocked. In the present case, the task seemed triply impossible.

In the first place, this was not to be just a lecture like any other; rather, it had to be something like an inaugural address. Of course, Cornell University has welcomed me generously many times since I first came to speak here in 1975. I have many friends here, and Cornell is in fact the first American university I ever taught for. That was in Paris, in 1967–68, as David Grossvogel will undoubtedly remember: he was in charge of a program that had also been directed by Paul de Man. But today, for the first time, I am taking the floor to speak as an Andrew Dickson White Professor-at-Large. In French, "Au large" is the expression a great ship uses to hail a small craft about to cross her course: "Wear off. Give way." In this case, the title with which your university has honored me at once brings me closer to you and adds to the anguish of the cornered animal. Was this inaugural lecture a well-chosen moment to ask whether the University has a reason for being? Wasn't I about to act with the unseemliness of a stranger who in return for noble hospitality plays prophet of doom with his hosts, or at best eschatological harbinger, like Elijah denouncing the power of kings or announcing the end of the realm?

A second cause for worry is that I find myself involved already, quite imprudently, that is, blindly and without foresight, in an act of dramaturgy, writing out the play of that view in which Cornell, from its beginnings, has felt so much to be at stake. The question of the view has informed the writing-out of the institutional scene, the landscape of your university, the alternatives of expansion and enclosure, life and death. From the first it was considered vital not to close off the view. This was recognized by Andrew Dickson White, Cornell's first president: may I pay him this homage? At a moment when the trustees wanted to locate the university closer to town, Ezra Cornell took them to the top of East Hill to show them the sights, and the site, he had in mind. "We viewed the land-scape," writes Andrew Dickson White. "It was a beautiful day and the panorama was magnificent. Mr. Cornell urged reasons on behalf of the upper site, the main one being that there was so much more room for expansion."[2] Ezra Cornell gave good reasons, and since the Board of Trustees, reasonably enough, concurred with them, reason won out. But in this case was reason quite simply on the side of life? Drawing on K. C. Parsons' account of the planning of the Cornell campus, James Siegel observes (and I quote) that

> for Ezra Cornell the association of the view with the university had something to do with death. Indeed Cornell's plan seems to have been shaped by the thematics of the Romantic sublime, which practically guaranteed that a cultivated man in the presence of certain landscapes would find his thoughts drifting metonymically through a series of topics—solitude, ambition, melancholy, death, spirituality, "classical inspiration"—which could lead, by an easy extension, to questions of culture and pedagogy. [p. 69]

A matter of life and death. The question arose once again in 1977, when the university administration proposed to erect protective railings on the College-town bridge and the Fall Creek suspension bridge to check thoughts of suicide inspired by the view of the gorge. "Barriers" was the term used; we could say "diaphragm," borrowing a word which in Greek literally means "partitioning fence." Beneath the bridges linking the university to its surroundings, connecting its inside to its outside, lies the abyss. In testimony before the Campus Council, one member of the faculty did not hesitate to express his opposition to the barriers, those diaphragmatic eyelids, on the grounds that blocking the view would mean, to use his words, "destroying the essence of the university." What did he mean? What is the essence of the university?

Perhaps now you can better imagine with what shudders of awe I prepared myself to speak to you on the subject—quite properly sublime—of the essence of the University. Sublime in the Kantian sense of the term: in the *Conflict of the Faculties*, Kant averred that the University should be governed by "an idea of reason," the idea of the whole field of what is presently teachable [*das ganze gegenwärtige Feld der Gelehrsamkeit*]. As it happens, no experience in the present allows for an adequate grasp of that present, presentable totality of doctrine, of teachable theory. But the crushing sense of that inadequacy is the exalting, desperate sense of the sublime, suspended between life and death.

Kant says, too, that the approach of the sublime is first heralded by an inhibition. There was a third reason for the inhibition I myself felt as I thought about speaking to you today. I was resolved of course to limit myself to preliminary, preventive remarks—propedeutical remarks, to use the word German took over from Greek to designate the teaching that comes before teaching. I would speak only of the risks to be avoided, the abyss, and bridges, and boundaries as one struggles with such fearful questions. But that would still be too much, because I wouldn't know how to pick and choose. In my teaching in Paris I have devoted a yearlong seminar to the question of the University. Furthermore, I was recently asked by the French government to write a proposal for the establishment of an International College of Philosophy, a proposal which for literally hundreds of pages considers all of the difficulties involved. To speak of such things in an hour would be more than just a challenge. As I sought to encourage myself, daydreaming a bit, it occurred to me that I didn't know how many meanings were conveyed by the phrase "at large," as in "professor at large." I wondered whether a professor at large, not belonging to any department, nor even to the university, wasn't rather like the person who in the old days was called *un ubiquiste,* a "ubiquitist," if you will, in the University of Paris. A ubiquitist was a doctor of theology not attached to any particular college. Outside that context, in French, an *ubiquiste* is someone who travels a lot and travels fast, giving the illusion of being everywhere at once. Perhaps a professor at large, while not exactly a ubiquitist, is also someone who, having spent a long time on the high seas, *"au large,"* occasionally comes ashore, after an absence which has cut him off from everything. He is unaware of the context, the proper rituals, and the changed environment. He is given leave to consider matters loftily, from afar. People indulgently close their eyes to the schematic, drastically selective views he has to express in the rhetoric proper to an academic lecture about the academy. But they may be sorry that he spends so much time in a prolonged and awkward attempt to capture the benevolence of his listeners.

As far as I know, nobody has ever founded a university against reason. So we may reasonably suppose that the University's reason for being has always been reason itself, and some essential connection of reason to being. But what is called the principle of reason is not simply reason. We cannot for now plunge into the history of reason, its words and concepts, into the puzzling scene of translation which has shifted *logos* to *ratio* to *raison, reason, Grund,* ground, *Vernunft,* and so on. What for three centuries now has been called the principle of reason was thought out and formulated, several times, by Leibniz. His most often quoted statement holds that "Nothing is without reason, no effect is without cause." According to Heidegger, though, the only formulation Leibniz himself considered authentic, authoritative, and rigorous is found in a late essay, *Specimen inventorum:* "There are two first principles in all reasoning, the principle of non-contradiction, of course . . . and the principle of rendering reason." The second principle says that for any truth—for any true proposition, that is—a reasoned account is possible. *"Omnis veritatis reddi ratio potest."* Or, to translate more literally, for any true proposition, reason can be rendered.[3]

Beyond all those big philosophical words—reason, truth, principle—that generally command attention, the principle of reason also holds that reason must be rendered. (In French the expression corresponding to Leibniz's *reddere rationem* is *rendre raison de quelque chose;* it means to explain or account for something.) But what does "render" mean with respect to reason? Could reason be something that gives rise to exchange, circulation, borrowing, debt, donation, restitution? But in that case, who would be responsible for that debt or duty, and to whom? In the phrase *reddere rationem, "ratio"* is not the name of a faculty or power (*Logos, Ratio, Reason, Vernunft*) that is generally attributed by metaphysics to man, *zoon logon ekon,* the rational animal. If we had more time, we could follow out Leibniz's interpretation of the semantic shift which leads from the *ratio* of the *principium reddendae rationis,* the principle of rendering reason, to reason as the rational faculty—and in the end, to Kant's definition of reason as the faculty of principles. In any case, if "reason" in the principle of reason is not the rational faculty or power, that does not mean it is a thing, encountered somewhere among the beings and the objects in the world, which must be rendered up, given back. The question of this reason cannot be separated from a question about the modal verb "must" and the phrase "must be rendered." The "must" seems to cover the essence of our relationship to principle, it seems to mark out for us requirement, debt, duty, request, command, obligation, law, the imperative. Whenever reason can be rendered (*reddi potest*), it must. Can we, without further precautions, call this a moral imperative, in the Kantian sense of pure practical reason? It is not clear that the sense of "practical," as it is determined by a critique of pure practical reason, gets to the bottom of the "must," or reveals its origin, although such a critique has to presuppose such a "must." It could be shown, I think, that the critique of practical reason continually calls on the principle of reason, on its "must" which, although it is certainly not of a theoretical order, is nonetheless not simply "practical" or "ethical" in the Kantian sense.

A responsibility is involved here, however. We have to respond to the call of the principle of reason. In *Der Satz vom Grund* [*The Principle of Reason*], Heidegger names that call *Anspruch*: requirement, claim, request, demand, command, convocation; it always entails a certain addressing of speech. The word is not seen, it has to be heard and listened to, this apostrophe that enjoins us to respond to the principle of reason.

A question of responsibility, to be sure. But is answering *to* the principle of reason the same act as answering *for* the principle of reason? Is the scene the same? Is the landscape the same? And where is the university located within this space?

To respond to the call of the principle of reason is to "render reason," to explain effects through their causes, rationally; it is also to ground, to justify, to account for on the basis of principles or roots. Keeping in mind that Leibnizian moment whose originality should not be underestimated, the response to the call of the principle of reason is thus a response to the Aristotelian requirements, those of metaphysics, of primary philosophy, of the search for "roots," "principles," and "causes." At this point, scientific and techno-scientific requirements lead back to a common origin. And one of the most insistent questions in Heidegger's meditation is indeed that of the long "incubation" time that separated this origin from the emergence of the principle of reason in the seventeenth century. Not only does that principle constitute the verbal formulation of a requirement present since the dawn of Western science and philosophy, it provides the impetus for a new era of purportedly "modern" reason, metaphysics and technoscience. And one cannot *think* the possibility of the modern university, the one that is re-structured in the nineteenth century in all the Western countries, without inquiring into that event, that institution of the principle of reason.

But to answer for the principle of reason (and thus for the university), to answer for this call, to raise questions about the origin or ground of this principle of foundation (*Der Satz vom Grund*), is not simply to obey it or to respond in the face of this principle. We do not listen in the same way when we are responding to a summons as when we are questioning its meaning, its origin, its possibility, its goal, its limits. Are we obeying the principle of reason when we ask what grounds this principle which is itself a principle of grounding? We are not— which does not mean that we are disobeying it, either. Are we dealing here with a circle or with an abyss? The circle would consist in seeking to account for reason by reason, to render reason to the principle of reason, in appealing to the principle in order to make it speak of itself at the very point where, according to Heidegger, the principle of reason says nothing about reason itself. The abyss, the hole, the *Abgrund,* the empty "gorge" would be the impossibility for a principle of grounding to ground itself. This very grounding, then, like the university, would have to hold itself suspended above a most peculiar void. Are we to use reason to account for the principle of reason? Is the reason for reason rational? Is it rational to worry about reason and its principle? Not *simply;* but it would be over-hasty to seek to disqualify this concern and to refer those who experience it back to their own irrationalism, their obscurantism, their nihilism. Who is more faithful to reason's call, who hears it with a keener ear, who better sees the difference, the one who offers questions in return and tries to think through the possibility of that summons, or the one who does not want to hear any question about the reason of reason? This is all played out, along the path of the Heideggerian question, in a subtle difference of tone or stress, according to the particular words emphasized in the formula *nihil est sine ratione.* This statement has two different implications according to whether *"nihil"* and *"sine"* are stressed, or *"est"* and *"ratione."* I shall not attempt here, given the limits of this talk, to pursue all of the reckonings involved in this shift of emphasis. Nor shall I attempt— among other things, and for the same reasons—to reconstitute a dialogue between Heidegger and for example Charles Sanders Peirce. A strange and necessary dialogue on the compound theme, indeed, of the university and the principle of reason. In a remarkable essay on "The limits of Professionalism," Samuel Weber quotes Peirce who, in 1990, "in the context of a discussion on the role of higher education" in the United States, concludes as follows:

> Only recently have we seen an American man of science and of weight discuss the purpose of education, without once alluding to the only motive that animates the genuine scientific investigator. I am not guiltless in this matter myself, for in my youth I wrote some articles to uphold a doctrine called pragmatism, namely, that the meaning and essence of every conception lies in the application that is to be made of it. That is all very well, when properly understood. I do not intend to recant it. But the question arises, *what* is the ultimate application; and at that time I seem to have been inclined to subordinate the *conception* to the *act,* knowing to doing. Subsequent experience of life has taught me that the only thing that is really *desirable* without a reason for being so, is to render ideas and things reasonable. *One cannot well demand a reason for reasonableness itself.*[4]

To bring about such a dialogue between Peirce and Heidegger, we would have to go beyond the conceptual opposition between "conception" and "act," between "conception" and "application," theoretical view and praxis, theory and technique. This passage *beyond* is sketched out briefly by Peirce in the very movement of his dissatisfaction: what might the ultimate application be? What Peirce only outlines is the path where Heidegger feels the most to be at stake, especially in *Der Satz vom Grund.* Being unable to follow this path myself here in the way I have attempted to follow it elsewhere, I shall merely draw from it two assertions, at the risk of oversimplifying.

1. The modern dominance of the principle of reason had to go hand in hand with the interpretation of the essence of beings as objects, an object present as representation [*Vortsellung*], an object placed and positioned *before* a subject. This latter, a man who says "I," an ego certain of itself, thus ensures his own technical mastery over the totality of what is. The "re-" of *repraesentario* also expresses the movement that accounts for—"renders reason to"—a thing whose presence is encountered by rendering it present, by bringing it to the subject of representation, to the knowing self. This would be the place, if we only had the time, to consider the way Heidegger makes the language do its work (the interaction between *begegnen, entgegen, Gegenstand, Gegenwart* on the one hand. *Stellen, Vorstellen, Zustellen* on the other hand.)[5] This relation of representation—which in its whole extension is not merely a relation of knowing—has to be grounded, ensured, protected: that is what we are told by the principle of reason, the *Satz vom Grund.* A dominance is thus assured for representation, for *Vorstellen,* for the relation to the object, that is, to the being that is located *before* a subject that says "I" and assures itself of its own present existence. But this dominance of the "being-before" does not reduce to that of sight or of *theoria,* nor even to that of a metaphor of the optical (or indeed sklerophthalmic) dimension. It is in *Der Satz vom Grund* that Heidegger states all his reservations on the very presuppositions of such rhetoricizing interpretations. It is not a matter of distinguishing here between sight and nonsight, but rather between two ways of thinking of sight and of light, as well as between two conceptions of listening and voice. But it is true that a caricature of representational man, in the Heideggerian sense, would readily endow him with hard eyes permanently open to a nature that he is to dominate, to rape if necessary, by fixing it in front of himself, or by swooping down on it like a bird of prey. The principle of reason installs its empire only to the extent that the abyssal question of the being that is hiding within it remains hidden, and with it the question of the grounding of the ground itself, of grounding as *gruden* (to ground, to give or take ground: *Boden-nehmen*), as *begrunden* (to motivate, justify, authorize) or especially as *stitten* (to erect or institute, a meaning to which Heidegger accords a certain pre-eminence).[6]

2. Now that institution of modern technoscience that is the university *Stifung* is built both on the principle of reason and on what remains hidden in that principle. As if in passing, but in two passages that are important to us, Heidegger asserts that the modern university is "grounded" [*gegrundet*], "built" [*gebaut*] on the principle of reason, it "rests" [*ruht*] on this principle.[7] But if today's university, locus of modern science, "is grounded on the principle of grounding," that is, on reason [*grundet auf dem Satz vom Grund*], nowhere do we encounter within it the principle of reason itself, nowhere is this prin-

ciple thought through, scrutinized, interrogated as to its origin. Nowhere, within the university as such, is anyone wondering from where the call [*Anspruch*] of reason is voiced, nowhere is anyone inquiring into the origin of that demand for grounds, for reason that is to be provided, rendered, delivered: *"Woher spricht dieser Anspruch des Grundes aus seine Zustellung?"* And this dissimulation of its origin within what remains unthought is not harmful, quite the contrary, to the development of the modern university; indeed, Heidegger in passing makes certain laudatory remarks about that university: progress in the sciences, its militant interdisciplinarity, its discursive zeal, and so on. But all this is elaborated above an abyss, suspended over a "gorge"—by which we mean on grounds whose own grounding remains invisible and unthought.

Having reached this point in my reading, instead of involving you in a micrological study of Heidegger's *Der Satz vom Grund* or of his earlier texts on the University (in particular his inaugural less of 1929, *Was ist Metaphysik,* or the Rector's Speech of 1933, *Die Selbstbehauptung der deutschen Universitat*)—a study which I am attempting elsewhere, in Paris, and to which we shall doubtless refer in the discussions that come after this talk—instead of meditating at the edge of the abyss—even if on a bridge protected by "barriers"—I prefer to return to a certain concrete actuality in the problems that assail us in the university.

The framework of grounding, or foundation, and the dimension of the fundamental impose themselves on several counts in the space of the university, whether we are considering the question of its reason for being in general, or its specific missions, or the politics of teaching and research. Each time, what is at stake is the principle of reason as principle of grounding, foundation or institution. A major debate is under way today on the subject of the politics of research and teaching, and on the role that the university may play in this arena: whether this role is central or marginal, progressive or decadent, collaborative with or independent of that of other research institutions sometimes considered better suited to certain ends. The terms of this debate tend to be analogous—I am not saying they are identical—in all the highly industrialized countries, whatever their political regime, whatever role the State traditionally plays in this arena (and, as we all know, even the Western democracies vary considerably in this respect). In the so-called "developing countries," the problem takes shape according to models that are certainly different but in all events inseparable from the preceding ones.

Such a problematics cannot always—cannot any longer—be reduced to a problematics centered on the nation-state; it is now centered instead on multinational military-industrial complexes or techno-economic networks, or rather international technomilitary networks that are apparently multi- or transnational in form. In France, for some time, this debate has been organized around what is called the "orientation" [*finalisation*] of research. "Oriented" research is research that is programmed, focused, organized in an authoritarian fashion *in view* of its utilization (in view of "*ta khreia,*" Aristotle would say), whether we are talking about technology, economy, medicine, psychosociology, or military power—and in fact we are talking about all of these at once. There is doubtless greater sensitivity to this problem in countries where the politics of research depend closely upon state-managed or "nationalized" structures, but I believe that conditions are becoming more and more homogeneous among all the technologically advanced industrialized societies. We speak of "oriented" research where, not so long ago, we spoke—as Peirce did—of "application." For it growing more and more obvious that, without being immediately applied or applicable, research may "pay off," be usable, "end-oriented," in more or less deferred ways. And what is at stake is not merely what sometimes used to be called the techno-economic, medical, or military "by-products" of pure research. The detours, delays and relays of "orientation," its random aspects as well, are more disconcerting than ever. Hence the attempt, by every possible means, to take them into account, to integrate them to the rational calculus of programmed research. A term like "orient" is preferred to "apply," in addition, because the word is less "utilitarian," it leaves open the possibility that noble aims may be written into the program.

You may wonder what is being advocated, in France, in opposition to this concept of oriented research. The answer is basic, "fundamental" research, disinterested research with aims that would not be pledged in advance to some utilitarian purpose. Once upon a time it was possible to believe that pure mathematics, theoretical physics, philosophy (and, within philosophy, especially metaphysics and ontology) were basic disciplines shielded from power, inaccessible to programming by the pressures of the State or, under cover of the State, by civil society or capital interests. The sole concern of such basic research would be knowledge, truth, the disinterested exercise of reason, under the sole authority of the principle of reason.

And yet we know better than ever before what must have been true for all time, that this opposition between the basic and the end-oriented is of real but limited relevance. It is difficult to maintain this opposition with thoroughgoing conceptual as well as practical rigor, especially in the modern fields of the formal sciences, theoretical physics, astrophysics (consider the remarkable example of the science of astronomy, which is becoming useful after having been for so long the paradigm of disinterested contemplation), chemistry, molecular biology, and so forth. Within each of these fields—and they are more interrelated than ever— the so-called basic philosophical questions no longer simply take the form of abstract, sometimes epistemological questions raised after the fact; they arise at the very heart of scientific research in the widest variety of ways. One can no longer distinguish between technology on the one hand and theory, science and rationality on the other. The term techno-science has to be accepted, and its acceptance confirms the fact that an essential affinity ties together objective knowledge, the principle of reason, and a certain metaphysical determination of the relation to truth. We can no longer—and this is finally what Heidegger recalls and calls on us to think through—we can no longer dissociate the principle of reason from the very idea of technology in the realm of their modernity. One can no longer maintain the boundary that Kant, for example, sought to establish between the schema that he called "technical" and the one he called "architectonic" in the systematic organization of knowledge—which was also to ground a systematic organization of the university. The architectonic is the art of systems. "Under the government of reason, our knowledge in general," Kant says, "should not form a rhapsody, but it must form a system in which alone it can support and favor the essential aims of reason." To that pure rational unity of the architectonic, Kant opposes the scheme of the merely technical unity that is empirically oriented, according to views and ends that are incidental, not essential. It is thus a limit between two aims that Kant seeks to define, the essential and noble ends of reason that give rise to a fundamental science versus the incidental and empirical ends which can be systematized only in terms of technical schemas and necessities.

Today, in the orientation or "finalization" of research—forgive me for presuming to recall such obvious points—it is impossible to distinguish between these two sets of aims. It is impossible, for example, to distinguish programs that one would like to consider "worthy," or even technically profitable for humanity, from other programs that would be destructive. This is not new; but never before has so-called basic scientific research been so deeply committed to aims that are at the same time military aims. The very essence of the military, the limits of military technology and even the limits of its accountability are no longer definable. When we hear that two million dollars a minute are being spent in the world today for armaments, we may assume that this figure represents simply the cost of weapons manufacture. But military investments do not stop at that. For military power, even police power, and more generally speaking the entire defensive and offensive security establishment benefits from more than just the "byproducts" of basic research. In the advanced technological societies, this establishment programs, orients, orders, and finances, directly or indirectly, through the State or otherwise, the front-line research that is apparently the least "end-oriented" of all. This is all to obvious in such areas as physics, biology, medicine, biotechnology, bioprogramming, data processing and telecommunications. We have only to mention telecommunications and data processing to assess the extent of the phenomenon: the "orientation" of research is limitless, everything in these areas proceeds "in view" of technical and instrumental security. At the service of war, of national and international security, research programs have to encompass the entire field of information, the stockpiling of knowledge, the workings and thus also the essence of language and of all semiotic systems, translation, coding and decoding, the play of presence and absence, hermeneutics, semantics, structural and generative linguistics, pragmatics, rhetoric. I am accumulating all these disciplines in a haphazard way, on purpose, but I shall end with literature, poetry, the arts and fiction in general: the theory that has these disciplines as its object may be just as useful in ideological warfare as it is in experimentation with variables in all-too-familiar perversions of the referential function. Such a theory may always be put to work in communications strategy, the theory of commands, the most refined military pragmatics of jussive utterances (by what token, for example, will it be clear that an utterance is to be taken as a command in the new technology of telecommunications? How are the new resources of simulation and simulacrum to be controlled? And so on . . .). One can just as easily seek to use the theoretical formulations of sociology, psychology, even psychoanalysis in order to refine what was called in France during the Indochinese or Algerian wars the powers of "psychological action"—alternating with torture. From now on, so long as it has the means, a military budget can invest in anything at all, in view of deferred profits: "basic" scientific theory, the humanities, literary theory and philosophy. The compartment of philosophy which covered all this, and which Kant thought ought to be kept unavailable to any utilitarian purpose and to the orders of any power whatsoever in its search for truth, can no longer lay claim to such autonomy. What is produced in this field can always be used. And even if it should remain useless in its results, in its productions, it can always serve to keep the masters of discourse busy: the experts, professionals of rhetoric, logic or philosophy who might otherwise be applying their energy elsewhere. Or again, it may in certain situations secure an ideological bonus of luxury and gratuitousness for a society that can afford it, within certain limits. Furthermore, when certain random consequences of research are taken into account, it is always possible to have in view some eventual benefit that may ensue from an apparently useless research project (in philosophy or the humanities, for example). The history of the sciences encourages researchers to integrate that margin of randomness into their centralized calculation. They then proceed to adjust the means at their disposal, the available financial support, and the distribution of credits. A State power or the forces that it represents no longer need to prohibit research or to censor discourse, especially in the West. It is enough that they can limit the means, can regulate support for production, transmission, and diffusion. The machinery for this new "censorship" in the broad sense is much more complex and omnipresent than in Kant's day, for example, when the entire problematics and the entire topology of the university were organized around the exercise of royal censorship. Today, in the Western democracies, that form of censorship has almost entirely disappeared. The prohibiting limitations function through multiple channels that are decentralized, difficult to bring together into a system. The unacceptability of a discourse, the noncertification of a research project, the illegitimacy of a course offering are declared by evaluative actions: studying such evaluations is, it seems to me, one of the tasks most indispensable to the exercise of academic responsibility, most urgent for the maintenance of its dignity. Within the university itself, forces that are apparently external to it (presses, foundations, the mass media) are intervening in an ever more decisive way. University presses play a mediating role that entails the most serious responsibilities, since scientific criteria, in principle represented by the members of the university corporation, have to come to terms with many other aims. When the margin of randomness has to be narrowed, restrictions on support affect the disciplines that are the least profitable in the short run. And that provokes, within the professions, all kinds of effects, certain ones of which seem to have lost any direct relation to that causality—which is itself still largely overdetermined. The shifting determination of the margin of randomness always depends upon the techno-economic situation of a society in its relation to the entire world arena. In the United States, for example (and it is not just one example among others), without even mentioning the economic regulation that allows certain surplus values—through the channel of private foundations among others—to sustain research or creative projects that are not immediately or apparently profitable, we also know that military programs, especially those of the Navy, can very rationally subsidize linguistic, semiotic or anthropological investigations. These in turn are related to history, literature, hermeneutics, law, political science, psychoanalysis, and so forth.

The concept of information or informatization is the most general operator here. It integrates the basic to the oriented, the purely rational to the technical, thus bearing witness to that original intermingling of the metaphysical and the technical. The value of "form" is not foreign to it; but let us drop this difficult point for now. In *Der Satz vom Grund,* Heidegger locates this concept of "information" (understood and pronounced as in English, he says at the time when he is putting America and Russia side by side like two symmetrical and homogeneous continents of metaphysics as technique) in a dependence upon the principle of reason, as a principle of integral calculability. Even the principle of uncertainty (and he would have said the same thing of a certain interpretation of undecidability) continues to operate within the problematics of representation and of the subject–object relation. Thus he calls this the atomic era and quotes a book of popularization entitled "We shall live thanks to atoms" with prefaces both by Otto Hahn, Nobel prize-winner and "fundamentalist" physicist, and Franz Joseph Strauss, then minister of national defense. Information ensures the insurance of calculation and the calculation of insurance. In this we recognize the period of the principle of reason. Leibniz, as Heidegger recalls, is considered to have been the inventor of life insurance. In the form of information [in *der Gestalt der Information*], Heidegger says, the principle of reason dominates our entire representation [*Vorstellen*] and delineates a period for which everything depends upon the delivery of atomic energy. Delivery in German is *Zustellung,* a word that also applies, as Heidegger points out, to the delivery of mail. It belongs to the chain of *Gestell,* from the *Stellen* group [*Vorstellen, Nachstellen, Zustellen, Sicherstellen*] that characterizes technological modernity. "Information in this sense is the most economic, the most rapid and the clearest (univocal, *eindeutig*) stockpiling, recording and communication of news. It must instruct men about the safeguarding [*Sickerstellung*] of what will meet their needs, *ta khreia.* Computer technology, data banks, artificial intelligences, translating machines, and so forth, all these are constructed on the basis of that instrumental determination of a calculable language. Information does not inform merely by delivering an information content, it gives form, *"in-formiert," "formiert zugleich."* It installs man in a form that permits him to ensure his mastery on earth and beyond. All this has to be pondered as the effect of the principle of reason, or, put more rigorously, has to be analyzed as the effect of a dominant interpretation of that principle, of a certain emphasis in the way we heed its summons. But I have said that I cannot deal with the question of such stress here; it lies outside the scope of my topic.

What, then, is my topic? What do I have in view that has led me to present things as I have done so far? I have been thinking especially of the necessity to awaken or to resituate a responsibility, in the university or in face of the university, whether one belongs to it or not.

Those analysts who study the informative and instrumental value of language today are necessarily led to the very confines of the principle of reason thus interpreted. This can happen in any number of disciplines. But if the analysts end up for example working on the structures of the simulacrum or of literary fiction, on a poetic rather than an informative value of language, on the effects of undecidability, and so on, by that very token they are interested in possibilities that arise at the outer limits of the authority and the power of the principle of reason. On that basis, they may attempt to define new responsibilities in the face of the university's total subjection to the technologies of informatization. Not so as to refuse them; not so as to counter with some obscurantist irrationalism (and irrationalism, like nihilism, is a posture that is completely symmetrical to, thus dependent upon, the principle of reason). The theme of extravagance as an irrationalism—there is very clear evidence for this—dates from the period when the principle of reason was being formulated. Leibniz denounced it in his *New Essays on Human Understanding*. To raise these new questions may sometimes protect an aspect of philosophy and the humanities that has always resisted the influx of knowledge; it may also preserve the memory of what is much more deeply buried and ancient than the principle of reason. But the approach I am advocating here is often felt by certain guardians of the "humanities" or of the positive sciences as a threat. It is interpreted as such by those who most often have never sought to understand the history and the system of norms specific to their own institution, the deontology of their own profession. They do not wish to know how their discipline has been constituted, particularly in its modern professional form, since the beginning of the nineteenth century and under the watchful vigilance of the principle of reason. For the principle of reason may have obscurantist and nihilist effects. They can be seen more or less everywhere, in Europe and in America among those who believe they are defending philosophy, literature and the humanities against these new modes of questioning that are also a new relation to language and tradition, a new *affirmation,* and new ways of taking responsibility. We can easily see on which side obscurantism and nihilism are lurking when on occasion great professors or representatives of prestigious institutions lose all sense of proportion and control; on such occasions they forget the principles that they claim to defend in their work and suddenly begin to heap insults, to say whatever comes into their heads on the subject of texts that they obviously have never opened or that they have encountered through a mediocre journalism that in other circumstances they would pretend to scorn.[8]

It is possible to speak of this new responsibility that I have invoked only by sounding a call to practice it. It would be the responsibility of a community of thought for which the frontier between basic and oriented research would no longer be secured, or in any event not under the same conditions as before. I call it a community of thought in the broad sense—"at large"—rather than a community of research, of science or philosophy, since these values are most often subjected to the unquestioned authority of a principle of reason. Now reason is only one species of thought—which does not mean that thought is "irrational." Such a community would interrogate the essence of reason and of the principle of reason, the values of the basic, of the principial, of radicality, of the *arkhe* in general, and it would attempt to draw out all the possible consequences of this questioning. It is not certain that such thinking can bring together a community or found an institution in the traditional sense of these words. What is meant by community and institution must be rethought. This thinking must also unmask—an infinite task—all the ruses of end-orienting reason, the paths by which apparently disinterested research can find itself indirectly reappropriated, reinvested by programs of all sorts. That does not mean that "orientation" is bad in itself and that it must be combatted, far from it. Rather, I am defining the necessity for a new way of educating students that will prepare them to undertake new analyses in order to evaluate these ends and to choose, when possible, among them all.

As I mentioned earlier, along with some colleagues I was asked last year by the French government to prepare a report in view of the creation of an International College of Philosophy. I insisted, in that report, on stressing the dimension that in this context I am calling "thought"—a dimension that is not reducible to technique, nor to science, nor to philosophy. This International College would not only be a College of Philosophy but also a place where philosophy itself would be questioned. It would be open to types of research that are not perceived as legitimate today, or that are insufficiently developed in French or foreign institutions, including some research that could be called "basic"; but it would not stop there. We would go one step further, providing a place to work on the *value and meaning* of the basic, the fundamental, on its opposition to goal-orientation, on the ruses of orientation in all its domains. As in the seminar that I mentioned earlier, the report confronts the political, ethical, and juridical consequences of such an undertaking. I cannot go into more detail here without keeping you much too long.

These new responsibilities cannot be purely academic. If they remain extremely difficult to assume, extremely precarious and threatened, it is because they must at once keep alive the memory of a tradition and make an opening beyond any program, that is, toward what is called the future. And the discourse, the works, or the position-taking that these responsibilities inspire, as to the institution of science and research, no longer stem solely from the sociology of knowledge, from sociology or politology. These disciplines are doubtless more necessary than ever; I would be the last to want to disqualify them. But whatever conceptual apparatus they may have, whatever axiomatics, whatever methodology (Marxist or neo-Marxist, Weberian or neo-Weberian, Mannheimian, some combination of these or something else entirely), they never touch upon that which, in themselves, continues to be based on the principle of reason and thus on the essential foundation of the modern university. They never question scientific normativity, beginning with the value of objectivity or of objectivation, which governs and authorizes their discourse. Whatever may be their scientific value—and it may be considerable—these sociologies of the institution remain in this sense internal to the university, intra-institutional, controlled by the deepseated standards, even the programs, of the space that they claim to analyze. This can be observed, among other things, in the rhetoric, the rites, the modes of presentation and demonstration that they continue to respect. Thus I shall go so far as to say that the discourse of Marxism and psychoanalysis, including those of Marx and Freud, inasmuch as they are standardized by a project of scientific practice and by the principle of reason, are intra-institutional, in any event homogeneous with the discourse that dominates the university in the last analysis. And the fact that this discourse is occasionally proffered by people who are not professional academics changes nothing essential. It simply explains, to a certain extent, the fact that even when it claims to be revolutionary, this discourse does not always trouble the most conservative forces of the university. Whether it is understood or not, it is enough that it does not threaten the fundamental axiomatics and deontology of the institution, its rhetoric, its rites and procedures. The academic landscape easily accommodates such types of discourse more easily within its economy and its ecology; however, when it does not simply exclude those who raise questions at the level of the foundation or non-foundation of the foundation of the university, it reacts much more fearfully to those that address sometimes the same questions to Marxism, to psychoanalysis, to the sciences, to philosophy and the humanities. It is not a matter simply of questions that one formulates while submitting oneself, as I am doing here, to the principle of reason, but also of preparing oneself thereby to transform the modes of writing, approaches to pedagogy, the procedures of academic exchange, the relation to languages, to other disciplines, to the institution in general, to its inside and its outside. Those who venture forth along this path, it seems to me, need not set themselves up in opposition to the principle of reason, nor need they give way to "irrationalism." They may continue to assume within the university, along with its memory and tradition, the imperative of professional rigor and competence. There is a double gesture here, a double postulation: to ensure professional competence and the most serious tradition of the university even while going as far as possible, theoretically and practically, in the most directly underground thinking about the abyss beneath the university, to think at one and the same time the entire "Cornellian" landscape—the campus on the heights, the bridges, and if necessary the barriers above the abyss—and the abyss itself. It is this double gesture that appears unsituatable and thus unbearable to certain university professionals in every country who join ranks to foreclose or to censure it by all available means, simultaneously denouncing the "professionalism" and the "antiprofessionalism" of those who are calling others to these new responsibilities.

I shall not venture here to deal with the debate on "professionalism" that is developing in your country. Its features are, to a certain extent at least, specific to the history of the American university. But I shall conclude on this general theme of "professions." At the risk of contradicting what I have been urging here, I should like to caution against another kind of precipitous reaction. For the responsibility that I am trying to situate cannot be simple. It implies multiple sites, a stratified terrain, postulations that are undergoing continual displacement, a sort of strategic rhythm. I said earlier that I would be speaking only of a certain rhythm, for example that of the blinking of an eye, and that I would only be playing one risk off against another, the barrier against the abyss, the abyss against the barrier, the one with the other and the one under the other.

Beyond technical goal-orientation, even beyond the opposition between technical goal-orientation and the principle of sufficient reason, beyond the affinity between technology and metaphysics, what I have here called "thought" risks in its turn (but I believe this risk is unavoidable—it is the risk of the future itself) being reappropriated by socio-political forces that could find it in their own interest in certain situations. Such a "thought" indeed cannot be produced outside of certain historical, techno-economic, politico-institutional and linguistic conditions. A strategic analysis that is to be as vigilant as possible must thus with its eyes wide open attempt to ward off such reappropriations. (I should have liked to situate at this point certain questions about the "politics" of Heideggerian thought, especially as elaborated prior to *Der Satz vom Grund,* for example in the two inaugural discourses of 1929 and 1933.)

I shall limit myself, however, to the double question of "professions." First: does the university have as its essential mission that of producing professional competencies, which may sometimes be external to the university? Second: is the task of the university to ensure within itself—and under what conditions—the reproduction of professional competence by preparing professors for pedagogy and for research who have respect for a certain code? One may answer the second question in the affirmative without having done so for the first, and seek to keep professional forms and values internal to the university outside the market place while keeping the goal-orientation of social work outside of the university. The new responsibility of the "thought" of which we are speaking cannot fail to be accompanied at least by a movement of suspicion, even of rejection with respect to the professionalization of the university in these two senses, and especially in the first, which regulates university life according to the supply and demand of the marketplace and according to a purely technical ideal of competence. To this extent at least, such "thought" may, at a minimum, result in reproducing a highly traditional politics of knowledge. And the effects may be those that belong to a social hierarchy in the exercise of technopolitical power. I am not saying that this "thought" is identical with that politics, and that it is therefore necessary to abstain from it; I am saying that under certain conditions it can serve that politics, and that everything thus comes down to the analysis of those conditions. In modern times, Kant, Nietzsche, Heidegger and numerous others have all said as much, quite unmistakably: the essential feature of academic responsibility must not be professional education (and the pure core of academic autonomy, the essence of the university, is located in the philosophy department, according to Kant). Does this affirmation not repeat the profound and hierarchizing political evaluation of Metaphysics, I mean of Aristotle's *Metaphysics?* Shortly after the passage that I read at the beginning (981b and following), one sees a theoretico-political hierarchy being put into place. At the top, there is theoretical knowledge. It is not sought after in view of its utility; and the holder of this knowledge, which is always a knowledge of causes and of principles, is the leader of *arkhitekton* of a society at work, is positioned above the manual laborer [*kheiroteknes*] who acts without knowing, just as a fire burns. Now this theoretician leader, this knower of causes who has no need of "practical" skill, is in essence a *teacher*. Beyond the fact of knowing causes and of possessing reason [*to logon ekhein*], he bears another mark [*semeion*] of recognition: the "capacity to teach" [*to dunasthai didaskein*]. To teach, then, and at the same time to direct, steer, organize the empirical work of the laborers. The theoretician-teacher or "architect" is a leader because he is on the side of the *arkhe*, of beginning and commanding. He commands—he is the premier or the prince—because he knows causes and principles, the "whys" and thus also the "wherefores" of things. Before the fact, and before anyone else, he answers to the principle of reason which is the first principle, the principle of principles. And that is why he takes orders from no one; it is he, on the contrary, who orders, prescribes, lays down the law (982a 18). And it is normal that this superior science, with the power that it confers by virtue of its very lack of utility, is developed in places [*topoi*], in regions where leisure is possible. Thus Aristotle points out that the mathematical arts were developed in Egypt owing to the leisure time enjoyed by the priestly caste [*to ton iereon ethnos*], the priestly folk.

Kant, Nietzsche and Heidegger, speaking of the university, premodern or modern, do not say exactly what Aristotle said, nor do all three of them say exactly the same thing. But they also do say the same thing. Even though he admits the industrial model of the division of labor into the university, Kant places the so-called "lower" faculty, the faculty of philosophy—a place of pure rational knowledge, a place where truth has to be spoken without controls and without concern for "utility," a place where the very meaning and the autonomy of the university meet—Kant places this faculty above and outside professional education: the architectonic schema of pure reason is above and outside the technical schema. In his *Lectures on the Future of our Educational Establishments*, Nietzsche condemns the division of labor in the sciences, condemns utilitarian and journalistic culture in the service of the State, condemns the professional ends of the University. The more one does [*tut*] in the area of training, the more one has to think [*denken*]. And, still in the first Lecture: *"Man muss nicht nur Standpunkte, sondern auch Gedanken haben!"*; one must not have viewpoints alone, but also thoughts! As for Heidegger, in 1929, in his inaugural lesson entitled "What is Metaphysics," he deplores the henceforth technical organization of the university and its compartmentalizing specialization. And even in his Rector's Speech, at the very point where he makes an appeal on behalf of the three services (*Arbeitsdienst, Wehrdienst, Wissensdienst,* the service of work, the military, and knowledge), at the very point where he is recalling that these services are of equal rank and equally original (he had recalled earlier that for the Greeks *theoria* was only the highest form of *praxis* and the mode, par excellence, of *energeia*), Heidegger nevertheless violently condemns disciplinary compartmentalization and "exterior training in view of a profession," as "an idle and inauthentic thing" [*Das Mussige und Unechte ausserlicher Berufsabrichtung . . .*].

Desiring to remove the university from "useful" programs and from professional ends, one may always, willingly or not, find oneself serving unrecognized ends, reconstituting powers of caste, class, or corporation. We are in an implacable political topography: one step further in view of greater profundity or radicalization, even going beyond the "profound" and the "radical," the principal, the *arkhe,* one step further toward a sort of original an-archy risks producing or reproducing the hierarchy. "Thought" requires *both* the principle of reason *and* what is beyond the principle of reason, the *arkhe* and an-archy. Between the two, the difference of a breath or an accent, only the *enactment* of this "thought" can decide. That decision is always risky, it always risks the worst. To claim to eliminate that risk by an institutional program is quite simply to erect a barricade against a future. The decision of thought cannot be an intra-institutional event, an academic moment.

All this does not define a politics, nor even a responsibility. Only, at best, some negative conditions, a "negative wisdom," as the Kant of *The Conflict of the Faculties* would say: preliminary cautions, protocols of vigilance for a new *Aufklärung,* what must be seen and kept in sight in a modern re-elaboration of that old problematics. Beware of the abysses and the gorges, but also of the bridges and the barriers. Beware of what opens the university to the outside and the bottomless, but also of what, closing it in on itself, would create only an illusion of closure, would make the university available to any sort of interest, or else render it perfectly useless. Beware of ends; but what would a university be without ends?

Neither in its medieval nor in its modern form has the university disposed freely of its own absolute autonomy and of the rigorous conditions of its own unity. During more than eight centuries, "university" has been the name given by a society to a sort of supplementary body that at one and the same time it wanted to project outside itself and to keep jealously to itself, to emancipate and to control. On this double basis, the university was supposed to *represent* society. And in a certain way it has done so: it has reproduced society's scenography, its views, conflicts, contradictions, its play and its differences, and also its desire for organic union in a total body. Organicist language is always associated with "techno-industrial" language in "modern" discourse on the university. But with the relative autonomy of a technical apparatus, indeed that of a machine and of a prosthetic body, this artifact that is the university has *reflected society* only in giving it the chance for reflection, that is, also, for *dissociation.* The time for reflection, here, signifies not only that the internal rhythm of the university apparatus is relatively independent of social time and relaxes the urgency of command, ensures for it a great and precious freedom of play. An empty place for chance: the invagination of an inside pocket. The time for reflection is also the chance for turning back on the very conditions of reflection, in all the senses of that word, as if with the help of a new optical device one could finally see sight, could not only view the natural landscape, the city, the bridge and the abyss, but could view viewing. As if through an acoustical device one could hear hearing, in other words, seize the inaudible in a sort of poetic telephony. Then the time of reflection is also an other time, it is heterogeneous with what it reflects and perhaps gives time for what calls for and is called thought. It is the chance for an event about which one does not know whether or not, presenting itself *within* the university, it belongs to the history of the university. It may also be brief and paradoxical, it may tear up time, like the instant invoked by Kierkegaard, one of those thinkers who are foreign, even hostile to the university, who give us more to think about, with respect to the essence of the university, than academic reflections themselves. The chance for this event is the chance of an instant, an *Augenblick,* a "wink" or a "blink," it takes place "in the twinkling of an eye." I would say, rather, "in the twilight of an eye," for it is in the most crepuscular, the most westerly situation of the Western university that the chances of this "twinkling" of thought are multiplied. In a period of "crisis," as we say, a period of decadence and renewal, when the institution is "on the blink," provocation to think brings together in the *same* instant the desire for memory and exposure to the future, the fidelity of a guardian faithful enough to want to keep even the chance of a future, in other words the singular responsibility of what he does not have and of what is not yet. Neither in his keeping nor in his purview. Keep the memory and keep the chance—is this possible? And chance—can it be kept? Is it not, as its name indicates, the risk or the advent of the fall, even of decadence, the falling due that befalls you at the bottom of the "gorge"? I don't know. I don't know if it is possible to keep both memory and chance. I am tempted to think, rather, that the one cannot be kept without the other, without keeping the other and being kept from the other. Differently. That double guard will be assigned, as its responsibility, to the strange destiny of the university. To its law, to its reason for being and to its truth. Let us risk one more etymological wink: truth is what keeps, that is, both preserves and is preserved. I am thinking here of *Wahrheit,* of the *Wahren* of *Wahrheit* and of *veritas*—whose name figures on the coat of arms of so many American universities. It institutes guardians and calls upon them to watch faithfully—truthfully—over itself.

Let me recall my *incipit* and the single question that I raised at the outset: how can we not speak, today, of the university? Have I said it, or done it? Have I said how one must not speak, today, of the university? Or have I rather spoken as one should not do today, within the University? Only others can answer. Beginning with you.

Translated by Catherine Porter and Edward P. Morris

Notes

1. In regard to this "naturalism" (a frequent, but not general phenomenon that Kant, for example, eludes at the beginning of the *Conflict of the Faculties*), and also to the classic motif of interdisciplinarity as an effect of the architectonic totality; see, for example, Schleiermacher's 1808 essay "Geregenther Gedanken über Universitaten in deutschem Sinn, nepst einem Annang über ein neu zu errontence." French translation of this text appears in a noteworthy collection, *Philosophies de l'université l'idéalism allemand et la question de l'Université,* ed. Ferry, Pesron, Renault [Paris: Pavon, 1979].

2. James Siegel, "Academic Work: The View from Cornell," *Diacritics* 11:1 [Spring 1981], 68–83; the quotation, on page 69, is taken from Kermit Parsons, *The Cornell Campus: A History of Its Planning and Development* [Ithaca: Cornell University Press, 1968].

3. Translator's Note. About national idioms and idioms which, like Latin, aspire to greater catholicity: Leibniz's *rationem reddere*—a phrase by no means his exclusive property, but common to philosophy at large—is easily carried over into ordinary

French as *rendre raison, rendre raison de quelque chose;* but in English, today, "render reason" sounds outlandish. The Oxford dictionary shows that English had the idiom at one time; setting aside a willfully archaic and dialectical sentence from Walter Scott, the most recent example adduced is from *An Exposition of the Creed,* by John Pearson, bishop of Chester, published in London in 1659, and it is an example not without interest for our purposes. "Thus," says Pearson as he expounds Article IX, "the Church of Christ in it's [sic] primary institution was made to be of a diffusive nature, to spread and extend itself from the City of *Jerusalem,* where it first began, to all the parts and corners of the earth. This reason did the ancient fathers render why the Church was called Catholick." [*An Exposition* . . . , (Ann Arbor, Michigan: University Microfilms, 1968), p. 697.] He then goes on to say that for a second reason the church is called catholic because it teaches everything, or at least everything necessary to Christian faith. Apparently, there was a whole teaching of diffusion and dissemination well before our own time. To judge from the quotations given by OED, *to render reason* (to give it back, as it were) worked in exchange and concert with *to yield reason* and *to give reason:* any one of the three could mean to give grounds for one's thoughts and assertions, but also, to give an account of one's acts or conduct, when summoned to do so: to be held accountable and to speak accordingly. In 1690, writing not of reason but only of understanding, Locke argued that we rank things under distinct names "according to complex ideas in us," as he says, "and not according to precise, distinct, real essences in them." We cannot denominate things by their real essences, as Locke puts the matter, for the good reason that "we know them not." Even the familiar objects of our everyday world are composed we know not how; they must have their reason, but we cannot give it back to them. Thus, for all his practical bent, Locke is drawn to say, and I quote him once again, "When we come to examine the stones we tread on, or the iron we daily handle, we presently find that we know not their make, and can give no reason of the different qualities we find in them" [*An Essay concerning Human Understanding,* III, vi, 8–9]. In English, as in French or Latin, at one time people could give reason, or render it, or not be able to render it.—E.P.M.

4. In this quotation from Peirce's *Values in a Universe of Chance* [(Stanford, Ca.: Stanford University Press, 1958), p. 332], in addition to the last sentence, I have italicized the allusion to *desire* in order to echo the opening words of Aristotle's *Metaphysics.* Weber's article appeared in a double issue of *The Oxford Literary Review* 5: 1–2 (1982), pp. 59–79.

5. Here is but one example: "Rationem reddere heisst: den Grund zurückgeben. Weshal zurück und wohin zurück? Weil es sich in den Bewisgängen, allgemein gesprochen im Erkennen um das *Vor*-stellen der Gegenstände handelt, kommt dieses zurück ins Spiel. Die lateinische Sprache der Philosophie sagt es deutlicher: das Vorstellen is repraesentatio. Das Begegnende wird auf das vorstellende Ich zu, auf es zurück und ihm entgegen praesentiert, in eine Gegenwart gestellt. Gemäss dem principium reddendae rationis muss das Vorstellen, wenn es ein erkennendes sein soll, den Grund des Gegegnenden auf das Vorstellen zu un d.h. ihm zurückgeben (reddere). Im erkennenden Vorstellen wird dem erkennenden Ich der Grund zu-gestellt. Dies Verlangt das principium rationis. Des Satz vom Grund is darum für Leibniz der Grundsatz des zuzustellenden Grundes" [*Der Satz vom Grund* (Pfullingen: G. Neske, 1957), p. 45].

6. In "Vom Wesen des Grundes," *Wegmarken* [Frankfurt am Main: Klostermann, 1976], pp. 60–61.

7. "And yet, without this all powerful principle there would be no modern science, and without such a science there would be no university today. The latter rests upon the principle of reason [*Diese gründet auf dem Satz vom Grund*]. How should we

represent that to ourselves [*Wie sollen wir uns dies vorstellen*], the university founded *gegründet* on a sentence (a primary proposition: *auf einen Satz*)? Can we risk such an assertion [*Dürfen wir eine solche Behauptung wagen*]" [*Der Satz vom Grund. Dritte Stunde,* p. 49].

8. Among many possible examples, I shall mention only two recent articles. They have at least one trait in common: their authors are highly placed representatives of two institutions whose power and influence hardly need to be recalled. I refer to "The Crisis in English Studies" by Walter Jackson Bate, Kingsley Porter University Professor at Harvard [*Harvard Magazine,* Sept./Oct. 1982], and to "The Shattered Humanities" by Willis J. Bennett, Chairman of the National Endowment for the Humanities [*Wall Street Journal,* Dec. 31, 1982]. The latter of these articles carries ignorance and irrationality so far as to write the following: "A popular movement in literary criticism called "Deconstruction" denies that there are any texts at all. If there are no texts, there are no great texts, and no argument for reading." The former makes remarks about deconstruction—and this is not by chance—that are, we might say, just as unnerved. As Paul de Man notes in an admirable short essay ["The Return to Philogy," *Times Literary Supplement,* December 10, 1982], Professor Bate "has this time confined his sources of information to *Newsweek* magazine. . . . What is left is a matter of law-enforcement rather than a critical debate. One must be feeling very threatened indeed to become so aggressively defensive."

Pierre Bourdieu (1930–2002)

Bourdieu was a French sociologist. In the forthcoming text, the introduction to his book *Distinction: A Social Critique of the Judgment of Taste,* Bourdieu examines relations between aesthetic taste and social status. Challenging Immanuel Kant's famous theory about the disinterested nature of artistic judgments, Bourdieu argues that aesthetic taste is a social construction tied to class privileges. Many people in the humanities and social sciences have found Bourdieu's discussions of "cultural capital" and *habitus* particularly helpful. Cultural capital signifies educationally acquired knowledge and sensibilities such as taste. And *habitus,* according to Derek Robbins in *The Works of Pierre Bourdieu,* signifies "a process of socialization whereby the dominant modes of thought and experience inherent in the social and physical world (both of which are symbolically constructed) are internalized by social agents" (84). As you read Bourdieu, consider some of the relations between the concept of ideology on the one hand and the concepts of cultural capital and *habitus* on the other hand.

Bourdieu attended college with Jacques Derrida, and both received degrees in philosophy. In the early 1960s, however, Bourdieu shifted his intellectual focus to anthropology and sociology, and in 1968, he became the director of the Centre de Sociologie Européenne. Bourdieu is very interested in how classifications are made in society, but deciding just how to classify his own critical practices and theoretical orientation is not easy. Some scholars see him as a structuralist, others see him as working within the Marxist traditions, and yet others see in his work a stance that might be termed post-Marxist. In an interview with Kevin Ovenden, Bourdieu himself rejected the structuralist identification. Of one thing we are sure, however: Bourdieu was born in southern France, in Dengvin. He taught in colonial French Algeria, and his experiences there helped spur his disciplinary shift from philosophy to anthropology and sociology. Some of Bourdieu's best known books include *The Logic of Practice* (trans. 1990), *Distinction: A Social Critique of the Judgment of Taste* (trans. 1987), *Language and Symbolic Power* (trans. 1991), *Homo Academicus* (1988), *The Rules of Art: Genesis and Structure of the Literary Field* (trans. 1995), and *The Field of Cultural Production* (trans. 1993).

Introduction

You said it, my good knight! There ought to be laws to protect the body of acquired knowledge.
Take one of our good pupils, for example: modest and diligent, from his earliest grammar classes he's kept a little notebook full of phrases.
After hanging on the lips of his teachers for twenty years, he's managed to build up an intellectual stock in trade; doesn't it belong to him as if it were a house, or money?

Paul Claudel, *Le soulier de satin*, Day III, Scene ii

There is an economy of cultural goods, but it has a specific logic. Sociology endeavours to establish the conditions in which the consumers of cultural goods, and their taste for them, are produced, and at the same time to describe the different ways of appropriating such of these objects as are regarded at a particular moment as works of art, and the social conditions of the constitution of the mode of appropriation that is considered legitimate. But one cannot fully understand cultural practices unless 'culture', in the restricted, normative sense of ordinary usage, is brought back into 'culture' in the anthropological sense, and the elaborated taste for the most refined objects is reconnected with the elementary taste for the flavours of food.

Whereas the ideology of charisma regards taste in legitimate culture as a gift of nature, scientific observation shows that cultural needs are the product of upbringing and education: surveys establish that all cultural practices (museum visits, concert-going, reading etc.), and preferences in literature, painting or music, are closely linked to educational level (measured by qualifications or length of schooling) and secondarily to social origin.[1] The relative weight of home background and of formal education (the effectiveness and duration of which are closely dependent on social origin) varies according to the extent to which the different cultural practices are recognized and taught by the educational system, and the influence of social origin is strongest—other things being equal—in 'extra-curricular' and avant-garde culture. To the socially recognized hierarchy of the arts, and within each of them, of genres, schools or periods, corresponds a social hierarchy of the consumers. This predisposes tastes to function as markers of 'class'. The manner in which culture has been acquired lives on in the manner of using it: the importance attached to manners can be understood once it is seen that it is these imponderables of practice which distinguish the different—and ranked—modes of culture acquisition, early or late, domestic or scholastic, and the classes of individuals which they characterize (such as 'pedants' and *mondains*). Culture also has its titles of nobility—awarded by the educational system—and its pedigrees, measured by seniority in admission to the nobility.

The definition of cultural nobility is the stake in a struggle which has gone on unceasingly, from the seventeenth century to the present day, between groups differing in their ideas of culture and of the legitimate relation to culture and to works of art, and therefore differing in the conditions of acquisition of which these dispositions are the product.[2] Even in the classroom, the dominant definition of the legitimate way of appropriating culture and works of art favours those who have had early access to legitimate culture, in a cultured household, outside of scholastic disciplines, since even within the educational system it devalues scholarly knowledge and interpretation as 'scholastic' or even 'pedantic' in favour of direct experience and simple delight.

The logic of what is sometimes called, in typically 'pedantic' language, the 'reading' of a work of art, offers an objective basis for this opposition. Consumption is, in this case, a stage in a process of communication, that is, an act of deciphering, decoding, which presupposes practical or explicit mastery of a cipher or code. In a sense, one can say that the capacity to see (*voir*) is a function of the knowledge (*savoir*), or concepts, that is, the words, that are available to name visible things, and which are, as it were, programmes for perception. A work of art has meaning and interest only for someone who possesses the cultural competence, that is, the code, into which it is encoded. The conscious or unconscious implementation of explicit or implicit schemes of perception and appreciation which constitutes pictorial or musical culture is the hidden condition for recognizing the styles characteristic of a period, a school or an author, and more generally, for the familiarity with the internal logic of works that aesthetic enjoyment presupposes. A beholder who lacks the specific code feels lost in a chaos of sounds and rhythms, colours and lines, without rhyme or reason. Not having learnt to adopt the adequate disposition, he stops short at what Erwin Panofsky calls the 'sensible properties', perceiving a skin as downy or lace-work as delicate, or at the emotional resonances arouses by these properties, referring to 'austere' colours or a 'joyful' melody. He cannot move from the 'primary stratum of the meaning we can grasp on the basis of our ordinary experience' to the 'stratum of secondary meanings', i.e., the 'level of the meaning of what is signified', unless he possesses the concepts which go beyond the sensible properties and which identify the specifically stylistic properties of the work.[3] Thus the encounter with a work of art is not 'love at first sight' as is generally supposed, and the act of empathy, *Einfühlung,* which is the art-lover's pleasure, presupposes an act of cognition, a decoding operation, which implies the implementation of a cognitive acquirement, a cultural code.[4]

This typically intellectualist theory of artistic perception directly contradicts the experience of the art-lovers closest to the legitimate definition; acquisition of legitimate culture by insensible familiarization within the family circle tends to favour an enchanted experience of culture which implies forgetting the acquisition.[5] The 'eye' is a product of history reproduced by education. This is true of the mode of artistic perception now accepted as legitimate, that is, the aesthetic disposition, the capacity to consider in and for themselves, as form rather than function, not only the works designated for such apprehension, i.e., legitimate works of art, but everything in the world, including cultural objects which are not yet consecrated—such as, at one time, primitive arts, or, nowadays, popular photography or kitsch—and natural objects. The 'pure' gaze is a historical invention linked to the emergence of an autonomous field of artistic production, that is, a field capable of imposing its own norms on both the production and the consumption of its products.[6] An art which, like all Post-Impressionist painting, is the product of an artistic intention which asserts the primacy of the mode of representation over the object of representation demands categorically an attention to form which previous art only demanded conditionally.

The pure intention of the artist is that of a producer who aims to be autonomous, that is, entirely the master of his product, who tends to reject not only the 'programmes' imposed a priori by scholars and scribes, but also—following the old hierarchy of doing and saying—the interpretations superimposed a posteriori on his work. The production of an 'open work', intrinsically and deliberately polysemic, can thus be understood as the final stage in the conquest of artistic autonomy by poets and, following in their footsteps, by painters, who had long been reliant on writers and their work of 'showing' and 'illustrating'. To assert the autonomy of production is to give primacy to that of which the artist is master, i.e., form, manner, style, rather than the 'subject', the external referent, which involves subordination to functions—even if only the most elementary one, that of representing, signifying, saying something. It also means a refusal to recognize any necessity other than that inscribed in the specific tradition of the artistic discipline in question: the shift from an art which imitates nature to an art which imitates art, deriving from its own history the exclusive source of its experiments and even of its breaks with tradition. An art which ever increasingly contains reference to its own history demands to be perceived historically; it asks to be referred not to an external referent, the represented or designated 'reality', but to the universe of past and present works of art. Like artistic production, in that it is generated in a field, aesthetic perception is necessarily historical, inasmuch as it is differential, relational, attentive to the deviations (*écarts*) which make styles. Like the so-called naive painter who, operating outside the field and its specific traditions, remains external to the history of the art, the 'naive' spectator cannot attain a specific grasp of works of art which only have meaning—or value—in relation to the specific history of an artistic tradition. The aesthetic disposition demanded by the products of a highly autonomous field of production is inseparable from a specific cultural competence. This historical culture functions as a principle of pertinence which enables one to identify, among the elements offered to the gaze, all the distinctive features and only these, by referring them, consciously or unconsciously, to the universe of possible alternatives. This mastery is, for the most part, acquired simply by contact with works of art—that is, through an implicit learning analogous to that which makes it possible to recognize familiar faces without explicit rules or criteria—and it generally remains at a practical level; it is what makes it possible to identify styles, i.e., modes of expression characteristic of a period, a civilization or a school, without having to distinguish clearly, or state explicitly, the features which constitute their originality. Everything seems to suggest that even among professional valuers, the criteria which define the stylistic properties of the 'typical works' on which all their judgements are based usually remain implicit.

The pure gaze implies a break with the ordinary attitude towards the world, which, given the conditions in which it is performed, is also a social separation. Ortega y Gasset can be believed when he attributes to modern art a systematic refusal of all that is 'human', i.e., generic, common—as opposed to distinctive, or distinguished—namely, the passions, emotions and feelings which 'ordinary' people invest in their 'ordinary' lives. It is as if the 'popular aesthetic' (the quotation marks are there to indicate that this is an aesthetic 'in itself' not 'for itself') were based on the affirmation of the continuity between art and life, which implies the subordination of form to function. This is seen clearly in the case of the novel and especially the theatre, where the working-class audience refuses any sort of formal experimentation and all the effects which, by introducing a distance from the accepted conventions (as regards scenery, plot etc.), tend to distance the spectator, preventing him from getting involved and fully identifying with the characters (I am thinking of Brechtian 'alienation' or the disruption of plot in the *nouveau roman*). In contrast to the detachment and disinterestedness which aesthetic theory regards as the only way of recognizing the work of art for what it is, i.e., autonomous, *selbständig,* the 'popular aesthetic' ignores or refuses the refusal of 'facile' involvement and 'vulgar' enjoyment, a refusal which is the basis of the taste for formal experiment. And popular judgements of paintings or photographs spring from an 'aesthetic' (in fact it is an ethos) which is the exact opposite of the Kantian aesthetic. Whereas, in order to grasp the specificity of the aesthetic judgement, Kant strove to distinguish that which pleases from that which gratifies and, more generally, to distinguish disinterestedness, the sole guarantor of the specifically aesthetic quality of contemplation, from the interest of reason which defines the Good, working-class people expect every image to explicitly perform a function, if only that of a sign, and their judgements make reference, often explicitly, to the norms of morality or agreeableness. Whether rejecting or praising, their appreciation always has an ethical basis.

Popular taste applies the schemes of the ethos, which pertain in the ordinary circumstances of life, to legitimate works of art, and so performs a systematic reduction of the things of art to the things of life. The very seriousness (or naivety) which this taste invests in fictions and representations demonstrates a contrario that pure taste performs a suspension of 'naive' involvement which is one dimension of a 'quasi-ludic' relationship with the necessities of the world. Intellectuals could be said to believe in the representation—literature, theatre, painting—more than in the things represented, whereas the people chiefly expect representations and the conventions which govern them to allow them to believe 'naively' in the things represented. The pure aesthetic is rooted in an ethic, or rather, an ethos of elective distance from the necessities of the natural and social world, which may take the form of moral agnosticism (visible when ethical transgression becomes an artistic *parti pris*) or of an aestheticism which presents the aesthetic disposition as a universally valid principle and takes the bourgeois denial of the social world to its limit. The detachment of the pure gaze cannot be dissociated from a general disposition towards the world which is the paradoxical product of conditioning by negative economic necessities—a life of ease—that tends to induce an active distance from necessity.

Although art obviously offers the greatest scope to the aesthetic disposition, there is no area of practice in which the aim of purifying, refining and sublimating primary needs and impulses cannot assert itself, no area in which the stylization of life, that is, the primacy of forms over function, of manner over matter, does not produce the same effects. And nothing is more distinctive, more distinguished, than the capacity to confer aesthetic status on objects that are banal or even 'common' (because the 'common' people make them their own, especially for aesthetic purposes), or the ability to apply the principles of a 'pure' aesthetic to the most everyday choices of everyday life, e.g., in cooking, clothing or decoration, completely reversing the popular disposition which annexes aesthetics to ethics.

In fact, through the economic and social conditions which they presuppose, the different ways of relating to realities and fictions, of believing in fictions and the realities they simulate, with more or less distance and detachment, are very closely linked to the different possible positions in social space and, consequently, bound up with the systems of dispositions (habitus) characteristic of the different classes and class fractions. Taste classifies, and it classifies the classifier. Social subjects, classified by their classifications, distinguish themselves by the distinctions they make, between the beautiful and the ugly, the distinguished and the vulgar, in which their position in the objective classifications is expressed or betrayed. And statistical analysis does indeed show that oppositions similar in structure to those found in cultural practices also appear in eating habits. The antithesis between quantity and quality, substance and form, corresponds to the opposition—linked to different distances from necessity—between the taste of necessity, which favours the most 'filling' and most economical foods, and the taste of liberty—or luxury—which shifts the emphasis to the manner (of presenting, serving, eating etc.) and tends to use stylized forms to deny function.

The science of taste and of cultural consumption begins with a transgression that is in no way aesthetic: it has to abolish the sacred frontier which makes legitimate culture a separate universe, in order to discover the intelligible relations which unite apparently incommensurable 'choices', such as preferences in music and food, painting and sport, literature and hairstyle. This barbarous reintegration of aesthetic consumption into the world of ordinary consumption abolishes the opposition, which has been the basis of high aesthetics since Kant, between the 'taste of sense' and the 'taste of reflection', and between facile pleasure, pleasure reduced to a pleasure of the senses, and pure pleasure, pleasure purified of pleasure, which is predisposed to become a symbol of moral excellence and a measure of the capacity for sublimation which defines the truly human man. The culture which results from this magical division is sacred. Cultural consecration does indeed confer on the objects, persons and situations it touches, a sort of ontological promotion akin to a transubstantiation. Proof enough of this is found in the two following quotations, which might almost have been written for the delight of the sociologist:

'What struck me most in this: nothing could be obscene on the stage of our premier theatre, and the ballerinas of the Opera, even as naked dancers, sylphs, sprites or Bacchae, retain an inviolable purity.'[7]

'There are obscene postures: the stimulated intercourse which offends the eye. Clearly, it is impossible to approve, although the interpolation of such gestures in dance routines does give them a symbolic and aesthetic quality which is absent from the intimate scenes the cinema daily flaunts before its spectators' eyes . . . As for the nude scene, what can one say, except that it is brief and theatrically not very effective? I will not say it is chaste or innocent, for nothing commercial can be so described. Let us say it is not shocking, and that the chief objection is that it serves as a box-office gimmick. . . . In *Hair,* the nakedness fails to be symbolic.'[8]

The denial of lower, coarse, vulgar, venal, servile—in a word, natural—enjoyment, which constitutes the sacred sphere of culture, implies an affirmation of the superiority of those who can be satisfied with the sublimated, refined, disinterested, gratuitous, distinguished pleasures forever closed to the profane. That is why art and cultural consumption are predisposed, consciously and deliberately or not, to fulfil a social function of legitimating social differences.

Notes

1. Bourdieu et al., *Un art moyen: essai sur les usages sociaux de la photographie* (Paris, Ed. de Minuit, 1965); P. Bourdieu and A. Darbel, *L'Amour de l'art: les musées et leur public* (Paris, Ed. de Minuit, 1966).

2. The word *disposition* seems particularly suited to express what is covered by the concept of habitus (defined as a system of dispositions)—used later in this chapter. It expresses first the *result of an organizing action,* with a meaning close to that of words such as structure; it also designates a way of being, a habitual state (especially of the body) and, in particular, a *predisposition, tendency, propensity* or *inclination.* [The semantic cluster of 'disposition' is rather wider in French than in English, but as this note—translated literally—shows, the equivalence is adequate. Translator.] P. Bourdieu, *Outline of a Theory of Practice* (Cambridge, Cambridge University Press, 1977), p. 214, n. 1.

3. E. Panofsky, 'Iconography and Iconology: An Introduction to the Study of Renaissance Art', *Meaning in the Visual Arts* (New York, Doubleday, 1955), p. 28.

4. It will be seen that this internalized code called culture functions as cultural capital owing to the fact that, being unequally distributed, it secures profits of distinction.

5. The sense of familiarity in no way excludes the ethnocentric misunderstanding which results from applying the wrong code. Thus, Michael Baxandall's work in historical ethnology enables us to measure all that separates the perceptual schemes that now

tend to be applied to Quattrocento paintings and those which their immediate addressees applied. The 'moral and spiritual eye' of Quattrocento man, that is, the set of cognitive and evaluative dispositions which were the basis of his perception of the world and his perception of pictorial representation of the world, differs radically from the 'pure' gaze (purified, first of all, of reference to economic value) with which the modern cultivated spectator looks at works of art. As the contracts show, the clients of Filippo Lippi, Domenico Ghirlandaio or Piero della Francesca were concerned to get 'value for money'. They approached works of art with the mercantile dispositions of a businessman who can calculate quantities and prices at a glance, and they applied some surprising criteria of appreciation, such as the expense of the colours, which sets gold and ultramarine at the top of the hierarchy. The artists, who shared this world view, were led to include arithmetical and geometrical devices in their compositions so as to flatter this taste for measurement and calculation; and they tended to exhibit the technical virtuosity which, in this context, is the most visible evidence of the quantity and quality of the labour provided; M. Baxandall, *Painting and Experience in Fifteenth-Century Italy: A Primer in the Social History of Pictorial Style* (Oxford, Oxford University Press, 1972).

6. See P. Bourdieu, 'Le marché des biens symboliques', *L'Année Sociologique,* 22 (1973), 49–126; and 'Outline of a Sociological Theory of Art Perception', *International Social Science Journal,* 20 (Winter 1968), 589–612.
7. O. Merlin, 'Mlle. Thibon dans la vision de Marguerite', *Le Monde,* 9 December 1965.
8. F. Chenique, '*Hair* est-il immoral?' *Le Monde,* 28 January 1970.

Mary Louise Pratt (1948–)

Canadian born, Pratt is currently the Silver Professor of Spanish and Portuguese Languages and Literatures and professor of comparative literature at New York University. For the year 2003, Pratt served as the president of the Modern Language Association (MLA), the largest organization of scholars and teachers of literature and language in North America. Pratt earned the prestigious position of MLA president because of her impeccable scholarship, which focuses primarily on Latin American literatures. In her 1992 book *Imperial Eyes: Travel Writings and Transculturation,* Pratt examines relationships between European imperialism, travel writing, and ideology. Scholars and students alike have found Pratt's idea of the "contact zone" important. In her introduction to *Imperial Eyes,* Pratt defines "contact zone" as "the space of colonial encounters, the space in which peoples geographically and historically separated come into contact with each other and establish ongoing relations, usually involving conditions of coercion, radical inequality, and intractable conflict (6)." In the preface to *Imperial Eyes,* Pratt writes, "This is a book marked by the global realignments and ideological upheavals that began in the 1980s and continue in the present. It was begun during the anguish of the Reagan–Thatcher years, when demystifying imperialism seemed more urgent than ever, and also more hopeless (xi)." To what degree is the forthcoming reading selection, "Humanities for the Future: Reflections on the Western Culture Debate at Stanford," also illustrative of Pratt's desire to "demystify[] imperialism?"

Pratt received her undergraduate degree from the University of Toronto, her M.A. degree in linguistics from the University of Illinois, and her Ph.D. in comparative literature from Stanford University. She has taught Spanish and Portuguese at both Stanford University and New York University. In addition to *Imperial Eyes,* Pratt has also written *Toward a Speech Act Theory of Literary Discourse* (1977). "Humanities for the Future" was first published in the *South Atlantic Quarterly* in 1990.

Humanities for the Future: Reflections on the Western Culture Debate at Stanford

SWM, 38, 5' 10", N/S, Stanford scientist, average-looking, a bit eccentric, blindingly brilliant, phenomenally funny, amazingly humble, likes jogging, bicycling, all things done with racquet-like instruments, movies, literature and most aspects of western civilization, but most interested in a reasonably attractive and intelligent 25–45 PA female capable of being interested in me. Send photo & brief description of your life, liberty and pursuits of happiness. Box 65C.

This singles ad appeared late last summer in the personals column of a local weekly serving the communities of Palo Alto, California, and neighboring Stanford University. Apart from its intriguing characterization of the "Stanford scientist," I quote it here to suggest the extent to which Stanford's long and intense debate over its Western culture curriculum last year permeated local life. In the semiotics of representation and identity, "Western civilization" remains a constant and intensely meaningful point of reference.

The debate which took place at Stanford during the winter of 1988 and the resulting reform of the Western culture requirement received a great deal of national attention, largely due to the involvement of then Secretary of Education William Bennett, who chose to use the Stanford case as a platform to advocate his views, quite literally making a federal case out of it. Perhaps because of Bennett's own partisanship, the account of the Stanford debate in the national press had a shape somewhat different from the local experience. As other institutions face similar struggles, fuller accounts of the workings of change at Stanford may be helpful. At the same time, there is an urgent need to formulate the concerns that so unexpectedly made freshman book lists an object of wide public concern. What nerves had been touched?

Histories of Western culture curricula in the United States point to the Western civilization course instituted at Columbia University in 1919 as a main antecedent for such courses all over the country. One recent account, however, notes that the Columbia course had a direct antecedent of its own, a War Issues course instituted in 1918 at various universities, including Columbia. Its aim was "to educate recently conscripted American soldiers about to fight in France . . . to introduce [them] to the European heritage in whose defense they were soon to risk their lives."[1] A new tie to Europe was constituted in relation to a national imperative.

Current struggles over Western culture curricula—both challenges to them and reactionary attempts to reassert them—also emerge from urgently felt national imperatives. Among these is an imperative to reimagine cultural and civic identity in the United States in the wake of vast changes produced by the decline of its global hegemony, the rapid internationalization of capital and industry, the immigrant implosion of the "third world" onto the "first," and the democratization of American institutions and political processes that occurred in the two decades prior to 1980. The question can be posed in Pierre Bourdieu's sometimes helpful language: What is to count as "cultural capital" in a culturally plural nation and a globalized human world? How will that capital be constructed and deployed, how will people be asked to identify with it? How might the United States project itself into the future as a cultural and political entity? In the words (a few of which I've emphasized) of one speaker in the Stanford debate:

> The character of U.S. society is changing. More and more North Americans insist on affirming the specificity of their class, ethnicity, gender, region, race, or sexual orientation, rather than melting into the homogenizing pot. They see such affirmations as *intrinsic to their citizenship*. Culture, literature, and the academy have been important sites for these affirmations: it will be neither productive nor comfortable to commit ourselves only to resisting these developments, rather than engaging with them.

Having acquiesced to change, by what visions will United Statesians be guided into a future where they and their society will be different from what they are now? What is the United States trying to become? What are the options?

The world is full of multicultural, multi-ethnic, multilingual nations, so there are plenty of models around. Indeed, Bloom, Bennett, Bellow, and the rest (known by now in some quarters as the Killer B's) are advocating one of them: to create a narrowly specific cultural capital that will be the normative *referent* for everyone, but will remain the *property* of a small and powerful caste that is linguistically and ethnically unified. It is this caste that is referred to by the "we" in Saul Bellow's astoundingly racist remark that "when the Zulus have a Tolstoy, *we* will read him." Few doubt that behind the Bennett–Bloom program is a desire to close not the American mind, but the American university, to all but a narrow and highly uniform elite with no commitment to either multiculturalism or educational democracy. Thus while the Killer B's (plus a C—Lynne Cheney, the Bennett mouthpiece now heading the National Endowment for the Humanities) depict themselves as returning to the orthodoxies of yesteryear, their project must not be reduced to nostalgia or conservatism. Neither of these explain the blanket contempt they express for the country's universities. They are fueled not by reverence for the past, but by an aggressive desire to lay hold of the present and future. The B's act as they do not because they are unaware of the cultural and demographic diversification underway in the country; they are utterly aware.

That is what they are trying to shape; that is why they are seeking, and using, national offices and founding national foundations.

Many citizens are attracted to Bloom's and Bennett's pronouncements, on the other hand, out of fairly unreflected attachments to the past (including their own college experience), and simply have trouble seeing how good books could possibly do any harm. Many people are perfectly ready for change but remain deeply anxious about where it is all supposed to be heading. Other visions of the cultural and educational future in the United States, then, are likely to generate as much interest as the Killer B's', if they can be effectively introduced into the national discussion. The attention drawn by Bloom's intellectually deplorable *Closing of the American Mind* and Bennett's intellectually more deplorable "To Reclaim a Legacy" most directly reflects not levels of enthusiasm for their programs (though much enthusiasm does exist), but levels of anxiety that have developed around the issue of national cultural identity. Even among the many people ready for change, one seems to hear voices asking, "If I give up white supremacy, who am I? Am I still American? Am I still white? If I give up homophobia, who am I? Am I the same as gay? If I give up misogyny, am I still a man? a woman? an American? If I learn Spanish, does it make me Mexican? What ties me to these gays, these feminists, these Salvadorans, these Vietnamese, these Navaho, these white people?" And perhaps more acutely, "What ties them to me?" The sooner answers to these questions are attempted, the better. What, indeed, would it mean to adopt the "nonhierarchical, intercultural perspective on the study of culture and the West" called for by one Stanford humanist (a classicist, at that)? What can cultural citizenship and identity be in a radically plural society enmeshed in relentlessly globalizing relations? Can there be transnational national culture? Can it be good?

Alongside the understandable apprehensions such questions generate (especially late in a century), it should be possible to create some excitement and curiosity. After all, this could become, perhaps has become, a fabulously energetic and revealing cultural experiment. It has tremendous imaginative appeal. Does the United States not badly need to revitalize its image and understanding of itself? Is there not much to be learned about the fluid global cultureways that bring the music of Soweto into living rooms across the United States, and make *The Cosby Show* the most popular TV program in South Africa? Is there not much to be learned about the past by rereading it in the light of contemporary intercultural understanding?

Stanford adopted its first Western civilization course in 1935, and, like many other universities, abolished it around 1970. Efforts to restore a requirement began around 1975 on the part of a group of senior faculty in literature, classics, and history. By 1978 a two-year pilot program had been approved and in 1980 a new year-long required course began for all incoming students. It consisted of several tracks corresponding roughly to different departments and schools, and sharing a core reading list that became the focus of the controversy. It is interesting to note that the notorious reading list was not part of the original proposal for the requirement. The list evolved during the pilot program out of desire to guarantee a "common intellectual experience," a phrase that acquired great importance in the subsequent debate without acquiring any greater specificity of meaning. Here is the much-discussed list:

ANCIENT WORLD

Required:
Hebrew Bible, Genesis
Plato, *Republic,* major portions
   of books 1–7
Homer, major selections from
   Iliad, Odyssey, or both
At least one Greek tragedy
New Testament, selections
   including a gospel

Strongly recommended:
Thucydides
Aristotle, *Nicomachean Ethics,*
   Politics
Cicero
Virgil, *Aeneid*
Tacitus

MEDIEVAL AND RENAISSANCE

Required:
Augustine, *Confessions,* 1–9
Dante, *Inferno*
More, *Utopia*
Machiavelli, *The Prince*
Luther, *Christian Liberty*
Galileo, *The Starry Messenger,*
   The Assayer

Strongly recommended:
Boethius, *Consolation of Philosophy*
Aquinas, some selection which
   illustrates the structure of
   a Thomistic question
A Shakespearean tragedy
Cervantes, *Don Quixote*
Descartes, *Discourse on Method,*
   Meditations
Hobbes, *Leviathan*
Locke, *Second Treatise of Civil*
   Government

MODERN

Required:
Voltaire, *Candide*
Marx and Engels, *Communist*
   Manifesto
Freud, *Outline of*
   Psychoanalysis,
   Civilization and Its
   Discontents
Darwin, *Selections*

Strongly recommended:
Roussesau, *Social Contract,*
   Confessions, Emile
Hume, *Enquiries, Dialogues on*
   Natural Religion
Goethe, *Faust, Sorrows of Young*
   Werther
Nineteenth-century novel
Mill, *Essay on Liberty,*
   The Subjection of Women
Nietzsche, *Genealogy of Morals,*
   Beyond Good and Evil

Participants in developing the course say that in its specifics the list was not intended to be written in stone. It represented a series of compromises rather painfully hammered out by a committee, inevitably through some of the crudest kind of horse-trading—Catholics for Protestants, poets for scientists, Italians for Germans. In the end, ironically, the difficulty of negotiating the list was one source of its permanence: the process had been so painful and so lacking in intellectual integrity that no one expressed the slightest desire to repeat it.

In any case, regardless of its specific content, the list did the job of shaping the requirement in, for many people, unnecessarily narrow ways. Indeed, its extreme narrowness clearly contributed to the breakdown of the program at Stanford. Most conspicuously, the list installed a specific historical paradigm: one quarter for ancient world, one for medieval–renaissance, and one for the past five hundred years. Implicit in the sequence was the canonical narrative of origins deriving the present from classical Greece via the Italian Renaissance and the Franco–German Enlightenment, a narrative that begins and ends with European lettered high culture. (Where is America?) Clearly, teachers of the course could question that implicit narrative, and some did. But to do so in a consistent or structured way involved teaching against the grain of the syllabus, an extremely difficult pedagogical task that often confused students more than it empowered them.

Second, the list not only lays down a Eurocentric paradigm, but also embodies a very restricted sense of Europe. France and even England are barely represented in the required readings; Iberia, Eastern Europe, and Scandinavia not at all. Only "high" culture is represented, an exclusion that has long been under challenge not just by the Black Students' Union, but by whole schools of mainstream literary and historical scholarship. One thinks of the scholars at Princeton's Center for European Studies, or the Berkeley-based new historicism, movements that are in no way radical or critical of the West, but which refuse to give "high" culture or belles lettres a monopoly on cultural understanding. Many Stanford scholars were troubled by the fact that the course organized itself around authors and orthodoxies rather than around problematics or issues, and that it therefore took *as* orthodoxies matters that were actually under serious debate in their fields. Translated into practice, this amounted to a structure of exclusion of faculty who took other perfectly legitimate approaches to culture and to the West, as well as of faculty who worked in non-European literatures and cultures. "For some scholars," said one colleague, "to see a book or an entire cultural tradition as if it were a self-contained whole is like listening to only one side of a phone conversation. For these scholars there is no place in the current program."

Third, the list implicitly suggests a monumentalist attitude to the texts as great works whose interest and value were sui generis. Again, teachers were of course not forbidden to adopt a critical attitude, but to do so required teaching from the negative position of a counter-discourse or a heresy. What you couldn't do was embark positively on a different project or way of thinking, even one that was equally celebratory and equally Eurocentric. An attempt was made to set up a critical track, a course titled "Conflict and Change in Western Culture." In many ways this course was extremely successful, but its founders were constantly hampered by the structure of center and periphery into which they were locked. To bring in other texts was always to bring in "Other" texts. In the end, this structure of otherness comprises, depending on your perspective, the main *obstacle to* or the main *bulwark against* relational approaches to culture. "The *notion* of a core list," argued one teacher in the history track,

> is inherently flawed, regardless of what kinds of works it includes or excludes. It
> is flawed because such a list undermines the critical stance that we wish students
> to take toward the materials they read. . . . A course with such readings creates
> two sets of books, those privileged by being on the list and those not worthy of
> inclusion. Regardless of the good intentions of those who create such lists, the
> students have not viewed and will not view these separate categories as equal.

The asymmetry can be exemplified by a remark made in support of retaining the
core list. Referring to the autobiography of the West African Olaudah Equiano,
published in England in the late eighteenth century, one English scholar argued
that students "who have studied Genesis, Aquinas, and Rousseau have a good
chance of understanding with some precision what the ex-slave Olaudah
Equiano meant when he spoke of 'that first natural right of mankind . . . inde-
pendency.'" The remark, true enough in a way, easily invites some troubling
inferences. Would one want to suggest that students who have *not* studied Genesis, Aquinas, and Rousseau have *no* chance of understanding Equiano? That
Equiano himself would not have understood liberty without his European education? Neither inference is true in the slightest. There are plenty of readings that
can serve to illuminate Equiano to American students, and these certainly include
Rousseau, Aquinas, and Genesis. As for Equiano himself, no slave ever needed
Rousseau or anybody else to know the difference between freedom and slavery,
though a slave might find Rousseau helpful (as Equiano did) in attempting to
argue matters with the enslavers. It is not from Europeans that enslaved peoples
have learned how to construct cultures that conserve a sense of humanity, meaningful life, and an abiding vision of freedom in the face of the West's relentless
imperial expansion. Indeed, it is essential to reverse the direction of inference and
note that students who have read Equiano have a good chance of understanding
what Rousseau meant in talking about human rights and equality. From there
follows the question many find deeply but unnecessarily disturbing: To what
extent was Rousseau influenced indirectly by the African slaves, whose fearsome
rebellions and unquenchable demands for change echoed constantly back to
Europe from the colonial frontier? From an intercultural perspective, the initial
statement about Equiano taken by itself reproduces a monumentalist cultural
hierarchy that is historically as well as morally distortive.

Many critics felt that the Western culture program set a tone for the humanities as a whole at Stanford, in the words of one Latin Americanist, making
"second-class citizens out of faculty whose work focuses on non-European literatures, on noncanonical writers, on European literatures not included in the core,
or on the West in dialogue with other parts of the world." In terms of faculty, in
the years the Western culture program was in place, classics outgrew all the
departments of modern languages and literatures; a Europeanist comparative literature department was founded; the English department continued to boast four
medievalists while African, African-American, and Caribbean literatures in English were represented by a single half-time faculty member (whose tenure was
hotly contested), and so-called "Commonwealth" literature not at all. The curriculum in French continued to include not a single course in Franco-African or
even Quebecois literature. The number of Chicano faculty remained the same in
1988 as it was in 1972. A new humanities center, on the other hand, did assert a

broader range, successfully seeking out interdisciplinary scholars and grants to fund minority and third world fellows.

The opposition to the Western culture curriculum that eventually coalesced at Stanford was there pretty much from the beginning. In the planning stages, it turned out, no fewer than seven other proposals for a culture requirement had been made and set aside. Several of these involved intercultural perspectives and heavily non-European materials. Right from the start many faculty in relevant fields chose not to participate in the course, including what was described as a near boycott by minority, women, and younger faculty. Then a beginning assistant professor, I recall vividly being asked to teach a section in one of the tracks. When I objected to the absence of the Iberian world and the Americas from the core list, I was told I might be invited to give a lecture on things written in Spanish since *Don Quixote*, "if I thought there was anything worth talking about." But really, the senior historian said, the advantage of the assignment was that it would help me avoid getting caught in a "Hispanic rut."

The fact that the course excluded or marginalized the work of many of the university's own humanities faculty made it a good deal more expensive than anticipated. Several hundred thousand dollars a year were needed to pay instructors on short-term contracts, most of them recent Ph.D.'s in the humanities. Many of these teachers did not share the monumentalist project, and they too became an impetus for change, as they introduced other materials and perspectives in their sections. By the time the reform was proposed, the core list was widely tampered with and no longer enforced. Some people were teaching against the grain—but the grain was still very much there. Organized student advocacy of reform was a consistent and essential component throughout the three-year process. Student momentum began to coalesce during Rainbow Coalition activity for the 1984 election, and through the intense anti-apartheid activity of 1985–86. A coalition of student groups, including the Black Students' Union, the Movimiento Estudiantil Chicano de Aztlan (MEChA), the Stanford American Indian Organization, the Asian American Student Association, and Students United for Democracy in Education formed to exert continuous pressure on the reform process, from within and without.

The chronology of the reform process ran roughly as follows:

1. In the spring of 1986 the dean of undergraduate studies, a European historian and the first woman to hold the position, appointed a task force to review the Western culture requirement and produce recommendations for the faculty senate's Committee on Undergraduate Studies. The task force consisted of three undergraduate students, two senior historians (one Europeanist and one African-Americanist), a senior philosopher (who had helped draft the original requirement), a senior woman classicist (who had taught in the "critical" track of the course), a senior Chicano administrator, and one of the lecturers in the program.

2. Throughout the 1986–87 academic year the task force met regularly, speaking with all the relevant parties and anyone else who wished to address them. In the spring of 1987 they released an interim report calling for a

reconception and restructuring of the requirement. This trial balloon provoked a great deal of discussion and response that was quite polarized.

3. In the late autumn of 1987, believing it has the support of all relevant parties, the task force released a revised report and recommendations to the Committee on Undergraduate Studies. The report argued (in passages later deleted) that "courses that do not acknowledge in some degree both the cultural diversity of Europe and the even greater diversity of our present American society have increasingly come to seem intellectually inadequate"; such courses, moreover, "have been open to the charge of being socially irresponsible, however unintentionally and inadvertently, for they seem to perpetuate racist and sexist stereotypes and to reinforce notions of cultural superiority that are wounding to some and dangerous to all in a world of such evident diversity." The report recommended a modified requirement called Culture/Ideas/Values (CIV) structured around a series of ground rules rather than a core list. Four instructional objectives were proposed which can be summarized as follows: increasing understanding of cultural diversity and interaction within the United States and elsewhere; engaging students with works that have intellectual importance "by virtue of the ideas they express, their mode of expression, or their influence"; developing critical thinking; and increasing skills in reading, reasoning, arguing, and analyzing texts. Requirements for social, geographical, and historical diversity would mean courses designed to "confront issues relating to class, ethnicity, race, religion, gender, and sexual orientation; to include the study of works by women, minorities, and persons of color"; to study works from at least one European and at least one non-European culture in their own historical and cultural context; and to involve at least six to eight centuries of historical depth.

4. In January of 1988 the new recommendations headed for the floor of the faculty senate with committee approval. At this juncture, opponents of the reform surprised many by introducing counterlegislation which retained the status quo but added one woman and one black writer to the core list for the third quarter of the course. This polarizing move set the stage for the debate that went on through the winter and into the spring. The faculty senate at Stanford is an elected body of fifty-five faculty members which inevitably includes a high proportion of senior scholars and former administrators. Given Stanford's composition, the senate is dominated numerically by faculty from the sciences and professional schools. Advocates of the reform were unprepared for a floor fight in the senate, most of whose members had not been educated as to the stakes and the issues. Senators were prone to support the familiar status quo. On the other hand, the election of this particular senate had involved, for the first time, a small effort to promote women candidates. Though this was not done with the Western culture debate in mind, the four women elected each made crucial contributions on behalf of the reform.

It would be absurd to summarize the untold hours of meetings, statement writing and reading, corridor talk, cynical maneuvering, and brutal negotiating sessions that followed. Despite the Machiavellian dimensions, two decisions in particular gave the process a democratic character that lends credence to the outcome. First, the weekly faculty/staff newspaper announced that it would print all statements on the matter that it received, from any person. An extraordinary number and range of people responded, making this newspaper the main medium for the community debate. Within the senate, it was likewise decided that anyone who signed up to make a statement would be permitted to do so, whether or not they were a member of the senate, and again many people responded, including student representatives. Thus, within the local taboos on, say, openly racist or openly Marxist language, a fairly full range of views was expressed, with deep conviction and eloquence on all sides. (The scientists, one should note, showed no reservations about expressing themselves on the matter, though it proved extremely difficult to communicate the issues to them.) The five senate meetings on the subject were opened to anyone who requested visitor status, though visitors could not participate. As a result, senate meetings uncannily reproduced the very core–periphery structure that was under debate. In a large round amphitheater, the senators, overwhelmingly senior white men, sat in the middle while up around the outside were gathered the women faculty, the minority faculty, the students, the black and Chicano administrators, all the "other Americans" not authorized to speak, but speaking powerfully through their bodily presence. There we were on the margins, we said, but *we were in the room*, and something had to be constructed that came to grips with that fact.

Perhaps the biggest surprise for naive observers like myself as we listened and read was what some of us came to call the "willful ignorance" factor. It was saddening to hear academics saying please don't make me read anything new, I refuse to agree there are things I am ignorant of that are important and worthwhile. "Does that make me a racist?" one old friend and colleague asked. What would Aretha Franklin reply, I wondered. At the same time, especially given the rantings of the official right, it is important to affirm the thoughtfulness and intellectual quality of the discussion that took place at Stanford, and to give you some examples. It was, for example, George Will and not an academic colleague who, amazingly, called for courses that "affirm this fact: America is predominantly a product of the Western tradition and is predominantly good because that tradition is good." It was William F. Buckley, and not a Stanford professor, who displayed his ignorance by declaring that "from Homer to the nineteenth century no great book has emerged from any non-European source." Below I offer some excerpts from what Stanford faculty and students did say, for and against the reform (the quotations are taken from statements published in the campus newspaper):

CON: Education is an exercise of modesty, a process whereby we give up some of ourselves to gain an understanding of that which is *not* ourselves, an understanding of things still shaping us. It's a kind of surrender; we learn that some things are superior in consequence to us, even to our particular gender, to our particular ethnic heritage, to all the parochialisms to which we are subject. Then the apparent foreignness of the past, its record of people seemingly *unlike* ourselves, becomes much less foreign and those people much less strange and irrelevant.

PRO: The famous texts of the past cannot continue to live for us if we simply place them on a pedestal and teach our students to worship them. Only if we see them as engaged with the stuff of history, both of the times in which they were written and of those later times, can we give a continuing life to these texts and to our cultural tradition as a whole. Only if we understand how the idea of a Western culture took shape in differing ways over the centuries and how it defined itself in relation to other forms of culture, can we justify giving it the prime consideration . . . to our students.

CON: As a historian of the United States I would be the last person to deny the ethnic, racial, and cultural complexity of American society. But, from the same perspective, I find it puzzling, if not troubling, to learn that some of the dominant and influential ideas in modern America are to be seen [in the new legislation] as originating outside the West. Few historians of the United States believe that the culture of this country has been seriously influenced by ideas from Africa, China, Japan or indigenous North America. . . . There is no direct connection between the dominant ideas and institutions in American culture and the cultures of Africa or Eastern Asia. [The roots of American culture], if one is talking about ideas and institutions, are derived overwhelmingly from Europe. To contend otherwise, I think would cause American historians to scratch their heads in amazement.

PRO: A "liberal education" for our time should expand beyond the culture-bound, basically colonialist, horizon that relies, albeit subtly, on the myth of the cultural superiority of the "West" (an ill-defined entity, in any event, whose borders are ludicrously artificial). . . . Does the new, integrated vision of Area One entail our teaching the Greek Hermes and Prometheus alongside the North American Indian Coyote or the West African Anansi and Legba as paradigms of trickster heroes, or Japanese Noh alongside Greek drama or Indian philosophy alongside Plato? If the answer is yes, so much the better.

PRO: I was never taught in Western Culture the fact that the Khemetic or "Egyptian" Book of the Dead contained many of the dialectic principles attributed to Greece, but was written three thousand years earlier, or the fact that Socrates, Herodotus, Pythagoras, and Solon studied in Egypt and acknowledged that much of their knowledge of astronomy, geometry, medicine, and building came from the African civilizations in and around Egypt. . . . I was never told that algebra came from Moslem Arabs, or numbers from India. I was never informed when it was found that the "very dark and wooly haired" Moors in Spain preserved, expanded, and reintroduced the classical knowledge that the Greeks had collected, which led to the "renaissance." . . . I read the Bible without knowing St. Augustine looked black like me, that the ten commandments were almost direct copies from the 147 negative confessions of Egyptian initiates, or that many of the words of Solomon came from the black pharaoh Amen-En-Eope. I didn't learn that Toussaint L'Ouverture's defeat of Napoleon in Haiti directly influenced the French Revolution or that the Iroquois Indians in America had a representative democracy which served as a model for the American system. . . . I'm damned if my children have to go to a school that preaches diversity, then refuses to practice its own values because it was scared.

In the end, the reform legislation was passed, with some substantial amendments. One, for instance, required courses to "include treatment of ancient and medieval cultures"; another required faculty teaching in the program to agree each spring on a set of "common elements" which all tracks would share the following year. The latter amendment, which finally broke the deadlock, is a very big loophole. It leaves open the unlikely possibility of faculty agreeing to restore the entire core list, or of the whole battle being fought over in miniature every spring. At the moment, it seems more likely that the parties will learn to understand each other better through this compulsory conversation. The actual consequences of the reform remain uncertain, however. With only minor alterations, the standard Great Books course *can* continue to exist at Stanford, and nobody is being required to reeducate him or herself. You can certainly talk about gender without challenging sexism, or race without challenging racism, or class without challenging classism. On the other hand, a space has been made for much greater change by those who desire it. Tracks constructed around other understandings of culture and broader perspectives on the West are now possible. Their existence and survival depend, however, on the presence of sufficient faculty to teach them, and the hiring and tenuring of such faculty is not possible without the acquiescence of those who opposed the reform. It is no accident that the final amendment passed by the senate deleted a phrase calling for the recruitment of minority faculty to teach in the new program. In the larger national picture, it seems fair to say that the new program puts Stanford in the vanguard of the rear guard, for other schools have long since left our modest reform behind. (Write, for example, for the catalog of Oglala College in Pine Ridge, South Dakota.)

Three faculty have jointly prepared a course according to the new guidelines. It is a course called Europe and the Americas which studies the European, African, and native American strands of American cultures, and the history of their interaction in the Americas. Canonical European texts retain a place in the course, but rather than forming its center of gravity, they simply coexist with American, Caribbean, Spanish-American, native-American and Anglo-American materials. "The complex interactions of colonialism, slavery, migration and immigration," says the course's preamble, "have produced on this side of the Atlantic societies that are highly diverse in origin, and in many cases multicultural and syncretic. European traditions play a prominent and indeed decisive role in these societies, *though by no means the same roles they play in Europe.*" At times the course adopts a comparative perspective—Haitian Vodun and Greek Dionysus are brought together, for instance, in a section on religious syncretism and ecstatic cults; a section on representations of the self juxtaposes the extroverted, historicized self-representation of a Navaho oral history with the confessional modes of St. Augustine and Freud. Historical dialogues are pursued—the legacy of Shakespeare's *The Tempest* in Aimé Césaire's *A Tempest,* José Enrique Rodó's *Ariel,* and Roberto Fernández Retamar's *Calibán* are examined; the give-and-take between European enlightenment discourse on human rights, American independence movements, abolitionism, and slave rebellions is considered; indigenous traditions are traced, from the ancient Mayan *Popul Vuh,* for instance, to the contemporary *testimonio* by Guatemalan indigenous activist Rigoberta Menchu, or from the pre-Colombian Inca state to the Spanish conquest (through Andean eyes) to the great Andean rebellions of the 1780s to the contemporary Quechua poetry of José María Arguedas. Terms like creolization, transculturation, and syncretism are used to develop an approach to culture that is relational and at the same time recognizes the internal fullness and integrity of particular moments and formations.

Approaches to culture and to United States culture such as those this course adopts are widespread in higher education, but are scarcely to be found in official discourse on education, nor in the national media's depictions of the curricular controversy. Partisans of reform have so far had little success at getting across in the public discourse the modes of understanding against which the monumentalist approach seems narrow and impoverished. Few people reading Bloom or Bennett, even those critical of them, can bring to bear a picture of what nonhierarchical, relational approaches to culture are or what people stand to gain from learning them. Stanford's scientists, in being asked to vote for reform, had little idea of what they were voting *for.* How could they not fall back on the common sense of the man in the personals ad I quoted at the beginning who simply likes most aspects of Western civilization? (As the West Texan is supposed to have said against daylight saving time, "If central time was good enough for Jesus Christ, it's good enough for me!") When then Secretary Bennett and Stanford President Donald Kennedy debated the issue on the *MacNeil/Lehrer Report,* neither party possessed a clear picture of alternative visions of culture, the West, or the United States. Bennett knew only vaguely what he was opposing, and Kennedy what he was defending. Lehrer also seemed to be groping for an unknown. And yet, one goes on to wonder, why should the discussion remain in the hands of those three people, a remarkably uniform group? Where are the voices of those who have the most fundamental, bodily stakes in efforts for change? For the moment, those voices are not authorized to speak for "us" all, the way Bennett, Kennedy, and Lehrer can. When they are, change will have occurred.

The final amendments-to-the-amendments on the Stanford reform were resolved in the last week of May 1988. In the days that followed, a series of local events suggested with unexpected clarity the need for the experiment Stanford had embarked on. A student was expelled from his dormitory after a year of disruptive activity directed especially toward a gay resident assistant, culminating in an assault on the resident and the vandalizing of the dormitory lounge. The following evening, ten fraternity brothers, in defense of the expelled student's freedom of speech, staged a silent vigil at midnight outside the dormitory lounge wearing masks and carrying candles, a gesture that seemed to deliberately invoke the customs of the Ku Klux Klan. The reactions of black students who assembled at the site ranged from terror to outrage, and the action was treated by the university as a serious racial and homophobic incident. The ten demonstrators, however, claimed complete ignorance of the associations their vigil invoked. They did not know, they said, that masks and candles at midnight had any connotations—it is just what they thought a vigil was. The following day a group of sorority women, as part of a rush ritual, performed a mock "Indian dance" around a fountain which happened to stand in the doorway of the native American student center. Asked to stop, they refused, later saying they did not intend to offend, or see the dance as offensive. It was just a tradition.

Many people did not believe these students' pleas of ignorance. But either way, the call for educational change was reinforced. If it is possible for young adults to leave the American educational system ignorant of the history of race relations in the United States (not part of standard Western culture curricula), then something needs to change. And if a person who knows the history of race relations and their symbolizations feels free to reenact racist rituals of mockery or intimidation, something needs to change. At the same time, blame must be placed where it belongs. In pleading ignorance, the students were following the example of many of the country's own leaders, for whom ignorance had become an acceptable standard of public life. Throughout their high school and college years these students had looked to a president who consistently showed himself to be both ignorant and utterly comfortable with his ignorance. (The Stanford incidents coincided with Reagan's extraordinary remarks in Moscow about the "coddling" of native Americans.) For many of us exhausted by conflict that spring, these discouraging incidents reminded us of what we were fighting for.

A week later a less weighty event drew local attention, when two California students turned up as the two finalists in the National Spelling Bee. Their names were Rageshree Ramachandran, an Indian-born American from Fair Oaks (who won), and Victor C. Wang, a Chinese American from Camarillo (who came in second). Nothing could have suggested more clearly the multicultural, multiethnic future taking shape on the West Coast. The final words in the spelling bee, the report noted, were these: buddleia (from an Englishman's surname), araucaria (from South American indigenous language), mhometer (from a German electrician's surname, spelled backwards), ovoviviparous (from Latin), caoutchouc (from another South American indigenous language, via French), stertorous (from Latin), and elegiacal (from Greek). "Who makes up these words?" asked Victor Wang as he went down to defeat on "stertorous." Good question, Victor. And as you head on up the educational ladder, I hope you find a system that will give you an honest and imaginative answer.

Note

1. See Gilbert Allardyce, "The Rise and Fall of the Western Civilization Course," *American Historical Review* 87 (1982): 695–743, cited by Herbert Lindenberger in his admirable essay, "On the Sacrality of Reading Lists: The Western Culture Debate at Stanford University," to appear in the British journal *Comparative Criticism*, Fall 1989.

Richard Rorty (1931–)

Rorty is one of the most influential philosophers in the humanities. After a long and distinguished career as a philosophy professor at such renowned schools as Wellesley College, Princeton University, and the University of Virginia, Rorty is himself blurring genres in terms of his professional identity, as he is now a professor of comparative literature and of philosophy at Stanford University. Like the critic Stanley Fish, Rorty focuses on pragmatism and has been particularly influential in English studies in this respect, and like another literary critic, Harold Bloom, Rorty criticizes contemporary theorists who attack literature and trivialize the idea of artistic genius. A self-identified leftist, Rorty does not, however, identify himself with Marxism. His leftist intellectual tradition has its roots in American writers such as Walt Whitman and John Dewey. In his 1998 book *Achieving Our Country: Leftist Thought in Twentieth-Century America*, Rorty offers two suggestions for leftists to help revitalize the Left: "the Left should put a moratorium on theory. It should try to kick the philosophy habit," and "the Left should try to mobilize what remains of our pride in being Americans. It should ask the public to consider how the country of Lincoln and Whitman might be achieved" (91–92). The essay presented next, "The Inspirational Value of Great Works of Literature," is also from *Achieving Our Country* and extends these two suggestions in provocative ways. What is it like, in a theory class, to read a theorist who urges a "moratorium on theory"? Rorty's views may strike many readers as akin to blasphemy.

The always controversial Rorty was born in New York City and lives in Stanford, California. After earning his undergraduate degree in 1949 and his M.A. degree in 1952 from the University of Chicago, Rorty earned his Ph.D. from Yale University in 1956 and then served for two years in the U.S. Army. After being discharged, he began his career as a professor of philosophy. Rorty's many books are required reading throughout courses on the humanities. His best known books include *The Linguistic Turn* (1967), *Philosophy and the Mirror of Nature* (1979), *Consequences of Pragmatism* (1982), *Contingency, Irony, and Solidarity* (1988), and *Achieving Our Country: Leftist Thought in Twentieth-Century America* (1998).

The Inspirational Value of Great Works of Literature

> Nil admirari prope res est una, Numici,
> Solaque quae possit facere et servare beatum.
> (To stand in awe of nothing, Numicius,
> is practically the only way to feel really good about yourself.)
>
> Horace, *Epistles*, I. vi. 1–2

The self-protective project described in this familiar Horatian tag is exemplified by one strain of thought in Fredric Jameson's influential *Postmodernism, or The Cultural Logic of Late Capitalism*. In one of the most depressing passages of that profoundly antiromantic book, Jameson says that "the end of the bourgeois ego, or monad, . . . means . . . the end . . . of style, in the sense of the unique and the personal, the end of the distinctive individual brush stroke."[1] Later he says that

> if the poststructuralist motif of the "death of the subject" means anything socially, it signals the end of the entrepreneurial and inner-directed individualism with its "charisma" and its accompanying categorial panoply of quaint romantic values such as that of the "genius" . . . Our social order is richer in information

and more literate . . . This new order no longer needs prophets and seers of the high modernist and charismatic type, whether among its cultural products or its politicians. Such figures no longer hold any charm or magic for the subjects of a corporate, collectivized, post-individualistic age; in that case, goodbye to them without regret, as Brecht might have put it: woe to the country that needs geniuses, prophets, Great Writers, or demiurges![2]

Adoption of this line of thought produces what I shall call "knowingness." Knowingness is a state of soul which prevents shudders of awe. It makes one immune to romantic enthusiasm.

This state of soul is found in the teachers of literature in American colleges and universities who belong to what Harold Bloom calls the "School of Resentment." These people have learned from Jameson and others that they can no longer enjoy "the luxury of the old-fashioned ideological critique, the indignant moral denunciation of the other."[3] They have also learned that hero-worship is a sign of weakness, and a temptation to elitism. So they substitute Stoic endurance for both righteous anger and social hope. They substitute knowing theorization for awe, and resentment over the failures of the past for visions of a better future.

Although I prefer "knowingness" to Bloom's word "resentment," my view of these substitutions is pretty much the same as his. Bloom thinks that many rising young teachers of literature can ridicule anything but can hope for nothing, can explain everything but can idolize nothing. Bloom sees them as converting the study of literature into what he calls "one more dismal social science"—and thereby turning departments of literature into isolated academic backwaters. American sociology departments, which started out as movements for social reform, ended up training students to clothe statistics in jargon. If literature departments turn into departments of cultural studies, Bloom fears, they will start off hoping to do some badly needed political work, but will end up training their students to clothe resentment in jargon.

I think it is important to distinguish know-nothing criticisms of the contemporary American academy—the sort of thing you get from columnists like George Will and Jonathan Yardley, and politicians like William Bennett and Lynne Cheney—from the criticisms currently being offered by such insiders as Bloom and Christopher Ricks. The first set of critics believe everything they read in scandalmongering books by Dinesh D'Souza, David Lehman, and others. They do not read philosophy, but simply search out titles and sentences to which they can react with indignation. Much of their work belongs to the current conservative attempt to discredit the universities—which itself is part of a larger attempt to discredit all critics of the cynical oligarchy that has bought up the Republican Party. The insiders' criticism, on the other hand, has nothing to do with national politics. It comes from people who are careful readers, and whose loathing for the oligarchy is as great as Jameson's own.

I myself am neither a conservative nor an insider. Because my own disciplinary matrix is philosophy, I cannot entirely trust my sense of what is going on in literature departments. So I am never entirely sure whether Bloom's gloomy predictions are merely peevish, or whether he is more far-sighted than those who dismiss him as a petulant eccentric. But in the course of hanging around literature departments over the past decade or so, I have acquired some suspicions that parallel his.

The main reason I am prey to such suspicions is that I have watched, in the course of my lifetime, similarly gloomy predictions come true in my own discipline. Philosophers of my generation learned that an academic discipline can become almost unrecognizably different in a half-century—different, above all, in the sort of talents that get you tenure. A discipline can quite quickly start attracting a new sort of person, while becoming inhospitable to the kind of person it used to welcome.

Bloom is to Jameson as A. N. Whitehead was to A. J. Ayer in the 1930s. Whitehead stood for charisma, genius, romance, and Wordsworth. Like Bloom, he agreed with Goethe that the ability to shudder with awe is the best feature of human beings. Ayer, by contrast, stood for logic, debunking, and knowingness. He wanted philosophy to be a matter of scientific teamwork, rather than of imaginative breakthroughs by heroic figures. He saw theology, metaphysics, and literature as devoid of what he called "cognitive significance," and Whitehead as a good logician who had been ruined by poetry. Ayer regarded shudders of awe as neurotic symptoms. He helped create the philosophical tone which Iris Murdoch criticized in her celebrated essay "Against Dryness."

In the space of two generations, Ayer and dryness won out over Whitehead and romance. Philosophy in the English-speaking world became "analytic," antimetaphysical, unromantic, and highly professional. Analytic philosophy still attracts first-rate minds, but most of these minds are busy solving problems which no nonphilosopher recognizes as problems: problems which hook up with nothing outside the discipline.[4] So what goes on in anglophone philosophy departments has become largely invisible to the rest of the academy, and thus to the culture as a whole. This may be the fate that awaits literature departments.

Analytic philosophy is not exactly one more dismal social science, but its desire to be dryly scientific, and thereby to differentiate itself from the sloppy thinking it believes to be prevalent in literature departments, has made it stiff, awkward, and isolated. Those who admire this kind of philosophy often claim that philosophy professors are not only a lot drier but also a lot smarter nowadays than in the past. I do not think this is so. I think they are only a little meaner. Philosophy is now more adversarial and argumentative than it used to be, but I do not think that it is pursued at a higher intellectual level.

As philosophy became analytic, the reading habits of aspiring graduate students changed in a way that parallels recent changes in the habits of graduate students of literature. Fewer old books were read, and more recent articles. As early as the 1950s, philosophy students like myself who had, as undergraduates, been attracted to philosophy as a result of falling in love with Plato or Hegel or Whitehead, were dutifully writing Ph.D. dissertations on such Ayer-like topics as the proper analysis of subjunctive conditional sentences. This was, to be sure, an interesting problem. But it was dear to me that if I did not write on some such respectably analytic problem I would not get a very good job. Like the rest of my generation of philosophy Ph.D.'s, I was not exactly cynical, but I did know on which side my bread was likely to be buttered. I am told, though I cannot vouch for the fact, that similar motives are often at work when today's graduate students of literature choose dissertation topics.

Nowadays, when analytic philosophers are asked to explain their cultural role and the value of their discipline, they typically fall back on the claim that the study of philosophy helps one see through pretentious, fuzzy thinking. So it does. The intellectual moves which the study of analytic philosophy trained me to make have proved very useful. Whenever, for example, I hear such words as "problematize" and "theorize," I reach for my analytic philosophy.

Still, prior to the rise of analytic philosophy, ridiculing pretentious fuzziness was only *one* of the things that philosophy professors did. Only some philosophers made this their specialty: Hobbes, Hume, and Bentham, for example, but not Spinoza, Hegel, T. H. Green, or Dewey. In the old days, there was another kind of philosopher—the romantic kind. This is the kind we do not get any more, at least in the English-speaking world. Undergraduates who want to grow up to be the next Hegel, Nietzsche, or Whitehead are not encouraged to go on for graduate work in anglophone philosophy departments. This is why my discipline has undergone both a paradigm shift and a personality change. Romance, genius, charisma, individual brush strokes, prophets, and demiurges have been out of style in anglophone philosophy for several generations. I doubt that they will ever come back into fashion, just as I doubt that American sociology departments will ever again be the centers of social activism they were in the early decades of the century.

So much for my analogy between the rise of cultural studies within English departments and of logical positivism within philosophy departments. I have no doubt that cultural studies will be as old hat thirty years from now as was logical positivism thirty years after its triumph. But the victory of logical positivism had irreversible effects on my discipline—it deprived it of romance and inspiration, and left only professional competence and intellectual sophistication. Familiarity with these effects makes me fear that Bloom may be right when he predicts that the victory of cultural studies would have irreversibly bad effects upon the study of literature.

To make clearer the bad effects I have in mind, let me explain what I mean by the term "inspirational value." I can do so most easily by citing an essay by the novelist Dorothy Allison: "Believing in Literature." There she describes what she calls her "atheist's religion"—a religion shaped, she says, by "literature" and by "her own dream of writing." Toward the close of this essay, she writes:

> There is a place where we are always alone with our own mortality, where we must simply have something greater than ourselves to hold onto—God or history or politics or literature or a belief in the healing power of love, or even righteous anger. Sometimes I think they are all the same. A reason to believe, a way to take the world by the throat and insist that there is more to this life than we have ever imagined.[5]

When I attribute inspirational value to works of literature, I mean that these works make people think there is more to this life than they ever imagined. This sort of effect is more often produced by Hegel or Marx than by Locke or Hume, Whitehead than Ayer, Wordsworth than Housman, Rilke than Brecht, Derrida than de Man, Bloom than Jameson.

Inspirational value is typically *not* produced by the operations of a method, a science, a discipline, or a profession. It is produced by the individual brush strokes of unprofessional prophets and demiurges. You cannot, for example, find inspirational value in a text at the same time that you are viewing it as the product of a mechanism of cultural production. To view a work in this way gives understanding but not hope, knowledge but not self-transformation. For knowledge is a matter putting a work in a familiar context—relating it to things already known.

If it is to have inspirational value, a work must be allowed to recontexualize much of what you previously thought you knew; it cannot, at least at first, be itself recontextualized by what you already believe. Just as you cannot be swept off your feet by another human being at the same time that you recognize him or her as a good specimen of a certain type, so you cannot simultaneously be inspired by a work and be knowing about it. Later on—when first love has been replaced by marriage—you may acquire the ability to be both at once. But the really good marriages, the inspired marriages, are those which began in wild, unreflective infatuation.

A humanistic discipline is in good shape only when it produces both inspiring works and works which contextualize, and thereby deromanticize and debunk, those inspiring works. So I think philosophy, as an academic discipline, was in better shape when it had room for admirers of Whitehead as well as admirers of Ayer. I think that literature departments were in better shape when people of Bloom's and Allison's sort had a better chance than, I am told, they now have of being allowed to spend their teaching lives reiterating their idiosyncratic enthusiasms for their favorite prophets and demiurges. People of that sort are the ones Jameson thinks outdated, because they are still preoccupied with what he calls the "bourgeois ego." They are people whose motto is Wordsworth's "What we have loved/Others will love, and we will teach them how." This kind of teaching is different from the kind that produces knowingness, or technique, or professionalism.

Of course, if such connoisseurs of charisma were the *only* sort of teacher available, students would be short-changed. But they will also be short-changed if the only sort of teacher available is the knowing, debunking, *nil admirari* kind. We shall always need people in every discipline whose talents suit them for understanding rather than for hope, for placing a text in a context rather than celebrating its originality, and for detecting nonsense rather than producing it. But the natural tendency of professionalization and academicization is to favor a talent for analysis and problem-solving over imagination, to replace enthusiasm with dry, sardonic knowingness. The dismalness of a lot of social science, and of a lot of analytic philosophy, is evidence of what happens when this replacement is complete.

Within the academy, the humanities have been a refuge for enthusiasts. If there is no longer a place for them within either philosophy or literature departments, it is not clear where they will find shelter in the future. People like Bloom and Allison—people who began devouring books as soon as they learned to read, whose lives were saved by books—may get frozen out of those departments. If they are, the study of the humanities will continue to produce knowledge, but it may no longer produce hope. Humanistic education may become what it was in Oxbridge before the reforms of the 1870s: merely a turnstile for admission to the overclass.

I hope that I have made clear what I mean by "inspirational value." Now I should like to say something about the term "great works of literature." This term is often thought to be obsolete, because Platonism is obsolete. By "Platonism" I mean the idea that great works of literature all, in the end, say the same thing—and are great precisely because they do so. They inculcate the same eternal "humanistic" values. They remind us of the same immutable features of human experience. Platonism, in this sense, conflates inspiration and knowledge by saying that only the eternal inspires—that the source of greatness has always been out there, just behind the veil of appearances, and has been described many times before. The best a prophet or a demiurge can hope for is to say once again what has often been said, but to say it in a different way, to suit a different audience.

I agree that these Platonist assumptions are best discarded. But doing so should not lead us to discard the hope shared by Allison, Bloom, and Matthew Arnold—the hope for a religion of literature, in which works of the secular imagination replace Scripture as the principal source of inspiration and hope for each new generation. We should cheerfully admit that canons are temporary, and touchstones replaceable. But this should not lead us to discard the idea of greatness. We should see great works of literature as great because they have inspired many readers, not as having inspired many readers because they are great.

This difference may seem a quibble, but it is the whole difference between pragmatist functionalism and Platonist essentialism. For a functionalist, it is no surprise that some putatively great works leave some readers cold; functionalists do not expect the same key to open every heart. For functionalists like Bloom, the main reason for drawing up a literary canon, "ordering a lifetime's reading," is to be able to offer suggestions to the young about where they might find excitement and hope. Whereas essentialists take canonical status as indicating the presence of a link to eternal truth, and lack of interest in a canonical work as a moral flaw, functionalists take canonical status to be as changeable as the historical and personal situations of readers. Essentialist critics like de Man think that philosophy tells them how to read nonphilosophy. Functionalist critics like M. H. Abrams and Bloom read philosophical treatises in the same way they read poems—in search of excitement and hope.

The Platonist subordination of time to eternity, and of hope and inspiration to knowledge, produces the attitude which Mark Edmundson criticizes in his *Literature against Philosophy: Plato to Derrida.* "To the degree that your terminology claims to encompass a text, to know it better than it knows itself," Edmundson says, "to that degree you give up the possibility of being read by it."[6] Edmundson's target is the assumption that one's reading is insufficiently informed if one is unable to put the text one is reading within a previously formulated theoretical context—a context which enables one, in the manner of Jameson, to treat the latest birth of time as just another specimen, reiterating a known type.

It is this assumption against which Shelley, in his *Defence of Poetry,* protested. "Poets," he said, "are the hierophants of an unapprehended inspiration; the mirrors of the gigantic shadows which futurity casts upon the present." There was, to be sure, still plenty of Platonism in Shelley, even more than there was in Arnold. But, since Shelley's day, there has been less Platonism in every succeeding generation, thanks to figures like Marx, Whitman, and Dewey—romantic utopians who prophesied a human future which would be patterned neither on the past nor on the eternal.

Though I think of Derrida as just such a romantic utopian, I cannot interpret either Foucault or Jameson in this way. I think that Bloom is right when he refers to the present "odd blend of Foucault and Marx" as "a very minor episode in the endless history of Platonism"—the endless attempt to make the intellect sovereign over the imagination.[7] Edmundson seems to me right in describing much of what is going on in anglophone literature departments as part of the latest attempt by knowing philosophers to gain supremacy over inspired poets. I hope that the philosophers never succeed in this attempt. But I do not think that literature will succeed in resisting philosophy unless literary critics think of it as Bloom does: as having nothing to do with eternity, knowledge, or stability, and everything to do with futurity and hope—with taking the world by the throat and insisting that there is more to this life than we have ever imagined.

Unfortunately, in contemporary American academic culture, it is commonly assumed that once you have seen through Plato, essentialism, and eternal truth you will naturally turn to Marx. The attempt to take the world by the throat is still, in the minds of Jameson and his admirers, associated with Marxism. This association seems to me merely quaint, as does Jameson's use of the term "late capitalism"—a term which equivocates nicely between economic history and millenarian hope. The main thing contemporary academic Marxists inherit from Marx and Engels is the conviction that the quest for the cooperative commonwealth should be scientific rather than utopian, knowing rather than romantic.

This conviction seems to me entirely mistaken. I take Foucault's refusal to indulge in utopian thinking not as sagacity but as a result of his unfortunate inability to believe in the possibility of human happiness, and his consequent inability to think of beauty as the promise of happiness. Attempts to imitate Foucault make it hard for his followers to take poets like Blake or Whitman seriously. So it is hard for these followers to take seriously people inspired by such poets—people like Jean Jaurès, Eugene Debs, Vaclav Havel, and Bill Bradley. The Foucauldian academic Left in contemporary America is exactly the sort of Left that the oligarchy dreams of: a Left whose members are so busy unmasking the present that they have no time to discuss what laws need to be passed in order to create a better future.

Emerson famously distinguished between the party of memory and the party of hope. Bloom has remarked that this distinction is now, in its application to American academic politics, out of date: the party of memory, he says, *is* the party of hope. His point is that, among students of literature, it is only those who agree with Hölderlin that "what abides was founded by poets" who are still capable of social hope. I suspect he is right at least to this extent: it is only those who still read for inspiration who are likely to be of much use in building a cooperative commonwealth. So I do not see the disagreement between Jamesonians and Bloomians as a disagreement between those who take politics seriously and those who do not. Instead, I see it as between people taking refuge in self-protective knowingness about the present and romantic utopians trying to imagine a better future.

Notes

1. Fredric Jameson, *Postmodernism, or The Cultural Logic of Late Capitalism* (Durham, N.C.: Duke University Press, 1991), p. 15.
2. *ibid.,* p. 306.
3. Jameson, *Postmodernism,* p. 46.
4. The best of these minds, however, are more inclined to dissolve problems than to solve them. They challenge the presuppositions of the problems with which the profession is currently occupied. This is what Ludwig Wittgenstein did in his *Philosophical Investigations,* and similar challenges are found in the work of the contemporary analytic philosophers I most admire—for example, Annette Baier, Donald Davidson, and Daniel Dennett. Such innovators are always viewed with some suspicion: those brought up on the old problems would like to think that their clever solutions to those problems are permanent contributions to human knowledge. Forty-odd years after its publication, *Philosophical Investigations* still makes many philosophers nervous. They view Wittgenstein as a spoilsport.
5. Dorothy Allison, "Believing in Literature," in Allison, *Skin: Talking about Sex, Class, and Literature* (Ithaca, N.Y.: Firebrand Books, 1994), p. 181.
6. Mark Edmundson, *Literature against Philosophy: Plato to Derrida* (New York: Cambridge University Press, 1995), p. 128.
7. Harold Bloom, *The Western Canon: The Books and School of the Ages* (New York: Harcourt Brace, 1994), p. 18. Unfortunately, Bloom attributes this latest version of Platonism to "our current New Historicists." I think it is absent from the work of Stephen Greenblatt, who is too good a critic to be buffaloed by theory. But lesser Foucauldians do indeed think of Foucault and Marx as providing keys sufficient to unlock any text.

Questions to Consider

1. Many English departments continue to separate reading ("literature") from writing ("rhetoric and composition"). To what extent does this disciplinary split seem to be evident in your own department and courses? How has your own course work followed one path or the other? Would you like to see a more integrated approach to the building of knowledge in the English curriculum? What might such an approach look like?
2. Pratt's argument, like many multiculturalist or revisionist arguments about the literary canon and the Eurocentric curriculum, has been attacked from

the Right as "mere PC rhetoric" or "white-male bashing." No doubt you have heard some of these arguments. How does Pratt (or any of the other writers in this section) help you to formulate a response to the argument that canon revision is only politically correct or even a "dumbing down" of the canon? How would you use these essays to redefine "great literature"?

3. The essays in this section all speak to a broad shift in disciplinarity and knowledge, which some have defined as a "cultural turn." This turn generally is seen as a rejection of scientificity in favor of language, culture, and metaphor. How would Derrida describe this phenomenon? What differences do you see among these thinkers? What similarities do you see? Can you see this turn affecting your own education?

4. How do the essays in this section speak to questions of "taste," not only in terms of an aesthetic disposition, but also in terms of intellectual dispositions? Are questions of taste factors in Derrida's discussion of basic and oriented research? What relationships do you see between taste and "knowingness" in Rorty's text? What relationships do you see between taste and the blurring of genres that Geertz discusses? Do you value taste as an important personal quality?

5. Think about the term "literature." How do you understand this term? What are some of the different ways the essays in this section may help you to rethink or challenge common assumptions about literature? Who decides what counts as literature? How are these decisions institutionalized? Why?

6. Questions about high versus low art and culture raise issues of privilege, greatness, seriousness, and value. How do the texts in this section help you to examine such value judgments? What texts, television shows, or movies have you seen recently that support, challenge, or blur distinctions? How important are these distinctions in your own life?

III

MONEY AND POWER

Money and power. The two seem as compatible as peanut butter and jelly or milk and cookies, though not nearly so innocent. Even the most cursory glance at the origin of the word "money" confirms the snug relationship between these two terms: "money" comes from the Latin *moneta,* which means "a mint" and which was also a surname of the Roman goddess Juno, in whose temple money was coined. *Moneta,* in turn, comes from *monere,* meaning to advise, warn, or admonish.

The idea of coining money in a religious temple may strike some of us as odd, since many of us are familiar with the story of Jesus driving the money changers out of the temple, as if money, or a particular way of handling it, had no place there. And yet if we examine a dollar bill, we find on its back the motto "In God We Trust," a reference to the ultimate power and authority of what Robert Bellah calls America's "civil religion." We can also draw certain conclusions about the relationship between money and power when we examine the face of a dollar bill, for what stares back at us is the placid visage of George Washington, our nation's first president, a role in which executive power is vested. And, of course, we have the word "pecuniary," which pertains to money but also to legal offenses involving a monetary penalty or fine, a word suggesting in no uncertain terms the connection between money and the power to penalize or punish. Is it any wonder people are inclined to take money so seriously? And yet there are those who don't.

In the late eighteenth century, for example, a book appeared in which the narrator states quite unequivocally his disdain for money:

> None of my prevailing tastes centre in things that can be bought. I want nothing but unadulterated pleasures, and money poisons all. . . . Money tempts me less

156

> than things, because between money and the possession of the desired object there is always an intermediary, whereas between the thing itself and the enjoyment of it there is none. If I see the thing, it tempts me; if I only see the means of gaining possession of it, it does not. (431)

This book was Jean-Jacques Rousseau's *Confessions,* an autobiographical account of an extraordinary individual in conflict with a world full of people whose only desire is to accumulate wealth and power. The money we possess, says Rousseau, "is the instrument of freedom[,]" but the money "we eagerly pursue is the instrument of slavery" (431). In Rousseau's view, because we are alienated from our original nature and prevented from becoming our true selves, we vainly grasp at objects outside ourselves in order to pursue the illusion of public acceptance. Appearance thus becomes more important than reality, and the artificial more important than the natural.

There are many ways we could begin a discussion of the relationship between money and power, but mention of Rousseau seems especially appropriate, as he is best known for social ideas and political treatises articulating his belief in the destructiveness of institutions and the antithesis between contemporary society and the nature of man, a view that you will find expressed sometimes directly and sometimes indirectly in the essay selections in this section. One of Rousseau's most powerful indictments was of European civilization for its imposition of behavioral uniformity on people, an imposition that causes them to ignore "the duties of man and the needs of nature." According to Rousseau, a particularly serious outcome of this imposition is the creation of a society whose central feature is an unnatural inequality based on wealth and power.

Born 32 years after Rousseau was another philosopher and social reformer, the Englishman Jeremy Bentham. What Bentham saw during his study of law was incoherence in both the theory and practice of the legal system, and thus he took as his life's work the articulation and advocacy of a clear, coherent, humane, and simplified legal system, part of which entailed designing a model prison called the Panopticon. The prison was circular in design, with a tower positioned at its center so that a single guard could always have each inmate in plain view. Like the tower at the center of this model prison, a discussion of Bentham's Panopticon occupies the center of Michel Foucault's "Panopticism," the third chapter of *Discipline and Punish,* which was published in 1975. Like Rousseau and Bentham, Foucault was politically active, his book a direct result of his work on prison reform.

When you first begin reading "Panopticism," you will find a description of an order, published at the end of the seventeenth century, that lays out in minute detail the measures to be taken by a town infected with the plague. It makes for interesting reading, for there's something positively Orwellian or Huxleyesque about it, but you may wonder how Foucault is going to get from the late seventeenth century's concern with plague to a discussion of the prison system and, further, how a history of the prison system is going to have any bearing on everyday life in the early twenty-first century. Foucault himself indirectly poses and then partially addresses this question in Chapter One of his book, when he asks himself why he has written a history of the prison: "Simply because I am interested in the past? No, if one means by that writing a history of the past in terms of the present. Yes, if one means writing the history of the present." Although the phrase "history of the present" may scramble our usual sense of time, which equates history with the past rather than the present, it clearly indicates where Foucault's concerns lie: to be both a political activist and an historian, he must have his feet securely planted in the present. And the leap from plague to prison is not really that great when you think about our current attitudes toward those we label sick and those we label criminal. In fact, the mental health of a person found guilty of a crime is often called into question for sentencing purposes. Is this person sick (insane and thus not culpable), the courts ask, or is this person sound (sane and thus culpable)? On occasion, we even consider illness a divine punishment for bad behavior. And thus the line between the sick and the criminal is rather blurry, the word "sick" being used frequently enough in an accusatory manner.

What will surely catch your attention as you read Foucault's description of the seventeenth-century order is its concern with surveillance and documentation. But what is perhaps really noteworthy—chilling, even—is the odd resemblance between measures to fight the plague and the operations of the contemporary classroom. Peppering the description are words and phrases such as "permanent registration"; "reports"; "documents" bearing name, age, and sex; "daily roll call"; note taking; and "a written note" from the physician in charge. And this resemblance is precisely what Foucault wishes to point out, for "Panopticism" ends with this question: "Is it surprising that prisons resemble factories, schools, barracks, hospitals, which all resemble prisons?"

If what Foucault says is true, that schools resemble prisons, how has this come to be? According to Foucault, the plague gave rise to a particular political dream, that of the disciplined society, while the leper gave rise to the political dream of the pure community. The plague called for disciplinary projects such as correct training, segmentation, analysis, and distribution, while the leper called for "rituals of exclusion" such as confinement, separation, and branding. So we have the disciplined society and the pure community—two different but not incompatible political dreams that Foucault sees as having merged in the nineteenth century. The formula to which this merger gives rise is to treat lepers as plague victims by identifying the "abnormal" and then altering it through corrective training. For Foucault, Bentham's Panopticon represents an architectural version of the marriage of these mechanisms of power, and its beauty, if such a thing can be called beautiful, is that it can function successfully in any number of institutional settings, "normalizing" everything that falls under its gaze. Here, of course, we see echoes of Rousseau and his indictment of European civilization for its imposition of behavioral uniformity.

While it would seem that Bentham's intentions were good when he designed his model prison, the way Foucault describes its operation sounds downright sinister. Subjected to constant surveillance that is visible but not verifiable, the prisoners (or workers, orphans, schoolchildren, the insane, etc.) are separated from one another, each occupying a private cell with no possibility of communication or even visual contact among them. The Panopticon, which Foucault refers to as a "laboratory of power," and which reverses the principle of the dungeon, operates under the notion that darkness protects and visibility is a trap. It also disrupts the dialectical nature of vision, for the prisoners are seen without being able to see, while the occupant of the tower sees everything without being seen. Foucault speaks of the panoptic society as perverse, but we might also speak of it as paranoid. It is marked by constant surveillance, examination, interrogation, and behavior modification—the stuff of nightmares and horror movies.

After Foucault's bleak vision of a modern society permeated by panopticism, a society that lodges power not in a monarch but in a machine whose disciplinary arms reach into every aspect of our lives, you will probably find Paul Fussell's witty and tongue-in-cheek discussion of class a welcome relief. And yet, even in "An Anatomy of the Classes," published in 1983 as the second chapter of *Class,* you may find evidence supporting some of Foucault's conclusions. Fussell begins his book by asserting that the subject of class is a touchy one for most Americans. We like the illusion that America is a classless society, and yet most of us secretly suspect, argues Fussell, that "an extremely complicated system of social classes" is very much in operation. As Fussell reports, when he mentions to people that he is writing a book on class, it is as if he has said, "I am working on a book urging the beating to death of baby whales using the dead bodies of baby seals." People get nervous and edgy, and many of them move quickly away as if in fear that Fussell will immediately identify the class to which they belong through some detail such as hair style, clothing, demeanor, table manners, or speech. In this respect, Fussell himself seems to operate rather like the Panopticon, restlessly observing, analyzing, dividing, segmenting, classifying, and branding.

Although the simplest division of class suggests the existence of only two classes—rich and poor—Fussell's careful observation of American society has led him to propose nine: top out-of-sight, upper, upper middle, middle, high proletarian, mid-proletarian, low proletarian, destitute, and bottom out-of-sight. Of course, money defines class, says Fussell, but it is certainly not the only thing that does so. Style, taste, and awareness play an important role, too. According to Fussell, it's the *way* people have money that counts, not their mere possession of it.

If you keep Foucault in mind as you read Fussell, you will begin to notice significant connections. Take Fussell's discussion of the top out-of-sight class, for instance. One of the interesting features of this class is its invisibility. Perhaps members of this class can be said to exercise the most power precisely because their money and status allow them a privacy that the other classes do not enjoy. In other words, the top out-of-sight class escapes the panoptic gaze. The middle class, on the other hand, appears to operate as if it's always under observation. "Status panic" is the affliction of the middle class, remarks Fussell, for the middle class lives in constant fear of doing something wrong or offending someone and thereby losing status. Its members are nervous and self-conscious not because they know they are being observed but because they know they *might* be. As Bentham theorized, the inmate of the Panopticon "must never know whether he is being looked at any one moment; but he must be sure that he may always be so." It's as if members of the middle class have been thoroughly "panopticized," for they avoid oddity, introversion, and privacy. The members of the middle class are team players, says Fussell, and no latitude is permitted to individuality or eccentricity. As an IBM executive bragged to Fussell, "The training makes our men interchangeable."

"Corrective training," on the other hand, can be used to achieve, or attempt to achieve, a shift in class status. People may dream of winning the lottery or becoming millionaires, but Fussell argues that, if given the opportunity, most members of the middle class would choose to be upper middle class rather than upper class or top out-of-sight class because while upper middle class is grander than middle class, it is still familiar territory. If a member of the middle class were suddenly transferred to one of the two highest classes, there would be too many opportunities to make mistakes—being asked to order a dinner entrée and the proper wine from a French menu might prove embarrassing, for example. Apparently, in making the shift from middle to upper middle class, simple surface alterations rather than substantive changes suffice, for not only can clothing and living and office space be "cosmeticized" toward the upper middle class, but also faces, bodies, gestures, and postures can be adjusted accordingly. Discipline and training may not change our essence, but they can change our appearance and thus certain class markers that betray our status.

Only five years after the publication of Fussell's *Class,* Fredric Jameson published "Postmodernism and Consumer Society," an article that seems to contradict or, at the very least, call into question some of Fussell's assumptions about class and to suggest a disruption in Foucault's panoptic machine. While Foucault argues that the disciplinary mechanisms of the panoptic society gave rise to the emergence of disciplines as we now know them in academia, and while Fussell's discussion of class implies a disciplinary model (people are disciplined to fit a particular class and are trained to dress and act in accordance with their class status or with the class status they wish to occupy), Jameson's discussion of postmodernism and consumer society suggests a breakdown in this disciplinary system. One of the central features of postmodernism (when Jameson uses this term, he uses it not simply to describe a style but to characterize a period) is its erasure of "some key boundaries or separations, most notably the erosion of the older distinction between high culture and so-called mass or popular culture."

Even theory itself is a manifestation of postmodernism, argues Jameson, for its discourse is a blend of many disciplines rather than a distinct discipline, and he cites none other than Michel Foucault as an example. Is Foucault's work to be called philosophy, history, social theory, or political science? asks Jameson. His answer is that it's undecidable; it is all these things and yet none. According to Jameson, this erosion of boundaries is perhaps most upsetting from an academic standpoint, for academia has traditionally wished to maintain a distinction between high and low culture—between, for example, the novels of Proust and the stories found in *Reader's Digest.* One of the questions that Jameson's assertion raises is a troubling one: *why* might academia have such a vested interest in maintaining these distinctions? Is it motivated by aesthetic snobbery? Or is it motivated by power? Is academia one of the dying arms of the Panopticon?

Jameson locates the shift from the modern period to the postmodern in the 1960s, referring to the sixties as a key transitional period. Given his definition of postmodernism, this location seems appropriate, for it was during the 1960s that gains made by the civil rights and women's movements were breaking down certain barriers that had existed between blacks and whites, women and men. Unfortunately, alongside positive social changes came rather ambiguous changes in the economic order: multinational capitalism ushered in the era of what we call "consumer society." Although Jameson doesn't put it this way, his argument seems to imply that we have consumed ourselves right out of meaningful existence. Our continual demand for the new has exhausted our storehouses of innovation, and now all we can do is ransack the past, but it is a past to which we have no access except through pop images and stereotypes. Out of touch with the past and unable to achieve aesthetic representation of our current experience, we have lost all sense of perspective regarding space and time. Having transformed reality into images and fragmented time into "a series of perpetual presents," we have become a schizophrenic society. Just as Fussell argues that the way an individual has money defines his or her class, Jameson argues that the way a society uses money shapes its collective psyche.

In some sense, each of the theorists we've discussed so far has been talking about money, power, or both in terms of identity. Foucault speaks of identity formed through oppositional or binary terms, the panoptic project being to sort out the normal from the abnormal, the sane from the insane. Fussell speaks of identity in terms of class markers or features. Jameson speaks of a cultural identity lodged in a world of images divorced from space and time. And John Guillory continues this discussion by introducing terms such as "social identity" and "identity politics." Even though the words "money" and "power" may not appear in "Canonical and Noncanonical: The Current Debate," they hover just behind the scenes in Guillory's discussion of cultural capital, the name of the book from which this essay has been drawn.

If Jameson sees a fragmentation of consumer society so profound that any sense of a linguistic norm has been lost, each group or profession speaking its own private language and each individual becoming "a kind of linguistic island," Guillory sees a similar phenomenon occurring in the realm of politics. According to Guillory, liberal pluralist thought conceives of individuals "in their relation to the state as members of groups whose interests are assumed to conflict," and thus representation is seen as an important objective. The problem, however, is that since World War II, there has been such a proliferation of diverse social groups in America that an apparent limit has been reached in the ability of political institutions to represent them all. The reason for this proliferation, argues Guillory, is that differences and antagonisms existing within and between dominated groups become the impetus for creating new groups and subgroups, each clamoring for representation, instead of the impetus for analyzing the causes of difference and resolving the antagonisms. With so many groups seeking representation, the representational barrel has run dry, and with the demise of liberalism in the political arena, a new venue of representation has had to be found. The university, then, has taken over where political institutions have left off. The question Guillory asks is what the political means in the context of the university. For many liberal academics, it means canon revision, opening up the canon to include writers from groups that have been unrepresented or underrepresented. But how, asks Guillory, does canon revision affect the social domain?

Obviously, Guillory is not against canon revision, but you might say that he sees solving political problems through canon revision as akin to putting a Band-Aid on a broken arm. The Band-Aid doesn't hurt—it may even give a modicum of comfort—but it doesn't adequately address the problem. The way the canon debate is currently articulated misses the point, says Guillory, because it is articulated in terms of inclusion and exclusion, as if there have been many great writers of all stripes and colors throughout the centuries who have been purposely excluded because of their social identity. This is simply not the case, argues Guillory. People have been denied not representation but access to the means of cultural production—denied access to literacy itself, a far more profound form of exclusion than lack of representation in the literary canon.

Of all the theorists in this section, Jeannette Winterson offers the harshest but also, perhaps, the most hopeful critique of a consumer society such as ours. It is appropriate that "Imagination and Reality," published in 1996, appears last, for her brief essay is wide ranging enough in its commentary that it manages to intersect with the ideas expressed by each of the other theorists in this section, and thus reading Winterson may provide you with an opportunity for synthesis. When Winterson speaks of governments, mass education, and mass media as powerful agencies that have no regard for individuality and that pay lip service to "freedom of choice" while promoting "streamlined homogeneity," you will surely hear echoes of Foucault's account of panoptic society and its "normalizing" goals. When Winterson mentions her mother's lowly social status and her need to buy things in order to feel better about herself, you will probably be reminded of what Fussell says about the middle class: "The desire to belong, and to belong by some mechanical act like purchasing something, is another sign of the middle class." When Winterson speaks of art, on the other hand, you will find her diverging from Jameson, for if he sees in postmodernism an imprisonment in the past and a failure of the new, Winterson sees the artist's potential as unlimited in its ability to invent: "Invention is the shaping spirit that re-forms fragments into new wholes, so that even what has been familiar can be seen fresh." And when Winterson speaks of the artist as a visionary, not a court photographer, you may wonder what the literary canon would look like if Winterson were in charge of revising it—or, better yet, what our culture would look like if everyone had equal access to literacy and the means of cultural production, if the world of the imagination were still valued, and if the only thing that counts were not money.

Michel Foucault (1926–1984)

It can easily be argued that the title of leading European thinker and writer of the second half of the twentieth century belongs to Foucault, for his influence has thoroughly permeated discourses as diverse as poststructuralism, New Historicism, cultural studies, and queer theory. The son of a doctor, he was born in Poitiers, France. Instead of studying medicine, as his family wished, Foucault chose to specialize in the philosophy of psychology, earning his degree at

France's top university, the École Normale Supérieure. Whereas Foucault's brother become a doctor, Foucault distressed his family still further, no doubt, by becoming a fierce critic of modern medical practices and institutions. During the 1950s, Foucault taught first in France and then in Sweden, Poland, and Germany. His first book was an outgrowth of his graduate thesis, part of which was translated into English as *Madness and Civilization* (1961). The follow-up to his first book was *The Birth of the Clinic,* which appeared in 1963, but it was in 1966 that his reputation was made with the publication of *The Order of Things,* an examination of how the disciplines of economics, linguistics, and biology emerged. Although Foucault was a member of the Communist party from 1950 until 1953, he became a serious political activist after his involvement with student unrest in Tunisia, where he taught for two years, and the student-led revolt against the French government in May of 1968. His work on prison reform led to the publication of *Discipline and Punish* (1975), from which "Panopticism" is taken. After tackling the history of the prison, Foucault turned his attention to the history of sexuality. Three volumes on this subject were published, but the project was left unfinished when Foucault died of complications from AIDS. At his death, he was only 57 years old.

Panopticism

The following, according to an order published at the end of the seventeenth century, were the measures to be taken when the plague appeared in a town.[1]

First, a strict spatial partitioning: the closing of the town and its outlying districts, a prohibition to leave the town on pain of death, the killing of all stray animals; the division of the town into distinct quarters, each governed by an intendant. Each street is placed under the authority of a syndic, who keeps it under surveillance; if he leaves the street, he will be condemned to death. On the appointed day, everyone is ordered to stay indoors: it is forbidden to leave on pain of death. The syndic himself comes to lock the door of each house from the outside; he takes the key with him and hands it over to the intendant of the quarter; the intendant keeps it until the end of the quarantine. Each family will have made its own provisions; but, for bread and wine, small wooden canals are set up between the street and the interior of the houses, thus allowing each person to receive his ration without communicating with the suppliers and other residents; meat, fish and herbs will be hoisted up into the houses with pulleys and baskets. If it is absolutely necessary to leave the house, it will be done in turn, avoiding any meeting. Only the intendants, syndics and guards will move about the streets and also, between the infected houses, from one corpse to another, the "crows," who can be left to die: these are "people of little substance who carry the sick, bury the dead, clean, and do many vile and abject offices." It is a segmented, immobile, frozen space. Each individual is fixed in his place. And, if he moves, he does so at the risk of his life, contagion, or punishment.

Inspection functions ceaselessly. The gaze is alert everywhere: "A considerable body of militia, commanded by good officers and men of substance," guards at the gates, at the town hall, and in every quarter to ensure the prompt obedience of the people and the most absolute authority of the magistrates, "as also to observe all disorder, theft and extortion." At each of the town gates there will be an observation post; at the end of each street sentinels. Every day, the intendant visits the quarter in his charge, inquires whether the syndics have carried out their tasks, whether the inhabitants have anything to complain of; they "observe their actions." Every day, too, the syndic goes into the street for which he is responsible; stops before each house: gets all the inhabitants to appear at the windows (those who live overlooking the courtyard will be allocated a window looking onto the street at which no one but they may show themselves); he calls each of them by name; informs himself as to the state of each and every one of them—"in which respect the inhabitants will be compelled to speak the truth under pain of death"; if someone does not appear at the window, the syndic must ask why: "In this way he will find out easily enough whether dead or sick are being concealed." Everyone locked up in his cage, everyone at his window, answering to his name and showing himself when asked—it is the great review of the living and the dead.

This surveillance is based on a system of permanent registration: reports from the syndics to the intendants, from the intendants to the magistrates or mayor. At the beginning of the "lock up," the role of each of the inhabitants present in the town is laid down, one by one; this document bears "the name, age, sex of everyone, notwithstanding his condition": a copy is sent to the intendant of the quarter, another to the office of the town hall, another to enable the syndic to make his daily roll call. Everything that may be observed during the course of the visits—deaths, illnesses, complaints, irregularities—is noted down and transmitted to the intendants and magistrates. The magistrates have complete control over medical treatment; they have appointed a physician in charge; no other practitioner may treat, no apothecary prepare medicine, no confessor visit a sick person without having received from him a written note "to prevent anyone from concealing and dealing with those sick of the contagion, unknown to the magistrates." The registration of the pathological must be constantly centralized. The relation of each individual to his disease and to his death passes through the representatives of power, the registration they make of it, the decisions they take on it.

Five or six days after the beginning of the quarantine, the process of purifying the houses one by one is begun. All the inhabitants are made to leave; in each room "the furniture and goods" are raised from the ground or suspended from the air; perfume is poured around the room; after carefully scaling the windows, doors, and even the keyholes with wax, the perfume is set alight. Finally, the entire house is closed while the perfume is consumed; those who have carried out the work are searched, as they were on entry, "in the presence of the residents of the house, to see that they did not have something on their persons as they left that they did not have on entering." Four hours later, the residents are allowed to reenter their homes.

This enclosed, segmented space, observed at every point, in which the individuals are inserted in a fixed place, in which the slightest movements are supervised, in which all events are recorded, in which an uninterrupted work of writing links the center and periphery, in which power is exercised without division, according to a continuous hierarchical figure, in which each individual is constantly located, examined, and distributed among the living beings, the sick and the dead—all this constitutes a compact model of the disciplinary mechanism. The plague is met by order; its function is to sort out every possible confusion: that of the disease, which is transmitted when bodies are mixed together; that of the evil, which is increased when fear and death overcome prohibitions. It lays down for each individual his place, his body, his disease, and his death, his well-being, by means of an omnipresent and omniscient power that subdivides itself in a regular, uninterrupted way even to the ultimate determination of the individual, of what characterizes him, of what belongs to him, of what happens to him. Against the plague, which is a mixture, discipline brings into play its power, which is one of analysis. A whole literary fiction of the festival grew up around the plague: suspended laws, lifted prohibitions, the frenzy of passing time, bodies mingling together without respect, individuals unmasked, abandoning their statutory identity and the figure under which they had been recognized, allowing a quite different truth to appear. But there was also a political dream of the plague, which was exactly its reverse: not the collective festival, but strict divisions; not laws transgressed, but the penetration of regulation into even the smallest details of everyday life through the mediation of the complete hierarchy that assured the capillary functioning of power; not masks that were put on and taken off, but the assignment to each individual of his "true" name, his "true" place, his "true" body, his "true" disease. The plague as a form, at once real and imaginary, of disorder had as its medical and political correlative discipline. Behind the disciplinary mechanisms can be read the haunting memory of "contagions," of the plague, of rebellions, crimes, vagabondage, desertions, people who appear and disappear, live and die in disorder.

If it is true that the leper gave rise to rituals of exclusion, which to a certain extent provided the model for and general form of the great Confinement, then the plague gave rise to disciplinary projects. Rather than the massive, binary division between one set of people and another, it called for multiple separations, individualizing distributions, an organization in depth of surveillance and control, an intensification and a ramification of power. The leper was caught up in a practice of rejection, of exile-enclosure; he was left to his doom in a mass among which it was useless to differentiate; those sick of the plague were caught up in a meticulous tactical partitioning in which individual differentiations were the constricting effects of a power that multiplied, articulated, and subdivided itself; the great confinement on the one hand; the correct training on the other. The leper and his separation; the plague and its segmentations. The first is marked; the second analyzed and distributed. The exile of the leper and the arrest of the plague do not bring with them the same political dream. The first is that of a pure community, the second that of a disciplined society. Two ways of exercising power over men, of controlling their relations, of separating out their dangerous mixtures. The plague-stricken town, traversed throughout with hierarchy, surveillance, observation, writing; the town immobilized by the functioning of an extensive power that bears in a distinct way over all individual bodies—this is the utopia of the perfectly governed city. The plague (envisaged as a possibility at least) is the trial in the course of which one may define ideally the exercise of disciplinary power. In order to make rights and laws function according to pure theory, the jurists place themselves in imagination in the state of nature; in order to see perfect disciplines functioning, rulers dreamed of the state of plague. Underlying disciplinary projects the image of the plague stands for all forms of confusion and disorder; just as the image of the leper, cut off from all human contact, underlies projects of exclusion.

They are different projects, then, but not incompatible ones. We see them coming slowly together, and it is the peculiarity of the nineteenth century that it applied to the space of exclusion of which the leper was the symbolic inhabitant (beggars, vagabonds, madmen, and the disorderly formed the real population) the technique of power proper to disciplinary partitioning. Treat "lepers" as "plague victims," project the subtle segmentations of discipline onto the confused space of internment, combine it with the methods of analytical distribution proper to power, individualize the excluded, but use procedures of individualization to mark exclusion—this is what was operated regularly by disciplinary power from the beginning of the nineteenth century in the psychiatric asylum, the penitentiary, the reformatory, the approved school and, to some extent, the hospital. Generally speaking, all the authorities exercising individual control function according to a double mode; that of binary division and branding (mad/sane; dangerous/harmless; normal/abnormal); and that of coercive assignment, of differential distribution (who he is; where he must be; how he is to be characterized; how he is to be recognized; how a constant surveillance is to be exercised over him in an individual way, etc.). On the one hand, the lepers are treated as plague victims; the tactics of individualizing disciplines are imposed on the excluded; and, on the other hand, the universality of disciplinary controls makes it possible to brand the "leper" and to bring into play against him the dualistic mechanisms of exclusion. The constant division between the normal and the abnormal, to which every individual is subjected, brings us back to our own time, by applying the binary branding and exile of the leper to quite different objects; the existence of a whole set of techniques and institutions for measuring, supervising, and correcting the abnormal brings into play the disciplinary mechanisms to which the fear of the plague gave rise. All the mechanisms of power which, even today, are disposed around the abnormal individual, to brand him and to alter him, are composed of those two forms from which they distantly derive.

Bentham's *Panopticon* is the architectural figure of this composition. We know the principle on which it was based: at the periphery, an annular building; at the center, a tower; this tower is pierced with wide windows that open onto the inner side of the ring; the peripheric building is divided into cells, each of which extends the whole width of the building; they have two windows, one on the inside, corresponding to the windows of the tower; the other, on the outside, allows the light to cross the cell from one end to the other. All that is needed, then, is to place a supervisor in a central tower and to shut up in each cell a madman, a patient, a condemned man, a worker, or a schoolboy. By the effect of backlighting, one can observe from the tower, standing out precisely against the light, the small captive shadows in the cells of the periphery. They are like so many cages, so many small theatres, in which each actor is alone, perfectly individualized and constantly visible. The panoptic mechanism arranges spatial unities that make it possible to see constantly and to recognize immediately. In short, it reverses the principle of the dungeon; or rather of its three functions—to enclose, to deprive of light, and to hide—it preserves only the first and eliminates the other two. Full lighting and the eye of a supervisor capture better than darkness, which ultimately protected. Visibility is a trap.

To begin with, this made it possible—as a negative effect—to avoid those compact, swarming, howling masses that were to be found in places of confinement, those painted by Goya or described by Howard. Each individual, in his place, is securely confined to a cell from which he is seen from the front by the supervisor; but the side walls prevent him from coming into contact with his companions. He is seen, but he does not see; he is the object of information, never a subject in communication. The arrangement of his room, opposite the central tower, imposes on him an axial visibility; but the divisions of the ring, those separated cells, imply a lateral invisibility. And this invisibility is a guarantee of order. If the inmates are convicts, there is no danger of a plot, an attempt at collective escape, the planning of new crimes for the future, bad reciprocal influences; if they are patients, there is no danger of contagion; if they are madmen, there is no risk of their committing violence upon one another; if they are school-children, there is no copying, no noise, no chatter, no waste of time; if they are workers, there are no disorders, no theft, no coalitions, none of those distractions that slow down the rate of work, make it less perfect, or cause accidents. The crowd, a compact mass, a locus of multiple exchanges, individualities merging together, a collective effect, is abolished and replaced by a collection of separated individualities. From the point of view of the guardian, it is replaced by a multiplicity that can be numbered and supervised; from the point of view of the inmates, by a sequestered and observed solitude (Bentham 60–64).

Hence the major effect of the Panopticon: to induce in the inmate a state of conscious and permanent visibility that assures the automatic functioning of power. So to arrange things that the surveillance is permanent in its effects, even if it is discontinuous in its action; that the perfection of power should tend to render its actual exercise unnecessary; that this architectural apparatus should be a machine for creating and sustaining a power relation independent of the person who exercises it; in short, that the inmates should be caught up in a power situation of which they are themselves the bearers. To achieve this, it is at once too much and too little that the prisoner should be constantly observed by an inspector: too little, for what matters is that he knows himself to be observed; too much, because he has no need in fact of being so. In view of this, Bentham laid down the principle that power should be visible and unverifiable. Visible: the inmate will constantly have before his eyes the tall outline of the central tower from which he is spied upon. Unverifiable: the inmate must never know whether he is being looked at at any one moment; but he must be sure that he may always be so. In order to make the presence or absence of the inspector unverifiable, so that the prisoners, in their cells, cannot even see a shadow, Bentham envisaged not only venetian blinds on the windows of the central observation hall, but, on the inside, partitions that intersected the hall at right angles and, in order to pass from one quarter to the other, not doors but zigzag openings; for the slightest noise, a gleam of light, a brightness in a half-opened door would betray the presence of the guardian.[2] The Panopticon is a machine for dissociating the see/being seen dyad: in the peripheric ring, one is totally seen, without ever seeing; in the central tower, one sees everything without ever being seen.[3]

It is an important mechanism, for it automatizes and disindividualizes power. Power has its principle not so much in a person as in a certain concerted distribution of bodies, surfaces, lights, gazes; in an arrangement whose internal mechanisms produce the relation in which individuals are caught up. The ceremonies, the rituals, the marks by which the sovereign's surplus power was manifested are useless. There is a machinery that assures dissymmetry, disequilibrium, difference. Consequently, it does not matter who exercises power. Any individual, taken almost at random, can operate the machine: in the absence of the director, his family, his friends, his visitors, even his servants (Bentham 45). Similarly, it does not matter what motive animates him: the curiosity of the indiscreet, the malice of a child, the thirst for knowledge of a philosopher who wishes to visit this museum of human nature, or the perversity of those who take pleasure in spying and punishing. The more numerous those anonymous and temporary observers are, the greater the risk for the inmate of being surprised and the greater his anxious awareness of being observed. The Panopticon is a marvelous machine which, whatever use one may wish to put it to, produces homogeneous effects of power.

A real subjection is born mechanically from a fictitious relation. So it is not necessary to use force to constrain the convict to good behavior, the madman to calm, the worker to work, the schoolboy to application, the patient to the observation of the regulations. Bentham was surprised that panoptic institutions could be so light: there were no more bars, no more chains, no more heavy locks; all that was needed was that the separations should be clear and the openings well arranged. The heaviness of the old "houses of security," with their fortresslike architecture, could be replaced by the simple, economic geometry of a "house of certainty." The efficiency of power, its constraining force have, in a sense, passed over to the other side—to the side of its surface of application. He who is subjected to a field of visibility, and who knows it, assumes responsibility for the constraints of power; he makes them play spontaneously upon himself; he inscribes in himself the power relation in which he simultaneously plays both roles; he becomes the principle of his own subjection. By this very fact, the external power may throw off its physical weight; it tends to the noncorporal; and, the more it approaches this limit, the more constant, profound, and permanent are its effects: it is a perpetual victory that avoids any physical confrontation and which is always decided in advance.

Bentham does not say whether he was inspired, in his project, by Le Vaux's menagerie at Versailles: the first menagerie in which the different elements are not, as they traditionally were, distributed in a park (Loisel 104–7). At the center was an octagonal pavilion which, on the first floor, consisted of only a single room, the king's *salon;* on every side large windows looked out onto seven cages (the eighth side was reserved for the entrance), containing different species of animals. By Bentham's time, this menagerie had disappeared. But one finds in the program of the Panopticon a similar concern with individualizing observation, with characterization and classification, with the analytical arrangement of space. The Panopticon is a royal menagerie; the animal is replaced by man, individual distribution by specific grouping, and the king by the machinery of a furtive power. With this exception, the Panopticon also does the work of a naturalist. It makes it possible to draw up differences: among patients, to observe the symptoms of each individual, without the proximity of beds, the circulation of miasmas, the effects of contagion confusing the clinical tables; among schoolchildren, it makes it possible to observe performances (without there being any imitation or copying), to map aptitudes, to assess characters, to draw up rigorous classifications, and in relation to normal development, to distinguish "laziness and stubbornness" from "incurable imbecility"; among workers, it makes it possible to note the aptitudes of each worker, compare the time he takes to perform a task, and if they are paid by the day, to calculate their wages (Bentham 60–64).

So much for the question of observation. But the Panopticon was also a laboratory; it could be used as a machine to carry out experiments, to alter behavior, to train or correct individuals. To experiment with medicines and monitor their effects. To try out different punishments on prisoners, according to their crimes and character, and to seek the most effective ones. To teach different techniques simultaneously to the workers, to decide which is the best. To try out pedagogical experiments—and in particular to take up once again the well-debated problem of secluded education, by using orphans. One would see what would happen when, in their sixteenth or eighteenth year, they were presented with other boys or girls; one could verify whether, as Helvetius thought, anyone could learn anything; one would follow "the genealogy of every observable idea"; one could bring up different children according to different systems of thought, making certain children believe that two and two do not make four or that the moon is a cheese, then put them together when they are twenty or twenty-five years old; one would then have discussions that would be worth a great deal more than the sermons or lectures on which so much money is spent; one would have at least an opportunity of making discoveries in the domain of metaphysics. The Panopticon is a privileged place for experiments on men, and for analyzing with complete certainty the transformations that may be obtained from them. The Panopticon may even provide an apparatus for supervising its own mechanisms. In this central tower, the director may spy on all the employees that he has under his orders: nurses, doctors, foremen, teachers, warders; he will be able to judge them continuously, alter their behavior, impose upon them the methods he thinks best; and it will even be possible to observe the director himself. An inspector arriving unexpectedly at the center of the Panopticon will be able to judge at a glance, without anything being concealed from him, how the entire establishment is functioning. And, in any case, enclosed as he is in the middle of this architectural mechanism, is not the director's own fate entirely bound up with it? The incompetent physician who has allowed contagion to spread, the incompetent prison governor or workshop manager will be the first victims of an epidemic or a revolt. "'By every tie I could devise,' said the master of the Panopticon, 'my own fate had been bound up by me with theirs'" (Bentham 177). The Panopticon functions as a kind of laboratory of power. Thanks to its mechanisms of observation, it gains in efficiency and in the ability to penetrate into men's behavior; knowledge follows the advances of power, discovering new objects of knowledge over all the surfaces on which power is exercised.

The plague-stricken town, the panoptic establishment—the differences are important. They mark, at a distance of a century and a half, the transformations of the disciplinary program. In the first case, there is an exceptional situation: against an extraordinary evil, power is mobilized; it makes itself everywhere present and visible; it invents new mechanisms; it separates, it immobilizes, it partitions; constructs for a time what is both a counter-city and the perfect society; it imposes an ideal functioning, but one that is reduced, in the final analysis, like the evil that it combats, to a simple dualism of life and death: that which moves brings death, and one kills that which moves. The Panopticon, on the other hand, must be understood as a generalizable model of functioning; a way of defining power relations in terms of the everyday life of men. No doubt Bentham presents it as a particular institution, closed in upon itself. Utopias, perfectly closed in upon themselves, are common enough. As opposed to the ruined prisons, littered with mechanisms of torture, to be seen in Piranese's engravings, the Panopticon presents a cruel, ingenious cage. The fact that it should have given rise, even in our own time, to so many variations, projected or realized, is evidence of the imaginary intensity that it has possessed for almost two hundred years. But the Panopticon must not be understood as a dream building: it is the diagram of a mechanism of power reduced to its ideal form; its functioning, abstracted from any obstacle, resistance, or friction, must be represented as a pure architectural and optical system: it is in fact a figure of political technology that may and must be detached from any specific use.

It is polyvalent in its applications; it serves to reform prisoners, but also to treat patients, to instruct schoolchildren, to confine the insane, to supervise workers, to put beggars and idlers to work. It is a type of location of bodies in space, of distribution of individuals in relation to one another, of hierarchical organization, of disposition of centers and channels of power, of definition of the instruments and modes of intervention of power, which can be implemented in hospitals, workshops, schools, prisons. Whenever one is dealing with a multiplicity of individuals on whom a task or a particular form of behavior must be imposed, the panoptic schema may be used. It is—necessary modifications apart—applicable "to all establishments whatsoever, in which, within a space not too large to be covered or commanded by buildings, a number of persons are meant to be kept under inspection" (Bentham 40; although Bentham takes the penitentiary house as his prime example, it is because it has many different functions to fulfil—safe custody, confinement, solitude, forced labor, and instruction).

In each of its applications, it makes it possible to perfect the exercise of power. It does this in several ways: because it can reduce the number of those who exercise it, while increasing the number of those on whom it is exercised. Because it is possible to intervene at any moment and because the constant pressure acts even before the offenses, mistakes, or crimes have been committed. Because, in these conditions, its strength is that it never intervenes, it is exercised spontaneously and without noise, it constitutes a mechanism whose effects follow from one another. Because, without any physical instrument other than architecture and geometry, it acts directly on individuals; it gives "power of mind over mind." The panoptic schema makes any apparatus of power more intense: it assures its economy (in material, in personnel, in time); it assures its efficacity by its preventative character, its continuous functioning and its automatic mechanisms. It is a way of obtaining from power "in hitherto unexampled quantity," "a great and new instrument of government . . . ; its great excellence consists in the great strength it is capable of giving to *any* institution it may be thought proper to apply it to" (Bentham 66).

It's a case of "it's easy once you've thought of it" in the political sphere. It can in fact be integrated into any function (education, medical treatment, production, punishment); it can increase the effect of this function, by being linked closely with it; it can constitute a mixed mechanism in which relations of power (and of knowledge) may be precisely adjusted, in the smallest detail, to the processes that are to be supervised; it can establish a direct proportion between "surplus power" and "surplus production." In short, it arranges things in such a way that the exercise of power is not added on from the outside, like a rigid, heavy constraint, to the functions it invests, but is so subtly present in them as to increase their efficiency by itself increasing its own points of contact. The panoptic mechanism is not simply a hinge, a point of exchange between a mechanism of power and a function; it is a way of making power relations function in a function, and of making a function function through these power relations. Bentham's Preface to *Panopticon* opens with a list of the benefits to be obtained from his "inspection-house": "*Morals reformed—health preserved—industry invigorated—instruction diffused—public burthens lightened*—Economy seated, as it were, upon a rock—the gordian knot of the Poor-Laws not cut, but untied— all by a simple idea in architecture!" (Bentham 39).

Furthermore, the arrangement of this machine is such that its enclosed nature does not preclude a permanent presence from the outside: we have seen that anyone may come and exercise in the central tower the functions of surveillance, and that, this being the case, he can gain a clear idea of the way in which the surveillance is practiced. In fact, any panoptic institution, even if it is as rigorously closed as a penitentiary, may without difficulty be subjected to such irregular and constant inspections: and not only by the appointed inspectors, but also by the public; any member of society will have the right to come and see with his own eyes how the schools, hospitals, factories, prisons function. There is no risk, therefore, that the increase of power created by the panoptic machine may degenerate into tyranny; the disciplinary mechanism will be democratically controlled, since it will be constantly accessible "to the great tribunal committee of the world."[4] This Panopticon, subtly arranged so that an observer may observe, at a glance, so many different individuals, also enables everyone to come and observe any of the observers. The seeing machine was once a sort of dark room into which individuals spied; it has become a transparent building in which the exercise of power may be supervised by society as a whole.

The panoptic schema, without disappearing as such or losing any of its properties, was destined to spread throughout the social body; its vocation was to become a generalized function. The plague-stricken town provided an exceptional disciplinary model: perfect, but absolutely violent; to the disease that brought death, power opposed its perpetual threat of death; life inside it was reduced to its simplest expression; it was, against the power of death, the meticulous exercise of the right of the sword. The Panopticon, on the other hand, has a role of amplification; although it arranges power, although it is intended to make it more economic and more effective, it does so not for power itself, nor for the immediate salvation of a threatened society: its aim is to strengthen the social forces—to increase production, to develop the economy, spread education, raise the level of public morality; to increase and multiply.

How is power to be strengthened in such a way that, far from impeding progress, far from weighing upon it with its rules and regulations, it actually facilitates such progress? What intensificator of power will be able at the same time to be a multiplicator of production? How will power, by increasing its forces, be able to increase those of society instead of confiscating them or impeding them? The Panopticon's solution to this problem is that the productive increase of power can be assured only if, on the one hand, it can be exercised continuously in the very foundations of society, in the subtlest possible way, and if, on the other hand, it functions outside these sudden, violent, discontinuous forms that are bound up with the exercise of sovereignty. The body of the king, with its strange material and physical presence, with the force that he himself deploys or transmits to some few others, is at the opposite extreme of this new physics of power represented by panopticism; the domain of panopticism is, on the contrary, that whole lower region, that region of irregular bodies, with their details, their multiple movements, their heterogeneous forces, their spatial relations; what are required are mechanisms that analyze distributions, gaps, series, combinations, and which use instruments that render visible, record, differentiate, and compare: a physics of a relational and multiple power, which has its maximum intensity not in the person of the king, but in the bodies that can be individualized by these relations. At the theoretical level, Bentham defines another way of analyzing the social body and the power relations that traverse it; in terms of practice, he defines a procedure of subordination of bodies and forces that must increase the utility of power while practicing the economy of the prince. Panopticism is the general principle of a new "political anatomy" whose object and end are not the relations of sovereignty but the relations of discipline.

The celebrated, transparent, circular cage, with its high tower, powerful and knowing, may have been for Bentham a project of a perfect disciplinary institution; but he also set out to show how one may "unlock" the disciplines and get them to function in a diffused, multiple, polyvalent way throughout the whole social body. These disciplines, which the classical age had elaborated in specific, relatively enclosed places—barracks, schools, workshops—and whose total implementation had been imagined only at the limited and temporary scale of a plague-stricken town, Bentham dreamed of transforming into a network of mechanisms that would be everywhere and always alert, running through society without interruption in space or in time. The panoptic arrangement provides the formula for this generalization. It programs, at the level of an elementary and easily transferable mechanism, the basic functioning of a society penetrated through and through with disciplinary mechanisms.

There are two images, then, of discipline. At one extreme, the discipline-blockade, the enclosed institution, established on the edges of society, turned inwards towards negative functions: arresting evil, breaking communications, suspending time. At the other extreme, with panopticism, is the discipline-mechanism: a functional mechanism that must improve the exercise of power by making it lighter, more rapid, more effective, a design of subtle coercion for a society to come. The movement from one project to the other, from a schema of exceptional discipline to one of a generalized surveillance, rests on a historical transformation: the gradual extension of the mechanisms of discipline throughout the seventeenth and eighteenth centuries, their spread throughout the whole social body, the formation of what might be called in general the disciplinary society.

A whole disciplinary generalization—the Benthamite physics of power represents an acknowledgement of this—had operated throughout the classical age. The spread of disciplinary institutions, whose network was beginning to cover an ever larger surface and occupying above all a less and less marginal position, testifies to this: what was an islet, a privileged place, a circumstantial measure, or a singular model, became a general formula; the regulations characteristic of the Protestant and pious armies of William of Orange or of Gustavus Adolphus were transformed into regulations for all the armies of Europe; the model colleges of the Jesuits, or the schools of Batencour or Demia, following the example set by Sturm, provided the outlines for the general forms of educational discipline; the ordering of the naval and military hospitals provided the model for the entire reorganization of hospitals in the eighteenth century.

But this extension of the disciplinary institutions was no doubt only the most visible aspect of various, more profound processes.

1. *The functional inversion of the disciplines.* At first, they were expected to neutralize dangers, to fix useless or disturbed populations, to avoid the inconveniences of over-large assemblies; now they were being asked to play a positive role, for they were becoming able to do so, to increase the possible utility of individuals. Military discipline is no longer a mere means of preventing looting, desertion, or failure to obey orders among the troops; it has become a basic technique to enable the army to exist, not as an assembled crowd, but as a unity that derives from this very unity an increase in its forces; discipline increases the skill of each individual, coordinates these skills, accelerates movements, increases firepower, broadens the fronts of attack without reducing their vigor, increases the capacity for resistance, etc. The discipline of the workshop, while remaining a way of enforcing respect for the regulations and authorities, of preventing thefts or losses, tends to increase aptitudes, speeds, output, and therefore profits; it still exerts a moral influence over behavior, but more and more it treats actions in terms of their results, introduces bodies into a machinery, forces into an economy. When, in the seventeenth century, the provincial schools or the Christian elementary schools were founded, the justifications given for them were above all negative: those poor who were unable to bring up their children left them "in ignorance of their obligations: given the difficulties they have in earning a

living, and themselves having been badly brought up, they are unable to communicate a sound upbringing that they themselves never had"; this involves three major inconveniences: ignorance of God, idleness (with its consequent drunkenness, impurity, larceny, brigandage), and the formation of those gangs of beggars, always ready to stir up public disorder and "virtually to exhaust the funds of the Hôtel-Dieu" (Demia 60–61). Now, at the beginning of the Revolution, the end laid down for primary education was to be, among other things, to "fortify," to "develop the body," to prepare the child "for a future in some mechanical work," to give him "an observant eye, a sure hand and prompt habits" (Talleyrand's Report to the Constituent Assembly, 10 September 1791, quoted by Léon 106). The disciplines function increasingly as techniques for making useful individuals. Hence their emergence from a marginal position on the confines of society, and detachment from the forms of exclusion or expiation, confinement, or retreat. Hence the slow loosening of their kinship with religious regularities and enclosures. Hence also their rooting in the most important, most central, and most productive sectors of society. They become attached to some of the great essential functions: factory production, the transmission of knowledge, the diffusion of aptitudes and skills, the war-machine. Hence, too, the double tendency one sees developing throughout the eighteenth century to increase the number of disciplinary institutions and to discipline the existing apparatuses.

2. *The swarming of disciplinary mechanisms.* While, on the one hand, the disciplinary establishments increase, their mechanisms have a certain tendency to become "de-institutionalized," to emerge from the closed fortresses in which they once functioned and to circulate in a "free" state; the massive, compact disciplines are broken down into flexible methods of control, which may be transferred and adapted. Sometimes the closed apparatuses add to their internal and specific function a role of external surveillance, developing around themselves a whole margin of lateral controls. Thus the Christian School must not simply train docile children; it must also make it possible to supervise the parents, to gain information as to their way of life, their resources, their piety, their morals. The school tends to constitute minute social observatories that penetrate even to the adults and exercise regular supervision over them: the bad behavior of the child, or his absence, is a legitimate pretext, according to Demia, for one to go and question the neighbors, especially if there is any reason to believe that the family will not tell the truth; one can then go and question the parents themselves, to find out whether they know their catechism and the prayers, whether they are determined to root out the vices of their children, how many beds there are in the house and what the sleeping arrangements are; the visit may end with the giving of alms, the present of a religious picture, or the provision of additional beds (Demia 39–40). Similarly, the hospital is increasingly conceived of as a base for the medical observation of the population outside; after the burning down of the Hôtel-Dieu in 1772, there were several demands that the large buildings, so heavy and so disordered, should be replaced by a series of smaller hospitals; their function would be to take in the sick of the

quarter, but also to gather information, to be alert to any endemic or epidemic phenomena, to open dispensaries, to give advice to the inhabitants, and to keep the authorities informed of the sanitary state of the region.[5]

One also sees the spread of disciplinary procedures, not in the form of enclosed institutions, but as centers of observation disseminated throughout society. Religious groups and charity organizations had long played this role of "disciplining" the population. From the Counter-Reformation to the philanthropy of the July monarchy, initiatives of this type continued to increase; their aims were religious (conversion and moralization), economic (aid and encouragement to work), or political (the struggle against discontent or agitation). One has only to cite by way of example the regulations for the charity associations in the Paris parishes. The territory to be covered was divided into quarters and cantons and the members of the associations divided themselves up along the same lines. These members had to visit their respective areas regularly. "They will strive to eradicate places of ill-repute, tobacco shops, life-classes, gaming house, public scandals, blasphemy, impiety, and any other disorders that may come to their knowledge." They will also have to make individual visits to the poor; and the information to be obtained is laid down in regulations: the stability of the lodging, knowledge of prayers, attendance at the sacraments, knowledge of a trade, morality (and "whether they have not fallen into poverty through their own fault"); lastly, "one must learn by skillful questioning in what way they behave at home. Whether there is peace between them and their neighbors, whether they are careful to bring up their children in the fear of God . . . , whether they do not have their older children of different sexes sleeping together and with them, whether they do not allow licentiousness and cajolery in their families, especially in their older daughters. If one has any doubts as to whether they are married, one must ask to see their marriage certificate."[6]

3. *The state-control of the mechanisms of discipline.* In England, it was private religious groups that carried out, for a long time, the functions of social discipline (cf. Radzinovitz 203–14); in France, although a part of this role remained in the hands of parish guilds or charity associations, another—and no doubt the most important part—was very soon taken over by the police apparatus.

The organization of a centralized police had long been regarded, even by contemporaries, as the most direct expression of royal absolutism; the sovereign had wished to have "his own magistrate to whom he might directly entrust his orders, his commissions, intentions, and who was entrusted with the execution of orders and orders under the King's private seal" (a note by Duval, first secretary at the police magistrature, quoted in Funck-Brentano I). In effect, in taking over a number of preexisting functions—the search for criminals, urban surveillance, economic and political supervision—the police magistratures and the magistrature-general that presided over them in Paris transposed them into a single, strict, administrative machine: "All the radiations of force and information that spread from

the circumference culminate in the magistrate-general. . . . It is he who operates all the wheels that together produce order and harmony. The effects of
his administration cannot be better compared than to the movement of the
celestial bodies" (Des Essarts 344, 528).

But, although the police as an institution were certainly organized in the
form of a state apparatus, and although this was certainly linked directly to
the center of political sovereignty, the type of power that it exercises, the
mechanisms it operates, and the elements to which it applies them are specific. It is an apparatus that must be coextensive with the entire social body
and not only by the extreme limits that it embraces, but by the minuteness of
the details it is concerned with. Police power must bear "over everything": it
is not, however, the totality of the state nor of the kingdom as visible and
invisible body of the monarch; it is the dust of events, actions, behavior,
opinions—"everything that happens";[7] the police are concerned with "those
things of every moment," those "unimportant things," of which Catherine II
spoke in her Great Instruction (Supplement to the *Instruction for the Drawing Up of a New Code,* 1769, article 535). With the police, one is in the
indefinite world of a supervision that seeks ideally to reach the most elementary particle, the most passing phenomenon of the social body: "The min-
istry of the magistrates and police officers is of the greatest importance; the
objects that it embraces are in a sense definite, one may perceive them only
by a sufficiently detailed examination" (Delamare, unnumbered preface):
the infinitely small of political power.

And, in order to be exercised, this power had to be given the instrument
of permanent, exhaustive, omnipresent surveillance, capable of making all
visible, as long as it could itself remain invisible. It had to be like a faceless
gaze that transformed the whole social body into a field of perception: thousands of eyes posted everywhere, mobile attentions ever on the alert, a long,
hierarchized network which, according to Le Maire, comprised for Paris the
forty-eight *commissaires,* the twenty *inspecteurs,* then the "observers," who
were paid regularly, the *"basses mouches,"* or secret agents, who were paid
by the day, then the informers, paid according to the job done, and finally
the prostitutes. And this unceasing observation had to be accumulated in a
series of reports and registers; throughout the eighteenth century, an
immense police text increasingly covered society by means of a complex
documentary organization (on the police registers in the eighteenth century,
cf. Chassaigne). And, unlike the methods of judicial or administrative writing, what was registered in this way were forms of behavior, attitudes, possibilities, suspicions—a permanent account of individuals' behavior.

Now, it should be noted that, although this police supervision was
entirely "in the hands of the king," it did not function in a single direction.
It was in fact a double-entry system: it had to correspond, by manipulating
the machinery of justice, to the immediate wishes of the king, but it was also
capable of responding to solicitations from below; the celebrated *lettres de
cachet,* or orders under the king's private seal, which were long the symbol
of arbitrary royal rule and which brought detention into disrepute on politi-

cal grounds, were in fact demanded by families, masters, local notables, neighbors, parish priests; and their function was to punish by confinement a whole infrapenality, that of disorder, agitation, disobedience, bad conduct; those things that Ledoux wanted to exclude from his architecturally perfect city and which he called "offenses of nonsurveillance." In short, the eighteenth-century police added a disciplinary function to its role as the auxiliary of justice in the pursuit of criminals and as an instrument for the political supervision of plots, opposition movements, or revolts. It was a complex function since it linked the absolute power of the monarch to the lowest levels of power disseminated in society; since, between these different, enclosed institutions of discipline (workshops, armies, schools), it extended an intermediary network, acting where they could not intervene, disciplining the nondisciplinary spaces; but it filled in the gaps, linked them together, guaranteed with its armed force an interstitial discipline and a metadiscipline. "By means of a wise police, the sovereign accustoms the people to order and obedience" (Vattel 162).

The organization of the police apparatus in the eighteenth century sanctioned a generalization of the disciplines that became coextensive with the state itself. Although it was linked in the most explicit way with everything in the royal power that exceeded the exercise of regular justice, it is understandable why the police offered such slight resistance to the rearrangement of the judicial power; and why it has not ceased to impose its prerogatives upon it, with ever-increasing weight, right up to the present day; this is no doubt because it is the secular arm of the judiciary; but it is also because, to a far greater degree than the judicial institution, it is identified, by reason of its extent and mechanisms, with a society of the disciplinary type. Yet it would be wrong to believe that the disciplinary functions were confiscated and absorbed once and for all by a state apparatus.

"Discipline" may be identified neither with an institution nor with an apparatus; it is a type of power, a modality for its exercise, comprising a whole set of instruments, techniques, procedures, levels of application, targets; it is a "physics" or an "anatomy" of power, a technology. And it may be taken over either by "specialized" institutions (the penitentiaries or "houses of correction" of the nineteenth century), or by institutions that use it as an essential instrument for a particular end (schools, hospitals), or by preexisting authorities that find in it a means of reinforcing or reorganizing their internal mechanisms of power (one day we should show how intrafamilial relations, essentially in the parents-children cell, have become "disciplined," absorbing since the classical age external schemata, first educational and military, then medical, psychiatric, psychological, which have made the family the privileged locus of emergence for the disciplinary question of the normal and the abnormal), or by apparatuses that have made discipline their principle of internal functioning (the disciplinarization of the administrative apparatus from the Napoleonic period), or finally by state apparatuses whose major, if not exclusive, function is to assure that discipline reigns over society as a whole (the police).

On the whole, therefore, one can speak of the formation of a disciplinary society in this movement that stretches from the enclosed disciplines, a sort of social "quarantine," to an indefinitely generalizable mechanism of "panopticism." Not because the disciplinary modality of power has replaced all the others; but because it has infiltrated the others, sometimes undermining them, but serving as an intermediary between them, linking them together, extending them, and above all making it possible to bring the effects of power to the most minute and distant elements. It assures an infinitesimal distribution of the power relations.

A few years after Bentham, Julius gave this society its birth certificate (Julius 384–86). Speaking of the panoptic principle, he said that there was much more there than architectural ingenuity: it was an event in the "history of the human mind." In appearance, it is merely the solution of a technical problem; but, through it, a whole type of society emerges. Antiquity had been a civilization of spectacle. "To render accessible to a multitude of men the inspection of a small number of objects": this was the problem to which the architecture of temples, theaters, and circuses responded. With spectacle, there was a predominance of public life, the intensity of festivals, sensual proximity. In these rituals in which blood flowed, society found new vigor and formed for a moment a single great body. The modern age poses the opposite problem: "To procure for a small number, or even for a single individual, the instantaneous view of a great multitude." In a society in which the principal elements are no longer the community and public life, but, on the one hand, private individuals and, on the other, the state, relations can be regulated only in a form that is the exact reverse of the spectacle: "It was to the modern age, to the ever-growing influence of the state, to its ever more profound intervention in all the details and all the relations of social life, that was reserved the task of increasing and perfecting its guarantees, by using and directing towards that great aim the building and distribution of buildings intended to observe a great multitude of men at the same time."

Julius saw as a fulfilled historical process that which Bentham had described as a technical program. Our society is one not of spectacle, but of surveillance; under the surface of images, one invests bodies in depth; behind the great abstraction of exchange, there continues the meticulous, concrete training of useful forces; the circuits of communication are the supports of an accumulation and a centralization of knowledge; the play of signs defines the anchorages of power; it is not that the beautiful totality of the individual is amputated, repressed, altered by our social order, it is rather that the individual is carefully fabricated in it, according to a whole technique of forces and bodies. We are much less Greeks than we believe. We are neither in the amphitheater, nor on the stage, but in the panoptic machine, invested by its effects of power, which we bring to ourselves since we are part of its mechanism. The importance, in historical mythology, of the Napoleonic character probably derives from the fact that it is at the point of junction of the monarchical, ritual exercise of sovereignty and the hierarchical, permanent exercise of indefinite discipline. He is the individual who looms over everything with a single gaze which no detail, however minute, can escape: "You may consider that no part of the Empire is without surveillance, no crime, no offense, no contravention that remains unpunished, and that the eye of the genius who can enlighten all embraces the whole of this vast machine, without, however, the slightest detail escaping his attention" (Treilhard 14). At the moment of its full blossoming, the disciplinary society still assumes with the Emperor the old aspect of the power of spectacle. As a monarch who is at one and the same time a usurper of the ancient throne and the organizer of the new state, he combined into a single symbolic, ultimate figure the whole of the long process by which the pomp of sovereignty, the necessarily spectacular manifestations of power, were extinguished one by one in the daily exercise of surveillance, in a panopticism in which the vigilance of intersecting gazes was soon to render useless both the eagle and the sun.

The formation of the disciplinary society is connected with a number of broad historical processes—economic, juridico-political and, lastly, scientific—of which it forms part.

1. Generally speaking, it might be said that the disciplines are techniques for assuring the ordering of human multiplicities. It is true that there is nothing exceptional or even characteristic in this; every system of power is presented with the same problem. But the peculiarity of the disciplines is that they try to define in relation to the multiplicities a tactics of power that fulfills three criteria: firstly, to obtain the exercise of power at the lowest possible cost (economically, by the low expenditure it involves; politically, by its discretion, its low exteriorization, its relative invisibility, the little resistance it arouses); secondly, to bring the effects of this social power to their maximum intensity and to extend them as far as possible, without either failure or interval; thirdly, to link this "economic" growth of power with the output of the apparatuses (educational, military, industrial or medical) within which it is exercised; in short, to increase both the docility and the utility of all the elements of the system. This triple objective of the disciplines corresponds to a well-known historical conjuncture. One aspect of this conjuncture was the large demographic thrust of the eighteenth century; an increase in the floating population (one of the primary objects of discipline is to fix; it is an antinomadic technique); a change of quantitative scale in the groups to be supervised or manipulated (from the beginning of the seventeenth century to the eve of the French Revolution, the school population had been increasing rapidly, as had no doubt the hospital population; by the end of the eighteenth century, the peacetime army exceeded 200,000 men). The other aspect of the conjuncture was the growth in the apparatus of production, which was becoming more and more extended and complex, it was also becoming more costly and its profitability had to be increased. The development of the disciplinary methods corresponded to these two processes, or rather, no doubt, to the new need to adjust their correlation. Neither the residual forms of feudal power nor the structures of the administrative monarchy, nor the local mechanisms of supervision, nor the unstable, tangled mass they all formed together could carry out this role: they were hindered from doing so by the irregular and inadequate extension of their network, by their often conflicting functioning, but above all by the "costly" nature of the power that was exercised in them. It was costly in several

senses: because directly it cost a great deal to the Treasury; because the system of corrupt offices and farmed-out taxes weighed indirectly, but very heavily, on the population; because the resistance it encountered forced it into a cycle of perpetual reinforcement; because it proceeded essentially by levying (levying on money or products by royal, seigniorial, ecclesiastical taxation; levying on men or time by *corvées* of press-ganging, by locking up or banishing vagabonds). The development of the disciplines marks the appearance of elementary techniques belonging to a quite different economy: mechanisms of power which, instead of proceeding by deduction, are integrated into the productive efficiency of the apparatuses from within, into the growth of this efficiency and into the use of what it produces. For the old principle of "levying-violence," which governed the economy of power, the disciplines substitute the principle of "mildness-production-profit." These are the techniques that make it possible to adjust the multiplicity of men and the multiplication of the apparatuses of production (and this means not only "production" in the strict sense, but also the production of knowledge and skills in the school, the production of health in the hospitals, the production of destructive force in the army).

In this task of adjustment, discipline had to solve a number of problems for which the old economy of power was not sufficiently equipped. It could reduce the inefficiency of mass phenomena: reduce what, in a multiplicity, makes it much less manageable than a unity; reduce what is opposed to the use of each of its elements and of their sum; reduce everything that may counter the advantages of number. That is why discipline fixes; it arrests or regulates movements; it clears up confusion; it dissipates compact groupings of individuals wandering about the country in unpredictable ways; it establishes calculated distributions. It must also master all the forces that are formed from the very constitution of an organized multiplicity; it must neutralize the effects of counterpower that spring from them and which form a resistance to the power that wishes to dominate it: agitations, revolts, spontaneous organizations, coalitions—anything that may establish horizontal conjunctions. Hence the fact that the disciplines use procedures of partitioning and verticality, that they introduce, between the different elements at the same level, as solid separations as possible, that they define compact hierarchical networks, in short, that they oppose to the intrinsic, adverse force of multiplicity the technique of the continuous, individualizing pyramid. They must also increase the particular utility of each element of the multiplicity, but by means that are the most rapid and the least costly, that is to say, by using the multiplicity itself as an instrument of this growth. Hence, in order to extract from bodies the maximum time and force, the use of those overall methods known as timetables, collective training, exercises, total and detailed surveillance. Furthermore, the disciplines must increase the effect of utility proper to the multiplicities, so that each is made more useful than the simple sum of its elements: it is in order to increase the utilizable effects of the multiple that the disciplines define tactics of distribution, reciprocal adjustment of bodies, gestures, and rhythms, differentiation of capacities, reciprocal coordination in relation to apparatuses or tasks. Lastly, the disciplines have to bring into play the power relations, not above but inside the very texture of the multiplicity, as discreetly as possible, as well articulated on the other functions of these multiplicities and also in the least expensive way possible: to this correspond anonymous instruments of power, coextensive with the multiplicity that they regiment, such as hierarchical surveillance, continuous registration, perpetual assessment, and classification. In short, to substitute for a power that is manifested through the brilliance of those who exercise it, a power that insidiously objectifies those on whom it is applied; to form a body of knowledge about these individuals, rather than to deploy the ostentatious signs of sovereignty. In a word, the disciplines are the ensemble of minute technical inventions that made it possible to increase the useful size of multiplicities by decreasing the inconveniences of the power which, in order to make them useful, must control them. A multiplicity, whether in a workshop or a nation, an army or a school, reaches the threshold of a discipline when the relation of the one to the other becomes favorable.

If the economic take-off of the West began with the techniques that made possible the accumulation of capital, it might perhaps be said that the methods for administering the accumulation of men made possible a political take-off in relation to the traditional, ritual, costly, violent forms of power, which soon fell into disuse and were superseded by a subtle, calculated technology of subjection. In fact, the two processes—the accumulation of men and the accumulation of capital—cannot be separated; it would not have been possible to solve the problem of the accumulation of men without the growth of an apparatus of production capable of both sustaining them and using them; conversely, the techniques that made the cumulative multiplicity of men useful accelerated the accumulation of capital. At a less general level, the technological mutations of the apparatus of production, the division of labor and the elaboration of the disciplinary techniques sustained an ensemble of very close relations (cf. Marx, *Capital,* vol. 1, chapter XIII and the very interesting analysis in Guerry and Deleule). Each makes the other possible and necessary; each provides a model for the other. The disciplinary pyramid constituted the small cell of power within which the separation, coordination, and supervision of tasks was imposed and made efficient; and analytical partitioning of time, gestures, and bodily forces constituted an operational schema that could easily be transferred from the groups to be subjected to the mechanisms of production; the massive projection of military methods onto industrial organization was an example of this modeling of the division of labor following the model laid down by the schemata of power. But, on the other hand, the technical analysis of the process of production, its "mechanical" breaking-down, were projected onto the labor force whose task it was to implement it: the constitution of those disciplinary machines in which the individual forces that they bring together are composed into a whole and therefore increased is the effect of this projection. Let us say that discipline is the unitary technique by which the body is reduced as a "political" force at the least cost and maximized as a useful force. The growth of a capitalist economy gave rise to the specific modality of disciplinary power whose general formulas, techniques of submitting forces and bodies, in short, "political anatomy," could be operated in the most diverse political regimes, apparatuses, or institutions.

2. The panoptic modality of power—at the elementary, technical, merely phys-ical level at which it is situated—is not under the immediate dependence or a direct extension of the great juridico-political structures of a society; it is nonetheless not absolutely independent. Historically, the process by which the bourgeoisie became in the course of the eighteenth century the politically dominant class was masked by the establishment of an explicit, coded, and formally egalitarian juridical framework, made possible by the organization of a parliamentary, representative regime. But the development and general-ization of disciplinary mechanisms constituted the other, dark side of these processes. The general juridical form that guaranteed a system of rights that were egalitarian in principle was supported by these tiny, everyday, physical mechanisms, by all those systems of micropower that are essentially non-egalitarian and asymmetrical that we call the disciplines. And although, in a formal way, the representative regime makes it possible, directly or indi-rectly, with or without relays, for the will of all to form the fundamental authority of sovereignty, the disciplines provide, at the base, a guarantee of the submission of forces and bodies. The real, corporal disciplines consti-tuted the foundation of the formal, juridical liberties. The contract may have been regarded as the ideal foundation of law and political power; panopti-cism constituted the technique, universally widespread, of coercion. It con-tinued to work in depth on the juridical structures of society, in order to make the effective mechanisms of power function in opposition to the for-mal framework that it had acquired. The "Enlightenment," which discov-ered the liberties, also invented the disciplines.

   In appearance, the disciplines constitute nothing more than an infralaw. They seem to extend the general forms defined by law to the infinitesimal level of individual lives; or they appear as methods of training that enable individuals to become integrated into these general demands. They seem to constitute the same type of law on a different scale, thereby making it more meticulous and more indulgent. The disciplines should be regarded as a sort of counterlaw. They have the precise role of introducing insuperable asym-metries and excluding reciprocities. First, because discipline creates between individuals a "private" link, which is a relation of constraints entirely differ-ent from contractual obligation; the acceptance of a discipline may be underwritten by contract; the way in which it is imposed, the mechanisms it brings into play, the nonreversible subordination of one group of people by another, the "surplus" power that is always fixed on the same side, the inequality of position of the different "partners" in relation to the common regulation, all these distinguish the disciplinary link from the contractual link, and make it possible to distort the contractual link systematically from the moment it has as its content a mechanism of discipline. We know, for example, how many real procedures undermine the legal fiction of the work contract: workshop discipline is not the least important. Moreover, whereas the juridical systems define juridical subjects according to universal norms, the disciplines characterize, classify, specialize; they distribute along a scale, around a norm, hierarchize individuals in relation to one another and, if necessary, disqualify and invalidate. In any case, in the space and during the time in which they exercise their control and bring into play the asymmetries of their power, they effect a suspension of the law that is never total, but is never annulled either. Regular and institutional as it may be, the discipline, in its mechanism, is a "counterlaw." And, although the universal juridicism of modern society seems to fix limits on the exercise of power, its universally widespread panopticism enables it to operate, on the underside of the law, a machinery that is both immense and minute, which supports, reinforces, multiplies the asymmetry of power and undermines the limits that are traced around the law. The minute disciplines, the panopticisms of every day may well be below the level of emergence of the great apparatuses and the great political struggles. But, in the genealogy of modern society, they have been, with the class domination that traverses it, the political counterpart of the juridical norms according to which power was redistributed. Hence, no doubt, the importance that has been given for so long to the small techniques of discipline, to those apparently insignificant tricks that it has invented, and even to those "sciences" that give it a respectable face; hence the fear of abandoning them if one cannot find any substitute; hence the affirmation that they are at the very foundation of society, and an element in its equilibrium, whereas they are a series of mechanisms for unbalancing power relations definitively and everywhere; hence the persistence in regarding them as the humble, but concrete form of every morality, whereas they are a set of physico-political techniques.

To return to the problem of legal punishments, the prison with all the corrective technology at its disposal is to be resituated at the point where the codified power to punish turns into a disciplinary power to observe; at the point where the universal punishments of the law are applied selectively to certain individuals and always the same ones; at the point where the redefinition of the juridical subject by the penalty becomes a useful training of the criminal; at the point where the law is inverted and passes outside itself, and where the counterlaw becomes the effective and institutionalized content of the juridical forms. What generalizes the power to punish, then, is not the universal consciousness of the law in each juridical subject; it is the regular extension, the infinitely minute web of panoptic techniques.

3. Taken one by one, most of these techniques have a long history behind them. But what was new, in the eighteenth century, was that, by being combined and generalized, they attained a level at which the formation of knowledge and the increase of power regularly reinforce one another in a circular process. At this point, the disciplines crossed the "technological" threshold. First the hospital, then the school, then, later, the workshop were not simply "reordered" by the disciplines; they became, thanks to them,

apparatuses such that any mechanism of objectification could be used in them as an instrument of subjection, and any growth of power could give rise in them to possible branches of knowledge; it was this link, proper to the technological systems, that made possible within the disciplinary element the formation of clinical medicine, psychiatry, child psychology, educational psychology, the rationalization of labor. It is a double process, then: an epistemological "thaw" through a refinement of power relations; a multiplication of the effects of power through the formation and accumulation of new forms of knowledge.

The extension of the disciplinary methods is inscribed in a broad historical process: the development at about the same time of many other technologies—agronomical, industrial, economic. But it must be recognized that, compared with the mining industries, the emerging chemical industries or methods of national accountancy, compared with the blast furnaces or the steam engine, panopticism has received little attention. It is regarded as not much more than a bizarre little utopia, a perverse dream—rather as though Bentham had been the Fourier of a police society, and the Phalanstery had taken on the form of the Panopticon. And yet this represented the abstract formula of a very real technology, that of individuals. There were many reasons why it received little praise; the most obvious is that the discourses to which it gave rise rarely acquired, except in the academic classifications, the status of sciences; but the real reason is no doubt that the power that it operates and which it augments is a direct, physical power that men exercise upon one another. An inglorious culmination had an origin that could be only grudgingly acknowledged. But it would be unjust to compare the disciplinary techniques with such inventions as the steam engine or Amici's microscope. They are much less; and yet, in a way, they are much more. If a historical equivalent or at least a point of comparison had to be found for them, it would be rather in the "inquisitorial" technique.

The eighteenth century invented the techniques of discipline and the examination, rather as the Middle Ages invented the judicial investigation. But it did so by quite different means. The investigation procedure, an old fiscal and administrative technique, had developed above all with the reorganization of the Church and the increase of the princely states in the twelfth and thirteenth centuries. At this time it permeated to a very large degree the jurisprudence first of the ecclesiastical courts, then of the lay courts. The investigation as an authoritarian search for a truth observed or attested was thus opposed to the old procedures of the oath, the ordeal, the judicial duel, the judgement of God or even of the transaction between private individuals. The investigation was the sovereign power arrogating to itself the right to establish the truth by a number of regulated techniques. Now, although the investigation has since then been an integral part of western justice (even up to our own day), one must not forget either its political origin, its link with the birth of the states and of monarchical sovereignty, or its later extension and its role in the formation of knowledge. In fact, the investigation has been the no doubt crude, but fundamental element in the constitution of the empirical sciences; it has been the juridico-political matrix of this experimental knowledge, which, as we know, was very rapidly released at the end of the Middle Ages. It is perhaps true to say that, in Greece, mathematics were born from techniques of measurement; the sciences of nature, in any case, were born, to some extent, at the end of the Middle Ages, from the practices of investigation. The great empirical knowledge that covered the things of the world and transcribed them into the ordering of an indefinite discourse that observes, describes, and establishes the "facts" (at a time when the Western world was beginning the economic and political conquest of this same world) had its operating model no doubt in the Inquisition—that immense invention that our recent mildness has placed in the dark recesses of our memory. But what this politico-juridical, administrative, and criminal, religious and lay, investigation was to the sciences of nature, disciplinary analysis has been to the sciences of man. These sciences, which have so delighted our "humanity" for over a century, have their technical matrix in the petty, malicious minutiae of the disciplines and their investigations. These investigations are perhaps to psychology, psychiatry, pedagogy, criminology, and so many other strange sciences, what the terrible power of investigation was to the calm knowledge of the animals, the plants, or the earth. Another power, another knowledge. On the threshold of the classical age, Bacon, lawyer and statesman, tried to develop a methodology of investigation for the empirical sciences. What Great Observer will produce the methodology of examination for the human sciences? Unless, of course, such a thing is not possible. For, although it is true that, in becoming a technique for the empirical sciences, the investigation has detached itself from the inquisitorial procedure, in which it was historically rooted, the examination has remained extremely close to the disciplinary power that shaped it. It has always been and still is an intrinsic element of the disciplines. Of course it seems to have undergone a speculative purification by integrating itself with such sciences as psychology and psychiatry. And, in effect, its appearance in the form of tests, interviews, interrogations and consultations is apparently in order to rectify the mechanisms of discipline: educational psychology is supposed to correct the rigors of the school, just as the medical or psychiatric interview is supposed to rectify the effects of the discipline of work. But we must not be misled; these techniques merely refer individuals from one disciplinary authority to another, and they reproduce, in a concentrated or formalized form, the schema of power-knowledge proper to each discipline (on this subject, cf. Tort). The great investigation that gave rise to the sciences of nature has become detached from its politico-juridical model; the examination, on the other hand, is still caught up in disciplinary technology.

In the Middle Ages, the procedure of investigation gradually superseded the old accusatory justice, by a process initiated from above; the disciplinary technique, on the other hand, insidiously and as if from below, has invaded a penal justice that is still, in principle, inquisitorial. All the great movements of extension that characterize modern penality—the problematization of the criminal behind his crime, the concern with a punishment that is a correction, a therapy, a normalization, the division of the act of judgement between various authorities that are supposed to measure, assess, diagnose, cure, transform individuals—all this betrays the penetration of the disciplinary examination into the judicial inquisition.

What is now imposed on penal justice as its point of application, its "useful" object, will no longer be the body of the guilty man set up against the body of the king; nor will it be the juridical subject of an ideal contract; it will be the disciplinary individual. The extreme point of penal justice under the Ancien Régime was the infinite segmentation of the body of the regicide: a manifestation of the strongest power over the body of the greatest criminal, whose total destruction made the crime explode into its truth. The ideal point of penality today would be an indefinite discipline: an interrogation without end, an investigation that would be extended without limit to a meticulous and ever more analytical observation, a judgment that would at the same time be the constitution of a file that was never closed, the calculated leniency of a penalty that would be interlaced with the ruthless curiosity of an examination, a procedure that would be at the same time the permanent measure of a gap in relation to an inaccessible norm and the asymptotic movement that strives to meet in infinity. The public execution was the logical culmination of a procedure governed by the Inquisition. The practice of placing individuals under "observation" is a natural extension of a justice imbued with disciplinary methods and examination procedures. Is it surprising that the cellular prison, with its regular chronologies, forced labor, its authorities of surveillance and registration, its experts in normality, who continue and multiply the functions of the judge, should have become the modern instrument of penality? Is it surprising that prisons resemble factories, schools, barracks, hospitals, which all resemble prisons?

Notes

1. Archives militaires de Vincennes, A 1,516 91 sc. Pièce. This regulation is broadly similar to a whole series of others that date from the same period and earlier.
2. In the *Postscript to the Panopticon*, 1791, Bentham adds dark inspection galleries painted in black around the inspector's lodge, each making it possible to observe two stories of cells.
3. In his first version of the *Panopticon*, Bentham had also imagined an acoustic surveillance, operated by means of pipes leading from the cells to the central tower. In the *Postscript* he abandoned the idea, perhaps because he could not introduce into it the principle of dissymmetry and prevent the prisoners from hearing the inspector as well as the inspector hearing them. Julius tried to develop a system of dissymmetrical listening (Julius 18).
4. Imagining this continuous flow of visitors entering the central tower by an underground passage and then observing the circular landscape of the Panopticon, was Bentham aware of the Panoramas that Barker was constructing at exactly the same period (the first seems to have dated from 1787) and in which the visitors, occupying

the central place, saw unfolding around them a landscape, a city, or a battle. The visitors occupied exactly the place of the sovereign gaze.

5. In the second half of the eighteenth century, it was often suggested that the army should be used for the surveillance and general partitioning of the population. The army, as yet to undergo discipline in the seventeenth century, was regarded as a force capable of instilling it. Cf., for example, Servan, *Le Soldat citoyen*, 1780.

6. Arsenal, MS. 2565. Under this number, one also finds regulations for charity associations of the seventeenth and eighteenth centuries.

7. Le Maire in a memorandum written at the request of Sartine, in answer to sixteen questions posed by Joseph II on the Parisian police. This memorandum was published by Gazier in 1879.

Bibliography

Archives militaires de Vincennes, A 1,516 91 sc.

Bentham, J., *Works,* ed. Bowring, IV, 1843.

Chassaigne, M., *La Lieutenance générale de police*, 1906.

Delamare, N., *Traité de police*, 1705.

Demia, C., *Règlement pour les écoles de la ville de Lyon*, 1716.

Des Essarts, T. N., *Dictionnaire universel del police*, 1787.

Funck-Brentano, F., *Catalogue des manuscrits de la bibliothèque de l'Arsenal*, IX.

Guerry, F., and Deleule, D., *Le Corps productif*, 1973.

Julius, N. H., *Leçons sur les prisons*, I, 1831 (Fr. trans.).

Léon, A., *La Révolution française et l'éducation technique*, 1968.

Loisel, G., *Histoire des ménageries*, II, 1912.

Marx, Karl, *Capital,* vol. I, ed. 1970.

Radzinovitz, L., *The English Criminal Law,* II, 1956.

Servan, J., *Le Soldat citoyen*, 1780.

Tort, Michel, *Q.I.,* 1974.

Treilhard, J. B., *Motifs du code d'instruction criminelle*, 1808.

Vattel, E. de, *Le Droit des gens*, 1768.

Paul Fussell (1924–)

As book reviewer Dwight Garner has said, "the great thing about Fussell—besides his lean, witty, no-nonsense prose—has always been his knack for pissing people off. His contrarian streak is a mile wide, and . . . he can be counted upon to blast cant, pretense and sloppy thinking wherever he finds them" (Salon 1999). Raised in an upper-middle-class family in Pasadena, California, Fussell earned his B.A. at Pomona College and his M.A. and Ph.D. at Harvard. During his stint as an infantry officer in World War II, he was gravely wounded when a German shell exploded, transforming him, as Fussell writes in *Doing Battle: The Making of a Skeptic,* from "a fat boy into a thing that would be called, in later wars, a lean, mean killing machine." Although he received a Bronze Star and Purple Heart for his military service, he became so sick of the army's "institutional fraud, boredom and futility" that he vowed never to place himself in the position of taking orders again: "In literature I fled the farthest possible distance from the simplifications and conformity demanded by the military," he writes. "I am entirely serious when I assert that if I have ever developed into a passable literary scholar, editor, and critic, the credit belongs to the United States Army."

Now retired, Fussell was the Donald T. Regan professor of English literature at the University of Pennsylvania. He has edited 6 books and authored 13 others, including *Poetic Meter and Poetic Form* (1965), *The Great War and Modern Memory* (1977), *Class* (1983), *Wartime: Understanding and Behavior in the Second World War* (1989), *BAD, or, The Dumbing of America* (1992), and *Uniforms: Why We Are What We Wear* (2002).

An Anatomy of the Classes

Nobody knows for sure what the word *class* means. Some people, like Vance Packard, have tried to invoke more objective terms, and have spoken about *status systems*. Followers of the sociologist Max Weber tend to say *class* when they're talking about the amount of money you have and the kind of leverage it gives you; they say *status* when they mean your social prestige in relation to your audience; and they say *party* when they're measuring how much political power you have, that is, how much built-in resistance you have to being pushed around by shits. By *class* I mean all three, with perhaps extra emphasis on *status*. I do wish the word *caste* were domesticated in the United States, because it nicely conveys the actual rigidity of class lines here, the difficulty of moving—either upward or downward—out of the place where you were nurtured.

How many classes are there?

My researches have persuaded me that there are nine classes in this country, as follows:

> Top out-of-sight
> Upper
> Upper middle
>
> ———
>
> Middle
> High proletarian
> Mid-proletarian
> Low proletarian
>
> ———
>
> Destitute
> Bottom out-of-sight

One thing to get clear at the outset is this: it's not riches alone that defines these classes. "It can't be money," one working man says quite correctly, "because nobody ever knows that about you for sure." Style and taste and awareness are as important as money. "Economically, no doubt, there are only two classes, the rich and the poor," says George Orwell, "but socially there is a whole hierarchy of classes, and the manners and traditions learned by each class in childhood are not only very different but—this is the essential point—generally persist from birth to death. . . . It is . . . very difficult to escape, culturally, from the class into which you have been born." When John Fitzgerald Kennedy, watching Richard Nixon on television, turned to his friends and, horror-struck, said, "The guy has no class," he was not talking about money.

Anyone who imagines that large assets or high income confer high class can take comfort from a little book titled *Live a Year with a Millionaire,* written by Cornelius Vanderbilt Whitney and distributed by him (free) to his friends for Christmas 1981. Not to put too fine a point on it, the banality, stupidity, complacency, and witlessness of this author can remind a reader only of characters in Ring Lardner or in such satires by Sinclair Lewis as *The Man Who Knew Coolidge.* "They are a cosmopolitan group," says Whitney of people he meets at one party. "Come from places all over the States." The more he goes on, the more his reader will perceive that, except for his money, Whitney is a profoundly middle-class fellow, committed without any self-awareness to every cliché of that social rank.

And down below, the principle still holds: money doesn't matter that much. To illustrate the point, John Brooks compares two families living in adjoining houses in a suburb. One man is "blue-collar," a garage mechanic. The other is "white-collar," an employee in a publishing house. They make roughly the same amount of money, but what a difference. "Mr. Blue" bought a small, neat "ranch house." "Mr. White" bought a beat-up old house and refurbished it himself. Mrs. Blue uses the local shops, especially those in the nearby shopping center, and thinks them wonderful, "so convenient." Mrs. White goes to the city to buy her clothes. The Blues drink, but rather furtively, and usually on Saturday night with the curtains closed. The Whites drink openly, often right out in the backyard. "The Blues shout to each other, from room to room of their house or from corner to corner of their lot, without self-consciousness; the Whites modulate their voices to the point where they sometimes can't hear each other." As household objects, books are a crucial criterion. There's not a book in the Blues' house, while the Whites' living room contains numerous full bookshelves. Brooks concludes: "Here, in sum, are two families with hardly anything in common . . . , yet their . . . incomes are practically identical." Likewise, it was Russell Lynes's awareness that it's less money than taste and knowledge and perceptiveness that determine class that some years ago prompted him to set forth the tripartite scheme of *highbrow, middlebrow,* and *lowbrow.*

Not that the three classes at the top don't have money. The point is that money alone doesn't define them, for the *way* they have their money is largely what matters. That is, as a class indicator the amount of money is less significant than the source. The main thing distinguishing the top three classes from each other is the amount of money inherited in relation to the amount currently earned. The top-out-of-sight class (Rockefellers, Pews, DuPonts, Mellons, Fords, Vanderbilts) lives on inherited capital entirely. No one whose money, no matter how copious, comes from his own work—film stars are an example—can be a member of the top-out-of-sight class, even if the size of his income and the extravagance of his expenditure permit him to simulate identity with it. Inheritance—"old money" in the vulgar phrase—is the indispensable principle defining the top three classes, and it's best if the money's been in the family for three or four generations. There are subtle local ways to ascertain how long the money's been there. Touring middle America, the British traveler Jonathan Raban came upon the girl Sally, who informed him that "New Money says Missouri; Old Money says Missoura."

"When I think of a really rich man," says a Boston blue-collar, "I think of one of those estates where you can't see the house from the road." Hence the name of the top class, which could just as well be called "the class in hiding." Their houses are never seen from the street or road. They like to hide away deep in the hills or way off on Greek or Caribbean islands (which they tend to own), safe, for the moment, from envy and its ultimate attendants, confiscatory taxation and finally expropriation. It was the Great Depression, Vance Packard speculates, that badly frightened the very rich, teaching them to be "discreet, almost reticent, in exhibiting their wealth." From the 1930s dates the flight of money from such exhibitionistic venues as the mansions of upper Fifth Avenue to hideaways in Virginia, upper New York State, Connecticut, Long Island, and New Jersey. The situation now is very different from the one in the 1890s satirized by Thorstein Veblen in *The Theory of the Leisure Class*. In his day the rich delighted to exhibit themselves conspicuously, with costly retainers and attendants much in evidence. Now they hide, not merely from envy and revenge but from exposé journalism, much advanced in cunning and ferocity since Veblen's time, and from an even worse threat, virtually unknown to Veblen, foundation mendicancy, with its hordes of beggars in three-piece suits constantly badgering the well-to-do. Showing off used to be the main satisfaction of being very rich in America. Now the rich must skulk and hide. It's a pity.

And it's not just that the individual houses and often the persons of the top-out-of-sights are removed from scrutiny. Their very class tends to escape the down-to-earth calculations of sociologists and poll takers and consumer researchers. It's not studied because it's literally out of sight, and a questionnaire proffered to a top-out-of-sight person will very likely be hurled to the floor with disdain. Very much, in fact, the way it would be ignored by a bottom-out-of-sight person. And it's here that we begin to perceive one of the most wonderful things about the American class system—the curious similarity, if not actual brotherhood, of the top- and bottom-out-of-sights. Just as the tops are hidden away on their islands or behind the peek-a-boo walls of their distant estates, the bottoms are equally invisible, when not put away in institutions or claustrated in monasteries, lamaseries, or communes, then hiding from creditors, deceived bail-bondsmen, and gulled merchants intent on repossessing cars and furniture. (This bottom-out-of-sight class is visible briefly at one place and time, muttering its wayward fancies on the streets of New York in the spring. But after this ritual yearly show of itself it retreats into invisibility again.) In aid of invisibility, members of both classes feel an equal anxiety to keep their names out of the papers. And the bottoms—"the lower or spurious leisure class," Veblen calls them— share something more with the top-out-of-sights. They do not earn their money.

They are given it and kept afloat not by their own efforts or merits but by the welfare machinery or the correctional system, the way the tops owe it all to their ancestors. And a further similarity: members of both classes carry very little cash on their persons. We can say, in summary, that the virtual identity, in important respects, of top- and bottom-out-of-sights is a remarkable example of the time-proven principle that Extremes Meet.

The next class down, the upper class, differs from the top-out-of-sight class in two main ways. First, although it inherits a lot of its money, it earns quite a bit too, usually from some attractive, if slight, work, without which it would feel bored and even ashamed. It's likely to make its money by controlling banks and the more historic corporations, think tanks, and foundations, and to busy itself with things like the older universities, the Council on Foreign Relations, the Foreign Policy Association, the Committee for Economic Development, and the like, together with the executive branch of the federal government, and often the Senate. In the days when ambassadors were amateurs, they were selected largely from this class, very seldom from the top-out-of-sight. And secondly, unlike the top-out-of-sights, the upper class is visible, often ostentatiously so. Which is to say that the top-out-of-sights have spun off and away from Veblen's scheme of conspicuous exhibition, leaving the mere upper class to carry on its former role. When you pass a house with a would-be impressive façade visible from the street or highway, you know it's occupied by a member of the upper class. The White House is probably the best example. Its residents, even on those occasions when they are Franklin D. Roosevelts or even John F. Kennedys, can never be designated top-out-of-sight but only upper-class. The house is simply too showy, being pure white and carefully positioned on high ground, and temporary residence there usually constitutes a come-down for most of its occupants. It is a hopelessly upper-class place—or even lower than that, as when the Harry Trumans lived there.

Like all the classes, the upper class has its distinct stigmata. It will be in the *Social Register,* for example, whereas the mere upper-middle class will not be, although it will slaver to get in. Having streets named after you is a signal that you are probably upper-class. At least if the street name's your surname: if it's your first name (like *Kathy Street*), you are middle-class or worse. Speaking French fluently, even though French is irrelevant to one's actual life, business, interests, and the like, is an upper-class sign, although it's important not to speak it with anything resembling a correct, or "French," accent.

Not smoking at all is very upper-class, but in any way calling attention to one's abstinence drops one to middle-class immediately. The constant coming and going of "houseguests" is an all but infallible upper-class sign, implying as it does plenty of spare bedrooms to lodge them in and no anxiety about making them happy, what with all the drinks, food, games, parties, etc. It is among members of the upper class that you have to refrain from uttering compliments, which are taken to be rude, possessions there being of course beautiful, expensive, and impressive, without question. The paying of compliments is a middle-class convention, for this class needs the assurance compliments provide. In the upper class there's never any doubt of one's value, and it all goes without saying. A British peer of a very old family was once visited by an artistic young man who, entering the dining room, declared that he'd never seen a finer set of Hepplewhite chairs. His host had him ejected instantly, explaining "Fellow praised my chairs! Damned cheek!" Dining among the uppers, one does not normally praise the food, because it goes without saying that the hostess would put forth nothing short of excellent. Besides, she's not cooked it. Likewise, if you spill a glass of wine, don't fret: the staff will clean it up.

Although not an infallible sign, because the upper-middle class has learned to ape it, devotion to horses—owning them, breeding them, riding them, racing them, chasing small animals while sitting on them—is, the way backgammon was before it became popular and lost caste, a fairly trustworthy upper-class mark. But it is, finally, by a characteristic the American upper class shares with all aristocracies that ye shall know them: their imperviousness to ideas and their total lack of interest in them. (A mark of the top-out-of-sights too, as Cornelius Vanderbilt Whitney's literary performance attests.) Their inattention to ideas is why Matthew Arnold calls them Barbarians, and he imputes their serenity specifically to their "never having had any ideas to trouble them. " Still, they are a nice class, and the life among them is comfortable and ample and even entertaining, so long as you don't mind never hearing anyone saying anything intelligent or original.

We now come to the upper-middle class. It may possess virtually as much as the two classes above it. The difference is that it has earned most of it, in law, medicine, oil, shipping, real estate, or even the more honorific kinds of trade, like buying and selling works of art. Although they may enjoy some inherited money and use inherited "things" (silver, Oriental rugs), the upper-middles suffer from a bourgeois sense of shame, a conviction that to live on the earnings of others, even forebears, is not quite nice.

Caste marks of the upper-middles would include living in a house with more rooms than you need, except perhaps when a lot of "overnight guests" are present to help you imitate upper-class style. Another sign of the upper-middle class is its chastity in sexual display: the bathing suits affected by the women here are the most sexless in the world, Britain and Canada included. They feature boy-pants legs, in imitation of the boxer shorts favored by upper-middle-class men. Both men's and women's clothes here are designed to conceal, rather than underline, anatomical differences between the sexes. Hence, because men's shoulders constitute a secondary sexual characteristic, the natural-shoulder jacket. Epaulets emphasize the shoulders. They are thus associated with the lower classes, whose shoulders are required for physical work. The military makes much of epaulets, betraying instantly its prole associations. If you know someone who voted for John Anderson at the last presidential election, ten to one she's (or he's) upper-middle. This class is also the most "role-reversed" of all: men think nothing of cooking and doing housework, women of working out of the house in journalism, the theater, or real estate. (If the wife stays home all the time, the family's middle-class only.) Upper-middles like to show off their costly educations by naming their cats Spinoza, Clytemnestra, and Candide, which means, as you'll have inferred already, that it's in large part the class depicted in Lisa Birnbach and others' *Official Preppy Handbook,* that significantly popular artifact of 1980.

And it is the class celebrated also in the 1970 Ivy-idyllic film *Love Story*. The vast popularity of these two products suggests the appeal of the upper-middle style to all Americans who don't possess it. Indeed, most people of the middle classes and below would rather be in the upper-middle class than even the upper or the top-out-of-sight. A recent Louis Harris poll showed that when asked what class they'd like to be in, most said the middle class, and when asked what *part* of the middle class they'd like to be in, most said the upper-middle class. Being in the upper-middle class is a familiar and credible fantasy: its usages, while slightly grander than one's own, are recognizable and compassable, whereas in the higher classes you might be embarrassed by not knowing how to eat caviar or use a finger bowl or discourse in French. It's a rare American who doesn't secretly want to be upper-middle class.

We could gather as much, if in a coarser way, from a glance at two books by John T. Molloy, *Dress for Success* (1975) and *Molloy's Live for Success* (1981). Molloy, whose talents are not at all contemptible, designates himself "America's first wardrobe engineer," in which capacity he is hired by businesses to advise them on principles of corporate dress. The ideal is for everyone in business to look upper-middle-class, because upper-middle-class equals Success. As he puts it with significant parallelism, "Successful dress is really no more than achieving good taste and the look of the upper-middle class." Even executives' offices can be tinkered with until they too emit an air of habitual success, which means, as Molloy says, that "the successful office exudes the qualities of the upper-middle class." That is, "It is (or looks) spacious and uncrowded. It is rich. It is well kept. It is tasteful. It is impressive. It is comfortable. It is private." And the waiting room too: it, "like the rest of your office, must immediately spell 'upper-middle class' to every visitor."

For Molloy, it's not just people's clothes and offices and waiting rooms that can be cosmeticized toward the upper-middle look. It's their faces, bodies, gestures, and postures as well. In *Molloy's Live for Success,* by the aid of line drawings he distinguishes between the male profile of the prole and the male profile of the upper-middle class. The prole either has his jaw set in bitterness and defiance or his mouth open in doltish wonder. The upper-middle-class male, on the other hand, has his mouth closed but not too firmly set, and his shoulders avoid the hangdog, whip-me-again-master slouch Molloy finds characteristic of the unsuccessful. "Upper-middle-class and lower-middle-class people not only stand and sit differently," Molloy points out, "they move differently. Upper-middle-class people tend to have controlled precise movements. The way they use their arms and where their feet fall is dramatically different from lower-middle-class people, who tend to swing their arms out rather than hold them in closer to their bodies."

The middle class is distinguishable more by its earnestness and psychic insecurity than by its middle income. I have known some very rich people who remain stubbornly middle-class, which is to say they remain terrified at what others think of them, and to avoid criticism are obsessed with doing everything right. The middle class is the place where table manners assume an awful importance and where net curtains flourish to conceal activities like hiding the salam' (a phrase no middle-class person would indulge in, surely: the fatuous *making love* is the middle-class equivalent). The middle class, always anxious about offending, is the main market for "mouthwashes," and if it disappeared the whole "deodorant" business would fall to the ground. If physicians tend to be upper-middle-class, dentists are gloomily aware that they're middle, and are said to experience frightful status anxieties when introduced socially to "physicians"— as dentists like to call them. (Physicians call themselves *doctors,* and enjoy doing this in front of dentists, as well as college professors, chiropractors, and divines.)

"Status panic": that's the affliction of the middle class, according to C. Wright Mills, author of *White Collar* (1951) and *The Power Elite* (1956). Hence the middles' need to accumulate credit cards and take in *The New Yorker,* which it imagines registers upper-middle taste. Its devotion to that magazine, or its ads, is a good example of Mills's description of the middle class as the one that tends "to borrow status from higher elements." *New Yorker* advertisers have always known this about their audience, and some of their pseudo-upper-middle gestures in front of the middles are hilarious, like one recently flogging expensive stationery, here, a printed invitation card. The pretentious Anglophile spelling of the second word strikes the right opening note:

> In honour of
> Dr and Mrs Leonard Adam Westman,
> Dr and Mrs Jeffrey Logan Brandon
> request the pleasure of your company for
> [at this point the higher classes might say *cocktails,* or, if
> thoroughly secure, *drinks.* But here, "Dr." and Mrs. Brandon
> are inviting you to consume specifically—]
> Champagne and Caviar
> on Friday, etc., etc.
> Valley Hunt Club,
> Stamford, Conn., etc.

The only thing missing is the brand names of the refreshments.

If the audience for that sort of thing used to seem the most deeply rooted in time and place, today it seems the class that's the most rootless. Members of the middle class are not only the sort of people who buy their own heirlooms, silver, etc. They're also the people who do most of the moving long-distance (generally to very unstylish places), commanded every few years to pull up stakes by the corporations they're in bondage to. They are the geologist employed by the oil company, the computer programmer, the aeronautical engineer, the salesman assigned a new territory, and the "marketing" (formerly *sales*) manager deputed to keep an eye on him. These people and their families occupy the suburbs and developments. Their "Army and Navy," as William H. Whyte, Jr., says, is their corporate employer. IBM and DuPont hire these people from second-rate colleges and teach them that they are nothing if not members of the team. Virtually no latitude is permitted to individuality or the milder forms of eccentricity, and these employees soon learn to avoid all ideological statements, notably, as we'll see, in the furnishing of their living rooms. Terrified of losing their jobs, these people grow passive, their humanity diminished as they perceive themselves mere parts of an infinitely larger structure. And interchangeable parts, too. "The training makes our men interchangeable," an IBM executive was once heard to say.

It's little wonder that, treated like slaves most of the time, the middle class lusts for the illusion of weight and consequence. One sign is their quest for heraldic validation ("This beautiful embossed certificate will show your family tree"). Another is their custom of issuing annual family newsletters announcing the most recent triumphs in the race to become "professional":

> John, who is now 22, is in his first year at the Dental School of Wayne State University.
>   Caroline has a fine position as an executive secretary for a prestigious firm in Boise, Idaho.

Sometimes these letters really wring the heart, with their proud lists of new "affiliations" achieved during the past year: "This year Bob became a member of the Junior Chamber of Commerce, the Beer Can Collectors League of North America, the Alumni Council of the University of Evansville, and the Young Republicans of Vanderburgh County." (Cf. Veblen: "Since conservatism is a characteristic of the wealthier and therefore more reputable portion of the community, it has acquired a certain honorific or decorative value.") Nervous lest she be considered nobody, the middle-class wife is careful to dress way up when she goes shopping. She knows by instinct what one middle-class woman told an inquiring sociologist: "You know there's class when you're in a department store and a well-dressed lady gets treated better."

"One who makes birth or wealth the sole criterion of worth": that's a conventional dictionary definition of a *snob*, and the place to look for the snob is in the middle class. Worried a lot about their own taste and about whether it's working for or against them, members of the middle class try to arrest their natural tendency to sink downward by associating themselves, if ever so tenuously, with the imagined possessors of money, power, and taste. "Correctness" and doing the right thing become obsessions, prompting middle-class people to write thank-you notes after the most ordinary dinner parties, give excessively expensive or correct presents, and never allude to any place—Fort Smith, Arkansas, for example—that lacks known class. It will not surprise readers who have traveled extensively to hear that Neil Mackwood, a British authority on snobbery, finds the greatest snobs worldwide emanating from Belgium, which can also be considered world headquarters of the middle class.

The desire to belong, and to belong by some mechanical act like purchasing something, is another sign of the middle class. Words like *club* and *guild* (as in Book-of-the-Month Club and Literary Guild) extend a powerful invitation. The middle class is thus the natural target for developers' ads like this:

> You Belong
>   in Park Forest!
> The moment you come to our town you know:
>   You're Welcome.
>   You're part of a big group. . . .

Oddity, introversion, and the love of privacy are the big enemies, a total reversal of the values of the secure upper orders. Among the middles there's a convention that erecting a fence or even a tall hedge is an affront. And there's also a convention that you may drop in on neighbors or friends without a telephone inquiry first. Being naturally innocent and well disposed and aboveboard, a member of the middle class finds it hard to believe that all are not. Being timid and conventional, no member of the middle class would expect that anyone is copulating in the afternoon instead of the evening, clearly, for busy and well-behaved corporate personnel, the correct time for it. When William H. Whyte, Jr., was poking around one suburb studying the residents, he was told by one quintessentially middle-class woman: "The street behind us is nowhere near as friendly. They knock on doors over there."

If the women treasure "friendliness," the men treasure having a genteel occupation (usually more important than money), with emphasis on the word (if seldom the thing) *executive*. (As a matter of fact, an important class divide falls between those who feel veneration before the term *executive* and those who feel they want to throw up.) Having a telephone-answering machine at home is an easy way of simulating (at relatively low cost) high professional desirability, but here you wouldn't think of a facetious or eccentric text (delivered in French, for example, or in the voice of Donald Duck or Richard Nixon) asking the caller to speak his bit after the beeping sound. For the middle-class man is scared. As C. Wright Mills notes, "He is always somebody's man, the corporation's, the government's, the army's. . . ." One can't be too careful. One "management adviser" told Studs Terkel: "Your wife, your children have to behave properly. You've got to fit in the mold. You've got to be on guard." In *Coming Up for Air* (1939) George Orwell, speaking for his middle-class hero, gets it right:

> There's a lot of rot talked about the sufferings of the working class. I'm not so sorry for the proles myself. . . . The prole suffers physically, but he's a free man when he isn't working. But in every one of those little stucco boxes there's some poor bastard who's *never* free except when he's fast asleep.

Because he is essentially a salesman, the middle-class man develops a salesman's style. Hence his optimism and his belief in the likelihood of self-improvement if you'll just hurl yourself into it. One reason musicals like *Annie* and *Man of La Mancha* make so much money is that they offer him and his wife songs, like "Tomorrow" and "The Impossible Dream," that seem to promise that all sorts of good things are on their way. A final stigma of the middle class, an emanation of its social insecurity, is its habit of laughing at its own jests. Not entirely certain what social effect he's transmitting, and yet obliged, by his role as "salesman," to promote goodwill and optimism, your middle-class man serves as his own enraptured audience. Sometimes, after uttering some would-be clever formulation in public, he will look all around to gauge the response of the audience. Favorable, he desperately hopes.

The young men of the middle class are chips off the old block. If you want to know who reads John T. Molloy's books, hoping to break into the upper-middle class by formulas and mechanisms, they are your answer. You can see them on airplanes especially, being forwarded from one corporate training program to another. Their shirts are implausibly white, their suits are excessively dark, their neckties resemble those worn by undertakers, and their hair is cut in the style of the 1950s. Their talk is of *the bottom line*, and for *no* they are likely to say *no way*. Often their necks don't seem long enough, and their eyes tend to be too much in motion, flicking back and forth rather than up and down. They will enter adult life as corporate trainees and, after forty-five faithful years, leave it as corporate personnel, wondering whether this is all.

So much for the great middle class, to which, if you innocently credit people's descriptions of their own status, almost 80 percent of our population belongs. Proceeding downward, we would normally expect to meet next the lower-middle class. But it doesn't exist as such any longer, having been pauperized by the inflation of the 1960s and 1970s and transformed into the high-proletarian class. What's the difference? A further lack of freedom and self-respect. Our former lower-middle class, the new high proles, now head "the masses," and even if they are positioned at the top of the proletarian classes, still they are identifiable as people things are done to. They are in bondage—to monetary policy, rip-off advertising, crazes and delusions, mass low culture, fast foods, consumer schlock. Back in the 1940s there was still a real lower-middle class in this country, whose solid high-school education and addiction to "saving" and "planning" maintained it in a position—often precarious, to be sure—above the working class. In those days, says C. Wright Mills,

> there were fewer little men, and in their brief monopoly of high-school education they were in fact protected from many of the sharper edges of the workings of capitalist progress. They were free to entertain deep illusions about their individual abilities and about the collective trustworthiness of the system. As their number has grown, however, they have become increasingly subject to wage-worker conditions.

Their social demotion has been the result. These former low-white-collar people are now simply working machines, and the wife usually works as well as the husband.

The kind of work performed and the sort of anxiety that besets one as a result of work are ways to divide the working class into its three strata. The high proles are the skilled workers, craftsmen, like printers. The mid-proles are the operators, like Ralph Kramden, the bus driver. The low proles are unskilled labor, like longshoremen. The special anxiety of the high proles is fear about loss or reduction of status: you're proud to be a master carpenter, and you want the world to understand clearly the difference between you and a laborer. The special anxiety of the mid-proles is fear of losing the job. And of the low proles, the gnawing perception that you're probably never going to make enough or earn enough freedom to have and do the things you want.

The kind of jobs high-prole people do tempt them to insist that they are really "professionals," like "sanitation men" in a large city. A mail carrier tells Studs Terkel why he likes his work: "They always say, 'Here comes the mailman.' . . . I feel it is one of the most respected professions there is throughout the nation." Prole women who go into nursing never tire of asserting how professional they are, and the same is true of their daughters who become air stewardesses, a favorite high-prole occupation. Although Army officers, because they are all terrified of the boss, are probably more middle-class than high-prole, they seem the lower the more they insist that they are "professionals," and since their disgrace in Vietnam, and their subsequent anxiety about their social standing, that insistence has grown more mechanical. An Army wife says, "Some like to speak of doctors, lawyers, etc., as professionals. All [Army] officers are professionals." And then, a notable deviation from logic: "Who could be more professional than the man who has dedicated his whole life to the defense of his country?"

One way to ascertain whether a person is middle-class or high-prole is to apply the principle that the wider the difference between one's working clothes and one's "best," the lower the class. Think not just of laborers and blue-collar people in general, but of doormen and bellboys, farmers and railway conductors and trainmen, and firemen. One of these once said: "I wish I was a lawyer. Shit, I wish I was a doctor. But I just didn't have it. You gotta have the smarts."

But high proles are quite smart, or at least shrewd. Because often their work is not closely supervised, they have pride and a conviction of independence, and they feel some contempt for those who have not made it as far as they have. They are, as the sociologist E. E. LeMasters calls them and titles his book, *Blue-Collar Aristocrats* (1975), and their disdain for the middle class is like the aristocrat's from the other direction. One high prole says: "If my boy wants to wear a god-damn necktie all his life and bow and scrape to some boss, that's his right, but by God he should also have the right to earn an honest living with his hands if that is what he likes." Like other aristocrats, says LeMasters, these "have gone to the top of their social world and need not expend time or energy on 'social climbing.'" They are aristocratic in other ways, like their devotion to gambling and their fondness for deer hunting. Indeed, the antlers with which they decorate their interiors give their dwellings in that respect a resemblance to the lodges of the Scottish peerage. The high prole resembles the aristocrat too, as Ortega y Gasset notes, in "his propensity to make out of games and sports the central occupation of his life," as well as in his unromantic attitude toward women.

Since they're not consumed with worry about choosing the correct status emblems, these people can be remarkably relaxed and unself-conscious. They can do, say, wear, and look like pretty much anything they want without undue feelings of shame, which belong to their betters, the middle class, shame being largely a bourgeois feeling. John Calvin, observes Jilly Cooper, is the prophet of the middle class, while Karl Marx is the prophet of the proles, even if most of them don't know it.

There are certain more or less infallible marks by which you can identify high proles, They're the ones who "belong" to Christmas and Channukah Clubs at banks, and they always buy big objects on installments. High proles are likely to spend money on things like elaborate color TVs, stereos, and tricky refrigerators, unlike the middles who tend to invest in furniture of "good taste" to display in the living and dining room. Riding in sedans, high-prole men sit in front, with their wives planted in back. (As you move up to the middle class, one couple will be in front, one in back. But among upper-middles, you're likely to see a man and woman of different couples sharing a seat.) High proles arrive punctually at social events, social lateness of twenty minutes or so being a mark of the higher orders. If you're in a bar and you want to estimate the class of a man, get him, on some pretext, to take out his wallet. The high-prole wallet always bulges, not just with snaps of wife, children, and grandchildren to exhibit when the bearer grows maudlin, but with sentimental paper memorabilia like important sports-ticket stubs and letters and other documents which can be whipped out to "prove" things. The definitive high-prole wallet has a wide rubber band around it.

All proles have a high respect for advertising and brand names. By knowing about such things you can display smartness and up-to-dateness, as well as associate yourself with the success of the products advertised. Drinking an identifiable bottle of Coca-Cola outside on a hot day is not just drinking a Coke: it's participating in a paradigm deemed desirable not just by your betters—the Cola-Cola Company—but by your neighbors, who perceive that you are doing something all-American and super-wonderful. John Brooks has observed that the graffiti inscribers in the New York subway cars tend to write everywhere but on the advertising cards, "as if advertising were the one aspect of . . . society that the writers can respect." Philip Roth's Sophie Portnoy hovers between middle-class and high-prole. If her habit of vigorous self-praise is middle, her respect for advertised brand names and her acute knowledge of prices is high-prole. "I'm the only one who's good to her," she tells her son, referring to the black cleaning woman. "I'm the only one who gives her a whole can of tuna for lunch, and I'm not talking dreck either, I'm talking Chicken of the Sea, Alex . . . 2 for 49!" *True Story*, aimed at "blue-collar women," assures its advertisers, doubtless correctly, that its readers are "the most brand-loyal group there is." If you're a high prole you do the things a commercial society has decreed you're supposed to do. In the Southwest, a place whose usages all of us are apparently expected to embrace in order to avoid "elitism," a popular high-prole family entertainment in the evening is going out to the car wash, with a stop-in at the local franchised food establishment on the way home. Or you might go to the Ice Show, titled, say, "Bugs Bunny in Space."

High proles are nice. It's down among the mid- and low proles that features some might find offensive begin to show themselves. These are the people who feel bitter about their work, often because they are closely supervised and regulated and generally treated like wayward children. "It's just like the Army," says an auto-assembly-plant worker. "No, it's worse. . . . You just about need a pass to piss." Andrew Levison, author of *The Working-Class Majority* (1974), invites us to imagine what it would be like to be under the constant eye of a foreman, "a figure who has absolutely no counterpart in middle-class society. Salaried professionals do often have people above them, but it is impossible to imagine professors or executives being required to bring a doctor's note if they are absent a day or having to justify the number of trips they take to the bathroom." Mid- and low proles are perceived to be so because they perform the role of the victims in that "coercive utilization of man by man" that Veblen found so objectionable. (Imposing the coercion, instead of having it imposed on you, is the prerogative of the more fortunate: managers, teachers, writers, journalists, clergy, film directors.)

The degree of supervision, indeed, is often a more eloquent class indicator than mere income, which suggests that the whole class system is more a recognition of the value of freedom than a proclamation of the value of sheer cash. The degree to which your work is overseen by a superior suggests your real class more accurately than the amount you take home from it. Thus the reason why a high-school teacher is "lower" than a tenured university professor. The teacher is obliged to file weekly "lesson plans" with a principal, superintendent, or "curriculum coordinator," thus acknowledging subservience. The professor, on the other hand, reports to no one, and his class is thus higher, even though the teacher may be smarter, better-mannered, and richer. (It is in public schools, the postal service, and police departments that we meet terms like *supervisor* and *inspector:* the prole hunter will need to know no more.) One is a mid- or low prole if one's servitude is constantly emphasized. Occupational class depends very largely on doing work for which the consequences of error or failure are distant or remote, or better, invisible, rather than immediately apparent to a superior and thus instantly humiliating to the performer.

Constantly demeaned at work, the lower sorts of proles suffer from poor morale. As one woman worker says, "Most of us . . . have jobs that are too small for our spirit." A taxi driver in St. Louis defended the Vietnam War by saying, "We can't be a pitiful, helpless giant. We gotta show 'em we're number one." "Are you number one?" Studs Terkel asked him. Pause. "I'm number nothin'," he said. There's a prole tendency to express class disappointment by self-simplification, and when examining proles it's well to be mindful of the observation of British critic Richard Hoggart: "There are no simple people. The 'ordinary' is complex too."

"A click": that's who runs things, say mid- and low proles, retreating into their private pursuits: home workshops and household repairs, washing and polishing the car; playing poker; hunting, fishing, camping; watching sports and Westerns on TV and identifying with quarterback or hero; visiting relatives (most upper-middles and uppers, by contrast, are in flight from their relatives and visit friends instead); family shopping at the local mall on Saturday or Sunday.

At the bottom of the working class, the low prole is identifiable by the gross uncertainty of his employment. This class would include illegal aliens like Mexican fruit pickers as well as other migrant workers. Social isolation is the norm here, and what Hoggart says of the lower working class in Britain applies elsewhere as well: "Socially . . . each day and each week is almost unplanned. There is no diary, no book of engagements, and few letters are sent or received." Remoteness and isolation, as in the valleys of Appalachia, are characteristics, and down here we find people who, trained for nothing, are likely out of sheer wayward despair to join the Army.

Still, they're better off than the destitute, who never have even seasonal work and who live wholly on welfare. They differ from the bottom-out-of-sights less because they're much better off than because they're more visible, in the form of Bowery bums, bag ladies, people who stand in public places lecturing and delivering harangues about their grievances, people who drink out of paper bags, people whose need for some recognition impels them to "act" in front of audiences in the street. When delinquency and distress grow desperate, you sink into the bottom-out-of-sight class, staying all day in your welfare room or contriving to get taken into an institution, whether charitable or correctional doesn't matter much.

Thus the classes. They are usefully imagined as a line of theaters running side by side down a long street. Each has a marquee and lots of posters on the front. Plays about self-respect are running constantly in all of them, from the most comfortable to the barest and meanest. But the odd thing is that there's no promotion from one theater to the next one up. And the important point is this: there's no one playing in any of these theaters, no matter how imposing, who isn't, much of the time, scared to death that he's going to stumble, muff his lines, appear in the wrong costume, or otherwise bomb. If you find an American who feels entirely class-secure, stuff and exhibit him. He's a rare specimen.

Fredric Jameson (1934–)

Jameson was born in Cleveland, Ohio. He earned his B.A. from Haverford College in 1954 and his Ph.D. in French and comparative literature from Yale University in 1959. During this period, Marxist aesthetics and literary criticism had almost completely died out because of the Cold War and the stigma attached to communism or anything associated with it. But it was Jameson who brought Marxist literary studies back to life in American academia with the publication of *Marxism and Form* (1971), a book recovering major Marxist thinkers, and his highly original *The Political Unconscious: Narrative as a Socially Symbolic Act* (1981), which opened with the now famous line "Always historicize!" and went on to sketch out Jameson's approach to Marxist literary criticism. Before settling at Duke University in 1986 as a distinguished professor of comparative literature and director of the Center for Critical Theory, he taught at Harvard, the University of California at San Diego, Yale, and the University of California at Santa Cruz.

Although Jameson is considered the leading contemporary Marxist critic in the United States and an important poststructuralist thinker, he has drawn a good deal of criticism as well as a significant following. Part of the reason for the criticism is that his work is sometimes seen as unnecessarily difficult and obscure, which makes it inaccessible to some readers. He has also been criticized, rightly or wrongly, for ignoring feminism and gender dynamics and for his lack of attention to ongoing political struggles. Fellow Marxist Terry Eagleton, for example, questions how Jameson's theory translates into concrete political practices and policies. The answer provided by Jameson is that his intention is to redefine Marxism in light of contemporary thought and give it a central place in intellectual circles. This he has accomplished with great success, and the fact that he has come under such fire merely serves to emphasize the critical power of his work.

Postmodernism and Consumer Society[1]

The concept of postmodernism is not widely accepted or even understood today. Some of the resistance to it may come from the unfamiliarity of the works it covers, which can be found in all the arts: the poetry of John Ashbery, for instance, but also the much simpler talk poetry that came out of the reaction against complex, ironic, academic modernist poetry in the 1960s; the reaction against modern architecture and in particular against the monumental buildings of the International Style, the pop buildings and decorated sheds celebrated by Robert Venturi in his manifesto, *Learning from Las Vegas;* Andy Warhol and Pop art, but also the more recent Photorealism; in music, the moment of John Cage but also the later synthesis of classical and 'popular' styles found in composers like Philip Glass and Terry Riley, and also punk and new-wave rock with such groups as the Clash, Talking Heads and the Gang of Four; in film, everything that comes out of Godard—contemporary vanguard film and video—but also a whole new style of commercial or fiction films, which has its equivalent in contemporary novels as well, where the works of William Burroughs, Thomas Pynchon and Ishmael Reed on the one hand, and the French new novel on the other, are also to be numbered among the varieties of what can be called postmodernism.

This list would seem to make two things clear at once: first, most of the postmodernisms mentioned above emerge as specific reactions against the established forms of high modernism, against this or that dominant high modernism which conquered the university, the museum, the art gallery network, and the foundations. Those formerly subversive and embattled styles—Abstract Expressionism; the great modernist poetry of Pound, Eliot or Wallace Stevens; the International Style (Le Corbusier, Frank Lloyd Wright, Mies); Stravinsky; Joyce, Proust and Mann—felt to be scandalous or shocking by our grandparents are, for the generation which arrives at the gate in the 1960s, felt to be the establishment and the enemy—dead, stifling, canonical, the reified monuments one has to destroy to do anything new. This means that there will be as many different forms of postmodernism as there were high modernisms in place, since the former are at least initially specific and local reactions *against* those models. That obviously does not make the job of describing postmodernism as a coherent thing any easier, since the unity of this new impulse—if it has one—is given not in itself but in the very modernism it seeks to displace.

The second feature of this list of postmodernisms is the effacement in it of some key boundaries or separations, most notably the erosion of the older distinction between high culture and so-called mass or popular culture. This is perhaps the most distressing development of all from an academic standpoint, which has traditionally had a vested interest in preserving a realm of high or elite culture against the surrounding environment of philistinism, of schlock and kitsch, of TV series and *Reader's Digest* culture, and in transmitting difficult and complex skills of reading, listening and seeing to its initiates. But many of the newer postmodernisms have been fascinated precisely by that whole landscape of advertising and motels, of the Las Vegas strip, of the Late Show and Grade-B Hollywood film, of so-called paraliterature with its airport paperback categories of the gothic and the romance, the popular biography, the murder mystery and the science fiction or fantasy novel. They no longer 'quote' such 'texts' as a Joyce might have done, or a Mahler; they incorporate them, to the point where the line between high art and commercial forms seems increasingly difficult to draw.

A rather different indication of this effacement of the older categories of genre and discourse can be found in what is sometimes called contemporary theory. A generation ago there was still a technical discourse of professional philosophy—the great systems of Sartre or the phenomenologists, the work of Wittgenstein or analytical or common language philosophy—alongside which one could still distinguish that quite different discourse of the other academic disciplines—of political science, for example, or sociology or literary criticism. Today, increasingly, we have a kind of writing simply called 'theory' which is all or none of those things at once. This new kind of discourse, generally associated with France and so-called French theory, is becoming widespread and marks the end of philosophy as such. Is the work of Michel Foucault, for example, to be called philosophy, history, social theory or political science? It's undecidable, as they say nowadays; and I will suggest that such 'theoretical discourse' is also to be numbered among the manifestations of postmodernism.

Now I must say a word about the proper use of this concept: it is not just another word for the description of a particular style. It is also, at least in my use, a periodizing concept whose function is to correlate the emergence of new formal features in culture with the emergence of a new type of social life and a new economic order—what is often euphemistically called modernization, postindustrial or consumer society, the society of the media or the spectacle, or multinational capitalism. This new moment of capitalism can be dated from the postwar boom in the United States in the late 1940s and early 1950s or, in France, from the establishment of the Fifth Republic in 1958. The 1960s are in many ways the key transitional period, a period in which the new international order (neo-colonialism, the Green Revolution, computerization and electronic information) is at one and the same time set in place and is swept and shaken by its own internal contradictions and by external resistance. I want here to sketch a few of the ways in which the new postmodernism expresses the inner truth of that newly emergent social order of late capitalism, but will have to limit the description to only two of its significant features, which I will call pastiche and schizophrenia; they will give us a chance to sense the specificity of the postmodernist experience of space and time respectively.

Pastiche Eclipses Parody

One of the most significant features or practices in postmodernism today is pastiche. I must first explain this term, which people generally tend to confuse with or assimilate to that related verbal phenomenon called parody. Both pastiche and parody involve the imitation or, better still, the mimicry of other styles and particularly of the mannerisms and stylistic twitches of other styles. It is obvious that modem literature in general offers a very rich field for parody, since the great modem writers have all been defined by the invention or production of rather unique styles: think of the Faulknerian long sentence or of D. H. Lawrence's characteristic nature imagery; think of Wallace Stevens's peculiar way of using abstractions; think also of mannerisms of the philosophers, of Heidegger for example, or Sartre; think of the musical styles of

Mahler or Prokofiev. All of these styles, however different from one another, are comparable in this: each is quite unmistakable; once one of them is learned, it is not likely to be confused with something else.

Now parody capitalizes on the uniqueness of these styles and seizes on their idiosyncrasies and eccentricities to produce an imitation which mocks the original. I won't say that the satiric impulse is conscious in all forms of parody. In any case, a good or great parodist has to have some secret sympathy for the original, just as a great mimic has to have the capacity to put himself/herself in the place of the person imitated. Still, the general effect of parody is—whether in sympathy or with malice—to cast ridicule on the private nature of these stylistic mannerisms and their excessiveness and eccentricity with respect to the way people normally speak or write. So there remains somewhere behind all parody the feeling that there is a linguistic norm in contrast to which the styles of the great modernists can be mocked.

But what would happen if one no longer believed in the existence of normal language, of ordinary speech, of the linguistic norm (the kind of clarity and communicative power celebrated by Orwell in his famous essay, say)? One could think of it in this way; perhaps the immense fragmentation and privatization of modern literature—its explosion into a host of distinct private styles and mannerisms—foreshadows deeper and more general tendencies in social life as a whole. Supposing that modern art and modernism—far from being a kind of specialized aesthetic curiosity—actually anticipated social developments along these lines; supposing that in the decades since the emergence of the great modern styles society had itself begun to fragment in this way, each group coming to speak a curious private language of its own, each profession developing its private code or idiolect, and finally each individual coming to be a kind of linguistic island, separated from everyone else? But then in that case, the very possibility of any linguistic norm in terms of which one could ridicule private languages and idiosyncratic styles would vanish, and we would have nothing but stylistic diversity and heterogeneity.

That is the moment at which pastiche appears and parody has become impossible. Pastiche is, like parody, the imitation of a peculiar or unique style, the wearing of a stylistic mask, speech in a dead language: but it is a neutral practice of such mimicry, without parody's ulterior motive, without the satirical impulse, without laughter, without that still latent feeling that there exists something *normal* compared with which what is being imitated is rather comic. Pastiche is blank parody, parody that has lost its sense of humor: pastiche is to parody what that curious thing, the modern practice of a kind of blank irony, is to what Wayne Booth calls the stable and comic ironies of, say, the eighteenth century.

The Death of the Subject

But now we need to introduce a new piece into this puzzle, which may help to explain why classical modernism is a thing of the past and why postmodernism should have taken its place. This new component is what is generally called the 'death of the subject' or, to say it in more conventional language, the end of individualism as such. The great modernisms were, as we have said, predicated on the invention of a personal, private style, as unmistakable as your fingerprint, as incomparable as your own body. But this means that the modernist aesthetic is in some way organically linked to the conception of a unique self and private identity, a unique personality and individuality, which can be expected to generate its own unique vision of the world and to forge its own unique, unmistakable style.

Yet today, from any number of distinct perspectives, the social theorists, the psychoanalysts, even the linguists, not to speak of those of us who work in the area of culture and cultural and formal change, are all exploring the notion that this kind of individualism and personal identity is a thing of the past; that the old individual or individualist subject is 'dead'; and that one might even describe the concept of the unique individual and the theoretical basis of individualism as ideological. There are in fact two positions on all this, one of which is more radical than the other. The first one is content to say: yes, once upon a time, in the classic age of competitive capitalism, in the heyday of the nuclear family and the emergence of the bourgeoisie as the hegemonic social class, there was such a thing as individualism, as individual subjects. But today, in the age of corporate capitalism, of the so-called organization man, of bureaucracies in business as well as in the state, of demographic explosion—today, that older bourgeois individual subject no longer exists.

Then there is a second position, the more radical of the two, what one might call the poststructuralist position. It adds: not only is the bourgeois individual subject a thing of the past, it is also a myth; it *never* really existed in the first place; there have never been autonomous subjects of that type. Rather, this construct is merely a philosophical and cultural mystification which sought to persuade people that they 'had' individual subjects and possessed some unique personal identity.

For our purposes, it is not particularly important to decide which of these positions is correct (or rather, which is more interesting and productive). What we have to retain from all this is rather an aesthetic dilemma: because if the experience and the ideology of the unique self, an experience and ideology which informed the stylistic practice of classical modernism, is over and done with, then it is no longer clear what the artists and writers of the present period are supposed to be doing. What is clear is merely that the older models—Picasso, Proust, T. S. Eliot—do not work any more (or are positively harmful), since nobody has that kind of unique private world and style to express any longer. And this is perhaps not merely a 'psychological' matter: we also have to take into account the immense weight of seventy or eighty years of classical modernism itself. This is yet another sense in which the writers and artists of the present day will no longer be able to invent new styles and worlds—they've already been invented; only a limited number of combinations are possible; the unique ones have been thought of already. So the weight of the whole modernist aesthetic tradition—now dead—also 'weighs like a nightmare on the brain of the living', as Marx said in another context.

Hence, once again, pastiche: in a world in which stylistic innovation is no longer possible, all that is left is to imitate dead styles, to speak through the masks and with the voices of the styles in the imaginary museum. But this means that contemporary or postmodernist art is going to be about art itself in a new kind of way; even more, it means that one of its essential messages will involve the necessary failure of art and the aesthetic, the failure of the new, the imprisonment in the past.

The Nostalgia Mode

As this may seem very abstract, I want to give a few examples, one of which is so omnipresent that we rarely link it with the kinds of developments in high art discussed here. This particular practice of pastiche is not high-cultural but very much within mass culture, and it is generally known as the 'nostalgia film, (what the French neatly call *la mode rétro*—retrospective styling). We must conceive of this category in the broadest way: narrowly, no doubt, it consists merely of films about the past and about specific generational moments of that past. Thus, one of the inaugural films in this new 'genre' (if that's what it is) was Lucas's *American Graffiti,* which in 1973 set out to recapture all the atmosphere and stylistic peculiarities of the 1950s United States: the United States of the Eisenhower era. Polanski's great film *Chinatown* does something similar for the 1930s, as does Bertolucci's *The Conformist* for the Italian and European context of the same period, the fascist era in Italy; and so forth. We could go on listing these films for some time: But why call them pastiche? Are they not rather, work in the more traditional genre known as the historical film—work which can more simply be theorized by extrapolating that other well-known form, the historical novel?

I have my reasons for thinking that we need new categories for such films. But let me first add some anomalies: supposing I suggested that *Star Wars* is also a nostalgia film. What could that mean? I presume that we can agree that this is not a historical film about our own intergalactic past. Let me put it somewhat differently: one of the most important cultural experiences of the generations that grew up from the 1930s to the 1950s was the Saturday afternoon serial of the Buck Rogers type—alien villains, true American heroes, heroines in distress, the death ray or the doomsday box, and the cliffhanger at the end whose miraculous resolution was to be witnessed next Saturday afternoon. *Star Wars* reinvents this experience in the form of a pastiche: that is, there is no longer any point to a parody of such serials since they are long extinct. *Star Wars,* far from being a pointless satire of such now dead forms, satisfies a deep (might I even say repressed?) longing to experience them again: it is a complex object in which on some first level children and adolescents can take the adventures straight, while the adult public is able to gratify a deeper and more properly nostalgic desire to return to that older period and to live its strange old aesthetic artifacts through once again. This film is thus *metonymically* a historical or nostalgia film. Unlike *American Graffiti,* it does not reinvent a picture of the past in its lived totality; rather, by reinventing the feel and shape of characteristic art objects of an older period (the serials), it seeks to reawaken a sense of the past associated with those objects. *Raiders of the Lost*

Ark, meanwhile, occupies an intermediary position here: on some level it is *about* the 1930s and 1940s, but in reality it too conveys that period metonymically through its own characteristic adventure stories (which are no longer ours).

Now let me discuss another interesting anomaly which may take us further towards understanding nostalgia film in particular and pastiche generally. This one involves a recent film called *Body Heat,* which, as has abundantly been pointed out by the critics, is a kind of distant remake of *The Postman Always Rings Twice* or *Double Indemnity.* (The allusive and elusive plagiarism of older plots is, of course, also a feature of pastiche.) Now *Body Heat* is technically not a nostalgia film, since it takes place in a contemporary setting, in a little Florida village near Miami. On the other hand, this technical contemporaneity is most ambiguous indeed: the credits—always our first cue—are lettered and scripted in a 1930s Art-Deco style which cannot but trigger nostalgic reactions (first to *Chinatown,* no doubt, and then beyond it to some more historical referent). Then the very style of the hero himself is ambiguous: William Hurt is a new star but has nothing of the distinctive style of the preceding generation of male superstars like Steve McQueen or even Jack Nicholson, or rather, his persona here is a kind of mix of their characteristics with an older role of the type generally associated with Clark Gable So here too there is a faintly archaic feel to all this. This spectator begins to wonder why this story, which could have been situated anywhere, is set in a small Florida town, in spite of its contemporary reference. One begins to realize after a while that the small town setting has a crucial strategic function: it allows the film to do without most of the signals and references which we might associate with the contemporary world, with consumer society—the appliances and artifacts, the high rises, the object world of late capitalism. Technically, then, its objects (its cars, for instance) are 1980s products, but everything in the film conspires to blur that immediate contemporary reference and to make it possible to receive this too as nostalgia work—as a narrative set in some indefinable nostalgic past, an eternal 1930s, say, beyond history. It seems to me exceedingly symptomatic to find the very style of nostalgia films invading and colonizing even those movies today which have contemporary settings, as though, for some reason, we were unable today to focus our own present, as though we had become incapable of achieving aesthetic representations of our own current experience. But if that is so, then it is a terrible indictment of consumer capitalism itself—or, at the very least, an alarming and pathological symptom of a society that has become incapable of dealing with time and history.

So now we come back to the question of why nostalgia film or pastiche is to be considered different from the older historical novel or film. (I should also include in this discussion the major literary example of all this, to my mind: the novels of E. L. Doctorow—*Ragtime,* with its turn-of-the-century atmosphere, and *Loon Lake,* for the most part about our 1930s. But these are, in my opinion, historical novels in appearance only. Doctorow is a serious artist and one of the few genuinely left or radical novelists at work today. It is no disservice to him, however, to suggest that his narratives do not represent our historical past so much as they represent our ideas or cultural stereotypes about that past.) Cultural production has been driven back inside the mind, within the monadic subject: it can no longer look directly out of its eyes at the real world for the referent but must, as in Plato's cave, trace its mental images of the world on its confining walls. If there is any realism left here, it is a 'realism' which springs from the shock of grasping that confinement and of realizing that, for whatever peculiar reasons, we seem condemned to seek the historical past through our own pop images and stereotypes about the past, which itself remains forever out of reach.

Postmodernism and the City

Now, before I try to offer a somewhat more positive conclusion, I want to sketch the analysis of a full-blown postmodern building—a work which is in many ways uncharacteristic of that postmodern architecture whose principal names are Robert Venturi, Charles Moore, Michael Graves and more recently Frank Gehry, but which to my mind offers some very striking lessons about the originality of postmodernist space. Let me amplify the figure which has run through the preceding remarks, and make it even more explicit: I am proposing the notion that we are here in the presence of something like a mutation in built space itself. My implication is that we ourselves, the human subjects who happen into this new space, have not kept pace with that evolution; there has been a mutation in the object, unaccompanied as yet by any equivalent mutation in the subject; we do not yet possess the perceptual equipment to match this new hyperspace, as I will call it, in part because our perceptual habits were formed in that older kind of space I have called the space of high modernism. The newer architecture therefore—like many of the other cultural products I have evoked in the preceding remarks—therefore stands as something like an imperative to grow new organs to expand our sensorium and our body to some new, as yet unimaginable, perhaps ultimately impossible, dimensions.

The Bonaventure Hotel

The building whose features I will very rapidly enumerate in the next few moments is the Bonaventure Hotel, built in the new Los Angeles downtown by the architect and developer John Portman, whose other works include the various Hyatt Regencies, the Peachtree Center in Atlanta, and the Renaissance Center in Detroit. I must mention the populist aspect of the rhetorical defence of postmodernism against the elite (and utopian) austerities of the great architectural modernisms: it is generally affirmed, in other words, that these newer buildings are popular works on the one hand; and that they respect the vernacular of the American city fabric on the other, that is to say, that they no longer attempt, as did the masterworks and monuments of high modernism, to insert a different, a distinct, an elevated, a new utopian language into the tawdry and commercial sign-system of the surrounding city, but rather, on the contrary, seek to speak that very language, using its lexicon and syntax that has been emblematically 'learned from Las Vegas'.

On the first of these counts, Portman's Bonaventure fully confirms the claim: it is a popular building, visited with enthusiasm by locals and tourists alike (although Portman's other buildings are even more successful in this respect). The populist insertion into the city fabric is, however, another matter, and it is with this that we will begin. There are three entrances to the Bonaventure: one from Figueroa, and the other two by way of elevated gardens on the other side of the hotel, which is built into the remaining slope of the former Beacon Hill. None of these is anything like the old hotel marquee, or the monumental *porte-cochère* with which the sumptuous buildings of yesteryear were wont to stage your passage from city street to the older interior. The entryways of the Bonaventure are as it were lateral and rather backdoor affairs: the gardens in the back admit you to the sixth floor of the towers, and even there you must walk down one flight to find the elevator by which you gain access to the lobby. Meanwhile, what one is still tempted to think of as the front entry, on Figueroa, admits you, baggage and all, onto the second-story balcony, from which you must take an escalator down to the main registration desk. More about these elevators and escalators in a moment. What I first want to suggest about these curiously unmarked ways-in is that they seem to have been imposed by some new category of closure governing the inner space of the hotel itself (and this over and above the material constraints under which Portman had to work). I believe that, with a certain number of other characteristic postmodern buildings, such as the Beaubourg in Paris, or the Eaton Centre in Toronto, the Bonaventure aspires to being a total space, a complete world, a kind of miniature city (and I would want to add that to this new total space corresponds a new collective practice, a new mode in which individuals move and congregate, something like the practice of a new and historically original kind of hyper-crowd). In this sense, then, ideally the mini-city of Portman's Bonaventure ought not to have entrances at all, since the entryway is always the seam that links the building to the rest of the city that surrounds it: for it does not wish to be a part of the city, but rather its equivalent and its replacement or substitute. That is, however, obviously not possible or practical, hence the deliberate downplaying and reduction of the entrance function to its bare minimum. But this disjunction from the surrounding city is very different from that of the great monuments of the International Style: there, the act of disjunction was violent, visible, and had a very real symbolic significance—as in Le Corbusier's great *pilotis* whose gesture radically separates the new utopian space of the modern from the degraded and fallen city fabric, which it thereby explicitly repudiates (although the gamble of the modern was that this new utopian space, in the virulence of its Novum, would fan out and transform that eventually by the power of its new spatial language). The Bonaventure, however, is content to 'let the fallen city fabric continue to be in its being' (to parody Heidegger); no further effects, no larger protopolitical utopian transformation, is either expected or desired.

This diagnosis is to my mind confirmed by the great reflective glass skin of the Bonaventure, whose function I will now interpret rather differently that I did a moment ago when I saw the phenomenon of reflexion generally as developing a thematics of reproductive technology (the two readings are however not incompatible). Now one would want rather to stress the way in which the glass skin repels the city outside; a repulsion for which we have analogies in those reflective sunglasses which make it impossible for your interlocutor to see your own eyes and thereby achieve a certain aggressivity towards and power over the Other. In a similar way, the glass skin achieves a peculiar and placeless dissociation of the

Bonaventure from its neighborhood: it is not even an exterior, inasmuch as when you seek to look at the hotel's outer walls you cannot see the hotel itself, but only the distorted images of everything that surrounds it.

Now I want to say a few words about escalators and elevators: given their very real pleasures in Portman, particularly these last, which the artist has termed 'gigantic kinetic sculptures' and which certainly account for much of the spectacle and the excitement of the hotel interior, particularly in the Hyatts, where like great Japanese lanterns or gondolas they ceaselessly rise and fall—given such a deliberate marking and foregrounding in their own right, I believe one has to see such 'people movers' (Portman's own term, adapted from Disney) as something a little more than mere functions and engineering components. We know in any case that recent architectural theory has begun to borrow from narrative analysis in other fields, and to attempt to see our physical trajectories through such buildings as virtual narratives or stories, as dynamic paths and narrative paradigms which we as visitors are asked to fulfil and to complete with our own bodies and movements. In the Bonaventure, however, we find a dialectical heightening of this process: it seems to me that the escalators and elevators here henceforth replace movement but also and above all designate themselves as new reflexive signs and emblems of movement proper (something which will become evident when we come to the whole question of what remains of older forms of movement in this building, most notably walking itself). Here the narrative stroll has been underscored, symbolized, reified and replaced by a transportation machine which becomes the allegorical signifier of that older promenade we are no longer allowed to conduct on our own: and this is a dialectical intensification of the autoreferentiality of all modern culture, which tends to turn upon itself and designate its own cultural production as its content.

I am more at a loss when it comes to conveying the thing itself, the experience of space you undergo when you step off such allegorical devices into the lobby or atrium, with its great central column, surrounded by a miniature lake, the whole positioned between the four symmetrical residential towers with their elevators, and surrounded by rising balconies capped by a kind of greenhouse roof at the sixth level. I am tempted to say that such space makes it impossible for us to use the language of volume of volumes any longer, since these last are impossible to seize. Hanging streamers indeed suffuse this empty space in such a way as to distract systematically and deliberately from whatever form it might be supposed to have; while a constant busyness gives the feeling that emptiness is here absolutely packed, that it is an element within which you yourself are immersed, without any of that distance that formerly enabled the perception of perspective or volume. You are in this hyperspace up to your eyes and your body; and if it seemed to you before that that suppression of depth I spoke of in postmodern painting or literature would necessarily be difficult to achieve in architecture itself, perhaps you may now be willing to see this bewildering immersion as its formal equivalent in the new medium.

Yet escalator and elevator are also in this context dialectical opposites; and we may suggest that the glorious movement of the elevator gondolas is also a dialectical compensation for this filled space of the atrium—it gives us the chance at a radically different, but complementary, spatial experience, that of rapidly shoot-ing up through the ceiling and outside, along one of the four symmetrical towers, with the referent, Los Angeles itself, spread out breathtakingly and even alarm-ingly before us. But even this vertical movement is contained: the elevator lifts you to one of those revolving cocktail lounges, in which you, seated, are again pas-sively rotated about and offered a contemplative spectacle of the city itself, now transformed into its own images by the glass windows through which you view it.

Let me quickly conclude all this by returning to the central space of the lobby itself (with the passing observation that the hotel rooms are visibly marginalized: the corridors in the residential sections are low-ceilinged and dark, most depress-ingly functional indeed: while one understands that the rooms are in the worst of taste). The descent is dramatic enough, plummeting back down through the roof to splash down in the lake; what happens when you get there is something else, which I can only try to characterize as milling confusion, something like the vengeance this space takes on those who still seek to walk through it. Given the absolute symmetry of the four towers, it is quite impossible to get your bearings in this lobby; recently, colour coding and directional signals have been added in a pitiful and revealing, rather desperate attempt to restore the coordinates of an older space. I will take as the most dramatic practical result of this spatial muta-tion the notorious dilemma of the shopkeepers on the various balconies: it has been obvious, since the very opening of the hotel in 1977, that nobody could ever find any of these stores, and even if you located the appropriate boutique, you would be most unlikely to be as fortunate a second time; as a consequence, the commercial tenants are in despair and all the merchandise is marked down to bargain prices. When you recall that Portman is a businessman as well as an architect, and a millionaire developer, an artist who is at one and the same time a capitalist in his own right, you cannot but feel that here too something of a 'return of the repressed' is involved.

So I come finally to my principal point here, that this latest mutation in space—postmodern hyperspace—has finally succeeded in transcending the capac-ities of the individual human body to locate itself, to organize its immediate sur-roundings perceptually, and cognitively to map its position in a mappable external world. And I have already suggested that this alarming disjunction between the body and its built environment—which is to the initial bewilderment of the older modernism as the velocities of spacecraft are to those of the automobile—can itself stand as the symbol and analog of that even sharper dilemma which is the incapacity of our minds, at least at present, to map the great global multinational and decentered communicational network in which we find ourselves caught as individual subjects.

The New Machine

But as I am anxious that Portman's space not be perceived as something either exceptional or seemingly marginalized and leisure-specialized on the order of Disneyland, I would like in passing to juxtapose this complacent and entertain-ing (although bewildering) leisure-time space with its analog in a very different area, namely the space of postmodern warfare, in particular as Michael Herr evokes it in his great book on the experience of Vietnam, called *Dispatches*. The extraordinary linguistic innovations of this work may be considered postmodern, in the eclectic way in which its language impersonally fuses a whole range of contemporary collective idiolects, most notably rock language and black language: but the fusion is dictated by problems of content. This first terrible postmodernist war cannot be told in any of the traditional paradigms of the war novel or movie—indeed that breakdown of all previous narrative paradigms is, along with the breakdown of any shared language through which a veteran might convey such experience, among the principal subjects of the book and may be said to open up the place of a whole new reflexivity. Benjamin's account of Baudelaire, and of the emergence of modernism from a new experience of city technology which transcends all the older habits of bodily perception, is both singularly relevant here, and singularly antiquated, in the light of this new and virtually unimaginable quantum leap in technological alienation:

> He was a moving-target-survivor subscriber, a true child of the war, because except for the rare times when you were pinned or stranded the system was geared to keep you mobile, if that was what you thought you wanted. As a technique for staying alive it seemed to make as much sense as anything, given naturally that you were there to begin with and wanted to see it close; it started out sound and straight but it formed a cone as it progressed, because the more you moved the more you saw, the more you saw the more besides death and mutilation you risked, and the more you risked of that the more you would have to let go of one day as a 'survivor'. Some of us moved around the war like crazy people until we couldn't see which way the run was taking us anymore, only the war all over its surface with occasional, unexpected penetration. As long as we could have choppers like taxis it took real exhaustion or depression near shock or a dozen pipes of opium to keep us even apparently quiet, we'd still be running around inside our skins like something was after us, ha, ha, La Vida Loca. In the months after I got back the hundreds of helicopters I'd flown in begin to draw together until they'd formed a collective meta-chopper, and in my mind it was the sexiest thing going; saver-destroyer, provider-waster, right hand-left hand, nimble, fluent, canny and human; hot steel, grease, jungle-saturated canvas webbing, sweat cooling and warming up again, cassette rock and roll in one ear and door-gun fire in the other, fuel, heat, vitality and death, death itself, hardly an intruder.

In this new machine, which does not, like the older modernist machinery of the locomotive or the airplane, represent motion, but which can only be represented *in motion*, something of the mystery of the new postmodernist space is concentrated.

The Aesthetic of Consumer Society

Now I must try very rapidly in conclusion to characterize the relationship of cultural production of this kind to social life in this country today. This will also be the moment to address the principal objection to concepts of postmodernism of the type I have sketched here: namely that all the features we have enumerated are not new at all but abundantly characterized modernism proper or what I call high modernism. Was not Thomas Mann, after all, interested in the idea of pastiche, and are not certain chapters of *Ulysses* its most obvious realization? Can Flaubert, Mallarmé and Gertrude Stein not be included in an account of postmodernist temporality? What is so new about all of this? Do we really need the concept of *post*modernism?

One kind of answer to this question would raise the whole issue of periodization and of how a historian (literary or other) posits a radical break between two henceforth distinct periods. I must limit myself to the suggestion that radical breaks between periods do not generally involve complete changes of content but rather the restructuring of a certain number of elements already given: features that in an earlier period or system were subordinate now become dominant, and features that had been dominant again become secondary. In this sense, everything we have described here can be found in earlier periods and most notably within modernism proper: my point is that until the present day those things have been secondary or minor features of modernist art, marginal rather than central, and that we have something new when they become the central features of cultural production.

But I can argue this more concretely by turning to the relationship between cultural production and social life generally. The older or classical modernism was an oppositional art; it emerged within the business society of the gilded age as scandalous and offensive to the middle-class public—ugly, dissonant, bohemian, sexually shocking. It was something to make fun of (when the police were not called in to seize the books or close the exhibitions): an offense to good taste and to common sense, or, as Freud and Marcuse would have put it, a provocative challenge to the reigning reality- and performance-principles of early twentieth-century middle-class society. Modernism in general did not go well with over-stuffed Victorian furniture, with Victorian moral taboos, or with the conventions of polite society. This is to say that whatever the explicit political content of the great high modernisms, the latter were always in some mostly implicit ways dangerous and explosive, subversive within the established order.

If then we suddenly return to the present day, we can measure the immensity of the cultural changes that have taken place. Not only are Joyce and Picasso no longer weird and repulsive, they have become classics and now look rather realistic to us. Meanwhile, there is very little in either the form or the content of contemporary art that contemporary society finds intolerable and scandalous. The most offensive forms of this art—punk rock, say, or what is called sexually explicit material—are all taken in stride by society, and they are commercially successful, unlike the productions of the older high modernism. But this means that even if contemporary art has all the same formal features as the older modernism, it has still shifted its position fundamentally within our culture. For one thing, commodity production and in particular our clothing, furniture, buildings and other artifacts are now intimately tied in with styling changes which derive from artistic experimentation; our advertising, for example, is fed by postmodernism in all the arts and inconceivable without it. For another, the classics of high modernism are now part of the so-called canon and are taught in schools and universities—which at once empties them of any of their older subversive power. Indeed, one way of marking the break between the periods and of dating the emergence of postmodernism is precisely to be found there: at the moment (the early 1960s, one would think) in which the position of high modernism and its dominant aesthetics become established in the academy and are henceforth felt to be academic by a whole new generation of poets, painters and musicians.

But one can also come at the break from the other side, and describe it in terms of periods of recent social life. As I have suggested, non-Marxists and Marxists alike have come around to the general feeling that at some point following World War II a new kind of society began to emerge (variously described as postindustrial society, multinational capitalism, consumer society, media society and so forth). New types of consumption; planned obsolescence; an ever more rapid rhythm of fashion and styling changes; the penetration of advertising, television and the media generally to a hitherto unparalleled degree throughout society; the replacement of the old tension between city and country, center and province, by the suburb and by universal standardization; the growth of the great networks of superhighways and the arrival of automobile culture—these are some of the features which would seem to mark a radical break with that older prewar society in which high modernism was still an underground force.

I believe that the emergence of postmodernism is closely related to the emergence of this new moment of late, consumer or multinational capitalism. I believe also that its formal features in many ways express the deeper logic of this particular social system. I will only be able, however, to show this for one major theme: namely the disappearance of a sense of history, the way in which our entire contemporary social system has little by little begun to lose its capacity to retain its own past, has begun to live in a perpetual present and in a perpetual change that obliterates traditions of the kind which all earlier social information have had in one way or another to preserve. Think only of the media exhaustion of news: of how Nixon and, even more so, Kennedy are figures from a now distant past. One is tempted to say that the very function of the news media is to relegate such recent historical experiences as rapidly as possible into the past. The informational function of the media would thus be to help us forget, to serve as the very agents and mechanisms for our historical amnesia.

But in that case the two features of postmodernism on which I have dwelt here—the transformation of reality into images, the fragmentation of time into a series of perpetual presents—are both extraordinarily consonant with this process. My own conclusion here must take the form of a question about the critical value of the newer art. There is some agreement that the older modernism functioned against its society in ways which are variously described as critical, negative, contestatory, subversive, oppositional and the like. Can anything of the sort be affirmed about postmodernism and its social moment? We have seen that there is a way in which postmodernism replicates or reproduces—reinforces—the logic of consumer capitalism; the more significant question is whether there is also a way in which it resists that logic. But that is a question we must leave open.

1988

Note

1. The present text combines elements of two previously published essays: "Postmodernism and Consumer Society," in *The Anti-Aesthetic* (Port Townsend, Wash.: Bay Press, 1983), and "Postmodernism: The Cultural Logic of Late Capitalism," in *New Left Review*, no. 146 (1984).

John Guillory (1952–)

Guillory received his B.A. from Tulane in 1974 and his Ph.D. from Yale in 1979. Before joining the faculty of New York University as an English professor in 1999, Guillory taught at Yale, Johns Hopkins, and Harvard. His research and teaching interests are many and varied: Renaissance poetry, Shakespeare, Milton, literature and science in the Renaissance, the history of criticism, the sociology of literary study, and twentieth-century literary theory. His highly influential *Cultural Capital: The Problem of Literary Canon Formation* (1993) dealt with a constellation of issues such as the history of criticism, the sociology of literary study, and the canon debate, and for it he was awarded the prestigious René Wellek Award by the American Comparative Literature Association in 1994. Guillory has been and continues to be on the cutting edge of discussions concerning the evolving position of literary studies and the academic profession in societies both past and present. Aside from his 1983 book *Poetic Authority: Spenser, Milton and Literary History*, Guillory has edited, along with Judith Butler and Kendall Thomas, *What's Left of Theory? New Work on the Politics of Literary Theory* (2000). As Guillory and his fellow editors write in their introduction to this collection, "For several years a debate on the politics of theory has been conducted energetically within literary studies. The terms of the debate, however, are far from clear. What is meant by politics? What is meant by theory?" In order to answer this question, the collection brings together some of the most prominent contemporary literary theorists to examine and illuminate crucial issues facing the study of literature and its relationship to politics.

Canonical and Noncanonical: The Current Debate

The Imaginary Politics of Representation

> *Not only in their answers but in their very questions there was a mystification.*
>
> —Marx, *The German Ideology*

Social Identity

In recent years the debate about the literary canon has entered a new phase, with the emergence in the university and in the popular media of a strong conservative backlash against revisions of the curriculum.[1] Given the renewal and even intensification of the debate after what had seemed a successful transition to an expanded syllabus of literary study, the moment may now have arrived for a reassessment of the debate, and particularly of the theoretical assumptions upon which the practice of canonical revision has been based. These assumptions derive without question from the political discourse—liberal pluralism—to which we owe the most successful progressive agendas of the last three decades. It will not be my intention to question social objectives whose realization is both necessary and urgent, but to demonstrate that a certain impasse in the debate about the canon follows from the fundamental assumptions of liberal pluralism itself. This impasse is visible, for example, when the distinction between "canonical" and "noncanonical" works is institutionalized in two very different and even contradictory ways: as the canonization of formerly noncanonical works, and as the development of distinct and separate noncanonical programs of study. I shall argue in this chapter that the vulnerability of curricular revision to attack from the right is one consequence of the contradiction between integrationist and separatist conceptions of curricular revision, a contradiction that can be traced to theoretical problems with pluralism itself, and that threatens to disable an effective response to the conservative backlash.

While the explicitly political ends of canonical revision are obvious, it has not been sufficiently acknowledged how much the language of revision owes to a political culture which is specifically American. It will be my contention that however easy it has been for both progressive academics and their reactionary critics to conflate the critique of the canon with the forms of leftist and even Marxist thought, the terms and methods of canonical revision must be situated squarely within the prevailing conventions of American pluralism. These conventions have been usefully summarized by Gregor McLennan, in his *Marxism, Pluralism, and Beyond*, as follows:

- a sociology of competing interest groups;
- a conception of the state as a political mechanism responsive to the balance of societal demands;
- an account of the democratic civic culture which sets a realistic minimum measure for the values of political participation and trust;
- an empiricist and multi-factorial methodology of social science.[2]

Within traditional liberal pluralist thought, individuals are conceived in their relation to the state as members of groups whose interests are assumed to conflict. Hence the object of representing these groups within the legislative institutions of the state is to negotiate among the interests of particular social groups or constituencies. "Representation" in political institutions now describes an important objective for many social groups, defined by a variety of forms of association: women, trade union members, the elderly, consumers, the sick, the disabled, veterans, and most recently members of minority ethnic or racial groups, the communities which constitute our pluralist society. In the context of the long-term development of democratic culture, the pluralist version of liberalism emergent in post–World War II American society registers a certain deepening crisis in the institutions of political representation, the sense (not necessarily conscious) of having reached an apparent limit in the capacity of these institutions to represent diverse social groups.[3] This crisis has reached a new stage with the decline of postwar liberalism in American political culture and the resurgence of a strongly reactionary politics which now designs to purge liberalism from political culture in the same way that it formerly (and successfully) purged socialism. In response to an increasingly hostile climate of opinion, it would seem that the political culture of liberalism has established a last redoubt in the university, where the very extremity of its situation has deformed its discourse by rigidifying certain defensive postures.[4] The deterioration of what was in the United States always a very limited program of economic socialization, along with a general decline in the credibility of democratic political institutions, constitute the immediate conditions for the development of a political critique of "representation" in contexts other than those formerly conceived as political. In retrospect it was only in the wake of liberalism's apparent defeat in American political culture that such agendas as "representation in the canon" could come to occupy so central a place within the liberal academy.[5] The new curricular critique made it possible for the university to become a new venue of representation, one in which new social identities might be represented more adequately, if also differently, than in existing political institutions of American society.

If the politics of canon formation has been understood as a politics of representation—the representation or lack of representation of certain social groups in the canon—this circumstance may well be a consequence of that fact that, as McLennan points out, the "whole relationship between subjects, individuals and their identity as members of certain social categories is one which has been dramatically unsettled in recent social theory."[6] Because the concept of "social identity" has undergone a kind of mutation, with which democratic institutions have not yet caught up, the venue of representation can be displaced to new arenas of contestation. But that displacement, while it reconceives a process such as canon formations as "political," leaves unclarified the question of the precise relation between a politics of representation in the canon and a democratic representational politics. In order to answer the question of what "representation in the canon" means within the larger context of American political culture, we must acknowledge at the outset that our concept of "social identity" is a product of that culture, and that only within that culture can the category of an author's racial, ethnic, or gender identity found a politics of curricular revision. Any reconsideration, then, of canon critique in its political context must begin with the notion of "social identity."

I propose to offer here a critique of the assumptions underlying the current understanding of the canon, a critique which derives its premises from a set of terms and arguments closer to Marxism than to liberal pluralism. But the point of such a reorientation is not to argue for the mutual exclusivity of Marxism and pluralism. I take it for granted that Marxism itself has theoretical limitations, which recent "post-Marxist" confrontations with pluralist methodology (for example, that of Laclau and Mouffe) have had to confront, with important theoretical results.[7] The major terms of my analysis are drawn from the arguably post-Marxist theory of "cultural capital" elaborated in the works of Pierre

Bourdieu.[8] Insofar as the concept of cultural capital presupposes the concept of capital, and inasmuch as it foregrounds the category of class, Bourdieu's theory must be located within the Marxist rather than the pluralist critical tradition. The object at the present moment of advancing a Marxist critique (however qualified) of liberal pluralist revisions of the canon would be to indicate the inherent limitations in pluralist analysis in order to bring to light certain questions occluded by the current problematic of "representation." These questions concern the *distribution* of cultural capital, of which canonical works constitute one form. I will assume, following Bourdieu, that the distribution of cultural capital in such an institution as the school reproduces the structure of social relations, a structure of complex and ramifying inequality. However, it will not be possible to explore the relation between the canon and access to the forms of cultural capital, until we have first demonstrated the inherent limitations in the problematic of representation, in the very questions it asks.

For the purposes of that critique, we can extract from the current debate about the canon two pervasive theoretical assumptions: The first of these assumptions is implicit in the word "canon" itself, not until recently a common term in critical discourse.[9] The word "canon" displaces the expressly honorific term "classic" precisely in order to isolate the "classics" as the object of critique. The concept of the canon names the traditional curriculum of literary texts by analogy to that body of writing historically characterized by an inherent logic of *closure*—the scriptural canon. The scriptural analogy is continuously present, if usually tacit, whenever canonical revision is expressed as "opening the canon." We may begin to interrogate this first assumption by raising the question of whether the process by which a selection of texts functions to define a religious practice and doctrine is really similar *historically* to the process by which literary texts come to be preserved, reproduced, and taught in the schools. This question concerns the historicity of a particular kind of written text, the "literary." Since the hypothesis of closure is a historical conjecture, it is subject to historical proof or disproof, a task I shall undertake in this and subsequent chapters.

The first assumption of canonical revision operates in concert with a second, which posits a homology between the process of *exclusion*, by which socially defined minorities are excluded from the exercise of power or from political representation, and the process of *selection*, by which certain works are designated canonical, others noncanonical. The second assumption clearly requires the first—literature as quasi-scripture—in order to make the claim that the process of canonical selection is always also a process of social exclusion, specifically the exclusion of female, black, ethnic, or working-class authors from the literary canon. The unrepresentative content of the canon is described in the rhetoric of canonical critique as a kind of scandal, after two millennia a scandal which has gone on long enough. If the forces of exclusion have been so powerful as to prevail without challenge until recent years, the strategy for their defeat has been surprisingly obvious, even simple. It has only been necessary to "open" the canon by adding works of minority authors to the syllabus of literary study. In this way the socially progressive agenda of liberal pluralism could be effected in a particular institution—the university—by transforming the literary syllabus into an inclusive or "representative" set of texts.

   Again, it will not be necessary to dissent from the larger aims of the progressive social agenda (far from it) in order to raise a question as the level of theoretical assumptions about the relation between the literary curriculum and "representation." The movement to open the canon to noncanonical authors submits the syllabus to a kind of demographic oversight. Canonical and noncanonical authors are supposed to *stand for* particular social groups, dominant or subordinate. One can easily concede that there must be *some* relation between the representation of minorities in positions of power and the representation of minorities in the canon, but what is that relation? The difficulty of describing this relation is in part a consequence of the fact that a particular social institution—the university—intervenes between these two sites of representation. Given the only partially successful social agenda of educational democratization in the last three decades, we may conclude that it is much easier to make the canon representative than the university. More to the point, those members of social minorities who enter the university do not "represent" the social groups to which they belong in the same way in which minority legislators can be said to represent their constituencies. The sense in which a social group is "represented" by an author or text is more tenuous still. The latter sense of representation conceives the literary canon as a hypothetical *image* of social diversity, a kind of mirror in which social groups either see themselves, or do not see themselves, reflected. In the words of Henry Louis Gates, Jr., the "teaching of literature" has always meant "the teaching of an aesthetic and political order, in which no women and people of color were ever able to discover the reflection or representation of their images, or hear the resonances of their cultural voices."[10] I shall argue that the sense of representation as *reflection* or image inhabits what may be called the field of "imaginary" politics. But by the latter term I do not mean what is opposed to the real but a politics which is manifestly a politics *of the image*. Such a politics belongs to the same political domain as the ongoing critique of minority images in the national media, to the project of correcting these images for stereotyping, or for a failure to represent minorities at all. Such a politics has real work to do, as complex and interesting as images themselves, but it is also inherently limited by its reduction of the political to the instance of representation, and of representation to the image. It is only the first step toward a political critique of the literary curriculum to say that it is a *medium* of cultural images. This mode of canonical critique reduces the curriculum to such a medium, and thus, as we shall see, to a mass cultural form. In this sense the critique of the canon betrays its determination by certain postmodern conditions, by those conditions in which media images have the central ideological function of organizing our responses to virtually all aspects of our lives.[11] If there is any difference worth considering between the politics of image-critique and the politics of canonical revision, this difference must inhere in the latter's institutional location. The literary curriculum is precisely not the site of mass cultural production and consumption, but the critique of the canon has proceeded as though it were, as though canon formation were like the Academy Awards. Clearly a "representative" canon does not redress the effects of social exclusion, or lack of representation, either within or without the university; nor would the project of canonical revision need to make this claim in order to justify the necessity of curricular revision.

But in construing the process of canon formation as an exclusionary process essentially the same as the exclusion of socially defined minorities from power, the strategy of opening the canon aims to reconstruct it as a true image (a true representation) of social diversity. In so specifying "representation" as the political effect of the canon, the liberal pluralist critique fails to consider what other effects, even political effects, the canon may have at its institutional site.

Whatever effects the canon as an image of equal or unequal representation may actually produce within the university, we must nevertheless insist that the politics of canonical revision is in its present form an imaginary politics, a politics of the image. That is just the reason why the social effects of a representative canon are so difficult to determine.[12] What the project of canon-critique still lacks is an analysis of how the institutional site of canonical revision mediates its political effects in the social domain. There is no question that the literary curriculum is the site of a political practice; but one must attempt to understand the politics of this practice according to the specificity of its social location. The specificity of the political here cannot mean simply a replication of the problem of "representation" in the sphere of democratic politics, and therefore it cannot mean simply importing into the school the same strategies of progressive politics which sometimes work at the legislative level.[13] Should we not rather rethink the whole question of what the "political" means in the context of the school as an institution? The institutional question bears directly, I shall argue, on the current impasse at which the pluralist agenda is lodged, its vacillation between integrationist and separatist institutional strategies, between the incorporation of noncanonical works into the curriculum on the grounds that such works ought to be canonical, and the establishment of separate or alternative curricula of works which continue to be presented as "noncanonical" in relation to the traditional curriculum.

With respect to the latter alternative, it is relatively easy to see why it has seemed necessary to many progressive critics to present certain texts by minority authors as *intrinsically* noncanonical, as unassimilable to the traditional canon. The separatist strategy follows from the same basic assumption of pluralist canonical critique as the integrationist, that the process of the inclusion or exclusion of texts is identical to the representation or nonrepresentation of social groups. In the context of curricular revision, the category of the noncanonical loses its empty significance as merely the sum total of what is not included in the canon, and takes on a content specified by the contemporary critique: the noncanonical must be conceived as the *actively* excluded, the object of a historical repression. But paradoxically, the most surprising aspect of the current legitimation crisis is the fact that the "noncanonical" is not what fails to appear in the classroom, but what, in the context of liberal pedagogy, *signifies exclusion*. The noncanonical is a newly constituted category of text production and reception, permitting certain authors and texts to be *taught* as noncanonical, to have the status of noncanonical works in the classroom. This effect is quite different from the effect of total absence, of nonrepresentation *tout court*. What it means is that the social referents of inclusion and exclusion—the dominant or subordinate groups defined by race, gender, class, or national status—are now represented in the discourse of canon formation by two groups of authors and texts: the canonical and the noncanonical. It is only *as* canonical works that certain texts can be said to represent hegemonic social groups. Conversely, it is only *as* noncanonical works that certain other texts can truly represent socially subordinated groups. This fact must be grasped in order to understand why the critique of the canon has proceeded in recent years to reinstate at the level of institutional practice, of curriculum, the same opposition—between the canonical and the noncanonical— that its early agenda of "opening the canon" called into question.

If the objective of representation in the syllabus is the expression of an imaginary politics, this objective does not exhaust the agenda of the liberal pluralist critique. The sense in which a canonical author represents a dominant social group, or a noncanonical author a socially defined minority, is continuous with the sense in which the work is perceived to be immediately expressive of the author's *experience* as a representative member of some social group. The primacy of the social identity of the author in the pluralist critique of the canon means that the revaluation of works on this basis will inevitably seek its ground in the author's experience, conceived as the experience of a marginalized race, class, or gender identity. The author returns in the critique of the canon, not as the genius, but as the representative of a social identity. We scarcely need to be reminded of the fact that just as the first wave of theory called into question such categories as that of the author (along with notions of genius, tradition, etc.), much other contemporary theory calls the valorization of experience itself into question, in order to critique the very concept of representation. Laclau and Mouffe, for example, set out from the recognition that the coherent identity demanded by a practice assuming the perfect fit of identity and experience is in fact unavailable to anyone:

> there is no social identity fully protected from a discursive exterior that deforms
> it and prevents it becoming fully sutured. Both the identities and their relations
> lose their necessary character. As a systematic structural ensemble the relations
> are unable to absorb the identities; but as the identities are purely relational,
> this is but another way of saying that there is no identity which can be fully
> constituted.[14]

Such theoretical arguments (which evoke the vexed question of "essentialism") have surprisingly coexisted in the present debate with an otherwise incompatible rhetoric of canonical revision in which it is precisely the fit between the author's social identity and his or her experience that is seen to determine canonical or noncanonical status. The typical valorization of the noncanonical author's experience as a marginalized social identity necessarily reasserts the transparency of the text to the experience it represents.[15] If the practice of canonical revision cannot pause to indulge theoretical scruples about such assertions, its urgency betrays an apparently unavoidable discrepancy between theory and practice, an incapacity as yet to translate theory into political practice *at the site of institutional practices*. Hence the critique of the canon remains quite vulnerable to certain elementary theoretical objections, but this fact is itself symptomatic of a political dilemma generated by the very logic of liberal pluralism. It suggests that the category of social identity is too important politically to yield any ground to theoretical arguments which might complicate the status of representation in literary texts, for the simple reason that the latter mode of representation is *standing in for* representation in the political sphere. We must speak here (and perhaps generally in postmodern culture) of a certain displacement of the political which is the condition for the new politics of representation. Hence the *theory* of representation, and the *politics* of representation, have begun to move in quite different directions.

While we may readily acknowledge that the relation of theory to practice is never easy to specify, we may also wonder whether practice is really condemned to invoke theoretical assumptions so manifestly deficient as those which govern liberal pluralist practice, in its present incarnation as "identity politics." Consider, for example, the invocation of "race, class, and gender" as the categories which are supposed to explain the historical process of canon formation. It would be difficult to deny that the canon critique's assumption of the text's transparency to the race, gender, or class experience of the author has been instrumental in the short term, in that this assumption has served as the immediate basis for canonical revision; but the ubiquitous invocation of these categories of social identity continually defers their theoretical discrimination from each other on behalf of whatever political work is being done by pronouncing their names in the same breath as practice. But what work is that? What political work requires the deferral of theory, despite the fact that one must always gesture to some future, as yet unelaborated, analysis of the *relations* between race, class, or gender? It is not so much that such analyses are presently unavailable—in fact, they are[16]—but that in the context of canonical critique and revision they have no obvious application. In that context the equation of all minority writers as "non-canonical" brings their social identities into ontological correspondence, and equates their works as the expression of analogous experiences of marginalization. For the present, it would appear that there is much greater pressure to equate the social identities of minority authors than to distinguish them in a systemic analysis of the modes of domination specific to different social groups.

The telegraphic invocation of race/class/gender is the symptom of just the failure to develop a systemic analysis that would integrate the distinctions and nuances of social theory into the practice of canonical revision. We can indicate briefly here what is at stake in the difference between a Marxist/post-Marxist and a liberal critique of the canon by insisting upon the theoretical and practical incommensurability of the terms race, class, and gender: the modes of domination and exploitation specific to each of these socially defined minorities thus cannot be redressed by the *same* strategy of representation. It is by no means evident that the representation of blacks in the literary canon, for example, has quite the same social effects as the representation of women, precisely because the representation of blacks *in the university* is not commensurable with the representation of women. It remains difficult, if not impossible, within a pluralist critique to express the practical political implications of the fact that race and gender do not merely signify analogous experiences of marginalization but incommensurable modes of social identification.[17] Even within the category of race, socially constructed racial identities are as different as the modes of racism specific to the oppression of different races (and these modes are obviously very different). A politics presuming the ontological indifference of all minority social identities as defining oppressed or dominated groups, a politics in which differences are sublimated in the constitution of a minority identity (the identity politics which is increasingly being questioned within feminism itself)[18] can recover the differences between social identities only on the basis of common and therefore commensurable experiences of marginalization, which experiences in turn yield a political practice that consists largely of *affirming* the identities specific to those experiences. For this reason the differences or antagonisms that exist within and between dominated social groups tend to become the basis for the constitution of new social identities or subgroups, rather than the occasion for an analysis of the systemic nature of social antagonisms. This point has been made with particular persuasiveness by Peter Osborne, whose discussion of Laclau and Mouffe's version of identity politics is worth quoting at some length:

> Claiming an "identity" on the basis of the experience of a specific oppression is seen here as the ground for a wholly new kind of politics, for which the affirmation and validation of experiences of "difference" are at least as important as the analysis of the basis of oppression and its location within the perspective of a wider oppositional movement—if not more so. On this model, oppressed social identities are transformed *directly* into oppositional political identities through a celebration of difference which inverts the prevailing structure of value but leaves the structure of differences untouched.
>   . . . . the problem with [this] position is that it tends to reduce radical politics to the expression of oppressed subjectivities, and thereby to lead to the construction of moralistic, and often simply additive, "hierarchies of oppression," whereby the political significance attributed to the views of particular individuals is proportional to the sum of their oppressions. Such a tendency both positively encourages a fragmentation of political agency and harbours the danger of exacerbating conflicts between oppressed groups. It also makes group demands readily recuperable by the competitive interest-group politics of a liberal pluralism.[19]

Granted the theoretical perspicacity of Laclau and Mouffe's analysis of the category of social identity, that analysis, in Osborne's view, fails to produce anything like a practical politics; hence the gesture toward the coalition politics of "hegemony" provides no indication of any expressly *political* means for the formation of such coalitions and falls back upon the same practice of affirming discrete and autonomous social identities their own theory subjects to a definitive critique. In Osborne's formulation, such a politics "ends up *reducing* political to social identities."[20] This reservation is worth emphasizing, not because it vitiates every aspect of Laclau and Mouffe's theoretical argument, but because it calls attention to the symptomatic discrepancy between the theory of social identity and the practice of identity politics. If liberal pluralism has discovered that the cultural is always also the political (which it is), it has seldom escaped the trap of reducing the political to the cultural.[21] There is surely no more exemplary instance of this trajectory of pluralist critique than the canon debate, which remains preeminently an expression of identity politics.

The above argument may explain why a culturalist politics, though it glances worriedly at the phenomenon of class, has in practice never devised a politics that would arise from a class "identity." For while it is easy enough to conceive of a self-affirmative racial or sexual identity, it makes very little sense to posit an affirmative lower-class identity, as such an identity would have to be grounded in the experience of deprivation per se. Acknowledging the existence of admirable and even heroic elements of working-class culture, the *affirmation* of lower-class identity is hardly compatible with a program for the abolition of want. The incommensurability of the category of class with that of race or gender (class cannot be constructed as a social identity in the *same way* as race or gender because it is not, in the current affirmative sense, a "social identity" at all) does not, on the other hand, disenable a description of the relation between these social modalities. This was after all the problem sociology once addressed by means of the distinction between class and *status*. The current equation of gender, race, and class as commensurable minority identities effaces just this structural distinction.

The underlying theoretical problem here, one might speculate, is the result of an as yet unacknowledged theoretical slippage between the concepts of "subject" and "identity." While it is typical enough for current practice to use these terms interchangeably, it is worth recalling that the problematic of the subject derives from theoretical projects which were at the time of their inception (in the 1960s) explicitly Marxist or psychoanalytic. As these projects were assimilated into American liberal pluralist discourse, the problematic of the subject was more or less displaced by that of identity, or simply confused with that concept. This confusion is evident in the argument sometimes expressed within feminist thought, that theory's overthrow of the autonomous subject somehow conflicts with a feminist political practice. That overthrow might on the contrary have been the *basis* for such a practice. Without reprising at this point the various debates within the critique of the subject, we can say that the problematic of the subject always emphasized the complex formation of subject positions by unconscious processes or by impersonal forms of social structuration. The politics implied by such a theoretical problematic was always addressed to the exposure of these unconscious or structural modes of subject formation. The problematic of identity, on the other hand, insofar as it has developed a voluntarist politics of self-affirmation, has little use for the subject of Marxist or psychoanalytic theory. This is not to say that the latter theories do not continue to circulate alongside a liberal pluralist practice, but that their actual incompatibility with that practice tends to go unrecognized. The fact that identity politics is brought up short before the concept of class suggests the limit, in one direction, of the concept of identity, but it also argues for the urgency of theorizing the relation between subject and identity, since "identification" (whether affirmative, negative, or in Laclau and Mouffe's view, constitutively incomplete) belongs to the process of subject formation as one of its moments.[22]

Meanwhile, we may say that the incommensurability of different subject formations (and, likewise, the "experiences" of these subjects) is the condition for an accurate description of the systemic relations between race, class, and gender.

In the context of the present critique of the canon, the actual incommensurability of these categories as *author*-identities remains to be acknowledged. The fact of incommensurability explains why the revisionist critique of the canon has in practice been incapable of identifying "noncanonical" works by lower-class writers who are not already identified by race or gender. For how would such "identities" be registered as self-affirmative? The name of "D. H. Lawrence," for example, may signify in the discourse of canonical critique a white author or a European author, but it does not usually signify a writer whose origins are working-class. Within the discourse of liberal pluralism, with its voluntarist politics of self-affirmation, the category of class in the invocation of race/class/gender is likely to remain merely empty. But this fact only confirms that the critique of the canon does indeed belong to a liberal pluralist discourse, within which, as Gregor McLennan has pointed out, the category of class has been systematically repressed.[23]

Canon Revision or Research Program?

We are in a position now to make the even stronger claim that the category of "social identity" is entirely inadequate to explain how particular works become canonical in the first place, in a particular set of historical conditions. Let us approach this question first from its end point, from the canonical history currently being made in the classroom: What does it mean in the real conditions of institutional practice to open the syllabus of canonical works to works regarded as "noncanonical," that is, to works by authors belonging to socially defined minorities? I would suggest that the objective of canonical revision entails in practice shifting the weight of the syllabus from older works to *modern* works, since what is in question for us are *new* social identities and new writers. In fact, the history of the literary curriculum has always been characterized by a tendency to modernize the syllabus at the expense of older works. The "opening" of the classical curriculum to vernacular writing in the eighteenth-century primary-school system, in response to certain cultural demands of the nascent bourgeoisie, is one momentous example, ultimately responsible for displacing many Greek and Roman works from the curriculum altogether. Closer at hand, and slightly less momentous, are the generic modernizations of the canon, the inclusion of the novel in syllabi of the later nineteenth century, or film since the 1960s. By defining canonicity as determined by the social identity of the author, the current critique of the canon both discovers, and misrepresents, the obvious fact that the older the literature, the less likely it will be that texts by socially defined minorities exist in sufficient numbers to produce a "representative" canon. Yet the historical reasons for this fact are insufficiently acknowledged for their theoretical and practical implications. The reason more women authors, for example, are not represented in older literatures is not primarily that their works were routinely excluded by invidious or prejudicial standards of evaluation, "excluded" as a consequence of their social identity as women. The historical reason is that, with few exceptions before the eighteenth century, women were routinely excluded from *access to literacy,* or were proscribed from composition or publication in the genres considered to be serious rather than ephemeral. If current research has recovered a number of otherwise forgotten women writers from the period before the eighteenth century, this fact is not directly related to canon formation as a process of selection or exclusion on the basis of social identity, but to the present institutional context of a valid and interesting *research program* whose subject is the history of women writers and writing. No other defense is required for studying these writers than the aims of the research program (and these could well be *political* aims). It is not necessary to claim canonical status for noncanonical works in order to justify their study, as the archive has always been the resource of historical scholarship. If the feminist research program has recovered from the archives the works of a number of women writers now all but forgotten, such as Lady Mary Wroth or Katherine Philips, it must also be borne in mind that the archives preserve (and bury) hundreds and thousands of writers, of various social origins and identities. The question for us, in reconsidering the rhetoric of canon revision, is why any particular noncanonical author discovered by a research program has to be presented as *excluded* from the canon. The hypothesis of exclusion has more to do with a misrecognition of the political work accomplished by the research program than with any actual historical circumstances of judgment.[24] But this misrecognition itself has certain political consequences, since it effaces the historical significance of literacy in the history of writers and writing.

The social conditions governing access to literacy before the emergence of the middle-class educational system determined that the greater number of writers, *canonical or noncanonical,* were men. The number of canonical texts represents in turn only the minutest percentage of these works, and the body of canonical authors could never in that case have reflected the actual social diversity of their times or places—not even, it might be added, in the case of women writers of the early modern period, who were literate by and large as a consequence of being aristocratic.[25] The retroconstruction of early modern women writers as expressing the marginalized experience of women in general, as though the difference between an aristocratic woman and a peasant were indifferent, is thus only the obverse of the error identifying the writings of these women as excluded from the canon merely as a consequence of the fact that they were written by women. If much feminist theory now problematizes the category of "woman" itself, what theoretical inhibition disallows the problematization of the "woman writer" in the canon debate?[26]

One might nevertheless want to object here that even if the most socially consequential process of exclusion occurs primarily at the level of access to literacy, it might still be the case that canon formation functions to exclude works by minority writers who do manage to acquire the means of literary production. For reasons I shall now indicate, even this qualified hypothesis is in crucial ways inaccurate. It is without question true that some past writers have suffered an undeserved oblivion; indeed the history of canon formation offers many examples of writers rediscovered after periods of obscurity. What seems dubious in historical context is that such cases can be *generally* explained by invoking the categories of race, class, or gender as the immediate criteria of inclusion or exclusion. These categories might well explain at the present time why some writers have been recovered from the archive, but not necessarily why they ceased to be read. Nor does the circumstance of their being read now mean that they have become canonical—only that they are read now.

Let us consider once again the category of gender as a hypothetical criterion for exclusion from the canon: The existence of canonical women authors, even before the revisionary movement of the last decade, invalidates in strictly logical terms the category of gender as a *general* criterion of exclusion; which is to say that in the case of an excluded woman author, it will not be sufficient merely to invoke the category of gender in order to explain the lack of canonical status. The principle that explains the exclusion of Harriet Beecher Stowe from the canon on the basis of gender cannot really account for the complexity of the historical circumstances governing the reception of Stowe's work, for the same reason that it cannot account for the counterexample of Jane Austen's canonical status. This is not to say that the category of gender is not a *factor* in the subsequent reputation of Stowe, or of any woman author. We can expect that many factors will enter into the situation of the reception of a given author's work, and that these factors will advance and recede at different moments in the history of the work's reception. This point can be briefly underscored by citing the famous opening sentence of F. R. Leavis's *The Great Tradition*, whose canonical intentions are entirely explicit: "The great English novelists are Jane Austen, George Eliot, Henry James and Joseph Conrad—to stop for the moment at that comparatively safe point in history."[27] Leavis seems not to be thinking of gender at all in pronouncing his canonical judgments. His project rather has to do, as readers of Leavis know, with defining a High Cultural novelistic canon in opposition to the depredations of what he sees as the emergence concurrently of modern mass culture and the novel (his canonical list excludes Dickens on the grounds of his mass cultural affiliations, despite his "great genius"). We can hardly attribute the apparently equal representation of men and women authors in Leavis's novelistic canon to the absence of bias, much less to any feminist sympathies. The point of the example is that the historical process of canon formation, even or especially at the moment of institutional judgment, is too complex to be reduced to determination by the single factor of the social identity of the author.

If the social identity of the author appears to us now as the condition of canonicity or noncanonicity, this is as much as to say that the categories of race and gender are contemporary conditions of canon formation; they are historically specific. These categories will not bind future critics either to the canonical choices of the present or to the categories of liberal pluralist critique. Social identities are themselves historically constructed; they mean different things at different historical moments, and thus the relation of different social groups to such cultural entitlements as literacy will be differently constructed at different times. Acknowledging the conditional force of literacy in the history of canon formation would thus disallow us from ever assuming that the field of writing is a kind of *plenum*, a textual repetition of social diversity, where everyone has access to the means of literary production and works ask only to be judged fairly. The fact that the field of writing is not such a *plenum* is a social fact but also an *institutional* fact. Linda Nochlin arrives at much the same conclusion in rejecting the premise of the question, "Why are there no great women artists?" The answer to this question lies not in the supposition that there must exist many unjustly forgotten great women artists but in reckoning the social consequences for women of "our institutions and our education."[28] An "institutional" fact such as literacy has everything to do with the relation of "exclusion" to social identity; but exclusion should be defined not as exclusion from representation but from access to the *means of cultural production*. I will define literacy accordingly throughout this book not simply as the capacity to read but as the *systematic regulation of reading and writing*, a complex social phenomenon corresponding to the following set of questions: Who reads? What do they read? How do they read? In what social and institutional circumstances? Who writes? In what social and institutional contexts? For whom?[29]

The question of literacy foregrounds what is at stake in the difference between a pluralist and a Marxist/post-Marxist conception of canon formation: for literacy is a question of the distribution of cultural goods rather than of the representation of cultural images.[30] From the point of view of such a materialist critique, it would seem that pluralism can only apprehend the history of canon formation as a history of consumption, the history of the judgment of cultural products. But if the socially unrepresentative content of the canon really has to do in the first place with how access to the means of literary production is socially regulated, a different history of canon formation will be necessary, one in which social identities are historical categories determined as much by the system of production as by consumption. The present tendency to restrict canonical critique to the reception of images attests to the absence of any theoretical understanding of the relation between a real historical silence—exclusion from the means of literary production—and the sphere of reception, in this case, the university. What becomes visible there is an immense collection of works, among which only a few can be "canonical," selected from inclusion within the curriculum of literary study. A critique which is confined to the level of consumption must necessarily misrepresent the historicity of literary production, the systemic effects of the *educational system* in the determination of who writes and who reads, as well as what gets read, and in what contexts. The educational institution performs the social function of systematically regulating the practices of reading and writing by governing access to the means of literary production as well as to the means of consumption (the knowledge required to read historical works). Nothing confirms the failure to ground the critique of the canon in a systemic analysis of the educational system more than the failure to reflect upon the most salient fact of the canon debate, its locus in the university. No one speaks there of the relation between canonical revision and the primary levels of the educational system, where for a much larger part of the population the content of the university curriculum is simply irrelevant. If literacy is a problem of the distribution of cultural resources, this problem is very much larger than the problem addressed by a politics of "representation in the canon."

Canonical and Noncanonical Values

In recent years the distinction between canonical and noncanonical works has been invoked to organize the curriculum in a new way, by institutionalizing that distinction in distinct syllabi. It would be difficult to overestimate the significance of this second phase of canonical critique, since it discovered a new project of representation for the curriculum. While the category of social identity continued to be employed to account for the historical lack of representation in the canon, it was no longer necessary to rectify that circumstance solely by the strategy of inclusion. In the second phase of canonical critique, the curriculum became representative in another sense, by reflecting the *actual* division of the social order into dominant and dominated social groups, each now represented by its own syllabus of works. In this context of representation, the "values" according to which works were canonized could themselves be called into question or declared to be simply incommensurable with the "values" embodied in subordinate cultures. This phase of canonical critique was raised to the level of theory in Barbara Herrnstein Smith's *Contingencies of Value*, which argues that works cannot become canonical unless they are seen to endorse the hegemonic or ideological values of dominant social groups:

> since those with cultural power tend to be members of socially, economically, and politically established classes . . . the texts that survive will tend to be those that appear to reflect and reinforce establishment ideologies. . . . they would not be found to please long and well if they were seen *radically* to undercut establishment interests, or *effectively* to subvert the ideologies that support them.[31]

Conversely, noncanonical works can be seen to express values which are transgressive, subversive, antihegemonic. While it would be easy enough to demonstrate that most historically noncanonical works are not characterized by any such political effectivity, we need to remember that the critique of the canon was never concerned with most noncanonical works, only with those works already marked by the socially defined minority identity of their authors. If one can successfully extend the critique of the canon from the category of social identity to the category of *cultural value,* then it would indeed follow that the inclusion of the noncanonical works in the canon misrepresents the social significance of the canon by failing to recognize it as the inevitable embodiment of hegemonic cultural values. On this account canonical and noncanonical works are by definition mutually exclusive; they confront each other in an internally divided curriculum in the same way that hegemonic culture confronts nonhegemonic subcultures in the larger social order.

The canon debate has given rise in recent years to a general critique of values, particularly "aesthetic" value, on grounds both philosophical and sociopolitical, a critique well exemplified by Herrnstein Smith's neorelativist position; but I should like to postpone until a later chapter a full consideration of that theoretical by-product of the debate, since what is at issue in the reassertion of cultural "relativism" is the very possibility of a specifically aesthetic value. It will not be necessary here either to dismiss or to defend that possibility in order to register a large reservation about the mapping of the distinction between canonical and noncanonical texts onto specific cultures and their values. It will suffice to open the terrain of this reservation to note a certain peculiar convergence in the characterization of the canon in the rhetoric of both progressive critique and reactionary defense. Here, for example, is the egregious William Bennett, whose polemics in the 1980s as director of the NEH, and later as secretary of education, popularized the revanchist reaction to curricular revision:

> For some 15 to 20 years now there had been a serious degree of embarrassment, of distancing, even of repudiation of that culture on the part of many of the people whose responsibility, one would think, is to transmit it. Many people in our colleges and universities aren't comfortable with the ideals of Western civilization.
>
> Bennett stands up and says, "You know, I really think people should be familiar with Homer and Shakespeare and George Eliot and Jane Austen," and they say, "We don't do that anymore. Why should we have to do that?" All right, if the purpose of the institution is not to transmit that culture, then what is the institution's purpose?[32]

Such remarks, presented more formally in the NEH publication "To Reclaim a Legacy," have been widely provoking, but not because Bennett's conception of what constitutes cultural value has itself been contested. On the contrary, pluralist critics of the canon would agree that canonical works do represent the "ideals of Western civilization," and that these ideals or values constitute a "culture." Whether Homer, Shakespeare, Eliot, and Austen actually express in some homogeneous way a culture of "Western civilization" is not in question on either side of the debate.

In this circumstance it has become surprisingly difficult to define a progressive political rationale for the teaching of canonical texts. Leaving aside the option of not teaching them at all (an entirely logical alternative, if the teaching of canonical texts actually disseminates hegemonic values), progressively inclined teachers of these texts must reground the politics of their pedagogy on assumptions that are themselves theoretically weak. Hence it might seem necessary to assume that a politically progressive reading will consist of *exposing* the hegemonic values of canonical works. Whenever liberal pluralist critique slides into such a characterization of its object, we can say that it has found its way back to what was once considered to be a "vulgar" Marxism; but the more important point is that such a rediscovery of "reflection theory" is determined by the internal logic of pluralism itself, by its theory of representation as reflection, as image.

Just as weak theoretically is the liberal position that claims for canonical texts an intrinsic subversiveness, that discovers in the intrinsically "liberating" effect of these texts the reason of their canonicity.[33] The deficiency of this compromise with the rhetoric of canonical critique is apparent as soon as its genealogical relation to the liberalism of the old bourgeoisie is revealed. For that apparently egalitarian ideology was always implicitly "elitist," in the sense that it divided the population into those who were capable of being so liberated and those who were not. Thus the defense of the canon on these grounds will inevitably resurrect the charge of elitism, as the bad conscience of its own bad theory, as in the following statement: "If we are alert to these elements of freedom in the canon of great literature, the charge of elitism will be less destructive of cultural values, and we will not have to stand mute before claims that inarticulateness, ignorance, occult mumbling, and loutishness are just as good as fine literature."[34] The latter author fears becoming what he has been made to behold: the condition of muteness is nothing other than exclusion from literary *production*. But why should the coming-into-writing of those formerly excluded from the means of literary production be experienced as the degeneration of cultural values? Or, on the other hand, why must the writing of minority authors be considered *intrinsically* subversive, as the overturning of supposedly hegemonic values represented by Homer or Shakespeare? These alternatives are only enjoined upon us by the supposition that canonical works can be characterized politically in some universal way, as either progressive or regressive in their social effects.

The virtual agreement of the progressive and the reactionary participants in the canon debate about the relation between culture and value suggests that the positions of these antagonists are more complexly interrelated than a narrative of hegemony and resistance would imply. We will have to say rather that the two positions are mutually constitutive, and even more that they both fall well within the normative assumptions of American political culture, even within the normative principles of liberal pluralism. (It is important to remember in this context that even the reactionary defenders of the canon are scrupulous to "include" token minority works in their conception of "Western civilization").[35] Here I would like to consider briefly three propositions about cultural value to which both progressive and reactionary critics would presumably assent, in order to demonstrate that these propositions are questionable, on whatever side of the debate they happen to be argued.

1. *Canonical texts are the repositories of cultural values.* The equation of the values expressed in a work with the value *of* the work is assumed by both the revanchists and the revisionists when they conceive literary texts as the means of transmitting specific values in the classroom. It is certainly the case that at the primary levels of the educational system "values" are simply decanted from carefully chosen texts which are not always the same texts taught at higher levels. In the stratosphere of pluralist pedagogy, the same reified values are often exposed and ritually qualified, subverted, or rejected, as though the work were simply the container of such values. What fails to be noted about this institutional arrangement is that the pedagogic relation between value and the literary work is very much keyed to the level of the educational system. At the level of the graduate school and the professional conference, the educational capital specific to that level can be signalled by a certain refusal of the rhetoric of "great works" characteristic of the lower levels of the system. Hence Michael Ryan, commenting on the surprising number of sessions at the 1984 MLA convention critical of the canonical epic tradition, can present the thesis that the epic is "a renowned bastion of male self-aggrandizement" as merely the consensus of these sessions.[36] Yet, as I hope to demonstrate more fully at a later point in this argument, the meaning of patriarchal or misogynist values, in contradistinction to "Homeric"

values, is enormously attenuated when spread over thousands of years and dozens of social formations. "Homeric values" are not transmitted to students any more than Homer expresses immediately the "ideals of Western civilization." The latter ideals are specific to individual social formations, to successive ideologies of tradition, and they are expressed in determinate social conditions of reading. These conditions are of course pedagogic, but it is a measure of the theoretical deficiency of the canon critique that "values" transmitted in the classroom can simply be conflated with the contents of historical works.[37]

2. *The selection of texts is the selection of values.* Within the world of reified and ahistorical values, aesthetic value confronts the reader, the consumer of values, as just another value, not in any conceivable way more important than the value of justice or social equality. Thus Lillian Robinson writes of the feminist critique of the canon: "At its angriest, none of this reinterpretation offers a fundamental challenge to the canon *as canon;* although it posits new values, it never suggests that, in the light of those values, we ought to reconsider whether the great monuments are really so great, after all."[38] The desirability of such a reconsideration is hinted by Nina Baym, on behalf of a version of feminist criticism operating vigorously in the last two decades in the field of canon revision: "it is time perhaps . . . to reexamine the grounds upon which certain hallowed American classics have been called great."[39] The distinction between masculine and feminine values has been relatively easy to superimpose upon the field of writing, especially as women writers in the modern European languages emerged earlier than writers of other minority groups. There is accordingly a larger body of writing by women to organize in alternative canonical form, and in such a way as to confirm the alignment of canonical and noncanonical texts with hegemonic and anti-hegemonic values.

The entrance of women into literary culture, however, is not a simple transition to an unambiguous literacy, as though writing were the neutral medium for the conveyance of gendered values. To acknowledge only the most conspicuous complication of the transition, for example, one might invoke, as does Myra Jehlen in her critique of Nina Baym, the historical relation between writing by women and the division of public writing into "serious" and "popular" genres; for Jehlen this is a question of women's "relationship to writing as such."[40] The distinction between serious and popular writing is a condition of canonicity; it belongs to the history of literacy, of the systematic regulation of reading and writing, as the adaptation of that system's regulatory procedures to social conditions in which the practice of writing is no longer confined to a scribal class. The explosion of popular writing in the eighteenth century was an effect of the fact that writing itself was becoming "popular." Thus the generic category of the popular continues to bear the stigma of nonwriting, of mere orality, within writing itself, since popular works are consumed, from the point of view of High Culture, as the textual simulacra of ephemeral speech. This is not to say anything of the actual importance of popular writing, of its multiple social effects, or of why one may wish to read it or study it. It should also be stressed that the distinction between serious and popular is a far less stable mechanism for enforcing social stratification than the sexual hierarchy itself, and it thus permits (because it cannot always prevent) the production of "serious" works by strategically placed members of groups to whom it means to assign devalorized textual practices—a contradiction marking the history of writing by women as the relation between their writing and the novel, itself a noncanonical genre until the end of the nineteenth century. The canonization of novels written by women was thus conditional upon the legitimation of the novel form, the canonization of a popular genre.

Considerably more would need to be said here in order to give even a brief creditable account of hierarchizing procedures within the field of writing and their complex relation to social stratification; but the above remarks should indicate at the least how unhistorical it is to claim, as Jane Tompkins does in *Sensational Designs: The Cultural Work of American Fiction,* that popular fiction "has been rigorously excluded from the ranks of 'serious' literary works,"[41] as though the two categories did not define *each other* in a system of literary production. Or to claim that the evaluation of popular writing by women can be subjected to a canonical reversal simply by revaluing the values expressed in these works: "My own embrace of the conventional led me to value everything that criticism taught me to despise" (xvi). Tompkins's project of "reconstituting the notion of value in literary works" dissolves the aesthetic, in a gesture now foundational in the critique of canon formation, by substituting for it a pseudo-historicism disguising the fact that the values being "revalued" are very simply *contemporary* values: "Instead of asking whether a work is unified or discontinuous, subtle, complex, or profound, one wants to know, first, whether it was successful in achieving its aims; and second, whether its aims were good or bad" (xvii). Hence the assertion that Susan Warner and Harriet Beecher Stowe offer "in certain cases a critique of American society far more devastating than any delivered by better-known critics such as Hawthorne and Melville" is defended not on the basis of a symptomatic reading of their texts in historical context, but on explicitly moral grounds, namely the affirmation of such values as the "sanctity of motherhood and the family" or "the saving power of Christian love" (145). If one demurs at endorsing these values, one need not look beneath this ground of value for a mythical elephant or tortoise, a fact perhaps not interesting with respect to the values in question but immediately indicative that values in this context always mean *moral* values.

The reversion to moralism is determined by the equation of text-selection with value-selection. For this reason much of what passes for political analysis of historically canonical works is nothing more than the passing of moral judgment on them. The critique of the canon moves quickly to reassert absolute notions of good and evil; the overturning of Kant's autonomous aesthetic is brought up short before Nietzsche's critique of morality. One need only compare Tompkins's theory of canon formation with Hans Robert Jauss's equally revisionary concept of "horizontal change" to see that a fall into moralism will occur regardless of what values are set against the category of the aesthetic. Tompkins argues that the "text succeeds or fails on the basis of the 'fit' with features of its immediate context, on the degree to which it provokes the desired response, and not in relation to unchanging formal, psychological, or philosophical standards of complexity, or truth, or correctness" (xviii). Her statement yields a spectacular but in the end illusory contrast to Jauss's historicization of literary tradition:

> The distance between the horizon of expectations and the work, between the familiarity of previous aesthetic experience and the "horizonal change" demanded by reception of the new work, determines the artistic character of a literary work, according to an aesthetics of reception: to the degree that this distance decreases, and no turn toward the horizon of yet-unknown experience is demanded of this receiving consciousness, the closer the work comes to the sphere of "culinary" or entertainment art.[42]

The difference between Jauss and Tompkins disappears entirely when Jauss comes to define how it is that a work can frustrate the expectations of its initial readers. The formal innovation Jauss admires rather more than Tompkins (his example is Flaubert's *style indirect libre*, valued over the conventionality of Feydeau) is finally only the vehicle for the introduction of new moral values, which may be "immoral" from the standpoint of the old: "If one looks at the moments in history when literary works toppled the taboos of the ruling morals or offered readers new solutions for the moral casuistry of his lived praxis, which thereafter could be sanctioned by the consensus of all readers in the society, then a still little-studied area of research opens itself up to the literary historian" (454). Whatever pleasure is produced by *style indirect libre,* or style as such, is thoroughly chastened in this Whiggish history of "the competitive relationship between literature and canonized morals." If Jauss's theory can then be used to *devalue* the same popular works Tompkins desires to revalue as the embodiment of excluded, counterhegemonic values, this paradox has less to do with any absolute difference between these two critics than with the inadequacy of reductively moralistic theories to account for the process of canon formation.

3. *Value must be either intrinsic or extrinsic to the work.* As we have just noted, the Kantian aesthetic is distantly engaged in the critique of canon formation by the argument that value is not intrinsic but rather relative, contingent, subjective, contextual, or, in other words, extrinsic. The distinction between intrinsic and extrinsic value accords well at the level of pluralist theory with a historical narrative of inclusion or exclusion. According to that narrative, the canonical judgments of dominant groups have been typically justified by an appeal to transcendent norms of judgment, as though history itself were the judge of works, or as though individuals could really transcend the conditions of their specific judgments. Yet the exploding of such fictions of intrinsic, universal, or transcendent value, which was a nec-

essary means of recovering a sense of the historicity of judgment, does not necessarily clarify the actual circumstances in which judgments are made and have effect. Further, the strategy of exposing intrinsic value as simply extrinsic has the curious effect of disabling at the outset any project of revaluation, where the object revalued is the work, and not (as in Tompkins) other extrinsic (moral) values. In the case of devalued or forgotten works, revaluation typically appeals to the "real" value or quality of the work; nothing other than a strong assertion of such value is likely to succeed in the actual institutional circumstances of canonical revision. Recently it has been possible to argue that the process of valuation is grounded in the consensus of a particular community where, for the members of such a community, such values function as though they were absolute. On this account values are indeed extrinsic to the work but they are at the same time intrinsic or internal to what Stanley Fish calls, in the most prominent version of this argument, an "interpretive community."[43] Hence it is only in the *absence* of consensus that a distinction between intrinsic and extrinsic value need arise at all with reference to particular works. Elizabeth Meese discovers the answer to the vexing question of "the failure of so many feminist commentaries aimed at demonstrating the stature of neglected works by women" in Fish's unapologetic observation that "the act of recognizing literature . . . proceeds from a collective decision as to what will count as literature, a decision that will be in force only so long as a community of readers and believers continues to abide by it."[44] Such an argument implies that a different community of readers—women readers, for example—will very likely express different values by valuing different works, that is, by positing a different canon of "literature." Having faced the fact that judgments cannot be reconciled under a universal norm of value, or by a surreptitious appeal to a transcendent court of judgment, advocates of this theory need no longer be troubled by the distinction between intrinsic and extrinsic value: judgment can always be grounded in some community or other.[45]

One can see in retrospect that the formulation of such notions as that of the "interpretive community" provided an early theoretical justification for the separatist phase of canon critique, since it is only necessary to claim that the university is host to more than one "interpretive community" in order to justify the institutionalization of different canons—canons of the noncanonical. One consensus is achieved by any "community of readers," however, that community enters into what looks like a state of mass delusion, in which valuation can proceed without reference to any constraints imposed by the social function of the school itself or by the difficulty of constituting a community sufficiently homogeneous in its interests or identity to operate by consensus. Hence those who dissent from a given consensus are compelled either to fall back upon assertions of the innate value of the cultural products they value or to constitute themselves as another distinct "community of readers"—a sequence of action and reaction repeatedly characterizing the canon debate. Shall we not say in this circumstance that "consensus" has the same relation to value within a particular "interpretive community" as the notion of transcendent value once had for a "community of readers" which imagined itself to be the only such community? But one only has to consider the fact that value judgments can and do come into conflict *within* an interpretive community in order to call into question the notion of consensus as the name for how judgments achieve canonizing force. Literary culture in general, and the university in particular, are by no means structurally organized to express the consensus of a community; these social and institutional sites are complex hierarchies in which the position and privilege of judgment are objects of competitive struggles.

The problem of value is scarcely resolved by recourse to the notion of the community as its hypothetical ground. On the contrary, consensus is the pleasant ideological shift by which social determinations are mystified as "collective decisions" that are finally only the sum of individual decisions. In this polity texts confront readers in an artificial social vacuum like the space of the voting booth, behind the curtain of private judgment. Disagreements about value within such a pseudodemocracy are comfortably absorbed in a continuous plebiscite within which even the coming to power of the loyal opposition changes nothing structurally, since there is no theoretical limit to the number of "interpretive communities," and since each one believes itself to function in exactly the same way, by consensus. The democratic metaphor is quite potent here, since the conflation of judgment with a kind of election betrays the fact that the terms of the canon debate are entirely determined by the basic assumptions of liberal pluralism.[46] This is why the critique of the canon has always constructed the history of canon formation as a conspiracy of judgment, a secret and exclusive ballot by which literary works are chosen for canonization because their authors belong to the same social group as the judges themselves, or because these works express the values of the dominant group.[47] The poverty of this historical reconstruction determines the limits of the response to it—the notion that dominated groups must choose their own canonical works by a kind of pseudoelection or "consensus." If the process of judgment is more complicated than the electoral analogy suggests, this model of canon formation will have to be discarded. While the selection of texts for preservation certainly does presuppose acts of judgment, which are indeed complex psychic and social events subject to many kinds of determination, these acts are necessary rather than sufficient to constitute a process of canon formation. An individual's judgment that a work is great does nothing in itself to preserve that work, unless that judgment is made in a certain institutional context, a setting in which it is possible to insure the *reproduction* of the work, its continual reintroduction to generations of readers. The work of preservation has other, more complex social contexts than the immediate responses of readers, even communities of readers, to texts; as we shall see, these institutional contexts shape and constrain judgments according to *institutional* agendas, and in such a way that the selection of texts never represents merely the consensus of a community of readers, either dominant or subordinate. The scene in which a group of readers, defined by a common social identity and common values, confronts a group of texts with the intention of making a judgment as to canonicity, is an *imaginary* scene. That imaginary scene must now be set against what happens in a real place, the school.

___

Notes

1. See, for example, Allan Bloom, *The Closing of the American Mind* (New York: Simon and Schuster, 1987); Roger Kimball, *Tenured Radicals: How Politics Has Corrupted Our Higher Education* (New York: Harper and Row, 1990); Dinesh D'Souza, *Illiberal Education: The Politics of Race and Sex on Campus* (New York: The Free Press, 1991); and Alvin Kernan, *The Death of Literature* (New Haven: Yale University Press, 1990). These texts have provided the popular media with the handful of arguments and anecdotes with which it has prosecuted the case against the liberal academy, in articles now too numerous to list. E. D. Hirsch, Jr.'s *Cultural Literacy: What Every American Needs to Know* (New York: Houghton Mifflin, 1987) is often cited in association with this backlash, although its agenda is rather more complicated than that of the texts mentioned above. See pages 35–36 below.
2. Gregor McLennan, *Marxism, Pluralism, and Beyond* (Cambridge, Mass.: Polity Press in association with Basil Blackwell, 1989), 18.
3. As McLennan remarks, in ibid., "[W]hen the state is brought into this picture of competing, exchanging groups, the polity is represented as driven by a tendency to equilibrium, one in which the 'preferences' of interest groups can be expressed and to a large extent satisfied" (22).
4. The phenomenon of "political correctness," recently the object of so much complaint in the right-wing media, can be seen in this context as the paradoxical triumph in the university of an otherwise defeated liberalism. It is not surprising that a progressive discourse, more or less routed in American culture, should find itself driven to police the borders of its diminished territory. As everyone on the left knows, the concept of political correctness was formulated within left discourse itself to critique the tendency to moralistic posturing provoked by the dire situation of an increasingly reactionary social order. The usefulness of that concept is certainly at an end, but one may continue to speak of "identity politics" or what I would call "radical liberalism," a specific style of political discourse and practice distinct from the historical forms of socialism and Marxism. The argument of this chapter with liberalism, both traditional and radical, is not with any of its progressive objectives, but with those assumptions of its theory and practice which, because they are uncritically shared with American political culture in general, have disabled an effective response to the resurgence of reactionary politics. Taking the long view historically, there is considerable evidence for arguing that "identity politics" *is* now American politics, and that what we call identity politics exists on the same continuum of "interest-group" politics with positions that are manifestly conservative or reactionary. Identity politics makes no conceptual break as a *politics* with its precursors, even in its radical forms. I do not doubt that to those who are traumatized by the demise of liberalism, the alternative of a class-critique will seem even more quixotic; but it seems to me that it is in just this circumstance that a mode of systemic analysis recommends itself, and that certain foreclosed truths may become visible once again.
5. The emergence of this topos into institutional prominence is marked by the publication of *English Literature: Opening Up the Canon*, selected papers from the English

Institute, ed. Leslie Fiedler and Houston Baker (Baltimore: Johns Hopkins University Press, 1981). See also Paul Lauter, "History and the Canon," *Social Text* 12 (Fall 1985), 94–101, and William Cain, *Crisis in Criticism: Theory, Literature and Reform in English Studies* (Baltimore: Johns Hopkins University Press, 1984). Among feminist critiques of the canon are the following (others will be cited at later points in the chapter): Lillian Robinson, "Treason Our Text: Feminist Challenges to the Literary Canon," in *Critical Theory since 1965,* ed. Hazard Adams and Leroy Searle (Tallahassee: Florida State University Press), 572–85; Deborah Rosenfelt, "The Politics of Bibliography: Women's Studies and the Literary Canon," in *Women in Print,* ed. Joan Hartman and Ellen Messer-Davidow (New York: Modern Language Association, 1982), 11–31; Florence Howe, "Those We Still Don't Read," *College English* 43 (January 1981), 12–16. Howe writes: "What do we want? Nothing less than the transformation of the literary curriculum and the revision of critical theory and literary history that such a transformation would require" (16). See also Christine Froula, "When Eve Reads Milton: Undoing the Canonical Economy," *Critical Inquiry* 10 (December 1983), 321–48, and Adrienne Munich, "Notorious Signs, Feminist Criticism, and Literary Tradition," in *Making a Difference: Feminist Literary Criticism,* ed. Gayle Greene and Coppelia Kahn (London: Methuen 1985), 238–59.

6. *Marxism, Pluralism, and Beyond,* 33.

7. See Ernesto Laclau and Chantal Mouffe, *Hegemony and Socialist Strategy: Towards a Radical Democratic Politics* (London: Verso, 1985). Also interesting in this context, and perhaps neglected by literary postmodernists, is the work of Samuel Bowles and Herbert Gintis, particularly their *Democracy and Capitalism: Property, Community, and the Contradictions of Modern Social Thought* (New York: Basic Books, 1986). Because Bowles and Gintis, unlike Laclau and Mouffe, are writing in response to an indigenous liberal tradition, they tend to emphasize the necessity for socializing the economy at the same time that it is democratized. Laclau and Mouffe do not disagree, but the very intimacy of their struggle with the Continental Marxist tradition, and the consequent vehemence of their post-Marxism, has had the unfortunate effect of underemphasizing for American readers the socialist commitments they also claim as their own.

8. Basic statements of Bourdieu's theory of cultural capital may be found in his *Reproduction in Education, Society and Culture,* trans. Richard Nice (London: Sage Publications, 1977); "The Market of Symbolic Goods," *Poetics* 14 (1985), 13–44; *Outline of a Theory of Practice,* trans. Richard Nice (Cambridge: Cambridge University Press, 1977); "The Production of Belief: Contribution to an Economy of Symbolic Goods," trans. Richard Nice, *Media, Culture and Society* 2, no 3. (1980), 261–93; *Distinction: A Social Critique of the Judgment of Taste,* trans. Richard Nice (Cambridge: Harvard University Press, 1984); "The Field of Cultural Production or: the Economic World Reversed," trans. Richard Nice, *Poetics* 12 (1983), 331–56; *The Logic of Practice,* trans. Richard Nice (Stanford: Stanford University Press, 1990); *In Other Words: Essays towards a Reflexive Sociology,* trans. Matthew Adamson (Stanford: Stanford University Press, 1990).

9. Rudolph Pfeiffer notes in his *History of Classical Scholarship from the Beginning to the End of the Hellenistic Age* (Oxford: Oxford University Press, 1968), that the analogy between the classics and the scriptural canon makes its first appearance in the work of the German philologist David Rühnken, in 1768. As late as Frank Kermode's *The Classic: Literary Images of Permanence and Change* (London: Viking Press, 1975), it was still possible to discuss what we call canon formation exclusively by reference to the word "classic."

10. Henry Louis Gates, Jr., "The Master's Pieces: On Canon Formation and the African-American Tradition," *South Atlantic Quarterly* 89 (1990), 105. Elsewhere, it should be noted, Gates has produced very effective critique of certain aspects of the "representation" view of canon formation, among them the fetishizing of authenticity and individual experience. For a more complete view of the complex evolution of Gate's thinking on the subject of the canon, see his *Loose Canons: Notes on the Culture Wars* (New York: Oxford University Press, 1992).

11. In this context, see David Harvey, "Flexibility: Threat or Opportunity?" in *Socialist Review* 21 (1991), 74: "The postmodern embrace of ephemeral images, spectacle-type events, 'invented' traditions and heritages of all sorts, and perpetual novelty in the realm of cultural production deserves to be understood. . . . In recent years the cultural mass has pursued a whole host of political and ideological struggles that have general significance: anti-racism, feminism, and struggles concerning ethnic identity, religious tolerance, cultural decolonization, and the like. Because postmodernism is associated with a democratization of voice within the cultural mass, many of the struggles against a central source of authority and power (white, male, elitist, and Protestant, for example) have enlisted under the postmodern banner. I think it is fair to say that efforts to counter various forms of gender, racial, ethnic, or religious oppression have been more successful within the cultural mass than in many other segments of society. The problem is that these fights are being waged within a relatively homogeneous class context, where issues of class oppression, though always on the agenda for political reasons, are by no means as strongly and personally felt as they would be among, say, women factory workers in the Philippines or Mexico." Harvey's understanding of the socioeconomic forces driving postmodern culture leads him to a thoroughgoing skepticism about the "ideological struggles" of the newly constituted cultural minorities. While I do not share the degree of Harvey's skepticism about the political significance of these struggles, there is a sense in which we might see the critique of the canon in the context of the new social movements as the latest version of a kind of left Hegelianism. The idealism of this critique consists in the belief that in order to change the world it is only necessary to change our image of the world. This is a question not of the reality of images but of the virtual absence of economic or class analysis in liberal pluralist theory. The absence of such analysis permits First World pluralists to construe the question of postcolonialism, for example, primarily as one of rehabilitating our images of the native cultures and identities of postcolonial populations, a program that does not begin to address the steadily worsening effects of what Immanuel Wallerstein has called the "capitalist world-system." See also Harvey's *The Condition of Postmodernity: An Enquiry into the Origins of Cultural Change* (London: Basil Blackwell, 1980); also Immanuel Wallerstein, *Geopolitics and Geoculture: Essays on the Changing World-System* (Cambridge: Cambridge University Press, 1991).

12. We are very far from being able to give a good account of the effects of images even within mass culture; this is one meaning, I take it, of the controversy over Spike Lee's film, *Do the Right Thing*. The provoking circumstance in that film's narrative of the absence of images of black Americans (the "brothers") from the wall of Sal's pizzaria (adorned with pictures of the heroes of Italian-American culture) suggests a rather obvious allegory of canon formation; but the subtler point, recently made by W. J. T. Mitchell, is that the provocation is beside the point when the narrative arrives at its complexly overdetermined moment of social violence. To see the images as the *cause* of the violence is to miss everything that overdetermines the social relations Lee is at

such pains to evoke in their real complexity. Among its other accomplishments, the film suggests, then, not an allegory for the process of canon formation but for the liberal critique of the canon, that is, for our postmodern tendency to reduce the social to images of the social. See W. J. T. Mitchell, "The Violence of Public Art: *Do the Right Thing*," *Critical Inquiry* 16 (1990), 880–99.

13. Hence the temptation to understand the process of canonical revision according to such political models as "affirmative action," a very dubious analogy which trivializes a necessary, fragile, and altogether too limited political practice whose site is very different—the site of employment. See, for example, Lillian Robinson, "Treason Our Text," on the necessity of including more female writers in the canon: "It is up to feminist scholars, when we determine that this is indeed the right course to pursue, to demonstrate that such an inclusion would constitute a genuinely affirmative action for all of us" (572). The fact that the "affirmative action" analogy is usually tacit in the rhetoric of canon revision indicates some uneasiness with it, an uneasiness that needs to be honestly acknowledged.

14. Laclau and Mouffe, *Hegemony and Socialist Strategy*, 111. See also Joan W. Scott's judicious reconsideration of this question in "The Evidence of Experience," *Critical Inquiry* 17 (1991), 773–97. Scott argues that "A refusal of essentialism seems particularly important once again these days within the field of history, as disciplinary pressure builds to defend the unitary subject in the name of his or her 'experience'" (791).

15. In his more recent *New Reflections on the Revolution of Our Time* (London: Verso, 1990), 231, Laclau relates social identity to the context of representation as follows: "The notion of representation as the transparency of the identity between representer and represented identity was always incorrect, of course: but it is even more so when applied to contemporary societies in which the instability of social identities makes the constitution of the latter around solid and permanent interests much more ill-defined." For the latest of many attempts to "reanimate the author" on behalf of a "politics of author recognition," see Cheryl Walker, "Feminist Literary Criticism and the Author," *Critical Inquiry* 16 (1990), 551–71. Walker wants to reassert the "antifeminist implications" of theory's notion of the death of the author (560).

16. For a good summary statement of the issues involved in this articulation, with extensive bibliography, see Ann Ferguson, "The Intersection of Race, Gender, and Class in the United States Today," *Rethinking Marxism* 3 (1990), 45–64.

17. The concept of a "minority author" should itself be submitted to critique. The unresolved contradiction between the assertion of equivalence vis-à-vis the experience of marginalization or oppression and the assertion of difference at the level of specific gender, racial, or ethnic identity is one consequence of identity politics, and accounts for at least some of the tensions expressed between different minority groups over the actually quite limited resources available for compensating disadvantaged groups. These tensions follow from the fact that the name of "minority" is superimposed upon specific gender, racial, or ethnic identities as *another* identity, a general identity which paradoxically effaces the very specificity which is the basis for the claim to that general identity. This contradiction can only be superseded in the recognition that the concept of "minority" names a historically determinate relation between dominant and subordinate social groups in a specific social context. The tensions between such groups in the practice of identity politics suggests that in identity politics' practice of traditional interest-group politics, the interest of the group is defined on the basis of a hypothetically *preexistent* identity (essential, if not natural), and not on the basis of an analysis of the objective conditions giving rise to that identity. Hence the apparent absence of analogy between, say, one's racial identity, and one's identity as a "consumer"—but

the obvious contingency of such "identities" as the latter is also the reason why it is so difficult to translate class position into the identity of "minority author."

18. See for example Judith Butler's dismantling of some of the metaphysical presuppositions of identity politics in her *Gender Trouble: Feminism and the Subversion of Identity* (New York: Routledge, 1990): "Indeed, the fragmentation within feminism and the paradoxical opposition to feminism from 'women' whom feminism claims to represent suggest the necessary limits of identity politics. The suggestion that feminism can seek wider representation for a subject that it itself constructs has the ironic consequence that feminist goals risk failure by refusing to take account of the constitutive powers of their own representational claims. This problem is not ameliorated through an appeal to the category of women for merely 'strategic' purposes, for strategies always have meanings that exceed the purposes for which they are intended" (4). Still powerful too is Alice Echols's early warning against the essentialist politics of cultural separatism, "The New Feminism of Yin and Yang," in *Powers of Desire: The Politics of Sexuality,* ed. Ann Snitow et al. (New York: Monthly Review Press, 1983), 439–59.

19. Peter Osborne, "Radicalism without Limit? Discourse, Democracy, and the Politics of Identity," in *Socialism and the Limits of Liberalism,* ed. Peter Osborne (New York: Verso, 1991), 216–17.

20. The social-institutional sites at which the articulation of different identities—or the coalition of minorities—can occur is actually very limited. For this reason we need to be cautious about generalizing the possibilities for such coalition from the experience of solidarities in the university. The latter version of solidarity is constructed on the basis of a common *institutional* affiliation, the very strong tendency of teachers or students to affiliate strongly on the basis of their "identities" as teachers or students. The question is what social basis of affiliation might create the possibility for such political coalitions outside the university. The conditions that really determine relations *between* minorities in our culture are more accurately invoked by the names of Bensonhurst and Crown Heights than by the university's version of identity politics, with its Puritan wing of the politically correct. If the formulation and expression of a cultural identity are undeniably political acts, with political consequences, these consequences are at present very ambiguous. We do not know yet what kind of politics a real articulation of different identities would produce, what kind of "hegemony." Nor do we know of what mechanisms such a politics would consist. We only know that the bad conscience of identity politics about the identities always being "left out" of any community of common identities betrays the inability of radical liberalism to transcend the strategies of traditional liberal interest-group politics.

21. The fact that liberal pluralism, in its current radical incarnation, has often been accused falsely of reducing the cultural to the political prevents one from seeing the fact that liberal pluralism's more serious problem is the reduction of the political to the cultural.

22. Here we may note the precedent of Michel Pêcheux's work on identification, as yet largely unassimilated in American cultural theory. See his *Language, Semantics, Ideology,* trans. Harbans Nagpal (New York: St. Martin's Press, 1982). In his *New Reflections* Laclau also has some interesting comments on this question, which in my view go beyond the conclusions of *Hegemony and Socialist Strategy*: "the incorporation of the individual into the symbolic order occurs through *identifications*. The individual is not simply an identity within the structure but is transformed by it into a subject, and this requires acts of identification." Such a statement clearly implies a necessary distinction between identity and subject. In context (Lauclau's remarks are

in reference to Lacan), that distinction points to the concept of the subject as defining what the individual does not know about the formation of his or her identity. Is it not one of the peculiarities of identity politics that it has everything to say about identity and little to say about identification as a moment in a *process,* a process which gives birth to the *subject* (always, of course, the subject-in-process)? It was of course never the project of theory to make the subject simply disappear but to make its claim to rational self-determination (its free affirmation of its identity) suspect. Even Foucault's most radical statement on the subject, "What Is an Author?" which has been read incorrectly as arguing that authors do not exist (just when women authors and black authors were being discovered or rediscovered) clearly says just the opposite: "But the subject should not be entirely abandoned. It should be reconsidered, not to restore the theme of an originating subject, but to seize its functions, its intervention in discourse, and its system of dependencies." It will prove to be a rich irony of our post-theoretical era if our new prize of "identity" should prove in the end to be nothing other than the old Cartesian subject, the subject as it was conceived before theory called its self-determination into question and exposed its social and psychological determinations.

23. See McLennan, *Marxism, Pluralism, and Beyond,* 21. Giving class its due does not, it should be emphasized, reduce the phenomena of race and gender to aspects of class; the point of insisting upon the incommensurability of these categories is only that nothing explains class but class.

24. The difference between a research program and canonical revaluation is symptomatically confused in such statements as that by Marilyn L. Williamson, *Raising Their Voices: British Women Writers, 1650–1750* (Detroit: Wayne State University Press, 1990), which I quote for its representative puzzlement: "I do not therefore make aesthetic judgments the goal of my reading, and some readers will doubtless find much of the writing covered in this study deficient in quality and therefore not worth much attention. My work and that of other feminist critics offers the possibility of breaking out of the cycle of assuming that what is unknown or obscure deserves to be so. I do not claim to have discovered inglorious Miltons among the score of writers in this study, but I believe their work deserves attention nonetheless. The neglect is historical: most were well-known, some quite famous, in their own time. Just as historians are beginning to read popular pamphlets along with Hobbes and Locke, so literary historians are reading far beyond the canon and the taste and values it informs" (9). Historians will be surprised to learn that they are just beginning to read archival material in connection with the study of major authors. But historical scholarship has sometimes been practiced by literary critics too, and in the university it has, historically speaking, been the norm. The dovetailing of new forms of historical scholarship with a critique of the canon has produced the quite interesting misapprehension that writing about a given author is equivalent to canonization of that author.

25. This fact remains an unspoken in such arguments as Lillian Robinson's "Treason Our Text," which grapples with the meaning of the feminist research program in the following terms: "The emergence of feminist literary study has been characterized, at the base, by scholarship devoted to the discovery, republication, and reappraisal of 'lost' or undervalued writers and their work. From Rebecca Harding Davis and Kate Chopin through Zora Neale Hurston and Mina Loy to Meridel LeSueur and Rebecca West, reputations have been reborn or remade and a female counter-canon has come into being, out of components that were largely unavailable even a dozen years ago." A footnote supplies a bibliography for the authors cited, but appends the qualification: "The examples are all from the nineteenth and twentieth centuries" (575). There follows a statement to the effect that "Valuable work has also been

done on women writers before the Industrial Revolution," along with a somewhat briefer bibliography of this work. From such an argument one can glean no understanding of why so many women writers have been recovered from the period following the Industrial Revolution, and indeed whether this factor has anything to do with the Industrial Revolution. It is simply taken for granted that any woman writer not currently canonical is ipso facto "lost or undervalued," as though it really did not matter how such texts came to be, or what social conditions enabled or constrained the practice of writing for different social groups.

While I have not undertaken to give a full account in the text of the relation between the distribution of cultural capital (access to the means of literary production) and the position of women in the system of distributions, the lineaments of such an account can be briefly indicated. We might begin by reconsidering two leading questions guiding the current account of women writers in the history of canon formation: First, is the fact of the transhistorical oppression of women sufficient to explain the exclusion of women from the means of literary production, if not from the canon itself? And second, does this fact imply that such oppression operates autonomously from class structure? Fortunately history does not enjoin upon us any choice between a transhistorical sexism and a historical class analysis. A properly historical question would be: What determines women's access or lack of access to the means of literary production at any given historical moment? While transhistorical sexism always makes women available to occupy disadvantaged locations in the social order, it is only the historical class system which determines how they will be so disadvantaged. In the premodern sexual division of labor, women occupy a different site in the system of production than they do after the emergence of generalized commodity production. The same system which "commodifies" women in new ways also permits them to produce new commodities (such as novels), to become new kinds of cultural producers. The historical class system of capitalism produces a new sexual division of labor, or a rearticulation of transhistorical sexism on the system by which material and cultural capital is distributed.

26. See for example the argument of Denise Riley, *Am I That Name? Feminism and the Category of "Women" in History* (Minneapolis: University of Minnesota Press, 1988).

27. F. R. Leavis, *The Great Tradition* (New York: New York University Press, 1964), 1.

28. Linda Nochlin, *Women, Art, and Power, and other Essays* (New York: Harper and Row, 1988), 150.

29. I have generally followed the lead of Brian Street's *Literacy in Theory and Practice* (Cambridge: Cambridge University Press, 1984) in his critique of Jack Goody's "autonomous" model of literacy. Street emphasizes the ambiguous effects of literacy in any given set of social conditions, effects I have attempted to invoke continually by defining literacy as the systematic regulation of reading and writing. Literacy is now the subject of new and rather intense debate, centering on the very concrete and practical matter of how children are taught to read (or not to read) in our schools. See for example, Michael Stubbes, *Language and Literacy: The Sociolinguistics of Reading and Writing* (London: Routledge and Kegan Paul, 1980); W. Ross Winterowd, *The Culture and Politics of Literacy* (New York: Oxford University Press, 1989); John Willinsky, *The New Literacy: Redefining Reading and Writing in the Schools* (New York: Routledge, 1990); James W. Tollefson, *Planning Language, Planning Inequality: Language Policy in the Community* (London: Longman, 1991); and Tony Crowley, *Standard English and the Politics of Language* (Urbana: University of Illinois Press, 1989).

30. I shall pose the question of distribution throughout this book as one of *access* to literacy; but the concept of "access" should not be confused with the ideological

notion of "opportunity." We are not speaking here of providing individuals with the cultural capital necessary for "success." That notion is of course the cornerstone of American ideology, which employs a fiction of "equal opportunity" as the ideological means of justifying a system in which some individuals fail and others succeed— through their own fault. Access to literacy should be considered on the contrary an absolute right, not a means to success in any other cultural or economic sense.

31. Barbara Herrnstein Smith, *Contingencies of Value: Alternative Perspectives for Literary Theory* (Cambridge: Harvard University Press, 1988), 51.

32. *New York Times*, February 17, 1985.

33. See, for example, Charles Altieri in "An Idea and an Ideal of a Literary Canon," *Critical Inquiry* 10 (September 1983), 55: "On this model, works do not address social life directly but elicit fundamental forms of desire and admiration that can motivate efforts to produce social change."

34. Jeffrey Sammons, *Literary Sociology and Practical Criticism* (Bloomington: Indiana University Press, 1977), 134.

35. See William Bennett, "To Reclaim a Legacy: Text of Report on Humanities in Education," *The Chronicle of Higher Education,* November 28, 1984, 18, where Bennett proposes his list of candidates for the canon of Western writers. The list contains a now obligatory nod to several minority texts, such as Martin Luther King's "Letter from a Birmingham Jail," and his "I Have a Dream" speech.

36. Michael Ryan, "Loaded Canons: Politics and Literature at the MLA," *Boston Review* (July 1985).

37. This mistake is pervasive, even among the most theoretically enlightened advocates of left pedagogy in the United States. Here I would cite, as an example, the otherwise judicious study of Patrick Brantlinger, *Crusoe's Footprints: Cultural Studies in Britain and America* (New York: Routledge, 1990). In his discussion of American literature in the context of "gender, class, race," Brantlinger remarks that "Great literature, my own education taught me, is not about public life or politics; it is instead about the experiences, lives, values of private, usually 'refined' individuals (lyric romantic poetry, portraits of the artist, remembrances of things past, etc.) How then does one begin to understand and value literature which ignores refinement, etiquette, and 'taste' to tell the truth about a nation's past and to represent the struggles of majorities [sic] against slavery, sexism, poverty?" (155). But is it really the case that Melville's *Benito Cerino*, Twain's *Huckleberry Finn,* or Faulkner's novels "to tell the truth" about the centrality of race and racism in the American experience, even if in the mode of sometimes expressing that racism? Or that they advertise hegemonic principles of taste and etiquette by habitually choosing to represent the lives of "refined" individuals? When Brantlinger cites Frederick Douglass's *The Narrative of the Life of Frederick Douglass* as a noncanonical text, he betrays the fact that the canon critique really does construe every literary work preferentially as *autobiography.* Yet even the canonicity of Douglass cannot finally be established on these grounds alone, because any text, even an autobiographical text which witnesses to the fact of racial repression, has to be *read.*

38. Lillian Robinson, "Treason Our Text," 574.

39. Nina Baym, *Women's Fiction: A Guide to Novels by and about Women* (Ithaca: Cornell University Press, 1978), 15.

40. Myra Jehlen, "Archimedes and the Paradox of Feminist Criticism," *Signs* 6 (1981), 575–601.

41. Jane Tompkins, *Sensational Designs: The Cultural Work of American Fiction, 1970–1860* (New York: Oxford University Press, 1985), xiv. On the subject of the distinction between serious and popular, see the argument of Peter Bürger in *Theory*

of the Avant-Garde, trans. Michael Shaw (Minneapolis: University of Minnesota Press, 1984), liii: "For once the institution of art/literature has been thematized, the question about the mechanisms that make it possible to exclude certain works as pulp literature necessarily arises." One might add that "pulp literature" *as such* necessarily emerges simultaneously with the institution of the High Culture canon.

42. Hans Robert Jauss, "Literary History as Challenge to Literary Theory," in *Toward an Aesthetic of Reception,* trans. Timothy Bahti (Minneapolis: University of Minnesota Press, (1982), 25.

43. Stanley Fish, *Is There a Text in This Class?: The Authority of Interpretive Communities* (Cambridge: Harvard University Press), 11.

44. Elizabeth Meese, "Sexual Politics and Critical Judgment," in *After Strange Texts: The Role of Theory in the Study of Literature,* ed. Gregory S. Jay and David L. Miller (Birmingham: University of Alabama Press, 1985), 90.

45. The argument for a less anxious response to this state of affairs is exemplified in the several essays and books of Frank Kermode on issues relating to canon formation, most typically in "The Institutional Control of Interpretation," in his *The Art of Telling: Essays on Fiction* (Cambridge: Harvard University Press, 1983), *Forms of Attention* (Chicago: University of Chicago Press, 1985), and *History and Value* (Oxford: The Clarendon Press, 1989).

46. On the issue of consensus and community I shall have more to say in Chapter 5. In the meanwhile we can concur with Gregor McLennan's observation that liberal pluralist theory tends to posit consensus as the ideal resolution to the competitive politics of interest groups (*Marxism, Pluralism, and Beyond,* 26). The canon critique follows faithfully in the logic of this politics by positing countercanons which are supposed to be consensual for given social subcommunities. For a very effective critique of the separatist tendencies in the institutionalized forms of canon revision, and the pluralist bases of those tendencies, see Cornell West, "Minority Discourse and the Pitfalls of Canon Formation," *Yale Journal of Criticism* 1 (1987), 193–202.

47. We might also note here that the very American style of liberal pluralist critique has made the entire debate about the canon seem rather mystifying to European critics. See, for example, Alice Jardine's and Anne Menke's interviews with fourteen French feminists in a recent issue of *Yale French Studies* 75 (1988). Jardine and Menke discovered to their surprise that French feminist writers found it difficult to become exercised over the problem of the canon, and that they were even incredulous that it had become a feminist issue in America: "It was hard for us to understand how so many could profess indifference to inclusion of their own work in the canon. And inclusion was not the only problem: for many of these women the word 'canon' does not refer to the literary tradition, and few of them see it as an area of feminist concern" (230). Here, to cite one response, are Monique Wittig's remarks, which are not untypical: "To say that writers have been excluded from the canon because they are women seems to me not only inexact, but the very idea proceeds from a trend toward theories of victimization. There are few great writers in any century. Each time there was one, not only was she welcome within the canon, but she was acclaimed, applauded, and praised in her time— sometimes *especially* because she was a woman. I'm thinking of Sand and Colette. I do not think that real innovators have been passed by. In the university, we ruin the purpose of what we do if we make a special category for women—especially when teaching. When we do that as feminists, we ourselves turn the canon into a male edifice" (257).

Jeanette Winterson (1959–)

An acclaimed writer of fiction who has published novels, essays, and short stories, Winterson grew up in a home where books were few and far between. She
was born in Manchester, England, but was adopted by working-class parents
who brought her up in a Pentecostal home in the nearby mill town of Accring-
ton. Although the Bible was the book favored by her parents, Malory's *Morte
d'Arthur* was the one that captured Winterson's imagination and set her on the
course of becoming a writer. Her parents had hoped that she would become a
missionary, but Winterson had other plans in mind. After attending Oxford University, Winterson did odd jobs in the theater while writing her first novel,
Oranges Are Not The Only Fruit, which was published in 1985. Around the
same time, she published a comic book with pictures, *Boating for Beginners,* and
then began working for her publishers at Pandora Press. Aside from jobs in the
theater and as a publisher, Winterson has worked as a makeup artist at a funeral
parlor and as a domestic in a mental hospital. But when *The Passion* appeared in
1987, Winterson became a full-time writer, publishing several books in rapid
succession: *Sexing the Cherry* (1989), *Written on the Body* (1992), *Art and Lies*
(1994), *Art Objects* (1995), *Gut Symmetries* (1997), *The World and Other
Places* (1998), and *The Powerbook* (2000). In addition to publishing books,
Winterson has dramatized *Oranges Are Not The Only Fruit* for the BBC-TV
(1990); written a television film, *Great Moments in Aviation,* for the BBC-2
(1994); and completed a screenplay of *The Passion* for Miramax Films. She is
currently working on an Internet venture with the BBC.

Imagination and Reality

The reality of art is the reality of the imagination.

What do I mean by reality of art?

What do I mean by reality of imagination?

My statement, and the questions it suggests, are worth considering now that the
fashionable approach to the arts is once again through the narrow gate of subjective experience. The charge laid on the artist, and in particular on the writer, is
not to bring back visions but to play the Court photographer.

Is this anathema to art? Is it anti-art? I think so. What art presents is much
more than the daily life of you and me, and the original role of the artist as
visionary is the correct one. 'Real' is an old word, is an odd word. It used to
mean a Spanish sixpence; a small silver coin, money of account in the days when
the value of a coin was the value of its metal. We are used to notional money but
'real' is an honest currency.

The honest currency of art is the honest currency of the imagination.

The small silver coin of art cannot be spent; that is, it cannot be exchanged or exhausted. What is lost, what is destroyed, what is tarnished, what is misappropriated, is ceaselessly renewed by the mining, shaping, forging imagination that exists beyond the conjectures of the everyday. Imagination's coin, the infinitely flexible metal of the Muse, metal of the moon, in rounded structure offers new universes, primary worlds, that substantially confront the pretences of notional life.

Notional life is the life encouraged by governments, mass education and the mass media. Each of those powerful agencies couples an assumption of its own importance with a disregard for individuality. Freedom of choice is the catch phrase but streamlined homogeneity is the objective. A people who think for themselves are hard to control and what is worse, in a money culture, they may be sceptical of product advertising. Since our economy is now a consumer economy, we must be credulous and passive. We must believe that we want to earn money to buy things we don't need. The education system is not designed to turn out thoughtful individualists, it is there to get us to work. When we come home exhausted from the inanities of our jobs we can relax in front of the inanities of the TV screen. This pattern, punctuated by birth, death and marriage and a new car, is offered to us as real life.

Children who are born into a tired world as batteries of new energy are plugged into the system as soon as possible and gradually drained away. At the time when they become adult and conscious they are already depleted and prepared to accept a world of shadows. Those who have kept their spirit find it hard to nourish it and between the ages of twenty and thirty, many are successfully emptied of all resistance. I do not think it an exaggeration to say that most of the energy of most of the people is being diverted into a system which destroys them. Money is no antidote. If the imaginative life is to be renewed it needs its own coin.

We have to admit that the arts stimulate and satisfy a part of our nature that would otherwise be left untouched and that the emotions art arouses in us are of a different order to those aroused by experience of any other kind.

We think we live in a world of sense-experience and what we can touch and feel, see and hear, is the sum of our reality. Although neither physics nor philosophy accepts this, neither physics nor philosophy has been as successful as religion used to be at persuading us of the doubtfulness of the seeming-solid world. This is a pity if only because while religion was a matter of course, the awareness of other realities was also a matter of course. To accept God was to accept Otherness, and while this did not make the life of the artist any easier (the life of the artist is never easy), a general agreement that there is more around us than the mundane allows the artist a greater licence and a greater authority than he or she can expect in a society that recognises nothing but itself.

An example of this is the development of the visual arts under Church patronage during the late medieval and Renaissance periods in Europe. This was much more than a patronage of money, it was a warrant to bring back visions.

Far from being restricted by Church rhetoric, the artist knew that he and his audience were in tacit agreement; each went in search of the Sublime.

Art is visionary; it sees beyond the view from the window, even though the window is its frame. This is why the arts fare much better alongside religion than alongside either capitalism or communism. The god-instinct and the art-instinct both apprehend more than the physical biological material world. The artist need not believe in God, but the artist does consider reality as multiple and complex. If the audience accepts this premise it is then possible to think about the work itself. As things stand now, too much criticism of the arts concerns itself with attacking any suggestion of art as Other, as a bringer of realities beyond the commonplace. Dimly, we know we need those other realities and we think we can get them by ransacking different cultures and rhapsodising work by foreign writers simply because they are foreign writers. We are still back with art as the mirror of life, only it is a more exotic or less democratic life than our own. No doubt this has its interests but if we are honest, they are documentary. Art is not documentary. It may incidentally serve that function in its own way but its true effort is to open to us dimensions of the spirit and of the self that normally lie smothered under the weight of living.

It is in Victorian England that the artist first becomes a rather suspect type who does not bring visions but narcotics and whose relationship to different levels of reality is not authoritative but hallucinatory. In Britain, the nineteenth century recovered from the shock of Romanticism by adopting either a manly Hellenism, with an interest in all things virile and Greek, or a manly philistinism, which had done with sweet Jonney Keats and his band and demanded of the poet, if he must be a poet, that he be either declamatory or decorative. Art could be rousing or it could be entertaining. If it hinted at deeper mysteries it was effeminate and absurd. The shift in sensibility from early to late Wordsworth is the shift of the age. For Tennyson, who published his first collection in 1830, the shift was a painful one and the compromises he made to his own work are clear to anyone who flicks through the collected poems and finds a visionary poet trying to hide himself in legend in order to hint at sublimities not allowed to his own time. Like Wordsworth before him, Tennyson fails whenever he collapses into the single obsessive reality of the world about him. As a laureate we know he is lying. As a visionary we read him now and find him true.

And what are we but our fathers' sons and daughters? We are the Victorian legacy. Our materialism, our lack of spirituality, our grossness, our mockery of art, our utilitarian attitude to education, even the dull grey suits wrapped around the dull grey lives of our eminent City men, are Victorian hand-me-downs. Many of our ideas of history and society go back no further than Victorian England. We live in a money culture because they did. Control by plutocracy is a nineteenth-century phenomenon that has been sold to us as a blueprint for reality. But what is real about the values of a money culture?

Money culture recognises no currency but its own. Whatever is not money, whatever is not making money, is useless to it. The entire efforts of our government as directed through our society are efforts towards making more and more money. This favours the survival of the dullest. This favours those who prefer to live in a notional reality where goods are worth more than time and where things are more important than ideas.

For the artist, any artist, poet, painter, musician, time in plenty and an abundance of ideas are the necessary basics of creativity. By dreaming and idleness and then by intense self-discipline does the artist live. The artist cannot perform between 9 and 6, five days a week, or if she sometimes does, she cannot guarantee to do so. Money culture hates that. It must know what it is getting, when it is getting it, and how much it will cost. The most tyrannical of patrons never demanded from their protegés what the market now demands of artists; if you can't sell your work regularly and quickly, you can either starve or do something else. The time that art needs, which may not be a long time, but which has to be its own time, is anathema to a money culture. Money confuses time with itself. That is part of its unreality.

Against this golden calf in the wilderness where all come to buy and sell, the honest currency of art offers quite a different rate of exchange. The artist does not turn time into money, the artist turns time into energy, time into intensity, time into vision. The exchange that art offers is an exchange in kind; energy for energy, intensity for intensity, vision for vision. This is seductive and threatening. Can we make the return? Do we want to? Our increasingly passive diversions do not equip us, mentally, emotionally, for the demands that art makes. We know we are dissatisfied, but the satisfactions that we seek come at a price beyond the resources of a money culture. Can we afford to live imaginatively, contemplatively? Why have we submitted to a society that tries to make imagination a privilege when to each of us it comes as a birthright?

It is not a question of the money in your pocket. Money can buy you the painting or the book or the opera seat but it cannot expose you to the vast energies you will find there. Often it will shield you from them, just as a rich man can buy himself a women but not her love. Love is reciprocity and so is art. Either you abandon yourself to another world that you say you seek or you find ways to resist it. Most of us are art-resisters because art is a challenge to the notional life. In a money culture, art, by its nature, objects. It fields its own realities, lives by its own currency, aloof to riches and want. Art is dangerous.

FOR SALE: MY LIFE. HIGHEST BIDDER COLLECTS.

The honest currency of art is the honest currency of the imagination.

In Middle English, 'real' was a variant of 'royal'.

Can we set aside images of our own dishonoured monarchy and think instead about the ancientness and complexity of the word 'royal'?

To be royal was to be distinguished in the proper sense; to be singled out, by one's fellows and by God or the gods. In both the Greek and the Hebraic traditions, the one who is royal is the one who has special access to the invisible world. Ulysses can talk to Hera, King David can talk to God. Royalty on earth is expected to take its duties on earth seriously but the King should also be a bridge between the terrestrial and the supernatural.

Perhaps it seems strange to us that in the ancient world the King was more accessible to his people than were the priests. Although King and priest worked together, priesthood, still allied to magic, even by the Hebrews, was fully mysterious. The set-apartness of the priest is one surrounded by ritual and taboo. The priest did not fight in battle, take concubines, hoard treasure, feast and riot, sin out of humanness, or if he did, there were severe penalties. The morality of the priesthood was not the morality of Kingship and whether you read *The Odyssey* or The Bible, the difference is striking. The King is not better behaved than his subjects, essentially he was (or should have been) the nobler man.

In Britain, royalty was not allied to morality until the reign of Queen Victoria. Historically, the role of the King or Queen had been to lead and inspire, this is an imaginative role, and it was most perfectly fulfilled by Elizabeth the First, Gloriana, the approachable face of Godhead. Gloriana is the Queen whose otherness is for the sake of her people, and it is important to remember that the disciplines she laid upon her own life, in particular her chastity, were not for the sake of example but for the sake of expediency. The Divine Right of Kings was not a good conduct award; it was a mark of favour. God's regent upon earth was expected to behave like God and anyone who studies Greek or Hebrew literature will find that God does not behave like a Christian schoolmistress. God is glorious, terrifying, inscrutable, often capricious to human eyes, extravagant, victorious, legislative but not law-abiding, and, the supreme imagination. 'In the beginning was the Word.'

At its simplest and at its best, royalty is an imaginative function; it must embody in its own person, subtle and difficult concepts of Otherness. The priest does not embody these concepts, the priest serves them. The priest is a functionary, the King is a function.

Shakespeare is preoccupied with Kingship as a metaphor for the imaginative life. Leontes and Lear, Macbeth and Richard II, are studies in the failure of the imagination. In *The Winter's Tale*, the redemption of Leontes is made possible through a new capacity in him; the capacity to see outside of his own dead vision into a chance as vibrant as it is unlikely. When Paulina says to him, 'It is required you do awake your faith' she does not mean religious faith. If the statue of Hermione is to come to life, Leontes must believe it *can* come to life. This is not common sense. It is imagination.

In the earliest Hebrew creation stories Yahweh makes himself a clay model of a man and breathes on it to give it life. It is this supreme confidence, this translation of forms, the capacity to recognise in one thing the potential of another, and the willingness to let that potential realise itself, that is the stamp of creativity and the birthright that Yahweh gives to humans. Leontes' failure to acknowledge any reality other than his own is a repudiation of that birthright, a neglect of humanness that outworks itself into the fixed immobility of his queen. When Hermione steps down and embraces Leontes it is an imaginative reconciliation.

I hope it is clear that as I talk about King and priest I am dealing in abstracts and not actualities. I do not wish to upset republicans anywhere. What I do want to do is to move the pieces across the chessboard to see if that gives us a different view.

By unravelling the word 'real' I hope to show that it contains in itself, and without any wishful thinking on my part, those densities of imaginative experience that belong to us all and that are best communicated through art. I see no conflict between reality and imagination. They are not in fact separate. Our real lives hold within them our royal lives; the inspiration to be more than we are, to find new solutions, to live beyond the moment. Art helps us to do this because it fuses together temporal and perpetual realities.

To see outside of a dead vision is not an optical illusion.

The realist (from the Latin *res* = thing) who thinks he deals in things and not images and who is suspicious of the abstract and of art, is not the practical man but a man caught in a fantasy of his own unmaking.

The realist unmakes the coherent multiple world into a collection of random objects. He thinks of reality as that which has an objective existence, but understands no more about objective existence than that which he can touch and feel, sell and buy. A lover of objects and of objectivity, he is in fact caught in a world of symbols and symbolism, where he is unable to see the thing in itself, as it really is, he sees it only in relation to his own story of the world.

The habit of human beings is to see things subjectively or not to see them at all. The more familiar a thing becomes the less it is seen. In the home, nobody looks at the furniture, they sit on it, eat off it, sleep on it and forget it until they buy something new. When we do look at other people's things, we are usually thinking about their cachet, their value, what they say about their owner. Our minds work to continually label and absorb what we see and to fit it neatly into our own pattern. That done, we turn away. This is a sound survival skill but it makes it very difficult to let anything have an existence independent of ourselves, whether furniture or people. It makes it easier to buy symbols, things that have a particular value to us, than it does to buy objects.

My mother, who was poor, never bought objects, she bought symbols. She used to save up to buy something hideous to put in the best parlour. What she bought was factory made and beyond her purse. If she had even been able to see it in its own right, she could never have spent money on it. She couldn't see it, and nor could any of the neighbours dragged in to admire it. They admired the effort it had taken to save for it. They admired how much it cost. Above all, they admired my mother; the purchase was a success.

I know that when my mother sat in her kitchen that had only a few pieces of handmade furniture, she felt depressed and conscious of her lowly social status. When she sat in her dreadful parlour with a china cup and a bought biscuit, she felt like a lady. The parlour, full of objects unseen but hard won, was a fantasy chamber, a reflecting mirror. Like Mrs Joe, in *Great Expectations*, she finally took her apron off.

Money culture depends on symbolic reality. It depends on a confusion between the object and what the object represents. To keep you and me buying and upgrading an overstock of meaningless things depends on those things having an acquisitional value. It is the act of buying that is important. In our society, people who cannot buy things are the underclass.

Symbolic man surrounds himself with objects as tyrants surround themselves with subjects: 'These will obey me. Through them I am worshipped. Through them I exercise control.' These fraudulent kingdoms, hard-headed and practical, are really the soft-centre of fantasy. They are wish fulfilment nightmares where more is piled on more to manufacture the illusion of abundance. They are lands of emptiness and want. Things do not satisfy. In part they fail to satisfy because their symbolic value changes so regularly and what brought whistles of admiration one year is next year's car boot sale bargain. In part they fail to satisfy because much of what we buy is gadgetry and fashion, which makes objects temporary and the need to be able to purchase them, permanent. In part they fail to satisfy because we do not actually want the things we buy. They are illusion, narcotic, hallucination.

To suggest that the writer, the painter, the musician, is the one out of touch with the real world is a doubtful proposition. It is the artist who must apprehend things fully, in their own right, communicating them not as symbols but as living realities with the power to move.

To see outside of a dead vision is not an optical illusion.

According to the science of optics, if an image consists of points through which light actually passes, it is called real. Otherwise it is called virtual.

The work of the artist is to see into the life of things; to discriminate between superficialities and realities; to know what is genuine and what is a make-believe. The artist through the disciplines of her work, is one of the few people who does see things as they really are, stripped of associative value. I do not mean that artists of whatever sort have perfect taste or perfect private lives, I mean that when the imaginative capacity is highly developed, it is made up of invention and discernment. Invention is the shaping spirit that re-forms fragments into new wholes, so that even what has been familiar can be seen fresh. Discernment is to know how to test the true and the false and to reveal objects, emotions, ideas in their own coherence. The artist is a translator; one who has learned how to pass into her own language the languages gathered from stones, from birds, from dreams, from the body, from the material world, from the invisible world, from sex, from death, from love. A different language is a different reality; what is the language, the world, of stones? What is the language, the world, of birds? Of atoms? Of microbes? Of colours? Of air? The material world is closed to those who think of it only as a commodity market.

> How do you know but every bird that cuts the airy way
> Is an immense world of delight closed by your senses five?
> William Blake, *The Marriage of Heaven and Hell* (c. 1790)

To those people every object is inanimate. In fact they are the ones who remain unmoved, fixed rigidly within their own reality.

The artist is moved.

The artist is moved through multiple realities. The artist is moved by empty space and points of light. The artist tests the image. Does light pass through it? Is it illuminated? Is it sharp, clear, its own edges, its own form?

The artist is looking for real presences. I suppose what the scientist Rupert Sheldrake would call 'morphic resonance'; the inner life of the thing that cannot be explained away biologically, chemically, physically. In the Catholic Church 'real presence' is the bread and wine that through transubstantiation becomes the living eucharist; the body and blood of Christ. In the Protestant Church the bread and wine are symbols only, one of the few places where we recognise that we are asking one thing to substitute for another. For the average person, this substitution is happening all the time.

The real presence, the image transformed by light, is not rare but it is easily lost or mistaken under clouds of subjectivity. People who claim to like pictures and books will often only respond to those pictures and books in which they can clearly find themselves. This is ego masquerading as taste. To recognise the worth of a thing is more than recognising its worth to you. Our responses to art are conditioned by our insistence that it present to us realities we can readily accept, however virtual those realities might be. Nevertheless art has a stubborn way of cutting through the subjective world of symbols and money and offering itself as a steady alternative to the quick change act of daily life.

We are naturally suspicious of faculties that we do not ourselves possess and we do not quite believe that the poet can read the sermons in stones or the painter know the purple that bees love. Still we are drawn to books and pictures and music, finding in ourselves an echo of their song, finding in ourselves an echo of their sensibility, an answering voice through the racket of the day.

Art is for us a reality beyond now. An imaginative reality that we need. The reality of art is the reality of the imagination.

The reality of art is not the reality of experience.

The charge laid on the artist is to bring back visions.

In Shakespeare's *Othello,* we find that the Moor wins Desdemona's heart by first winning her imagination. He tells her tales of cannibals and of the Anthropophagi whose heads grow beneath their shoulders. What he calls his 'round unvarnished tale' is a subtle mixture of art and artfulness. When a Shakespearean hero apologises for his lack of wit we should be on our guard. Shakespeare always gives his heroes the best lines, even when the hero is Richard II.

Othello's untutored language is in fact powerful and wrought. He is more than a master of arms, he is a master of art. It is his words that win Desdemona. She says 'I saw Othello's visage in his mind.' His face, like his deeds, belongs to the world of sense-experience, but it is his wit that makes both dear to her. For Desdemona, the reality of Othello is his imaginative reality.

OTHELLO
> she thank'd me,
> And bade me, if I had a friend that lov'd
> her,
> I should but teach him how to tell my story,
> And that would woo her.

The clue here is not the story but the telling of it. It is not Othello the action man who has taught Desdemona to love him, it is Othello the poet.

We know that Shakespeare never bothered to think of a plot. As a good drama-tist and one who earned his whole living by his work, he had to take care to make his historical ransackings stage-satisfactory. The engineering of the plays gives pleasure even to those who are not interested in the words. But the words are the thing. The words are what interested Shakespeare and what should closely interest us. Shakespeare is a dramatic poet. He is not a chronicler of experience.

I have to say something so obvious because of the multitude of so called real-ists, many making money out of print, who want art to be as small as they are. For them, art is a copying machine busily copying themselves. They like the doc-umentary version, the 'life as it is lived'. To support their opinions they will either point to Dickens or Shakespeare. I have never understood why anyone calls Dickens a realist, but I have dealt with that myth elsewhere in these essays. As for Shakespeare, they will happily disregard the pervading spirit behind the later plays, and quote *Hamlet* Act III, Scene II 'the purpose of playing . . . is, to hold, as 'twere, the mirror up to nature.'

But what is nature?

From the Latin *Natura*, it is my birth, my characteristics, my condition.
It is my nativity, my astrology, my biology, my physiognomy, my geography, my cartography, my spirituality, my sexuality, my mentality, my corporeal, intellec-tual, emotional, imaginative self. And not just my self, every self and the Self of the world. There is no mirror I know that can show me all of these singularities, unless it is the strange distorting looking-glass of art where I will not find my reflection nor my representation but a nearer truth than I prefer. *Natura* is the whole that I am. The multiple reality of my existence.

The reality of the imagination leaves out nothing. It is the most complete reality that we can know. Imagination takes in the world of sense experience, and rather than trading it for a world of symbols, delights in it for what it is. The artist is physical and it is in the work of true artists in any medium, that we find the most moving and the most poignant studies of the world that we can touch and feel. It is the writer, the painter, and not the realist, who is intimate with the material world, who knows its smells and tastes because they are fresh in her nostrils, full in her mouth. What her hand touches, she feels. R. A. Collingwood said that Cézanne painted like a blind man (critics at the time agreed though for different reasons). He meant that the two-dimensional flimsy world of what is overlooked by most of us, suddenly reared out of the canvas, massy and tough. Cézanne seems to have hands in his eyes and eyes in his hands. When Cézanne paints a tree or an apple, he does not paint a copy of a tree or an apple, he paints its nature. He paints the whole that it is, the whole that is lost to us as we pass it, eat is, chop it down. It is through the painter, writer, compose, who lives more intensely than the rest of us, that we can rediscover the intensity of the physical world.

And not only the physical world. There is no limit to new territory. The gate is open. Whether or not we go through is up to us, but to stand mockingly on the threshold, claiming that nothing lies beyond, is something of a flat earth theory.

The earth is not flat and neither is reality. Reality is continuous, multiple, simultaneous, complex, abundant and partly invisible. The imagination alone can fathom this and it reveals its fathomings through art.

The reality of art is the reality of the imagination.

Questions to Consider

1. Foucault argues that schools resemble prisons and vice versa. Does your own educational experience bear this argument out? Is it plausible to think of the classroom as a "laboratory of power" and, if so, is the knowledge or information gathered or dispensed there ever innocent or neutral? Is it possible to separate power and knowledge? If so, how might we go about doing this? Would this separation change the look of the contemporary classroom? If so, how? Describe the relations between power and knowledge as you have seen them worked out within a specific class in which you have participated.

2. How might Foucault's description of panopticism be applied to other areas of social or political life? What institutions beyond the prison are shaped by visual surveillance? For example, does Fussell's discussion of class and the emphasis placed on visual markers make him a panopticon of sorts? Does Winterson's discussion of mass education imply the continuing operation of Foucault's panopticon?

3. If, as Foucault argues, the plague gave rise to a particular political dream that has helped shape institutions such as prisons and schools, how are new medical concerns such as the spread of AIDS affecting these institutions? In our society, has a connection been drawn (however speciously) between disease and identity? Between disease and class? If so, why is this the case? Who benefits and who suffers from these sorts of connections?

4. While Jameson speaks of postmodernism as a failure of the new, our zeal for the latest fad ironically forcing us to ransack the past, Winterson argues that the artist's potential is unlimited in its ability to invent. With which view do you agree? Can you think of examples from your everyday life that support one view or the other? What is your own attitude with respect to the new or the inventive? Is the new or the inventive always connected to consumerism? Why or why not? Does placing a monetary value on an art object diminish or enhance its artistic value? Why?

5. While Foucault speaks of the panoptic society as "perverse," Jameson argues that we have become a "schizophrenic" society. Both of these designations suggest a deviation from the norm, but as we know from the history of these words, each carries a different connotative value and force. How do we conceptualize what is normal and what is abnormal, and who gets to do this conceptualizing, i.e., who gets to institutionalize it? How does the way we speak of ourselves shape who we are? And what would it mean to call ourselves a paranoid, neurotic, depressive, or bipolar society? Do you see contemporary society as sick in any of these ways? Provide a specific example of such a diagnosis from your own experience.

6. We all understand money as a currency of exchange, but are there other currencies of exchange used in our society? If so, what are they, and which ones seem most closely linked with power? What are the currencies of exchange suggested by each of the essayists in this section? For example, for Guillory, the currency of exchange might be cultural capital. Are some currencies of exchange more "honest" than others, as Winterson argues? What currency of exchange do you feel best describes your own interactions? Does it alter your own behavior to think with different currencies of exchange?

IV

CULTURE AND ETHNICITY

Perhaps the best way to introduce the essays that appear in this section, each of which discusses the history of Western colonialism (where colonialism is defined most simply as the direct conquest and control of other people's land), is to sketch out the attitudes that prevailed among whites during the first half of the twentieth century, known as the Age of Empires. How is it possible that roughly half of the world's population was subject to alien rule during this time? How is it possible that one eighth of the world's population—the four core states of the United States, Great Britain, France, and Germany—was able to justify the direct control of over 4 million people (or one fourth of the world's population) and the indirect control through economic influence of hundreds of millions more? The answer may not surprise you, but it will probably disturb you: a perceived racial superiority, measured not just in mechanical, economic, and military terms but in moral terms as well.

The scientific, technical, and industrial advances being made in western Europe and the United States in the nineteenth century seemed (and "seemed" is the operant word here) to lend legitimacy to these states' perceived right to rule the rest of the world. What else could their myriad successes suggest, if not superiority? And thus, in 1901, we find British professor Karl Pearson stating the following with a confidence and lack of apology that many of us would find stunning if it were articulated in today's world:

> the scientific view of the nation is that of the organised whole, kept up to a pitch
> of internal efficiency by insuring that its numbers are substantially recruited
> from the *better stocks*, and kept to a high pitch of external efficiency by contest,
> chiefly by way of war with *inferior races*, and with *equal races* by the struggle

257

for trade routes and for the sources of raw material and of food supply. (my
emphasis, quoted in Ponting, 18–19)

Not explicitly stated, but implicit in this excerpt, is a belief in the "science" of
eugenics, a term coined in 1883 by Francis Galton, Charles Darwin's cousin.
Why not improve the human stock, Galton proposed, by eliminating the "unde-
sirables" and multiplying the "desirables"? Who, you might wonder, qualified as
"desirable" and who as "undesirable"? Generally, the members of the white middle class were seen as "good human stock" and thus "desirable." By implication,
then, anyone falling outside this category could be seen as "undesirable."

While most of us know the part played by eugenics in Nazi Germany, perhaps few of us know its role in the United States at the turn of the century. In
1896, for example, over twenty states passed laws prohibiting marriage and
extramarital relationships with those labeled "eugenically unfit," and in 1899 the
state of Indiana began forcibly sterilizing criminals in prison, a practice that had
spread by 1941 to 16 other states and resulted in over 36,000 sterilizations.
Laws such as these were passed not just in the United States, however, but in
many parts of Europe as well. Given this type of legislation, it is hardly surprising that a 1903 edition of the *Encyclopaedia Britannica* contained an entry for
"Negro" reading thus: "weight of brain, as indicating cranial capacity, 35 ounces
(highest gorilla 20, average European 45) . . . thick epidermis . . . emitting a
peculiar rancid odour, compared . . . to that of a buck goat" (quoted in Ponting,
24). The entry further stated that not only did the Negro and white develop differently but also the Negro brain ceased to develop at an early age, thereby
accounting for the Negro's inferiority.

Clearly, this kind of thinking is what allowed the four core states to control
the world as if it were their own private Monopoly board; the more they were
able to dominate, the more justified the domination seemed. "Might makes
right" was the prevalent attitude. Nor was it simply a matter of controlling what
already existed; it was also a matter of *creating* new realities. In other words,
many ex-colonial states, particularly those in Africa and the Middle East, came
into existence because of artificial "lines drawn on a map somewhere in Europe
in the late nineteenth century or at the end of the First World War[,]" lines that
"cut across tribal and ethnic boundaries with little regard for the people
involved" (Ponting 216).

Given this degree of disregard, the events that occurred in Kenya in 1905
were appalling but inevitable. The land was forcibly taken from the Kenyans by
the British and given to white settlers. Those who objected to this injustice not
only lost their land but also had their cattle confiscated. Once their land was taken
away, the Kenyans were moved to overcrowded "reserves," and although we have
plenty of data illustrating the detrimental effects of overcrowding, the evidence
Kenya provides is overwhelming: in 1902, the native population was 4 million,
but by 1922 it had dropped to 2.5 million. To make matters worse, the burden of
financially supporting the colonial government was put on the Kenyans by the
imposition of one tax after another, many of which they could barely afford to
pay. An import tax, for example, was imposed on agricultural implements used by
the native population, but for the white settlers the same implements were duty

free. In short, not only were the Kenyans forced to accept a government that had taken away their means of economic production, but they were also forced to actively support it.

The British were not the only ones guilty of colonial abuses, however, and we have the United States's handling of the Philippines as proof. After the Spanish–American war of 1898, the United States acquired the Philippines, but perhaps because the Filipinos did not wish to be treated as pawns shuttled from one colonial power to another, they waged a three-year war of independence with U.S. troops. In this brutal war, 4,200 U.S. soldiers were killed and 200,000 Filipinos, over four fifths of whom were civilians. The strange lopsidedness of these losses can perhaps be explained by the following excerpt, taken from a letter written by a U.S. soldier to his parents:

> Last night one of our boys was found shot and his stomach cut open. Immediate orders were received . . . to burn the town and kill every native in sight. . . . About 1,000 men, women and children were reported killed. . . . I am in my glory when I can sight my gun on some dark skin and pull the trigger. (quoted in Ponting, 174–175)

This kind of retaliation indicates something more than a simple will to dominate; the hatred and the racism ring loud and clear. And yet the justification given by President McKinley for holding onto the Philippines masquerades as humanitarianism: "we could not leave them to themselves—they were unfit for self government and would soon have anarchy and misrule over there worse than Spain's was [sic]" (quoted in Ponting, 180). Most chilling of all, when set against the soldier's letter, is McKinley's rhetorical question, "Did we need their consent to perform a great act of humanity?" (quoted in Ponting, 180).

When William Howard Taft became the first civilian governor of the Philippines, he spoke in terms very similar to those of McKinley:

> it is absolutely necessary, in order that the people be taught self-government, that a firm, stable government under American guidance and control . . . should be established. Nothing but such a government can educate the people into a knowledge of what self-government is. (quoted in Ponting, 180)

One of the questions raised by Taft's philosophy is this: Can we learn self-governance if we have no autonomy, if we are given no opportunity to make decisions for ourselves? There can be little doubt that this question was very much on the minds of many colonized peoples, but it was not until 1947 that affirmative answers to this question began to arise. Following various campaigns of anticolonial resistance, 1947 marked the beginning of the formal dissolution of colonial empires and the granting of independence to previously colonized countries. In some cases, independence was won through legal and diplomatic maneuvers, but in other cases such as that of Kenya and Algeria, it was won through war, through which the colonizers were opposed on what many saw as the real ground of colonial power: military might.

The Algerian war of independence, which began in 1954 with the revolt of the Algerian National Liberation Front, is the backdrop against which Frantz Fanon delivered "On National Culture" at the Second National Congress of Black Artists and Writers in Rome. When Fanon wrote this essay, in 1959, Algeria was still three years away from winning independence from France. Fanon actually participated in this war, and thus he speaks from experience when he describes what happens when native intellectuals begin to fight colonialism. Because a nation under colonial rule cannot develop culturally, the native intellectual often looks to the past to find evidence that a valuable cultural heritage existed before the colonial era. Although Fanon sympathizes with this backward-glancing impulse, pointing out that colonialism is not satisfied with imposing its dominion over a colonized people's present and future, but must do so with their past as well, he argues that this excavation of the past is ultimately ineffectual, for what the native intellectual finds are simply the "mummified fragments" of culture, its "outworn contrivances," "the cast-offs of thought, its shells and corpses." And, as Fanon points out, when native intellectuals dig up these cultural relics, they are behaving very much like foreigners in their own country, exoticizing their own people and history. Trotting out these cultural relics will not win a colonized people its freedom, argues Fanon; instead, "[t]o fight for national culture means in the first place to fight for the liberation of the nation, that material keystone which makes the building of a culture possible."

Using Algeria as an example, Fanon argues that in the very fight for freedom, where battles are fought with bare hands in prisons, under the guillotine, and in French outposts captured or destroyed, the Algerian people are creating a national culture. For Fanon, then, the question of national identity comes before that of cultural identity. When he speaks of national identity, however, he is not talking about the kind of jingoism associated with nationalism but about national consciousness. For when a nation casts off colonialism, he argues, it also casts off "the colonized man." The implication here is that when we become free of oppression, we regain our humanity, a humanity that "cannot do otherwise than define a new humanism both for [ourselves] and others." In Fanon's model, national consciousness gives rise not to head-in-the-sand isolationism, but to communication with and responsibility toward our neighbors: we cannot be free without wishing and working for the freedom of others.

As you finish reading Fanon's essay, one of the questions you might ask is why Fanon would be so heavily invested in the idea of *national* culture, given that many African nations were artificially constructed by colonial powers. In other words, why would Fanon want to keep intact and fight for something that was created by the very forces he seeks to oppose? Further, will there come, or has there already come, a time when the model of the discrete nation is no longer useful? Although the latter question is not directly posed by James Clifford, it seems to hover on the outskirts of his essay. Almost thirty years after Fanon delivered "On National Culture," Clifford published *The Predicament of Culture,* the introductory chapter of which appears in this section. The title, "The Pure Products Go Crazy," is taken from a William Carlos Williams poem written around 1920, during the Age of Empires.

According to Clifford, the impetus for the poem was Williams's observation of a girl he calls Elsie helping his wife in the kitchen or laundry room. Because Elsie is "an ambiguous person of questionable origins" who is no longer outside but inside his house, no longer a distant, irrelevant other but connected to Williams through the intimacy of shared domestic space, what his encounter with her represents is a confrontation with modernity itself, a modernity defined by "scattered traditions," "rootlessness," "mobility," "cultural breakdown," "cultural incest," and "lost authenticity"—in short, Elsie represents a pure product gone crazy. But, as Clifford argues, this confrontation is not necessarily a negative one for Williams. Instead, it calls for creative imagination. Williams's world may be changing in strange and unpredictable ways, and yet he views the future not as something to be endured but as something to be invented. For Clifford, Elsie's "invasion" of private bourgeois space anticipates the fight against colonial relationships that began occurring after World War II. With the end of colonialism, the previously colonized "other" could no longer be kept in its (traditional) place. Suddenly, so much depends on Elsie.

During the colonial era, it was easy for the West to speak with privileged authority about its culture and others, but, as Clifford points out, once previously colonized peoples began speaking for themselves, this position of privileged authority was impossible to maintain. And thus a crisis arose in Western ethnographic discourse, out of which emerged important questions: "Who has the authority to speak for a group's identity or authenticity? What are the essential elements and boundaries of a culture?" In other words, how do we engage in ethnographic activity—the scientific description of individual cultures—when we stand not outside culture but inside it, and when the boundaries of individual cultures have begun to blur and shift? Clifford answers this question in a number of interesting ways. First, he emphasizes the collaborative nature of ethnographic texts, referring to them as "orchestrations of multivocal exchanges" that produce "constructed domains of truth, serious fictions." Second, in this description of the ethnographic text as "constructed" truth or "serious fiction," he replaces overblown notions of transcendent truth, authenticity, and authority with historical contingency. In other words, any ethnographic collection that claims to be authoritative is situated locally and temporarily, not universally and transhistorically, and thus always open to revision. Third, Clifford proposes that whenever we intervene in a world that has become as interconnected as ours has, we are always, "to varying degrees, 'inauthentic': caught between cultures, implicated in others."

As you read Clifford, the question you might ask is where he crosses paths with Fanon. Certainly, the two men have important ethnic, historical, and political differences. For example, Fanon, who is Martinican, is writing during the heyday of colonialism, while Clifford, who is American, is writing during what is rather ambiguously referred to as the postcolonial era (the term is ambiguous because Western influence continues, located in fluid combinations of the economic, the political, the military, and the ideological). And while the issue for Clifford is how to operate as an ethnographer in a postcolonial world, the issue for Fanon is how *not* to behave as an ethnographer in one's own country, how to talk *to* one's people rather than *about* them in order to become liberated from colonial rule.

Despite the obvious differences between Fanon and Clifford, perhaps we could nevertheless argue that what is at stake for both is liberation. For Fanon, it is liberation from a hegemonic narrative that would dehumanize and thus exclude him, while for Clifford it is liberation from a hegemonic narrative that configures change as disorder and modernity as the shipwreck of authenticity, essence, or purity. What Clifford proposes instead is an historical vision that no longer thinks of identity as something pure and thus subject to corruption but as something that is always "mixed, relational, inventive." For Clifford, identity is no longer something lost through homogenization or recovered as "archaic survival" but an ongoing process. Here, we encounter echoes of Fanon, for Fanon, too, sees identity as dynamic rather than static:

> It is not enough to try to get back to the people in that past out of which they have already emerged; rather we must join them in that fluctuating movement which they are just giving a shape to, and which, as soon as it has started, will be the signal for everything to be called in question. Let there be no mistake about it; it is to this zone of occult instability where the people dwell that we must come. . . .

In Stuart Hall's "Cultural Identity and Diaspora," published in 1990, we find a good deal of overlap with both Fanon and Clifford. Hall was born in the Caribbean during the colonial era, like Fanon, but moved to Britain in 1951 when he won a Rhodes scholarship. He writes, then, from the uncanny position of "familiar stranger," intimately acquainted with both colonizer (Britain) and colonized (Jamaica) but wholly identified with neither. Could we say that Hall himself is, to use Clifford's terminology, a kind of ethnographic "orchestration," occupying the position of both "native" and "visiting participant-observer"? For even if he writes from a perspective unlike Clifford's, Hall, too, wishes to complicate or problematize "the very authority and authenticity to which the term 'cultural identity' lays claim." Given Clifford's definition of ethnography—"diverse ways of thinking and writing about culture from a standpoint of participant observation"—Hall, it seems, would qualify as an ethnographer in his own right.

Like Clifford, Hall suggests thinking of identity not as "an already accomplished fact" but as "a 'production' which is never complete, always in process, and always constituted within, not outside, representation." Perhaps this is why Hall begins his essay with reference to a new cinema emerging from the Caribbean. For if identity is a "production" constituted within representation, then it is necessary for those whose identity is at stake to take charge of the production, to control the movie camera. Instead of being spoken about, they must speak (of) themselves.

Just who is this emergent, new subject of the cinema? Hall asks. The simple answer is that it is the new postcolonial subject, but how is this new postcolonial subject attempting to represent itself? According to Hall, there are two ways of thinking about representation or cultural identity, and he refers to them as axes or vectors that have a dialogic relationship. The first vector emphasizes the importance of similarity and continuity (being), while the second emphasizes the importance of difference and rupture (becoming).

For Hall, the first vector is exemplified by the artistic work of Armet Francis, whose photographs, taken in Africa, the Caribbean, the United States, and the United Kingdom, "attempt to reconstruct in visual terms 'the underlying unity of the black people whom colonisation and slavery distributed across the African diaspora'. His text is an act of imaginary reunification." While Fanon uses the mother as a metaphor for colonial rule, Hall uses the mother as a metaphor for Africa: Africa as the mother of these disparate civilizations, Africa as the missing term that gives them meaning, Africa as the unifying link. Because the blacks of the Caribbean were taken from Africa and scattered throughout the islands, they are like children separated from their mother at an early age, children who have lost their identity. And, thus, to give them back their mother, metaphorically speaking, is to heal the "rift of separation" that is the Caribbean experience. (In Hall's discussion of diaspora, you will probably be reminded of slave narratives such as those of Olaudah Equiano or Frederick Douglass, both of which mention what might be called "familial diaspora," or the painful separation and dispersal of families when sold into bondage.)

The second vector, however, recognizes that although the blacks of the Caribbean share many similarities, they also have many critical differences, and Hall uses as an example the differences between Martinique, colonized by the French, and Jamaica, colonized by the British. Their differences, according to Hall, are not simply topographical or climatic but cultural and historical as well. For peoples of the Caribbean, both vectors are important, for "being" creates stability and continuity, while "becoming" prevents "being" from ossifying or stagnating. Any attempt to represent cultural identity must take into account the dialogic relationship between "same as" and "different from."

Although Hall briefly makes reference to himself at the beginning of his essay, you'll find Gloria Anzaldúa's essay far more personal than the others in this section. Situating herself at the Denver Museum of Natural History, she begins "Chicana Artists: Exploring *Nepantla, el Lugar de la Frontera*" in the present tense, the effect of which is to place us beside her as she looks at the dismembered body of Coyolxauhqui, an Aztec warrior goddess who was decapitated by her brother. Why, you might ask, does Anzaldúa stop in front of this particular artifact? Why does she give us a detailed description of this one rather than another one? A possible answer is that, as a Mexican-American lesbian, she identifies with the warrior goddess, for, like Coyolxauhqui, Anzaldúa, too, has been decapitated (metaphorically) by a culture that has failed to recognize her existence, by a culture that has "dismembered" her cultural heritage. As she says, she belongs to "a people who have been stripped of [their] history, language, identity and pride." Her essay, then, might be seen as an attempt to write herself into existence, to put her dismembered body back together again—hence the need for the personal pronoun "I."

The anger Anzaldúa feels can be heard loudly and clearly when she comments on her fellow exhibition-goers, the whites who "gape in vicarious wonder and voraciously consume the exoticized images" while making "censorious, culturally ignorant" remarks. Although she recognizes that she, too, is a "gaping consumer," she makes the argument that her consumption is different from that of the "outsiders," for the Aztec civilization is part of her cultural heritage, and reflecting upon these ancient Mexican art forms is a way of gaining access and remaining connected to her historical Indian identity. In the world of her essay, the whites become the "outsiders" and Anzaldúa the "insider." Upsetting our usual notions of inside and outside, the included and the excluded, she speaks of *nepantla,* the Nahuatl word for an in-between state, as the borderland where women artists work and compares it to Jorge Luis Borges's *Aleph:*

> . . . the one spot on earth which contains all other places within. All people in it, whether natives or immigrants, colored or white, queer or heterosexual, from this side of the border or *del otro lado,* are *personas del lugar,* local people—all of whom relate to the border and to *nepantla* in different ways.

Normally, we think of a border as empty of content, but Anzaldúa's border is full of content. Normally, we think of a border as a divider, but Anzaldúa's border is a unifier. In this respect, Anzaldúa's border offers the same fullness and plenitude as Hall's "mother" Africa, for, like "mother" Africa, which heals the "rift of separation" described in Hall's essay, the border becomes a site of healing in Anzaldúa's essay. Instead of separating or creating a barrier, the border transforms "the two home territories, Mexico and the United States[,]" into one.

Appropriately enough, the concept of border bleeds directly into Homi Bhabha's "Border Lives: The Art of the Present," not just in the title but in the epigraph Bhabha uses to introduce his essay: "A boundary is not that at which something stops but, as the Greeks recognized, the boundary is that from *which something begins its presencing.*" This is a quotation taken from Martin Heidegger's "Building, dwelling, thinking," but it could just as easily have come from Anzaldúa's essay. When Anzaldúa speaks of inhabiting the borderland of *nepantla,* however, she speaks specifically of Chicana artists. Bhabha, on the other hand, speaks of our general existence at the century's edge as life lived "on the borderlines of the 'present'." What he means is that, these days, we are less concerned with beginnings and endings than with the in-between, which he describes as "a moment of transit where space and time cross to produce complex figures of difference and identity, past and present, inside and outside, inclusion and exclusion."

You have only to refer back to Clifford, Hall, and Anzaldúa to see very similar ideas being expressed, for when Bhabha speaks of the in-between or the "beyond" as a "back and forth" movement, it is easy to locate a parallel movement in Clifford's articulation of modern ethnography's oscillation between two meta-narratives: "one of homogenization, the other of emergence; one of loss, the other of invention." Similar parallels can be found in Hall's dialogic relation between "being" (similarity and continuity) and "becoming" (difference and rupture) and in Anzaldúa's border *mestizo* culture, "a site where many different cultures 'touch' each other and the permeable, flexible, and ambiguous shifting grounds lend themselves to hybrid images." In each of these conceptions, identity is not something that can be located at one pole or the other, but something that emerges out of the back-and-forth movement itself. And thus we have Bhabha's reference to African-American artist Renée Green, who uses the stairwell as an architectural representation of this in-between space: "The hither and thither of the stairwell, the temporal movement and passage that it allows, prevents identities at either end of it from settling into primordial polarities." For each of these theorists, then, identity is an ongoing process of negotiating what lies between beginnings and endings, the top of the stairwell and the bottom.

One of the most interesting points made by Bhabha, a point that Anzaldúa might appreciate but contest, is that, increasingly, "'national' cultures are being produced from the perspective of disenfranchised minorities," not because these minorities are producing "alternative histories of the excluded"—that is, not because they are simply adding another story to the plurality of stories that already exist—but because their narratives are radically revising the concept of human community itself. According to Bhabha, "the Western Metropole must confront its postcolonial history, told by its influx of postwar migrants and refugees, as an indigenous or native narrative *internal to its national identity* . . . ." Is this not, once again, a confrontation with Elsie, who is inside, not outside, and internal, not external? Is this not the "mixed, relational, inventive" identity that Clifford theorizes? Is this not the *mestiza* experience in which we become, as Anzaldúa says, "both *nos* (us) and *otras* (others)—*nos/otras?*"

Frantz Fanon (1925–1961)

A leading third-world intellectual, Fanon was born into a middle-class black family on the island of Martinique, which was then a French colony. Growing up among descendants of African slaves brought to the Caribbean to work on sugar plantations, he was able to observe the problems of colonialism and racism at very close range. As a teenager, these observations led to his political activism, first in the guerilla struggle against supporters of the pro-Nazi Vichy government and, after 1943, when the Free French forces had gained control in Martinique, in Europe. At the end of World War II, Fanon emerged a decorated war hero. He remained in France to finish his education and to train as a psychiatrist, and it was there that he began his career as a writer. His first book, *Black Skin, White Masks* (1952; trans. 1967), movingly describes his experience as a black man in a white society, regarded not as a human being, but as a specimen of an exotic and savage race.

In 1953, Fanon was appointed head of the psychiatric department of a hospital in Algeria, a French colony in North Africa. Because of his sympathy for Algerians revolting against French rule, he resigned his medical post in 1956 to become editor of the National Liberation Front newspaper. Much of what he wrote during this period centered on the Algerian revolution, the result of which was the publication of *A Dying Colonialism* (1959, trans. 1965). He continued to be involved in the Algerian fight for liberation until his death from leukemia in 1961. He was 36 when he died, but just weeks before his death, he solidified his reputation as a leading revolutionary thinker of the twentieth century with his publication of *The Wretched of the Earth*. This book, which includes an impassioned introduction by existentialist philosopher Jean-Paul Sartre, combines Marxist thought with an anticolonial perspective that shows the complex relationship between class and race in the colonial situation. Fanon's work has been and continues to be important for intellectuals and writers, but it was also inspirational to those involved in the Black Power movement in the United States during the 1960s.

On National Culture

To take part in the African revolution it is not enough to write a revolutionary song; you must fashion the revolution with the people. And if you fashion it with the people, the songs will come by themselves, and of themselves.

In order to achieve real action, you must yourself be a living part of Africa and her thought; you must be an element of that popular energy which is entirely called forth for the freeing, the progress, and the happiness of Africa. There is no place outside that fight for the artist or for the intellectual who is not himself concerned with and completely at one with the people in the great battle of Africa and of suffering humanity.

Sékou Touré.*

Each generation must out of relative obscurity discover its mission, fulfill it, or betray it. In underdeveloped countries the preceding generations have both resisted the work or erosion carried by colonialism and also helped on the maturing of the struggles of today. We must rid ourselves of the habit, now that we are in the thick of the fight, of minimizing the action of our fathers or of feigning incomprehension when considering their silence and passivity. They fought as well as they could, with the arms that they possessed then; and if the echoes of their struggle have not resounded in the international arena, we must realize that the reason for this silence lies less in their lack of heroism than in the fundamentally different international situation of our time. It needed more than one native to say "We've had enough"; more than one peasant rising crushed, more than one demonstration put down before we could today hold our own, certain in our victory. As for we who have decided to break the back of colonialism, our historic mission is to sanction all revolts, all desperate actions, all those abortive attempts drowned in rivers of blood.

In this chapter we shall analyze the problem, which is felt to be fundamental, of the legitimacy of the claims of a nation. It must be recognized that the political party which mobilizes the people hardly touches on this problem of legitimacy. The political parties start from living reality and it is in the name of this reality, in the name of the stark facts which weigh down the present and the future of men and women, that they fix their line of action. The political party may well speak in moving terms of the nation, but what it is concerned with is that the people who are listening understand the need to take part in the fight if, quite simply, they wish to continue to exist.

. . .

Inside the political parties, and most often in offshoots from these parties, cultured individuals of the colonized race make their appearance. For these individuals, the demand for a national culture and the affirmation of the existence of such a culture represent a special battlefield. While the politicians situate their action in actual present-day events, men of culture take their stand in the field of

---

*"The political leader as the representative of a culture." Address to the second Congress of Black Writers and Artists, Rome, 1959.

history. Confronted with the native intellectual who decides to make an aggressive response to the colonialist theory of pre-colonial barbarism, colonialism will
react only slightly, and still less because the ideas developed by the young colonized intelligentsia are widely professed by specialists in the mother country. It is
in fact a commonplace to state that for several decades large numbers of research
workers have, in the main, rehabilitated the African, Mexican, and Peruvian civilizations. The passion with which native intellectuals defend the existence of
their national culture may be a source of amazement; but those who condemn
this exaggerated passion are strangely apt to forget that their own psyche and
their own selves are conveniently sheltered behind a French or German culture
which has given full proof of its existence and which is uncontested.

I am ready to concede that on the plane of factual being the past existence of
an Aztec civilization does not change anything very much in the diet of the Mexican peasant of today. I admit that all the proofs of a wonderful Songhai civilization will not change the fact that today the Songhais are underfed and illiterate,
thrown between sky and water with empty heads and empty eyes. But it has been
remarked several times that this passionate search for a national culture which
existed before the colonial era finds its legitimate reason in the anxiety shared by
native intellectuals to shrink away from that Western culture in which they all
risk being swamped. Because they realize they are in danger of losing their lives
and thus becoming lost to their people, these men, hotheaded and with anger in
their hearts, relentlessly determine to renew contact once more with the oldest
and most pre-colonial springs of life of their people.

Let us go further. Perhaps this passionate research and this anger are kept up
or at least directed by the secret hope of discovering beyond the misery of today,
beyond self-contempt, resignation, and abjuration, some very beautiful and
splendid era whose existence rehabilitates us both in regard to ourselves and in
regard to others. I have said that I have decided to go further. Perhaps unconsciously, the native intellectuals, since they could not stand wonderstruck before
the history of today's barbarity, decided to back further and to delve deeper
down; and, let us make not mistake, it was with the greatest delight that they discovered that there was nothing to be ashamed of in the past, but rather dignity,
glory, and solemnity. The claim to a national culture in the past does not only
rehabilitate that nation and serve as a justification for the hope of a future
national culture. In the sphere of psycho-affective equilibrium, it is responsible
for an important change in the native. Perhaps we have not sufficiently demonstrated that colonialism is not simply content to impose its rule upon the present
and the future of a dominated country. Colonialism is not satisfied merely with
holding a people in its grip and emptying the native's brain of all form and content. By a kind of perverted logic, it turns to the past of the oppressed people,
and distorts, disfigures, and destroys it. This work of devaluing pre-colonial history takes on a dialectical significance today.

When we consider the efforts made to carry out the cultural estrangement so
characteristic of the colonial epoch, we realize that nothing has been left to
chance and that the total result looked for by colonial domination was indeed to
convince the natives that colonialism came to lighten their darkness. The effect
consciously sought by colonialism to drive into the natives' heads the idea that if

the settlers were to leave, they would at once fall back into barbarism, degradation, and bestiality.

On the unconscious plane, colonialism therefore did not seek to be considered by the native as a gentle, loving mother who protects her child from a hostile environment, but rather as a mother who unceasingly restrains her fundamentally perverse offspring from managing to commit suicide and from giving free reign to its evil instincts. The colonial mother protects her child from itself, from its ego, and from its physiology, its biology, and its own unhappiness which is its very essence.

In such a situation the claims of the native intellectual are not a luxury but a necessity in any coherent program. The native intellectual who takes up arms to defend his nation's legitimacy and who wants to bring proofs to bear out that legitimacy, who is willing to strip himself naked to study the history of his body, is obliged to dissect the heart of his people.

Such an examination is not specifically national. The native intellectual who decides to give battle to colonial lies fights on the field of the whole continent. The past is given back its value. Culture, extracted from the past to be displayed in all its splendor, is not necessarily that of his own country. Colonialism, which has not bothered to put too fine a point on its efforts, has never ceased to maintain that the Negro is a savage; and for the colonist, the Negro was neither an Angolan nor a Nigerian, for he simply spoke of "the Negro." For colonialism, this vast continent was the haunt of savages, a country riddled with superstitions and fanaticism, destined for contempt, weighed down by the curse of God, a county of cannibals—in short, the Negro's country. Colonialism's condemnation is continental in its scope. The contention by colonialism that the darkest night of humanity lay over pre-colonial history concerns the whole of the African continent. The efforts of the native to rehabilitate himself and to escape from the claws of colonialism are logically inscribed from the same point of view as that of colonialism. The native intellectual who has gone far beyond the domains of Western culture and who has got it into his head to proclaim the existence of another culture never does so in the name of Angola or of Dahomey. The culture which is affirmed is African culture. The Negro, never so much a Negro as since he has been dominated by the whites, when he decides to prove that he has a culture and to behave like a cultured person, comes to realize that history points out a well-defined path to him: he must demonstrate that a Negro culture exists.

And it is only too true that those who are most responsible for this radicalization of thought, or at least for the first movement toward that thought, are and remain those Europeans who have never ceased to set up white culture to fill the gap left by the absence of other cultures. Colonialism did not dream of wasting its time in denying the existence of one national culture after another. Therefore the reply of the colonized peoples will be straight away continental in its breadth. In Africa, the native literature of the last twenty years is not a national literature but a Negro literature. The concept of negritude, for example, was the emotional if not the logical antithesis of that insult which the white man flung at humanity. This rush of negritude against the white man's contempt showed itself in certain spheres to be the one idea capable of lifting interdictions and anathemas. Because the New Guinean or Kenyan intellectuals found themselves above all up against a general ostracism and delivered to the combined contempt of their overlords, their reaction was to sing praises in admiration of each other. The unconditional affirmation of African culture has succeeded the unconditional affirmation of European culture. On the whole, the poets of negritude oppose the idea of an old Europe to a young Africa, tiresome reasoning to lyricism, oppressive logic to a high-stepping nature, and on one side stiffness, ceremony, etiquette, and skepticism, while on the other frankness, liveliness, liberty, and—why not?—luxuriance: but also irresponsibility.

The poets of negritude will not stop at the limits of the continent. From America, black voices will take up the hymn with fuller unison. The "black world" will see the light and Busia from Ghana, Birago Diop from Senegal, Hampaté Ba from the Soudan, and Saint-Clair Drake from Chicago will not hesitate to assert the existence of common ties and a motive power that is identical.

The example of the Arab world might equally well be quoted here. We know that the majority of Arab territories have been under colonial domination. Colonialism has made the same effort in these regions to plant deep in the minds of the native population the idea that before the advent of colonialism their history was one which was dominated by barbarism. The struggle for national liberty has been accompanied by a cultural phenomenon known by the name of the awakening of Islam. The passion with which contemporary Arab writers remind their people of the great pages of their history is a reply to the lies told by the occupying power. The great names of Arabic literature and the great past of Arab civilization have been brandished about with the same ardor as those of the African civilizations. The Arab leaders have tried to return to the famous Dar El Islam which shone so brightly from the twelfth to the fourteenth century.

Today, in the political sphere, the Arab League is giving palpable form to this will to take up again the heritage of the past and to bring it to culmination. Today, Arab doctors and Arab poets speak to each other across the frontiers, and strive to create a new Arab culture and a new Arab civilization. It is in the name of Arabism that these men join together, and that they try to think together. Everywhere, however, in the Arab world, national feeling has preserved even under colonial domination a liveliness that we fail to find in Africa. At the same time that spontaneous communion of each with all, present in the African movement, is not to be found in the Arab League. On the contrary, paradoxically, everyone tries to sing the praises of the achievement of his nation. The cultural process is freed from the indifferentiation which characterized it in the African world, but the Arabs do not always manage to stand aside in order to achieve their aims. The living culture is not national but Arab. The problem is not as yet to secure a national culture, not as yet to lay hold of a movement differentiated by nations, but to assume an African or Arabic culture when confronted by the all-embracing condemnation pronounced by the dominating power. In the African world, as in the Arab, we see that the claims of the man of culture in a colonized country are all-embracing, continental, and in the case of the Arabs, worldwide.

This historical necessity in which the men of African culture find themselves to racialize their claims and to speak more of African culture than of national culture will tend to lead them up a blind alley. Let us take for example the case of the African Cultural Society. This society had been created by African intellectuals who wished to get to know each other and to compare their experiences and the results of their respective research work. The aim of this society was therefore to affirm the existence of an African culture, to evaluate this culture on the plane of distinct nations, and to reveal the internal motive forces of each of their national cultures. But at the same time this society fulfilled another need: the need to exist side by side with the European Cultural Society, which threatened to transform itself into a Universal Cultural Society. There was therefore at the bottom of this decision the anxiety to be present at the universal trysting place fully armed, with a culture springing from the very heart of the African continent. Now, this Society will very quickly show its inability to shoulder these different tasks, and will limit itself to exhibitionist demonstrations, while the habitual behavior of the members of this Society will be confined to showing Europeans that such a things as African culture exists, and opposing their ideas to those of ostentatious and narcissistic Europeans. We have shown that such an attitude is normal and draws its legitimacy from the lies propagated by men of Western culture, but the degradation of the aims of this Society will become more marked with the elaboration of the concept of negritude. The African Society will become the cultural society of the black world and will come to include the Negro dispersion, that is to say the tens of thousands of black people spread over the American continents.

The Negroes who live in the United States and in Central or Latin America in fact experience the need to attach themselves to a cultural matrix. Their problem is not fundamentally different from that of the Africans. The whites of America did not mete out to them any different treatment from that of the whites who ruled over the Africans. We have seen that the whites were used to putting all Negroes in the same bag. During the first congress of the African Cultural Society which was held in Paris in 1956, the American Negroes of their own accord considered their problems from the same standpoint as those of their African brothers. Cultured Africans, speaking of African civilizations, decreed that there should be a reasonable status within the state for those who had formerly been slaves. But little by little the American Negroes realized that the essential problems confronting them were not the same as those that confronted the African Negroes. The Negroes of Chicago only resemble the Nigerians or the Tanganyikans in so far as they were all defined in relation to the whites. But once the first comparisons had been made and subjective feelings are assuaged, the American Negroes realized that the objective problems were fundamentally heterogeneous. The test cases of civil liberty whereby both whites and blacks in America try to drive back racial discrimination have very little in common in their principles and objectives with the heroic fight of the Angolan people against the detestable Portuguese colonialism. Thus, during the second congress of the African Cultural Society the American Negroes decided to create an American society for people of black cultures.

Negritude therefore finds its first limitation in the phenomena which take account of the formation of the historical character of men. Negro and African-Negro culture broke up into different entities because the men who wished to incarnate these cultures realized that every culture is first and foremost national, and that the problems which kept Richard Wright or Langston Hughes on the alert were fundamentally different from those which might confront Leopold Senghor or Jomo Kenyatta. In the same way certain Arab states, though they had chanted the marvelous hymn of Arab renaissance, had nevertheless to realize that their geographical position and the economic ties of their region were stronger even than the past that they wished to revive. Thus we find today the Arab states organically linked once more with societies which are Mediterranean in their culture. The fact is that these states are submitted to modern pressure and to new channels to trade while the network of trade relations which was dominant during the great period of Arab history has disappeared. But above all there is the fact that the political regimes of certain Arab states are so different, and so far away from each other in their conceptions, that even a cultural meeting between these states is meaningless.

Thus we see that the cultural problem as it sometimes exists in colonized countries runs the risk of giving rise to serious ambiguities. The lack of culture of the Negroes, as proclaimed by colonialism, and the inherent barbarity of the Arabs ought logically to lead to the exaltation of cultural manifestations which are not simply national but continental, and extremely racial. In Africa, the movement of men of culture is a movement toward the Negro-African culture or the Arab-Moslem culture. It is not specifically toward a national culture. Culture is becoming more and more cut off from the events of today. It finds its refuge beside a hearth that glows with passionate emotion, and from there makes its way by realistic paths which are the only means by which it may be made fruitful, homogeneous, and consistent.

. . .

If we wanted to trace in the works of native writers the different phases which characterize this evolution we would find spread out before us a panorama on three levels. In the first phase, the native intellectual gives proof that he has assimilated the culture of the occupying power. His writings correspond point by point with those of his opposite numbers in the mother country. His inspiration is European and we can easily link up these works with definite trends in the literature of the mother country. This is the period of unqualified assimilation. We find in this literature coming from the colonies the Parnassians, the Symbolists, and the Surrealists.

In the second phase we find the native is disturbed; he decides to remember what he is. This period of creative work approximately corresponds to that immersion which we have just described. But since the native is not a part of his people, since he only has exterior relations with his people, he is content to recall their life only. Past happenings of the byegone days of his childhood will be brought up out of the depths of his memory; old legends will be reinterpreted in the light of a borrowed estheticism and of a conception of the world which was discovered under other skies.

Sometimes this literature of just-before-the-battle is dominated by humor and by allegory; but often too it is symptomatic of a period of distress and difficulty, where death is experienced, and disgust too. We spew ourselves up; but already underneath laughter can be heard.

Finally, in the third phase, which is called the fighting phase, the native, after having tried to lose himself in the people and with the people, will on the contrary shake the people. Instead of according the people's lethargy an honored place in his esteem, he turns himself into an awakener of the people; hence comes a fighting literature, a revolutionary literature, and an national literature. During this phase a great many men and women who up till then would never have thought of producing a literary work, now that they find themselves in exceptional circumstances—in prison, with the Maquis, or on the eve of their execution—feel the need to speak to their nation, to compose the sentence which expresses the heart of the people, and to become the mouthpiece of a new reality in action.

The native intellectual nevertheless sooner or later will realize that you do not show proof of your nation from its culture but that you substantiate its existence in the fight which the people wage against the forces of occupation. No colonial system draws its justification from the fact that the territories it dominates are culturally non-existent. You will never make colonialism blush for shame by spreading out little-known cultural treasures under its eyes. At the very moment when the native intellectual is anxiously trying to create a cultural work he fails to realize that he is utilizing techniques and language which are borrowed from the stranger in his country. He contents himself with stamping these instruments with a hallmark which he wishes to be national, but which is strangely reminiscent of exoticism. The native intellectual who comes back to his people by way of cultural achievements behaves in fact like a foreigner. Sometimes he has no hesitation in using a dialect in order to show his will to be as near as possible to the people; but the ideas that he expresses and the preoccupations he is taken up with have no common yardstick to measure the real situation which the men and the women of his country know. The culture that the intellectual leans toward is often no more than a stock of particularisms. He wishes to attach himself to the people; but instead he only catches hold of their outer garments. And these outer garments are merely the reflection of a hidden life, teeming and perpetually in motion. That extremely obvious objectivity which seems to characterize a people is in fact only the inert, already forsaken result of frequent, and not always very coherent, adaptations of a much more fundamental substance which itself is continually being renewed. The man of culture, instead of setting out to find this substance, will let himself be hypnotized by these mummified fragments which because they are static are in fact symbols of negation and outworn contrivances. Culture has never the translucidity of custom; it abhors all simplification. In its essence it is opposed to custom, for custom is always the deterioration of culture. The desire to attach oneself to tradition or bring abandoned traditions to life again does not only mean going against the current of history but also opposing one's own people. When a people undertakes an armed struggle or even a political struggle against a relentless colonialism, the significance of tradition changes. All that has made up the technique of passive resistance in the past may, during this phase, be radically condemned. In an underdeveloped country during the period of struggle traditions are fundamentally unstable and are shot through by centrifugal tendencies. This is why the intellectual often runs the risk of being out of date. The peoples who have carried on the struggle are more and more impervious to demagogy; and those who wish to follow them reveal themselves as nothing more than common opportunists, in other words, latecomers.

In the sphere of plastic arts, for example, the native artist who wishes at whatever cost to create a national work of art shuts himself up in a stereotyped reproduction of details. These artists who have nevertheless thoroughly studied modern techniques and who have taken part in the main trends of contemporary painting and architecture, turn their backs on foreign culture, deny it, and set out to look for a true national culture, setting great store on what they consider to be the constant principles of national art. But these people forget that the forms of thought and what it feeds on, together with modern techniques of information, language, and dress have dialectically reorganized the people's intelligences and that the constant principles which acted as safeguards during the colonial period are now undergoing extremely radical changes.

The artist who has decided to illustrate the truths of the nation turns paradoxically toward the past and away from actual events. What he ultimately intends to embrace are in fact the castoffs of thought, its shells and corpses, a knowledge which has been stabilized once and for all. But the native intellectual who wishes to create an authentic work of art must realize that the truths of a nation are in the first place its realities. He must go on until he has found the seething pot out of which the learning of the future will emerge.

Before independence, the native painter was insensible to the national scene. He set a high value on non-figurative art, and more often specialized in still lifes. After independence his anxiety to rejoin his people will confine him to the most detailed representation of reality. This is representative art which has no internal rhythms, an art which is serene and immobile, evocative not of life but of death. Enlightened circles are in ecstasies when confronted with this "inner truth" which is so well expressed; but we have the right to ask if this truth is in fact a reality, and if it is not already outworn and denied, called in question by the epoch through which the people are treading out their path toward history.

In the realm of poetry we may establish the same facts. After the period of assimilation characterized by rhyming poetry, the poetic tom-tom's rhythms break through. This is a poetry of revolt; but it is also descriptive and analytical poetry. The poet ought however to understand that nothing can replace the reasoned, irrevocable taking up of arms on the people's side.

. . .

Yes, the first duty of the native poet is to see clearly the people he has chosen as the subject of his work of art. He cannot go forward resolutely unless he first realizes the extent of his estrangement from them. We have taken everything from the other side; and the other side gives us nothing unless by a thousand detours we swing finally round in their direction, unless by ten thousand wiles and a hundred thousand tricks they manage to draw us toward them, to seduce us, and to imprison us. Taking means in nearly every case being taken: thus it is not enough to try to free oneself by repeating proclamations and denials. It is not enough to try to get back to the people in that past out of which they have already emerged; rather we must join them in that fluctuating movement which they are just giving a shape to, and which, as soon as it has started, will be the signal for everything to be called in question. Let there be no mistake about it; it is to this zone of occult instability where the people dwell that we must come; and it is there that our souls are crystallized and that our perceptions and our lives are transfused with light.

· · ·

The responsibility of the native man of culture is not a responsibility vis-à-vis his national culture, but a global responsibility with regard to the totality of the nation, whose culture merely, after all, represents one aspect of that nation. The cultured native should not concern himself with choosing the level on which he wishes to fight or the sector where he decides to give battle for his nation. To fight for national culture means in the first place to fight for the liberation of the nation, that material keystone which makes the building of a culture possible. There is no other fight for culture which can develop apart from the popular struggle. To take an example: all those men and women who are fighting with their bare hands against French colonialism in Algeria are not by any means strangers to the national culture of Algeria. The national Algerian culture is taking on form and content as the battles are being fought out, in prisons, under the guillotine, and in every French outpost which is captured or destroyed.

We must not therefore be content with delving into the past of a people in order to find coherent elements which will counteract colonialism's attempts to falsify and harm. We must work and fight with the same rhythm as the people to construct the future and to prepare the ground where vigorous shoots are already springing up. A national culture is not a folklore, nor an abstract populism that believes it can discover the people's true nature. It is not made up of the inert dregs of gratuitous actions, that is to say actions which are less and less attached to the ever-present reality of the people. A national culture is the whole body of efforts made by a people in the sphere of thought to describe, justify, and praise the action through which that people has created itself and keeps itself in existence. A national culture in underdeveloped countries should therefore take its place at the very heart of the struggle for freedom which these countries are carrying on. Men of African cultures are still fighting in the name of African-Negro culture and who have called many congresses in the name of the unity of that culture should today realize that all their efforts amount to is to make comparisons between coins and sarcophagi.

There is no common destiny to be shared between the national cultures of Senegal and Guinea; but there *is* a common destiny between the Sengalese and Guinean nations which are both dominated by the same French colonialism. If it is wished that the national culture of Senegal should come to resemble the national culture of Guinea, it is not enough for the rulers of the two peoples to decide to consider their problems—whether the problem of liberation is concerned, or the trade-union question, or economic difficulties—from similar viewpoints. And even here there does not seem to be complete identity, for the rhythm of the people and that of their rulers are not the same. There can be no two cultures which are completely identical. To believe that it is possible to create a black culture is to forget that niggers are disappearing, just as those people who brought them into being are seeing the breakup of their economic and cultural supremacy.* There will never be such a things as black culture because there is not a single politician who feels he has a vocation to bring black republics into being. The problem is to get to know the place that these men mean to give their people, the kind of social relations that they decide to set up, and the conception that they have of the future of humanity. It is this that counts; everything else is mystification, signifying nothing.

In 1959, the cultured Africans who met at Rome never stopped talking about unity. But one of the people who was loudest in the praise of this cultural unity, Jacques Rabemananjara, is today a minister in the Madagascan government, and as such has decided, with his government, to oppose the Algerian people in the General Assembly of the United Nations. Rabemananjara, if he had been true to himself, ought to have resigned from the government and denounced those men who claim to incarnate the will of the Madagascan people. The ninety thousand dead of Madagascar have not given Rabemananjara authority to oppose the aspirations of the Algerian people in the General Assembly of the United Nations.

It is around the peoples' struggles that African-Negro culture takes on substance, and not around songs, poems, or folklore. Senghor, who is also a member of the Society of African Culture and who has worked with us on the question of African culture, is not afraid for his part either to give the order to his delegation to support French proposals on Algeria. Adherence to African-Negro culture and to the cultural unity of Africa is arrived at in the first place by upholding unconditionally the peoples' struggle for freedom. No one can truly wish for the spread of African culture if he does not give practical support to the creation of the conditions necessary to the existence of that culture; in other words, to the liberation of the whole continent.

I say again that no speech-making and no proclamation concerning culture will turn us from our fundamental tasks: the liberation of the national territory; a continual struggle against colonialism in its new forms; and an obstinate refusal to enter the charmed circle of mutual admiration at the summit.

Reciprocal Bases of National Culture and the Fight for Freedom

Colonial domination, because it is total and tends to oversimplify, very soon manages to disrupt in spectacular fashion the cultural life of a conquered people. This cultural obliteration is made possible by the negation of national reality, by new legal relations introduced by the occupying power, by the banishment of the

---

*At the last school prize giving in Dakar, the president of the Sengalese Republic, Leopold Senghor, decided to include the study of the idea of negritude in the curriculum. If this decision was due to a desire to study historical causes, no one can criticize it. But if on the other hand it was taken in order to create black self-consciousness, it is simply a turning of his back upon history which has already taken cognizance of the disappearance of the majority of Negroes.

natives and their customs to outlying districts by colonial society, by expropriation, and by the systematic enslaving of men and women.

Three years ago at our first congress I showed that, in the colonial situation,
dynamism is replaced fairly quickly by a substantification of the attitudes of the
colonizing power. The area of culture is then marked off by fences and signposts.
These are in fact so many defense mechanisms of the most elementary type, comparable for more than one good reason to the simple instinct for preservation.
The interest of this period for us is that the oppressor does not manage to convince himself of the objective non-existence of the oppressed nation and its culture. Every effort is made to bring the colonized person to admit the inferiority of
his culture which has been transformed into instinctive patterns of behavior, to
recognize the unreality of his "nation," and, in the last extreme, the confused
and imperfect character of his own biological structure.

Vis-à-vis this state of affairs, the native's reactions are not unanimous. While
the mass of the people maintain intact traditions which are completely different
from those of the colonial situation, and the artisanal style solidifies into a formalism which is more and more stereotyped, the intellectual throws himself in
frenzied fashion into the frantic acquisition of the culture of the occupying power
and takes every opportunity of unfavorably criticizing his own national culture,
or else takes refuge in setting out and substantiating the claims of that culture in
a way that is passionate but rapidly becomes unproductive.

The common nature of these two reactions lies in the fact that they both lead
to impossible contradictions. Whether a turncoat or a substantialist, the native is
ineffectual precisely because the analysis of the colonial situation is not carried
out on strict lines. The colonial situation calls a halt to national culture in almost
every field. Within the framework of colonial domination there is not and there
will never be such phenomena as new cultural departures or changes in the
national culture. Here and there valiant attempts are sometimes made to reanimate the cultural dynamic and to give fresh impulses to its themes, its forms, and
its tonalities. The immediate, palpable, and obvious interest of such leaps ahead
is nil. But if we follow up on the consequences to the very end we see that prepa-
rations are being thus made to brush the cobwebs off national consciousness, to
question oppression, and to open up the struggle for freedom.

A national culture under colonial domination is a contested culture whose
destruction is sought in systematic fashion. It very quickly becomes a culture
condemned to secrecy. This idea of a clandestine culture is immediately seen in
the reactions of the occupying power which interprets attachment to traditions as
faithfulness to the spirit of the nation and as a refusal to submit. This persistence
in following forms of cultures which are already condemned to extinction is
already a demonstration of nationality; but it is a demonstration which is a
throwback to the laws of inertia. There is no taking of the offensive and no
redefining of relationships. There is simply a concentration on a hard core of culture which is becoming more and more shriveled up, inert, and empty.

By the time a century or two of exploitation has passed there comes about a
veritable emaciation of the stock of national culture. It becomes a set of automatic habits, some traditions of dress, and a few broken-down institutions. Little
movement can be discerned in such remnants of culture; there is no real creativity

and no overflowing life. The poverty of the people, national oppression, and the inhibition of culture are one and the same thing. After a century of colonial domination we find a culture which is rigid in the extreme, or rather what we find are the dregs of culture, its mineral strata. The withering away of the reality of the nation and the death pangs of the national culture are linked to each other in mutual dependence. This is why it is of capital importance to follow the evolution of these relations during the struggle for national freedom. The negation of the native's culture, the contempt for any manifestation of culture whether active or emotional, and the placing outside the pale of all specialized branches of organization contribute to breed aggressive patterns of conduct in the native. But these patterns of conduct are of the reflexive type; they are poorly differentiated, anarchic, and ineffective. Colonial exploitation, poverty, and endemic famine drive the native more and more to open, organized revolt. The necessity for an open and decisive breach is formed progressively and imperceptibly, and comes to be felt by the great majority of the people. Those tensions which hitherto were non-existent come into being. International events, the collapse of whole sections of colonial empires and the contradictions inherent in the colonial system strengthen and uphold the native's combativity while promoting and giving support to national consciousness.

These new-found tensions which are present at all stages in the real nature of colonialism have their repercussions on the cultural plane. In literature, for example, there is relative overproduction. From being a reply on a minor scale to the dominating power, the literature produced by natives becomes differentiated and makes itself into a will to particularism. The intelligentsia, which during the period of repression was essentially a consuming public, now themselves become producers. This literature at first chooses to confine itself to the tragic and poetic style; but later on novels, short stories, and essays are attempted. It is as if a kind of internal organization or law of expression existed which wills that poetic expression become less frequent in proportion as the objectives and the methods of the struggle for liberation become more precise. Themes are completely altered; in fact, we find less and less of bitter, hopeless recrimination and less also of that violent, resounding, florid writing which on the whole serves to reassure the occupying power. The colonialists have in former times encouraged these modes of expression and made their existence possible. Stinging denunciations, the exposing of distressing conditions and passions which find their outlet in expression are in fact assimilated by the occupying power in a cathartic process. To aid such processes is in a certain sense to avoid their dramatization and to clear the atmosphere.

But such a situation can only be transitory. In fact, the progress of national consciousness among the people modifies and gives precision to the literary utterances of the native intellectual. The continued cohesion of the people constitutes for the intellectual an invitation to go further than his cry of protest. The lament first makes the indictment; and then it makes an appeal. In the period that follows, the words of command are heard. The crystallization of the national consciousness will both disrupt literary styles and themes, and also create a completely new public. While at the beginning the native intellectual used to produce his work to be read exclusively by the oppressor, whether with the intention of charming him or of denouncing him through ethnic or subjectivist means, now the native writer progressively takes on the habit of addressing his own people.

It is only from that moment that we can speak of a national literature. Here there is, at the level of literary creation, the taking up and clarification of themes which are typically nationalist. This may be properly called a literature of combat, in the sense that it calls on the whole people to fight for their existence as a nation. It is a literature of combat, because it molds the national consciousness, giving it form and contours and flinging open before it new and boundless horizons; it is a literature of combat because it assumes responsibility, and because it is the will to liberty expressed in terms of time and space.

On another level, the oral tradition—stories, epics, and songs of the people—which formerly were filed away as set pieces are now beginning to change. The storytellers who used to relate inert episodes now bring them alive and introduce into them modifications which are increasingly fundamental. There is a tendency to bring conflicts up to date and to modernize the kinds of struggle which the stories evoke, together with the names of heroes and the types of weapons. The method of allusion is more and more widely used. The formula "This all happened long ago" is substituted with that of "What we are going to speak of happened somewhere else, but it might well have happened here today, and it might happen tomorrow." The example of Algeria is significant in this context. From 1952–53 on, the storytellers, who were before that time stereotyped and tedious to listen to, completely overturned their traditional methods of storytelling and the contents of their tales. Their public, which was formerly scattered, became compact. The epic, with its typified categories, reappeared; it became an authentic form of entertainment which took on once more a cultural value. Colonialism made no mistake when from 1955 on it proceeded to arrest these storytellers systematically.

The contact of the people with the new movement gives rise to a new rhythm of life and to forgotten muscular tensions, and develops the imagination. Every time the storyteller relates a fresh episode to his public, he presides over a real invocation. The existence of a new type of man is revealed to the public. The present is no longer turned in upon itself but spread out for all to see. The storyteller once more gives free rein to him imagination; he makes innovations and he creates a work of art. It even happens that the characters, which are barely ready for such a transformation—highway robbers or more or less antisocial vagabonds—are taken up and remodeled. The emergence of the imagination and of the creative urge in the songs and epic stories of a colonized country is worth following. The storyteller replies to the expectant people by successive approximations, and makes his way, apparently alone but in fact helped on by his public, toward the seeking out of new patterns, that is to say national patterns. Comedy and farce disappear, or lose their attraction. As for dramatization, it is no longer placed on the plane of the troubled intellectual and his tormented conscience. By losing its characteristics of despair and revolt, the drama becomes part of the common lot of the people and forms part of an action in preparation or already in progress.

Where handicrafts are concerned, the forms of expression which formerly were the dregs of art, surviving as if in a daze, now begin to reach out. Woodwork, for example, which formerly turned out certain faces and attitudes by the million, begins to be differentiated. The inexpressive or overwrought mask comes to life and the arms tend to be raised from the body as if to sketch an action. Compositions containing two, three, or five figures appear. The traditional schools are led on to creative efforts by the rising avalanche of amateurs or of critics. This new vigor in this sector of cultural life very often passes unseen; and yet its contribution to the national effort is of capital importance. By carving figures and faces which are full of life, and by taking as his theme a group fixed on the same pedestal, the artist invites participation in an organized movement.

If we study the repercussions of the awakening of national consciousness in the domains of ceramics and pottery-making, the same observations may be drawn. Formalism is abandoned in the craftsman's work. Jugs, jars, and trays are modified, at first imperceptibly, then almost savagely. The colors, of which formerly there were but few and which obeyed the traditional rules of harmony, increase in number and are influenced by the repercussion of the rising revolution. Certain ochres and blues, which seemed forbidden to all eternity in a given cultural area, now assert themselves without giving rise to scandal. In the same way the stylization of the human face, which according to sociologists is typical of very clearly defined regions, becomes suddenly completely relative. The specialist coming from the home country and the ethnologist are quick to note these changes. On the whole such changes are condemned in the name of a rigid code of artistic style and of a cultural life which grows up at the heart of the colonial system. The colonialist specialists do not recognize these new forms and rush to the help of the traditions of the indigenous society. It is the colonialists who become the defenders of the native style. We remember perfectly, and the example took on a certain measure of importance since the real nature of colonialism was not involved, the reactions of the white jazz specialists when after the Second World War new styles such as the be-bop took definite shape. The fact is that in their eyes jazz should only be the despairing, broken-down nostalgia of an old Negro who is trapped between five glasses of whiskey, the curse of his race, and the racial hatred of the white men. As soon as the Negro comes to an understanding of himself, and understands the rest of the world differently, when he gives birth to hope and forces back the racist universe, it is clear that his trumpet sounds more clearly and his voice less hoarsely. The new fashions in jazz are not simply born of economic competition. We must without any doubt see in them one of the consequences of the defeat, slow but sure, of the southern world of the United States. And it is not utopian to suppose that in fifty years' time the type of jazz howl hiccuped by a poor misfortunate Negro will be upheld only by the whites who believe in it as an expression of negritude, and who are faithful to this arrested image of a type of relationship.

We might in the same way seek and find in dancing, singing, and traditional rites and ceremonies the same upward-springing trend, and make out the same changes and the same impatience in this field. Well before the political or fighting phase of the national movement, an attentive spectator can thus feel and see the manifestation of new vigor and feel the approaching conflict. He will note unusual forms of expression and themes which are fresh and imbued with a power which is no longer that of invocation but rather of the assembling of the people, a summoning together for a precise purpose. Everything works together to awaken the native's sensibility and to make unreal and inacceptable the contemplative attitude, or the acceptance of defeat. The native rebuilds his perceptions because he renews the purpose and dynamism of the craftsmen, of dancing and music, and of literature and the oral tradition. His world comes to lose its accursed character. The conditions necessary for the inevitable conflict are brought together.

We have noted the appearance of the movement in cultural forms and we have seen that this movement and these new forms are linked to the state of maturity of the national consciousness. Now, this movement tends more and more to express itself objectively, in institutions. From thence comes the need for a national existence, whatever the cost.

A frequent mistake, and one which is moreover hardly justifiable, is to try to find cultural expressions for and to give new values to native culture within the framework of colonial domination. This is why we arrive at a proposition which at first sight seems paradoxical: the fact that in a colonized country the most elementary, most savage, and the most undifferentiated nationalism is the most fervent and efficient means of defending national culture. For culture is first the expression of a nation, the expression of its preferences, of its taboos and of its patterns. It is at every stage of the whole of society that other taboos, values, and patterns are formed. A national culture is the sum total of all these appraisals; it is the result of internal and external tensions exerted over society as a whole and also at every level of that society. In the colonial situation, culture, which is doubly deprived of the support of the nation and of the state, falls away and dies. The condition for its existence is therefore national liberation and the renaissance of the state.

The nation is not only the condition of culture, its fruitfulness, its continuous renewal, and its deepening. It is also a necessity. It is the fight for national existence which sets culture moving and opens to it the doors of creation. Later on it is the nation which will ensure the conditions and framework necessary to culture. The nation gathers together the various indispensable elements necessary for the creation of a culture, those elements which alone can give it credibility, validity, life, and creative power. In the same way it is its national character that will make such a culture open to other cultures and which will enable it to influence and permeate other cultures. A non-existent culture can hardly be expected to have bearing on reality, or to influence reality. The first necessity is the reestablishment of the nation in order to give life to national culture in the strictly biological sense of the phrase.

Thus we have followed the breakup of the old strata of culture, a shattering which becomes increasingly fundamental; and we have noticed, on the eve of the decisive conflict for national freedom, the renewing of forms of expression and the rebirth of the imagination. There remains one essential question: what are the relations between the struggle—whether political or military—and culture? Is there a suspension of culture during the conflict? Is the national struggle an expression of a culture? Finally, ought one to say that the battle for freedom however fertile *a posteriori* with regard to culture is in itself a negation of culture? In short, is the struggle for liberation of a cultural phenomenon or not?

We believe that the conscious and organized undertaking of a colonized people to re-establish the sovereignty of that nation constitutes the most complete and obvious cultural manifestation that exists. It is not alone the success of the struggle which afterward gives validity and vigor to culture; culture is not put into cold storage during the conflict. The struggle itself in its development and in its internal progression sends culture along different paths and traces out entirely new ones for it. The struggle for freedom does not give back to the national culture its former values and shapes; this struggle which aims at a fundamentally different set of relations between men cannot leave intact either the form or the content of the people's culture. After the conflict there is not only the disappearance of colonialism but also the disappearance of the colonized man.

This new humanity cannot do otherwise than define a new humanism both for itself and for others. It is pre-figured in the objectives and methods of the conflict. A struggle which mobilizes all classes of the people and which expresses their aims and their impatience, which is not afraid to count almost exclusively on the people's support, will of necessity triumph. The value of this type of conflict is that it supplies the maximum of conditions necessary for the development and aims of culture. After national freedom has been obtained in these conditions, there is no such painful cultural indecision which is found in certain countries which are newly independent, because the nation by its manner of coming into being and in the terms of its existence exerts a fundamental influence over culture. A nation which is born of the people's concerted action and which embodies the real aspirations of the people while changing the state cannot exist save in the expression of exceptionally rich forms of culture.

The natives who are anxious for the culture of their country and who wish to give to it a universal dimension ought not therefore to place their confidence in the single principle of inevitable, undifferentiated independence written into the consciousness of the people in order to achieve their task. The liberation of the nation is one thing; the methods and popular content of the fight are another. It seems to us that the future of national culture and its riches are equally also part and parcel of the values which have ordained the struggle for freedom.

And now it is time to denounce certain pharisees. National claims, it is here and there stated, are a phase that humanity has left behind. It is the day of great concerted actions, and retarded nationalists ought in consequence to set their mistakes aright. We however consider that the mistake, which may have very serious consequences, lies in wishing to skip the national period. If culture is the expression of national consciousness, I will not hesitate to affirm that in the case with which we are dealing it is the national consciousness which is the most elaborate form of culture.

The consciousness of self is not the closing of a door to communication. Philosophic thought teaches us, on the contrary, that it is its guarantee. National consciousness, which is not nationalism, is the only things that will give us an international dimension. This problem of national consciousness and of national culture takes on in Africa a special dimension. The birth of a national consciousness in Africa has a strictly contemporaneous connection with the African consciousness. The responsibility of the African as regards national culture is also a responsibility with regard to African Negro culture. This joint responsibility is not the fact of a metaphysical principle but the awareness of a simple rule which wills that every independent nation in an Africa where colonialism is still entrenched is an encircled nation, a nation which is fragile and in permanent danger.

If man is known by his acts, then we will say that the most urgent thing today for the intellectual is to build up his nation. If this building up is true, that is to say if it interprets the manifest will of the people and reveals the eager African peoples, then the building of a nation is of necessity accompanied by the discovery and encouragement of universalizing values. Far from keeping aloof from other nations, therefore, it is national liberation which leads the nation to play its part of the stage of history. It is at the heart of consciousness that international consciousness lives and grows. And this two-fold emerging is ultimately only the source of all culture.

Statement made at the Second Congress
of Black Artists and Writers, Rome, 1959

James Clifford (1945–)

Trained in social and intellectual history at Harvard during the 1970s, Clifford currently teaches in the History of Consciousness Program at the University of California–Santa Cruz. Although he says in an interview published in the Italian version of AVATAR that it now seems to him he became an historian quite by chance, he is nevertheless best known for his historical and literary critiques of anthropological practice, travel literature, and Western exoticism. During his graduate study, one of the most influential works for Clifford was Raymond Williams's *Culture and Society,* a book that impressed Clifford because it offered "a way of talking about ideas, like 'culture,' not simply at the level of intellectuals influencing other great intellectuals but as implicated and entangled with historical process" (AVATAR March 2001, 124–136). While Williams had "historicized the idea of culture in its more literary humanist versions," says Clifford, what he wanted to do was historicize the idea of culture from an ethnographical and anthropological standpoint.

Clifford's first book, *Person and Myth: Maurice Leenhardt in the Melanesian World* (1982), was an exploration of cross-cultural translation and transformation in the ongoing colonial situation of New Caledonia. His second book, *Writing Culture: the Poetics and Politics of Ethnography* (1986), coedited with George Marcus, created considerable controversy in sociocultural anthropology and related fields. "The Pure Products Go Crazy," which appears next, is the introductory chapter to *The Predicament of Culture* (1988), a collection of Clifford's essays on twentieth-century ethnography, literature, and art. Because of its wide appeal and influence, this collection has been translated into seven languages. Clifford's most recent book, *Routes: Travel and Translation in the Late Twentieth Century* (1997), explores issues of dwelling and travel in anthropology, travel, tourism, and a range of cultural performances.

Introduction:
The Pure Products Go Crazy

> *We were once the masters of the earth, but since the gringos arrived we have become veritable pariahs . . . We hope that the day will come when they realize that we are their roots and that we must grow together like a giant tree with its branches and flowers.*
>
> Francisco Servin, Pai-Tavytera, at the Congress of Indians, Paraguay, 1974

Sometime around 1920 in a New Jersey suburb of New York City, a young doctor wrote a poem about a girl he called Elsie. He saw her working in his kitchen or laundry room, helping his wife with the house cleaning or the kids. Something about her brought him up short. She seemed to sum up where everything was going—his family, his fledgling practice, his art, the modern world that surrounded and caught them all in its careening movement.

The poem William Carlos Williams wrote was a rush of associations, beginning with a famous assertion:

> The pure products of America
> go crazy—

and continuing almost without stopping for breath . . .

> mountain folk from Kentucky
>
> or the ribbed north end of
> Jersey
> with its isolate lakes and
>
> valleys, its deaf-mutes, thieves
> old names
> and promiscuity between
>
> devil-may-care men who have taken
> to railroading
> out of sheer lust for adventure—
>
> and young slatterns, bathed
> in filth
> from Monday to Saturday
>
> to be tricked out that night
> with gauds
> from imaginations which have no

peasant traditions to give them
character
but flutter and flaunt

sheer rags—succumbing without
emotion
save numbed terror

under some hedge of choke-cherry
or viburnum—
which they cannot express—

Unless it be that marriage
perhaps
with a dash of Indian blood

will throw up a girl so desolate
so hemmed round
with disease or murder

that she'll be rescued by an
agent—
reared by the state and

sent out at fifteen to work in
some hard pressed
house in the suburbs—

some doctor's family, some Elsie—
voluptuous water
expressing with broken

brain the truth about us—
her great
ungainly hips and flopping breasts

addressed to cheap
jewelry
and rich young men with fine eyes

when suddenly the angry description veers:

as if the earth under our feet
were
an excrement of some sky

and we degraded prisoners
destined
to hunger until we eat filth

while the imagination strains
after deer
going by fields of goldenrod in

> the stifling heat of September
> Somehow
> it seems to destroy us
>
> It is only in isolate flecks that
> something
> is given off
>
> No one
> to witness
> and adjust, no one to drive the car

These lines emerged en route in Williams' dada treatise on the imagination, *Spring & All* (1923). I hope they can serve as a pretext for this book, a way of starting in with a predicament. Call the predicament ethnographic modernity: ethnographic because Williams finds himself off center among scattered traditions; modernity since the condition of rootlessness and mobility he confronts is an increasingly common fate. "Elsie" stands simultaneously for a local cultural breakdown and a collective future. To Williams her story is inescapably his, everyone's. Looking at the "great/ungainly hips and flopping breasts" he feels things falling apart, everywhere. All the beautiful, primitive places are ruined. A kind of cultural incest, a sense of runaway history pervades, drives the rush of associations.

This feeling of lost authenticity, of "modernity" ruining some essence or source, is not a new one. In *The Country and the City* (1973) Raymond Williams finds it to be a repetitive, pastoral "structure of feeling." Again and again over the millennia change is configured as disorder, pure products go crazy. But the image of Elsie suggests a new turn. By the 1920s a truly global space of cultural connections and dissolutions has become imaginable: local authenticities meet and merge in transient urban and suburban settings—settings that will include the immigrant neighborhoods of New Jersey, multicultural sprawls like Buenos Aires, the townships of Johannesburg. While William Carlos Williams invokes the pure products of America, the "we" careening in his driverless car is clearly something more. The ethnographic modernist searches for the universal in the local, the whole in the part. Williams' famous choice of an American (rather than English) speech, his regionally based poetic and medical practice must not cut him off from the most general human processes. His cosmopolitanism requires a perpetual veering between local attachments and general possibilities.

Elsie disrupts the project, for her very existence raises *historical* uncertainties underlining the modernist doctor-poet's secure position.[1] His response to the disorder she represents is complex and ambivalent. If authentic traditions, the pure products, are everywhere yielding to promiscuity and aimlessness, the option of nostalgia holds no charm. There is no going back, no essence to redeem. Here, and throughout his writing, Williams avoids pastoral, folkloristic appeals of the sort common among other liberals in the twenties—exhorting, preserving, collecting a true rural culture in endangered places like Appalachia. Such authenticities would be at best artificial aesthetic purifications (Whisnant 1983). Nor does Williams settle for two other common ways of confronting the rush of history.

He does not evoke Elsie and the idiocy of rural life to celebrate a progressive, technological future. He shares her fate, for there really is "no one to drive the car"—a frightening condition. Nor does Williams resign himself sadly to the loss of local traditions in an entropic modernity—a vision common among prophets of cultural homogenization, lamenters of the ruined tropics. Instead, he claims that "something" is still being "given off"—if only in "isolate flecks."

It is worth dwelling on the discrepancy between this emergent, dispersed "something" and the car in which "we" all ride. Is it possible to resist the poem's momentum, its rushed inevitability? To do so is not so much to offer an adequate reading (of a poetic sequence abstracted from *Spring & All*) as it is to reflect on several readings, on several historical "Elsies." Let this problematic figure with her "dash of Indian blood," her ungainly female form, her inarticulateness stand for groups marginalized or silenced in the bourgeois West: "natives," women, the poor. There is violence, curiosity, pity, and desire in the poet's gaze. Elsie provokes very mixed emotions. Once again a female, possibly colored body serves as a site of attraction, repulsion, symbolic appropriation. Elsie lives only for the eyes of privileged men. An inarticulate muddle of lost origins, she is going nowhere. Williams evokes this with his angry, bleak sympathy—and then turns it all into modern history. Two-thirds of the way through the poem, Elsie's personal story shifts toward the general; her own path through the suburban kitchen vanishes. She, Williams, all of us are caught in modernity's inescapable momentum.

Something similar occurs whenever marginal peoples come into a historical or ethnographic space that has been defined by the Western imagination. "Entering the modern world," their distinct histories quickly vanish. Swept up in a destiny dominated by the capitalist West and by various technologically advanced socialisms, these suddenly "backward" peoples no longer invent local futures. What is different about them remains tied to traditional pasts, inherited structures that either resist or yield to the new but cannot produce it.

This book proposes a different historical vision. It does not see the world as populated by endangered authenticities—pure products always going crazy. Rather, it makes space for specific paths through modernity, a recognition anticipated by Williams' discrepant question: what is "given off" by individual histories like Elsie's? Are the "isolate flecks" dying sparks? New beginnings? Or . . . ? "Compose. (No ideas/but in things) Invent!" This was Williams' slogan (1967:7). In *Spring & All* the human future is something to be creatively imagined, not simply endured: "new form dealt with as reality itself . . . To enter a new world, and have there freedom of movement and newness" (1923:70, 71). But geopolitical questions must now he asked of every inventive poetics of reality, including that urged by this book: Whose reality? Whose new world? Where exactly does anyone stand to write "as if the earth under *our* feet/were an excrement of some sky/and *we* . . . destined . . ."?

People and things are increasingly out of place. A doctor-poet-fieldworker, Williams watches and listens to New Jersey's immigrants, workers, women giving birth, pimply-faced teenagers, mental cases. In their lives and words, encountered through a privileged participant observation both poetic and scientific, he finds material for his writing. Williams moves freely out into the homes of his patients, keeping a medical-aesthetic distance (though sometimes with great difficulty, as in the "beautiful thing" sequences of *Paterson,* book 3). The meeting with Elsie is somehow different: a troubling outsider turns up *inside* bourgeois domestic space. She cannot be held at a distance.

This invasion by an ambiguous person of questionable origin anticipates developments that would become widely apparent only after the Second World War. Colonial relations would be pervasively contested. After 1950 peoples long spoken for by Western ethnographers, administrators, and missionaries began to speak and act more powerfully for themselves on a global stage. It was increasingly difficult to keep them in their (traditional) places. Distinct ways of life once destined to merge into "the modern world" reasserted their difference, in novel ways. We perceive Elsie differently in light of these developments.

Reading against the poem's momentum, from new positions, we are able to wonder: What becomes of this girl after her stint in William Carlos Williams' kitchen? Must she symbolize a dead end? What does Elsie prefigure? As woman: her ungainly body is either a symbol of failure in a world dominated by the male gaze or the image of a powerful, "disorderly" female form, an alternative to sexist definitions of beauty. As impure product: this mix of backgrounds is either an uprooted lost soul or a new hybrid person, less domestic than the suburban family home she passes through. As American Indian: Elsie is either the last all-but-assimilated remnant of the Tuscaroras who, according to tradition, settled in the Ramapough hills of Northern New Jersey, *or* she represents a Native American past that is being turned into an unexpected future. (During the last decade a group of Elsie's kin calling themselves the Ramapough Tribe have actively asserted an Indian identity.)[2] Williams' assimilation of his symbolic servant to a shared destiny seems less definitive now.

"Elsie," read in the late twentieth century, is both more specific and less determined. Her possible futures reflect an unresolved set of challenges to Western visions of modernity—challenges that resonate throughout this book. Elsie is still largely silent here, but her disturbing presences—a plurality of emergent subjects—can be felt.[3] The time is past when privileged authorities could routinely "give voice" (or history) to others without fear of contradiction. "Croce's great dictum that all history is contemporary history does not mean that all history is *our* contemporary history . . ." (Jameson 1981:18) When the prevailing narratives of Western identity are contested, the political issue of history as emergence becomes inescapable. Juliet Mitchell writes in *Women: The Longest Revolution* (1984): "I do not think that we can live as human subjects without in some sense taking on a history; for us, it is mainly the history of being men or women under bourgeois capitalism. In deconstructing that history, we can only construct other histories. What are we in the process of becoming?" (p. 294). We are not all together in Williams' car.

Only one of Elsie's emergent possibilities, the one connected with her "dash of Indian blood," is explored in this book. During the fall of 1977 in Boston Federal Court the descendants of Wampanoag Indians living in Mashpee, "Cape Cod's Indian Town," were required to prove their identity. To establish a legal right to sue for lost lands these citizens of modern Massachusetts were asked to demonstrate continuous tribal existence since the seventeenth century. Life in Mashpee had changed dramatically, however, since the first contacts between English Pilgrims at Plymouth and the Massachusett-speaking peoples of the region. Were the plaintiffs of 1977 the "same" Indians? Were they something more than a collection of individuals with varying degrees of Native American ancestry? If they were different from their neighbors, how was their "tribal" difference manifested? During a long, well-publicized trial scores of Indians and whites testified about life in Mashpee. Professional historians, anthropologists, and sociologists took the stand as expert witnesses. The bitter story of New England Indians was told in minute detail and vehemently debated. In the conflict of interpretations, concepts such as "tribe," "culture," "identity," "assimilation," "ethnicity," "politics," and "community" were themselves on trial. I sat through most of the forty days of argument, listening and taking notes.

It seemed to me that the trial—beyond its immediate political stakes—was a crucial experiment in cross-cultural translation. Modern Indians, who spoke in New England–accented English about the Great Spirit, had to convince a white Boston jury of their authenticity. The translation process was fraught with ambiguities, for all the cultural boundaries at issue seemed to be blurred and shifting. The trial raised far-reaching questions about modes of cultural interpretation, implicit models of wholeness, styles of distancing, stories of historical development.

I began to see such questions as symptoms of a pervasive postcolonial crisis of ethnographic authority. While the crisis has been felt most strongly by formerly hegemonic Western discourses, the questions it raises are of global significance. Who has the authority to speak for a group's identity or authenticity? What are the essential elements and boundaries of a culture? How do self and other clash and converse in the encounters of ethnography, travel, modern interethnic relations? What narratives of development, loss, and innovation can account for the present range of local oppositional movements? During the trial these questions assumed a more than theoretical urgency.

My perspective in the courtroom was an oblique one. I had just finished a Ph.D. thesis in history with a strong interest in the history of the human sciences, particularly cultural anthropology. At the time of the trial I was rewriting my dissertation for publication. The thesis was a biography of Maurice Leenhardt, a missionary and ethnographer in French New Caledonia and an ethnologist in Paris (Clifford 1982a). What could be farther from New England Indians? The connections turned out to be close and provocative.

In Melanesia Leenhardt was deeply involved with tribal groups who had experienced a colonial assault as extreme as that inflicted in Massachusetts. He was preoccupied with practical and theoretical problems of cultural change, syncretism, conversion, and survival. Like many American Indians the militarily defeated Kanaks of New Caledonia had "tribal" institutions forced on them as a restrictive reservation system. Both groups would make strategic accommodations with these external forms of government. Native Americans and Melanesians would survive periods of acute demographic and cultural crisis, as well as periods of change and revival. Over the last hundred years New Caledonia's Kanaks have managed to find powerful, distinctive ways to live as Melanesians in an invasive world. It seemed to me that the Mashpee were struggling toward a similar goal, reviving and inventing ways to live as Indians in the twentieth century.

Undoubtedly what I heard in the New England courtroom influenced my sense of Melanesian identity, something I came to understand not as an archaic survival but as an ongoing process, politically contested and historically unfinished. In my studies of European ethnographic institutions I have cultivated a similar attitude.

This book is concerned with Western visions and practices. They are shown, however, responding to forces that challenge the authority and even the future identity of "the West." Modern ethnography appears in several forms, traditional and innovative. As an academic practice it cannot be separated from anthropology. Seen more generally, it is simply diverse ways of thinking and writing about culture from a standpoint of participant observation. In this expanded sense a poet like Williams is an ethnographer. So are many of the people social scientists have called "native informants." Ultimately my topic is a pervasive condition of off-centeredness in a world of distinct meaning systems, a state of being in culture while looking at culture, a form of personal and collective self-fashioning. This predicament—not limited to scholars, writers, artists, or intellectuals—responds to the twentieth century's unprecedented overlay of traditions. A modern "ethnography" of conjunctures, constantly moving *between* cultures, does not, like its Western alter ego "anthropology," aspire to survey the full range of human diversity or development. It is perpetually displaced, both regionally focused and broadly comparative, a form both of dwelling and of travel in a world where the two experiences are less and less distinct.

This book migrates between local and global perspectives, constantly recontextualizing its topic. Part One focuses on strategies of writing and representation, strategies that change historically in response to the general shift from high colonialism around 1900 to postcolonialism and neocolonialism after the 1950s. In these chapters I try to show that ethnographic texts are orchestrations of multivocal exchanges occurring in politically charged situations. The subjectivities produced in these often unequal exchanges—whether of "natives" or of visiting participant-observers—are constructed domains of truth, serious fictions. Once this is recognized, diverse inventive possibilities for postcolonial ethnographic representation emerge, some of which are surveyed in this book. Part Two portrays ethnography in alliance with avant-garde art and cultural criticism, activities with which it shares modernist procedures of collage, juxtaposition, and estrangement. The "exotic" is now nearby. In this section I also probe the limits of Western ethnography through several self-reflexive forms of travel writing, exploring the possibilities of a twentieth-century "poetics of displacement." Part Three turns to the history of collecting, particularly the classification and display of "primitive" art and exotic "cultures." My general aim is to displace any transcendent regime of authenticity, to argue that all authoritative collections, whether made in the name of art or science, are historically contingent and subject to local reappropriation. In the book's final section I explore how non-Western historical experiences—those of "orientals" and "tribal" Native Americans—are hemmed in by concepts of continuous tradition and the unified self. I argue that identity, considered ethnographically, must always be mixed, relational, and inventive.

Self-identity emerges as a complex cultural problem in my treatment of two polyglot refugees, Joseph Conrad and Bronislaw Malinowski, Poles shipwrecked in England and English. Both men produced seminal meditations on the local fictions of collective life, and, with different degrees of irony, both constructed identities based on the acceptance of limited realities and forms of expression. Embracing the serious fiction of "culture," they wrote at a moment when the ethnographic (relativist and plural) idea began to attain its modern currency. Here and elsewhere in the book I try to historicize and see beyond this currency, straining for a concept that can preserve culture's differentiating functions while conceiving of collective identity as a hybrid, often discontinuous inventive process. Culture is a deeply compromised idea I cannot yet do without.

Some of the political dangers of culturalist reductions and essences are explored in my analysis of Edward Said's polemical work *Orientalism* (1978a). What emerges is the inherently discrepant stance of a post-colonial "oppositional" critic, for the construction of simplifying essences and distancing dichotomies is clearly not a monopoly of Western Orientalist experts. Said himself writes in ways that simultaneously assert and subvert his own authority. My analysis suggests that there can be no final smoothing over of the discrepancies in his discourse, since it is increasingly difficult to maintain a cultural and political position "outside" the Occident from which, in security, to attack it. Critiques like Said's are caught in the double ethnographic movement I have been evoking. Locally based and politically engaged, they must resonate globally; while they engage pervasive postcolonial processes, they do so without overview, from a blatantly partial perspective.

Intervening in an interconnected world, one is always, to varying degrees, "inauthentic": caught between cultures, implicated in others. Because discourse in global power systems is elaborated vis-à-vis, a sense of difference or distinctness can never be located solely in the continuity of a culture or tradition. Identity is conjunctural, not essential. Said addresses these issues most affectingly in *After the Last Sky,* a recent evocation of "Palestinian Lives" and of his own position among them (1986a:150): "A part of something is for the foreseeable future going to be better than all of it. Fragments over wholes. Restless nomadic activity over the settlements of held territory. Criticism over resignation. The Palestinian as self-consciousness in a barren plain of investments and consumer appetites. The heroism of anger over the begging bowl, limited independence over the status of clients. Attention, alertness, focus. To do as others do, but somehow to stand apart. To tell your story in pieces, as *it is.*" This work appeared as I was finishing my own book. Thus my discussion of *Orientalism* merely anticipates Said's ongoing search for nonessentialist forms of cultural politics. *After the Last Sky* actively inhabits the discrepancy between a specific conditions of Palestinian exile and a more general twentieth-century range of options. It is (and is not only) as a Palestinian that Said movingly accepts "our wanderings," pleading for "the open secular element, and not the symmetry of redemption" (p. 150).

I share this suspicion of "the symmetry of redemption." Questionable acts of purification are involved in any attainment of a promised land, return to "original" sources, or gathering up of a true tradition. Such claims to purity are in any event always subverted by the need to stage authenticity *in opposition to* external, often dominating alternatives. Thus the "Third World" plays itself against the "First World," and vice versa. At a local level, Trobriand Islanders invent *their* culture within and against the contexts of recent colonial history and the new nation of Papua–New Guinea. If authenticity is relational, there can be no essence except as a political, cultural invention, a local tactic.

In this book, I question some of the local tactics of Western ethnography, focusing on redemptive modes of textualization and particularly of collecting. Several chapters analyze in some detail the systems of authenticity that have been imposed on creative works of non-Western art and culture. They look at collecting and authenticating practices in contemporary settings: for example the controversy surrounding an exhibition at the Museum of Modern Art in New York City over the relations between "tribal" and "modern" art. How have exotic objects been given value as "art" and "culture" in Western collecting systems? I do not argue, as some critics have, that non-Western objects are properly understood only with reference to their original milieux. Ethnographic contextualizations are as problematic as aesthetic ones, as susceptible to purified, ahistorical treatment.

I trace the modern history of both aesthetic and ethnographic classifications in an earlier setting: avant-garde Paris of the 1920s and 1930s, a radical context I call ethnographic surrealism. Two influential museums, the Musée d'Ethnographie du Trocadéro and its scientific successor, the Musée de l'Homme, symbolize distinct modes of "art and culture collecting." Their juxtaposition forces the question: How are ethnographic worlds and their meaningful artifacts cut up, salvaged, and valued? Here culture appears not as a tradition to be saved but as assembled codes and artifacts always susceptible to critical and creative recombination. Ethnography is an explicit form of cultural critique sharing radical perspectives with dada and surrealism. Instead of acquiescing in the separation of avant-garde experiment from disciplinary science, I reopen the frontier, suggesting that the modern division of art and ethnography into distinct institutions has restricted the former's analytic power and the latter's subversive vocation.

Since 1900 inclusive collections of "Mankind" have become institutionalized in academic disciplines like anthropology and in museums of art or ethnology. A restrictive "art-culture system" has come to control the authenticity, value, and circulation of artifacts and data. Analyzing this system, I propose that any collection implies a temporal vision generating rarity and worth, a metahistory. This history defines which groups or things will be redeemed from a disintegrating human past and which will be defined as the dynamic, or tragic, agents of a common destiny. My analysis works to bring out the local, political contingency of such histories and of the modern collections they justify. Space is cleared, perhaps, for alternatives.

This book is a spliced ethnographic object, an incomplete collection. It consists of explorations written and rewritten over a seven-year period. Its own historical moment has been marked by rapid changes in the terms—scientific, aesthetic, and textual—governing cross-cultural representation. Written from within a "West" whose authority to represent unified human history is now widely challenged and whose very spatial identity is increasingly problematic, the explorations gathered here cannot—should not—add up to a seamless vision. Their partiality is apparent. The chapters vary in form and style, reflecting diverse conjunctures and specific occasions of composition. I have not tried to rewrite those already published to produce a consistent veneer. Moreover, I have included texts that actively break up the book's prevailing tone, hoping in this way to manifest the rhetoric of my accounts. I prefer sharply focused pictures, composed in ways that show the frame or lens.

Ethnography, a hybrid activity, thus appears as writing, as collecting, as modernist collage, as imperial power, as subversive critique. Viewed most broadly, perhaps, my topic is a mode of travel, a way of understanding and getting around in a diverse world that, since the sixteenth century, has become cartographically unified. One of the principal functions of ethnography is "orientation" (a term left over from a time when Europe traveled and invented itself with respect to a fantastically unified "East"). But in the twentieth century ethnography reflects new "spatial practices" (De Certeau 1984), new forms of dwelling and circulating.

This century has seen a drastic expansion of mobility, including tourism, migrant labor, immigration, urban sprawl. More and more people "dwell" with the help of mass transit, automobiles, airplanes. In cities on six continents foreign populations have come to stay—mixing in but often in partial, specific fashions. The "exotic" is uncannily close. Conversely, there seem no distant places left on the planet where the presence of "modern" products, media, and power cannot be felt. An older topography and experience of travel is exploded. One no longer leaves home confident of finding something radically new, another time or space. Difference is encountered in the adjoining neighborhood, the familiar turns up at the ends of the earth. This dis-"orientation" is reflected throughout the book. For example twentieth-century academic ethnography does not appear as a practice of interpreting distinct, whole ways of life but instead as a series of specific dialogues, impositions, and inventions. "Cultural" difference is no longer a stable, exotic otherness; self-other relations are matters of power and rhetoric rather than of essence. A whole structure of expectations about authenticity in culture and in art is thrown in doubt.

The new relations of ethnographic displacement were registered with precocious clarity in the writings of Victor Segalen and Michel Leiris. Both would have to unlearn the forms that once organized the experience of travel in a time when "home" and "abroad," "self" and "other," "savage" and "civilized" seemed more clearly opposed. Their writings betray an unease with narratives of escape and return, of initiation and conquest. They do not claim to know a distanced "exotic," to bring back its secrets, to objectively describe its landscapes, customs, languages. Everywhere they go they register complex encounters. In Segalen's words the new traveler expresses "not simply his vision, but through an instantaneous, constant *transfer*, the echo of his presence." China becomes an allegorical mirror. Leiris' fieldwork in a "phantom Africa" throws him back on a relentless self-ethnography—not autobiography but an act of writing his existence in a present of memories, dreams, politics, daily life.

Twentieth-century identities no longer presuppose continuous cultures or traditions. Everywhere individuals and groups improvise local performances from (re)collected pasts, drawing on foreign media, symbols, and languages. This existence among fragments has often been portrayed as a process of ruin and cultural decay, perhaps most eloquently by Claude Lévi-Strauss in *Tristes tropiques* (1955). In Lévi-Strauss's global vision—one widely shared today—authentic human differences are disintegrating, disappearing in an expansive commodity culture to become, at best, collectible "art" or "folklore." The great narrative of entropy and loss in *Tristes tropiques* expresses an inescapable, sad truth. But it is too neat, and it assumes a questionable Eurocentric position at the "end" of a unified human history, gathering up, memorializing the world's local historicities. Alongside this narrative of progressive monoculture a more ambiguous "Caribbean" experience may be glimpsed. In my account Aimé Césaire, a practitioner of "neologistic" cultural politics, represents such a possibility—organic culture reconceived as inventive process or creolized "interculture" (Wagner 1980; Drummond 1981).[4] The roots of tradition are cut and retied, collective symbols appropriated from external influences. For Césaire culture and identity are inventive and mobile. They need not take root in ancestral plots; they live by pollination, by (historical) transplanting.

The "filth" that an expansive West, according to the disillusioned traveler of *Tristes tropiques* (p. 38), has thrown in the face of the world's societies appears as raw material, compost for new orders of difference. It is also filth. Modern cultural contacts need not be romanticized, erasing the violence of empire and continuing forms of neocolonial domination. The Caribbean history from which Césaire derives an inventive and tactical "negritude" is a history of degradation, mimicry, violence, and blocked possibilities. It is also rebellious, syncretic, and creative. This kind of ambiguity keeps the planet's local futures uncertain and open. There is no master narrative that can reconcile the tragic and comic plots of global cultural history.

It is easier to register the loss of traditional orders of difference than to perceive the emergence of new ones. Perhaps this book goes too far in its concern for ethnographic presents-becoming-futures. Its utopian, persistent hope for the reinvention of difference risks downplaying the destructive, homogenizing effects of global economic and cultural centralization. Moreover, its Western assumption that assertions of "tradition" are always responses to the new (that there is no real recurrence in history) may exclude local narratives of cultural continuity and recovery. I do not tell all the possible stories. As an Igbo saying has it, "You do not stand in one place to watch a masquerade."

My primary goal is to open space for cultural futures, for the recognition of emergence. This requires a critique of deep-seated Western habits of mind and systems of value. I am especially skeptical of an almost automatic reflex—in the service of a unified vision of history—to relegate exotic peoples and objects to the collective past (Fabian 1983). The inclusive orders of modernism and anthropology (the "we" riding in Williams' car, the Mankind of Western social science) are always deployed at the end point or advancing edge of History. Exotic traditions appear as archaic, purer (and more rare) than the diluted inventions of a syncretic present. In this temporal setup a great many twentieth-century creations can only appear as imitations of more "developed" models. The Elsies of the planet are still traveling nowhere their own.

Throughout the world indigenous populations have had to reckon with the forces of "progress" and "national" unification. The results have been both destructive and inventive. Many traditions, languages, cosmologies, and values are lost, some literally murdered; but much has simultaneously been invented and revived in complex, oppositional contexts. If the victims of progress and empire are weak, they are seldom passive. It used to be assumed, for example, that conversion to Christianity in Africa, Melanesia, Latin America, or even colonial Massachusetts would lead to the extinction of indigenous cultures rather than to their transformation. Something more ambiguous and historically complex has occurred, requiring that we perceive *both* the end of certain orders of diversity and the creation or translation of others (Fernandez 1978). More than a few "extinct" peoples have returned to haunt the Western historical imagination.[5] It is difficult, in any event, to equate the future of "Catholicism" in New Guinea with its current prospects in Italy; and Protestant Christianity in New Caledonia is very different from its diverse Nigerian forms. The future is not (only) monoculture.[6]

To reject a single progressive or entropic metanarrative is not to deny the existence of pervasive global processes unevenly at work. The world is increasingly connected, though not unified, economically and culturally. Local particularism offers no escape from these involvements. Indeed, modern ethnographic histories are perhaps condemned to oscillate between two metanarratives: one of homogenization, the other of emergence; one of loss, the other of invention. In most specific conjunctures both narratives are relevant, each undermining the other's claim to tell "the whole story," each denying to the other a privileged, Hegelian vision. Everywhere in the world distinctions are being destroyed *and* created; but the new identities and orders of difference are more reminiscent of Williams' Elsie than of Edward Curtis' idealized "vanishing" American Indians. The histories of emergent differences require other ways of telling: Césaire's impure cultural poetics, Said's dispersed "Palestinian Lives," Mashpee's reinvented tradition—there is no single model. This book surveys several hybrid and subversive forms of cultural representation, forms that prefigure an inventive future. In the last decades of the twentieth century, ethnography begins from the inescapable fact that Westerners are not the only ones going places in the modern world.

But have not travelers always encountered worldly "natives"? Strange anticipation: the English Pilgrims arrive at Plymouth Rock in The New World only to find Squanto, a Patuxet, just back from Europe.

Notes

1. "Elsie" also displaces a literary tradition. In Western writing servants have always performed the chore of representing "the people"—lower classes and different races. Domesticated outsiders of the bourgeois imagination, they regularly provide fictional epiphanies, recognition scenes, happy endings, utopic and distopic transcendences. A brilliant survey is provided by Bruce Robbins 1986.

2. The Native American ancestry of the isolated and inbred Ramapough mountain people ("old names" . . . from "the ribbed north end of/Jersey") is debatable. Some, like the folklorist David Cohen (1974), deny it altogether, debunking the story of a Tuscarora offshoot. Others believe that this mixed population (formerly called Jackson's Whites, and drawing on black, Dutch, and English roots) probably owes more to

Delaware than to Tuscarora Indian blood. Whatever its real historical roots, the tribe as presently constituted is a living impure product.

3. "Natives," women, the poor: this book discusses the ethnographic construction of only the first group. In the dominant ideological systems of the bourgeois West they are interrelated, and a more systematic treatment than mine would bring this out. For some beginnings see Duvignaud 19793; Alloula 1981; Trinh 1987; and Spivak 1987.

4. For recent work on the historical-political invention of cultures and traditions see, among others, Comaroff 1985; Guss 1986; Handler 1985; Handler and Linnekin 1984; Hobsbawm and Ranter 1983; Taussig 1980, 1987; Whisnant 1983; and Cantwell 1984. Familiar approaches to "culture-contact," "syncretism," and "acculturation" are pressed farther by the concepts of "interference" and "interreference" (Fischer 1986:219, 232; Baumgarten 1982: 154), "transculturation" (Rama 1982; Pratt 1987), and "intercultural intertexts" (Tedlock and Tedlock 1985).

5. The continued tribal life of California Indians is a case in point. Even, most notorious of all, the genocidal "extinction" of the Tasmanians now seems a much less definitive "event." After systematic decimations, with the 1876 death of Truganina, the last "pure" specimen (playing a mythic role similar to that of Ishi in California), the race was scientifically declared dead. But Tasmanians did survive and intermarried with aboriginals, whites, and Maori. In 1978 a committee of inquiry reported between four and five thousand persons eligible to make land claims in Tasmania (Stocking 1987:283).

6. Research specifically on this issue is being conducted by Ulf Hannerz and his colleagues at the University of Stockholm on "the world system of culture." In an early statement Hannerz confronts the widespread assumption that "cultural diversity is waning, and the same single mass culture will soon be everywhere." He is skeptical: "I do not think it is only my bias as an anthropologist with a vested interest in cultural variation which makes it difficult for me to recognize that the situation for example in Nigeria could be anything like this. The people in my favorite Nigerian town drink Coca Cola, but they drink *burukutu* too; and they can watch *Charlie's Angels* as well as Hausa drummers on the television sets which spread rapidly as soon as electricity has arrived. My sense is that the world system, rather than creating massive cultural homogeneity on a global scale, is replacing one diversity with another; and the new diversity is based relatively more on interrelations and less on autonomy" (Hannerz n. d.: 6).

Stuart Hall (1932–)

Widely recognized as the single most prominent and influential theorist of British cultural studies, Hall was born in Jamaica but left in 1951 when he accepted a Rhodes scholarship in Great Britain, and there he has remained. As Hall explains, a combination of circumstances personal, political, and professional hampered his return to Jamaica. Perhaps, however, it was precisely his hybrid identity as black colonial subject in white British society that allowed him an especially insightful stance from which to work. He became involved in the formation of Great Britain's New Left, helping found the influential *New Left Review* and striving to create a form of socialism that would look beyond mere economic factors in attempting to understand people's allegiances, attitudes, and beliefs. Hall's interest in popular culture and his work with the education department of the British Film Institute led, in 1961, to his appointment at the University of London as the first lecturer in film and mass media studies in Great Britain. Until his retirement in 1998, he was known as an immensely charismatic teacher, his impact and charisma only partially captured in his writing.

Because Hall is a writer whose essays are scattered in various journals and collections, it is sometimes difficult to find his work. The only volume that brings some of these essays together in one collection is his *Hard Road to Renewal* (1988). He has, however, edited a number of collections that usually include an essay of his own: *The Popular Arts,* edited by Hall and Paddy Whannel (1964); *Resistance Through Rituals: Youth Subcultures in Post-War Britain,* edited by Hall and Tony Jefferson (1976); *Policing the Crisis: Mugging, the State, and Law and Order,* edited by Hall et al. (1978); *Culture, Media, Language: Working Papers in Cultural Studies,* edited by Hall et al. (1980); *New Times: The Changing Face of Politics in the 1990s,* edited by Hall and Martin Jacques (1990); *Questions of Cultural Identity,* edited by Hall and Paul du Gay (1996); and *Representation: Cultural Representations and Signifying Practices,* edited by Hall (1997).

Cultural Identity and Diaspora

A new cinema of the Caribbean is emerging, joining the company of the other 'Third Cinemas'. It is related to, but different from, the vibrant film and other forms of visual representation of the Afro-Caribbean (and Asian) 'blacks' of the diasporas of the West—the new post-colonial subjects. All these cultural practices and forms of representation have the black subject at their centre, putting the issue of cultural identity in question. Who is this emergent, new subject of the cinema? From where does he/she speak? Practices of representation always implicate the positions from which we speak or write—the positions of *enunciation.* What recent theories of enunciation suggest is that, though we speak, so to say 'in our own name', of ourselves and from our own experience, nevertheless who speaks, and the subject who is spoken of, are never identical, never exactly in the same place. Identity is not as transparent or unproblematic as we think. Perhaps instead of thinking of identity as an already accomplished fact, which the new cultural practices then represent, we should think, instead, of identity as a 'production' which is never complete, always in process, and always constituted within, not outside, representation. This view problematises the very authority and authenticity to which the term 'cultural identity' lays claim.

We seek, here, to open a dialogue, an investigation, on the subject of cultural identity and representation. Of course, the 'I' who writes here must also be thought of as, itself, 'enunciated'. We all write and speak from a particular place and time, from a history and a culture which is specific. What we say is always 'in context', *positioned.* I was born into and spent my childhood and adolescence in a lower-middle-class family in Jamaica. I have lived all my adult life in England, in the shadow of the black diaspora—'in the belly of the beast'. I write against the background of a lifetime's work in cultural studies. If the paper seems preoccupied with the diaspora experience and its narratives of displacement, it is worth remembering that all discourse is 'placed', and the heart has its reasons.

There are at least two different ways of thinking about 'cultural identity'. The first position defines 'cultural identity' in terms of one, shared culture, a sort of collective 'one true self', hiding inside the many other, more superficial or artificially imposed 'selves', which people with a shared history and ancestry hold in common. Within the terms of this definition, our cultural identities reflect the common historical experiences and shared cultural codes which provide us, as 'one people', with stable, unchanging and continuous frames of reference and meaning, beneath the shifting divisions and vicissitudes of our actual history. This 'oneness', underlying all the other, more superficial differences, is the truth, the essence, of 'Caribbeanness', of the black experience. It is this identity which a Caribbean or black diaspora must discover, excavate, bring to light and express through cinematic representation.

Such a conception of cultural identity played a critical role in all post-colonial struggles which have so profoundly reshaped our world. It lay at the centre of the vision of the poets of 'Negritude', like Aimé Césaire and Léopold Senghor, and of the Pan-African political project, earlier in the century. It continues to be a very powerful and creative force in emergent forms of representation amongst hitherto marginalised peoples. In post-colonial societies, the rediscovery of this identity is often the object of what Frantz Fanon once called a

> passionate research . . . directed by the secret hope of discovering beyond the misery of today, beyond self-contempt, resignation and abjuration, some very beautiful and splendid era whose existence rehabilitates us both in regard to ourselves and in regard to others.

New forms of cultural practice in these societies address themselves to this project for the very good reason that, as Fanon puts it, in the recent past,

> Colonisation is not satisfied merely with holding a people in its grip and emptying the native's brain of all form and content. By a kind of perverted logic, it turns to the past of oppressed people, and distorts, disfigures and destroys it.[1]

The question which Fanon's observation poses is, what is the nature of this 'profound research' which drives the new forms of visual and cinematic representation? Is it only a matter of unearthing that which the colonial experience buried and overlaid, bringing to light the hidden continuities it suppressed? Or is a quite different practice entailed—not the rediscovery but the *production* of identity. Not an identity grounded in the archaeology, but in the *re-telling* of the past?

We should not, for a moment, underestimate or neglect the importance of the act of imaginative rediscovery which this conception of a rediscovered, essential identity entails. 'Hidden histories' have played a critical role in the emergence of many of the most important social movements of our time—feminist, anti-colonial and anti-racist. The photographic work of a generation of Jamaican and Rastafarian artists, or of a visual artist like Armet Francis (a Jamaican-born photographer who has lived in Britain since the age of eight) is a testimony to the continuing creative power of this conception of identity within the emerging practices of representation. Francis's photographs of the peoples of The Black Triangle, taken in Africa, the Caribbean, the USA and the UK, attempt to reconstruct in visual terms 'the underlying unity of the black people whom colonisation and slavery distributed across the African diaspora'. His text is an act of imaginary reunification.

Crucially, such images offer a way of imposing an imaginary coherence on the experience of dispersal and fragmentation, which is the history of all enforced diasporas. They do this by representing or 'figuring' Africa as the mother of these different civilisations. This Triangle is, after all, 'centred' in Africa. Africa is the name of the missing term, the great aporia, which lies at the centre of our cultural identity and gives it a meaning which, until recently, it lacked. No one who looks at these textural images now, in the light of the history of transportation, slavery and migration, can fail to understand how the rift of separation, the 'loss of identity', which has been integral to the Caribbean experience only begins to be healed when these forgotten connections are once more set in place. Such texts restore an imaginary fullness or plentitude, to set against the broken rubric of our past. They are resources of resistance and identity, with which to confront the fragmented and pathological ways in which that experience has been reconstructed within the dominant regimes of cinematic and visual representation of the West.

There is, however, a second, related but different view of cultural identity. This second position recognises that, as well as the many points of similarity, there are also critical points of deep and significant *difference* which constitute 'what we really are'; or rather—since history has intervened—'what we have become'. We cannot speak for very long, with any exactness, about 'one experience, one identity', without acknowledging its other side—the ruptures and discontinuities which constitute, precisely, the Caribbean's 'uniqueness'. Cultural identity, in this second sense, is a matter of 'becoming' as well as of 'being'. It belongs to the future as much as to the past. It is not something which already exists, transcending place, time, history and culture. Cultural identities come from somewhere, have histories. But, like everything which is historical, they undergo constant transformation. Far from being eternally fixed in some essentialised past, they are subject to the continuous 'play' of history, culture and power. Far from being grounded in mere 'recovery' of the past, which is waiting to be found, and which when found, will secure our sense of ourselves into eternity, identities are the names we give to the different ways we are positioned by, and position ourselves within, the narratives of the past.

It is only from this second position that we can properly understand the traumatic character of 'the colonial experience'. The ways in which black people, black experiences, were positioned and subject-ed in the dominant regimes of representation were the effects of a critical exercise of cultural power and normalisation. Not only, in Said's 'Orientalist' sense, were we constructed as different and other within the categories of knowledge of the West by those regimes. They had the power to make us see and experience *ourselves* as 'Other'. Every regime of representation is a regime of power formed, as Foucault reminds us, by the fatal couplet 'power/ knowledge'. But this kind of knowledge is internal, not external. It is one thing to position a subject or set of peoples as the Other of a dominant discourse. It is quite another thing to subject them to that 'knowledge', not only as a matter of imposed will and domination, by the power of inner compulsion and subjective con-formation to the norm. That is the lesson—the sombre majesty—of Fanon's insight into the colonising experience in *Black Skin, White Masks*.

This inner expropriation of cultural identity cripples and deforms. If its silences are not resisted, they produce, in Fanon's vivid phrase, 'individuals without an anchor, without horizon, colourless, stateless, rootless—a race of angels'.[2] Nevertheless, this idea of otherness as an inner compulsion changes our conception of 'cultural identity'. In this perspective, cultural identity is not a fixed essence at all, lying unchanged outside history and culture. It is not some universal and transcendental spirit inside us on which history has made no fundamental mark. It is not once-and-for-all. It is not a fixed origin to which we can make some final and absolute Return. Of course, it is not a mere phantasm either. It is *something*—not a mere trick of the imagination. It has its histories—and histories have their real, material and symbolic effects. The past continues to speak to us. But it no longer addresses us as a simple, factual 'past', since our relation to it, like the child's relation to the mother, is always-already 'after the break'. It is always constructed through memory, fantasy, narrative and myth. Cultural identities are the points of identification, the unstable points of identification or suture, which are made, within the discourses of history and culture. Not an essence but a *positioning*. Hence, there is always a politics of identity, a politics of position, which has no absolute guarantee in an unproblematic, transcendental 'law of origin'.

This second view of cultural identity is much less familiar, and more unsettling. If identity does not proceed, in a straight unbroken line, from some fixed origin, how are we to understand its formation? We might think of black Caribbean identities as 'framed' by two axes or vectors, simultaneously operative: the vector of similarity and continuity; and the vector of difference and rupture. Caribbean identities always have to be thought of in terms of the dialogic relationship between these two axes. The one gives us some grounding in, some continuity with, the past. The second reminds us that what we share is precisely the experience of a profound discontinuity: the peoples dragged into slavery, transportation, colonisation, migration, came predominantly from Africa—and when that supply ended, it was temporarily refreshed by indentured labour from the Asian subcontinent. (This neglected fact explains why, when you visit Guyana or Trinidad, you see, symbolically inscribed in the faces of their peoples, the paradoxical 'truth' of Christopher Columbus's mistake: you *can* find 'Asia' by sailing west, if you know where to look!) In the history of the modern world, there are few more traumatic ruptures to match these enforced separations from Africa—already figured, in the European imaginary, as 'the Dark Continent'. But the slaves were also from different countries, tribal communities, villages, languages and gods. African religion, which has been so profoundly formative in

Caribbean spiritual life, is precisely *different* from Christian monotheism in believing that God is so powerful that he can only be known through a proliferation of spiritual manifestations, present everywhere in the natural and social world. These gods live on, in an underground existence, in the hybridised religious universe of Haitian voodoo, pocomania, Native pentacostalism, Black baptism, Rastafarianism and the black Saints Latin American Catholicism. The paradox is that it was the uprooting of slavery and transportation and the insertion into the plantation economy (as well as the symbolic economy) of the Western world that 'unified' these peoples across their differences, in the same moment as it cut them off from direct access to their past.

Difference, therefore, persists—in and alongside continuity. To return to the Caribbean after any long absence is to experience again the shock of the 'doubleness' of similarity and difference. Visiting the French Caribbean for the first time, I also saw at once how different Martinique is from, say, Jamaica: and this is no mere difference of topography or climate. It is a profound difference of culture and history. And the difference *matters*. It positions Martiniquains and Jamaicans as *both* the same *and* different. Moreover, the boundaries of difference are continually repositioned in relation to different points of reference. Vis-à-vis the developed West, we are very much 'the same'. We belong to the marginal, the underdeveloped, the periphery, the 'Other'. We are at the outer edge, the 'rim', of the metropolitan world—always 'South' to someone else's *El Norte*.

At the same time, we do not stand in the same relation of the 'otherness' to the metropolitan centres. Each has negotiated its economic, political and cultural dependency differently. And this 'difference', whether we like it or not, is already inscribed in our cultural identities. In turn, it is this negotiation of identity which makes us, vis-à-vis other Latin American people, with a very similar history, different—Caribbeans, *les Antilliennes* ('islanders' to their mainland). And yet, vis-à-vis one another, Jamaican, Haitian, Cuban, Guadeloupean, Barbadian, etc. . . . .

How, then, to describe this play of 'difference' within identity? The common history—transportation, slavery, colonisation—has been profoundly formative. For all these societies, unifying us across our differences. But it does not constitute a common *origin*, since it was, metaphorically as well as literally, a translation. The inscription of difference is also specific and critical. I use the word 'play' because the double meaning of the metaphor is important. It suggests, on the one hand, the instability, the permanent unsettlement, the lack of any final resolution. On the other hand, it reminds us that the place where this 'doubleness' is most powerfully to be heard is 'playing' within the varieties of Caribbean musics. This cultural 'play' could not therefore be represented, cinematically, as a simple, binary opposition—'past/present', 'them/us'. Its complexity exceeds this binary structure of representation. At different places, times, in relation to different questions, the boundaries are re-sited. They become, not only what they have, at times, certainly been—mutually excluding categories, but also what they sometimes are—differential points along a sliding scale.

One trivial example is the way Martinique both *is* and *is not* 'French'. It is, of course, a *department* of France, and this is reflected in its standard and style of life: Fort de France is a much richer, more 'fashionable' place than Kingston—which is not only visibly poorer, but itself at a point of transition between being 'in fashion' in an Anglo-African and Afro-American way—for those who can afford to be in any sort of fashion at all. Yet, what is distinctively 'Martiniquais' can only be described in terms of that special and peculiar supplement which the black and mulatto skin adds to the 'refinement' and sophistication of a Parisian-derived *haute couture*: that is, a sophistication which, because it is black, is always transgressive.

To capture this sense of difference which is not pure 'otherness', we need to deploy the play on words of a theorist like Jacques Derrida. Derrida uses the anomalous 'a' in his way of writing 'difference'—*differance*—as a marker which sets up a disturbance in our settled understanding or translation of the word/concept. It sets the word in motion to new meanings without erasing the *trace* of its other meanings. His sense of *differance*, as Christopher Norris puts it, thus

> remains suspended between the two French verbs 'to differ' and 'to defer' (postpone), both of which contribute to its textual force but neither of which can fully capture its meaning. Language depends on difference, as Saussure showed . . . the structure of distinctive propositions which make up its basic economy. Where Derrida breaks new ground . . . is in the extent to which 'differ' shades into 'defer' . . . the idea that meaning is always deferred, perhaps to this point of an endless supplementarity, by the play of signification.[3]

This second sense of difference challenges the fixed binaries which stabilise meaning and representation and show how meaning is never finished or completed, but keeps on moving to encompass other, additional or supplementary meanings, which, as Norris puts it elsewhere,[4] 'disturb the classical economy of language and representation'. Without relations of difference, no representation could occur. But what is then constituted within representation is always open to being deferred, staggered, serialised.

Where, then, does identity come in to this infinite postponement of meaning? Derrida does not help us as much as he might here, though the notion of the 'trace' goes some way towards it. This is where it sometimes seems as if Derrida has permitted his profound theoretical insights to be reappropriated by his disciples into a celebration of formal 'playfulness', which evacuates them of their political meaning. For if signification depends upon the endless repositioning of its differential terms, meaning, in any specific instance, depends on the contingent and arbitrary stop—the necessary and temporary 'break' in the infinite semiosis of language. This does not detract from the original insight. It only threatens to do so if we mistake this 'cut' of identity—this *positioning*, which makes meaning possible—as a natural and permanent, rather than an arbitrary and contingent 'ending'—whereas I understand every such position as 'strategic' and arbitrary, in the sense that there is no permanent equivalence between the particular sentence we close, and its true meaning, as such. Meaning continues to unfold, so to speak, beyond the arbitrary closure which makes it, at any moment, possible. It is always either over- or under-determined, either an excess or a supplement. There is always something 'left over'.

It is possible, with this conception of 'difference', to rethink the positioning and repositioning of Caribbean cultural identities in relation to at least three 'presences', to borrow Aimé Césaire's and Léopold Senghor's metaphor: *Présence*

Africaine, Présence Européenne, and the third, most ambiguous, presence of all—the sliding term, *Présence Americaine.* Of course, I am collapsing, for the moment, the many other cultural 'presences' which constitute the complexity of Caribbean identity (Indian, Chinese, Lebanese, etc). I mean America, here, not in its 'first-world' sense—the big cousin to the North whose 'rim' we occupy, but in the second, broader sense: America, the 'New World', *Terra Incognita.*

Présence Africaine is the site of the repressed. Apparently silenced beyond memory by the power of the experience of slavery, Africa was, in fact, present everywhere: in the everyday life and customs of the slave quarters, in the languages and patois of the plantations, in names and words, often disconnected from their taxonomies, in the secret syntactical structures through which other languages were spoken, in the stories and tales told to children, in religious practices and beliefs in the spiritual life, the arts, crafts, musics and rhythms of slave and post-emancipation society. Africa, the signified which could not be represented directly in slavery, remained and remains the unspoken unspeakable 'presence' in Caribbean culture. It is 'hiding' behind every verbal inflection, every narrative twist of Caribbean cultural life. It is the secret code with which every Western text was 're-read'. It is the ground-bass of every rhythm and bodily movement. *This* was—is—the 'Africa' that 'is alive and well in the diaspora'.[5]

When I was growing up in the 1940s and 1950s as a child in Kingston, I was surrounded by the signs, music and rhythms of this Africa of the diaspora, which only existed as a result of a long and discontinuous series of transformations. But, although almost everyone around me was some shade of brown or black (Africa 'speaks'!), I never once heard a single person refer to themselves or to others as, in some way, or as having been at some time in the past, 'African'. It was only in the 1970s that this Afro-Caribbean identity became historically available to the great majority of Jamaican people, at home and abroad. In this historic moment, Jamaicans discovered themselves to be 'black'—just as, in the same moment, they discovered themselves to be the sons and daughters of 'slavery'.

This profound cultural discovery, however, was not, and could not be, made directly, without 'mediation'. It could only be made *through* the impact on popular life of the post-colonial revolution, the civil rights struggles, the culture of Rastafarianism and the music of reggae—the metaphors, the figures or signifiers of a new construction of 'Jamaican-ness'. These signified a 'new' Africa of the New World, grounded in an 'old' Africa: a spiritual journey of discovery that led, in the Caribbean, to an indigenous cultural revolution; this is Africa, as we might say, necessarily 'deferred'—as a spiritual, cultural and political metaphor.

It is the presence/absence of Africa, in this form, which has made it the privileged signifier of new conceptions of Caribbean identity. Everyone in the Caribbean, of whatever ethnic background, must sooner or later come to terms with this African presence. Black, brown, mulatto, white—all must look *Présence Africaine* in the face, speak its name. But whether it is, in this sense, an *origin* of our identities, unchanged by four hundred years of displacement, dismemberment, transportation, to which we could in any final or literal sense return, is more open to doubt. The original 'Africa' is no longer there. It too has been transformed. History is, in that sense, irreversible. We must not collude with the West which, precisely, normalizes and appropriates Africa by freezing it into some timeless zone of the primitive, unchanging past. Africa must at last be reckoned with by Caribbean people, but it cannot in any simple sense be merely recovered.

It belongs irrevocably, for us, to what Edward Said once called an 'imaginative geography and history', which helps 'the mind to intensify its own sense of itself by dramatising the difference between what is close to it and what is far away'.[6] It 'has acquired an imaginative or figurative value we can name and feel'.[7] Our belongingness to it constitutes what Benedict Anderson calls 'an imagined community'.[8] To *this* 'Africa', which is a necessary part of the Caribbean imaginary, we can't literally go home again.

The character of this displaced 'homeward' journey—its length and complexity—comes across vividly, in a variety of texts. Tony Sewell's documentary archival photographs, 'Garvey's Children: the Legacy of Marcus Garvey' tell the story of a 'return' to an African identity which went, necessarily, by the long route through London and the United States. It 'ends', not in Ethiopia but with Garvey's statue in front of the St Ann Parish Library in Jamaica: not with a traditional tribal chant but with the music of Burning Spear and Bob Marley's 'Redemption Song'. This is our 'long journey' home. Derek Bishton's courageous visual and written text, *Black Heart Man*—the story of the journey of a *white* photographer 'on the trail of the promised land'—starts in England, and goes, through Shashemene, the place in Ethiopia to which many Jamaican people have found their way on their search for the Promised Land, and slavery; but it ends in Pinnacle, Jamaica, where the first Rastafarian settlements were established, and 'beyond'—among the dispossessed of 20th-century Kingston and the streets of Handsworth, where Bishton's voyage of discovery first began. These symbolic journeys are necessary for us all—and necessarily circular. This is the Africa we must return to—but 'by another route': what Africa has *become* in the New World, what we have made of 'Africa': 'Africa'—as we re-tell it through politics, memory and desire.

What of the second, troubling, term in the identity equation—the European presence? For many of us, this is a matter not of too little but of too much. Where Africa was a case of the unspoken, Europe was a case of that which is endlessly speaking—and endlessly speaking *us*. The European presence interrupts the innocence of the whole discourse of 'difference' in the Caribbean by introducing the question of power. 'Europe' belongs irrevocably to the 'play' of power, to the lines of force and consent, to the role of the *dominant,* in Caribbean culture. In terms of colonalism, underdevelopment, poverty and the racism of colour, the European presence is that which, in visual representation, has positioned the black subject within its dominant regimes of representation: the colonial discourse, the literatures of adventure and exploration, the romance of the exotic, the ethnographic and travelling eye, the tropical languages of tourism, travel brochure and Hollywood and the violent, pornographic languages of *ganja* and urban violence.

Because *Présence Européenne* is about exclusion, imposition and expropriation, we are often tempted to locate that power as wholly external to us—an extrinsic force, whose influence can be thrown off like the serpent sheds its skin. What Frantz Fanon reminds us, in *Black Skin, White Masks,* is how this power has become a constitutive element in our own identities.

> The movements, the attitudes, the glances of the other fixed me there in the sense in which a chemical solution is fixed by a dye. I was indignant; I demanded an explanation. Nothing happened. I burst apart. Now the fragments have been put together again by another self.[9]

This 'look', from—so to speak—the place of the Other, fixes us, not only in its violence, hostility and aggression, but in the ambivalence of its desire. This brings us face to face with the dominating European presence not simply as the site or 'scene' of integration where those other presences which it had actively disaggregated were recomposed—re-framed, put together in a new way; but as the site of a profound splitting and doubling—what Homi Bhabha has called 'this ambivalent identification of the racist world . . . the "Otherness" of the Self inscribed in the perverse palimpsest of colonial identity'.[10]

The dialogue of power and resistance, of refusal and recognition, with and against *Présence Européenne* is almost as complex as the 'dialogue' with Africa. In terms of popular cultural life, it is nowhere to be found in its pure, pristine state. It is always-already fused, syncretised, with other cultural elements. It is always-already creolised—not lost beyond the Middle Passage, but ever-present: from the harmonics in our musics to the ground-bass of Africa, traversing and intersecting our lives at every point. How can we stage this dialogue so that, finally, we can place it, without terror or violence, rather than being forever placed by it? Can we ever recognise its irreversible influence, whilst resisting its imperialising eye? The enigma is impossible, so far, to resolve. It requires the most complex of cultural strategies. Think, for example, of the dialogue of every Caribbean filmmaker or writer, one way or another, with the dominant cinemas and literature of the West—the complex relationship of young black British filmmakers with the 'avant-gardes' of European and American filmmaking. Who could describe this tense and tortured dialogue as a 'one way trip'?

The Third, 'New World' presence, is not so much power, as ground, place, territory. It is the juncture-point where the many cultural tributaries meet, the 'empty' land (the European colonisers emptied it) where strangers from every other part of the globe collided. None of the people who now occupy the islands—black, brown, white, African, European, American, Spanish, French, East Indian, Chinese, Portuguese, Jew, Dutch—originally 'belonged' there. It is the space where the creolisations and assimilations and syncretisms were negotiated. The New World is the third term—the primal scene—where the fateful/fatal encounter was staged between Africa and the West. It also has to be understood as the place of many, continuous displacements: of the original pre-Columbian inhabitants, the Arawaks, Caribs and Amerindians, permanently displaced from their homelands and decimated; of other peoples displaced in different ways from Africa, Asia and Europe; the displacements of slavery, colonisation and conquest. It stands for the endless ways in which Caribbean people have been destined to 'migrate'; it is the signifier of migration itself—of travelling, voyaging and return as fate, as destiny; of the Antillean as the prototype of the modern or postmodern New World nomad, continually moving between centre and periphery. This preoccupation with movement and migration Caribbean cinema shares with many other 'Third Cinemas', but it is one of our defining themes, and it is destined to cross the narrative of every film script or cinematic image.

Présence Americaine continues to have its silences, its suppressions. Peter Hulme, in his essay on 'Islands of enchantment'[11] reminds us that the word 'Jamaica' is the Hispanic form of the indigenous Arawak name—'land of wood and water'—which Columbus's renaming ('Santiago') never replaced. The Arawak presence remains today a ghostly one, visible in the islands mainly in museums and archeological sites, part of the barely knowable or usable 'past'. Hulme notes that it is not represented in the emblem of the Jamaican National Heritage Trust, for example, which chose instead the figure of Diego Pimienta, 'an African who fought for his Spanish masters against the English invasion of the island in 1655'—a deferred, metonymic, sly and sliding representation of Jamaican identity if ever there was one! He recounts the story of how Prime Minister Edward Seaga tried to alter the Jamaican coat-of-arms, which consists of two Arawak figures holding a shield with five pineapples, surmounted by an alligator. 'Can the crushed and extinct Arawaks represent the dauntless character of Jamaicans. Does the low-slung, near extinct crocodile, a cold-blooded reptile, symbolise the warm, soaring spirit of Jamaicans?' Prime Minister Seaga asked rhetorically.[12] There can be few political statements which so eloquently testify to the complexities entailed in the process of trying to represent a diverse people with a diverse history through a single, hegemonic 'identity'. Fortunately, Mr Seaga's invitation to the Jamaican people, who are overwhelmingly of African descent, to start their 'remembering' by first 'forgetting' something else, got the comeuppance it so richly deserved.

The 'New World' presence—America, *Terra Incognita*—is therefore itself the beginning of diaspora, of diversity, of hybridity and difference, what makes Afro-Caribbean people already people of a diaspora. I use this term here metaphorically, not literally: diaspora does not refer us to those scattered tribes whose identity can only be secured in relation to some sacred homeland to which they must at all costs return, even if it means pushing other people into the sea. This is the old, the imperialising, the hegemonising, form of 'ethnicity'. We have seen the fate of the people of Palestine at the hands of this backward-looking conception of diaspora—and the complicity of the West with it. The diaspora experience as I intend it here is defined, not by essence or purity, but by the recognition of a necessary heterogeneity and diversity; by a conception of 'identity' which lives with and through, not despite, difference; by *hybridity*. Diaspora identities are those which are constantly producing and reproducing themselves anew, through transformation and difference. One can only think here of what is uniquely—'essentially'—Caribbean: precisely the mixes of colour, pigmentation, physiognomic type; the 'blends' of tastes that is Caribbean cuisine; the aesthetics of the 'cross-overs', of 'cut-and-mix', to borrow Dick Hebdige's telling phrase, which is the heart and soul of black music. Young black cultural practitioners and critics in Britain are increasingly coming to acknowledge and explore in their work this 'diaspora aesthetic' and its formations in the post-colonial experience:

> Across a whole range of cultural forms there is a 'syncretic' dynamic which critically appropriates elements from the master-codes of the dominant culture and 'creolises' them, disarticulating given signs and re-articulating their symbolic meaning. The subversive force of this hybridising tendency is most apparent at the level of language itself where creoles, patois and black English decentre, destabilise and carnivalise the linguistic domination of 'English'—the nation-language of master-discourse—through strategic inflections, re-accentuations and other performative moves in semantic, syntactic and lexical codes.[13]

It is because this New World is constituted for us as place, a narrative of displacement, that it gives rise so profoundly to a certain imaginary plentitude, re-creating the endless desire to return to 'lost origins', to be one again with the mother, to go back to the beginning. Who can ever forget, when once seen rising up out of that blue-green Caribbean, those islands of enchantment. Who has not known, at this moment, the surge of an overwhelming nostalgia for lost origins, for 'times past'? And yet, this 'return to the beginning' is like the imaginary in Lacan—it can neither be fulfilled nor requited, and hence is the beginning of the symbolic, of representation, the infinitely renewable source of desire, memory, myth, search, discovery—in short, the reservoir of our cinematic narratives.

We have been trying, in a series of metaphors, to put in play a different sense of our relationship to the past, and thus a different way of thinking about cultural identity, which might constitute new points of recognition in the discourses of the emerging Caribbean cinema and black British cinemas. We have been trying to theorize identity as constituted, not outside but within representation; and hence of cinema, not as a second-order mirror held up to reflect what already exists, but as that form of representation which is able to constitute us as new kinds of subjects, and thereby enable us to discover places from which to speak. Communities, Benedict Anderson argues in *Imagined Communities,* are to be distinguished, not by their falsity/genuineness, but by the style in which they are imagined.[14] This is the vocation of modern black cinemas: by allowing us to see and recognise the different parts and histories of ourselves, to construct those points of identification, those positionalities we call in retrospect our 'cultural identities'.

We must not therefore be content with delving into the past of a people in order to find coherent elements which will counteract colonialism's attempts to falsify and harm. . . . A national culture is not a folk-lore, nor an abstract populism that believes it can discover a people's true nature. A national culture is the whole body of efforts made by a people in the sphere of thought to describe, justify and praise the action through which that people has created itself and keeps itself in existence.[15]

Notes

1. Frantz Fanon, 'On national culture', in *The Wretched of the Earth,* London, 1963, p. 170. [See also p. 37 above.]
2. *ibid.,* p. 176.
3. Christopher Norris, *Deconstruction: Theory and practice,* London, 1982, p. 32.
4. *idem, Jacques Derrida,* London, 1987, p. 15.
5. Stuart Hall, *Resistance Through Rituals,* London, 1976.
6. Edward Said, *Orientalism,* London, 1985, p. 55.
7. *ibid.*
8. Benedict Anderson, *Imagined Communities: Reflections on the origin and rise of nationalism,* London, 1982.
9. Frantz Fanon, *Black Skin, White Masks,* London, 1986, p. 109.
10. Homi Bhabha, 'Foreword' to Fanon, *ibid.,* pp. xiv–xv. [See also p. 116 above.]
11. In *New Formations,* 3, Winter 1987.
12. *Jamaica Hansard,* 9, 1983–4, p. 363. Quoted in Hulme, *ibid.*
13. Kobena Mercer, 'Diaspora culture and the dialogic imagination', in M. Cham and C. Watkins (eds), *Blackframes: Critical perspectives on black independent cinema,* 1988, p. 57.
14. Anderson, *op. cit.,* p. 15.
15. Fanon, *Black Skin, White Masks,* p. 188.

Gloria Anzaldúa (1942–2004)

A self-described "chicana dyke-feminist, *tejana patlache* poet, writer, and cultural theorist," Anzaldúa was born into a seventh-generation Mexican American family that settled in the Rio Grande Valley in southern Texas. When Anzaldúa was 15, her father died, and she began to work as a farm laborer in order to help support her family financially. Although the death of her father meant that Anzaldúa was forced to divide her time between school and farmwork, she received a B.A. from Pan-American University in 1969 and an M.A. in English and education from the University of Texas at Austin in 1972. As a teacher, Anzaldúa has had a wide variety of classroom experiences, which include teaching not only in universities and colleges but also in a bilingual preschool program, a special-education program for mentally and emotionally handicapped students, and a high school for migrant workers in Indiana. Her academic life, however, has not been struggle free. For example, when she returned to Texas to pursue a Ph.D. in comparative literature, her intention was to focus on Chicano literature, but she met with such resistance that she finally quit. No doubt, experiences such as this have helped shape the kind of writing she engages in, a mélange of disparate genres and languages that is intensely personal, sometimes angry, and always poetic.

Anzaldúa has won numerous awards for her work such as a National Endowment for the Arts Fiction Award and the 1991 Lesbian Rights Award, and in 1987, her *Borderlands/La Frontera: The New Mestiza* was selected by the *Literary Journal* as one of the year's 38 best books. Much of Anzaldúa's work revolves around a cultural politics that operates on two levels: as a simple call for recognition and as a revision of how we understand identity. Aside from *Borderlands/La Frontera*, she has written *Speaking in Tongues: A Letter to Third World Women Writers* (1983); *Towards a New Consciousness* (1990); and two children's books, *Friends from the Other Side/Amigos del otro lado* (1993) and *Prietita and the Ghost Woman/Prietita y la Llorona* (1996). She has also coedited, with Cherríe Moraga, *This Bridge Called My Back: Writings by Radical Women of Color* (1981) and edited *Making Face, Making Soul: Creative and Critical Perspectives by Women of Color* (1990), both of which have been highly influential collections.

Chicana Artists: Exploring *Nepantla, el Lugar de la Frontera*

I stop before the dismembered body of *la diosa de la luna,* Coyolxauhqui, daughter of Coatlicue. The warrior goddess' eyes are closed, she has bells on her cheeks, and her head is in the form of a snail design. She was decapitated by her brother, Huitzilopochtle, the Left-Handed Hummingbird. Her bones jut from their sockets. I stare at the huge round stone of *la diosa.* She seems to be pushing at the restraining orb of the moon. Though I sense a latent whirlwind of energy, I also sense a timeless stillness—one patiently waiting to explode into activity.

Here before my eyes, on the opening day of the "Aztec: The World of Moctezuma" exhibition at the Denver Museum of Natural History, is the culture of *neustros antepasados indígenas.* I ask myself, What does it mean to me *esta jotita,* this queer Chicana, this *mexicatejana* to enter a museum and look at indigenous objects that were once used by my ancestors? Will I find my historical Indian identity here at this museum among the ancient artifacts and their *mestisaje lineage?*

As I pull out a pad to take notes on the clay, stone, jade, bone, feather, straw, and cloth artifacts, I am disconcerted with the knowledge that I am passively consuming and appropriating an indigenous culture. I arrive at the serpentine base of a reconstructed 16-foot temple where the Aztecs flung down human sacrifices, leaving bloodied steps. Around me I hear the censorious, culturally ignorant words of the Whites who, while horrified by the bloodthirsty Aztecs, gape in vicarious wonder and voraciously consume the exoticized images. Though I too am a gaping consumer, I feel that these artworks are part of my legacy—my appropriation differs from the misappriopriation of "outsiders."

I am again struck by how much Chicana artists and writers feel the impact of ancient Mexican art forms, foods, and customs. *Sus símbolos ye metáforas todavía viven en la gente chicana/mexicana.* This sense of connection and community compels Chicana writers/artists to delve into, sift through, and rework native imagery. We consistently reflect back these images in revitalized and modernized versions in theater, film, performance art, painting, dance, sculpture, and literature. *La negación sistemática de la cultura mexicana-chicana en los Estados Unidos impide su desarrollo haciéndolo este un acto de colonización.* As a people who have been stripped of our history, language, identity and pride, we attempt again and again to find what we have lost by imaginatively digging into our cultural roots and making art out of our findings.

I recall Yolanda López' *Portrait of the Artist as the Virgin of Guadalupe* (1978), which depicts a Chicana/*mexicana* woman emerging and running from the oval halo of rays that looks to me like thorns, with the mantle of the traditional *virgen* in one hand and a serpent in the other. She wears running shoes, has short hair, and her legs are bare and look powerful—a very dykey-looking woman. *Portrait* represents the cultural rebirth of the Chicana struggling to free herself from oppressive gender roles.[1]

I remember visiting Chicana *tejana* artist Santa Barraza in her Austin studio in the mid 1970s and talking about the merger and appropriation of cultural symbols and techniques by artists in search of their spiritual and cultural roots. As I walked around her studio, I was amazed at the vivid *Virgen de Guadalupe* iconography on her walls and on the drawings strewn on tables and shelves.

La gentle chicana tiene tres madres. All three are mediators: *Guadalupe,* the virgin mother who has not abandoned us, *la Chingada (Malinche),* the raped mother whom we have abandoned, and *la Llorona,* the mother who seeks her lost children and is a combination of the other two. *Guadalupe* has been used by the Church to mete out institutionalized oppression: to placate the Indians and *mexicanos* and Chicanos. In part, the true identity of all three has been subverted—*Guadalupe* to make us docile and enduring, *la Chingada* to make us ashamed of our Indian side, and *la Llorona* to make us long-suffering people. This obscuring has encouraged the *virgen/puta* dichotomy. The three *madres* are cultural figures that Chicana writers and artists "reread" in our works.

Now, 16 years later, Barraza is focusing on interpretations of Pre-Columbian codices as a reclamation of cultural and historical mestiza identity. Her "codices" are edged with *milagros* and *ex votos.*[2] Using the folk-art format, Barraza is now painting tin testimonials known as *retablos*. These are traditional popular miracle paintings on metal, a medium introduced to colonial Mexico by the Spaniards. One of her devotional *retablos* is of *la Malinche,* made with *maguey.* (The *maguey* cactus is Barraza's symbol of rebirth). Like that of many Chicana artists, her work, she says, explores indigenous Mexican "symbols and myths in a historical and contemporary context as a mechanism of resistance to oppression and assimilation."[3]

I wonder about the genesis of *el arte de la frontera.* Border art remembers its roots—sacred and folk art are often still one and the same. I recall the *nichos* (niches or recessed areas) and *retablos* that I had recently seen in several galleries and museums. The *retablos* are placed inside open boxes of wood, tin, or cardboard. the *cajitas* contain three dimensional figures such as *la virgen,* photos of ancestors, candles, and sprigs of herbs tied together. They are actually tiny installations. I make mine out of cigar boxes or vegetable crates that I find discarded on the street before garbage pickups. The *retablos* range from the strictly traditional to modern, more abstract forms. Santa Barraza, Yolanda López, Marcia Gómez, Carmen Lomas Garza and other Chicana artists connect their art to everyday life, instilling both with political, sacred and aesthetic values. *Haciendo tortillas* becomes a sacred ritual in literary, visual, and performance arts.[4]

Border art, in critiquing old, traditional, and erroneous representations of the Mexico–United States border, attempts to represent the "real world" *de la gente* going about their daily lives. But it renders that world and its people in more than mere surface slices of life. If one looks beyond the tangible, one sees a connection to the spirit world, to the underworld, and to other realities. In the "old world," art was/is functional and sacred as well as aesthetic. When folk and fine art separated, the *metate* (a flat porous volcanic stone with rolling pin used to make corn tortillas) and the *huipil* (a Guatemalan blouse) were put in museums by Western curators of art.[5]

I come to a glass case where the skeleton of a jaguar with a stone in its open mouth nestles on cloth. The stone represents the heart. My thoughts trace the jaguar's spiritual and religious symbolism from its Olmec origins to present-day jaguar masks worn by people who no longer know that the jaguar was connected to rain, who no longer remember that Tlaloc and the jaguar and the serpent and rain are tightly intertwined.[6] Through the centuries a culture touches and influences another, passing on its metaphors and its gods before it dies. (Metaphors *are* gods.) The new culture adopts, modifies, and enriches these images, and it, in turn, passes them on changed. The process is repeated until the original meanings of images are pushed into the unconscious. What surfaces are images more significant to the prevailing culture and era. The artist on some level, however, still connects to that unconscious reservoir of meaning, connects to that *nepantla* state of transition between time periods, and the border between cultures.

Nepantla is the Nahuatl word for an in-between state, that uncertain terrain one crosses when moving from one place to another, when changing from one class, race, or gender position to another, when traveling from the present identity into a new identity. The Mexican immigrant at the moment of crossing the barbed-wire fence into the hostile "paradise" of *el norte,* the United States, is caught in a state of *nepantla.* Others who find themselves in this bewildering transitional space may be those people caught in the midst of denying their projected/assumed heterosexual identity and coming out, presenting and voicing their lesbian, gay, bi-, or transsexual selves. Crossing class lines—especially from working class to middle class-ness and privilege—can be just as disorienting. The marginalized, starving Chicana artist who suddenly finds her work exhibited in mainstream museums, or being sold for thousands of dollars in prestigious galleries, as well as the once-neglected writer whose work is on every professor's syllabus for a time inhabit *nepantla.* For women artists, *nepantla* is a constant state; dislocation is the norm. Chicana artists are engaged in "reading" that *nepantla,* that border.

I think of the borderlands as Jorge Luis Borges' *Aleph,* the one spot on earth which contains all other places within it. All people in it, whether natives or immigrants, colored or white, queer or heterosexual, form this side of the border or *del otro lado,* are *personas del lugar,* local people—all of whom relate to the border and to *nepantla* in different ways.

The border is a historical and metaphorical site, *un sitio ocupado,* an occupied borderland where individual artists and collaborating groups transform space, and the two home territories, Mexico and the United States, become one. Border art deals with shifting identities, border crossings, and hybridism. But there are other borders besides the actual Mexico/US *frontera*. Chilean-born artist Juan Davila's *Wuthering Heights* (1990) oil painting depicts Juanito Leguna, a half-caste, mixed breed transvestite. Juanito's body is a simulacrum parading as the phallic mother with hairy chest and hanging tits.[7] Another Latino artist, Rafael Barajas (who signs his work as "El Fisgón"), has a mixed-media piece entitled *Pero eso si . . . soy muy macho* (1989). It shows a Mexican male wearing the proverbial sombrero taking a siesta against the traditional cactus, tequila bottle on the ground, gunbelt hanging from a nopal branch. But the leg sticking out from beneath the sarape-like mantle is wearing a highheeled shoe, pantyhose, and a garter belt. It suggests another kind of border crossing— gender-bending.[8]

According to anthropologist Edward Hall, early in life we become oriented to space in a way that is tied to survival and sanity. When we become disoriented from that sense of space we fall in danger of becoming psychotic.[9] I question this—to be disoriented in space is the "normal" way of being for us mestizas living in the borderlands. It is the sane way of coping with the accelerated pace of this complex, interdependent, and multicultural planet. To be disoriented in space is to be *en nepantla*, to experience bouts of disassociation of identity, identity breakdowns and buildups. The border is in a constant *nepantla* state, and it is an analog of the planet.

This is why the border is a persistent metaphor in *el arte de la frontera*, an art that deals with such themes as identity, border crossings, and hybrid imagery. The Mexico–United States border is a site where many different cultures "touch" each other and the permeable, flexible, and ambiguous shifting grounds lend themselves to hybrid images. The border is the locus of resistance, of rupture, of implosion and explosion, and of putting together the fragments and creating a new assemblage. Border artists *cambian el punto de referencia*. By disrupting the neat separations between cultures, they create a culture mix, *una mestizada* in their artworks. Each artist locates herself in this border "*lugar*" and tears apart then rebuilds the "place" itself. "Imagenes de la Frontera" was the title of the Centro Cultural Tijuana's June 1992 exhibition.[10] Malaquís Montoya's Frontera Series and Irene Pérez' Dos Mundos monoprint are examples of the multi-subjectivity, split-subjectivity, and refusal-to-be-split themes of the border artist creating a counter-art.

The *nepantla* state is the natural habitat of women artists, most specifically for the mestiza border artists who partake of the traditions of two or more worlds and who may be binational. They thus create a new artistic space—a border mestizo culture. Beware of *el romance del mestazaje*, I hear myself saying silently. *Puede ser una fición*. But I and other writers/artists of *la frontera* have invested ourselves in it. *Mestizaje*, not Chicanismo, is the reality of our lives. *Mestizaje* is at the heart of our art. We bleed in *mestazaje*, we eat and sweat and cry in *mestizaje*. But the Chicana is inside the mestiza.

There are many obstacles and dangers in crossing into *nepantla*. Popular culture and the dominant art institutions threaten border artists from the outside with appropriation. "Outsiders" jump on the border artists' bandwagon and work their territory. The present unparalleled economic depression in the arts gutted by government funding cutbacks threatens *los artistas de la frontera*. Sponsoring corporations that judge projects by "family values" criteria force multi-cultural artists to hang tough and brave out financial and professional instability.

I walk into the Aztec Museum shop and see feathers, paper flowers, and ceramic statues of fertility goddesses selling for ten times what they sell for in Mexico. Border art is becoming trendy in these neo-colonial times that encourage art tourism and pop-culture ripoffs. Of course, there is nothing new about colonizing, commercializing, and consuming the art of ethnic people (and of queer writers and artists) except that now it is being misappropriated by pop culture. Diversity is being sold on TV, billboards, fashion runways, department-store windows, and yes, airport corridors and "regional" stores where you can take home a jar of Tex-Mex *picante* sauce along with Navaho artist R. C. Gorman's "Saguro" or Robert Arnold's "Chili Dog," and drink a margarita at Rosie's Cantina.

I touch the armadillo pendant hanging from my neck and think, *frontera* artists have to grow protective shells. We enter the silence, go inward, attend to feelings and to that inner *cenote,* the creative reservoir where earth, female, and water energies merge. We surrender to the rhythm and the grace of our artworks. Through our artworks we cross the border into other subjective levels of awareness, shift into different and new terrains of *mestizaje*. Some of us have a highly developed *facultad* and many intuit what lies ahead. Yet the political climate does not allow us to withdraw completely. In fact, border artists are engaged artists. Most of us are politically active in our communities. If disconnected from *la gente,* border artists would wither in isolation. The community feeds our spirits and the responses from our "readers" inspire us to continue struggling with our art and aesthetic interventions that subvert cultural genocide. Border art challenges and subverts the imperialism of the United States, and combats assimilation by either the United State or Mexico, yet it acknowledges its affinities to both cultures.[11]

"Chicana" artist, "border" artist. These are adjectives labeling identities. Labeling creates expectations. White poets don't write "white" in front of their names, nor are they referred to as white by others. Is "border" artist just another label that strips legitimacy from the artist, signaling that she is inferior to the adjectiveless artist, a label designating that she is only capable of handling ethnic, folk, and regional subjects and art forms? Yet the dominant culture consumes, swallows whole the ethnic artist, sucks out her vitality, and then spits out the hollow husk along with its labels (such as Hispanic). The dominant culture shapes the ethnic artist's identity if she does not scream loud enough and fight long enough to name herself. Until we live in a society where all people are more or less equal, we need these labels to resist the pressure to assimilate.

Artistic ideas that have been incubating and developing at their own speed have come into their season—now is the time of border art. Border *arte* is an art that supersedes the pictorial. It depicts both the soul *del artista* and the soul *del pueblo*. It deals with who tells the stories and what stories and histories are told. I call this form of visual narrative *autohistoria*. This form goes beyond the traditional self-portrait or autobiography; in telling the writer/artist's personal story, it also includes the artist's cultural history. The *retablos* I make are not just representations of myself, they are representations of Chicana culture. *El arte de la frontera* is community and academically based—many Chicana artists have M.A.s and Ph.D.s and hold precarious teaching positions on the fringes of universities. They are overworked, overlooked, passed over for tenure, and denied the support they deserve. To make, exhibit, and sell their artwork, and to survive, *los artistas* have had to band together collectively.[12]

I cross the exhibit room. Codices hang on the walls. I stare at the hieroglyphics. The ways of a people, their history and culture put on paper beaten from maguey leaves. Faint traces of red, blue, and black ink left by their artists, writers, and scholars. The past is hanging behind glass. We, the viewers in the present, walk around and around the glassboxed past. I wonder who I used to be, I wonder who I am. The border artist constantly reinvents herself. Through art she is able to reread, reinterpret, re-envision and reconstruct her culture's present as well as its past. This capacity to construct meaning and culture privileges the artist. As cultural icons for her ethnic communities, she is highly visible.

But there are drawbacks to having artistic and cultural power—the relentless pressure to produce, being put in the position of representing her entire *pueblo* and carrying all the ethnic culture's baggage on her *espalda* while trying to survive in a gringo world. Power and the seeking of greater power may create a self-centered ego or a fake public image, one the artist thinks will make her acceptable to her audience. It may encourage self-serving hustling—all artists have to sell themselves in order to get grants, get published, secure exhibit spaces, and get good reviews. But for some, the hustling outdoes the art-making.

The Chicana border writer/artist has finally come to market. The problem now is how to resist corporate culture while asking for and securing its patronage; how to get the dollars without resorting to "mainstreaming" the work. Is the border artist complicit in the appropriation of her at by the dominant art dealers? And if so, does this constitute a self-imposed imperialism? The artist, in making *plata* from the sale of her sculpture, "makes it." Money means power. The access to privilege that comes with the bucks and the recognition can turn the artist on her ear in a *nepantla* spin.

Finally, I find myself before the reconstructed statue of the newly unearthed *el dios murciélago,* the bat god with his big ears, fangs, and protruding tongue representing the vampire bat associated with night, blood sacrifice, and death. I make an instantaneous association of the bat man with the stage of border artists—the dark cave of creativity where they hang upside down, turning the self upside down in order to see from another point of view, one that brings a new state of understanding. Or it may mean transposing the former self into a new one—the death of the old self and the old ways, breaking down former notions of who you are. Night fear, *susto,* when every button is pushed. The border person constantly moves through that birth canal, *nepantla*. If you stay too long in *nepantla* you are in danger of being blocked, resulting from a breech birth or being stillborn.

I wonder what meaning this bat figure will have for other Chicanas, what artistic meaning they will make of it and what political struggle it will represent. Perhaps the *murciélago* questions the viewer's unconscious collective and personal identity and its ties to her ancestors, *los muertos*. In border art there is always the specter of death in the background. Often *las calaveras* (skeletons and skulls) take a prominent position—and not just on *el día de los muertos* (November 2). *De la tierra nacemos,* from earth we are born, *a la tierra regresaremos,* to earth we shall return, *a dar lo que ella nos dió,* to give back to her what she has given. Yes, I say to myself, the earth eats the dead, *la tierra se come los muertos.*

I walk out of the Aztec exhibit hall. It is September 28, *mi cumpleaños.* I seek out the table with the computer, key in my birthdate and there on the screen is my Aztec birth year and ritual day name: 8 Rabbit, 12 Skull. In that culture I would have been named Matlactli Omome Mizuitzli. I stick my chart under the rotating rubber stamps, press down, pull it out and stare at the imprint of the rabbit (symbol of fear and of running scared) pictograph and then of the skull (night, blood sacrifice, and death). Very appropriate symbols in my life, I mutter. It's so *raza. ¿y qué?*

I ask myself, What direction will *el arte fronterizo* take in the future? The multi-subjectivity and split-subjectivity of the border artist creating various counter arts will continue, but with a parallel movement where a polarized us/them, insiders/outsiders culture clash is not the main struggle, where a refusal to be split will be a given. We are not *nos* (us) and *otras* (others)—*nos/otras.*

My mind reviews image after image. Something about who and what I am and the 200 "artifacts" I have just seen does not feel right. I pull out my "birth chart." Yes, cultural roots are important *but I was not born at Tenochitlán in the ancient past nor in an Aztec village in modern times. I was born and live in that in-between space,* nepantla, *the borderlands.* Hay muchas razas *running in my veins,* mescladas dentro de mi, otras culturas *that my body lives in and out of.* Mi cuerpo vive dentro y fuera de otras culturas *and a white man who constantly whispers inside my skull. For me, being Chicana is not enough. It is only one of my multiple identities. Along with other* border gente, *it is this site and time,* en este tiempo y lugar *where and when, I create my identity* con mi arte.

1993

Notes

I thank Dianna Williamson and Clarisa Rojas, my literary assistants, for their invaluable and incisive critical comments, and Deidre McFadyen.

1. See Amalia Mesa-Bains, *"El Mundo Feminino:* Chicana Artists of the Movement—A Commentary on Development and Production," in Richard Griswold Del Castillo, Teresa McKenna, and Yvonne Yarbo Bejarano (eds), CARA, *Chicano Art: Resistance and Affirmation* (Los Angeles: Wight Gallery, University of California, 1991).

2. See Luz María and Ellen J. Stekert's untitled art catalog essay in *Santa Baraza*, March 8–April 1, 1992, La Raza/Galería Posada, Sacramento, CA.

3. Quoted in Jennifer Heath's "Women Artists of Color Share World of Struggle," *Sunday Camera*, March 8, 1992, p. 9C.

4. See Carmen Lomas Garza's children's bilingual book, *Family Pictures/Cuadros de familia* (San Francisco: Children's Book Press, 1990), in particular *"Camas para sonar*/Beds for Dreaming."

5. The Maya huipiles are large rectangular blouses which describe the Maya cosmos. They portray the world as a diamond. the four sides of the diamond represent the boundaries of space and time; the smaller diamonds at each corner, the cardinal points. The weaver maps the heavens and underworld.

6. Roberta H. Markman and Peter T. Markman (eds), *Masks of the Spirit: Image and Metaphor in Mesoamerica* (Berkley: University of California Press, 1989).

7. See Guy Brett, *Transcontinental: An Investigation of Reality* (London: Verso, 1990).

8. See *ex profeso, recuento de afinidades colectiva plástica contemporánea: imágenes: gay-lésbicas-éroticas* put together by Circulo Cultural Gay in Mexico City and exhibited at Museuo Universatario del Chope during Gay Cultural Week, June 14–23, 1989.

9. The exact quote is: "We have an internalization of fixed space learned early in life. One's orientation in space is tied to survival and sanity. To be disoriented in space is to be psychotic," See Edward T. Hall and Mildred Reed Hall, "The Sounds of Silence," in James P. Spradley and David W. McCurdy (eds), *Conformity and Conflict: Readings in Cultural Anthropology* (Boston: Little Brown, 1987).

10. The exhibition was part of Festival Internacional de la Raza '92. The artworks were produced in the Silkscreen Studios of Self Help Graphics, Los Angeles, and in the studios of Strike Editions in Austin, Texas. Self Help Graphics and the Galería Sin Fronteras, Austin, Texas, organized the exhibitions.

11. Among the alternative galleries and art centers that combat assimilation are the Guadalupe Cultural Arts Center in San Antonio, Mexic-Arte Museum and Sin Fronteras Gallery in Austin, Texas, and the Mission Cultural Center in San Francisco.

12. For a discussion of Chicano posters, almanacs, calendars, and cartoons that join "images and texts to depict community issues as well as historical and cultural themes," and that metaphorically link Chicano struggles for self-determination with the Mexican Revolution, and establish "a cultural and visual continuum across borders," see Tomás Ybarra-Fausto's "Gráfica/Urban Iconography" in *Chicano Expressions: A New View in American Art, April 14–July 31, 1986* (New York: INTAR Latin American Gallery, 1986), pp. 21–4.

Homi Bhabha (1949–)

If feminists have declared that the personal is the political, then Bhabha has declared that the theoretical is the political, that we can use theory to make political interventions. A prominent figure in postcolonial studies, Bhabha was born just two years after India gained independence from Great Britain. The son of an important constitutional lawyer, he grew up in Bombay, and it was from Bombay University that he received his B.A. After finishing his undergraduate work, he left Bombay for England, where he earned his M.A., M. Phil., and D.Phil.

from Oxford University. Bhabha currently teaches at Harvard University, but he has held visiting positions at a number of American universities, including Princeton and the University of Pennsylvania, where he delivered the Richard Wright lecture series. Before moving to Harvard in 2001, he was the Chester D. Tripp Professor in the Humanities at the University of Chicago, where he taught in both the English and the art departments.

One of the concepts that Bhabha is best known for is "hybridity," a way of thinking about cultural identity that opposes more restrictive notions of identity politics, which, as many argue, too easily result in separatism or aggressive nationalism. Although Bhabha's concept of hybridity has been criticized as being too broad and amorphous, it has nevertheless radically changed the way postcolonial studies understands nation and identity. As W. J. T. Mitchell said in an interview published in *Artforum* in 1995, it's hard "to remember what life was like before terms like 'multiculturalism' and 'the postcolonial' became the lingua franca, not only of the academy, but of an international realm of public discourse," and the reason Bhabha's work has been so important is that "he has made it difficult to use those words thoughtlessly or complacently" (80–84).

Bhabha is best known for his essays, many of which are collected in his book *The Location of Culture* (1994). He edited an influential anthology, *Nation and Narration* (1990), and he coedited *Cosmopolitanism* (2002).

Border Lives: The Art of the Present

A boundary is not that at which something stops but, as the Greeks recognized, the boundary is that from which something begins its presencing.

Martin Heidegger, 'Building, dwelling, thinking'

It is the trope of our times to locate the question of culture in the realm of the *beyond*. At the century's edge, we are less exercised by annihilation—the death of the author—or epiphany—the birth of the 'subject'. Our existence today is marked by a tenebrous sense of survival, living on the borderlines of the 'present', for which there seems to be no proper name other than the current and controversial shiftiness of the prefix 'post': *postmodernism, postcolonialism, postfeminism. . . .*

The 'beyond' is neither a new horizon, nor a leaving behind of the past. . . . Beginnings and endings may be the sustaining myths of the middle years; but in the *fin de siècle,* we find ourselves in the moment of transit where space and time cross to produce complex figures of difference and identity, past and present, inside and outside, inclusion and exclusion. For there is a sense of disorientation, a disturbance of direction, in the 'beyond': an exploratory, restless movement caught so well in the French rendition of the words *au-delà*—here and there, on all sides, *fort/da,* hither and thither, back and forth.[1]

The move away from the singularities of 'class' or 'gender' as primary conceptual and organizational categories, has resulted in an awareness of the subject positions—of race, gender, generation, institutional location, geopolitical locale, sexual orientation—that inhabit any claim to identity in the modern world. What is theoretically innovative, and politically crucial, is the need to think beyond narratives of originary and initial subjectivities and to focus on those moments or processes that are produced in the articulation of cultural differences. These 'in-between' spaces provide the terrain for elaborating strategies of selfhood—singular or communal—that initiate new signs of identity, and innovative sites of collaboration, and contestation, in the act of defining the idea of society itself.

It is in the emergence of the interstices—the overlap and displacement of domains of difference—that the intersubjective and collective experiences of *nationness*, community interest, or cultural value are negotiated. How are subjects formed 'in-between', or in excess of, the sum of the 'parts' of difference (usually intoned as race/class/gender, etc.)? How do strategies of representation or empowerment come to be formulated in the competing claims of communities where, despite shared histories of deprivation and discrimination, the exchange of values, meanings and priorities may not always be collaborative and dialogical, but may be profoundly antagonistic, conflictual and even incommensurable?

The force of these questions is borne out by the 'language' of recent social crises sparked off by histories of cultural difference. Conflicts in South Central Los Angeles between Koreans, Mexican-Americans and African-Americans focus on the concept of 'disrespect'—a term forged on the borderlines of ethnic deprivation that is, at once, the sign of racialized violence and the symptom of social victimage. In the aftermath of the the *Satanic Verses* affair in Great Britain, Black and Irish feminists, despite their different constituencies, have made common cause against the 'racialization of religion' as the dominant discourse through which the State represents their conflicts and struggles, however secular or even 'sexual' they may be.

Terms of cultural engagement, whether antagonistic or affiliative, are produced performatively. The representation of difference must not be hastily read as the reflection of *pre-given* ethnic or cultural traits set in the fixed tablet of tradition. The social articulation of difference, from the minority perspective, is a complex, on-going negotiation that seeks to authorize cultural hybridities that emerge in moments of historical transformation. The 'right' to signify from the periphery of authorized power and privilege does not depend on the persistence of tradition; it is resourced by the power of tradition to be reinscribed through the conditions of contingency and contradictoriness that attend upon the lives of those who are 'in the minority'. The recognition that tradition bestows is a partial form of identification. In restaging the past it introduces other, incommensurable cultural temporalities into the invention of tradition. This process estranges any immediate access to an originary identity or a 'received' tradition. The borderline engagements of cultural difference may as often be consensual as conflictual; they may confound our definitions of tradition and modernity; realign the customary boundaries between the private and the public, high and low; and challenge normative expectations of development and progress.

> I wanted to make shapes or set up situations that are kind of open. . . . My work has a lot to do with a kind of fluidity, a movement back and forth, not making a claim to any specific or essential way of being.[2]

Thus writes Renée Green, the African-American artist. She reflects on the need to understand cultural difference as the production of minority identities that 'split'—are estranged unto themselves—in the act of being articulated into a collective body:

> Multiculturalism doesn't reflect the complexity of the situation as I face it
> daily. . . . It requires a person to step outside of him/herself to actually see what
> he/she is doing. I don't want to condemn well-meaning people and say (like
> those T-shirts you can buy on the street) 'It's a black thing, you wouldn't under-
> stand.' To me that's essentialising blackness.[3]

Political empowerment, and the enlargement of the multiculturalist cause, come
from posing questions of solidarity and community from the interstitial perspective. Social differences are not simply given to experience through an already
authenticated cultural tradition; they are the signs of the emergence of community envisaged as a project—at once a vision and a construction—that takes you
'beyond' yourself in order to return, in a spirit of revision and reconstruction, to
the political *conditions* of the present:

> Even then, it's still a struggle for power between various groups within ethnic
> groups about what's being said and who's saying what, who's representing who?
> What is a community anyway? What is a black community? What is a Latino
> community? I have trouble with thinking of all these things as monolithic fixed
> categories.[4]

If Renée Green's questions open up an interrogatory, interstitial space
between the act of representation—who? what? where?—and the presence of
community itself, then consider her own creative intervention within this in-
between moment. Green's 'architectural' site-specific work, *Sites of Genealogy*
(Out of Site, The Institute of Contemporary Art, Long Island City, New York),
displays and displaces the binary logic through which identities of difference are
often constructed—Black/White, Self/Other. Green makes a metaphor of the
museum building itself, rather than simply using the gallery space:

> I used architecture literally as a reference, using the attic, the boiler room, and
> the stairwell to make associations between certain binary divisions such as
> higher and lower and heaven and hell. The stairwell became a liminal space, a
> pathway between the upper and lower areas, each of which was annotated with
> plaques referring to blackness and whiteness.[5]

The stairwell as liminal space, in-between the designations of identity, becomes
the process of symbolic interaction, the connective tissue that constructs the difference between upper and lower, black and white. The hither and thither of the
stairwell, the temporal movement and passage that it allows, prevents identities
at either end of it from settling into primordial polarities. This interstitial passage
between fixed identifications opens up the possibility of a cultural hybridity that
entertains difference without an assumed or imposed hierarchy:

> I always went back and forth between racial designations and designations from
> physics or other symbolic designations. All these things blur in some way . . . To
> develop a genealogy of the way colours and noncolours function is interesting
> to me.[6]

'Beyond' signifies spatial distance, marks progress, promises the future; but our intimations of exceeding the barrier or boundary—the very act of going *beyond*—are unknowable, unrepresentable, without a return to the 'present' which, in the process of repetition, becomes disjunct and displaced. The imaginary of spatial distance—to live somehow beyond the border of our times—throws into relief the temporal, social differences that interrupt our collusive sense of cultural contemporaneity. The present can no longer be simply envisaged as a break or a bonding with the past and the future, no longer a synchronic presence: our proximate self-presence, our public image, comes to be revealed for its discontinuities, its inequalities, its minorities. Unlike the dead hand of history that tells the beads of sequential time like a rosary, seeking to establish serial, causal connections, we are now confronted with what Walter Benjamin describes as the blasting of a monadic moment from the homogenous course of history, 'establishing a conception of the present as the "time of the now"'.[7]

If the jargon of our times—postmodernity, postcoloniality, postfeminism—has any meaning at all, it does not lie in the popular use of the 'post' to indicate sequentiality—*after*-feminism; or polarity—*anti*-modernism. These terms that insistently gesture to the beyond, only embody its restless and revisionary energy if they transform the present into an expanded and ex-centric site of experience and empowerment. For instance, if the interest in postmodernism is limited to a celebration of the fragmentation of the 'grand narratives' of postenlightenment rationalism then, for all its intellectual excitement, it remains a profoundly parochial enterprise.

The wider significance of the postmodern condition lies in the awareness that the epistemological 'limits' of those ethnocentric ideas are also the enunciative boundaries of a range of other dissonant, even dissident histories and voices—women, the colonized, minority groups, the bearers of policed sexualities. For the demography of the new internationalism is the history of post-colonial migration, the narratives of cultural and political diaspora, the major social displacements of peasant and aboriginal communities, the poetics of exile, the grim prose of political and economic refugees. It is in this sense that the boundary becomes the place from which *something begins its presencing* in a movement not dissimilar to the ambulant, ambivalent articulation of the beyond that I have drawn out: 'Always and ever differently the bridge escorts the lingering and hastening ways of men to and fro, so that they may get to other banks.... The bridge *gathers* as a passage that crosses.'[8]

The very concepts of homogenous national cultures, the consensual or contiguous transmission of historical traditions, or 'organic' ethnic communities—*as the grounds of cultural comparativism*—are in a profound process of redefinition. The hideous extremity of Serbian nationalism proves that the very idea of a pure, 'ethnically cleansed' national identity can only be achieved through the death, literal and figurative, of the complex interweavings of history, and the culturally contingent borderlines of modern nationhood. This side of the psychosis of patriotic fervour, I like to think, there is overwhelming evidence of a more transnational and translational sense of the hybridity of imagined communities. Contemporary Sri Lankan theatre represents the deadly conflict between the

Tamils and the Sinhalese through allegorical references to State brutality in South Africa and Latin America; the Anglo-Celtic canon of Australian literature and cinema is being rewritten from the perspective of Aboriginal political and cultural imperatives; the South African novels of Richard Rive, Bessie Head, Nadine Gordimer, John Coetzee, are documents of a society divided by the effects of apartheid that enjoin the international intellectual community to meditate on the unequal, assymetrical worlds that exist elsewhere; Salman Rushdie writes the fabulist historiography of post-Independence India and Pakistan in *Midnight's Children* and *Shame,* only to remind us in *The Satanic Verses* that the truest eye may now belong to the migrant's double vision; Toni Morrison's *Beloved* revives the past of slavery and its murderous rituals of possession and self-possession, in order to project a contemporary fable of a woman's history that is at the same time the narrative of an affective, historic memory of an emergent public sphere of men and women alike.

What is striking about the 'new' internationalism is that the move from the specific to the general, from the material to the metaphoric, is not a smooth passage of transition and transcendence. The 'middle passage' of contemporary culture, as with slavery itself, is a process of displacement and disjunction that does not totalize experience. Increasingly, 'national' cultures are being produced from the perspective of disenfranchised minorities. The most significant effect of this process is not the proliferation of 'alternative histories of the excluded' producing, as some would have it, a pluralist anarchy. What my examples show is the changed basis for making international connections. The currency of critical comparativism, or aesthetic judgement, is no longer the sovereignty of the national culture conceived as Benedict Anderson proposes as an 'imagined community' rooted in a 'homogeneous empty time' of modernity and progress. The great connective narratives of capitalism and class drive the engines of social reproduction, but do not, in themselves, provide a foundational frame for those modes of cultural identification and political affect that form around issues of sexuality, race, feminism, the lifeworld of refugees or migrants, or the deathly social destiny of AIDS.

The testimony of my examples represents a radical revision in the concept of human community itself. What this geopolitical space may be, as a local or transnational reality, is being both interrogated and reinitiated. Feminism, in the 1990s, finds its solidarity as much in liberatory narratives as in the painful ethical position of a slavewoman, Morrison's Sethe, in *Beloved,* who is pushed to infanticide. The body politic can no longer contemplate the nation's health as simply a civic virtue; it must rethink the question of rights for the entire national, and international, community, from the AIDS perspective. The Western metropole must confront its postcolonial history, told by its influx of postwar migrants and refugees, as an indigenous or native narrative *internal to its national identity;* and the reason for this is made clear in the stammering, drunken words of Mr. 'Whisky' Sisodia from *The Satanic Verses:* 'The trouble with the Engenglish is that their hiss hiss history happened overseas, so they dodo don't know what it means.'[9]

Postcoloniality, for its part, is a salutary reminder of the persistent 'neocolonial' relations within the 'new' world order and the multinational division of labour. Such a perspective enables the authentication of histories of exploitation and the evolution of strategies of resistance. Beyond this, however, postcolonial critique bears witness to those countries and communities—in the North and the South, urban and rural—constituted, if I may coin a phrase, 'otherwise than modernity'. Such cultures of a postcolonial *contra-modernity* may be contingent to modernity, discontinuous or in contention with it, resistant to its oppressive, assimilationist technologies; but they also deploy the cultural hybridity of their borderline conditions to 'translate', and therefore reinscribe, the social imaginary of both metropolis and modernity. Listen to Guillermo Gomez-Peña, the performance artist who lives, amongst other times and places, on the Mexico/US border:

> *hello America*
> *this is the voice of* Gran Vato Charollero
> broadcasting from the hot deserts of Nogales, Arizona
> *zona libre cogercio*
> *2000 megaherz en todas direciones*
>
> *you are celebrating Labor Day in Seattle*
> *while the Klan demonstrates*
> *against Mexicans in Georgia*
> ironia, 100% ironia[10]

Being in the 'beyond', then, is to inhabit an intervening space, as any dictionary will tell you. But to dwell 'in the beyond' is also, as I have shown, to be part of a revisionary time, a return to the present to redescribe our cultural contemporaneity; to reinscribe our human, historic commonality; *to touch the future on its hither side.* In that sense, then, the intervening space 'beyond', becomes a space of intervention in the here and now. To engage with such invention, and intervention, as Green and Gomez-Peña enact in their distinctive work, requires a sense of the new that resonates with the hybrid chicano aesthetic of '*rasquachismo*' as Tomas Ybarra-Frausto describes it:

> the utilization of available resources for syncretism, juxtaposition, and integration. *Rasquachismo* is a sensibility attuned to mixtures and confluence . . . a delight in texture and sensuous surfaces . . . self-conscious manipulation of materials or iconography . . . the combination of found material and satiric wit . . . the manipulation of *rasquache* artifacts, code and sensibilities from both sides of the border.[11]

The borderline work of culture demands an encounter with 'newness' that is not part of the continuum of past and present. It creates a sense of the new as an insurgent act of cultural translation. Such art does not merely recall the past as social cause or aesthetic precedent; it renews that past, refiguring it as a contingent 'in-between' space, that innovates and interrupts the performance of the present. The 'past-present' becomes part of the necessity, not the nostalgia, of living.

Pepon Osorio's *objets trouvés* of the Nuyorican (New York/Puerto Rican) community—the statistics of infant mortality, or the silent (and silenced) spread of AIDS in the Hispanic community—are elaborated into baroque allegories of social alienation. But it is not the high drama of birth and death that captures Osorio's spectacular imagination. He is the great celebrant of the migrant act of survival, using his mixed-media works to make a hybrid cultural space that forms contingently, disjunctively, in the inscription of signs of cultural memory and sites of political agency. *La Cama (The Bed)* turns the highly decorated four-poster into the primal scene of lost-and-found childhood memories, the memorial to a dead nanny Juana, the *mise-en-scène* of the eroticism of the 'emigrant' everyday. Survival, for Osorio, is working in the interstices of a range of practices: the 'space' of installation, the spectacle of the social statistic, the transitive time of the body in performance.

Finally, it is the photographic art of Alan Sekula that takes the borderline condition of cultural translation to its global limit in *Fish Story*, his photographic project on harbours: 'the harbour is the site in which material goods appear in bulk, in the very flux of exchange'.[12] The harbour and the stockmarket become the *paysage moralisé* of a containerized, computerized world of global trade. Yet, the non-synchronous time-space of transnational 'exchange', and exploitation, is embodied in a navigational allegory:

> Things are more confused now. A scratchy recording of the Norwegian national anthem blares out from a loudspeaker at the Sailor's Home on the bluff above the channel. The container ship being greeted flies a Bahamian flag of convenience. It was built by Koreans working long hours in the giant shipyards of Ulsan. The underpaid and the understaffed crew could be Salvadorean or Filipino. Only the Captains hear a familiar melody.[13]

Norway's nationalist nostalgia cannot drown out the babel on the bluff. Transnational capitalism and the impoverishment of the Third World certainly create the chains of circumstance that incarcerate the Salvadorean or the Filipino/a. In their cultural passage, hither and thither, as migrant workers, part of the massive economic and political diaspora of the modern world, they embody the Benjaminian 'present': that moment blasted out of the continuum of history. Such conditions of cultural displacement and social discrimination—where political survivors become the best historical witnesses—are the grounds on which Frantz Fanon, the Martinican psychoanalyst and participant in the Algerian revolution, locates an agency of empowerment:

> As soon as I *desire* I am asking to be considered. I am not merely here-and-now, sealed into thingness. I am for somewhere else and for something else. I demand that notice be taken of my *negating activity* [my emphasis] insofar as I pursue something other than life; insofar as I do battle for the creation of a human world—that is a world of reciprocal recognitions.
>
> I should constantly remind myself that the real *leap* consists in introducing invention into existence.
>
> In the world in which I travel, I am endlessly creating myself. And it is by going beyond the historical, instrumental hypothesis that I will initiate my cycle of freedom.[14]

Once more it is the desire for recognition, 'for somewhere else and for something else' that takes the experience of history *beyond* the instrumental hypothesis. Once again, it is the space of intervention emerging in the cultural interstices that introduces creative invention into existence. And one last time, there is a return to the performance of identity as iteration, the re-creation of the self in the world of travel, the resettlement of the borderline community of migration. Fanon's desire for the recognition of cultural presence as 'negating activity' resonates with my breaking the time-barrier of a culturally collusive 'present'.

Unhomely Lives: The Literature of Recognition

Fanon recognizes the crucial importance, for subordinated peoples, of asserting their indigenous cultural traditions and retrieving their repressed histories. But he is far too aware of the dangers of the fixity and fetishism of identities within the calcification of colonial cultures to recommend that 'roots' be struck in the celebratory romance of the past or by homogenizing the history of the present. The negating activity is, indeed, the intervention of the 'beyond' that establishes a boundary: a bridge, where 'presencing' begins because it captures something of the estranging sense of the relocation of the home and the world—the unhomeliness—that is the condition of extra-territorial and cross-cultural initiations. To be unhomed is not to be homeless, nor can the 'unhomely' be easily accommodated in that familiar division of social life into private and public spheres. The unhomely moment creeps up on you stealthily as your own shadow and suddenly you find yourself with Henry James's Isabel Archer, in *The Portrait of a Lady,* taking the measures of your dwelling in a state of 'incredulous terror'.[15] And it is at this point that the world first shrinks for Isabel and then expands enormously. As she struggles to survive the fathomless waters, the rushing torrents, James introduces us to the 'unhomeliness' inherent in that rite of extra-territorial and cross-cultural initiation. The recesses of the domestic space become sites for history's most intricate invasions. In that displacement, the borders between home and world become confused; and, uncannily, the private and the public become part of each other, forcing upon us a vision that is as divided as it is disorienting.

Although the 'unhomely' is a paradigmatic colonial and post-colonial condition, it has a resonance that can be heard distinctly, if erratically, in fictions that negotiate the powers of cultural difference in a range of transhistorical sites. You have already heard the shrill alarm of the unhomely in that moment when Isabel Archer realizes that her world has been reduced to one high, mean window, as her house of fiction becomes 'the house of darkness, the house of dumbness, the house of suffocation.'[16] If you hear it thus at the Palazzo Roccanera in the late 1870s, then a little earlier in 1873 on the outskirts of Cincinnati, in mumbling houses like 124 Bluestone Road, you hear the undecipherable language of the black and angry dead; the voice of Toni Morrison's *Beloved,* 'the thoughts of the women of 124, unspeakable thoughts, unspoken'.[17] More than a quarter of a century later in 1905, Bengal is ablaze with the Swadeshi or Home Rule movement when 'home-made Bimala, the product of the confined space', as Tagore describes her in *The Home and the World,* is aroused by 'a running undertone of melody, low down in the bass . . . the true manly note, the note of power.' Bimala is possessed and drawn forever from the zenana, the secluded women's quarters, as she crosses that fated verandah into the world of public affairs—'over to another shore and the ferry had ceased to ply.'[18] Much closer to our own times in contemporary South Africa, Nadine Gordimer's heroine Aila in *My Son's Story* emanates a stilling atmosphere as she makes her diminished domesticity into the perfect cover for gun-running: suddenly the home turns into another world, and the narrator notices that 'It was as if everyone found that he had unnoticingly entered a strange house, *and it was hers* . . .'[19]

The historical specificities and cultural diversities that inform each of these texts would make a global argument purely gestural; in any case, I shall only be dealing with Morrison and Gordimer in any detail. But the 'unhomely' does provide a 'non-continuist' problematic that dramatizes—in the figure of woman— the ambivalent structure of the civil State as it draws its rather paradoxical boundary between the private and the public spheres. If, for Freud, the *unheimlich* is 'the name for everything that ought to have remained . . . secret and hidden but has come to light', then Hannah Arendt's description of the public and private realms is a profoundly unhomely one: 'it is the distinction between things that should be hidden and things that should be shown', she writes, which through their inversion in the modern age 'discovers how rich and manifold the hidden can be under conditions of intimacy'.[20]

This logic of reversal, that turns on a disavowal, informs the profound revelations and reinscriptions of the unhomely moment. For what was 'hidden from sight' for Arendt, becomes in Carole Pateman's *The Disorder of Women* the 'ascriptive domestic sphere' that is *forgotten* in the theoretical distinctions of the private and public spheres of civil society. Such a forgetting—or disavowal— creates an uncertainty at the heart of the generalizing subject of civil society, compromising the 'individual' that is the support for its universalist aspiration. By making visible the forgetting of the 'unhomely' moment in civil society, feminism specifies the patriarchal, gendered nature of civil society and disturbs the symmetry of private and public which is now shadowed, or uncannily doubled, by the difference of genders which does not neatly map on to the private and the public, but becomes disturbingly supplementary to them. This results in redrawing the domestic space as the space of the normalizing, pastoralizing, and individuating techniques of modern power and police: the personal-*is*-the-political; the world-*in*-the-home.

The unhomely moment relates the traumatic ambivalences of a personal, psychic history to the wider disjunctions of political existence. Beloved, the child murdered by her own mother, Sethe, is a daemonic, belated repetition of the violent history of black infant deaths, during slavery, in many parts of the South, less than a decade after the haunting of 124 Bluestone Road. (Between 1882 and 1895 from one-third to a half of the annual black mortality rate was accounted for by children under five years of age.) But the memory of Sethe's act of infanticide emerges through 'the holes—the things the fugitives did not say; the questions they did not ask . . . the unnamed, the unmentioned'.[21] As we reconstruct the narrative of child murder through Sethe, the slave mother, who is herself the victim of social death, the very historical basis of our ethical judgement undergoes a radical revision.

Such forms of social and psychic existence can best be represented in that tenuous survival of literary language itself, which allows memory to speak:

> while knowing Speech can (be) at best, a shadow echoing
> the silent light, bear witness
> To the truth, it is not . . .

W. H. Auden wrote those lines on the powers of *poesis* in *The Cave of Making,* aspiring to be, as he put it, 'a minor Atlantic Goethe'.[22] And it is to an intriguing suggestion in Goethe's final 'Note on world literature' (1830) that I now turn to find a comparative method that would speak to the 'unhomely' condition of the modern world.

Goethe suggests that the possibility of a world literature arises from the cultural confusion wrought by terrible wars and mutual conflicts. Nations

> could not return to their settled and independent life again without noticing that they had learned many foreign ideas and ways, which they had unconsciously adopted, and come to feel here and there previously unrecognized spiritual and intellectual needs.[23]

Goethe's immediate reference is, of course, to the Napoleonic wars and his concept of 'the feeling of neighborly relations' is profoundly Eurocentric, extending as far as England and France. However, as an Orientalist who read Shakuntala at seventeen years of age, and who writes in his autobiography of the 'unformed and overformed'[24] monkey god Hanuman, Goethe's speculations are open to another line of thought.

What of the more complex cultural situation where 'previously unrecognized spiritual and intellectual needs' emerge from the imposition of 'foreign' ideas, cultural representations, and structures of power? Goethe suggests that the 'inner nature of the whole nation as well as the individual man works all unconsciously'.[25] When this is placed alongside his idea that the cultural life of the nation is 'unconsciously' lived, then there may be a sense in which world literature could be an emergent, prefigurative category that is concerned with a form of cultural dissensus and alterity, where nonconsensual terms of affiliation may be established on the grounds of historical trauma. The study of world literature might be the study of the way in which cultures recognize themselves through their projections of 'otherness'. Where, once, the transmission of national traditions was the major theme of a world literature, perhaps we can now suggest that transnational histories of migrants, the colonized, or political refugees—these border and frontier conditions—may be the terrains of world literature. The centre of such a study would neither be the 'sovereignty' of national cultures, nor the universalism of human culture, but a focus on those 'freak social and cultural displacements' that Morrison and Gordimer represent in their 'unhomely' fictions. Which leads us to ask: can the perplexity of the unhomely, intrapersonal world lead to an international theme?

If we are seeking a 'worlding' of literature, then perhaps it lies in a critical act that attempts to grasp the sleight of hand with which literature conjures with historical specificity, using the medium of psychic uncertainty, aesthetic distancing, or the obscure signs of the spirit-world, the sublime and the subliminal. As literary creatures and political animals we ought to concern ourselves with the understanding of human action and the social world as a moment when *something is beyond control, but it is not beyond accommodation*. This act of writing the world, of taking the measure of its dwelling, is magically caught in Morrison's description of her house of fiction—art as 'the fully realized presence of a haunting'[26] of history. Read as an image that describes the relation of art to social reality, my translation of Morrison's phrase becomes a statement on the political responsibility of the critic. For the critic must attempt to fully realize, and take responsibility for, the unspoken, unrepresented pasts that haunt the historical present.

Our task remains, however, to show how historical agency is transformed through the signifying process; how the historical event is represented in a discourse that is *somehow beyond control*. This is in keeping with Hannah Arendt's suggestion that the author of social action may be the initiator of its unique meaning, but as agent he or she cannot control its outcome. It is not simply what the house of fiction contains or 'controls' *as content*. What is just as important is the metaphoricity of the houses of racial memory that both Morrison and Gordimer construct—those subjects of the narrative that mutter or mumble like 124 Bluestone Road, or keep a still silence in a 'grey' Cape Town suburb.

Each of the houses in Gordimer's *My Son's Story* is invested with a specific secret or a conspiracy, an unhomely stirring. The house in the ghetto is the house of the collusiveness of the coloureds in their antagonistic relations to the blacks; the lying house is the house of Sonny's adultery; then there is the silent house of Aila's revolutionary camouflage; there is also the nocturnal house of Will, the narrator, writing of the narrative that charts the phoenix rising in his home, while the words must turn to ashes in his mouth. But each 'unhomely' house marks a deeper historical displacement. And that is the condition of being 'coloured' in South Africa, or as Will describes it, 'halfway between . . . being not defined—and it was this lack of definition in itself that was never to be questioned, but observed like a taboo, something which no one, while following, could ever admit to'.[27]

This halfway house of racial and cultural origins bridges the 'in-between' diasporic origins of the coloured South African and turns it into the symbol for the disjunctive, displaced everyday life of the liberation struggle: 'like so many others of this kind, whose families are fragmented in the diaspora of exile, code names, underground activity, people for whom a real home and attachments are something for others who will come after'.[28]

Private and public, past and present, the psyche and the social develop an interstitial intimacy. It is an intimacy that questions binary divisions through which such spheres of social experience are often spatially opposed. These spheres of life are linked through an 'in-between' temporality that takes the measure of dwelling at home, while producing an image of the world of history. This is the moment of aesthetic distance that provides the narrative with a double edge, which like the coloured South African subject represents a hybridity, a difference 'within', a subject that inhabits the rim of an 'in-between' reality. And the inscription of this borderline existence inhabits a stillness of time and a strangeness of framing that creates the discursive 'image' at the crossroads of history and literature, bridging the home and the world.

Such a strange stillness is visible in the portrait of Aila. Her husband Sonny, now past his political prime, his affair with his white revolutionary lover in abeyance, makes his first prison visit to see his wife. The wardress stands back, the policeman fades, and Aila emerges as an unhomely presence, on the opposite side from her husband and son:

> but through the familiar beauty there was a vivid strangeness. . . . It was as if some chosen experience had seen in her, as a painter will in his subject, what she was, what was there to be discovered. In Lusaka, in secret, in prison—who knows where—she had sat for her hidden face. *They had to recognise her.*[29]

Through this painterly distance a vivid strangeness emerges; a partial or double 'self' is framed in a climactic political moment that is also a contingent historical event—'some chosen experience . . . who knows where . . . or what there was to be discovered'.[30] They had to recognize her, but *what* do they recognize in her?

Words will not speak and the silence freezes into the images of apartheid: identity cards, police frame-ups, prison mug-shots, the grainy press pictures of terrorists. Of course, Aila is not judged, nor is she judgemental. Her revenge is much wiser and more complete. In her silence she becomes the unspoken 'totem' of the taboo of the coloured South African. She displays the unhomely world, 'the halfway between . . . not defined' world of the coloured as the 'distorted place and time in which they—all of them—Sonny, Aila, Hannah—lived'.[31] The silence that doggedly follows Aila's dwelling now turns into an image of the 'interstices', the in-between hybridity of the history of sexuality and race.

> The necessity for what I've done—She placed the outer edge of each hand, fingers extended and close together, as a frame on either sides of the sheets of testimony in front of her. And she placed herself before him, to be judged by him.[32]

Aila's hidden face, the outer edge of each hand, these small gestures through which she speaks describe another dimension of 'dwelling' in the social world. Aila as coloured woman defines a boundary that is at once inside and outside, the insider's outsideness. The stillness that surrounds her, the gaps in her story, her hesitation and passion that speak between the self and its acts—these are moments where the private and public touch in contingency. They do not simply transform the content of political ideas; the very 'place' from which the political is spoken—the public sphere itself, becomes an experience of liminality which questions, in Sonny's words, what it means to speak 'from the centre of life'.[33]

The central political preoccupation of the novel—till Aila's emergency—focuses on the 'loss of absolutes', the meltdown of the cold war, the fear 'that if we can't offer the old socialist paradise in exchange for the capitalist hell here, we'll have turned traitor to our brothers'.[34] The lesson Aila teaches requires a movement away from a world conceived in binary terms, away from a notion of the people's aspirations sketched in simple black and white. It also requires a

shift of attention from the political as a pedagogical, idealogical practice to politics as the stressed necessity of everyday life—politics as a performativity. Aila
leads us to the unhomely world where, Gordimer writes, the banalities are
enacted—the fuss over births, marriages, family affairs with their survival rituals
of food and clothing.[35] But it is precisely in these banalities that the unhomely
stirs, as the violence of a racialized society falls most enduringly on the details of
life: where you can sit, or not; how you can live, or not; what you can learn, or
not; who you can love, or not. Between the banal act of freedom and its historical denial rises the silence: 'Aila emanated a stilling atmosphere; the parting jab-
ber stopped. It was as if everyone found he had unnoticingly entered a strange
house, and it was hers; she stood there.'[36]

In Aila's stillness, its obscure necessity, we glimpse what Emmanuel Levinas
has magically described as the twilight existence of the aesthetic image—art's
image as 'the very event of obscuring, a descent into night, an invasion of the
shadow'.[37] The 'completion' of the aesthetic, the distancing of the world in the
image, is precisely not a transcendental activity. The image—or the metaphoric,
'fictional' activity of discourse—makes visible 'an interruption of time by a
movement going on on the hither side of time, in its interstices'.[38] The complexity
of this statement will become clearer when I remind you of the stillness of time
through which Aila surreptitiously and subversively interrupts the ongoing presence of political activity, using her interstitial role, her domestic world to both
'obscure' her political role and to articulate it the better. Or, as *Beloved,* the continual eruption of 'undecipherable languages' of slave memory obscures the historical narrative of infanticide only to articulate the unspoken: that ghostly
discourse that enters the world of 124 'from the outside' in order to reveal the
transitional world of the aftermath of slavery in the 1870s, its private and public
faces, its historical past and its narrative present.

The aesthetic image discloses an ethical time of narration because, Levinas
writes, 'the real world appears in the image as it were between parentheses'.[39]
Like the outer edges of Aila's hands holding her enigmatic testimony, like
124 Bluestone Road which is a fully realized presence haunted by undecipherable
languages, Levinas's parenthetical perspective is also an ethical view. It effects an
'externality of the inward' as the very enunciative position of the historical and
narrative subject, 'introducing into the heart of subjectivity a radical and anarchical reference to the other which in fact constitutes the inwardness of the subject'.[40] Is it not uncanny that Levinas's metaphors for this unique 'obscurity' of
the image should come from those Dickensian unhomely places—those dusty
boarding schools, the pale light of London offices, the dark, dank second-hand
clothes shops?

For Levinas the 'art-magic' of the contemporary novel lies in its way of 'seeing inwardness from the outside', and it is this ethical-aesthetic positioning that
returns us, finally, to the community of the unhomely, to the famous opening
lines of *Beloved:* '124 was spiteful. The women in the house knew it and so did
the children.'

It is Toni Morrison who takes this ethical and aesthetic project of 'seeing
inwardness from the outside' furthest or deepest—right into *Beloved*'s naming of
her desire for identity: 'I want you to touch me on my inside part and call me my

name.'[41] There is an obvious reason why a ghost should want to be so realized. What is more obscure—and to the point—is how such an inward and intimate desire would provide an 'inscape' of the memory of slavery. For Morrison, it is precisely the signification of the historical and discursive boundaries of slavery that is the issue.

Racial violence is invoked by historical dates—1876, for instance—but Morrison is just a little hasty with the events 'in-themselves', as she rushes past 'the true meaning of the Fugitive Bill, the Settlement Fee, God's Ways, antislavery, manumission, skin voting'.[42] What has to be endured is the knowledge of doubt that comes from Sethe's eighteen years of disapproval and a solitary life, her banishment in the unhomely world of 124 Bluestone Road, as the pariah of her post-slavery community. What finally causes the thoughts of the women of 124 'unspeakable thoughts to be unspoken' is the understanding that the victims of violence are themselves 'signified upon': they are the victims of projected fears, anxieties and dominations that do not originate within the oppressed and will not fix them in the circle of pain. The stirring of emancipation comes with the knowledge that the racially supremacist belief 'that under every dark skin there was a jungle' was a belief that grew, spread, touched every perpetrator of the racist myth, turned them mad from their own untruths, and was then expelled from 124 Bluestone Road.

But before such an emancipation from the ideologies of the master, Morrison insists on the harrowing ethical repositioning of the slave mother, who must be the enunciatory site for seeing the inwardness of the slave world from the outside— when the 'outside' is the ghostly return of the child she murdered; the double of herself, for 'she is the laugh I am the laughter I see her face which is mine'.[43] What could be the ethics of child murder? What historical knowledge returns to Sethe, through the aesthetic distance or 'obscuring' of the event, in the phantom shape of her dead daughter Beloved?

In her fine account of forms of slave resistance in *Within the Plantation Household*, Elizabeth Fox-Genovese considers murder, self-mutilation and infanticide to be the core psychological dynamic of all resistance. It is her view that 'these extreme forms captured the essence of the slave woman's self-definition'.[44] Again we see how this most tragic and intimate act of violence is performed in a struggle to push back the boundaries of the slave world. Unlike acts of confrontation against the master or the overseer which were resolved within the household context, infanticide was recognized as an act against the system and at least acknowledged the slavewoman's legal standing in the public sphere. Infanticide was seen to be an act against the master's property—against his surplus profits—and perhaps that, Fox-Genovese concludes, 'led some of the more desperate to feel that, by killing an infant they loved, they would be in some way reclaiming it as their own'.[45]

Through the death and the return of Beloved, precisely such a reclamation takes place: the slave mother regaining through the presence of the child, the property of her own person. This knowledge comes as a kind of self-love that is also the love of the 'other': Eros and Agape together. It is an ethical love in the Levinasian sense in which the 'inwardness' of the subject is inhabited by the 'radical and anarchical reference to the other'. This knowledge is visible in those intriguing chapters[46] which lay over each other, where Sethe, Beloved, and Denver perform a fugue-like ceremony of claiming and naming through intersecting and interstitial subjectivities: 'Beloved, she my daughter'; 'Beloved is my sister'; 'I am Beloved and she is mine.' The women speak in tongues, from a space 'in-between each other' which is a communal space. They explore an 'interpersonal' reality: a social reality that appears within the poetic image as if it were in parentheses—aesthetically distanced, held back, and yet historically framed. It is difficult to convey the rhythm and the improvization of those chapters, but it is impossible not to see in them the healing of history, a community reclaimed in the making of a name. We can finally ask ourselves:

> Who is Beloved?

Now we understand: she is the daughter that returns to Sethe so that her mind will be homeless no more.

> Who is Beloved?

Now we may say: she is the sister that returns to Denver, and brings hope of her father's return, the fugitive who died in his escape.

> Who is Beloved?

Now we know: she is the daughter made of murderous love who returns to love and hate and free herself. Her words are broken, like the lynched people with broken necks; disembodied, like the dead children who lost their ribbons. But there is no mistaking what her live words say as they rise from the dead despite their lost syntax and their fragmented presence.

> My face is coming   I have to have it   I am looking for the join
> I am loving my face so much   I want to join   I am loving my
> face so much   my dark face is close to me   I want to join.[47]

Looking for the Join

To end, as I have done, with the nest of the phoenix, not its pyre is, in another way, to return to my beginning in the *beyond*. If Gordimer and Morrison describe the historical world, forcibly entering the house of art and fiction in order to invade, alarm, divide and dispossess, they also demonstrate the contemporary compulsion to move beyond; to turn the present into the 'post'; or, as I said earlier, to touch the future on its hither side. Aila's in-between identity and Beloved's double lives both affirm the borders of culture's insurgent and interstitial existence. In that sense, they take their stand with Renée Green's pathway between racial polarities; or Rushdie's migrant history of the English written in the margins of satanic verses; or Osorio's bed—*La Cama*—a place of dwelling, located between the unhomeliness of migrancy and the baroque belonging of the metropolitan, New York/Puerto-Rican artist.

When the public nature of the social event encounters the silence of the word it may lose its historical composure and closure. At this point we would do well to recall Walter Benjamin's insight on the disrupted dialectic of modernity: 'Ambiguity is the figurative appearance of the dialectic, the law of the dialectic at a standstill.'[48] For Benjamin that stillness is Utopia; for those who live, as I described it, 'otherwise' than modernity but not outside it, the Utopian moment is not the necessary horizon of hope. I have ended this argument with the woman framed—Gordimer's Aila—and the woman renamed—Morrison's Beloved—because in both their houses great world events erupted—slavery and apartheid—and their happening was turned, through that peculiar obscurity of art, into a second coming.

Although Morrison insistently repeats at the close *Beloved,* 'This is not a story to pass on,' she does this only in order to engrave the event in the deepest resources of our amnesia, of our unconsciousness. When historical visibility has faded, when the present tense of testimony loses its power to arrest, then the displacements of memory and the indirections of art offer us the image of our psychic survival. To live in the unhomely world, to find its ambivalencies and ambiguities enacted in the house of fiction, or its sundering and splitting performed in the work of art, is also to affirm a profound desire for social solidarity: 'I am looking for the join . . . I want to join . . . I want to join.'

Notes

1. For an interesting discussion of gender boundaries in the *fin de siècle,* see E. Showalter, *Sexual Anarchy: Gender and Culture in the Fin de Siècle* (London: Bloomsbury, 1990), especially 'Borderlines', pp. 1–18.
2. Renée Green interviewed by Elizabeth Brown, from catalogue published by Allen Memorial Art Museum, Oberlin College, Ohio.
3. Interview conducted by Miwon Kwon for the exhibition 'Emerging New York Artists', Sala Mendonza, Caracas, Venezuela (xeroxed manuscript copy).
4. Ibid., p. 6.
5. Renée Green in conversation with Donna Harkavy, Curator of Contemporary Art at the Worcester Museum.
6. Ibid.
7. W. Benjamin, 'Theses on the philosophy of history', in his *Illuminations* (London: Jonathan Cape, 1970), p. 265.
8. M. Heidegger, 'Building, dwelling, thinking', in *Poetry, Language, Thought* (New York: Harper & Row, 1971), pp. 152–3.
9. S. Rushdie, *The Satanic Verses* (London: Viking, 1988), p. 343.
10. G. Gomez-Peña, *American Theatre,* vol. 8, no. 7, October 1991.
11. T. Ybarra-Frausto, 'Chicano movement/chicano art,' in I. Karp and S.D. Lavine (eds.) (Washington and London: Smithsonian Institution Press, 1991), pp. 133–4.
12. A. Sekula, *Fish Story,* manuscript, p. 2.
13. Ibid., p. 3.
14. F. Fanon, *Black Skin, White Masks,* Introduction by H. K. Bhabha (London: Pluto, 1986), pp. 218, 229, 231.
15. H. James, *The Portrait of a Lady* (New York: Norton, 1975), p. 360.
16. Ibid., p. 361.
17. T. Morrison, *Beloved* (London: Chatto & Windus, 1987), p. 198–9.
18. R. Tagore, *The Home and the World* (Harmondsworth: Penguin, 1985), pp. 70–1.
19. N. Gordimer, *My Son's Story* (London: Bloomsbury, 1990), p. 249.
20. S. Freud, 'The uncanny', Standard Edition XVII, p. 225; H. Arendt, *The Human Condition* (Chicago: Chicago University Press, 1958), p. 72.

21. Morrison, *Beloved*, p. 170.
22. W. H. Auden, 'The cave of making', in his *About the House* (London: Faber, 1959), p. 20.
23. *Goethe's Literary Essays*, J. E. Spingarn (ed.) (New York: Harcourt, Brace, 1921), pp. 98–9.
24. *The Autobiography of Goethe*, J. Oxenford (ed.) (London: Henry G. Bohn, 1948), p. 467.
25. Goethe, 'Note on world literature', p. 96.
26. T. Morrison, *Honey and Rue* programme notes, Carnegie Hall Concert, January 1991.
27. Gordimer, *My Son's Story*, pp. 20–1.
28. Ibid., p. 21.
29. Ibid., p. 230
30. Ibid.
31. Ibid., p. 241.
32. Ibid.
33. Ibid.
34. Ibid., p. 214.
35. Ibid., p. 243.
36. Ibid., p. 249.
37. E. Levinas, 'Reality and its shadow', in *Collected Philosophical Papers* (Dordrecht: Martinus Nijhoff, 1987), pp. 1–13.
38. Ibid.
39. Ibid., pp. 6–7.
40. Robert Bernasconi quoted in 'Levinas's ethical discourse, between individuation and universality', in *Re-Reading Levinas*, R. Bernasconi and S. Critchley, (eds.) (Bloomington: Indiana University Press, 1991), p. 90.
41. Morrison, *Beloved*, p. 116.
42. Ibid., p. 173.
43. Ibid., p. 213.
44. E. Fox-Genovese, *Within the Plantation Household* (Chapel Hill, N.C.: University of North Carolina Press, 1988), p. 329.
45. Ibid., p. 324.
46. Morrison, *Beloved*, Pt. II, pp. 200–17.
47. Ibid., p. 213.
48. W. Benjamin, *Charles Baudelaire: A Lyric Poet in the Era of High Capitalism* (London: NLB, 1973), p. 171.

Questions to Consider

1. Is your ethnic identity important to you? Why so? Is your cultural identity important to you? Why so? What is the relationship between your ethnic and cultural identity? Are they one and the same? Are they different, even opposed?

2. What would you say is the most fundamental difference between people: race, class, culture, economic status, or gender? Which difference gives rise to the most fraught misunderstandings and violent forms of antagonism? What evidence can you find in historical events or literary texts to support your view?

3. Fanon argues that Negro-ism failed to achieve its aims because the concerns of the postcolonial subject are different from those of the former slave. In other words, the institutions of colonialism and slavery may have much in common, but they also have important differences. What common ground is shared by these institutions, and where do they diverge? What narratives or novels might you read to explore this issue?

4. Much of postcolonial criticism revolves around the twin poles of authenticity and hybridization. In these debates, the standard for authenticity is Kenyan writer Ngugi wa Thiong'o, who rejects English in favor of his native Gikuyu for the language of his novels. Advocates of creolization, on the other hand, celebrate the "exuberant mutual contamination of styles" (to use Neil ten Kortenaar's words), arguing that authenticity is quixotic and that some degree of interfertilization has always been a fact of life everywhere. Where would you place yourself in this debate? Where would you place the writers in this section?

5. Several of the theorists in this section use the mother as a metaphor. Since this metaphor is feminine, does its use suggest something significant about the writer's gender politics? If so, what? If you replaced the mother metaphor with a father metaphor, how would that change the sense of the writer's discussion? Do you see such gendered dimensions in the contemporary political realities of the world? If so, where?

6. While Fanon speaks of cultural identity in terms of the nation or national boundaries, many of the writers in this section speak of the blurring, breakdown, or shifting of boundaries and borders. How and where do you see such breakdowns and blurrings happening in your own experience? How might Fanon have responded to Clifford's notion of cultural identity as "mixed, relational, inventive," Hall's conception of "a 'production' which is never complete," Anzaldúa's concept of *Nepantla,* or Bhabha's concepts of hybridity and the "join"? Would these new understandings of identity have made Fanon's fight for liberation easier or harder? Why?

V

POLITICS AND RHETORIC

In a general sense, politics means the art or science of government, and rhetoric signifies the art of persuasive speech or writing. In everyday discourse, however, the meanings of politics and rhetoric often expand. We routinely hear that everything from television commercials and literature to hairstyles and cuisine is political. Similarly, politicians and pundits often accuse each other of offering the American public the "smoke and mirrors" of mere rhetoric instead of real substance, that is, facts or the truth. In other words, in its negative or pejorative sense of lie, fantasy, or pipe dream, the term "rhetoric" is used to dismiss or demonize someone's view of reality or explanation of a problem. By this same logical fallacy, an accurate or truthful view or explanation is presumably unrhetorical. But is it even possible to be unrhetorical? Can a presentation of "just the facts" or "the truth and nothing but the truth" be shorn of bias or spin? Likewise, is it any more possible to be unpolitical? People have debated these questions every day for thousands of years. Just as Aristotle long ago said humans are political animals by nature, we can say that humans are rhetorical animals as well.

Despite the necessity of politics and rhetoric, many people view them cynically, which may help to explain why most eligible voters in the United States do not go to the polls and cast their ballots despite the fact that, on holidays such as July Fourth, people take great pride in our country's democratic heritage: families and friends gather for barbecues, folks sing the national anthem with added vigor at baseball games, and fireworks crown the festivities. Like freedom of speech, voting is a bedrock of our republic, a political act to be cherished. Given conventional cynicism, however, what language or rhetoric might folks use to

334

inspire and persuade at least half the eligible voters to go to the polls for local and national elections? What eloquent metaphors might help bring people from different walks of life together to overturn injustices?

These overtly political questions may seem antithetical to or remote from issues and practices associated with critical theory. For example, Nina Baym's 1981 essay "Melodramas of Beset Manhood" focuses on theories of American literature. What could be more remote from elections and injustice than questions about what books we should read? While common sense might prompt some of us to agree with this sentiment, a closer look at Baym's thesis about the politics of canon formation reveals concerns about elections and injustices. A literary canon is a group of texts accorded prestige by scholars and by society at large. From one perspective, canonical texts are supposedly the very best and, therefore, the most important written works that a culture has to offer. The plays of William Shakespeare, for example, are typically recognized as central to the English literary canon and to Anglo-American culture. The presumed inherent quality of canonical texts signifies their merit; in other words, the merit is self-evident and not conferred extrinsically by critics and scholars according to their agendas and political biases. Hence, canonical texts have traditionally been the works most often taught to students in literature courses.

From another perspective, however, critics such as Baym have questioned arguments about intrinsic merit and the unpolitical nature of canon formation. Rather than focusing on the particular literary texts of the American canon, Baym analyzes how and why influential post–World War II scholars accorded canonical status to certain texts authored primarily by men. She questions why the scholars constructed theories of American literature that "led to the exclusion of women authors from the canon." Because many people today are not persuaded by the argument that literature and the arts generally are unpolitical, analyses like Baym's help us ask important questions: Why were theories of American literature that tended to exclude women from the canon authoritative and persuasive? And why were poems and stories by some writers considered more American than poems and stories by other writers?

In offering answers to such questions, Baym develops her own theory about the major canonical theories of American literature. Developing a theory about theory, or a metatheory, may seem abstract or divorced from the practical. However, what has happened culturally, intellectually, and politically to the way we think about literature and other arts may, indeed, relate to how we think about everyday concerns such as equal access to and opportunities for jobs, education, housing, and health care. You yourself already use theories and, perhaps, metatheories daily. Think about the politics of your job and whether you have ever considered the politics of the politics at work. What is approved of and what is excluded, repressed, or off limits, and why? When you begin to ask and answer such questions, you begin to theorize about the politics of your job. Similarly, we employ theories when we think about fashion and how we define what is in style and what is out of style. Since there are theories of fashion, it makes sense that there are also theories about the theories.

Making your theories about work, fashion, or the arts explicit can be very exciting. Such reflection can help you enhance or enrich your understanding of your public and private lives. Nevertheless, some people may find theories and metatheories alienating. Like Steven Knapp and Walter Benn Michaels in "Against Theory," some people may wonder whether the politics and rhetoric of theory are much ado about nothing. Unlike Baym, who looks at large questions of canon formation, Knapp and Michaels examine the seemingly narrower debate about theories of interpretative practice. According to one major theory, readers can objectively arrive at a valid interpretation of a literary work by relying on the author's expressed intention about the aims and meaning of her or his text; according to a major opposing theory, the "authorial intention" approach is invalid because readers can never arrive at a single, definitive, "valid" interpretation. In other words, the author's expressed intention carries no more weight than a reader's interpretation about a text's meaning; correct or valid interpretation is a myth because readers will not universally agree on the "correct" interpretation. In their essay, Knapp and Michaels challenge the validity of both theories. In fact, they reject "the idea of doing theory at all." Theory, for Knapp and Michaels, is "the attempt to govern interpretations of particular texts by appealing to an account of interpretation in general." Overall, Knapp and Michaels's polemical or controversial argument is informed by traditions of pragmatist philosophy, which emphasize discourse about practice over that of theory when trying to speak or write about large questions such as truth in a useful way.

If we see Baym as attempting to turn on their head theories of American literature once viewed as unquestionable because they are unpolitical, then can we also see Knapp and Michaels as attempting to upend orthodoxy, albeit a relatively new one? Interestingly, Knapp and Michaels's neopragmatist insights can be understood as a theory. What, we might ask, are the politics of an antitheoretical orientation or movement? What is persuasive about neopragmatist rhetoric? What do Knapp and Michaels offer to literary criticism specifically and to readers generally? Do their criticisms of Stanley Fish's arguments about practice and theory accord with your own sense of Fish's orientation in his essay "Rhetoric?"

The articles by Knapp and Michaels and by Baym examine and put forth arguments about authority and interpretation: what gets included and excluded, and who says so and why? Such arguments necessarily highlight the politics and rhetoric of some specific aspects of literary study. Edward Said also discusses literary criticism, but he widens the field of vision with respect to authority and interpretation in his 1989 essay "The Politics of Knowledge." Said links authority and interpretation in literature to questions about national politics and to globalization. A seemingly large topic like nationalism can be, paradoxically, cramped and limiting when people engage in what Said calls the "politics of identity": the belief that each one of us belongs exclusively to a specific group by virtue of ethnicity, race, gender, class, sexuality, or nationality. In narrow-minded or parochial versions of identity politics, each of us is sympathetic to the members of our own group and suspicious and potentially antagonistic toward members of other groups who do not, we suspect, have our best interests in mind.

Said admonishes academics who carelessly or shortsightedly focus not on the evidence and logic of an argument but instead on whether writers and authorities from historically marginalized groups are cited. Such identity politics is a problem, Said says, because it "asserts a sort of separatism that wishes only to draw attention to itself" and thereby fails to integrate itself into a socially global consciousness.

Said's metaphor for the larger collectivity is "worldliness," which means, for example, looking at specific literary texts not as African texts, American texts, Chicana texts, or queer texts, but as works within a global or transnational network. In this sense, we can see Said's essay within the everyday context of globalization that has been restructuring business, communications, economics, education, foreign policies, technology, and travel. Said's theory of worldliness may help you think about texts—new texts as well as familiar ones—in some unexpected ways. Do the theorists Baym analyzes justify their canonical criteria in terms of worldliness? Do Baym's own criteria include worldliness, or do her criteria suggest alternatives to or provide you with arguments against worldliness?

While the context of Said's arguments takes us outward from the more particular English-studies focus of Baym, Knapp, and Michaels, can we read Said's conclusion as turning back toward some of the specific concerns about politics and rhetoric in "Melodramas of Beset Manhood" and "Against Theory"? For example, Said says, "It does not finally matter *who* wrote what, but rather *how* a work is written and *how* it is read." Said's point is fairly clear: we shouldn't read or value a text simply because it is written by a woman; we should be reading the text because of what it is. In other words, the text, not the author, is of primary concern. But why do the "how," not the "who," questions "finally matter"? By what authority does Said make his claim? Would Knapp and Michaels likely approve of Said's approach?

Neither Said's ideas about literature and worldliness, nor Baym's ideas, nor Knapp and Michaels's arguments are insular or ivory-tower concerns. They not only highlight different perspectives on the politics and rhetoric of authority and interpretation in literary studies but also give us an idea of the breadth of critical theory's general engagement with rhetoric and politics. This inclusiveness is vividly detailed in the last two readings in this section, Stanley Fish's 1989 essay "Rhetoric" and Chantal Mouffe's 1992 essay "Feminism, Citizenship and Radical Democratic Politics."

Though it begins with a close reading of a passage from John Milton's epic poem *Paradise Lost*, Fish's essay expands the relevance of rhetoric from literature to nonartistic everyday concerns and seems to give the devil his due in describing two antithetical attitudes toward rhetoric. On the one hand, some people have been criticizing rhetoric as biased, duplicitous, and therefore dangerous since at least the time of Plato; on the other hand, other people have always been defending and promoting rhetoric as a necessary and, indeed, a natural part of our everyday lives. As you read Fish's discussion of both sides, you will no doubt wonder where Fish's allegiances lay. By presenting the strengths and weaknesses of both arguments, Fish may seem impartial. But try to determine Fish's politics in "Rhetoric." Is he with the foundationalists, the antirhetorical folks who believe in "truth with a capital T" and that rhetoric's power must be resisted, or is he with the antifoundationalists, those who believe that truths are contingent and who recognize in rhetoric's power the development and practical functioning of political processes? Or is Fish simply describing—objectively or scientifically—the two sides of the dispute without himself taking sides?

Considering how Fish's own essay form—its structure and effect—enacts the very topic or theme of his essay might help you decide Fish's politics of rhetoric. Compare your own politics of rhetoric with his. Are you a member of "the species *homo seriosus* or *homo rhetoricus*"? How about your friends and members of your family? See how useful the opposing perspectives of *homo seriosus* and *homo rhetoricus* are to other theorists you have read, and examine how Fish's discussion of rhetoric relates to debates about canons, interpretation, identity politics, the politics of knowledge, theory, and practical political action.

Unlike the other texts in this section, Chantal Mouffe's "Feminism, Citizenship and Radical Democratic Politics" does not specifically engage literary criticism. Mouffe focuses instead on competing feminist political theories and offers her own theory for political action. Reading Mouffe reminds us that feminism is not simply a homogenous political program; there are many feminist theories—one size does not fit all. For some feminists, successful political action necessitates an essentialist model of identity. Like the word "essence," essentialism refers to the intrinsic nature of something or someone. For many feminists, the concept of woman implies an essential difference from the concept of man. Essentialism, however, is not visible only in theory or in academia. In popular culture, we see essentialism at work as well. We see it, for instance, in the playful title of John Gray's 1992 book *Men are from Mars, Women are from Venus*. For many folks, the essential distinction of sexual difference just seems to be common sense, and therefore it seems practical for women to highlight their essential, shared identity as they band together politically to combat sexism and other forms of male dominance.

However, common sense is not always accurate or helpful. Indeed, we might see in essentialism pitfalls like those Said identifies in identity politics. In contrast to the arguably narrow politics and rhetoric of sexual difference, Mouffe proposes feminist political theories of action linked to larger mutual concerns of citizenship and democratic practices: her "collective, inclusive, and generalized" antiessentialist program entails female and male identification to challenge "situations of domination." Mouffe finds essentialist-based theories of feminism too restrictive for a radical democratic project. In this sense, essentialism might be said to lack something like the worldliness that Said identified as absent in the politics of knowledge and identity. You might consider possible links not only between Mouffe's and Said's arguments but also between Mouffe's antiessentialist politics of "radical and plural democracy" and Baym's analysis of canon formation, Knapp and Michaels's antitheory, and Fish's explanations of *homo seriosus* and *homo rhetoricus*. Ask yourself if the ideas presented in the other essays in this section engage with feminism, citizenship, and radical democratic politics. How might you use Mouffe's ideas as a lens to help you see other dimensions of politics and rhetoric in one or more of the essays from this section? For example, what relationship, if any, do you see between sexual difference and citizenship in the literary canon? Should a literary canon exemplify the "political principles of modern pluralist democracy, namely, the assertion of liberty and justice for all"? Or, moving from literature to your everyday life, use Mouffe's ideas as a lens to help you focus on your own politics. What relationship, if any, do you see between sexual difference and citizenship? What do you include and exclude in your understanding, and why? Or consider your understanding of citizenship and of feminism in terms of Mouffe's understanding of radical democratic politics. Engaging your ideas with Mouffe's and with those of the other theorists in this section can be exciting and can inspire you to examine intensively the different and sometimes contradictory meanings that come to mind when you think about politics and rhetoric.

Nina Baym (1936–)

Baym was born in Princeton, New Jersey, and earned her Ph.D. from Harvard University in 1963. For the past 30 years, she has masterfully written and edited influential articles and books while teaching English at the University of Illinois at Urbana–Champaign, and her immense reputation in American literary studies continues to grow. Indeed, since 1998, she has been the general editor for the prestigious *Norton Anthology of American Literature.* Under Baym's editorship, the *Norton Anthology of American Literature* has been productively revised to reflect the impressive breadth of American writing. The increase in the number of texts by women and minorities in the anthology suggests a richer canon, as does the increase in the types of texts included. Such changes mirror, but also help to spur further, changes in English studies. At the University of Illinois at Urbana–Champaign, Baym holds the prestigious titles of Swanlund Endowed Chair for the Center for Advanced Study and Jubilee Professor of Liberal Arts and Sciences. Well versed in critical theory, Baym nevertheless describes herself as an empirical feminist literary critic. In other words, she emphasizes the practices of literary scholarship and textual analysis as opposed to critical theory, which has often challenged such practices as naïve and old fashioned.

In addition to her work on the *Norton Anthology of American Literature,* Baym has written over 60 articles on a variety of American writers, including Nathaniel Hawthorne, James Fenimore Cooper, Emily Dickinson, Lydia Sigourney, and Robert Frost. She has also written the following books: *The Shape of Hawthorne's Career* (1976), *Woman's Fiction: A Guide to the Novels by and about Women in America (1820–1870)* (1978), *Novels, Readers, and Reviewers: Responses to Fiction in Antebellum America* (1984), and *Feminism and American Literary History* (1992). The selection given next, "Melodramas of Beset Manhood," first appeared in *American Quarterly* 33 (1981).

Melodramas of Beset Manhood

This paper is about American literary criticism rather than American literature. It proceeds from the assumption that we never read American literature directly or freely, but always through the perspective allowed by theories.

Theories account for the inclusion and exclusion of texts in anthologies, and theories account for the way we read them. My concern is with the fact that the theories controlling our reading of American literature have led to the exclusion of women authors from the canon.

Let me use my own practice as a case in point. In 1977 there was published a collection of essays on images of women in major British and American literature, to which I contributed.[1] The American field was divided chronologically among six critics, with four essays covering literature written prior to World War II. Taking seriously the charge that we were to focus only on the major figures, the four of us—working quite independently of each other—selected altogether only four women writers. Three of these were from the earliest period, a period which predates the novel: the poet Anne Bradstreet and the two diarists Mary Rowlandson and Sarah Kemble Knight. The fourth was Emily Dickinson. For the period between 1865 and 1940 no women were cited at all. The message that we—who were taking women as our subject—conveyed was clear: there have been almost no major women writers in America; the major novelists have all been men.

Now, when we wrote our essays we were not undertaking to reread all American literature and make our own decisions as to who the major authors were. That is the point: we accepted the going canon of major authors. As late as 1977, that canon did not include any women novelists. Yet, the critic who goes beyond what is accepted and tries to look at the totality of literary production in America quickly discovers that women authors have been active since the earliest days of settlement. Commercially and numerically they have probably dominated American literature since the middle of the nineteenth century. As long ago as 1854, Nathaniel Hawthorne complained to his publisher about the "damn'd mob of scribbling women" whose writings—he fondly imagined—were diverting the public from his own.

Names and figures help make this dominance clear. In the years between 1774 and 1799—from the calling of the First Continental Congress to the close of the eighteenth century—a total of thirty-eight original works of fiction were published in this country.[2] Nine of these, appearing pseudonymously or anonymously, have not yet been attributed to any author. The remaining twenty-nine are the work of eighteen individuals, of whom four are women. One of these women, Susannah Rowson, wrote six of them, or more than a fifth of the total. Her most popular work, *Charlotte* (also known as *Charlotte Temple),* was printed three times in the decade it was published, nineteen times between 1800 and 1810, and eighty times by the middle of the nineteenth century. A novel by a second of the four women, Hannah Foster, was called *The Coquette* and had thirty editions by mid-nineteenth century. *Uncle Tom's Cabin,* by a woman, is probably the all-time biggest seller in American history. A woman, Mrs. E.D.E.N. Southworth, was probably the most widely read novelist in the nineteenth century. How is it possible for a critic or historian of American literature to leave these books, and these authors, out of the picture?

I see three partial explanations for the critical invisibility of the many active women authors in America. The first is simple bias. The critic does not like the idea of women as writers, does not believe that women can be writers, and hence does not see them even when they are right before his eyes. His theory or his standards may well be nonsexist but his practice is not. Certainly, an *a priori* resistance to recognizing women authors as serious writers has functioned powerfully in the mindset of a number of influential critics. One can amusingly demonstrate the inconsistencies between standard and practice in such critics, show how their minds slip out of gear when they are confronted with a woman author. But this is only a partial explanation.

A second possibility is that, in fact, women have not written the kind of work that we call "excellent," for reasons that are connected with their gender although separable from it. This is a serious possibility. For example, suppose we required a dense texture of classical allusion in all works that we called excellent. Then, the restriction of a formal classical education to men would have the effect of restricting authorship of excellent literature to men. Women would not have written excellent literature because social conditions hindered them. The reason, though gender-connected, would not be gender per se.

The point here is that the notion of the artist, or of excellence, has efficacy in a given time and reflects social realities. The idea of "good" literature is not only a personal preference, it is also a cultural preference. We can all think of species of women's literature that do not aim in any way to achieve literary excellence as society defines it: e.g., the "Harlequin Romances." Until recently, only a tiny proportion of literary women aspired to artistry and literary excellence in the terms defined by their own culture. There tended to be a sort of immediacy in the ambitions of literary women leading them to professionalism rather than artistry, by choice as well as by social pressure and opportunity. The gender-related restrictions were really operative, and the responsible critic cannot ignore them. But again, these restrictions are only partly explanatory.

There are, finally, I believe, gender-related restrictions that do not arise out of cultural realities contemporary with the writing woman, but out of later critical theories. These theories may follow naturally from cultural realities pertinent to their own time, but they impose their concerns anachronistically, after the fact, on an earlier period. If one accepts current theories of American literature, one accepts as a consequence—perhaps not deliberately but nevertheless inevitably—a literature that is essentially male. This is the partial explanation that I shall now develop.

Let us begin where the earliest theories of American literature begin, with the hypothesis that American literature is to be judged less by its form than its content. Traditionally, one ascertains literary excellence by comparing a writer's work with standards of performance that have been established by earlier authors, where formal mastery and innovation are paramount. But from its historical beginnings, American literary criticism has assumed that literature produced in this nation would have to be ground-breaking, equal to the challenge of the new nation, and completely original. Therefore, it could not be judged by referring it back to earlier achievements. The earliest American literary critics began to talk about the "most American" work rather than the "best" work because they knew no way to find out the best other than by comparing American to British writing. Such a criticism struck them as both unfair and unpatriotic. We had thrown off the political shackles of England; it would not do for us to be servile in our literature. Until a tradition of American literature developed its own inherent forms, the early critic looked for a standard of Americanness rather than a standard of excellence. Inevitably, perhaps, it came to seem that the quality of "Americanness," whatever it might be, *constituted* literary excellence for American authors. Beginning as a nationalistic enterprise, American literary criticism and theory has retained a nationalist orientation to this day.

Of course, the idea of Americanness is even more vulnerable to subjectivity than the idea of the best. When they speak of "most American," critics seldom mean the statistically most representative or most typical, the most read or the most sold. They have some qualitative essence in mind, and frequently their work develops as an explanation of this idea of "American" rather than a description and evaluation of selected authors. The predictable recurrence of the term "America" or "American" in works of literary criticism treating a dozen or fewer authors indicates that the critic has chosen his authors on the basis of their conformity to his idea of what is truly American. For examples: *American Renaissance, The Romance in America, Symbolism and American Literature, Form and Fable in American Fiction, The American Adam, The American Novel and Its Tradition, The Place of Style in American Literature* (a subtitle), *The Poetics of American Fiction* (another subtitle). But an idea of what is American is no more than an idea, needing demonstration. The critic all too frequently ends up using his chosen authors as demonstrations of Americanness, arguing through them to his definition.

So Marius Bewley explains in *The Eccentric Design* that "for the American artist there was no social surface responsive to his touch. The scene was crude, even beyond successful satire," but later, in a concluding chapter titled "The Americanness of the American Novel," he agrees that "this 'tradition' as I have set it up here has no room for the so-called realists and naturalists."[3] F. O. Matthiessen, whose *American Renaissance* enshrines five authors, explains that "the one common denominator of my five writers, uniting even Hawthorne and Whitman, was their devotion to the possibilities of democracy."[4] The jointly written *Literary History of the United States* proclaims in its "address to the reader" that American literary history "will be a history of the books of the great and the near-great writers in a literature which is most revealing when studied as a by-product of American experience."[5] And Joel Porte announces confidently in *The Romance in America* that "students of American literature . . . have provided a solid theoretical basis for establishing that the rise and growth of fiction in this country is dominated by our authors' conscious adherence to a tradition of non-realistic romance sharply at variance with the broadly novelistic mainstream of English writing. When there has been disagreement among recent critics as to the contours of American fiction, it has usually disputed, not the existence *per se* of a romance tradition, but rather the question of which authors, themes, and stylistic strategies *deserve* to be placed with certainty at the heart of that tradition" (emphasis added).[6]

Before he is through, the critic has had to insist that some works in America are much more American than others, and he is as busy excluding certain writers as "un-American" as he is including others. Such a proceeding in the political arena would be extremely suspect, but in criticism it has been the method of choice. Its final result goes far beyond the conclusion that only a handful of American works are very good. *That* statement is one we could agree with, since very good work is rare in any field. But it is odd indeed to argue that only a handful of American works are really American.[7]

Despite the theoretical room for an infinite number of definitions of Americanness, critics have generally agreed on it—although the shifting canon suggests that agreement may be a matter of fad rather than fixed objective qualities.[8] First, America as a nation must be the ultimate subject of the work. The author must be writing about aspects of experience and character that are American only, setting Americans off from other people and the country from other nations. The author must be writing his story specifically to display these aspects, to meditate on them, and to derive from them some generalizations and conclusions about "the" American experience. To Matthiessen the topic is the possibilities of democracy; Sacvan Bercovitch (in *The Puritan Origins of the American Self*) finds it in American identity. Such content excludes, at one extreme, stories about universals, aspects of experience common to people in a variety of times and places—mutability, mortality, love, childhood, family, betrayal, loss. Innocence versus experience is an admissible theme *only* if innocence is the essence of the American character, for example.

But at the other extreme, the call for an overview of America means that detailed, circumstantial portrayals of some aspect of American life are also, peculiarly, inappropriate: stories of wealthy New Yorkers, Yugoslavian immigrants, southern rustics. Jay B. Hubbell rather ingratiatingly admits as much when he writes, "in both my teaching and my research I had a special interest in literature as a reflection of American life and thought. This circumstance may explain in part why I found it difficult to appreciate the merits of the expatriates and why I was slow in doing justice to some of the New Critics. I was repelled by the sordid subject matter found in some of the novels written by Dreiser, Dos Passos, Faulkner, and some others."[9] Richard Poirier writes that "the books which in my view constitute a distinctive American tradition . . . resist within their pages forces of environment that otherwise dominate the world" and he distinguishes this kind from "the fiction of Mrs. Wharton, Dreiser, or Howells."[10] The *Literary History of the United States* explains that "historically, [Edith Wharton] is likely to survive as the memorialist of a dying aristocracy" (1211). And so on. These exclusions abound in all the works which form the stable core of American literary criticism at this time.

Along with Matthiessen, the most influential exponent of this exclusive Americanness is Lionel Trilling, and his work has particular applicability because it concentrates on the novel form. Here is a famous passage from his 1940 essay, "Reality in America," in which Trilling is criticizing Vernon Parrington's selection of authors in *Main Currents in American Thought*:

> A culture is not a flow, nor even a confluence; the form of its existence is struggle—or at least debate—it is nothing if not a dialectic. And in any culture there are likely to be certain artists who contain a large part of the dialectic within themselves, their meaning and power lying in their contradictions; they contain within themselves, it may be said, the very essence of the culture. To

> throw out Poe because he cannot be conveniently fitted into a theory of American culture . . . to find his gloom to be merely personal and eccentric . . . as Hawthorne's was . . . to judge Melville's response to American life to be less noble than that of Bryant or of Greeley, to speak of Henry James as an escapist . . . this is not merely to be mistaken in aesthetic judgment. Rather it is to examine without attention and from the point of view of a limited and essentially arrogant conception of reality the documents which are in some respects the most suggestive testimony to what America was and is, and of course to get no answer from them.[11]

Trilling's immediate purpose is to exclude Greeley and Bryant from the list of major authors and to include Poe, Melville, Hawthorne, and James. We probably share Trilling's aesthetic judgment. But note that he does not base his judgment on aesthetic grounds; indeed, he dismisses aesthetic judgment with the word "merely." He argues that Parrington has picked the wrong artists because he doesn't understand the culture. Culture is his real concern.

But what makes Trilling's notion of culture more valid than Parrington's? Trilling really has no argument; he resorts to such value-laden rhetoric as "a limited and essentially arrogant conception of reality" precisely because he cannot objectively establish his version of culture over Parrington's. For the moment, there are two significant conclusions to draw from this quotation. First, the disagreement is over the nature of our culture. Second, there is no disagreement over the value of literature—it is valued as a set of "documents" which provide "suggestive testimony to what America was and is."

One might think that an approach like this which is subjective, circular, and in some sense nonliterary or even antiliterary would not have had much effect. But clearly Trilling was simply carrying on a longstanding tradition of searching for cultural essence, and his essays gave the search a decided and influential direction toward the notion of cultural essence as some sort of tension. Trilling succeeded in getting rid of Bryant and Greeley, and his choice of authors is still dominant. They all turn out—and not by accident—to be white, middle-class, male, of Anglo-Saxon derivation or at least from an ancestry which has settled in this country before the big waves of immigration which began around the middle of the nineteenth century. In every case, however, the decision made by these men to become professional authors pushed them slightly to one side of the group to which they belonged. This slight alienation permitted them to belong, and yet not to belong, to the so-called "mainstream." These two aspects of their situation—their membership in the dominant middle-class white Anglo-Saxon group, and their modest alienation from it—defined their boundaries, enabling them to "contain within themselves" the "contradictions" that, in Trilling's view, constitute the "very essence of the culture." I will call the literature they produced, which Trilling assesses so highly, a "consensus criticism of the consensus."

This idea plainly excludes many groups but it might not seem necessarily to exclude women. In fact, nineteenth-century women authors were overwhelmingly white, middle-class, and anglo-Saxon in origin. Something more than what is overtly stated by Trilling (and others cited below) is added to exclude them. What critics have done is to assume, for reasons shortly to be expounded, that the women writers invariably represented the consensus, rather than the criticism of it; to assume that their gender made them part of the consensus in a way that prevented them from partaking in the criticism. The presence of these women and their works is acknowledged in literary theory and history as an impediment and obstacle, that which the essential American literature had to criticize as its chief task.

So, in his lively and influential book of 1960, *Love and Death in the American Novel,* Leslie Fiedler describes women authors as creators of the "flagrantly bad best-seller" against which "our best fictionists"—all male—have had to struggle for "their integrity and their livelihoods."[12] And, in a 1978 reader's introduction to an edition of Charles Brockden Brown's *Wieland,* Sydney J. Krause and S. W. Reid write as follows:

> What it meant for Brown personally, and belles lettres in America historically, that he should have decided to write professionally is a story unto itself. Americans simply had no great appetite for serious literature in the early decades of the Republic—certainly nothing of the sort with which they devoured . . . the ubiquitous melodramas of beset womanhood, "tales of truth," like Susanna Rowson's *Charlotte Temple* and Hannah Foster's *The Coquette.*[13]

There you see what has happened to the woman writer. She has entered literary history as the enemy. The phrase "tales of truth" is put in quotes by the critics, as though to cast doubt on the very notion that a "melodrama of beset womanhood" could be either true or important. At the same time, ironically, they are proposing for our serious consideration, as a candidate for intellectually engaging literature, a highly melodramatic novel with an improbable plot, inconsistent characterizations, and excesses of style that have posed tremendous problems for all students of Charles Brockden Brown. But, by this strategy it becomes possible to begin major American fiction historically with male rather than female authors. The certainty here that stories about women could not contain the essence of American culture means that the matter of American experience is inherently male. And this makes it highly unlikely that American women would write fiction encompassing such experience. I would suggest that the theoretical model of a story which may become the vehicle of cultural essence is: "a melodrama of beset manhood." This melodrama is presented in a fiction which, as we'll later see, can be taken as representative of the author's literary experience, his struggle for integrity and livelihood against flagrantly bad best-sellers written by women. Personally beset in a way that epitomizes the tensions of our culture, the male author produces his melodramatic testimony to our culture's essence— so the theory goes.

Remember that the search for cultural essence demands a relatively uncircumstantial kind of fiction, one which concentrates on national universals (if I may be pardoned the paradox). This search has identified a sort of nonrealistic narrative, a romance, a story free to catch an essential, idealized American character, to intensify his essence and convey his experience in a way that ignores details of an actual social milieu. This nonrealistic or antisocial aspect of American fiction is noted—as a fault—by Trilling in a 1947 essay, "Manners, Morals, and the Novel." Curiously, Trilling here attacks the same group of writers he had rescued from Parrington in "Reality in America." But, never doubting that his selection represents "the" American authors, he goes ahead with the task that really interests him—criticizing the culture through its representative authors. He writes:

> The novel in America diverges from its classic [i.e., British] intention which . . . is the investigation of the problem of reality beginning in the social field. The fact is that American writers of genius have not turned their minds to society. Poe and Melville were quite apart from it; the reality they sought was only tangential to society. Hawthorne was acute when he insisted that he did not write novels but romances—he thus expressed his awareness of the lack of social texture in his work. . . . In America in the nineteenth century, Henry James was alone in knowing that to scale the moral and aesthetic heights in the novel one had to use the ladder of social observation.[14]

Within a few years after publication of Trilling's essay, a group of Americanists took its rather disapproving description of American novelists and found in this nonrealism or romanticism the essentially American quality they had been seeking. The idea of essential Americanness then developed in such influential works of criticism as *Virgin Land* by Henry Nash Smith (1950), *Symbolism and American Literature* by Charles Feidelson (1953), *The American Adam* by R.W.B. Lewis (1955), *The American Novel and Its Tradition* by Richard Chase (1957), and *Form and Fable in American Fiction* by Daniel G. Hoffman (1961). These works, and others like them, were of sufficiently high critical quality, and sufficiently like each other, to compel assent to the picture of American literature that they presented. They used sophisticated New Critical close-reading techniques to identify a myth of America which had nothing to do with the classical fictionist's task of chronicling probable people in recognizable social situations.

The myth narrates a confrontation of the American individual, the pure American self divorced from specific social circumstances, with the promise offered by the idea of America. This promise is the deeply romantic one that in this new land, untrammeled by history and social accident, a person will be able to achieve complete self-definition. Behind this promise is the assurance that individuals come before society, that they exist in some meaningful sense prior to, and apart from, societies in which they happen to find themselves. The myth also holds that, as something artificial and secondary to human nature, society exerts an unmitigatedly destructive pressure on individuality. To depict it at any length would be a waste of artistic time; and there is only one way to relate it to the individual—as an adversary.

One may believe all this and yet look in vain for a way to tell a believable story that could free the protagonist from society or offer the promise of such freedom, because nowhere on earth do individuals live apart from social groups. But in America, given the original reality of large tracts of wilderness, the idea seems less a fantasy, more possible in reality or at least more believable in literary treatment. Thus it is that the essential quality of America comes to reside in its unsettled wilderness and the opportunities that such a wilderness offers to the individual as the medium on which he may inscribe, unhindered, his own destiny and his own nature.

As the nineteenth century wore on, and settlements spread across the wilderness, the struggle of the individual against society became more and more central to the myth; where, let's say, Thoreau could leave in Chapter I of *Walden*, Huckleberry Finn has still not made his break by the end of Chapter XLII (the conclusion) of the book that bears his name. Yet, one finds a struggle against society as early as the earliest Leatherstocking tale *(The Pioneers*, 1823). In a sense, this supposed promise of America has always been known to be delusory. Certainly by the twentieth century the myth has been transmuted into an avowedly hopeless quest for unencumbered space *(On the Road)*, or the evocation of flight for its own sake *(Rabbit, Run* and *Henderson the Rain King)*, or as pathetic acknowledgment of loss—e.g., the close of *The Great Gatsby* where the narrator Nick Carraway summons up "the old island here that flowered once for Dutch sailors' eyes—a fresh, green breast of the new world . . . the last and greatest of all human dreams" where man is "face to face for the last time in history with something commensurate to his capacity for wonder."

We are all very familiar with this myth of America in its various fashionings and owing to the selective vision that has presented this myth to us as the whole story, many of us are unaware of how much besides it has been created by literary Americans. Keeping our eyes on this myth, we need to ask whether anything about it puts it outside women's reach. In one sense, and on one level, the answer is no. The subject of this myth is supposed to stand for human nature, and if men and women alike share a common human nature, then all can respond to its values, its promises, and its frustrations. And in fact as a teacher I find women students responsive to the myth insofar as its protagonist is concerned. It is true, of course, that in order to represent some kind of believable flight into the wilderness, one must select a protagonist with a certain believable mobility, and mobility has until recently been a male prerogative in our society. Nevertheless, relatively few men are actually mobile to the extent demanded by the story, and hence the story is really not much more vicarious, in this regard, for women than for men. The problem is thus not to be located in the protagonist or his gender per se; the problem is with the other participants in his story—the entrammeling society and the promising landscape. For both of these are depicted in unmistakably feminine terms, and this gives a sexual character to the protagonist's story which does, indeed, limit its applicability to women. And this sexual definition has melodramatic, misogynist implications.

In these stories, the encroaching, constricting, destroying society is represented with particular urgency in the figure of one or more women. There are several possible reasons why this might be so. It seems to be a fact of life that we all—women and men alike—experience social conventions and responsibilities and obligations first in the persons of women, since women are entrusted by society with the task of rearing young children. Not until he reaches midadolescence does the male connect up with other males whose primary task is socialization; but at about this time—if he is heterosexual—his lovers and spouses become the agents of a permanent socialization and domestication. Thus, although women are not the source of social power, they are experienced as such. And although not all women are engaged in socializing the young, the young do not encounter women who are not. So from the point of view of the young man, the only kind of women who exist are entrappers and domesticators.

For heterosexual man, these socializing women are also the locus of powerful attraction. First, because everybody has social and conventional instincts; second, because his deepest emotional attachments are to women. This attraction gives urgency and depth to the protagonist's rejection of society. To do it, he must project onto the woman those attractions that he feels, and cast her in the melodramatic role of temptress, antagonist, obstacle—a character whose mission in life seems to be to ensnare him and deflect him from life's important purposes of self-discovery and self-assertion. (A Puritan would have said: from communion with Divinity.) As Richard Chase writes in *The American Novel and Its Tradition,* "The myth requires celibacy." It is partly against his own sexual urges that the male must struggle, and so he perceives the socializing and domesticating woman as a doubly powerful threat; for this reason, Chase goes on to state, neither Cooper nor "any other American novelist until the age of James and Edith Wharton" could imagine "a fully developed woman of sexual age."[15] Yet in making this statement, Chase is talking about his myth rather than Cooper's. (One should add that, for a homosexual male, the demands of society that he link himself for life to a woman make for a particularly misogynist version of this aspect of the American myth, for the hero is propelled not by a rejected attraction, but by true revulsion.) Both heterosexual and homosexual versions of the myth cooperate with the hero's perceptions and validate the notion of woman as threat.

Such a portrayal of women is likely to be uncongenial, if not basically incomprehensible, to a woman. It is not likely that women will write books in which women play this part; and it is by no means the case that most novels by American men reproduce such a scheme. Even major male authors prominent in the canon have other ways of depicting women; e.g., Cooper's *Pathfinder* and *The Pioneers,* Hemingway's *For Whom the Bell Tolls,* Fitzgerald's *The Beautiful and Damned.* The novels of Henry James and William Dean Howells pose a continual challenge to the masculinist bias of American critical theory. And in one work— *The Scarlet Letter*—a "fully developed woman of sexual age" who is the novel's protagonist has been admitted into the canon, but only by virtue of strenuous critical revisions of the text that remove Hester Prynne from the center of the novel and make her subordinate to Arthur Dimmesdale.

So Leslie Fiedler, in *Love and Death in the American Novel,* writes this of *The Scarlet Letter:*

> It is certainly true, in terms of the plot, that Chillingworth drives the minister toward confession and penance, while Hester would have lured him to evasion and flight. But this means, for all of Hawthorne's equivocations, that the eternal feminine does not draw us on toward grace, rather that the woman promises only madness and damnation. . . . [Hester] is the female temptress of Puritan mythology, but also, though sullied, the secular madonna of sentimental Protestantism (236).

In the rhetorical "us" Fiedler presumes that all readers are men, that the novel is an act of communication among and about males. His characterization of Hester as one or another myth or image makes it impossible for the novel to be in any way about Hester as a human being. Giving the novel so highly specific a gender reference, Fiedler makes it inaccessible to women and limits its reference to men in comparison to the issues that Hawthorne was treating in the story. Not the least of these issues was, precisely, the human reference of a woman's tale.

Amusingly, then, since he has produced this warped reading, Fiedler goes on to condemn the novel for its sexual immaturity. *The Scarlet Letter* is integrated into Fiedler's general exposure of the inadequacies of the American male— inadequacies which, as his treatment of Hester shows, he holds women responsible for. The melodrama here is not Hawthorne's, but Fiedler's—the American critic's melodrama of beset manhood. Of course, women authors as major writers are notably and inevitably absent from Fiedler's chronicle.

In fact many books by women—including such major authors as Edith Wharton, Ellen Glasgow, and Willa Cather—project a version of the particular myth we are speaking of but cast the main character as a woman. When a woman takes the central role, it follows naturally that the socializer and domesticator will be a man. This is the situation in *The Scarlet Letter*. Hester is beset by the male reigning oligarchy and by Dimmesdale, who passively tempts her and is responsible for fathering her child. Thereafter, Hester (as the myth requires) elects celibacy, as do many heroines in versions of this myth by women: Thea in Cather's *The Song of the Lark*, Dorinda in Glasgow's *Barren Ground*, Anna Leath in Wharton's *The Reef*. But what is written in the criticism about these celibate women? They are said to be untrue to the imperatives of their gender, which require marriage, childbearing, domesticity. Instead of being read as a woman's version of the myth, such novels are read as stories of the frustration of female nature. Stories of female frustration are not perceived as commenting on, or containing, the essence of our culture, and so we don't find them in the canon.

So the role of entrapper and impediment in the melodrama of beset manhood is reserved for women. Also, the role of the beckoning wilderness, the attractive landscape, is given a deeply feminine quality. Landscape is deeply imbued with female qualities, as society is; but where society is menacing and destructive, landscape is compliant and supportive. It has the attributes simultaneously of a virginal bride and a nonthreatening mother; its female qualities are articulated with respect to a male angle of vision: what can nature do for me, asks the hero, what can it give me?

Of course, nature has been feminine and maternal from time immemorial, and Henry Nash Smith's *Virgin Land* picks up a timeless archetype in its title. The basic nature of the image leads one to forget about its potential for imbuing any story in which it is used with sexual meanings, and the gender implications of a female landscape have only recently begun to be studied. Recently, Annette Kolodny has studied the traditional canon from this approach.[16] She theorizes that the hero, fleeing a society that has been imagined as feminine, then imposes on nature some ideas of women which, no longer subject to the correcting influence of real-life experience, become more and more fantastic. The fantasies are infantile, concerned with power, mastery, and total gratification: the all-nurturing mother, the all-passive bride. Whether one accepts all the Freudian or Jungian implications of her argument, one cannot deny the way in which heroes of American myth turn to nature as sweetheart and nurture, anticipating the satisfaction of all desires through her and including among these the desires for mastery and power. A familiar passage that captures these ideas is one already quoted: Carraway's evocation of the "fresh green breast" of the new world. The fresh greenness is the virginity that offers itself to the sailors, but the breast promises maternal solace and delight. *The Great Gatsby* contains our two images of women: while Carraway evokes the impossible dream of a maternal landscape, he blames a nonmaternal woman, the socialite Daisy, for her failure to satisfy Gatsby's desires. The true adversary, of course, is Tom Buchanan, but he is hidden, as it were, behind Daisy's skirts.

I have said that women are not likely to cast themselves as antagonists in a man's story; they are even less likely, I suggest, to cast themselves as virgin land. The lack of fit between their own experience and the fictional role assigned to them is even greater in the second instance than in the first. If women portray themselves as brides or mothers it will not be in terms of the mythic landscape. If a woman puts a female construction on nature—as she certainly must from time to time, given the archetypal female resonance of the image—she is likely to write of it as more active, or to stress its destruction or violation. On the other hand, she might adjust the heroic myth to her own psyche by making nature out to be male—as, for example, Willa Cather seems to do in *O Pioneers!* But a violated landscape or a male nature does not fit the essential American pattern as critics have defined it, and hence these literary images occur in an obscurity that criticism cannot see. Thus, one has an almost classic example of the "double bind." When the woman writer creates a story that conforms to the expected myth, it is not recognized for what it is because of a superfluous sexual specialization in the myth as it is entertained in the critics' minds. (Needless to say, many male novelists also entertain this version of the myth, and do not find the masculinist bias with which they imbue it to be superfluous. It is possible that some of these novelists, especially those who write in an era in which literary criticism is a powerful influence, have formed their ideas from their reading in criticism.) But if she does not conform to the myth, she is understood to be writing minor or trivial literature.

Two remaining points can be treated much more briefly. The description of the artist and of the act of writing which emerges when the critic uses the basic American story as his starting point contains many attributes of the basic story itself. This description raises the exclusion of women to a more abstract, theoretical—and perhaps more pernicious—level. Fundamentally, the idea is that the artist writing a story of this essential American kind is engaging in a task very much like the one performed by his mythic hero. In effect, the artist writing his narrative is imitating the mythic encounter of hero and possibility in the safe confines of his study; or, reversing the temporal order, one might see that mythic encounter of hero and possibility as a projection of the artist's situation.

Although this idea is greatly in vogue at the moment, it has a history. Here, for example, is Richard Chase representing the activity of writing in metaphors of discovery and exploration, as though the writer were a hero in the landscape: "The American novel has usually seemed content to explore . . . the remarkable and in some ways unexampled territories of life in the New World and to reflect its anomalies and dilemmas. It has . . . wanted . . . to discover a new place and a new state of mind."[17] Richard Poirier takes the idea further:

> The most interesting American books are an image of the creation of America itself. . . . They carry the metaphoric burden of a great dream of freedom—of the expansion of national consciousness into the vast spaces of a continent and the absorption of those spaces into ourselves. . . . The classic American writers try through style temporarily to free the hero (and the reader) from systems, to free them from the pressures of time, biology, economics, and from the social forces which are ultimately the undoing of American heroes and quite often of their creators. . . . The strangeness of American fiction has . . . to do . . . with the environment [the novelist] tries to create for his hero, usually his surrogate.[18]

The implicit union of creator and protagonist is made specific and overt at the end of Poirier's passage here. The ideas of Poirier and Chase, and others like them, are summed up in an anthology called *Theories of American Literature*, edited by Donald M. Kartiganer and Malcolm A. Griffith.[19] The editors write, "It is as if with each new work our writers feel they must invent again the complete world of a literary form." (Yet, the true subject is not what the writers feel, but what the critics think they feel.) "Such a condition of nearly absolute freedom to create has appeared to our authors both as possibility and liability, an utter openness suggesting limitless opportunity for the imagination, or an enormous vacancy in which they create from nothing. For some it has meant an opportunity to play Adam, to assume the role of an original namer of experience" (4–5). One can see in this passage the transference of the American myth from the Adamic hero *in* the story, to the Adamic creator *of* the story, and the reinterpretation of the American myth as a metaphor for the American artist's situation.

This myth of artistic creation, assimilating the act of writing novels to the Adamic myth, imposes on artistic creation all the gender-based restrictions that we have already examined in that myth. The key to identifying an "Adamic writer" is the formal appearance, or, more precisely the *informal* appearance, of his novel. The unconventionality is interpreted as a direct representation of the open-ended experience of exploring and taming the wilderness, as well as a rejection of "society" as it is incorporated in conventional literary forms. There is no place for a woman author in this scheme. Her roles in the drama of creation are those allotted to her in a male melodrama: either she is to be silent, like nature; or she is the creator of conventional works, the spokesperson of society. What she might do as an innovator in her own right is not to be perceived.

In recent years, some refinements of critical theory coming from the Yale and Johns Hopkins and Columbia schools have added a new variant to the idea of creation as a male province. I quote from a 1979 book entitled *Home as Found* by Eric Sundquist. The author takes the idea that in writing a novel the artist is really writing a narrative about himself and proposes this addition:

> Writing a narrative about oneself may represent an extremity of Oedipal usurpation or identification, a bizarre act of self fathering. . . . American authors have been particularly obsessed with *fathering* a tradition of their own, with becoming

their "own sires." . . . The struggle . . . is central to the crisis of representation, and hence of style, that allows American authors to find in their own fantasies those of a nation and to make of those fantasies a compelling and instructive literature.[20]

These remarks derive clearly from the work of such critics as Harold Bloom, as any reader of recent critical theory will note. The point for our purpose is the facile translation of the verb "to author" into the verb "to father," with the profound gender-restrictions of that translation unacknowledged. According to this formulation, insofar as the author writes about a character who is his surrogate—which, apparently, he always does—he is trying to become his own father.

We can scarcely deny that men think a good deal about, and are profoundly affected by, relations with their fathers. The theme of fathers and sons is perennial in world literature. Somewhat more spaciously, we recognize that intergenerational conflict, usually perceived from the point of view of the young, is a recurrent literary theme, especially in egalitarian cultures. Certainly, this idea involves the question of authority, and "authority" is a notion related to that of "the author." And there is some gender-specific significance involved since authority in most cultures that we know tends to be invested in adult males. But the theory has built from these useful and true observations to a restriction of literary creation to a sort of therapeutic act that can only be performed by men. If literature is the attempt to *father* oneself by the author, then every act of writing by a woman is both perverse and absurd. And, of course, it is bound to fail.

Since this particular theory of the act of writing is drawn from psychological assumptions that are not specific to American literature, it may be argued that there is no need to confine it to American authors. In fact, Harold Bloom's *Anxiety of Influence,* defining literature as a struggle between fathers and sons, or the struggle of sons to escape from their fathers, is about British literature. And so is Edward Said's book *Beginnings,* which chronicles the history of the nineteenth-century British novel as exemplification of what he calls "filiation." His discussion omits Jane Austen, George Eliot, all three Brontë sisters, Mrs. Gaskell, Mrs. Humphrey Ward—not a sign of a woman author is found in his treatment of Victorian fiction. The result is a revisionist approach to British fiction that recasts it in the accepted image of the American myth. Ironically, just at the time that feminist critics are discovering more and more important women, the critical theorists have seized upon a theory that allows the women less and less presence. This observation points up just how significantly the critic is engaged in the act of *creating* literature.

Ironically, then, one concludes that in pushing the theory of American fiction to this extreme, critics have "deconstructed" it by creating a tool with no particular American reference. In pursuit of the uniquely American, they have arrived at a place where Americanness has vanished into the depths of what is alleged to be the universal male psyche. The theory of American fiction has boiled down to the phrase in my title: a melodrama of beset manhood. What a reduction this is of the enormous variety of fiction written in this country, by both women and men! And, ironically, nothing could be further removed from Trilling's idea of the artist as embodiment of a culture. As in the working out of all theories, its weakest link has found it out and broken the chain.

Notes

1. Marlene Springer, ed., *What Manner of Woman: Essays on English and American Life and Literature* (New York: New York Univ. Press, 1977). [All notes are Baym's.]
2. See Lyle Wright, *American Fiction 1774–1850* (San Marino, Calif.: Huntington Library Press, 1969).
3. Marius Bewley, *The Eccentric Design* (New York: Columbia Univ. Press, 1963), 15, 291.
4. F. O. Matthiessen, *American Renaissance* (New York: Oxford Univ. Press, 1941), ix.
5. Robert E. Spiller et al., eds., *Literary History of the United States* (New York: Macmillan, 1959), xix.
6. Joel Porte, *The Romance in America* (Middletown, Conn.: Wesleyan Univ. Press, 1969), ix.
7. A good essay on this topic is William C. Spengemann's "What Is American Literature?" *CentR*, 22 (1978), 119–38.
8. See Jay B. Hubbell, *Who Are the Major American Authors?* (Durham, N.C.: Duke Univ. Press, 1972).
9. Ibid., 335–36.
10. Richard Poirier, *A World Elsewhere: The Place of Style in American Literature* (New York: Oxford Univ. Press, 1966), 5.
11. Lionel Trilling, *The Liberal Imagination* (New York: Anchor, 1950), 7–9.
12. Leslie Fiedler, *Love and Death in the American Novel* (New York: Criterion Books, 1960), 93.
13. Charles Brockden Brown, *Wieland*, ed. Sydney J. Krause and S. W. Reid (Kent, Ohio: Kent State Univ. Press, 1978), xii.
14. *The Liberal Imagination*, 206.
15. Richard Chase, *The American Novel and Its Tradition* (New York: Anchor, 1957), 55, 64.
16. Annette Kolodny, *The Lay of the Land* (Chapel Hill: Univ. of North Carolina Press, 1975).
17. Chase, *American Novel*, 5.
18. Poirier, *A World Elsewhere*, 3, 5, 9.
19. Donald M. Kartiganer and Malcolm A. Griffith, eds., *Theories of American Literature* (New York: Macmillan, 1962).
20. Eric Sundquist, *Home as Found* (Baltimore: Johns Hopkins Univ. Press, 1979), xviii–xix.

Stephen Knapp (1951–) and Walter Benn Michaels (1948–)

After working from 1978 to 1994 as a professor of English at the University of California at Berkeley, Knapp left for the East coast to become Vice President of Academic Affairs and Dean of the Krieger School of Arts and Sciences at Johns Hopkins University. A British literature scholar by training, Knapp has written two books, *Personification and the Sublime: Milton to Coleridge* (1985) and *Literary Interests: The Limits of Anti-Formalism* (1993), and in 1981 he was one of the inaugural coeditors of the influential interdisciplinary journal *Representations*. Like Knapp, Michaels also has shifted schools. Before becoming a professor of English at the University of Illinois at Chicago, Michaels was a professor of English at Johns Hopkins University. Michaels is one of the premier American literature scholars working today, as is evidenced by his acclaimed books *The Gold Standard and the Logic of Naturalism: American Literature at the Turn of the Century* (1987), *Our America: Nativism, Modernism, and Pluralism* (1995), and *The American Renaissance Reconsidered* (1985), the latter of which he coedited with Donald E. Pease.

The selection given next, "Against Theory," first appeared in the journal *Critical Inquiry* in 1982 and presents "neopragmatism" as an alternative to poststructuralist theories such as the deconstruction practiced by Paul De Man and to hermeneutical approaches such as those offered by E. D. Hirsch in the late 1970s and early 1980s. In addition to being polemical or controversial in "Against Theory," Knapp and Michaels can be understood as helping to make room for theorists and critics who wanted to practice scholarship beyond the pale of poststructuralist theories of textuality, which emphasize undecidability as the human condition. Indeed, much of Michaels's post–"Against Theory" work can be characterized as a version of New Historicism.

Against Theory

I

By "theory" we mean a special project in literary criticism: the attempt to govern interpretations of particular texts by appealing to an account of interpretation in general. The term is sometimes applied to literary subjects with no direct bearing on the interpretation of individual works, such as narratology, stylistics, and prosody. Despite their generality, however, these subjects seem to us essentially empirical, and our argument against theory will not apply to them.

Contemporary theory has taken two forms. Some theorists have sought to ground the reading of literary texts in methods designed to guarantee the objectivity and validity of interpretations. Others, impressed by the inability of such procedures to produce agreement among interpreters, have translated that failure into an alternative mode of theory that denies the possibility of correct interpretation. Our aim here is not to choose between these two alternatives but rather to show that both rest on a single mistake, a mistake that is central to the notion of theory per se. The object of our critique is not a particular way of doing theory but the idea of doing theory at all.

Theory attempts to solve—or to celebrate the impossibility of solving—a set of familiar problems: the function of authorial intention, the status of literary language, the role of interpretive assumptions, and so on. We will not attempt to solve these problems, nor will we be concerned with tracing their history or surveying the range of arguments they have stimulated. In our view, the mistake on which all critical theory rests has been to imagine that these problems are real. In fact, we will claim such problems only seem real—and theory itself only seems possible or relevant—when theorists fail to recognize the fundamental inseparability of the elements involved.

The clearest example of the tendency to generate theoretical problems by splitting apart terms that are in fact inseparable is the persistent debate over the relation between authorial intention and the meaning of texts. Some theorists have claimed that valid interpretations can only be obtained through an appeal to authorial intentions. This assumption is shared by theorists who, denying the possibility of recovering authorial intentions, also deny the possibility of valid interpretations. But once it is seen that the meaning of a text is simply identical to the author's intended meaning, the project of *grounding* meaning in intention becomes incoherent. Since the project itself is incoherent, it can neither succeed nor fail; hence both theoretical attitudes toward intention are irrelevant. The mistake made by theorists has been to imagine the possibility or desirability of moving from one term (the author's intended meaning) to a second term (the text's meaning), when actually the two terms are the same. One can neither succeed nor fail in deriving one term from the other, since to have one is already to have them both.

In the following two sections we will try to show in detail how theoretical accounts of intention always go wrong. In the fourth section we will undertake a similar analysis of an influential account of the role interpretive assumptions or beliefs play in the practice of literary criticism. The issues of belief and intention are, we think, central to the theoretical enterprise; our discussion of them is thus directed not only against specific theoretical arguments but against theory in general. Our examples are meant to represent the central mechanism of all theoretical arguments, and our treatment of them is meant to indicate that all such arguments will fail and fail in the same way. If we are right, then the whole enterprise of critical theory is misguided and should be abandoned.

2. Meaning and Intention

The fact that what a text means is what its author intends is clearly stated by E. D. Hirsch when he writes that the meaning of a text "is, and can be, nothing other than the author's meaning" and "is determined once and for all by the character of the speaker's intention."[1] Having defined meaning as the author's intended meaning, Hirsch goes on to argue that all literary interpretation "must stress a reconstruction of the author's aims and attitudes in order to evolve guides and norms for construing the meaning of his text." Although these guides and norms cannot guarantee the correctness of any particular reading—nothing can—they nevertheless constitute, he claims, a "fundamentally sound" and "objective" method of interpretation (pp. 224, 240).

What seems odd about Hirsch's formulation is the transition from definition to method. He begins by defining textual meaning as the author's intended meaning and then suggests that the best way to find textual meaning is to look for authorial intention. But if meaning and intended meaning are already the same, it's hard to see how looking for one provides an objective method—or any sort of method—for looking for the other; looking for one just *is* looking for the other. The recognition that what a text means and what its author intends it to mean are identical should entail the further recognition that any appeal from one to the other is useless. And yet, as we have already begun to see, Hirsch thinks the opposite; he believes that identifying meaning with the expression of intention has the supreme theoretical usefulness of providing an objective method of choosing among alternative interpretations.

Hirsch, however, has failed to understand the force of his own formulation. In one moment he identifies meaning and intended meaning; in the next moment he splits them apart. This mistake is clearly visible in his polemic against formalist critics who deny the importance of intention altogether. His argument against these critics ends up invoking their account of meaning at the expense of his own. Formalists, in Hirsch's summary, conceive the text as a "'piece of language,'" a "public object whose character is defined by public norms." The problem with this account, according to Hirsch, is that "no mere sequence of words can represent an actual verbal meaning with reference to public norms alone. Referred to these alone, the text's meaning remains indeterminate." Hirsch's example, "My car ran out of gas," is, as he notes, susceptible to an indeterminate range of interpretations. There are no public norms which will help us decide whether the sentence means that my automobile lacks fuel or "my Pullman dash[ed] from a cloud of Argon." Only by assigning a particular intention to the words "My car ran out of gas" does one arrive at a determinate interpretation. Or, as Hirsch himself puts it, "The array of possibilities only begins to become a more selective system of *probabilities* when, instead of confronting merely a word sequence, we also posit a speaker who very likely means something" (p. 225).[2]

This argument seems consistent with Hirsch's equation of meaning and intended meaning, until one realizes that Hirsch is imagining a moment of interpretation before intention is present. This is the moment at which the text's meaning "remains indeterminate," before such indeterminacy is cleared up by the *addition* of authorial intention. But if meaning and intention really are inseparable, then it makes no sense to think of intention as an ingredient that needs to be added; it must be present from the start. The issue of determinacy or indeterminacy is irrelevant. Hirsch thinks it's relevant because he thinks, correctly, that the movement from indeterminacy to determinacy involves the addition of information, but he also thinks, incorrectly, that adding information amounts to adding intention. Since intention is already present, the only thing added, in the movement from indeterminacy to determinacy, is information *about* the intention, not the intention itself. For a sentence like "My car ran out of gas" even to be recognizable as a sentence, we must already have posited a speaker and hence an intention. Pinning down an interpretation of the sentence will not involve adding a speaker but deciding among a range of possible speakers. Knowing that the speaker inhabits a planet with an atmosphere of inert gases and on which the primary means of transportation is railroad will give one interpretation; knowing that the speaker is an earthling who owns a Ford will give another. But even if we have none of this information, as soon as we attempt to interpret at all we are already committed to a characterization of the speaker as a speaker of language. We know, in other words, that the speaker intends to speak; otherwise we wouldn't be interpreting. In this latter case, we have less information about the speaker than in the other two (where we at least knew the speaker's planetary origin), but the relative lack of information has nothing to do with the presence or absence of intention.

This mistake no doubt accounts for Hirsch's peculiar habit of calling the proper object of interpretation the "author's meaning" and, in later writings, distinguishing between it and the "reader's meaning."[3] The choice between these two kinds of meaning becomes, for Hirsch, an ethical imperative as well as an "operational" necessity. But if all meaning is always the author's meaning, then the alternative is an empty one, and there is no choice, ethical or operational, to be made. Since theory is designed to help us make such choices, all theoretical arguments on the issue of authorial intention must at some point accept the premises of anti-intentionalist accounts of meaning. In debates about intention, the movement of imagining intentionless meaning constitutes the theoretical movement itself. From the standpoint of an argument against critical theory, then, the only important question about intention is whether there can in fact be intentionless meanings. If our argument against theory is to succeed, the answer to this question must be no.

The claim that all meanings are intentional is not, of course, an unfamiliar one in contemporary philosophy of language. John Searle, for example, asserts that "there is no getting away from intentionality," and he and others have advanced arguments to support this claim.[4] Our purpose here is not to add another such argument but to show how radically counterintuitive the alternative would be. We can begin to get a sense of this simply by noticing how difficult it is to imagine a case of intentionless meaning.

Suppose that you're walking along a beach and you come upon a curious sequence of squiggles in the sand. You step back a few paces and notice that they spell out the following words.

> A slumber did my spirit seal;
>   I had no human fears;
> She seemed a thing that could not feel
>   The touch of earthly years.[5]

This would seem to be a good case of intentionless meaning: you recognize the writing as writing, you understand what the words mean, you may even identify them as constituting a rhymed poetic stanza—and all this without knowing anything about the author and indeed without needing to connect the words to any notion of an author at all. You can do all these things without thinking of anyone's intention. But now suppose that, as you stand gazing at this pattern in the sand, a wave washes up and recedes, leaving in its wake (written below what you now realize was only the first stanza) the following words:

> No motion has she now, no force;
>   She neither hears nor sees;
> Rolled round in earth's diurnal course,
>   With rocks, and stones, and trees.

One might ask whether the question of intention still seems as irrelevant as it did seconds before. You will now, we suspect, feel compelled to explain what you have just seen. Are these marks mere accidents, produced by the mechanical operation of the waves on the sand (through some subtle and unprecedented process of erosion, percolation, etc.)? Or is the sea alive and striving to express its pantheistic faith? Or has Wordsworth, since his death, become a sort of genius of the shore who inhabits the waves and periodically inscribes on the sand his elegiac sentiments? You might go on extending the list of explanations indefinitely, but you would find, we think, that all the explanations fall into two categories. You will either be ascribing these marks to some agent capable of intentions (the living sea, the haunting Wordsworth, etc.), or you will count them as nonintentional effects of mechanical processes (erosion, percolation, etc.). But in the second case—where the marks now seem to be accidents—will they still seem to be words?

Clearly not. They will merely seem to *resemble* words. You will be amazed, perhaps, that such an astonishing coincidence could occur. Of course, you would have been no less amazed had you decided that the sea or the ghost of Wordsworth was responsible. But it's essential to recognize that in the two cases your amazement would have two entirely different sources. In one case, you would be amazed by the identity of the author—who would have thought that the sea can write poetry? In the other case, however, in which you accept the hypothesis of natural accident, you're amazed to discover that what you thought was poetry turns out not to be poetry at all. It isn't poetry because it isn't language; that's what it means to call it an accident. As long as you thought the marks were poetry, you were assuming their intentional character. You had no idea who the author was, and this may have tricked you into thinking that positing an author was irrelevant to your ability to read the stanza. But in fact you had, without realizing it, already posited an author. It was only with the mysterious arrival of the second stanza that your tacit assumption (e.g., someone writing with a stick) was challenged and you realized that you had made one. Only now, when positing an author seems impossible, do you genuinely imagine the marks as authorless. But to deprive them of an author is to convert them into accidental likenesses of language. They are not, after all, an example of intentionless meaning; as soon as they become intentionless they become meaningless as well.

The arrival of the second stanza made clear that what had seemed to be an example of intentionless language was either not intentionless or not language. The question was whether the marks counted as language; what determined the answer was a decision as to whether or not they were the product of an intentional agent. If our example has seemed farfetched, it is only because there is seldom occasion in our culture to wonder whether the *sea* is an intentional agent. But there *are* cases where the question of intentional agency might be an important and difficult one. Can computers speak? Arguments over this question reproduce exactly the terms of our example. Since computers are machines, the issue of whether they can speak seems to hinge on the possibility of intentionless language. But our example shows that there is no such thing as intentionless language; the only real issue is whether computers are capable of intentions. However this issue may be decided—and our example offers no help in deciding it—the decision will not rest on a theory of meaning but on a judgment as to whether computers can be intentional agents. This is not to deny that a great deal—morally, legally, and politically—might depend on such judgments. But no degree of practical importance will give these judgments theoretical force.

The difference between theoretical principle and practical or empirical judgments can be clarified by one last glance at the case of the wave poem. Suppose, having seen the second stanza wash up on the beach, you have decided that the "poem" is really an accidental effect of erosion, percolation, and so on and therefore not language at all. What would it now take to change your mind? No theoretical argument will make a difference. But suppose you notice, rising out of the sea some distance from the shore, a small submarine, out of which clamber a half dozen figures in white lab coats. One of them trains his binoculars on the beach and shouts triumphantly, "It worked! It worked! Let's go down and try it again." Presumably, you will now once again change your mind, not because you have a new account of language, meaning, or intention but because you now have new evidence of an author. The question of authorship is and always was an empirical question; it has now received a new empirical answer. The theoretical temptation is to imagine that such empirical questions must, or should, have theoretical answers.

Even a philosopher as committed to the intentional status of language as Searle succumbs to this temptation to think that intention is a theoretical issue. After insisting, in the passage cited earlier, on the inescapability of intention, he goes on to say that "in serious literal speech the sentences are precisely the realizations of the intentions" and that "there need be no *gulf* at all between the illocutionary intention and its expression."[6] The point, however, is not that there *need* be no gulf between intention and the meaning of its expression but that there *can* be no gulf. Not only in serious literal speech but in *all* speech what is intended and what is meant are identical. In separating the two Searle imagines the possibility of expression without intention and so, like Hirsch, misses the point of his own claim that when it comes to language "there is no getting away from intentionality." Missing this point, and hence imagining the possibility of two different *kinds* of meaning, is more than a theoretical mistake; it is the sort of mistake that makes theory possible. It makes theory possible because it creates the illusion of a choice between alternative methods of interpreting.[7]

To be a theorist is only to think that there is such a choice. In this respect intentionalists and anti-intentionalists are the same. They are also the same in another respect: neither can really escape intention. But this doesn't mean the intentionalists win, since what intentionalists want is a guide to valid interpretation; what they get, however, is simply a description of what everyone always does. In practical terms, then, the stakes in the battle over intention are extremely low—in fact, they don't exist. Hence it doesn't matter who wins. In theoretical terms, however, the stakes are extremely high, and it still doesn't matter who wins. The stakes are high because they amount to the existence of theory itself; it doesn't matter who wins because as long as one thinks that a position on intention (either for or against) makes a difference in achieving valid interpretations, the ideal of theory itself is saved. Theory wins. But as soon as we recognize that there are no theoretical choices to be made, then the point of theory vanishes. Theory loses.[8]

3. Language and Speech Acts

We have argued that what a text means and what its author intends it to mean are identical and that their identity robs intention of any theoretical interest. A similar account of the relation between meaning and intention has recently been advanced by P. D. Juhl. According to Juhl, "there is a logical connection between statements about the meaning of a literary work and statements about the author's intention such that a statement about the meaning of a work *is* a statement about the author's intention." Juhl criticizes Hirsch, as we do, for believing that critics "*ought* to . . . try to ascertain the author's intention," when in fact, Juhl argues, "they are necessarily doing so already" (*Interpretation,* p. 12). But for Juhl, these claims serve in no way to discredit theory; rather, they themselves constitute a theory that "makes us aware of what we as critics or readers are doing in interpreting literature" and, more crucially, "provides the basis for a principled acceptance or rejection of an interpretation of a literary work" (p. 10). How is it that Juhl derives a theory from arguments which seem to us to make theory impossible?

What makes this question particularly intriguing is the fact that Juhl's strategy for demonstrating the centrality of intention is apparently identical to ours; it consists "in contrasting statements about the meaning of a literary work created by a person with statements about the meaning of a text produced by chance, such as a computer poem" (p. 13).[9] But Juhl's treatment of examples like our wave poem reveals that his sense of the relation between language and intention is after all radically different from ours. Like Hirsch, but at a further level of abstraction, Juhl ends up imagining the possibility of language prior to and independent of intention and thus conceiving intention as something that must be added to language to make it work. Like Hirsch, and like theorists in general, Juhl thinks that intention is a matter of choice. But where Hirsch recommends that we choose intention to adjudicate among interpretations, Juhl thinks no recommendation is necessary—not because we need never choose intention but only because our concept of a literary work is such that to read literature is already to have chosen intention.

Discussing the case of a "poem" produced by chance ("marks on [a] rock" or "a computer poem"), Juhl points out that there is "something odd about *interpreting* [such a] 'text.'" However one might understand this text, one could not understand it as a representation of "the meaning of a particular utterance." We agree with this—if it implies that the random marks mean nothing, are not language, and therefore cannot be interpreted at all. But for Juhl the implications are different. He thinks that one *can* interpret the random marks, though only in the somewhat specialized sense "in which we might be said to 'interpret' a sentence when we explain its meaning to a foreigner, by explaining to him what the individual words mean, how they function in the sentence, and thus how the sentence *could* be used or what it *could* be used to express or convey" (pp. 84–86).

Our point is that marks produced by chance are not words at all but only resemble them. For Juhl, the marks remain words, but words detached from the intentions that would make them utterances. Thus he can argue that when a "parrot utters the words 'Water is pouring down from the sky,'" one can understand that "the words mean 'It is raining'" but deny that the "'parrot *said* that it is raining'"(p. 109).[10] It is clear that, for Juhl, the words continue to mean even when devoid of intention. They mean *"in abstracto"* and thus constitute the condition of language prior to the addition of intention, that is, prior to "a speaker's utterance or speech act." In literary interpretation, this condition of language is never operative because, Juhl claims, "our notion of the meaning of a literary work" is "like our notion of the meaning of a person's speech act," not "like our notion of the meaning of a word in a language" (p. 41).[11]

Implicit in Juhl's whole treatment of meaning and intention is the distinction made here between language and speech acts. This distinction makes possible a methodological prescription as strong as Hirsch's, if more general: when confronted with a piece of language, read it as a speech act. The prescriptive force of Juhl's argument is obscured by the fact that he has pushed the moment of decision one step back. Whereas Hirsch thinks we have to add intention to *literature* in order to determine what a text means, Juhl thinks that adding intentions to *language* gives us speech acts (such as literary works) whose meaning is already determinate. Juhl recognizes that as soon as we think of a piece of language as literature, we already regard it as a speech act and hence the product of intention; his prescription tells us how to get from language in general to a specific utterance, such as a literary work.[12]

But this prescription only makes sense if its two terms (language and speech acts) are not already inseparable in the same way that meaning and intention are. Juhl is right of course to claim that marks without intention are not speech acts, since the essence of a speech act is its intentional character. But we have demonstrated that marks without intention are not language either. Only by failing to see that linguistic meaning is always identical to expressed intention can Juhl imagine language without speech acts. To recognize the identity of language and speech acts is to realize that Juhl's prescription—when confronted with language, read it as a speech act—can mean nothing more than: when confronted with language, read it as language.

For Hirsch and Juhl, the goal of theory is to provide an objectively valid method of literary interpretation. To make method possible, both are forced to imagine intentionless meanings or, in more general terms, to imagine a separation between language and speech acts.[13] The method then consists in adding speech acts to language; speech acts bring with them the particular intentions that allow interpreters to clear up the ambiguities intrinsic to language as such. But this separation of language and speech acts need not be used to establish an interpretive method; it can in fact be used to do just the opposite. For a theorist like Paul de Man, the priority of language to speech acts suggests that all attempts to arrive at determinate meanings by adding intentions amount to a violation of the genuine condition of language. If theory in its positive or methodological mode rests on the choice of speech acts over language, theory in its negative or antimethodological mode tries to preserve what it takes to be the purity of language from the distortion of speech acts.

The negative theorist's hostility to method depends on a particular account of language, most powerfully articulated in de Man's "The Purloined Ribbon." The essay concerns what de Man sees as a crucial episode in Rousseau's *Confessions,* in which Rousseau attempts to interpret, and thereby to justify, a particularly incriminating speech act. While working as a servant, he had stolen a ribbon from his employers. When accused of the theft, he blamed it on a fellow servant, Marion. In the passage that interests de Man, Rousseau is thus concerned with two crimes, the theft itself and the far more heinous act of excusing himself by accusing an innocent girl. This second act, the naming of Marion, is the one that especially needs justifying.

Rousseau offers several excuses, each an explanation of what he meant by naming Marion. But the explanation that intrigues de Man is the surprising one that Rousseau perhaps meant nothing at all when he said "Marion." He was merely uttering the first sound that occurred to him: "Rousseau was making whatever noise happened to come into his head; he was saying nothing at all."[14] Hence, de Man argues, "In the spirit of the text, one should resist all temptation to give any significance whatever to the sound 'Marion.'" The claim that "Marion" was meaningless gives Rousseau his best defense: "For it is only if . . . the utterance of the sound 'Marion' is truly without any conceivable motive that the total arbitrariness of the action becomes the most effective, the most efficaciously performative excuse of all" (p. 37). Why? Because, "if the essential non-signification of the statement had been properly interpreted, if Rousseau's accusers had realized that Marion's name was 'le premier objet qui s'offrit,' they would have understood his lack of guilt as well as Marion's innocence" (p. 40).

But de Man is less interested in the efficacy of the "excuse" than he is in what it reveals about the fundamental nature of language. The fact that the sound "Marion" can mean nothing reminds us that language consists of inherently meaningless sounds to which one adds meanings—in other words, that the relation between signifier and signified is arbitrary. Why does de Man think this apparently uncontroversial description of language has any theoretical interest? The recognition that the material condition of language is inherently meaningless has no theoretical force in itself. But de Man thinks that the material condition of language is not simply meaningless but is also already "linguistic," that is, sounds are signifiers even before meanings (signifieds) are added to them. As a collection of "pure signifier[s]," in themselves "devoid of meaning and function," language is primarily a meaningless structure to which meanings are secondarily (and in de Man's view illegitimately) added (p. 32). Thus, according to de Man, Rousseau's accusers mistakenly added a meaning to the signifier "Marion"—hearing a speech act where they should have heard only language. This separation of language and speech act is the precondition for de Man's version of the theoretical choice.

De Man's separation of language and speech acts rests on a mistake. It is of course true that sounds in themselves are meaningless. It is also true that sounds become signifiers when they function in language. But it is not true that sounds in themselves are signifiers; they become signifiers only when they acquire meanings, and when they lose their meanings they stop being signifiers. De Man's mistake is to think that the sound "Marion" remains a signifier even when emptied of all meaning.[15] The fact is that the meaningless noise "Marion" only *resembles* the signifier "Marion," just as accidentally uttering the sound "Marion" only *resembles* the speech act of naming Marion. De Man recognizes that the accidental emission of the sound "Marion" is not a speech act (indeed, that's the point of the example), but he fails to recognize that it's not language either. What reduces the signifier to noise and the speech act to an accident is the absence of intention. Conceiving linguistic activity as the accidental emission of phonemes, de Man arrives at a vision of "the absolute randomness of language, prior to any figuration or meaning": "There can be no use of language which is not, within a certain perspective thus radically formal, i.e., mechanical, no matter how deeply this aspect may be concealed by aesthetic, formalistic delusions" (pp. 44, 41).

By conceiving language as essentially random and mechanical, de Man gives a new response to the dilemma of the wave poem and suggests a fuller account of why that dilemma is central to theory in general. Our earlier discussion of the wave poem was intended to show how counter-intuitive it is to separate language and intention. When the second stanza washed up on the beach, even the theorist should have been ready to admit that the poem was not a poem because the marks were not language. But our subsequent discussions of Juhl and de Man have revealed that theory precisely depends on not making this admission. For Juhl, the accidental marks remain language, but language *in abstracto* and hence inherently ambiguous. The wave poem thus presents a positive theorist like Juhl with a choice between the multiple meanings of intentionless marks and the determinate meaning of an intentional speech act. Since the point of positive theory is to ground the practice of determining particular meanings, the positive theorist chooses to read the marks as an intentional act. But when a negative theorist like de Man encounters the second (accidental) stanza, it presents him with a slightly different version of the same choice. For de Man the marks are not multiply meaningful but essentially meaningless, and the choice is not between one intentional meaning and many intentionless meanings but between intentional meaning and no meaning at all. Since, in de Man's view, all imputations of meaning are equally groundless, the positive theorist's choice of intention seems to him pointless. In apparent hostility to interpretive method, the negative theorist chooses the meaningless marks. But the negative theorist's choice in fact provides him with a positive methodology, a methodology that grounds the practice of interpretation in the single decisive truth about language. The truth about language is its accidental and mechanical nature: any text, "properly interpreted," will reveal its "essential nonsignification" (p. 40). For both Juhl and de Man, proper interpretation depends upon following a methodological prescription. Juhl's prescription is: when confronted with language, read it as a speech act. De Man's prescription is: when confronted with what seems to be a speech act, read it as language.

The wave poem, as encountered by a theorist, presents a choice between two kinds of meaning or, what comes to the same thing, two kinds of language. The issue in both cases is the presence or absence of intention; the positive theorist adds intention, the negative theorist subtracts it.[16] In our view, however, the relation between meaning and intention or, in slightly different terms, between language and speech acts is such that intention can neither be added nor subtracted. Intention cannot be added to or subtracted from meaning because meanings are always intentional; intention cannot be added to or subtracted from language because consists of speech acts, which are also always intentional. Since language has intention already built into it, no recommendation about what to do with intention has any bearing on the question of how to interpret any utterance or text. For the nontheorist, the only question raised by the wave poem is not *how* to interpret but whether to interpret. Either the marks are a poem and hence a speech act, or they are not a poem and just happen to resemble a speech act. But once this empirical question is decided, no further judgments—and therefore no theoretical judgments—about the status of intention can be made.

4. Theory and Practice

Our argument so far has concerned what might be called the ontological side of theory—its peculiar claims about the nature of its object. We have suggested that those claims always take the form of generating a difference where none in fact exists, by imagining a mode of language devoid of intention—devoid, that is, of what makes it language and distinguishes it from accidental or mechanical noises and marks. But we have also tried to show that this strange ontological project is more than a spontaneous anomaly; it is always in the service of an epistemological goal. That goal is the goal of method, the governance of interpretive practice by some larger and more principled account. Indeed, theoretical controversy in the Anglo-American tradition has more often taken the form of arguments about the epistemological situation of the interpreter than about the ontological status of the text. If the ontological project of theory has been to imagine a condition of language before intention, its epistemological project has been to imagine a condition of knowledge before interpretation.

The aim of theory's epistemological project is to base interpretation on a direct encounter with its object, an encounter undistorted by the influence of the interpreter's particular beliefs. Several writers have demonstrated the impossibility of escaping beliefs at any stage of interpretation and have concluded that theory's epistemological goal is therefore unattainable. Some have gone on to argue that the unattainability of an epistemologically neutral stance not only undermines the claims of method but prevents us from ever getting any correct interpretations. For these writers the attack on method thus has important practical consequences for literary criticism, albeit negative ones.[17]

But in discussing theory from the ontological side, we have tried to suggest that the impossibility of method has no practical consequences, positive or negative. And the same conclusion has been reached from the epistemological side by the strongest critic of theoretical attempts to escape belief, Stanley Fish. In his last essay in *Is There a Text in This Class?*, Fish confronts the "final question" raised by his critique of method, namely, "what implications it has for the practice of literary criticism." His answer is, "none whatsoever":

> That is, it does not follow from what I have been saying that you should go out
> and do literary criticism in a certain way or refrain from doing it in other ways.
> The reason for this is that the position I have been presenting is not one that you

(or anyone else) could live by. Its thesis is that whatever seems to you to be obvious and inescapable is only so within some institutional or conventional structure, and that means that you can never operate outside some such structure, even if you are persuaded by the thesis. As soon as you descend from theoretical reasoning about your assumptions, you will once again inhabit them and you will inhabit them without any reservations whatsoever; so that when you are called on to talk about Milton or Wordsworth or Yeats, you will do so from within whatever beliefs you hold about these authors.[18]

At the heart of this passage is the familiar distinction between "theoretical reasoning" and the "assumptions" or "beliefs" that inform the concrete "practice of literary criticism." Where most theorists affirm the practical importance of their theories, Fish's originality lies in his denial that his theory has any practical consequences whatsoever. But once theory gives up all claims to affect practice, what is there left for theory to do? Or, since Fish's point is that there is nothing left for theory to *do*, what is there left for theory to *be*? Understood in these terms, Fish's work displays the theoretical impulse in its purest form. Stripped of the methodological project either to ground or to undermine practice, theory continues to imagine a position outside it. While this retreat to a position outside practice looks like theory's last desperate attempt to save itself, it is really, as we hope to show, the founding gesture of all theoretical argument.

Fish's attack on method begins with an account of belief that is in our view correct. The account's two central features are, first, the recognition that beliefs cannot be grounded in some deeper condition of knowledge and, second, the further recognition that this impossibility does not in any way weaken their claims to be true. "If one believes what one believes," Fish writes, "then one believes that what one believes is *true,* and conversely, one believes that what one doesn't believe is not true" (p. 361). Since one can neither escape one's beliefs nor escape the sense that they are true, Fish rejects both the claims of method and the claims of skepticism. Methodologists and skeptics maintain that the validity of beliefs depends on their being grounded in a condition of knowledge prior to and independent of belief; they differ only about whether this is possible. The virtue of Fish's account is that it shows why an insistence on the inescapability of belief is in no way inimical to the ordinary notions of truth and falsehood implicit in our sense of what knowledge is. The character of belief is precisely what gives us those notions in the first place; having beliefs just *is* being committed to the truth of what one believes and the falsehood of what one doesn't believe. But to say all this is, as Fish asserts, to offer no practical help or hindrance to the task of acquiring true beliefs. We can no more get true beliefs by looking for knowledge than we can get an author's meaning by looking for his or her intention, and for the same reason: knowledge and true belief are the same.

So far, this argument seems to us flawless. But Fish, as it turns out, fails to recognize the force of his own discussion of belief, and this failure is what makes him a theorist. It commits him, ultimately, to the ideal of knowledge implicit in all epistemological versions of theory, and it leads him to affirm, after all, the methodological value of his theoretical stance. Fish's departure from his account of belief shows up most vividly in his response to charges that his arguments lead to historical relativism. The fear of relativism is a fear that the abandonment of method must make all inquiry pointless. But, Fish rightly says, inquiry never seems pointless; our present beliefs about an object always seem better than any previous beliefs about the same object: "In other words, the idea of progress is inevitable, not, however, because there *is* a progress in the sense of a clearer and clearer sight of an independent object but because the *feeling* of having progressed is an inevitable consequence of the firmness with which we hold our beliefs" (pp. 361–62).

As an account of the inevitable psychology of belief, this is irreproachable. But when he later turns from the general issue of intellectual progress to the particular case of progress in literary criticism, Fish makes clear that he thinks our psychological assurance is unfounded. Our present beliefs only *seem* better than earlier ones; they never really *are*. And, indeed, the discovery of this truth about our beliefs gives us, Fish thinks, a new understanding of the history of literary criticism and a new sense of how to go about studying it. According to what Fish calls the "old model" for making sense of the history of criticism, the work of critics "like Sidney, Dryden, Pope, Coleridge, Arnold" could only be seen as "the record of the rather dismal performances of men . . . who simply did not understand literature and literary values as well as we do." But Fish's new model enables us to "regard those performances not as unsuccessful attempts to approximate our own but as extensions of a literary culture whose assumptions were *not inferior but merely different*" (pp. 367–68; our emphasis).

To imagine that we can see the beliefs we hold as no better than but "merely different" from opposing beliefs held by others is to imagine a position from which we can see our beliefs without really believing them. To be in this position would be to see the truth about beliefs without actually having any—to know without believing. In the moment in which he imagines this condition of knowledge outside belief, Fish has forgotten the point of his own earlier identification of knowledge and true belief.

Once a theorist has reached this vision of knowledge, there are two epistemological ways to go: realism and idealism. A realist thinks that theory allows us to stand outside our beliefs in a neutral encounter with the objects of interpretation; an idealist thinks that theory allows us to stand outside our beliefs in a neutral encounter with our beliefs themselves. The issue in both cases is the relation between objects and beliefs. For the realist, the object exists independent of beliefs, and knowledge requires that we shed our beliefs in a disinterested quest for the object. For the idealist, who insists that we can never shed our beliefs, knowledge means recognizing the role beliefs play in *constituting* their objects. Fish, with his commitment to the primacy of beliefs, chooses idealism: "objects," he thinks, "are made and not found"; interpretation "is not the art of construing but the art of constructing" (pp. 331, 327). Once he arrives at epistemological idealism, Fish's methodological payoff immediately follows. Knowing that "interpreters do not decode poems" but "make them," "we are free to consider the various forms the literary institution has taken and to uncover the interpretive strategies by which its canons have been produced and understood" (pp. 327, 368). By thinking of the critic as an idealist instead of a realist, Fish is able to place literary criticism at the very center of all literary practice:

> No longer is the critic the humble servant of texts whose glories exist independently of anything he might do; it is what he does, within the constraints embedded in the literary institution, that brings texts into being and makes them available for analysis and appreciation. The practice of literary criticism is not something one must apologize for; it is absolutely essential not only to the maintenance of, but to the very production of, the objects of its attention. (p. 368)

We began this section by noting that Fish, like us, thinks that no general account of belief can have practical consequences. But, as we have just seen, *his* account turns out to have consequences after all. Why, then, is Fish led both to assert that his argument has no practical consequences and to proclaim its importance in providing a new model for critical practice? The answer is that, despite his explicit disclaimers, he thinks a true account of belief must be a *theory* about belief, whereas we think a true account of belief can only be a *belief* about belief.[19] The difference between these two senses of what it means to have a true account of something is the difference between theory and the kind of pragmatist argument we are presenting here. These two kinds of positions conceive their inconsequentiality in two utterly different ways. A belief about the nature of beliefs is inconsequential because it merely tells you what beliefs are, not whether they are true or false in particular or in general. From this point of view, knowing the truth about belief will no more help you in acquiring true beliefs than knowing that meaning is intentional will help you find correct meanings. This is not in the least to say that you can't have true beliefs, only that you can't get them by having a good account of what beliefs are.

Fish's *theory* about beliefs, on the other hand, strives to achieve inconsequentiality by standing outside all the practical commitments that belief entails. It is perfectly true that one can achieve inconsequentiality by going outside beliefs but only because, as Fish himself insists, to be outside beliefs is to be nowhere at all. But of course Fish doesn't think that his theory about beliefs leaves him nowhere at all; he thinks instead that it gives him a way of arriving at truth, not by choosing some beliefs over others but by choosing beliefless knowledge over all beliefs. The truth of knowledge, according to Fish, is that no beliefs are, in the long run, truer than others; all beliefs, in the long run, are equal. But, as we have noted, it is only from the standpoint of a theory about belief which is not itself a belief that this truth can be seen. Hence the descent from "theoretical reasoning" about our beliefs to the actual practice of believing—from neutrality to commitment—demands that we forget the truth theory has told us. Unlike the ordinary methodologist, Fish wants to repudiate the attempt to derive practice from theory, insisting that the world of practice must be founded not on theoretical truth but on the repression of theoretical truth. But the sense that practice can only begin with the repression of theory already amounts to a methodological prescription: when confronted with beliefs, forget that they are not really true. This prescription gives Fish everything theory always wants: knowledge of the truth-value of beliefs and instructions on what to do with them.[20]

We can now see why Fish, in the first passage quoted, says that his position is "not one that you (or anyone else) could live by . . . even if you [were] persuaded" by it. Theory, he thinks, can have no practical consequences; it cannot be lived because theory and practice—the truth about belief and belief itself—can never in principle be united. In our view, however, the only relevant truth about belief is that you can't go outside it, and, far from being unlivable, this is a truth you can't help but live. It has no practical consequences not because it can never be *united* with practice but because it can never be *separated* from practice.

The theoretical impulse, as we have described it, always involves the attempt to separate things that should not be separated: on the ontological side, meaning from intention, language from speech acts; on the epistemological side, knowledge from true belief. Our point has been that the separated terms are in fact inseparable. It is tempting to end by saying that theory and practice too are inseparable. But this would be a mistake. Not because theory and practice (unlike the other terms) really are separate but because theory is nothing else but the attempt to escape practice. Meaning is just another name for expressed intention, knowledge just another name for true belief, but theory is not just another name for practice. It is the name for all the ways people have tried to stand outside practice in order to govern practice from without. Our thesis has been that no one can reach a position outside practice, that theorists should stop trying, and that the theoretical enterprise should therefore come to an end.

Notes

1. E. D. Hirsch, Jr., *Validity in Interpretation* (New Haven, Conn., 1967), pp. 216, 219. Our remarks on Hirsch are in some ways parallel to criticisms offered by P. D. Juhl in the second chapter of his *Interpretation: An Essay in the Philosophy of Literary Criticism* (Princeton, N. J., 1980). Juhl's position will be discussed in the next section. All further citations to these works will be included in the text.

2. The phrase "piece of language" goes back, Hirsch notes, to the opening paragraph of William Empson's *Seven Types of Ambiguity,* 3rd ed. (New York, 1955).

3. See Hirsch, *The Aims of Interpretation* (Chicago, 1976), p. 8.

4. John R. Searle, "Reiterating the Differences: A Reply to Derrida," *Glyph* I (1977): 202.

5. Wordsworth's lyric has been a standard example in theoretical arguments since its adoption by Hirsch; see *Validity in Interpretation,* pp. 227–30 and 238–40.

6. Searle, "Reiterating," p. 202.

7. In conversation with the authors, Hirsch mentioned the case of a well-known critic and theorist who was persuaded by new evidence that his former reading of a poem was mistaken but who, nevertheless, professed to like his original reading better than what he now admitted was the author's intention. Hirsch meant this example to show the importance of choosing intention over some other interpretive criterion. But the critic in Hirsch's anecdote was not choosing among separate methods of interpretation; he was simply preferring his mistake. Such a preference is surely irrelevant to the theory of interpretation; it might affect what one does *with* an interpretation, but it has no effect on how one *gets* an interpretation.

8. The arguments presented here against theoretical treatments of intention at the local utterance level would apply, virtually unaltered, to accounts of larger-scale intentions elsewhere in Hirsch; they would apply as well to the theoretical proposals of such writers as M. H. Abrams, Wayne C. Booth, R. S. Crane, and Ralph W. Rader—all associated, directly or indirectly, with the Chicago School. Despite variations of approach and emphasis, these writers tend to agree that critical debates about the

meaning of a particular passage ought to be resolved through reference to the broader structural intentions informing the work in which the passage appears. Local meanings, in this view, should be deduced from hypothetical constructions of intentions implicit, for example, in an author's choice of genre; these interpretive hypotheses should in turn be confirmed or falsified by their success or failure in explaining the work's details. But this procedure would have methodological force only if the large-scale intentions were different in theoretical status from the local meanings they are supposed to constrain. We would argue, however, that all local meanings are always intentional and that structural choices and local utterances are therefore related to intention in exactly the same fashion. While an interpreter's sense of one might determine his sense of the other, neither is available to interpretation— or amenable to interpretive agreement—in a specially objective way. (Whether interpretations of intention at any level are best conceived as hypotheses is another, though a related, question.)

9. In fact, Juhl employs the same poem we do—Wordsworth's "A Slumber Did My Spirit Seal"—in his own treatment of accidental "language" (*Interpretation*, pp. 70–82). The device of contrasting intentional speech acts with marks produced by chance is a familiar one in speech-act theory.

10. Juhl briefly acknowledges the strangeness of the sort of distinction he makes here when he asks whether words produced by chance could even be called "words" (*Interpretation*, p. 84). But he drops the question as abruptly as he raises it.

11. For additional remarks on meaning "*in abstracto,*" see Juhl, *Interpretation*, pp. 25 n, 55–57, 203, 223, 238, 288–89.

12. Juhl's motives are, in fact, not far from Hirsch's. For both theorists, meaning *in abstracto* is indeterminate or ambiguous ("indeterminate" for Hirsch, "ambiguous" for Juhl); both appeal to intention in order to achieve determinate or particular meanings or, as Juhl says, to "disambiguate" the text (*Interpretation*, p. 97). This theoretical interest in the problem of indeterminacy derives in part from the widespread notion that words and sentences have a range of "linguistically possible" meanings, the ones recorded in dictionaries and grammar books. But a dictionary is an index of frequent usages in particular speech acts—not a matrix of abstract, preintentional possibilities. (For Hirsch's terminological distinction between ambiguity and indeterminacy, see *Validity in Interpretation*, p. 230.)

13. This distinction, in one form or another, is common among speech-act theorists. H. P. Grice, for example, distinguishes between "locutions of the form 'U (utterer) meant that . . .'" and "locutions of the form 'X (utterance-type) means . . . ,'" characterizing the first as "occasion-meaning" and the second as "applied timeless meaning" (H. P. Grice, "Utterer's Meaning, Sentence-Meaning, and Word-Meaning," in *The Philosophy of Language*, ed. Searle [London, 1971], pp. 54–56). And Searle, citing Wittgenstein ("*Say* 'it's cold here' and *mean* 'it's warm here'"), distinguishes between meaning as a "matter of intention" and meaning as a "matter of convention" (*Speech Acts* [Cambridge, 1969], p. 45).

14. Paul de Man, "The Purloined Ribbon," *Glyph* 1 (1977): 39; all further citations to this work will be included in the text.

15. Another, perhaps more usual, way of reaching this notion of the pure signifier is by observing that one signifier can be attached to many different meanings and concluding from this that the signifier has an identity of its own, independent of meaning in general. But the conclusion doesn't follow. Far from attaining its true identity when unrelated to any meaning, a signifier in this condition merely ceases to be a signifier.

16. At least this is true of the present generation of theorists. For earlier theorists such as W. K. Wimsatt and Monroe C. Beardsley, the objective meanings sought by positive

theory were to be acquired precisely by *subtracting* intention and relying on the formal rules and public norms of language. This, of course, is the view they urge in "The Interntional Fallacy" (*The Verbal Icon: Studies in the Meaning of Poetry* [Lexington, Ky., 1954], pp. 3–18.

17. Negative theory rests on the perception of what de Man calls "an insurmountable obstacle in the way of any reading or understanding" (*Allegories of Reading* [New Haven, Conn., 1979], p. 131). Some theorists (e.g., David Bleich and Norman Holland) understand this obstacle as the reader's subjectivity. Others (like de Man himself and J. Hillis Miller) understand it as the aporia between constative and performative language, between demonstration and persuasion. In all cases, however, the negative theorist is committed to the view that interpretation is, as Jonathan Culler says," necessary error" (*The Pursuit of Signs* [Ithaca, N.Y., 1981], p. 14).

18. Stanley Fish, *Is There a Text in This Class? The Authority of Interpretive Communities* (Cambridge, Mass., 1980), p. 370; all further citations to this work will be included in the text.

19. Fish calls his account a "general or metacritical belief" (*Is There a Text in This Class?* p. 359; cf. pp. 368–70).

20. In one respect Fish's prescription is unusual: it separates the two theoretical goals of grounding practice and reaching objective truth. It tells us what is true and how to behave—but not how to behave in order to find out what is true.

Edward Said (1935–2003)

Said was born in Jerusalem, Palestine, in 1935 and moved with his well-to-do family to Cairo, Egypt, in 1947. He came to the United States to attend prep school in Massachusetts, went to college at Princeton University, and earned his Ph.D. in literature from Harvard University. From 1963 to 2003, Said taught English and comparative literature at Columbia University, where he was a renowned scholar and theorist. As a celebrated and controversial public intellectual, however, Said was even more famous. Indeed, he was generally recognized as the leading spokesperson for Palestinian rights and nationhood in the United States. The place of politics in Said's literary criticism and theory is a central concern, as is evidenced by the reading given next, "The Politics of Knowledge," which first appeared in the prestigious journal *Raritan* in 1991. Politics is also a key concern in Said's most famous book, *Orientalism* (1978), which examines Western imperialism, particularly its literary constructions of the Middle and Far East. Many critics today view *Orientalism* as a foundational text in the growing field of postcolonial studies. Said's early literary scholarship was also influential because his examinations of Jacques Derrida's and Michel Foucault's theories helped introduce these preeminent poststructuralists to students and scholars in the United States. Throughout his scholarly career, Said consistently argued for critical practices that engage social realities, as opposed to abstract and insular focuses on linguistics or on art as a self-contained entity.

In addition to *Orientalism,* Said's other major books include *Beginnings: Intention and Method* (1975), *The World, the Text, and the Critic* (1983), *After the Last Sky: Palestinian Lives* (1986), *Culture and Imperialism* (1993), *Out of Place: A Memoir* (1999), and *Reflections on Exile and Other Essays* (2002).

The Politics of Knowledge

Last fall I was invited to participate in a seminar at a historical studies center of a historically renowned American university. The subject of the seminar for this and the next academic year is imperialism, and the seminar discussions are chaired by the center's director. Outside participants are asked to send a paper before their arrival; it is then distributed to the members of the seminar, who are graduate students, fellows, and faculty. They will have read the paper in advance, precluding any reading of a lecture to them by the visitor, who is instead asked to summarize its main points for about ten minutes. Then for an hour and a half, there is an open discussion of the paper—a fairly rigorous but stimulating exercise. Since I have been working for some years on a sequel to *Orientalism*—it will be a long book that deals with the relationship between modern culture and imperialism—I sent a substantial extract from the introduction, in which I lay out the main lines of the book's argument. I there begin to describe the emergence of a global consciousness in Western knowledge at the end of the nineteenth century, particularly in such apparently unrelated fields as geography and comparative literature. I then go on to argue that the appearance of such cultural disciplines coincides with a fully global imperial perspective, although such a coincidence can only be made to seem significant from the point of view of later history, when nearly everywhere in the colonized world there emerged resistance to certain oppressive aspects of imperial rule like theories of subject races and peripheral regions, and the notions of backward, primitive, or undeveloped cultures. *Because* of that native resistance—for instance, the appearance of many nationalist and independence movements in India, the Caribbean, Africa, the Middle East—it is now evident that culture and imperialism in the West could be understood as offering support, each to the other. Here I referred to the extraordinary work of a whole range of non-Western writers and activists, including Tagore, Fanon, C. L. R. James, Yeats, and many others, figures who have given integrity to anti-imperialist cultural resistance.

The first question after my brief resumé was from a professor of history, a black woman of some eminence who had recently come to the university, but whose work was unfamiliar to me. She announced in advance that her question was to be hostile, "a very hostile one in fact." She then said something like the following: for the first thirteen pages of your paper you talked only about white European males. Thereafter, on page fourteen, you mention some names of non-Europeans. "How could you do such a thing?" I remonstrated somewhat, and tried to explain my argument in greater detail—after all, I said, I was discussing European imperialism, which would not have been likely to include in its discourse the work of African American women. I pointed out that in the book I say quite a bit about the response to imperialism all over the world; that point was a place in my argument where it would be pertinent to focus on the work of such writers as—and here I again mentioned the name of a great Caribbean writer and intellectual whose work has a special importance for my own—C. L. R. James. To this my critic replied with a stupefying confidence that my answer was not satisfactory since C. L. R. James was dead! I must admit that I was nonplussed by the severity of this pronouncement. James indeed *was* dead, a fact that needn't, to a historian, have made further discussion impossible. I waited for her to resume, hoping that she might expatiate on what she meant by having suggested that even in discussions of what dead white European males said on a given topic it was inappropriate to confine oneself to what they said while leaving out the work of living African American, Arab, and Indian writers.

But she did not proceed, and I was left to suppose that she considered her point sufficiently and conclusively made: I was guilty of not mentioning living non-European nonmales, even when it was not obvious to me or, I later gathered, to many members of the seminar, what their pertinence might have been. I noted to myself that my antagonist did not think it necessary to enumerate what specifically in the work of living non-Europeans I should have used, or which books and ideas by them she found important and relevant. All I had been given to work with was the asserted necessity to mention some approved names—which names did not really matter—as if the very act of uttering them was enough. I was also left unmistakably with the impression that as a nonwhite—a category incidentally to which as an Arab I myself belong—she was saying that to affirm the existence of non-European "others" took the place of evidence, argument, discussion.

It would be pointless to deny that the exchange was unsettling. Among other things I was chagrined at the distortions of my position and for having responded to the distortions so clumsily. It did not seem to matter that a great deal of my own work has concerned itself with just the kind of omission with which I was being charged. What apparently mattered now was that having contributed to an early trend, in which Western and European intellectuals were arraigned for having their work constructed out of the suffering and deprivations of so many people of color, I was now allegedly doing what such complicit intellectuals had always done. For if in one place you criticize the exclusion of Orientals, as I did in *Orientalism,* the exclusion of "others" from your work in another place becomes, on one level, difficult to justify or explain. I was disheartened not because I was being attacked, but because the general validity of the point made in *Orientalism* still obtained and yet was now being directed at me. It was *still* true that various Others—the word has acquired a sheen of modishness that has become extremely objectionable—were being represented unfairly, their reality distorted, their truth either denied or twisted with malice. Yet instead of joining in their behalf, I felt I was being asked to get involved in an inconsequential academic contest. I had wanted to say, but didn't, "Is all that matters about the issue of exclusion and misrepresentation the fact that *names* were left out? Why are you detaining us with such trivialities?"

To make matters worse, a few minutes later in the discussion I was attacked by a retired professor of Middle Eastern studies, himself an Orientalist. Like me, he was an Arab, but he had consistently identified himself with intellectual tendencies of which I had always been critical. He now intervened to defend imperialism, saying in tones of almost comic reverence, that it had accomplished things that natives couldn't have done for themselves. It had taught them, among other things, he said, how to appreciate the cuneiform and hieroglyphics of their own traditions. As he droned on about the imperial schools, railroads, hospitals, and telegraphs in the Third World that stood for examples of British and French largesse, the irony of the whole thing seemed overpowering. It appeared to me that there had to be something to say that surrendered neither to the caricatural reductiveness of the two positions by then arrayed against me, and against each other, nor to that verbal quality in each that was determined to remain ideologically correct and little else.

I was being reminded by such negative flat-minded examples of thinking, that the one thing that intellectuals *cannot* do without is the full intellectual process itself. Into it goes historically informed research as well as the presentation of a coherent and carefully argued line that has taken account of alternatives. In addition, there must be, it seems to me, a theoretical presumption that in matters having to do with human history and society any rigid theoretical ideal, any simple additive or mechanical notion of what is or is not factual, must yield to the central factor of human work, the actual participation of peoples in the making of human life. If that is so then it must also be true that, given the very nature of human work in the construction of human society and history, it is impossible to say of it that its products are so rarefied, so limited, so beyond comprehension as to exclude most other people, experiences, and histories. I mean further, that this kind of human work, which is intellectual work, is worldly, that it is situated in the world, and about that world. It is not about things that are so rigidly constricted and so forbiddingly arcane as to exclude all but an audience of likeminded, already fully convinced persons. While it would be stupid to deny the importance of constituencies and audiences in the construction of an intellectual argument, I think it has to be supposed that many arguments can be made to more than one audience and in different situations. Otherwise we would be dealing not with intellectual argument but either with dogma, or with a technological jargon designed specifically to repel all but a small handful of initiates or coteries.

Lest I fall into the danger myself of being too theoretical and specialized, I shall be more specific now and return to the episode I was discussing just a moment ago. At the heart of the imperial cultural enterprise I analyzed in *Orientalism* and also in my new book, was a politics of identity. That politics has needed to assume, indeed needed firmly to believe, that what was true about Orientals or Africans was *not* however true about or for Europeans. When a French or German scholar tried to identify the main characteristics of, for instance, the Chinese mind, the work was only partly intended to do that; it was also intended to show how different the Chinese mind was from the Western mind.

Such constructed things—they have only an elusive reality—as the Chinese mind or the Greek spirit have always been with us; they are at the source of a great deal that goes into the making of individual cultures, nations, traditions, and peoples. But in the modern world considerably greater attention has generally been given to such identities than was ever given in earlier historical periods, when the world was larger, more amorphous, less globalized. Today a fantastic emphasis is placed upon a politics of national identity, and to a very great degree, this emphasis is the result of the imperial experience. For when the great modern Western imperial expansion took place all across the world, beginning in the late eighteenth century, it accentuated the interaction between the identity of the French or the English and that of the colonized native peoples. And this mostly antagonistic interaction gave rise to a separation between people as members of homogenous races and exclusive nations that was and still is one of the characteristics of what can be called the epistemology of imperialism. At its core is the supremely stubborn thesis that everyone is principally and irreducibly a member of some race or category, and that race or category cannot ever be assimilated to or accepted by others—except as itself. Thus came into being such invented essences as the Oriental or Englishness, as Frenchness, Africanness, or American exceptionalism, as if each of those had a Platonic idea behind it that guaranteed it as pure and unchanging from the beginning to the end of time.

One product of this doctrine is nationalism, a subject so immense that I can treat it only very partially here. What interests me in the politics of identity that informed imperialism in its global phase is that just as natives were considered to belong to a different category—racial or geographical—from that of the Western white man, it also became true that in the great anti-imperialist revolt represented by decolonization this same category was mobilized around, and formed the resisting identity of, the revolutionaries. This was the case everywhere in the Third World. Its most celebrated instance is the concept of *négritude,* as developed intellectually and poetically by Aimé Césaire, Leopold Senghor, and, in English, W. E. B. Du Bois. If blacks had once been stigmatized and given inferior status to whites, then it has since become necessary not to deny blackness, and not to aspire to whiteness, but to accept and celebrate blackness, to give it the dignity of poetic as well as metaphysical status. Thus *négritude* acquired positive Being where before it had been a mark of degradation and inferiority. Much the same revaluation of the native particularity occurred in India, in many parts of the Islamic world, China, Japan, Indonesia, and the Philippines, where the denied or repressed native essence emerged as the focus of, and even the basis for, nationalist recovery.

It is important to note that much of the early cultural resistance to imperialism on which nationalism and independence movements were built was salutary and necessary. I see it essentially as an attempt on the part of oppressed people who had suffered the bondage of slavery, colonialism, and—most important—spiritual dispossession, to reclaim their identity. When that finally occurred in places such as Algeria, the grander nationalist efforts amounted to little short of a reconstructed communal political and cultural program of independence. Where the white man had once only seen lazy natives and exotic customs, the insurrection against imperialism produced, as in Ireland for example, a national revolt, along with political parties dedicated to independence, which, like the Congress party in India, was headed by nationalist figures, poets, and military heroes. There were remarkably impressive results from this vast effort at cultural reclamation, most of which are well known and celebrated.

But while the whole movement toward autonomy and independence produced in effect newly independent and separate states constituting the majority of new nations in the postcolonial world today, the nationalist politics of identity has nonetheless quickly proved itself to be insufficient for the ensuing period.

Inattentive or careless readers of Frantz Fanon, generally considered one of the two or three most eloquent apostles of anti-imperialist resistance, tend to forget his marked suspicions of unchecked nationalism. So while it is appropriate to draw attention to the early chapters on violence in *The Wretched of the Earth*, it should be noticed that in subsequent chapters he is sharply critical of what he called the pitfalls of national consciousness. He clearly meant this to be a paradox. And for the reason that while nationalism is a necessary spur to revolt against the colonizer, national consciousness must be immediately transformed into what he calls "social consciousness," just as soon as the withdrawal of the colonizer has been accomplished.

Fanon is scathing on the abuses of the postindependence nationalist party, on, for instance, the cult of the Grand Panjandrum (or maximum leader), or the centralization of the capital city, which Fanon said flatly needed to be deconsecrated, and most importantly, on the hijacking of common sense and popular participation by bureaucrats, technical experts, and jargon-wielding obfuscators. Well before V. S. Naipaul, Fanon was arguing against the politics of mimicry and separatism which produced the Mobutus, Idi Amins, and Saddams, as well as the grotesqueries and pathologies of power that gave rise to tyrannical states and praetorian guards while obstructing democratic freedoms in so many countries of the Third World. Fanon also prophesied the continuing dependency of numerous postcolonial governments and philosophies, all of which preached the sovereignty of the newly independent people of one or another new Third World state, and, having failed to make the transition from nationalism to true liberation, were in fact condemned to practice the politics, and the economics, of a new oppression as pernicious as the old one.

At bottom, what Fanon offers most compellingly is a critique of the separatism and mock autonomy achieved by a pure politics of identity that has lasted too long and been made to serve in situations where it has become simply inadequate. What invariably happens at the level of knowledge is that signs and symbols of freedom and status are taken for the reality; you want to be named and considered for the sake of being named and considered. In effect this really means that just to be an independent postcolonial Arab, or black, or Indonesian is not a program, nor a process, nor a vision. It is no more than a convenient starting point from which the real work, the hard work, might begin.

As for that work, it is nothing less than the reintegration of all those people and cultures, once confined and reduced to peripheral status, with the rest of the human race. After working through *négritude* in the early sections of *Cahier d'un retour*, Aimé Césaire states this vision of integration in his poem's climatic moment: "no race possesses the monopoly of beauty, of intelligence, of force, and there is a place for all at the rendez-vous of victory."

Without this concept of "place for all at the rendez-vous of victory," one is condemned to an impoverishing politics of knowledge based only upon the assertion and reassertion of identity, an ultimately uninteresting alternation of presence and absence. If you are weak, your affirmation of identity for its own sake amounts to little more than saying that you want a kind of attention easily and superficially granted, like the attention given an individual in a crowded room at a roll call. Once having such recognition, the subject has only to sit there silently as the proceedings unfold as if in his or her absence. And, on the other hand, though the powerful get acknowledged by the sheer force of presence, this commits them to a logic of displacement, as soon as someone else emerges who is as, or more, powerful.

This has proved a disastrous process, whether for postcolonials, forced to exist in a marginal and dependent place totally outside the circuits of world power, or for powerful societies, whose triumphalism and imperious willfulness have done so much to devastate and destabilize the world. What has been at issue between Iraq and the United States is precisely such a logic of exterminism and displacement, as unedifying as it is unproductive. It is risky, I know, to move from the realm of interpretation to the realm of world politics, but it seems to me true that the relationship between them is a real one, and the light that one realm can shed on the other is quite illuminating. In any case the politics of knowledge that is based principally on the affirmation of identity is very similar, is indeed directly related to, the unreconstructed nationalism that has guided so many postcolonial states today. It asserts a sort of separatism that wishes only to draw attention to itself; consequently it neglects the integration of that earned and achieved consciousness of self within "the rendez-vous of victory." On the national and on the intellectual level the problems are very similar.

Let me return therefore to one of the intellectual debates that has been central to the humanities in the past decade, and which underlies the episode with which I began. The ferment in minority, subaltern, feminist, and postcolonial consciousness has resulted in so many salutary achievements in the curricular and theoretical approach to the study of the humanities as quite literally to have produced a Copernican revolution in all traditional fields of inquiry. Eurocentrism has been challenged definitively; most scholars and students in the contemporary American academy are now aware, as they were never aware before, that society and culture have been the heterogenous product of heterogenous people in an enormous variety of cultures, traditions, and situations. No longer does T.S. Eliot's idea of the great Western masterpieces enduring together in a constantly redefining pattern of monuments have its old authority; nor do the sorts of patterns elucidated with such memorable brilliance in formative works like *Mimesis* or *The Anatomy of Criticism* have the same cogency for today's student or theorist as they did even quite recently.

And yet the great contest about the canon continues. The success of Allan Bloom's *The Closing of the American Mind,* the subsequent publication of such works as Alvin Kernan's *The Death of Literature,* and Roger Kimball's *Tenured Radicals* as well as the rather posthumous energies displayed in journals like *The American Scholar* (now a neoconservative magazine), *The New Criterion,* and *Commentary*—all this suggests that the work done by those of us who have tried to widen the area of awareness in the study of culture is scarcely finished or secure. But our point, in my opinion, cannot be simply and obdurately to reaffirm the paramount importance of formerly suppressed or silenced forms of knowledge and leave it at that, nor can it be to surround ourselves with the sanctimonious piety of historical or cultural victimhood as a way of making our intellectual presence felt. Such strategies are woefully insufficient. The whole effort to deconsecrate Eurocentrism cannot be interpreted, least of all by those who participate in the enterprise, as an effort to supplant Eurocentrism with, for instance, Afrocentric or Islamocentric approaches. On its own, ethnic particularity does not provide for intellectual process—quite the contrary. At first, you will recall, it was a question, for some, of adding Jane Austen to the canon of male Western writers in humanities courses; then it became a matter of displacing the entire canon of American writers like Hawthorne and Emerson with best-selling writers of the same period like Harriet Beecher Stowe and Susan Warner. But after that the logic of displacement became even more attenuated, and the mere names of politically validated living writers became more important than anything about them or their works.

I submit that these clamorous dismissals and swooping assertions are in fact caricatural reductions of what the great revisionary gestures of feminism, subaltern or black studies, and anti-imperialist resistance originally intended. For such gestures it was never a matter of replacing one set of authorities and dogmas with another, nor of substituting one center for another. It was always a matter of opening and participating in a central strand of intellectual and cultural effort and of showing what had always been, though indiscernibly, a part of it, like the work of women, or of blacks and servants—but which had been either denied or derogated. The power and interest of—to give two examples particularly dear to me—Tayib Salih's *Season of Migration to the North* is not only how it memorably describes the quandary of a gifted young Sudanese who has lived in London but then returns home to his ancestral village alongside the Nile; the novel is also a rewriting of Conrad's *Heart of Darkness,* seen now as the tale of someone who voyages into the heart of light, which is modern Europe, and discovers there what had been hidden deep within him. To read the Sudanese writer is of course to interpret an Arabic novel written during the late sixties at a time of nationalism and a rejection of the West. The novel is therefore affiliated with other Arabic novels of the postwar period including the works of Mahfouz and Idriss; but given the historical and political meaning of a narrative that quite deliberately recalls and reverses Conrad—something impossible for a black man at the time *Heart of Darkness* was written—Tayib Salih's masterpiece is necessarily to be viewed as, along with other African, Indian, and Caribbean works, enlarging, widening, refining the scope of a narrative form at the center of which had heretofore always been an exclusively European observer or center of consciousness.

There is an equally complex resonance to Ghassan Kanafani's *Men in the Sun,* a compelling novella about the travails of three Palestinian refugees who are trying to get from Basra in Iraq to Kuwait. Their past in Palestine is evoked in order to contrast it with the poverty and dispossession of which they are victims immediately after 1948. When they find a man in Basra whose occupation is in part to smuggle refugees across the border in the belly of his empty watertruck, they strike a deal with him, and he takes them as far as the border post where he is detained in conversation in the hot sun. They die of asphyxiation, unheard and forgotten. Kanafani's novella belongs to the genre of immigrant literature contributed to by an estimable number of postwar writers—Rushdie, Naipaul, Berger, Kundera, and others. But it is also a poignant meditation on the Palestinian fate, and of course eerily prescient about Palestinians in the current Gulf crisis. And yet it would do the subject of the work and its literary merit an extraordinary disservice were we to confine it to the category of national allegory, to see in it only a mirroring of the actual plight of Palestinians in exile. Kanafani's work is literature connected both to its specific historical and cultural situations as well as to a whole world of other literatures and formal articulations, which the attentive reader summons to mind as the interpretation proceeds.

The point I am trying to make can be summed up in the useful notion of worldliness. By linking works to each other we bring them out of the neglect and secondariness to which for all kinds of political and ideological reasons they had previously been condemned. What I am talking about therefore is the opposite of separatism, and also the reverse of exclusivism. It is only through the scrutiny of these works as literature, as style, as pleasure and illumination, that they can be brought in, so to speak, and kept in. Otherwise they will be regarded only as informative ethnographic specimens, suitable for the limited attention of experts and area specialists. *Worldliness* is therefore the restoration to such works and interpretations of their place in the global setting, a restoration that can only be accomplished by an appreciation not of some tiny, defensively constituted corner of the world, but of the large, many-windowed house of human culture as a whole.

It seems to me absolutely essential that we engage with cultural works in this unprovincial, interested manner while maintaining a strong sense of the contest for forms and values which any decent cultural work embodies, realizes, and contains. A great deal of recent theoretical speculation has proposed that works of literature are completely determined as such by their situation, and that readers themselves are totally determined in their responses by their respective cultural situations, to a point where no value, no reading, no interpretation can be anything other than the merest reflection of some immediate interest. All readings and all writing are reduced to an assumed historical emanation. Here the indeterminacy of deconstructive reading, the airy insouciance of postaxiological criticism, the casual reductiveness of some (but by no means all) ideological schools are principally at fault. While it is true to say that because a text is the product of an unrecapturable past, and that contemporary criticism can to some extent afford a neutral disengagement or opposed perspective impossible for the text in its own time, there is no reason to take the further step and exempt the interpreter from *any* moral, political, cultural, or psychological commitments. All of these remain in play. The attempt to read a text in its fullest and most integrative context commits the reader to positions that are educative, humane, and engaged, positions that depend on training and taste and not simply on a technologized professionalism, or on the tiresome playfulness of "postmodern" criticism, with its repeated disclaimers of anything but local games and pastiches. Despite Lyotard and his acolytes, we are still in the era of large narratives, of horrendous cultural clashes, and of appallingly destructive war—as witness the recent conflagration in the Gulf—and to say that we are against theory, or beyond literature, is to be blind and trivial.

I am not arguing that every interpretive act is equivalent to a gesture either for or against life. How could anyone defend or attack so crudely general a position? I am saying that once we grant intellectual work the right to exist in a relatively disengaged atmosphere, and allow it a status that isn't disqualified by partisanship, we ought then to reconsider the ties between the text and the world in a serious and uncoercive way. Far from repudiating the great advances made when Eurocentrism and patriarchy began to be demystified, we should consolidate these advances, using them so as to reach a better understanding of the degree to which literature and artistic genius belong to and are some part of the world where all of us also do other kinds of work.

This wider application of the ideas I've been discussing cannot even be attempted if we simply repeat a few names or refer to a handful of approved texts ritualistically or sanctimoniously. Victimhood, alas, does not guarantee or necessarily enable an enhanced sense of humanity. To testify to a history of oppression is necessary, but it is not sufficient unless that history is redirected into intellectual process and universalized to include all sufferers. Yet too often testimony to oppression becomes only a justification for further cruelty and inhumanity, or for high sounding cant and merely "correct" attitudes. I have in mind, for instance, not only the antagonists mentioned at the beginning of this essay but also the extraordinary behavior of an Elie Wiesel who has refused to translate the lessons of his own past into consistent criticisms of Israel for doing what it has done and is doing right now to Palestinians.

So while it is not necessary to regard every reading or interpretation of a text as the moral equivalent of a war or a political crisis it does seem to me to be important to underline the fact that whatever else they are, works of literature are not merely texts. They are in fact differently constituted and have different values, they aim to do different things, exist in different genres, and so on. One of the great pleasures for those who read and study literature is the discovery of long-standing norms in which all cultures known to me concur: such things as style and performance, the existence of good as well as lesser writers, and the exercise of preference. What has been most unacceptable during the many harangues on both sides of the so-called Western canon debate is that so many of the combatants have ears of tin, and are unable to distinguish between good writing and politically correct attitudes, as if a fifth-rate pamphlet and a great novel have more or less the same significance. Who benefits from leveling attacks on the canon? Certainly not the disadvantaged person or class whose history, if you bother to read it at all, is full of evidence that popular resistance to injustice has always derived immense benefits from literature and culture in general, and very few from invidious distinctions made between ruling-class and subservient cultures. After all, the crucial lesson of C. L. R. James's *Black Jacobins,* or of E. P. Thompson's *Making of the English Working Class* (with its reminder of how important Shakespeare was to nineteenth-century radical culture), is that great antiauthoritarian uprisings made their earliest advances, not by denying the humanitarian and universalist claims of the general dominant culture, but by attacking the adherents of that culture for failing to uphold their own declared standards, for failing to extend them to all, as opposed to a small fraction, of humanity. Toussaint L'Ouverture is the perfect example of a downtrodden slave whose struggle to free himself and his people was informed by the ideas of Rousseau and Mirabeau.

Although I risk oversimplification, it is probably correct to say that it does not finally matter *who* wrote what, but rather *how* a work is written and *how* it is read. The idea that because Plato and Aristotle are male and the products of a slave society they should be disqualified from receiving contemporary attention is as limited an idea as suggesting that *only* their work, because it was addressed to and about elites, should be read today. Marginality and homelessness are not, in my opinion, to be gloried in; they are to be brought to an end, so that more, and not fewer, people can enjoy the benefits of what has for centuries been denied the victims of race, class, or gender.

Stanley Fish (1938–)

Stanley Fish is one of the most provocative and influential literary scholars and critical theorists in the United States. One hardly knows where to start when enumerating Fish's accomplishments. Does one begin with his influential scholarship on John Milton and Renaissance literature? How about with his reader-response theories? Or should one foreground Fish's neopragmatist approaches to sense making and questions of belief? As if these accomplishments were not enough, Fish is also a legal scholar and theorist. In the selection given next, "Rhetoric," Fish surveys attitudes for and against a topic that has elicited both praise and blame at least since the time of Plato's Socratic dialogues. Perhaps Fish has been so influential precisely because of his own rhetorical skills.

Fish was born in Providence, Rhode Island, went to college at the University of Pennsylvania, and received his Ph.D. from Yale University. He has taught English at the University of California at Berkeley, Johns Hopkins University, and Duke University. Most recently, Fish has served as the dean of arts and sciences at the University of Illinois at Chicago. Fish's books include *Surprised by Sin: The Reader in "Paradise Lost"* (1967), *Self-Consuming Artifacts: The Experience of Seventeenth-Century Literature* (1972), *Is There a Text in This Class? The Authority of Interpretive Communities* (1980), and *Doing What Comes Naturally: Change, Rhetoric, and the Practice of Theory in Literary and Legal Studies* (1989). The next reading selection, "Rhetoric," comes from *Doing What Comes Naturally.*

Rhetoric

> ... up rose
> *Belial,* in act more graceful and humane;
> A fairer person lost not Heav'n; he seem'd
> For dignity compos'd and high exploit:
> But all was false and hollow; though his Tongue
> Dropt Manna, and could make the worse appear
> The better reason, to perplex and dash
> Maturest counsels: for his thoughts were low; ...

> . . . yet he pleas'd the ear,
> And with persuasive accent thus began.
>
> *Paradise Lost*, II, 108–15, 117–18

I

For Milton's seventeenth-century readers this passage, introducing one of the more prominent of the fallen angels, would have been immediately recognizable as a brief but trenchant essay on the art and character of the rhetorician. Indeed, in these few lines Milton has managed to gather and restate with great rhetorical force (a paradox of which more later) all of the traditional arguments against rhetoric. Even Belial's gesture of rising is to the (negative) point: he catches the eye even before he begins to speak, just as Satan will in book IX when he too raises himself and moves so that "each part, / Motion, each act won audience ere the tongue" (673–74). That is, he draws attention to his appearance, to his surface, and the suggestion of superficiality (a word to be understood in its literal meaning) extends to the word "act"; that is, that which can be seen. That act is said to be "graceful," the first in a succession of double meanings (one of the stigmatized attributes of rhetorical speech) we find in the passage. Belial is precisely *not* full of grace; that is simply his outward aspect, and the same is true for "humane" and "fairer." The verse's judgment on all of his apparent virtues is delivered in the last two words of line 110—"he seem'd"—and the shadow of "seeming" falls across the next line which in isolation might "seem" to be high praise. But under the pressure of what precedes it, the assertion of praise undoes itself with every Janus-faced word (the verse now begins to imitate the object of its criticism by displaying a pervasive disjunction between its outer and inner meanings; indicting seeming, it itself repeatedly seems): "compos'd" now carries its pejorative meaning of affected or made-up; "high" at once refers to the favored style of bombastic orators and awaits its ironic and demeaning contrast with the lowness of his thoughts; "dignity" is an etymological joke, for Belial is anything but worthy; in fact, he is just what the next line says he is, "false and hollow," an accusation that repeats one of the perennial antirhetorical topoi, that rhetoric, the art of fine speaking, is all show, grounded in nothing but its own empty pretensions, unsupported by any relation to truth. "There is no need," declares Socrates in Plato's *Gorgias*, "for rhetoric to know the facts at all, for it has hit upon a means of persuasion that enables it to appear in the eyes of the ignorant to know more than those who really know" (459),[1] and in the *Phaedrus* the title figure admits that the "man who plans to be an orator" need not "learn what is really just and true, but only what seems so to the crowd" (260).[2]

This reference to the vulgar popular ear indicates that rhetoric's deficiencies are not only epistemological (sundered from truth and fact) and moral (sundered from true knowledge and sincerity) but social: it panders to the worst in people and moves them to base actions, exactly as Belial is said to do in the next famous run-on statement, "and could make the worse appear/The better reason." This is an explicit reference to a nest of classical sources: the most familiar is Aristotle, *Rhetoric*, II, 1402, 23, condemning the skill of being able to make arguments on either side of a question: "This . . . illustrates what is meant by making the worse argument appear the better. Hence people were right in objecting to the training Protagoras undertook to give them."[3] Socrates makes the same point in the *Phaedrus*: "an orator who knows nothing about good or evil undertakes to persuade a city in the same state of ignorance . . . by recommending evil as though it were good" (260). Behind Belial (or descending from him; the direction of genealogy in *Paradise Lost* is always problematic) is the line of sophists— Protagoras, Hippias, Gorgias, shadowy figures known to us mostly through the writings of Plato where they appear always as relativist foils for the idealistic Socrates. The judgment made on them by a philosophic tradition dominated by Plato is the judgment here made on Belial; their thoughts were low, centered on the suspect skills they taught for hire; the danger they represented is the danger Belial represents: despite the lowness of their thoughts, perhaps *because* of the lowness of their thoughts, they pleased the ear, at least the ear of the promiscuous crowd (there is always just beneath the surface of the antirhetorical stance a powerful and corrosive elitism), and the explanation of their unfortunate success is the power Belial now begins to exercise, the power of "persuasive accent." Encoded in this phrase is a continuing debate about the essence of rhetoric, a debate whose two poles are represented by Gorgias's praise in the *Encomium of Helen* of rhetoric as an irresistible force and the stoic Cato's characterization of the rhetorician as a good man skilled at speaking *("vir bonus, dicendi peritus")*. The difference is that for Gorgias the skill is detached from any necessary moral center and represents a self-sustaining power ("persuasion allied to words can mould men's minds"), while for Cato the skill is a by-product of a focus on goodness and truth (thus the other of his famous aphorisms, "seize the thing, the words will follow"—*"rem tene, verba sequentur"*—which later flowers in the Renaissance distinction between res et verba.[4] In one position eloquence is the hard-won creation of a special and technical facility, a facility one acquires by mastering a set of complicated—and morally neutral—rules; in the other eloquence is what naturally issues when a man is in close touch with the Truth and allows it to inspire him. Born, it would seem, in a posture of defensiveness, rhetoric has often gravitated toward this latter view in an effort to defuse the charge that it is amoral. Quintilian's formulation (itself gathered from the writings of Cicero) is one that will later be echoed in countless treatises: "no man can speak well who is not good himself" *("bene dicere non possit nisi bonus," Institutes, II, xv, 34)*. As a defense, however, this declaration has the disadvantage of implying the superfluousness of rhetoric, an implication fully realized in Augustine's *On Christian Doctrine* where eloquence is so much subordinated to wisdom that it disappears as a distinct and separable property. Belial, in contrast, is wholly defined by that property, by his ability to produce "persuasive accents." "Accent" here is a powerfully resonant word, one of whose relevant meanings is "mode of utterance peculiar to an individual, locality or nation" (OED). He who speaks "in accent" speaks from a particular *angled* perspective into which he tries to draw his auditors: he also speaks in the rhythms of song (etymologically, accent means "song added to speech") which as Milton will soon observe *"charms* the sense" (II, 556). "Persuasive accent," then, is almost a redundancy: the two words mean the same thing and what they tell the reader is that he is about to be exposed to a force whose exercise is unconstrained by any sense of responsibility either to the Truth or to the Good. Indeed, so dangerous does Milton consider this force that he feels it necessary to provide a corrective gloss as soon as Belial stops speaking: "Thus *Belial* with words cloth'd in reason's garb/Counsell'd ignoble ease and peaceful sloth" (II, 226–27). Just in case you hadn't noticed.

I have lingered so long over this passage because we can extrapolate from it almost all of the binary oppositions in relation to which rhetoric has received its (largely negative) definition: inner/outer, deep/surface, essential/peripheral, unmediated/mediated, clear/colored, necessary/contingent, straightforward/angled, abiding/fleeting, reason/passion, things/words, realities/illusions, fact/opinion, neutral/partisan. Underlying this list, which is by no means exhaustive, are three basic oppositions: first, between a truth that exists independently of all perspectives and points of view and the many truths that emerge and seem perspicuous when a particular perspective or point of view has been established and is in force; second, an opposition between true knowledge, which is knowledge as it exists apart from any and all systems of belief, and the knowledge, which because it flows from some or other system of belief, is incomplete and partial (in the sense of biased); and third, an opposition between a self or consciousness that is turned outward in an effort to apprehend and attach itself to truth and true knowledge and a self or consciousness that is turned inward in the direction of its own prejudices, which, far from being transcended, continue to inform its every word and action. Each of these oppositions is attached in turn to an opposition between two kinds of language: on the one hand, language that faithfully reflects or reports on matters of fact uncolored by any personal or partisan agenda or desire; and on the other hand, language that is infected by partisan agendas and desires, and therefore colors and distorts the facts which it purports to reflect. It is use of the second kind of language that makes one a rhetorician, while adherence to the first kind makes one a seeker after truth and an objective observer of the way things are. It is this distinction that, as Thomas Kuhn notes, underwrites the claims of science to be a privileged form of discourse because it has recourse to a "neutral observation language,"[5] a language uninflected by any mediating presuppositions or preconceptions; and it is the same distinction that informs Aristotle's observation (*Rhetoric*, III, 1404, 13) that "Nobody uses fine language when teaching geometry." The language of geometry—of formal rules with no substantive content—is contrasted by Aristotle to all those languages that are intended only to "charm the hearer," the languages of manipulation, deception, and self-consciously deployed strategy.

It is this understanding of linguistic possibilities and dangers that generates a succession of efforts to construct a language from which all perspectival bias (a redundant phrase) has been eliminated, efforts that have sometimes taken as a model the notations of mathematics, at other times the operations of logic, and more recently the purely formal calculations of a digital computer. Whether it issues in the elaborate linguistic machines of seventeenth-century "projectors" like Bishop Wilkins (*An Essay Towards a Real Character and a Philosophical*

Language, 1668), or in the building (à la Chomsky) of a "competence" model of language abstracted from any particular performance, or in the project of Esperanto or some other artificial language claiming universality,[6] or in the fashioning of a Habermasian "ideal speech situation" in which all assertions express "a 'rational will' in relation to a common interest ascertained without deception,"[7] the impulse behind the effort is always the same: to establish a form of communication that escapes partiality and aids us in first determining and then affirming what is absolutely and objectively true, a form of communication that in its structure and operations is the very antithesis of rhetoric, of passionate partisan discourse.

That desideratum and the fears behind it have received countless articulations, but never have they been articulated with more precision than in these sentences from Bishop Sprat's *History of the Royal Society of London,* 1667:

> When I consider the means of *happy living,* and the causes of their *corruption,* I can hardly forbear . . . concluding that *eloquence* ought to be banish'd out of all *civil societies,* as a thing fatal to Peace and good Manners. . . . They [the ornaments of speaking] are in open defiance against *Reason;* professing not to hold much correspondence with that; but with its slaves, the *Passions:* they give the mind a motion too changeable, and bewitching, to consist with *right practice.* Who can behold without indignation, how many mists and uncertainties, these specious *Tropes* and *Figures* have brought on our Knowledge? How many rewards, which are due to more profitable, and difficult arts, have been snatch'd away by the easie vanity of *fine speaking?* (pp. 111–13)

The terms of banishment are exactly those invoked by Plato against the poets in book X of his *Republic:* Homer, Socrates says, may be "the most poetic of poets and the first of tragedians, but we must know the truth [and] we can admit no poetry into our city save only hymns to the gods and the praises of good men; for if you grant admission to the honeyed Muse . . . pleasure and pain will be lords of your city instead of law and that which shall . . . have approved itself to the general reason as the best" (607a). The "honeyed muse" is precisely what Belial becomes when his tongue drops Manna (113), a quintessentially idolatrous act in which he substitutes his own word for the word sent down to us by God and therefore deprives us of the direction that God's word might have given us. Although the transition from classical to Christian thought is marked by many changes, one thing that does not change is the status of rhetoric in relation to a foundational vision of truth and meaning. Whether the center of that vision is a personalized deity or an abstract geometric reason, rhetoric is the force that pulls us away from that center and into its own world of ever-shifting shapes and shimmering surfaces.

Of course, the allure of surfaces and shapes, of "specious *Tropes* and *Figures,*" would not be felt if there were not something already in us that inclined to it. Rhetoric may be a danger that assaults us from without, but its possible success is a function of an *inner* weakness. The entire art, as Aristotle explains regretfully, is predicated on "the defect of our hearers" (*Rhetoric,* III, 1404, 8), on the assumption that members of the audience will be naturally susceptible to the rhetorician's appeal. The anti-rhetorical stance can only be coherent if it posits an *in*coherence at the heart (literally) of the self that is both rhetoric victim and its source. That self is always presented as divided, as the site of contesting forces; in Christian terms the forces are named the carnal and the spiritual; in secular psychologies the names are passed and reason or the willful and the rational; but whatever the names, the result is a relationship of homology between the inner and outer landscapes, both of which contain a core element of truth and knowledge that is continually threatened by a penumbra of irrationality.[8] If tropes and figures "give the mind a motion too changeable," it is because the principle of change, in the form of the passions, already lives in the mind, and it follows then that banishing eloquence and the poets from your republic will only do half the job. As Miltion puts it in the *Areopagitica,* "they are not skillful considerers of human things who imagine to remove sin by removing the matter of sin";[9] policing the outer landscape will be of little effect if the inner landscape remains host to the enemy, to sin, to error, to show.

It is the view of the anti-rhetoricians that this double task of inner and outer regulation can be accomplished by linguistic reform, by the institution of conditions of communication that at once protect discourse from the irrelevancies and contingencies that would compromise its universality and insulate the discoursing mind from those contingencies and irrelevancies it itself harbors. Wilkins proposes to fashion a language that will admit neither *Superfluities*—plural signifiers of a single signified, more than one word for a particular thing—nor *Equivocal*—signifiers doing multiple duty, single words that refer to several things—nor *Metaphor*—a form of speech that interposes itself between the observer and the referent and therefore contributes "to the disguising of it with false appearances" (pp. 17–18). The idea is that such language, purged of ambiguity, redundancy, and indirection, will be an appropriate instrument for the registering of an independent reality, and that if men will only submit themselves to that language and remain within the structure of its stipulated definitions and exclusions, they will be incapable of formulating and expressing wayward, subjective thoughts and will cease to be a danger either to themselves or to those who hearken to them. In this way, says Wilkins, they will be returned to that original state in which the language spoken was the language God gave Adam, a language in which every word perfectly expressed its referent (on the model of Adam's simultaneously understanding the nature of the animals and conferring upon them their names), a language that in the course of time and "emergencies" has unfortunately "admitted various and *casual alterations*" (p. 19).

In the twentieth century Wilkins's program is echoed point for point (absent the theological scaffolding) by Rudolf Carnap: Carnap would admit into the lexicon only words that can be tied firmly to "protocol" or "observation" sentences, sentences that satisfy certain truth conditions and are therefore verifiable by reference to the facts of the world. The stipulation of this criterion, Carnap asserts, "takes away one's freedom to decide what one wishes to 'mean' by [a] word."[10] The freedom of individual speakers and hearers would be further taken away if the words of a verifiable lexicon were embedded in a grammar that "corresponded exactly to logical syntax," for if that were the case "pseudo-statements could not arise" (p.68). That is, no one could be misled either by the words of another or by that part of his consciousness inclined to wander from the path of truth; the tendency of language to perform in excess of its proper duty—to report or reflect matters of fact—would be curbed in advance, and the mind's susceptibility to the power of a language unconstrained by its empirical moorings would be neutralized. In short, the danger posed by rhetoric, both to the field of discourse and the discoursing consciousness, would have been eliminated. Of course, there are important differences to be noted between the idealism of Plato, the antienthusiasm of a Restoration bishop, and the logical positivism of a member of the Vienna Circle, but together (and in the company of countless others) they stand on the same side of a quarrel that Plato was already calling "old" in the fifth century before Christ. That quarrel, the quarrel between philosophy and rhetoric, survives every sea change in the history of Western thought, continually presenting us with the (skewed) choice between the plain unvarnished truth straightforwardly presented and the powerful but insidious appeal of "fine language," language that has transgressed the limits of representation and substituted its own forms for the forms of reality.[11]

II

To this point my presentation has been as skewed as this choice, because it has suggested that rhetoric has received only negative characterizations. In fact, there have always been friends of rhetoric, from the sophists to the antifoundationalists of the present day, and in response to the realist critique they have devised (and repeated) a number of standard defenses. Two of these defenses are offered by Aristotle in the *Rhetoric*. First, he defines rhetoric as a faculty or art whose practice will help us to observe "in any given case the available means of persuasion" (I, 1355, 27) and points out that as a faculty it is not in and of itself inclined away from truth. Of course, bad men may abuse it, but that after all "is a charge which may be made in common against all good things." "What makes a man a 'sophist,'" he declares, "is not his faculty, but his moral purpose" (I, 1355, 17). To the anticipated objection that rhetoric's potential for misuse is a reason for eschewing it, Aristotle replies that it is sometimes a necessary adjunct to the cause of truth, first, because if we leave the art to be cultivated by deceivers, they will lead truth-seekers astray, and, second, because, regrettable though it may be, "before some audiences not even the possession of the exactest knowledge will make it easy for what we say to produce conviction" and on those occasions "we must use, as our modes of persuasion and argument, notions possessed by everybody" (I, 1355, 27). That is, because of the defects of our hearers the truth itself must often be rhetorically dressed so that it will gain acceptance.[12]

Aristotle's second defense is more aggressively positive and responds directly to one of the most damaging characterizations of rhetoric: "We must be able to employ persuasion, just as strict reasoning can be employed, on opposite sides of a question, not in order that we may in practice employ it in both ways (for we must not make people believe what is wrong), but in order that we may see clearly what the facts are" (I, 1355, 28–33). In short, properly used, rhetoric is a heuristic, helping us not to distort the facts, but to discover them; moreover, adds Aristotle, the setting forth of contrary views of a matter will have the beneficial effect of showing us which of those views most accords with the truth because "the underlying facts do not lend themselves equally well to the contrary views." By this argument, as Peter Dixon has pointed out, Aristotle "removes rhetoric from the realm of the haphazard and the fanciful"[13] and rejoins it to that very realm of which it was said to be the great subverter.

But if this is the strength of Aristotle's defense, it is also its weakness, for in making it he reinforces the very assumptions in relation to which rhetoric will always be suspect, assumptions of an independent reality whose outlines can be perceived by a sufficiently clear-eyed observer who can then represent them in a transparent verbal medium. The stronger defense, because it hits at the heart of the opposing tradition, is one that embraces the accusations of that tradition and makes of them a claim. The chief accusation, as we have seen, is that rhetoricians hold "the probable (or likely-seeming, plausible) in more honour than the true" (*Phaedrus*, 267a). The sophist response is to assert that the realm of the probable—of what is likely to be so given particular conditions within some local perspective—is the only relevant realm of consideration for human beings. The argument is contained in two statements attributed famously to Protagoras. The first declares the unavailability (not the unreality) of the gods: "About gods I cannot say either that they are or that they are not."[14] And the second follows necessarily from the absence of godly guidance: "Man is the measure of all things, of the things that are that they are, and of the things that are not that they are not" (quoted in Plato, *Theaetetus*, 152a). What this means, as W. K. C. Guthrie has pointed out, is "that the Sophists recognized only accidental as opposed to essential being, . . . the conditional and relative as opposed to the self-existent."[15] This is not to say that the categories of the true and good are abandoned, but that in different contexts they will be filled differently and that there exists no master context (for that could only be occupied by the unavailable gods) from the vantage point of which the differences could be assessed and judged.

The result is to move rhetoric from the disreputable periphery to the necessary center: for if the highest truth for any man is what he believes it to be (*Theaetetus*, 152a), the skill which produces belief and therefore establishes what, in a particular time and particular place, is true, is the skill essential to the building and maintaining of a civilized society. In the absence of a revealed truth, rhetoric is that skill, and in teaching it the sophists were teaching "the one thing that mattered, how to take care of one's own affairs and the business of the state."[16] The rhetorician is like a physician; it is his job "to diagnose the particular institution and prescribe the best course of action for a man or a state under given conditions"[17] (see Plato, *Theaetetus*, 167b-d, *Protagoras*, 318e-19a); and when Socrates asks Protagoras if he is "promising to make men good citizens," the reply is firm: "That . . . is exactly what I profess to do" (*Protagoras*, 319a). Of course, in this context words like "good" and "best" do not have the meanings a Plato or Socrates would want them to have—good and best in any and all circumstances; rather, they refer to what would appear to be the better of the courses that seem available in what are generally understood to be the circumstantial constraints of a particular situation; but since, according to the sophist view, particular situations are the only kind there are, circumstantial determinations of what is good are as good as you're going to get.

That is, as I have already said, the strongest of the defenses rhetoric has received because it challenges the basic premise of the anti-rhetorical stance, the premise that any discourse must be measured against a stable and independent reality. To the accusation that rhetoric deals only with the realms of the probable and contingent and forsakes truth, the sophists and their successors respond that truth itself is a contingent affair and assumes a different shape in the light of differing local urgencies and the convictions associated with them. "Truth was individual and temporary, not universal and lasting, for the truth for any man was . . . what he could be persuaded of."[18] Not only does this make rhetoric— the art of analyzing and presenting local exigencies—a form of discourse no one can afford to ignore, it renders the opposing discourse—formal philosophy— beside the point. This is precisely Isocrates' thesis in his *Antidosis*. Abstract studies like geometry and astronomy, he says, do not have any "useful application either to private or public affairs; . . . after they are learned . . . they do not attend us through life nor do they lend aid in what we do, but are wholly divorced from our necessities."[19] Indeed, he goes so far as to deny to such disciplines the label "philosophy," for "I hold that man to be wise who is able by his powers of conjecture to arrive generally at the best course, and I hold that man to be a philosopher who occupies himself with the studies from which he will most quickly gain that kind of insight"(p. 271). Men who want to do some good in the world, he concludes, "must banish utterly from their interests all vain speculations and all activities which have no bearing on our lives."

What Isocrates does (at least rhetorically) is shift the balance of power between philosophy and rhetoric by putting philosophy on the defensive. This same strategy is pursued after him by Cicero and Quintilian, the most influential of the Roman rhetoricians. In the opening pages of his *De Inventione* Cicero elaborates the myth that will subsequently be invoked in every defense of humanism and belles lettres. There was a time, he says, when "men wandered at large in the field like animals," and there was "as yet no ordered system of religious worship nor of social duties."[20] It was then that a "great and wise" man "assembled and gathered" his uncivilized brothers and "introduced them to every useful and honorable occupation, though they cried out against it at first because of its novelty." Nevertheless, he gained their attention through "reason and eloquence" (*"propter rationem atque orationem"*) and by these means he "transformed them from wild savages into a kind and gentle folk." Nor would it have been possible, Cicero adds, to have "turned men . . . from their habits" if wisdom had been "mute and voiceless"; only "a speech at the same time powerful and entrancing could have induced one who had great physical strength to submit to justice without violence." From that time on, "many cities have been founded, . . . the flames of a multitude of wars have been extinguished, and . . . the strongest alliances and most sacred friendships have been formed not only by the use of reason, but also more easily by the use of eloquence" (I, 1). Whereas in the foundationalist story an original purity (of vision, purpose, procedure) is corrupted when rhetoric's siren song proves too sweet, in Cicero's story (later to be echoed by countless others)[21] all the human virtues, and indeed humanity itself, are wrested by the arts of eloquence from a primitive and violent state of nature. Significantly (and this is a point to which we shall return), both stories are stories of power, rhetoric's power; it is just that in one story that power must be resisted lest civilization fall, while in the other that power brings order and a genuine political process where before there was only the rule of "physical strength."

The contrast between the two stories can hardly be exaggerated because what is at stake is not simply a matter of emphasis or priority (as it seems to be in Aristotle's effort to demonstrate an *alliance* between rhetoric and truth) but a difference in worldviews. The quarrel between rhetorical and foundational thought is itself foundational; its content is a disagreement about the basic constituents of human activity and about the nature of human nature itself. In Richard Lanham's helpful terms, it is a disagreement as to whether we are members of the species *homo seriosus* or *homo rhetoricus*. *Homo seriosus* or Serious Man

> possesses a central self, an irreducible identity. These selves combine into a single, homogeneously real society which constitutes a referent reality for the men living in it. This referent society is in turn contained in a physical nature itself referential, standing "out there" independent of man. Man has invented language to communicate with his fellow man. He communicates facts and concepts about both nature and society. He can also communicate a third category of response, emotions. When he is communicating facts or concepts, success is measured by something we call *clarity*. When he is communicating feelings, success is measured by something we call *sincerity, faithfulness to the self* who is doing the feeling.[22]

Homo rhetoricus or rhetorical man, on the other hand,

> is an actor; his reality public, dramatic. His sense of identity, depends on the reassurance of daily histrionic reenactment. He is thus centered in time and concrete local event. The lowest common denominator of his life is a social situation. . . . He assumes a natural agility in changing orientations. . . . From birth, almost, he has dwelt not in a single value-structure but in several. He is thus committed to no single construction of the world; much rather, to prevailing in the game at hand. . . . He accepts the present paradigm and explores its resources. Rhetorical man is trained not to discover reality but to manipulate it. Reality is what is accepted as reality, what is useful. (p. 4)

As rhetorical man manipulates reality, establishing through his words the imperatives and urgencies to which he and his fellows must respond, he manipulates or fabricates himself, simultaneously conceiving of and occupying the roles that become first possible and then mandatory given the social structure his rhetoric has put in place. By exploring the available means of persuasion in a particular situation, he tries them on, and as they begin to suit him, he becomes them.[23] "I hold," says Isocrates, "that people can become better and worthier if they conceive an ambition to speak well," for in the setting forth of his position the orator "will select from all the actions of men . . . those examples which are the most illustrious and the most edifying; and habituating himself to contemplate and appraise such examples, he will feel their influence not only in the preparation of a given discourse but in all the actions of his life" (pp. 275, 277). What serious man fears—the invasion of the fortress of essence by the contingent, the protean, and the unpredictable—is what rhetorical man celebrates and incarnates. In the philosopher's vision of the world rhetoric (and representation in general) is merely the (disposable) form by which a prior and substantial content is conveyed; but in the world of *homo rhetoricus* rhetoric is *both* form and content, the manner of presentation and what is presented; the "improvising power of the rhetor" is at once all-creating and the guarantee of the impermanence of its creations: "to make a thing beautiful or unbeautiful, just or unjust, good or bad is both a human power and a sign of the insubstantiality of these attributes."[24] Having been made they can be made again.

Which of these views of human nature is the correct one? The question can only be answered from within one or the other, and the evidence of one party will be regarded by the other either as illusory or as grist for its own mill. When presented with the ever-changing panorama of history, serious man will see variation on a few basic themes; and when confronted with the persistence of essentialist questions and answers, rhetorical man will reply as Lanham does by asserting that serious man is himself a supremely fictional achievement; seriousness is just another style, not the state of having escaped style:

> In a fallen cosmetic world, [plain Jane] is asking *not* to be considered, wants to be overlooked—or perhaps to claim attention by contrast. She is as rhetorical as her made up sister, proclaims as loudly an attitude. Thus the whole range of ornament from zero to 100 is equally rhetorical, equally deep or equally superficial. (p. 30)

That is to say, for rhetorical man the distinctions (between form and content, periphery and core, ephemeral and abiding) invoked by serious man are nothing more than the scaffolding of the theater of seriousness, are themselves instances of what they oppose. And on the other side, if serious man were to hear *that* argument, he would regard it as one more example of rhetorical manipulation and sleight of hand, an outrageous assertion that flies in the face of common sense, the equivalent in debate of "so's your old man." And so it would go, with no prospect of ever reaching accord, an endless round of accusation and counteraccusation in which truth, honesty, and linguistic responsibility are claimed by everyone: "from serious premises, all rhetorical language is suspect; from a rhetorical point of view, transparent language seems dishonest; false to the world."[25]

And so it *has* gone; the history of Western thought could be written as the history of this quarrel. And, indeed, such histories have been written and with predictably different emphases. In one version written many times, the mists of religion, magic, and verbal incantation (all equivalently suspect forms of fantasy) are dispelled by the Enlightenment rediscovery of reason and science; enthusiasm and metaphor alike are curbed by the refinement of method, and the effects of difference (point of view) are bracketed and held in check by a procedural rigor. In another version (told by a line stretching from Vico to Foucault) a carnivalesque world of exuberance and possibility is drastically impoverished by the ascendency of a soulless reason, a brutally narrow perspective that claims to be objective and proceeds in a repressive manner to enforce its claim. It is not my intention here to endorse either history or to offer a third or to argue as some have for a nonhistory of discontinuous *episteme* innocent of either a progressive or lapsarian curve; rather, I only wish to point out that the debate continues to this very day and that its terms are exactly those one finds in the dialogues of Plato and the orations of the sophists.

III

As I write, the fortunes of rhetorical man are on the upswing, as in discipline after discipline there is evidence of what has been called the interpretive turn, the realization (at least for those it seizes) that the givens of any field of activity— including the facts it commands, the procedures it trusts in, and the values it expresses and extends—are socially and politically constructed, are fashioned by man rather than delivered by God or Nature. The most recent (and unlikely) field to experience this revolution, or at least to hear of its possibility, is economics. The key text is Donald McCloskey's *The Rhetoric of Economics* (Wisconsin, 1985), a title that is itself polemical since, as McCloskey points out, mainstream economists don't like to think of themselves as employing a rhetoric; rather, they regard themselves as scientists whose methodology insulates them from the appeal of special interests or points of view. They think, in other words, that the procedures of their discipline will produce "knowledge free from doubt, free from metaphysics, morals and personal conviction" (p. 16). To this, McCloskey responds by declaring (in good sophistic terms) that no such knowledge is available, and that while economic method promises to deliver it, "what it is able to deliver [and] renames as scientific methodology [are] the scientist's and especially the economic scientist's metaphysics, moral, and personal convictions" (p. 16). Impersonal method, then, is both an illusion and a danger (as a kind of rhetoric it masks its rhetorical nature), and as an antidote to it McCloskey offers rhetoric, which he says, deals not with abstract truth, but with the truth that emerges in the context of distinctly human conversations (pp. 28–29). Within those conversations there are always

> particular arguments good or bad. After making them there is no point in asking
> a last, summarizing question: "Well, is it True?" It's whatever it is—persuasive,
> interesting, useful, and so forth. . . . There is no reason to search for a general
> quality called Truth, which answers only the unanswerable question, "What is it
> in the mind of God?" (p. 47)

The answerable questions are always asked within the assumptions of particular situations, and both question and answer "will always depend on one's audience and the human purposes involved" (p. 150). The real truth, concludes McCloskey, is that "assertions are made for purposes of persuading some audience" and that, given the unavailability of a God's-eye view, "this is not a shameful fact," but the bottom line fact in a rhetorical world.

At the first conference called to consider McCloskey's arguments, the familiar anti-rhetorical objections were heard again in the land, and the land might have been fifth-century Athens as well as Wellesley, Massachusetts, in 1986. One participant spoke of "the primrose path to extreme relativism" which proceeds from "Kuhn's conception of the incommensurability of paradigms" to the "contention that there are no objective and unambiguous procedures for applying . . . rules since the meanings of particular actions and terms are entirely . . . context-dependent." Other voices proclaimed that nothing in McCloskey's position was new (an observation certainly true), that everyone already knew it, and that at any rate it didn't touch the core of the economists's practice. Still others invoked a set of related (and familiar) distinctions between empirical and interpretive activities, between demonstration and persuasion, between verifiable procedures and anarchic irrationalism. Of course, each of these objections had already been formulated (or reformulated) in those disciplines that had heard rhetoric's siren song long before it reached the belated ears of economists. The name that everyone always refers to (in praise or blame) is Thomas Kuhn. His *The Structure of Scientific Revolutions* is arguably the most frequently cited work in the humanities and social sciences in the past twenty-five years, and it is rhetorical through and through. Kuhn begins by rehearsing and challenging the orthodox model of scientific inquiry in which independent facts are first collected by objective methods and then built up into a picture of nature, a picture that he himself either confirms or rejects in the context of controlled experiments. In this model, science is a "cumulative process" (p. 3) in which each new discovery adds "one more item to the population of the scientist's world" (p. 7). The shape of that world—of the scientist's professional activities— is determined by the shapes (of fact and structure) already existing in the larger world of nature, shapes that constrain and guide the scientist's work.

Kuhn challenges this story by introducing the notion of a paradigm, a set of tacit assumptions and beliefs within which research goes on, assumptions which rather than deriving from the observation of facts are determinative of the facts that could possibly be observed. It follows, then, that when observations made within different paradigms conflict, there is no principled (i.e., nonrhetorical) way to adjudicate the dispute. One cannot put the competing accounts to the test of fact, because the specification of fact is precisely what is at issue between them; a fact cited by one party would be seen as a mistake by the other. What this means is that science does not proceed by offering its descriptions to the independent judgment of nature; rather, it proceeds when the proponents of one paradigm are able to present their case in a way that the adherents of other paradigms find compelling. In short, the "motor" by which science moves is not verification or falsification, but persuasion. Indeed, says Kuhn, in the end the force of scientific argument "is *only* that of persuasion" (p. 94). In the case of disagreement, "each party must try, by persuasion, to convert the other" (p. 198), and when one party succeeds there is no higher court to which the outcome might be referred: "there is no standard higher than the assent of the relevant community" (p. 94). "What better criterion," asks Kuhn, "could there be?" (p. 170).

The answer given by those who were horrified by Kuhn's rhetoricization of scientific procedure was predictable: a better criterion would be one that was not captive to a particular paradigm but provided a neutral space in which competing paradigms could be disinterestedly assessed. By denying such a criterion, Kuhn leaves us in a world of epistemological and moral anarchy. The words are Israel Scheffler's:

> Independent and public controls are no more, communication has failed, the common universe of things is a delusion, reality itself is made . . . rather than discovered. . . . In place of a community of rational men following objective procedures in the pursuit of truth, we have a set of isolated monads, within each of which belief forms without systematic constraints.[26]

Kuhn and those he has persuaded have, of course, responded to these accusations, but, needless to say, the debate continues in terms readers of this essay could easily imagine; and the debate has been particularly acrimonious because the area of contest—science and its procedures—is so heavily invested in as the one place where the apostles of rhetorical interpretivism would presumably fear to tread.

At one point in his argument Kuhn remarks that in the tradition he is critiquing scientific research is "reputed to proceed" from "raw data" or "brute experience"; but, he points out, if that were truly the mode of proceeding, it would require a "neutral observation language" (p. 125), a language that registers facts without any mediation by paradigm-specific assumptions. The problem is that "philosophical investigation has not yet provided even a hint of what a language able to do that would be like" (p. 127). Even a specially devised language "embodies a host of expectations about nature," expectations that limit in advance what can be described. Just as one cannot (in Kuhn's view) have recourse to neutral facts in order to settle a dispute, so one cannot have recourse to a neutral language in which to report those facts or even to report on the configuration of the dispute. The difference that divides men "is prior to the application of the languages in which it is nevertheless reflected" (p. 201). Whatever reports a particular language (natural or artificial) offers us will be the report on the world as it is seen from within some particular situation; there is no other aperspectival way to see and no language other than a situation-dependent language—an interested, rhetorical language—in which to report.

This same point was being made with all the force of philosophical authority by J. L. Austin in a book published, significantly, in the same year (1962) that saw the publication of *The Structure of Scientific Revolutions*. Austin begins *How to Do Things with Words* by observing that traditionally the center of the philosophy of language has been just the kind of utterance Kuhn declares unavailable, the context-independent statement that offers objective reports on an equally independent world in sentences of the form "He is running" and "Lord Raglan won the battle of Alma" (pp. 47, 142). Such utterances, which Austin calls "constative," are answerable to a requirement of truth and verisimilitude ("the truth of the constative . . . 'he is running' depends on his being running"); the words must match the world, and if they do not they can be criticized as false and inaccurate. There are, however, innumerable utterances that are not assessable in this way. If, for example, I say to you, "I promise to pay you five dollars" or "Leave the room," it would be odd were you to respond by saying "true" or "false"; rather, you would say to the first "good" or "that's not enough" or "I won't hold my breath" and to the second "yes, sir" or "but I'm expecting a phone call" or "who do you think you are?" These and many other imaginable responses would not be judgments on the truth or accuracy of my utterance but on its appropriateness given our respective positions in some social structure of understanding (domestic, military, economic, etc.). It is only if the circumstances are of a certain kind—that is, if five dollars is a reasonable rather than an insulting amount, if the room I order you to leave is mine not yours— that the utterances will "take" and achieve the meaning of being a promise or a command. Thus the very identity, and therefore the meaning, of this type of utterance—Austin names it "performative"—depends on the context in which it is produced and received. There is no regular—in the sense of reliable and predictable—relationship between the form of the linguistic marks (the words and their order) and their significance. Nothing guarantees that "I promise to pay you five dollars" will be either intended or heard as a promise; in different circumstances it could be received as a threat or a joke (as when I utter it from debtors' prison), and in many circumstances it will be intended as one act and understood as another (as when your opinion of my trustworthiness is much lower than my own). When the criterion of verisimilitude has been replaced by the criterion of appropriateness, meaning becomes radically contextual, potentially as variable as the situated (and shifting) understandings of countless speakers and hearers.

It is, of course, precisely this property of performatives—their force is contingent and cannot be formally constrained—that is responsible for their being consigned by philosophers of language to the category of the "derived" or "parasitic," where, safely tucked away, they are prevented from contaminating the core category of the constative. But it is this act of segregation and quarantining that Austin undoes in the second half of his book when he extends the analysis of performatives to constatives and finds that they too mean differently in the light of differing contextual circumstances. Consider the exemplary constative, "Lord Raglan won the battle of Alma." Is it true, accurate, a faithful report? It depends, says Austin, on the context in which it is uttered and received (pp. 142–43). In a high school textbook it might be accepted as true because of the in-place assumptions as to what, exactly, a battle is, what constitutes winning, what the function of a general is, etc., while in a work of "serious" historical research all of these assumptions may have been replaced by others, with the result that the very notions "battle" and "won" would have a different shape. The properties that supposedly distinguish constatives from performatives— fidelity to preexisting facts, accountability to a criterion of truth—turn out to be as dependent on particular conditions of production and reception as performatives. "True" and "false," Austin concludes, are not names for the possible relationships between freestanding (constative) utterances and an equally freestanding state of affairs; rather, they are situation-specific judgments on the relationship between contextually produced utterances and states of affairs that are themselves no less contextually produced. At the end of the book constatives are "discovered" to be a subset of performatives, and with this discovery the formal core of language disappears entirely and is replaced by a world of utterances vulnerable to the sea change of every circumstance, the world, in short, of rhetorical (situated) man.

This is a conclusion Austin himself resists when he attempts to isolate (and thereby contain) the rhetorical by invoking another distinction between serious and nonserious utterance. Serious utterances are utterances for which the speaker takes responsibility; he means what he says, and therefore you can infer his meaning by considering his words in context. A nonserious utterance is an utterance produced in circumstances that "abrogate" (p. 21) the speaker's responsibility, and therefore one cannot with any confidence—that is, without the hazard of ungrounded conjecture—determine what he means:

> a performative utterance will, for example, be . . . hollow or void if said by an actor on the stage, or if introduced in a poem, or spoken in a soliloquy. . . . Language in such circumstances is in special ways . . . used not seriously, but in ways *parasitic* upon its normal use. . . . All this we are *excluding* from consideration. Our performative utterances . . . are to be understood as issued in ordinary circumstances. (p. 22)

The distinction, then, is between utterances that are, as Austin puts it later, "tethered to their origin" (p. 61), anchored by a palpable intention, and utterances whose origin is hidden by the screen of a theatrical or literary stage setting. This distinction and the passage in which it appears were taken up in 1967 by Jacques Derrida in a famous (and admiring) critique of Austin. Derrida finds Austin working against his own best insights and forgetting what he has just acknowledged, that "infelicity [communication going astray, in an unintended direction] is an ill to which *all* [speech] acts are heir."[27] Despite this acknowledgment, Austin continues to think of infelicity—of those cases in which the tethering origin of utterances is obscure and must be constructed by interpretive conjecture—as special, whereas, in Derrida's view, infelicity is itself the originary state in that any determination of meaning must always proceed within an interpretive construction of a speaker's intention. The origin that supposedly tethers the interpretation of an utterance will always be the product of that interpretation; the special circumstances in which meaning must be inferred through a screen rather than directly are the circumstances of every linguistic transaction. In short, there are no ordinary circumstances, merely those myriad and varied circumstances in which actors embedded in stage settings hazard interpretations of utterances produced by actors embedded in other stage situations. All the world, as Shakespeare says, is a stage, and on that stage "the quality of risk admitted by Austin" is not something one can avoid by sticking close to ordinary language in ordinary circumstances, but is rather "the internal and positive condition" of any act of communication."[28]

In the same publication in which the English translation of Derrida's essay appeared, John Searle, a student of Austin's, replied in terms that make clear the affiliation of this particular debate to the ancient debate whose configurations we have been tracing. Searle's strategy is basically to repeat Austin's points and declare that Derrida has missed them: "Austin's idea is simply this: if we want to know what it is to make a promise we had better not *start* our investigations with promises made by actors on stage . . . because in some fairly obvious way such utterances are not standard cases of promises" (p. 204). But in Derrida's argument, the category of the "obvious" is precisely what is being challenged or "deconstructed." Although it is true that we consider promises uttered in every-day contexts more direct—less etiolated—than promises made on a stage, this (Derrida would say) is only because the stage settings within which everyday life proceeds are so powerfully—that is, rhetorically—in place that they are in effect invisible, and therefore the meanings they make possible are experienced as if they were direct and unmediated by any screens. The "obvious" cannot be opposed to the "staged," as Searle assumes, because it is simply the achievement of a staging that has been particularly successful. One does not escape the rhetor-ical by fleeing to the protected area of basic communication and common sense because common sense in whatever form it happens to take is always a rhetorical—partial, partisan, interested—construction. This does not mean, Derrida hastens to add, that all rhetorical constructions are equal, just that they are equally rhetorical, equally the effects and extensions of some limited and challengeable point of view. The "citationality"—the condition of being in quotes, of being *in*direct—of an utterance in a play is not the same as the cita-tionality of a philosophical reference or a deposition before a court; it is just that no one of these performatives is more serious—more direct, less mediated, less rhetorical—than any other. Whatever opposition there is takes place within a "general" citationality which "constitutes a violation of the allegedly rigorous purity of every event of discourse or every *speech act*" (p. 192).

Searle points out (p. 205) that in order to achieve a "general theory of speech acts," one must perform acts of exclusion or idealization like Austin's; but it is the possibility of a general theory—of an account that is itself more than an extension of some *particular* context or perspective—that Derrida denies. His is the familiar world of Rhetorical Man, teeming with roles, situations, strategies, interventions, but containing no master role, no situation of situations, no strat-egy for outflanking all strategies, no intervention in the arena of dispute that does not expand the arena of dispute, no neutral point of rationality from the vantage point of which the "merely rhetorical" can be identified and held in check. That is why deconstructive or post-structuralist thought is supremely rhetorical: it sys-tematically asserts and demonstrates the mediated, constructed, partial, socially constituted nature of all realities, whether they be phenomenal, linguistic, or psy-chological. To deconstruct a text, says Derrida, is to "work through the struc-tured genealogy of its concepts in the most scrupulous and immanent fashion, but at the same time to determine from a certain external perspective that it can-not name or describe what this history may have concealed or excluded, consti-tuting itself as history through this repression in which it has a stake."[29] The "external perspective" is the perspective from which the analyst knows in advance (by virtue of his commitment to the rhetorical or anti-foundational worldview) that the coherences presented by a text (and an institution or an economy can in this sense be a text) rests on a contradiction it cannot acknowledge, rests on the suppression of the challengeable rhetoricity of its own standpoint, a standpoint that offers itself as if it came from nowhere in particular and simply delivered things as they really (i.e., nonperspectivally) are. A deconstructive reading will surface those contradictions and expose those suppressions and thus "trouble" a unity that is achieved only by covering over all the excluded emphases and interests that might threaten it. These exclusions are part of the text in that the success of its totalizing effort depends on them. Once they are made manifest, the hitherto manifest meaning of the text is undermined—indeed, is shown to have always and already been undermined—as "the rhetorical operations that produce the supposed ground of argument, the key concept or premise," are deprived of the claim to be *un*rhetorical, serious, disinterested.[30]

Nor is this act performed in the service of something beyond rhetoric. Derridean deconstruction does not uncover the operations of rhetoric in order to reach the Truth; rather, it continually uncovers the truth of rhetorical operations, the truth that all operations, including the operation of deconstruction itself, are rhetorical. If, as Paul de Man asserts, "a deconstruction always has for its target to reveal the existence of hidden articulations and fragmentations within assumedly monadic totalities," care must be taken that a new monadic totality is not left as the legacy of the deconstructive gesture. Since the course of a deconstruction is to uncover a "fragmented stage that can be called natural with regard to the system that is being undone," there is always the danger that the "natural" pattern will "substitute *its* relational system for the one it helped to dissolve."[31] The only way to escape this danger is to perform the deconstructive act again and again, submitting each new emerging constellation to the same suspicious scrutiny that brought it to light, and resisting the temptation to put in place of the truths it rhetoricizes the truth that everything is rhetorical. One cannot rest even in the insight that there is no place to rest. "Rhetoric," says de Man, "suspends logic and opens up vertiginous possibilities of referential aberration" (p. 10). But the rhetorical vision is foreclosed on and made into a new absolute if those "vertiginous possibilities" are celebrated as the basis of a new wisdom. The rhetorical beat must by definition go on, endlessly repeating the sequence by which "the lure of solid ground" is succeeded by "the ensuing demystification."[32] When de Man approvingly quotes Nietzsche's identification of truth with "a moving army of metaphors, metonymies and anthropomorphisms," a rhetorical construction whose origin has been (and must be) forgotten, he does not exempt Nietzsche's text from its own corrosive effects. If Nietzsche declares (well in advance of Kuhn and Austin, but well after Gorgias and Protagoras) that "there is no such thing as an unrhetorical, 'natural' language," for "tropes are not something that can be added or subtracted from language at will," the insight must be extended to that very declaration: "A text like *On Truth and Lie*, although it presents itself legitimately as a demystification of literary rhetoric, remains entirely literary, and deceptive itself" (p. 113). The "rhetorical mode," the mode of deconstruction, is a mode of "endless reflection," since it is "unable ever to escape from the rhetorical deceit it announces" (p. 115).

IV

That, however, is just what is wrong with deconstructive practice from the viewpoint of the intellectual left, many of whose members subscribe to Nietzsche's account of truth and reality as rhetorical but find that much of post-structuralist discourse uses that account as a way of escaping into new versions of idealism and formalism. Frank Lentricchia, for example, sees in some of de Man's texts an intention to place "discourse in a realm where it can have no responsibility to historical life" and fears that we are being invited into "the realm of the thoroughly predictable linguistic transcendental," the "rarified region of the undecidable," where every text "speaks synchronically and endlessly the same tale . . . of its own duplicitous self-consciousness."[33] Terry Eagleton's judgment is even harsher. Noting that in the wake of Nietzschean thought, rhetoric, "mocked and berated for centuries by an abrasive rationalism," takes its "terrible belated revenge" by finding itself in every rationalist project, Eagleton complains that many rhetoricians seem content to stop there, satisfied with the "Fool's function of unmasking all power as self-rationalization, all knowledge as a mere fumbling with metaphor."[34] Operating as a "vigorous demystifier of all ideology," rhetoric functions only as a form of thought and ends up by providing "the final ideological rationale for political inertia." In retreat "from market place to study, politics to philology, social practice to semiotics," deconstructive rhetoric turns the emancipatory promise of Nietzschean thought into "a gross failure of ideological nerve," allowing the liberal academic the elitist pleasure of repeatedly exposing "vulgar commercial and political hectorings" (pp. 108–9). In both his study of Benjamin and his influential *Literary Theory: An Introduction*, Eagleton urges a return to the Ciceronian-Isocratic tradition in which the rhetorical arts are inseparable from the practice of a politics, "techniques of persuasion indis\sociable from the substantive issues and audiences involved," techniques whose employment is "closely determined by the pragmatic situation at hand."[35] In short, he calls for a rhetoric that will do real work and cites as an example the slogan "black is beautiful," which he says is "paradigmatically rhetorical since it employs a figure of equivalence to produce particular discursive and extra-discursive effects without direct regard for truth."[36] That is, someone who says "black is beautiful" is not so much interested in the accuracy of the assertion (it is not constatively intended) as he is in the responses it may provoke—surprise, outrage, urgency, solidarity—responses that may in turn set in motion "practices that are deemed, in the light of a particular set of falsifiable hypotheses, to be desirable."[37]

For Eagleton, the desirable practices are Marxist-socialist and the rhetoric that will help establish them has three tasks:

> First, to participate in the production of works and events which . . . so fictionalize the "real" as to intend those effects conducive to the victory of socialism. Second, as "critic" to expose the rhetorical structures by which non-socialist works produce politically undesirable effects. . . . Third, to interpret such words where possible "against the grain," so as to appropriate from them whatever may be valuable for socialism.[38]

It is, of course, the second of these tasks that presents conceptual and cognitive problems. If all cultural work is, as Eagleton says in the sentence just before this passage, rhetorical, then how does one's own rhetoric escape the inauthenticity it discovers in the rhetoric of others? Eagleton's answer is contained in his assumption of the superiority of the socialist program; any rhetorical work in the service of that program will be justified in advance, while conversely any rhetorical work done in opposition to socialist urgencies will flow from "false consciousness" and will deserve to be exposed. This confidence in his objectives makes Eagleton impatient with those for whom the rhetoricity of all discourse is something to be savored for itself, something to be lovingly and obsessively demonstrated again and again. It is not, he says, "a matter of starting from certain theoretical or methodological problems; it is a matter of starting from what we want to *do*, and then seeing which methods and theories will best help us to achieve these ends."[39] Theories, in short, are themselves rhetorics whose usefulness is a function of contingent circumstances. It is ends—specific goals in local contexts—that rule the invocation of theories, not theories that determine goals and the means by which they can be reached.

There are those on the left, however, for whom the direction is the other way around, from the theoretical realization of rhetoric's pervasiveness to a vision and a program for implementing it. In their view the discovery (or rediscovery) that all discourse and therefore all knowledge is rhetorical leads or should lead to the adoption of a *method* by which the dangers of rhetoric can be at least mitigated and perhaps extirpated. This method has two stages: the first is a stage of debunking, and it issues from the general suspicion in which all orthodoxies and arrangements of power are held once it is realized that their basis is not reason or nature but the success of some rhetorical/political agenda. Armed with this realization, one proceeds to expose the contingent and therefore challengeable basis of whatever presents itself as natural and inevitable. So far this is precisely the procedure of deconstruction; but whereas deconstructive practice (at least of the Yale variety) seems to produce nothing but the occasion for its endless repetition, some cultural revolutionaries discern in it a more positive residue, the loosening or weakening of the structures of domination and oppression that now hold us captive. The reasoning is that by repeatedly uncovering the historical and ideological basis of established structures (both political and cognitive), one becomes sensitized to the effects of ideology and begins to clear a space in which those effects can be combated; and as that sensitivity grows more acute, the area of combat will become larger until it encompasses the underlying structure of assumptions that confers a spurious legitimacy on the powers that currently be. The claim, in short, is that the radically rhetorical insight of Nietzschean/Derridean thought can do radical political work; becoming aware that everything is rhetorical is the first step in countering the power of rhetoric and liberating us from its force. Only if deeply entrenched ways of thinking and acting are made the objects of suspicion will we be able "even to *imagine* that life could be different and better."

This last sentence is taken from an essay by Robert Gordon entitled "New Developments in Legal Theory."[40] Gordon is writing as a member of the Critical

Legal Studies Movement, a group of legal academics who have discovered the rhetorical nature of legal reasoning and are busily exposing as interested the supposedly disinterested operations of legal procedures. Gordon's pages are replete with the vocabulary of enclosure or prison; we are "locked into" a system of belief we did not make; we are "demobilized" (that is, rendered less mobile); we must "break out" (p. 291), we must "unfreeze the world as it appears to common sense" (p. 289). What will help us to break out, to unfreeze, is the discovery "that the belief-structures that rule our lives are not found in nature but are historically contingent," for that discovery, says Gordon, "is extraordinarily liberating" (p. 289). What it will liberate are the mental energies that were before prevented by the "paralysis-inducing" effects of received systems of thought from even imagining that "life could be different and better." In the words of Roberto Unger (another prominent member of the movement), if you start with an awareness of the insight "that no one scheme of human association has conclusive authority" and come to an understanding of the "flawed" nature of the schemes now in place, you can then "imagine the actualizations [i.e., present-day arrangements of things] transformed" and in time "transform them in fact."[41] The result will be a "cultural-revolutionary practice" that will bring about the "progressive emancipation from a background plan of social division and hierarchy" (p. 587). To the question, what is the *content* of that emancipation, given a world that is rhetorical through and through, those who work Gordon's and Unger's side of the street usually reply that emancipation will take the form of a strengthening and enlarging of a capacity of mind that stands to the side of, and is therefore able to resist, the appeal of the agenda that would enslave us. That capacity of mind has received many names, but the one most often proposed is "critical self-consciousness." Critical self-consciousness is the ability (stifled in some, developed in others) to discern in any "scheme of association," including those one finds attractive and compelling, the partisan aims it hides from view; and the claim is that as it performs this negative task, critical self-consciousness participates in the positive task of formulating schemes of associations (structures of thought and government) that are in the service not of a particular party but of all mankind.

It need hardly be said that this claim veers back in the direction of the rationalism and universalism that the critical/deconstructive projects sets out to demystify. That project begins by rejecting the rationalities of present life as rationalizations and revealing the structure of reality to be rhetorical, that is, partial; but then it turns around and attempts to use the insight of partiality to build something that is less partial, less hostage to the urgencies of a particular vision and more responsive to the needs of men and women in general. Insofar as this "turn" is taken to its logical conclusion, it ends up reinventing at the conclusion of a rhetorically informed critique the entire array of antirhetorical gestures and exclusions. One sees this clearly in the work of Jürgen Habermas, a thinker whose widespread influence is testimony to the durability of the tradition that began (at least) with Plato. Habermas's goal is to bring about something he calls the "ideal speech situation," a situation in which all assertions proceed not from the perspective of individual desires and strategies, but from the perspective of a general rationality upon which all parties are agreed. In such a situation nothing would count except the claims to universal validity of all assertions. "No force except that of the better argument is exercised; and, . . . as a result, all motives except that of the cooperative search for truth are excluded."[42] Of course, in the world we now inhabit there is no such purity of motive; nevertheless, says Habermas, even in the most distorted of communicative situations there remains something of the basic impulse behind all utterance, "the intention of communicating a true *[wahr]* proposition . . . so that the hearer can share the knowledge of the speaker."[43] If we could only eliminate from our discourse performances those intentions that reflect baser goals—the intentions to deceive, to manipulate, to persuade—the ideal speech situation could be approximated.

What stands in our way is the fact that many of our speech acts issue from the perspective of local and historically contingent contexts, and these by definition cannot contribute to the building up of a general rationality. Therefore, it is incumbent upon us to choose and proffer utterances that satisfy (or at least claim and desire to satisfy) *universal* conditions of validity. This is the project Habermas names "Universal Pragmatics" and the name tells its own story. Habermas recognizes, as all modern and postmodern contextualists do, that language is a social and not a purely formal phenomenon, but he thinks that the social/pragmatic aspect of language use is itself "accessible to formal analysis" (p. 6) and that therefore it is possible to construct a universal "communicative competence" (p. 29) parallel to Chomsky's linguistic competence. Sentences produced according to the rules and norms of this communicative competence would be tied not to "particular epistemic presuppositions and changing contexts" (p. 29), but to the unchanging context (the context of contexts) in which one finds the presuppositions underlying the general possibility of successful speech. "A *general* theory of speech acts would . . . describe . . . that fundamental system of rules that adult subjects master to the extent that they can fulfill *the conditions of happy employment of sentences in utterances* no matter to which particular language the sentences may belong and in which accidental contexts the utterances may be embedded" (p. 26). If we can operate on the level of that fundamental system, the distorting potential of "accidental contexts" will be neutralized because we will always have one eye on what is essential, the establishing by rational cooperation of an interpersonal (nonaccidental) truth. Once speakers are oriented to this goal and away from others, oriented toward *general* understanding, they will be incapable of deception and manipulation: "Truthfulness guarantees the transparency of a subjectivity representing itself in language" (p. 57). A company of transparent subjectivities will join together in the fashioning of a transparent truth and of a world in which the will to power has been eliminated.

In his book *Textual Power* (New Haven, 1985), Robert Scholes examines the rationalist epistemology in which a "complete self confronts a solid world, perceiving it directly and accurately, . . . capturing it perfectly in a transparent language" and declares it to be so thoroughly discredited that it now "is lying in ruins around us" (pp. 132–33). Perhaps so, in some circles, but the fact of Habermas's work and of the audience he commands suggests that even now those ruins are collecting themselves and rising again into the familiar anti-rhetorical structure. It would seem that any announcement of the death of either position will always be premature, slightly behind the institutional news that in some corner of the world supposedly abandoned questions are receiving what at least appear to be new answers. Only recently the *public* fortunes of rationalist-foundationalist thought have taken a favorable turn with the publication of books like Allan Bloom's *The Closing of the American Mind* and E. D. Hirsch's *Cultural Literacy,* both of which (Bloom's more directly) challenge the "new Orthodoxy" of "extreme cultural relativism" and reassert, albeit in different ways, the existence of normative standards. In many quarters these books have been welcomed as a return to the common sense that is necessary if civilization is to avoid the dark night of anarchy. One can expect administrators and legislators to propose reforms (and perhaps even purges) based on Bloom's arguments (the rhetorical force of anti-rhetoricalism is always being revived), and one can expect too a host of voices raised in opposition to what will surely be called the "new positivism." Those voices will include some that have been mentioned here and some others that certainly merit recording but can only be noted in a list that is itself incomplete. The full story of rhetoric's twentieth-century resurgence would boast among its cast of characters: Kenneth Burke, whose "dramatism" anticipates so much of what is considered avant-garde today; Wayne Booth, Whose *The Rhetoric of Fiction* was so important in legitimizing the rhetorical analysis of the novel; Mikhail Bakhtin, whose contrast of monologic to dialogic and heteroglossic discourse sums up so many strands in the rhetorical tradition; Roland Barthes, who in the concept of "jouissance" makes a (non) constitutive principle of the tendency of rhetoric to resist closure and extend play; the ethnomethodologists (Harold Garfinkel and company) who discover in every supposedly rule-bound context the operation of a principle (exactly the wrong word) of "ad-hocing"; Chaim Perelman and L. Olbrechts-Tyeca whose *The New Rhetoric: A Treatise on Argumentation* provides a sophisticated modern source book for would-be rhetoricians weary of always citing Aristotle; Barbara Herrnstein Smith who, in the course of espousing an unashamed relativism, directly confronts and argues down the objections of those who fear for their souls (and more) in a world without objective standards; Fredric Jameson and Hayden White who teach us (among other things) that "history . . . is unaccessible to us except in textual form, and that our approach to it and to the Real itself necessarily passes through its prior textualization";[44] reader-oriented critics like Norman Holland, David Bleich, Wolfgang Iser, and H. R. Jauss who, by shifting the emphasis from the text to its reception, open up the act of interpretation to the infinite variability of contextual circumstance; innumerable feminists who relentlessly unmark male hegemonic structures and expose as rhetorical the rational posturings of the legal and political systems; equally innumerable theorists of composition who, under the slogan "process, not product," insist on the rhetorical nature of communication and argue for far-reaching changes in the way writing is taught. The list is already formidable, but it could go on and on, providing support for Scholes's contention that the rival epistemology has been vanquished and for Clifford Geertz's announcement (and he too is a contributor to the shift he reports) that "Something is happening to the way we think about the way we think."[45]

But it would seem, from the evidence marshaled in this essay, that something is always happening to the way we think, and that it is always the same something, a tug-of-war between two views of human life and its possibilities, no one of which can ever gain complete and lasting ascendancy because in the very moment of its triumphant articulation each turns back in the direction of the other. Thus Wayne Booth feels obliged in both *The Rhetoric of Fiction* and *A Rhetoric of Irony* to confine the force of rhetoric by sharply distinguishing its legitimate uses from two extreme-limit cases (the "unreliable narrator" and "unstable irony"); some reader-response critics deconstruct the autonomy and self-sufficiency of the text, but in the process end up privileging the autonomous and self-sufficient subject; some feminists challenge the essentialist claims of "male reason" in the name of a female rationality or nonrationality apparently no less essential; Jameson opens up the narrativity of history in order to proclaim one narrative the true and unifying one. Here one might speak of the return of the repressed (and thereby invoke Freud whose writings and influence would be still another chapter in the story I have not even begun to tell) were it not that the repressed—whether it be the fact of difference or the desire for its elimination—is always so close to the surface that it hardly need be unearthed. What we seem to have is a tale full of sound and fury, and signifying itself, signifying a durability rooted in inconclusiveness, in the impossibility of there being a last word.

In an essay, however, someone must have the last word and I give it to Richard Rorty. Rorty is himself a champion of the antiessentialism that underlies rhetorical thinking; his neo-pragmatism makes common cause with Kuhn and others who would turn us away from the search for transcendental absolutes and commend to us (although it would seem superfluous to do so) the imperatives and goals already informing our practices. It is, however, not the polemicist Rorty whom I call upon to sum up, but the Rorty who is the brisk chronicler of our epistemological condition:

> There . . . are two ways of thinking about various things. . . . The first . . . thinks of truth as a vertical relationship between representations and what is represented. The second . . . thinks of truth horizontally—as the culminating reinterpretation of our predecessors' reinterpretation of their predecessors' reinterpretation. . . . It is the difference between regarding truth, goodness, and beauty as eternal objects which we try to locate and reveal, and regarding them as artifacts whose fundamental design we often have to alter.[46]

It is the difference between serious and rhetorical man. It is the difference that remains.

Notes

1. *Gorgias,* ed. and trans. W. C. Helmbold (Indianapolis, 1952), p. 18.
2. Plato, *Phaedrus,* ed. and trans. W. C. Helmbold and W. G. Rabinowitz (Indianapolis, 1956), p. 46.
3. *The Works of Aristotle,* vol. II, ed. and trans. W. Rhys Roberts (Oxford, 1946).
4. See A. C. Howell, "*Res et Verba:* Words and Things," in *Seventeenth Century Prose: Modern Essays and Criticism,* ed. S. Fish (Oxford, 1971).

5. Thomas Kuhn, *The Structure of Scientific Revolutions* (Chicago, 1962), p. 125.
6. See Andrew Lange, *The Artificial Language Movement* (Oxford, New York, and London, 1985).
7. Jürgen Habermas, *Legitimation Crisis* (Boston, 1975), p. 108.
8. This is the language of H. L. A. Hart's *The Concept of Law* (Oxford, 1961).
9. John Milton, "Areopagitica," in *Milton's Prose*, ed. J. Max Patrick et al. (New York, 1968), p. 297.
10. Rudolf Carnap, "The Elimination of Metaphysics," in *Logical Positivism*, ed. A. J. Ayer (Glenco, Ill., 1959), p. 63.
11. See on this point George Kennedy, *The Art of Persuasion in Greece* (Princeton, N.J., 1963), p. 23.
12. See John Milton, "Reason of Church Government," in *The Complete Prose Works of John Milton*, ed. D. M. Wolfe et al., vol. 1 (New Haven, Conn., 1953), pp. 817–18.
13. *Rhetoric* (London, 1971), p. 14.
14. *Die Fragmente der Vorsokratiker*, ed. H. Diels and W. Kranz (Berlin, 1960), 371:80, B4.
15. William K. Guthrie, *The Sophists* (Cambridge, 1971), p. 193.
16. Ibid., p. 186.
17. Ibid., p. 187.
18. Ibid., p. 51.
19. Isocrates, "Antidosis," in *Isocrates*, vol. 2, ed. and trans. George Norlin (Cambridge: Harvard University Press, 1962), pp. 275, 277.
20. Cicero, "De Inventione," in *Cicero*, vol. 2, ed. and trans. H. M. Hubbell (Cambridge: Harvard University Press, 1968), I, 2.
21. See, for example, John Lawson, *Lectures Concerning Oratory*, ed. E. N. Claussen and K. R. Wallace (Carbondale and Edwardsville: Southern Illinois University Press, 1972), p. 27.
22. *The Motives of Eloquence* (New Haven, Conn., 1976), p. 1.
23. See Thomas Sloane, *Donne, Milton, and the End of Humanist Rhetoric* (Berkeley, Los Angeles, and London, 1985), p. 87: "Rhetoric succeeded in humanism's great desideratum, the artistic creation of adept personhood." See also Stephen Greenblatt, *Renaissance Self-Fashioning* (Chicago, 1980).
24. Nancy Streuver, *The Language of History in the Renaissance* (Princeton, N.J., 1970), pp. 15, 12.
25. Lanham, *Motives*, p. 28.
26. *Science and Subjectivity* (Indianapolis, 1967), p. 19.
27. Jacques Derrida, "Signature Event Context," *Glyph* 1 (1977): 190.
28. Ibid.
29. Jacques Derrida, *Positions* (Chicago: University of Chicago Press, 1981), p. 6.
30. Jonathan Culler, *On Deconstruction* (Ithaca, N.Y., 1982), p. 86.
31. *Allegories of Reading* (New Haven, Conn., 1979), p. 249.
32. *William Ray, Literary Meaning* (Oxford, 1984), p. 195.
33. *After the New Criticism* (Chicago, 1980), pp. 310, 317.
34. *Walter Benjamin or Towards a Revolutionary Criticism* (London, 1981), p. 108.
35. Ibid., p. 104.
36. Ibid., p. 112.
37. Ibid., p. 113.
38. Ibid.
39. *Literary Theory* (Minneapolis, 1983), p. 211.
40. *The Politics of Law* (New York, 1983), p. 287.

41. "The Critical Legal Studies Movement," *Harvard Law Review* 96 (1983): 580.
42. *Legitimation Crisis* (Boston, 1975), pp. 107–8.
43. *Communication and the Evolution of Society* (Boston, 1979), p. 2.
44. *The Political Unconscious* (Ithaca, 1981), p. 35.
45. "Blurred Genres: The Refiguration of Social Thought," *The American Scholar* 49 (Spring 1980).
46. *Consequences of Pragmatism* (Minneapolis, 1982), p. 92.

Chantal Mouffe (1943–)

Belgian born, Mouffe is professor of political theory at the University of Westminster's Centre for the Study of Democracy. She was educated at the University of Louvain, the University of Paris, and the University of Essex. Mouffe's extensive scholarship is grounded in political philosophy. Although her training was guided by Marxist theories, Mouffe has, for quite a while, sought a post-Marxist orientation that emphasizes what she calls radical democratic politics, as detailed in the reading selection given next. In Mouffe's wide-ranging scholarship, readers will find analyses of contemporary philosophy, feminism, democracy, sovereignty, and political liberalism. She has written two books—*The Return of the Political* (1993) and *The Democratic Paradox* (2000)—and edited four others: *Gramsci and Marxist Theory* (1979), *Dimensions of Radical Democracy* (1996), *Deconstruction and Pragmatism* (1996), and *The Challenge of Carl Schmitt* (1999). In addition, Mouffe and Ernesto Laclau have coauthored the influential book *Hegemony and Socialist Strategy: Towards a Radical Democratic Politics* (1985). "Feminism, Citizenship, and Radical Democratic Politics" provides a good overview of many of Mouffe's theoretical concerns and of her desire to help make political theory more relevant to more people's lives.

Feminism, Citizenship, and Radical Democratic Politics

Two topics have recently been the subject of much discussion among Anglo-American feminists: postmodernism and essentialism. Obviously they are related since the so-called "postmoderns" are also presented as the main critics of essentialism, but it is better to distinguish them since some feminists who are sympathetic to postmodernism have lately come to the defense of essentialism.[1] I consider that, in order to clarify the issues that are at stake in that debate, it is necessary to recognize that there is not such a thing as "postmodernism" understood as a coherent theoretical approach and that the frequent assimilation between poststructuralism and postmodernism can only lead to confusion. Which is not to say that we have not been witnessing through the twentieth century a progressive questioning of the dominant form of rationality and of the premises of the modes of thought characteristic of the Enlightenment. But this critique of universalism, humanism, and rationalism has come from many different quarters and it is far from being limited to the authors called "poststructuralists" or "postmodernists." From that point of view, all the innovative currents of this century—Heidegger and the post-Heideggerian philosophical hermeneutics of Gadamer, the later Wittgenstein and the philosophy of language inspired by his work, psychoanalysis and the reading of Freud proposed by Lacan, American pragmatism—all have from diverse standpoints criticized the idea of a universal human nature, of a universal canon of rationality through which that human nature could be known as well as the traditional conception of truth. Therefore, if the term "postmodern" indicates such a critique of Enlightenment's universalism and rationalism, it must be acknowledged that it refers to the main currents of twentieth-century philosophy and there is no reason to single out poststructuralism as a special target. On the other side, if by "postmodernism" one wants to designate only the very specific form that such a critique takes in authors such as Lyotard and Baudrillard, there is absolutely no justification for putting in that category people like Derrida, Lacan, or Foucault, as has generally been the case. Too often a critique of a specific thesis of Lyotard or Baudrillard leads to sweeping conclusions about "the postmoderns" who by then include all the authors loosely connected with poststructuralism. This type of amalgamation is completely unhelpful when not clearly disingenuous.

Once the conflation between postmodernism and poststructuralism has been debunked, the question of essentialism appears in a very different light. Indeed, it is with regard to the critique of essentialism that a convergence can be established among many different currents of thought and similarities found in the work of authors as different as Derrida, Wittgenstein, Heidegger, Dewey, Gadamer, Lacan, Foucault, Freud, and others. This is very important because it means that such a critique takes many different forms and that if we want to scrutinize its relevance for feminist politics we must engage with all its modalities and implications and not quickly dismiss it on the basis of some of its versions.

My aim in this article will be to show the crucial insights that an antiessentialist approach can bring to the elaboration of a feminist politics which is also informed by a radical democratic project. I certainly do not believe that essentialism necessarily entails conservative politics and I am ready to accept that it can be formulated in a progressive way. What I want to argue is that it presents some inescapable shortcomings for the construction of a democratic alternative whose objective is the articulation of the struggles linked to different forms of oppression. I consider that it leads to a view of identity that is at odds with a conception of radical and plural democracy and that it does not allow us to construe the new vision of citizenship that is required by such a politics.

The Question of Identity and Feminism

One common tenet of critics of essentialism has been the abandoning of the category of the subject as a rational transparent entity that could convey a homogeneous meaning on the total field of her conduct by being the source of her action. For instance, psychoanalysis has shown that far from being organized around the transparency of an ego, personality is structured in a number of levels which lie outside of the consciousness and the rationality of the agents. It has therefore undermined the idea of the unified character of the subject. Freud's central claim is that the human mind is necessarily subject to division between two systems of which one is not and cannot be conscious. Expanding the Freudian vision, Lacan has shown the plurality of registers—the Symbolic, the Real, and the Imaginary—which penetrate any identity, and the place of the subject as the place of the lack which—though represented within the structure—is the empty place which at the same time subverts and is the condition of constitution of any identity. The history of the subject is the history of his/her identifications and there is no concealed identity to be rescued beyond the latter. There is thus a double movement. On the one hand, a movement of decentering which prevents the fixation of a set of positions around a preconstituted point. On the other hand, and as a result of this *essential* nonfixity, the opposite movement: the institution of nodal points, partial fixations which limit the flux of the signified under the signifier. But this dialectics at nonfixity/fixation is possible only because fixity is not given beforehand, because no center of subjectivity precedes the subject's identifications.

In the philosophy of language of the later Wittgenstein, we also find a critique of the rationalist conception of the subject that indicates that the latter cannot be the source of linguistic meanings since it is through participation in different language games that the world is disclosed to us. We encounter the same idea in Gadamer's philosophical hermeneutics in the thesis that there is a fundamental unity between thought, language, and the world and that it is within language that the horizon of our present is constituted. A similar critique of the centrality of the subject in modern metaphysics and of its unitary character can be found under several forms in the other authors mentioned earlier. However, my purpose here is not to examine those theories in detail but simply to indicate some basic convergences. I am not overlooking the fact that there are important differences among all those very diverse thinkers. But from the point of view of the argument that I want to make, it is important to grasp the consequences of their common critique of the traditional status of the subject and of its implications for feminism.

It is often said that the deconstruction of essential identities, which is the result of acknowledging the contingency and ambiguity of every identity, renders feminist political action impossible. Many feminists believe that, without seeing women as a coherent identity, we cannot ground the possibility of a feminist political movement in which women could unite as women in order to formulate and pursue specific feminist aims. Contrary to that view, I will argue that, for those feminists who are committed to a radical democratic politics, the deconstruction of essential identities should be seen as the necessary condition for an adequate understanding of the variety of social relations where the principles of liberty and equality should apply. It is only when we discard the view of the subject as an agent both rational and transparent to itself, and discard as well the supposed unity and homogeneity of the ensemble of its positions, that we are in the position to theorize the multiplicity of relations of subordination. A single individual can be the bearer of this multiplicity and be dominant in one relation while subordinated in another. We can then conceive the social agent as constituted by an ensemble of "subject positions" that can never be totally fixed in a closed system of differences, constructed by a diversity of discourses among which there is no necessary relation, but a constant movement of overdetermination and displacement. The "identity" of such a multiple and contradictory subject is therefore always contingent and precarious, temporarily fixed at the intersection of those subject positions and dependent on specific forms of identification. It is therefore impossible to speak of the social agent as if we were dealing with a unified, homogeneous entity. We have rather to approach it as a plurality, dependent on the various subject positions through which it is constituted within various discursive formations. And to recognize that there is no a priori, necessary relation between the discourses that construct its different subject positions. But, for the reasons pointed out earlier, this plurality does not involve the *coexistence,* one by one, of a plurality of subject positions but rather the constant subversion and overdetermination of one by the others, which make possible the generation of "totalizing effects" within a field characterized by open and indeterminate frontiers.

Such an approach is extremely important to understand feminist as well as other contemporary struggles. Their central characteristic is that an ensemble of subject positions linked through inscription in social relations, hitherto considered as apolitical, have become loci of conflict and antagonism and have led to political mobilization. The proliferation of these new forms of struggle can only be theoretically tackled when one starts with the dialectics and decentering/ recentering described earlier.

In *Hegemony and Socialist Strategy,*[2] Ernesto Laclau and I have attempted to draw the consequences of such a theoretical approach for a project of radical and plural democracy. We argued for the need to establish a chain of equivalence among the different democratic struggles so as to create an equivalent articulation between the demands of women, blacks, workers, gays, and others. On this point our perspective differs from other nonessentialist views where the aspect of detotalization and decentering prevails and where the dispersion of subject positions is transformed into an effective separation, as is the case with Lyotard and to some extent with Foucault. For us, the aspect of articulation is crucial. To deny the existence of an a priori, necessary link between subject positions does not mean that there are not constant efforts to establish between them historical, contingent, and variable links. This type of link, which establishes between various positions a contingent, unpredetermined relation is what we designated as "articulation." Even though there is no necessary link between different subject positions, in the field of politics there are always discourses that try to provide an articulation from different standpoints. For that reason every subject position is constituted within an essentially unstable discursive structure since it is submitted to a variety of articulatory practices that constantly subvert and transform it. This is why there is no subject position whose links with others is definitively assured and, therefore, no social identity that would be fully and permanently acquired. This does not mean, however, that we cannot retain notions like "working-class," "men," "women," "blacks," or other signifiers referring to collective subjects. However, once the existence of a common essence has been discarded, their status must be conceived in terms of what Wittgenstein designates as "family resemblances" and their unity must be seen as the result of the partial fixation of identities through the creation of nodal points.

For feminists to accept such an approach has very important consequences for the way we formulate our political struggles. If the category "woman" does not correspond to any unified and unifying essence, the question can no longer be to try to unearth it. The central issues become: how is "woman" constructed as a category within different discourses? how is sexual difference made a pertinent distinction in social relations? and how are relations of subordination constructed through such a distinction? The whole false dilemma of equality versus difference is exploded since we no longer have a homogeneous entity "woman" facing another homogeneous entity "man," but a multiplicity of social relations in which sexual difference is always constructed in very diverse ways and where the struggle against subordination has to be visualized in specific and differential forms. To ask if women should become identical to men in order to be recognized as equal, or if they should assert their difference at the cost of equality, appears meaningless once essential identities are put into question.[3]

Citizenship and Feminist Politics

In consequence, the very question of what a feminist politics should be, has to be posed in completely different terms. So far, most feminists concerned with the contribution that feminism could make to democratic politics have been looking either for the specific demands that could express women's interests or for the specific feminine values that should become the model for democratic politics. Liberal feminists have been fighting for a wide range of new rights for women to make them equal citizens, but without challenging the dominant liberal models of citizenship and politics. Their view has been criticized by other feminists who argue that the present conception of the political is a male one and that women's concerns cannot be accommodated within such a framework. Following Carol Gilligan, they oppose a feminist "ethics of care" to the male and liberal "ethics of justice." Against liberal individualist values, they defend a set of values based on the experience of women *as* women, that is, their experience of motherhood and care exercised in the private realm of the family. They denounce Liberalism for having constructed modern citizenship as the realm of the public, identified with men, and for having excluded women by relegating them to the private realm. According to this view, feminists should strive for a type of politics that is guided by the specific values of love, care, the recognition of needs, and friendship. One of the clearest attempts to offer an alternative to liberal politics grounded in feminine values is to be found in "Maternal Thinking" and "Social Feminism" principally represented by Sara Ruddick and Jean Bethke Elshtain.[4] Feminist politics, they argue, should privilege the identity of "women as mothers" and the private realm of the family. The family is seen as having moral superiority over the public domain of politics because it constitutes our common humanity. For Elshtain "the family remains the locus of the deepest and most resonant human ties, the most enduring hopes, the most intractable conflicts."[5] She considers that it is in the family that we should look for a new political morality to replace liberal individualism. In women's experience in the private realm as mothers, she says, a new model for the activity of citizenship is to be found. The maternalists want us to abandon the male liberal politics of the public informed by the abstract point of view of justice and the "generalized other" and adopt instead a feminist politics of the private, informed by the virtues of love, intimacy, and concern for the "concrete other" specific to the family.

An excellent critique of such an approach has been provided by Mary Dietz[6] who shows that Elshtain fails to provide a theoretical argument which links maternal thinking and the social practice of mothering to democratic values and democratic politics. Dietz argues that maternal virtues cannot be political because they are connected with and emerge from an activity that is special and distinctive. They are the expression of an unequal relation between mother and child which is also an intimate, exclusive, and particular activity. Democratic citizenship, on the contrary, should be collective, inclusive, and generalized. Since democracy is a condition in which individuals aim at being equals, the mother–child relationship cannot provide an adequate model of citizenship.

Yet a different feminist critique of liberal citizenship is provided by Carole Pateman.[7] It is more sophisticated, but shares some common features with "Maternal Thinking." Pateman's tone bears the traces of radical feminism, for the accent is put, not on the mother/child relation, but on the man/woman antagonism.

Citizenship is, according to Pateman, a patriarchal category: who a "citizen" is, what a citizen does and the arena within which he acts have been constructed in the masculine image. Although women in liberal democracies are now citizens, formal citizenship has been won within a structure of patriarchal power in which women's qualities and tasks are still devalued. Moreover, the call for women's distinctive capacities to be integrated fully into the public world of citizenship faces what she calls the "Wollstonecraft dilemma": to demand equality is to accept the patriarchal conception of citizenship which implies that women must become like men while to insist that women's distinctive attributes, capacities, and activities be given expression and valued as contributing to citizenship is to demand the impossible because such difference is precisely what patriarchal citizenship excludes.

Pateman sees the solution to this dilemma in the elaboration of a "sexually differentiated" conception of citizenship that would recognize women *as* women, with their bodies and all that they symbolize. For Pateman this entails giving political significance to the capacity that men lack: to create life, which is to say, *motherhood*. She declares that this capacity should be treated with equal political relevance for defining citizenship as what is usually considered the ultimate test of citizenship: a man's willingness to fight and to die for his country. She considers that the traditional patriarchal way of posing an alternative, where either the separation or the sameness of the sexes is valorized, needs to be overcome by a new way of posing the question of women. This can be done through a conception of citizenship that recognizes both the specificity of womanhood and the common humanity of men and women. Such a view "that gives due weight to sexual difference in a context of civil equality, requires the rejection of a unitary (i.e., masculine) conception of the individual, abstracted from our embodied existence and from the patriarchal division between the private and the public."[8] What feminists should aim for is the elaboration of a sexually differentiated conception of individuality and citizenship that would include "women *as* women in a context of civil equality and active citizenship."[9]

Pateman provides many very interesting insights into the patriarchal bias of the social contract theorists and the way in which the liberal individual has been constructed according to the male image. I consider that her own solution, however, is unsatisfactory. Despite all her provisos about the historically constructed aspects of sexual difference, her view still postulates the existence of some kind of essence corresponding to women *as* women. Indeed, her proposal for a differentiated citizenship that recognizes the specificity of womanhood rests on the identification of women *as* women with motherhood. There are for her two basic types of individuality that should be expressed in two different forms of citizenship: men *as* men and women *as* women. The problem according to her is that the category of the "individual," while based on the male model, is presented as the universal form of individuality. Feminists must uncover that false universality by asserting the existence of two sexually differentiated forms of universality; this is the only way to resolve the "Wollstonecraft dilemma" and to break free from the patriarchal alternatives of "othering" and "saming."

I agree with Pateman that the modern category of the individual has been constructed in a manner that postulates a universalist, homogeneous "public" that relegates all particularity and difference to the "private" and that this has very negative consequences for women. I do not believe, however, that the remedy is to replace it by a sexually differentiated, "bi-gendered" conception of the individual and to bring women's so-called specific tasks into the very definition of citizenship. It seems to me that such a solution remains trapped in the very problematic that Pateman wants to challenge. She affirms that the separation between public and private is the founding moment of modern patriarchalism because

> the separation of private and public is the separation of the world of natural subjection, i.e. women, from the world of conventional relations and individuals, i.e. men. The feminine, private world of nature, particularity, differentiation, inequality, emotion, love and ties of blood is set apart from the public, universal—and masculine—realm of convention, civil equality and freedom, reason, consent and contract.[10]

It is for that reason that childbirth and motherhood have been presented as the antithesis of citizenship and that they have become the symbol of everything natural that cannot be part of the "public" but must remain in a separate sphere. By asserting the political value of motherhood, Pateman intends to overcome that distinction and contribute to the deconstruction of the patriarchal conception of citizenship and private and public life. As a result of her essentialism, however, she never deconstructs the very opposition of men/women. This is the reason that she ends up, like the maternalists, proposing an inadequate conception of what should be a democratic politics informed by feminism. This is why she can assert that "the most profound and complex problem for political theory and practice is how the two bodies of humankind and feminine and masculine individuality can be fully incorporated into political life."[11]

My own view is completely different. I want to argue that the limitations of the modern conception of citizenship should be remedied, not by making sexual difference politically relevant to its definition, but by constructing a new conception of citizenship where sexual difference should become effectively nonpertinent. This, of course, requires a conception of the social agent in the way that I have defended earlier, as the articulation of an ensemble of subject positions, corresponding to the multiplicity of social relations in which it is inscribed. This multiplicity is constructed within specific discourses which have no necessary relation but only contingent and precarious forms of articulation. There is no reason why sexual difference should be pertinent in all social relations. To be sure, today many different pratices, discourses and institutions do construct men and women (differentially), and the masculine/feminine distinction exists as a pertinent one in many fields. But this does not imply that it should remain the case, and we can perfectly imagine sexual difference becoming irrelevant in many social relations where it is currently found. This is indeed the objective of many feminist struggles.

I am not arguing in favor of a total disappearance of sexual difference as a pertinent distinction; I am not saying either that equality between men and women requires gender-neutral social relations, and it is clear that, in many cases, to treat men and women equally implies treating them differentially. My thesis is that, in the domain of politics, and as far as citizenship is concerned, sexual difference should not be a pertinent distinction. I am at one with Pateman in criticizing the liberal, male conception of modern citizenship but I believe that what a project of radical and plural democracy needs is not a sexually differentiated model of citizenship in which the specific tasks of both men and women would be valued equally, but a truly different conception of what it is to be a citizen and to act as a member of a democratic political community.

A Radical Democratic Conception of Citizenship

The problems with the liberal conception of citizenship are not limited to those concerning women, and feminists committed to a project of radical and plural democracy should engage with all of them. Liberalism has contributed to the formulation of the notion of universal citizenship, based on the assertion that all individuals are born free and equal, but it has also reduced citizenship to a merely legal status, indicating the rights that the individual holds against the state. The way those rights are exercised is irrelevant as long as their holders do not break the law or interfere with the rights of others. Notions of public-spiritedness, civic activity and political participation in a community of equals are alien to most liberal thinkers. Besides, the public realm of modern citizenship was constructed in a universalistic and rationalistic manner that precluded the recognition of division and antagonism and that relegated to the private all particularity and difference. The distinction public/private, central as it was for the assertion of individual liberty, acted therefore as a powerful principle of exclusion. Through the identification between the private and the domestic, it played indeed an important role in the subordination of women. Recently, several feminists and other critics of liberalism have been looking to the civic republican tradition for a different, more active conception of citizenship that emphasizes the value of political participation and the notion of a common good, prior to and independent of individual desires and interests.

Nevertheless, feminists should be aware of the limitations of such an approach and of the potential dangers that a communitarian type of politics presents for the struggle of many oppressed groups. The communitarian insistence on a substantive notion of the common good and shared moral values is incompatible with the pluralism that is constitutive of modern democracy and that I consider to be necessary to deepen the democratic revolution and accommodate the multiplicity of present democratic demands. The problems with the liberal construction of the public/private distinction would not be solved by discarding it, but only by reformulating it in a more adequate way. Moreover, the centrality of the notion of rights for a modern conception of the citizen should be acknowledged, even though these must be complemented by a more active sense of political participation and of belonging to a political community.[12]

The view of radical and plural democracy that I want to put forward sees citizenship as a form of political identity that consists in the identification with the political principles of modern pluralist democracy, namely, the assertion of liberty and equality for all. It would be a common political identity of persons who might be engaged in many different purposive enterprises and with differing conceptions of the good, but who are bound by their common identification with a given interpretation of a set of ethico-political values. Citizenship is not just one identity among others, as it is in Liberalism, nor is it the dominant identity that overrides all others, as it is in Civic Republicanism. Instead, it is an articulating principle that affects the different subject positions of the social agent while allowing for a plurality of specific allegiances and for the respect of individual liberty. In this view, the public/private distinction is not abandoned, but constructed in a different way. The distinction does not correspond to discrete, separate spheres; every situation is an encounter between "private" and "public" because every enterprise is private while never immune from the public conditions prescribed by the principles of citizenship. Wants, choices and decisions are private because they are the responsibility of each individual, but performances are public because they have to subscribe to the conditions specified by a specific understanding of the ethico-political principles of the regime which provide the "grammar" of the citizen's conduct.[13]

It is important to stress here that if we affirm that the exercise of citizenship consists in identifying with the ethico-political principles of modern democracy, we must also recognize that there can be as many forms of citizenship as there are interpretations of those principles and that a radical democratic interpretation is one among others. A radical democratic interpretation will emphasize the numerous social relations in which situations of domination exist that must be challenged if the principles of liberty and equality are to apply. It indicates the common recognition by the different groups struggling for an extension and radicalization of democracy that they have a common concern. This should lead to the articulation of the democratic demands found in a variety of movements:

women, workers, blacks, gays, ecological, as well as other "new social move-ments." The aim is to construct a "we" as radical democratic citizens, a collective political identity articulated through the principle of democratic *equivalence*. It must be stressed that such a relation of *equivalence* does not eliminate *difference*—that would be simple identity. It is only insofar as democratic differences are opposed to forces or discourses which negate all of them that these differences are substitutable for each other.

The view that I am proposing here is clearly different from the liberal as well as the civic republican one. It is not a gendered conception of citizenship, but neither is it a neutral one. It recognizes that every definition of a "we" implies the delimitation of a "frontier" and the designation of a "them." That definition of a "we" always takes place, then, in a context of diversity and conflict. Contrary to Liberalism, which evacuates the idea of the common good, and Civic Republicanism, which reifies it, a radical democratic approach views the common good as a "vanishing point," something to which we must constantly refer when we are acting as citizens, but that can never be reached. The common good functions, on the one hand, as a "social imaginary": that is, as that for which the very impossibility of achieving full representation gives to it the role of an horizon which is the condition of possibility of any representation within the space that it delimits. On the other hand, it specifies what I have designated, following Wittgenstein, as a "grammar of conduct" that coincides with the allegiance to the constitutive ethico-political principles of modern democracy: liberty and equality for all. Yet, since those principles are open to many competing interpretations, one has to acknowledge that a fully inclusive political community can never be realized. There will always be a "constitutive outside," an exterior to the community that is the very condition of its existence. Once it is accepted that there cannot be a "we" without a "them" and that all forms of consensus are by necessity based on acts of exclusion, the question cannot be any more the creation of a fully inclusive community where antagonism, division, and conflict will have disappeared. Hence, we have to come to terms with the very impossibility of a full realization of democracy.

Such a radical democratic citizenship is obviously at odds with the "sexually differentiated" view of citizenship of Carole Pateman, but also with another feminist attempt to offer an alternative to the liberal view of the citizen: the "group differentiated" conception put forward by Iris Young.[14] Like Pateman, Young argues that modern citizenship has been constructed on a separation between "public" and "private" that presented the public as the realm of homogeneity and universality and relegated difference to the private. But she insists that this exclusion affects not only women but many other groups based on differences of ethnicity, race, age, disabilities, and so forth. For Young, the crucial problem is that the public realm of citizenship was presented as expressing a general will, a point of view that citizens held in common and that transcended their differences. Young argues in favor of a repoliticization of public life that would not require the creation of a public realm in which citizens leave behind their particular group affiliation and needs in order to discuss a presumed general interest or common good. In its place she proposes the creation of a "heterogeneous public" that provides mechanisms for the effective representation and recognition of the distinct voices and perspectives of those constituent groups that are oppressed or disadvantaged. In order to make such a project possible, she looks for a conception of normative reason that does not pretend to be impartial and universal and that does not oppose reason to affectivity and desire. She considers that, despite its limitations, Habermas's communicative ethics can contribute a good deal to its formulation.

Whereas I sympathize with Young's attempt to take account of other forms of oppression than the ones suffered by women, I nevertheless find her solution of "group differentiated citizenship" highly problematic. To begin with, the notion of a group that she identifies with comprehensive identities and ways of life might make sense for groups like Native Americans, but is completely inadequate as a description for many other groups whose demands she wants to take into account like women, the elderly, the differently abled, and others. She has an ultimately essentialist notion of "group," and this accounts for why, in spite of all her disclaimers, her view is not so different from the interest-group pluralism that she criticizes: there are groups with their interests and identities already given, and politics is not about the construction of new identities, but about finding ways to satisfy the demands of the various parts in a way acceptable to all. In fact, one could say that hers is a kind of "Habermasian version of interest group pluralism," according to which groups are not viewed as fighting for egoistic private interests but for justice, and where the emphasis is put on the need for argumentation and publicity. So politics in her work is still conceived as a process of dealing with already-constituted interests and identities while, in the approach that I am defending, the aim of a radical democratic citizenship should be the construction of a common political identity that would create the conditions for the establishment of a new hegemony articulated through new egalitarian social relations, practices and institutions. This cannot be achieved without the transformation of existing subject positions; this is the reason why the model of the rainbow coalition favored by Young can be seen only as a first stage toward the implementation of a radical democratic politics. It might indeed provide many opportunities for a dialogue among different oppressed groups, but for their demands to be construed around the principle of democratic equivalence, new identities need to be created: in their present state many of these demands are antithetical to each other, and their convergence can only result from a political process of hegemonic articulation, and not simply of free and undistorted communication.

Feminist Politics and Radical Democracy

As I indicated at the outset, there has been a great deal of concern among feminists about the possibility of grounding a feminist politics once the existence of women *as* women is put into question. It has been argued that to abandon the idea of a feminine subject with a specific identity and definable interests was to pull the rug from under feminism as politics. According to Kate Soper,

> feminism, like any other politics, has always implied a banding together, a movement based on the solidarity and sisterhood of women, who are linked by perhaps very little else than their *sameness* and "common cause" as women. If this sameness itself is challenged on the ground that there is no "presence" of

womanhood, nothing that the term "woman" immediately expresses, and nothing instantiated concretely except particular women in particular situations, then the idea of a political community built around women—the central aspiration of the early feminist movement— collapses.[15]

I consider that Soper here construes an illegitimate opposition between two extreme alternatives: either there is an already given unity of "womanhood" on the basis of some a priori belonging or, if this is denied, no forms of unity and feminist politics can exist. The absence of a female essential identity and of a pre-given unity, however, does not preclude the construction of multiple forms of unity and common action. As the result of the construction of nodal points, partial fixations can take place and precarious forms of identification can be established around the category "women" that provide the basis for a feminist identity and a feminist struggle. We find in Soper a type of misunderstanding of the antiessentialist position that is frequent in feminist writings and that consists in believing that the critique of an essential identity must necessarily lead to the rejection of any concept of identity whatsoever.[16]

In *Gender Trouble*,[17] Judith Butler asks, "What new shape of politics emerges when identity as a common ground no longer constrains the discourse of feminist politics?" My answer is that to visualize feminist politics in that way opens much greater opportunity for a democratic politics that aims at the articulation of the various different struggles against oppression. What emerges is the possibility of a project of radical and plural democracy.

To be adequately formulated, such a project requires discarding the essentialist idea of an identity of women *as* women as well as the attempt to ground a specific and strictly feminist politics. Feminist politics should be understood not as a separate form of politics designed to pursue the interests of women *as* women, but rather as the pursuit of feminist goals and aims within the context of a wider articulation of demands. Those goals and aims should consist in the transformation of all the discourses, practices and social relations where the category "woman" is constructed in a way that implies subordination. Feminism, for me, is the struggle for the equality of women. But this should not be understood as a struggle for realizing the equality of a definable empirical group with a common essence and identity, women, but rather as a struggle against the multiple forms in which the category "woman" is constructed in subordination. However, we must be aware of the fact that those feminist goals can be constructed in many different ways, according to the multiplicity of discourses in which they can be framed: Marxist, liberal, conservative, radical-separatist, radical-democratic, and so on. There are, therefore, by necessity many feminisms and any attempt to find the "true" form of feminist politics should be abandoned. I believe that feminists can contribute to politics a reflection on the conditions for creating an effective equality of women. Such a reflection is bound to be influenced by the existing political and theoretical discourses. Instead of trying to prove that a given form of feminist discourse is the one that corresponds to the "real" essence of womanhood, one should intend to show how it opens better possibilities for an understanding of women's multiple forms of subordination.

My main argument here has been that, for feminists who are committed to a political project whose aim is to struggle against the forms of subordination which exist in many social relations, and not only in those linked to gender, an approach that permits us to understand how the subject is constructed through different discourses and subject positions is certainly more adequate than one that reduces our identity to one single position—be it class, race, or gender. This type of democratic project is also better served by a perspective that allows us to grasp the diversity of ways in which relations of power are constructed and helps us to reveal the forms of exclusion present in all pretensions to universalism and in claims to have found the true essence of rationality. This is why the critique of essentialism and all its different forms: humanism, rationalism, universalism, far from being an obstacle to the formulation of a feminist democratic project is indeed the very condition of its possibility.

Notes

1. See the issue of the journal *Differences,* 1 (September 1989), entitled "The Essential Difference: Another Look at Essentialism" as well as the recent book by Diana Fuss, *Essentially Speaking* (New York: Routledge, 1989).
2. Ernesto Laclau and Chantal Mouffe, *Hegemony and Socialist Strategy. Towards a Radical Democratic Politics* (London: Verso, 1985).
3. For an interesting critique of the dilemma of equality versus difference which is inspired by a similar *problématique* from the one I am defending here, see Joan W. Scott, *Gender and The Politics of History* (New York: Columbia Univ. Press, 1988), Part IV. Among feminists the critique of essentialism was first developed by the journal *m/f* which during its eight years of existence (1978–1986) made an invaluable contribution to feminist theory. I consider that it has not yet been superseded and that the editorials as well as the articles by Parveen Adams still represent the most forceful exposition of the antiessentialist stance. A selection of the best articles from the 12 issues of *m/f* are reprinted in *The Woman In Question,* edited by Parveen Adams and Elisabeth Cowie (Cambridge, Mass.: MIT Press, 1990 and London: Verso, 1990).
4. Sara Ruddick, *Maternal Thinking* (London: Verso, 1989); Jean Bethke Elshtain, *Public Man, Private Woman* (Princeton: Princeton University Press, 1981).
5. Jean Bethke Elshtain, "On 'The Family Crisis,'" *Democracy,* 3, 1 (Winter 1983) p. 138.
6. Mary G. Dietz, "Citizenship with a Feminist Face. The Problem with Maternal Thinking," *Political Theory,* 13, 1 (February 1985).
7. Carole Pateman, *The Sexual Contract* (Stanford: Stanford University Press, 1988), and *The Disorder of Women* (Cambridge: Polity Press, 1989), as well as numerous unpublished papers on which I will also be drawing, especially the following: "Removing Obstacles to Democracy: The Case of Patriarchy"; "Feminism and Participatory Democracy: Some Reflections on Sexual Difference and Citizenship"; "Women's Citizenship: Equality, Difference, Subordination."
8. Carole Pateman, "Feminism and Participatory Democracy," unpublished paper presented to the Meeting of the American Philosophical Association, St. Louis, Missouri, May 1986, p. 24.
9. Ibid., p. 26.
10. Carole Pateman, "Feminism and Participatory Democracy," pp. 7–8.
11. Carole Pateman, *The Disorder of Women,* p. 53.

12. I analyze more in detail the debate between liberals and communitarians in my article "American Liberalism and Its Critics: Rawls, Taylor, Sandel and Walzer," *Praxis International*, 8, 2 (July 1988).

13. The conception of citizenship that I am presenting here is developed more fully in my "Democratic Citizenship and The Political Community," in *Community at Loose Ends*, edited by the Miami Theory Collective (Minneapolis, MN: University of Minnesota Press, 1991).

14. Iris Marion Young, "Impartiality and the Civic Public," in *Feminism as Critique*, edited by Seyla Benhabib and Drucilla Cornell (Minneapolis: University of Minnesota Press, 1987) and "Polity and Group Difference: A Critique of the Ideal of Universal Citizenship," *Ethics*, 99 (January 1989).

15. Kate Soper, "Feminism, Humanism and Postmodernism," *Radical Philosophy, 55* (Summer 1990), pp. 11–17.

16. We find a similar confusion in Diana Fuss who, as Anna Marie Smith indicates in her review of *Essentially Speaking, Feminist Review*, 38 (Summer 1991), does not realize that the repetition of a sign can take place without an essentialist grounding. It is for that reason that she can affirm that constructionism is essentialist as far as it entails the repetition of the same signifiers across different contexts.

17. Judith Butler, *Gender Trouble, Feminism and the Subversion of Identity* (New York: Routledge, 1990). p. xi.

Questions to Consider

1. How do you understand the terms "politics" and "rhetoric"? What are some of the different ways that the essays in this section help you revise some of your own thinking about these two terms? How do the essays in this section intersect with or contextualize your own experiences not only in literature classes, but also in daily life outside the classroom?

2. Do you have an essential identity? If so, what accounts for that identity in your eyes? What might account for it in the eyes of others? If your attitude is antiessentialist, how have you arrived at that understanding of yourself? What practical consequences might there be in your own life if you either have or do not have an essential identity?

3. In "Rhetoric," Stanley Fish discusses *homo seriosus* and *homo rhetoricus*, terms Richard Lanham uses to distinguish broadly contrasting attitudes toward conceptions of truth and how we generally understand our world. How do you define the politics of *homo seriosus* and *homo rhetoricus?* Do you see the study of literature as closer to the attitudes Lanham identifies with *homo seriosus* or with *homo rhetoricus?* Do you see yourself as closer to one or the other? Which is each of the theorists in this section closest to?

4. Fish's essay "Rhetoric" describes a back-and-forth debate or battle between people antagonistic to rhetoric as artificial and manipulative and people who accept rhetoric as a natural part of our lives. Where would you place Baym and Said in this debate, and why? Are they likely to lean toward antagonism toward rhetoric or toward acceptance of rhetoric? Which way do you lean?

5. Debates about literary canons highlight questions not only about what educated people should presumably know about literature but also about what approaches or methodologies people can use to examine texts. What methodologies do Baym, Knapp and Michaels, Said, and Fish favor, and why? What are the politics of these methodologies? In other words, what do the respective theorists' methodologies or approaches favor or emphasize, and what do the methodologies disapprove of or call into question?

6. Knapp and Michaels's essay is titled "Against Theory." Each of the other essays in this section might similarly be titled "Against _____" (fill in the blank). What are the other theorists against? What common threads do you see? What rhetoric does each theorist employ to make her or his case against _____? What kind of theory or practice are you against, and why?

VI

ART AND
ENTERTAINMENT

Long ago, Aristotle characterized us as political animals, but he could have said that we are performing animals as well. Indeed, Shakespeare's memorable lines from *As You Like It*—"All the world's a "stage,/And all the men and women merely players"—signal our performing nature. Notice also how Shakespeare's choice of title calls attention to the play as entertainment, which is no small point. For quite a long time, Shakespeare has represented "art with a capital *A*," and for much of the twentieth century, entertainment meant simply an amusing public performance or show. In fact, entertainment was often trivialized as escapism and understood as the opposite of "art with a capital *A*," which has traditionally signified beautiful or refined skills or techniques. For example, critics have typically hailed as high art Vincent Van Gogh's brilliant colors and distinctive brush strokes, Luis Bunuel's cinematic surrealism, Martha Graham's modern dance choreography, and Emily Dickinson's range of metaphor and stylistic idiosyncrasies in poetry. Similarly, appreciation of such artists has long signaled social distinction, whereas appreciation of cartoons, graffiti, popular songs, and soap operas has not. Only recently have university courses in popular culture rubbed shoulders with classes in art history and renaissance literature, traditional staples of a liberal arts education. Today, the existence of college seminars devoted to such topics as Madonna or a collection of scholarly essays about philosophy in *The Simpsons* signals reconfigurations of what counts as knowledge. Only a generation ago, however, few scholars would have challenged the following assertions: Pablo Picasso is an artist, but Norman Rockwell is not; likewise, Virginia Woolf writes literature, but Mary Corelli does not.

Much changes in a generation, as university classes in popular culture suggest. The art of entertainment now commands serious scholarly attention, and many people find aesthetic distinctions between elite art and mass entertainment much less appropriate and persuasive in light of progressive social changes (for instance, the Civil Rights and women's rights movements) and democratizing and radical critical theories that challenge traditional understandings of culture. Clearly, the refined distinction between art and entertainment seems as blurry as the line between network news and the Daily Show on Comedy Central. Can news anchor Dan Rather be both a serious journalist and a celebrity? Are Bugs Bunny cartoons merely children's entertainment or artifacts of larger cultural relevance? Is the renowned cellist Yo-Yo Ma an artist, an entertainer, or both? If beauty is in the eye of the beholder, how do we arrive at a consensus about art? Reflect on your own preferences, your own tastes, and your own interpretive practices. What appeals to you, and why? Much critical theory similarly reflects on how we respond to human creativity and to labels like art and entertainment.

It should hardly surprise you that critical theory focusing on our responses to art and entertainment often emphasizes strategies of interpretation. The title of Susan Sontag's 1964 essay "Against Interpretation," however, may catch you flat footed. What kind of critic argues against interpretation? We routinely think of interpretation as a critic's job, just as a doctor's job is to diagnose or interpret illness. Moreover, professors ask students to interpret poems, fiction, plays, and films in English classes every day. Sontag is troubled, however, by the widespread practice of focusing on a work of art's content instead of its form and style. In his influential theory of mimesis, or imitation, Plato says the purpose of art is to mirror reality, and Sontag says critical engagement with art since Plato has typically meant offering an interpretation, that is, translating the content by detecting a meaning hidden or buried within the content. From Sontag's perspective, content gets in the way of experiencing art; content is a kind of shield or screen that separates and alienates us from artistic sensation. Ironically, the theory of mimesis—art imitates reality—makes art unreal. According to Sontag, "the aim of all commentary on art should be to make works of art—and, by analogy, our own experience—more, rather than less, real to us."

Strip mining for coal decimates the landscape, and Sontag would similarly argue that interpretation ravages literature, film, and painting. Hermeneutical activity, that is, interpretation, not only destroys texts; it also enervates or weakens us, according to Sontag: "The effusion of interpretations of art today poisons our sensibilities." "Real art," Sontag claims, "has the capacity to make us nervous. By reducing the work of art to its content and then interpreting that, one tames the work of art. Interpretation makes art manageable, conformable." Her emphasis on how interpretation atrophies or withers both art and our own "sensibilities" suggests our loss of what makes us human: unique emotional responses. From her perspective, scientific precision and probing leave us artistically unconscious, like T. S. Eliot's "patient etherised upon a table," unaware of the excitement and sensuous pleasures of art.

Particularly critical of psychoanalytic and Marxist critics for profaning or despoiling art, Sontag says, "The modern style of interpretation excavates, and as it excavates, destroys; it digs 'behind' the text, to find a sub-text which is the true one. The most celebrated and influential modern doctrines, those of Marx and Freud, actually amount to elaborate systems of hermeneutics, aggressive and impious theories of interpretation." What approach to art does Sontag advocate? If "real art" make us "nervous," then what is the value of such art, from Sontag's perspective? Why will emphasis on form rather than content arouse us to "recover our senses" and "learn to *see* more, to *hear* more, to *feel* more," assuming that Sontag's interpretation of interpretation is accurate? Her provocative conclusion suggests that sensations rather than deep messages best convey the effect of art: "In place of a hermeneutics we need an erotics of art." If so, how does an "erotics of art" resist Plato's mimetic theory? Why is it necessarily a better approach than Marxist and psychoanalytic theories? Might someone accuse Sontag of formalistic blindness, of sacrificing attention to content and context for the sake of elite aesthetic pleasure in formal ingenuity?

Laura Mulvey's approach in her 1973 essay "Fears, Fantasies and the Male Unconscious *or* 'You Don't Know What is Happening, Do You, Mr. Jones?'" contrasts with Sontag's antihermeneutic message. For example, Mulvey opens her essay, which is about the sculpture of pop artist Allen Jones, with an epigraph from Sigmund Freud. Sontag, of course, harshly criticizes the use of Freud as a critical framework for the analysis of art in "Against Interpretation." Mulvey's use of Freud signals a key development in art and cultural criticism: the turn to psychoanalytic theory by many feminist scholars in the 1970s and 1980s as a means of demystifying the objectification of women in patriarchal societies.

Mulvey uses Freud's theory of fetishism as a critical lens for viewing representations of women's bodies such as Jones's sculpture series, "Women as Furniture." Jones' life-sized sculptures represent scantily clad women as chairs, tables, and hat stands. Hardly the "erotics of art" Sontag longs for, the sculpture series, according to Mulvey, reveals how representations of women paradoxically function in the patriarchal unconscious as signs of phallic or male identity and castration anxiety. Mulvey views the paradox in terms of fetishism, which Freud defined as a substitution of an object such as a foot, a shoe, a hand, or a ring for the "missing" maternal penis. The fetishistic object becomes the site of libidinal or sexual energy, and Mulvey believes that fetishistic discourse and visual imagery address our unconscious every day through popular media. What is more, Mulvey argues that such discourse and imagery are not really about the women represented but instead about narcissistic male fears of castration: "Man and his phallus are the real subject of Allen Jones's paintings and sculptures, even though they deal exclusively with images of women on display." Compare such a critical perspective with Sontag's objection to critical practices that "excavate" or "dig 'behind' the text, to find a sub-text which is the true one." To argue, as Mulvey does, that representations of women are paradoxically best understood as representations of male identity exemplifies a version of the hermeneutical approach

Sontag disparages: the argument that what appears to be *X*—in this case, visual displays of women—is really, instead, not *X*, but *Y* (or anti-*X*)—in this case, representations of male identity that also imply castration anxiety.

Reflecting on the following quotation and Mulvey's other uses of Freud can help you understand how Mulvey's approach helps her—and you, too, potentially—to open up new vistas or views on art and entertainment: "Freud's analysis of the male unconscious is crucial for any understanding of the myriad ways in which the female form has been used as a mould into which meanings have been poured by a male-dominated culture." Many critics and theorists find such psychoanalytic insights enlightening, and Mulvey is particularly well known for her groundbreaking use of psychoanalytic theories to analyze the objectification of women in traditional Hollywood cinema. Think as well, however, about possible pitfalls of psychoanalytic approaches: tidy, predictable, reductionist conclusions. How does Mulvey seek to avoid oversimplifying her analysis? What might Sontag say about Mulvey's method of argument, and why?

Now that we have emphasized the differences between Mulvey's and Sontag's approaches, it makes sense to look for places where their critical paths might cross and head in similar directions. For example, in her conclusion, Mulvey urges replacing the popular media's everyday displays of women, which, according to her, actually reflect male or phallic identity, with art that presents women's "own fears and desires." What kind of erotics does Mulvey seem to have in mind, and might it be akin to Sontag's desire for "an erotics of art"? As you think about these questions, also reflect on whether there can be an "erotics of art" exclusive of psychoanalytic theories of desire, the erotic, and the sexual.

Mulvey's concern about the representation of women in art reflects concerns of the women's liberation movement of the 1970s, a movement preceded and empowered by the gains of the civil rights movement of the 1960s. The movement for civil rights helped usher in profound social changes in a variety of institutions, particularly education. As more minorities and women entered colleges and universities in the '60s and '70s, they encountered curricula focusing primarily on great cultural achievements of white males of European descent. Why were so few works by women and other minorities studied in college during those years? How were social inequalities mirrored in attitudes toward art and entertainment? Just as Mulvey attacks obstacles to female empowerment, Houston Baker's 1984 book *Blues, Ideology, and Afro-American Literature,* challenges the system of exclusions by using critical theory to demonstrate the centrality of black experience to the origins of the American self.

In the introduction to his book, Baker shows blues music to be a significant cultural achievement that is well deserving of serious analysis. Throughout the twentieth century, popular art forms like the blues were typically deemed to be entertainment and therefore unworthy of scholarly study. Moreover, other cultural performances by African-Americans were routinely dismissed, as were the productions of women. Higher education focused on "serious" cultural accomplishments: on Mozart and Beethoven, but not on Muddy Waters and Howling Wolf; on Nathaniel Hawthorne and Robert Frost, but not on Frederick Douglass and Zora Neale Hurston. In the blues rather than in a symphony, Baker finds "forceful and indigenous American creativity." He says, "Afro-American culture is a complex, reflexive enterprise which finds its proper figuration in blues conceived as a matrix." The abstract language of Baker's assertion is, paradoxically, part of his larger "vernacular theory" of American culture. Vernacular is the language or idiom of one's native country. It also signifies homely speech, and, in its Latin root meaning, vernacular pertains to slaves. Like the energy of blues music, the vernacular is transitional: while it has sometimes meant the marginal (e.g., slave), paradoxically it has also come to occupy the center (in its meaning as one's national linguistic norm). Long ago, Latin was the elite language while English, a vernacular, lacked prestige. Over time, the hegemony or supremacy of Latin has collapsed as vernacular languages such as English have risen in prestige, moving from the margins to the center. In Shakespeare's mastery of the English language, for example, England could boast of a national literary treasure; Shakespeare's greatness presumably signaled Britain's greatness on the world political stage. Similarly, in the blues, the United States can celebrate a priceless cultural achievement.

Like Mulvey, Baker also finds powerful intellectual weaponry in critical theory, which helps him turn back and vanquish racist stereotypes and dismissals of black cultural achievement. His "blues matrix" metaphor grounds his vernacular theory. According to Baker, "Afro-American culture is a complex, reflexive enterprise which finds its proper figuration in blues conceived as a matrix. A matrix is a womb, a network, a fossil-bearing rock, . . . a principle metal in an alloy, a mat or plate for reproducing print or photographic records. The matrix is a point of ceaseless input and output. . . . Afro-American blues constitute such a vibrant network." Blues musicians transform collective oppression into song; their translation of experience into the blues "constitutes a lively scene, a robust matrix, where endless antinomies are mediated and understanding and explanation find conditions of possibility." Unlike some popular art such as Hollywood films whose patriarchal support needs uncovering and disabling through critical analysis, the blues are already oppositional or critical of inequalities fostered by the dominant society. Hence, Baker's analysis praises rather than blames the popular art form.

In praising the musicians, Baker also lauds the critics who interpret blues music. Just as blues musicians are translators, so are blues critics, according to Baker: "The matrix effectively functions toward cultural understanding . . . only when an investigator brings an inventive attention to bear." Both the blues musician and the critic are virtuosi. As oppression gets transformed in the matrix into "the energies of rhythmic song," the song is also transformed through the creativity of the blues critic. What do you think of Baker's argument that the critic, too, shares the stage, so to speak, with the blues artists? How are a critic's performances improvisational, jam sessions of sorts? Can you connect Baker's claim that his theory involves "a willingness . . . to do more than merely hear, read, or see the blues," that he "must also play (with and on) them," with Sontag's imperative that "we must learn to *see* more, to *hear* more, to *feel* more"? How might Baker's theory connect with an "erotics of art" or with Mulvey's goal of women exhibiting their own "fears and desires"?

Like Baker's praise of blues music, Arthur Danto's writing celebrates pop art as another "properly American achievement." In "Pop Art and Past Futures," Danto examines how avant-garde works such as Andy Warhol's *Brillo Box* and paintings of Campbell's soup cans initiated an artistic sea change in the 1960s, rendering abstract expressionism, realism, and modernism exhausted, empty styles. Pop art signals "a cataclysmic moment" of "profound social and political shifts" as well as, according to Danto, equally "profound philosophical transformations in the concept of art." Danto provocatively claims that the twentieth century really begins, paradoxically, in 1964 with signs of social and artistic liberation: the civil rights protests, The Beatles's pop music, and the advent of pop art.

The artistic revolution of the 1960s is particularly remarkable because pop art seemed to come out of nowhere. Abstract expressionist works such as Jackson Pollock's antimimetic amalgamation, or mixing, of colors seemed preeminent and suffocating to artists and patrons who favored realistic painting, a style considered old fashioned and conservative in the '60s. Pop art stunningly vanquished abstract expressionism and realistic painting by parodying Plato's mimetic theories, according to Danto. What are Warhol's reproductions of a brillo box saying about hitherto respected theories of art? "What makes the difference between an artwork and something which is not an artwork," Danto asks, "if in fact they look exactly alike? Such a question could never occur when one *could* teach the meaning of 'art' by examples, or when the distinction between art and reality seemed perceptual, like the difference between a picture on a vase of a bed and a real bed."

Think about possible relationships between the ordinary, say Warhol's soup cans, and Baker's theory of the vernacular. Ask yourself whether you are seeing something akin to an "erotics of art" or women's "fears and desires" when Warhol features the popular film icon Marilyn Monroe in his work. Someone might argue that pop art participates in the blurring of the lines between art and entertainment. Do you agree or disagree? Does Danto grant to pop art "the capacity to make us nervous," the criterion of "real art" according to Sontag? Think about how you might use Danto's discussion of "transfiguration" to analyze Sontag's discussion of content, Mulvey's criticisms of Jones's art, or Baker's analysis of blues lyrics.

Today, as Danto notes, video technologies provide artistic avenues that make more traditional practices such as painting seem old fashioned. Like one of the hundreds of channels on cable or satellite television, painting has become "just one of a large number of artistic possibilities." Are we seeing in new video technologies the "end of art"? Is it true that "the history of art, structured narratively, ha[s] come to an end"? Likewise, might new computer technologies suggest the possibility of our own obsolescence or our own enslavement? Rather than machines serving us, might we one day serve them? Such a vision might be a new twist or turn on the old signification of the vernacular, returning to its Latin meaning of slave born on the master's estate. Dystopic or nightmarish visions of technology have long been a staple of art and entertainment, and the film *The Matrix,* which has received both critical and popular approval, extends the nightmare.

In "The Matrix: Or, The Two Sides of Perversion," Slavoj Žižek examines *The Matrix*'s bleak futuristic reality, the "desert of the real," which is invisible to most humans in the film because they are suspended in virtual reality, unaware of their function as batteries powering a massive computer network. The blurring of actual, material existence and virtual reality that Žižek explores raises theoretical questions about relationships between virtual reality and mimetic theories. How does technology extend, but also revise, theories of art while at the same time extending and revising what we have come to call our real world? What are art and entertainment in the "desert of the real"?

Žižek uses Lacanian psychoanalytic theory to frame his analysis of *The Matrix.* In particular, he examines relationships between virtual reality and Lacan's theory of the "big Other," which Žižek identifies with the software directing the super computer, the Matrix, in the film: both represent "the virtual symbolic order, the network that structures reality for us." Although Žižek identifies and discusses problems and inconsistencies in the film, his focus is processes of domination—that is, "the network"—as evidenced by the "central image of millions of human beings leading a claustrophobic life in water-filled cradles, kept alive in order to generate energy for the Matrix." He interprets this unaesthetic image as a postmodern twist, "combining utopia with dystopia." Unaware of their passive status as batteries, people in the film interpret the Matrix-generated virtual reality, a computer fantasy, to be their actual, active, complex lives. Such a state of affairs raises significant questions about art and entertainment. What roles, for instance, do art and entertainment play in either fostering misapprehensions of reality or fostering insight about dystopic aspects of society? You might consider how cinematic apparatus can be understood as a kind of matrix.

After reading and reviewing Žižek's essay, think about how his general discussion of postmodernism relates to Sontag's "erotics of art," Mulvey's "analysis of fetishism," Baker's transfiguration of the blues critic as a blues artist, or Danto's provocative "end of art" thesis. Some folks see *The Matrix* as primarily mainstream Hollywood entertainment, whereas others see it as "art with a capital *A.*" Indeed, someone might want to argue that the film's formal explorations of cybernetics and virtual reality reveal intellectual sophistication akin to the alternative or radical cinema that Sontag praises. If you have seen the film, what do you think? You might also consider what Žižek's discussion of the "desert of the real" tell us about our techno-consumerist society and about ourselves as political and performing animals. Is all the world still a stage in *The Matrix?* Is our world not a stage but a Matrix? Is that how we like it?

Susan Sontag (1933–)

A writer, a critic, and a human rights activist, Sontag exemplifies the notion of a public intellectual. In the 1960s and 1970s, Sontag's cutting-edge articles about drama, film, literature, and philosophy helped introduce avant-garde European theorists such as Roland Barthes to readers in the United States. She was born in, and now lives in, New York City, but she grew up in Tucson, Arizona, and Los Angeles, California. A prodigy, she was only 18 years old when she graduated from the University of Chicago with a philosophy degree in 1951. While she has taught at universities such as Harvard, Rutgers, and Columbia, Sontag has earned her living by and large through her writing. Her novels include the best-seller *The Volcano Lover* (1993), and her most influential nonfiction works include *Against Interpretation and Other Essays* (1966), *On Photography* (1977), *Illness as Metaphor* (1978), and, most recently, *Regarding the Pain of Others* (2003). In addition to her fiction and nonfiction, Sontag has written and directed films, including *Duets for Cannibals* (1969) and *Promised Lands* (1974). The reading selection given next, "Against Interpretation," first appeared in 1964 and challenges what might appear to be common sense or common practice in English departments: interpretive practices designed to determine what a text or visual image means.

Against Interpretation

Content is a glimpse of something, an encounter like a flash. It's very tiny—very tiny, content.

Willem De Kooning, in an interview

It is only shallow people who do not judge by appearances. The mystery of the world is the visible, not the invisible.

Oscar Wilde, in a letter

1

The earliest *experience* of art must have been that it was incantatory, magical; art was an instrument of ritual. (Cf. the paintings in the caves at Lascaux, Altamira, Niaux, La Pasiega, etc.) The earliest *theory* of art, that of the Greek philosophers, proposed that art was mimesis, imitation of reality.

It is at this point that the peculiar question of the *value* of art arose. For the mimetic theory, by its very terms, challenges art to justify itself.

Plato, who proposed the theory, seems to have done so in order to rule that the value of art is dubious. Since he considered ordinary material things as themselves mimetic objects, imitations of transcendent forms or structures, even the best painting of a bed would be only an "imitation of an imitation." For Plato, art is neither particularly useful (the painting of a bed is no good to sleep on), nor, in the strict sense, true. And Aristotle's arguments in defense of art do not really challenge Plato's view that all art is an elaborate *trompe l'oeil,* and therefore a lie. But he does dispute Plato's idea that art is useless. Lie or no, art has a certain value according to Aristotle because it is a form of therapy. Art is useful, after all, Aristotle counters, medicinally useful in that it arouses and purges dangerous emotions.

In Plato and Aristotle, the mimetic theory of art goes hand in hand with the assumption that art is always figurative. But advocates of the mimetic theory need not close their eyes to decorative and abstract art. The fallacy that art is necessarily a "realism" can be modified or scrapped without ever moving outside the problems delimited by the mimetic theory.

The fact is, all Western consciousness of and reflection upon art have remained within the confines staked out by the Greek theory of art as mimesis or representation. It is through this theory that art as such—above and beyond given works of art—becomes problematic, in need of defense. And it is the defense of art which gives birth to the odd vision by which something we have learned to call "form" is separated off from something we have learned to call "content," and to the well-intentioned move which makes content essential and form accessory.

Even in modern times, when most artists and critics have discarded the theory of art as representation of an outer reality in favor of the theory of art as subjective expression, the main feature of the mimetic theory persists. Whether we conceive of the work of art on the model of a picture (art as a picture of reality) or on the model of a statement (art as the statement of the artist), content still comes first. The content may have changed. It may now be less figurative, less lucidly realistic. But it is still assumed that a work of art *is* its content. Or, as it's usually put today, that a work of art by definition says something. ("What X is saying is . . . ," "What X is trying to say is . . . ," "What X said is . . ." etc., etc.)

2

None of us can ever retrieve that innocence before all theory when art knew no need to justify itself, when one did not ask of a work of art what it *said* because one knew (or thought one knew) what it *did*. From now to the end of consciousness, we are stuck with the task of defending art. We can only quarrel with one or another means of defense. Indeed, we have an obligation to overthrow any means of defending and justifying art which becomes particularly obtuse or onerous or insensitive to contemporary needs and practice.

This is the case, today, with the very idea of content itself. Whatever it may have been in the past, the idea of content is today mainly a hindrance, a nuisance, a subtle or not so subtle philistinism.

Though the actual developments in many arts may seem to be leading us away from the idea that a work of art is primarily its content, the idea still exerts an extraordinary hegemony. I want to suggest that this is because the idea is now perpetuated in the guise of a certain way of encountering works of art thoroughly ingrained among most people who take any of the arts seriously. What the overemphasis on the idea of content entails is the perennial, never consummated project of *interpretation*. And, conversely, it is the habit of approaching works of art in order to *interpret* them that sustains the fancy that there really is such a thing as the content of a work of art.

3

Of course, I don't mean interpretation in the broadest sense, the sense in which Nietzsche (rightly) says, "There are no facts, only interpretations." By interpretation, I mean here a conscious act of the mind which illustrates a certain code, certain "rules" of interpretation.

Directed to art, interpretation means plucking a set of elements (the X, the Y, the Z, and so forth) from the whole work. The task of interpretation is virtually one of translation. The interpreter says, Look, don't you see that X is really—or, really means—A? That Y is really B? That Z is really C?

What situation could prompt this curious project for transforming a text? History gives us the materials for an answer. Interpretation first appears in the culture of late classical antiquity, when the power and credibility of myth had been broken by the "realistic" view of the world introduced by scientific enlightenment. Once the question that haunts post-mythic consciousness—that of the *seemliness* of religious symbols—had been asked, the ancient texts were, in their pristine form, no longer acceptable. Then interpretation was summoned, to reconcile the ancient texts to "modern" demands. Thus, the Stoics, to accord with their view that the gods had to be moral, allegorized away the rude features of Zeus and his boisterous clan in Homer's epics. What Homer really designated by the adultery of Zeus with Leto, they explained, was the union between power and wisdom. In the same vein, Philo of Alexandria interpreted the literal historical narratives of the Hebrew Bible as spiritual paradigms. The story of the exodus from Egypt, the wandering in the desert for forty years, and the entry into the promised land, said Philo, was really an allegory of the individual soul's emancipation, tribulations, and final deliverance. Interpretation thus presupposes a discrepancy between the clear meaning of the text and the demands of (later) readers. It seeks to resolve that discrepancy. The situation is that for some reason a text has become unacceptable; yet it cannot be discarded. Interpretation is a radical strategy for conserving an old text, which is thought too precious to repudiate, by revamping it. The interpreter, without actually erasing or rewriting the text, *is* altering it. But he can't admit to doing this. He claims to be only making it intelligible, by disclosing its true meaning. However far the interpreters alter the text (another notorious example is the Rabbinic and Christian "spiritual" interpretations of the clearly erotic Song of Songs), they must claim to be reading off a sense that is already there.

Interpretation in our own time, however, is even more complex. For the contemporary zeal for the project of interpretation is often prompted not by piety toward the troublesome text (which may conceal an aggression), but by an open aggressiveness, an overt contempt for appearances. The old style of interpretation was insistent, but respectful; it erected another meaning on top of the literal one. The modern style of interpretation excavates, and as it excavates, destroys; it digs "behind" the text, to find a sub-text which is the true one. The most celebrated and influential modern doctrines, those of Marx and Freud, actually amount to elaborate systems of hermeneutics, aggressive and impious theories of interpretation. All observable phenomena are bracketed, in Freud's phrase, as *manifest content*. This manifest content must be probed and pushed aside to find the true meaning—the *latent content*—beneath. For Marx, social events like revolutions and wars; for Freud, the events of individual lives (like neurotic symptoms and slips of the tongue) as well as texts (like a dream or a work of art)— all are treated as occasions for interpretation. According to Marx and Freud, these events only *seem* to be intelligible. Actually, they have no meaning without interpretation. To understand *is* to interpret. And to interpret is to restate the phenomenon, in effect to find an equivalent for it.

Thus, interpretation is not (as most people assume) an absolute value, a gesture of mind situated in some timeless realm of capabilities. Interpretation must itself be evaluated, within a historical view of human consciousness. In some cultural contexts, interpretation is a liberating act. It is a means of revising, of transvaluing, of escaping the dead past. In other cultural contexts, it is reactionary, impertinent, cowardly, stifling.

4

Today is such a time, when the project of interpretation is largely reactionary, stifling. Like the fumes of the automobile and of heavy industry which befoul the urban atmosphere, the effusion of interpretations of art today poisons our sensibilities. In a culture whose already classical dilemma is the hypertrophy of the intellect at the expense of energy and sensual capability, interpretation is the revenge of the intellect upon art.

Even more. It is the revenge of the intellect upon the world. To interpret is to impoverish, to deplete the world—in order to set up a shadow world of "meanings." It is to turn *the* world into *this* world. ("This world"! As if there were any other.)

The world, our world, is depleted, impoverished enough. Away with all duplicates of it, until we again experience more immediately what we have.

5

In most modern instances, interpretation amounts to the philistine refusal to leave the work of art alone. Real art has the capacity to make us nervous. By reducing the work of art to its content and then interpreting *that,* one tames the work of art. Interpretation makes art manageable, comfortable.

This philistinism of interpretation is more rife in literature than in any other art. For decades now, literary critics have understood it to be their task to translate the elements of the poem or play or novel or story into something else. Sometimes a writer will be so uneasy before the naked power of his art that he will install within the work itself—albeit with a little shyness, a touch of the good taste of irony—the clear and explicit interpretation of it. Thomas Mann is an example of such an overcooperative author. In the case of more stubborn authors, the critic is only too happy to perform the job.

The work of Kafka, for example, has been subjected to a mass ravishment by no less than three armies of interpreters. Those who read Kafka as a social allegory see case studies of the frustrations and insanity of modern bureaucracy and its ultimate issuance in the totalitarian state. Those who read Kafka as a psychoanalytic allegory see desperate revelations of Kafka's fear of his father, his castration anxieties, his sense of his own impotence, his thralldom to his dreams. Those who read Kafka as a religious allegory explain that K. in *The Castle* is trying to gain access to heaven, that Joseph K. in *The Trial* is being judged by the inexorable and mysterious justice of God. . . . Another *oeuvre* that has attracted interpreters like leeches is that of Samuel Beckett. Beckett's delicate dramas of the withdrawn consciousness—pared down to essentials, cut off, often represented as physically immobilized—are read as a statement about modern man's alienation from meaning or from God, or as an allegory of psychopathology.

Proust, Joyce, Faulkner, Rilke, Lawrence, Gide . . . one could go on citing author after author; the list is endless of those around whom thick encrustations of interpretation have taken hold. But it should be noted that interpretation is not simply the compliment that mediocrity pays to genius. It is, indeed, *the* modern way of understanding something, and is applied to works of every quality. Thus, in the notes that Elia Kazan published on his production of *A Streetcar Named Desire,* it becomes clear that, in order to direct the play, Kazan had to discover that Stanley Kowalski represented the sensual and vengeful barbarism that was engulfing our culture, while Blanche Du Bois was Western civilization, poetry, delicate apparel, dim lighting, refined feelings and all, though a little the worse for wear to be sure. Tennessee Williams' forceful psychological melodrama now became intelligible: it was *about* something, about the decline of Western civilization. Apparently, were it to go on being a play about a handsome brute named Stanley Kowalski and a faded mangy belle named Blanche Du Bois, it would not be manageable.

6

It doesn't matter whether artists intend, or don't intend, for their works to be interpreted. Perhaps Tennessee Williams thinks *Streetcar* is about what Kazan thinks it to be about. It may be that Cocteau in *The Blood of a Poet* and in *Orpheus* wanted the elaborate readings which have been given these films, in terms of Freudian symbolism and social critique. But the merit of these works certainly lies elsewhere than in their "meanings." Indeed, it is precisely to the extent that Williams' plays and Cocteau's films do suggest these portentous meanings that they are defective, false, contrived, lacking in conviction.

From interviews, it appears that Resnais and Robbe-Grillet consciously designed *Last Year at Marienbad* to accommodate a multiplicity of equally plausible interpretations. But the temptation to interpret *Marienbad* should be resisted. What matters in *Marienbad* is the pure, untranslatable, sensuous immediacy of some of its images, and its rigorous if narrow solutions to certain problems of cinematic form.

Again, Ingmar Bergman may have meant the tank rumbling down the empty night street in *The Silence* as a phallic symbol. But if he did, it was a foolish thought. ("Never trust the teller, trust the tale," said Lawrence.) Taken as a brute object, as an immediate sensory equivalent for the mysterious abrupt armored happenings going on inside the hotel, that sequence with the tank is the most striking moment in the film. Those who reach for a Freudian interpretation of the tank are only expressing their lack of response to what is there on the screen.

It is always the case that interpretation of this type indicates a dissatisfaction (conscious or unconscious) with the work, a wish to replace it by something else.

Interpretation, based on the highly dubious theory that a work of art is composed of items of content, violates art. It makes art into an article for use, for arrangement into a mental scheme of categories.

7

Interpretation does not, of course, always prevail. In fact, a great deal of today's art may be understood as motivated by a flight from interpretation. To avoid interpretation, art may become parody. Or it may become abstract. Or it may become ("merely") decorative. Or it may become non-art.

The flight from interpretation seems particularly a feature of modern painting. Abstract painting is the attempt to have, in the ordinary sense, no content; since there is no content, there can be no interpretation. Pop Art works by the opposite means to the same result; using a content so blatant, so "what it is," it, too, ends by being uninterpretable.

A great deal of modern poetry as well, starting from the great experiments of French poetry (including the movement that is misleadingly called Symbolism) to put silence into poems and to reinstate the *magic* of the word, has escaped from the rough grip of interpretation. The most recent revolution in contemporary taste in poetry—the revolution that has deposed Eliot and elevated Pound—represents a turning away from content in poetry in the old sense, an impatience with what made modern poetry prey to the zeal of interpreters.

I am speaking mainly of the situation in America, of course. Interpretation runs rampant here in those arts with a feeble and negligible avant-garde: fiction and the drama. Most American novelists and playwrights are really either journalists or gentlemen sociologists and psychologists. They are writing the literary equivalent of program music. And so rudimentary, uninspired, and stagnant has been the sense of what might be done with *form* in fiction and drama that even when the content isn't simply information, news, it is still peculiarly visible, handier, more exposed. To the extent that novels and plays (in America), unlike poetry and painting and music, don't reflect any interesting concern with changes in their form, these arts remain prone to assault by interpretation.

But programmatic avant-gardism—which has meant, mostly, experiments with form at the expense of content—is not the only defense against the infestation of art by interpretations. At least, I hope not. For this would be to commit art to being perpetually on the run. (It also perpetuates the very distinction between form and content which is, ultimately, an illusion.) Ideally, it is possible to elude the interpreters in another way, by making works of art whose surface is so unified and clean, whose momentum is so rapid, whose address is so direct that the work can be . . . just what it is. Is this possible now? It does happen in films, I believe. This is why cinema is the most alive, the most exciting, the most important of all art forms right now. Perhaps the way one tells how alive a particular art form is, is by the latitude it gives for making mistakes in it, and still being good. For example, a few of the films of Bergman—though crammed with lame messages about the modern spirit, thereby inviting interpretations—still triumph over the pretentious intentions of their director. In *Winter Light* and *The*

Silence, the beauty and visual sophistication of the images subvert before our eyes the callow pseudo-intellectuality of the story and some of the dialogue. (The most remarkable instance of this sort of discrepancy is the work of D. W. Griffith.) In good films, there is always a directness that entirely frees us from the itch to interpret. Many old Hollywood films, like those of Cukor, Walsh, Hawks, and countless other directors, have this liberating anti-symbolic quality, no less than the best work of the new European directors, like Truffaut's *Shoot the Piano Player* and *Jules and Jim,* Godard's *Breathless* and *Vivre Sa Vie,* Antonioni's *L' Avventura,* and Olmi's *The Fiancés.*

The fact that films have not been overrun by interpreters is in part due simply to the newness of cinema as an art. It also owes to the happy accident that films for such a long time were just movies; in other words, that they were understood to be part of mass, as opposed to high, culture, and were left alone by most people with minds. Then, too, there is always something other than content in the cinema to grab hold of, for those who want to analyze. For the cinema, unlike the novel, possesses a vocabulary of forms—the explicit, complex, and discussable technology of camera movements, cutting, and composition of the frame that goes into the making of a film.

8

What kind of criticism, of commentary on the arts, is desirable today? For I am not saying that works of art are ineffable, that they cannot be described or paraphrased. They can be. The question is how. What would criticism look like that would serve the work of art, not usurp its place?

What is needed, first, is more attention to form in art. If excessive stress on *content* provokes the arrogance of interpretation, more extended and more thorough descriptions of *form* would silence. What is needed is a vocabulary— a descriptive, rather than prescriptive, vocabulary—for forms.* The best criticism, and it is uncommon, is of this sort that dissolves considerations of content into those of form. On film, drama, and painting respectively, I can think of Erwin Panofsky's essay, "Style and Medium in the Motion Pictures," Northrop Frye's essay "A Conspectus of Dramatic Genres," Pierre Francastel's essay "The Destruction of a Plastic Space." Roland Barthes' book *On Racine* and his two essays on Robbe-Grillet are examples of formal analysis applied to the work of a single author. (The best essays in Erich Auerbach's *Mimesis,* like "The Scar of Odysseus," are also of this type.) An example of formal analysis applied

---

*One of the difficulties is that our idea of form is spatial (the Greek metaphors for form are all derived from notions of space). This is why we have a more ready vocabulary of forms for the spatial than for the temporal arts. The exception among the temporal arts, of course, is the drama; perhaps this is because the drama is a narrative (i.e., temporal) form that extends itself visually and pictorially, upon a stage. . . . What we don't have yet is a poetics of the novel, any clear notion of the forms of narration. Perhaps film criticism will be the occasion of a breakthrough here, since films are primarily a visual form, yet they are also a subdivision of literature.

simultaneously to genre and author is Walter Benjamin's essay, "The Story Teller: Reflections on the Works of Nicolai Leskov."

Equally valuable would be acts of criticism which would supply a really accurate, sharp, loving description of the appearance of a work of art. This seems even harder to do than formal analysis. Some of Manny Farber's film criticism, Dorothy Van Ghent's essay "The Dickens World: A View from Todgers'," Randall Jarrell's essay on Walt Whitman are among the rare examples of what I mean. These are essays which reveal the sensuous surface of art without mucking about in it.

9

Transparence is the highest, most liberating value in art—and in criticism—today. Transparence means experiencing the luminousness of the thing in itself, of things being what they are. This is the greatness of, for example, the films of Bresson and Ozu and Renoir's *The Rules of the Game.*

Once upon a time (say, for Dante), it must have been a revolutionary and creative move to design works of art so that they might be experienced on several levels. Now it is not. It reinforces the principle of redundancy that is the principal affliction of modern life.

Once upon a time (a time when high art was scarce), it must have been a revolutionary and creative move to interpret works of art. Now it is not. What we decidedly do not need now is further to assimilate Art into Thought, or (worse yet) Art into Culture.

Interpretation takes the sensory experience of the work of art for granted, and proceeds from there. This cannot be taken for granted, now. Think of the sheer multiplication of works of art available to every one of us, superadded to the conflicting tastes and odors and sights of the urban environment that bombard our senses. Ours is culture based on excess, on overproduction; the result is a steady loss of sharpness in our sensory experience. All the conditions of modern life—its material plenitude, its sheer crowdedness—conjoin to dull our sensory faculties. And it is in the light of the condition of our senses, our capacities (rather than those of another age), that the task of the critic must be assessed.

What is important now is to recover our senses. We must learn to *see* more, to *hear* more, to *feel* more.

Our task is not to find the maximum amount of content in a work of art, much less to squeeze more content out of the work than is already there. Our task is to cut back content so that we can see the thing at all.

The aim of all commentary on art now should be to make works of art—and, by analogy, our own experience—more, rather than less, real to us. The function of criticism should be to show *how it is what it is,* even *that it is what it is,* rather than to show *what it means.*

10

In place of a hermeneutics we need an erotics of art.

Laura Mulvey (1941–)

A British theorist and filmmaker, Mulvey was born in Oxford, England. She earned a degree in history from Oxford University in 1963. In 1999 she was appointed Professor of Film and Media Studies at Birbeck College, University of London. Before her appointment at Birbeck, Mulvey taught at several British universities and also lecturered in the United States and in Europe. Her well-known essay, "Visual Pleasure and Narrative Cinema," has long been recognized as a major text in feminist criticism. Using psychoanalytic theories from both Sigmund Freud and Jacques Lacan, Mulvey examined how Hollywood cinematic form and content reinforce patriarchal norms for audiences. In "Fears, Fantasies and the Male Unconscious *or* 'You Don't Know What is Happening, Do You, Mr. Jones?'" Mulvey applies Freudian psychoanalytic theory as a lens for examining the artwork of Allen Jones. Mulvey's use of psychoanalytic theory in the 1970s for critical analysis offered many readers in the United States novel or new approaches for analyzing art, cinema, literature, and culture. Along with her husband, Peter Wollen, Mulvey has co-directed several avant-garde films, including *Penthesilea: Queen of the Amazons* (1974) and *Riddles of the Sphinx* (1977). Her books include *Visual and Other Pleasures* (1989) and *Fetishism and Curiosity* (1996).

Fears, Fantasies, and the Male Unconscious *or* 'You Don't Know What Is Happening, Do You, Mr. Jones?'

To decapitate equals to castrate. The terror of the Medusa is thus a terror of castration that is linked to the sight of something. The hair upon the Medusa's head is frequently represented in works of art in the form of snakes, and these once again are derived from the castration complex. It is a remarkable fact that, however frightening they may be in themselves, they nevertheless serve actually as a mitigation of the horror, for they replace the penis, the absence of which is the cause of the horror. This is a confirmation of the technical rule according to which a multiplication of penis symbols signifies castration.

Freud, "The Medusa's Head"

In 1970 Tooth's Gallery in London held a one-man show of sculptures by Allen Jones which gained him the notoriety he now enjoys throughout the Women's Movement. The sculptures formed a series, called 'Women as Furniture', in which life-size effigies of women, slave-like and sexually provocative, double as hat-stands, tables and chairs. The original of *Chair* is now in the Düsseldorf home of a West German tycoon, whose complacent form was recently photographed for a *Sunday Times* article, sitting comfortably on the upturned and upholstered female figure. Not surprisingly, members of Women's Liberation noticed the exhibition and denounced it as supremely exploitative of women's already exploited image. Women used, women subjugated, women on display: Allen Jones did not miss a trick.

Since 1970 Allen Jones's work has developed and proliferated in the same vein. It has won increasing international acclaim, with exhibitions in Italy, Germany, Belgium and the United States, as well as Britain. He is one of the shining properties in the stable of Marlborough Fine Art, the heaviest and most prestige-conscious of the international art traders. He has expanded his interests beyond painting and sculpture proper into stage design, coffee-table books, luxury editions, film and television. The Allen Jones artistic octopus extends its tentacles into every nook and cranny where the image of woman can be inserted and spotlighted.

At first glance Allen Jones seems simply to reproduce the familiar formulas which have been so successfully systematised by the mass media. His women exist in a state of suspended animation, without depth or context, withdrawn from any meaning other than the message imprinted by their clothes, stance and gesture. The interaction between his images and those of the mass media is made quite explicit by the collection of source material which he has published. *Figures*[1] is a scrapbook of cuttings out of magazines, both respectable (*Nova*, *Harper's Bazaar*, *Life*, *Vogue*, *Sunday Times* supplement and so on) and non-respectable (*Exotique*, *Female Mimics*, *Bound*, *Bizarre* and so on). There are also postcards, publicity material, packaging designs and film stills (*Gentlemen Prefer Blondes*, *Barbarella*, *What's New, Pussycat?*). *Projects*,[2] his second book, records, sketches and concepts (some unfinished) for stage, film and TV shows, among them *Oh Calcutta!* and Kubrick's *A Clockwork Orange* and includes more source material as an indication of the way his ideas developed.

By publishing these clippings Allen Jones gives vital clues, not only to the way he sees women, but to the place they occupy in the male unconscious in general. He has chosen images which clearly form a definite pattern, which have their own visual vocabulary and grammar. The popular visuals he produces go beyond an obvious play on the exhibitionism of women and the voyeurism of men. Their imagery is that of a fetishism. Although every single image is a female form, not one shows the actual female genitals. Not one is naked. The female genitals are always concealed, disguised or supplemented in ways which alter the significance of female sexuality. The achievement of Allen Jones is to throw an unusually vivid spotlight on the contradiction between woman's fantasy presence and real absence from the male unconscious world. The language which he speaks is the language of fetishism, which speaks to all of us every day, but whose exact grammar and syntax we are usually only dimly aware of. Fetishistic obsession reveals the meaning behind popular images of women.

It is Allen Jones's mastery of the language of 'basic fetishism' that makes his work so rich and compelling. His use of popular media is important not because he echoes them stylistically (pop art) but because he gets to the heart of the way in which the female image has been requisitioned, to be recreated in the image of man. The fetishist image of women has three aspects, all of which come across clearly in his books and art objects. First: woman plus phallic substitute. Second: woman minus phallus, punished and humiliated, often by woman plus phallus.

Third: woman as phallus. Women are displayed for men as figures in an amazing masquerade, which expresses a strange male underworld of fear and desire.

The Language of Castration Anxiety

The nearer the female figure is to genital nakedness, the more flamboyant the phallic distraction. The only example of frontal nudity in his work, a sketch for *Oh Calcutta!,* is a history of knickers, well-worn fetishist items, in which the moment of nakedness is further retrieved by the fact that the girls are carrying billiard cues and an enormous phallus is incorporated into the scenery. In the source material, a girl from *Playboy* caresses a dog's head on her lap; another, on the cover of a movie magazine, clutches an enormous boa constrictor as it completely and discreetly entwines her. Otherwise there is an array of well-known phallic extensions to divert the eye: guns, cigarettes, erect nipples, a tail, whips, strategically placed brooches (Marilyn Monroe and Jane Russell in *Gentlemen Prefer Blondes*), a parasol, and so on, and some, more subtle, which depend on the visual effect of shadows or silhouettes.

Women without a phallus have to undergo punishment by torture and fetish objects ranging from tight shoes and corsetry, through rubber goods to leather. Here we can see the *sadistic* aspect of male fetishism, but it still remains fixated on objects with phallic significance. An ambiguous tension is introduced within the symbolism. For instance, a whip can be simultaneously a substitute phallus and an instrument of punishment. Similarly, the high heel on high-heeled shoes, a classic fetishist image, is both a phallic extension and a means of discomfort and constriction. Belts and necklaces, with buckles and pendants, are both phallic symbols and suggest bondage and punishment. The theme of *woman bound* is one of the most consistent in Allen Jones's source material: at its most vestigial, the limbs of pin-up girls are bound with shiny tape, a fashion model is loaded with chains, underwear advertisements, especially for corsets, proliferate, as do rubber garments from fetishistic magazines. Waists are constricted by tight belts, necks by tight bands, feet by the ubiquitous high-heeled shoes. For the television show illustrated in *Projects* Allen Jones exploits a kind of evolved garter of black shiny material round the girls' thighs, which doubles, openly in one case, as a fetter. The most effective fetish both constricts and uplifts, binds and raises, particularly high-heeled shoes, corsets or bras and, as a trimming, high neck bands holding the head erect.

In *Projects* the theme of punishment can be seen in the abandoned plan for the milkbar in the film of *A Clockwork Orange* (infinitely more subtle in its detailed understanding of fetishism than the kitsch design Kubrick finally used for the movie). The waitress is dressed from neck to fingertip to toe in a rubber garment with an apron, leaving only her buttocks bare, ready for discipline, while she balances a tray to imply service. The same theme can be traced in his women-as-furniture sculptures. In *Figures,* the background and evolution of the sculptures is made clear. Gesture, bodily position and clothing are all of equal importance. *Hat-Stand* is based on the crucial publicity still from *Barbarella,* which unites boots, binding, leather and phallic *cache-sexe* in the image of a girl captive who hangs ready for torture, her hands turned up in a gesture which finally becomes the hat-peg. A similar design for an hors-d'oeuvre stand derives from a Vargas drawing of a waitress who sums up the spirit of service and depersonalisation.

Another aspect of the theme of punishment is that the castrated woman should suffer spanking and humiliation at the hands of the man–woman, the great male hope. Characterised in Eneg's drawings for *Bound* (reproduced in *Figures*) by tight belt, tight trousers, mask and constricted neck (while a female woman carries a soon-abandoned handbag), the man–woman emerges with full force of vengeance in *Projects* as Miss Beezley in *Homage to St. Dominic's* ('to be played by a 7-foot woman—*or a man would do*. With 6-inch platform heels "she" would be 18 inches taller than the school "girls"'). And again in *The Playroom* (another abandoned stage project) the transvestite owner, 'an elderly "woman"' chases the children. A series of paintings shows sexually ambiguous figures in which a man walks into female clothing to become a woman or male and female legs are locked as one.

Finally, in *Männer Wir Kommen,* a show for West German television, which is illustrated in *Projects* by stills, notes and sketches, Allen Jones adds yet another dimension to his use of fetishistic vocabulary. The close-ups and superimpositions possible on television give him the chance to exploit ambiguities of changed scale and proportion. The spectator is stripped of normal perceptual defences (perspective, normal size relationships) and exposed to illusion and fantasy on the screen. As sections of the female body are isolated from the whole and shown in close-up, or as the whole body shrinks in size and is superimposed on a blown-up section, Allen Jones develops even further the symbolic references of woman to man and subjects her form to further masculinisation.

His previous work preserved the normal scale of the female body physically, although it distorted it symbolically. *Männer Wir Kommen* contains some imagery of this kind: *Homage to Harley* uses the motorcycle and the nozzle in their classic role as phallic extensions, with the women in natural proportion to them (women with boots and bound necks and black bands around their thighs). But by far the most striking image is that of the entire figure of one girl, shrunk in scale though symbolically erect, superimposed as a phallic substitute on the tight black shiny shorts of another. A series of freeze-frames from the show, female manikins strategically poised, makes Allen Jones's point blindingly clear.

More close-ups in the television sketch carry the female body further into phallic suggestion. Girls like human pillars supporting a boxing ring have bared breasts divided by shiny pink material fastened to their necks. A single frame, from breast to neck only, makes the breasts look like testicles with the pink material functioning as a penis. Female bodies and fragments of bodies are redeployed to produce fantasy male anatomies. A similar emphasis on breasts divided by a vertical motif can be seen in the source material: the torture harness in the *Barbarella* still, Verushka's single-strap bikini in a fashion photograph. There is a strong overlap between the imagery of bondage and the imagery of woman as phallus built into fetishism. The body is unified to a maximum extent into a single, rigid whole, with an emphasis on texture, stiffness caused by tight clothing and binding, and a general restriction of free movement.

In *Figures* there is a consistent theme of women as automata, with jerking, involuntary, semaphore-like movements, suggestive of erection. These automata often have rhythmic movements (Ursula Andress dancing in a series of stills like an animated doll, the Rockettes, Aquamaid water-skiers in Florida), uniforms in which the conception of duty and service is combined with strictness and rigidity (for instance, a cutting from the *Daily Express* in which 'Six Model Girls Step Smartly Forward for Escort Duty') and, most important of all, the stiffness induced by wearing tight clothes which constitute a second slithery skin (rubber garments transforming the body into a solid mass from fingertip to toe, one-piece corsets, synthetic garments ranging from perspex to nylon). An identification develops between the phallus and woman herself. She must be seen in her full phallic glory.

The Fetishist's Collection of Signs

To understand the paradoxes of fetishism, it is essential to go back to Freud. Fetishism, Freud first pointed out, involves displacing the sight of woman's imaginary castration onto a variety of reassuring but often surprising objects—shoes, corsets, rubber gloves, belts, knickers and so on—which serve as *signs* for the lost penis but have no direct connection with it. For the fetishist, the sign itself becomes the source of fantasy (whether actual fetish objects or else pictures or descriptions of them) and in every case the sign is the sign of the phallus. It is man's narcissistic fear of losing his own phallus, his most precious possession, which causes shock at the sight of the female genitals and the subsequent fetishistic attempt to disguise or divert attention from them.

A world which revolves on a phallic axis constructs its fears and fantasies in its own phallic image. In the drama of the male castration complex, as Freud discovered, women are no more than puppets; their significance lies first and foremost in their lack of a penis and their star turn is to symbolise the castration which men fear. Women may seem to be the subjects of an endless parade of pornographic fantasies, jokes, day-dreams and so on, but fundamentally most male fantasy is a closed-loop dialogue with itself, as Freud conveys so well in the quotation about the Medusa's head. Far from being a woman, even a monstrous woman, the Medusa is the sign of a male castration anxiety. Freud's analysis of the male unconscious is crucial for any understanding of the myriad ways in which the female form has been used as a mould into which meanings have been poured by a male-dominated culture.

Man and his phallus are the real subject of Allen Jones's paintings and sculptures, even though they deal exclusively with images of women on display. From his scrapbooks we see how the mass media provide material for a 'harem cult' (as Wilhelm Stekel describes the fetishist's penchant for collections and scrapbooks in his classic psychoanalytic study) in which the spectre of the castrated female, using a phallic substitute to conceal or distract attention from her wound, haunts the male unconscious. The presence of the female form by no means ensures that the message of pictures or photographs or posters is about women. We could say that the image of woman comes to be used as a sign, which does not necessarily signify the meaning 'woman' any more than does the Medusa's head. The harem cult which dominates our culture springs from the male unconscious and woman becomes its narcissistic projection.

Freud saw the fetish object itself as phallic replacement so that a shoe, for instance, could become the object on which the scandalised denial of female castration was fixated. But, on a more obvious level, we could say with Freud in 'The Medusa's Head' that a *proliferation* of phallic symbols must symbolise castration. This is the meaning of the parade of phallic insignia borne by Allen Jones's harem, ranging from precisely poised thighs, suggestive of flesh and erection, through to enormous robots and turrets. Castration itself is only rarely alluded to in even indirect terms. In one clipping an oriental girl brandishes a large pair of scissors, about to cut the hair of a man holding a large cigar. In another, a chocolate biscuit is described in three consecutive pictures: *c'est comme un doigt* (erect female finger), *avec du chocolat autour* (ditto plus chocolate), *Ça disparaît très vite* (empty frame), then larger frame and triumphal return, *c'est un biscuit: Finger de Cadbury* (erect biscuit held by fingers).

There is one exception to this: the increasingly insistent theme of women balancing. Female figures hang suspended, on the point of coming down (the phallic reference is obvious). Anything balanced upright—a woman walking a tightrope or balancing a tray or poised on the balls of her feet—implies a possible catastrophe that may befall. The sculptures of women as furniture, especially the hat-stand, freeze the body in time as the erect pose seems to capture a moment, and also they are suspended, cut off from any context, to hang in space. In addition, the formal structure of some of Jones's earlier paintings—three-dimensional flights of steps leading steeply up to two-dimensional paintings of women's legs poised on high heels—describe an ascension: erect posture and suspension and balance are fused into one illusionistic image.

In his most recent paintings, exhibited this summer at the Marlborough Galleries, Allen Jones develops the theme of balance much further. A number of the paintings are of women circus performers, objects of display and of balance. Here the equation 'woman = phallus' is taken a step further, almost as if to illustrate Freud's dictum that 'the remarkable phenomenon of erection which constantly occupies the human phantasy, cannot fail to be impressive as an apparent suspension of the laws of gravity (of the winged phalli of the ancients)'. In *Bare Me,* for example, the phallic woman, rigid and pointing upwards, holding her breasts erect with her hands, is standing in high heels on a tray-like board balanced on two spheres. She is on the way up, not down. Loss of balance is possible, but is not immediate.

But in other paintings this confidence is undercut. The defiance of gravity is more flamboyant than convincing. The same devices—high heels, walking on spheres—which compel an upright, erect posture can also point to its precariousness. The painting *Whip* is derived from a brilliant Eneg drawing of two women, castrator and castrated: a woman lassoed by a whipcord is slipping off a three-legged stool. In the painting, we can see only the toppling stool, but there can be no doubt from comparison with the Eneg source that the real absence—symbolic castration—is intended. In another painting, *Slip,* both figures from the same

Eneg drawing are combined into one and loss of balance becomes the explicit theme. Dancers on points, waitresses carrying trays, women acrobats teetering on high heels or walking the tightrope—all are forced to be erect and to thrust vertically upwards. But this phallic deportment carries the threat of its own undoing: the further you strive up, the further you may fall.

In *Männer Wir Kommen* the reverse side of the phallic woman, the true horror of the fetishist, can be seen in one startling sequence. The female body, although still bound in a tight corset and with a snake necklace wound around her neck, has a flamboyant, scarlet scar over her genitals. The surrounding *mise en scène* consists of enormous eggs, containing bound women rising from a foetus-like position while, in another sequence, maggot-like women's limbs emerge from equally enormous apples. The scar breeds the putrescence of pregnancy and nothing but decay can come out of the apple. The apple and the egg are the only non-fetishistic images of women to appear in Allen Jones's work. Infested by manikin maggots, they are the eternal companions of the scar.

Most people think of fetishism as the private taste of an odd minority, nurtured in secret. By revealing the way in which fetishistic images pervade not just specialised publications but the *whole of the mass media*, Allen Jones throws a new light on woman as spectacle. The message of fetishism concerns not woman, but the narcissistic wound she represents for man. Women are constantly confronted with their own image in one form or another, but what they see bears little relation or relevance to their own unconscious fantasies, their own hidden fears and desires. They are being turned all the time into objects of display, to be looked at and gazed at and stared at by men. Yet, in a real sense, women are not there at all. The parade has nothing to do with woman, everything to do with man. The true exhibit is always the phallus. Women are simply the scenery onto which men project their narcissistic fantasies. The time has come for us to take over the show and exhibit our own fears and desires.

Notes

1. Allen Jones, *Figures* (Berlin: Galerie Mikro, and Milan: Edizioni O, 1969).
2. Allen Jones, *Projects* (London: Matheus Miller Dunbar, and Milan: Edizioni O, 1971).

Houston Baker (1943–)

Baker has long been an influential critic and scholar of African-American and U.S. literatures. Through his scholarship, Baker has helped folks inside and outside of academia recognize traditions of African-American literature. That Baker is an astute theorist and a sensitive reader of texts is evidenced by his supple analysis of the "blues matrix" in the reading selection given next, the introduction to his 1984 book *Blues, Ideology, and Afro-American Literature: A Vernacular*

Theory. Baker was born and raised in Louisville, Kentucky, and he attended college at Howard University in Washington, D.C., and earned his Ph.D. at the University of California at Los Angeles in 1968. After teaching at Yale University and the University of Virginia, Baker became director of the Afro-American Studies Program at the University of Pennsylvania in 1974. In 1998, he moved from Penn to Duke University, where he is the Susan Fox Beischer and George D. Beischer Arts & Sciences Professor of English and Professor of African and African American Studies. A leader in the field of literary studies, Baker has served as president of the Modern Language Association and is currently the editor of *American Literature,* one of the premier scholarly journals in the humanities. His books include *Long Black Song: Essays in Black American Literature and Culture* (1972), *A Many Colored Coat of Dreams: The Poetry of Countee Cullen* (1974), *Modernism and the Harlem Renaissance* (1987), *Black Studies, Rap, and the Academy* (1995), *Afro-American Poetics: Revisions of Harlem and the Black Aesthetic* (1996), *Turning South Again: Rethinking Modernism/Rereading Booker T* (2001), and *Critical Memory: Public Spheres, African American Writing, and Black Fathers and Sons in America* (2001).

Introduction

Vernacular, adj.: Of a slave: That is born on his master's estate; home-born
Of arts, or features
of these: Native or peculiar to a particular country or locality
Other states indicate themselves in their deputies . . . but the genius of the
United States is not best or most in its executives or legislatures, nor in its
ambassadors or authors or colleges or churches or parlors, nor even in its
newspapers or inventors . . . but always most in the common
people . . . these . . . are unrhymed poetry. It awaits the gigantic and
generous treatment worthy of it.

Walt Whitman

If you see me coming, better open up your door,
If you see me coming, better open up your door,
I ain't no stranger, I been here before.

Traditional Blues

Standing at the crossroads, tried to flag a ride,
Standing at the crossroads, tried to flag a ride,
Ain't nobody seem to know me, everybody passed me by.

Crossroad Blues

In every case the result of an untrue mode of knowledge must not be
allowed to run away into an empty nothing, but must necessarily be
grasped as the nothing of that from which it results—a result which
contains what was true in the preceding knowledge.

Hegel, *Phenomenology of Spirit*

So perhaps we shy from confronting our cultural wholeness because it
offers no easily recognizable points of rest, no facile certainties as to who,

what, or where (culturally or historically) we are. Instead, the whole is
always in cacophonic motion.

Ralph Ellison, "The Little Man at the Chehaw Station"

. . . maybe one day, you'll find they actually do understand exactly what
you are talking about, all these fantasy people. All these blues people.

Amiri Baraka, *Dutchman*

From Symbol to Ideology

In my book *The Journey Back: Issues in Black Literature and Criticism* (1980),[1]
I envisioned the "speaking subject" creating language (a code) to be deciphered
by the present-day commentator. In my current study, I envision language (the
code) "speaking" the subject. The subject is "decentered." My quest during the
past decade has been for the distinctive, the culturally specific aspects of Afro-
American literature and culture. I was convinced that I had found such specificity in a peculiar subjectivity, but the objectivity of economics and the sound
lessons of poststructuralism arose to reorient my thinking. I was also convinced
that the symbolic, and quite specifically the symbolically anthropological,
offered avenues to the comprehension of Afro-American expressive culture in
its plenitude.[2] I discovered that the symbolic's antithesis—practical reason, or
the material—is as necessary for understanding Afro-American discourse as the
cultural-in-itself.

My shift from a centered to a decentered subject, from an exclusively symbolic to a more inclusively expressive perspective, was prompted by the curious
force of dialectical thought. My access to the study of such thought came from
attentive readings of Fredric Jameson, Hayden White, Marshall Sahlins, and others. While profiting from observations by these scholars, I also began to attend
meetings of a study group devoted to Hegel's *Phenomenology of Spirit*.

Having journeyed with the aid of symbolic anthropology to what appeared
to be the soundest possible observations on Afro-American art, I found myself
confronted suddenly by a figure-to-ground reversal. A fitting image for the effect
of my reorientation is the gestalt illustration of the Greek hydria (a water vase
with curved handles) that transforms itself into two faces in profile. John Keats's
"Ode on a Grecian Urn," with its familiar detailing of the economies of "art"
and human emotion, can be considered one moment in the shift. Contrasting
with Keats's romantic figurations are the emergent faces of a venerable ancestry.
The shift from Greek hydrias to ancestral faces is a shift from high art to vernacular expression.

The "vernacular" in relation to human beings signals "a slave born on his
master's estate." In expressive terms, vernacular indicates "arts native or peculiar
to a particular country or locale." The material conditions of slavery in the
United States and the rhythms of Afro-American blues combined and emerged
from my revised materialistic perspective as an ancestral matrix that has produced a forceful and indigenous American creativity. The moment of emergence
of economic and vernacular concerns left me, as the French say, *entre les deux:*

suspended somewhere between symbolic anthropology and analytical strategies that Fredric Jameson calls the "ideology of form."[3]

Ideology, Semiotics, and the Material

In acknowledging a concern for the ideology of form, however, I do not want to imply that my symbolic-anthropological orientation was untrue, in the sense of deluded or deceived.[4] This symbolic orientation was simply one moment in my experiencing of Afro-American culture—a moment superseded now by a prospect that constitutes its determinate negation.[5] What was true in my prior framework remains so in my current concern for the ideology of form. Certainly the mode of ideological investigation proposed by Jameson is an analysis that escapes all hints of "vulgar Marxism" through its studious attention to modern critiques of political economy, and also through its shrewd incorporation of post-structuralist thought.[6]

In chapters that follow, I too attempt to avoid a naive Marxism. I do not believe, for example, that a fruitful correlation exists when one merely claims that certain black folk seculars are determinate results of agricultural gang labor. Such attributions simply privilege the material as a substrate while failing to provide detailed accounts of processes leading from an apparent substrate to a peculiar expressive form. A faith of enormous magnitude is required to accept such crude formulations as adequate explanations. The "material" is shifty ground, and current critiques of political economy suggest that postulates based on this ground can be understood only in "semiotic" terms. Hence, the employment of ideology as an analytical category begins with the awareness that "production" as well as "modes of production" must be grasped in terms of the sign. An example of a persuasive case for "political economy" as a code existing in a relationship of identity with language can be found in Jean Baudrillard's *For a Critique of the Political Economy of the Sign*.[7] To read economics as a semiotic process leads to the realization that ideological analyses may be as decidedly intertextual as, say, analyses of the relationship between Afro-American vernacular expression and more sophisticated forms of verbal art. If what is normally categorized as *material* (e.g., "raw material," "consumer goods") can be interpreted semiotically, then any collection of such entities and their defining interrelationships may be defined as a *text*.[8]

In the chapters in this book, however, I do not write about or interpret the *material* in exclusively semiotic terms. Although I am fully aware of insights to be gained from semiotics, my analyses focus directly on the living and laboring conditions of people designated as "the desperate class" by James Weldon Johnson's narrator in *The Autobiography of an Ex-Colored Man*. Such people constitute the vernacular in the United States. Their lives have always been sharply conditioned by an "economics of slavery" as they worked the agricultural rows, searing furnaces, rolling levees, bustling roundhouses, and piney-woods logging camps of America. A sense of "production" and "modes of production" that foregrounds such Afro-American labor seems an appropriate inscription of the material.

The Matrix as Blues

The guiding presupposition of the chapters that follow is that Afro-American culture is a complex, reflexive enterprise which finds its proper figuration in blues conceived as a matrix. A matrix is a womb, a network, a fossil-bearing rock, a rocky trace of a gemstone's removal, a principal metal in an alloy, a mat or plate for reproducing print or phonograph records. The matrix is a point of ceaseless input and output, a web of intersecting, crisscrossing impulses always in productive transit. Afro-American blues constitute such a vibrant network. They are what Jacques Derrida might describe as the "always already" of Afro-American culture.[9] They are the multiplex, enabling *script* in which Afro-American cultural discourse is inscribed.

First arranged, scored, and published for commercial distribution early in the twentieth century when Hart Wand, Arthur "Baby" Seals, and W. C. Handy released their first compositions, the blues defy narrow definition. For they exist, not as a function of formal inscription, but as a forceful condition of Afro-American inscription itself. They were for Handy a "found" folk signifier, awakening him from (perhaps) a dream of American form in Tutwiler, Mississippi, in 1903.[10] At a railroad juncture deep in the southern night, Handy dozed restlessly as he awaited the arrival of a much-delayed train. A guitar's bottleneck resonance suddenly jolted him to consciousness, as a lean, loose-jointed, shabbily clad black man sang:

> Goin' where the Southern cross the Dog.
> Goin' where the Southern cross the Dog.
> Goin' where the Southern cross the Dog.

This haunting invocation of railroad crossings in bottleneck tones left Handy stupified and inspired. In 1914, he published his own Yellow Dog Blues.

But the autobiographical account of the man who has been called the "Father of the Blues" offers only a simplistic detailing of *a progress,* describing, as it were, the elevation of a "primitive" folk ditty to the status of "art" in America. Handy's rendering leaves unexamined, therefore, myriad corridors, mainroads, and way-stations of an extraordinary and elusive Afro-American cultural phenomenon.

Defining Blues

The task of adequately describing the blues is equivalent to the labor of describing a world class athlete's awesome gymnastics. Adequate appreciation demands comprehensive attention. An investigator has to *be* there, to follow a course recommended by one of the African writer Wole Soyinka's ironic narrators to a London landlord: "See for yourself."

The elaborations of the blues may begin in an austere self-accusation: "Now this trouble I'm having, I brought it all on myself." But the accusation seamlessly fades into humorous acknowledgment of duplicity's always duplicitous triumph: "You know the woman that I love, I stoled her from my best friend, / But you know that fool done got lucky and stole her back again." Simple provisos for the troubled mind are commonplace, and drear exactions of crushing manual labor are objects of wry, *in situ* commentary. Numinous invocation punctuates a guitar's resonant back beat with: "Lawd, Lawd, Lawd . . . have mercy on me / Please send me someone, to end this misery." Existential declarations of lack combine with lustily macabre prophecies of the subject's demise. If a "matchbox" will hold his clothes, surely the roadside of much-traveled highways will be his memorial plot: "You can bury my body down by the highway side / So my old devil sprit can catch a Greyhound bus and ride." Conative formulations of a brighter future (sun shining in the back door some day, wind rising to blow the blues away) join with a slow-moving *askesis* of present, amorous imprisonment: "You leavin' now, baby, but you hangin' crepe on my door," or "She got a mortgage on my body, and a lien on my soul." Self-deprecating confession and slack-strumming growls of violent solutions combine: "My lead mule's cripple, you know my off mule's blind / You know I can't drive nobody / Bring me a loaded .39 (I'm go'n pop him, pop that mule!)." The wish for a river of whiskey where if a man were a "divin' duck" he would submerge himself and never "come up" is a function of a world in which "when you lose yo' eyesight, yo' best friend's gone / Sometimes yo' own dear people don't want to fool with you long."

Like a streamlined athlete's awesomely dazzling explosions of prowess, the blues song erupts, creating a veritable playful festival of meaning. Rather than a rigidly personalized form, the blues offer a phylogenetic recapitulation—a nonlinear, freely associative, nonsequential meditation—of species experience. What emerges is not a filled subject, but an anonymous (nameless) voice issuing from the black (w)hole.[11] The blues singer's signatory coda is always *atopic,* placeless: "If anybody ask you who sang this song / Tell 'em X done bee'n here and gone." The "signature" is a space already "X" (ed), a trace of the already "gone"—a fissure rejoined. Nevertheless, the "you" (audience) addressed is always free to invoke the X(ed) spot in the body's absence.[12] For the signature comprises a scripted authentication of "your" feelings. Its mark is an invitation to energizing intersubjectivity. Its implied (in)junction reads: Here is my body meant for (a phylogenetically conceived) you.

The blues are a synthesis (albeit one always synthesizing rather than one already hypostatized). Combining work songs, group seculars, field hollers, sacred harmonies, proverbial wisdom, folk philosophy, political commentary, ribald humor, elegiac lament, and much more, they constitute an amalgam that seems always to have been in motion in America—always becoming, shaping, transforming, displacing the peculiar experiences of Africans in the New World.

Blues as Code and Force

One way of describing the blues is to claim their amalgam as a code radically conditioning Afro-America's cultural signifying. Such a description implies a prospect in which any aspect of the blues—a guitar's growling vamp or a stanza's sardonic boast of heroically back-breaking labor—"stands," in Umberto Eco's words, "for something else" in virtue of a systematic set of conventional procedures.[13] The materiality of any blues manifestation, such as a guitar's walking bass or a French harp's "whoop" of motion seen, is, one might say, enciphered in ways that enable the material to escape into a named or coded, blues signification. The material, thus, slips into irreversible difference. And as phenomena named and set in meaningful relation by a blues code, both the harmonica's whoop and the guitar's bass can recapitulate vast dimensions of experience. For such discrete blues instances are always intertextually related by the blues code as a whole. Moreover, they are involved in the code's manifold interconnections with other codes of Afro-American culture.

A further characterization of blues suggests that they are equivalent to Hegelian "force."[14] In the *Phenomenology,* Hegel speaks of a flux in which there is "only *difference* as a *universal* difference, or as a difference into which the many antitheses have been resolved. This difference, as a *universal* difference, is consequently the *simple element in the play of Force itself* and what is true in it. It is the *law of Force*" (p. 90). Force is thus defined as a relational matrix where *difference* is the law. Finally the blues, employed as an image for the investigation of culture, represents a *force* not unlike electricity. Hegel writes:

> Of course, given *positive* electricity, negative too is given *in principle;* for the positive *is,* only as related to a negative, or, the positive is *in its own self* the difference from itself; and similarly with the negative. But that electricity as such should divide itself in this way is not in itself a necessity. Electricity, as *simple Force,* is indifferent to its law—*to be* positive and negative; and if we call the former its *Notion* but the latter its being, then its Notion is indifferent to its being. It merely *has* this property, which just means that this property is not *in itself* necessary to it. . . . It is only with law as law that we are to compare its *Notion* as Notion, or its necessity. But in all these forms, necessity has shown itself to be only an empty word. [p. 93]

Metaphorically extending Hegel's formulation vis-à-vis electricity, one might say that a traditional property of cultural study may well be the kind of dichotomy inscribed in terms like "culture" and "practical reason." But even if such dichotomies are raised to the status of law, they never constitute the necessity or "determinant instances" of cultural study and explanation conceived in terms of *force*—envisioned, that is, in the analytic notion of a blues matrix as force. The blues, therefore, comprise a mediational site where familiar antinomies are resolved (or dissolved) in the office of adequate cultural understanding.

Blues Translation at the Junction

To suggest a trope for the blues as a forceful matrix in cultural understanding is to summon an image of the black blues singer at the railway junction lustily transforming experiences of a durative (unceasingly oppressive) landscape into the energies of rhythmic song. The railway juncture is marked by transience. Its inhabitants are always travelers—a multifarious assembly in transit. The "X" of crossing roadbeds signals the multi-directionality of the juncture and is simply a single instance in a boundless network that redoubles and circles, makes sidings and ladders, forms Y's and branches over the vastness of hundreds of thousands of American miles. Polymorphous and multidirectional, scene of arrivals and departures, place betwixt and between (ever *entre les deux*), the juncture is the way-station of the blues.

The singer and his production are always at this intersection, this crossing, codifying force, providing resonance for experience's multiplicities. Singer and song never arrest transience—fix it in "transcendent form." Instead they provide expressive equivalence for the juncture's ceaseless flux. Hence, they may be conceived as translators.[15]

Like translators of written texts, blues and its sundry performers offer interpretations of the experiencing of experience. To experience the juncture's ever-changing scenes, like successive readings of ever-varying texts by conventional translators, is to produce vibrantly polyvalent interpretations encoded as blues. The singer's product, like the railway juncture itself (or a successful translator's original), constitutes a lively scene, a robust matrix, where endless antinomies are mediated and understanding and explanation find conditions of possibility.

The durative—transliterated as lyrical statements of injustice, despair, loss, absence, denial, and so forth—is complemented in blues performance by an instrumental energy (guitar, harmonica, fiddle, gut-bucket bass, molasses jug, washboard) that employs locomotive rhythms, train bells, and whistles as onomatopoeic references. In *A Theory of Semiotics,* Eco writes:

> Music presents, on the one hand, the problem of a semiotic system without a semantic level (or a content plane): on the other hand, however, there are musical "signs" (or syntagms) with an explicit denotative value (trumpet signals in the army) and there are syntagms or entire "texts" possessing pre-culturalized connotative value ("pastoral" or "thrilling" music, etc.). [p. 111]

The absence of a content plane noted by Eco implies what is commonly referred to as the "abstractness" of instrumental music. The "musical sign," on the other hand, suggests cultural signals that function onomatopoeically by calling to mind "natural" sounds or sounds "naturally" associated with common human situations. Surely, though, it would be a mistake to claim that onomatopoeia is in any sense "natural," for different cultures encode even the "same" natural sounds in varying ways. (A rooster onomatopoeically sounded in Puerto Rican Spanish is phonically unrecognizable in United States English, as a classic Puerto Rican short story makes hilariously clear.)

If onomatopoeia is taken as cultural mimesis, however, it is possible to apply the semiotician's observations to blues by pointing out that the dominant blues syntagm in America is an instrumental imitation of *train-wheels-over-track-junctures*. This sound is the "sign," as it were, of the blues, and it combines an intriguing melange of phonics: rattling gondolas, clattering flatbeds, quilling whistles, clanging bells, rumbling boxcars, and other railroad sounds. A blues text may thus announce itself by the onomatopoeia of the train's whistle sounded on the indrawn breath of a harmonica or a train's bell tinkled on the high keys of an upright piano. The blues stanzas may then roll through an extended meditative repertoire with a steady train-wheels-over-track-junctures guitar back beat as a traditional, syntagmatic complement. If desire and absence are driving conditions of blues performance, the amelioration of such conditions is implied by the onomatopoeic *training* of blues voice and instrument. Only a *trained* voice can sing the blues.[16]

At the junctures, the intersections of experience where roads cross and diverge, the blues singer and his performance serve as codifiers, absorbing and transforming discontinuous experience into formal expressive instances that bear only the trace of origins, refusing to be pinned down to any final, dualistic significance. Even as they speak of paralyzing absence and ineradicable desire, their instrumental rhythms suggest change, movement, action, continuance, unlimited and unending possibility. Like signification itself, blues are always nomadically wandering. Like the freight-hopping hobo, they are ever on the move, ceaselessly summing novel experience.

Antinomies and Blues Mediation

The blues performance is further suggestive if economic conditions of Afro-American existence are brought to mind. Standing at the juncture, or railhead, the singer draws into his repertoire hollers, cries, whoops, and moans of black men and women working in fields without recompense. The performance can be cryptically conceived, therefore, in terms suggested by the bluesman Booker White, who said, "The foundation of the blues is working behind a mule way back in slavery time."[17] As a force, the blues matrix defines itself as a network mediating poverty and abundance in much the same manner that it reconciles durative and kinetic. Many instances of the blues performance contain lyrical inscriptions of both lack and commercial possibility. The performance that sings of abysmal poverty and deprivation may be recompensed by sumptuous food and stimulating beverage at a country picnic, amorous favors from an attentive listener, enhanced Afro-American communality, or Yankee dollars from representatives of record companies traveling the South in search of blues as commodifiable entertainment. The performance, therefore, mediates one of the most prevalent of all antimonies in cultural investigation—creativity and commerce.

As driving force, the blues matrix thus avoids simple dualities. It perpetually achieves its effects as a fluid and multivalent network. It is only when "understanding"—the analytical work of a translator who translates the infinite changes of the blues—converges with such blues "force," however, that adequate explanatory perception (and half-creation) occurs. The matrix effectively functions toward cultural understanding, that is, only when an investigator brings an inventive attention to bear.

The Investigator, Relativity, and Blues Effect

The blues matrix is a "cultural invention": a "negative symbol" that generates (or obliges one to invent) its own referents.[18] As an inventive trope, this matrix provides for my following chapters the type of image or model that is always present in accounts of culture and cultural products. If the analyses that I provide are successful, the blues matrix will have *taken effect* (and *affect*) through me.

To "take effect," of course, is not identical with to "come into existence" or to "demonstrate serviceability for the first time." Because what I have defined as a blues matrix is so demonstrably anterior to any single instance of its cultural-explanatory employment, my predecessors as effectors are obviously legion. "Take effect," therefore, does not signify discovery in the traditional sense of that word. Rather, it signals the tropological nature of my uses of an already extant matrix.

Ordinarily, accounts of art, literature, and culture fail to acknowledge their governing theories; further, they invariably conceal the *inventive* character of such theories. Nevertheless, all accounts of art, expressive culture, or culture in general are indisputably functions of their creators' tropological energies. When such creators talk of "art," for example, they are never dealing with existential givens. Rather, they are summoning objects, processes, or events defined by a model that they have created (by and for themselves) as a picture of art. Such models, or tropes, are continually invoked to constitute and explain phenomena inaccessible to the senses. Any single model, or any complementary set of inventive tropes, therefore, will offer only a selective account of experience—a partial reading, as it were, of the world. While the single account temporarily reduces chaos to ordered plan, all such accounts are eternally troubled by "remainders."

Where literary art is concerned, for example, a single, ordering, investigative model or trope will necessarily exclude phenomena that an alternative model or trope privileges as a definitive artistic instance. Recognizing the determinacy of "invention" in cultural explanation entails the acknowledgment of what might be called a *normative relativity*. To acknowledge relativity in our post-Heisenbergian universe is, of course, far from original. Neither, however, is it an occasion for the skeptics or the conservatives to heroically assume the critical stage.

The assumption of normative relativity, far from being a call to abandonment or retrenchment in the critical arena, constitutes an invitation to speculative explorations that are aware both of their own partiality and their heuristic transitions from suggestive (sometimes dramatic) images to inscribed concepts. The openness implied by relativity enables, say, the literary critic to *re-cognize* his endeavors, presupposing from the outset that such labors are not directed toward independent, observable, empirical phenomena but rather toward processes, objects, and events that he or she half-creates (and privileges as "art") through his or her own speculative, inventive energies and interests.

One axiological extrapolation from these observations on invention and relativity is that no object, process, or single element possesses *intrinsic aesthetic value*. The "art object" as well as its value are selective *constructions* of the critic's tropes and models. A radicalizing uncertainty may thus be said to mark cultural explanation. This uncertainty is similar in kind to the always selective endeavors of, say, the particle physicist.[19]

The physicist is always compelled to choose between velocity and position.[20] Similarly, an investigator of Afro-American expressive culture is ceaselessly compelled to forgo manifold variables in order to apply intensive energy to a selected array.

Continuing the metaphor, one might say that if the investigator's efforts are sufficiently charged with blues energy,[21] he is almost certain to remodel elements and events appearing in traditional, Anglo-American space-time in ways that make them "jump" several rings toward blackness and the vernacular. The blues-oriented observer (the *trained* critic) necessarily "heats up" the observational space by his or her very presence.[22]

An inventive, tropological, investigative model such as that proposed by *Blues, Ideology, and Afro-American Literature* entails not only awareness of the metaphorical nature of the blues matrix, but also a willingness on my own part to do more than merely hear, read, or see the blues. I must also play (with and on) them. Since the explanatory possibilities of a blues matrix—like analytical possibilities of a delimited set of forces in unified field theory—are hypothetically unbounded, the blues challenge investigative *understanding* to an unlimited play.

Blues and Vernacular Expression in America

The blues should be privileged in the study of American culture to precisely the extent that inventive understanding successfully converges with blues force to yield accounts that persuasively and playfully refigure expressive geographies in the United States. My own ludic uses of the blues are various, and each figuration implies the valorization of vernacular facets of American culture. The Afro-American writer James Alan McPherson is, I think, the commentator who most brilliantly and encouragingly coalesces blues, vernacular, and cultural geographies of the United States in his introduction to *Railroad: Trains and Train People in American Culture.*[23]

Having described a fiduciary reaction to the steam locomotive by nineteenth-century financiers and an adverse artistic response by such traditional American writers as Melville, Hawthorne, and Thoreau, McPherson details the reaction of another sector of the United States population to the railroad:

> To a third group of people, those not bound by the assumptions of either business or classical traditions in art, the shrill whistle might have spoken of new possibilities. These were the backwoodsmen and Africans and recent immigrants—the people who comprised the vernacular level of American society. To them the machine might have been loud and frightening, but its whistle and its wheels promised movement. And since a commitment to both freedom and movement was the basic promise of democracy, it was probable that such people would view the locomotive as a challenge to the integrative powers of their imaginations. [p. 6]

Afro-Americans—at the bottom even of the vernacular ladder in America—responded to the railroad as a "meaningful symbol offering both economic progress and the possibility of aesthetic expression" (p. 9). This possibility came from the locomotive's drive and thrust, its promise of unrestrained mobility and unlimited freedom. The blues musician at the crossing, as I have already suggested, became an expert at reproducing or translating these locomotive energies. With the birth of the blues, the vernacular realm of American culture acquired a music that had "wide appeal because it expressed a toughness of spirit and resilience, a willingness to transcend difficulties which was strikingly familiar to those whites who remembered their own history" (p. 16). The signal expressive achievement of blues, then, lay in their translation of technological innovativeness, unsettling demographic fluidity, and boundless frontier energy into expression which attracted avid interest from the American masses. By the 1920s, American financiers had become aware of commercial possibilities not only of railroads but also of black music deriving from them.

A "race record" market flourished during the twenties. Major companies issued blues releases under labels such as Columbia, Vocalion, Okeh, Gennett, and Victor. Sometimes as many as ten blues releases appeared in a single week; their sales (aided by radio's dissemination of the music) climbed to hundreds of thousands. The onset of the Great Depression ended this phenomenal boom. During their heyday, however, the blues unequivocally signified a ludic predominance of the vernacular with that sassy, growling, moaning, whooping confidence that marks their finest performances.

McPherson's assessment seems fully justified. It serves, in fact, as a suggestive play in the overall project of refiguring American expressive geographies. Resonantly complementing the insights of such astute commentators as Albert Murray, Paul Oliver, Samuel Charters, Amiri Baraka, and others,[24] McPherson's judgments highlight the value of a blues matrix for cultural analysis in the United States.

In harmony with other brilliant commentators on the blues already noted, Ralph Ellison selects the railroad way-station (the "Chehaw Station") as his topos for the American "little man."[25] In "The Little Man at the Chehaw Station,"[26] he autobiographically details his own confirmation of his Tuskegee music teacher's observation that in the United States

> You must *always* play your best, even if it's only in the waiting room at Chehaw Station, because in this country there'll always be a little man hidden behind the stove . . . and he'll know the *music,* and the *tradition,* and the standards of *musicianship* required for whatever you set out to perform [p. 25].

When Hazel Harrison made this statement to the young Ellison, he felt that she was joking. But as he matured and moved through a diversity of American scenes, Ellison realized that the inhabitants of the "drab, utilitarian structure" of the American vernacular do far more than respond in expressive ways to "blues-echoing, train-whistle rhapsodies blared by fast express trains as they thundered past" the junction. At the vernacular level, according to Ellison, people possess a "cultivated taste" that asserts its "authority out of obscurity" (p. 26). The "little man" finally comes to represent, therefore, "that unknown quality which renders the American audience far more than a receptive instrument that may be dominated through a skillful exercise of the sheerly 'rhetorical' elements—the flash and filigree—of the artist's craft" (p. 26).

From Ellison's opening gambit and wonderfully illustrative succeeding examples, I infer that the vernacular (in its expressive adequacy and adept critical facility) always *absorbs* "classical" elements of American life and art. Indeed, Ellison seems to imply that expressive performers in America who ignore the judgments of the vernacular are destined to failure.

Although his injunctions are intended principally to advocate a traditional "melting pot" ideal in American "high art," Ellison's observations ultimately valorize a comprehensive, vernacular expressiveness in America. Though he seldom loses sight of the possibilities of a classically "transcendent" American high art, he derives his most forceful examples from the vernacular: Blues seem implicitly to comprise the *All* of American culture.

Blues Moments in Afro-American Expression

In the chapters that follow, I attempt to provide suggestive accounts of moments in Afro-American discourse when personae, protagonists, autobiographical narrators, or literary critics successfully negotiate an obdurate "economics of slavery" and achieve a resonant, improvisational, expressive dignity. Such moments and successful analyses of them provide cogent examples of the blues matrix at work.

The expressive instances that I have in mind occur in passages such as the conclusion of the *Narrative of the Life of Frederick Douglass*. Standing at a Nantucket convention, riffing (in the "break" suddenly confronting him) on the *personal* troubles he has seen and successfully negotiated in a "prisonhouse of American bondage," Douglass achieves a profoundly dignified blues voice. Zora Neale Hurston's protagonist Janie in the novel *Their Eyes Were Watching God*— as she lyrically and idiomatically relates a tale of personal suffering and triumph that begins in the sexual exploitations of slavery—is a blues artist par excellence. Her wisdom might well be joined to that of Amiri Baraka's Walker Vessels (a "locomotive container" of blues?), whose chameleon code-switching from academic philosophy to blues insight makes him a veritable incarnation of the absorptively vernacular. The narrator of Richard Wright's *Black Boy* inscribes a black blues life's lean desire (as I shall demonstrate in chapter 3) and suggests yet a further instance of the blues matrix's expressive energies. Ellison's invisible man and Baraka's narrator in *The System of Dante's Hell* (whose blues book produces dance) provide additional examples. Finally, Toni Morrison's Milkman Dead in *Song of Solomon* discovers through "Sugarman's" song that an awesomely expressive blues response may well consist of improvisational and serendipitous surrender to the air: "As fleet and bright as a lodestar he wheeled toward Guitar and it did not matter which one of them would give up his ghost in the killing arms of his brother. For now he knew what Shalimar knew: If you surrendered to the air, you could *ride* it."[27]

Such blues moments are but random instances of the blues matrix at work in Afro-American cultural expression. In my study as a whole, I attempt persuasively to demonstrate that a blues matrix (as a vernacular trope for American cultural explanation in general) possesses enormous force for the study of literature, criticism, and culture. I know that I have appropriated the vastness of the vernacular in the United States to a single matrix. But I trust that my necessary selectivity will be interpreted, not as a sign of myopic exclusiveness, but as an invitation to inventive play. The success of my efforts would be effectively signaled in the following chapters, I think, by the transformation of my "I" into a juncture where readers could freely improvise their own distinctive tropes for cultural explanation. A closing that in fact opened on such inventive possibilities (like the close of these introductory remarks) would be appropriately marked by the crossing sign's inviting "X."

Notes

1. Chicago: University of Chicago Press, 1980.
2. Though a great many sources were involved in my reoriented cultural thinking, certainly the terminology employed in my discussion at this point derives from Marshall Sahlins's wonderfully lucid *Culture and Practical Reason* (Chicago: University of Chicago Press, 1976). Sahlins delineates two modes of thinking that have characterized anthropology from its inception. These two poles are "symbolic" and "functionalist." He resolves the dichotomy suggested by these terms through the middle term "cultural proposition," a phrase that he defines as a cultural mediating ground where the material and symbolic, the useful and the ineffable, ceaselessly converge and depart.
3. The "ideology of form" as a description of Jameson's project derives from the essay "The Symbolic Inference; or, Kenneth Burke and Ideological Analysis," *Critical Inquiry* 4 (1978): 507–23. Surely, though, Jameson's most recent study, *The Political Unconscious: Narrative as a Socially Symbolic Act* (Ithaca, N.Y.: Cornell University Press, 1981), offers the fullest description of his views on ways in which cultural texts formally inscribe material/historical conditions of their production, distribution, and consumption.
4. In *The Journey Back,* I define my project as follows: "The phrase ['the anthropology of art'] expresses for me the notion that art must be studied with an attention to the methods and findings of disciplines which enable one to address such concerns as the status of the artistic object, the relationship of art to other cultural systems, and the nature and function of artistic creation and perception in a given society" (p. xvi). The project's privileging of "symbolic anthropology" and "art" under the sign *interdisciplinary* involved exclusions that were ironical and (I now realize) somewhat disabling where a full description of expressive culture is sought.
5. The Hegelian epigraph that marks the beginning of these introductory remarks offers the best definition I know of "determinate negation." The epigraph is taken from the *Phenomenology of Spirit.*
6. I have in mind Louis Althusser and Étienne Balibar, *Reading Capital* (London: New Left Books, 1977), and Jean Baudrillard's *For a Critique of the Political Economy of the Sign* (1972; St. Louis: Telos Press, 1981) and *The Mirror of Production* (1973; St. Louis: Telos Press, 1975). By "poststructuralist" thought, I have in mind the universe of discourse constituted by *deconstruction*. Jacques Derrida's *Of Grammatology* (1967; Baltimore: Johns Hopkins University Press, 1976) is perhaps the locus classicus of the deconstructionist project. One of the more helpful accounts of deconstruction is Christopher Norris's *Deconstruction: Theory and Practice* (London: Methuen, 1982). Of course, there is a certain collapsing of poststructuralism and political economy in the sources cited previously.
7. For a full citation of Baudrillard, see note 6.
8. Ibid.
9. In *Of Grammatology*, Derrida defines a problematic in which *writing*, conceived as an iterable *differe(a)nce*, is held to be *always already* instituted (or, in motion) when a traditionally designated *Man* begins to speak. Hence, *script* is anterior to speech,

and absence and *differe(a)nce* displace presence and identity (conceived as "Intention") in philosophical discourse.

10. The story appears in W. C. Handy, *Father of the Blues,* ed. Arna Bontemps (New York: Macmillan Co., 1941), p.78. Other defining sources of blues include: Paul Oliver, *The Story of the Blues* (London: Chilton, 1969); Samuel B. Charters, *The Country Blues* (New York: Rinehart, 1959); Giles Oakley, *The Devil's Music: A History of the Country Blues* (New York: Harcourt Brace Jovanovich, 1976); Amiri Baraka, *Blues People: Negro Music in White America* (New York: William E. Morrow, 1963); Albert Murray, *Stomping the Blues* (New York: McGraw-Hill Book Co., 1976); and William Ferris, *Blues from the Delta* (New York: Anchor Books, 1979).

11. The description at this point is coextensive with the "decentering" of the subject mentioned at the outset of my introduction. What I wish to effect by noting a "subject" who is not *filled* is a displacement of the notion that knowledge, or "art," or "song," are manifestations of an ever more clearly defined individual consciousness of *Man.* In accord with Michel Foucault's explorations in his *Archaeology of Knowledge* (1969; New York: Harper & Row, 1972), I want to claim that blues is like a discourse that comprises the "already said" of Afro-America. Blues' governing statements and sites are thus vastly more interesting in the process of cultural investigation than either a history of ideas or a history of individual, subjective consciousness vis-á-vis blues. When I move to the "X" of the trace and the body as host, I am invoking Mark Taylor's formulations in a suggestive deconstructive essay toward radical christology called "The Text as Victim," in *Deconstruction and Theology* (New York: Crossroad, 1982), pp. 58–78.

12. The terms used in "The Text as Victim," ibid., are "host" and "parasite." The words of the blues are hostlike in the sense of a christological Logos-as-Host. But without the dialogical action of the parasite, of course, there could be no Host. Host is, thus, parasitic on a parasite's citation. Both, in Taylor's statement of the matter, are *para-sites.*

13. The definition of "code" is drawn from *A Theory of Semiotics* (Bloomington: Indiana University Press, 1976). All references to Eco refer to this work and are hereafter marked by page numbers in parentheses.

14. *The Phenomenology of Spirit,* trans. A. V. Miller (New York: Oxford University Press, 1977). While it is true that the material dimensions of the dialectic are of primary importance to my current study, it is also true that the locus classicus of the dialectic, in and for itself, is the *Phenomenology.* Marx may well have stood Hegel on his feet through a materialist inversion of the *Phenomenology,* but subsequent generations have always looked at that uprighted figure—Hegel himself—as an authentic host.

15. Having heard John Felstiner in a session at the 1982 Modern Language Association Convention present a masterful paper defining "translation" as a process of preserving "something of value" by keeping it in motion, I decided that the blues were apt translators of experience. Felstiner, it seemed to me, sought to demonstrate that *translation* was a process equivalent to gift-giving in Mauss's classic definition of that activity. The value of the gift of translation is never fixed because, say, the poem, is always in a transliterational motion, moving from one alphabet to another, always renewing and being *re-newed* in the process. Translation forestalls fixity. It calls attention always to the *translated's* excess—to its complex multivalence.

16. One of the most inspiring and intriguing descriptions of the relationship between blues voice and sounds of the railroad is Albert Murray's lyrical exposition in *Stomping the Blues.*

17. Quoted in Oakley, *The Devil's Music,* p. 7.

18. I have appropriated the term "negative symbol" from Roy Wagner's *The Invention of Culture* (Chicago: University of Chicago Press, 1975), p. xvi.

19. My references to a "post-Heisenbergian universe" and to the "particle physicist" were made possible by a joyful reading of Gary Zukav's *The Dancing Wu Li Masters: An Overview of the New Physics* (New York: William E. Morrow, 1979).

20. Zukav, ibid., writes: "According to the uncertainty principle, we cannot measure accurately, at the same time, both the position *and* the momentum of a moving particle. The more precisely we determine one of these properties, the less we know about the other. If we precisely determine the position of the particle, then, strange as it sounds, there is *nothing* that we can know about its momentum. If we precisely determine the momentum of the particle, there is no way to determine its position" (p. 111). Briefly, if we bring to bear enough energy actually to "see" the imagined "particle," that energy has always already *moved* the particle from its *position* (which is one of the aspects of its existence that one attempts to *determine*) when we take our measurement. Indeterminacy thus becomes normative.

21. The "blues force" is my translational equivalent in investigative "energy" for the investigative energy delineated by Heisenberg's formulations. See note 20.

22. Eco (*A Theory of Semiotics,* p. 29) employs the metaphor of "ecological variation" in his discussions of the semiotic investigation of culture to describe observer effect in the mapping of experience.

23. New York: Random House, 1976. All citations refer to this edition and are hereafter marked by page numbers in parentheses.

24. See n. 9 above.

25. The Chehaw Station is a whistle-stop near Tuskegee, Alabama. It was a feature of the landscape of Tuskegee Institute, where Ellison studied music (and much else).

26. *American Scholar* 47 (1978): 24–48. All citations refer to this version and are hereafter marked by page numbers in parentheses.

27. *Song of Solomon* (New York: Alfred A. Knopf, 1977), p. 337.

Arthur Danto (1924–)

Danto has been teaching philosophy at Columbia University for over 50 years, beginning in 1951, and he has also, for some time now, been the art critic for *The Nation,* a weekly political and cultural magazine. Danto graduated from Wayne State University in 1948 and earned his M.A. in 1949 and his Ph.D. in 1952 from Columbia University. A keen intellect, creativity, and range are evident in his scholarship, just as eloquence, wit, and substance are hallmarks of his writing. He is renowned both for his texts on Friedrich Nietzsche, Jean-Paul Sartre, and analytic philosophy and for his many books examining works of art and theories of art. His philosophical investigations of art often focus on questions of interpretation and questions of why something may or may not be considered art. For example, what makes Andy Warhol's 1960s brillo boxes art? Should one or should one not interpret Warhol's paintings of Campbell's soup cans?

Of Danto's many books, the following are some of the most influential: *Analytical Philosophy in History* (1965), *Analytical Philosophy of Action* (1973), *The Philosophical Disenfranchisement of Art* (1986), *Connections to the*

World: The Basic Concepts of Philosophy (1989), The Transfiguration of the Commonplace: A Philosophy of Art (1990), Beyond the Brillo Box: The Visual Arts in Post-Historical Perspective (1992), and After the End of Art: Contemporary Art and the Pale of History (1997). The reading selection given next, "Pop Art and Past Futures," comes from After the End of Art.

Pop Art and Past Futures

If we attempt to return to the perspective of artists and critics in the early 1960s, putting in brackets, as it were, the history of art as it worked itself out between then and now, and attempt to reconstruct the *vergangene Zukunft*—the future as it appeared in that past moment to those whose present it was—it must have seemed to the abstract expressionists and their supporters alike, that the future was very much theirs. The Renaissance paradigm had lasted for over six hundred years, and there seemed reason enough to suppose that the New York paradigm might last at least as long. To be sure, the Renaissance paradigm turned out to be developmental and progressive—to sustain a narrative—and though modernism, in the thought of Clement Greenberg, was itself developmental and progressive, it is difficult to suppose that this aspect of Greenberg's thought was widely shared or even widely known. But perhaps an argument for longevity could have been induced from the diversity of the New York School itself, made up, as it was, of figures of such distinctive artistic manners. Pollock, de Kooning, Kline, Newman, Rothko, Motherwell, Still—each was distinctively himself and sufficiently unlike the rest that one would never have been able even to deduce the possibility of Rothko's style, had Rothko himself not found it, from the disjunction of other styles which defined the New York School. So it must have seemed that as new personalities became part of the school, new and utterly unimagined styles, as different from the existing styles as they were from one another, would as a matter of course emerge, with no internal limit to their number and variety.

But if abstraction held the future in its grip, what was to happen to the realists, who still existed in large numbers in America, and indeed in New York? The realists were not prepared to surrender the future to abstract expressionism, and that meant that their present was one of protest and aesthetic battle. They felt their back to the wall, not merely of art history, but of the practical production of art—for abstract expressionism was sweeping the institutional infrastructure of the art world and it seemed as if abstraction was an enemy to be defeated, or at least repelled, and that one's entire future as an artist—indeed the very question of whether one was going to have a future as an artist—depended upon what one did here and now.

Let us consider the case of Edward Hopper. There is a direct line of descent from Thomas Eakins through Robert Henri to Hopper, in that Henri was Eakins's student and Hopper was Henri's—and Eakins himself descended from the Beaux Arts Academy in Paris and the painter Gérôme. Abstract expressionism, indeed high modernism, intersects this history the way a meteor intersects the orderly swing of planets in the solar system. Hopper would have been altogether content to work out the further implications of Eakins's agenda, just as

Henri did. Henri led a battle of the so-called Independent Artists against the practices of the National Academy. In 1913, and even earlier, at Stieglitz's gallery, artists like Picasso and Matisse were but marginal presences, too wild in a way to constitute a serious threat to art as Henri, his followers, and his enemies understood it. But in Hopper's era, abstract expressionism was hardly marginal. Hopper and the artists who understood him, and whom he understood, were marginal, and in danger of being pushed off the board altogether. And the Academy represented no threat or obstacle whatsoever, as it had done for Henri, and, in a way for Eakins. Eakins, indeed, set the agenda that Henri transformed into an aesthetic ideology and which Hopper merely adopted as a matter of course.

Let's just consider the treatment of the nude figure. Eakins reacted, while still a student at the Beaux Arts Academy in Paris, against the artificial way in which the paintings in the Salon of 1868 presented the nude: "The pictures are of naked women, standing, sitting, lying down, flying, dancing, doing nothing," he wrote, "which they call Phrynes, Venuses, nymphs, hermaphrodites, houris, and Greek proper names." He more or less vowed to paint the nude in a real situation, rather than as "smirking goddesses of many complexions, amidst the delicious arsenic green trees and gentle wax flowers. . . . I hate affectation."[1] So he painted the great *William Rush Carving his Allegorical Figure of the Skuylkill River* after his return to Philadelphia, for the Centennial Exhibition of 1876. It showed the nude as model, one of the ways in which a woman might naturally appear undressed. Henri, who founded the so-called Ash Can School, not only showed models as naked women, but did so in an altogether natural way, that is, showing the way real as against idealized women look with their clothes off. And Hopper, when he painted the nude, did so in erotic situations in which a woman might naturally be undressed, such as *Girlie Show* of 1941 or *Morning Sunshine* of 1952, where one feels the woman is fantasizing. There is nothing especially modern in these paintings of Hopper's: it was, virtually, as if the late nineteenth century continued on, encapsulated in the twentieth century, as if modernism, as we have come to understand it, had never happened—though of course, with their shadows and golden lights, Eakins's pictures have the look of Old Master paintings in a way that Hopper's pictures never do: his pictures are spare and clear, with no unexplained, or so to speak, *metaphysical* shadows.

But modernism is a concept which has itself evolved. Hopper was in fact included in the Museum of Modern Art's second show, "Paintings by Nineteen Living Americans," in 1929. Alfred Barr thought Hopper "the most exciting painter in America" when he gave him a retrospective at that museum in 1933. The show was criticized as "the reverse of that which characterized the modern movement" by the critic Ralph Pearson;[2] and Barr gives us a deep insight into how modernism was understood by the institution most closely associated with it in America and, certainly in 1929, in the world: he accused Pearson of trying "to transform a popular and temporary implication of the word modern into an academic and comparatively permanent lable."[3] Modernism circa 1933 was very different from modernism circa 1960, when Clement Greenberg wrote his canonical essay "Modernist Painting." But by then modernism was very nearly over with, and its demise has to be distinguished from the demise of abstract expressionism: Greenberg took a certain pleasure in noting the death of the latter in 1962, but modernism, he felt, would go on, even if it seemed to have become stalled when I heard him speak in 1992. Whatever the case, in 1933, the "modern" stood for a tremendous diversity of art: the impressionists and post-impressionists, including Rousseau; the surrealists, the fauves, the cubists. And of course, there were the abstractionists and suprematists and the nonobjectivists. But they were felt merely part of modernity, which also included Hopper, and as such modernism was no threat to realism. But by the 1950s, and especially in consequence of the immense critical success of abstract expressionism, art of the sort Hopper exemplified was in danger of being swamped by a modernism narrowly defined in terms of abstraction. What had been a part now threatened to become the whole. And the future seemed bleak for art as Hopper and his peers understood it. That defined their present as a field of battle in the style wars of the twentieth century.

Gail Levin narrates the Hoppers' involvement in the campaign against abstraction, or "gobbledegook," as they called it. They supported the action taken by a group of realist painters against the Museum of Modern Art, felt to favor abstraction and "nonobjective art" to the exclusion of realism. They were appalled by the way the Whitney annual of 1959–1960 was marked by the sparsity of realist canvases (a protest reenacted on 29 September 1995). They banded together with other artists, Jo Hopper wrote in her diary, "to preserve existence of realism in art against the wholesale usurpation of the abstract by Mod, Mus., Whitney, and thru them spread thru most of the universities for those who cannot abide not subscribing to le dernier cri from Europe."[4] They helped put out a magazine called *Reality,* which ran through several issues. They felt sincerely that if they did not prevail in these efforts, realist painting was a doomed thing.

I do not think it possible to convey the moral energy that went into this division between abstraction and realism, from both sides, in those years. It had an almost theological intensity, and in another stage of civilization there would certainly have been burnings at the stake. In those days a young artist who did the figure did so with the sense of espousing a dangerous and heretical practice. "Aesthetic correctness" filled the role which has come to be filled by political correctness today, and the actions of the Hoppers and their cohorts convey the indignation and shock that all the conservative books on political correctness do today, although it has to be remembered how the realists were freely consigned to artistic oblivion by those who idelogized abstraction. The realists of course felt their very existence threatened, which is perhaps matched by the way in which professors have been threatened with loss of tenure, or at least have been made fearful of such loss, unless their syllabus and their classroom vocabulary is brought into line.

Whatever the merits of the analogy, the conflict was essentially over in five or six years. Greenberg is an interesting case to examine in this light. In 1939 he saw abstraction as an historical inevitability: abstraction was, as we saw him argue in "Towards a Newer Laocoön," an "imperative [that] comes from history." In

"The Case for Abstract Art" of 1959, he implied that representation is irrelevant, that "the abstract formal unity of a picture by Titian is more important to its quality than what that picture images"—a point made earlier in the century by Roger Fry. "It is a fact," Greenberg continues, "that representational paintings are essentially and most fully appreciated when the identifications of what they represent are only secondarily present to our consciousness." He largely repeated this invidious characterization in his canonical essay "Modernist Painting" of 1960, where he wrote that "modernist painting in its latest phase has not abandoned the representation of recognizable objects in principle. What it has abandoned in principle is the representation of the kind of space that recognizable objects can inhabit." Painting did this in order to set itself logically apart from sculpture, he famously argues, and it is only fair to observe that this distinction, while it might give credibility to an artist like Stuart Davis or Miró, situates Hopper and the realists on a lower rung of historical evolution. But by 1961 he had ascended to a level from which he could say that there is good and bad in all of us, so that even abstraction has lost its note of historical destiny: "there is both bad and good in abstract art." And by 1962 abstract expressionism was all but finished, though this was not in any obvious way immediately apparent to anyone in that year.

Hopper and the realists saw the future as empty of their presence if they did not fight for it, the way, I suppose, the factions in Bosnia must feel about their country. But in just a few years Greenberg was able to say that there was no basic difference at all between the abstractionist and the realist, since there was a level at which all that mattered was quality, not kind, which is very much the situation today. Just as the Armory Show of 1913 made it plain that the differences between the Independents and the academicians were of small moment by contrast with the difference between both of them and cubism or fauvism, so, today, the difference between figuration and abstraction, since both are modes of painting, is of vastly lesser importance than the difference between painting in whatever mode, and video, say, or performance art. By 1911 the future both of the Ash Can painters and the academicians was a *vergangenes Zukunft,* as was, by 1961, the future of the realists and the abstractionists. They identified the future of art with the future of painting. And the future, as it happens, all at once put painting in the position abstraction had occupied in the early years of modernism as defined by the Museum of Modern Art: it was just one of a large number of artistic possibilities. The entire shape of art history had undergone change, however difficult it was to perceive in the early sixties when art and painting were virtually synonymous. And it is striking that neither abstract expressionism's advocates, like Greenberg, nor its opponents, were able to perceive the historical present in which they lived, because each saw the future in a way that proved irrelevant to the way things were.

The cause of the change, in my view, was the emergence of the somewhat unfortunately named pop art, again in my view the most critical art movement of the century. It began somewhat insidiously in the early sixties—insidiously in the sense that its impulses were disguised under drips and dribbles of paint in the manner of abstract expressionism, the emblem of artistic legitimacy at that time. But by 1964 it had thrown off the disguises and stood, in its full reality, as what it was. Interestingly enough, the Whitney decided to mount a Hopper retrospective in 1964. This had certainly little to do with the efforts of the realists, or their magazine *Reality,* or their picket lines in front of museums, or their letters in defense of John Canaday's attacks on abstract expressionism in the *New York Times.* "The decision to organize the retrospective came at a time when younger artists, especially among the pop and the photorealist movements, were taking a renewed interest in realism and in one of its leading exponents."[5] "At a time when younger artists . . . were taking a renewed interest" leaves it open whether this was a cause or merely a coincidence. Even the abstract expressionists "took an interest" in Hopper; at least de Kooning did, though he might be considered a compromised member of the movement due to the use of the figure. "You're doing the figure," Pollock charged. "You're still doing the same goddamn thing. You know you never go out of being a figure painter."[6] And the critical uproar when de Kooning exhibited his *Women* at Sidney Janis Gallery in 1953 is legendary: he had betrayed, or at least imperiled "our [abstract] revolution in painting." But de Kooning said to Irving Sandler in 1959. "Hopper is the only American I know who could paint the Merritt Parkway."[7] Once popular graphic imagery became thematic in pop, scholars found in Hopper a "predecessor," thinking of the way he painted the words "Ex Lax" in his picture of a drugstore, or the logo of Mobil Gas in his celebrated image of a gas station. But these are all externalities. They throw light neither on Hopper nor on pop. We really have to try to think of pop—or at least I think we have to think of pop—in a more philosophical way. I subscribe to a narrative of the history of modern art in which pop plays the philosophically central role. In my narrative, pop marked the end of the great narrative of Western art by bringing to self-consciousness the philosophical truth of art. That it was a most unlikely messenger of philosophical depth is something I readily acknowledge.

I want at this point to insert myself into this narrative, for I am now discussing an event I lived through. Artists, when they show their slides and talk about their work, characteristically report turning points in their development. It is less common for historians or philosophers to do this, but perhaps it is justified, since my experience of the pop movement was a set of philosophical responses that led to the body of thought that occasioned my having been invited to deliver the lectures on which this book is based. My own *vergangene Zukunft* in the 1950s, so far as painting was concerned, was one in which reality was represented gesturally, exactly in the manner of de Kooning's *Women* and his subsequent landscapes, such as *Merritt Parkway.* So, to the degree that I participated in the controversies, which were in any case unavoidable if one associated with artists in those years, I was too abstract for realists and too realist for abstractionists. I was myself attempting an artistic career in the fifties, and my own work sought to make that future present. But I was also attempting a philosophical career, and I have the most vivid recollection of seeing my first pop work—it was in the spring of 1962. I was living in Paris and working on a book which appeared a few years later under the somewhat daunting title *Analytical Philoso-phy of History*. I stopped one day at the American Center to read some periodi-cals, and I saw Roy Lichtenstein's *The Kiss* (printed sideways) in *Art News*, the crucial art publication of those years. I found out about pop the way almost everyone in Europe found out about it—through art magazines, which were, then as now, the main carriers of artistic influence. And I must say I was stunned. I knew that it was an astonishing and an inevitable moment, and in my own mind I understood immediately that if it was possible to paint something like this—and have it taken seriously enough by a leading art publication to be reviewed—then everything was possible. And, though it did not immediately occur to me, if everything was possible, there really was no specific future; if everything was possible, nothing was necessary or inevitable including my own vision of an artistic future. For me, that meant that it was all right, as an artist, to do whatever one wanted. It also meant that I lost interest in doing art and pretty much stopped. From that point on I was single-mindedly a philosopher, and so I remained until 1984, when I began to be an art critic. When I returned to New York, I was keen to see the new work, and began to see the shows at Castelli's and the Green Gallery, though pop paintings and other works were turning up everywhere, including the Guggenheim Museum. And there was a singular exhi-bition at Janis's. My great experience, often enough described, was my encounter with Warhol's *Brillo Box* at the Stable Gallery, in April of 1964, the year of Hop-per's Whitney retrospective. It was a most exciting moment, not least of all because the entire structure of debate which had defined the New York art scene up to that point had ceased having application. A whole new theory was called for other than the theories of realism, abstraction, and modernism which had defined the argument for Hopper and his allies and his opponents.

As luck would have it, I was invited that year to read a paper on aesthetics for the American Philosophical Association meeting in Boston. The person who had been scheduled to give it dropped out, and the program chairman thought to invite me as substitute. The paper was titled "The Art World," and it was the first philosophical effort to deal with the new art.[8] I take a certain pride that Warhol, Lichtenstein, Rauschenberg, and Oldenberg were discussed in *The Journal of Philosophy*—which published the symposium papers of the APA meeting—well before they were featured in what used to be called "the slicks." And that paper, not once so far as I know cited in the copious bibliographies on pop in later years, really did become the basis for philosophical aesthetics in the second half of this century. Another sign of how distant from one another the worlds of art and philosophy have continued to stand, however deeply related art and philoso-phy as such must be in the philosophy of what Hegel terms Absolute Spirit.

What struck me in particular with pop at that time was the way it sub-verted an ancient teaching, that of Plato, who famously relegated art, construed mimetically, to the lowest imaginable rung of reality. The notorious example is set forth in book ten of *The Republic*, where Plato specifies the three modes of reality of the bed: as idea or form, as what a carpenter might make, and then as what a painter might make, imitating the carpenter who has imitated the form. There are Greek vases on which the artist shows Achilles in bed, with the corpse of Hektor prone on the floor beneath it, or Penelope and Odysseus in conversation beside the bed Odysseus had built for his bride. Since you can imitate, Plato wanted to say, without knowing the first thing about the thing you are imitating (as Socrates sought to make plain in an infuriating dialogue with Ion the Rhapsode), artists lack knowledge. They "know" only the appearances of appearances. And now, all at once, one began to see actual beds in the art world of the early sixties—Rauschenberg's, Oldenberg's, and, not long after that, George Segal's. It was, I argued, as if artists were beginning to close the gap between art and reality. And the question now was what made these beds art if they were after all beds. But nothing in the literature explained that. I began to develop something of a theory in "The Art World," which gave rise, among other things, to George Dickie's institutional theory of art. The *Brillo Box* made the question general. Why was it a work of art when the objects which resemble it exactly, at least under perceptual criteria, are mere things, or, at best, mere artifacts? But even if artifacts, the parallels between them and what Warhol made were exact. Plato could not discriminate between them as he could between pictures of beds and beds. In fact, the Warhol boxes were pretty good pieces of carpentry. The example made it clear that one could not any longer understand the difference between art and reality in purely visual terms, or teach the meaning of "work of art" by means of examples. But philosophers had always supposed one could. So Warhol, and the pop artists in general, rendered almost worthless everything written by philosophers on art, or at best rendered it of local significance. For me, through pop, art showed what the proper philosophical question about itself really was. It was this: What makes the difference between an artwork and something which is not an artwork if in fact they look exactly alike? Such a question could never occur when one *could* teach the meaning of "art" by examples, or when the distinction between art and reality seemed perceptual, like the difference between a picture on a vase of a bed and a real bed.

It seemed to me that now that the philosophical problem of art had been clarified from within the history of art, that history had come to an end. The history of Western art divides into two main episodes, what I call the Vasari episode and what I call the Greenberg episode. Both are progressive. Vasari, construing art as representational, sees it getting better and better over time at the "conquest of visual appearance." That narrative ended for painting when moving pictures proved far better able to depict reality than painting could. Modernism began by asking what painting should do in the light of that? And it began to probe its own identity. Greenberg defined a new narrative in terms of an ascent to the identifying conditions of the art, specifically what differentiates the art of painting from every other art. And he found this in the material conditions of the medium. Greenberg's narrative is very profound, but it comes to an end with pop, about which he was never able to write other than disparagingly. It came to an end when art came to an end, when art, as it were, recognized that there was no special way a work of art had to be. Slogans began to appear like "Everything is an artwork" or Beuys's "Everyone is an artist," which would never have occurred to anyone under either of the great narratives I have identified.

The history of the art's quest for philosophical identity was over. And now that it was over, artists were liberated to do whatever they wanted to do. It was like Rabelais's Abbaye de Theleme, whose injunction was the counterinjunction "Fay ce que voudras" (do what you like). Paint lonely New England houses or make women out of paint or do boxes or paint squares. Nothing is more right than anything else. There is no single direction. There are indeed no directions. And that is what I meant by the end of art when I began to write about it in the mid-1980s. Not that art died or that painters stopped painting, but that the history of art, structured narratively, had come to an end.

A few years ago I gave a talk in Munich titled "Thirty Years after the End of Art." A student raised an interesting question. For her, she said, 1964 was really not an interesting year, and she was astonished that I made so much of it. The uprisings of 1968 were what interested her, and the emergence of the counterculture. But she would not have found 1964 nondescript had she been an American. It was the year of our "Summer of Freedom," during which blacks, with the support of thousands of whites, busloads of whom converged on the South to register black voters, worked to make civil rights real for an entire disenfranchised race. Racism in the United States did not end in 1964, but a form of apartheid which had sullied political life in our country ended that year. In 1964 a congressional committee on women's rights released its findings, giving support to the tremendous feminist movement detonated with the publication of Betty Friedan's *Feminine Mystique* of 1963. Both liberationist movements became radicalized by 1968, to be sure, but 1964 was the year of liberation. And it cannot be forgotten that the Beatles made their first personal appearance in the United States on the Ed Sullivan show in 1964, and they were emblems and facilitators of the spirit of liberation which swept the country and in time the world. Pop fit into this entirely. It really was a singularly liberating movement outside the United States, via the same channels of transmission as the one through which I first learned about it—the art magazines. In Germany Sigmar Polke and Gerhard Richter's powerful capitalist realist movement was directly inspired by pop. In the then Soviet Union, Komar and Melamid invented Sots art, and appropriated as a painting the design of a cigarette pack logo of the face of the dog named Laika who died in outer space. The painting was a realistic portrait of a stylized representation of a dog, and satisfied the stylistic imperatives of Soviet realist painting while subverting them by portraying a dog as Soviet hero. In terms of art-world strategies, American pop, German capitalist realism, and Russian Sots art could be seen as so many strategies for attacking official styles—socialist realism in the Soviet Union, of course, but abstract painting in Germany, where abstraction was itself heavily politicized and felt to be the only acceptable way of painting (easily understandable in terms of the way figuration was itself politicized under Nazism), and then abstract expressionism in the United States, which also had become an official style. Only in the Soviet Union, so far as I know, was pop art the object of a repressive attack—in the celebrated "bulldozer" show of 1974, when artists and journalists were chased by police using bulldozers. It is worth mention that it was the worldwide coverage of the event which seemed to bring about a policy of artistic detente in the Soviet Union, allowing in principle everyone to do as they liked, just as it was the intense television coverage of the beatings of civil rights protesters in Alabama which stopped them, the South somehow not being able to tolerate the image of itself that was being internalized by the rest of the world. In any case, it would hardly have been consistent with the liberating spirit of pop art that its artists should have allowed themselves to become victims of their own style. One mark, it seems to me, of artists after the end of art is that they adhere to no single avenue of creativity: Komar and Melamid's work has a spirit of impishness, but no visually identifying style. America has been conservative in this, but Warhol made films, sponsored a form of music, revolutionized the concept of the photograph, as well as made paintings and sculpture, and of course he wrote books and achieved fame as an aphorist. Even his style of dress, jeans and leather jacket, became the style of an entire generation. At this point I enjoy invoking the celebrated vision of history after the end of history that Marx and Engels put forward in *The German Ideology*, under which one can farm, hunt, fish, or write literary criticism, without *being* a farmer, a hunter, a fisherman, or a literary critic. And, if I may bring forward alongside them a true piece of philosophical artillery, this refusal to be any particular thing is what Jean-Paul Sartre calls being truly human. It is inconsistent with what Sartre calls *mauvaise foi* (bad faith), or regarding oneself as an object, and hence as having an identity as a waiter if a waiter, or a woman if a woman. That the ideal of Sartrian freedom is not necessarily easy to live by is I think testified to by the search for identity that is part of the popular psychology of our time, and by the effort to absorb oneself into the group to which one belongs, as in the political psychology of multiculturalism, and certain forms of feminism and of "queer" ideology, all so much part of this moment. But it is exactly the mark of the post-historical moment that the quest for identity is undertaken by those who are after all distant from their target—who, in a kind of Sartrian way of putting things, are not what they are and are what they are not. The Jews of the *stetel* were what they were, and did not have to *establish* an identity.

The term pop was invented by Lawrence Alloway, my immediate predecessor as art critic for *The Nation*, and though I feel it captures only certain surface features of the movement, it was not a bad designation in terms of its irreverence. Its sound is the noise of abrupt deflation, as of an exploding balloon. "We discovered," Alloway writes,

> that we had in mind a vernacular culture that persisted beyond any special interests or skills in art, architecture, design, or art criticism that any of us might possess. The area of contact was mass-produced urban culture: movies, advertising, science fiction, Pop music. [This, one might observe, is the standard bill of fare in each issue of ArtForum today.] We felt none of the dislike of commercial culture standard among most intellectuals, but accepted it as a fact, discussed it in detail, and consumed it enthusiastically. One result of our discussions was to take Pop culture out of the realm of "escapism," "sheer entertainment," "relaxation," and to treat it with the seriousness of art.[9]

I certainly think these discussions prepared the way for the acceptance of pop, but I would like to draw a few distinctions. There is a difference between pop *in* high art, pop *as* high art, and pop art as such. We must think of this when we try to seek predecessors for pop. When Motherwell used the Gauloise cigarette package in certain of his collages, or Hopper and Hockney used elements from the world of advertising in paintings which were themselves far from pop, this is pop *in* high art. To treat popular arts *as* serious art is really what Alloway is describing; "I used the term, and also 'Pop culture,' to refer to the products of the mass media, not to works of art that draw upon popular culture."[10] Pop art as such consists in what I term transfiguring emblems from popular culture into high art. It requires recreating the logo as socialist realist art, or making the Campbell's soup can the subject of a genuine oil painting which uses commercial art as a painterly style. Pop art was so exciting because it was transfigurative. There were plenty of buffs who treated Marilyn Monroe in the same way they would treat one of the great stage or opera stars. Warhol transfigured her into an icon by setting her beautiful face on a field of gold paint. Pop art as such was a properly American achievement, and I think it was the transfigurativeness of its basic stance that made it so subversive abroad. Transfiguration is a religious concept. It means the adoration of the ordinary, as, in its original appearance, in the Gospel of Saint Matthew it meant adoring a man as a god. I tried to convey this idea in the title of my first book on art, *The Transfiguration of the Commonplace,* a title I appropriated from a fictional title in a novel by the Catholic novelist Muriel Spark. It seems to me now that part of the immense popularity of pop lay in that fact that it transfigured the things or kinds of things that meant most to people, raising them to the status of subjects of high art.

Erwin Panofsky, among others, has argued that there is a certain unity in a culture's various manifestations, a common tincture affecting its painting and philosophy, for example. Positivistically, it is easy to be skeptical about such notions, but I do think there is a degree of confirmation of Panofsky's basic intuition in the state of the visual arts and of philosophy at the middle of the twentieth century. This is rather rarely commented upon, and I want to sketch the philosophical counterpart of pop. It too is something I lived through and, within limits, believed in.

The prevailing philosophy in the post World War II years, in the English speaking world at least, was something loosely designated "analytical philosophy," which divided into two branches with rather different views of language, and both of which descended in one way or another from different stages in the thought of Ludwig Wittgenstein. However they may have differed, both modes of analytical philosophy were committed to the view that philosophy as it had been traditionally practiced, and most particularly that part of philosophy known as metaphysics, was intellectually suspect if not downright bogus, and that the negative task of both branches of analytical philosophy was to exhibit, to demonstrate, the emptiness and nonsense of metaphysics. The one branch was inspired by formal logic, and was dedicated to the rational reconstruction of language—rebuilding language on solid foundations, themselves defined in terms of direct sensory experience (or observation), so that there would be no way in which metaphysics—which was not based on experience—could infect the system with its cognitive rot. Metaphysics was nonsense because it was radically disconnected from experience, or from observation.

The other branch thought language in no great need of reconstruction, so long as it was employed in a correct way: "Philosophy begins when language goes on holiday" is one of the things Wittgenstein says in his posthumous masterpiece, *Philosophical Investigations*. Under both its aspects, analytical philosophy was tied to common human experience at the most basic level, and ordinary discourse of the kind everyone is master of. Its philosophy was in effect what everybody always knows. J.L. Austin was for a time the leader of the school of ordinary language philosophy at Oxford, and here is something he said which bears on my speculation. It was something of a credo:

> Our common stock of words embodies all the distinctions men have found
> worth drawing, and the connexions they have found worth making, in the life-
> times of many generations: these surely are likely to be more numerous, more
> sound, since they have stood up to the long test of the survival of the fittest, and
> more subtle, at least in all ordinary and reasonably practical matters, than any
> you or I are likely to think up in our arm-chairs of an afternoon.[11]

I think that pop art too transfigures into art what everybody knows: the objects and icons of common cultural experience, the common furnishing of the group mind at the current moment of history. Abstract expressionism, by contrast, was concerned with hidden processes and was predicated on surrealist premises. Its practitioners sought to be shamans, in touch with primordial forces. It was metaphysical through and through, whereas pop celebrated the most ordinary things of the most ordinary lives—corn flakes, canned soup, soap pads, movie stars, comics. And by the processes of transfiguration, it gave them an almost transcendental air. Something in the 1960s explains, has to explain, why the ordinary things of the common world suddenly became the bedrock of art and philosophy. The abstract expressionists despised the world the pop artist apotheosized. Analytical philosophy felt that traditional philosophy had come to an end, having radically misconceived the possibilities of cognition. What philosophy was to do henceforward, after the end, is difficult to say, but presumably something useful and of direct human service. Pop art meant the end of art, as I have argued, and what artists were to do after the end of art is also difficult to say, but it was at least a possibility that art, too, might be enlisted in the direct service of humanity. Both faces of the culture were liberationist—Wittgenstein spoke of how to show the fly the way out of the fly bottle. It was then up to the fly where to go and what to do, just so long as it kept out of fly bottles in the future.

The temptation, of course, is to see both art and philosophy at mid-century as reactive—as reactions against. For example, there is a level of taunting of abstract expressionist pretensions in Lichtenstein. But I think both movements were really on a new level altogether, largely because they viewed the philosophy and the art before them as wholes. Analytical philosophy set itself against the whole of philosophy, from Plato through Heidegger. Pop set itself against art as a whole in favor of real life. But I think, beyond that, that both of them answered to something very deep in the human psychology of the moment, and that this is what made them so liberating outside the American scene. What they answered to was some universal sense that people wanted to enjoy their lives now, as they were, and not on some different plane or in some different world or in some later stage of history for which the present was a preparation. They did not want to defer or to sacrifice, which is why the black movement and the women's movement in America were so urgent, and why, in the Soviet Union, one had to stop celebrating the heros of a distant utopia. Nobody wanted to wait to go to Heaven for their reward, or to take joy in members of the classless society living in a future socialist utopia. Just being left alone to live in the world pop raised to consciousness was as good a life as anyone could want. Whatever social programs there were to be had to be consistent with that. "We don't need another hero," Barbara Kruger writes on one of her posters, putting into a nut-shell what Komar and Melamid sought in Sots. It was the perception, through television, that others were enjoying the benefits of ordinary life *now* that brought the Berlin Wall down in 1989.

House Speaker Newt Gingrich, in *To Renew America,* has a sense of history not unlike mine. For him 1965 was the pivotal year, but the precise year can hardly matter. What took place in 1965, according to him was "a calculated effort by cultural elites to discredit this civilization and replace it with a culture of irresponsibility."[12] I cannot believe it was a calculated effort, nor can I believe that artists and philosophers should have effected a revolution which, to the contrary, explains the art and the philosophy. There was a tremendous change in the fabric of society, a demand for liberation which has not ended yet. People decided that they wanted to be left in peace to "pursue happiness," which is on the short list of fundamental human rights according to the enabling documents of our country. It is not likely that a populace dedicated to this can be reconciled to an earlier form of life, however nostalgic some may be for the law and order that defined it, and it is even arguable that wanting to be left alone by a government perceived as overbearing forms part of Representative Gingrich's agenda.

I have sought here to situate pop art in a far wider context than the common art-historical contexts of causal influence and iconographic innovation. In my view pop was not just a movement which followed one movement and was replaced by another. It was a cataclysmic moment which signaled profound social and political shifts and which achieved profound philosophical transformations in the concept of art. It really proclaimed the twentieth century, which had languished for so long a time—sixty-four years—in the field of the nineteenth century, as we can see in the *vergangene Zukunft* I began with. One by one the terrible ideas of the nineteenth century have been exhausting themselves, though many of the nineteenth-century institutions of repression remain. What will the twentieth century be like once it gets under way? I would like to see an image by Barbara Kruger that says, "We don't need another narrative."

One possible advantage of seeing art in the widest context we can manage is, at least in the present case, that it helps us with a rather narrow problem of differentiating between Duchamp's ready-mades and such pop works as Warhol's *Brillo Box.* Whatever he achieved, Duchamp was not celebrating the ordinary. He was, perhaps, diminishing the aesthetic and testing the boundaries of art. There really is, in history, no such thing as having done something before. That there is an outward resemblance between Duchamp and pop is one of the things it is the achievement of pop to help us see through. The resemblances are far less striking than those between *Brillo Box* and ordinary Brillo cartons. What makes the difference between Duchamp and Warhol is similarly far less difficult to state than what is the difference between art and reality. Situating pop in its deep cultural moment helps show us how different its causes were than those that drove Duchamp half a century earlier.

Notes

1. Thomas Eakins, quoted in Lloyd Goodrich, *Thomas Eakins: His Life and Work* (New York: Whitney Museum of American Art, 1933), 20.
2. Gail Levin, *Edward Hopper: An Intimate Biography* (New York: Knopf, 1995), 251.
3. Ibid., 252.
4. Ibid., 469.
5. Ibid., 567.
6. *Willem de Kooning Paintings* (Washington, D.C.: National Gallery of Art, 1994), 131.
7. Levin, *Edward Hopper,* 549.
8. Arthur C. Danto, "The Art World," *Journal of Philosophy* 61, no. 19 (1964). 571–84. This was my first philosophical publication on art as well, and remained so until, with a few minor exceptions, the appearance of my *The Transfiguration of the Commonplace* (Cambridge: Harvard University Press, 1981).
9. Lawrence Alloway, "The Development of British Pop," in Lucy R. Lippard, *Pop Art* (London: Thames and Hudson, 1985), 29–30.
10. Ibid., 27.
11. J. L. Austin, "A Plea for Excuses," *in Philosophical Papers,* ed. J. O. Urmson and G. J. Warnock (Oxford: Clarendon Press, 1961), 130.
12. Newt Gingrich, *To Renew America* (New York: HarperCollins, 1995), 29.

Slavoj Žižek (1949–)

Born in Ljubljana, Slovenia, Žižek is a theorist, philosopher, cultural critic, and prolific writer. In Žižek's writing, one sees particularly the influence of Jacques Lacan's psychoanalytic theories. In the reading given next, "The Matrix: Or, The Two Sides of Perversion," Žižek links Lacan's theories with the first of the three popular *Matrix* science fiction movies. In this selection, as well as in many other of his articles and books, Žižek examines how technologies such as virtual reality and digitalization affect our environment and our sense of our environment. Žižek is currently a professor at the Institute for Sociology in Ljubljana. He earned a B.A. in philosophy and sociology in 1971, an M.A. in philosophy in 1975, and two different doctor-of-arts degrees, one in philosophy in 1981 and a second in psychoanalysis in 1985. He has taught in the United States as a visiting professor at SUNY Buffalo, the University of Minnesota, Tulane University, Columbia University, Princeton University, the University of Michigan, and Georgetown University. He was a candidate for president of the Republic of

Slovenia in 1990. His research interests include German philosophy, psycho-analysis, and political philosophy. Some of his most thought-provoking books are *The Sublime Object of Ideology* (1989), *Looking Awry* (1991), *The Ticklish Subject* (1999), *Enjoy Your Symptom!* (1992), and *The Plague of Fantasies* (1997). "The Matrix: Or, the Two Sides of Perversion" appears in the book *The Matrix and Philosophy* (2002), edited by William Irwin.

The Matrix: Or, the Two Sides of Perversion

When I saw *The Matrix* at a local theater in Slovenia, I had the unique opportunity of sitting close to the ideal spectator of the film—namely, to an idiot. A man in his late twenties at my right was so absorbed in the movie that he continually disturbed the other viewers with loud exclamations, like "My God, wow, so there is no reality!"

I definitely prefer such naive immersion to the pseudo-sophisticated intellec-tualist readings which project refined philosophical or psychoanalytic conceptual distinctions into the film.[1] It is nonetheless easy to understand this intellectual attraction of *The Matrix:* Isn't *The Matrix* one of those films which function as a kind of Rorschach test [http://rorschach.test.at/], setting in motion the universal-ized process of recognition, like the proverbial painting of God which seems always to stare directly at you, from wherever you look at it—practically every orientation seems to recognize itself in it?

My Lacanian friends tell me that the authors must have read Lacan; the Frankfurt School partisans see in *The Matrix* the extrapolated embodiment of *Kulturindustrie,* the alienated-reified social Substance (of Capital) directly taking over, colonizing our inner life itself, using us as the source of energy; New Agers see in it a source of speculations on how our world is just a mirage generated by a global Mind embodied in the World Wide Web.

This series goes back to Plato's *Republic.* Doesn't *The Matrix* exactly repeat Plato's device of the cave (ordinary humans as prisoners, tied firmly to their seats and compelled to watch the shadowy performance of (what they falsely consider to be) reality)? The important difference, of course, is that when some individu-als escape their cave predicament and step out onto the surface of the Earth, what they find there is no longer a bright surface illuminated by the rays of the Sun, the supreme Good, but the desolate "desert of the real."

The key opposition here is the one between the Frankfurt School and Lacan: Should we historicize *The Matrix* into the metaphor of Capital that has colo-nized culture and subjectivity, or is it the reification of the symbolic order as such? However, what if this very alternative is false? What if the virtual character of the symbolic order "as such" is the very condition of historicity?

Reaching the End of the World

The idea of the hero living in a totally manipulated and controlled artificial uni-verse is hardly original: *The Matrix* just radicalizes it by bringing in virtual reality

(VR). The point here is the radical ambiguity of VR with regard to the problematic of iconoclasm. On the one hand, VR marks the radical reduction of the wealth of our sensory experience to—not even letters, but—the minimal digital series of 0 and 1, of the transmission and non-transmission of an electrical signal. On the other hand, this very digital machine generates the "simulated" experience of reality which tends to become indistinguishable from the "real" reality, with the consequence of undermining the very notion of "real" reality. VR is thus at the same time the most radical assertion of the seductive power of images.

Is not the ultimate American paranoid fantasy that of an individual living in a small, idyllic Californian city, a consumerist paradise, who suddenly starts to suspect that the world he lives in is a fake, a spectacle staged to convince him that he lives in a real world, while all the people around him are effectively actors and extras in a gigantic show? The most recent example of this is Peter Weir's *The Truman Show* (1998), with Jim Carrey playing the small-town clerk who gradually discovers the truth that he is the hero of a 24-hour ongoing TV show: his hometown is constructed on a gigantic studio set, with cameras following him continually.

Sloterdijk's "sphere" is here literally realized, as the gigantic metal sphere that envelops and isolates the entire city. The final shot of *The Truman Show* may seem to enact the liberating experience of breaking out from the ideological suture of the enclosed universe into its outside, invisible from the ideological inside. However, what if it is precisely this "happy" denouement of the film (let us not forget: applauded by millions around the world watching the last minutes of the show), with the hero breaking out and, as we are led to believe, soon to join his true love (so that we have again the formula of the production of the couple!), that is ideology at its purest? What if ideology resides in the very belief that, outside the closure of the finite universe, there is some "true reality" to be entered?[2]

Among the predecessors of this notion is Phillip K. Dick's novel *Time Out of Joint* (1959), in which a man living a modest daily life in an idyllic Californian small town of the late 1950s, gradually discovers that the whole town is a fake staged to keep him satisfied. The underlying experience of *Time Out of Joint* and of *The Truman Show* is that the late-capitalist consumerist Californian paradise is, in its very hyper-reality, in a way irreal, substanceless, deprived of material inertia. So it's not only that Hollywood stages a semblance of real life deprived of the weight and inertia of materiality: In late-capitalist consumerist society, "real social life" itself somehow acquires the features of a staged fake, with our neighbors behaving in "real" life as stage actors and extras. The ultimate truth of the capitalist utilitarian despiritualized universe is the dematerialization of "real life" itself, its reversal into a spectral show.

In the realm of science-fiction, one should mention also Brian Aldiss's *Starship,* in which members of a tribe live in the closed world of a tunnel in a giant starship, isolated from the rest of the ship by thick vegetation, unaware that there is a universe beyond. Finally some children penetrate the bushes and reach the world beyond, populated by other tribes.

Among the older, more "naive" forerunners, one should mention George Seaton's *36 Hours,* the early 1960s movie about an American officer (James

Garner) who knows all the plans for the invasion of Normandy and is seized by the Germans just days before D-Day. Since he is taken prisoner unconscious following an explosion, the Germans quickly construct for him a replica of a small American military hospital, and try to convince him that he now lives in 1950, that America has already won the war and that he has no memory of the last six years—the intention being that he will reveal all he knows about the invasion plans. Cracks soon appear in this carefully constructed edifice . . . (Lenin, in the last two years of his life, lived in an almost similar controlled environment, in which, as we now know, Stalin had printed for him a specially-prepared one-copy edition of *Pravda,* censored of all news that would tell Lenin about the political struggles going on, with the justification that Comrade Lenin should take a rest and not be excited by unnecessary provocations.)

What lurks in the background is the pre-modern notion of "arriving at the end of the universe." In those well-known engravings, the surprised wanderers approach the screen or curtain of heaven, a flat surface with painted stars on it, pierce it and reach beyond—this is exactly what happens at the end of *The Truman Show.* No wonder that the last scene of this movie, when Truman steps up the stairs attached to the wall on which the "blue sky" horizon is painted and opens the door, has a distinctly Magrittean touch: Isn't this same sensitivity today returning with a vengeance? Do works like Syberberg's *Parsifal,* in which the infinite horizon is also blocked by the obviously "artificial" rear-projections, not signal that the time of the Cartesian infinite perspective is running out, and that we are returning to a kind of renewed medieval pre-perspective universe?

Fred Jameson perspicuously drew attention to the same phenomenon in some of Chandler's novels and Hitchcock's films. The shore of the Pacific Ocean in *Farewell, My Lovely* functions as a kind of "end or limit of the world," beyond which there is an unknown abyss; and it is similar with the vast open valley that stretches out in front of the Mount Rushmore heads when, on the run from their pursuers, Eva Marie Saint and Cary Grant reach the peak of the monument, and into which Eva Marie Saint almost falls, before being pulled up by Cary Grant.

One is tempted to add to this series the famous battle scene at a bridge on the Vietnamese-Cambodian frontier in *Apocalypse Now,* where the space beyond the bridge is experienced as the "beyond of our known universe." And the view that our Earth is not a planet floating in infinite space, but really a circular opening or hole, within the endless compact mass of eternal ice, with the sun in its center, was one of the favorite Nazi pseudo-scientific fantasies—according to some reports, they even considered putting some telescopes on the Sylt islands in order to observe America.

The "Really Existing" Big Other

What, then, is the Matrix? Simply the Lacanian "big Other," the virtual symbolic order, the network that structures reality for us. This dimension of the "big Other" is that of the constitutive alienation of the subject in the symbolic order: the big Other pulls the strings, the subject doesn't speak, he "is spoken" by the symbolic structure. In short, this "big Other" is the name for the social Substance, for all that on account of which the subject never fully dominates the effects of his acts, on account of which the final outcome of his activity is always something other than what he aimed at or anticipated.

However, in the key chapters of *Seminar XI,* Lacan struggles to delineate the operation that follows alienation and is in a sense its counterpoint, that of separation: Alienation *in* the big Other is followed by separation *from* the big Other. Separation takes place when the subject takes note of how the big Other is in itself inconsistent, purely virtual, "barred," deprived of the Thing—and fantasy is an attempt to fill out this lack of the Other, not of the subject, to (re)constitute the consistency of the big Other.

For that reason, fantasy and paranoia are inherently linked: Paranoia is at its most elementary a belief in an "Other of the Other", into another Other who, hidden behind the Other of the explicit social texture, programs (what appears to us as) the unforeseen effects of social life and thus guarantees its consistency: Beneath the chaos of the market, the degradation of morals, and so forth, there is the purposeful strategy of the Jewish plot . . . This paranoid stance has acquired a further boost with today's digitalization of our daily lives. When our entire social existence is progressively externalized-materialized in the big Other of the computer network, it's easy to imagine an evil programmer erasing our digital identity and thus depriving us of our social existence, turning us into non-persons.

Following the same paranoid twist, the thesis of *The Matrix* is that this big Other is externalized in the really existing Mega-Computer. There is—there *has* to be—a Matrix because "things are not right, opportunities are missed, something goes wrong all the time." In other words, the movie's suggestion that this is so because there is the Matrix obfuscates the true reality that is behind it all. Consequently, the problem with the film is that it is not "crazy" enough, because it supposes another "real" reality behind our everyday reality sustained by the Matrix.

However, to avoid a fatal misunderstanding, the inverse notion that "all there is is generated by the Matrix," that there is *no* ultimate reality, just the infinite series of virtual realities mirroring themselves in each other, is no less ideological. In the sequels to *The Matrix,* we shall probably learn that the very "desert of the real" is generated by another matrix. Much more subversive than this multiplication of virtual universes would have been the multiplication of realities themselves—something that would reproduce the paradoxical danger that some physicists see in recent high-accelerator experiments.

Scientists are now trying to construct an accelerator capable of smashing together the nuclei of very heavy atoms at nearly the speed of light. The idea is that such a collision will not only shatter the atom's nuclei into their constituent protons and neutrons, but will pulverize the protons and neutrons themselves, leaving a "plasma," a kind of energy soup consisting of loose quark and gluon particles, the building blocks of matter that have never before been studied in such a state, since such a state only existed briefly after the Big Bang.

However, this prospect has given rise to a nightmarish scenario. What if the success of this experiment created a doomsday machine, a kind of world-devouring monster that would with inexorable necessity annihilate the ordinary matter around itself and thus abolish the world as we know it? The irony of it is that this end of the world, the disintegration of the universe, would be the ultimate irrefutable proof that the tested theory were true, since it would suck all matter into a black hole and then bring about a new universe, perfectly recreating the Big Bang scenario.

The paradox is thus that both versions—(1) a subject freely floating from one to another VR, a pure ghost aware that every reality is a fake; (2) the paranoiac supposition of the real reality beneath the Matrix—are false. They both miss the Real. The film is not wrong in insisting that there *is* a Real beneath the Virtual Reality simulation—as Morpheus puts it to Neo when he shows him the ruined Chicago landscape: "Welcome to the desert of the real."

However, the Real is not the "true reality" behind the virtual simulation, but the void which makes reality incomplete or inconsistent, and the function of every symbolic Matrix is to conceal this inconsistency. One of the ways to effectuate this concealment is precisely to claim that, behind the incomplete/inconsistent reality we know, there is another reality with no deadlock of impossibility structuring it.

"The Big Other Doesn't Exist"

"Big Other" also stands for the field of common sense at which one can arrive after free deliberation; philosophically, its last great version is Habermas's communicative community with its regulative ideal of agreement. And it is this "big Other" that progressively disintegrates today.

What we have today is a certain radical split. On the one hand, there is the objectivized language of experts and scientists which can no longer be translated into the common language accessible to everyone, but is present in common language in the mode of fetishized formulas that no one really understands, but which shape our artistic and popular imaginary universes (Black Hole, Big Bang, Superstrings, Quantum Oscillation . . .). Not only in the natural sciences, but also in economics and other social sciences, the expert jargon is presented as an objective insight with which one cannot really argue, and which is simultaneously untranslatable into our common experience. In short, the gap between scientific insight and common sense is unbridgeable, and it is this very gap which elevates scientists into the popular cult figures of the "subjects supposed to know" (the Stephen Hawking phenomenon).

And on the other hand, the strict obverse of this objectivity is the way in which, in cultural matters, we are confronted with the multitude of lifestyles which we cannot translate into each other. All we can do is secure the conditions for their tolerant co-existence in a multicultural society. The icon of today's subject is perhaps the Indian computer programmer who, during the day, excels in his expertise, while in the evening, upon returning home, he lights the candle to the local Hindu divinity and respects the sanctity of the cow.

This split is perfectly rendered in the phenomenon of cyberspace. Cyberspace was supposed to bring us all together in a Global Village. Yet what effectively happens is that we are bombarded with the multitude of messages belonging to inconsistent and incompatible universes. Instead of the Global Village, the big Other, we get the multitude of "small others," of tribal particular identifications at our choice. To avoid a misunderstanding: Lacan is here far from relativizing science into just one of the arbitrary narratives, ultimately on an equal footing with Politically Correct myths, and so forth: Science *does* "touch the Real," its knowledge *is* "knowledge in the real." The deadlock resides simply in the fact that scientific knowledge cannot serve as the *symbolic* "big Other." The gap between modern science and Aristotelian common-sense philosophical ontology is here insurmountable. This gap emerges with Galileo, and is brought to an extreme in quantum physics, where we're dealing with laws which do work, though they cannot ever be retranslated into our experience of representable reality.

The theory of the risk society and its global reflexivization is right in its emphasis on how, today, we are at the opposite end of the classical Enlightenment universalist ideology which presupposed that, in the long run, the fundamental questions can be resolved by way of reference to the "objective knowledge" of the experts. When we're confronted with conflicting opinions about the environmental consequences of a certain new product (say, of genetically modified vegetables), we search in vain for the ultimate expert opinion. And the point is not simply that the real issues are blurred because science is corrupted through financial dependence on large corporations and state agencies. Even in themselves, the sciences cannot provide the answer.

Fifteen years ago ecologists predicted the death of the Earth's forests, but we now learn that the problem is too large an increase of forest growth. Where this theory of the risk society falls short is in emphasizing the irrational predicament into which this puts us, common subjects. We are again and again compelled to decide, although we are well aware that we are in no position to decide, that our decision will be arbitrary. Ulrich Beck and his followers refer to the democratic discussion of all options and consensus-building. However this does not resolve the immobilizing dilemma: Why should the democratic discussion in which the majority participates lead to better results, when, cognitively, the ignorance of the majority remains?

The political frustration of the majority is thus understandable. They are called upon to decide, while, at the same time, receiving the message that they are in no position effectively to decide, to objectively weigh the pros and cons. The recourse to "conspiracy theories" is a desperate way out of this deadlock, an attempt to regain a minimum of what Fred Jameson calls "cognitive mapping."

Jodi Dean[3] drew attention to a curious phenomenon clearly observable in the "dialogue of the mutes" between the official ("serious," academically institutionalized) science and the vast domain of so-called pseudo-sciences, from ufology to those who want to decipher the secrets of the pyramids. One cannot but be struck by how it is the official scientists who proceed in a dogmatic, dismissive way, while the pseudo-scientists refer to facts and argumentation, disregarding common prejudices. The answer, of course, will be that established scientists speak with the authority of the big Other, of science as an institution, but the problem is that, precisely, this scientific big Other is again and again revealed as a consensual symbolic fiction. So when we are confronted with conspiracy theories, we should proceed in a strict homology to the proper reading of Henry James's *The Turn of the Screw*. We should neither accept the existence of ghosts as part of the narrative reality nor reduce them, in a pseudo-Freudian way, to the "projection" of the heroine's hysterical sexual frustrations.

Conspiracy theories are of course not to be accepted as "fact." However one should also not reduce them to the phenomenon of modern mass hysteria. Such a notion still relies on the "big Other," on the model of "normal" perception of shared social reality, and thus does not take into account how it is precisely this notion of reality that is undermined today. The problem is not that ufologists and conspiracy theorists regress to a paranoid attitude unable to accept (social) reality; the problem is that this reality itself is becoming paranoiac.

Contemporary experience again and again confronts us with situations in which we are compelled to take note of how our sense of reality and normal attitude towards it is grounded in a symbolic fiction—how the "big Other" that determines what counts as normal and accepted truth, what is the horizon of meaning in a given society, is in no way directly grounded in "facts" as rendered by the scientific "knowledge in the real."

Let us take a traditional society in which modern science is not yet elevated into the "master discourse." If, in its symbolic space, an individual advocates propositions of modern science, he will be dismissed as a "madman." And the key point is that it is not enough to say that he is not "really mad," that it is merely the narrow, ignorant society which puts him in this position. In a certain way, being treated as a madman, being excluded from the social big Other, effectively *equals* being mad. "Madness" is not the designation which can be grounded in a direct reference to "facts" (in the sense that a madman is unable to perceive things the way they really are, since he is caught in his hallucinatory projections), but only with regard to the way an individual relates to the "big Other."

Lacan usually emphasizes the opposite aspect of this paradox: "The madman is not only a beggar who thinks he is a king, but also a king who thinks he is a king." In other words, madness designates the collapse of the distance between the Symbolic and the Real, an immediate identification with the symbolic mandate; or, to take his other exemplary statement, when a husband is pathologically jealous, obsessed by the idea that his wife sleeps with other men, his obsession remains a pathological feature even if it is proved that he is right and that his wife in fact sleeps with other men.

The lesson of such paradoxes is clear. Pathological jealously is not a matter of getting the facts wrong, but of the way these facts are integrated into the subject's libidinal economy. However, what we should assert here is that the same paradox should also be performed as it were in the opposite direction: The society (its socio-symbolic field, the big Other) is "sane" and "normal" even when it is proven factually wrong. Maybe it was in this sense that the late Lacan designated himself as "psychotic." He effectively was psychotic insofar as it was not possible to integrate his discourse into the field of the big Other. One is tempted to claim, in the Kantian mode, that the mistake of the conspiracy theory is somehow homologous to the "paralogism of pure reason," to the confusion between the two levels: the suspicion (of the received scientific, social, etc. common sense) as the formal methodological stance, and the positing of this suspicion in another all-explaining global para-theory.

Screening the Real

From another standpoint, the Matrix also functions as the "screen" that separates us from the Real, that makes the "desert of the real" bearable. However, it is here that we should not forget the radical ambiguity of the Lacanian Real: it is not the ultimate referent to be covered-gentrified-domesticated by the screen of fantasy. The Real is also and primarily the screen itself as the obstacle that always distorts our perception of the referent, of the reality out there.

In philosophical terms, therein resides the difference between Kant and Hegel: For Kant, the Real is the noumenal domain that we perceive "schematized" through the screen of transcendental categories; for Hegel, on the contrary, as he asserts exemplarily in the *Introduction* to his *Phenomenology,* this Kantian gap is false. Hegel introduces here *three* terms: when a screen intervenes between ourselves and the Real, it always generates a notion of what is In-itself, beyond the screen (of the appearance), so that the gap between appearance and the In-itself is always-already "for us." Consequently, if we subtract from the Thing the distortion of the Screen, we lose the Thing itself (in religious terms, the death of Christ is the death of the God in himself, not only of his human embodiment)—which is why, for Lacan, who here follows Hegel, the Thing in itself is ultimately the gaze, not the perceived object. So, back to the Matrix: the Matrix itself is the Real that distorts our perception of reality.

A reference to Lévi-Strauss's exemplary analysis, from his *Structural Anthropology,* of the spatial disposition of buildings in the Winnebago, one of the Great Lake tribes, might be of some help here. The tribe is divided into two sub-groups ("moieties"), "those who are from above" and "those who are from below"; when we ask an individual to draw on a piece of paper, or on sand, the ground-plan of his or her village (the spatial disposition of cottages), we obtain two quite different answers, depending on his or her belonging to one or the other sub-group. Both perceive the village as a circle; but for one sub-group, there is within this circle another circle of central houses, so that we have two concentric circles, while for the other sub-group, the circle is split into two by a clear dividing line. In other words, a member of the first sub-group (let us call it "conservative-corporatist") perceives the ground-plan of the village as a ring of houses more or less symmetrically disposed around the central temple, whereas a member of the second ("revolutionary-antagonistic") sub-group perceives his or her village as two distinct heaps of houses separated by an invisible frontier . . .[4]

Lévi-Strauss's main point is that this example should in no way entice us into cultural relativism, according to which the perception of social space depends on the observer's group-membership. The very splitting into the two "relative" perceptions implies a hidden reference to a constant—not the objective, "actual" disposition of buildings but a traumatic kernel, a fundamental antagonism the inhabitants of the village were unable to symbolize, to account for, to "internalize," to come to terms with, an imbalance in social relations that prevented the community from stabilizing itself into a harmonious whole.

The two perceptions of the ground-plan are simply two mutually exclusive endeavors to cope with this traumatic antagonism, to heal its wound via the imposition of a balanced symbolic structure. Is it necessary to add that things stand exactly the same with respect to sexual difference, that "masculine" and "feminine" are, like the two configurations of houses in the Lèvi-Straussian village? And in order to dispel the illusion that our "developed" universe is not dominated by the same logic, suffice it to recall the splitting of our political space into left and right: a leftist and a rightist behave exactly like members of the opposite sub-groups of the Lévi-Straussian village. They not only occupy different places within the political space; each of them perceives differently the very disposition of the political space—a leftist as the field that is inherently split by some fundamental antagonism, a rightist as the organic unity of a community disturbed only by foreign intruders.

However, Lévi-Strauss makes a further crucial point: since the two subgroups nonetheless form one and the same tribe, living in the same village, this identity somehow has to be symbolically inscribed. But how is this possible, if the entire symbolic articulation, all social institutions, of the tribe are not neutral, but are overdetermined by the fundamental and constitutive antagonistic split? By what Lévi-Strauss ingeniously calls the "zero-institution," a kind of institutional counterpart to the famous *mana,* the empty signifier with no determinate meaning, since it signifies only the presence of meaning as such, in opposition to its absence: a specific institution which has no positive, determinate function—its only function is the purely negative one of signalling the presence and actuality of social institution as such, in opposition to its absence, to pre-social chaos.

It's the reference to such a zero-institution that enables all members of the tribe to experience themselves as such, as members of the same tribe. Is, then, this zero-institution not ideology at its purest—the direct embodiment of the ideological function of providing a neutral all-encompassing space in which social antagonism is obliterated, in which all members of society can recognize themselves? And is the struggle for hegemony not precisely the struggle for how this zero-institution will be overdetermined, colored by some particular signification?

To provide a concrete example: is not the modern notion of nation such a zero-institution that emerged with the dissolution of social links grounded in direct family or traditional symbolic matrixes, when, with the onslaught of modernization, social institutions were less and less grounded in naturalized tradition and more and more experienced as a matter of "contract."[5] Of special importance here is the fact that national identity is experienced as at least minimally "natural," as a belonging grounded in "blood and soil," and as such opposed to the "artificial" belonging to social institutions proper (state, profession . . .). Premodern institutions functioned as "naturalized" symbolic entities (as institutions grounded in unquestionable traditions), and the moment institutions were conceived as social artifacts, the need arose for a "naturalized" zero-institution that would serve as their neutral common ground.

And, back to sexual differences, I am tempted to risk the hypothesis that, perhaps, the same logic of zero-institution should be applied not only to the unity of a society, but also to its antagonistic split: what if sexual difference is ultimately a kind of zero-institution of the social split of humankind, the naturalized minimal zero-difference, a split that, prior to signalling any determinate social difference, signals this difference as such? The struggle for hegemony is then, again, the struggle for how this zero-difference will be overdetermined by other particular social difference. It is against this background that one should read an important, although usually overlooked, feature of Lacan's schema of the signifier: Lacan replaces the standard Saussurean scheme (above the bar the word "arbre," and beneath it the drawing of a tree) with, above the bar, two words one alongside the other, "homme" and "femme," and, beneath the bar, two identical drawings of a door.

In order to emphasize the differential character of the signifier, Lacan first replaces Saussure's single scheme with a signifier's couple, with the opposition man-woman, with the sexual difference; but the true surprise resides in the fact that, at the level of the imaginary referent, *there is no difference* (we do not get some graphic index of the sexual difference, the simplified drawing of a man and a woman, as is usually the case in most of today's restrooms, but *the same* door reproduced twice). Is it possible to state in clearer terms that sexual difference does not designate any biological opposition grounded in "real" properties, but a purely symbolic opposition to which nothing corresponds in the designated objects—nothing but the Real of some undefined X which cannot ever be captured by the image of the signified?

Back to Lévi-Strauss's example of the two drawings of the village. Here one can see in what precise sense the Real intervenes through anamorphosis. We have first the "actual," "objective," arrangement of the houses, and then their two different symbolizations which both distort in an anamorphic way the actual arrangement. However, the "real" here is not the actual arrangement, but the traumatic core of the social antagonism which distorts the tribe members' view of the actual antagonism. The Real is thus the disavowed X on account of which our vision of reality is anamorphically distorted. (And, incidentally, this three-levels device is strictly homologous to Freud's three-level device of the interpretation of dreams: The real kernel of the dream is not the dream's latent thought, which is displaced or translated into the explicit texture of the dream, but the unconscious desire which inscribes itself through the very distortion of the latent thought into the explicit texture.)

The same goes for today's art scene, in which the Real does *not* return primarily in the guise of the shocking brutal intrusion of excremental objects, mutilated corpses, shit, and so forth. These objects are, to be sure, out of place—but in order for them to be out of place, the (empty) place must already be here, and this place is rendered by "minimalist" art, starting from Malevitch. Therein resides the complicity between the two opposed icons of high modernism,

Kazimir Malevitch's "Black Square on White Surface" and Marcel Duchamp's display of ready-made objects as works of art.

The underlying notion of Malevitch's elevation of an everyday object into a work of art is that being a work of art is not an inherent property of the object: It is the artist himself who, by pre-empting the (or, rather, *any*) object and locating it at a certain place, makes it the work of art. Being a work of art is not a question of "why" but "where." And what Malevitch's minimalist disposition does is simply to render—to isolate—this place as such, the empty place (or frame) with the proto-magic property of transforming any object that finds itself within its scope into the work of art.

In short, there is no Duchamp without Malevitch. Only after the art practice isolates the frame/place as such, emptied of all its content, can one indulge in the ready-made procedure. Before Malevitch, a urinal would have remained just a urinal, even if it were to be displayed in the most distinguished gallery.

The emergence of excremental objects which are out of place is thus strictly correlative to the emergence of the place without any object in it, of the empty frame as such. Consequently, the Real in contemporary art has three dimensions, which somehow repeat within the Real the triad of Imaginary-Symbolic-Real. The Real is first here as the anamorphotic stain, the anamorphotic distortion of the direct image of reality—as a distorted image, as a pure semblance that "subjectivizes" objective reality. Then, the Real is here as the empty place, as a structure, a construction which is never here, experiences as such, but can only be retroactively constructed and has to be presupposed as such—the Real as symbolic construction.

Finally, the Real is the obscene excremental Object out of place, the Real "itself." This last Real, if isolated, is a mere fetish whose fascinating or captivating presence masks the structural Real, in the same way that, in Nazi anti-Semitism, the Jew as the excremental Object is the Real that masks the unbearable "structural" Real of the social antagonism.

These three dimensions of the Real result from the three modes of setting distance from "ordinary" reality: One submits this reality to anamorphic distortion; one introduces an object that has no place in it; or one subtracts or erases all content (objects) of reality, so that all that remains is the very empty place these objects were filling in.

The Freudian Touch

The falsity of *The Matrix* is perhaps most directly discernable in its designation of Neo as "the One." Who is the One? There effectively is such a place in the social link. There is, first, the One of the Master-Signifier, the symbolic authority. Even in social life in its most horrifying form, the memories of concentration camp survivors invariably mention the One, an individual who did not break down, who, in the midst of the unbearable conditions which reduced all others to the egoistic struggle for bare survival, miraculously maintained and radiated an "irrational" generosity and dignity. In Lacanian terms, we are dealing here with the function of *Y'a de l'Un*: even here, there was the One who served as the support of the minimum of solidarity that defines the social link proper as opposed to collaboration within the frame of the pure strategy of survival.

Two features are crucial here. First, this individual was always perceived as one (there was never a multitude of them, as if, following some obscure necessity, this excess of the inexplicable miracle of solidarity has to be embodied in a One); secondly, it was not so much what this One effectively did for the others which mattered, but rather his very presence among them (what enabled the others to survive was the awareness that, even if they are for most of the time reduced to survival-machines, there is the One who maintained human dignity). In a way homologous to canned laughter, we have here something like canned dignity, where the Other (the One) retains my dignity for me, in my place, or, more precisely, where I retain my dignity *through* the Other. I may be reduced to the cruel struggle for survival, but the very awareness that there is One who retains his dignity enables *me* to maintain a minimal link to humanity.

Often, when this One broke down or was unmasked as a fake, the other prisoners lost their will to survive and turned into indifferent living dead—paradoxically, their very readiness to struggle for bare survival was sustained by its exception, by the fact that there was the One *not* reduced to this level, so that, when this exception disappeared, the struggle for survival itself lost its force.

What this means is that this One was not defined exclusively by his "real" qualities (at this level, there may well have been more individuals like him, or it may even have been that he was not really unbroken, but a fake, just playing that role). His exceptional role was rather that of transference: He occupied a place constructed (presupposed) by the others.

In *The Matrix,* on the contrary, the One is he who is able to see that our everyday reality is not real, but just a codified virtual universe, and who therefore is able to unplug from it, to manipulate and suspend its rules (fly in the air, stop bullets, and so forth). Crucial for the function of this One is his virtualization of reality. Reality is an artificial construct whose rules can be suspended or at least rewritten—therein resides the properly paranoid notion that the One can suspend the resistance of the Real ("I can walk through a thick wall, if I really decide to . . ."—the impossibility for most of us to do this is reduced to the failure of the subject's will).

Here again, the film does not go far enough. In the memorable scene in the waiting room of the Oracle who will decide if Neo is the One, a child who is seen bending a spoon with his mere thoughts tells the surprised Neo that the way to do it is not to convince myself that I can bend the spoon, but to convince myself that *there is no spoon* . . . However, what about *myself*? Shouldn't the movie have taken the further step of accepting the Buddhist proposition that I, *myself,* the subject, do not exist?

In order to further specify what is false in *The Matrix,* one should distinguish simple technological impossibility from phantasmic falsity: Time-travel is (probably) impossible, but phantasmic scenarios about it are nonetheless "true" in the way they render libidinal deadlocks. Consequently, the problem with *The Matrix* is not the scientific naivety of its tricks. The idea of passing from reality to VR through the phone makes sense, since all we need is a gap or hole through which we can escape.

Perhaps, an even better solution would have been the toilet. Is not the domain where excrements vanish after we flush the toilet effectively one of the metaphors for the horrifyingly sublime Beyond of the primordial, pre-ontological Chaos into which things disappear? Although we rationally know what goes on with the excrements, the imaginary mystery nonetheless persists—shit remains an excess which does not fit our daily reality, and Lacan was right in claiming that we pass from animals to humans the moment an animal has problems with what to do with its excrements, the moment they turn into an excess that annoys it. The Real is thus not primarily the horrifyingly-disgusting stuff re-emerging from the toilet sink, but rather the hole itself, the gap which serves as the passage to a different ontological order—the topological hole or torsion which "curves" the space of our reality so that we perceive/imagine excrements as disappearing into an alternative dimension which is not part of our everyday reality.

The problem is a more radical phantasmic inconsistency, which erupts most explicitly when Morpheus (the African-American leader of the resistance group who believe that Neo is the One) tries to explain to the still perplexed Neo what the Matrix is. He quite consequently links it to a failure in the structure of the universe:

MORPHEUS:

> *It's that feeling you have had all your life. That feeling that something was wrong with the world. You don't know what it is but it's there, like a splinter in your mind, driving you mad. . . . The Matrix is everywhere, it's all around us, here even in this room. . . . It is the world that has been pulled over your eyes to blind you from the truth.*

NEO:

> *What truth?*

MORPHEUS:

> *That you are a slave, Neo. That you, like everyone else, was born into bondage . . . kept inside a prision that you cannot smell, taste, or touch. A prison of your mind.*

Here the film encounters its ultimate inconsistency: the experience of the lack/inconsistency/obstacle is supposed to bear witness of the fact that what we experience as reality is a fake—however, towards the end of the film, Smith, the Agent of the Matrix, gives a different, much more Freudian explanation:

> *Did you know that the first Matrix was designed to be a perfect human world? Where none suffered, where everyone would be happy? It was a disaster. No one would accept the program. Entire crops [of the humans serving as batteries] were lost. Some believed we lacked the programming language to describe your perfect world. But I believe that, as a species, human beings define their reality*

through suffering and misery. The perfect world was a dream that your primi-
tive cerebrum kept trying to wake up from. Which is why the Matrix was re-
designed to this: the peak of your civilization.

The imperfection of our world is thus at the same time the sign of its virtuality *and* the sign of its reality. One could effectively claim that Agent Smith (let us not forget: not a human being as others, but the direct virtual embodiment of the Matrix—the big Other—itself) is the stand-in for the figure of the analyst within the universe of the film: His lesson is that the experience of an insurmountable obstacle is the positive condition for us, humans, to perceive something as reality—reality is ultimately that which resists.

Malebranche in Hollywood

Another inconsistency concerns death: *Why* does one "really" die when one dies in the VR regulated by the Matrix? The film provides the obscurantist answer: "Neo: If you are killed in the Matrix, you die here [not only in the VR, but also in real life]? Morpheus: The body cannot live without the mind." The logic of this solution is that your "real" body can only function in conjunction with the mind, the mental universe into which you are immersed. So if you are in a VR and killed there, this death affects also your real body . . . The obvious opposite solution (you only really die when you are killed in reality) is also too short.

The catch is: Is the subject *wholly* immersed in the Matrix-dominated VR or does he know or at least *suspect* the actual state of things? If the answer to the former question is *yes,* then a simple withdrawal into a prelapsarian Adamic state of distance would render us immortal *in the* VR and, consequently, Neo who is already liberated from the full immersion in the VR should *survive* the struggle with Agent Smith which takes place *within* the VR controlled by the Matrix (in the same way he is able to stop bullets, he should also have been able to derealize blows that wound his body). This brings us back to Malebranche's occasionalism. Much more than Berkeley's God who sustains the world in his mind, the *ultimate* Matrix is Malebranche's occasionalist God.

Malebranche was undoubtedly the philosopher who provided the best conceptual apparatus to account for Virtual Reality. Malebranche, a disciple of Descartes, drops Descartes's ridiculous reference to the pineal gland in order to explain the co-ordination between the material and the spiritual substance, body and soul. How, then, are we to explain their co-ordination, if there is no contact between the two, no point at which a soul can act causally on a body or vice versa? Since the two causal networks (that of ideas in my mind and that of bodily interconnections) are totally independent, the only solution is that a third, true Substance (God) continuously co-ordinates and mediates between the two, sustaining the semblance of continuity. When I think about raising my hand and my hand effectively raises, my thought causes the raising of my hand not directly but only "occasionally." Upon noticing my thought directed at raising my hand, God sets in motion the other, material, causal chain which leads to my hand effectively being raised. If we replace "God" with the big Other, the symbolic order, we can see the closeness of occasionalism to Lacan's position: As Lacan put it in his polemics against Aristotle in "Television,"[6] the relationship between soul and body is never direct, since the big Other always interposes itself between the two.

Occasionalism is thus essentially a name for the "arbitrary of the signifier," for the gap that separates the network of ideas from the network of bodily (real) causality, for the fact that it is the big Other which accounts for the co-ordination of the two networks, so that, when my body bites an apple, my soul experiences a pleasurable sensation. This same gap is targeted by the ancient Aztec priest who organizes human sacrifices to ensure that the sun will rise again: The human sacrifice is here an appeal to God to sustain the co-ordination between the two series, the bodily necessity and the concatenation of symbolic events. "Irrational" as the Aztec priest's sacrificing may appear, its underlying premise is far more insightful than our commonplace intuition according to which the co-ordination between body and soul is direct—it's "natural" for me to have a pleasurable sensation when I bite an apple since this sensation is caused directly by the apple: what gets lost is the intermediary role of the big Other in guaranteeing the co-ordination between reality and our mental experience of it.

And is it not the same with our immersion in Virtual Reality? When I raise my hand in order to push an object in virtual space, this object effectively moves—my illusion, of course, is that it was the movement of my hand which directly caused the dislocation of the object; in my immersion, I overlooked the intricate mechanism of computerized co-ordination, homologous to the role of God guaranteeing the co-ordination between the two series in occasionalism.[7]

It is a well-known fact that the "Close the door" button in most elevators is a totally redundant placebo, placed there just to give the individuals the impression that they are somehow participating, contributing to the speed of the elevator journey—when we push this button, the door closes in exactly the same time as when we just pressed the floor button without "speeding up" the process by pressing also the "Close the door" button. This extreme and clear case of fake participation is an appropriate metaphor of the participation of individuals in our "postmodern" political process. And this is occasionalism at its purest: according to Malebranche, we are all the time pressing such buttons, and it is God's incessant activity that co-ordinates between them and the event that follows (the door closing), while we think the event results from our pushing the button . . .

For that reason, it is crucial to keep open the radical ambiguity of how cyberspace will affect our lives: this does not depend on technology as such but on the mode of its social inscription. Immersion into cyberspace can intensify our bodily experience (new sensuality, new body with more organs, new sexes . . .), but it also opens up the possibility for the one who manipulates the machinery which runs the cyberspace literally to steal our own (virtual) body, depriving us of control over it, so that one no longer relates to one's body as to "one's own." What one encounters here is the constitutive ambiguity of the notion of mediatization.[8] Originally this notion designated the gesture by means of which a subject was stripped of its direct, immediate right to make decisions; the great master of political mediatization was Napoleon who left to the conquered monarchs the appearance of power, while they were effectively no longer in a position to exercise it. At a more general level, one could say that such a "mediatization" of the monarch defines the constitutional monarchy: In it, the monarch is reduced to the point of a purely formal symbolic gesture of "dotting the i's," of signing and thus conferring the performative force on the edicts whose content is determined by the elected governing body. And does not, mutatis mutandis, the same hold for today's progressive computerization of our everyday lives, in the course of which the subject is also more and more "mediatized," imperceptibly stripped of his power, under the false guise of its increase? When our body is mediatized (caught in the network of electronic media), it is simultaneously exposed to the threat of a radical "proletarization": the subject is potentially reduced to the pure dollar sign, since even my own personal experience can be stolen, manipulated, regulated by the mechanical Other. One can see, again, how the prospect of radical virtualization bestows on the computer the position which is strictly homologous to that of God in Malebrancheian occasionalism. Since the computer co-ordinates the relationship between my mind and (what I experience as) the movement of my limbs (in the virtual reality), one can easily imagine a computer which runs amok and starts to act like an Evil God, disturbing the co-ordination between my mind and my bodily self-experience—when the signal of my mind to raise my hand is suspended or even counteracted in (the virtual) reality, the most fundamental experience of the body as "mine" is undermined. It seems thus that cyberspace effectively realizes the paranoiac fantasy elaborated by Schreber, the German judge whose memoirs were analyzed by Freud.[9] The "wired universe" is psychotic insofar as it seems to materialize Schreber's hallucination of the divine rays through which God directly controls the human mind.

In other words, does the externalization of the big Other in the computer not account for the inherent paranoiac dimension of the wired universe? Or, to put it in yet another way, the commonplace is that, in cyberspace, the ability to download consciousness into a computer finally frees people from their bodies—but it also frees the machines from "their" people . . .

Staging the Fundamental Fantasy

The final inconsistency concerns the ambiguous status of the liberation of humanity announced by Neo in the last scene. As the result of Neo's intervention, there is a "SYSTEM FAILURE" in the Matrix; at the same time, Neo addresses people still caught in the Matrix as the Savior who will teach them how to liberate themselves from the constraints of the Matrix—they will be able to break the physical laws, bend metals, fly in the air . . . However, the problem is that all these "miracles" are possible only if we remain *within* the VR sustained by the Matrix and merely bend or change its rules: our "real" status is still that of the slaves of the Matrix, we as it were are merely gaining additional power to change our mental prison rules—so what about exiting from the Matrix altogether and entering the "real reality" in which we are miserable creatures living on the destroyed earth surface?

In an Adornian way, one should claim that these inconsistencies[10] are the film's moment of truth: they signal the antagonisms of our late-capitalist social experience, antagonisms concerning basic ontological couples like reality and pain (reality as that which disturbs the reign of the pleasure-principle), freedom and system (freedom is only possible within the system that hinders its full deployment). However, the ultimate strength of the film is nonetheless to be located at a different level. Years ago, a series of science-fiction films like *Zardoz* or *Logan's Run* forecast today's postmodern predicament: The isolated group living an aseptic life in a secluded area longs for the experience of the real world of material decay. Till postmodernism, utopia was an endeavor to break out of the real of historical time into a timeless Otherness. With postmodern overlapping of the "end of history" with full availability of the past in digitalized memory, in this time where we *live* the atemporal utopia as everyday ideological experience, utopia becomes the longing for the Reality of History itself, for memory, for the traces of the real past, the attempt to break out of the closed dome into smell and decay of the raw reality. *The Matrix* gives the final twist to this reversal, combining utopia with dystopia: the very reality we live in, the atemporal utopia staged by the Matrix, is in place so that we can be effectively reduced to a passive state of living batteries providing the Matrix with the energy.

The unique impact of the film thus resides not so much in its central thesis (what we experience as reality is an artificial virtual reality generated by the "Matrix," the mega-computer directly attached to all our minds), but in its central image of millions of human beings leading a claustrophobic life in water-filled cradles, kept alive in order to generate energy for the Matrix. So when (some of) the people "awaken" from their immersion into the Matrix-controlled virtual reality, this awakening is not the opening into the wide space of the external reality, but first the horrible realization of this enclosure, where each of us is effectively just a fetus-like organism, immersed in the pre-natal fluid . . . This utter passivity is the foreclosed fantasy that sustains our conscious experience as active, self-positing subjects—it is the ultimate perverse fantasy, the notion that we are ultimately instruments of the Other's (Matrix's) *jouissance,* sucked out of our life-substance like batteries.

Therein resides the true libidinal enigma of this device. *Why* does the Matrix need human energy? The purely energetic solution is, of course, meaningless. The Matrix could have easily found another, more reliable, source of energy which would have not demanded the extremely complex arrangement of virtual reality co-ordinated for millions of human units. Another question is discernible here. Why does the Matrix not immerse each individual into his or her own solipsistic artificial universe? Why complicate matters by co-ordinating the programs so that all humanity inhabits one and the same virtual universe? The only consistent answer is that the Matrix feeds on the humans' *jouissance*—so we are back at the fundamental Lacanian thesis that the big Other itself, far from being an anonymous machine, needs the constant influx of *jouissance*. This is how we should turn around the state of things presented by the film. What this movie depicts as the scene of our awakening into our true situation, is effectively its exact opposition, the very fundamental fantasy that sustains our being.

The intimate connection between perversion and cyberspace is today a commonplace. According to the standard view, the perverse scenario stages the "disavowal of castration." Perversion can be seen as a defense against the motif of "death and sexuality," against the threat of mortality as well as the contingent imposition of sexual difference. What the pervert enacts is a universe in which, as in cartoons, a human being can survive any catastrophe; in which adult sexuality is reduced to a childish game; in which one is not forced to die or to choose one of the two sexes. As such, the pervert's universe is the universe of pure symbolic order, of the signifier's game running its course, unencumbered by the Real of human finitude.

As a first approach, it may seem that our experience of cyberspace fits perfectly this universe: Isn't cyberspace also a universe unencumbered by the inertia of the Real, constrained only by its self-imposed rules? And is not the same true of Virtual Reality in *The Matrix*? The "reality" in which we live loses its inexorable character; it becomes a domain of arbitrary rules (imposed by the Matrix) that one can violate if one's Will is strong enough . . . However, according to Lacan, what this standard notion leaves out of consideration is the unique relationship between the Other and the *jouissance* in perversion. What, exactly, does this mean?

In "Le prix du progrès," one of the fragments that conclude *The Dialectic of Enlightenment,* Adorno and Horkheimer quote the argument of the nineteenth-century French physiologist Pierre Flourens against medical anesthesia with chloroform. Flourens claims that it can be proven that the anesthetic works only on our memory's neuronal network. In short, while we are butchered alive on the operating table, we fully feel the terrible pain, but later, after awakening, we do not remember it . . . For Adorno and Horkheimer, this, of course, is the perfect metaphor of the fate of Reason based on the repression of nature in itself: his body, the part of nature in the subject, fully feels the pain, it is only that, due to repression, the subject does not remember it. Therein resides the perfect revenge of nature for our domination over it: Unknowingly, we are our own greatest victims, butchering ourselves alive . . . Isn't it also possible to read this as the perfect fantasy scenario of inter-passivity, of the Other Scene in which we pay the price for our active intervention into the world? There is no active free agent without this phantasmic support, without this Other Scene in which he is totally manipulated by the Other.[11] A sado-masochist willingly assumes this suffering as the access to Being.

Perhaps, it is along these lines that one can also explain the obsession of Hitler's biographers with his relationship to his niece Geli Räubel, who was found dead in Hitler's Munich apartment in 1931, as if the alleged Hitler's sexual perversion will provide the "hidden variable," the intimate missing link, the phantasmic support that would account for his public personality. Here is this scenario as reported by Otto Strasser:

> Hitler made her undress [while] he would lie down on the floor. Then she would have to squat down over his face where he could examine her at close range, and this made him very excited. When the excitement reached its peak, he demanded that she urinate on him, and that gave him his pleasure. (Ron Rosenbaum, *Explaining Hitler* [New York: Harper, 1999], p. 134)

Crucial here is the utter passivity of Hitler's role in this scenario as the phantasmic support that pushed him into his frenetically destructive public political activity—no wonder Geli was desperate and disgusted at these rituals.

Therein resides the correct insight of *The Matrix*: in its juxtaposition of the two aspects of perversion: on the one hand, reduction of reality to a virtual domain regulated by arbitrary rules that can be suspended; on the other hand, the concealed truth of this freedom, the reduction of the subject to an utter instrumentalized passivity.[12]

Notes

1. Comparing the original script (available on the internet) with the movie itself, we can see that the Wachowski brothers were intelligent enough to throw out the clunky pseudo-intellectual references: "Look at 'em. Automatons. Don't think about what they're doing or why. Computer tells 'em what to do and they do it." "The banality of evil." This pretentious reference to Arendt misses the point: People immersed in the VR of the Matrix are in an entirely different, almost opposite, position compared with the executioners of the Holocaust. Another wise move was to drop the all too obvious references to Eastern techniques of emptying your mind as the way to escape the control of the Matrix: "You have to learn to let go of that anger. You must let go of everything. You must empty yourself to free your mind."

2. It's also crucial that what enables the hero of *The Truman Show* to see through and exit his manipulated world is the unforeseen intervention of his father. There are two paternal figures in the film, the actual symbolic-biological father and the paranoiac "real" father, played by Ed Harris, the director of the TV show who totally manipulates his life and protects him in the closed environment.

3. On whom I rely extensively here. See Dean's *Aliens in America: Conspiracy Cultures from Outerspace to Cyberspace* (Ithaca: Cornell University Press, 1998).

4. Claude Lévi-Strauss, "Do Dual Organizations Exist?", in *Structural Anthropology* (New York: Basic Books, 1963), pp. 131–163. The drawings are on pp. 133–34.

5. See Rastko Mocnik, "Das 'Subjekt, dem unterstellt wird zu glauben' und die Nationals eine Null-Institution," in H. Boke, ed., *Denk-Prozesse nach Althusser* (Hamburg: Argument Verlag, 1994).

6. See Jacques Lacan, "Television," *October* 40 (1987).

7. The main work of Nicolas Malebranche is *Recherches de la Vérité* (1674–75; the most available edition is Paris: Vrin, 1975).

8. As to this ambiguity, see Paul Virilio, *The Art of the Motor,* Minneapolis: University of Minnesota Press, 1995).

9. The connection between cyberspace and Schreber's psychotic universe was suggested to me by Wendy Chun, Princeton.

10. A further pertinent inconsistency also concerns the status of intersubjectivity in the universe run by the Matrix: do all individuals share *the same* virtual reality? Why? Why not to each its preferred own?

11. What Hegel does is to "traverse" this fantasy by demonstrating its function of filling in the pre-ontological abyss of freedom—reconstituting the positive Scene in which the subject is inserted into a positive noumenal order. In other words, for Hegel, Kant's vision is meaningless and inconsistent, since it secretly reintroduces the ontologically fully constituted divine totality, a world conceived *only* as Substance, *not* also as Subject.

12. An earlier version of this chapter was delivered to the international symposium "Inside *The Matrix*," Center for Art and Media, Karlsruhe, Germany.

Questions to Consider

1. What distinctions, if any, do you see between art and entertainment? What counts as art for you and why? Why do you suppose that many people have set up a distinction between art and entertainment? What purposes, if any, are served?

2. Review Baker's definition of the vernacular. How has your own education emphasized and/or deemphasized your vernacular?

3. Sontag is "against interpretation." What does this mean to you? Are Mulvey, Baker, Danto, and Žižek similarly writing against something: some practice, some ideas, some power? Are they "against interpretation," too?

4. Baker ("the blues matrix") and Žižek (the film, *The Matrix*) use the matrix metaphor. Compare their use of the metaphor. What seems to attract theorists and artists to this metaphor? Do you see the matrix as a useful configuration of your understanding of important dimensions of the contemporary world?

5. Danto sees a link between pop art and "a tremendous change in the fabric of society, a demand for liberation which has not yet ended." Think about the phrase, "fabric of society," and the "demand for liberation." What are some of the different ways that theorists in this section examine the "fabric of society" and "demand for liberation"?

6. So-called reality television shows have been quite popular for the past few years. What do these shows tell us about the categories of art and entertainment? Which theorists in this section of *Everyday Theory* present ideas/arguments most relevant from your perspective to the issues reality television raises and why? Do the theorists in this section help to clarify your own attitudes about and understanding of these shows? Would such clarification affect the way you view them?

VII

Desire and Sexuality

We deal with issues and events involving desire and sexuality every day. We get turned on, and we get turned off; we find one person highly attractive and another hideous; we have feelings of disgust, arousal, ambivalence, and affection, feelings we sometimes have explanations for and sometimes find completely inexplicable; we fall in love, and we fall out of love; we marry, and we divorce, sometimes repeatedly; we come out of the closet, and we remain in the closet; we consume pornography, and we campaign against it; we label some people perverts, putting certain ones in jail and killing others with only the most travestied semblance of judge and jury present; we get our hearts broken, and we break hearts; we hook up on the rebound, and we swear off romance; we look for soul mates, playmates, father figures, and a girl like mom; we get our egos wounded, our feelings hurt, our trust betrayed, and our faith shaken; we are frigid, impotent, neurotic, perverse, hot, cold, uptight, loose, monogamous, flirtatious, androgynous, heterosexual, homosexual, bisexual, transsexual, metrosexual, and asexual. And this list just barely scratches the surface.

If the field of desire and sexuality offers us the most profound joy and pleasure, it also offers us the most abject fear and suffering. In nearly every Hollywood movie, whether it's the main plot or a subplot, there is a situation involving conflicted love interests, and TV shows dealing with sexual relationships abound, some along the lines of *Divorce Court* and others along the lines of *Elimi-Date* but all showing in one way or another the difficulties presented by human couplings. Would it, then, be an exaggeration to say that desire and sexuality are terms belonging to one of the realms of human experience most fraught with perplexity? Probably not. Even the terms themselves are troubling, desire sometimes referring to need or demand and sometimes used synonymously with longing, wish, or want. However we use the term, it seems fairly clear that we associate desire with the carnal, occasionally linking it to love, but more frequently, perhaps, to lust. Sexuality, too, covers a wide field. We sometimes use the term to speak of sexual practice, sometimes to speak of sexual identity, but we generally connect it in one way or another with gender roles and gender politics. In the essays in this section, you will find yourself bumping into discussions of castration and narcissism, the homosexual and the homosocial, masochism and sadism, hysterics and obsessionals, love and language—discussions that overlap, that contradict, that question, and that jostle against one another in both comfortable and uncomfortable ways.

The first selection, Barbara Johnson's "The Critical Difference: BartheS/ BalZac," published in 1980, may puzzle you. What, you might ask, is it doing here? How does an explanation of deconstruction or a discussion of readerly, as opposed to writerly, texts have any bearing on desire and sexuality? One thing that may help you to see the logic of its placement more clearly is a bit of background information on the subject of Johnson's essay: Roland Barthes's reading practice. In 1973, Barthes published a book called *The Pleasure of the Text* in which he theorized an erotics of reading. Accordingly, when he speaks of the relationship between a reader, writer, or text, he speaks of it in sexually charged terms:

> Does writing in pleasure guarantee—guarantee me, the writer—my reader's pleasure? Not at all. I must seek out this reader (must "cruise" him) *without knowing where he is*. A site of bliss is then created. It is not the reader's "person" that is necessary to me, it is this site: the possibility of a dialectics of desire, of an *unpredictability* of bliss. . . . (his emphasis, 4)

Note the language Barthes uses a little bit later in the text: " . . . this prattling text is then a frigid text, as any demand is frigid until desire, until neurosis forms in it" (5). Or note Barthes's wording when he says that " . . . the texts . . . contain within themselves, *if they want to be read,* that bit of neurosis necessary to the seduction of their readers: these terrible texts are *all the same* flirtatious texts" (his emphasis, 5–6). And if any doubt remains about the way Barthes uses terms such as "pleasure" or "bliss," we have this passage to guide us: "The pleasure of the text is like that untenable, impossible, purely *novelistic* instant so relished by Sade's libertine when he manages to be hanged and then to cut the rope at the very moment of his orgasm, his bliss" (his emphasis, 7). According to Barthes, pleasure is like orgasm is like bliss.

Given Barthes's notion of an erotics of reading, it is easy to see why he would have chosen to write about a Balzac story that involves desire, castration, narcissism, and failed love, and why Johnson would have felt equally compelled to write about Barthes. Interestingly, the heavily layered or mediated quality of Johnson's essay—Johnson is writing about Barthes, who is writing about Balzac, who is writing about a narrator, who is telling someone else's story—suggests a kind of voyeuristic pleasure at work. In other, rather cruder, words, if Barthes is getting off on writing about Balzac, perhaps Johnson is getting off on writing about Barthes's writing about Balzac.

Johnson begins casually enough, however, by asserting that literary criticism is the art of rereading. No doubt, you have been well steeped in a pedagogy that advocates the necessity of reading and rereading, writing and rewriting, so Johnson's assertion may not sound particularly striking at first glance, but when the term "difference" gets introduced, she puts a whole new spin on the act of rereading. In Johnson's discussion of Barthes's comments, "difference" means difference *within* a single book, not difference *between* two or more books. You could say that reading a text only once is a narcissistic experience because "what we can see in the text the first time is already in us, not in it." When we read a book only once, it becomes a mere echo or reflection of ourselves. We see what we already know, and thus the text we read is none other than our own. In order to see the text as "other," as well as to differentiate the text's otherness from itself, we must reread it rather than tossing it aside and consuming a new one. Is there not an interesting parallel between fidelity to one text, reading it many times over, and a monogamous relationship? and an equally interesting parallel between the consumption of many texts and what we call "playing the field" in dating?

What Johnson gives us, then, is both theory and practice: theory in that she provides us with an explanation of how to do a deconstructive reading, and practice in that she actually provides us with a deconstructive reading. Unfortunately for Sarrasine, a character in Balzac's story, he had neither Barthes's nor Johnson's guidance when reading La Zambinella, his "love interest," and thus his failure to reread the castrato's "text" resulted in his own death. It may sound rather hyperbolic to say that a failure to reread leads to death, and yet it may be precisely our narcissism, our failure to reread, that leads to the death of many a relationship. Is it possible that theoretical insights, if applied to interpersonal relationships, can actually help us "read" friends, family members, and lovers more generously and more effectively?

After reading Johnson's essay, in which the concept of difference as difference *within* rather than *between* plays a central role, you will probably be struck by the title of Eve Kosofsky Sedgwick's book *Between Men: English Literature and Male Homosocial Desire,* the introduction to which appears in this section. "Between men": do the words themselves suggest a problem in the way men are conceptualized? Is it possible to apply the deconstructive principles you've just learned to Sedgwick's remarks about the male homosocial continuum? According to Sedgwick, the male homosocial continuum is invisible, while the female homosocial continuum is not. Because of the way power and sexual relationships are organized in our culture, the female homosocial continuum can easily accommodate heterosexual women who promote the interests of women and homosexual women who love women. The male homosocial continuum, however, is neither so fluid nor so flexible. In fact, there seems to be a powerful investment in maintaining differences *between* men rather than acknowledging the wide spectrum of experience that the category "man" encompasses—hence the continued invisibility of the male continuum and the paradox of a discontinuous continuum. Because an opposition is created *between* men rather than *within* the category itself, the attitude seems to be this: "I'm one kind of man, a heterosexual man; and you're a different kind of man, a homosexual man. There is a difference between us, a gulf so wide it can never be bridged." As Sedgwick points out, however, this attitude is culturally and historically specific, not universal and timeless.

One of the points Sedgwick raises is whether patriarchy structurally requires homophobia. Put more simply, the question is this: Our culture may be viciously homophobic, but does it have to be? Does its organization of power and sexual relationships necessarily require homophobia? Sedgwick's answer is that while patriarchy requires heterosexuality, it need not require homophobia, and she cites the ancient Greeks as an example of a patriarchal culture that embraced both heterosexuality and male homosexual practices. What ancient Greece suggests to Sedgwick is that "the structure of homosocial continuums is culturally contingent, not an innate feature of either 'maleness' or 'femaleness'." Her project, then, is to explore why social and political relationships, when sexualized, become problematic.

Like Johnson, Sedgwick offers a particular theoretical methodology for her exploration, a blend of "Marxist feminism" and "radical feminism." According to Sedgwick, these two approaches represent the outer extremes of the feminist-theory spectrum, Marxist feminism engaging in the most historicizing and radical feminism, the least. As she explains, radical feminism is called radical not because of its leftist orientation but because "it takes gender itself, gender alone, to be the most radical division of human experience, and a relatively unchanging one." Since Marxist feminism has traditionally lacked a theory of sexuality, frequently reducing female sexuality to its reproductive function, and since radical feminism has failed to bring history into its account of sexuality, universalizing the problem of gender difference in a transhistorical manner, neither one provides an adequate methodology for Sedgwick's task. Put the two together, however, and—voila!—you have a hybrid theory that can more effectively analyze that "most fertile space of ideological formation": the place where the political and the sexual meet. What Sedgwick's essay illustrates is the dynamism of theory; in the hands of a creative reader such as Sedgwick, theory is not static, but highly malleable.

In Gilles Deleuze's discussion of the Marquis de Sade and Leopold von Sacher-Masoch, we see a convergence of the issues and questions raised by Johnson and Sedgwick, for the literary works of both Sade and Masoch suggest an erotics of reading at the same time that they articulate a certain set of power and sexual relations. "The Language of Sade and Masoch" is the first chapter of Deleuze's *Masochism: Coldness and Cruelty,* a book which argues that the literary works of the eighteenth-century Sade have overshadowed the literary works of the nineteenth-century Masoch because of a mistaken understanding of sadism and masochism, which are frequently collapsed into one "syndrome" called sadomasochism. Deleuze's project, then, is to separate sadism from masochism, demonstrating their different structures, and thus their lack of complementarity, in order to resurrect the works of Masoch and show their importance to the literary and clinical fields. Although Deleuze's approach is more philosophical than political, it does raise interesting questions: First, what is perversion? And second, why do we treat it with such ambivalence, being at once appalled and fascinated by it?

Until quite recently, homosexuality itself was classified as a clinical perversion, and therapists saw it as their job to "cure" people of their homosexual desires, to "normalize" them. And yet, given Freud's definition of the perverse, anything that doesn't lead quickly and directly to reproductive sexual intercourse qualifies as perverse. On this model, foreplay itself, which delays the sexual act, can be seen as a perverse activity. Perhaps the definition of perversion and the politics behind it become a little less obscure when we note that the word "perversion" was not defined by the *Oxford English Dictionary* in its sexological sense until the publication of the 1933 supplement, but in the numerous citations that come before that, two other kinds of so-called pervert show up: the wayward woman and the religious heretic, both of whom interrupt (and thus pervert) the smooth workings of patriarchy's two most powerful institutions, the family and the church.

While few of us may wish to identify with Eve, the first "wayward woman," or Satan, the first "religious heretic," if we are honest with ourselves, we can probably find a fault line or contradiction in our own desires. We wish to follow rules and to break them. We wish to create and to destroy. Think, for example, of the pleasure young children get when they build elaborate structures out of blocks and then knock them down. Could it be that in the heart of each of us resides an imp of perversion?

If you read Deleuze's comments on Sade and Masoch with Sedgwick in mind, it might be helpful to note what the French psychoanalyst Jean Clavreul has to say about the field of perversion:

> Is it not patent that on the whole, erotic literature has been made up of writings by perverts? Again we must add that from the point of view of eroticism, the "normal individual" is presented, next to the pervert, as an inept yokel unable to elevate his love above a routine. The sexual good health that he brags about appears to derive from a lack of imagination. We cannot fail to notice that the ordinary hetrosexual [sic] seems very often to be a prisoner of this "vulgar love" denounced by the participants in the *Symposium,* who themselves do not hesitate to dismiss as uninteresting the bestial coupling that is only good for assuring the necessary and uninteresting mission of the perpetuation of the species. (216)

Clavreul's commentary thrusts us back to Sedgwick's historical analysis of sexuality, for we see here that our cultural ancestors, the ancient Greeks, denounced heterosexual intercourse as "vulgar love," as uninteresting "bestial coupling," while contemporary Western culture does quite the reverse. Why is this? What is gained, and by whom, when we privilege one type of sexuality over another or when we call one type of sexual activity "normal" and another type "abnormal," "perverse," or "sick"?

As you begin reading Renata Salecl's "Love: Providence or Despair," an essay that appeared in 1994 in a special issue of *New Formations* on the subject of Jacques Lacan and love, you may begin to see how strangely desire operates. Following Lacan's articulation of desire, Salecl explains that desire arises out of lack; because it is linked to the law in a very essential way (the law as assertions of "No"), desire always searches for what is unavailable or prohibited. For example, when we cannot have something, or when we are told we cannot have something, our desire for that thing is not diminished but enhanced; we want what we want all the more. But if, by chance, we manage to obtain the desired object, it ceases to interest us, and we soon begin to desire something else that appears just out of reach. We see the dialectical nature of desire expressed every day in pop music, in songs with lyrics that tell of a breakup and the ensuing resurgence of love, such as Sugar Ray's "When It's Over": "When it's over/That's the time I fall in love again/When it's over/Can I still come over?" What these lyrics suggest is that desire itself is transgressive and even, perhaps, perverse in the most general sense of the term, for when the singer's girlfriend is available, he doesn't want her (they break up), but as soon as she becomes unavailable, his desire returns (he falls in love again).

When you read a great tale of love such as William Shakespeare's *Romeo and Juliet* or Alexander Pope's *Eloisa to Abelard,* you may think to yourself how tragic it is that external forces so frequently intervene to prevent or disrupt the union of young lovers, but if what Salecl says is true, that "one of the greatest illusions of love is that prohibitions and social codes prevent its realization," you may find yourself having to revise your usual notion of the tragic. Perhaps these couples were lucky to have experienced, if only briefly, the kind of passionate love that prohibition produces rather than prevents. If, for example, there had been no antagonism between the Montagues and the Capulets, if the way had been paved for the two families to unite, would love have developed between Romeo and Juliet? Or if Eloisa and Abelard's secret marriage had not been discovered, if Abelard had not been castrated, and if the two had not been sent to separate monasteries, would we have had the exchange of love letters that led to Pope's heroic epistle?

Like Johnson, Salecl engages in both theory and practice, for as she explains various psychoanalytic concepts, she illustrates how they function through her analysis of two movies, *The Remains of the Day* and *The Age of Innocence.* Some of the questions you might ask yourself after reading Salecl's essay are these: Does the explanation she gives of desire explain why sexual relationships are so fraught with difficulty? What is the relationship between love and desire? How do you suppose Salecl would answer the question implicit in her title: Is love providence or despair? And, finally, drawing on Deleuze's discussion of masochist and sadist and Salecl's discussion of hysteric and obsessional, would you say that desire operates differently in the fields of perversion and neurosis? If so, how?

The final essay in this section, Luce Irigaray's "I Love To You," from her book of the same name, puts the question of love—how we are to do it and speak it—at front and center. While Salecl sees psychoanalysis as a valuable tool for understanding love, Irigaray says that, in its standard formation and application, psychoanalysis is not of much use to us. And yet her concern with language and sexual difference does locate her within a psychoanalytic orbit, for those are two of the biggest concerns of psychoanalysis, especially as it has been articulated by Lacan. Her project, however, is radically different from that of Salecl, for if Salecl is trying to explain how the structures of desire and love function in our culture, Irigaray is trying to go beyond explanation to a reconfiguration of the current structures. Another way to think about the difference between Salecl's and Irigaray's projects is through architectural terms. One is telling how a building that already exists has been put together, and the other is trying to envision an entirely new building. What would happen if we began to speak love differently—not speak *about* love differently, but speak love itself differently? This is Irigaray's question, and thus it is no surprise that the subtitle of the book is *Sketch of a Possible Felicity in History*.

"*I love to you* means I maintain a relation of indirection to you." This is Irigaray's opening line, and it may sound wrong to you on first reading. Aren't we supposed to be direct—as in, honest or straight forward—with one another? Isn't indirection a way of skirting the issue, a form of dialogic cowardice? These are good questions, but Irigaray puts indirection in the most positive light when, in the next paragraph, she says, "The 'to' prevents the relation of transitivity, bereft of the other's irreducibility and potential reciprocity." The key to understanding this statement is the word "transitivity," which is closely connected to the word "transitive" and which the dictionary defines as expressing an action that is thought of as passing over to and taking effect on some person or thing. In the sentence, "I hit you," for example, "hit" is a transitive verb. My action of hitting passes over to you, has an effect on you—probably a negative one. In the sentence, "I fall," on the other hand, there is no transitive verb, only an intransitive verb, which is to say that my action does not pass over to another, nor does it have an effect on anyone but me.

The concept of "transitivism" can also be used to explain the behavior of very young children who have not yet established a clear division between self and other. For example, a child who hits will say that he or she has been hit, and a child who sees another fall will cry. Is the one who hits lying? No. Is the one who cries feeling compassion? No. In both cases, there is a merging of self and other that skews perception. Most children grow out of this mindset when they begin to understand that they are their own separate beings and that others, too, are their own separate beings. And yet a residue of transitivism always remains, a residue whose troubling effects can be observed when adults argue: "You hurt me," one will say, to which the other will reply, "No, you hurt me. I simply reacted to that."

If this section began with rereading as a possible avenue by which to escape narcissism, one might say that it ends with rewriting as a possible avenue by which to escape transitivism. To reduce the other to the same or to dominate the other is to erase the other, but, as Irigaray argues, to respect the other's radical alterity (i.e., otherness or difference) and to have our own alterity respected would be a felicitous way to rewrite the future of sexual relations.

Barbara Johnson (1947–)

A celebrated translator and critic of French poststructuralist theory, Johnson has made the often difficult works of Jacques Derrida, Roland Barthes, and Jacques Lacan accessible to students and teachers of literature. Born near Boston, she earned her B.A. in French from Oberlin College in 1969 and her Ph.D. in French from Yale in 1977. Johnson's book *The Critical Difference: Essays in the Contemporary Rhetoric of Reading* (1980) argues for theory as a subgenre of literature. Rather than viewing theory as something that is applied to a text, she argues that theory is already an integral part of the text itself. Johnson made a similar case in 1982 with *The Pedagogical Imperative: Teaching as a Literary Genre* (1982), a collection of essays discussing the links between the literary and the pedagogical. In later works, Johnson continued to be committed to interdisciplinarity, bringing pedagogy, law, and feminism into conversation with literature. From 1977 until 1983, she taught French and comparative literature at Yale, after which she moved to Harvard, where she now teaches French, comparative literature, and English. She has been named the Fredric Wertham Professor of Law and Psychiatry in Society. Johnson's other works include *Défigurations du langage poétique* (1979); *A World of Difference* (1987); *Consequences of Theory* (1990), coauthored with Jonathan Arac; *Freedom and Interpretation* (1993); *The Wake of Deconstruction* (1994); and a translation of Derrida's *Dissemination* (1981).

The Critical Difference: BartheS/BalZac

Literary criticism as such can perhaps be called the art of rereading. I would therefore like to begin by quoting the remarks about rereading made by Roland Barthes in S/Z:

> Rereading, an operation contrary to the commercial and ideological habits of our society, which would have us "throw away" the story once it has been consumed ("devoured"), so that we can then move on to another story, buy another book and which is tolerated only in certain marginal categories of readers (children, old people, and professors), rereading is here suggested at the outset, for it alone saves the text from repetition (*those who fail to reread are obliged to read the same story everywhere*).[1] (Emphasis mine)

What does this paradoxical statement imply? First, it implies that a single reading is composed of the already-read, that what we can see in a text the first time is already in us, not in it; in us insofar as we ourselves are a stereotype, an already-read text; and in the text only to the extent that the already-read is that aspect of a text that it must have in common with its reader in order for it to be readable at all. When we read a text once, in other words, we can see in it only what we have already learned to see before.

Secondly, the statement that those who do not reread must read the same story everywhere involves a reversal of the usual properties of the words *same* and *different*. Here, it is the consuming of different stories that is equated with the repetition of the same, while it is the rereading of the same that engenders what Barthes calls the "text's difference." This critical concept of difference, which has been valorized both by Saussurian linguistics and by the Nietzschean tradition in philosophy—particularly the work of Jacques Derrida—is crucial to the practice of what is called deconstructive criticism. I would therefore like to examine here some of its implications and functions.

In a sense, it could be said that to make a critical difference is the object of all criticism as such. The very word *criticism* comes from the Greek verb *krinein,* "to separate or choose," that is, to differentiate. The critic not only seeks to establish standards for evaluating the differences between texts but also tries to perceive something uniquely different within each text he reads and in so doing to establish his own individual difference from other critics. But this is not quite what Barthes means when he speaks of the text's difference. On the first page of S/Z, he writes:

> This difference is not, obviously, some complete, irreducible quality (according to a mythic view of literary creation), it is not what designates the individuality of each text, what names, signs, finishes off each work with a flourish; on the contrary, it is a difference which does not stop and which is articulated upon the infinity of texts, of languages, of systems: a difference of which each text is the return. (p. 3)

In other words, a text's difference is not its uniqueness, its special identity. It is the text's way of differing from itself. And this difference is perceived only in the act of rereading. It is the way in which the text's signifying energy becomes unbound, to use Freud's term, through the process of repetition, which is the return not of sameness but of difference. Difference, in other words, is not what distinguishes one identity from another. It is not a difference between (or at least not between independent units), but a difference within. Far from constituting the text's unique identity, it is that which subverts the very idea of identity, infinitely deferring the possibility of adding up the sum of a text's parts or meanings and reaching a totalized, integrated whole.

Let me illustrate this idea further by turning for a moment to Rousseau's *Confessions.* Rousseau's opening statement about himself is precisely an affirmation of difference: "I am unlike anyone I have ever met; I will even venture to say that I am like no one in the whole world. I may be no better, but at least I am different" (Penguin edition, 1954, p. 17). Now, this can be read as an unequivocal assertion of uniqueness, of difference between Rousseau and the whole rest of the world. This is the boast on which the book is based. But in what does the uniqueness of this self consist? It is not long before we find out: "There are times when I am so unlike myself that I might be taken for someone else of an entirely opposite character" (p. 126). "In me are united two almost irreconcilable characteristics, though in what way I cannot imagine" (p. 112). In other words, this story of the self's difference from others inevitably becomes the story of its own unbridgeable difference from itself. Difference is not engendered in the space between identities; it is what makes all totalization of the identity of a self or the meaning of a text impossible.

It is this type of textual difference that informs the process of deconstructive criticism. *Deconstruction* is not synonymous with *destruction,* however. It is in fact much closer to the original meaning of the word *analysis,* which etymologically means "to undo"—a virtual synonym for "to de-construct." The de-construction of a text does not proceed by random doubt or arbitrary subversion, but by the careful teasing out of warring forces of signification within the text itself. If anything is destroyed in a deconstructive reading, it is not the text, but the claim to unequivocal domination of one mode of signifying over another. A deconstructive reading is a reading that analyzes the specificity of a text's critical difference from itself.

I have chosen to approach this question of critical difference by way of Barthes's S/Z for three reasons:

1. Barthes sets up a critical value system explicitly based on the paradigm of difference, and in the process works out one of the earliest, most influential, and most lucid and forceful syntheses of contemporary French theoretical thought;

2. The Balzac story that Barthes chooses to analyze in S/Z is itself in a way a study of difference—a subversive and unsettling formulation of the question of sexual difference;

3. The confrontation between Barthes and Balzac may have something to say about the critical differences between theory and practice, on the one hand, and between literature and criticism, on the other.

I shall begin by recalling the manner in which Barthes outlines the value system:

> Our evaluation can be linked only to a practice, and this practice is that of writing. On the one hand, there is what it is possible to write, and on the other, what is no longer possible to write. . . . What evaluation finds is precisely this value: what can be written (rewritten) today: the *writerly* [*le scriptible*]. Why is the writerly our value? Because the goal of literary work (of literature as work) is to make the reader no longer a consumer, but a producer of the text. . . . Opposite the writerly text is its countervalue, its negative, reactive value: what can be read, but not written: the *readerly* [*le lisible*]. We call any readerly text a classic text. (p. 4)

Here, then, is the major polarity that Barthes sets up as a tool for evaluating texts: the readerly versus the writerly. The readerly is defined as a product consumed by the reader; the writerly is a process of production in which the reader becomes a producer: it is "ourselves writing." The readerly is constrained by considerations of representation: it is irreversible, "natural," decidable, continuous, totalizable, and unified into a coherent whole based on the signified. The writerly is infinitely plural and open to the free play of signifiers and of difference, unconstrained by representative considerations, and transgressive of any desire for decidable, unified, totalized meaning.

With this value system, one would naturally expect to find Barthes going on to extoll the play of infinite plurality in some Joycean or Mallarméan piece of writerly obscurity, but no; he turns to Balzac, one of the most readerly of readerly writers, as Barthes himself insists. Why then does Barthes choose to talk about Balzac? Barthes skillfully avoids confronting this question. But perhaps it is precisely the way in which Barthes's choice of Balzac does not follow logically from his value system—that is, the way in which Barthes somehow differs from himself—which opens up the critical difference we must analyze here.

Although Balzac's text apparently represents for Barthes the negative, readerly end of the hierarchy, Barthes's treatment of it does seem to illustrate all the characteristics of the positive, writerly end. In the first place, one cannot help but be struck by the plurality of Barthes's text, with its numerous sizes of print, its "systematic use of digression," and its successive superposable versions of the same but different story, from the initial reproduction of Girodet's *Endymion* to the four appendixes, which repeat the book's contents in different forms. The reading technique proper also obeys the demand for fragmentation and pluralization, and consists of "manhandling" the text:

> What we seek is to sketch the stereographic space of writing (which will here be a classic, readerly writing). The commentary, based on the affirmation of the plural, cannot work with "respect" to the text; the tutor text will ceaselessly be broken, interrupted without any regard for its natural divisions . . . the work of the commentary, once it is separated from any ideology of totality, consists precisely in *manhandling* the text, *interrupting* it [lui couper la parole]. What is thereby denied is not the *quality* of the text (here incomparable) but its "naturalness." (p. 15)

Barthes goes on to divide the story diachronically into 561 fragments called *lexias* and synchronically into five so-called voices or codes, thus transforming the text into a "complex network" with "multiple entrances and exits."

The purposes of these cuts and codes is to pluralize the reader's intake, to effect a resistance to the reader's desire to restructure the text into large, ordered masses of meaning: "If we want to remain attentive to the plural of a text . . . we must renounce structuring this text in large masses, as was done by classical rhetoric and by secondary-school explication: no construction of the text" (pp. 11–12). In leaving the text as heterogeneous and discontinuous as possible, in attempting to avoid the repressiveness of the attempt to dominate the message and force the text into a single ultimate meaning, Barthes thus works a maximum of disintegrative violence and a minimum of integrative violence. The question to ask is whether this "anti-constructionist" (as opposed to "deconstructionist") fidelity to the fragmented signifier succeeds in laying bare the functional plurality of Balzac's text or whether in the final analysis a certain systematic level of textual difference is not also lost and flattened by Barthes's refusal to reorder or reconstruct the text.

Let us now turn to Balzac's *Sarrasine* itself. The story is divided into two parts: the story of the telling and the telling of the story. In the first part, the narrator attempts to seduce a beautiful Marquise by telling her the second part; that is, he wants to exchange narrative knowledge for carnal knowledge. The lady wants to know the secret of the mysterious old man at the party, and the narrator wants to know the lady. Story-telling, as Barthes points out, is thus not an innocent, neutral activity, but rather part of a bargain, an act of seduction. But here the bargain is not kept; the deal backfires. The knowledge the lady has acquired, far from bringing about her surrender, prevents it. In fact, the last thing she says is: "No one will have *known* me."

It is obvious that the key to this failure of the bargain lies in the content of the story used to fulfill it. That story is about the passion of the sculptor Sarrasine for the opera singer La Zambinella, and is based not on knowledge but on ignorance: the sculptor's ignorance of the Italian custom of using castrated men instead of women to play the soprano parts on the operatic stage. The sculptor, who had seen in La Zambinella the perfect female body for the first time realized in one person, a veritable Pygmalion's statue come to life, finds out that this image of feminine perfection literally has been carved by a knife, not in stone but in the flesh itself. He who had proclaimed his willingness to die for his love ends up doing just that, killed by La Zambinella's protector.

How is it that the telling of this sordid little tale ends up subverting the very bargain it was intended to fulfill? Barthes's answer to this is clear: "castration is contagious"—"contaminated by the castration she has just been told about, [the Marquise] impels the narrator into it" (p. 36).

What is interesting about this story of seduction and castration is the way in which it unexpectedly reflects upon Barthes's own critical value system. For in announcing that "the tutor text will ceaselessly be broken, interrupted without any regard for its natural divisions," is Barthes not implicitly privileging something like castration over what he calls the "ideology of totality"? "If the text is subject to some form," he writes, "this form is not unitary. . . . finite; it is the fragment, the slice, the cut up or erased network" (p. 20; translation modified). Indeed, might it not be possible to read Balzac's opposition between the ideal woman and the castrato as metaphorically assimilable to Barthes's opposition between the readerly and the writerly? Like the readerly text, Sarrasine's deluded image of La Zambinella is a glorification of perfect unity and wholeness:

> At that instant he marveled at the ideal beauty he had hitherto sought in life, seeking in one often unworthy model the roundness of a perfect leg; in another, the curve of a breast; in another, white shoulders; finally taking some girl's neck, some woman's hands, and some child's smooth knees, without ever having encountered under the cold Parisian sky the rich, sweet creations of ancient Greece. La Zambinella displayed to him, *united*, living, and delicate, those exquisite female forms he so ardently desired. (pp. 237–38; emphasis mine)

But like the writerly text, Zambinella is actually fragmented, unnatural, and sexually undecidable. Like the readerly, the soprano is a product to be "devoured" ("With his eyes, Sarrasine devoured Pygmalion's statue, come down from its pedestal" [p. 238]), while, like the writerly, castration is a process of production, an active and violent indetermination. The soprano's appearance seems to embody the very essence of "woman" as a *signified* ("This was woman herself . . ." [p. 248]), while the castrato's reality, like the writerly text, is a mere play of signifiers, emptied of any ultimate signified, robbed of what the text calls a "heart": "I have no heart," says Zambinella, "the stage where you saw me . . . is my life, I have no other" (p. 247).

Here, then, is the first answer to the question of why Barthes might have chosen this text; it explicitly thematizes the opposition between unity and fragmentation, between the idealized signified and the discontinuous empty play of signifiers, which underlies his opposition between the readerly and the writerly. The traditional value system that Barthes is attempting to reverse is thus already mapped out within the text he analyzes. Three questions, however, immediately present themselves: (1) Does

Balzac's story really uphold the unambiguousness of the readerly values to which Barthes relegates it? (2) Does Balzac simply regard ideal beauty as a lost paradise and castration as a horrible tragedy? (3) If Barthes is really attempting to demystify the ideology of totality, and if his critical strategy implicitly gives a positive value to castration, why does his analysis of Balzac's text still seem to take castration at face value as an unmitigated and catastrophic horror?

In order to answer these questions, let us take another look at Balzac's story. To regard castration as the ultimate narrative revelation and as the unequivocal cause of Sarrasine's tragedy, as Barthes repeatedly does, is to read the story more or less from Sarrasine's point of view. It is in fact Barthes's very attempt to pluralize the text which thus restricts his perspective; however "disrespectfully" he may cut up or manhandle the story, his reading remains to a large extent dependent on the linearity of the signifier and thus on the successive unfoldings of the truth of castration to Sarrasine and to the reader. Sarrasine's ignorance, however, is not only a simple lack of knowledge but also blindness to the injustice that is being done to him and that he is also potentially doing to the other. This does not mean that Balzac's story is a plea for the prevention of cruelty to castrati, but that the failure of the couple to unite can perhaps not simply be attributed to the literal fact of castration. Let us therefore examine the nature of Sarrasine's passion more closely.

Upon seeing La Zambinella for the first time, Sarrasine exclaims: "To be loved by her, or to die!" (p. 238). This alternative places all of the energy of the passion not in the object, La Zambinella, but on the subject, Sarrasine. To be loved, or to die; to exist as the desired object, or not to exist at all. What is at stake is not the union between two people, but the narcissistic awakening of one. Seeing La Zambinella is Sarrasine's first experience of *himself* as an object of love. By means of the image of sculpturesque perfection, Sarrasine thus falls in love with none other than himself. Balzac's fictional narrator makes explicit the narcissistic character of Sarrasine's passion and at the same time nostalgically identifies with it himself when he calls it "this golden age of love, during which we are happy almost by ourselves" (p. 240). Sarrasine contents himself with La Zambinella as the product of his own sculptor's imagination ("This was more than a woman, this was a masterpiece!" [p. 238]) and does not seek to find out who she is in reality ("As he began to realize that he would soon have to act ... to ponder, in short, on ways to see her, speak to her, these great, ambitious thoughts made his heart swell so painfully that he put them off until later, deriving as much satisfaction from his physical suffering as he did from his intellectual pleasures" [p. 240]). When the sculptor is finally forced into the presence of his beloved, he reads in her only the proof of his own masculinity—she is the ideal woman, therefore he is the ideal man. When Sarrasine sees La Zambinella shudder at the pop of a cork, he is charmed by her weakness and says, "My strength [puissance] is your shield" [p. 244]. La Zambinella's weakness is thus the inverted mirror image of Sarrasine's potency. In this narcissistic system, the difference between the sexes is based on symmetry, and it is precisely the castrato that Sarrasine does indeed love—the image of the lack of what he thereby thinks he himself possesses. When Sarrasine says that he would be able to love a strong woman, he is saying in effect that he would be unable to love anyone who was not his symmetrical opposite and the proof of his masculinity. This is to say that even if La Zambinella *had* been a real woman, Sarrasine's love would be a refusal to deal with her as a real other. This type of narcissism is in fact just as contagious in the story as castration: the Marquise sees the narcissistic delusion inherent in the narrator's own passion, and, banteringly foreshadowing one of the reasons for her ultimate refusal, protests: "Oh, you fashion me to your own taste, What tyranny! You don't want me for myself!" (p. 233).

Sarrasine cannot listen to the other as other. Even when Zambinella suggests the truth by means of a series of equivocal remarks culminating in the question (directed toward Sarrasine's offers to sacrifice everything for love)—"And if I were not a woman?"—Sarrasine cries: "What a joke! Do you think you can deceive an artist's eye?" (p. 247). Sarrasine's strength is thus a shield *against* La Zambinella, not *for* her. He creates her as his own symmetrical opposite and through her loves only himself. This is why the revelation of the truth is fatal. The castrato is simultaneously outside the difference between the sexes as well as representing the literalization of its illusory symmetry. He subverts the desire for symmetrical, binary difference by fulfilling it. He destroys Sarrasine's reassuring masculinity by revealing that it is based on castration. But Sarrasine's realization that he himself is thereby castrated, that he is looking at his true mirror image, is still blind to the fact that he had never been capable of loving in the first place. His love was from the beginning the cancellation and castration of the other.

What Sarrasine dies of, then, is precisely a failure to *reread* in the exact sense with which we began this chapter. What he devours so eagerly in La Zambinella is actually located within himself: a collection of sculpturesque clichés about feminine beauty and his own narcissism. In thinking that he knows where difference is located—between the sexes—he is blind to a difference that cannot be situated between, but only within. In Balzac's story, castration thus stands as the literalization of the "difference within" which prevents any subject from coinciding with itself. In Derrida's terms, Sarrasine reads the opera singer as pure voice ("his passion for La Zambinella's voice [p. 241], as an illusion of imaginary immediacy ("The distance between himself and La Zambinella had ceased to exist, he possessed her" [p. 239]), as a perfectly readable, motivated sign ("Do you think you can deceive an artist's eye?"), as full and transparent Logos, whereas she is the very image of the empty and arbitrary sign, of writing inhabited by its own irreducible difference from itself. And it can be seen that the failure to reread is hardly a trivial matter: for Sarrasine, it is fatal.

Balzac's text thus itself demystifies the logocentric blindness inherent in Sarrasine's reading of the Zambinellian text. But if Sarrasine's view of La Zambinella as an image of perfect wholeness and unequivocal femininity is analogous to the classic, readerly conception of literature according to Barthes's definition, then Balzac's text has already worked out the same type of deconstruction of the readerly ideal as that which Barthes is trying to accomplish as if it stood in opposition to the classic text. In other words, Balzac's text already "knows" the limits and blindnesses of the readerly, which it personifies in Sarrasine. Balzac has already in a sense done Barthes's work for him. The readerly text is itself nothing other than a deconstruction of the readerly text.

But at the same time, Balzac's text does not operate a simple reversal of the readerly hierarchy; Balzac does not proclaim castration as the truth behind the readerly blindness in as unequivocal a way as Barthes's own unequivocality would lead one to believe. For every time Balzac's text is about to use the word *castration,* it leaves a blank instead. "Ah, you are a woman," cries Sarrasine in despair; "for even a . . ." He breaks off. "No," he continues, "he would not be so cowardly" (p. 251). Balzac repeatedly castrates his text of the word *castration.* Far from being the unequivocal answer to the text's enigma, castration is the way in which the enigma's answer is withheld. Castration is what the story must, and cannot, say. But what Barthes does in his reading is to label these textual blanks "taboo on the word castrato" (pp. 75, 177, 195, 210). He fills in the textual gaps with a name. He erects castration into *the* meaning of the text, its ultimate signified. In so doing, however, he makes the idea of castration itself into a readerly fetish, the supposed answer to all the text's questions, the final revelation in the "hermeneutic" code. Balzac indeed shows that the answer cannot be this simple, not only by eliminating the word *castration* from his text but also by suppressing the name of its opposite. When Sarrasine first feels sexual pleasure, Balzac says that this pleasure is located in "what we call the heart, for lack of any other word" (p. 238). Later Zambinella says "I have no heart" (p. 247). Barthes immediately calls "heart" a euphemism for the sexual organ, but Balzac's text, in stating that what the heart represents cannot be named, that the word is lacking, leaves the question of sexuality open, as a rhetorical problem which the simple naming of parts cannot solve. Balzac's text thus does not simply reverse the hierarchy between readerly and writerly by substituting the truth of castration for the delusion of wholeness; it deconstructs the very possibility of naming the difference.

On the basis of this confrontation between a literary and a critical text, we could perhaps conclude that while both involve a study of difference, the literary text conveys a difference from itself which it "knows" but cannot say, while the critical text, in attempting to say the difference, reduce it to identity. But in the final analysis, Barthes's text, too, displays a strange ambivalence. For although every metaphorical dimension in Barthes's text *proclaims castration as the desirable essence of the writerly*—the writerly about which "there may be nothing to say" (p. 4) just as the castrato is one "about whom there is nothing to say" (p. 214)—the literal concept of castration is loudly disavowed by Barthes as belonging to the injustices of the readerly: "To reduce the text to the unity of meaning, by a deceptively univocal reading, is . . . to sketch the castrating gesture" (p. 160). By means of this split, Barthes's own text reveals that it, like Balzac's, cannot with impunity set up any unequivocal value in opposition to the value of unequivocality. Just as Balzac's text, in its demystificaiton of idealized beauty, reveals a difference not between the readerly and the writerly, but within the very ideals of the readerly, Barthes's text, in its ambivalence toward castration, reveals that the other of the readerly cannot but be subject to its own difference from itself. Difference as such cannot ever be affirmed as an ultimate value because it is that which subverts the very foundations of any affirmation of value. Castration can neither be assumed nor denied, but only enacted in the return of unsituable difference in every text. And the difference between literature and criticism consists perhaps only in the fact that criticism is more likely to be blind to the way in which its own critical difference from itself makes it, in the final analysis, literary.

Note

1. Roland Barthes, S/Z, trans. Richard Miller (New York: Hill and Wang, 1974), pp. 15–16.

Eve Kosofsky Sedgwick (1950–)

With *Between Men: English Literature and Male Homosocial Desire,* published in 1985, Sedgwick helped introduce to literary studies a new approach to gender and sexuality now known as queer theory. The aim of queer theory was to unsettle conventional categories of sexual difference and lesbian and gay identity. Referred to by many as a pioneer in queer theory and literary studies, Sedgwick continued to address the performativity and politics of sexuality and desire in literature and art in her later critical works. Her works employ a range of genres, including poetry and autobiography. Born in Dayton, Ohio, she received her B.A. and M.Phil. from Cornell and her Ph.D. from Yale in 1975. She is now Distinguished Professor of English at the Graduate Center at the City University of New York. Her works include *The Coherence of Gothic Conventions* (1980), *Epistemology of the Closet* (1990), *Tendencies* (1993), *A Dialogue on Love* (1999), and a book of poetry, *Fat Art, Thin Art* (1994). She has also edited, with Andrew Parker, *Performativity and Performances* (1994) and *Novel Gazing: Queer Readings in Fiction* (1997), the latter of which has the distinction of being the first collection of essays that deal with the novel from a queer-theory perspective. Her most recent book, *Touching Feeling: Affect, Pedagogy, Performativity,* coauthored with Adam Frank, interrogates emotion in many forms and raises interesting questions about issues such as what connections can be found between the work of teaching and the experience of illness, and how shame can become an engine for queer politics, performance, and pleasure. As one editorial reviewer from *Publishers Weekly* has said of the book, "Sedgwick's unfashionable commitment to the truth of happiness propels a book as open-hearted as it is intellectually daring."

Introduction

i. Homosocial Desire

The subject of this book is a relatively short, recent, and accessible passage of English culture, chiefly as embodied in the mid-eighteenth to mid-nineteenth-century novel. The attraction of the period to theorists of many disciplines is obvious: condensed, self-reflective, and widely influential change in economic, ideological, and gender arrangements. I will be arguing that concomitant changes in the structure of the continuum of male "homosocial desire" were tightly, often causally bound up with the other more visible changes; that the emerging pattern of male friendship, mentorship, entitlement, rivalry, and hetero- and homosexuality was in an intimate and shifting relation to class; and that no element of that pattern can be understood outside of its relation to women and the gender system as a whole.

"Male homosocial desire": the phrase in the title of this study is intended to mark both discriminations and paradoxes. "Homosocial desire," to begin with, is a kind of oxymoron. "Homosocial" is a word occasionally used in history and the social sciences, where it describes social bonds between persons of the same sex; it is a neologism, obviously formed by analogy with "homosexual," and just as obviously meant to be distinguished from "homosexual." In fact, it is applied to such activities as "male bonding," which may, as in our society, be characterized by intense homophobia, fear and hatred of homosexuality.[1] To draw the "homosocial" back into the orbit of "desire," of the potentially erotic, then, is to hypothesize the potential unbrokenness of a continuum between homosocial and homosexual—a continuum whose visibility, for men, in our society, is radically disrupted. It will become clear, in the course of my argument, that my hypothesis of the unbrokenness of this continuum is not a *genetic* one— I do not mean to discuss genital homosexual desire as "at the root of" other forms of male homosociality—but rather a strategy for making generalizations about, and marking historical differences in, the *structure* of men's relations with other men. "Male homosocial desire" is the name this book will give to the entire continuum.

I have chosen the word "desire" rather than "love" to mark the erotic emphasis because, in literary critical and related discourse, "love" is more easily used to name a particular emotion, and "desire" to name a structure; in this study, a series of arguments about the structural permutations of social impulses fuels the critical dialectic. For the most part, I will be using "desire" in a way analogous to the psychoanalytic use of "libido"—not for a particular affective state or emotion, but for the affective or social force, the glue, even when its manifestation is hostility or hatred or something less emotively charged, that shapes an important relationship. How far this force is properly sexual (what, historically, it means for something to be "sexual") will be an active question.

The title is specific about *male* homosocial desire partly in order to acknowledge from the beginning (and stress the seriousness of) a limitation of my subject; but there is a more positive and substantial reason, as well. It is one of the main projects of this study to explore the ways in which the shapes of sexuality, and what *counts* as sexuality, both depend on and affect historical power relationships.[2] A corollary is that in a society where men and women differ in their access to power, there will be important gender differences, as well, in the structure and constitution of sexuality.

For instance, the diacritical opposition between the "homosocial" and the "homosexual" seems to be much less thorough and dichotomous for women, in our society, than for men. At this particular historical moment, an intelligible continuum of aims, emotions, and valuations links lesbianism with the other forms of women's attention to women: the bond of mother and daughter, for instance, the bond of sister and sister, women's friendship, "networking," and the active struggles of feminism.[3] The continuum is crisscrossed with deep discontinuities—with much homophobia, with conflicts of race and class—but its intelligibility seems now a matter of simple common sense. However agonistic the politics, however conflicted the feelings, it seems at this moment to make an obvious kind of sense to say that women in our society who love women, women who teach, study, nurture, suckle, write about, march for, vote for, give jobs to, or otherwise promote the interests of other women, are pursuing congruent and closely related activities. Thus the adjective "homosocial" as applied to women's bonds (by, for example, historian Carroll Smith-Rosenberg)[4] need not be pointedly dichotomized as against "homosexual"; it can intelligibly denominate the entire continuum.

The apparent simplicity—the unity—of the continuum between "women loving women" and "women promoting the interests of women," extending over the erotic, social, familial, economic, and political realms, would not be so striking if it were not in strong contrast to the arrangement among males. When Ronald Reagan and Jesse Helms get down to serious logrolling on "family policy," they are men promoting men's interests. (In fact, they embody Heidi Hartmann's definition of patriarchy: "relations between men, which have a material base, and which, though hierarchical, establish or create interdependence and solidarity among men that enable them to dominate women.")[5] Is their bond in any way congruent with the bond of a loving gay male couple? Reagan and Helms would say no—disgustedly. Most gay couples would say no—disgustedly. But why not? Doesn't the continuum between "men-loving-men" and "men-promoting-the-interests-of-men" have the same intuitive force that it has for women?

Quite the contrary: much of the most useful recent writing about patriarchal structures suggests that "obligatory heterosexuality" is built into male-dominated kinship systems, or that homophobia is a *necessary* consequence of such patriarchal institutions as heterosexual marriage.[6] Clearly, however convenient it might be to group together all the bonds that link males to males, and by which males enhance the status of males—usefully symmetrical as it would be, that grouping meets with a prohibitive structural obstacle. From the vantage point of our own society, at any rate, it has apparently been impossible to imagine a form of patriarchy that was not homophobic. Gayle Rubin writes, for instance, "The suppression of the homosexual component of human sexuality, and by corollary, the oppression of homosexuals, is . . . a product of the same system whose rules and relations oppress women."[7]

The historical manifestations of this patriarchal oppression of homosexuals have been savage and nearly endless. Louis Crompton makes a detailed case for describing the history as genocidal.[8] Our own society is brutally homophobic; and the homophobia directed against both males and females is not arbitrary or gratuitous, but tightly knit into the texture of family, gender, age, class, and race relations. Our society could not cease to be homophobic and have its economic and political structures remain unchanged.

Nevertheless, it has yet to be demonstrated that, because most patriarchies structurally include homophobia, therefore patriarchy structurally *requires* homophobia. K. J. Dover's recent study, *Greek Homosexuality,* seems to give a strong counterexample in classical Greece. Male homosexuality, according to Dover's evidence, was a widespread, licit, and very influential part of the culture. Highly structured along lines of class, and within the citizen class along lines of age, the pursuit of the adolescent boy by the older man was described by stereotypes that we associate with romantic heterosexual love (conquest, surrender, the "cruel fair," the absence of desire in the love object), with the passive part going to the boy. At the same time, however, because the boy was destined in turn to grow into manhood, the assignment of roles was not permanent.[9] Thus the love relationship, while temporarily oppressive to the object, had a strongly educational function; Dover quotes Pausanias in Plato's *Symposium* as saying "that it would be right for him [the boy] to perform any service for one who improves him in mind and character."[10] Along with its erotic component, then, this was a bond of mentorship; the boys were apprentices in the ways and virtues of Athenian citizenship, whose privileges they inherited. These privileges included the power to command the labor of slaves of both sexes, and of women of any class including their own. "Women and slaves belonged and lived together," Hannah Arendt writes. The system of sharp class and gender subordination was a necessary part of what the male culture valued most in itself: "Contempt for laboring originally [arose] out of a passionate striving for freedom from necessity and a no less passionate impatience with every effort that left no trace, no monument, no great work worthy to remembrance";[11] so the contemptible labor was left to women and slaves.

The example of the Greeks demonstrates, I think, that while heterosexuality is necessary for the maintenance of any patriarchy, homophobia, against males at any rate, is not. In fact, for the Greeks, the continuum between "men loving men" and "men promoting the interests of men" appears to have been quite seamless. It is as if, in our terms, there were no perceived discontinuity between the male bonds at the Continental Baths and the male bonds at the Bohemian Grove[12] or in the board room or Senate cloakroom.

It is clear, then, that there is an asymmetry in our present society between, on the one hand, the relatively continuous relation of female homosocial and homosexual bonds, and, on the other hand, the radically discontinuous relation of male homosocial and homosexual bonds. The example of the Greeks (and of other, tribal cultures, such as the New Guinea "Sambia" studied by G. H. Herdt) shows, in addition, that the structure of homosocial continuums is culturally contingent, not an innate feature of either "maleness" or "femaleness." Indeed, closely tied though it obviously is to questions of male vs. female power, the explanation will require a more exact mode of historical categorization than "patriarchy," as well, since patriarchal power structures (in Hartmann's sense) characterize both Athenian and American societies. Nevertheless, we may take as an explicit axiom that the historically differential shapes of male and female homosociality—much as they themselves may vary over time—will always be articulations and mechanisms of the enduring inequality of power between women and men.

Why should the different shapes of the homosocial continuum be an interesting question? Why should it be a *literary* question? Its importance for the practical politics of the gay movement as a minority rights movement is already obvious from the recent history of strategic and philosophical differences between lesbians and gay men. In addition, it is theoretically interesting partly as a way of approaching a larger question of "sexual politics": What does it mean—what difference does it make—when a social or political relationship is sexualized? If the relation of homosocial to homosexual bonds is so shifty, then what theoretical framework do we have for drawing any links between sexual and power relationships?

ii. Sexual Politics and Sexual Meaning

This question, in a variety of forms, is being posed importantly by and for the different gender-politics movements right now. Feminist along with gay male theorists, for instance, are disagreeing actively about how direct the relation is between power domination and sexual sadomasochism. Start with two arresting images: the naked, beefy motorcyclist on the front cover, or the shockingly battered nude male corpse on the back cover, of the recent so-called "Polysexuality" issue of *Semiotext(e)* (4, no. 1 [1981])—which, for all the women in it, ought to have been called the semisexuality issue of *Polytext*. It seemed to be a purpose of that issue to insist, and possibly not only for reasons of radical-chic titillation, that the violence imaged in sadomasochism is not mainly theatrical, but is fully continuous with violence in the real world. Women Against Pornography and the framers of the 1980 NOW Resolution on Lesbian and Gay Rights share the same view, but without the celebratory glamour: to them too it seems intuitively clear that to sexualize violence or an image of violence is simply to extend, unchanged, its reach and force.[13] But, as other feminist writers have reminded us, another view is possible. For example: is a woman's masochistic sexual fantasy really only an internalization and endorsement, if not a cause, of her more general powerlessness and sense of worthlessness? Or may not the sexual drama stand in some more oblique, or even oppositional, relation to her political experience of oppression?[14]

The debate in the gay male community and elsewhere over "man-boy love" asks a cognate question: can an adult's sexual relationship with a child be simply a continuous part of a more general relationship of education and nurturance? Or must the inclusion of sex qualitatively alter the relationship, for instance in the direction of exploitiveness? In this case, the same NOW communiqué that had assumed an unbroken continuity between sexualized violence and real, social violence, came to the opposite conclusion on pedophilia: that the injection of the sexual charge *would* alter (would corrupt) the very substance of the relationship. Thus, in moving from the question of sadomasochism to the question of pedophilia, the "permissive" argument and "puritanical" argument have essentially exchanged their assumptions about how the sexual relates to the social.

So the answer to the question "what difference does the inclusion of sex make" to a social or political relationship, is—it varies: just as, for different groups in different political circumstances, homosexual activity can be either supportive of or oppositional to homosocial bonding. From this and the other examples I have mentioned, it is clear that there is not some ahistorical *Stoff* of sexuality, some sexual charge that can be simply added to a social relationship to "sexualize" it in a constant and predictable direction, or that splits off from it unchanged. Nor does it make sense to *assume* that the sexualized form epitomizes or simply condenses a broader relationship. (As, for instance, Kathleen Barry, in *Female Sexual Slavery,* places the Marquis de Sade at the very center of all forms of female oppression, including traditional genital mutilation, incest, and the economic as well as the sexual exploitation of prostitutes.)

Instead, an examination of the relation of sexual desire to political power must move along two axes. First, of course, it needs to make use of whatever forms of analysis are most potent for describing historically variable power asymmetries, such as those of class and race, as well as gender. But in conjunction with that, an analysis of representation itself is necessary. Only the model of representation will let us do justice to the (broad but not infinite or random) range of ways in which sexuality functions as a signifier for power relations. The importance of the rhetorical model in this case is not to make the problems of sexuality or of violence or oppression sound less immediate and urgent; it is to help us analyze and use the really very disparate intuitions of political immediacy that come to us from the sexual realm.

For instance, a dazzling recent article by Catherine MacKinnon, attempting to go carefully over and clear out the grounds of disagreement between different streams of feminist thought, arrives at the following summary of the centrality of sexuality per se for every issue of gender:

> Each element of the female *gender* stereotype is revealed as, in fact, *sexual.* Vulnerability means the appearance/reality of easy sexual access; passivity means receptivity and disabled resistance. . . ; softness means pregnability by something hard. . . . Woman's infantilization evokes pedophilia; fixation on dismembered body parts . . . evokes fetishism; idolization of vapidity, necrophilia. Narcissism insures that woman identifies with that image of herself that man holds up. . . . Masochism means that pleasure in violation becomes her sensuality.

And MacKinnon sums up this part of her argument: "Socially, femaleness means feminity, which means attractiveness to men, which means sexual attractiveness, which means sexual availability on male terms."[15]

There's a whole lot of "mean"-ing going on. MacKinnon manages to make every manifestation of sexuality mean the same thing, by making every instance of "meaning" mean something different. A trait can "mean" as an element in a semiotic system such as fashion ("softness means pregnability"); or anaclitically, it can "mean" its complementary opposite ("Woman's infantilization evokes pedophilia"); or across time, it can "mean" the consequence that it enforces ("Narcissism insures that woman identifies. . . . Masochism means that pleasure in violation becomes her sensuality"). MacKinnon concludes, "What defines woman as such is what turns men on." But what defines "defines"? That every node of sexual experience is in *some* signifying relation to the whole fabric of gender oppression, and vice versa, is true and important, but insufficiently exact to be of analytic use on specific political issues. The danger lies, of course, in the illusion that we do know from such a totalistic analysis where to look for our sexuality and how to protect it from expropriation when we find it.

On the other hand, one value of MacKinnon's piece was as a contribution to the increasing deftness with which, over the last twenty years, the question has been posed, "Who or what is the subject of the sexuality we (as women) enact?" It has been posed in terms more or less antic or frontal, phallic or gyno-, angry or frantic—in short, perhaps, Anglic or Franco-. But in different terms it is this same question that has animated the compliant of the American "sex object" of the 1960s, the claim since the 70s for "women's control of our own bodies," and the recently imported "critique of the subject" as it is used by French feminists.

Let me take an example from the great ideological blockbuster of white bourgeois feminism, its apotheosis, the fictional work that has most resonantly thematized for successive generations of American women the constraints of the "feminine" role, the obstacles to and the ravenous urgency of female ambition, the importance of the economic motive, the compulsiveness and destructiveness of romantic love, and (what MacKinnon would underline) the centrality and the total alienation of female sexuality. Of course, I am referring to *Gone with the Wind*. As MacKinnon's paradigm would predict, in the life of Scarlett O'Hara, it is expressly clear that to be born female is to be defined entirely in relation to the role of "lady," a role that does take its shape and meaning from a sexuality of which she is not the subject but the object. For Scarlett, to survive as a woman does mean learning to see sexuality, male power domination, and her traditional gender role as all meaning the same dangerous thing. To absent herself silently from each of them alike, and learn to manipulate them from behind this screen as objects or pure signifiers, as men do, is the numbing but effective lesson of her life.

However, it is *only* a white bourgeois feminism that this view apotheosizes. As in one of those trick rooms where water appears to run uphill and little children look taller than their parents, it is only when viewed from one fixed vantage in any society that sexuality, gender roles, and power domination can seem to line up in this perfect chain of echoic meaning. From an even slightly more eccentric or disempowered perspective, the *dis*placements and *dis*continuities of the signifying chain come to seem increasingly definitive. For instance, if it is true in this novel that all the woman characters exist in some meaning-ful relation to the role of "lady," the signifying relation grows more tortuous—though at the same time, in the novel's white bourgeois view, more totally determining—as the women's social and racial distance from that role grows. Melanie is a woman as she is a lady; Scarlett is a woman as she is required to be and pretends to be a lady; but Belle Watling, the Atlanta prostitute, is a woman not in relation to her own role of "lady," which is exiguous, but only negatively, in a compensatory and at the same time parodic relation to Melanie's and Scarlett's. And as for Mammy, her mind and life, in this view, are *totally* in thrall to the ideal of the "lady," but in a relation that excludes herself entirely: she is the template, the support, the enforcement, of Scarlett's "lady" role, to the degree that her personal femaleness loses any meaning whatever that is not in relation to Scarlett's role. Whose mother is Mammy?

At the precise intersection of domination and sexuality is the issue of rape. *Gone with the Wind*—both book and movie—leaves in the memory a most graphic image of rape:

> As the negro came running to the buggy, his black face twisted in a leering grin, she fired point-blank at him. . . . The negro was beside her, so close that she could smell the rank odor of him as he tried to drag her over the buggy side. With her own free hand she fought madly, clawing at his face, and then she felt his big hand at her throat and, with a ripping noise, her basque was torn open from breast to waist. Then the black hand fumbled between her breasts, and terror and revulsion such as she had never known came over her and she screamed like an insane woman.[16]

In the wake of this attack, the entire machinery by which "rape" is signified in this culture rolls into action. Scarlett's menfolk and their friends in the Ku Klux Klan set out after dark to kill the assailants and "wipe out that whole Shantytown settlement," with the predictable carnage on both sides. The question of how much Scarlett is to blame for the deaths of the white men is widely mooted, with Belle Watling speaking for the "lady" role—"She caused it all, prancin' bout Atlanta by herself, enticin' niggers and trash"—and Rhett Butler, as so often, speaking from the central vision of the novel's bourgeois feminism, assuring her that her desperate sense of guilt is purely superstitious (chs. 46,47). In preparation for this central incident, the novel had even raised the issue of the legal treatment of rape victims (ch. 42). And the effect of that earlier case, the classic effect of rape, had already been to abridge Scarlett's own mobility and, hence, personal and economic power: it was to expedite her business that she had needed to ride by Shantytown in the first place.

The attack on Scarlett, in short, fully means rape, both *to her* and to all the forces in her culture that produce and circulate powerful meanings. It makes no difference at all that one constituent element of rape is missing; but the missing constituent is simply sex. The attack on Scarlett had been for money; the black hands had fumbled between the white breasts because the man had been told that was where she kept her money; Scarlett knew that; there is no mention of any other motive; but it does not matter in the least, the absent sexuality leaves no gap in the character's, the novel's, or the society's discourse of rape.

Nevertheless, *Gone with the Wind* is not a novel that omits enforced sexuality. We are shown one actual rape in fairly graphic detail; but when it is white hands that scrabble on white skin, its idelogical name is "blissful marriage." "[Rhett] had humbled her, used her brutally through a wild mad night and she had gloried in it" (ch. 54). The sexual predations of white men on Black women are also a presence in the novel, but the issue of force vs. consent is never raised there; the white male alienation of a Black woman's sexuality is shaped differently from the alienation of the white woman's, to the degree that rape ceases to be a meaningful term at all. And if forcible sex ever did occur between a Black male and female character in this world, the sexual event itself would have no signifying power, since Black sexuality "means" here only as a grammatic transformation of a sentence whose true implicit subject and object are white.

We have in this protofeminist novel, then, in this ideological microcosm, a symbolic economy in which both the meaning of rape and rape itself are insistently circulated. Because of the racial fracture of the society, however, *rape and its meaning circulate in precisely opposite directions*. It is an extreme case; the racial fracture is, in America, more sharply dichotomized than other except perhaps for gender. Still, other symbolic fractures such as class (and by fractures I mean the lines along which quantitative differentials of power may in a given society be read as qualitative differentials with some other name) are abundant and actively disruptive in every social constitution. The signifying relation of sex to power, of sexual alienation to political oppression, is not the most stable, but precisely the most volatile of social nodes, under this pressure.

Thus, it is of serious political importance that our tools for examining the signifying relation be subtle and discriminate ones, and that our literary knowledge of the most crabbed or oblique paths of meaning not be oversimplified in the face of panic-inducing images of real violence, especially the violence of, around, and to sexuality. To assume that sex signifies power in a flat, unvarying relation of metaphor or synecdoche will always entail a blindness, not to the rhetorical and pyrotechnic, but to such historical categories as class and race. Before we can fully achieve and use our intuitive grasp of the leverage that sexual relations seem to offer on the relations of oppression, we need more—more different, more complicated, more diachronically apt, more off-centered—more daring and prehensile applications of our present understanding of what it may mean for one thing to signify another.

iii. Sex or History?

It will be clear by this point that the centrality of sexual questions in this study is important to its methodological ambitions, as well. I am going to be recurring to the subject of sex as an especially charges leverage-point, or point for the exchange of meanings, *between* gender and class (and in many societies, race), the sets of categories by which we ordinarily try to describe the divisions of human labor. And methodologically, I want to situate these readings as a contribution to a dialectic within feminist theory between more and less historicizing views of the oppression of women.

In a rough way, we can label the extremes on this theoretical spectrum "Marxist feminism" for the most historicizing analysis, "radical feminism" for the least. Of course, "radical feminism" is so called not because it occupies the farthest "left" space on a conventional political map, but because it takes gender itself, gender alone, to be the most radical division of human experience, and a relatively unchanging one.

For the purposes of the present argument, in addition, and for reasons that I will explain more fully later, I am going to be assimilating "French" feminism—deconstructive and/or Lacanian-oriented feminism—to the radical-feminist end of this spectrum. "French" and "radical" feminism differ on very many very important issues, such as how much respect they give to the brute fact that everyone gets categorized as either female or male; but they are alike in seeing all human culture, language, and life as structured in the first place—structured radically, transhistorically, and essentially *similarly,* however coarsely or finely—by a drama of gender difference. (Chapter 1 discusses more fully the particular terms by which this structuralist motive will be represented in the present study.) French-feminist and radical-feminist prose tend to share the same vatic, and perhaps imperialistic, uses of the present tense. In a sense, the polemical energy behind my arguments will be a desire, through the rhetorically volatile subject of sex, to recruit the representational finesse of deconstructive feminism in the service of a more historically discriminate mode of analysis.

The choice of sexuality as a thematic emphasis of this study makes salient and problematical a division of thematic emphasis between Marxist-feminist and radical-feminist theory as they are now practiced. Specifically, Marxist feminism, the study of the deep interconnections between on the one hand historical and economic change, and on the other hand the vicissitudes of gender division, has typically proceeded in the absence of a theory of sexuality and without much interest in the meaning or experience of sexuality. Or more accurately, it has held implicitly to a view of female sexuality as something that is essentially of a piece with reproduction, and hence appropriately studied with the tools of demography; or else essentially of a piece with a simple, prescriptive hegemonic ideology, and hence appropriately studied through intellectual or legal history. Where important advances have been made by Marxist-feminist-oriented research into sexuality, it has been in areas that were already explicitly distinguished as deviant by the society's legal discourse: signally, homosexuality for men and prostitution for women. Marxist feminism has been of little help in unpacking the historical meanings of women's experience of heterosexuality, or even, until it becomes legally and medically visible in this century, of lesbianism.[17]

Radical feminism, on the other hand, in the many different forms I am classing under that head, has been relatively successful in placing sexuality in a prominent and interrogative position, one that often allows scope for the decentered and the contradictory. Kathleen Barry's *Female Sexual Slavery,* Susan Griffin's *Pornography and Silence,* Gilbert and Gubar's *The Madwoman in the Attic,* Jane Gallop's *The Daughter's Seduction,* and Andrea Dworkin's *Pornography: Men Possessing Women* make up an exceedingly heterogeneous group of texts in many respects—in style, in urgency, in explicit feminist identification, in French or American affiliation, in "brow"-elevation level. They have in common, however, a view that sexuality is centrally problematical in the formation of women's experience. And in more or less sophisticated formulations, the subject as well as the ultimate object of female heterosexuality within what is called patriarchal culture are seen as male. Whether in literal interpersonal terms or in internalized psychological and linguistic terms, this approach privileges sexuality and often sees it within the context of the structure that Lévi-Strauss analyzes as "the male traffic in women."

This family of approaches has, however, shared with other forms of structuralism a difficulty in dealing with the diachronic. It is the essence of structures viewed as such to reproduce themselves; and historical change from this point of view appears as something outside of structure and threatening—or worse, *not* threatening—to it, rather than in a formative and dialectical relation with it. History tends thus to be either invisible or viewed in an impoverishingly glaring and contrastive light.[18] Implicitly or explicitly, radical feminism tends to deny that the meaning of gender or sexuality has ever significantly changed; and more damagingly, it can make future change appear impossible, or necessarily apocalyptic, even though desirable. Alternatively, it can radically oversimplify the prerequisites for significant change. In addition, history even in the residual, synchronic form of class or racial difference and conflict becomes invisible or excessively coarsened and dichotomized in the universalizing structuralist view.

As feminist readers, then, we seem poised for the moment between reading sex and reading history, at a choice that appears (though, it must be, wrongly) to be between the synchronic and the diachronic. We know that it must be wrongly viewed in this way, not only because in the abstract the synchronic and the diachronic must ultimately be considered in relation to one another, but because specifically in the disciplines we are considering they are so mutually inscribed: the narrative of Marxist history is so graphic, and the schematics of structuralist sexuality so narrative.

I will be trying in this study to activate and use some of the potential congruences of the two approaches. Part of the underpinning of this attempt will be continuing meditation on ways in which the category *ideology* can be used as part of an analysis of *sexuality*. The two categories seem comparable in several important ways: each mediates between the material and the representational, for instance; ideology, like sexuality as we have discussed it, *both* epitomizes *and* itself influences broader social relations of power; and each, I shall be arguing, mediates similarly between diachronic, narrative structures of social experience and synchronic, graphic ones. If commonsense suggests that we can roughly group historicizing, "Marxist" feminism with the diachronic and the narrative, and "radical," structuralist, deconstructive, and "French" feminisms with the synchronic and the graphic, then the methodological promise of these two mediating categories will be understandable.

In *The German Ideology,* Marx suggests that the function of ideology is to conceal contradictions in the status quo by, for instance, recasting them into a diachronic narrative of origins. Corresponding to that function, one important structure of ideology is an idealizing appeal to the outdated values of an earlier system, in defense of a later system that in practice undermines the material basis of those values.[19]

For instance, Juliet Mitchell analyzes the importance of the family in ideologically justifying the shift to capitalism, in these terms:

> The peasant masses of feudal society had individual private property; their ideal was simply more of it. Capitalist society seemed to offer more because it stressed the *idea* of individual private property in a new context (or in a context of new ideas). Thus it offered individualism (an old value) plus the apparently new means for its greater realization—freedom and equality (values that are conspicuously absent from feudalism). However, the only place where this ideal could be given an apparently concrete base was in the maintenance of an old institution:

> the family. Thus the family changed from being the economic basis of individual private property under feudalism to being the focal point of the *idea* of individual private property under a system that banished such an economic form from its central mode of production—capitalism. . . . The working class work socially in production for the private property of a few capitalists *in the hope of* individual private property for themselves and their families.[20]

The phrase "A man's home is his castle" offers a nicely condensed example of ideological construction in this sense. It reaches *back* to an emptied-out image of mastery and integration under feudalism in order to propel the male wage-worker *forward* to further feats of alienated labor, in the service of a now atomized and embattled, but all the more intensively idealized home. The man who has this home is a different person from the lord who has a castle; and the forms of property implied in the two possessives (his [mortgaged] home/ his [inherited] castle) are not only different but, as Mitchell points out, mutually contradictory. The contradiction is assuaged and filled in by transferring the lord's political and economic control over the *environs* of his castle to an image of the father's personal control over the *inmates* of his house. The ideological formulation thus permits a criss-crossing of agency, temporality, and space. It is important that ideology in this sense, even when its form is flatly declarative ("A man's home is his castle"), is always at least implicitly narrative, and that, in order for the reweaving of ideology to be truly invisible, the narrative is necessarily chiasmic in structure: that is, that the subject of the beginning of the narrative is different from the subject at the end, and that the two subjects cross each other in a rhetorical figure that conceals their discontinuity.

It is also important that the sutures of contradiction in these ideological narratives become most visible under the disassembling eye of an alternative narrative, ideological as that narrative may itself be. In addition, the diachronic opening-out of contradictions within the status quo, even when the project of that diachronic recasting is to conceal those very contradictions, can have just the opposite effect of making them newly visible, offering a new leverage for critique. For these reasons, distinguishing between the construction and the critique of ideological narrative is not always even a theoretical possibility, even with relatively flat texts; with the fat rich texts we are taking for examples in this project, no such attempt will be made.

Sexuality, like ideology, depends on the mutual redefinition and occlusion of synchronic and diachronic formulations. The developmental fact that, as Freud among others has shown, even the naming of sexuality as such is always retroactive in relation to most of the sensations and emotions that constitute it,[21] is *historically* important. What *counts* as the sexual is, as we shall see, variable and itself political. The exact, contingent space of indeterminacy—the place of shifting over time—of the mutual boundaries between the political and the sexual is, in fact, the most fertile space of ideological formation. This is true because ideological formation, like sexuality, depends on retroactive change in the naming or labeling of the subject.[22]

The two sides, the political and the erotic, necessarily obscure and misrepresent each other—but in ways that offer important and shifting affordances to all parties in historical gender and class struggle.

Notes

1. The notion of "homophobia" is itself fraught with difficulties. To being with, the word is etymologically nonsensical. A more serious problem is that the linking of fear and hatred in the "phobia" suffix, and in the word's usage, does tend to prejudge the question of the cause of homosexual oppression: it is attributed to fear, as opposed to (for example) a desire for power, privilege, or material goods. An alternative term that is more suggestive of collective, structurally inscribed, perhaps materially based oppression is "heterosexism." This study will, however, continue to use "homophobia," for three reasons. First, it will be an important concern here to question, rather than to reinforce, the presumptively symmetrical opposition between homo- and heterosexuality, which seems to be implicit in the term "heterosexism." Second, the etiology of individual people's attitudes toward male homosexuality will not be a focus of discussion. And third, the ideological and thematic treatments of male homosexuality to be discussed from the late eighteenth century onward do combine fear and hatred in a way that is appropriately called phobic. For a good summary of social science research on the concept of homophobia, see Morin and Garfinkle, "Male Homophobia."

2. For a good survey of the background to this assertion, see Weeks, *Sex*, pp. 1–18.

3. Adrienne Rich describes these bonds as forming a "lesbian continuum," in her essay, "Compulsory Heterosexuality and Lesbian Existence," in Stimpson and Person, *Women*, pp. 62–91, especially pp. 79–82.

4. "The Female World of Love and Ritual," in Cott and Pleck, *Heritage*, pp. 311–42; usage appears on, e.g., pp. 316, 317.

5. "The Unhappy Marriage of Marxism and Feminism: Towards a More Progressive Union," in Sargent, *Women and Revolution*, pp. 1–41; quotation is from p. 14.

6. See, for example, Rubin, "Traffic," pp. 182–83.

7. Rubin, "Traffic," p. 180.

8. Crompton, "Gay Genocide"; but see chapter 5 for a discussion of the limitations of "genocide" as an understanding of the fate of homosexual men.

9. On this, see Miller, *New Psychology*, ch. 1.

10. Dover, *Greek Homosexuality*, p. 91.

11. Arendt, *Human Condition*, p. 83, quoted in Rich, *On Lies*, p. 206.

12. On the Bohemian Grove, an all-male summer camp for American ruling-class men, see Domhoff, *Bohemian Grove*; and a more vivid, although homophobic, account, van der Zee, *Men's Party*.

13. The NOW resolution, for instance, explicitly defines sadomasochism, pornography, and "pederasty" (meaning pedophilia) as issues of "exploitation and violence," *as opposed to* "affectional/sexual preference/orientation." Quoted in *Heresies 12*. vol. 3 no. 4 (1981), p. 92

14. For explorations of these viewpoints, see *Heresies, ibid.*; Snitow et al., *Powers*, and Samois, *Coming*.

15. Mackinnon, "Feminism," pp. 530–31.

16. Mitchell, *Gone*, p. 780. Further citations will be incorporated within the text and designated by chapter number.

17. For a discussion of these limitations, see Vicinus, "Sexuality." The variety of useful work that is possible within these boundaries is exemplified by the essays in Newton et al., *Sex and Class*.

18. On this, see McKeon, "'Marxism.'"

19. Juliet Mitchell discusses this aspect of *The German Ideology* in *Woman's Estate*, pp. 152–58.

20. Mitchell, *Woman's Estate,* p. 154.
21. The best and clearest discussion of this aspect of Freud is Laplanche, *Life and Death,* especially pp. 25–47.
22. On this, see ch. 8.

Gilles Deleuze (1925–1995)

Deleuze is probably best known for *Anti-Oedipus: Capitalism and Schizophrenia* (1972), a book he coauthored with Félix Guattari that was an immediate hit in France. Once it was translated into English in 1983, it became an academic bestseller in England, Canada, and the United States. Born into a middle-class Parisian family, Deleuze received his education in the French university system, after which he taught philosophy at the University of Paris at Vincennes from 1969 until his retirement in 1987. Like many writers and intellectuals, Deleuze was profoundly affected by the student-led revolt against the French government in May of 1968, and the effects were most notable in his writing. He abandoned the bureaucratic voice of academia and orthodox philosophy, which he felt had been present in his earlier works on Hume and Bergson, for what he called his "own" voice and a new way of writing philosophy. This project led to a productive alliance with the practicing psychoanalyst and political activist Guattari and the publication of their highly polemical *Anti-Oedipus,* in which they attack not only state philosophy, but also orthodox Marxism and institutional Freudianism. They argue that when psychoanalysis allies itself with capitalism, it controls desire instead of liberating it. For Deleuze and Guattari, words such as "affirmation" and "action" were key to their writing and their lives, each man asserting that philosophy is not just a way of thinking but a mode of action. In *Negotiations* (1990), Deleuze argues that philosophy is a form of guerilla warfare that takes place not just in the street but also within the self. In 1992, Deleuze found himself fighting another kind of enemy: cancer. He continued to write and teach for the next three years, but in 1995 he jumped to his death from his apartment window.

The Language of Sade and Masoch

"It is too idealistic . . . and therefore cruel."

Doestoevsky, *The Insulted and Injured*

What are the uses of literature? The names of Sade and Masoch have been used to denote two basic perversions, and as such they are outstanding examples of the efficiency of literature. Illnesses are sometimes named after typical patients, but more often it is the doctor's name that is given to the disease (Roger's disease, Parkinson's disease, etc.). The principles behind this labeling deserve closer analysis. The doctor does not invent the illness, he dissociates symptoms that were previously grouped together, and links up others that were dissociated. In shorts he builds up a profoundly original clinical picture. The history of medicine can therefore be regarded under at least two aspects. The first is the history of illnesses, which may disappear, become less frequent, reappear or alter their form according to the state of the society and the development of therapeutic methods. Intertwined with this history is the history of symptomatology, which sometimes precedes and sometimes follows changes in therapy or in the nature of diseases: symptoms are named, renamed and regrouped in various ways. Progress from this point of view generally means a tendency toward greater specificity, and indicates a refinement of symptomatology. (Thus the plague and leprosy were more common in the past not only for historical and social reasons but because one tended to group under these headings various types of diseases now classified separately.) Great clinicians are the greatest doctors: when a doctor gives his name to an illness this is a major linguistic and semiological step, inasmuch as a proper name is linked to a given group of signs, that is, *a proper name is made to connote signs.*

Should we therefore class Sade and Masoch among the great clinicians? It is difficult to treat sadism and masochism on a level with the plague, leprosy and Parkinsons's disease; the word disease is clearly inappropriate. Nevertheless, Sade and Masoch present unparalleled configurations of symptoms and signs. In coining the term masochism, Krafft-Ebing was giving Masoch credit for having redefined a clinical entity not merely in terms of the link between pain and sexual pleasure, but in terms of something more fundamental connected with bondage and humiliation (there are limiting cases of masochism without algolagnia and even algolagnia without masochism).[1] Another question we should ask is whether Masoch does not present a symptomatology that is more refined than Sade's in that it enables us to discriminate between disturbances which were previously regarded as identical. In any case whether Sade and Masoch are "patients" or clinicians or both, they are also great anthropologists, of the type whose work succeeds in embracing a whole conception of man, culture and nature; they are also great artists in that they discovered new forms of expressions, new ways of thinking and feeling and an entirely original language.

In principle, violence is something that does not speak, or speaks but little, while sexuality is something that is little spoken about. Sexual modesty cannot be related to biological fear, otherwise it would not be formulated as its is: "I am less afraid of being touched and even of being seen than of being put into words." What is the meaning of the meeting of violence and sexuality in such excessive and abundant language as that of Sade and Masoch? How are we to account for the violent language linked with eroticism? In a text that ought to invalidate all theories relating Sade to Nazism, Georges Bataille explains that the language of Sade is paradoxical *because it is essentially that of a victim.* Only the victim can describe torture; the torturer necessarily uses the hypocritical language of established order and power. "As a general rule the torturer does not use the language of the violence exerted by him in the name of an established authority; he uses the language of the authority. . . . The violent man is willing to keep quiet and connives at cheating. . . . Thus Sade's attitude is diametrically opposed to that of the torturer. When Sade writes he refuses to cheat, but he attributes his own attitude to people who in real life could only have been silent and uses them to make self-contradictory statements to other people."[2]

Ought we to conclude that the language of Masoch is equally paradoxical in this instance because the victim speaks the language of the torturer he is to himself, with all the hypocrisy of the torturer?

What is known as pornographic literature is a literature reduced to a few imperatives (do this, do that) followed by obscene descriptions. Violence and eroticism do meet, but in a rudimentary fashion. Imperatives abound in the work of Sade and Masoch; they are issued by the cruel libertine or by despotic woman. Descriptions also abound (although the function of the descriptions as well as the nature of their obscenity are strikingly different in the two authors). It would appear that both for Sade and for Masoch language reaches its full significance when it acts directly on the senses. Sade's *The One Hundred and Twenty Days of Sodom* hinges on tales told to the libertines by "woman chroniclers," and in principle the heroes may not take any initiative in anticipation of these tales. Words are at their most powerful when they compel the body to repeat the movements they suggest, and "the sensations communicated by the ear are the most enjoyable and have the keenest impact." In Masoch's life as well as in his fiction, love affairs are always set in motion by anonymous letters, by the use of pseudonyms or by advertisements in newspapers. They must be regulated by contracts that formalize and verbalize the behavior of the partners. Everything must be stated, promised, announced and carefully described before being accomplished. However, the work of Sade and Masoch cannot be regarded as pornography; it merits the more exalted title of "pornology" because its erotic language cannot be reduce to the elementary functions of ordering and describing.

With Sade we witness an astonishing development of the demonstrative use of language. Demonstration as a higher function of language makes its appearance between sequences of description, while the libertines are resting, or in the interval between two commands. One of the libertines will read out a severe pamphlet, or expound inexhaustible theories, or draft a constitution. Alternatively he may agree to hold a conversation or a discussion with his victim. Such moments are frequent, particularly in *Justine*, where each of the heroine's torturers uses her as a listener and confidante. The libertine may put on an act of trying to convince and persuade; he may even proselytize and gain new recruits (as in *Philosophy in the Bedroom*). But the intention to convince is merely apparent, for nothing is in fact more alien to the sadist that the wish to convince, to persuade, in short to educate. He is interested in something quite different, namely to demonstrate that reasoning itself is a form of violence, and that he is on the side of violence, however calm and logical he may be. He is not even attempting to prove anything to anyone, but to perform a demonstration related essentially to the solitude and omnipotence of its author. The point of the exercise is to show that the demonstration is identical to violence. It follows that the reasoning does not have to be shared by the person to whom it is addressed any more than pleasure is meant to be shared by the object from which it is derived. The acts of violence inflicted on the victims are a mere reflection of a higher form of violence to which the demonstration testifies. Whether he is among his accomplices or among his victims, each libertine, while engaged in reasoning, is caught in the hermetic circle of his own solitude and uniqueness—even if the argumentation is the same for all the libertines. In every respect, as we shall see, the sadistic "instructor" stands in contrast to the masochistic "educator."

Here, again, Bataille says of Sade: "It is a language which repudiates any relationship between speaker and audience." Now if it is true that this language is the supreme realization of a demonstrative function to be found in the relation between violence and eroticism, then the other aspect, the language of imperatives and descriptions, appears in a new light. It still remains, but in an entirely dependent role, steeped in the demonstrative element, as it were, floating in it. The descriptions, the attitudes of the bodies, are merely living diagrams illustrating the abominable description; similarly the imperatives uttered by the libertines are like the statements of problems referring back to the more fundamental chain of sadistic theorems: "I have demonstrated it theoretically," says Noirceuil, "let us now put it to the test of practice."

We have therefore to distinguish two factors constituting a dual language. The first, the imperative and descriptive factor, represent the *personal* element; it directs and describes the personal violence of the sadist as well as his individual tastes; the second and higher factor represents the *impersonal* element in sadism and identifies the impersonal violence with an Idea of pure reason, with a terrifying demonstration capable of subordinating the first element. In Sade we discover a surprising affinity with Spinoza—a naturalistic and mechanistic approach imbued with the mathematical spirit. This accounts for the endless repetitions, the reiterated quantitative process of multiplying illustrations and adding victims upon victim, again and again retracing the thousand circles of an irreducibly solitary argument. Krafft-Ebing sensed the essential nature of such a process: "In certain cases the personal element is almost entirely absent. The subject gets sexual enjoyment from beating boys and girls, but the purely impersonal element of his perversion is much more in evidence. . . . While in most individuals of this type the feelings of power are experienced in relation to specific persons, we are dealing here with a pronounced form of sadism operating to a great extent in geographical and mathematical patterns."[3]

In the work of Masoch there is a similar transcendence of the imperative and the descriptive toward a higher function. But in this case it is all persuasion and education. We are no longer in the presence of a torturer seizing upon a victim and enjoying her all the more because she is unconsenting and unpersuaded. We are dealing instead with a victim in search of a torturer and who needs to educate, persuade and conclude an alliance with the torturer in order to realize the strangest of schemes. This is why advertisements are part of the language of masochism while they have no place in true sadism, and why the masochist draws up contracts while the sadist abominates and destroys them. The sadist is in need of institutions, the masochist of contractual relations. The middle ages distinguished with considerable insight between two types of commerce with the devil: the first resulted from possession, the second from a pact of alliance. The sadist thinks in terms of institutionalized possession, the masochist in terms of contracted alliance. Possession is the sadist's particular form of madness just as the pact is the masochist's. It is essential to the masochist that he should fashion the woman into a despot, that he should persuade her to cooperate and get her to "sign." He is essentially an educator and thus runs the risk inherent in educational undertakings. In all Masoch's novels, the woman, although persuaded, is still basically doubting, as though she were afraid: she is forced to commit herself to a role to which she may prove inadequate, either by overplaying or by falling short of expectations. In *The Divorced Woman*, the heroine complains: "Julian's ideal was a cruel woman, a woman like Catherine the Great, but alas, I was cowardly and weak. . . ." In *Venus*, Wanda says: "I am afraid of not being capable of it, but for you, my beloved, I am willing to try." Or again: "Beware, I might grow to enjoy it."

The educational undertaking of Masoch's heroes, their submission to a woman, the torments they undergo, are so many steps in their climb toward the Ideal. *The Divorced Woman* is subtitled *The Calvary of an Idealist*. Severin, the hero of *Venus*, takes as a motto for his doctrine of "supersensualism" the words of Mephistopheles to Faust: "Thou sensual, supersensual libertine, a little girl can lead thee by the nose." (*Übersinnlich* in Goethe's text does not means "supersensitive" but "supersensual," "supercarnal," in conformity with theological tradition, where *Sinnalichkeit* denotes the *flesh, sensualitas*). It is therefore not surprising that masochism should seek historical and cultural confirmation in mystical or idealistic initiation rites. The naked body of a woman can only be contemplated in a mystical frame of mind, as is the case in *Venus*. This fact is illustrated more clearly still in *The Divorced Woman*, where the hero, Julian, under the disturbing influence of a friend, desires for the first time to see his mistress naked. He begins by invoking a "need" to "observe," but finds that he is overcome by a religious feeling "without anything sensual about it" (we have here the two basic stages of fetishism). The ascent from the human body to the work of art and from the work of art to the Idea must take place under the shadow of the whip. Masoch is animated by a dialectical spirit. In *Venus* the story is set in motion by a dream that occurs during an interrupted reading of Hegel. But the primary influence is that of Plato. While Sade is spinozistic and employs demonstrative reason, Masoch is platonic and proceeds by dialectical imagination. One of Masoch's stories is entitled *The Love of Plato* and was at the origin of his adventure with Ludwig II.[4] Masoch's relation to Plato is evidenced not only by the ascent to the realm of the intelligible, but by the whole technique of dialectical reversal, disguise and reduplication. In the adventure with Ludwig II Masoch does not know at first whether his correspondent is a man or a woman; he is not sure at the end whether he is one or two people, nor does he know during the episode what part his wife will play, but he is prepared for anything, a true dialectician who knows the opportune moment and seizes it. Plato showed that Socrates appeared to be the lover but that fundamentally he was the loved one. Likewise the masochistic hero appears to be educated and fashioned by the authoritarian woman whereas basically it is he who forms her, dresses her for the part and prompts the harsh words she addresses to him. It is the victim who speaks through the mouth of his torturer, without sparing himself. Dialectic does not simply mean the free interchange of discourse, but implies transpositions or displacements of this kind, resulting in a scene being enacted simultaneously on several levels with reversals and reduplications in the allocation of roles and discourse.

Pornological literature is aimed above all at confronting language with its own limits, with what is in sense a "nonlanguage" (violence that does not speak, eroticism that remains unspoken). However this task can only be a accomplished by an internal splitting of language: the imperative and descriptive function must transcend itself toward a higher function, the personal element turning by reflection upon itself into the impersonal. When Sade invokes a universal analytical Reason to explain that which is most particular in desire, we must not merely take this as evidence that he is a man of the eighteenth century; particularity and the corresponding delusion must also represent an Idea of pure reason. Similarly when Masoch invokes the dialectical spirit, the spirit of Mephistopheles and that of Plato in one, this must not merely be taken as proof of his romanticism; here too particularity is seen reflectively in the impersonal Ideal of the dialectical spirit. In Sade the imperative and descriptive function of language transcends itself toward a pure demonstrative, instituting function, and in Masoch toward a dialectical, mythical and persuasive function. These two transcendent functions essentially characterize the two perversions, they are twin ways in which the monstrous exhibits itself in reflection.

Notes

1. Krafft-Ebing himself points out the existence of "passive flagellation" independently from masochism. Cf. *Psychopathia Sexualis* (revised by Moll, 1963).
2. Georges Bataille, *Eroticism,* Engl. tr. M. Dalwood (Calderbooks, 1965), pp. 187, 188, 189.
3. Krafft-Ebing, *Psychopathia Sexualis,* pp. 208–9.
4. Cf. Appendix III.

Renata Salecl (1962–)

One of the most important and prolific of the "New Lacanians," Salecl studied philosophy and sociology in Slovenia at the University of Ljubljana, where she received her B.A. in 1986, her M.A. in 1988, and her Ph.D. in 1991. She is now a senior researcher at the Institute of Criminology with the University of Ljubljana's faculty of law. She has also been a visiting professor at Duke University, where she taught in the literature department; the Centennial Professor in the

Department of Law at the London School of Economics; and a visiting professor at the Cordozo School of Law in New York and at George Washington University in Washington, D.C. Her many works, which bring together the areas of feminism, psychoanalysis, and political theory, include *Discipline as the Condition of Freedom* (1991); *Why do we Obey Power? Social Control, Ideology, and Ideological Fantasies* (1993); *The Spoils of Freedom: Psychoanalysis and Feminism After the Fall of Socialism* (1994); *Des Politik des Phantasmas: Nationalismus, Feminismus und Psychoanalyse* (1994); *Gaze and Voice as Love Objects*, coedited with Slavoj Žižek (1996); *(Per)Versions of Love and Hate* (1998); and *Sexuation* (2000). She is on the editorial board of the British journal *New Formations*, in which the essay "Love: Providence or Despair" appeared, and she is a contributing editor to the American journal *Lacanian Ink*. What makes her work so compelling is the ease and lucidity with which she writes about complex subjects—and her obvious sense of humor, which is suggested by "Love me, love my dog: psychoanalysis and the animal/human divide," the title of an essay that appeared in *Interpol: the art show which divided East and West*, edited by Eda Cufer and Victor Misiano.

Love: Providence or Despair

I can't love you unless I give you up.

Edith Wharton, *The Age of Innocence*

Love for oneself knows only one barrier
—love for others, love for objects.

Sigmund Freud, *Group Psychology and the Analysis of the Ego*

One of the greatest illusions of love is that prohibition and social codes prevent its realization. The illusionary character of this proposition is unveiled in every self-help manual: the advice people desperately in love usually get is to establish artificial barriers, prohibitions and make themselves temporarily inaccessible in order to provoke their love-object to return love. Or, as Freud said: 'Some obstacle is necessary to swell the tide of the libido to its heights; and in all periods of history, wherever natural barriers in the way of satisfaction have not sufficed, mankind has erected conventional ones in order to be able to enjoy love.'[1] What is the nature of these barriers? What is the role of institutions, rituals and social codes in relation to the subject's innermost passions, their love?

I will try to answer these questions by taking the example of two novels, Kazuo Ishiguro's *The Remains of the Day* and Edith Wharton's *The Age of Innocence*. Both novels deal with the problem of love relations in the context of ideological institutions. The plots of the two novels offer an aesthetic presentation of what Louis Althusser named Ideological State Apparatuses (ISA): 'a certain number of realities which present themselves to the immediate observer in the form of distinct and specialist institutions' and are primarily part of the private domain, like families, some schools, churches, parties, cultural ventures, etc.[2] In the two novels, it is precisely two of the most important ISAs, the family and society, in the sense of codified social norms, and the hierarchy of social relations, that dominate the private life of the protagonists: their love affairs are supposedly restrained by the influence of the oppressive ISAs that organize their lives.

The Age of Innocence is set in an extremely hierarchical nineteenth-century New York high society where every social act or movement is codified, and where there is a constant struggle not to misinterpret the unwritten rules and become an outcast. The extent of the codification in this society is visible from the way people organize their public and private lives: from the type of china they use at dinner parties, the way they dress, the location of their houses, the respect they pay to the people higher on the social ladder, and so on. *The Remains of the Day* is set in an equally hierarchical English aristocratic society just before and after the Second World War with the central role being played by the highest of servants—the butler. This is also a society of unwritten codes, in which every part of life is fully organized. And the butler is the one upon whom the perfection and maintenance of this order depends. As the butler, Stevens, points out, by doing his service in the most dignified and perfectionist manner he contributes significantly to the major historical events in which his master is involved. Stevens is the prototype of an 'ideological servant': he never questions his role in the machinery, he never opposes his boss even when he makes obvious mistakes, he does not think but obeys.

Behind this ideological machinery, in both novels, there is supposed to be something suppressed or hidden—and this concerns passions of the individuals engaged in rituals, their secret 'true' loves. The films of the two novels especially stress this hidden terrain 'beneath' the institution, the 'real' emotions behind the fake, public ones. The main trauma of *The Age of Innocence* is thus the impossibility of love between Newland Archer, young aristocrat, and Countess Ellen Olenska, the eccentric woman whose behaviour is very much under the scrutiny of New York society. Newland who is engaged to be married to the 'proper' woman of this society, tacitly, because of the high society rules, gives up his hopes of fulfilling his desire for Ellen and becomes a devoted husband. In *The Remains of the Day* we have the unspoken passion between Stevens and the housekeeper Miss Kenton, both of whom are obedient to the social codes to let their feelings out and to find some personal happiness for themselves. In short, both novels reveal the oppressiveness of the institutions in which their protagonists live, and which prevent them from finding love. The question is, however, is it really the institution that prevents love? Is it not actually the institution that, in a paradoxical way, produces love?

The Remains of the Day

The Remains of the Day is the story of a butler, Stevens, who has spent his whole life serving in the house of Lord Darlington. In his old age, Stevens takes a trip to visit the housekeeper Miss Kenton, who used to work in the house twenty years previously, with a view to convincing her to return to serve there again. During this trip, Stevens writes a diary in which he remembers his relationship with Miss

Kenton and the life in the house before the Second World War. Stevens's memories are primarily a tribute to the principles of dignity and moral greatness that define a perfect servant wholly devoted to his master. The subtle character of the novel concerns the fact that emotions are never expressed: although Stevens and Miss Kenton care about each other in more than a professional way, they never admit this to each other. Even at the end, when they finally meet after all these years and when there is no actual barrier to their relationship, nothing happens between them. Ritual stays intact and emotions never fully come out—why not?

One of the interpretations of Stevens's behaviour, of his complete repression of emotions, is that he is, in some way, non-human. This is exemplified by his attitude towards his father's death: even at the time of his father's dying, it is more important for Stevens to perform his service in an impeccable way than to grieve. Such a humanist interpretation, of course, misses the point of the novel. To understand the logic of the novel, one should proceed in the opposite direction: rather than trying to discern the repressed passions which do not come out because of the rigidity of the social system and because of the butler's all too impeccable service, it would be better to begin by taking the ritual and institution seriously and then determine the place which love has in it.

How should one understand the title of the novel? There are a number of explanations that are hinted at in the novel. 'The remains of the day' might simply be the memories Stevens records in his diary every evening of his journey. Or it could be that both protagonists of the novel are already in their later years, so the 'remains' are the few years they still have of life. However, if we take the analogy between remains of the day and the Freudian 'day's residues', a more interesting explanation can be given. In Freud's theory of dreams, 'day's residues' are the events, the residues of the previous day, that acquire a new meaning in dreams because of the unconscious structure in which they get embedded. By reading Stevens's memories with the help of this Freudian concept, it can be said that the remains of the day concern primarily the memory of his relationship with Miss Kenton. In the memories that Stevens cherishes the most, he and Miss Kenton used to meet every evening in their private quarters for a cocoa and to discuss the events of the day. These meetings were 'the remains of the day' which in Stevens's memories function as residues that he cannot incorporate into the perfect construction of his obsessional style of life. Stevens's relationship with Miss Kenton is therefore the residue around which his unconscious braids, the residue that forces him to confront his desire.

Lacan characterizes the obsessional as one who installs himself in the place of the Other from where he then acts in such a way that he prevents any risk of encountering his desire. That is why they invent a number of rituals, self-imposed rules, and organize their life in a compulsive way. The obsessional also constantly delays decisions in order to escape the risk and to avoid the uncertainty that pertains to the desire of the Other, the symbolic order as well as the concrete other, the opposite sex.

Stevens never admits to himself that he is taking the trip because he wishes to meet Miss Kenton. He finds an excuse for the trip in the lack of the servants in the house and in the possibility that he might solve his staff plan by convincing Miss Kenton to return to the house.

> You may be amazed that such an obvious shortcoming to a staff plan should have continued to escape my notice, but then you will agree that such is often the way with matters one has given abiding thought to over a period of time; one is not struck by the truth until prompted quite accidentally by some external event. So it was in this instance; that is to say my receiving the letter from Miss Kenton, containing as it did, along with its long, rather unrevealing passages, an unmistakable nostalgia for Darlington Hall, and—I am quite sure of this— distinct hints of her desire to return here, obliged me to see my staff plan afresh. Only then did it strike me that there was indeed a role that a further staff member could crucially play here; that it was, in fact, this very shortage that had been at the heart of all my recent troubles. And the more I considered it, the more obvious it became that Miss Kenton, with her great affection for this house, with her exemplary professionalism—the sort almost impossible to find nowadays— was just the factor needed to enable me to complete a fully satisfactory staff plan for Darlington Hall.[3]

This passage is the most profound example of obsessional discourse. To understand Stevens's 'real' desire, we have to turn each sentence upside down. The obsessional's speech always suggests meaning that desperately tries to cover his desire, or, more precisely, the obsessional speaks and thinks compulsively only to avoid his desire. When Stevens speaks about the need to solve the staff problem or when he detects in Miss Kenton's letter her wish to return to Darlington Hall, he creates excuses that would prevent him from recognizing his own desire. Stevens deposits his desire into the Other: he presents it as the desire of Miss Kenton. The obsessional thus substitutes thought for action and believes that the events in the real are determined by what he thinks. But this omnipotence of thought is linked with a fundamental impotence: 'His actions are impotent because he is incapable of engaging himself in an action where he will be recognized by other people.'[4] Freud observed that with the obsessional the thought process itself becomes sexualized, 'for the pleasure which is normally attached to the content of thought becomes shifted onto the act of thinking itself, and the satisfaction derived from reaching the conclusion of a line of thought is experienced as a sexual satisfaction.'[5] Stevens thus gets sexual satisfaction from the plan to solve the staff problem by taking the trip to visit Miss Kenton, not out of thoughts about Miss Kenton herself.

When Stevens informs his master about his plan to visit Miss Kenton, the master mockingly comments that he did not expect his butler to be still interested in women at his age. This remark touches the core of Stevens's desire and he immediately has to organize a ritual to contradict its implication. His conclusion is that Darlington expects Stevens to exchange banter as part of his professional service. Stevens, of course, fails in this task, so he tries to learn the art of witticism: '. . . I have devised a simple exercise which I try to perform at least once a day; whenever an odd moment presents itself, I attempt to formulate three witticisms based on my immediate surroundings at that moment.'[6] This is a difficult task because it presents the danger of encountering his desire. Stevens knows the danger witticism brings with it, the fact that its effects are uncontrollable, which means a real horror for an obsessional: 'By the very nature of a witticism, one is given very little time to assess its various possible repercussions before one is called to give voice to it, and one gravely risks uttering all manner of unsuitable things if one has not first acquired the necessary skill and experience.'[7]

This avoidance of desire is linked to the profession of butler. The high principles of serving as a butler take, for Stevens, the form of his Ego-Ideal. The most important among them is 'dignity' which concerns the 'butler's ability not to abandon the professional being he inhabits'.[8] While the lesser butler easily abandons his professional being for the private one, the great butler never does this regardless of the situation: 'A butler of any quality must be seen to *inhabit* his role, utterly and fully; he cannot be seen casting it aside one moment simply to do it again the next as though it were nothing more as a pantomime constume.'[9] The butler thus has to put duty first. Jacques-Alain Miller defined the noble as the master who sacrifices his desire to the Ego-Ideal. The Ego-Ideal is the place in the symbolic with which the subject identifies. It is the place from which the subject observes him or herself in the way he or she would like to be seen. For Stevens this place is that of the principles or code of the butler's service, or, more precisely, his dignity. When the subject sacrifices his desire to the ideal, when he completely subordinates himself to symbolic identity and takes on some symbolic mask, it is in this mask that one can discern his desire. So when Stevens totally devotes himself to his profession, gives up his private life, and renounces any sexual contact with women, when he, therefore, unites himself with the Ideal, it is in this Ideal, in this social mask of decency that his desire reveals itself. The ideal which has the meaning of adopting the figure of the Other is also the other of the subject's desire: the traits of the masks of decency, professionalism, and asexuality which form the Ideal are thus co-relative to Stevens's desire. For example, his intended, active ignorance of women can be read as the desire for a woman: 'What the subject dissimulates and by means of which he dissimulates, is also the very form of its disclosure.'[10]

There is nothing behind the mask; it is in the mask, in the veil that seemingly covers the essence of the subject, that we have to search for this essence. In the case of Stevens there is no 'beyond', no suppressed world of passions hidden behind his mask of proper Englishness.[11] It is useless to search in Stevens for some hidden love which could not come out because of the rigid ritual in which he engaged—all of his love is in the rituals. Inasmuch as it can be said that he loves Miss Kenton, he loves her from the perspective of submission to the codes of their profession. Miss Kenton is also a very competent servant, but what actually attracts Stevens to her is her periodical hysterical resistance to the rituals when she suddenly questions the codes, but eventually subordinates herself to them again.

For that reason, it would be a mistake to depict Stevens as the only culprit in the non-realization of the love affair. It is a naïve conclusion to make that Miss Kenton would realize her love towards Stevens if only he had been different, more human. Miss Kenton is an example of the hysteric restrained by her paradoxical desire. On the one hand she wants Stevens to change, to reveal his love for her, but, on the other hand, she loves him only for what he actually is—a bureaucrat who tries by all available means to avoid his desire. If Stevens changed, one could predict that Miss Kenton would quickly abandon him and would have despised him, in the same way she despises her husband.

Miss Kenton develops her first hysterical reaction when a young maid informs her that she is going to marry a fellow servant. The reaction of Miss Kenton to this news is very emotional as she herself identifies with the young woman in her wish to find love. The young servants realize what Miss Kenton would like to happen between her and Stevens. The next hysterical gesture is Miss Kenton's announcement of her intention to marry Mr. Benn. By this act, as she admits at the end of the novel, Miss Kenton intended to provoke a reaction from Stevens. The hysteric always deals with the question: 'What will happen to him, if he loses me?' The paradox of the hysteric's desire is that she wants to have a master, the Other, that she herself can control.

Paradoxically, it could thus be said that it is Miss Kenton who is actually the support of the institution. She is the *desire* of the institution. This is obvious from her relationship with her husband. When her husband abandons the institution she despises him. She herself cannot endure being outside it. At the end of the book she returns to the institution of the family, although giving reasons outside herself—the husband, daughter. Nonetheless, this is her true desire.

The Age of Innocence

At first sight, *The Age of Innocence,* appears to be a novel of unfulfilled romantic love, of the desperate longing of two people deeply in love (Newland and Ellen) who are unable to pursue their happiness because of the rigid society in which they live. Newland is a conformist, a decent member of New York high society, engaged to be married to May, one of the most eligible girls of this same society. By encountering the eccentric Ellen and falling in love with her, Newland discovers that there might be something 'outside' the societal codes to which he so dutifully relates. This 'outside' is presumably the world of pure passions, a world where love reigns unconditionally.

The external constraints of the society codes, and the fact that both lovers are married, produce the conditions for romantic love to develop. Newland himself admits that the image of Ellen in his memory is stronger than the 'real' Ellen. Ellen thus has a special value precisely as absent, inaccessible, as the object of Newland's constant longings. That is why he does not even intend to realize this relationship with her in any sexual form. During one of their emotional encounters, he says:

> Don't be afraid: you needn't squeeze yourself back into your corner like that. A stolen kiss isn't what I want. Look: I'm not even trying to touch the sleeve of your jacket. Don't suppose that I don't understand your reasons for not wanting to let this feeling between us dwindle into an ordinary hole-and-corner love-affair. I couldn't have spoken like this yesterday, because when we've been apart, and I'm looking forward to seeing you, every thought is burnt up in a

great flame. But then you come; and you're so much more than I remembered,
and what I want of you is so much more than an hour or two every now and
then, with wastes of thirsty waiting between, that I can sit perfectly still beside
you, like this, with that other vision in my mind, just quietly trusting to it to
come true.[12]

For romantic love to emerge, one does not need the real person present, what is
necessary is the existence of the image. Lacan first defines love in terms of a narcissistic relationship of the subject: what is at work in falling in love is the recognition of the narcissistic image that forms the substance of the ego ideal. When
we fall in love, we position the person who is the object of our love in the place
of the ideal ego. We love this object because of the perfection which we have
striven to reach for our own ego. However, it is not only that the subject loves in
the other the image it would like to inhabit him or herself. The subject simultaneously posits the object of his or her love in the place of the Ego-Ideal, from
which the subject would like to see him or herself in a likeable way. When we are
in love, the love object placed in the Ego-Ideal enables us to perceive ourselves in
a new way—compassionate, lovable, beautiful, decent. Because of the ideal
invested in the person we love, we feel shame in front of her or him or we try to
fascinate this person.

However, to understand the mechanisms of love, one has to go beyond the
Ideal. Lacan's famous definition of love is that the object gives to the other what
he or she does not have. This object is the traumatic *objet petit a*, the object
cause of desire. Behind the narcissistic relationship towards the love-object we
encounter the Real, the traumatic object in ourselves, as well as in the other:
'Analysis proves that love is in its essence Narcissistic, and reveals the substance
of the presumably—fallaciously—objectal as that which is in the desire its
residue, i.e. its cause: the support of its dissatisfaction, even its impossibility.'[13]

How does the subject relate to the object of his or her desire in romantic
love? Newland wants to escape with Ellen to a place where they would be able
freely to enjoy their love, where they would be 'simply two human beings who
love each other; and nothing else on earth will matter.' Significantly, it is Newland, the conformist, who believes in the possibility of this place of fulfilment
outside institutions, and it is Ellen, the nonconformist half-outcast, who dispels
his illusions when she answers him by saying:

'Oh, my dear—where is that country? Have you ever been there? . . . I know
of so many who've tried to find it; and believe me, they all got out by mistake
at wayside stations; at places like Boulogne, or Pisa, or Monte-Carlo—and it
wasn't at all different from the old world they'd left, but only rather smaller
and dingier and more promiscuous . . . Ah, believe me, it's a miserable little
country! . . .'

'Then what, exactly, is your plan for us?' he asked. 'For *us*? But there is no
us in that sense! We're near each other only if we stay far from each other. Then
we can be ourselves. Otherwise we're only Newland Archer, the husband of
Ellen Olenska's cousin, and Ellen Olenska, the cousin of Newland Archer's wife,
trying to be happy behind the backs of the people who trust them.'

'Ah, I'm beyond that,' he groaned.

'No, you're not! You've never been beyond. And *I* have, and I know what it looks like there.'[14]

It is only at the very end of the novel that this message—and thereby the truth of Newland's desire—is brought home to him. Lacan points out that 'desire is formed as something . . . the demand means beyond whatever it is able to formulate.'[15] On the level of *demand,* Newland's passion could be perceived as his wish to unite with Ellen, however, his *desire* is to renounce this unification: Newland submits himself to the social code in order to maintain Ellen as the inaccessible object that sets his desire in motion. This logic enables us to understand the ending of the novel when Newland, now widowed, during his trip to Paris decides not to see Ellen and thus finally gives up the realization of his great love. When Newland, sitting in front of Ellen's house, tries to imagine what goes on in the apartment, he contemplates:

> 'It's more real to me here than if I went up,' he suddenly heard himself say; and the fear lest that last shadow of reality should lose its edge kept him routed to his seat as the minutes succeeded each other.
>
> He sat for a long time on the bench in the thickening dusk, his eyes never turning from the balcony. At length a light shone through the windows, and a moment later a man-servant came out on the balcony, drew up the awnings, and closed the shutters.
>
> At that, as if it had been the signal he waited for, Newland Archer got up slowly and walked back alone to his hotel.[16]

This last act is an ethical one in the Lacanian sense of 'not giving up on one's desire.' All previous renunciations of the love-affair between Newland and Ellen depended on an 'ethics with the excuse.' Thus we can read Ellen's statement, 'I can't love you unless I give you up,'[17] as the declaration of romantic love and not as an ethical act: love becomes romantic because of the suffering that pertains to it. Similarly, Newland's giving up on Ellen in his youth is still linked to the expectation of a 'future' when he will stop lying to his wife and when the reality (of his love) will get a true form. Only the last renunciation has the meaning of an ethical act because there is no utilitarian demand any more. From a pragmatic point of view, this renunciation is stupid: Newland is celibate, the same goes for Ellen, he still loves her, presumably she is also far from indifferent to him, even Newland's son wishes his father to finally find his great love. Not only are there no social obstacles to their relationship, on the contrary, it is the expectation of Newland's society that a young widower would find a new life companion.

Why did Newland decide not to see Ellen? The answer could be traced in 'the fear lest that last shadow of reality should lose its edge.' Our perception of reality is linked to the fact that something has to be precluded from it: the object as the point of the gaze. Every screen of reality includes a constitutive 'stain', the trace of what had to be precluded from the field of reality in order that this field can acquire its consistency; this stain appears in the guise of a void Lacan names *object petit a*. It is the point that I, the subject, cannot see: it eludes me insofar as it is the point from which the screen itself 'returns the gaze', or watches me, that is, the point where the gaze itself is inscribed into the visual field of reality. For Newland, this object has to stay closed in the room in Paris, for his reality to retain consistency. That is why he can leave the scene, when the man-servant closes the window. This gesture of closing the window is a sign for Newland: a sign that the object is securely precluded so that his reality may remain intact.

Throughout his life, Newland perceived his married life with May as a necessity to which he must submit because of society as well as the 'innocence' and 'purity' of his lovely wife. He thus obeyed society's codes and acted as was expected. At the very end of the novel, there is however another duty he encounters: the recognition that there is no 'other country', that there is no 'beyond' of the codes and rituals that suppressed him throughout his life.

The other person that was aware of there being no 'beyond' is May. After May's death, Newland learns that she knew about his great love for Ellen. However, May responded to this fact in her 'innocent' way: she never revealed her knowledge or made reproaches to Newland, but manipulated the situation with the help of society rules and codes. This recognition of the nonexistence of the 'beyond' of the institutions is what May, paradoxically, has in common with Ellen.

The Big Other in Love

How does it happen that people subordinate themselves to the logic of the institution and obey all kinds of social rituals that are supposedly against their well-being? Althusser points out that individuals in their relation to other individuals function in the mode of transference.[18] Transference is thus the 'stuff' of social relations. But what is transference other than a specific form of love? What then is the function of love as a social bond?

In this writings on psychoanalysis, Althusser refers to Stendhal's *Red and Black*. This novel is an aesthetic discourse composed of a series of utterances, presented in a certain order. This discourse is the very existence of Julien and his 'passions': Julien's passion in its affective violence does not precede the discourse, it is also not something uttered between the lines—his passion is discourse itself: 'The constraints which define this *discourse* are the very existence of this "passion".'[19] The same goes for the discourse of the unconscious: 'the unconscious is structured as language' means that the unconscious is the constraint that is at work in this discourse, this constraint is the very existence of the unconscious— there is no unconscious hidden behind the discursive constraints that 'express' themselves in the discourse.

The effect (of the unconscious, of 'passions') is therefore not exterior to the mechanism that produces the effect: 'The effect is nothing other than the discourse itself.'[20] For each discourse can be said to be defined by a system of specific constraints which function as the law of the language and the effects of this discourse are the products of the constraints. In the case of the unconscious, the constraints that function in this discourse produce the libido as its effect; in the

case of ideological discourse, the constraints produce the effect of recognition/
misrecognition.

Along the same lines, we can say that it is the constraint (of discourse, of the
social symbolic structure) that actually produces love. This institution concerns
what Lacan names 'the big Other'. In his seminar on transference, Lacan pointed
out the role that the big Other plays in love: 'the divine place of the Other' gives
a consecrated nature to the relationship between subjects, as long as the providence of the desire of the loved one inscribes itself in this divine place.[21]

In Lacanian psychoanalysis, the Other is a symbolic structure in which the
subject has always been embedded. This symbolic structure is not a positive
social fact: it is of a quasi-transcendental nature, it forms the very frame structuring our perception of reality; its status is normative, it is a world of symbolic
rules and codes. As such, it also does not belong to the psychic level: it is a radically external, non-psychological universe of symbolic codes regulating our psychic self-experience. It is a mistake either to internalize the big Other and to
reduce it to a psychological fact, or to externalize the big Other and reduce it to
institutions in social reality. By doing this we miss the fact that language is in
itself an institution to which the subject is submitted.

How is love connected to the big Other? There is no love outside speech:
non-speaking beings do not love. As La Rochefoucauld observed, people do not
love if they do not speak about it. Love emerges out of speech as a demand that is
not linked to any need. Love is a demand that constitutes itself as such only
because the subject is the subject of the signifier.[22] As such the subject is split,
barred, marked by a fundamental lack. And it is in this lack that one encounters
the object cause of desire. This object has a paradoxical status: it is what the subject lacks, and at the same time what fills this lack. The enchantment of love is
how the subject deals, on the one hand, with his or her own lack, and, on the
other hand, with the lack in the loved one. As such, love does not call for an
answer, although we usually think so: 'From the times men write about love, it is
clear that they survived far better the longer the beauty remained mute, the
longer she did not answer at all—which provokes the thought that the discourse
on love itself engenders a kind of enjoyment, that it makes the extreme limit at
which speech becomes enjoyment, an enjoyment of the speech itself.'[23]

The fact that love does not expect an answer can be understood as bearing
witness to its imaginary, narcissistic character: any possible answer from the
beloved object would undermine this narcissistic relationship, it would disturb
the mirroring of the subject's ego in the beloved object. In the case of *The
Remains of the Day*, for example, Miss Kenton does not expect Stevens's answer,
she actually escapes from the possible answer. Her act of marriage is a kind of
acting-out that tried to resolve the dilemma of her love for Stevens. However, her
intention was not to hear a confession of Stevens's love for her: for a hysteric the
world collapses if the master loses his sacred place and becomes human.

However, the perception of love as a narcissistic relation loses ground the
moment we take into account that 'love is a demand (although it remains without the answer) that addresses being . . . some being that is inaccessible as long as

it does not answer. Love addresses that point in speech where the word fails. Confronted with his experience, the subject has two solutions at hand: the point at which he no longer has any words, he can either try to encircle or to stuff it with a stopper.[24] What love as a demand targets in the other is therefore the object in him or herself, the Real, non-symbolizable kernel around which the subject organizes his or her desire. What gives to the beloved his dignity, what leads the loving subject to the survalorisation of the beloved, is the presence of the object in him or her:

> ... by being survalorised, it (the object) has the task of saving the dignity of the subject, that is, of making something else out of us than a subject submitted to the endless sliding of the signifier. It makes of us something other from the subject of speech, and exactly this something other is unique, invaluable, irreplaceable, it is the true point at which we can finally mark what I have named the dignity of the subject.[25]

As we have already seen, there are two relations of the subject to this object. On the one hand, we can use the object as the stopper which, by its fascinating and *eblouissante* presence, renders invisible the lack in the Other: such as is the case in the elevation of the object in romantic love. On the other hand, we can deal with the object in the terms of sublimation, of a circulation around the object that never touches its core. Sublimation is not a form of romantic love kept alive by the endless striving for the inaccessible love-object. In sublimation, the subject confronts the horrifying dimension of the object, the object as *das Ding*, the traumatic foreign body in the symbolic structure. Sublimation circles around the object, it is driven by the fact that the object can never be reached because of its impossible, horrifying nature. Whereas romantic love strives to enjoy the Whole of the Other, of the partner, the true sublime love renounces, since it is well aware that we can 'only enjoy a part of the body of the Other . . . That is why we are limited in this to a little contact, to touch only the forearm or whatever else—ouch!'[26]

Such a sublimation is well exemplified in Jane Campion's film *The Piano*. What I have in mind here is not only the slow advance of the two lovers to the sexual act, their endless foreplay in which the body of the other is accessible only part by part and never as a whole (the little piece of skin that can be reached through the hole in Holly Hunter's stocking, for example), but the contractual relationship that exists between the characters played by Harvey Keitel and Holly Hunter. The two make a deal under which she can earn back her piano by allowing Keitel to touch her. This contract is so specified that is even defines how many piano-keys are worth a certain touch. The miracle is that out of this subordination to the sexual contract the most passionate and sublime love emerges.

A similar development is at work in Pedor Almodovar's film *Atame (Tie me Up, Tie me Down)*, in which the kidnapper ties the actress but never sexually abuses her: their daily ritual unexpectedly produces love—the actress falls in love with her kidnapper and even plans to marry him. Here, the partial discovery of the body of the loved one goes on through the act of tying: when the kidnapper carefully chooses the appropriate tie or when he buys masking tape that allows the woman to breathe, by doing this he discovers her body (part by part). The kidnapper does not do what might be expected, he does not take the woman by force, he does not try to take her by 'whole'. Through the ritual of tying he remains all the time distanced and thus he inflames her desire for him.

This, then, is the supreme paradox of love and the institution: the true sublime love can only emerge against the background of an external, contractual, symbolic exchange mediated by the institution. Love is not only the guise for the impossibility of relationship with other fellow beings, but the dissimulation which covers the subject's own radical lack. Freud's motto: 'love for oneself knows only one barrier—love for others, love for objects,' can thus be paraphrased into: 'love for others knows only one barrier—love for oneself, love for the object in oneself.'

Notes

1. Sigmund Freud, *Sexuality and the Psychology of Love,* Macmillan, New York, 1963, p. 57.
2. Louis Althusser, *Lenin and Philosophy and Other Essays,* trans. Ben Brewster, Monthly Review Press, New York, 1971, p. 136.
3. Kazuo Ishiguro, *The Remains of the Day,* Faber and Faber, London, p. 9–10.
4. Stuart Schneiderman, *Rat Man,* New York University Press, New York. 1986, p. 35.
5. Sigmund Freud, *Standard Edition,* Volume X, p. 245.
6. Ishiguro, *op. cit.,* p. 131
7. *Ibid.*
8. *Ibid.,* p. 42.
9. *Ibid.,* p. 169.
10. Jacques-Alain Miller, 'Sur le Gide de Lacan', *Le Cause freudienne: Revue de Psychanalyse* 25, p. 37.
11. Significantly, Stevens points out that butlers only truly exist in England. "Continentals are unable to be butlers because they are as a breed incapable of the emotional restraint which only the English race are capable of.' Ishiguro, *op. cit.,* p. 43.
12. Edith Wharton, *The Age of Innocence,* Macmillan, New York, 1986, p. 289.
13. Jacques Lacan, *Le Séminair, livre XX: Encore,* Editions du Seuil, Paris, 1975, p. 12.
14. Wharton, *op. cit.,* pp. 290–291.
15. Jacques Lacan, *The Ethics of Psychoanalysis* (1959–60), trans. Dennis Porter, Routledge, London, 1992, p. 294.
16. Wharton, *op. cit.,* p. 362.
17. *Ibid.,* p. 172.
18. Louis Althusser, *Ecrits sur la psychanalyse: Freud et Lacan,* Stock/Imec, Paris, 1993, p. 176.
19. *Ibid.,* p. 157.
20. *Ibid.,* p. 158.
21. See Jacques Lacan, *Le seminaire, livre VIII: Le transfert,* Editions du Seuil, Paris, 1991.
22. Jacques Lacan, *Ecrits: A Selection,* trans. Alan Sheridan, Tavistock, London, 1977, p. 270.
23. Michel Silvestre, *Demain le psychanalyse,* Navarin Editeur, Paris, 1987, pp. 300–301.
24. *Ibid.,* p. 301.
25. Jacques Lacan, *Le Séminaire, livre VIII: Le transfert,* Editions du Seuil, Paris, 1991, p. 203.
26. Jacques Lacan, *Le Séminaire, livre XX: Encore,* Editions du Seuil, Paris, 1975, p. 26.

Luce Irigaray (1930–)

Often misunderstood but never ignored, Irigaray is known as one of the most important of the "French feminists." Born in Belgium, she earned her M.A. from the University of Louvain in 1955 and then taught high school in Brussels from 1956 until 1959. She moved to France in the early 1960s and in 1961 received an M.A. in psychology from the University of Paris. One year later, she received a diploma in psychopathology. During the 1960s, Irigaray attended the famous seminars of psychoanalyst Jacques Lacan, later training as and becoming an analyst herself. In 1968, she received a Ph.D. in linguistics, and from 1970 until 1974 she taught at the University of Vincennes. Shortly after the publication of *Speculum of the Other Woman,* a disturbing and subversive look at Western culture, Irigaray was expelled from Lacan's École Freudienne de Paris and from her teaching position at Vincennes. Although she had provoked the wrath of Lacan and other male authorities, Irigaray was able to find a willing audience for her work in feminist circles. In addition to being invited to give seminars and speak at conferences throughout Europe, Irigaray has been involved in demonstrations for contraception and abortion rights. She is now the director of research at the Centre National de Recherche Scientifique, Paris. One of the foremost contemporary scholars in the fields of feminist thought and linguistics, she is the author of many books, including *This Sex Which Is Not One* (1985), *Elemental Passions* (1992), *Sexes and Genealogies* (1993), *Je, Tu, Nous: Toward a Culture of Difference* (1993), *An Ethics of Sexual Difference* (1993), *Thinking the Difference: For a Peaceful Revolution* (1994), *I Love To You: Sketch of a Possible Felicity in History* (1996), *Democracy Begins Between Two* (2001), and *Between East and West: From Singularity to Community* (2001).

I Love to You

I *love to you* means I maintain a relation of indirection to you.[1] I do not subjugate you or consume you. I respect you (as irreducible). I hail you: in you I hail. I praise you: in you I praise. I give you thanks: to you I give thanks for . . . I bless you for . . . I speak *to* you, not just about something; rather I speak to you, not so much this or that, but rather I tell *to* you.

The "to" is the guarantor of indirection. The "to" prevents the relation of transitivity, bereft of the other's irreducibility and potential reciprocity. The "to" maintains intransitivity between persons, between the interpersonal question, speech or gift: I speak to you, I ask of you, I give to you (and not: I give *you* to another).

The "to" is the sign of non-immediacy, of mediation between us. Thus, it is not: I order you or command you to do some particular thing, which could mean or imply: I prescribe this for you, I subject you to these truths, to this order— whether these amount to a form of labor or to a form of human or divine pleasure. Nor is it: I seduce you to me, the you becoming (what belongs) to me; the "I love to you" becoming "I love (what belongs) to me." Any more than it is: I marry you, in the sense that I am making you my wife or my husband, that is: I take you, I am making you mine. Rather it is: I hope to be attentive to you now and in the future, I ask you if I may stay with you, and I am faithful to you.

The "to" is the site of non-reduction of the person to the object. I love you, I desire you, I take you, I seduce you, I order you, I instruct you, and so on, always risk annihilating the alterity of the other, of transforming him/her into my property, my object, of reducing him/her to what is mine, into mine, meaning what is already a part of my field of existential or material properties.

The "to" is also a barrier against alienating the other's freedom in my subjectivity, my world, my language.

I love to you thus means: I do not take you for a direct object, nor for an indirect object by revolving around you. It is, rather, around myself that I have to revolve in order to maintain the *to you* thanks to the return to me. Not with my prey—you become mine—but with the intention of respecting my nature, my history, my intentionality, while also respecting yours. Hence, I do not return to me by way of: I wonder if I am loved. That would result from an introverted intentionality, going toward the other so as to return ruminating, sadly and endlessly, over solipsistic questions in a sort of cultural cannibalism.

The "to" is the guarantor of two intentionalities: mine and yours. In you I love that which can correspond to my own intentionality and to yours.

It could be that what I love in you—"to you"—is not consciously willed by you and escapes your intentions: a certain mannerism, a particular expression, a feature of your body, your sensibility. We have to see if we can build a *we* on the basis of what, of *you*, is thus compatible with my intentions but escapes your own (less conscious as it may be for you). On the basis of this *to you*—more a property of yours than an intention, assuming this distinction holds—can we construct a temporality?

The problem of *we* is that of meeting which occurs through fortune, good fortune, as it were (a *kairos?*), or partly that of a coincidence whose necessity escapes us, but it is also or especially that of constituting a temporality: together, with, between. All too often, sacramental or juridical commitment and the obligation to reproduce have compensated for this problem: how to construct a temporality between us? How to unite two temporalities, two subjects, in a lasting way?

For making you my property, my possession, my *mine* does not accomplish the alliance between us. This act sacrifices one subjectivity to another. The "to" becomes a possessive, a sign of possession and not of an existential property. But what if it is claimed that man is a possessor who transforms his instincts into laws? In that case, the "to" of possession is no longer bilateral. You are (what belongs) to me, often without any reciprocity. In this mine that you are, you lose the freedom of reciprocity; never mind the fact that the possessor is scarcely available to belong to someone. Active and passive are divided between the possessor and the possessed, the lover and the beloved, for example. With that, we no longer have two subjects in a loving relationship.

The "to" is an attempt to avoid falling back into the horizon of the reduction of the subject to the object, to an item of property.

But how can a subject attach him or herself or be attached to another on a long-term basis? How can we prevent the length of this attachment from being dependent upon the judgment of a God-the-Father or King, upon the decisions of a civil authority, upon a genealogical kind of power or knowledge—whether dictated or elected? And how can the relationship between the lovers be saved from alienation through the family?

It could be that, behind the sacramental or juridical mirages of "Thou art mine," and I am thine, forever, there lies something natural, unresolved, which is projected onto the celestial or the law.

In my view, *I love to you* cannot be temporalized in this fashion: I love to you your natural subsistence, even if this "to" does not imply the sacrifice of the latter. For can what I love turn out to be obedience to a nature?

In our culture, this is still the fate that befalls the definition and condition of women, and those of men, too, insofar as he has to be a citizen whose nature is neutralized, as he also has to be the "head" for human kind (and for woman particularly), as well as the "image" of divinity. All of this is to be expected with the lack of a culture of sexuality.

But am I able to love subjection to a nature, be it animal, human, or divine? Isn't freedom of movement lacking on both sides, a movement that constructs the one and the other and enables a common temporality to be constituted? If I am attentive to your intentionality, to your fidelity to yourself and to its/your becoming, then it is permissible for me to imagine whether there can be anything long-lasting between us, whether our intentionalities can come into accordance.

These intentionalities cannot be reduced to *one*. It is not enough to look ahead in the same direction, as Saint-Exupéry says, or even to ally rather than abolish differences. Man and woman, faithful to their identity, do not have the same intentionality, as they are not of the same gender, and do not occupy the same genealogical position. But they can make commitments to act together according to terms of agreement that render their intentionalities compatible: to build a culture of sexuality together, for example, or to construct a politics of difference.

In realizing our intentionality, each one of us can find support from alliances such as these.

And so: you do not know me, but you know something of my appearance. You can also perceive the directions and dimensions of my intentionality. You cannot know who I am but you can help me to be by perceiving that in me which escapes me, my fidelity or infidelity to myself. In this way you can help me get away from inertia, tautology, repetition, or even from errancy, from error. You can help me become while remaining myself.

Nothing here, then, suggests marriage through a contract that snatches me away from one family to chain to another, nothing subjects me like a disciple to a master, nothing takes away my virginity, or halts my becoming within submission to another (supported by an Other or the State); nor is there anything to force my nature to reproduce. What we are dealing with, rather, is a new stage in my existence, one enabling me to accomplish my gender in a specific identity, related to my history and to a period of History.

For the generic universal is not transhistorical. It is to be hoped that it will be realized progressively, and by extension, that this occurs throughout the world. It is now possible for the culture of sexual difference to spread throughout different peoples and traditions. Such an extension should be accompanied by (qualitative) progress, by a progressive distancing from animality and from the subjection of sexuality to reproduction or pornography.

This progress needs language. Not just the language of information, as I have suggested, but the language of communication, too. What we particularly need is a syntax of communication. For communication amounts to establishing links, and that is a matter for syntax.

Thus: how am I to speak to you? And: how am I to listen to you?

_____

Note

1. See note 3, p. 102 (Tr.)

_____

Questions to Consider

1. How might the acts of rereading (as suggested by Barthes via Johnson) and rewriting (as suggested by Irigaray in her discussion of the language of love) help build better interpersonal relationships, especially those that operate within the fields of desire and sexuality? Can you think of words, phrases, types of questions, or statements used in everyday conversation that cause problems in your own interpersonal relationships? If you were to revise your way of listening and speaking to others, would that lead to a revision of your interpersonal relationships?

2. If you were to use Barthes's notion of an erotics of reading, how would you rate the erotic value of the essays that appear in this section? Are some more erotic than others? How would you go about locating the erotic elements and effects, or lack thereof, in a text?

3. In our society, many arguments have arisen over the definition of terms such as "erotic" and "pornographic." Is there a difference between the two? If so, how might you articulate the difference? Would the works of Sade and Masoch be categorized as erotic? as pornographic? Why? Is the perverse literary artist more capable of erotic writing than the "normal" artist, as Clavreul argues?

4. Would Sedgwick argue that masochism and sadism have a social and political basis as well as a sexual one? Would Irigaray see masochism and sadism as transitive acts?

5. Salecl speaks of prohibition as creating desire, not inhibiting it. If love arises at the very site of its impossibility, what implications does this phenomenon have for the institution of marriage as it is practiced in our culture? How do you think Salecl would answer the question posed by her title, "Love: Providence or Despair"? How would you answer the question? Can you think of films set in contemporary times that would support or refute Salecl's argument?

6. It could be argued that Deleuze uses Barthes's concept of "difference within" to interrogate the concept of sadomasochism, a deconstructive move that allows him to split up something that has generally been understood as a unity. Are there other things considered unified or, at the very least, complementary that might benefit from separation or detachment? For example, would conceptualizing desire, love, and sexual identity not as totalizing unities, but as having differences within, assist us in understanding and coping with the ambivalence we experience vis-à-vis desire, love, and sex?

VIII

IDENTITY AND
SPIRITUALITY

To explore the links between identity and spirituality, this section's selections take you on a madcap journey through ancient Greece, Israel, and Egypt; medieval Europe; and contemporary America. Along the way, you'll read of things as disparate as pigeon gonads, automatons, paranoia, the sexless society, lesbians and runaway slaves, the cult of relics, levitating mystics, embryology and resurrection, the sub-body and the super-body, gods incognito and gods in drag, U.S. presidents and Christ figures, civil religion and civil war. What possible connection could there be, you might ask, between pigeon gonads and civil war? To answer this question, you will need to read each essay carefully so that you can locate the points of intersection. However, before you begin the reading and synthesizing process, you might want to brainstorm for a moment about the two terms "identity" and "spirituality" and see what connections immediately come to mind.

If you look up the word "identity" in Webster's dictionary, what you will find might surprise you: there is a contradiction. In one breath, identity is defined as "the condition or fact of being some specific person or thing, or individuality," while in the next breath it is defined as "the condition of being the same as someone or something assumed, described, or claimed." What this definition suggests is both difference from and sameness as. Identity, then, operates in much the same way the uncanny does, for the uncanny is something that is at once unfamiliar and familiar, different and same. In Freud's discussion of the uncanny, we find him stating that "among its different shades of meaning the word '*heimlich*' exhibits one which is identical with its opposite, '*unheimlich*'. What is *heimlich* . . . comes to be *unheimlich* . . . Thus *heimlich* is a word the meaning of which develops in the direction of ambivalence, until it finally coincides with its opposite, *unheimlich*" (224, 226). With the uncanny, then, we begin to find a possible link between identity and spirituality, for, like the uncanny, which is defined as something preternatural or even supernatural, the spiritual realm is often associated with miracles and wonders, things that cannot be seen or touched, things that operate and have their being outside the sensual, corporeal realm. In the Christian tradition, for example, we have the uncanny notion of the Trinity: God is at once Father, Son, and Holy Ghost. He is three in one, different from and same as, divine and human. We also see a link between identity and spirituality when we consider the names given to certain religions—Christianity and Buddhism, for example—that show the bodily identity of the master or teacher merging with the body of spiritual thought espoused. Or in the case of Taoism, there is a conflation of the master with the book of his teachings, both of which are referred to as Lao Tzu.

Questions of who or what we are always impinge on questions of how and why: How did we get here? Who or what made us? And why are we here? Can we know who or what we are without knowing how or why we were created? The sheer complexity and immensity of the universe—the red giants, white dwarfs, black holes, nebulae, the crazy tilt of Uranus, the extreme temperatures of Pluto—can give us pause. How did it all begin? When we try to answer this question, we find ourselves arguing endlessly about the big bang theory, evolution, and creationism. Clearly, what we believe regarding the force or forces that created us says a good deal about how we identify ourselves both culturally and personally.

Words such as "spirit" and "soul," which suggest the spiritual realm, are also used to talk about personality or character, both of which are intimately connected to identity. "He's got soul," we say, meaning that he has passion or deep feeling. Or to suggest pluck or fortitude, we say, "She's got spirit." We have hundreds of labels for ourselves and others, each of which suggests something about personality or character (identity) but also moral or ethical concerns (spirituality): bad girls and good old boys, fence-sitters and bridge builders, ne'er-do-wells and Goody Two-Shoes, troublemakers and tattletales, busy-bodies and bimbos, windbags and blowhards, double-crossers and two-timers, eggheads and good eggs, time bombs and tomboys, hotheads and pinheads, bad apples and snakes in the grass, Pollyannas and prima donnas, wimps and wet blankets, and the list goes on.

Perhaps an everyday object such as the mirror cannot tell us whether we are a bad apple or a snake in the grass, but it does suggest an intersection between identity and spirituality. At the most basic level, we have two important signs or markers of identity: name and body. The two things that always appear on a passport or a driver's license are our name and a photograph of our face. Like the photograph, the mirror allows us a glimpse of our visual image; it allows us to identify ourselves as a person with a certain set of features or physical characteristics. To exist is to have a mirror image and a shadow, neither of which the undead creatures of myth and legend have and both of which have given rise to speculations concerning the spiritual realm. The vampire, who is said to be soulless, has no mirror image. The mirror registers us as living beings, and, by holding it close to the mouth, we can even use it to determine whether an unconscious body still breathes. The mirror, then, is associated with the breath of life, the qi, the life force, our very essence.

It is with the mirror, then, that we take up our first selection, Jacques Lacan's "The Mirror Stage," which was published in 1949. In this brief but very dense essay, Lacan begins his discussion of the child's formation of identity with an attack on the concept of the cogito, which assumes a coincidence between thinking and being: "I think, therefore I am," said René Descartes. The concept of the cogito suggests that we are who we think ourselves to be; that there's an easy, one-to-one correspondence between the realms of being and thought; and that the coincidence between the two is a manifestation of reality. According to Lacan, however, what the concept of the cogito, and rationalism in general, fails to take into account is the fact that identity is based not on reality but on an illusion, a fiction, a mirror image with which we do not and can never truly coincide, for we cannot recognize ourselves at the same time that we are being ourselves. Because of this lack of coincidence, the mirror image immediately introduces us to the dimension of castration or alienation. In other words, at the very heart of our identity, there is a gap, fault line, or split: we are both self (a material body) and other (a mirror image), the two of which never quite match up.

It is during the mirror stage, which represents our first encounter with our own likeness, that the still-dependent child comes to recognize itself in its mirror image. What the child sees is a "whole" being, one whose limbs are unified or connected and work in tandem. This sight produces a moment of joyful recognition: "Hey, there I am! That's me!" But on the heels of this jubilation comes the disappointing realization that the child's lived experience of the body, an experience of fragmentation and lack of coordination, is radically different from its specular or mirror image. This disappointment gives rise to frustration and aggression because the image in the mirror is seen as far superior to, and thus more capable or more "together" than, the child itself.

From the very start, then, the child's identification with its mirror image structures the child as a rival with itself. The mirror stage situates the ego as a site of opposition, where self and other are always in conflict. For the ego, only two possibilities exist: to annihilate or to be annihilated. Even popular songs suggest the conflictual space of the ego, for as recording artist Pete Yorn sings, "Two is a crowd."

It is, however, this very split between the child and its image that allows the child to become inserted into the world, that connects the child's "I" to socially constructed situations. Without this split, there would be no lack and hence no desire, desire being set in motion at the moment the child takes on an image. Because the child is alienated from itself, it must seek validation or recognition from others. In other words, what we believe ourselves to be missing is something we believe can be found in another person. "You complete me," we say. Unfortunately, this, too, is a fiction, for just as the self is lacking, so, too, is the other. Because the thing we lack was never ours in the first place, searching for it either within or outside of ourselves is a lost cause. Thus, says Lacan, our "real journey" can begin only after psychoanalysis has made us aware of the "knot of imaginary servitude" at the core of our identity. If psychoanalysis can make us aware of the knot, however, the job of untying or severing it belongs to love—not desire, but love. Although the concept of love remains undefined or unexplored in this essay, its mere mention surely points us once again in the direction of the spiritual.

Love is never mentioned in Monique Wittig's "One Is Not Born a Woman," published in 1981, but questions of identity are central to her argument. While Lacan focuses on the formation of self-image, ego, and "I," Wittig focuses on the formation of gender. Wittig does not speak of a "real journey," but if she were to use that phraseology, she might say our real journey must begin with the recognition that men and women are different not because of biology, but because of ideology. If Lacan's project is to expose the fiction upon which our identity is based, Wittig's project is to expose the fiction that identifies men and women as "natural" groups. Her project is to show that women are a "class," a political and economic category, not an eternal one. Her argument is that when we naturalize history by giving biological explanations for the divisions that exist between men and women, we make any possibility of change impossible.

For Wittig, both our bodies and our minds are products of ideological manipulation, and thus, like the mirror image Lacan speaks of, the image held up for women is one with which they are compelled to identify, even if that image does not mesh with their lived experiences. Here, you might think of the television or movie screen as a kind of mirror that provides images for women and men to model themselves after, frequently to the detriment of one or both sexes. And just as aggression is produced by the binarism of the Imaginary, that realm in which self and other are pitted against each other, aggression is produced by the binarism of heterosexuality. Like self and other, men and women are structured as rivals, pitted against each other in a fight if not to the death, then at least for the disempowerment of the other.

Although identifying women as a class is an important gesture for Wittig, this is not her terminating point. According to Wittig, we must recognize our status before we can work to change it, and change is certainly what she advocates. The goal for Wittig is to create a sexless society by destroying the concept of "woman"—not women as individual people, but woman as myth. In her view, "what makes a woman is a specific social relation to a man, a relation that we have previously called servitude . . . ." To destroy this relation of servitude, Wittig argues, we must destroy heterosexuality as a social system, since it "is based on the oppression of women by men" and "produces the doctrine of difference between the sexes to justify this oppression." Clearly, Wittig's agenda is more political than spiritual, and yet she nevertheless insists upon the importance of understanding ourselves not just as isolated individuals but as part of something larger: the fight to eliminate oppression.

You may find Wittig's ideas startling and what she advocates unsettling or even distressing, for our culture is heavily invested in, and certainly accustomed to, thinking in terms of two groups of sexed beings: men and women. When you read Caroline Walker Bynum's "The Female Body and Religious Practice in the

Later Middle Ages," however, you may find that our contemporary understanding of categories such as "man" and "woman" is rather different from that of the Middle Ages. Just as Wittig argues that men and women are classes, not natural and eternal groups, Bynum argues that the body itself may have a history and that the body, particularly the female body, "seems to have begun to behave in new ways at a particular moment in the European past." Like Wittig, Bynum is hesitant to assign biological explanations for differences in men's and women's bodily experiences, for, as she argues, "biology and culture are almost impossible to distinguish in these matters, because men and women differ from each other consistently across societies in their social and psychological as well as their physiological experiences."

What Bynum finds noteworthy, however, is not so much the difference between men and women in the later Middle Ages but the medieval tendency to violate boundaries that contemporary Western culture considers inviolable, such as those between male and female, the spiritual and the physical, self and matter. If we carefully examine the medieval scientific tradition, says Bynum, it is not even clear that two sexes were thought to exist, for men and women were seen as having the same sex organs, one merely an inversion of the other. According to Bynum, "medieval thinkers used gender imagery fluidly, not literally." And thus we have medieval theologians and natural philosophers mixing and fusing the genders to such a profound degree that men are said to menstruate, Christ is called "mother" and shown suckling sinners at his breast, and the pain Christ suffers on the cross is described as birth pangs.

These days, we may be quite dualistic in our thinking, but dualism did not play the central role in medieval thinking with which it is often credited. Unlike Platonism, which views a person as a soul held captive in a body, medieval theology saw people as body *and* soul, a psychosomatic unity, and thus medieval spirituality was extraordinarily bodily. We can see evidence of the emphasis placed on the body as a sacred site in a number of medieval practices, some of which would be found repulsive or even sacrilegious by members of religious communities today: (1) the cult of relics; (2) acts of healing such as spitting or blowing into the mouths of the sick, kissing lepers, drinking or bathing in the lice-ridden bath water of would-be saints, and eating the pus that oozed from sick bodies; (3) the manipulation of one's body for religious purposes, such as driving knives or nails into one's flesh in order to identify with the pain Christ suffered on the cross; and (4) the reverence not only for Christ's body as a unified whole (he is, after all said to be God incarnate), but also for specific members of Christ's body such as the penis and foreskin. For example, Catherine of Siena claimed to have married Christ with a ring made of his circumcised flesh, while Agnes Blannbekin had a vision in which she received Christ's foreskin in her mouth like a communion wafer.

While the contemporary world tends to keep theology and science separate, medieval scholastic treatises often combined the two. Bynum reports that "a number of major theologians of the thirteenth century wrote both on embryology and on the resurrection of the body, and explicitly stated that there was a connection between the topics, for both bore on the question of the nature and identity of the human person." For the medieval world, attempts to understand the human body were also attempts to understand the sacred or the divine. Interestingly, in Jean-Pierre Vernant's "Dim Body, Dazzling Body," published in 1989, we see a similar concern with the body during the archaic Greek period. If the medieval world conceptualized the human as a tightly knit unit of body and soul, the Greeks of the archaic period did not even acknowledge a distinction between body and soul. For them, there was no radical break between the natural and the supernatural; in other words, human corporeality included "organic realities, vital forces, psychic activities, [and] divine inspiration or influxes."

"The body of the gods" may be an expression that poses a problem for us, says Vernant, but he suggests posing the problem otherwise, that is, positing the body not as a fact of nature or a constant and universal reality, but as an historical category "steeped in imagination." Posing the problem in this way puts Vernant's conception of the body very much in line with that proposed by Wittig and Bynum, who speak not of biology but of ideology, culture, and history. The question at the heart of Vernant's essay, then, is, What was the body for the Greeks? To answer this question, Vernant defines the function it assumes and the form it takes, a definition achieved, in part, through his examination of the ancient Greek language and the literature of Homer and Hesiod. What he finds in his examination is that no single word exists which represents the body as an organic unity. In fact, the word "soma," which we now think of as representing body at least in its material sense, originally meant "corpse." This plethora of words—none of which captures our contemporary sense of body as a scientific object defined in anatomical or physiological terms—suggests to Vernant that the body was understood by the ancient Greeks not as singular, but as plural: the body as a network of multiple relations to self, others, and the divine.

Vernant also finds that, for the Greeks, the tragedy of existence is not having a soul trapped in a body, but having a body that is not fully one. In other words, the human body is thought of as a sub-body because of its impermanent and fleeting nature, while the divine body is thought of as a super-body because of its permanence or immortality. For humans, blood suggests life, but it can also suggest death when it gushes from a wound. The gods, too, are said to bleed, and yet their wounds are never fatal. Is their immortal blood really blood? Or are the gods bloodless? And what of food? Humans must eat in order to replenish the body's energy, but the gods' bodies are never in need of nourishment. Given these differences between humans and gods, it would seem that the Greeks' traditional religious system would have taken the final rupturing step that severs the divine and the corporeal, but, according to Vernant, this does not happen. The gods' super-body touches upon the non-body, but it never merges with it.

In moving from Vernant's discussion to Robert Bellah's, we move from ancient Greece to contemporary America, and yet the terrain is not so different as it might appear, for what each author is talking about is the human connection to the divine, which the ancient Greeks work out through an articulation of the body and contemporary Americans examine through civil religion. Although Bellah's "Civil Religion in America" was first published in 1969, it reappeared in 1990 as part of a larger collection called *Culture and Society: Contemporary*

Debates, edited by Jeffrey C. Alexander and Steven Seidman. Its return after 21 years suggests that Bellah's final question suddenly became very pertinent as we entered the last decade of the twentieth century. If, as Bellah argues, America has what can be called a civil religion, a term first coined by Rousseau, and if the Judeo-Christian God has played a central role in that religion, what happens when the meaning or significance of that God changes? From the first days of the Puritan settlers, Americans have thought of themselves as God's chosen people, the flight from the Old Country, which culminated in the Revolutionary War, representing the great exodus out of Egypt. As Bellah points out, this kind of thinking can lead to positive change, and he uses the civil rights movement as an example, but it can also lead to arrogance, jingoism, colonialism, and, in colonialism's transformed state, imperialism. It's almost as if Bellah himself takes on a prophetic role when he says, "If the whole God symbolism requires reformulation, there will be obvious consequences for the civil religion, consequences perhaps of liberal alienation and of fundamentalist ossification." One of the questions we might ask ourselves is whether this prophecy has indeed come true.

Jacques Lacan (1901–1981)

The name Lacan has become synonymous with psychoanalysis. No one serious about the study of psychoanalysis can ignore the profound and thoroughgoing influence Lacan has had on the field, both as a clinician and as a theoretician. Known as the French Freud because of his return to the discoveries and lifelong study of Freud, Lacan is reported to have said to the members of his seminar, "You may call yourselves 'Lacanians,' but, as for me, I'm a Freudian." As biographer Elisabeth Roudinesco says of Lacan, he "was a kind of antihero, not at all cut out for a normal life, destined to eccentricity and incapable of knuckling under to the countless commonplace rules of behavior—hence his excessive interest in the discourse of madness, as the only key to understanding a crazy world" (71). If this description is accurate, which it may well be, as Roudinesco was part of Lacan's inner circle and thus knew him well, it would go a long way toward explaining the continual conflicts Lacan had with the European psychoanalytic community. In 1938, he became a member of the Société Psychanalytique de Paris (SPA), the official French branch of the International Psycho-Analytical Society (IPA), founded by Freud in 1910. By 1953, Lacan was president of the SPA, but when he was told to regularize his practice—he saw patients for variable lengths of time instead of the usual 50-minute period—he resigned and joined the newer Société Française de Psychanalyse (SFP). In 1963, the SFP was told that it could join the IPA if Lacan were banned. Unwilling to change his unorthodox teaching and clinical practices, Lacan decided to create his own school, L'École Freudienne de Paris. In 1966, when Lacan published his legendary 900-page collection of essays and conference papers, *Écrits* (*Writings*), it was an immediate hit, and crowds began flocking to his weekly seminars. In Lacan's final years, new controversies erupted within L'École Freudienne de Paris so ferocious that Lacan finally dissolved the school and set up yet a new one, "La Cause Freudienne," and this just one year before his death from cancer. Although much translation work remains to be done, some of the annual seminars of Lacan that have been translated into English are Book 1, *Freud's Papers on Technique, 1953–54* (1988); Book 2, *The Ego in Freud's Theory and in the Technique of Psychoanalysis, 1954–55* (1988); Book 3, *The Psychoses, 1955–56* (1993); Book 7, *The Ethics of Psychoanalysis, 1959–60* (1992); *The Four Fundamental Concepts of Psycho-Analysis* (1977); and Book 20, *On Feminine Sexuality: The Limits of Love and Knowledge, 1972–73* (1998).

The Mirror Stage as Formative of the Function of the I as Revealed in Psychoanalytic Experience

Delivered at the 16th International Congress of Psychoanalysis, Zürich, July 17, 1949

The conception of the mirror stage that I introduced at our last congress, thirteen years ago, has since become more or less established in the practice of the French group. However, I think it worthwhile to bring it again to your attention, especially today, for the light it sheds on the formation of the *I* as we experience it in psychoanalysis. It is an experience that leads us to oppose any philosophy directly issuing from the *Cogito*.

Some of you may recall that this conception originated in a feature of human behaviour illuminated by a fact of comparative psychology. The child, at an age when he is for a time, however short, outdone by the chimpanzee in instrumental intelligence, can nevertheless already recognize as such his own image in a mirror. This recognition is indicated in the illuminative mimicry of the *Aha-Erlebnis*, which Köhler sees as the expression of situational apperception, an essential stage of the act of intelligence.

This act, far from exhausting itself, as in the case of the monkey, once the image has been mastered and found empty, immediately rebounds in the case of the child in a series of gestures in which he experiences in play the relation between the movements assumed in the image and the play the relation between the movements assumed in the image and the reflected environment, and between this virtual complex and the reality it reduplicates—the child's own body, and the persons and things, around him.

This event can take place, as we have known since Baldwin, from the age of six months, and its repetition has often made me reflect upon the startling spectacle of the infant in front of the mirror. Unable as yet to walk, or even to stand up, and held tightly as he is by some support, human or artificial (what, in France, we call a '*trotte-bébé*'), he nevertheless overcomes, in a flutter of jubilant activity, the obstructions of his support and, fixing his attitude in a slightly leaning-forward position, in order to hold it in his gaze, brings back an instantaneous aspect of the image.

For me, this activity retains the meaning I have given it up to the age of eighteen months. This meaning discloses a libidinal dynamism, which has hitherto remained problematic, as well as an ontological structure of the human world that accords with my reflections on paranoiac knowledge.

We have only to understand the mirror stage *as an identification,* in the full sense that analysis gives to the term: namely, the transformation that takes place in the subject when he assumes an image—whose predestination to this phase-effect is sufficiently indicated by the use, in analytic theory, of the ancient term *imago.*

This jubilant assumption of his specular image by the child at the *infans* stage, still sunk in his motor incapacity and nursling dependence, would seem to exhibit in an exemplary situation the symbolic matrix in which the *I* is precipitated in a primordial from, before it is objectified in the dialectic of identification with the other, and before language restores to it, in the universal, its function as subject.

This form would have to be called the Ideal-I,[1] if we wished to incorporate it into our usual register, in the sense that it will also be the source of secondary identifications, under which term I would place the functions of libidinal normalization. But the important point is that this form situates the agency of the ego, before its social determination, in a fictional direction, which will always remain irreducible for the individual alone, or rather, which will only rejoin the coming-into-being (*le devenir*) of the subject asymptotically, whatever the success of the dialectical syntheses by which he must resolve as *I* his discordance with his own reality.

The fact is that the total form of the body by which the subject anticipates in a mirage the maturation of his power is given to him only as *Gestalt,* that is to say, in an exteriority in which this form is certainly more constituent than constituted, but in which it appears to him above all in a contrasting size (*un relief de stature*) that fixes it and in a symmetry that inverts it, in contrast with the turbulent movements that the subject feels are animating him. Thus, this *Gestalt*—whose pregnancy should be regarded as bound up with the species, though its motor style remains scarcely recognizable—by these two aspects of its appearance, symbolizes the mental permanence of the *I,* at the same time as it prefigures its alienating destination; it is still pregnant with the correspondences that unite the *I* with the statue in which man projects himself, with the phantoms that dominate him, or with the automation in which, in an ambiguous relation, the world of his own making tends to find completion.

Indeed, for the *imagos*—whose veiled faces it is our privilege to see in outline in our daily experience and in the penumbra of symbolic efficacity[2]—the mirror-image would seem to be the threshold of the visible world, if we go by the mirror disposition that the *imago of one's own body* presents in hallucinations or dreams, whether it concerns its individual features, or even its infirmities, or its object-projections; or if we observe the role of the mirror apparatus in the appearances of the *double,* in which psychical realities, however heterogeneous, are manifested.

That a *Gestalt* should be capable of formative effects in the organism is attested by a piece of biological experimentation that is itself so alien to the idea of psychical causality that it cannot bring itself to formulate its results in these terms. It nevertheless recognizes that it is a necessary condition for the maturation of the gonad of the female pigeon that it should see another member of its species, of either sex; so sufficient in itself is this condition that the desired effect may be obtained merely by placing the individual within reach of the field of reflection of a mirror. Similarly, in the case of the migratory locust, the transition within a generation from the solitary to the gregarious form can be obtained by exposing the individual, at a certain stage, to the exclusively visual action of a similar image, provided it is animated by movements of a style sufficiently close to that characteristic of the species. Such facts are inscribed in an order of homeomorphic identification that would itself fall within the larger question of the meaning of beauty as both formative and erogenic.

But the facts of mimicry are no less instructive when conceived as cases of heteromorphic identification, in as much as they raise the problem of the signification of space for the living organism—psychological concepts hardly seem less appropriate for shedding light on these matters than ridiculous attempts to reduce them to the supposedly supreme law of adaptation. We have only to recall how Roger Caillois (who was then very young, and still fresh from his breach with the sociological school in which he was trained) illuminated the subject by using the term '*legendary psychasthenia*' to classify morphological mimicry as an obsession with space in its derealizing effect.

I have myself shown in the social dialectic that structures human knowledge as paranoiac[3] why human knowledge has greater autonomy than animal knowledge in relation to the field of force of desire, but also why human knowledge is determined in that 'little reality' (*ce peu de réalité*), which the Surrealists, in their restless way, saw as its limitation. These reflections lead me to recognize in the spatial captation manifested in the mirror-stage, even before the social dialectic, the effect in man of an organic insufficiency in his natural reality—in so far as any meaning can be given to the word 'nature'.

I am led, therefore, to regard the function of the mirror-stage as a particular case of the function of the *imago,* which is to establish a relation between the organism and its reality—or, as they say, between the *Innenwelt* and the *Umwelt.*

In man, however, this relation to nature is altered by a certain dehiscence at the heart of the organism, a primordial Discord betrayed by the signs of uneasiness and motor unco-ordination of the neo-natal months. The objective notion of the anatomical incompleteness of the pyramidal system and likewise the presence of certain humoral residues of the maternal organism confirm the view I have formulated as the fact of a real *specific prematurity of birth* in man.

It is worth noting, incidentally, that this is a fact recognized as such by embryologists, by the term *foetalization,* which determines the prevalence of the so-called superior apparatus of the neurax, and especially of the cortex, which psycho-surgical operations lead us to regard as the intra-organic mirror.

This development is experienced as a temporal dialectic that decisively projects the formation of the individual into history. The *mirror stage* is a drama whose internal thrust is precipitated from insufficiency to anticipation—and which manufactures for the subject, caught up in the lure of spatial identification, the succession of phantasies that extends from a fragmented body-image to a form of its totality that I shall call orthopaedic—and, lastly, to the assumption of the armour of an alienating identity, which will mark with its rigid structure the subject's entire mental development. Thus, to break out of the circle of the *Innenwelt* into the *Umwelt* generates the inexhaustible quadrature of the ego's verifications.

This fragmented body—which term I have also introduced into our system of theoretical references—usually manifests itself in dreams when the movements of the analysis encounters a certain level of aggressive disintegration in the individual. It then appears in the form of disjointed limbs, or of those organs represented in exoscopy, growing wings and taking up arms for intestinal persecutions—the very same that the visionary Hieronymus Bosch has fixed, for all time, in painting, in their ascent from the fifteenth century to the imaginary zenith of modern man. But this form is even tangibly revealed at the organic level, in the lines of 'fragilization' that define the anatomy of phantasy, as exhibited in the schizoid and spasmodic symptoms of hysteria.

Correlatively, the formation of the *I* is symbolized in dreams by a fortress, or a stadium—its inner arena and enclosure, surrounded by marshes and rubbish-tips, dividing it into two opposed fields of contest where the subject flounders in quest of the lofty, remote inner castle whose form (sometimes juxtaposed in the same scenario) symbolizes the id in a quite startling way. Similarly, on the mental plane, we find realized the structures of fortified works, the metaphor of which arises spontaneously, as if issuing from the symptoms themselves, to designate the mechanisms of obsessional neurosis—inversion, isolation, reduplication, cancellation and displacement.

But if we were to build on these subjective givens alone—however little we free them from the condition of experience that makes us see them as partaking of the nature of a linguistic technique—our theoretical attempts would remain exposed to the charge of projecting themselves into the unthinkable of an absolute subject. This is why I have sought in the present hypothesis, grounded in a conjunction of objective data, the guiding grid for a *method of symbolic reduction*.

It establishes in the *defences of the ego* a genetic order, in accordance with the wish formulated by Miss Anna Freud, in the first part of her great work, and situates (as against a frequently expressed prejudice) hysterical repression and its returns at a more archaic stage than obsessional inversion and its isolating processes, and the latter in turn as preliminary to paranoic alienation, which dates from the deflection of the specular *I* into the social *I*.

This moment in which the mirror-stage comes to an end inaugurates, by the identification with the *imago* of the counterpart and the drama of primordial jealousy (so well brought out by the school of Charlotte Bühler in the phenomenon of infantile *transitivism*), the dialectic that will henceforth link the *I* to socially elaborated situations.

It is this moment that decisively tips the whole of human knowledge into mediatization through the desire of the other, constitutes its objects in an abstract equivalence by the co-operation of others, and turns the I into that apparatus for which every instinctual thrust constitutes a danger, even though it should correspond to a natural maturation—the very normalization of this maturation being henceforth dependent, in man, on a cultural mediation as exemplified, in the case of the sexual object, by the Oedipus complex.

In the light of this conception, the term primary narcissism, by which analytic doctrine designates the libidinal investment characteristic of that moment, reveals in those who invented it the most profound awareness of semantic latencies. But it also throws light on the dynamic opposition between this libido and the sexual libido, which the first analysts tried to define when they invoked destructive and, indeed, death instincts, in order to explain the evident connection between the narcissistic libido and the alienating function of the I, the aggressivity it releases in any relation to the other, even in a relation involving the most Samaritan of aid.

In fact, they were encountering that existential negativity whose reality is so vigorously proclaimed by the contemporary philosophy of being and nothingness.

But unfortunately that philosophy grasps negativity only within the limits of a self-sufficiency of consciousness, which, as one of its premises, links to the *méconnaissances* that constitute the ego, the illusion of autonomy to which it entrusts itself. This flight of fancy, for all that it draws, to an unusual extent, on borrowings from psychoanalytic experience, culminates in the pretention of providing an existential psychoanalysis.

At the culmination of the historical effort of a society to refuse to recognize that it has any function other than the utilitarian one, and in the anxiety of the individual confronting the 'concentrational'[4] form of the social bond that seems to arise to crown this effort, existentialism must be judged by the explanations it gives of the subjective impasses that have indeed resulted from it; a freedom that is never more authentic than when it is within the walls of a prison; a demand for commitment, expressing the impotence of a pure consciousness to master any situation; a voyeuristic–sadistic idealization of the sexual relation; a personality that realizes itself only in suicide; a consciousness of the other than can be satisfied only by Hegelian murder.

These propositions are opposed by all our experience, in so far as it teaches us not to regard the ego as centred on the *perception–consciousness system,* or as organized by the 'reality principle'—a principle that is the expression of a scientific prejudice most hostile to the dialectic of knowledge. Our experience shows that we should start instead from the *function of méconnaissance* that characterizes the ego in all its structures, so markedly articulated by Miss Anna Freud. For, if the *Verneinung* represents the patent form of that function, its effects will, for the most part, remain latent, so long as they are not illuminated by some light reflected on to the level of fatality, which is where the id manifests itself.

We can thus understand the inertia characteristic of the formations of the I, and find there the most extensive definition of neurosis—just as the captation of the subject by the situation gives us the most general formula for madness, not only the madness that lies behind the walls of asylums, but also the madness that deafens the world with its sound and fury.

The sufferings of neurosis and psychosis are for us a schooling in the passions of the soul, just as the beam of the psychoanalytic scales, when we calculate the tilt of its threat to entire communities, provides us with an indication of the deadening of the passions in society.

At this junction of nature and culture, so persistently examined by modern anthropology, psychoanalysis alone recognizes this knot of imaginary servitude that love must always undo again, or sever.

For such a task, we place no trust in altruistic feeling, we who lay bare the aggressivity that underlies the activity of the philanthropist, the idealist, the pedagogue, and even the reformer.

In the recourse of subject to subject that we preserve, psychoanalysis may accompany the patient to the ecstatic limit of the 'Thou art that', in which is revealed to him the cipher of his mortal destiny, but it is not in our mere power as practitioners to bring him to that point where the real journey begins.

Notes

1. Throughout this article I leave in its peculiarity the translation I have adopted for Freud's *Ideal-Ich* [i.e., 'je-idéal'], without further comment, other than to say I have not maintained it since.
2. Cf. Claude Lévi-Strauss, *Structural Anthropology*, Chapter X.
3. Cf. 'Aggressivity in Psychoanalysis', p. 8 and *Écrits*, p. 180.
4. *'Concentrationnaire'*, an adjective coined after World War II (this article was written in 1949) to describe the life of the concentration-camp. In the hands of certain writers it became, by extension, applicable to many aspects of 'modern' life [Tr.].

Monique Wittig (1935–2003)

Wittig was born in Germany on the Upper Rhine, but in order to escape the Nazi regime, her parents moved to Alsace, France. She studied Oriental languages, literatures, history, and philosophy at the Sorbonne in Paris, receiving her Ph.D. in 1986. She began her career as a writer long before her academic career was in full swing, however, winning the Prix Medici for her first novel, *The Opoponax* (1964; trans. 1966). Known as a writer and radical lesbian theorist, Wittig espoused political views that were shaped by the left-wing French intellectual milieu of Paris in the 1950s and 1960s. Her political views in turn shaped her writing, her second novel, *Les Guérillères* (1969), growing out of her participation in the May 1968 student–worker uprisings. In the same way that Wittig was unwilling to use standard categories of sex to talk about women and men, her writing shows an unwillingness to operate as one genre or another. She may be better known for her fiction than her theoretical writings, but her work frequently erodes the usual boundaries drawn between literature and theory. Thus, many feminists view her second novel, a book that describes a post-Holocaust world where Amazon fighters attempt to create a new society, as a source of theory about language and women's writing.

Wittig was active in the French women's movement from its beginning, cofounding the Women's Liberation Movement, founding the Féministes Révolutionaires, and participating in a group called the Red Dykes. In 1976, she moved to the United States, where she taught at Berkeley, the University of Southern California, Vassar College, Duke University, New York University, and the University of Arizona. Some of her works include *The Lesbian Body* (1973; trans. 1975); *Across the Acheron* (1985; trans. 1987); *Lesbian Peoples: Material for a Dictionary,* coauthored with Sande Zeig (1976; trans. 1987); and *The Straight Mind and Other Essays,* a collection of essays written mostly in English (1992).

One Is Not Born a Woman

A materialist feminist[1] approach to women's oppression destroys the idea that women are a "natural group": "a racial group of a special kind, a group perceived as *natural,* a group of men considered as materially specific in their bodies."[2] What the analysis accomplishes on the level of ideas, practice makes actual at the level of facts: by its very existence, lesbian society destroys the artificial (social) fact constituting women as a "natural group." A lesbian society[3] pragmatically reveals that the division from men of which women have been the object is a political one and shows that we have been ideologically rebuilt into a "natural group." In the case of women, ideology goes far since our bodies as well as our minds are the product of this manipulation. We have been compelled in our bodies and in our minds to correspond, feature by feature, with the *idea* of nature that has been established for us. Distorted to such an extent that our deformed body is what they call "natural," what is supposed to exist as such before oppression. Distorted to such an extent that in the end oppression seems to be a consequence of this "nature" within ourselves (a nature which is only an *idea*). What a materialist analysis does by reasoning, a lesbian society accomplishes practically: not only is there no natural group "women" (we lesbians are living proof of it), but as individuals as well we question "woman," which for us, as for Simone de Beauvoir, is only a myth. She said: "One is not born, but becomes a woman. No biological, psychological, or economic fate determines the figure that the human female presents in society: it is civilization as a whole that produces this creature, intermediate between male and eunuch, which is described as feminine."[4]

However, most of the feminists and lesbian-feminists in America and elsewhere still believe that the basis of women's oppression is *biological as well as* historical. Some of them even claim to find their sources in Simone de Beauvoir.[5] The belief in mother right and in a "prehistory" when women created civilization (because of a biological predisposition) while the coarse and brutal men hunted (because of a biological predisposition) is symmetrical with the biologizing interpretation of history produced up to now by the class of men. It is still the same method of finding in women and men a biological explanation of their division, outside of social facts. For me this could never constitute a lesbian approach to women's oppression, since it assumes that the basis of society or the beginning of society lies in heterosexuality. Matriarchy is no less heterosexual than patriarchy: it is only the sex of the oppressor that changes. Furthermore, not only is this conception still imprisoned in the categories of sex (woman and man), but it holds onto the idea that the capacity to give birth (biology) is what defines a woman. Although practical facts and ways of living contradict this theory in lesbian society, there are lesbians who affirm that "women and men are different species or races (the words are used interchangeably): men are biologically inferior to women; male violence is a biological inevitability . . . "[6] By doing this, by admitting that there is a "natural" division between women and men, we naturalize history, we assume that "men" and "women" have always existed and will always exist. Not only do we naturalize history, but also consequently we naturalize the social phenomena which express our oppression, making change impossible. For example, instead of seeing giving birth as a forced production, we see it as a "natural," "biological" process, forgetting that in our societies births are planned (demography), forgetting that we ourselves are programmed to produce children, while this is the only social activity "short of war"[7] that presents such a great danger of death. Thus, as long as we will be "unable to abandon by will or impulse a lifelong and centuries-old commitment to childbearing as *the* female creative act,"[8] gaining control of the production of children will mean much more than the mere control of the material means of this production: women will have to abstract themselves from the definition "woman" which is imposed upon them.

A materialist feminist approach shows that what we take for the cause or origin of oppression is in fact only the *mark*[9] imposed by the oppressor: the "myth of woman,"[10] plus its material effects and manifestations in the appropriated consciousness and bodies of women. Thus, this mark does not predate oppression: Colette Guillaumin has shown that before the socioeconomic reality of black slavery, the concept of race did not exist, at least not in its modern meaning, since it was applied to the lineage of families. However, now, race, exactly like sex, is taken as an "immediate given," a "sensible given," "physical features," belonging to a natural order. But what we believe to be a physical and direct perception is only a sophisticated and mythic construction, an "imaginary formation,"[11] which reinterprets physical features (in themselves as neutral as any others but marked by the social system) through the network of relationships in which they are perceived. (They are seen as *black,* therefore they *are* black; they are seen as *women,* therefore, they *are* women. But before being *seen* that way, they first had to be *made* that way.) Lesbians should always remember and acknowledge how "unnatural," compelling, totally oppressive, and destructive being "woman" was for us in the old days before the women's liberation movement. It was a political constraint, and those who resisted it were accused of not being "real" women. But then we were proud of it, since in the accusation there was already something like a shadow of victory: the avowal by the oppressor that "woman" is not something that goes without saying, since to be one, one has to be a "real" one. We were at the same time accused of wanting to be men. Today this double accusation has been taken up again with enthusiasm in the context of the women's liberation movement by some feminists and also, alas, by some lesbians whose political goal seems somehow to be becoming more and more "feminine." To refuse to be a woman, however, does not mean that one has to become a man. Besides, if we take as an example the perfect "butch," the classic example which provokes the most horror, whom Proust would have called a woman/man, how is her alienation different from that of someone who wants to become a woman? Tweedledum and Tweedledee. At least for a woman, wanting to become a man proves that she has escaped her initial programming. But even if she would like to, with all her strength, she cannot become a man. For becoming a man would demand from a woman not only a man's external appearance but his consciousness as well, that is, the consciousness of one who disposes by right of at least two "natural" slaves during his life span. This is impossible, and one feature of lesbian oppression consists precisely of making women out of reach for us, since women belong to men. Thus a lesbian *has* to be something else, a not-woman, a not-man, a product of society, not a product of nature, for there is no nature in society.

The refusal to become (or to remain) heterosexual always meant to refuse to become a man or a woman, consciously or not. For a lesbian this goes further than the refusal of the *role* "woman." It is the refusal of the economic, ideological, and political power of a man. This, we lesbians, and nonlesbians as well, knew before the beginning of the lesbian and feminist movement. However, as Andrea Dworkin emphasizes, many lesbians recently "have increasingly tried to transform the very ideology that has enslaved us into a dynamic, religious, psychologically compelling celebration of female biological potential."[12] Thus, some avenues of the feminist and lesbian movement lead us back to the myth of woman which was created by men especially for us, and with it we sink back into a natural group. Having stood up to fight for a sexless society,[13] we now find ourselves entrapped in the familiar deadlock of "woman is wonderful." Simone de Beauvoir underlined particularly the false consciousness which consists of selecting among the features of the myth (that women are different from men) those which look good and using them as a definition for women. What that concept "woman is wonderful" accomplishes is that it retains for defining women the best features (best according to whom?) which oppression has granted us, and it does not radically question the categories "man" and "woman," which are political categories and not natural givens. It puts us in a position of fighting within the class "women" not as the other classes do, for the disappearance of our class, but for the defense of "woman" and its reenforcement. It leads us to develop with complacency "new" theories about our specificity: thus, we call our passivity "nonviolence," when the main and emergent point for us is to fight our passivity (our fear, rather, a justified one). The ambiguity of the term "feminist" sums up the whole situation. What does "feminist" mean? Feminist is formed with the word "femme," "woman," and means: someone who fights for women. For many of us it means someone who fights for women as a class and for the disappearance of this class. For many others it means someone who fights for woman and her defense—for the myth, then, and its reenforcement. But why was the word "feminist" chosen if it retains the least ambiguity? We chose to call ourselves "feminists" ten years ago, not in order to support or reenforce the myth of woman, nor to identify ourselves with the oppressor's definition of us, but rather to affirm that our movement had a history and to emphasize the political link with the old feminist movement.

It is, then, this movement that we can put in question for the meaning that it gave to feminism. It so happens that feminism in the last century could never resolve its contradictions on the subject of nature/culture, woman/society. Women started to fight for themselves as a group and rightly considered that they shared common features as a result of oppression. But for them these features were natural and biological rather than social. They went so far as to adopt the Darwinist theory of evolution. They did not believe like Darwin, however, "that women were less evolved than men, but they did believe that male and female natures had diverged in the course of evolutionary development and that society at large reflected this polarization."[14]

"The failure of early feminism was that it only attacked the Darwinist charge of female inferiority, while accepting the foundations of this charge—namely, the view of woman as 'unique.'"[15] And finally it was women scholars—and not feminists—who scientifically destroyed this theory. But the early feminists had failed to regard history as a dynamic process which develops from conflicts of interests. Furthermore, they still believed as men do that the cause (origin) of their oppression lay within themselves. And therefore after some astonishing victories the feminists of this first front found themselves at an impasse out of a lack of reasons to fight. They upheld the illogical principle of "equality in difference," an idea now being born again. They fell back into the trap which threatens us once again: the myth of woman.

Thus it is our historical task, and only ours, to define what we call oppression in materialist terms, to make it evident that women are a class, which is to say that the category "woman" as well as the category "man" are political and economic categories not eternal ones. Our fight aims to suppress men as a class, not through a genocidal, but a political struggle. Once the class "men" disappears, "women" as a class will disappear as well, for there are no slaves without masters. Our first task, it seems, is to always thoroughly dissociate "women" (the class within which we fight) and "woman," the myth. For "woman" does not exist for us: it is only an imaginary formation, while "women" is the product of a social relationship. We felt this strongly when everywhere we refused to be called a *"woman's* liberation movement." Furthermore, we have to destroy the myth inside and outside ourselves. "Woman" is not each one of us, but the political and ideological formation which negates "women" (the product of a relation of exploitation). "Woman" is there to confuse us, to hide the reality "women." In order to be aware of being a class and to become a class we first have to kill the myth of "woman" including its most seductive aspects (I think about Virginia Woolf when she said the first task of a woman writer is to kill "the angel in the house"). But to become a class we do not have to suppress our individual selves, and since no individual can be reduced to her/his oppression we are also confronted with the historical necessity of constituting ourselves as the individual subjects of our history as well. I believe this is the reason why all these attempts at "new" definitions of woman are blossoming now. What is at stake (and of course not only for women) is an individual definition as well as a class definition. For once one has acknowledged oppression, one needs to know and experience the fact that one can constitute oneself as a subject (as opposed to an object of oppression), that one can become *someone* in spite of oppression, that one has one's own identity. There is no possible fight for someone deprived of an identity, no internal motivation for fighting, since, although I can fight only with others, first I fight for myself.

The question of the individual subject is historically a difficult one for everybody. Marxism, the last avatar of materialism, the science which has politically formed us, does not want to hear anything about a "subject." Marxism has rejected the transcendental subject, the subject as constitutive of knowledge, the "pure" consciousness. All that thinks per se, before all experience, has ended up in the garbage can of history, because it claimed to exist outside matter, prior to matter, and needed God, spirit, or soul to exist in such a way. This is what is called "idealism." As for individuals, they are only the product of social relations, therefore their consciousness can only be "alienated." (Marx, in *The German Ideology,* says precisely that individuals of the dominating class are also alienated, although they are the direct producers of the ideas that alienate the classes oppressed by them. But since they draw visible advantages from their own alienation they can bear it without too much suffering.) There exists such a thing as class consciousness, but a consciousness which does not refer to a particular subject, except as participating in general conditions of exploitation at the same time as the other subjects of their class, all sharing the same consciousness. As for the practical class problems—outside of the class problems as traditionally defined—that one could encounter (for example, sexual problems), they were considered "bourgeois" problems that would disappear with the final victory of the class struggle. "Individualistic," "subjectivist," "petit bourgeois," these were the labels given to any person who had shown problems which could not be reduced to the "class struggle" itself.

Thus Marxism has denied the members of oppressed classes the attribute of being a subject. In doing this, Marxism, because of the ideological and political power this "revolutionary science" immediately exercised upon the workers' movement and all other political groups, has prevented all categories of oppressed peoples from constituting themselves historically as subjects (subjects of their struggle, for example). This means that the "masses" did not fight for themselves but for *the* party or its organizations. And when an economic transformation took place (end of private property, constitution of the socialist state), no revolutionary change took place within the new society, because the people themselves did not change.

For women, Marxism had two results. It prevented them from being aware that they are a class and therefore from constituting themselves as a class for a very long time, by leaving the relation "women/men" outside of the social order, by turning it into a natural relation, doubtless for Marxists the only one, along with the relation of mothers to children, to be seen this way, and by hiding the class conflict between men and women behind a natural division of labor *(The German Ideology).* This concerns the theoretical (ideological) level. On the practical level, Lenin, *the* party, all the communist parties up to now, including all the most radical political groups, have always reacted to any attempt on the part of women to reflect and form groups based on their own class problem with an accusation of divisiveness. By uniting, we women are dividing the strength of the people. This means that for the Marxists women *belong* either to the bourgeois class or to the proletariat class, in other words, to the men of these classes. In addition, Marxist theory does not allow women any more than other classes of oppressed people to constitute themselves as historical subjects, because Marxism does not take into account the fact that a class also consists of individuals one by one.

Class consciousness is not enough. We must try to understand philosophically (politically) these concepts of "subject" and "class consciousness" and how they work in relation to our history. When we discover that women are the objects of oppression and appropriation, at the very moment that we become able to perceive this, we become subjects in the sense of cognitive subjects, through an operation of abstraction. Consciousness of oppression is not only a reaction to (fight against) oppression. It is also the whole conceptual reevaluation of the social world, its whole reorganization with new concepts, from the point of view of oppression. It is what I would call the science of oppression created by the oppressed. This operation of understanding reality has to be undertaken by every one of us: call it a subjective, cognitive practice. The movement back and forth between the levels of reality (the conceptual reality and the material reality of oppression, which are both social realities) is accomplished through language.

It is we who historically must undertake the task of defining the individual subject in materialist terms. This certainly seems to be an impossibility since materialism and subjectivity have always been mutually exclusive. Nevertheless, and rather than despairing of ever understanding, we must recognize the *need* to reach subjectivity in the abandonment by many of us to the myth "woman" (the myth of woman being only a snare that holds us up). This real necessity for everyone to exist as an individual, as well as a member of a class, is perhaps the first condition for the accomplishment of a revolution, without which there can be no real fight or transformation. But the opposite is also true; without class and class consciousness there are no real subjects, only alienated individuals. For women to answer the question of the individual subject in materialist terms is first to show, as the lesbians and feminists did, that supposedly "subjective," "individual," "private" problems are in fact social problems, class problems; that sexuality is not for women an individual and subjective expression, but a social institution of violence. But once we have shown that all so-called personal problems are in fact class problems, we will still be left with the question of the subject of each singular woman—not the myth, but each one of us. At this point, let us say that a new personal and subjective definition for all humankind can only be found beyond the categories of sex (woman and man) and that the advent of individual subjects demands first destroying the categories of sex, ending the use of them, and rejecting all sciences which still use these categories as their fundamentals (practically all social sciences).

To destroy "woman" does not mean that we aim, short of physical destruction, to destroy lesbianism simultaneously with the categories of sex, because lesbianism provides for the moment the only social form in which we can live freely. Lesbian is the only concept I know of which is beyond the categories of sex (woman and man), because the designated subject (lesbian) is *not* a woman, either economically, or politically, or ideologically. For what makes a woman is a specific social relation to a man, a relation that we have previously called servitude,[16] a relation which implies personal and physical obligation as well as economic obligation ("forced residence,"[17] domestic corvée, conjugal duties, unlimited production of children, etc.), a relation which lesbians escape by refusing to become or to stay heterosexual. We are escapees from our class in the same way as the American runaway slaves were when escaping slavery and becoming free. For us this is an absolute necessity; our survival demands that we contribute all our strength to the destruction of the class of women within which men appropriate women. This can be accomplished only by the destruction of heterosexuality as a social system which is based on the oppression of women by men and which produces the doctrine of the difference between the sexes to justify this oppression.

Notes

1. Christine Delphy, "Pour un féminisme matérialiste," *L'Arc* 61 (1975). Translated as "For a Materialist Feminism," *Feminist Issues* 1, no. 2 (winter 1981).
2. Colette Guillaumin, "Race et Nature: Système des marques, idée de groupe naturel et rapports sociaux," *Pluriel*, no. 11 (1977). Translated as "Race and Nature: The System of Marks, the Idea of a Natural Group and Social Relationships," *Feminist Issues* 8, no. 2 (fall 1988).
3. I use the word *society* with an extended anthropological meaning: strictly speaking, it does not refer to societies, in that lesbian societies do not exist completely autonomously from heterosexual social systems.
4. Simone de Beauvoir, *The Second Sex* (New York: Bantam, 1952), p. 249.
5. Redstockings, *Feminist Revolution* (New York: Random House, 1978), p. 18.
6. Andrea Dworkin, "Biological Superiority: The World's Most Dangerous and Deadly Idea," *Heresies* 6 (1989): 46.
7. Ti-Grace Atkinson, *Amazon Odyssey* (New York: Links Books, 1974), p. 15.
8. Dworkin, op. cit.
9. Guillaumin, op. cit.
10. Beauvior, op. cit.
11. Guillaumin, "Race and Nature."
12. Dworkin, op. cit.
13. Atkinson, p. 6: "If feminism has any logic at all, it must be working for a sexless society."
14. Rosalind Rosenberg, "In Search of Woman's Nature," *Feminist Studies* 3, nos. 1/2 (1975): 144.
15. Ibid., p. 146.
16. In an article published in *L'Idiot International* (mai 1970), whose original title was "Pour un mouvement de libération des femmes" (For a Woman's Liberation Movement).
17. Christiane Rochefort, *Les stances à Sophie* (Paris: Grasset, 1963).

Caroline Walker Bynum (1941–)

Bynum was born in Atlanta, Georgia, but she went north for her education, receiving a B.A. from the University of Michigan in 1962 and a Ph.D. from Harvard in 1969. She currently teaches at Columbia University, where she is Professor of Western Medieval History at the Institute for Advanced Studies. There, she teaches courses in medieval European history with a special interest in women's piety, the history of theology and philosophy, and the social background of ideas. As an article in the *Chronicle of Higher Education* says of Bynum, she is a product of the sixties, having submitted her dissertation "on the very day in 1969 that [Harvard] students occupied University Hall to protest the war in Vietnam." Further, as a young teacher and scholar, "she kept a slogan popular on Paris walls during the student rebellion of '68 tacked above her desk: . . . 'Every view of things that is not strange is false'" (June 22, 2001). This slogan may explain why the view Bynum takes of things medieval is so strangely interesting and provocative. One of her first books, *Jesus as Mother: Studies in the Spirituality of the High Middle Ages* (1982), turned the world of medieval scholarship upside down with its examination of male and female conceptions of Christ. Following on the heels of *Jesus as Mother,* Bynum published *Holy Feast and Holy Fast: The Religious Significance of Food to Medieval Women* (1987), *Fragmentation and Redemption: Essays on Gender and the Human Body in Medieval Religion* (1991), and *The Resurrection of the Body in Western Christianity: 200–1336* (1995). She has also edited three volumes: *Gender and Religion* (1986), *Body-Part Reliquaries* (1997), and *Last Things: Death and Apocalypse in the Middle Ages* (2000). In keeping with the strange view taken in her early work, her most recent publication, *Metamorphosis and Identity* (2001), begins with a discussion of a twelfth-century scholar, Gerald of Wales, who compared Christ to a werewolf.

The Female Body and Religious Practice in the Later Middle Ages

Introduction

One night in the early fifteenth century, as she prayed to the Virgin Mary, the Franciscan reformer Colette of Corbie received a vision of Christ. The Christ who came to Colette was not the sweet-faced bridegroom nor the adorable baby familiar to us from medieval paintings and illuminations. Christ appeared to Colette as a dish completely filled with "carved-up flesh like that of a child," while the voice of God warned her that it was human sin that minced his son into such tiny pieces.[1]

A hundred years earlier, in the Rhineland, a Dominican friend of the nun Lukardis of Oberweimar received a vision of the Crucifixion. Yet the figures he saw were not the executed bodies of Christ and two thieves common in both art and visionary experience. Rather the friar saw his friend Lukardis and two other nailed to crosses, and the voice of God informed him that it was Lukardis who was to be identified with Christ because she suffered most.[2]

These visions startle the modern reader. Conditioned by classic accounts such as Johann Huizinga's and recent popularizations such as Barbara Tuchman's to see the late Middle Ages as violent in its daily practice, morbid, graphic and literal-minded in its images, we are nonetheless surprised to find Christ depicted as chopped meat or to read of a crucified body as female.[3] The images seem, if not disgusting, at least distasteful. Boundaries appear to be violated here—boundaries between spiritual and physical, male and female, self and matter. There is something profoundly alien to modern sensibilities about the role of body in medieval piety.

It is not my purpose in this essay to explore our modern discomfort with such boundary crossing, but rather to provide a context for understanding the ease with which medieval people mixed categories. Nonetheless, we do well to being by recognizing the essential strangeness of medieval religious experience. The recent outpouring of work on the history of the body, especially the female body, has largely equated body with sexuality and understood discipline or control of body as the rejection of sex or of woman.[4] We must wipe away such assumptions before we come to medieval source material. Medieval images of the body have less to do with sexuality than with fertility and decay.[5] Control, discipline, even torture of the flesh is, in medieval devotion, not so much the rejection of physicality as the elevation of it—a horrible yet delicious elevation—into a means of access to the divine.[6]

In the discussion that follows, I wish first to illustrate the new religious significance body acquired in the period from 1200 to 1500, and second to argue that female spirituality in the same period was especially somatic—so much so that the emergence of certain bizarre miracles characteristic of women may actually mark a turning point in the history of the body in the West. Then I wish to explain briefly the ecclesiastical and social setting of women's somatic and visionary piety, before turning to an exploration of its context in two sets of medieval assumptions—assumptions about male/female and assumptions about soul/body. The final two sections of the essay discuss these assumptions at length in order to show that the very dualisms modern commentators have emphasized so much were far from absolute in the late Middle Ages. Not only did theology, natural philosophy and folk tradition mingle male and female in their understanding of human character and human physiology; theological and psychological discussion also sometimes mingled body and soul. The spirituality of medieval women owed its intense bodily quality in part to the association of the female with the fleshly made by philosophers and theologians alike. But its somatic quality also derived from the fact that by the thirteenth century the prevalent concept of person was of a psychosomatic unity, the orthodox position in eschatology required resurrection of body as well as soul at the end of time, and the philosophical, medical and folk understandings of body saw men and women as variations on a single physiological structure. Compared to other periods of Christian history and other world religions, medieval spirituality—especially female spirituality—was peculiarly bodily; this was so not only because medieval assumptions associated female with flesh, but also because theology and natural philosophy saw persons as in some real sense body as well as soul.[7]

The Body in Late Medieval Piety

One aspect of the medieval enthusiasm for body as means of religious access remains prominent in modern Catholic Europe. The cult of relics is well known. From the early Middle Ages down into modern times, pieces of dead holy people have been revered as the loci of the sacred. Medieval relics were jealously guarded, feared, fought for and sometimes even stolen from fellow Christians.[8] According to at least some learned and some popular opinion, relics were far more than mere aids to pious memory; they were the saints themselves, living already with God in the incorrupt and glorified bodies more ordinary mortals would attain only at the end of time.[9]

The cult of relics was only one of the ways in which late medieval piety emphasized body as the locus of the sacred. The graphic physical processes of living people were revered as well. Holy people spat or blew into the mouths of others to effect cures or convey grace.[10] The ill clamored for the bath water of would-be saints to drink or bathe in, and preferred it if these would-be saints themselves washed seldom and therefore left skin and lice floating in the water.[11] Following Francis of Assisi, who kissed lepers, several Italian saints ate pus or lice from poor or sick bodies, thus incorporating into themselves the illness and misfortune of others.[12] Holy virgins in the Low Countries lactated miraculously and cured their adherents with the breast milk they exuded.[13]

Medieval people, moreover, manipulated their own bodies for religious goals. Both male and female saints regularly engaged in what modern people call self torture—jumping into ovens or icy ponds, driving knives, nails or nettles into their flesh, whipping or hanging themselves in elaborate pantomimes of Christ's Crucifixion.[14] Understood sometimes as chastening of sexual urges or as punishment for sin, such acts were more frequently described as union with the body of Jesus. The fourteenth-century Dominican Henry Suso, for example, said of ascetic practices:

> If suffering brought with it no other gain than that by our griefs and pains we grow in likeness to Christ, our prototype, it would still be a priceless benefit. . . . Even if God should choose to give the same eternal reward to those who suffer and to those who do not, we should nevertheless prefer afflictions as our earthly portion in order to resemble our leader.[15]

The ecstatic, even erotic, overtones of such union are often quite clear. Starving her body into submission, the Italian tertiary Angela of Foligno spoke of encounter with Jesus as "love and inestimable satiety, which, although it satiated, generated at the same time insatiable hunger, so that all her members were unstrung. . . . "[16]

Pious folk in the later Middle Ages also gave extraordinary religious significance to the body of God. Not only did they believe that at the moment of consecration the bread on the altar became Christ; they also experienced miracles in which the bread turned into bloody flesh on the paten or in the mouth of the recipient.[17] Increasingly, therefore, eucharistic reception became symbolic cannibalism: devotees consumed and thus incorporated (as they are understood to do in other cannibal cultures, such as the Iroquois or Aztec) the power of the tortured god.[18] Moreover, pious practice came to revere the consecrated wafer as a physical remnant (or relic) of Christ—the only such relic that could exist on earth, Christ's body having been assumed into heaven. As the cult of the eucharistic host developed in the late twelfth century, consecrated wafers were reserved in reliquaries and honored with the sort of candles and lamps that burned before the relics of the saints.[19] Such an understanding of the host as relic is clearly illustrated by the story of Bishop Hugh of Lincoln, who chewed off a bit from the bone of Mary Magdalen preserved at Fécamp and defended himself to her outraged supporters by claiming that if he could touch Christ's body in the mass he could certainly chew the Magdalen's arm.[20]

Specific members of Christ's body were revered by the devout in ways that astonish and sometimes offend us. As Leo Steinberg has demonstrated, artists in the fifteenth century often called attention to the penis of the infant or the adult Christ.[21] And the cult of the holy foreskin was popular in the later Middle Ages. Although the hagiographer Raymond of Capua and the artists of early modern Europe depict Catherine of Siena as marrying Christ with a ring of gold and precious stones, Catherine herself says she married him with his circumcised flesh.[22] Birgitta of Sweden received a revelation from God saying where Christ's foreskin was preserved on earth; and the Viennese Beguine Agnes Blannbekin received the foreskin in her mouth in a vision and found it to taste as sweet as honey.[23]

The Female Body and Female Experience

Behavior in which bodiliness provides access to the sacred seems to have increased dramatically in frequency in the twelfth century and to have been more characteristic of women than of men. Although both men and women manipulated their bodies from the outside, so to speak, by flagellation and other forms of self-inflicted suffering, cases of psychosomatic manipulation (or manipulation from within) are almost exclusively female. I refer here to a number of phenomena that are sometimes called "paramystical" by modern scholars of religion and "hysterical" or "conversion phenomena" by modern psychologists.

Trances, levitations, catatonic seizures or other forms of bodily rigidity, miraculous elongation or enlargement of parts of the body, swellings of sweet mucus in the throat (sometimes known as the "globus hystericus") and ecstatic nosebleeds are seldom if at all reported of male saints but are quite common in the *vitae* of thirteenth- and fourteenth-century women. The inability to eat anything except the eucharistic host (which Rudolf Bell calls "holy anorexia") is reported only of women for most of the Middle Ages.[24] Although a few stories of fasting girls are told from Carolingian Europe, reports that see such inedia as a manifestation of sanctity begin to proliferate about 1200. These reports often include claims to other forms of miraculous bodily closure as well: women who do not eat are reputed neither to excrete nor to menstruate.

Despite the fame of Francis of Assisi's stigmata, he and the modern figure Padre Pio are the only males in history who have claimed all five visible wounds.

There are, however, dozens of such claims for late medieval women. Francis (d. 1226) may indeed have been the first case (although even this is uncertain); but stigmata rapidly became a female miracle, and only for women did the stigmatic wounds bleed periodically.[25] Miraculous lactation was, of course, female behavior, and it appears to have originated in the Low Countries in the early thirteenth century. Other kinds of holy exuding—particularly the exuding of sweet-smelling oil after death—seem more characteristic of women as well.[26] Bodily swelling understood as "mystical pregnancy" was usually (although not always) a female claim.[27] The most bizarre cases of pictures etched on hearts and discovered during preparation for burial are told of women.[28] Indeed, if we look outside the religious sphere, we find that writings by rather matter-of-fact fourteenth-century surgeons express an odd combination of reverence and almost prurient curiosity about what is contained inside women—that is, their "secrets."[29]

Although a number of blood prodigies are attributed to the bodies of male saints, female bodies provide a disproportionate percentage of the wonder-working relics in late medieval Europe.[30] As Claude Carozzi has argued, we can sometimes, in hagiographical accounts, see a woman turning into a relic even before her own death.[31] Moreover, incorruptibility either of the whole cadaver or of a part seems a virtual requirement for female sanctity by the early modern period. According to Thurston, incorruptibility (that is, remaining lifelike and supple for long years after death) has been claimed for all six of the female saints added to the universal Roman calendar between 1400 and 1900 (although it is mentioned for fewer than half of the male saints).[32] In short, women's bodies were more apt than men's to display unusual changes, closures, openings or exudings; such changes were either more common or much more frequently reported after 1200; religious significance was attached to such changes when they seemed to parallel either events in Christ's life or in the mass.

Another kind of bodily experience—illness or recurrent pain—was also more apt to be given religious significance in women's lives than in men's. In their statistical study of saints, Weinstein and Bell have pointed out that, although women were only seventeen and one-half percent of those canonized or revered as saints between 1000 and 1700, they were over fifty percent of those in whose lives patient suffering of illness was the major element of sanctity.[33] Ernst Benz, Richard Kieckhefer and Elizabeth Petroff have also pointed out the prominence of illness—as theme and as fact—in women's spirituality.[34] Some visionary women (such as Julian of Norwich) prayed for disease as a gift from God; some (such as Lidwina of Schiedam) at first desired to be cured. But, whatever the cause of disease or the saint's initial reaction to it, many medieval women—for example, Serafina of San Gimignano, Villana de' Botti, Margaret of Ypres, Dorothy of Montau, Gertrude of Helfta and Alpais of Cudot—made physical and mental anguish an opportunity for their own salvation and that of others.[35] Hagiographers fairly frequently described their female subjects as impelled to bodily frenzy by God's presence; Beatrice of Nazareth wondered whether it would be desirable to drive herself insane out of love for God.[36] Dauphine of Puimichel commented that if people knew how useful diseases were to the spirit, they would purchase them in the marketplace.[37] The leper Alice of Schaerbeke explained that illness could be offered for the redemption of one's neighbor:

> Dear sister, do not grieve [for me]; and do not think that I suffer for or expiate my own sins; I suffer rather for those who are already dead and in the place of penitence [i.e., purgatory] and for the sins of the world. . . . [38]

By 1500 there are extant women's *vitae,* such as Catherine of Genoa's, in which much of the account is devoted to physiological changes in the saint's dying body.

It is true that medieval writers, like modern ones, frequently saw disease as a condition to be avoided.[39] Indeed, cures of illness were the most common miracles performed by saints. But it is also true that sickness and suffering were sometimes seen by medieval people as conditions "to be endured" rather than "cured." Alpais of Cudot, for example, clearly indicated such an attitude when she saw the devil appear in a vision as a doctor. To Alpais, as to Elsbeth Achler and Catherine of Siena, the offer of cure was a temptation.[40] Indeed, a nun of the monastery of Töss composed a poem in which Christ said to her: "The sicker you are, the dearer you are to me."[41]

There is reason to believe that conditions that both we and medieval people would see as "illnesses" were given different meanings depending on whether they occurred in male or female bodies. Illness was more likely to be described as something "to be endured" when it happened to women. For example, in a ninth-century account of the posthumous miracles of Walburga, a man and a woman suffering from what we would term an "eating disorder" both present themselves before the saint's relics. The man in cured of his loathing for food when he is offered a chalice by three nuns; the woman, however, turns from voracious hunger to inability to eat—a condition of which she is not "cured." Rather, she is miraculously sustained for three years without eating.[42]

Statistics tell the same story. Sigal, in his recent study of miracles in eleventh- and twelfth-century France, finds that females account for only between eighteen and forty-two percent of recipients of miraculous cures. (The percentage varies with the disease cured.) Females are an even smaller percentage of the miraculous cures of children and adolescents, and of the cures that take place at shrines rather than at a distance. These facts cannot be accounted for by sex ratios in the population or by disproportionate percentage of men among those falling ill. Rather, they clearly indicate, as Sigal argues, that the society found it more valuable to cure one sex than the other. They also suggest that endurance of a condition of illness without supernatural amelioration was considered more appropriate to women, whether the endurance was a prelude to sanctity or not.[43]

The tendency of women to somatize religious experience and to give positive significance to bodily occurrences is related to what is generally recognized (for example, by scholars such as Dinzelbacher and Dronke) to be a more experiential quality in their mystical writing.[44] Male writers too, of course, use extremely physical and physiological language to speak of encounter with God. Indeed, the locus classicus for descriptions of eating God or being eaten by Him is Bernard of Clairvaux's sermons on the *Song of Songs,* later graphically echoed in John

Tauler's sermons for Corpus Christi.[45] But men's writing often lacks the immediacy of women's; the male voice is impersonal. It is striking to note that, however fulsome or startling their imagery, men write of "*the* mystical experience," giving a general description which may be used as a theory or yardstick, whereas women write of "*my* mystical experience," speaking directly of something that may have occurred to them alone.[46] This is true even when, as in the case of Hildegard of Bingen or Julian of Norwich, a highly sophisticated theology is elaborated over many years as a gloss on visionary experiences.

Women regularly speak of tasting God, of kissing Him deeply, of going into His heart or entrails, of being covered by His blood. Their descriptions of themselves or of other women often, from a modern point of view, hopelessly blur the line between spiritual or psychological, on the one hand, and bodily or even sexual, on the other. Lidwina of Schiedam and Gertrude of Delft, for example, felt such maternal desire for the Christ child that milk flowed from their breasts; Beatrice of Nazareth experienced a joy in Christ that contorted her face and racked her with hysterical laughter; Lukardis of Oberweimar and Margaret of Faenza kissed their spiritual sisters with open mouths and grace flowed from one to the other with an ardor that left both women shaken. The thirteenth-century poet and mystic Hadewijch spoke of Christ penetrating her until she lost herself in the ecstasy of love. She wrote:

> After that he came himself to me, took me entirely in his arms and pressed me to
> him; and all my members felt his in full felicity, in accordance with the desire of
> my heart and my humanity. So I was outwardly satisfied and fully transported.
> Also then, for a short while, I had the strength to bear this; but soon, after a
> short time, I lost that manly beauty outwardly in the sight of his form. I saw him
> completely come to naught and so fade and all at once dissolve that I could no
> longer distinguish him within me. That it was to me as if we were one without
> difference.[47]

Watching sisters sometimes saw the bodies of mystical women elongate or levitate or swoon in ecstatic trances; but the visionary women themselves often did not bother to make clear where the events happened—whether in body, heart or soul, whether in the eye of the mind or before the eyes of the body. Indeed, in the books of women's *Revelations,* which are really a new literary genre by the late fourteenth or early fifteenth century, the point is not to provide proof that one woman or a group of women received charismatic gifts so much as to communicate and share a piety in which spiritual-somatic experiences lie at the center.[48]

It would be wrong to draw an absolute contrast between male and female piety. Medieval men also saw visions, and their hagiographers described their affective experiences of God.[49] But those men (such as Bernard of Clairvaux, Francis of Assisi, Suso, Ruysbroeck or Richard Rolle) whose religiosity was most experiential and visionary often understood themselves in feminine images and learned their pious practices from women.[50] Moreover, whether they denigrated, admired or used the experiences of mystical women, men such as Albert the Great, Eckhart and Gerson spoke explicitly of somatic and visionary experiences as peculiarly female. David of Augsburg ridiculed them as "erotic ticklings."

John Tauler wrote more sympathetically, but even he made it clear that he was a bit suspicious of such piety.[51]

Thus, if we speak phenomenologically, it seems clear that when "the other" breaks through into the lives of individuals, it often throws men into profound stillness. Male mystics write repeatedly of being at a core or ground or inner point (as Eckhart or Walter Hilton put it).[52] Women, on the other hand, are "switched on" by "the other," heightened into an affectively or sensuality that goes beyond both the senses and our words for describing them. Even those female mystics, such as Hadewijch and Margaret Porete, who distrust or reject affectivity, speak with intimate knowledge of that which they wish to transmute or transcend.[53]

Women's sense that Christ is body, received and perceived by body, is vividly reflected in a vision given to the little-known French nun, Marguerite of Oingt (d. 1310). Marguerite saw herself as a withered tree which suddenly flowered when inundated by a great river of water (representing Christ). Marguerite then saw, written on the flowering branches of her self, the names of the five senses: sight, hearing, taste, smell and touch. It is hard to imagine a more pointed way of indicating that the effect of experiencing Christ is to "turn on," so to speak, the bodily senses of the receiving mystic.[54]

The Italian mystic Angela of Foligno (d. 1309), in words undoubtedly reworked by a scholastically educated redactor, expresses the same awareness when she says:

> [The soul in this present life knows] the lesser in the greater and the greater in the lesser, for it discovers uncreated God and "humanated" God, that is divinity and humanity, in Christ, united and conjoined in one person. . . . And sometimes . . . the soul receives greater delight in the lesser. . . . For the soul is more conformed and adapted to the lesser which it sees in Christ the incarnate God, than it is to that which it sees in Christ the uncreated God; because the soul is a creature who is the life of the flesh and of all the members of its body. Thus it discovers both God "humanated" and God uncreated, Christ the creator and Christ the creature, and in that Christ it discovers soul with flesh and blood and with all the members of his most sacred body. And this is why, when the human intellect discovers, sees, and knows in this mystery Christ the man and Christ-God . . . , this intellect feels delight and expands in him, because it sees God "humanated" and God uncreated conformed and made like itself—because, that is, the human soul sees the soul of Christ, his eyes, his flesh, and his body. But while it looks . . . , it should not forget also to turn to the higher . . . the divine. . . . [55]

To Angela, the encounter with the body of Christ into which grace lifts her is beyond ordinary affectivity, for it is simultaneously a transport of pain and of delight. Even filtered through the screen provided by her confessor-redactor, the exuberance of Angela's enthusiasm contrasts sharply with the moderation and hesitation of a Tauler or an Eckhart. She says:

> Once, when I was at Vespers and was contemplating the Crucifix . . . suddenly my soul was lifted into love, and all the members of my body felt a very great joy. And I saw and felt that Christ, within me, embraced my soul with that arm

> by which he was crucified . . . and I felt such great security that I could not doubt
> it was God. . . . So I rejoice when I see that hand which he holds out with the
> signs of the nails, saying to me: "Behold what I bore for you."
>
> Now I can feel no sadness at the Passion . . . for all my joy is in that suffer-
> ing God-Man. And it seems to my soul that it enters within that wound in the
> side of Christ and walks there with delight. . . .[56]

In such piety, body is not so much a hindrance to the soul's ascent as the opportunity for it. Body is the instrument upon which the mystic rings changes of pain
and of delight. It is from body—whether whipped into frenzy by the ascetic herself or gratified with an ecstasy given by God—that sweet melodies and aromas
rise to the very throne of heaven.[57]

Thus, as many recent scholars have argued, the spiritualities of male and
female mystics were different, and this difference has something to do with
body.[58] Women were more apt to somatize religious experience and to write in
intense bodily metaphors; women mystics were more likely than men to receive
graphically physical visions of God; both men and women were inclined to attribute to women and encourage in them intense asceticisms and ecstasies. Moreover,
the most bizarre bodily occurrences associated with women (e.g., stigmata, incorruptibility of the cadaver in death, mystical lactations and pregnancies, catatonic
trances, ecstatic nosebleeds, miraculous inedia, eating and drinking pus, visions
of bleeding hosts) either first appear in the twelfth and thirteenth centuries or
increase significantly in frequency at that time. These facts suggest—hard as it is
for sober modern historians to countenance such arguments—that the body itself
may actually have a history. The body, and in particular the female body, seems to
have begun to behave in new ways at a particular moment in the European past.[59]
The question is: Why is this so?

The Ecclesiastical and Social Context

Many explanations can be proposed for the bodily quality of female spirituality
in the later Middle Ages. I have written elsewhere about the importance of
charismatic authorization for women at a time when clerical control increased in
the Church, and it is customary now for scholars to emphasize women's mysticism as a form of female empowerment.[60] Since the Gregorian Reform of the late
eleventh century, priest and layperson had been sharply separated in status and
form of life; clerical dignity had become ever more elevated and awesome. Thus,
one might argue that women *had* to stress the experience of Christ and manifest
it outwardly in their flesh, because they did not have clerical office as an authorization for speaking. This argument must also recognize that the clergy themselves encouraged such female behavior both because female asceticism,
eucharistic devotion and mystical trances brought women more closely under the
supervision of spiritual directors, and because women's visions functioned for
males too as means of learning the will of God. Moreover, theologians and
prelates found women's experiential piety useful in the thirteenth-century fight
against heresy. The increased emphasis on bodily miracles and indeed the appearance of new miracles of bodily transformation came at exactly the time of the

campaign against Cathar dualism. Women whose bodies became one with the crucified man on the cross in stigmata, and visions in which the consecrated wafer suddenly turned into bleeding meat, were powerful evidence against the Cathar assertion that matter and flesh could not be the creations of a good God. Some of the earliest supporters of this bodily aspect of women's piety, James of Vitry and Thomas of Cantimpré, held it up explicitly as a reproach to the dualists.[61]

In addition, we must not forget the educational context. At least since the work of Grundmann in the 1930s, we have been aware of how much women's writing was shaped both by their lack of formal theological training and by the availability of the new vernacular languages with their characteristic literary genres.[62] In other words, part of the reason for the more open, experiential style of women's writings is the fact that women usually wrote not in the formal scholastic Latin taught in universities but in the vernaculars—that is, in the languages they grew up speaking. The major literary genres available in these languages were various kinds of love poetry and romantic stories: the vocabulary provided by such genres was therefore a vocabulary of feelings. A comparison of two women from much the same milieu, Mechtild of Hackeborn and Mechtild of Magdeburg, shows clearly that the one who wrote in Latin wrote more impersonally and to a much greater extent under the influence of the liturgy, whereas the vernacular poet wrote more experientially, with a greater sense both of personal vulnerability and of an immediate and special relationship to God.[63] Furthermore, women's works, especially their accounts of visions, were often dictated (that is, spoken) rather than penned—a fact that is clearly one of the explanations for women's more discursive, conversational, aggregative, tentative, empathetic and self-reflective style. As Elizabeth Petroff has recently pointed out, the prose of a female writer such as Julian of Norwich, which tends to circle around its point, evoking a state of being, displays exactly those traits Walter Ong has seen as characteristic of oral thought and expression.[64]

Social context also sheds light on the nature of women's piety. Secular society expected women to be intimately involved in caring for the bodies of others (especially the young, the sick and the dying). To some extent, women simply took these roles over into their most profound religious experiences. Not only did female mystics kiss, bathe and suckle babies in visions and grieve with Mary as she received her son's dead body for burial; they actually acted out maternal and nuptial roles in the liturgy, decorating lifesize statues of the Christ child for the Christmas crèche or dressing in bridal garb when going to receive their bridegroom in the Eucharist. Anyone who has stood before the lovely Beguine cradle on display in the Metropolitan Museum in New York and realized that it is a liturgical object must have thought, at least for a moment: "Why these nuns and Beguines were just little girls, playing with dolls!"[65]

It is possible that there is, in addition, a biological element in women's predisposition to certain kinds of bodily experiences. The fact that, in many cultures, women seem more given to spirit possession and more apt to somatize their inner emotional or spiritual states suggests a physiological explanation. In cultures as different as medieval Europe, medieval China and modern America, self-mutilation and self-starvation seem to be more characteristic of women than of men.[66] But we should be cautious about espousing biological explanations too hastily. Biology and culture are almost impossible to distinguish in these matters, because men and women differ from each other consistently across societies in their social and psychological as well as their physiological experiences. The various cultures in which women are more inclined than men to fast, to mutilate themselves, to experience the gift of tongues and to somatize spiritual states are all societies that associate the female with self-sacrifice and service.

Intellectual Traditions: Dualism and Misogyny

Basic assumptions about body and about gender provide another context against which we must place the new miracles of bodily transformation and the graphic physiological visions of the later Middle Ages. There were intellectual traditions that conditioned women *and men* to certain expectations of women's bodies. Medieval thinkers associated *body* with *woman;* they therefore expected women's expressiveness to be more physical and physiological than men's. They also associated body with God, through the doctrine of the Incarnation, and eschewed sharp soul/body dichotomies more than did either patristic theologians or those of the early modern period. They could, therefore, give to the bodily experiences of members of both sexes a deeply spiritual significance.

It may appear odd to emphasize the bodiliness of God, or the bodiliness of women as a means of approaching God, in a discussion of the Middle Ages. Standard accounts of the period are much more inclined to emphasize its misogyny and dualism. And there is no denying these aspects of medieval attitudes. The practical dualism of medieval Christianity is well known. As Jacques Le Goff has pointed out, twelfth- and thirteenth-century literature presented the body not merely as dust but as rottenness, a garment masking the food of worms.[67] Ascetic theologians often wrote of spirit and flesh warring with each other. Both in Latin and in the emerging vernaculars, the genre of the debate between body and soul became popular. In one Latin version, so well-known it survives in at least 132 manuscripts, Soul describes herself as a noble creature blackened by Flesh, which must be overcome by hunger, thirst and beatings.[68] Indeed, chastity for men and virginity for women were almost preconditions for sanctity. Even in the later Middle Ages, when some married saints were added to the calendar, rejection of actual conjugal sex was taken as a major sign of the saint's growth toward holiness.[69]

It is also clear that theological, scientific and folk traditions associated women with body, lust, weakness and irrationality, men with spirit or reason or strength.[70] Patristic exegetes, for example, argued that women (or Eve) represents the appetites, man (or Adam) represents soul or intellect.[71] As Weinstein and Bell have pointed out, hagiographers were inclined to see female sin as bodily or sexual, as arising from within the woman's body, whereas male sinners were depicted as tempted from without—often indeed as tempted by the proffered bodiliness of women.[72] In James of Voragine's *Golden Legend*, a collection of saints' lives retold for use by thirteenth-century preachers in edifying sermons, the major achievement of holy women is dying in defense of their virginity. Defense of chastity is an extremely infrequent theme in the male lives James tells. Resurrection from the dead is, however, a fairly common motif in accounts of holy men, and these men are raised in order to complete tasks or make reparation for deeds done on earth. This pattern suggests that women's lives can be complete only when death has assured perpetual virginity. In contrast, male lives are complete when virtue is won, evil defeated or restitution made. Whereas an early demise is advisable for women, assuring that their weak bodies can no longer be tempted or violated, death itself may be temporarily suspended to give men time to assert themselves and finish the job of winning salvation.[73]

As these examples demonstrate, medieval writers did associate body and flesh with woman, and they did sometimes draw from this dualist and misogynist conclusions. But what I would like to suggest here is that the impact of medieval conceptions of woman and of body was more complex than scholars have realized, because the concepts themselves were more complex. Medieval men and women did not take the equation of woman with body merely as the basis for misogyny. They also extrapolated from it to an association of woman with the body or the humanity of Christ. Indeed, they often went so far as to treat Christ's flesh as female, at least in certain of its salvific functions, especially its bleeding and nurturing. This fact helps us to understand why it was women more than men who imitated Christ bodily, especially in stigmata.

Moreover, if we look closely at the various traditions that associated woman with body or flesh, we find that neither medieval gender contrasts nor medieval notions of soul and body were as dichotomous as we have been led to think by projecting modern contrasts back onto them.[74] Thus, I would like to argue that we must consider not just the dichotomy but also the mixing or fusing of the genders implicit in medieval assumptions. Only in this way will we understand how mystical women could see themselves and be seen by men as especially apt to imitate and fuse with the male body of Christ. We must also consider the ways in which treatments of body and soul, particularly in the period after 1200, tended to mix rather than separate the two components of the person. Such background is necessary in order to comprehend how medieval people of both sexes could see the holy manifest in that same flesh which lured humans into lust and greed during their lives and, after death, putrefied in the grave.

Medieval traditions concerning male/female and body/soul are complex enough that I need to take them up separately and in some detail.

Women Is to Man as Body Is to Soul

As all medievalists are by now aware, the body of Christ was sometimes depicted as female in medieval devotional texts—partly, of course, because *ecclesia*, Christ's body, was a female personification, partly because the tender, nurturing aspect of God's care for souls was regularly described as motherly. Both male and female mystics called Jesus "mother" in his eucharistic feeding of Christians with liquid exuded from his breast and in his bleeding on the Cross which gave birth to our hope of eternal life.[75] In the thirteenth century Margaret of Oingt described Jesus' pain on the Cross as birth pangs; Guerric of Igny in the twelfth century, and Catherine of Siena and the anonymous monk of Farne in the fourteenth, wrote of Christ nursing the soul at his breast; the fourteenth-century English mystic Julian of Norwich spoke of creation as a maternal act because God, in taking on our humanity in the Incarnation, gives himself to us as a mother gives herself to the fetus she bears.[76]

Iconography illustrates the same theme. In the moralized Bibles of the thirteenth and fourteenth centuries, artists depicted the Church being born from Christ's side, as Eve is born of Adam.[77] Miniatures and panel paintings showed Christ, exuding wine or blood into chalices or even into hungry mouths and drew visual parallels between his wound and Mary's breast offered to suckle sinners.[78] We know that such traditions lie behind sixteenth-century depictions of Christ feeding Catherine of Siena from his side, because the various versions of Catherine's *vita* speak of Christ nursing her at his breast.[79] The motif of "Jesus as mother" may also help explain the unusual northern Renaissance paintings by Jan Gossaert that depict the infant Christ with engorged breasts.[80]

There were two separate strands on which medieval mystics drew in identifying woman with flesh and Christ's flesh with the female. Although it is easiest to cite these strands from treatises on theology, natural philosophy and medicine, recent work by French historians of medicine and anthropologists makes it abundantly clear that we have to deal here not merely with learned ideas but with assumptions widespread in the culture.[81] I have written about these elsewhere, but it seems advisable to repeat some of the material in order to make my argument clear.[82]

The first set of roots is theological. Medieval interpreters of the Bible regularly taught that "spirit is to flesh as male is to female"—that is, that the dichotomy male/female can serve as a symbol for the dichotomies strong/weak, rational/irrational, soul/body. This use of pairs of symbols led some medieval writers to see the male as symbol of Christ's divinity, the female as symbol of his humanity. Hildegard of Bingen, for example, argued that in Christ "divinity is to humanity as male is to female." Hildegard's association of women with Christ's humanity underlay her reiterated position that women were appropriately denied the priesthood because they had another way of joining with Christ. As Christ's brides in mystical union, women were the body of Christ, not merely his representatives. The analogy "male is to female as divinity is to humanity" also underlay Elisabeth of Schönau's vision—confusing even to its recipient—in which a female virgin, representing Christ's humanity, appeared sitting on the sun (his divinity). The analogy is reflected in the many medieval texts that say that Christ married human nature as a man marries a woman, and it lies behind miniatures that depict not only *ecclesia* but also *humanitas* as female.

Such an association of Christ's humanity with the female and the fleshly was also supported by the theological doctrine of the Virgin Birth and the emerging notions of the Immaculate Conception and bodily Assumption. Because Christ had no human father, his body came entirely from Mary and was therefore closely associated with female flesh. As Thomas Aquinas put it:

> According to Aristotle, the male semen does not play the role of "matter" in the conception of animals. It is rather prime agent, so to speak, while the female alone supplies the matter. So even if male semen were lacking in Christ's conception it does not follow that the necessary matter was missing.
>   . . . it is not given to the blessed Virgin to be father to Christ but mother. . . . So it is to be held that in the actual conception of Christ, the blessed Virgin did not actively effect anything in the conceiving, but ministered the matter only. But she actively effected something before the conception by preparing the matter to be apt for conception.

Associating the flesh of Christ with Mary in another way, Bonaventure wrote:

> Indeed she [Mary] is raised above the hierarchy of the perfect [in heaven]. . . . And thus it can be said that she is there corporeally, for she has a special sort of perfection in the celestial city. . . . The soul of Christ is not from her soul—since soul does not come by transmission [from the parents]—but his body is from her body. Therefore she will not be there [in heaven] in the mode of perfection unless she is there corporeally.[83]

Since some theologians increasingly stressed Mary's humanity as sinless from her conception, they were able to suggest that just as the Logos (the divinity of Christ separate from that of God) preexisted the Incarnation, so the humanity of Christ also preexisted the Incarnation in the sinless humanity of Mary. Such arguments could, of course, be carried to dubious theological lengths. But orthodox prayers and mass commentaries from the period also speak of Mary as the humanity of Christ, especially its bodily component or flesh. Catherine of Siena said that Christ's flesh was Mary's, sealed like hot wax by the Holy Spirit; Hildegard of Bingen wrote that Mary is the *tunica humanitatis* Christ puts on; Francis of Assisi called her Christ's robe or tabernacle. The notion is clearly depicted in eucharistic tabernacles which Mary surmounts as if she *were* the container, in monstrances made in her image, and in the so-called "opening Virgins"—small statues of *Maria lactans* which open to show the Trinity inside. As Carol Purtle and Barbara Lane have demonstrated, such a concept is also reflected in those late medieval paintings in which Mary takes on priestly characteristics. Such images of Mary as priest have nothing to do with claiming sacerdotal functions for ordinary women. Mary is priest because it is she who offers to ordinary mortals the saving flesh of God, which comes most regularly and predictably in the mass.[84]

Scientific ideas—especially theories of conception or generation—were a second set of roots for the medieval tendency to associate flesh with female, and God's body with woman's body.[85] According to the Aristotelian theory of conception, held by some medieval scientists and theologians, the mother provides the matter of the fetus and the father its form or life or spirit. This theory clearly associates woman with the unformed physical stuff of which the fully human is made. According to the competing theory of conception available at the time—Galen's theory—two seeds were necessary, one from the father and one from the mother. This theory in a sense associates both father and mother with the physiological stuff. But even according to Galen the mother is the oven or vessel in which the fetus cooks, and her body feeds the growing child, providing its stuff as it matures.[86] Moreover, Giles of Rome in the thirteenth century, who rejected the Galenic theory as mediated by Avicenna and turned to Aristotle, argued against Galen that if woman provided both the menstrual matter and seed then she might impregnate herself and the male would have no role at all. Such an argument shows not only the tendency to associate matter with woman, but also a fear that this threatens the importance of the male contribution to life.[87]

Physiological theory associated matter, food and flesh with female in another sense. All medieval biological thought the mother's blood fed the child in the womb and then, transmuted into breast milk, fed the baby outside the womb as well.[88] For example, a fourteenth-century surgeon wrote that milk is blood "twice cooked."[89] One of the Arab texts most frequently used by Western doctors argued: "Since the infant has just been nourished from menstrual blood [in the womb], it needs nurture whose nature is closest to menstrual blood, and the matter that has this quality is milk, because milk is formed from menstrual blood."[90] Thus, blood was the basic body fluid, and female blood was the fundamental support of human life. Medical theory also held that the shedding of blood purged or cleansed those who shed it.[91] Indeed, bleeding was held to be necessary for the washing away of superfluity, so much so that physiologists sometimes spoke of males as menstruating (presumably they meant hemorrhoidal bleeding) and recommended bleeding with leeches if they did not do so. Such medical conceptions of blood could lead to the association of Christ's bleeding on the Cross—which purges our sin in the Atonement and feeds our souls in the Eucharist—with female bleeding and feeding.

The sets of medieval assumptions just described associated female and flesh with the body of God. Not only was Christ enfleshed with flesh from a woman; his own flesh did womanly things; it bled, it bled food and it gave birth to new life. If certain key moments in the life of Christ were described by devotional writers as "female," it is no wonder that women's physiological processes were given religious significance. Such process were especially open to religious interpretation when they were not just ordinary but also extraordinary—that is, when they were continuations of normal physiology yet miracles as well (as in the cases of virgin lactation or periodic stigmatic bleeding). Not surprisingly, women strove to experience such bodily moments, which recapitulated events in the life of Christ. And, not surprisingly, men (for whom such experiences were not in any sense "ordinary") both revered these women and suspected them of fraud or collusion with the devil.[92]

The analysis I have just given seems, however, to beg an important question. For the human Christ was, after all, male. And, as we all know from the many medieval discussions of women's incapacity for the priesthood, the inferior female body was in certain contexts and by certain theologians prohibited from representing God.[93] How then did it happen that medieval women came more frequently than medieval men to literal, bodily *imitatio Christi,* both in stigmata and in other forms of miraculous sufferings and exudings?

The answer lies in part in the fact that—for all their application of male/female contrasts to organize life symbolically—medieval thinkers used gender imagery fluidly, not literally. Medieval theologians and natural philosophers often mixed and fused the genders, treating not just the body of Christ but all bodies as both male and female.

From the patristic period on, those who saw the female as representing flesh, while the male symbolized spirit, wrote of real people as both. To say this is not to deny that men were seen as superior in rationality and strength. Clearly they were. But existing, particular human beings were understood as having both feminine and masculine characteristics.[94] Moreover, because of the emphasis on reversal that lay at the heart of the Christian tradition, devotional writers sometimes used the description "woman" or "weak woman" in order to attribute an inferiority that would—exactly because it was inferior—be made superior by God.[95] For example, male mystics such as Bernard of Clairvaux, Eckhart and John Gerson spoke of devout men as fecund mothers or weak women. The women writers about whom Peter Dronke has written so sensitively sometimes used "weak woman" as an ironic self-description in order to underline their special standing before God.[96]

This mixing of the genders is even more apparent in the scientific tradition, where in one sense it is not even clear that there were two sexes. As Thomas Laqueur and Marie-Christine Pouchelle have recently pointed out, medieval natural philosophers argued that men and woman are really a superior and inferior version of the same physiology. Woman's reproductive system was just man's turned inside out. For example, the fourteenth-century surgeons Henri de Mondeville and Guy de Chauliac said: "The apparatus of generation in women is like the apparatus of generation in men, except that it is reversed"; "the womb is like a penis reversed or put inside." In the sixteenth century, Paré even suggested that women could turn into men if, owing to an accident, their internal organs were suddenly pushed outward.[97]

Medieval scientific ideas, especially in their Aristotelian version, made the male body paradigmatic. It was the form or pattern or definition of what we are as humans; what was particularly womanly was the unformedness, the "stuffness" or physicality of our humanness. Such a notion identified woman with breaches in boundaries, with lack of shape or definition, with openings and exudings and spillings forth.[98] But this conception also made men and women versions of the same thing. Men and women had the same sex organs; men's were just better arranged. These assumptions made the boundary between the sexes extremely permeable.

Permeability or interchangeability of the sexes is seen in a number of aspects of physiological theory. For example, all human exudings—menstruation, sweating, lactation, emission of semen, etc.—were seen as bleedings; and all bleedings—lactation, menstruation, nosebleeds, hemorrhoidal bleeding, etc.— were taken to be analogous. Thus, it was not far-fetched for a medical writer to refer to a man menstruating or lactating, or to a woman emitting seed.[99]

Because biological sex seemed so labile, the question of how to account for the observed sharpness of sexual difference—that is, for the fact that persons are distinctly male or female in gross anatomy—puzzled medieval writers. In discussions of generation, for example, natural philosophers held that the sex of the fetus resulted either from a combination of parts from both parents, or from the stronger or weaker impact of male seed on the menstruum, or from location of the fetus on the right or left side of the womb. Such explanations seem to put male and female along a continuum and leave it totally unclear why there are not at least as many hermaphrodites (midpoints on the spectrum) as there are males or females (endpoints on the spectrum).[100] Perhaps because of this uncertainty, the nature and cause of hermaphroditism, as of other embryological anomalies, was much discussed.[101]

Moreover, tales of pregnant men were fairly common in folklore and miracle stories from the twelfth to fifteenth centuries. These tales hardly suggest that doctors or ordinary folk actually thought male could become pregnant. Their purpose was either to ridicule the clergy (the pregnant male was often a cleric) or to warn against the dangers of unacceptable position in sexual intercourse. Nonetheless, the popularity of the satiric notion that woman-on-top sex might drive the seed down into the man, impregnating him, suggests that those telling the tale have no good explanation why such things in fact do not happen.[102]

Medieval assumptions about maleness and femaleness associated body—particularly in its fleshly, oozing, unformed physicality—with woman. But such assumptions saw the physiological structure of the body as paradigmatically male. Thus, medieval thinkers put actual men and women on a continuum and saw their bodies as functioning in essentially the same ways. Such ideas made it easy for writers and artists to fuse or interchange the genders and, therefore, to use both genders symbolically to talk about self and God. As mystics and theologians in the thirteenth, fourteenth and fifteenth centuries increasingly emphasized the human body of Christ, that body was seen both as the paradigmatic male body of Aristotelian physiological theory and as the womanly, nurturing flesh that Christ's holy mother received from her female forebear.[103]

Female *imitatio Christi* mingled the genders in its most profound metaphors and its most profound experiences. Women could fuse with Christ's body because they *were* in some sense body, yet women never forgot the maleness of Christ. Indeed, exactly because maleness was humanly superior, the God who especially redeemed and loved the lowly stooped to marry *female* flesh. Hildegard of Bingen saw *ecclesia* as both Christ's bride and Christ's body. Julian of Norwich, who forged the most sophisticated theology of the motherhood of God, never ceased to refer to "Christ our mother" with the male pronoun. Some mystics, such as Hadewijch and Angela of Foligno, met Christ erotically as female to his maleness; others, such as Catherine of Siena or Margery Kempe, met him maternally, nursing him in their arms. But women mystics often simply became the flesh of Christ, because their flesh could do what his could do: bleed, feed, die and give life to others.[104]

The Body/Soul Relationship and the Significance of Body

Before concluding this examination of the religious significance of the female body, one conceptual boundary remains to be considered—that between body and soul. For the theological writing of the thirteenth and fourteenth centuries came to treat the relationship between body and soul as much tighter and more integral than it had earlier been understood to be. It seems reasonable to suppose that the extraordinary importance given to body, especially female body, in thirteenth- to fifteenth-century religion, and what appear to be the historical beginnings of certain somatic events (such as stigmata or miraculous lactation), owe something to the fact that theorists in the High Middle Ages did not see body primarily as the enemy of soul, the container of soul or the servant of soul; rather, they saw the person as a psychosomatic unity, as body and soul together.

Received wisdom has held that pious folk in the Middle Ages were practical dualists who hated and attacked the body.[105] Moreover, some feminist analysis has recently claimed that the Thomistic-Aristotelian association of form/matter with male/female laid the basis for modern theories of sex polarity and male supremacy, and for a certain denigration of the bodily or experiential as well.[106] There is truth in all this, of course. But when one reads medieval discussions, one is struck less by the polarities and dichotomies than by the muddle theologians and natural philosophers made of them, either by inserting entities between body and soul or by obscuring differences. Those who wrote about body in the thirteenth and fourteenth centuries were in fact concerned to bridge the gap between material and spiritual and to give to body positive significance. Nor should we be surprised to find this so in a religion whose central tenet was the incarnation—the enfleshing—of its God.[107]

No scholastic theologian and no mystic (male or female) denied that the distinction between body and soul was in a technical, philosophical sense a real distinction. None rejected the Pauline idea that flesh (which, to Paul, means "sin" more than "body")[108] is a weight pulling spirit down. Nonetheless, theological speculation in the period of high scholasticism modified considerably the traditional platonic notion that the person is a soul, making use of a body.[109] A concept of person as soul *and* body (or, in modern parlance, a psychosomatic unity) undergirds scholastic discussions of such topics as bodily resurrection, miracles, embryology, asceticism, Christology and the Immaculate Conception. Indeed, it is because medieval thinkers felt it necessary to tie body and soul together, to bridge the gap between them while allowing body to retain a reality and significance of its own, that their writings in these areas are so extraordinarily difficult to understand. But, despite the obscurity of their theoretical writings, these theologians were in no way isolated from pious practice. They preached about miracles or trained other to preach; they inquired into accusation of heresy, claims for canonization and disputed over relics; they sometimes even supervised convents or advised other who did so. It thus seems likely that their attitudes toward the body shaped and reflected the environment within which holy women found it easy to experience bizarre bodily miracles and people of both sexes admired them.

The thirteenth and fourteenth centuries saw a proliferation of treatises and quodlibetal questions concerning various aspects of body.[110] (Quodlibetal disputations were debates by university students and masters on freely chosen rather than set topics; they are therefore an excellent index of which issues excited contemporary interest.) There was, for example, much discussion of the resurrection of the body;[111] and this fundamental tenet of Christian belief was treated not so much as a manifestation of divine power (as it had been in the patristic period) but as a consequence of human nature. Certain scholastic theologians (e.g., Peter of Capua) even questioned whether bodily resurrection after the Last Judgment might be natural—i.e., not a gift of divine grace but an implication of the fact that God created human nature as a body/soul unity.[112] Most theorists answered that resurrection was supernatural. But in several papal and conciliar pronouncements, Christians were required to hold that the damned as well as the saved rise bodily, nevermore to suffer corruption;[113] and moralists repeatedly explained this doctrine by arguing that body sinned or gained merit alongside soul and must, therefore, also receive reward or punishment eternally.[114] Such arguments imply that persons *are* in some sense their bodies, not merely souls temporarily inhabiting matter. As is well known, heretics of the twelfth to fourteenth centuries were castigated for holding the obverse opinion.[115] What most bothered orthodox polemicists about heretical opinions was not the moral argument (i.e., the idea that flesh drags spirit down) but the ontological-cosmological one (i.e., the idea that matter and body cannot be included in the human).[116]

Scholastic treatises often combined theological with scientific (i.e., natural philosophical) interests. The attention devoted to Mary's virgin conception of Christ, and the significantly larger amount of attention devoted to Mary's own Immaculate Conception and her bodily Assumption, suggest that religious writers were fascinated by those Christian doctrines that forced an examination of bodily processes.[117] Some even considered explicitly the physiological effects of religious practice. Albert the Great, for example, asked whether cessation of eating and of menstruation in holy women was damaging to their health.[118] A number of the major theologians of the thirteenth century (e.g., Albert the Great, Giles of Rome, Richard of Middleton) wrote both on embryology and on the resurrection of the body, and explicitly stated that there was a connection between the topics, for both bore on the question of the nature and identity of the human person.[119] A quick perusal of book 2, chapters 56 to 90, of the *Summa contra gentiles* convinces the reader that Aquinas assumed that questions of psychology, embryology and eschatology must be solved together. Moreover, a large section of Aquinas's long discussion of miracles in his *On the Power Of God* is concerned with whether demons or angels can make use of physical human bodies and, if so, exactly how they might do it. Since this kind of miracle did not loom large among those actually reported in Aquinas's day, one is tempted to attribute his interest in the question to the general fascination with which he and his contemporaries viewed the body/soul nexus.[120] Hagiographers too combined an interest in bodily miracles with exploration of medical lore, especially embryology. For example, Thomas of Cantimpré, the hagiographer who showed greatest interest in collecting somatic miracles, especially female ones,[121] wrote on gynecology as well.[122]

In theological treatments of psychology and embryology we see a tendency to confuse the body/soul boundary. Thirteenth- to fifteenth-century explorations into psychology used the Aristotelian conception of soul—that is, the idea that soul is the principle of life. According to such theory, plants and animals as well as humans have souls. This idea made it difficult for those who wrote about the biological process of conception to say at what point the fetus was ensouled with the rational soul given by God, or indeed whether it had one or several souls as it developed. Moreover, under the influence of Avicenna, theologians and natural philosophers tried to work out a theory of "spirits" or "powers" located between soul and body as a sort of rarefied instrument to connect the two. Such discussions drew a sharper line between levels of soul than between soul and body.[123]

One of the reasons for the obscuring of the body/soul boundary in these treatments lay in Aristotle's theory itself, which actually worked less well to explain embryological development than the Galenic two-seed theory preferred by doctors.[124] As part of their general adoption of Aristotelian philosophy, theologians were drawn to the idea that the father provides the form for the fetus and the mother the matter (or menstrual material), but the concept proved difficult to use in detail. How does the father's seed, which is material, carry form or vital spirit? It is hard to follow Giles of Rome's explanation, in the *De formatione corporis humani in utero,* of how the father's body concocts a seed with vital spirits, which in some sense engenders spirits in the menstrual matter, which in turn form organs. But one thing is clear: the line between soul and body, form and matter, disappears in a complex apparatus that obscures the transition point from one to the other.[125]

In discussions of eschatology from the same period, we find the human person treated as a similarly tight and integral union of soul and body. Indeed, the doctrine of the resurrection of the body seemed to require a theory of the person in which body was integral. Accounts of the history of philosophy have long seen it as one of Aquinas's greatest achievements to utilize the Aristotelian form/matter dichotomy as a way of explaining that bodily resurrection after the Last Judgment is philosophically necessay.[126] According to Aquinas's use of hylomorphic analysis, the soul as a substantial form survives the death of the body, but the full person does not exist until body (matter) is restored to its form at the end of time. "The soul . . . is not the full man and my soul is not I [*anima . . . non est totus homo et anima mea non est ego*]."[127]

What historians of philosophy have not fully realized, however, is that Aquinas's conservative opponents, as much as Aquinas himself, gave positive significance to body. Theologians in the second half of the thirteenth century debated whether material continuity was necessary for bodily resurrection. Did God have to reassemble in the resurrected body the same bits of matter that had before been animated by a particular soul? They also debated whether the human person was to be explained by a plurality of forms or by a single form.[128] These debated are too complex to explain fully here, but what is important for our purposes is that both conservative theologians and those who followed Aquinas wanted to make body integral to person. Aquinas made philosophically necessary, but in some sense telescoped body into form by holding both that soul is enough to account for individual continuity and that soul is the *forma corporeitatis*.[129] (In other words, it is soul that accounts for the "whatness" of body. Thus any matter that soul informs at the end of time will be *its* body.)[130] Those who opposed Thomas, following an older, platonic tradition, struggled to give body a greater substantial reality by positing a separate *forma corporeitatis* and arguing for material continuity in the resurrection. But to them too, the union of body and soul is necessary for personhood—and for happiness. Bonaventure wrote, in a sermon on the Assumption of the Virgin Mary:

> Her happiness would not be complete unless she [Mary] were there personally [i.e., bodily assumed into heaven]. The person is not the soul; it is a composite. Thus it is established that she must be there as a composite, that is, of soul and body. Otherwise she would not be there [in heaven] in perfect joy; for (as Augustine says) the minds of the saints [before their resurrections] are hindered, because of their natural inclination for their bodies, from being totally borne into God.[131]

Indeed, one can argue that those who differed with Aquinas, following a more Platonic, Augustinian or Franciscan tradition, gave even more importance to body than did the Thomists.[132] Henry of Ghent, for example, held to the theory of a separate *forma corporeitatis* so that the gifts of the glorified body could be understood as real change *of that body*, not merely as a consequence of change in the soul.[133] In general, Franciscan thinkers emphasized the yearning of soul and body for each other after death. Richard of Middleton and Bonaventure actually saw this yearning as a motive for the saints in heaven: the blessed supposedly pray all the harder for us sinners because they will receive again their own deeply desired bodies only when the number of the elect is filled up and the Judgment comes.[134] More than a hundred years before Bonaventure, Bernard of Clairvaux (the great Cistercian who anticipated many aspects of Franciscan piety) spoke thus of the joys of bodily resurrection:

> Do not be surprised if the glorified body seems to give the spirit something, for it was a real help when man was sick and mortal. How true that text is which says that all things turn to the good of those who love God [Rom. 8.28]. The sick, dead and resurrected body is a help to the soul who loves God; the first for the fruits of penance, the second for repose and the third for consummation. Truly the soul does not want to be perfected, without that from whose good services it feels it has benefited . . . in every way. . . . Listen to the bridegroom in the Canticle inviting us to this triple progress: 'Eat, friends, and drink; be inebriated, dearest ones.' He calls to those working in the body to eat; he invites those who have set aside their bodies to drink; and he impels those who have resumed their bodies to inebriate themselves, calling them his dearest one, as if they were filled with charity. . . . It is right to call them dearest who are drunk with love. . . . [135]

Discussions of eschatology emphasized the fascination and value of body in other ways as well, sometimes even obscuring differences between body and soul. In some of their more adventuresome explorations of the future life, theologians elevated aspects of body into the spiritual realm. They wondered, for example, whether the blessed in their glorified bodies would truly taste and smell, as well as see, the pleasures of heaven.[136] At other moments in theological discussion, soul seems almost to spill over into body. The gifts (*dotes*) of subtlety, impassibility, clarity and agility that characterize the bodies of the saved were understood to be a flowing over of the beatific vision—perhaps even a way in which soul expresses itself as body.[137]

A number of the issues theologians raised enabled them to explore the nature of bodiliness at its very boundaries. For example, they debated whether we can open and close our eyes in the glorified body, how old we will be in heaven, whether we will rise in two sexes, whether the wounds of the martyrs will still be present in the glorified body, and how the damned in their restored bodies (which are incorruptible but not impassible) can cry without losing any bodily matter through the dissolution of tears.[138] In such discussion, jejune though it has seemed to most modern commentators, a very profound conception of body is adumbrated—one in which both innate and acquired physical differences between persons, including biological sex and even the marks of human suffering, *are* the person for eternity. Theologians agreed that human beings rise in two sexes and with the traces not only of martyrdom but of other particularities as well.[139] Although defects will be repaired in glory and woman's sex can, in Aristotelian terms, be seen as a defect, theologians nonetheless asserted that, for reasons they could not fully explain, God's creation was more perfect in two sexes than in one.[140] What is temporary or temporal, according to this view, is not physical distinctiveness or gender, but the change we call corruption (or decay or dissolution) of material being.[141] This conception of body as integral to person—indeed, of body as being the conveyor of personal specificity—helps us understand how relics could in this culture be treated as if they *were* the saints.[142]

Moreover, the idea that body as well as soul is rewarded (or punished) at the end of time—an idea reflected not just in theology but also in the literary genre of the debate between Body and Soul—seemed to give significance to physical rewards that might come *before* death or the Last Judgment. The catatonic trances and miraculous inedia of living holy women, like the incorrupt bodies they sometimes displayed beyond the grave, could easily be understood as having achieved in advance the final incorruption and impassibility of the glorified body in heaven. Indeed, Christ was understood to have assumed all general defects of body in the Incarnation because, as Thomas said, "we know human nature only as it is subject to defect," and all particular defects are caused by the general defects of corruption and passibility.[143] Thus, even the ugliness of disease and suffering can be not only lifted up into the curative pangs of purgatory but also transmuted, through Christ's wondrous yet fully human body, into the beauty of heaven. (Presumably, stigmatics will still bear their marks before the throne of God, although the wounds will no longer bleed periodically.)[144]

By the 1330s the faithful were required to believe that the beatific vision could come to the blessed before the end of time; and theologians held, although in different ways, that the gifts of the glorified body were in some sense a consequence of the soul's vision of God.[145] Indeed, some theologians argued that a special miracle had been necessary to block the manifestation of God's glory in the human body of his son Jesus; the body Jesus displayed at the Transfiguration was, they held, his normal body, manifesting the beatific vision he constantly possessed.[146] Theologians were, of course, cautious about stating that any specific person had actually received the beatific vision. But in the context of such opinion, it is not surprising that hagiographers made extravagant claims, describing their holy subjects as rosy and beautiful despite (perhaps even because of) flagellation and self-starvation, excruciating disease and death itself.[147] Aquinas wrote that the martyrs were enabled to bear up under pain exactly because the beatific vision flows over naturally into the body.[148]

The widely shared assumption that bodies not only reflect the glory their souls receive in God's presence but are also the place where persons are rewarded or punished in their specificity underlies the many hagiographical stories and *exempla* from this period in which incorruption or other miraculous marks touch only part of a body. Caesarius of Heisterbach, for example, told of a master who copied many books; after death, his right hand was found undecayed although the rest of his body had turned to dust.[149] In another tale from Caesarius's collection, a pious man who said his prayers as he walked returned after death in a vision with the words *Ave Maria* written on his boots; God, says Caesarius, puts "the mark of glory most of all on those members by which it is earned."[150] Given the tremendous emphasis on female virginity as an avenue to sanctity, it is hardly surprising that the bodies of many female saints were found wholly intact many years after burial.[151] As Caesarius might have put it, God marked their unviolated bodies with permanent inviolability.

It is, moreover, hardly surprising that, as the doctrine of purgatory was elaborated, the experiences of souls there were imagined as bodily events, even though theologians taught that souls in this state subsisted without their bodies. Bodily metaphors for spiritual states are used in many societies. But more seems to be involved in these Christian ideas than mere convenience of metaphor. In technical theology as in popular miracle stories, pain was understood to be the experience of a psychosomatic unit. Aquinas said about the suffering of Christ's soul: "soul and body are one being. So when body is disturbed by some corporeal suffering, soul is of necessity disturbed indirectly as a result [*per accidens*]. . . ."[152] More generally in the culture, the reverse was assumed as well: when soul is disturbed, body is disturbed. Pain and imperviousness to it happen to a personal entity that is body and soul together.[153] So many forces in the religious life of the period conspired to suggest that persons *are* their bodies that preachers found it almost impossible to speak of immortal souls without clothing them in their quite particular flesh. The many tales of temporary resurrections of the dead, of corpses bleeding to accuse their murderers or sitting up to revere the Eucharist, of cadavers growing or smelling sweet or even exuding food after death, point to a widespread cultural assumption that person is body as well as soul, body integrally bound with soul.[154]

Conclusion

About the topics I have discussed above, much more could be said. But I have explained and explored enough to make it quite clear that the extraordinary bodily quality of women's piety between 1200 and 1500 must be understood in the context of attitudes toward woman and toward body peculiar to the later Middle Ages. Because preachers, confessors and spiritual directors assumed the person to be a psychosomatic unity, they not only read unusual bodily events as expressions of soul, but also expected body itself to offer a means of access to the divine. Because they worshiped a God who became incarnate and died for the sins of others, they viewed all bodily events—the hideous wounds of martyrs or stigmatics as well as the rosy-faced beauty of virgins—as possible manifestations of grace. Because they associated the female with the fleshly, they expected somatic expressions to characterize women's spirituality.

We must never forget the pain and frustration, the isolation and feelings of helplessness, that accompanied the quest of religious women. For all her charismatic empowerment, woman was inferior to man in the Middle Ages; her voice was often silenced, even more frequently ignored. Not every use of the phrase "weak woman" by a female writer was ironic; women clearly internalized the negative value placed on them by the culture in which they lived. Moreover, for all its expressiveness and lability, body was inferior to soul. The locus of fertility and of mystical encounter, it was also the locus of temptation and decomposition. Whereas soul was immortal, body rose again only after decay and as a result of the grace of Christ's Resurrection. Body was not always a friend or a tool or a gateway to heaven. Nonetheless, one of the most striking characteristics of this period in Western religious history is the extent to which female bodily experience was understood to be union with God.

The thirteenth-century Flemish Saint Christina the Astonishing, whose body lactated and levitated in mystical encounter, supposedly spoke of her own asceticism in a little dialogue that has many literary antecedents:

> Then wailing bitterly she began to beat her breast and her body ... "O miserable and wretched body! How long will you torment me ... ? Why do you delay me from seeing the face of Christ? When will you abandon me so that my soul can return freely to its Creator?" ... [T]hen, taking the part of the body, she would say... "O miserable soul! Why are you tormenting me in this way? What is keeping you in me and what is it that you love in me? Why do you not allow me to return to the earth from where I was taken and why do you not let me be at rest until I am restored to you on the Last Day of Judgment?" ... [S]he would then rest a little in silence. . . . Then, taking her feet with body hands, she would kiss the soles of her feet with greatest affection and would say, "O most beloved body! Why have I beaten you? Why have I reviled you? Did you not obey me in every good deed I undertook to do with God's help? You have endured the torment and hardships most generously and most patiently which the spirit placed on you. . . . Now, O best and sweetest body ... is an end of your hardship, now you will rest in the dust and will sleep for a little and then, at last, when the trumpet blows, you will rise again purified of all corruptibility and you will be joined in eternal happiness with the soul you have had as a companion in the present sadness."[155]

Christina's words express much of what a thirteenth-century woman and her hagiographer assumed about female body. Source of temptation and torment, body is also a beloved companion and helpmeet; delay and hindrance on earth, it is essential to the person herself and will be perfected and glorified in heaven.

Christina's words can be supplemented by a later and more gruesome dialogue, which is nonetheless descended from the genre in which Thomas of Cantimpré, her hagiographer, wrote. In the fifteenth-century *Disputacion Betwyx the Body and Wormes,* the anonymous author modifies the traditional debate between Body and Soul to dramatize death and decay.[156] Here a female body, so misled about the significance of flesh that she actually boasts of her descent from Eve, is forced to hear the message of Worms, who will strip the body of its stinking flesh, scouring the bones. Nonetheless, the poem does not end with the feast of Worms, not with the triumph of devils carrying Body off to hell. The poet argues for victory over death, not by denying the horrors of decay, but by identifying corruption with the suffering of Christ on the Cross.[157] As Christina says in Thomas's quite similar account: Body itself will rise again. Welcoming the "kys" of Worms and agreeing to "dwell to gedyr" with them in "lufl" until Judgment Day as "neghbors" and "frendes," Body arms herself with "gode sufferaunce" and anticipates the coming "blis of heuen" through the "mene and mediacione" of "our blissed Lord, our verry patrone."[158]

In such a dialogue, the modern reader glimpses the startling significance attributed to body, and especially female body, in the later Middle Ages. Clothing of decay and potential food for worms, female flesh was also an integral component of female person. Created and redeemed by God, it was a means of encounter with Him. Healed and elevated by grace, it was destined for glory at the Last Judgment. And in that Judgment it rose as female. Although medieval theologians did not fully understand why, they were convinced that God's creation was more perfect in two sexes than in one.

Notes

1. Peter of Vaux, "Life of Colette of Corbie," trans. Stephen Juliacus, ch. 10, par. 84, in *Acta sanctorum* (hereafter AASS), March, vol. 1 (Paris, 1865), p. 558. See Caroline Walker Bynum, *Holy Feast and Holy Fast: The Religious Significance of Food to Medieval Women* (hereafter HFHF) (Berkeley: University of California Press, 1987), p. 67.
2. Life of Lukardis, ch. 55, *Analecta Bollandiana* 18 (1899), p. 340.
3. Johann Huizinga, *The Waning of the Middle Ages: A Study of Forms of Life, Thought and Art in France and the Netherlands in the XIVth and XVth Centuries* (1924), trans. E Hopman (Pbk reprint: Garden City: Doubleday, 1956); Barbara W. Tuchman, *A Distant Mirror: The Calamitous Fourteenth Century* (New York: Knopf, 1978).
4. For discussion of the modern period, see Catherine Gallagher and Thomas Laqueur, eds., *The Making of the Modern Body; Sexuality and Society in the Nineteenth Century* (Berkeley: University of California Press, 1987). For discussion of the Middle Ages, see Danielle Jacquart and Claude Thomasset, *Sexualité et savoir médical au Moyen Age* (Paris: Presses universitaires de France, 1985); Jacques LeGoff, "Corps et idéologie dans l'Occident médiéval: La révolution corporelle," in *L'Imaginaire médiéval: Essais* (Paris: Gallimard, 1985), pp. 123–27; and Michel Sot, "Mépris du monde et résistance des corps aux XIe et XIIe siècles," and Jacques Dalarun, "Eve, Marie ou Madeleine? La dignité du corps feminin dans hagiographie médiévale," in *Médiévales* 8 (1985), *Le souci du corps*, pp. 6–32.
5. A close reading of the evidence LeGoff presents in "Corps et idéologie" makes this clear. In the twelfth- and thirteenth-century literature he cites, disease and deformity are symbols of sin or of the corruption of society (not primarily of sex); the disgust displayed toward body is ultimately a disgust toward the putrefaction that will be manifest most clearly in the grave.
6. I have discussed this in "Women Mystics and Eucharistic Devotion in the Thirteenth Century," *Women's Studies* 11 (1984), pp. 179–214; in "Fast, Feast and Flesh: The

Religious Significance of Food to Medieval Women," *Representations* 11 (Summer 1985), pp. 1–25; and in HFHF. The point is also made by Peter Dinzelbacher, "Europäische Frauenmystik des Mittelalters: Ein Überblick," in *Frauenmystik im Mittelalter,* ed. P. Dinzelbacher and D. Bauer, Wissenschaftliche Studientagung der Akademie der Diozese Rottenburg-Stuttgart 22–25. Februar 1984, in Weingarten (Ostfildern: Schwabenverlag, 1985), pp. 11–23; by Peter Brown, *The Cult of the Saints: Its Rise and Function in Latin Christianity* (Chicago: University of Chicago Press, 1981); by Jacques Gelis and Odile Redon, Preface, and Michel Bouvier, "De l'incorruptibilité des corps saints," in *Les miracles miroirs des corps,* eds. Gelis and Redon (Paris: Presses et publications de L'universite de Paris VIII, 1983), pp. 9–20, 193–221; by Marie-Christine Pouchelle, "Representations du corps dans la *Legende dorée,*" *Ethnologie française* 6 (1976), pp. 293–308; by Dominique de Courcelles, "Les corps des saints dans les cantiques catalans de la fin du moyen âge," *Médiévales* 8 (1985): *Le souci du corps,* pp. 43–56; and, in a different way, by Herbert Thurston, *The Physical Phenomena of Mysticism* (hereafter PP) (Chicago: Henry Regnery, 1952).

7. I have treated some of the material that follows in HFHF, although from a somewhat different point of view. I should, however, point out here that the material in the final two sections of this essay is new and goes considerably beyond anything touched on in HFHF.

8. P. Séjourné, "Reliques," *Dictionnaire de théologie catholique* (hereafter DTC) (Paris: Letouzey et Ané, 1903–72), vol. 13, pt. 2, cols. 2330–65; Patrick J. Geary, *Furta Sacra: Thefts of Relics in the Central Middle Ages* (Princeton, 1978), esp. pp. 152–54; and E.A.R. Brown, "Death and the Human Body in the Later Middle Ages: The Legislation of Boniface VIII on the Division of the Corpse," *Viator* 12 (1981), pp. 221–70, esp. pp. 223–24.

9. See Peter the Venerable, Sermon 4, *Patrologia latina,* ed. J.-P. Migne (hereafter PL), vol. 189 (Paris: 1890), cols. 1001–03; reedited by Giles Constable, "Petri Venerabilis Sermones Tres," *Revue Bénédictine* 64 (1954), pp. 269–70. See also Caesarius of Heisterbach, *Dialogus miraculorum,* ed. Joseph Strange, 2 vols. (Cologne: Heberle, 1851), bk. 8, ch. 87, vol. 2, pp. 145–46.

10. See, for example, the case of Lukardis, HFHF, pp. 113–14. See also, "Life of Lutgard of Aywières," bk. 1, chs. 1–2, and bk. 2, ch. 1, AASS, June, vol. 4 (Paris and Rome, 1867), pp. 192–94; and "Life of Benevenuta of Bojano," ch. 10, par. 82, AASS, October, vol. 13 (1883), p. 172.

11. Nicole Hermann-Mascard, *Les Reliques des saints: Formation coutumière d'un droit,* Société d'Histoire du Droit: collection d'histoire institutionnelle et sociale 6 (Paris: Edition Klincksieck, 1975), p. 274, n. 21. As examples, see the process of canonization of 1276 for Margaret of Hungary, in Vilmos Fraknói, *Monumenta romana episcopatus vesprimiensis (1103–1526),* vol. 1 (Budapest: Collegium Historicorum Hungarorum Romanum, 1896), pp. 237–38, 266, 267, 288; and the case of Lidwina of Schiedam, "Fast, Feast and Flesh," p. 5.

12. Angela of Foligno, *Le Livre de l'expérience des vrais fidèles: texte latin publié d'après le manuscrit d'Assise,* eds. and trans. M.-J. Ferré and L. Baudry (Paris: Editions E. Droz, 1927), par. 53, p. 106 (cf., *ibid.,* par. 80, p. 166); Raymond of Capua, *Legenda maior* of Catherine of Siena, AASS, April, vol. 3 (1866), pt. 2, ch. 4, pars. 155 and 162–63, and pt. 3, ch. 7, pars. 412 and 414, pp. 901–03, 963; Catherine of Genoa, *Il dialogo spirituale* and *Vita,* ch. 12, ed. Umile Bonzi da Genova, *S. Caterina Fieschi Adorno,* vol. 2, *Edizione critica dei manoscritti Cateriniani* (Turin: Marietti, 1962). pp. 422–27, 140–41. And see Thomas of Celano, "First Life of Francis of Assisi," bk. 1, ch. 7, par. 17, in *Analecta Franciscana* 10 (Quaracchi: Col-

legium S. Bonaventurae, 1941), p. 16; Celano, "Second Life," bk. 1, ch. 5, par. 9, in *ibid.,* pp. 135–63; Bonaventure, *Legenda maior* of Francis, pt. 1, ch. 1, pars. 5–6, in *ibid.,* pp. 562–63; and Bonaventure, *Leganda minor,* ch. 1, eighth lesson, in *ibid.,* pp. 657–58.

13. HFHF, pp. 122–23, 126, 211, 273–75.

14. Giles Constable, *Attitudes Toward Self-Inflicted Suffering in the Middle Ages,* The Ninth Stephen J. Brademas Sr. Lecture (Brookline, Mass.: Hellenic College Press, 1982); Richard Kieckhefer, *Unquiet Souls: Fourteenth-Century Saints and Their Religious Milieu* (Chicago: University of Chicago Press, 1984), chs. 3–5; Brenda Bolton, *"Mulieres sanctae," Studies in Church History* 10: *Sanctity and Secularity: The Church and the World,* ed. D. Baker (1973), pp. 77–93, and *idem, "Vitae Matrum:* A Further Aspect of the *Frauenfrage," Medieval Women: Dedicated and Presented to Professor Rosalind M.T. Hill . . . ,* ed. D. Baker, Studies in Church History: Subsidia 1 (Oxford, 1970), pp. 253–73.

15. "Life of Suso," ch. 31, in Henry Suso, *Deutsche Schriften im Auftrag der Württembergischen Kommission für Landesgeschichte,* ed. Karl Bihlmeyer (Stuttgart: Kohlhammer, 1907), pp. 91–92; trans. M. Ann Edwards, *The Exemplar: Life and Writings of Blessed Henry Suso, O.P.,* ed. Nicholas Heller, 2 vols. (Dubuque: Priory Press, 1962), vol. 1, pp. 87–88.

16. Angela of Foligno, *Le Livre,* par. 75, pp. 156–58.

17. Peter Browe, *Die Eucharistischen Wunder des Mittelalters,* Breslauer Studien zur historischen Theologie NF 4 (Breslau: Müller and Seiffert, 1938).

18. Peggy Reeves Sanday, *Divine Hunger: Cannibalism as a Cultural System* (New York: Cambridge University Press, 1986), and Louis-Vincent Thomas, *Le Cadavre: De la biologie à l'anthropologie* (Brussels: Editions complexe, 1980), pp. 159–69.

19. Ronald C. Finucane, *Miracles and Pilgrims: Popular Beliefs in Medieval England* (Totowa, N.J.: Rowan and Littlefield, 1977), pp. 197–98: Benedicta Ward, *Miracles and the Medieval Mind: Record and Event, 1000–1215* (Philadelphia: University of Pennsylvania Press, 1982), pp. 15–18; Gary Macy, *The Theologies of the Eucharist in the Early Scholastic Period: A Study of the Salvific Function of the Sacrament According to the Theologies, c.1080–c.1220* (Oxford: Oxford University Press, 1984), pp. 87–95; HFHF, p. 255.

20. Adam of Eynsham, *Life of Hugh of Lincoln,* eds. D. Douie and H. Farmer, 2 vols. (London: Thomas Nelson and Sons, 1961), bk. 5, ch. 15, vol. 2, p. 170.

21. Leo Steinberg, *The Sexuality of Christ in Renaissance Art and in Modern Oblivion* (New York, Pantheon, 1983).

22. See Louis Canet in Robert Fawtier and Louis Canet, *La double expérience de Catherine Benincasa (Sainte Catherine de Siene)* (Paris: Gallimard, 1948), pp. 245–46.

23. Peter Dinzelbacher, "Die 'Vita et Revelationes' der Wiener Begine Agnes Blannbekin (+1315) im Rahmen der Viten-und Offenbarungsliteratur ihrer Zeit," in Dinzelbacher and Bauer, eds., *Frauenmystik,* pp. 152–177.

24. See Thurston, PP; Dinzelbacher, "Überblick"; *idem, Vision und Visionsliteratur im Mittelalter* (Stuttgart: Hiersemann, 1981); Rudolph M. Bell, *Holy Anorexia* (Chicago: University of Chicago Press, 1985); and HFHF. As all four of the important recent books on saints make clear, these phenomena are particularly documented for Low Country women in the thirteenth century, for women in the Rhineland in the late thirteenth and early fourteenth centuries, and for north Italian women in the fourteenth to fifteenth centuries: see André Vauchez, *La sainteté en Occident aux derniers siècles du moyen âge d'après les procès de canonisation et les documents hagiographiques,* Bibliothèque des Ètudes Françaises d'Athènes et de Rome 241 (Rome: Ecole française de Rome, 1981); Donald Weinstein and Rudolph

M. Bell, *Saints and Society: The Two Worlds of Western Christendom, 1000–1700* (hereafter SS) (Chicago: University of Chicago Press, 1982); Michael Goodich, *Vita Perfecta: The Ideal of Sainthood in the Thirteenth Century,* Monographien zur Geschichtie des Mittelalters 25 (Stuttgart: Hiersemann, 1982); and Kieckhefer, *Unquiet Souls.*

25. Thurston, PP, esp. pp. 69, 95–99, 123; Antoine Imbert-Gourbeyre, *La Stigmatisation: L'Extase divine et les miracles de Lourdes: Réponse aux libres-penseurs,* 2 vols. (Clermont-Ferrand, 1894), which must be used with caution; Pierre Debongnie, "Essai critique sur l'histoire des stigmatisations au Moyen Age," *Etudes carmélitaines* 21.2 (1936), pp. 22–59: E. Amann, "Stigmatisation," DTC, vol. 14, pt. l, cols. 2617–19.

26. J.-K. Huysmans, *Sainte Lydwine de Schiedam* (Paris, 1901), pp. 288–91, which, however, contains no documentation; Thurston, PP. pp. 268–70; Hermann-Mascard, *Les Reliques,* pp. 68–69; Charles W. Jones, *Saint Nicolas of Myra, Bari and Manhattan: Biography of a Legend* (Chicago: University of Chicago Press, 1978), pp. 144–53; and Bynum, "Fast, Feast and Flesh," nn. 22, 81, 82, 85. Women also account for most of the cases of exuding sweet odors: see Thurston, PP, pp. 222–32.

27. HFHF, pp. 203–04, 257, 268–69; Bynum, "Women Mystics," p. 202.

28. Clare of Montefalco's spiritual sisters tore out her heart after her death and found the insignia of the Passion incised upon it; see Vauchez, *La sainteté,* p. 408. Three precious stones, with images of the Holy Family on them, were supposedly found in the heart of Margaret of Città di Castello; see "Life of Margaret," ch. 8, *Analecta Ballandiana* 19 (1900), pp. 27–28. On mystical espousal rings and miraculous bodily elongation, see Thurston, PP, pp. 139 and 200.

29. The point is Pouchelle's; see Marie-Christine Pouchelle, *Corps et chirurgie à l'apogée du Moyen Age* (Paris: Flammarion, 1983), pp. 132–36. She claims that the earliest official dissections (in 1315) were dissections of female bodies. The dissections to which she refers were clearly not the first dissections or autopsies of any sort. Dissections arising out of embalming or for the purpose of determining the cause of death in legal cases were practiced at least from the early thirteenth century; dissections of the human body for teaching purposes were practiced at Bologna about 1300. See Walter Artelt, *Die ältesten Nachrichten über die Sektion menschlicher Leichen im mittelalterlichen Abendland,* Abhandlungen zur Geschichte der Medizin und der Naturwissenschaften 34 (Berlin: Ebering, 1940), pp. 3–25: Mary Niven Alston, "The Attitude of the Church Towards Dissection Before 1500," *Bulletin of the History of Medicine* 16 (1944), pp. 221–38; Ynez Viole O'Neill, "Innocent III and the Evolution of Anatomy," *Medical History* 20.4 (1976), pp. 429–33; Nancy G. Siraisi, "The Medical Learning of Albertus Magnus," in James A. Weisheipl, ed., *Albertus Magnus and the Sciences: Commemorative Essays, 1980* (Toronto: Pontifical Institute of Medieval Studies, 1980), p. 395; and Jacquart and Thomasset, *Sexualité,* p. 49.

30. According to the tables in Weinstein and Bell, SS, women provide twenty-seven percent of the wonder-working relics, although only seventeen and one-half percent of the saints. On blood prodigies, see Thurston, PP, pp. 283–93.

31. Claude Carozzi, "Douceline et les autres," in *La religion populaire en Languedoc du XIIIe siècle à la moitié du XIVe siècle,* Cahiers de Fanjeaux ll (Toulouse, 1967), pp. 251–67; and see de Courcelles, "Les corps des saints," esp. p. 51.

32. Thurston, PP, pp. 233–82, esp. pp. 246–52. Of the forty-two saints living between 1400 and 1900 whose feasts are kept by the universal church, there are claims of incorruption in twenty-two cases, and in seven more there are reports of odd phenomena which imply non-decay. Seventeen of the incorrupt are male, but of the six

females among the forty-two, five are incorrupt and for the sixth (Jane Frances de Chantal), who was embalmed, there appears to be a claim for extraordinary survival. There are thus more incorrupt male bodies, but all the female bodies are claimed to be incorrupt. On incorruption, see also Bouvier, "De l'incorruptibilité"; João de Pina-Cabral, *Sons of Adam, Daughters of Eve: The Peasant World of the Alto Minho* (Oxford, 1986), pp. 230–38; and Bynum, "Holy Anorexia in Modern Portugal," in *Culture, Medicine and Phychiatry* 12 (1988), pp. 259–68. For examples of miraculous bodily closure in women saints, see Bynum, "Fast, Feast and Flesh," n. 54.

33. Weinstein and Bell, SS, pp. 234–35.

34. Ernst Benz, *Die Vision: Erfahrungsformen und Bilderwelt* (Stuttgart: Ernst Klett, 1969), pp. 17–34; Kieckhefer, *Unquiet Souls,* pp. 57–58; and Elizabeth A. Petroff, *Medieval Women's Visionary Literature* (Oxford: Oxford University Press, 1986), pp. 37–44.

35. Julian of Norwich, *A Book of Showings,* long text, chs. 2–4, eds. E. Colledge and J. Walsh, 2 vols., P.I.M.S. Studies and Texts 35 (Toronto: Pontifical Institute of Medieval Studies, 1978), vol. 2, pp. 285–98; "Life of Villana de' Botti," ch. 1, pars. 11–12, AASS, August, vol. 5 (1868), pp. 866–67; Caroline Walker Bynum, *Jesus as Mother: Studies in the Spirituality of the High Middle Ages* (Berkeley: University of California Press, 1982), pp. 192 and 253 n. 295; L. Reypens, ed., *Vita Beatricis: De autobiografie van de Z. Beatrys van Tienln O. Cist. 1200–1268* (Antwerp: Ruusbroec-Genootschap, 1964), p. 64; G.G. Meersseman, ed., "Life of Margaret of Ypres," in "Frères prêcheurs et mouvement dévot en Flandre au XIIIe siècle," *Archivum fratrum praedicatorum* 18 (1948), pp. 125–26; Bynum, "Fast, Feast and Flesh," pp. 4–8; Kiechkefer, *Unquiet Souls,* pp. 22–33; "Life of Alpais of Cudot," AASS, November, vol. 2.1 (1894), pp. 167–209; "Life of Serafina of San Gimignano," AASS, March, vol. 2 (1865), pp. 232–38.

36. *Vita Beatricis,* ed. Reypens, bk. 3, ch. 6, pp. 134–36. See also pp. 45–49, 63, 99, 154–55. The poet Hadewijch also speaks of ecstasy as "insanity"; see poem 15, Poems in Couples, in Hadewijch, *The Complete Works,* trans. C. Hart (New York: Paulist Press, 1980), pp. 350–52. Philip of Clairvaux in his "Life of Elisabeth of Spalbeek" calls her ecstasy *imbecillitas;* see *Catalogus codicum hagiographicorum Bibliothecae regiae Bruxellensis,* Subsidia hagiographica 1, vol. 1.1 (Brussels, 1886), p. 364.

37. Process of canonization, art. 33, in Jacques Cambell, ed., *Enquéte pour le procès de canonisation de Dauphine de Puimichel, comtesse d' Ariano (+26-xi-1360)* (Turin: Erasmo, 1978), p. 52.

38. "Life of Alice," ch. 3, para. 26, AASS, June, vol. 2 (1867), p. 476. And see "Life of Lutgard of Aywières," bk. 3, ch. l, AASS. p. 204. The emphasis on service is important. Even those women who languished alone in illness thought of themselves as saving others through their suffering. Although all recent works on saints (Vauchez, *La sainteté,* Weinstein and Bell, SS, Goodich, *Vita Perfecta* and Kieckhefer, *Unquiet Souls*) have contrasted contemplative women with active ones and have seen the active form of life to be more characteristic of Italian women, I take issue with this dichotomy; see HFHF, chs.1 and 4.

39. See Jerome Kroll and Bernard Bachrach, "Sin and the Etiology of Disease in Pre-Crusade Europe," *Journal of the History of Medicine and Allied Sciences* 41 (1986), pp. 395–414; Alain Saint-Denis, "Soins du corps et médecine contre la souffrance à l'Hôtel-Dieu de Laon au XIIIe siècle," *Médiévales* 8 (1985); *Le souci du corps,* pp. 33–42; Katharine Park, "Medicine and Society in Medieval Europe, 500–1500," in Andrew Wear, ed., *Medicine in Society* (Cambridge: Cambridge University Press), ch. 2, forthcoming.

40. "Life of Alpais," bk. 3, ch. 4, and bk. 4, ch. 1, AASS, pp. 196–97 and 198. For Elsbeth Achler, see Bihlmeyer, ed., "Die Schwäbische Mystikerin Elsbeth Achler von Reute († 1420) . . . ," *Festgabe Philipp Strauch zum 80. Geburtstag am 23, September 1932,* ed. G. Bäsecke and F.J. Schneider (Halle: Niemeyer, 1932), pp. 88–109. On Catherine, see Raymond of Capua, *Legenda maior,* pt. 2, ch. 5, par. 167, AASS, p. 904.

41. Elsbet Stagel, *Das Leben der Schwestern zu Töss beschrieben von Elsbet Stagel,* ed. Ferdinand Vetter, Deutsche Texte des Mittelalters 6 (Berlin: Weidmann, 1906). p. 37.

42. "Life of Walburga" (d. 799) by Wolfhard of Eichstadt, in AASS, February, vol. 3 (Antwerp, 1658), pp. 528 and 540–42.

43. Pierre-André Sigal, *L'homme et les miracles dans la France médièvale (XI-XIIe siècle),* (Paris: Editions du Cerf, 1985), esp. pp. 259–61.

44. Dinzelbacher, "Überblick"; and Peter Dronke, *Women Writers of the Middle Ages: A Critical Study of Texts from Perpetua († 203) to Marguerite Porete († 1310)* (Cambridge: Cambridge University Press, 1984), pp. x–xi.

45. See, for example, Bernard of Clairvaux, *Sermones super Cantica Canticorum,* sermon 71, *Sancti Barnardi opera,* ed. J. Leclercq, C.H. Talbot and H.M. Rochais (Rome: Editiones Cistercienses, 1958), vol. 2, pp. 214–24; John Tauler, sermon 31, in *Die Predigten Taulers,* ed. Ferdinand Vetter (Berlin: Wiedman, 1910), p. 310. See also Huizinga, *Waning,* pp. 197–200.

46. This point is made in a number of the papers in Dinzelbacher and Bauer, eds., *Frauenmystik.* See esp. Franz Wöhrer, "Aspekte der englischen Frauenmystik im späten 14. und beginnenden 15. Jahrhundert," pp. 431–40.

47. See above nn.10, 13, 26, 27, 36; and Hadewijch, vision 7, in *Complete Works,* trans. C. Hart, pp. 280–81.

48. See Siegfried Ringler, "Die Rezeption mittelalterlicher Frauenmystik als wissenschaftliches Problem, dargestellt am Werk der Christine Ebner," and Dinzelbacher, "Agnes Blannbekin," in Dinzelbacher and Bauer, eds., *Frauenmystik,* pp. 178–200 and 152–77; and Bynum, "Women Mystics," pp. 185–92. Miraculous elements tend to be more or less stressed in accounts of visions depending on the audience for which they are composed; see Simone Roisin, *L'Hagiographie Cistercienne dans le diocèse de Liège au XIIIe siècle* (Louvain, 1947).

49. For a comparison of male and female visions, see Dinzelbacher, *Vision,* pp. 151–55 and 226–28; Kieckhefer, *Unique Souls,* p. 172; Bynum, "Women Mystics," pp. 181–84.

50. Bynum, *Jesus as Mother,* pp. 110–69; HFHF, ch. 3; and Hester G. Gelber, "A Theatre of Virtue: The Exemplary World of St. Francis of Assisi," *Saints and Virtues,* ed. J.S. Hawley (Berkeley: University of California Press, 1987), pp.15–35.

51. Browe, *Die Wunder,* pp.110–11; Tauler, sermon 31, *Die Predigten,* pp. 310–11.

52. Wöhrer, "Aspekte der englischen Frauenmystik."

53. For Hadewijch, see *Complete Works,* trans. C. Hart. For Marguerite Porete, see Romana Guarnieri, ed., "Il 'Miroir des simples âmes' di Margherita Porete," *Archivio Italiano per la storia della pietà* 4 (1965), pp. 501–635, and Dronke, *Women Writers,* pp. 202–28.

54. Marguerite of Oingt, *Les oeuvres de Marguerite d'Oingt,* ed. and trans. Antonin Duraffour, Pierre Gardette and P. Durdilly (Paris: Société d'édition 'Les belles lettres,' 1965), p. 147.

55. Angela of Foligno, *Le livre,* par. 167, pp. 382–84.

56. *Ibid.,* pars. 66 and 151, pp. 138–40 and 326. For the contrast between Eckhart and women mystics, see Otta Langer, "Zur dominikanischen Frauenmystik im

spätmittelalterlichen Deutschland," in Dinzelbacher and Bauer, eds., *Frauenmystik*, pp. 341–46.

57. See HFHF, p. 210.

58. This difference cuts across differences of class or region. The few female saints we know of from poorer groups in society are remarkably similar in their pious practices to the saintly princesses and noblewomen of the period; see Weinstein and Bell, SS, pp. 216 and 220–38. On regional differences, see n. 38 above.

59. For helpful remarks on this topics, see Barbara Duden, "A Repertory of Body History," *Zone* 5 (1989).

60. *Jesus as Mother*, pp. 9–21 and 170–262; and "Women Mystics," pp. 192–96. The argument is implied in the title of a recent collection, *Women of Spirit: Female Leadership in the Jewish and Christian Traditions*, eds. Rosemary Reuther and Eleanor McLaughlin (New York: Simon and Schuster, 1979). Petroff, *Women's Visionary Literature*, p. 27, argues that writing itself was considered a male activity; therefore women needed direct divine inspiration to call a writing and speaking voice into existence.

61. HFHF, pp. 76–77, 229, 253. Eucharistic visions, especially visions of the bleeding host, occurred to women more frequently than to men; see Browe, *Die Wunder*.

62. Herbert Grundmann, "Die Frauen und die Literatur im Mittelalter: Ein Beitrag zur Frage nach der Entstehung des Schrifttums in der Volksprache," *Archiv für Kulturgeschichte* 26 (1936), pp. 129–61.

63. Margot Schmidt, "Elemente der Schau bei Mechtild von Magdeburg und Mechtild von Hackeborn: Zur Bedeutung der geistlichen Sinne," in Dinzelbacher and Bauer, eds., *Frauenmystik*, pp. 123–151.

64. Petroll, *Women's Visionary Literature*, pp. 28–32.

65. For Hildegard of Bingen dressing her nuns as brides to receive communion, see "Letter of Abbess T[engswich] of Andernach to Hildegard," epistle 116, PL 197, col. 336c. For examples of cradles and baby Christ figures used by women in the liturgy, see Elisabeth Vavra, "Bildmotiv und Frauenmystik—Funktion und Rezeption," in Dinzelbacher and Bauer, eds., *Frauenmystik*, pp. 201–30; Ursula Schlegel, "The Christchild as Devotional Image in Medieval Italian Sculpture: A Contribution to Ambrogio Lorenzetti Studies," *The Art Bulletin* 52.1 (March 1970), pp.1–10; and Petroff, *Women's Visionary Literature*, p. 54, n. 22. The crib in the Metropolitan Museum is fifteenth century and from the Grand Beguinage in Louvain.

66. Thurston, PP; I.M. Lewis, *Ecstatic Religion: An Anthropological Study of Spirit Possession and Shamanism* (Harmondsworth: Penguin, 1971); Bynum, "Holy Anorexia in Modern Portugal"; Katherine Carlitz, "Private Suffering as a Public Statement: Biographies of Virtuous Women in Sixteenth-Century China," paper delivered at the Seventh Berkshire Conference on the History of Women, June 1987; Robert McClory, "Cutters: Mutilation: The New Wave in Female Self-Abuse," *Reader: Chicago's Free Weekly* 15.48 (September 5, 1986), pp, 29–38.

67. Le Goff, "Corps et idéologie," pp, 123–25.

68. Robert W. Ackerman, "*The Debate of the Body and the Soul* and Parochial Christianity," *Speculum* 37 (1962), pp. 541–65, esp. pp. 552–53. In the dialogue, Flesh does try to retaliate by suggesting that sin lies rather in the will—i.e., that it should really be charged to Soul's account.

69. Clarissa Atkinson, "Precious Balsam in a Fragile Glass: The Ideology of Virginity in the Later Middle Ages," *Journal of Family History* 8.2 (Summer 1982), pp. 131–43; Marc Glasser, "Marriage in Medieval Hagiography," *Studies in Medieval and Renaissance History* n.s. 4 (1981), pp. 3–34.

70. Kari Elisabeth Børresen, *Subordination et équivalence: Nature et rôle de la femme d'après Augustin et Thomas d'Aquin* (Oslo, 1968); Vern L. Bullough, "Medieval Medical and Scientific Views of Women," *Viator* 4 (1973), pp. 487–93; Eleanor McLaughlin, "Equality of Souls, Inequality of Sexes: Women in Medieval Theology," *Religion and Sexism: Images of Women in the Jewish and Christian Traditions,* eds. Reuther and McLaughlin (New York: Simon and Schuster, 1974), pp. 213–66; Marie-Thérèse d'Alverny, "Comment les théologiens et les philosophes voient la femme?" *La femme dans les civilisations des Xe-XIIIe siècles: Actes du colloque tenu à Poitiers les 23–25 Septembre 1976, Cahiers de civilisation médiévale* 20 (1977), pp. 105–29; Natalie Z. Davis, *Society and Culture in Early Modern France* (Stanford: Stanford University Press, 1975), pp. 124–31.

71. Medieval theologians sometimes carried the dichotomy further, suggesting that the mother was responsible for the nurture of the child's body but the father was charged with its *educatio*—that is, the nourishing of its soul. See John T. Noonan, Jr., *Contraception: A History of Its Treatment by the Catholic Theologians and Canonists,* enlarged ed. (Cambridge, Mass.: Harvard University Press, 1986), p. 280. Female theologians agreed with male ones about the dichotomy but sometimes used it in unusual ways. See, for example, the discussion of Hildegard of Bingen in Prudence Allen, *The Concept of Woman: The Aristotelian Revolution 750 B.C–A.D. 1250* (Montreal and London: Eden Press, 1985), p. 297, and the works on Hildegard cited in n. 104 below.

72. Weinstein and Bell, SS, pp. 234–36; Dalarun, "Eve, Marie ou Madeleine?"

73. James of Voragine, *Legenda aurea vulgo historia lombardica dicta,* ed. T. Graesse (Dresden and Leipzig: Libraria Arnoldiana, 1846). According to my very rough count, twenty-three of twenty-four female martyrs defend their virginity. (Twelve die.) There are only six cases of male saints whose virginity is threatened. (Only one dies.) In contrast, there are forty-eight temporary resurrections of men, only nine of women. Such an emphasis on the inviolability of the living female body should be placed against the background of the culture's similar emphasis on the incorruptibility of the female dead and in the context also of various miraculous body closures; see above n. 32 and below n. 98. On the extraordinary popularity and diffusion of the Golden Legend, see Brenda Dunn-Lardeau, ed., *Legenda aurea: Sept siècles de diffusion* (Montreal and Paris: Bellarmin and J. Vrin, 1986).

74. For an influential article that projects back into the earlier Western tradition the modern nature/culture contrast, see Sherry Ortner, "Is Female to Male as Nature Is to Culture?" in Michelle Z. Rosaldo and Louise Lamphere, eds., *Women, Culture and Society* (Stanford: Stanford University Press, 1974,), pp. 67–86. For criticisms of Ortner's approach, on these and other grounds, see Eleanor Leacock and June Nash, "Ideologies of Sex: Archetypes and Stereotypes," *Issues in Cross-Cultural Research* 285 (New York: New York Academy of Sciences, 1977), pp. 618–45; and Carol P. MacCormack and M. Strathern, eds., *Nature, Culture and Gender* (Cambridge: Cambridge University Press, 1980). The point about the mixing of genders has been nicely made by Eleanor McLaughlin, "'Christ My Mother': Feminine Naming and Metaphor in Medieval Spirituality," *Nashota Review* 15 (1975).

75. See Valerie Lagorio, "Variations on the Theme of God's Motherhood in Medieval English Mystical and Devotional Writings," *Studia mystica* 8 (1985), pp. 15–37, which gives citations to earlier literature on the subject.

76. HFHF, pp. 266–67.

77. Gertrud Schiller, *Ikonographie der christlichen Kunst,* vol. 4, pt, 1: *Die Kirche* (Gütersloh: Gerd Mohn, 1976), plates 217–19; and Robert Zapperi, *L'Homme*

enceint: L'Homme, la femme et le pouvoir, trans. M.-A.M Vigueur (Paris: Presses Universitaires de France, 1983), pp. 19–46.

78. For Christ bleeding into the chalice (either in the so-called "Mass of St. Gregory" or the "Eucharistic Man of Sorrows"), see Gertrud Schiller, *Iconography of Christian Art,* trans. J. Seligman, vol. 2, *The Passion of Jesus Christ* (London: Humphries, 1972), plates 707, 708, 710, 806; and Ewald M. Vetter, "Mulier amicta sole und mater salvatoris," *Münchner Jahrbuch der bildenden Kunst,* ser. 3, vols. 9 and 10 (1958–59), pp. 32–71, esp. p. 51. For the so-called "Double Intercession," in which Christ's wound is made parallel to Mary's lactating breast, see Schiller, *Iconography,* vol. 2, *Passion,* pls. 798 and 802; Barbara G. Lane, *The Altar and the Altarpiece: Sacramental Themes in Early Netherlandish Painting* (New York: Harper & Row, 1984), pp, 7–8; and A. Monballieu, "Het Antonius Tsgrootentriptiekje (1507) uit Tongerloo van Goosen van der Weyden," *Jaarboek van het Koninklijl Museum voor Schone Kunsten Antwerpen* (1967), pp. 13–36. I am grateful to Stephen Wight and James Marrow for help with this point and with the material in the next two notes.

79. HFHF, pp. 165–80. By the sixteenth century, artists often showed Catherine drinking from Christ's side while he lifted the open wound toward her mouth with his fingers in the same gesture *Maria lactans* usually employs to present her nipple to her baby son. See engravings by M. Florini (1597) and Pieter de Jode (1600 or 1606), after Francisco Vanni; W. Pleister, "Katharina von Siena," *Lexikon der christlichen Ikonographie,* ed. W. Braunfels (Vienna: Herder, 1974), vol. 7, col. 305, pl. 4: and "Peeter de Jode l," *Wurzbuch Niederländisches Kunstler Lexikon* (Leipzig: Halm and Goldmann, 1906), vol. l, p. 759, item 12. See also the painting of Catherine's vision by Ludovico Gimignani (1643–97) reproduced in Jean-Noël Vuarnet, *Extases feminines* (Paris: Artuad, 1980), n.p., and the eighteenth-century painting of the same scene by Gaetano Lapis reproduced in Giuliana Zandri, "Documenti per Santa Caterina da Siena in Via Giulia," *Commentari* 22 (1971), p. 242, fig. 2.

80. The picture reproduced in figure 6 exists in at least four versions; the best (signed and dated to 1527) is in Munich. See *Le siècle de Bruegel: La peinture en Belgique au XVIe siècle,* 2nd ed. (Brussels: Musées Royaux des Beaux-Arts de Belgique, 1963), pp. 106–07, item 115; and Max J. Friedländer, *Early Netherlandish painting,* vol. 8, *Jan Gossart and Bernart van Orley,* notes by Pauwels and Herzog, trans. H. Norden (Leyden: Sijhoff, 1972), pl. 29. Several other depicitons of the Virgin and child by Gossart show a similar enlarging of the child's breasts: see Friedländer, *Jan Gossart,* pl. 31, no. 30, pl. 36, nos. 38a and b; and Larry Silver, "*Figure nude, historie e poesie:* Jan Gossaert and the Renaissance Nude in the Netherlands," *Nederlands kunsthistorisch Jaarboek* 36(1986), pp. 25–28. One of these uses the two-fingered lifting gesture by which the Virgin calls attention to the child's nipple: Friedländer, *Jan Gossart,* pl. 31, no. 30. Gossart also draws attention to the Virgin's breast, especially by having the child lean on it, stroke it or cuddle against it as he sleeps; see *ibid.,* pls. 33, 36, 38; and Silver, "*Figure nude,*" p. 28, pl. 45. It is possible that one should not seek a Christological explanation for this iconographic emphasis, since Gossart appears in at least one place to represent *putti* with engorged breasts; see the *putti* on the base of the columns depicted on shutters now in the Toledo Museum; Friedländer, *Jan Gossart,* pl. 17. Gossart shared the late medieval–Renaissance fascination with hermaphrodites; he drew the famous statue of the *Resting Apollo* or *Hermaphrodite* on his trip to Rome in 1508 and illustrated the story of Hermaphroditus and Salmacis: see Max Friedländer, *Early Netherlandish Paintings From Van Eyck to Bruegel,* trans. Marguerite Kay (New York: Phaidon, 1965), p. 96 and pl. 210; and Silver, "*Figure nude,*" p. 17. His hermaphroditic infants may reflect this interest or may

indeed simply be Mannerist efforts to shock. Critical discussion of Gossart always emphasizes the "massive," "heavy," "carnal" quality of the bodies he depicts; his attention to the breast and especially to the engorged male breast has not been commented on.

81. Pouchelle, *Corps,* pp. 157–60. It is a truism that medical and theological opinion were not, in the Middle Ages, fully compatible; this was especially true of opinion about sexual practice and abstinence, See Joan Cadden. "Medieval Scientific and Medical Views of Sexuality: Questions of Propriety," *Medievalia et Humanistica* n.s. 14 (1986), pp. 157–71; and Jacquart and Thomasset, *Sexualité,* p. 265ff. Nonetheless, in the ideas about gender which I discuss here, medical, theological and folk conceptions were quite often compatible and similar. See also Park, "Medicine and Society in Medieval Europe."

82. See HFHF and Bynum, "The Body of Christ in the Later Middle Ages: A Reply to Leo Steinberg," *Renaissance Quarterly* 39.3 (1986), pp. 399–439. In what follows, I shall not, for the most part, repeat documentation given in those two studies.

83. Thomas Aquinas, *Summa theologiae,* Blackfriars ed., 61 vols. (New York: McGraw-Hill, 1964–81), pt. 3a, q. 28, art. I, vol. 51, p. 41, and 3a, q. 32, art. 4, vol. 52, p. 55. Bonaventure, *De assumptione B. Virginis Mariae,* sermon 1, sec, 2, in *S. Bonaventurae opera omnia,* ed. Collegium S. Bonaventurae (Quarrachi: Collegium S. Bonaventurae, 1901), vol. 9, p. 690.

84. Lane, *Altar,* pp. 71–72; Carol J. Purtle, *The Marian Paintings of Jan van Eyck* (Princeton, 1982), pp. 13–15, 27–29 and passim; Vetter, "Mulier amicta sole und mater salvatoris"; and Bynum, "Reply to Steinberg," pl. 8.

85. Erna Lesky, *Die Zeugungs- und Vererbungslehren der Antike und ihr Nachwirken* (Mainz, 1950); Joseph Needham, *A History of Embryology,* 2nd ed. (Cambridge: Cambridge University Press, 1959), pp. 37–74; Anthony Preus, "Galen's Criticism of Aristotle's Conception Theory," *Journal of the History of Biology* 10 (1977), pp. 65–85; Thomas Laquer, "Orgasm, Generation and the Politics of Reproductive Biology," in *The Making of the Modern Body,* eds. Gallagher and Laqueur; *idem, The Female Orgasm and the Body Politic,* work in progress; and Pouchelle, *Corps.* Galen's two-seed theory holds that both male and female contribute to the matter of the fetus; Galen is unclear, however, on what the female seed is—i.e., on whether it is the menstruum or a female lubricant; see Preus, "Galen's Criticism." The situation in the Middle Ages was further complicated by the fact that Galen was known partly in spurious texts; see Luke Demaitre and Anthony A. Travill, "Human Embrology and Development in the Works of Albertus Magnus," in *Albertus Magnus and the Sciences,* ed. Weisheipl, pp, 414–16. The account of Galen and his influence in Allen, *Concept of Woman,* is oversimplified.

86. Pouchelle, *Corps,* p. 234 and passim.

87. M. Anthony Hewson, *Giles of Rome and the Medieval Theory of Conception: A Study of the* Deformatione corporis humani in utero (London: University of London, Athlone Press, 1975); and Jacquart and Thomasset, *Sexualité,* pp. 87–92.

88. See Mary McLaughlin, "Survivors and Surrogates: Children and Parents from the Ninth to the Thirteenth Centuries," *The History of Childhood,* ed. L. DeMause (New York: Psychohistory Press, 1974), pp. 115–18; Charles T. Wood, "The Doctors' Dilemma: Sin, Salvation and the Menstrual Cycle in Medieval Thought," *Speculum* 56 (1981), pp. 710–27, esp. p. 719; Pouchelle, *Corps,* pp. 263–66. The Aristotelian idea that blood is the basic fluid, concocted into milk, semen, etc., is a partial departure from the earlier theory of the four humors and not fully compatible with it; see Preus, "Galen's Criticism," pp. 76–78.

89. Pouchelle, *Corps,* p. 264. Some anatomists actually held that the womb and breasts were connected by a blood vessel; see Jacquart and Thomasset, *Sexualité,* pp. 59–60, 71–72.

90. *Ibid.,* p. 100.

91. Blood was a highly ambiguous symbol. But exactly because the culture held it to be in some ways impure, the shedding of blood, either naturally or through cauterization or leeching, was purgative. Thus, although menstrual blood was taboo, menstruation was a necessary and positive function. See Pouchelle, *Corps,* pp. 115–23; Jacquart and Thomasset, *Sexualité,* pp. 99–108; Kroll and Bachrach, "Sin and . . . Disease," esp. p. 409; and L. Gougaud, "La pratique de la phlébotomie dans les cloitres," *Revue Mabillon* 53 (1924), pp. 1–13.

92. Male suspicion of women's visionary and charismatic experiences, like male distrust of the female body, was never absent. It seems to have increased in the later fourteenth, fifteenth and sixteenth centuries. See Vauchez, *La Sainteté,* pp. 439–48; Weinstein and Bell, SS, pp. 228–32; and Edouard Dumoutet, *Corpus Domini: Aux sources de la pieté eucharistique médiévale* (Paris, 1942), p. 125. The increase in witchcraft accusations in the same period is an aspect of this mistrust.

93. Francine Cardman, "The Medieval Question of Women and Orders," *The Thomist* 42 (October 1978), pp. 582–99.

94. For examples of hagiographers who praise woman as "virile," see "Life of Ida of Louvain," AASS, April, vol. 2 (1865), p. 159; and "Life of Ida of Léau," AASS, October, vol. 13 (1883), p. 112. The compliment could, of course, cut both ways.

95. According to Christ and Paul, the first shall be last, the meek shall inherit the earth, and the foolishness of men is wisdom before God. See Bynum, *Jesus as Mother,* pp. 127–28, and *idem,* "Women's Stories, Women's Symbols: A Critique of Victor Turner's Theory of Liminality," *Anthropology and the Study of Religion,* ed. F. Reynolds and R. Moore (Chicago: Center for the Scientific Study of Religion, 1984), pp. 105–24.

96. Bynum, *Jesus as Mother,* pp. 110–69; HFHF, pp. 80 and 281; Vauchez, *La Sainteté,* p. 446 n. 511; Dronke, *Women Writers.*

97. Laqueur, *Female Orgasm;* Pouchelle, *Corps,* pp. 223–27, 307–10, 323–25; Jacquart and Thomasset, *Sexualité,* pp. 50–52; Claude Thomasset, "La répresentation de la sexualité et de la génération dans la pensée scientifique médiévale," in *Love and Marriage in the Twelfth Century,* eds. Willy Van Hoecke and A. Welkenhuysen, Mediavalia Lovaniensia, ser. l, studia 8 (Louvain: The University Press, 1981), pp. 1–17, esp. pp. 7–8.

98. In discussing women's right to drink wine in the monastery, Abelard claims that women are rarely inebriated because their bodies are humid and pierced with many holes. See Allen, *Concept of Woman,* p. 281. See also Pouchelle, *Corps,* pp. 310 and 323–27, and Jacquart and Thomasset, *Sexualité,* p. 66, on the general sense in the culture that the female body is full of openings. Such assumptions are part of the background to the emphasis in saints' lives on miraculous closure; see above nn. 29 and 32, and Pouchelle, *Corps,* pp. 224–28. To religious writers, the good female body is closed and intact; the bad woman's body is open, windy and breachable. At the same time, the closed, secret and virgin body of a woman is fascinating and threatening, inviting investigation.

99. See above n. 85.

100. There is much about this in Allen, *Concept of Woman* (although the individual accounts are not always correct). See also Jacquart and Thomasset, *Sexualité,* pp. 193–95; and Thomasset, "La répresentation."

101. See Demaitre and Travill, "Albertus Magnus," pp. 432–34; Thomasset, "La répresentation," pp. 5–7; J.M. Thijssen, "Twins as Monsters: Albertus Magnus's Theory of the Generation of Twins and Its Philosophical Context," *Bulletin of the History of Medicine* 61 (1967), pp. 237–46; and André Pecker, *Hygiène et maladie de la femme au cours des siècles* (Paris: Dacosta, 1961), c. 5—a quasi-popular account that nonetheless makes the interest in hermaphrodites quite clear. Stories of bearded women were also popular at the close of the Middle Ages.

102. Zapperi, *L'Homme enceint;* and Pouchelle, *Corps,* pp. 142 and 223.

103. On the increase attention to the physicality of Christ in the later Middle Ages, see Kieckhefer, *Unquiet Souls,* pp. 89–121. On the increasingly positive sense of body generally, see Alan E. Bernstein, "Political Anatomy," *University Publishing* (Winter 1978), pp. 8–9.

104. On Hildegard, see Barbara Newman, *Sister of Wisdom: St. Hildegard's Theology of the Feminine* (Berkeley: University of California Press, 1987); and Elisabeth Gössmann, "Das Menschenbild der Hildegard von Bingen und Elisabeth von Schoenau vor dem Hintergrund der frühscholastischen Anthropologie," in Dinzelbacher and Bauer, eds., *Frauenmystik,* pp. 24–27. On Julian, see E. McLaughlin, "'Christ Our Mother.'" On Margery Kempe, see Clarissa W. Atkinson, *Mystic and Pilgrim: The Book and the World of Margery Kempe* (Ithaca: Cornell University Press, 1983).

105. See above nn. 4, 5, 67–73.

106. Allen, *Concept of Woman.* See also Maryanne Cline Horowitz, "Aristotle and Women," *Journal of the History of Biology* 9 (1976), pp. 186–213.

107. A recent nonscholarly book that argues this position is Frank Bottomley, *Attitudes Toward the Body in Western Christendom* (London: Lepus Books, 1979).

108. See Oscar Cullman, "Immortality of the Soul or Resurrection of the Dead? The Witness of the New Testament," in Terence Penelhum, ed., *Immortality* (Belmont, Cal.: Wadsworth, 1973), pp. 53–84.

109. Richard Heinzmann, *Die Unsterblichkeit der Seele und die Auferstehung des Leibes: Eine problemgeschichtliche Untersuchung der frühscholastischen Sentenzen- und Summenliteratur von Anselm von Laon bis Wilhelm von Auxerre,* Beiträge zur Geschichte der Philosophie und Theologie des Mittelalters: Texte und Untersuchungen 40.3 (Münster: Aschedorff, 1965); and Hermann J. Weber, *Die Lehre von der Auferstehung der Toten in den Haupttraktaten der scholastischen Theologie von Alexander von Hales zu Duns Skotus,* Freiburger Theologische Studien (Freiburg: Herder, 1973). Thomas Aquinas, *Quaestiones disputatae de potentia Dei absolute,* q. 5, art. 10, ed. P.M. Pession, in Thomas Aquinas, *Quaestiones dispuatate,* vol. 2. ed. P. Bazzi et al., 8th ed. (Rome: Marietti, 1949), pp. 43–44, says explicitly that Porphyry's idea that the soul is happiest without the body, and Plato's idea that the body is a tool of the soul, are wrong; the soul is more like God when it is united to the body than when it is separated, because it is then more perfect.

110. Hewson, *Giles of Rome,* p. 56, n. 21.

111. See the works cited in n. 109 above.

112. Weber, *Auferstehung,* pp. 80–106.

113. A. Michel, "Résurrection des morts," DTC 13, pt. 2, cols. 2501–03. Benedict XII, in the bull *Benedictus Deus,* cited the profession of faith of Michael Paleologus at the Second Council of Lyon of 1274 which asserted that *omnes homines* appear before the tribunal of Christ in the Last Judgment *cum suis corporibus.* See below n. 144.

114. Michel, "Résurrection des morts," cols. 2501–71. And see Aquinas, *On the Truth of the Catholic Faith: Summa contra gentiles,* trans. Anton Pegis et al., 4 vols. in 5 (New York: Image Books, 1955–57), 4, ch. 85, par. 4, vol. 4, pp. 323–24; and Wilhelm Kübel, "Die Lehre von der Auferstehung der Toten nach Albertus Magnus,"

Studia Albertina: Festschrift für Bernhard Geyer zum 70. Geburstage, ed. H. Ostlender, Beiträge zur Geschichte der Philosophie und Theologie der Mittelalters, Supplementband 4 (Münster: Aschendorff, 1952), pp. 279–318. For the position that *all* must rise and that *body* must be rewarded or punished for good or evil deeds, theologians regularly cited 2 Cor. 5.10.

115. See, for example Moneta of Cremona, *Adversus Catharos et Valdenses libri quinque* (Rome, 1743. Reprint: Ridgewood, N. J.: Gregg Press, 1964), bk. 4, chs. 8–12, pp. 346–88; and on Moneta, Georg Schmitz-Valckenberg, *Grundlehren katharischer Sekten des 13. Jahrhunderts: Eine theologische Untersuchung mit besonderer Berücksichtigung von Adversus Catharos et Valdenses des Moneta von Cremona,* Münchener Universitäts-Schriften: Kath. Theologische Fakultät: Veröffentlichungen des Grabmann-Institutes zur Erforschung der mittelalterlichen Theologie und Philosophie, NF 11 (Munich: Schöningh, 1971), pp. 196–207.

116. Many of the extant sources on the Cathar position (both anti-Cathar polemic and Cathar material itself) suggest that the dualists' insistence on "spiritual body" and their denial of any resurrection of physical body was based on their abhorrence of matter—its tangibility, putrefiability, dissolvability. One has the sense that, to the Cathars (at least as they appeared to orthodox eyes), the paradigmatic body was the cadaver. See Walter L. Wakefield and Austin P. Evans, eds., *Heresies of the High Middle Ages: Selected Sources Translated and Annotated,* Record of Civilization 81 (New York: Columbia University Press, 1969), pp. 167, 231, 238–39, 297, 311–13, 321–23, 339–42, 343–45, 353, 357, 361, 380. See also M.D. Lambert, "The Motives of the Cathars: Some Reflections . . . ," *Religious Motivation: Biographical and Sociological Problems for the Church Historian,* Studies in Church History 15 (1978), pp. 49–59.

117. Wood, "Doctors' Dilemma"; *idem,* "Gynecological Aspects of the Annunciation," to appear in *Actes du colloque l'Annonciation à la Renaissance* (Florence: Casa Usher); Edward D. O' Connor, ed.; *The Dogma of the Immaculate Conception: History and Significance* (Notre Dame, Ind.: University of Notre Dame Press, 1958).

118. Albert the Great, *De animalibus libri XXVI nach der Cölner Urschrift,* vol. 1, Beiträge zur Geschichte der Philosophie der Mittelalters: Texte und Untersuchungen 15 (Münster: Aschendorff, 1916), bk. 9, tract. 1, ch. 2, p. 682.

119. Weber, *Auferstechung,* pp. 13–14 and 235–36; Hewson, *Giles of Rome,* pp. 38–58; Kübel, "Die Lehre . . . nach Albertus," esp. p. 299.

120. Aquinas, *De potentia Dei,* q. 6, arts. 5–10, pp. 49–54. Aquinas argues (art. 8) that Christ willed to eat after the Resurrection to show the reality of his body; angels cannot, however, really eat and speak (i.e., move the organs and the air or divide food and send it throughout the body). The analysis makes it quite clear that the human body/soul nexus is far closer than that suggested by any model of a spirit using a material object (as the angels do). See esp. art. 8, reply to obj. 8, where Aquinas explains why Christ's eating after the Resurrection is different from the angels' eating, even though in neither case can food be changed into flesh and blood.

121. Thomas wrote, probably in the following order, four lives of women saints, all of which are characterized by somatic miracles and highly experiential piety: a supplement to James of Vitry's "Life of Mary of Oignies," AASS, June, vol. 5 (1867), pp. 572–81; a "Life of Christina the Astonishing" (which contains the most remarkable somatic miracles of any thirteenth-century woman's *vita*), AASS, July, vol. 5 (1868), pp. 637–60; a "Life of Margaret of Ypres" (see above n. 35); and a "Life of Lutgard of Aywières" (which he composed in order to obtain her finger as a relic), AASS, June, vol. 4, pp. 187–210. He also composed a *vita* of John, first abbot of

Cantimpré. His *Bonum universale de apibus,* ed. Georges Colvener (Douai, 1627), is a collection of miracle stories, many of which display a concern for body. On this, see Henri Platelle, "Le recueil des miracles de Thomas de Cantimpré et la vie religieuse dans les Pays-Bas et le nord de la France au XIIIe siècle," in *Assistance et assistés jusqu'à 1610,* Actes du 97e Congrès National des Sociétés Savantes, Nantes, 1972 (Paris: Bibliothèque Nationale, 1979), pp. 469–98; and Alexander Murray, "Confession as a Historical Source in the Thirteenth Century," in *The Writing of History in the Middle Ages: Essays Presented to Richard William Southern* (Oxford: Clarendon Press, 1981), pp. 275–322, especially pp. 286–305.

122. *Die Gynäkologie des Thomas von Brabant: Ein Beitrag zur Kenntnis der mittelalterlichen Gynäkologie und ihrer Quellen,* ed. C. Ferckel (Munich: Carl Kuhn, 1912), an edition of part of bk. 1 of Thomas of Cantimpré's *De naturis rerum;* there is a new ed. by Helmut Boese, *Liber de natura rerum: Editio princeps secundum codices manuscriptos,* vol. 1, *Text* (New York and Berlin: De Gruyter, 1973). On Thomas's encyclopedia, see Pierre Michaud-Quantin, "Les petites encyclopédies du XIIIe siècle, "*Cahiers d'histoire mondiale* 9.2 (1966), *Encyclopédies et civilisations,* pp. 580–95; G.J.J. Walstra "Thomas de Cantimpré, *De naturis rerum:* Etat de la question, "*Vivarium* 5 (1967), pp. 146–71, and 6 (1968), pp. 46–61; and Helmut Boese, "Zur Textüberlieferung von Thomas Cantimpratensis' *Liber de natura rerum,*" *Archivum fratrum praedicatorum* 39 (1969), pp. 53–68.

123. See Katherine Park and Eckhart Kessler, "The Concept of Psychology," and K. Park, "The Organic Soul," in Charles B. Schmitt, ed., *The Cambridge History of Renaissance Philosophy* (Cambridge: Cambridge University Press) chs. 13 and 14, forthcoming; and E. Ruth Harvey, *The Inward Wits: Psychological Theory in the Middle Ages and the Renaissance,* Warburg Institute Surveys 6 (London: Warburg Institute, 1975).

124. See Preus, "Galen's Criticism." See also Michael Boylan, "The Galenic and Hippocratic Challenges to Aristotle's Conception Theory," *Journal of the History of Biology* 17 (1984), pp. 83–112.

125. See Hewson, *Giles of Rome.*

126. See the works cited in n. 109 above, and Michel, "Résurrection des morts." For a modern position on the survival questions that agrees with Thomas, see Peter Geach, "Immortality," in Penelhum, *Immortality,* p. 11ff.

127. Aquinas, Commentary on 1 Cor. 15, lect. 2, quoted in Emile Mersch and Robert Brunet, "Corps mystique et spiritualité," *Dictionnaire de spiritualité, ascétique et mystique: doctrine et histoire,* vol. 2, pt. 2 (Paris: Beauchesne, 1953), col. 2352.

128. In general, see Heinzmann, *Unsterblichkeit,* pt. 2 passim, and Weber, *Auferstehung,* passim, esp. pp. 125–57 and 217–54. On the question of the necessity of material continuity for numerical continuity, answers ranged from William of Auxerre (in the early thirteenth century), who argued that the ashes of Paul must rise as the body of Paul (Heinzmann, *Unsterblichkeit,* p. 243, n. 11), to Durandus (in the early fourteenth century) who held that God can make the body of Peter out of dust that was once the body of Paul (Weber, *Auferstehung,* p. 228ff., especially p. 241, n. 400).

129. Because of this telescoping of body into soul, some recent interpreters have debated how important body is to Thomas. Does it really add anything to the capacities of soul? See Norbert Luyten, "The Significance of the Body in a Thomistic Anthropology," *Philosophy Today* 7 (1963), pp. 175–93; J. Giles Milhaven, "Physical Experience: Contrasting Appraisals by Male Theologians and Women Mystics in the Middle Ages," paper given at the Holy Cross Symposium "The Word Becomes Flesh," November 9, 1985; Richard Swinburne, *The Evolution of the Soul* (Oxford:

Clarendon Press, 1986), pp. 299–306, esp. n. 9; and the article by Bazan cited in n. 130 below. Nonetheless, Aquinas did argue that, without body, the soul in heaven before the end of time would in a certain sense lack memory and other passions; see *Summa contra gentiles* 2, ch. 81, pars. 12, 14–15, vol. 2, pp. 264–66.

130. *Summa contra gentiles* 4, ch. 81, par. 7, vol. 4, p. 303: "Corporeity, however, can be taken in two ways. In one way, it can be taken as the substantial form of a body. . . . Therefore, copOreity, as the substantial form in man, cannot be other than the rational soul. . . ." See Bernardo C. Bazan, "La corporalité selon saint Thomas," *Revue philosophique de Louvain* 81, ser. 4.49 (1983), pp. 369–409, esp. pp. 407–08. Bazan says that, according to Thomas, "Notre corporalité est toute pénétrée de spiritualité, car sa source est 'áme rationnelle."

131. Bonaventure, *De assumptione B. Virginis Mariae*, sermon 1, sec 2, p. 690. See also Aquinas, *Summa contra gentiles* 4, ch. 79, par. 11, vol. 4, p. 299; and the passage from *De potentia Dei*, cited in n. 109 above.

132. Heinzmann, *Unsterblichkeit*, p. 188, quotes a passage from the *Summa called Breves dies hominis* in which Plato is represented as supporting the position that resurrection is natural because of the longing of soul for body. This suggests that contemporaries were aware that a Platonic position tends in some ways to give more weight to body than an Arisotelian one (and not necessarily negative weight).

133. Weber, *Auferestehung*, p. 326. The doctrine of the plurality of forms seems to lurk behind much of Franciscan teaching on the gifts (*dotes*) of the glorified body, for thinkers such as Bonaventure and Richard of Middleton hold that body is in some way predisposed for the flowing over of glory into it before it receives the *dotes;* see *ibid.*, p. 314ff. Such a position tends to give substantial reality to body.

134. Weber, *Auferstehung*, p. 304, n. 197; and see *ibid.*, pp. 266 and 135–36.

135. Bernard, *De diligendo Deo*, sec. 11, pars. 30–33, in *Tractatus et opuscula, Sancti Bernardi opera*, vol. 3 (1963), pp. 145–47; trans. Robert Walton, *The Works of Bernard of Clairvaux*, vol. 5, *Treatises*, vol. 2, Cistercian Fathers Series 13 (Washington D.C.: Cistercian Publications, 1974), pp. 122–24.

136. Weber, *Auferstehung*, pp. 255–63. Thomas held that risen bodies will have the capacity for touch; see *Summa contra gentiles* 4, ch. 84, par. 14, vol. 4, pp. 322–23. Risen bodies will not, however, eat: see *Summa contra gentiles* 4, ch. 83, vol. 4, pp. 311–20.

137. Nikolaus Wicki, *Die Lehre von der himmlischen Seligkeit in der mittelalterlichen Scholastik von Petrus Lombardus bis Thomas von Aquinas*, Studia Friburgensia NF 9 (Freiburg: Universitätsverlag, 1954); Joseph Göring, "The *De Dotibus* of Robert Grosseteste," *Mediaeval Studies* 44 (1982), pp. 83–109; and Weber, *Auferstehung*, pp. 314–42.

138. See, for example, Hugh of St. Victor, *De sacramentis* 2, pt. 18, ch. 18; Pl. 176 (1854), col. 616A; Peter Lombard, *Sententiae in IV libris distinctae*, vol. 2 , 3rd ed., Spieilegium, Bonaventurianum 5 (Grottaferrata: Collegium Bonaventurae ad Claras Aquas, 1981), bk. 4, distinctio 44, pp. 510–22; and *Summa contra gentiles* 4, ch. 90, par. 9, vol. 4, p. 334.

139. See, for example, *Summa contra gentiles* 4, ch. 88, vol. 4, pp. 328–30; and *Summa theologiae* 3a, q. 54, art. 4, vol. 55, pp. 30–35. See also Supplement to *Summa theologiae* 3, q. 96, art. 10, on whether the scars of the martyrs are an *aureole; Supplementum*, comp. and ed. by the Brothers of the Order, in *Sancti Thomae Aquinatis opera omnia*, vol. 12 (Rome: S.C. de Propaganda Fide, 1906), p. 238. In general, thirteenth-century theologians drew on Augustine's *City of God*, bk. 22, ch. 17 ("vitia detrahentur, natura servabitur") on this matter; see Weber, *Auferstehung*, p. 79, n. 194.

140. Allen, *Concept of Woman;* Weber, *Auferstehung,* pp. 256–59. Weber quotes Augustinus Triumphus, writing on the resurrection, to the effect that, if persons were to rise in the opposite sex, they would not be the same persons: "Non omnes resurgentes eundem sexum habebunt, nam masculinus sexus et femininus, quamvis non sint differentiae formales facientes differentiam in specie, sunt tamen differentiae materiales facientes differentiam in numero. Et quia in resurrectione quilibet resurget non solum quantum ad id quod est de identitate specifica, secundum habet esse in specie humana, verum etiam resurget quantum ad id, quod est de identitae numerali, secumdum quam habet esse in tali individuo. Ideo oportet unumquodque cum sexu proprio et cum aliis pertinentibus ad integritatem suae individualis naturae resurgere, propter quod femina resurget cum sexu femineo et homo cum masculino, remota omni libidine et omni vitiositate naturae." Moneta of Cremona, writing against the Cathars, argued that God created sex difference: see Moneta, *Adversus Catharos,* bk. 1, ch. 2, sec. 4, and bk. 4, ch. 7, sec. 1, pp. 121 and 315.

141. The resurrected bodies of the damned will be incapable of corruption (i.e., of dissolution or of loss of their matter) but not incapable of suffering. See n. 144 below.

142. Theologians were aware that some of the particular issues they raised in debates over eschatology had implications for the cult of relics—particularly the issue of whether the cadaver of John is still the body of John and whether its specific matter must rise in John at the Last Judgment. See Weber, *Auferstehung,* pp. 76–78, 150–53, 239, and n. 128 above.

143. *Summa theologiae* 3a, q. 14, arts. 1–4, vol. 49, pp. 170–87, esp. p. 174.

144. Indeed, scholastic theologians held that the damned also receive their bodies *whole* after the resurrection, because only the permanence (i.e., the perfect balance or wholeness) of these bodies ensures that their punishment will be permanent and perpetual; see Kübel, "Die Lehre . . . nach Albertus," pp. 316–17.

145. After fierce debate, the issue was finally settled by Benedict XII in the bull *Benedictus Deus* of January 29, 1336; see Henry Denzinger; *Enchirdion symbolorum: Definitionum et declarationum de rebus fidei et morum,* 31st ed., ed. C. Rahner (Freiburg: Herder, 1957), pp. 229–30. For a brief overview, see M.J. Redle, "Beatific Vision," *New Catholic Encyclopedia* (Washington D.C.: Catholic University of America, 1967), vol. 2, pp. 186–93.

146. A. Challet, "Corps glorieux," DTC 3, cols. 1879–1906.

147. See, for example, the cases of Jane Mary of Maillé and Columba of Rieti, in HFHF, pp. 131–134, 148.

148. *Summa theologiae* 3a, q. 15, art. 5, obj. 3 and reply, vol. 49, pp. 204–07; and see also *ibid.,* 3a, q. 14, art. 1, obj. 2 and reply, pp. 170–75. Bernard of Clairvaux expresses the same opinion in *De diligendo Deo,* sec. 10, par. 29, *Iractatus et opuscula,* p.144.

149. Caesarius, *Dialogue,* bk. 12, ch. 47, vol. 2, p. 354.

150. *Ibid.,* ch. 50, vol. 2, pp. 355–56; see also *ibid.,* ch. 54, p. 358. For the importance of marks of healing visible on the body, see Judith-Danielle Jacquet, "Le Miracle de la jambe noire," in Gelis and Redon, eds., *Les miracles miroirs des corps,* pp. 23–52.

151. See above, n. 32. A related issue concerning incorruptibility, which I do not have space to treat here, is the incorruptibility of the bodies of great sinners; see Thomas, *Le cadavre,* pp. 39–43, who however underestimates the importance of incorruptibility for sanctity.

152. *Summa theologiae* 3a, q. 15, art. 4, vol. 49, p. 202 (my translation).

153. Doctors showed their own awareness of such psychosomatic unity. For example, Henri de Mondeville, skeptical about miraculous cures, explained their apparent suc-

cess thus: "If the human spirit believes that a thing is useful (which in itself is of no help), it may happen that by the imagination alone this thing aids the body." See Pouchelle, *Corps,* p. 107. Mondeville shows by many examples how "in acting on the soul one acts on the body" (*ibid.,* p. 108).

154. Henri Platelle, "La Voix du sang: Le cadavre qui saigne en presence de son meutrier," *La piété populaire au moyen age,* Actes du 99e Congrès National des Sociétés Savantes, Besançon 1974 (Paris: Bibliothèque Nationale, 1977), pp. 161–79; Finucane, *Miracles and Pilgrims,* pp. 73–75; Bouvier, "De l'incorruptibilité; Philippe Aries, *The Hour of Our Death,* trans. Weaver (New York: Knopf, 1981), pp. 261–68 and 353ff. Jacques Gelis, "De la mort à la vie: Les 'sanctuaires à réprit,'" *Ethnologie française* 11 (1981), pp. 211–24.

155. "Life of Christina Mirabilis," ch.5, no. 36, par. 47–48, AASS, July, vol. 5, pp. 658–59; trans. Margot H. King, *The Life of Christina Mirabilis,* Matrologia latina 2 (Saskatoon: Peregrina, 1986), pp. 27–28. This little dialogue was supposedly witnessed by Thomas, abbot of St. Trond; see ch. 5, no. 36, par. 47, p. 658. See also, Petroff, *Women's Visionary Literature,* p. 36; and Ackerman, "*Debate of the Body and Soul* and Parochial Christianity."

156. For the text, see Karl Brunner, "Mittelenglische Todesgedichte," *Archiv für das Studium er neueren Sprachen* 167, n.s. 67 (1935), pp. 30–35. See also, Marjorie M. Malvern, "An Earnest 'Monyscyon' and 'thinge Delectabyll' Realized Verbally and Visually in 'A Disputacion Betwyx the Body and Wormes,' A Middle English Poem Inspired by Tomb Art and Northern Spirituality," *Viator* 13 (1982), pp. 415–43.

157. See Malvern, "'Monyscyon'," pp. 427 and 432ff.

158. Stanzas 24, 28–29 in Brunner, "Mittelenglische Todesgedichte," p. 34.

Jean-Pierre Vernant (1914–)

Often referred to as one of the most remarkable classicists of our time, Vernant is a French historian who has profoundly transformed our perceptions of ancient Greece. He was born in Provence, France, and by the time he was a teenager he was already involved in antifascist activity. He studied in Paris at the Sorbonne, where he received a degree in philosophy in 1937. That same year, he was called to military service, but when he was demobilized in July of 1940, he joined the French Resistance and took a position teaching philosophy at the College of Toulouse. For Vernant, resistance was a pedagogical as well as a political strategy. According to Vernant, the way he handled himself in the Resistance was the same as that in the classroom. "When I was a teacher," says Vernant, "all my behavior, all my way of being was to abolish the distance between the teacher and the pupils (E-interview)." To this end, he addressed his pupils as "tu," the familiar form of "you," and they in turn addressed Vernant as "tu." At bottom, says Vernant, "I am a utopian, I undoubtedly dream [of creating] groups linked by . . . friendship on a plan of equality"(E-interview).

A professor emeritus at the College of France in Paris, Vernant is the author of numerous publications on the subject of Greek mythology, including *Origins of Greek Thought* (1984); *Myth and Tragedy in Ancient Greece,* coauthored with Pierre Vidal-Naquet and Janet Lloyd (1990); *Myth and Society in Ancient Greece,* coauthored with Janet Lloyd (1990); *Mortals and Immortals* (1991); *The Gardens of Adonis,* coauthored with Marcel Detienne and Janet Lloyd (1994); *The Greeks,* coauthored with Charles Lambert and Teresa Lavender Fagan (1995); *Ancestor of the West: Writing, Reasoning, and Religion in Mesopotamia, Elam, and Greece,* coauthored with Jean Bottero, Clarisse Herrenschmidt, Francois Zabbal, and Teresa Lavender Fagan (2000); and *The Universe, the Gods, and Men: Ancient Greek Myth Told by Jean-Pierre Vernant* (2002).

Dim Body, Dazzling Body

From "Corps des dieux," Le temps de la réflexion, *vol. 7, Paris, Gallimard, 1986. Translated by Anne M. Wilson.*

The body of the gods. How does this expression pose a problem for us? Can gods who have bodies—anthropomorphic gods like those of the ancient Greeks—really be considered gods? Six centuries before Christ, Xenophanes already protested the possibility of such a thing, denouncing the foolishness of mortals who believe they can measure the divine by the yardstick of their own nature: "Men believe that, like themselves, the gods have clothing, language and a body."[1] An identical body for gods and men? "The Ethiopians claim that their gods are flat-nosed and black-skinned; the Thracians, that they are blue-eyed and have red hair."[2] Why not an animal's body, then, Xenophanes ironically asks: "If oxen, horses and lions had hands with which to draw and make works like men, horses would represent the gods in the likeness of a horse, oxen in that of an ox, and each one would make for them a body like the one he himself possessed."[3]

These remarks made by the Greek poet-philosopher are conveyed to us by Clement of Alexandra in his *Stromata,* written in the second century A.D. Clement wishes to show that through the light of reason the wisest of the ancients were able to recognize the vanity of idolatry and mock the gods of Homer—those puppets invented by man in his own image, with all his faults, vices, passions and weaknesses.

That in his polemic against "false gods" a Church Father should make use of criticisms voiced by a pagan philosopher who takes a distance from the collective beliefs of a religion in which divinity occasionally appears in a too human light, is fair play. But it is certainly not the surest and most suitable way to approach the problem of the body of the gods in ancient Greece. To do this, one must put oneself in the very framework of polytheism and adopt its perspective.

Would the Greeks, in representing the gods to themselves, really have attributed to them the form of corporeal existence that is proper to all perishable creatures here on earth? To pose the question in these terms would be to admit, from the outset, that for human beings "the body" is a given, a fact, one that is immediately evident, a "reality" inscribed in nature and, as such, beyond question. In the case of the Greeks, the difficulty arises only from their apparently having projected the notion of a body onto beings who, insofar as they are divine, are situated outside the body's legitimate sphere of application, since they are, by definition, supernatural and belong to the other world, the beyond.

But one can also approach the problem from the opposite angle and direct one's inquiry to the body itself, no longer posited as a fact of nature, a constant and universal reality, but as an entirely problematic notion, a historical category, steeped in imagination (to use Le Goff's expression), and one which must, in every case, be deciphered within a particular culture by defining the functions it assumes and the forms it takes on with that culture. Therefore, the real question can be formulated as: what was the body for the Greeks? Today the concept of the body gives us the illusion of self-evidence for essentially two reasons: first, because of the definitive opposition between soul and body, spiritual and material, that has established itself in our Western tradition. And consequently and correspondingly, because the body, reduced entirely to matter, depends on positivistic study; in other words, it has acquired the status of scientific object defined in anatomical and physiological terms.

The Greeks contributed to this "objectification" of the body in two ways. First of all, within the religious context of the sectarian cults—whose teaching was later taken up and transposed by Plato into the field of philosophy—they elaborated a new notion of the soul, an immortal soul which man must isolate and purify in order to separate it from a body whose role has now become nothing more than that of a receptacle or tomb. Then, through medical practice and medical literature, the Greeks investigated the body, observing, describing, theorizing about its visible aspects, its parts, the internal organs that compose it, their function and the diverse humors that circulate in it and direct its health or illness.

But the affirmation of the presence of a noncorporeal element within us which is related to the divine and which is "our selves," like the naturalistic approach to the body, marks more than just a turning point in Greek culture: it marks a kind of rupture.

In this respect, despite Clement, Xenophanes is a good witness to that which, in reference to the most ancient Greek philosophers, one might perhaps call the pre-Socratic body. Although he lampoons the heterogeneous and restless troop of Homeric gods in order to propose a more rigorous and refined conception of divinity, a conception that evokes the spherical One of Parmenides (who some believe was his student),[4] nevertheless, Xenophanes does not radically dissociate divine nature from corporeal reality. Just as he does not postulate the existence of a unique god when he writes, "One god, the greatest among gods and men," he also does not affirm that the gods do not have bodies. Xenophanes merely claims that the body of a god is not like that of a mortal. It is dissimilar for precisely the same reason that a god's thought (*noēma*)—with which he is abundantly endowed—is dissimilar to a man's thought.[5] Dissimilarity of body and dissimilarity of thought are jointly proclaimed in the unity of a formula in which gods' bodies and thoughts are fused by virtue of their common difference to human beings.[6] Like everybody and anybody, a god sees, hears, understands. But for all that, he does not require specialized organs like our eyes and ears. A god is "wholly" seeing, hearing, understanding.[7] He moves without effort or fatigue; without having to budge, without even changing his place, he shakes everything up.[8] In order to traverse the gulf separating god and man, Xenophanes is not led to oppose the corporeal to the noncorporeal, to an immateriality, a pure Spirit; for him, it is enough to acknowledge the contrast between the constant and the changing, the immutable and the mutable, the perfection of that which remains eternally accomplished in the plenitude of itself, and the incompleteness and imperfection of that which is divided, dispersed, partial, transitory, perishable.

The fact is that in the archaic period Greek "corporeity" still does not acknowledge a body/soul distinction, nor does it establish a radical break between the natural and the supernatural. Man's corporeality also includes organic realities, vital forces, psychic activities, divine inspirations or influxes. The same word can refer to these various domains. On the other hand, there is no term that designates the body as an organic unity which supports the individual in the multiplicity of his vital and mental functions. The word *sōma*, translated as body, originally designated a corpse, that is to say, what remains of an individual after his incarnated life and physical vitality have left him, reducing him to a pure inert figure, an effigy. He becomes an object of exhibition and lamentation of others, before he disappears, burned or buried, into invisibility. The term *demas*, used in the accusative, designates not the body but an individual's stature, his size, his build made up of assembled pieces (the verb *demō* signifies the erecting of a construction through superimposed rows, as in a brick wall). It is often used in connection with *eidos* and *phuē*: the visible aspect, the carriage, the imposing appearance of what has grown well. Nor is *chrōs* the body: rather, it is the external envelope, the skin, the surface where there is contact between oneself and an other; it also means flesh-tint, complexion.

To the extent the man is alive, inhabited by force and energy, traversed by drives that move and stir him, his body is plural. The Greek vocabulary of the corporeal is characterized by multiplicity, even when it is a matter of expressing it in its totality. The Greeks use the word *guia*: the bodily members in their suppleness, their articulated mobility, or *melea*, the limbs as bearers of force.

They also use the word *kara*, the head, with a metonymic value: a part for the whole. Even in this case, the head is not equivalent to the body; it is a way of saying "a man himself," as an individual. In death, men are called "heads," but they are heads hooded in night, enveloped in darkness, faceless. Among the living, heads have a countenance, a face, a *prosōpon*; they are there, present before your eyes just as you are present to their eyes. The head, the face is what one sees first in a being, what is revealed of him on the surface; it is what identifies him and makes him recognizable when he is present to the gaze of others.

When one wishes to speak of the body in terms of its vitality, its life force, its emotions, as well as its ability to reflect and know, a host of terms is available: *ste̅thos, e̅tor, kardia, phre̅n, prapides, thumos, menos, nous*. The values of these words are closely related. They designate, without always distinguishing among them very precisely, bodily parts or organs (heart, lungs, diaphragm, chest, guts); breaths, vapors or liquid juices; feelings, drives, desires; and thoughts, concrete operations of the intellect such as comprehension, recognition, naming and understanding.[9] This intertwining of the physical and the psychological within a self-consciousness that involves itself in the parts of the body is summarized in James Redfield's striking remark that for the Homeric heroes, "the interior I is none other than the organic I."[10]

This vocabulary of, if not the body, then at least the various dimensions or aspects of the corporeal, constitutes in its entirety the code that allowed a Greek to express and think about his relation to himself, his presence to himself, which, depending on the circumstances, was greater or smaller, more or less unified or dispersed. But it connotes equally his relations to others, to whom he is bound by all forms of bodily appearance: face, size, bearing, voice, gestures—what Mauss calls "body techniques"—not to mention all that is related to the olfactory and tactile senses. This vocabulary also encompasses the relation to the divine or supernatural, whose presence within oneself, in and through one's own body, like the outer manifestations in the case of a god's apparitions or epiphanies, expresses itself in the same symbolic register.

To pose the problem of the body of the gods is thus not to ask how the Greeks could have outfitted their gods with human bodies. It is rather an investigation of how this symbolic system functions, how the corporeal code permits one to think of the relation between man and god under the double figures of the same and the other, of the near and far, of contact and separation, while marking between the poles of the human and the divine that which associates them through a play of similitudes, mutual advances, overlapping areas, and dissociates them through the effects of contrast, opposition, incompatibility and mutual exclusion.

From this symbolic system that codifies the relation to oneself, to others and to the divine, I would like to draw attention to certain elements that are pertinent to our subject. Roughly, the problem consists of deciphering all the signs that mark the human body with the seal of limitation, deficiency, incompleteness, and that make it a sub-body. This sub-body cannot be understood except in reference to what it presupposes: corporeal plenitude, a super-body, the body of the gods. We will therefore examine the paradox of the sublimated body, of a divine super-body. By pushing to an extreme all the qualities and bodily values that are present in an always diminished, derivative, faltering and precarious form in man, one is led to endow the divinities with a set of traits which, even in their epiphanic manifestations here below, in their presence among mortals, locates them in an inaccessible beyond and causes them to transgress the corporeal code by means of which they are represented in their relation to humans.

Man and his body are embedded in the course of nature, of *phusis,* which causes all that is born here below to rise, mature, and disappear according to the rhythm of the days, seasons, years and the life span proper to each species.[11] Therefore, man and his body bear the mark of a congenital infirmity; like a stigma, the seal of the impermanent and fleeting is branded on them. In order to exist they must, like plants and other creatures living on the earth, pass through the successive phases of growth and decline: after childhood and youth, the body matures and expands in the strength of manhood, and then, when old age comes, it changes, weakens, becomes ugly and dilapidated, until it is engulfed forever in the night of death.

It is this inconstant body, vulnerable to the vicissitudes of time flowing without return, that makes human beings the creatures whom the Greeks, in order to be contrasted with "those who exist eternally"[12]—the gods endowed with the perpetuity of their full presence—have baptized with the term "the ephemeral ones," beings whose lives unfold in the quotidian, the day to day, in the narrow limits of a changing and unstable "now" whose continuity and future is always uncertain.

The human body is ephemeral. This does not merely signify that, no matter how beautiful, how strong, how perfect it may appear to be, it is destined for decrepitude and death; but, in a more essential way, it means that since nothing in it is immutable, the vital energies it deploys and the psychological and physical forces it puts into play can remain in a state of plenitude for only a brief moment. They are exhausted as soon as they become active. Like a fire that consumes itself as it burns and which must continuously be fed in order to keep it from going out, the human body functions in alternating phases of expenditure and recuperation. It does not function along a continuous line or at a constant level of intensity, but in cycles punctuated by more or less complete or lasting eclipses, pauses or fade-outs. Sleep follows waking as its necessary counterpart; every effort brings on lassitude and demands time for rest. When in any particular activity the body is put to task or strained, it must restore the inner loss, the decrease in energy that hunger soon signals and which finds only provisional remedy in the satiety of a meal. If, in order to survive, man must endlessly sit down to a meal and eat in order to abate the depletion of his forces, it is because those forces weaken with use. The more intensely arduous an activity, the more serious and difficult it is to overcome the consequent weakness.

In this way, death does not only stand out in the lives of men as the end that unremittingly limits the horizon of their existence: it is there every day, every moment, ensconced in life itself, like the hidden face of a condition of existence in which the two opposing positive and negative poles—being and its privation—are again inextricably intertwined: no birth without death, no waking without sleep, no lucidity without unconsciousness, no tension without relaxation. The other side of a luminous youthful body is an ugly faded one. The body is the agent and instrument of actions, powers and forces which can only deploy themselves at the price of a loss of energy, a failure, a powerlessness caused by a congenital weakness. *Thanatos,* Death, might borrow the mask of his twin brother *Hupnos,* Sleep, or assume the appearance of some of his sinister associates— *Ponos, Limos, Geras*—who incarnate the human ills of fatigue, hunger and old age. (Through their mother *Nux,* the Dark Night, they are all children of the same lineage, and like Death himself, they are the issue of *Chaos,* the original Chasm, the dark, primordial Abyss that existed before anything had form, solidity and foundation.)[13] But it is always Death, in person or by delegation, who sits within the intimacy of the human body, like a witness to its fragility. Tied to all the nocturnal powers of confusion, to a return to the indistinct and unformed, Death, associated with the tribe of his kin—Sleep, Fatigue, Hunger, Old Age— denounces the failure, the incompleteness of a body of which neither its visible aspect—contours, radiance, external beauty—nor its inner forces of desire, feeling, thoughts and plans are ever perfectly pure. They are never radically separated from that part of darkness and nonbeing which the world inherited from its "chaotic" origin and which remains, even in the cosmos organized and now presided over by Zeus, a stranger to the luminous domain of the divine, to its constant, inexhaustible vitality.

Thus, for the Greeks of the archaic period, man's misfortune is not that a divine and immortal soul finds itself imprisoned in the envelope of a material and perishable body, but that his body is not fully one. It does not possess, completely and definitively, that set of powers, qualities and active virtues which bring to an individual being's existence a constant, radiant, enduring life in a pure, totally alive state, a life that is imperishable because it is free from any seed of corruption and divorced from what could, from within or without, darken, wither and annihilate it.

Although they belong to the same universe as men, the gods are of a different race: they are the *athanatoi,* the nonmortals, the *ambrotoi,* the ones who do not perish. The designation is paradoxical because, in order to make a comparison with human beings, it defines those beings whose bodies and lives possess complete positivity—without lack or defect—through negation, absence. The paradox is instructive because it implies that in order to think of the divine life and body, the required reference or point of departure for the Greeks is this defective body—this mortal life which they themselves experienced each day. To be sure, the mortal body is their point of departure so that they might better disengage themselves from it, break free from it and, through a series of deviations and successive denials, constitute a kind of purified body, an ideal body incarnating divine efficiencies and sacred values which will forever appear as the source, the foundation, the model of that which is only its poor reflection, its feeble, deformed, paltry image on this earth: those phantoms of the body and life that are at a mortal's disposal in the course of his brief existence.

In the human body, blood is life. But when it gushes out of a wound,[14] flows over the ground, mixes with earth and dust,[15] coagulates and becomes putrid, then blood means death. Because the gods are alive, there is undoubtedly blood in their bodies. Yet, even when it trickles from an open wound, this divine blood cannot tip the scales toward the side of death. A blood that flows, but that does not mean the loss of life; a blood that does not hemorrhage, that is always intact, incorruptible; in short, an "immortal blood," *ambroton haima*—is it still blood? Since the gods bleed, one must admit that their bodies have blood in them, but it must be immediately added that this is so only on the condition that this blood is not really blood, since death, the other side of life, is not present in it. Letting blood that is not blood, the gods simultaneously appear to have "immortal blood" and to be "bloodless."

The same wavering, the same oscillation occurs with respect to meals. The gods dine just as men do. Men are mortal because their bodies, inhabited by a hunger that is endlessly reborn, cannot survive without eating. Men's vitality and blood are nourished by a sustenance that, whether it is meat, bread or wine, can be defined as "ephemeral food"[16] because it is itself marked by death, decomposition, decay. Meat is the dead flesh of an animal slaughtered during sacrifice and offered to the gods. Its life has departed, leaving the field open to the internal forces of corruption in those parts of the animal reserved for man (i.e., all that is edible). Bread represents human nourishment par excellence: it is the symbol of civilized life; men are "bread eaters," and for the Greeks, "to eat bread," "to live off the fruit of the plowed earth" is another way of saying "to be mortal." If the Ethiopians, who live at the edge of the world in that islet of the golden age which it is their privilege to inhabit, are of all humanity the closest to the gods by virtue of their striking physical beauty, the fragrance they exude and their exceptional longevity, it is because their diet knows no cereals, and they consider wheat to be a kind of manure.[17] And even wine, that confounding and ambiguous drink, is worked on by fermentation, so that it too is the result of corruption.

According to the Homeric formula, to enjoy imperishable life, to possess immortal blood (or not to have blood at all) implies "not to eat bread, not to drink wine." To be true to Hesiod, one must add that this also means not to touch the flesh of the sacrificial victim, to keep for oneself only the aroma of the herbs burned on the altar, the emanations of the charred bones that rise in smoke toward heaven. The gods are always observing a fast.

Under these conditions, why do the gods sit down to a meal? The first answer: they assemble as guests for the pleasure of it, for the splendor of the celebration and the radiant joy of the banquet. They do not gather in order to appease their appetites, to satisfy their stomachs or to fill up that belly, the *gastēr*, the cause of man's misfortune that dooms him to death.[18] The second answer: just as there is ephemeral nourishment, so there is a food and drink of immortality. Whoever eats and drinks or succeeds in procuring such repast for himself becomes a god, if he is not one already. But, jealous of their privilege, the gods are careful to keep exclusively for themselves this nourishment that is "ambrosian" like their own bodies. Thus, after the table is set at the summit of Mount Olympus, the gods are, at the same time, those who, nourished by nectar and ambrosia, eat the dishes of immortality and those whose immortal bodies know no hunger and have no need at all to eat.

These paradoxes are not really perverse. Beneath their contradictory appearance, the propositions they enunciate are really saying the same thing: whatever positive forces such as vitality, energy, power, luster, the human body may harbor, the gods possess these forces in a pure and unlimited state. In order to conceive of the divine body in its plenitude and its permanence, it is thus necessary to subtract from the human body all those traits that bind it to its mortal nature and betray its transitory, precarious and unfulfilled character.

It is also necessary to correct the commonly held view that the anthropomorphism of the Greek gods means they were conceived in the image of the human body. It is rather the reverse: in all its active aspects, in all the components of its physical and psychological dynamism, the human body reflects the divine model as the inexhaustible source of a vital energy when, for an instant, the brilliance of divinity happens to fall upon a mortal creature, illuminating him, as in a fleeting reflection, with a little of that splendor that always clothes the body of a god.

Splendor of the gods. That is what shows through in all the *dunameis,* the powers, that the body manifests when it is as it should be: radiating youth, vigor and beauty, "similar to a god, like unto the Immortals."[19] Let us look, with the

Homeric Hymns, at the Ionians on the island of Delos, as they engage in dance, song, wrestling, and in the Games to please Apollo: "An unexpected arrival would think them immortal and forever free from old age for he would see, in all, their grace."[20] Grace, *charis,* makes the body shine with a joyful luster that is like the emanation of life itself, like the charm that continually wells from it. First of all, then, there is *charis,* with it there is stature, breadth, presence, speed of leg, strength of arm, freshness of complexion, and a relaxation, suppleness and agility of the limbs. And all of these are no longer perceived through someone else's eyes but are grasped by everyone within himself, in his *stēthos, thumos, phrenes, nous,* fortitude, enthusiasm for combat, the warrior's frenzy, and the momentum of anger, fear, desire, self-mastery, prudent intellection and subtle guile—these are some of the powers for which the body is the depository, powers that can be read upon it like marks that attest to what a man is and what he is worth.

The Greek body of Antiquity did not appear as a group morphology of fitted organs in the manner of an anatomical drawing, nor in the form if physical particularities proper to each one of us, as in a portrait. Rather, it appears in the manner of coat of arms and presents through emblematic traits the multiple "values"—concerning his life, beauty and power—with which an individual is endowed, values which he bears and which proclaim his *timē,* his dignity and rank. To designate mobility of soul, the generosity of the hearts of the best men, the *aristoi,* the Greeks used the phrase *kalos kagathos,* underlining the indissolubility of physical beauty and moral superiority. The latter can be evaluated only through a comparison with the former. Through a combination of its qualities, powers and "vital" values, which in their reference to a divine model always bear a sacred dimension, and which each individual has in varying amounts, the body takes on the form of a sort of heraldic painting upon which each person's social and personal status is inscribed and decipherable: the admiration, fear, longing and respect he inspires, the esteem in which he is held, the honors to which he is entitled—in short, his value, his price, his place on a scale of "perfection" that rises as high as the gods encamped upon its summit, and whose lower rungs, at various levels, human beings share.

Two orders of remark will complete this sketch. The first concerns the body's frontiers. The human body is, of course, strictly delimited. It is circumscribed like the figure of a distinct being, separate, with its inside and outside: its skin marks the surface of contact, while its mouth, anus and genitals are the orifices that assure communication with the outside. Nevertheless, it is not shut up on itself, closed, isolated or cut off from the outside, like an empire within an empire. On the contrary, it is fundamentally permeable to the forces that animate it, accessible to the intrusion of the vital powers that make it act. When a man feels joy, irritation or pity, when he suffers, is bold or feels any emotion, he is inhabited by drives that he senses within himself, in his "organic consciousness," but which, breathed into him by a god, run through and across him like a visitor coming from the outside. By touching the Aiantes with his staff, Poseidon "fills them both with a powerful passion [*meneos krateroio*]; he makes their limbs agile, first the legs, then, rising, the arms."[21] *Menos,* vital ardor, *alkē,* fortitude, *kratos,* the power of domination, *phobos,* fear, *erōs,* the impetus of desire and *lussa,* the warrior's frenzy, are all localized in the body, tied to this body which they invest: but as "powers" they exceed and surpass every individual carnal envelope. They can abandon it just as they invaded it. In the same way, when a man's spirit is blinded or enlightened, it is most often because, in the intimacy of his *noos* or his *phrenes,* a god intervenes to inspire the aberration of error, *atē,* or a wise resolve.

The powers which, in penetrating the body, act upon the inner scene in order to move and animate it, find on its outside, in what a man wears or handles—clothing, cover, adornments, weapons, tools—extensions that permit them to enlarge their field of action and to reinforce their effects. Let us take an example. The ardor of *menos* burns in the warrior's breast; it shines in his eyes. Sometimes, in exceptional cases when it becomes incandescent, as with Achilles, it bursts into flames above his head. But it also manifests itself in the dazzling brilliance of the bronze worn by the warrior. Rising skyward, the gleam of weapons that incites panic in the enemy's ranks is like an exhalation of the fire that burns in the warrior's body. The hero's accoutrements, the prestigious arms that allude to his career, his exploits and his personal value, are a direct extension of his body. They adhere to him, form an alliance with him, are integrated into his unusual figure like every other trait of his bodily armory.[22]

What military panoplies are to the body of a warrior, rouge, ointment, jewelry, iridescent fabrics and bust-ribbons are to a woman's body. The grace and seductiveness, the power to attract that are part of these adornments, emanate from them like magical charms whose effect on others is no different than that exercised by the charms of the feminine body itself.

When the gods create Pandora, so that she, this "marvel to behold," will become the deep, inextricable trap where men will be caught, they create in the same gesture a virgin's body and the vestmental trappings that will make this body "operative": dress, veil, belt, necklaces, tiara. . . .[23] This provision of Pandora's clothing is integrated into her anatomy to compose the bodily physiognomy of a creature one cannot behold without admiring and loving because in the femininity of her appearance she is as beautiful as an immortal goddess. The lion's skin that Hercules wears on his shoulders, Ajax's bow, Peleus's javelin in Achilles' hand, the scepter of the Atreides carried by Agamemnon, and, among the gods, the aegis on Athena's breast, the dogskin cap worn by Hades, the thunder brandished by Zeus, the caduceus that Hermes waves—all these precious objects are efficacious symbols of powers held, functions exercised. Serving as a support or link to the inner energies with which a person is endowed, they belong to his "appurtenances," like his arms or his legs, and, together with the other parts of his body, they define his bodily configuration.

It is necessary to go one step further. Physical appearance itself, with all that it details and that seems to our eyes congenitally determined—size, stature, bearing, complexion, the brightness of the eyes, the liveliness and elegance of movements, in brief, a person's beauty—can be, on occasion, "poured" from the outside onto the body in order to modify, revivify and embellish one's appearance. These "salves" of youth, grace, power and radiance which the gods sometimes give their protégés by suddenly "clothing" them in supernatural beauty, and which operate at a more modest level in the activities of grooming, bathing, and applying oils, function to transfigure the body through cleaning and purifying, ridding it of everything that makes it blemished or dirty, of anything that pollutes, disfigures, defiles or soils it.[24] Suddenly made unrecognizable as if he had exchanged his sordid old rags for sumptuous apparel, the individual, newly clothed in strength and grace, appears radiant in the bloom of youthful vitality.

Thus, when Nausicaa discovers Odysseus on the beach where he has been deposited by the tide, his naked body swollen from the sea, Odysseus is fearful, terrible to look on *(smerdaleos)*.[25] The hero washes himself, rubs himself with oil and puts on new clothes. Athena makes him "taller and more massive, with his hair curling down over his forehead." When Nausicaa sees him again, "he is radiant with charm and beauty."[26] The same scenario, the same metamorphosis takes place in Odysseus's meeting with Telemachus. Odysseus is in the courtyard, like an old beggar with a withered body, bald and bleary-eyed.[27] Athena, touching him with her golden wand, "gives him back his handsome bearing and his youth"; his skin become ruddy, his cheeks fill out, his beard grows back blue-tinged on his chin. When Telemachus sees him like this, he is afraid, and turns his eyes away for fear of looking on a god. "Stranger, how you have changed," he confides to Odysseus. "A moments ago I saw you in other clothes and with a completely different skin [*chros*]. Are you perhaps some god, a lord of the heavens?"[28]

To this sudden beautification of the body through the exaltation of its positive qualities and the effacing of what taints and darkens it, may be contrasted mourning rituals and the brutalities leveled against the enemy's corpse, procedures that pollute the body, make it dirty, and commit outrage upon it. Here it is a matter of destroying all the values the body incarnates, all the vital, aesthetic, social and religious qualities it once bore, to make it ugly and to dishonor it by sending it, deprived of form and vitality, to the dark world of the formless.

Therefore, for a Greek of this period to conceive of the category of the body is less a matter of precisely determining its general morphology or the particular form nature gives to one individual or another than it is a matter of situating the body between the opposite poles of luminosity and darkness, beauty and ugliness, value and foulness. And it must be situated all the more rigorously, because when it does not have a definitively fixed position, it tends to oscillate between extremes, moving from one pole to the other. Not that in such a case a person would actually change bodies. Frightful or splendid, Odysseus always has the same body. But corporeal identity lends itself to these sudden mutations and changes in appearance. The young, strong body that becomes old and weak with age, that moves in action from enthusiasm to dejection, can also, without ceasing to be itself, rise or descend in that hierarchy of life's values which it reflects and to which it bears witness, from the darkness and ugliness of disgrace all the way to the brilliant beauty of glory.

This leads us to the second order of our remarks. Epic characters are often represented as being perfectly sure of their powers in the hour of combat. They overflow with confidence and enthusiasm or, as we would say today, they are in great shape, all keyed up. They express this feeling of corporeal plenitude and strength by saying that their *menos* is *atromon*,[29] unshakeable, that, similar in its inflexible ardor "to blazing iron [*aithōni sidērōi*],"[30] it remains *empedon*,[31] unalterable, sure within them. *Hēroisme oblige!* In reality, like everything human, like strength, suppleness or speed, the ardor of *menos* is subject to vicissitudes: it relaxes, waivers, weakens and disappears with death. In Hades, the dead form the troops of the *armenēna karēna*, the heads that are without *menos*.[32] With age, the physical and psychic qualities make a complete man, leave the body, delivering the old man up to nostalgia for his lost strength, his extinguished ardor: "Why isn't your strength intact [*biē empedos*]."[33] Agamemnon says to Nestor who is overwhelmed by the weight of years; and the old man, in a litany, exhales his regret at no longer being what he was: "My strength today is no longer the same as that which once inhabited my supple limbs. Oh! If only I were young now, if only my strength were still intact [*biē empedos*].[34] And again: "No, my limbs no longer have the same sureness [*empeda guia*], neither do my feet, nor my arms—no longer do you see them shoot out rapidly to the right and the left of my shoulders. Oh! If only I were young again, if only my strength were intact [*biē empedos*]."[35]

The nature of the bronze sky is, in fact, *empedos,* unshakeable above our heads like the gods who live there. No hero can change the fact that everything in the human body is consumed and destroyed and decays. This exhaustion of vital forces which must fade with time is translated by the root *phthi* in the verbs *phthinō, phthiō, phthinuthō.* Therefore, in order to make himself *empedos,* the hero cannot count on the body or on anything connected with it. Whatever his strength, passion or valor may have been, he, too, when the day comes, will become one of those heads emptied of *menos.* His corpse, his *sōma,* would rot as carrion if the funeral ritual, in consuming his flesh on the pyre, did not previously expedite it into invisibility, its skin intact, and smooth as in the case of the young warrior fallen as a hero on the field of battle, the bloom of his virile beauty still upon him.

When his body disappears, vanishes, what remains here below of the hero? Two things. First of all the *sēma,* or *mnēma,* the stele, the funeral memorial erected on his tomb, which will remind the generations of men to come of his name, his renown, his exploits. As the *Iliad* puts it, "once set up on the tomb of a man or a woman, the stele is immutable [*menei empedon*]."[36] It is a permanent witness to the identity of a being who, together with his body, finds his end in definitive absence—and even, it would seem, somewhat more than a witness. In the sixth century, when the stele began to bear a figurative representation of the deceased, or when a funeral statue—a *kouros,* a *korē*—was erected on the tomb, this *mnēma,* appeared as a kind of corporeal substitute that expressed in an immutable form the values of beauty and life that the person incarnated during his brief existence. Second, parallel to the funeral monument, there is the song of praise that faithfully remembers high deeds of the past. Endlessly conserved and revivified in the oral tradition, the poetic word, in celebrating the exploits of the warriors of yesteryear, snatches them from the anonymity of death, from the darkness of Hades where the common man disappears. Their constant remembrance in the course of epic recitation makes these vanished ones "shining heroes" whose figures, always present to the spirit of the living, radiate a splendor that nothing can dim, the splendor of *kleos aphthiton*, "imperishable glory."[37]

The mortal body must return and lose itself in the nature to which it belongs, a nature that only made the body appear in order to swallow it up again. The permanence of immortal beauty, the stability of undying glory: in its institutions, culture alone has the power to construct these by conferring upon ephemeral creatures the status of the "beautiful dead," the illustrious dead.[38] If the gods are immortal and imperishable, it is because, unlike men, their corporeality possesses, by nature and even in the very heart of nature, that constant beauty and glory which the social imagination strives to invent for mortals when they no longer have a body to display their beauty or an existence that can win them glory. Living always in strength and beauty, the gods have a super-body: a body made entirely and forever of beauty and glory.

Without claiming to be able to answer it, there is one last question one cannot avoid posing. What is a super-body? How does the splendor of a divine body manifest itself?

First of all, it is manifested by what one might call its superlative effect: the magnification or multiplication of all values which appear by comparison on the human body as diminished, paltry and laughable. The gods are much larger and "a hundred times stronger" than men. When they confront one another in hand-to-hand combat on the battlefield of Troy in order to settle their differences, the entire world trembles, shaken to its foundations: in the depths of his subterranean dwelling, Hades jumps from his throne and is alarmed. Will the earth break open, revealing the ghastly dwelling place of death and corruption hidden in its bowels?[39] When Apollo advances in front of the Trojans, he causes, with a simple playful kick of his foot, the collapse of the embankment that the Achaians have built to protect their ships. Then, effortlessly, he pulls down their wall: "As a child by the seashore makes childish playthings out of the sand and then wrecks them with a kick or a punch to amuse himself, in the same way, Phoebus, you destroy what cost the Argives so much pain and toil."[40] To Calypso, who takes pride in being equal in the beauty of her body and appearance *(demas, edios)* to the human wife whom Odysseus longs to see again, the hero answers that, in fact, next to the goddess, as perfect as Penelope may be, she would seem "inferior in appearance and size [*eidos, megethos*] by comparison, because she is only human and you are free from death and old age [*athanatos, agērōs*]."[41]

But the difference between the body of the gods and that of men is not essentially on the order of "more" as opposed to "less." The way the gods manifest themselves to mortals when they decide to personally intervene in their affairs varies greatly. It depends on whether the god concerned is a Power, like Hades, whose status requires that he must always remain hidden and invisible to human eyes; or whether, like Pan and the nymphs, he is given to appearing in broad daylight, or during the night in a dream, like Aschlepius; or whether it is a god who, like Hermes, normally enjoys human company and commerce; or, finally, whether, like Dionysus, he is one who appears by surprise, just as it pleases him, so that his presence be recognized as an imperious and baffling epiphany. Furthermore, the nature of our documents adds to this diversity: divine apparitions do not follow an analogous scenario, nor do they obey the same model in an epic narrative, a religious hymn or a scene of a tragedy.

Nevertheless, one might venture a typological schema of the forms assumed by the gods when they make corporeal appearances. The gamut of possibilities runs from complete incognito to the god's revelation in full majesty. There are two kinds of incognito: the first is for the god to hide himself by clothing his body in a fog, enveloping it in a mist so that it becomes (or remains) invisible. Master of the situation, he acts with all the more power and efficiency as the spectators, blind to his presence, neither see nor understand what is happening right under their noses. When Aphrodite wishes to save Paris from Menelaus's impending blow, she makes him vanish from the closed space where the two men are pitted against each other and deposits him in Helen's room. Everyone, both Greek and Trojan, is deceived. Paris is already resting next to his beloved while the Greek warriors are still searching the ranks of the enemy to see where the devil that Trojan could have hidden himself.[42]

Therefore, the gods have a body that they can at will make (or keep) totally invisible to mortal eyes—and it does not cease to be a body. The visibility that defines the nature of the human body (inasmuch as it necessarily has a form, *eidos*) is flesh-colored (*chroiē*), and it has a covering of skin (*chros*) that takes on a completely different meaning for the gods. In order to manifest his presence, the divinity chooses to make himself visible in the form of *a* body, rather than *his* body. From a divine perspective, the opposition visible/invisible is no longer entirely pertinent. Even in the framework of an epiphany, the god's body may appear to be perfectly visible and recognizable to one of the spectators while remaining, at the same time and in the same place, completely hidden to the eyes of others. Before the assembled Greek army, Achilles ponders in his heart whether to draw the sword and strike Agamemnon. Immediately, Athena dashes down from the heights of heaven. She stops short behind the son of Peleus and puts her hand on his blond hair, "visible to him alone; no one else sees her. The hero turns around and immediately recognizes Pallas Athena."[43]

The second type of incognito appearance is when a god gives his body a strictly human appearance. However, this frequently used trick has its limits. As well-camouflaged as a god may be in the skin of a mortal, there is something "off," something in the otherness of the divine presence that remains strange and disconcerting even when the god is in disguise. Rising from the sea, Poseidon gives himself the stature and the voice of Calchas, the diviner. He approaches the two Aiantes, exhorts them, and with his remarks he gives them confidence and an ardor that wells up in their breasts. His mission accomplished, he turns and departs. But the son of Oileus is not deceived. It is a god who has come to us in the guise of Calchas, he confides to his companion: "No, that is not Calchas the seer. Without difficulty, I recognized from behind, while he was going away, the trace of his feet and his legs. The gods are recognizable."[44] One detects a god by his trace, just as a hunter recognizes the marks of the game he pursues. In spite of his disguise, the imprint left by the god as he walks on the ground undoubtedly reveals the disorienting, paradoxical and prodigious character of a body that is "other," because, in the very effort to look as though nothing were wrong, it reveals itself to be both the heaviest and the lightest of bodies. When Athena climbs into her chariot, it creaks and buckles under her weight. But when she leaps from one place to another, the same goddess does not even touch the ground. Poseidon left the two Aiantes in the human appearance of Calchas, imitating his gait, but his step was like that of "a quick-winged falcon pursuing a bird across the plain."[45] The divine body, in all the concentrated mass of its being, weighs as much as the marble or bronze statue located in the gods' temple: yet, it is aerial, ethereal, impalpable and as weightless as a ray of light.

So that they will not be recognized when they mingle with the crowd of fighters, the gods take the precaution of throwing a mist over the warriors' eyes to prevent them from distinguishing the divine from the human. In order to support Diomedes, Athena is not content to inspire him with a passion three times greater than his usual ardor, to make his legs, then this arms and his whole body supple from top to bottom: she takes away the mist that covered his eyes so he can distinguish whether a god or a man is before him, and thus will not run the risk of hand-to-hand combat with immortal divinities.

The bandage of darkness that covers their eyes and causes them to confuse mortals and immortals not only gives men a disadvantage because it hides the divine presence from them, it also protects them. To see a god face-to-face, as he is authentically in his uncovered body, is far more than human strength can bear. For the experience of seeing Artemis bathe in the nude, Actaeon pays with his life; for seeing Athena, Tiresias pays with his sight. After having slept with an immortal, Aphrodite, but without fully knowing that he has been with a goddess (*ou saphra eidōs*),[46] the mortal Anchises is understandably frightened when upon waking he sees the deity. Her head touches the roof of the room; her body is dressed in all its best finery; her cheeks are "radiant with immortal beauty [*kallos ambroton*]."[47] It is enough to see Aphrodite's "neck and her lovely eyes." He turns his gaze away in terror, hides his face under the covers, and begs for mercy:[48] may the goddess spare him, may he not be made "*amenēnos*," forever deprived of *menos,* the fire of his vital ardor, for having approached too brilliant a flame. Metaneira also feels her knees weaken and is speechless, prostrate and terror-stricken when Demeter, shedding the guise of an old woman, reveals herself in all her majesty to Metaneira: tall and noble of stature, radiant with beauty, exhaling a lovely perfume, "the immortal body of the goddess gave out a light that was illuminated as if by a bolt of lightning."[49]

The body of the gods shines with such an intense brilliance that no human eye can bear it. Its splendor is blinding. Its radiance robs it of visibility through an excess of light the way darkness causes invisibility through a lack of light. Between the shadows of death where they finally must lose themselves and the pure luminosity of the divine which remains inaccessible to them, men live in a middle world, divided between day and night. Their perishable bodies stand out clearly in the light of the sun. Their mortal eyes are made to recognize that which, through the combination of light and shadow, presents a precise form with its own shape, color and solidity. The paradox of the divine body is that in order to appear to mortals, it must cease to be itself; it must clothe itself in a mist, disguise itself as a mortal, take the form of a bird, a star, a rainbow. Or, if the god chooses to be seen in all his majesty, only the tiniest bit of the splendor of the god's size, stature, beauty and radiance can be allowed to filter through, and this is already enough to strike the spectator with *thambos,* stupefaction, to plunge him into a state of reverential fear. But to show themselves openly, as they truly are—*enargeis*—is a terrible favor the gods accord no one.[50] Heracles himself, who very much wanted to see Zeus, was unable to look at the god's face. Zeus "who did not want to be seen by him," hid his face behind an animal skin.[51]

More than any other part of the body, the face, like a mirror, reveals what an individual is and what he stands for. When a human being disappears in death, he loses his face at the same instant that he loses his life. The dead, their heads covered with darkness, drowned in shadow, are "faceless" as they are "without *menos.*"

For a god to show his face openly would be to give himself up: the face-to-face encounter implies a relationship of parity between partners who look one another in the eyes. Looking away, lowering one's eyes to the ground, covering one's head: mortals have no other way to acknowledge their unworthiness and avoid the risk of confronting the unequaled, unbearable splendor of the divine countenance.

A body invisible in its radiance, a face that cannot be seen directly: the apparition, rather than revealing the being of a god, hides it behind the multiple disguises of a "seeming to be" that is adapted to feeble human vision. If a god's body can take on so many forms, it is because not one of them can encompass within itself the Power that surpasses each of them and would impoverish itself if it were to be identified with any one of the figures that lends it its appearance. It is not important that Athena, in her struggle with Odysseus against the suitors, initially approaches him in the guise of a very young boy taking his herd to pasture,[52] only to take on a little later the appearance of a tall and beautiful woman.[53] As boy or girl, Athena's visible body fails equally to express what the goddess is authentically. It fails to designate that invisible body made of undying energy, power and vitality, and, in the case of Athena, a sovereign mastery of the art of cunning intelligence, ingenious stratagems, skillful know-how, shrewd lies. These are capacities that all belong to her, that constitute her attributes and define her power among the gods, just as they are Odysseus's lot and glory among mankind. Confronted with a goddess who likes to "take all manner of shapes,"[54] the only authentic criteria the hero, however cunning he may be, has by which he can ascertain whether it is Athena in person who is really facing him, is to admit that in the game of cunning, in craftiness, in deceptive discourse, he is not her match and that he must take a back seat to one who, in divine Olympus, is intelligence incarnate.[55]

One of the functions of the human body is that it precisely positions every individual, assigning him one and only one location in space. A god's body escapes this limitation no less than it does that of form. The gods are here and there at the same time. They are on earth where they show themselves by exercising their actions, and in the heavens where they reside. When Poseidon goes to the Ethiopians to feast with them in the land of the rising and setting sun, he travels, in the same movement, to the two opposite extremities of the earth.[56] Certainly, each god is attached to a particular domain of action depending on his type of power: the underworld for Hades, the ocean depths for Poseidon, cultivated land for Demeter, woods, forests and peripheral wilderness for Artemis. Thus, the gods do not enjoy absolute ubiquity anymore than any one of them possesses omniscience or omnipotence. But by travelling at a speed as fast as thought, the constraints imposed by the externality of the divisions of space are child's play to them, just as, through the independence they enjoy from natural cycles and their successive phases, they do not know the externality of the divisions of time as they relate to one another. In a single impulse, the gods' corporeal vitality extends across past, present and future, in the same way that its energy is deployed to the ends of the Universe.

Thus, if the nature of the gods seems to belie rather than to exalt the traits that define the corporeal in human existence, why speak of the body of the gods? First of all, because the Greeks of the archaic period, in order to conceive of a being of whatever kind, had no alternative but to express that being within the framework of the body's vocabulary, even though it meant skewing this code through procedures of distortion and denial, contradicting it at the very moment they used it. We have observed that the gods have blood that is not blood; that they eat the food of immortality while continuing to fast; and that sometimes they even sleep without closing their eyes or letting their vigilance fall completely asleep.[57] Should we not add: they have a body that is not a body?

We may indeed, as long as we specify that in the traditional religious system the step that would finalize the rupture between the divine and the corporeal is never taken—the step that at the same time would sever the continuity between gods and human beings established by the presence of the same vital values, the same qualities of force, radiance and beauty whose reflection is worn by the bodies of both mortals and immortals.

Moreover, all the activities of the cult presuppose the incorporation of the divine: how could mankind institute regular exchange with the gods in which homages and benefits balance out, unless the Immortals appear in this world in a visible and specific form, in a particular place and at a particular time?

But another reason, one that relates to the very nature of polytheism, must also be taken into consideration. For the Greeks, the divine world is organized into a society of the beyond, with its hierarchies of rank, its scale of grades and functions, its distribution of competencies and specialized abilities. Thus, it gathers together a multiplicity of particular divine figures, each one has its place, its role, its privileges, its signs of honor, its particular mode of action, a domain of intervention reserved for it alone: in short, each one has an individual identity.

Individual identity has two aspects: a name and a body. The proper name is that particular social mark attributed to a subject in order to consecrate its uniqueness within the species to which it belongs. Generally, things and animals do not have proper names. All human beings—as human beings—have one, because each person, even the most unknown, has a form of individual existence. As Alcinous reminds Odysseus when he invites him to say who he is: "There has never been a man without a name; whether he is noble or a peasant, everyone receives one at the time of his birth."[58] Similarly, it is the body that gives a subject his identity, by distinguishing him from all of his peers through his appearance, his physiognomy, his clothing and his insignia. Like men, the gods have proper names. Like men, too, they have bodies—that is to say, a set of specific characteristics which make them recognizable by differentiating them from the other supernatural Powers with whom they are associated.

A divine world that is multiple and therefore divided within itself by the plurality of beings composing it. Gods, each one of whom has his own name and individual body, partake of a limited and particular form of existence: this conception has not failed to arouse questions, reservations or rejection in certain marginal religious currents and sects, as well as among philosophers. These hesitations, which have expressed themselves in widely divergent ways, proceed from a single conviction: the presence of evil, misfortune and negativity in the world results from the process of individuation to which it has been subjected and which has given rise to beings who are separate, isolated, individual. Perfection, plenitude and eternity are the exclusive attributes of totally unified Being. Every fragmentation of the One, every dispersion of Being, every distinction among parts signifies death's entrance on the stage, together with a multiplicity of individual existences and the finitude that necessarily delimits each of them. To rid themselves of death, to fulfill themselves in the permanence of their perfection, the gods of Olympus would therefore have to renounce their individual bodies, dissolve themselves in the unity of a great cosmic god or be absorbed into the person of the orphic Dionysus—the god who is divided up and later reunified by Apollo. Dionysus is the guarantor of the return to primordial indistinctness and the reconquest of a divine unity that must be found again after having been lost.[59]

Hesiod's orthodox *Theogony* gives the corporeal nature of the gods its theological foundation by categorically rejecting this perspective: it places the complete, perfect and immutable not in the confusion of an original unity, in the obscure indistinctness of chaos, but rather in its opposite, in the differentiated order of a cosmos whose parts and constitutive elements have bit by bit become separate, delimited and located. Here, the divine Powers that were at first included in vague cosmic forces took on in the third generation definitive form as celestial gods living in a constant ethereal light, with their particular personalities and figures, their functions articulated each in relation to the others, their powers balanced and adjusted under the unshakeable authority of Zeus. If the gods possess plenitude, perfection, immutability, it is because at the end of the process that led to the emergence of a stable, organized and harmonious cosmos, each divine person's individuality is clearly fixed.

The divine being is one who, endowed with an existence that, like human existence, is individual, nevertheless knows neither death nor what is associated with it, because in its very particularity it has the value of a general, atemporal essence, of a universal, inexhaustible power. Aphrodite is *one* beauty: she is that particular goddesses whose appearance makes her recognizable among all the others. When Aphrodite, Athena and Hera stand before Paris, it is by comparing and contrasting the bodies of the three goddesses, by registering their differences, that Helen's future seducer can divine the powers and privileges that belong to each one, privileges that will not fail to be granted him by the one whose favor he will win with his vote. If he chooses Aphrodite, if he hands her the palm, it is because she, the most beautiful one, is also Beauty itself, that Beauty by which every individual in the world, whether animal, human or divine, is made beautiful and desirable. In its splendor, the goddess's body is the very power of Eros to the extent that Eros is a universal force. Nor is Zeus any more only a king, the king of gods: he is royalty itself. A monarch who does not derive his power from Zeus does not exist, nor is there a king who does not exercise his function through him and who does not receive from him, by delegation, the honors and glory reserved for the supreme master. The power of sovereignty finds its anchor in Zeus in the particular figure wherein it is fixed and incarnate.

The splendor, glory and radiant brilliance of a permanent, cosmic, indestructible royalty, which no person can ever overturn, have a form and a body, even if the former escapes the limitations of form and the latter is beyond a body.

In many ways, the divine super-body evokes and touches upon the non-body. It points to it; it never merges with it. If it were to swing to one side, to turn itself into the absence of body, the denial of body, it would upset the very equilibrium of Greek polytheism in its constant, necessary tension between the darkness in which the visible human body is steeped and the radiant light with which the gods' invisible body shines.

Notes

1. Xenophanes, frag. 14, in Clement of Alexandria *Stromata* 5.109.2=fr.170 in *The Presocratic Philosophers,* eds. G.S. Kirk and J.E. Raven (Cambridge: Cambridge University Press, 1957) (hereafter cited as KR).
2. Xenophanes, frag. 16: *Stromata* 7.22.1=171 KR.
3. Xenophanes, frag. 15: *Stromata* 5.109.1=172 KR.
4. Aristotle, *Metaphysics* A5.986b21=177 KR: Diogenes Laertius 28AI in *Die Fragmente der Vorsokratiker,* comp. H. Diels, ed. W. Kranz (Berlin, 1954) (hereafter cited as DK).
5. Xenophanes, frag. 23: *Stromata* 5.109.1=173 KR.
6. *Outi demas thnetoisin homoiios oude noēma:* "like mortals neither in the body nor in thought."
7. Sextus, frag. 24=175 KR: "Wholly [*oulos*] he sees, wholly he understands, wholly he hears."
8. Simplicius, frags. 25, 26=171 KR. The text specifies that, without becoming tired, without difficulty and without moving, the god makes everything shake through the "desire of his intellection [*noou phreni*]." The association of the terms *nous* and *phrēn* is reminiscent of the Homeric expression *noein phresi,* to have a thought, or a project, in one's *phrenes* (*Iliad* 9.600 and 22.235). What are the *phrenes*? A part

of the body: the lungs or the membrane of the heart, and an interior place of thought, since it is through the *phrenes* that one knows; but also a site of feeling or of passion—in effect the *thumos*: ardor, anger and also breath, vapor, can, like intellection, be situated in the *phrenes* (*Iliad* 8.202, 13.487, 22.475, 24.321). Let us add that the *nous*, the intelligence insofar as it perceives, understands or projects, may itself be localized in the *thumos* (*Odyssey* 14.490).

9. On this vocabulary as a whole and the problem it raises concerning psychology, the person, and self-consciousness in Homer, James Redfield has recently published a penetrating *mise au point*, all the more useful in that the reader will find in its bibliographical notes a list of the principal books and articles dealing with these questions. The title of his study is "Le sentiment homérique du Moi," it appeared in *Le genre humain*, vol. 12, *Les usages de la nature*, pp. 93–111.

10. Redfied, *ibid.*, p. 100; and further, "organic consciousness is self-consciousness," p. 99; or, in speaking of the epic character, "his consciousness of himself is also a consciousness of his 'me' as an organism," p. 98.

11. Cf. *Iliad* 6.146ff.: "As with the generations of leaves, so with the generations of men: the wind scatters the leaves over the ground and the burgeoning forest makes them grow again when the spring season returns. Thus it is with men: one generation is born at the very instant that another disappears."

12. The gods are defined *hoi aei ontes*: "those who exist forever." On the value of *aei* and its relation to the *aion*, the continuity of being that characterizes the divine vitality, cf. E. Benvéniste, "Expression indo-européenne de l'éternité," *Bulletin de la Société de Linguistique* 38, fasc. 1, pp. 103–13.

13. Cf. Hesiod, *Theogony* 220ff., and Clémence Ramnoux, *La nuit et les enfants de la nuit dans la tradition grecque,* new ed. (Paris, 1986).

14. On the interplay of *brotos,* mortal, and *brotos,* the blood that flows from a wound, cf. the analysis of Nicole Loraux, "Le corps vulnérable d'Arès," in *Le temps de la réflexion,* vol. 7, *Corps des dieux (Paris, 1986),* p. 335.

15. On *to luthron,* mixed blood with dust, cf. J.-P. Vernant, "The Pure and the Impure," in *Myth and Society in Ancient Greece* (New York: Zone Books, 1989), pp. 121–41.

16. Cf. Apollodorus 1.6.3 on Typhon, weakened and conquered by Zeus after having eaten the *ephēmeroi karpoi,* the "ephemeral fruits," instead of the drug of immortality.

17. Herodotus 3.22.19. Having learned what wheat is and how it grows, the Ethiopian Long-Life *(makrobios)* observes "that he is not at all surprised if, nourishing themselves on the manure [*kopros*], they lived a short span of years."

18. On the *gastēr kakoergos* (the evil-doing belly), *stugerē* (odious), *lugrē* (despicable), *oulomene* (disastrous), cf. J.-P. Vernant, "A la table des hommes," in *La cuisine du sacrifice en pays grec,* ed. M. Detienne and J.-P. Vernant (Paris, 1979), p. 94ff.

19. Cf. Elena Cassin, *La Splendeur divine* (Paris, 1968).

20. *Homeric Hymn to Apollo* 1.151–53.

21. *Iliad* 13.59–61.

22. Cf. the description of Achilles putting on the warrior's equipment that Hephaestus forged for him: "the divine Achilles tries out his armor: Will it fit him well? Will his glorious limbs run easily with it? And then it is as if he grew wings and they lift up the shepherd of men." *Iliad* 19.384–86.

23. Hesiod, *Theogony* 570–85; *Works and Days* 70–75.

24. The care lavished on a god's statue, of course, falls into the same category: at its fabrication, an incorruptible material is selected and it is enhanced with precious stones and metals to make it shine with a thousand fires; as part of its upkeep, its decayed parts are replaced and it is smeared with oil to increase its brilliance.

25. *Odyssey* 6.137.

26. *Ibid.* 6.227–37.

27. *Ibid.* 13.429–35.

28. *Ibid.* 16.173–83.

29. *Iliad.* 17.157.

30. *Ibid.* 20.372.

31. *Ibid.* 5.527.

32. *Odyssey* 10.521.

33. *Iliad* 4.314.

34. *Ibid.* 11.668–70.

35. *Ibid.* 23.627–29.

36. *Ibid.* 17.434–35.

37. *Ibid.* 9.413.

38. Cf. J.-P. Vernant, "La belle mort et le cadavre outragé," in *La mort, les morts dans les sociétés anciennes,* eds. G. Gnioli and J.-P. Vernant (Cambridge and Paris, 1982), pp. 45–76.

39. *Iliad* 20.54–65.

40. *Ibid.* 15.361–65.

41. *Odyssey* 5.217–18. In the same way, when Alcinous wonders if Odyyseus might not be a god who has come to visit him and his people, Odysseus answers: "Do not have this thought. I have nothing, neither stature nor presence [*demas, phuē*], in common with the Immortals, masters of the vast sky; I am but a simple mortal" (7.208–10).

42. *Iliad* 3.373–82.

43. *Ibid.* 1.197–200. On the episode as a whole and the problems that Athena's appearance poses within the very text of the *Iliad* itself, cf. the excellent analysis by Pietro Pucci, "Epifanie testuali nell' *Iliade,*" *Studi italiani di filologia classica* 78 (1985), pp. 170–83.

44. *Iliad* 13.70–72.

45. *Ibid.* 13.62–65.

46. *Homeric Hymn to Aphrodite* 1.167.

47. *Ibid.* 172–75.

48. *Ibid.* 181–90.

49. *Homeric Hymn to Demeter* 1.275–80. Even animals react to the terrible strangeness of a divine presence: in Eumaeus's hut, Athena stands before the door in the guise of a tall and beautiful woman, a skilled craftswoman. She is invisible to the eyes of Odysseus; Telemachus faces her without seeing her; but like Odysseus, the dogs have perceived the goddess, but without barking, they take refuge, frightened, in a corner of the hut (*Odyssey* 16.157–63).

50. *Iliad* 20.131; *Odyssey* 16.161. If Alcinous on his Phaeacian isle can claim that his people's ancestors in the past saw the gods a hundred times appear *enargeis,* in flesh and blood, it is because in contrast to other men the Phaeacians, like the Cyclopes and the Giants, are of the same origin, the same family as the gods, who therefore do not need to "hide themselves from them" (*Odyssey* 7.201–05).

51. *Herodotus* 2.42.

52. *Odyssey* 13.221.

53. *Ibid.* 13.288.

54. *Ibid.* 13.312–14: "Goddess," Odysseus declares to Athena, "when mortal, however quick-witted he may be, could recognize you at once when he met you: you take all manner of shapes."

55. *Ibid.* 13.295–99.

56. *Ibid.* 1.22–25.
57. Zeus's eyes are always open, his vigilance is faultless. Nevertheless, when Zeus is asleep, Typhon takes advantage of the occasion to try to steal his thunder. The attempt goes badly for Typhon; before he is able to lay a hand on the royal weapon, Zeus's eyes have already struck him with lightning. On the god's sleep as a substitute for their impossible death, one can invoke the case of Cronus who, since having been dethroned by Zeus, is, according to some traditions, plunged in sleep and dreams. Especially noteworthy is the *kakon kōma,* the cruel torpor that, for the duration of a great year envelopes the gods who are at fault, who are guilty of perjury, "hiding" them (*kaluptei*) as death hides humans. For them there is no more council, no more banquet, no more nectar or ambrosia, no more contact, communication or exchange of words with other divinities. Without being dead, since they are immortal, those who are guilty are bracketed, they are out of the game (Hesiod, *Theogony* 793–804).
58. *Odyssey* 8.552–54.
59. On this theme, cf. Giulia Sissa, "Dionysos: corps divin, corps divisé," *Le temps de la réflexion* vol. 7, *Corps des dieux* (Paris, 1986), p. 355.

Robert Bellah (1927–)

As Bellah says of himself in an autobiographical essay, he decided to major in social anthropology when he was a student at Harvard because he felt alienated from American society, both culturally and politically. His hope was that by studying other cultures quite different from his own, he might begin to "feel a degree of cultural authenticity that [he] did not experience at home" (Religion Online). After receiving his B.A., he stayed on at Harvard to study East Asia, particularly Japan. He earned his Ph.D. in 1955, but because of his Marxist political involvements as an undergraduate, he felt vulnerable during the McCarthy period and thus moved to Canada. "For a while I did not know if I would ever return," (Religion Online) he said, but after the hysteria surrounding the "red scare" died down, he returned to the United States in 1957 to join the Harvard faculty as a sociology professor. Bellah remained at Harvard until 1967, when he moved to Berkeley to serve as the UC Berkeley Ford Professor of Sociology, a position he held until 1997. While at Berkeley, he also chaired the Center for Japanese and Korean Studies from 1968 to 1974. He is currently the Elliott Professor of Sociology Emeritus at Berkeley.

Bellah's books on the sociology of religion—*Beyond Belief: Essays on Religion in a Post-Traditional World* (1970), *The Broken Covenant* (1975), *Habits of the Heart* (1985), and *The Good Society* (1991)—have been more than influential; they have helped shape the discipline of sociology itself. In 1985, *Habits of the Heart,* a cultural analysis of American society written in collaboration with four other authors, won *The Los Angeles Times* book prize for "Current Interest," and, in 1986, the book was a jury nominee for the Pulitzer Prize in General Nonfiction. Since its publication in 1985, it has sold more than half a million copies. In 2000, Bellah was chosen by President Bill Clinton to receive

the prestigious National Humanities Medal. His essay "Civil Religion in America" is a selection from *Beyond Belief*.

Civil Religion in America

While some have argued that Christianity is the national faith, and others that church and synagogue celebrate only the generalized religion of "the American Way of Life," few have realized that there actually exists alongside of and rather clearly differentiated from the churches an elaborate and well-institutionalized civil religion in America. This [chapter] argues not only that there is such a thing, but also that this religion—or perhaps better, this religious dimension—has its own seriousness and integrity and requires the same care in understanding that any other religion does.

The Kennedy Inaugural

John F. Kennedy's inaugural address of January 20, 1961, serves as an example and a clue with which to introduce this complex subject. That address began:

> We observe today not a victory of party but a celebration of freedom—symbolizing an end as well as beginning—signifying renewal as well as change. For I have sworn before you and Almighty God the same solemn oath our forebears prescribed nearly a century and three quarters ago.
>
> The world is very different now. For man holds in his mortal hands the power to abolish all forms of human poverty and to abolish all forms of human life. And yet the same revolutionary beliefs for which our forebears fought are still at issue around the globe—the belief that the rights of man come not from the generosity of the state but from the hand of God.

And it concluded:

> Finally, whether you are citizens of America or of the world, ask of us the same high standards of strength and sacrifice that we shall ask of you. With a good conscience our only sure reward, with history the final judge of our deeds, let us go forth to lead the land we love, asking His blessing and His help, but knowing that here on earth God's work must truly be our own.

These are the three places in this brief address in which Kennedy mentioned the name of God. If we could understand why he mentioned God, the way in which he did it, and what he meant to say in those three references, we would understand much about American civil religion.

Considering the separation of church and state, how is a president justified in using the word "God" at all? The answer is that the separation of church and state has not denied the political realm a religious dimension. Although matters of personal religious belief, worship, and association are considered to be strictly private affairs, there are, at the same time, certain common elements of religious orientation that the great majority of Americans share. These have

played a crucial role in the development of American institutions and still provide a religious dimension for the whole fabric of American life, including the political sphere. This public religious dimension is expressed in a set of beliefs, symbols, and rituals that I am calling the American civic religion. The inauguration of a president is an important ceremonial event in this religion. It reaffirms, among other things, the religious legitimation of the highest political authority.

Let us look more closely at what Kennedy actually said. First he said, "I have sworn before you and almighty God the same solemn oath our forebears prescribed nearly a century and three quarters ago." The oath is the oath of office, including the acceptance of the obligation to uphold the Constitution. He swears it before the people (you) and God. Beyond the Constitution, then, the president's obligation extends not only to the people but to God. In American political theory, sovereignty rests, of course, with the people, but implicitly, and often explicitly, the ultimate sovereignty has been attributed to God. This is the meaning of the motto "In God we trust," as well as the inclusion of the phrase "under God" in the pledge to the flag. What difference does it make that sovereignty belongs to God? Though the will of the people as expressed in majority vote is carefully institutionalized as the operative source of political authority, it is deprived of an ultimate significance. The will of the people is not itself the criterion of right and wrong. There is a higher criterion in terms of which this will can be judged; it is possible that the people may be wrong. The president's obligation extends to the higher criterion.

When Kennedy says that "the rights of man come not from the generosity of the state but from the hand of God," he is stressing this point again. It does not matter whether the state is the expression of the will of an autocratic monarch or of the "people"; the rights of man are more basic than any political structure and provide a point of revolutionary leverage from which any state structure may be radically altered. That is the basis for his reassertion of the revolutionary significance of America.

But the religious dimension in political life as recognized by Kennedy not only provides a grounding for the rights of man that makes any form of political absolutism illegitimate, it also provides a transcendent goal for the political process. This is implied in his final words that "here on earth God's work must truly be our own." What he means here is, I think, more clearly spelled out in a previous paragraph, the wording of which, incidentally, has a distinctly biblical ring:

> Now the trumpet summons us again—not as a call to bear arms, though arms we need—not as a call to battle, though embattled we are—but a call to bear the burden of a long twilight struggle, year in and year out, "rejoicing in hope, patient in tribulation"—a struggle against the common enemies of man: tyranny, poverty, disease and war itself.

The whole address can be understood as only the most recent statement of a theme that lies very deep in the American tradition, namely the obligation, both collective and individual, to carry out God's will on earth. This was the motivating spirit of those who founded America, and it has been present in every genera-

tion since. Just below the surface throughout Kennedy's inaugural address, it becomes explicit in the closing statement that God's work must be our own. That this very activist and noncontemplative conception of the fundamental religious obligation, which has been historically associated with the Protestant position, should be enunciated so clearly in the first major statement of the first Catholic president seems to underline how deeply established it is in the American outlook. Let us now consider the form and history of the civil religious tradition in which Kennedy was speaking.

The Idea of a Civil Religion

The phrase "civil religion" is, of course, Rousseau's. In chapter 8, book 4 of *The Social Contract,* he outlines the simple dogmas of the civil religion: the existence of God, the life to come, the reward of virtue and the punishment of vice, and the exclusion of religious intolerance. All other religious opinions are outside the cognizance of the state and may be freely held by citizens. While the phrase "civil religion" was not used, to the best of my knowledge, by the founding fathers, and I am certainly not arguing for the particular influence of Rousseau, it is clear that . . . religion, particularly the idea of God, played a constitutive role in the thought of the early American statesmen.

Kennedy's inauguration pointed to the religious aspect of the Declaration of Independence, and it might be well to look at that document a bit more closely. There are four references to God. The first speaks of the "Laws of Nature and of Nature's God" that entitle any people to be independent. The second is the famous statement that all men "are endowed by their Creator with certain inalienable Rights." Here Jefferson is locating the fundamental legitimacy of the new nation in a conception of "higher law" that is itself based on both classical natural law and biblical religion. The third is an appeal to "the Supreme Judge of the world for the rectitude of our intentions," and the last indicates "a firm reliance on the protection of divine Providence." In these last two references, a biblical God of history who stands in judgment over the world is indicated.

The intimate relation of these religious notions with the self-conception of the new republic is indicated by the frequency of their appearance in early official documents. For example, we find in Washington's first inaugural address of April 30, 1789:

> It would be peculiarly improper to omit in this first official act my fervent supplications that the Almighty Being who rules over the universe, who presides in the councils of nations, and whose providential aids can supply every defect, that His benediction may consecrate to the liberties and happiness of the people of the United States a Government instituted by themselves for these essential purposes. . . .
>
> No people can be bound to acknowledge and adore the invisible Hand which conducts the affairs of man more than those of the United States. Every step by which we have advanced to the character of an independent nation seems to have been distinguished by some token of providential agency. . . .

Nor did these religious sentiments remain merely the personal expression of the president. At the request of both Houses of Congress, Washington proclaimed on October 3 of that same first year as president that November 26 should be "a day of public thanksgiving and prayer," the first Thanksgiving Day under the Constitution.

The words and acts of the founding fathers, especially the first few presidents, shaped the form and tone of the civil religion as it has been maintained ever since. Though much is selectively derived from Christianity, this religion is clearly not itself Christianity. For one thing, neither Washington nor Adams nor Jefferson mentions Christ in his inaugural address; nor do any of the subsequent presidents, although not one of them fails to mention God.[1] The God of the civil religion is not only rather "unitarian," he is also on the austere side, much more related to order, law, and right than to salvation and love. Even though he is somewhat deist in cast, he is by no means simply a watchmaker God. He is actively interested and involved in history, with a special concern for America. Here the analogy has much less to do with natural law than with ancient Israel; the equation of America with Israel in the idea of the "American Israel" is not infrequent. What was implicit in the words of Washington already quoted becomes explicit in Jefferson's second inaugural when he said: "I shall need, too, the favor of that Being in whose hands we are, who led our fathers, as Israel of old, from their native land and planted them in a country flowing with all the necessaries and comforts of life." Europe is Egypt; America, the promised land. God has led his people to establish a new sort of social order that shall be a light unto all the nations.

This theme, too, has been a continuous one in the civil religion. We have already alluded to it in the case of the Kennedy inaugural. We find it again in President Johnson's inaugural address:

> They came here—the exile and the stranger, brave but frightened—to find a place where a man could be his own man. They made a covenant with this land. Conceived in justice, written in liberty, bound in union, it was meant one day to inspire the hopes of all mankind; and it binds us still. If we keep its terms, we shall flourish.

What we have, then, from the earliest years of the republic is a collection of beliefs, symbols, and rituals with respect to sacred things and institutionalized in a collectivity. This religion—there seems no other word for it—while not antithetical to and indeed sharing much in common with Christianity, was neither sectarian nor in any specific sense Christian. At a time when the society was overwhelmingly Christian, it seems unlikely that this lack of Christian reference was meant to spare the feelings of the tiny non-Christian minority. Rather, the civil religion expressed what those who set the precedents felt was appropriate under the circumstances. It reflected their private as well as public views. Nor was the civil religion simply "religion in general." While generality was undoubtedly seen as a virtue by some . . . the civil religion was specific enough when it came to the topic of America. Precisely because of this specificity, the civil religion was saved from empty formalism and served as a genuine vehicle of national religious self-understanding.

But the civil religion was not, in the minds of Franklin, Washington, Jefferson, or other leaders, with the exception of a few radicals like Tom Paine, ever felt to be a substitute for Christianity. There was an implicit but quite clear division of function between the civil religion and Christianity. Under the doctrine of religious liberty, an exceptionally wide sphere of personal piety and voluntary social action was left to the churches. But the churches were neither to control the state nor to be controlled by it. The national magistrate, whatever his private religious views, operates under the rubrics of the civil religion as long as he is in his official capacity, as we have already seen in the case of Kennedy. This accommodation was undoubtedly the product of a particular historical moment and of a cultural background dominated by Protestantism of several varieties and by the Enlightenment, but it has survived despite subsequent changes in the cultural and religious climate[s].

Civil War and Civil Religion

Until the Civil War, the American civil religion focused above all on the event of the Revolution, which was seen as the final act of the Exodus from the old lands across the waters. The Declaration of Independence and the Constitution were the sacred scriptures and Washington the divinely appointed Moses who led his people out of the hands of tyranny. The Civil War, which Sidney Mead calls "the center of American history," was the second great event that involved the national self-understanding so deeply as to require expression in the civil religion. In 1835, Alexis de Tocqueville wrote that the American republic had never really been tried and that victory in the Revolutionary War was more the result of British preoccupation elsewhere and the presence of a powerful ally than of any great military success of the Americans. But in 1861 the time of testing had indeed come. Not only did the Civil War have the tragic intensity of fratricidal strife, but it was one of the bloodiest wars of the nineteenth century; the loss of life was far greater than any previously suffered by Americans.

The Civil War raised the deepest questions of national meaning. The man who not only formulated but in his own person embodied its meaning for Americans was Abraham Lincoln. For him the issue was not in the first instance slavery but "whether that nation, or any nation so conceived, and so dedicated, can long endure." He had said in Independence Hall in Philadelphia on February 22, 1861:

> All the political sentiments I entertain have been drawn, so far as I have been able to draw them, from the sentiments which originated in and were given to the world from this Hall. I have never had a feeling, politically, that did not spring from the sentiments embodied in the Declaration of Independence.

The phrases of Jefferson constantly echo in Lincoln's speeches. His task was, first of all, to save the Union—not for America alone but for the meaning of America to the whole world so unforgettably etched in the last phrase of the Gettysburg Address.

But inevitably the issue of slavery as the deeper cause of the conflict had to be faced. In his second inaugural, Lincoln related slavery and the war in an ultimate perspective:

> If we shall suppose that American slavery is one of those offenses which, in the providence of God, must needs come, but which, having continued through His appointed time, He now wills to remove, and that He gives to both North and South this terrible war as the woe due to those by whom the offense came, shall we discern therein any departure from those divine attributes which the believers in a living God always ascribe to Him? Fondly do we hope, fervently do we pray, that this mighty scourge of war may speedily pass away. Yet, if God wills that it continue until all the wealth piled by the bondsman's two hundred and fifty years of unrequited toil shall be sunk, and until every drop of blood drawn with the lash shall be paid by another drawn with the sword, as was said three thousand years ago, so still it must be said "the judgments of the Lord are true and righteous altogether."

But he closes on a note if not of redemption then of reconciliation—"With malice toward none, with charity toward all."

With the Civil War, a new theme of death, sacrifice, and rebirth enters the civil religion. It is symbolized in the life and death of Lincoln. Nowhere is it stated more vividly than in the Gettysburg Address, itself part of the Lincolnian "New Testament" among the civil scriptures. Robert Lowell has recently pointed out the "insistent use of birth images" in this speech explicitly devoted to "these honored dead": "brought forth," "conceived," "created," "a new birth of freedom". . . . The earlier symbolism of the civil religion had been Hebraic without in any specific sense being Jewish. The Gettysburg symbolism (". . . those who here gave their lives, that the nation might live") is Christian without having anything to do with the Christian church.

The new symbolism soon found both physical and ritualistic expression. The great number of the war dead required the establishment of a number of national cemeteries. Of these, the Gettysburg National Cemetery, which Lincoln's famous address served to dedicate, has been overshadowed only by the Arlington National Cemetery. Begun somewhat vindictively on the Lee estate across the river from Washington, partly with the end that the Lee family could never reclaim it, it has subsequently become the most hallowed monument of the civil religion. Not only was a section set aside for the Confederate dead, but it has received the dead of each succeeding American war. It is the site of the one important new symbol to come out of World War I, the Tomb of the Unknown Soldier; more recently it has become the site of the tomb of another martyred president and its symbolic eternal flame.

Memorial Day, which grew out of the Civil War, gave ritual expression to the themes we have been expressing. As Lloyd Warner has so brilliantly analyzed it, the Memorial Day observance, especially in the towns and smaller cities of America, is a major event for the whole community involving a rededication to the martyred dead, to the spirit of sacrifice, and to the American vision. Just as Thanksgiving Day, which incidentally was securely institutionalized as an annual national holiday only under the presidency of Lincoln, serves to integrate the family into the civil religion, so Memorial Day has acted to integrate the local community into the national cult. Together with the less overtly religious Fourth of July and the more minor celebrations of Veterans Day and the birthdays of Washington and Lincoln, these two holidays provide an annual ritual calendar for the civil religion. The public school system serves as a particularly important context for the cultic celebration of the civil rituals.

The Civil Religion Today

. . . The civil religion at its best is a genuine apprehension of universal and transcendent religious reality as seen in or, one could almost say, as revealed through the experience of the American people. Like all religions, it has suffered various deformations and demonic distortions. At its best, it has neither been so general that it has lacked incisive relevance to the American scene nor so particular that it has placed American society above universal human values. . . .

It is certainly true that the relation between religion and politics in America has been singularly smooth. This is in large part due to the dominant tradition. As de Tocqueville wrote:

> The greatest part of British America was peopled by men who, after having
> shaken off the authority of the Pope, acknowledged no other religious
> supremacy: they brought with them into the New World a form of Christianity
> which I cannot better describe than by styling it a democratic and republican
> religion.[2]

The churches opposed neither the Revolution nor the establishment of democratic institutions. Even when some of them opposed the full institutionalization of religious liberty, they accepted the final outcome with good grace and without nostalgia for an *ancien regime*. The American civil religion was never anticlerical or militantly secular. On the contrary, it borrowed selectively from the religious tradition in such a way that the average American saw no conflict between the two. In this way, the civil religion was able to build up without any bitter struggle with the church powerful symbols of national solidarity and to mobilize deep levels of personal motivation for the attainment of national goals.

Such an achievement is by no means to be taken for granted. It would seem that the problem of a civil religion is quite general in modern societies and that the way it is solved or not solved will have repercussions in many spheres. One need only think of France to see how differently things can go. The French Revolution was anticlerical to the core and attempted to set up an anti-Christian civil religion. Throughout modern French history, the chasm between traditional Catholic symbols and the symbolism of 1789 has been immense.

American civil religion is still very much alive. Just three years ago we participated in a vivid reenactment of the sacrifice theme in connection with the funeral of our assassinated president. The American Israel theme is clearly behind both Kennedy's New Frontier and Johnson's Great Society. Let me give just one recent illustration of how the civil religion serves to mobilize support for the attainment of national goals. On March 15, 1965, President Johnson went before Congress to ask for a strong voting-rights bill. Early in the speech he said:

> Rarely are we met with the challenge, not to our growth or abundance, or our welfare or our security—but rather to the values and the purposes and the meaning of our beloved nation.
>
> The issue of equal rights for American Negroes is such an issue. And should we defeat every enemy, and should we double our wealth and conquer the stars and still be unequal to this issue, then we will have failed as a people and as a nation.
>
> For with a country as with a person, "What is a man profited, if he shall gain the whole world, and lose his own soul?"

And in conclusion he said:

> Above the pyramid on the great seal of the United States it says in Latin, "God has favored our undertaking."
>
> God will not favor everything that we do. It is rather our duty to divine his will. I cannot help but believe that He truly understands and that He really favors the undertaking that we begin here tonight.

The civil religion has not always been invoked in favor of worthy causes. On the domestic scene, an American-Legion type of ideology that fuses God, country, and flag has been used to attack nonconformist and liberal ideas and groups of all kinds. Still, it has been difficult to use the words of Jefferson and Lincoln to support special interests and undermine personal freedom. The defenders of slavery before the Civil War came to reject the thinking of the Declaration of Independence. Some of the most consistent of them turned against not only Jeffersonian democracy but Reformation religion; they dreamed of a South dominated by medieval chivalry and divine-right monarchy. For all the overt religiosity of the radical right today, their relation to the civil religious consensus is tenuous, as when the John Birch Society attacks the central American symbol of Democracy itself.

With respect to America's role in the world, the dangers of distortion are greater and the built-in safeguards of the tradition weaker. The theme of the American Israel was used, almost from the beginning, as a justification for the shameful treatment of the Indians so characteristic of our history. It can be overtly or implicitly linked to the idea of manifest destiny that has been used to legitimate several adventures in imperialism since the early nineteenth century. Never has the danger been greater than today. The issue is not so much one of imperial expansion, of which we are accused, as of the tendency to assimilate all governments or parties in the world that support our immediate policies or call upon our help by invoking the notion of free institutions and democratic values. Those nations that are for the moment "on our side" become "the free world." A repressive and unstable military dictatorship in South Vietnam becomes "the free people of South Vietnam and their government." It is then part of the role of America as the New Jerusalem and "the last best hope of earth" to defend such governments with treasure and eventually with blood. When our soldiers are actually dying, it becomes possible to consecrate the struggle further by invoking the great theme of sacrifice. For the majority of the American people who are unable to judge whether the people in South Vietnam (or wherever) are "free like us," such arguments are convincing. Fortunately President Johnson has been less ready to assert that "God has favored our undertaking" in the case of Vietnam than with respect to civil rights. But others are not so hesitant. The civil religion has exercised long-term pressure for the humane solution of our greatest domestic problem, the treatment of the Negro American. It remains to be seen how relevant it can become for our role in the world at large, and whether we can effectively stand for "the revolutionary beliefs for which our forebears fought," in John F. Kennedy's words.

The civil religion is obviously involved in the most pressing moral and political issues of the day. But it is also caught in another kind of crisis, theoretical and theological, of which it is at the moment largely unaware. "God" has clearly been a central symbol in the civil religion from the beginning and remains so today. This symbol is just as central to the civil religion as it is to Judaism or Christianity. In the late eighteenth century this posed no problem; even Tom Paine, contrary to his detractors, was not an atheist. From left to right and regardless of church or sect, all could accept the idea of God. But today, as even *Time* has recognized, the meaning of "God" is by no means so clear or so obvious. There is no formal creed in the civil religion. We have had a Catholic president; it is conceivable that we could have a Jewish one. But could we have an agnostic president? Could a man with conscientious scruples about using the word "God" the way Kennedy and Johnson have used it be elected chief magistrate of our country? If the whole God symbolism requires reformulation, there will be obvious consequences for the civil religion, consequences perhaps of liberal alienation and of fundamentalist ossification that have not so far been prominent in this realm. The civil religion has been a point of articulation between the profoundest commitments of the Western religious and philosophical traditions and the common beliefs of ordinary Americans. It is not too soon to consider how the deepening theological crisis may affect the future of this articulation.

Notes

1. God is mentioned or referred to in all inaugural addresses but Washington's second, which is a very brief (two paragraphs) and perfunctory acknowledgment. It is not without interest that the actual word "God" does not appear until Monroe's second inaugural, March 5, 1821. In his first inaugural, Washington refers to God as "that Almighty Being who rules the universe," "Great Author of every public and private good," "Invisible Hand," and "benign Parent of the Human Race." John Adams refers to God as "Providence," "Being who is supreme over all," "Patron of Order," "Fountain of Justice," and "Protector in all ages of the world of virtuous liberty." Jefferson speaks of "that infinite Power which rules the destinies of the universe" and "that Being in whose hands we are." Madison speaks of "that Almighty Being whose

power regulates the destiny of nations" and "Heaven." Monroe uses "Providence" and "the Almighty" in his first inaugural and finally "Almighty God" in his second. See *Inaugural Addresses of the Presidents of the United States from George Washington 1789 to Harry S. Truman 1949*, 82d Congress, 2d Session, House Document No. 540, 1952.

2. Alexis de Tocqueville, *Democracy in America* Vol. 1 (New York: Doubleday, 1954), p. 311.

Questions to Consider

1. What role, if any, does the spiritual play in your life? Does the way you articulate your identity, whether cultural, ethnic, economic, religious, or sexual, ever come into conflict with what might be called the spiritual realm? If so, where and why? Bynum argues that medieval European society understood the body and the soul as a psychosomatic unity that was not in conflict with itself. Can you think of examples in contemporary society where the corporeal and the sacred are either in accord or in conflict?

2. What role does the body play in each of the essays in this section? What would Wittig say about the medieval fluidity of gender definition? Would Wittig like or trust the concept of Jesus as mother? If, as Wittig hopes, we someday become a sexless society, how would this change our conceptions of mother and father? How would this change our conception of feminine and masculine religious figures? Are such changes appealing to you? Why or why not?

3. Vernant conceives of the body as an historical category "steeped in imagination." Is it possible to conceive of the god of Bellah's civil religion in this way? If so, does our contemporary sense of the body as a scientific object defined in anatomical or physiological terms influence or affect our contemporary sense of god? How would you characterize the human body and the divine body?

4. Although Vernant speaks of the sub-body and the super-body in order to suggest the difference between the human and the divine body, might we also use his terms to characterize differences between one human body and another? For example, terms such as "supermodel," "superhero," and "superstar" are used every day to suggest the "dazzling body" of the fashion runway, the cartoon world, and the box-office hit, but do we also employ terms to suggest the "dim body"? In our culture, who might be said to have a sub-body?

5. As illustrated through Lacan's theory of the mirror stage, the visual field plays a powerful role in identity formation. In what other aspects of our lives does sight play a central role? Given that the eye is easily deceived, is our heavy reliance on it appropriate? Although the ear, too, plays a role in identity formation, other sensory fields such as taste, touch, and smell get short shrift. Would our identity formation be radically altered if less impor-

tance were placed on the eye and more importance on other sensory organs? If so, how?

6. Questions of identity are often bound up with questions of spirituality. In other words, who we are is often defined by how we articulate our origins. Is this concern with origins beneficial? How does this concern affect abandoned or adopted children, displaced peoples, hybridity or creolization, and experiences of diaspora or exile that leave one a stranger in a strange land? If, as Lacan argues, the mirror stage constitutes the ego as oppositional and rivalrous, what impact does this factor have on religious beliefs and tolerance for those who believe differently from us?

IX

TECHNOLOGY AND PROGRESS

Many people think of technology and progress in terms of the wonders of the Internet and the convenience of cell phones, which allow the sharing of information instantly on campus, across town, and around the globe. Other people think of technology and progress in terms of science-fiction-like labor-saving robots or fantastic medical advances such as those promised by genetic research through the Human Genome Project. Influencing our conceptions of work and of our bodies, these innovations affect our understanding of quality of life. Indeed, our portable commodities such as laptop computers, personal digital assistants, and digital cameras continue to refigure boundaries in marvelous ways. Miniaturization, for instance, means that we can hold complex commodities right in our hands, giving us a more personal sense of technology as equipment for living. Similarly, the conception and use of compact discs and DVDs, PDAs and video cell phones, instant messaging and plasma-screen televisions, measure progress in our consumer economy. Whether we are talking about robots or e-mail, we stereotypically understand technology as innovations that improve our lives by helping us do things better; similarly, we understand progress as the unceasing movement from worse to better. It is very comforting to think that things keep improving. As the old saying goes, "You can't stop progress." Who would want to?

Well, not everyone sees technology and progress as solely beneficial. For some people, the words "technology" and "progress" have become meaningless—unclear, obscure, impenetrable. If "technology" and "progress" can be used to signify anything from the latest Macintosh computer to the newest three-blade disposable razor, then what do the words really signify? The packaging for Wrigley's Eclipse Flash Strips offers advice for "your other immediate breath control needs." This language sounds high-tech. Apparently, these newfangled, thinner than thin, rectangular strips that dissolve in your mouth represent the latest in "breath control" technology. But, do "breath control" and technology really go together? Like "technology," the term "progress" is often bandied about as if it is an unalloyed or pure good. People don't object to progress, but they do object to the word being used as an unquestionable excuse for doing anything one wants, from tearing down perfectly good houses in order to build yet another drugstore or more ritzy condominiums for upscale professionals and their higher tax base to clearing forestland in order to construct a parking lot for yet another mall.

For many other people, unregulated technologies signify anything but progress. From sci-fi scenarios of biomolecular research into cloning to perhaps prosaic, but no less important, questions about who makes the high-tech consumer goods we buy and under what kinds of working conditions, a host of reasonable questions continues to dog the heels of innovation and progress. For example, how does a high-tech economy affect traditional industries and small businesses, and, similarly, what are the effects of technology on families and on education gaps between the rich and the poor in the United States? One is not necessarily being negative or cynical, or opposed to technological development or enterprising growth, when one wants to think carefully about how to balance innovation and civic accountability. Critical theory can help us think responsibly about technology and progress. Rather than believing that the world always progresses forward like a sprinter in a 50-meter dash, we can use theory wisely to help us clear unexpected hurdles. For instance, many people think that science, or someone—a politician, perhaps—will surely solve problems as they arise. However, such an attitude puts a lot of faith in the hands of experts and political leaders. Do we want to leave key decisions solely up to experts or politicians? Would lack of democratic participation in decision making signify progress?

The reading selections in this section are diverse, coming at technology and progress from distinct—and sometimes seemingly eccentric—angles. Kenneth Burke's essay "Literature as Equipment for Living" may appear to be particularly unusual or anomalous, because Burke discusses not technological novelties, but the old, folk wisdom of proverbs, as the basis for what he calls a sociological approach to the study of literature. Like photography, television, and movies, literature is a medium, and therefore we can understand it as a type of technology. Burke's title suggests another way to link technology with literature and language. "Equipment" certainly signifies intellectual resources, but it also means a thing or material object, such as a tool or apparatus, necessary for an expedition, job, or warfare. If you think of your cell phone or computer as equipment for living, can literature be, too? What does literature offer us, according to Burke, beyond aesthetic or artistic pleasure?

If you think of technologies as problem-solving devices, then think about how Burke views proverbs and literature: as strategies for sizing up situations, strategies that allow us to classify and chart "relationships involved in competitive and cooperative acts." Such classification is important, he argues, not simply for telling us about artistic form or "literary organization," but also for helping us better understand "social situations outside of art." In other words, viewing literature through Burke's proverbial lens reveals cultural insights, which suggest strategies for appropriate action, and which possibly lead to innovation. We might understand literature and arts generally as being, from Burke's perspective, symbolic technologies: "strategies for selecting enemies and allies, for socializing losses, for warding off evil eye, for purification, propitiation, and desanctification, consolation and vengeance, admonition and exhortation, implicit commands or instructions of one sort or another." Might we similarly speak of critical theory as a form or kind of technology?

Unlike Burke's perhaps unusual or irregular focus on literature, Thomas Kuhn's focus on X rays, electricity, and planets in "The Historical Structure of Scientific Discovery" likely will meet your expectations for a text dealing with issues of technology and progress. According to Kuhn, scientists have typically "seen the individual discovery as an appropriate unit with which to measure scientific progress and have devoted much time and skill to determining what man made which discovery at what point in time." Kuhn contests this approach, however, saying that we have an inappropriate "image of discovery." Rather than seeing discovery as a "unitary event" and seeking to identify when and where the discovery occurred and by whom, historians of science need, according to Kuhn, to refigure their approach. They should understand discovery as a structural process, "a complex development extended both in space and time."

In his discussion of the discovery of oxygen, for instance, Kuhn reveals a complex history of misdiagnosed observations, recalculations, and competing claims. For example, he says, "Though undoubtedly correct, the sentence 'Oxygen was discovered' misleads by suggesting that discovering something is a single simple act unequivocally attributable, if only we knew enough, to an individual and an instant in time. When the discovery is unexpected, however, the latter attribution is always impossible and the former often is as well." Kuhn offers, instead, a three-stage structural model for unexpected discoveries: what he labels the "prehistory," "internal history," and posthistory" phases of the discovery process. When recognition of an "anomaly," that is, an unexpected novelty, leads someone to refigure data, instruments, and thinking in order to account for the anomaly or make it "lawlike," then the result, a discovery, increases scientific knowledge. Such discoveries, according to Kuhn, "react back upon what has previously been known, providing a new view of some previously familiar objects and simultaneously changing the way in which even some traditional parts of science are practiced." Elsewhere, Kuhn calls this changing vision a paradigm shift. His theory of the discovery process and paradigm shifts has exerted great influence in the arts and sciences. Scholars and theorists from diverse fields have found Kuhn's keen formulation useful for sizing up, as Burke would say, a variety of situations—historical, literary, economic, anthropological, sociological, and philosophical, as well as scientific.

You might want to compare Kuhn's structural explanation of discovery and its aftermath with Stephen Greenblatt's historical and literary examination of European linguistic colonization of the New World in his 1976 essay "Learning to Curse." Following Kuhn's contention that scientific discovery is often not a unitary event, you might complicate or call into question history-book claims that Columbus discovered the Americas. What kind of structure or process gets flattened out in the claims of Columbus as discoverer? What progress does the European entrance into the Americas presumably signal? We might expect Greenblatt to emphasize the role of new European navigational instruments and military firepower in the "discovery" and colonization of the New World, but instead he emphasizes the role of language, focusing particularly on European conceptions of "savages" and their language, or lack thereof. As you read his essay, ask yourself if Greenblatt views language as a crucial colonial technology, as equipment for living and for conquering.

The role of language in legitimating European conquest raises questions about what counts as knowledge and about how we understand others who speak a language different from our own. For example, consider Greenblatt's discussion of the widely held European view that "savages" had "no language at all." Such a belief may seem old fashioned, but not too long ago Hollywood films—particularly Westerns—typically depicted Indians who screamed, grunted, or uttered monosyllables such "ugh" and "how"; such depictions implied an impassable gulf between the humanity of the white characters in the films and the debased savagery of the Native Americans. A more sympathetic, but no less stereotypical, image of the languageless Indian appeared in a very popular series of ecological commercials in the 1970s, which depicted a speechless Indian surveying some of the careless effects of technology and progress—polluted landscapes and streams—as an eloquent tear rolls down his cheek.

Just as the "discovery" of the languageless Indian is puzzling to us today, so is the opposite "discovery" that Europeans and indigenous peoples could miraculously understand each other during colonial encounters. As Greenblatt notes, Europeans and Indians spoke different languages, yet many Europeans wrote accounts of encounters in which there appear to be no problems with the colonists and Indians understanding one another. To assume a one-to-one correspondence between one language (e.g., Spanish or English) and another (e.g., Aztec or Pequod) in such situations naively or uncritically homogenizes social interactions and denies cultural specificity to other people. The replacement of difference or heterogeneity with homogenization is made possible by writing, publishing, and travel technologies. The scenarios Greenblatt describes—Indians are either inhuman brutes because they lack language, or they are completely transparent and understandable—are fantasies that serve the interests of the colonists at the expense of the indigenous peoples of the New World. Fantasies like the latter imply that another's customs and worldview are "naturally" and necessarily just like our own. However, one system of meaning does not "naturally" mirror another's, because there are many arbitrary factors at work—not the least of which is language. In other words, as Burke suggests, different cultures develop different linguistic strategies to size up situations. The words in the world's language systems are arbitrary: they derive from random choice and are not divinely ordained. This lesson is evident everywhere. For example, English speakers use the word "door," but Spanish speakers use the word "puerta." Neither is the better word or the truer one. As Greenblatt notes, "reality for each society is constructed to a significant degree out of the *specific* qualities of its language and symbols."

These distinctions should lead us to ask more questions about how and why certain linguistic strategies are approved of, while others are not. For example, why do political leaders praise and authorize certain visions of technology and progress while delegitimizing other visions or perspectives? As technology brings many aspects of the world closer together, perhaps one sign of progress would be the recognition, in Greenblatt's words, that there is not "a single faith, a single text, a single reality." There is, likewise, not a single set of proverbs: "equipment for living" varies, and heterogeneity is good. Indeed, a variety of strategies can help us when we encounter the unfamiliar or unexpected.

Some see Greenblatt's historical analysis of colonial contact between Old World Europeans and New World indigenous peoples as part of a paradigm shift in literary research and scholarship. Yet, his historical focus may seem starkly at odds with Donna Haraway's innovative and sci-fi-tinged 1985 essay "A Cyborg Manifesto: Science, Technology, and Socialist-Feminism in the Late Twentieth Century." Haraway defines a cyborg as "a hybrid of machine and organism, a creature of social reality as well as a creation of fiction." In Haraway's words, the cyborg identity "changes what counts as women's experience in the late twentieth century." Suggesting a world without gender, a postpatriarchal space where diverse coalitions can form, the cyborg identity helps us understand how and why technology and science are not necessarily masculine and patriarchal. Indeed, science and technology offer opportunities for women to rewrite accepted scripts of male domination, according to Haraway: "science and technology provide fresh sources of power," which cyborgs can marshal to improve their lives. The cyborg identity Haraway praises signals a potential paradigm shift—a revolution in understanding and social relations. As Kuhn notes, a paradigm shift can "provid[e] a new view of some previously familiar objects," which can help us to revalue them. What familiar objects does Haraway want us to observe with fresh eyes? You might examine her discussion of a revaluation of politics that resists the status quo: "Rearrangements of race, sex, and class rooted in high-tech-facilitated social relations can make socialist feminism more relevant to effective progressive politics." Why does Haraway believe that such rearrangements can effectively ally or make harmonious "socialist feminism" and "progressive politics"? What does Haraway mean by "socialist feminism," and how does this concept relate to the cyborg identity?

Linking Haraway's discussion of cyborgs and socialist feminism to Kuhn's theory of scientific revolution can be instructive, and so can comparing her discussion of cyborg resistance to the "informatics of domination" with Greenblatt's analysis of Caliban's resistance to Prospero's domination in Shakespeare's play *The Tempest*. Does the cyborg writing that Haraway praises demonstrate qualities similar to the "opacity" Greenblatt identifies and admires in Caliban's language? Does anything happen to this opacity in the change or "movement," in Haraway's words, "from an organic, industrial society to a polymorphous, information system?" You might also consider what technologies mark "a polymorphous, information system" and what kind(s) of progress does it signal, if any? Also, think about what counts as "equipment for living" in a "polymorphous, information system."

It is important to notice that Haraway, like Burke and Greenblatt, sees language as technology: "Writing is pre-eminently the technology of cyborgs, etched surfaces of the late twentieth century," and cyborg writing is "about the power to survive . . . on the basis of seizing the tools to mark the world that marked them as other." In other words, writing enables cyborg authors to size up situations in order to rework and undermine "central myths of origin of Western culture." While Haraway suggests that such subversion will signal progress, her view may seem anomalous or even threatening to some people. What attracts, puzzles, or worries you about her theory?

Greenblatt's historical focus ostensibly contrasts with Haraway's seemingly futuristic topic. Similarly, Haraway's cyborgs likely appear alien to the common, everyday event of a mother feeding her child a breakfast of hot oatmeal—the opening image of Arlie Russell Hochschild's 2003 text "From the Frying Pan into the Fire." Like Haraway, however, Hochschild examines subversion and paradigm shifts entailed in the processes by which the once profane spaces of the workplace and shopping mall reach into and redefine the formerly sacred intimacies of home and family. If you have a job, then you know how work, particularly the drive for efficiency, affects people's home life. According to Hochschild,

> increasingly, our belief that family comes first conflicts with the emotional draw of both workplace and mall. Indeed, I would argue that a constellation of pressures is pushing men and women further into the world of the workplace and mall. And television—a pipeline, after all, to the mall—is keeping them there. Family and community life have meanwhile become less central as places to talk and relate, and less the object of collective rituals.

Compare her assessment of the "constellation of pressures" with your own work experiences.

Hochschild's analysis of a Quaker Oats advertisement demonstrates how the efficiency principle infiltrates and directs private life. The caring, but on-the-go, mother in the advertisement makes sure that her child gets a hot, nutritious breakfast by serving Quaker Oats, which takes only 90 seconds to prepare. According to Hochschild, "the ad suggests that it is the cereal itself that solves the problem. It conveys love because it is hot, but it permits efficiency because it's quickly made. The cereal would seem to reconcile an image of American motherhood of the 1950s with the female work role of 2000 and beyond." Many of us can identify with the mother's "solution" to time constraints, given our hectic lives. Is the efficient mother the best mother, just as the efficient worker is presumably the best worker, from the perspective of management? As you think about answers to these questions, also compare Hochschild's analysis of efficiency with Haraway's discussion of the "homework economy." Is the "homework economy" a sign of progress? How has time-saving technology such as cell phones or work ideals such as multitasking refigured people's lives at home? Consider the implications of Hochschild's observation that, "the ethic of 'saving time' raises the question of what we want to save time for."

Hochschild's title refers to the shift from patriarchy (the "frying pan") to "the fire of market individualism under capitalism." According to Hochschild, capitalism is "a cultural as well as an economic system" with "symbols and rituals" that "compete with, however much they seem to serve, the symbols and rituals of community and family." What would Haraway identify as the "symbols and rituals" of the "informatics of domination"? We inquire into a system's symbols and rituals for many of the same reasons we might read proverbs: to better understand when and how to act and when and how to refrain from acting, and to understand better, in Burke's words, "the relationships involved in competitive and cooperative acts." Does the ideal of efficiency embedded in capitalism's symbols and rituals cooperate as well as compete with home and family? What technologies enable you to be more efficient, and what relationships do you see between efficiency and progress? Can efficiency threaten progress?

Finally, what happens if you apply the principle of efficiency to the study of literature or of history? What are the benefits and costs? Think about how the theorists in this section would likely respond to calls that they use the principle of efficiency to pursue knowledge and to do theory. Democracy and progress are not necessarily efficient; should they be? Could new technologies make them so, and if so, what would those technologies likely be? To answer these questions, we may need something like a fantastic crystal ball in order to see the shape of future paradigms. Or perhaps, we just need more theory.

Kenneth Burke (1897–1993)

Was there a more creative and unconventional twentieth-century U.S. critic than Kenneth Burke? He has influenced folks in a variety of fields, including English studies, anthropology, communications, and sociology; nevertheless, his theories have not proven portable in the sense of enabling a recognizably stable critical mass of scholars—that is, a School of Burke, so to speak—to coalesce and operate like some other recognized critical schools. Burke was born in Pittsburgh, Pennsylvania, and never graduated from college; yet he taught at Bennington College in Vermont for almost twenty years and lectured widely at other colleges and universities across the United States. Today, it is generally recognized that Burke's focus on rhetoric anticipates much contemporary theory of the last 30 years. Similarly, his sociological approach to literary texts intersects with many key concerns in contemporary "cultural studies." Burke's insight and creativity are also evident in his theory of "dramatism" and his discussion of the "Four Master Tropes" in *The Grammar of Motives* (1945), his arguments about "identification" and "consubstantiality" in *The Rhetoric of Motives* (1950), and his focus on people as "symbol-using animal[s]" in *Language as Symbolic Action* (1966). Burke's other major books include *Counter-Statement* (1931), *Permanence and Change* (1935), *Attitudes Toward History* (1937), *The Philosophy of*

Literary Form (1941), and *The Rhetoric of Religion* (1961). The selection given next, "Literature as Equipment for Living," appears in *The Philosophy of Literary Form*.

Literature as Equipment for Living

Here I shall put down, as briefly as possible, a statement in behalf of what might be catalogued, with a fair degree of accuracy, as a *sociological* criticism of literature. Sociological criticism in itself is certainly not new. I shall here try to suggest what partially new elements or emphasis I think should be added to this old approach. And to make the "way in" as easy as possible, I shall begin with a discussion of proverbs.

1

Examine random specimens in *The Oxford Dictionary of English Proverbs*. You will note, I think, that there is no "pure" literature here. Everything is "medicine." Proverbs are designed for consolation or vengeance, for admonition or exhortation, for foretelling.

Or they name typical, recurrent situations. That is, people find a certain social relationship recurring so frequently that they must "have a word for it." The Eskimos have special names for many different kinds of snow (fifteen, if I remember rightly) because variations in the quality of snow greatly affect their living. Hence, they must "size up" snow much more accurately than we do. And the same is true of social phenomena. Social structures give rise to "type" situations, subtle subdivisions of the relationships involved in competitive and coöperative acts. Many proverbs seek to chart, in more or less homey and picturesque ways, these "type" situations. I submit that such naming is done, not for the sheer glory of the thing, but because of its bearing upon human welfare. A different name for snow implies a different kind of hunt. Some names for snow imply that one should not hunt at all. And similarly, the names for typical, recurrent social situations are not developed out of "disinterested curiosity," but because the names imply a command (what to expect, what to look out for).

To illustrate with a few representative examples:

Proverbs designed for consolation: "The sun does not shine on both sides of the hedge at once." "Think of ease, but work on." "Little troubles the eye, but far less the soul." "The worst luck now, the better another time." "The wind in one's face makes one wise." "He that hath lands hath quarrels." "He knows how to carry the dead cock home." "He is not poor that hath little, but he that desireth much."

For vengeance: "At length the fox is brought to the furrier." "Shod in the cradle, barefoot in the stubble." "Sue a beggar and get a louse." "The higher the ape goes, the more he shows his tail." "The moon does not heed the barking of dogs." "He measures another's corn by his own bushel." "He shuns the man who knows him well." "Fools tie knots and wise men loose them."

Proverbs that have to do with foretelling: (The most obvious are those to do with the weather.) "Sow peas and beans in the wane of the moon, Who soweth them sooner, he soweth too soon." "When the wind's in the north, the skilful fisher goes not forth." "When the sloe tree is as white as a sheet, sow your barley whether it be dry or wet." "When the sun sets bright and clear, An easterly wind you need not fear. When the sun sets in a bank, A westerly wind we shall not want."

In short: "Keep your weather eye open": be realistic about sizing up today's weather, because your accuracy has bearing upon tomorrow's weather. And forecast not only the meteorological weather, but also the social weather: "When the moon's in the full, then wit's in the wane." "Straws show which way the wind blows." "When the fish is caught, the net is laid aside." "Remove an old tree, and it will wither to death." "The wolf may lose his teeth, but never his nature." "He that bites on every weed must needs light on poison." "Whether the pitcher strikes the stone, or the stone the pitcher, it is bad for the pitcher." "Eagles catch no flies." "The more laws, the more offenders."

In this foretelling category we might also include the recipes for wise living, sometimes moral, sometimes technical: "First thrive, and then wive." "Think with the wise but talk with the vulgar." "When the fox preacheth, then beware your geese." "Venture a small fish to catch a great one." "Respect a man, he will do the more."

In the class of "typical, recurrent situations" we might put such proverbs and proverbial expressions as: "Sweet appears sour when we pay." "The treason is loved but the traitor is hated." "The wine in the bottle does not quench thirst." "The sun is never the worse for shining on a dung hill." "The lion kicked by an ass." "The lion's share." "To catch one napping." "To smell a rat." "To cool one's heels."

By all means, I do not wish to suggest that this is the only way in which the proverbs could be classified. For instance, I have listed in the "foretelling" group the proverb, "When the fox preacheth, then beware your geese." But it could obviously be "taken over" for vindictive purposes. Or consider a proverb like, "Virtue flies from the heart of a mercenary man." A poor man might obviously use it either to console himself for being poor (the implication being, "Because I am poor in money I am rich in virtue") or to strike at another (the implication being, "When he got money, what else could you expect of him but deterioration?"). In fact, we could even say that such symbolic vengeance would itself be an aspect of solace. And a proverb like "The sun is never the worse for shining on a dunghill" (which I have listed under "typical recurrent situations") might as well be put in the vindictive category.

The point of issue is not to find categories that "place" the proverbs once and for all. What I want is categories that suggest their active nature. Here there is no "realism for its own sake." There is realism for promise, admonition, solace, vengeance, foretelling, instruction, charting, all for the direct bearing that such acts have upon matters of welfare.

2

Step two: Why not extend such analysis of proverbs to encompass the whole field of literature? Could the most complex and sophisticated works of art legitimately be considered somewhat as "proverbs writ large"? Such leads, if held admissible, should help us to discover important facts about literary organization (thus satisfying the requirements of technical criticism). And the kind of observation from this perspective should apply beyond literature to life in general (thus helping to take literature out of its separate bin and give it a place in a general "sociological" picture).

The point of view might be phrased in this way: Proverbs are *strategies* for dealing with *situations*. In so far as situations are typical and recurrent in a given social structure, people develop names for them and strategies for handling them. Another name for strategies might be *attitudes*.

People have often commented on the fact that there are contrary *proverbs*. But I believe that the above approach to proverbs suggests a necessary modification of that comment. The apparent contradictions depend upon differences in *attitude,* involving a correspondingly different choice of *strategy.* Consider, for instance, the *apparently* opposite pair: "Repentance comes too late" and "Never too late to mend." The first is admonitory. It says in effect: "You'd better look out, or you'll get yourself too far into this business." The second is consolatory, saying in effect: "Buck up, old man, you can still pull out of this."

Some critics have quarreled with me about my selection of the word "strategy" as the name for this process. I have asked them to suggest an alternative term, so far without profit. The only one I can think of is "method." But if "strategy" errs in suggesting to some people an overly *conscious* procedure, "method" errs in suggesting an overly *"methodical"* one. Anyhow, let's look at the documents:

Concise Oxford Dictionary: "Strategy: Movement of an army or armies in a compaign, art of so moving or disposing troops or ships as to impose upon the enemy the place and time and conditions for fighting preferred by oneself" (from a Greek word that refers to the leading of an army).

New English Dictionary: "Strategy: The art of projecting and directing the larger military movements and operations of a campaign."

André Cheron, *Traité Complet d'Echecs:* "*On entend par stratégie les manoeuvres qui ont pour but et la sortie et le bon arrangement des piéces.*"

Looking at these definitions, I gain courage. For surely, the most highly alembicated and sophisticated work of art, arising in complex civilizations, could be considered as designed to organize and command the army of one's thoughts and images, and to so organize them that one "imposes upon the enemy the time and place and conditions for fighting preferred by oneself." One seeks to "direct the larger movements and operations" in one's campaign of living. One "maneuvers," and the maneuvering is an "art."

Are not the final results one's "strategy"? One tries, as far as possible, to develop a strategy whereby one "can't lose." One tries to change the rules of the game until they fit his own necessities. Does the artist encounter disaster? He will "make capital" of it. If one is a victim of competition, for instance, if one is elbowed out, if one is willy-nilly more jockeyed against that jockeying, one can by the solace and vengeance of art convert this very "liability" into an "asset." One tries to fight on his own terms, developing a strategy for imposing the proper "time, place, and conditions."

But one must also, to develop a full strategy, be *realistic*. One must *size things up* properly. One cannot accurately know how things *will be,* what is promising and what is menacing, unless he accurately knows how things *are*. So the wise strategist will not be content with strategies of merely a self-gratifying sort. He will "keep his weather eye open." He will not too eagerly "read into" a scene an attitude that is irrelevant to it. He won't sit on the side of an active volcano and "see" it as a dormant plain.

Often, alas, he will. The great allurement in our present popular "inspirational literature," for instance, may be largely of this sort. It is a strategy for easy consolation. It "fills a need," since there is always a need for easy consolation— and in an era of confusion like our own the need is especially keen. So people are only too willing to "meet a man halfway" who will *play down* the realistic naming of our situation and *play up* such strategies as make solace cheap. However, I should propose a reservation here. We usually take it for granted that people who consume our current output of books on "How to Buy Friends and Bamboozle Oneself and Other People" are reading as *students* who will attempt applying the recipes given. Nothing of the sort. *The reading of a book on the attaining of success is in itself the symbolic attaining of that success*. It is *while they read* that these readers are "succeeding." I'll wager that, in by far the great majority of cases, such readers make no serious attempt to apply the book's recipes. The lure of the book resides in the fact that the reader, while reading it, is then living in the aura of success. What he wants is *easy* success; and he gets it in symbolic form by the mere reading itself. To attempt applying such stuff in real life would be very difficult, full of many disillusioning difficulties.

Sometimes a different strategy may arise. The author may remain realistic, avoiding too easy a form of solace—yet he may get as far off the track in his own way. Forgetting that realism is an aspect for foretelling, he may take it as an end in itself. He is tempted to do this by two factors: (1) an *ill-digested* philosophy of science, leading him mistakenly to assume that "relentless" naturalistic "truthfulness" is a proper end in itself, and (2) a merely *competitive* desire to outstrip other writers by being "more realistic" than they. Works thus made "efficient" by tests of competition internal to the book trade are a kind of academicism not so named (the writer usually thinks of it as the *opposite* of academicism). Realism thus stepped up competitively might be distinguished from the proper sort by the name of "naturalism." As a way of "sizing things up," the naturalistic tradition tends to become as inaccurate as the "inspirational" strategy, though at the opposite extreme.

Anyhow, the main point is this: A work like *Madame Bovary* (or its homely American translation, *Babbitt*) is the strategic naming of a situation. It singles out a pattern of experience that is sufficiently representative of our social structure, that recurs sufficiently often *mutandis mutatis,* for people to "need a word for it" and to adopt an attitude towards it. Each work of art is the addition of a word to an informal dictionary (or, in the case of purely derivative artists, the addition of a subsidiary meaning to a word already given by some originating artist). As of *Madame Bovary,* the French critic Jules de Gaultier proposed to add it to our *formal* dictionary by coining the word "Bovarysme" and writing a whole book to say what he meant by it.

Mencken's book on *The American Language,* I hate to say, is splendid. I console myself with the reminder that Mencken didn't write it. Many millions of people wrote it, and Mencken was merely the amanuensis who took it down from their dictation. He found a true "vehicle" (that is, a book that could be greater than the author who wrote it). He gets the royalties, but the job was done by a collectivity. As you read that book, you see a people who were up against a new set of typical recurrent situations, situations typical of their business, their politics, their criminal organizations, their sports. Either there were no words for these in standard English, or people didn't know them, or they didn't "sound right." So a new vocabulary arose, to "give us a word for it." I see no reason for believing that Americans are unusually fertile in word-coinage. American slang was not developed out of some exceptional gift. It was developed out of the fact that new typical situations had arisen and people needed names for them. They had to "size things up." They had to console and strike, to promise and admonish. They had to describe for purposes of forecasting. And "slang" was the result. It is, by this analysis, simply *proverbs not so named,* a kind of "folk criticism."

3

With what, then, would "sociological criticism" along these lines be concerned? It would seek to codify the various strategies which artists have developed with relation to the naming of situations. In a sense, much of it would even be "timeless," for many of the "typical, recurrent situations" are not peculiar to our own civilization at all. The situations and strategies framed in Aesop's Fables, for instance, apply to human relations now just as fully as they applied in ancient Greece. They are, like philosophy, sufficiently "generalized" to extend far beyond the particular combination of events named by them in any one instance. They name an "essence." Or, as Korzybski might say, they are on a "high level of abstraction." One doesn't usually think of them as "abstract," since they are usually so concrete in their stylistic expression. But they invariably aim to discern the "general behind the particular" (which would suggest that they are good Goethe).

The attempt to treat literature from the standpoint of situations and strategies suggests a variant of Spengler's notion of the "contemporaneous." By "contemporaneity" he meant corresponding stages of different cultures. For instance, if modern New York is much like decadent Rome, then we are "contemporaneous" with decadent Rome, or with some corresponding decadent city among the Mayas, etc. It is in this sense that situations are "timeless," "non-historical," "contemporaneous." A given human relationship may be at one time named in terms of foxes and lions, if there are foxes and lions about; or it may now be named in terms of salesmanship, advertising, the tactics of politicians, etc. But beneath the change in particulars, we may often discern the naming of the one situation.

So sociological criticism, as here understood, would seek to assemble and codify this lore. It might occasionally lead us to outrage good taste, as we sometimes found exemplified in some great sermon or tragedy or abstruse work of philosophy the same strategy as we found exemplified in a dirty joke. At this point, we'd put the sermon and the dirty joke together, thus "grouping by situation" and showing the range of possible particularizations. In his exceptionally discerning essay, "A Critic's Job of Work," R. P. Blackmur says, "I think on the whole his (Burke's) method could be applied with equal fruitfulness to Shakespeare, Dashiell Hammett, or Marie Corelli." When I got through wincing, I had to admit that Blackmur was right. This article is an attempt to say for the method what can be said. As a matter of fact, I'll go a step further and maintain: You can't properly put Marie Corelli and Shakespeare apart until you have first put them together. First genus, then differentia. The strategy in common is the genus. The *range* or *scale* or *spectrum* of particularizations is the differentia.

Anyhow, that's what I'm driving at. And that's why reviewers sometime find in my work "intuitive" leaps that are dubious as "science." They are not "leaps" at all. They are classifications, groupings, made on the basis of some strategic element common to the items grouped. They are neither more nor less "intuitive" than *any* grouping or classification of social events. Apples can be grouped with bananas as fruits, and they can be grouped with tennis balls as round. I am simply proposing, in the social sphere, a method of classification with reference to *strategies*.

The method has these things to be said in its favor: It gives definite insight into the organization of literary works; and it automatically breaks down the barriers erected about literature as a specialized pursuit. People can classify novels by reference to three kinds, eight kinds, seventeen kinds. It doesn't matter. Students patiently copy down the professor's classification and pass examinations on it, because the range of possible academic classifications is endless. Sociological classification, as herein suggested, would derive its relevance from the fact that it should apply both to works of art and to social situations outside of art.

It would, I admit, violate current pieties, break down current categories, and thereby "outrage good taste." But "good taste" has become *inert*. The classifications I am proposing would be *active*. I think that what we need is active categories.

These categories will lie on the bias across the categories of modern specialization. The new alignment will outrage in particular those persons who take the division of faculties in our universities to be an exact replica of the way in which God himself divided up the universe. We have had the Philosophy of the Being; and we have had the Philosophy of the Becoming. In contemporary specialization, we have been getting the Philosophy of the Bin. Each of these mental localities has had its own peculiar way of life, its own values, even its own special idiom for seeing, thinking, and "proving." Among other things, a sociological approach should attempt to provide a reintegrative point of view, a broader empire of investigation encompassing the lot.

What would such sociological categories be like? They would consider works of art, I think, as strategies for selecting enemies and allies, for socializing losses, for warding off evil eye, for purification, propitiation, and desanctification, consolation and vengeance, admonition and exhortation, implicit commands or instructions of one sort or another. Art forms like "tragedy" or "comedy" or "satire" would be treated as *equipments for living,* that size up situations in various ways and in keeping with correspondingly various attitudes. The typical ingredients of such forms would be sought. Their relation to typical situations would be stressed. Their comparative values would be considered, with the intention of formulating a "strategy of strategies," the "over-all" strategy obtained by inspection of the lot.

Thomas Kuhn (1922–1996)

Kuhn was professor of philosophy and the history of science at the Massachusetts Institute of Technology from 1979 to 1991. Calling Kuhn "the most influential philosopher to write in English since the Second World War," philosopher Richard Rorty went on to say, "Kuhn's major contribution to remapping culture was to help us see that the natural scientists do not have a special access to reality or to truth" ("Thomas Kuhn, Rocks and the Laws of Physics"). Kuhn's reputation results particularly from his celebrated 1962 book *The Structure of Scientific Revolutions*. It is hard to imagine too many other books that have had as much influence in academia during the twentieth century. Kuhn has been cheered by many, as well as scorned by more than a few people. About his famous book, *Structure,* one of Kuhn's admirers, anthropologist Clifford Geertz, asks, "Why has everyone, from particle physicists and philosophers to sociologists, historians, literary critics, and political theorists, not to speak of publicists, popularizers, and counterculture know-nothings, found in it [*Structure*] something either to turn excitedly toward their own ends or to react, equally excitedly, against?" ("The Legacy of Thomas Kuhn: The Right Text at the Right Time"). In *Structure,* Kuhn analyzes tensions between "normal science" and periods of scientific revolution. Such tensions signal paradigm shifts in understanding and what counts as knowledge.

Kuhn wrote the selection given next, "The Historical Structure of Scientific Discovery," while a graduate student at Harvard University. It illustrates some of the key ideas in *Structure*. Some of Kuhn's other key texts include *The Copernican Revolution: Planetary Astronomy and the Development of Western Thought* (1957) and *The Essential Tension: Selected Studies in Scientific Tradition and Change* (1977).

The Historical Structure of Scientific Discovery

My object in this article is to isolate and illuminate one small part of what I take to be a continuing historiographic revolution in the study of science. The structure of scientific discovery is my particular topic, and I can best approach it by pointing out that the subject itself may well seem extraordinarily odd. Both scientists and, until quite recently, historians have ordinarily viewed discovery as the sort of event which, though it may have preconditions and

---

"The Historical Structure of Scientific Discovery" by Thomas Kuhn from *Science,* Volume 136: 760–64, June 1, 1962. Copyright 1988 by American Association for the Advancement of Science. Reprinted by permission.

surely has consequences, is itself without internal structure. Rather than being seen as a complex development extended both in space and time, discovering something has usually seemed to be a unitary event, one which, like seeing something, happens to an individual at a specific time and place.

This view of the nature of discovery has, I suspect, deep roots in the nature of the scientific community. One of the few historical elements recurrent in the textbooks from which the prospective scientist learns his field is the attribution of particular natural phenomena to the historical personages who first discovered them. As a result of this and other aspects of their training, discovery becomes for many scientists an important goal. To make a discovery is to achieve one of the closest approximations to a property right that the scientific career affords. Professional prestige is often closely associated with these acquisitions.[1] Small wonder, then, that acrimonious disputes about priority and independence in discovery have often marred the normally placid tenor of scientific communication. Even less wonder that many historians of science have seen the individual discovery as an appropriate unit with which to measure scientific progress and have devoted much time and skill to determining what man made which discovery at what point in time. If the study of discovery has a surprise to offer, it is only that, despite the immense energy and ingenuity expended upon it, neither polemic nor painstaking scholarship has often succeeded in pinpointing the time and place at which a given discovery could properly be said to have "been made."

That failure, both of argument and of research, suggests the thesis that I now wish to develop. Many scientific discoveries, particularly the most interesting and important, are not the sort of event about which the questions "Where?" and, more particularly, "When?" can appropriately be asked. Even if all conceivable data were at hand, those questions would not regularly possess answers. That we are persistently driven to ask them nonetheless is symptomatic of a fundamental inappropriateness in our image of discovery. That inappropriateness is here my main concern, but I approach it by considering first the historical problem presented by the attempt to date and to place a major class of fundamental discoveries.

The troublesome class consists of those discoveries—including oxygen, the electric current, X rays, and the electron—which could not be predicted from accepted theory in advance and which therefore caught the assembled profession by surprise. That kind of discovery will shortly be my exclusive concern, but it will help first to note that there is another sort and one which presents very few of the same problems. Into this second class of discoveries fall the neutrino, radio waves, and the elements which filled empty places in the periodic table. The existence of all these objects had been predicted from theory before they were discovered, and the men who made the discoveries therefore knew from the start what to look for. That foreknowledge did not make their task less demanding or less interesting, but it did provide criteria which told them when their goal had been reached.[2] As a result, there have been few priority debates over discoveries of this second sort, and only a paucity of data can prevent the historian from ascribing them to a particular time and place. Those facts help to isolate the difficulties we encounter as we return to the troublesome discoveries of the first class. In the cases that most concern us here there are no benchmarks to inform either the scientist or the historian when the job of discovery has been done.

As an illustration of this fundamental problem and its consequences, consider first the discovery of oxygen. Because it has repeatedly been studied, often with exemplary care and skill, that discovery is unlikely to offer any purely factual surprises. Therefore it is particularly well suited to clarify points of principle.[3] At least three scientists—Carl Scheele, Joseph Priestley, and Antoine Lavoisier—have a legitimate claim to this discovery, and polemicists have occasionally entered the same claim for Pierre Bayen.[4] Scheele's work, though it was almost certainly completed before the relevant researches of Priestley and Lavoisier, was not made public until their work was well known.[5] Therefore it had no apparent causal role, and I shall simplify my story by omitting it.[6] Instead, I pick up the main route to the discovery of oxygen with the work of Bayen, who, sometime before March 1774, discovered that red precipitate of mercury (HgO) could, by heating, be made to yield a gas. That aeriform product Bayen identified as fixed air (CO_2), a substance made familiar to most pneumatic chemists by the earlier work of Joseph Black.[7] A variety of other substances were known to yield the same gas.

At the beginning of August 1774, a few months after Bayen's work had appeared, Joseph Priestley repeated the experiment, though probably independently. Priestley, however, observed that the gaseous product would support combustion and therefore changed the identification. For him the gas obtained on heating red precipitate was nitrous air (N_2O), a substance that he had himself discovered more than two years before.[8] Later in the same month Priestley made a trip to Paris and there informed Lavoisier of the new reaction. The latter repeated the experiment once more, both in November 1775 and in February 1774. But, because he used tests somewhat more elaborate than Priestley's, Lavoisier again changed the identification. For him, as of May 1775, the gas released by red precipitate was neither fixed air nor nitrous air. Instead, it was "[atmospheric] air itself entire without alteration . . . even to the point that . . . it comes out more pure."[9] Meanwhile, however, Priestley had also been at work, and, before the beginning of March 1775, he, too, had concluded that the gas must be "common air." Until this point all of the men who had produced a gas from red precipitate of mercury had identified it with some previously known species.[10]

The remainder of this story of discovery is briefly told. During March 1775 Priestley discovered that his gas was in several respects very much "better" than common air, and he therefore reidentified the gas once more, this time calling it "dephlogisticated air," that is, atmospheric air deprived of its normal complement of phlogiston.* This conclusion Priestley published in the *Philosophical Transactions,* and it was apparently that publication which led Lavoisier to reexamine his own results.[11] The reexamination began during February 1776 and within a year had led Lavoisier to the conclusion that the gas was actually a

---

***Phlogiston** Was once believed to be the element that caused combustion and that was given off by anything burning.

separable component of the atmospheric air which both he and Priestley had previously thought of as homogeneous. With this point reached, with the gas recognized as an irreducibly distinct species, we may conclude that the discovery of oxygen had been completed.

But to return to my initial question, when shall we say that oxygen was discovered and what criteria shall we use in answering that question? If discovering oxygen is simply holding an impure sample in one's hands, then the gas had been "discovered" in antiquity by the first man who ever bottled atmospheric air. Undoubtedly, for an experimental criterion, we must at least require a relatively pure sample like that obtained by Priestley in August 1774. But during 1774 Priestley was unaware that he had discovered anything except a new way to produce a relatively familiar species. Throughout that year his "discovery" is scarcely distinguishable from the one made earlier by Bayen, and neither case is quite distinct from that of the Reverend Stephen Hales, who had obtained the same gas more than forty years before.[12] Apparently to discover something one must also be aware of the discovery and know as well what it is that one has discovered.

But, that being the case, how much must one know? Had Priestley come close enough when he identified the gas as nitrous air? If not, was either he or Lavoisier significantly closer when he changed the identification to common air? And what are we to say about Priestley's next identification, the one made in March 1775? Dephlogisticated air is still not oxygen or even, for the phlogistic chemist, a quite unexpected sort of gas. Rather it is a particularly pure atmospheric air. Presumably, then, we wait for Lavoisier's work in 1776 and 1777, work which led him not merely to isolate the gas but to see what it was. Yet even that decision can be questioned, for in 1777 and to the end of his life Lavoisier insisted that oxygen was an atomic "principle of acidity" and that oxygen *gas* was formed only when that "principle" united with caloric, the matter of heat.[13] Shall we therefore say that oxygen had not yet been discovered in 1777? Some may be tempted to do so. But the principle of acidity was not banished from chemistry until after 1810 and caloric lingered on until the 1860s. Oxygen had, however, become a standard chemical substance long before either of those dates. Furthermore, what is perhaps the key point, it would probably have gained that status on the basis of Priestley's work alone without benefit of Lavoisier's still partial reinterpretation.

I conclude that we need a new vocabulary and new concepts for analyzing events like the discovery of oxygen. Though undoubtedly correct, the sentence "Oxygen was discovered" misleads by suggesting that discovering something is a single simple act unequivocally attributable, if only we knew enough, to an individual and an instant in time. When the discovery is unexpected, however, the latter attribution is always impossible and the former often is as well. Ignoring Scheele, we can, for example, safely say that oxygen had not been discovered before 1774; probably we would also insist that it had been discovered by 1777 or shortly thereafter. But within those limits any attempt to date the discovery or to attribute it to an individual must inevitably be arbitrary. Furthermore, it must be arbitrary just because discovering a new sort of phenomenon is necessarily a complex process which involves recognizing both *that* something is and *what* it is. Observation and conceptualization, fact and the assimilation of fact to theory, are inseparably linked in the discovery of scientific novelty. Inevitably, that process extends over time and may often involve a number of people. Only for discoveries in my second category—those whose nature is known in advance— can discovering *that* and discovering *what* occur together and in an instant.

Two last, simpler, and far briefer examples will simultaneously show how typical the case of oxygen is and also prepare the way for a somewhat more pre- cise conclusion. On the night of 13 March 1781, the astronomer William Her- schel made the following entry in his journal: "In the quartile near Zeta Tauri . . . is a curious either nebulous star or perhaps a comet."[14] That entry is generally said to record the discovery of the planet Uranus, but it cannot quite have done that. Between 1690 and Herschel's observation in 1781 the same object had been seen and recorded at least seventeen times by men who took it to be a star. Herschel differed from them only in supposing that, because in his tele- scope it appeared especially large, it might actually be a *comet!* Two additional observations on 17 and 19 March confirmed that suspicion by showing that the object he had observed moved among the stars. As a result, astronomers throughout Europe were informed of the discovery, and the mathematicians among them began to compute the new comet's orbit. Only several months later, after all those attempts had repeatedly failed to square with observation, did the astronomer Lexell suggest that the object observed by Herschel might be a planet. And only when additional computations, using a planet's rather than a comet's orbit, proved reconcilable with observation was that suggestion generally accepted. At what point during 1781 do we want to say that the planet Uranus was discovered? And are we entirely and unequivocally clear that it was Herschel rather than Lexell who discovered it?

Or consider still more briefly the story of the discovery of X rays, a story which opens on the day in 1895 when the physicist Roentgen interrupted a well- precedented investigation of cathode rays because he noticed that a barium platinocyanide screen far from his shielded apparatus glowed when the discharge was in process.[15] Additional investigations—they required seven hectic weeks during which Roentgen rarely left the laboratory—indicated that the cause of the glow traveled in straight lines from the cathode ray tube, that the radiation cast shadows, that it could not be deflected by a magnet, and much else besides. Before announcing his discovery Roentgen had convinced himself that his effect was not due to cathode rays themselves but to a new form of radiation with at least some similarity to light. Once again the question suggests itself: When shall we say that X rays were actually discovered? Not, in any case, at the first instant, when all that had been noted was a glowing screen. At least one other investiga- tor had seen that glow and, to his subsequent chagrin, discovered nothing at all. Nor, it is almost as clear, can the moment of discovery be pushed back to a point during the last week of investigation. By that time Roentgen was exploring the properties of the new radiation he had *already* discovered. We may have to settle for the remark that X rays emerged in Würzburg between 8 November and 28 December 1895.

The characteristics shared by these examples are, I think, common to all the episodes by which unanticipated novelties become subjects for scientific attention. I therefore conclude these brief remarks by discussing three such common characteristics, one which may help to provide a framework for the further study of the extended episodes we customarily call "discoveries."

In the first place, notice that all three of our discoveries—oxygen, Uranus, and X rays—began with the experimental or observational isolation of an anomaly, that is, with nature's failure to conform entirely to expectation. Notice, further, that the process by which that anomaly was educed displays simultaneously the apparently incompatible characteristics of the inevitable and the accidental. In the case of X rays, the anomalous glow which provided Roentgen's first clue was clearly the result of an accidental disposition of his apparatus. But by 1895 cathode rays were a normal subject for research all over Europe; that research quite regularly juxtaposed cathode-rays tubes with sensitive screens and films; as a result, Roentgen's accident was almost certain to occur elsewhere, as in fact it had. Those remarks, however, should make Roentgen's case look very much like those of Herschel and Priestley. Herschel first observed his oversized and thus anomalous star in the course of a prolonged survey of the northern heavens. That survey was, except for the magnification provided by Herschel's instruments, precisely of the sort that had repeatedly been carried through before and that had occasionally resulted in prior observations of Uranus. And Priestley, too—when he isolated the gas that behaved almost but not quite like nitrous air and then almost but not quite like common air—was seeing something unintended and wrong in the outcome of a sort of experiment for which there was much European precedent and which had more than once before led to the production of the new gas.

These features suggest the existence of two normal requisites for the beginning of an episode of discovery. The first, which throughout this paper I have largely taken for granted, is the individual skill, wit, or genius to recognize that something has gone wrong in ways that may prove consequential. Not any and every scientist would have noted that no unrecorded star should be so large, that the screen ought not to have glowed, that nitrous air should not have supported life. But that requisite presupposes another which is less frequently taken for granted. Whatever the level of genius available to observe them, anomalies do not emerge from the normal course of scientific research until both instruments and concepts have developed sufficiently to make their emergence likely and to make the anomaly which results recognizable as a violation of expectation.[16] To say that an unexpected discovery begins only when something goes wrong is to say that it begins only when scientists know well both how their instruments and how nature should behave. What distinguished Priestley, who saw an anomaly, from Hales, who did not, is largely the considerable articulation of pneumatic techniques and expectations that had come into being during the four decades which separate their two isolations of oxygen.[17] The very number of claimants indicates that after 1770 the discovery could not have been postponed for long.

The role of anomaly is the first of the characteristics shared by our three examples. A second can be considered more briefly, for it has provided the main theme for the body of my text. Though awareness of anomaly marks the beginning of a discovery, it marks only the beginning. What necessarily follows, if anything at all is to be discovered, is a more or less extended period during which the individual and often many members of his group struggle to make the anomaly lawlike. Invariably that period demands additional observation or experimentation as well as repeated cogitation. While it continues, scientists repeatedly revise their expectations, usually their instrumental standards, and sometimes their most fundamental theories as well. In this sense discoveries have a proper internal history as well as prehistory and a posthistory. Furthermore, within the rather vaguely delimited interval of internal history, there is no single moment or day which the historian, however complete his data, can identify as the point at which the discovery was made. Often, when several individuals are involved, it is even impossible unequivocally to identify any one of them as the discoverer.

Finally, turning to the third of these selected common characteristics, note briefly what happens as the period of discovery draws to a close. A full discussion of that question would require additional evidence and a separate paper, for I have had little to say about the aftermath of discovery in the body of my text. Nevertheless, the topic must not be entirely neglected, for it is in part a corollary of what has already been said.

Discoveries are often described as mere additions or increments to the growing stockpile of scientific knowledge, and that description has helped make the unit discovery seem a significant measure of progress. I suggest, however, that it is fully appropriate only to those discoveries which, like the elements that filled missing places in the periodic table, were anticipated and sought in advance and which therefore demanded no adjustment, adaptation, and assimilation from the profession. Though the sorts of discoveries we have here been examining are undoubtedly additions to scientific knowledge, they are also something more. In a sense that I can now develop only in part, they also react back upon what has previously been known, providing a new view of some previously familiar objects and simultaneously changing the way in which even some traditional parts of science are practiced. Those in whose area of special competence the new phenomenon falls often see both the world and their work differently as they emerge from the extended struggle with anomaly which constitutes the discovery of that phenomenon.

William Herschel, for example, when he increased by one the time-honored number of planetary bodies, taught astronomers to see new things when they looked at the familiar heavens even with instruments more traditional than his own. That change in the vision of astronomers must be a principal reason why, in the half century after the discovery of Uranus, twenty additional circumsolar bodies were added to the traditional seven.[18] A similar transformation is even clearer in the aftermath of Roentgen's work. In the first place, established techniques for cathode-ray research had to be changed, for scientists found they had failed to control a relevant variable. Those changes included both the redesign of old apparatus and revised ways of asking old questions. In addition, those scientists most concerned experienced the same transformation of vision that we have just noted in the aftermath of the discovery of Uranus. X rays were the first new sort of radiation discovered since infrared and ultraviolet at the beginning of the century. But within less than a decade after Roentgen's work, four more were disclosed by the new scientific sensitivity (for example, to fogged photographic plates) and by some of the new instrumental techniques that had resulted from Roentgen's work and its assimilation.[19]

Very often these transformations in the established techniques of scientific practice prove even more important than the incremental knowledge provided by the discovery itself. That could at least be argued in the cases of Uranus and of X rays; in the case of my third example, oxygen, it is categorically clear. Like the work of Herschel and Roentgen, that of Priestley and Lavoisier taught scientists to view old situations in new ways. Therefore, as we might anticipate, oxygen was not the only new chemical species to be identified in the aftermath of their work. But, in the case of oxygen, the readjustments demanded by assimilation were so profound that they played an integral and essential role—though they were not by themselves the cause—in the gigantic upheaval of chemical theory and practice which has since been known as the chemical revolution. I do not suggest that every unanticipated discovery has consequences for science so deep and so far-reaching as those which followed the discovery of oxygen. But I do suggest that every such discovery demands, from those most concerned, the sorts of readjustment that, when they are more obvious, we equate with scientific revolution. It is, I believe, just because they demand readjustments like these that the process of discovery is necessarily and inevitably one that shows structure and that therefore extends in time.

Notes

1. For a brilliant discussion of these points, see R. K. Merton, "Priorities in Scientific Discovery: A Chapter in the Sociology of Science," *American Sociological Review* 22 (1957): 635. Also very relevant, though it did not appear until this article had been prepared, is F. Reif, "The Competitive World of the Pure Scientist," *Science* 134 (1961): 1957.

2. Not all discoveries fall so neatly as the preceding into one or the other of my two classes. For example, Anderson's work on the positron was done in complete ignorance of Dirac's theory from which the new particle's existence had already been very nearly predicted. On the other hand, the immediately succeeding work by Blackett and Occhialini made full use of Dirac's theory and therefore exploited experiment more fully and constructed a more forceful case for the positron's existence than Anderson had been able to do. On this subject see N. R. Hanson, "Discovering the Positron," *British Journal for the Philosophy of Science* 12 (1961): 194; 12 (1962): 299. Hanson suggests several of the points developed here. I am much indebted to Professor Hanson for a preprint of this material.

3. I have adapted a less familiar example from the same viewpoint in "The Caloric Theory of Adiabatic Compression," *Isis* 49 (1958): 132. A closely similar analysis of the emergence of a new theory is included in the early pages of my essay "Energy Con-

servation as an Example of Simultaneous Discovery," in *Critical Problems in the History of Science*, ed. M. Clagett (Madison: University of Wisconsin Press, 1959), pp. 321–56. . . . Reference to these papers may add depth and detail to the following discussion.

4. The still classic discussion of the discovery of oxygen is A. N. Meldrum, *The Eighteenth Century Revolution in Science: The First Phase* (Calcutta, 1930), chap. 5. A more convenient and generally quite reliable discussion is included in J. B. Conant, *The Overthrow of the Phlogiston Theory: The Chemical Revolution of 1775–1789*, Harvard Case Histories in Experimental Science, case 2 (Cambridge: Harvard University Press, 1950). A recent and indispensable review which includes an account of the development of the priority controversy, is M. Daumas, *Lavoisier, théoricien et expérimentateur* (Paris, 1955), chaps. 2 and 3. H. Guerlac has added much significant detail to our knowledge of the early relations between Priestley and Lavoisier in his "Joseph Priestley's First Papers on Gases and Their Reception in France," *Journal of the History of Medicine* 12 (1957): 1 and in his very recent monograph, *Lavoisier: The Crucial Year* (Ithaca: Cornell University Press, 1961). For Scheele see J. R. Partington, *A Short History of Chemistry*, 2d ed. (London, 1951), pp. 104–109.

5. For the dating of Scheele's work, see A. E. Nordenskjöld, *Carl Wilhelm Scheele, Nachgelassene Briefe und Aufzeichnungen* (Stockholm, 1892).

6. U. Bocklund ("A Lost Letter from Scheele to Lavoisier," *Lychnos*, 1957 58, pp 39–62) argues that Scheele communicated his discovery of oxygen to Lavoisier in a letter of 30 Sept. 1774. Certainly the letter is important, and it clearly demonstrates that Scheele was ahead of both Priestley and Lavoisier at the time it was written. But I think the letter is not quite so candid as Bocklund supposes, and I fail to see how Lavoisier could have drawn the discovery of oxygen from it. Scheele describes a procedure for reconstituting common air, not for producing a new gas, and that, as we shall see, is almost the same information that Lavoisier received from Priestley at about the same time. In any case, there is no evidence that Lavoisier performed the sort of experiment that Scheele suggested.

7. P. Bayen, "Essai d'expériences chymiques, faites sur quelques précipités de mercure, dans la vue de découvrir leur nature, Second partie," *Observations sur la physique* 3 (1774): 280–295, particularly pp. 289–291.

8. J. B. Conant, *The Overthrow of the Phlogiston Theory*, pp. 34–40.

9. Ibid., p. 23. A useful translation of the full text is available in Conant.

10. For simplicity I use the term *red precipitate* throughout. Actually, Bayen used the precipitate; Priestley used both the precipitate and the oxide produced by direct calcination of mercury; and Lavoisier used only the latter. The difference is not without importance, for it was not unequivocally clear to chemists that the two substances were identical.

11. There has been some doubt about Priestley's having influenced Lavoisier's thinking at this point, but, when the latter returned to experimenting with the gas in February 1776, he recorded in his notebooks that he had obtained "l'air dephlogistique de M. Priestley" (M. Daumas, *Lavoisier*, p. 36).

12. J. R. Partington, *A Short History of Chemistry*, p. 91.

13. For the traditional elements in Lavoisier's interpretations of chemical reactions, see H. Metzger, *La philosophie de la matière chez Lavoisier* (Paris, 1935), and Daumas, *Lavoisier*, chap. 7.

14. P. Doig, *A Concise History of Astronomy* (London: Chapman, 1990), pp. 115–116.

15. L. W. Taylor, *Physics, the Pioneer Science* (Boston: Houghton Mifflin Co., 1941), p. 790.

16. Though the point cannot be argued here, the conditions which make the emergence of anomaly likely and those which make anomaly recognizable are to a very great extent the same. That fact may help us understand the extraordinarily large amount of simultaneous discovery in the sciences.

17. A useful sketch of the development of pneumatic chemistry is included in Partington, *A Short History of Chemistry,* chap. 6.

18. R. Wolf, *Geschichte der Astronomie* (Munich, 1877), pp. 513–515, 683–693. The prephotographic discoveries of the asteroids is often seen as an effect of the invention of Bode's law. But that law cannot be the full explanation and may not even have played a large part. Piazzi's discovery of Ceres, in 1801, was made in ignorance of the current speculation about a missing planet in the "hole" between Mars and Jupiter. Instead, like Herschel, Piazzi was engaged on a star survey. More important, Bode's law was old by 1800 (ibid., p. 683), but only one man before that date seems to have thought it worthwhile to look for another planet. Finally, Bode's law, by itself, could only suggest the utility of looking for additional planets; it did not tell astronomers where to look. Clearly, however, the drive to look for additional planets dates from Herschel's work on Uranus.

19. For α-, β-, and γ- radiation, discovery of which dates from 1896, see Taylor, *Physics,* pp. 800–804. For the fourth new form of radiation, N rays, see D. J. S. Price, *Science Since Babylon,* (New Haven: Yale University Press, 1961), pp. 84–89. That N rays were ultimately the source of a scientific scandal does not make them less revealing of the scientific community's state of mind.

Stephen Greenblatt (1943–)

Greenblatt has been a professor of English at the University of California, Berkeley, and is currently the Cogan University Professor of Humanities at Harvard University. A Renaissance scholar, Greenblatt coined the label "New Historicism" for the critical movement with which he is most associated. New Historicists reconstruct through interdisciplinary research the historical context that helps influence and shape literary texts. As a scholar, a founding coeditor of the journal *Representations,* and a former president of the Modern Language Association, Greenblatt has influenced countless numbers of people in English studies. In his 1989 essay "Towards a Poetics of Culture," which appears in the collection *The New Historicism,* edited by H. Aram Veeser, Greenblatt writes,

> One of the peculiar characteristics of the 'new historicism' in literary studies is precisely how unresolved and in some ways disingenuous it has been—I have been—about the relation to literary theory. On the one hand it seems to me that an openness to the theoretical ferment of the last few years is precisely what distinguishes the new historicism from the positivistic historical scholarship of the early twentieth century. . . . On the other hand the historicist critics have on the whole been unwilling to enroll themselves in one or the other of the dominant theoretical camps (1).

The selection given next, "Learning to Curse: Aspects of Linguistic Colonialism in the Sixteenth Century," originally appeared in the 1976 collection *First Images of America: The Impact of the New World on the Old,* edited by Fredi Chiappelli. Other major texts by Greenblatt include *Renaissance Self-Fashioning* (1980), *Shakespearean Negotiations: The Circulation of Social Energy in Renaissance England* (1988), and *Marvelous Possessions: The Wonder of the New World* (1991).

Learning to Curse: Aspects of Linguistic Colonialism in the Sixteenth Century

At the close of *Musophilus,* Samuel Daniel's brooding philosophical poem of 1599, the poet's spokesman, anxious and uncertain through much of the dialogue in the face of his opponent's skepticism, at last rises to a ringing defense of eloquence, and particularly English eloquence, culminating in a vision of its future possibilities:

> And who in time knowes whither we may vent
> The treasure of our tongue, to what strange shores
> This gaine of our best glorie shal be sent,
> T'inrich vnknowing Nations with our stores?
> What worlds in th'yet vnformed Occident
> May come refin'd with th'accents that are ours?[1]

For Daniel, the New World is a vast, rich field for the plantation of the English language. Deftly he reverses the conventional image and imagines argosies freighted with a cargo of priceless words, sailing west "T'inrich vnknowing Nations with our stores." There is another reversal of sorts here: the "best glorie" that the English voyagers will carry with them is not "the treasure of our faith" but "the treasure of our tongue." It is as if in place of the evangelical spirit, which in the early English voyages is but a small flame compared to the blazing mission of the Spanish friars, Daniel would substitute a linguistic mission, the propagation of English speech.

Linguistic colonialism is mentioned by continental writers as well but usually as a small part of the larger enterprise of conquest, conversion, and settlement. Thus Peter Martyr writes to Pope Leo X of the "large landes and many regyons whiche shal hereafter receaue owre nations, tounges, and maners: and therwith embrase owre relygion."[2] Occasionally, more substantial claims are made. In 1492, in the introduction to his *Gramática,* the first grammar of a modern European tongue, Antonio de Nebrija writes that language has always been the partner ("compañera") of empire. And in the ceremonial presentation of the volume to Queen Isabella, the bishop of Avila, speaking on the scholar's behalf, claimed a still more central role for language. When the queen asked flatly, "What is it for?" the bishop replied, "Your Majesty, language is the perfect instrument of empire."[3] But for Daniel, English is the neither partner nor instrument; its expansion is virtually the goal of the whole enterprise.

Daniel does not consider the spread of English a conquest but rather a gift of inestimable value. He hasn't the slightest sense that the natives might be reluctant to abandon their own tongue; for him, the Occident is "yet unformed," its nations "unknowing." Or, as Peter Martyr puts it, the natives are a *tabula rasa* ready to take the imprint of European civilization: "For lyke as rased or vnpaynted tables, are apte to receaue what formes soo euer are fyrst drawen theron by the hande of the paynter, euen soo these naked and simple people, doo soone receaue the customes of owre Religion, and by conuersation with owre men, shake of theyr fierce and natiue barbarousnes."[4] The mention of the nakedness of the Indians is typical; to a ruling class obsessed with the symbolism of dress, the Indian's physical appearance was a token of a cultural void. In the eyes of the Europeans, the Indians were culturally naked.

This illusion that the inhabitants of the New World are essentially without a culture of their own is both early and remarkably persistent, even in the face of overwhelming contradictory evidence. In his journal entry for the day of days, 12 October 1492, Columbus expresses the thought that the Indians ought to make good servants, "for I see that they repeat very quickly whatever was said to them." He thinks, too, that they would easily be converted to Christianity, "because it seemed to me that they belonged to no religion." And he continues: "I, please Our Lord, will carry off six of them at my departure to Your Highnesses, that they may learn to speak." The first of the endless series of kidnappings, then, was plotted in order to secure interpreters; the primal crime in the New Word was committed in the interest of language. But the actual phrase of the journal merits close attention: "that they may learn to speak" *(para que aprendan a hablar)*.[5] We are dealing, of course, with an idiom: Columbus must have known, even in that first encounter, that the Indians could speak, and he argued from the beginning that they were rational human beings. But the idiom has a life of its own; it implies that the Indians had no language at all.

This is, in part, an aspect of that linguistic colonialism we have already encountered in *Musophilus:* to speak is to speak one's own language, or at least a language with which one is familiar. "A man would be more cheerful with his dog for company," writes Saint Augustine, "than with a foreigner."[6] The unfamiliarity of their speech is a recurrent motif in the early accounts of the New World's inhabitants, and it is paraded forth in the company of all their other strange and often repellent qualities. The chronicler Robert Fabian writes of three savages presented to Henry VII that they "were clothed in beasts skins, & did eate raw flesh, and spake such speech that no man could understand them, and in their demeanour like to bruite beastes." Roy Harvey Pearce cites this as an example of the typical English view of the Indians as animals, but Fabian is far more ambiguous, for he continues: "Of the which upon two yeeres after, I saw two apparelled after the maner of Englishmen in Westminster pallace, which that time I could not discerne from Englishmen, til I was learned what they were, but as for speech, I heard none of them utter one word."[7] When he sees the natives again, are they still savages, now masked by their dress, or was his first impression misleading? And the seal of the ambiguity is the fact that he did not hear them utter a word, as if the real test of their conversion to civilization would be whether they had been able to master a language that "men" could understand.

In the 1570s the strangeness of Indian language can still be used in precisely the same way. In his first voyage to "Meta Incognita," as George Best reports, Frobisher captured a savage to take home with him as ". . . a sufficient witnesse of the captaines farre and tedious travell towards the unknowen parts of the world, as did well appeare by this strange infidell, whose like was never seene, read, nor heard of before, and whose language was neither knowen nor understood of any. . . ."[8] For Gregorio García, whose massive study of the origins of the Indians was published in 1607, there was something diabolical about the difficulty and variety of languages in the New World: Satan had helped the Indians to invent new tongues, thus impeding the labors of Christian missionaries.[9] And even the young John Milton, attacking the legal jargon of his time, can say in rhetorical outrage, "our speech is, I know not what, American, I suppose, or not even human!"[10]

Of course, there were many early attempts to treat Indian speech as something men could come to understand. According to John H. Parry, "All the early friars endeavoured to master Indian languages, usually Nahuatl, though some acquired other languages; the learned Andrés de Olmos, an early companion of Zumárraga, was credited with ten."[11] Traders and settlers also had an obvious interest in learning at least a few Indian words, and there are numerous word lists in the early accounts, facilitated as Peter Martyr points out by the fortuitous circumstance that "the languages of all the nations of these Ilandes, maye well be written with our Latine letters."[12] Such lists even suggested to one observer, Marc Lescarbot, the fact that Indian languages could change in time, just as French had changed from the age of Charlemagne. This, he explains, is why Cartier's dictionary of Indian words, compiled in the 1530s, in no longer of much use in the early seventeenth century.[13]

Indian languages even found some influential European admirers. In a famous passage, Montaigne approvingly quotes in translation several Indian songs, noting of one that "the invention hath no barbarism at all in it, but is altogether Anacreontic." In his judgement, "Their language is a kind of pleasant speech, and hath a pleasing sound and some affinity with the Greek terminations."[14] Ralegh, likewise, finds that the Tivitivas of Guiana have "the most manlie speech and most deliberate that euer I heard of what nation soeuer,"[15] while, in the next country, William Penn judges Indian speech "lofty" and full of words "of more sweetness or greatness" than most European tongues.[16] And the great Bartolomé de Las Casas, as he so often does, turns the tables on the Europeans:

> A man is apt to be called barbarous, in comparison with another, because he is
> strange in his manner of speech and mispronounces the language of the
> other. . . . According to Strabo, Book XIV, this was the chief reason the Greeks
> called other peoples barbarous, that is, because they were mispronouncing the
> Greek language. But from this point of view, there is no man or race which is not
> barbarous with respect to some other man or race. . . . Thus, just as we esteemed
> these peoples of these Indies barbarous, so they considered us, because of not
> understanding us.[17]

Simple and obvious as this point seems to us, it does not appear to have taken firm hold in the early years of conquest and settlement. Something of its spirit may be found in Oviedo's observation of an Indian interpreter failing to communicate with the members of another tribe: "[he] did not understand them better than a Biscayan talking Basque could make himself intelligible to a person speaking German or Arabic, or any other strange language."[18] But the view that Indian speech was close to gibberish remained current in intellectual as well as popular circles at least into the seventeenth century.[19] Indeed it is precisely in educated, and particularly humanist, circles that the view proved most tenacious and extreme. The rough, illiterate sea dog, bartering for gold trinkets on a far-away beach, was far more likely than the scholar to understand that the natives had their own tongue. The captains or lieutenants whose accounts we read had stood on the same beach, but when they sat down to record their experiences, powerful cultural presuppositions asserted themselves almost irresistibly.

For long before men without the full command of language, which is to say without eloquence, were thought to have been discovered in the New World, Renaissance humanists *knew* that such men existed, rather as modern scientists knew from the periodic table of the necessary existence of elements yet undiscovered. Virtually every Renaissance schoolboy read in Cicero's *De oratore* that only eloquence had been powerful enough "to gather scattered mankind together in one place, to transplant human beings from a barbarous life in the wilderness to a civilized social system, to establish organized communities, to equip them with laws and judicial safeguards and civic rights."[20] These lines, and similar passages from Isocrates and Quintilian, are echoed again and again in the fifteenth and sixteenth centuries as the proudest boast of the *stadium humanitatis*. Eloquence, wrote Andrea Ugo of Siena in 1421, led wandering humanity from a savage, bestial existence to civilized culture. Likewise, Andrea Brenta of Padua declared in 1480 that primitive men had led brutish and lawless lives in the fields until eloquence brought them together and converted barbaric violence into humanity and culture.[21] And more than a hundred years later, Puttenham can make the same claim, in the same terms, on behalf of poetry:

> Poesie was th'originall cause and occasion of their first assemblies, when before the people remained in the woods and mountains, vagarant and dipersed like the wild beasts, lawlesse and naked, or verie ill clad, and of all good and necessarie prouision for harbour or sustenance vtterly vnfurnished: so as they little differed for their maner of life, from the very brute beasts of the field.[22]

Curiously enough, a few pages later Puttenham cites the peoples of the New World as proof that poetry is more ancient than prose:

> This is proued by certificate of marchants & trauellers, who by late nauigations haue surueyed the whole world, and discouered large countries and strange peoples wild and sauage, affirming that the American, the Perusine & the very Canniball, do sing and also say, their highest and holiest matters in certaine riming versicles and not in prose.[23]

But it was more reasonable and logically consistent to conclude, as others did, that the savages of America were without eloquence or even without language.

To validate one of their major tenets, humanists needed to reach such as conclusion, and they clung to it, in the face of all the evidence, with corresponding tenacity.

Moreover, both intellectual and popular culture in the Renaissance had kept alive the medieval figure of the Wild Man, one of whose common characteristics is the absence of speech. Thus when Spenser's Salvage Man, in Book VI of the *Faerie Queene,* wishes to express his compassion for a distressed damsel, he kisses his hands and crouches low to the ground,

> For other language had he none, nor speach,
> But a soft murmure, and confused sound
> Of senselesse words, which Nature did him teach.[24]

To be sure, the Wild Man of medieval and Renaissance literature often turns out to be of gentle blood, having been lost, as an infant, in the woods; his language problem, then, is a consequence of his condition, rather than, as in Cicero, its prime cause. But this view accorded perfectly with the various speculations about the origins of the Indians, whether they were seen as lost descendants of the Trojans, Hebrews, Carthaginians, or Chinese. Indian speech, that speech no man could understand, could be viewed as the tattered remnants of a lost language.[25]

It is only a slight exaggeration, I think, to suggest that Europeans had, for centuries, rehearsed their encounter with the peoples of the New World, acting out, in their response to the legendary Wild Man, their mingled attraction and revulsion, longing and hatred. In the Christian Middle Ages, according to a recent account, "the Wild Man is the distillation of the specific anxieties underlying the three securities supposedly provided by the specifically Christian institutions of civilized life: the securities of *sex* (as organized by the institution of the family), *sustenance* (as provided by the political, social, and economic institutions), and *salvation* (as provided by the Church)."[26] These are precisely the areas in which the Indians most disturb their early observers. They appear to some to have no stable family life and are given instead to wantonness and perversion.[27] Nor, according to others, are they capable of political organization or settled social life. Against the campaign to free the enslaved Indians, it was argued that once given their liberty, they would return to their old ways: "For being idle and slothfull, they wander vp & downe, and returne to their olde rites and ceremonies, and foule and mischieuous actes."[28] And everywhere we hear of their worship of idols which, in the eyes of the Europeans, strikingly resemble the images of devils in Christian art.[29]

Certainly the Indians were again and again identified as Wild Men, as wild, in the words of Francis Pretty, "as ever was a bucke or any other wilde beast."[30] "These men may very well and truely be called Wilde," writes Jacques Cartier, at once confirming and qualifying the popular name, "because there is no poorer people in the world."[31] Peter Martyr records tales of Wild Men in the New World, but he distinguishes them from the majority of the inhabitants:

> They say there are certeyne wyld men whiche lyue in the caues and dennes of the montaynes, contented onely with wilde fruites. These men neuer vsed the companye of any other: nor wyll by any meanes becoome tame. They lyue without any

certain dwellynge places, and with owte tyllage or culturynge of the grounde, as
wee reade of them whiche in oulde tyme lyued in the golden age. They say also
that these men are withowte any certaine language. They are sumtymes seene.
But owre men haue yet layde handes on none of them.[32]

As Martyr's description suggests, Wild Men live beyond the pale of civilized
life, outside all institutions, untouched by the long, slow development of human
culture. If their existence is rude and repugnant, it also has, as Martyr's curious
mention of the Golden Age suggests, a disturbing allure. The figure of the Wild
Man, and the Indians identified as Wild Men, serve as a screen onto which
Renaissance Europeans, bound by their institutions, project their darkest and
yet most compelling fantasies. In the words of the earliest English tract on
America:

the people of this lande haue no kynge nor lorde nor theyr god. But all thinges is
comune/this people goeth all naked. . . . These folke lyuen lyke bestes without
any resonablenes and the wymen be also as comon. And the men hath conuer-
sacyon with the wymen/who that they ben or who they fyrst mete/is she his sys-
ter/his mother/his daughter/or any other kyndred. And the wymen be very hoote
and dysposed to lecherdnes. And they ete also on[e] a nother. The man etethe his
wyfe his chylderne. . . . And that lande is ryght full of folke/for they lyue commonly, iii.C. [300] yere and more as with sykenesse they dye nat.[33]

This bizarre description is, of course, an almost embarrasingly clinical delin-
eation of the Freudian id. And the id, according to Freud, is without language.

At the furthest extreme, the Wild Man shades into the animal—one possible
source of the medieval legend being European observation of the great apes.[34]
Language is, after all, one of the crucial ways of distinguishing between men and
beasts: "The one special advantage we enjoy over animals," writes Cicero, "is
our power to speak with one another, to express our thoughts in words."[35] Not
surprisingly, then, there was some early speculation that the Indians were subhu-
man and thus, among other things, incapable of receiving the true faith. One of
the early advocates on their behalf, Bernadino de Minaya, recalls that, on his
return to Spain from the New World,

I went on foot, begging, to Valladolid, where I visited the cardinal and informed
him that Friar Domingo [de Betanzos, an exponent of the theory that the Indians
were beasts] knew neither the Indians' language nor their true nature. I told him
of their ability and the right they had to become Christians. He replied that I was
much deceived, for he understood that the Indians were no more than parrots,
and he believed that Friar Domingo spoke with prophetic spirit. . . .[36]

The debate was dampened but by no means extinguished by Pope Paul III's
condemnation, in the bull *Sublimis Deus* (1537), of the opinion that the Indians
are "dumb brutes created for our service" and "incapable of receiving the
Catholic faith."[37] Friar Domingo conceded in 1544 that the Indians had language but argued against training them for the clergy on the grounds that their
language was defective, lacking the character and copiousness necessary to
explain Christian doctrine without introducing great improprieties which could
easily lead to great errors.[38] Similarly, Pierre Massée observes that the Brazilian

Indians lack the letters F, L, and R, which they could only receive by divine inspiration, insofar as they have neither "Foy, Loy, ne Roy."[39] Ironically, it is here, in these virtual slanders, that we find some of the fullest acknowledgement of the enormous cultural gap between Europeans and Indians, and of the near impossibility of translating concepts like conversion, Incarnation, or the Trinity into native speech.[40]

Perhaps the profoundest literary exploration of these themes in the Renaissance is to be found in Shakespeare. In *The Tempest* the startling encounter between a lettered and an unlettered culture is heightened, almost parodied, in the relationship between a European whose entire source of power is his library and a savage who had no speech at all before the European's arrival. "Remember/First to possess his books," Caliban warns the lower-class and presumably illiterate Stephano and Trinculo,

> for without them
> He's but a sot, as I am, nor hath not
> One spirit to command: they all do hate him
> As rootedly as I. Burn but his books.[41]

This idea my well have had some historical analogue in the early years of conquest. In his *Thresor de l'histoire des langves de cest univers (1607)*, Claude Duret reports that the Indians, fearing that their secrets would be recorded and revealed, would not approach certain trees whose leaves the Spanish used for paper, and Father Chaumonot writes in 1640 that the Hurons "were convinced that we were sorcerers, imposters come to take possession of their country, after having made them perish by our spells, which were shut up in our inkstands, in our books, etc.,—inasmuch that we dared not, without hiding ourselves, open a book or write anything.[42]

The link between *The Tempest* and the New World has often been noted, as, for example, by Terence Hawkes who suggests, in his book *Shakespeare's Talking Animals,* that in creating Prospero, the playwright's imagination was fired by the resemblance he perceived between himself and a colonist. "A colonist," writes Hawkes,

> acts essentially as a dramatist. He imposes the 'shape' of his own culture, *embodied in his speech,* on the new world, and makes that world recognizable, habitable, 'natural,' able to speak his language.[43]

Conversely,

> the dramatist is metaphorically a colonist. His art penetrates new areas of experience, his language expands the boundaries of our culture, and makes the new territory over in its own image. His 'raids on the inarticulate' open up new worlds for the imagination. (212)[44]

The problem for critics has been to accommodate this perceived resemblance between dramatist and colonist with a revulsion that reaches from the political critiques of colonialism in our own century back to the moral outrage of Las Casas and Montaigne. Moreover, there are many aspects of the play itself that make colonialism a problematical model for the theatrical imagination: if *The*

Tempest holds up a mirror to empire, Shakespeare would appear deeply ambivalent about using the reflected image as a representation of his own practice.

Caliban enters in Act I, cursing Prospero and protesting bitterly: "This island's mine, by Sycorax my mother, / Which thou tak'st from me" (I. ii. 333–34). When he first arrived, Prospero made much of Caliban, and Caliban, in turn, showed Prospero "all the qualities o'th'isle." But now, Caliban complains. "I am all the subjects that you have, / Which first was mine own King." Prospero replies angrily that he had treated Caliban "with human care" until he tried to rape Miranda, a charge Caliban does not deny. At this point, Miranda herself chimes in, with a speech Dryden and others have found disturbingly indelicate:

> Abhorred slave,
> Which any print of goodness wilt not take,
> Being capable of all ill! I pitied thee,
> Took pains to make thee speak, taught thee each hour
> One thing or other: when thou didst not, savage,
> Know thine own meaning, but wouldst gabble like
> A thing most brutish, I endow'd thy purposes
> With words that made them known. But thy vile race,
> Though thou didst learn, had that in't which good natures
> Could not abide to be with; therefore wast thou
> Deservedly confin'd into this rock,
> Who hadst deserv'd more than a prison.[45]

To this, Caliban replies:

> You taught me language; and my profit on't
> Is, I know how to curse. The red plague rid you
> For learning me your language!
>   (I. ii. 353–67)

Caliban's retort might be taken as self-indictment: even with the gift of language, his nature is so debased that he can only learn to curse. But the lines refuse to mean this; what we experience instead is a sense of their devastating justness. Ugly, rude, savage, Caliban nevertheless achieves for an instant an absolute if intolerably bitter moral victory. There is no reply; only Prospero's command: "Hagseed, hence! / Fetch us in fuel," coupled with an ugly threat:

> If you neglect'st, or dost unwillingly
> What I command, I'll rack thee with old cramps,
> Fill all thy bones with aches, make thee roar,
> That beasts shall tremble at thy din.
>   (I. ii. 370–73)

What makes this exchange so powerful, I think, is that Caliban is anything but a Noble Savage. Shakespeare does not shrink from the darkest European fantasies about the Wild Man; indeed he exaggerates them: Caliban is deformed, lecherous, evil-smelling, idle, treacherous, naive, drunken, rebellious, violent, and devil-worshipping.[46] According to Prospero, he is not even human: a "born devil," "got by the devil himself / Upon thy wicked dam" (I. ii. 321–22). *The Tempest* utterly rejects the uniformitarian view of the human race, the view that would later triumph in the Enlightenment and prevail in the West to this day. All men, the play seems to suggest, are *not* alike; strip away the adornments of culture and you will *not* reach a single human essence. If anything, *The Tempest* seems closer in spirit to the attitude of the present-day inhabitants of Java who, according to Clifford Geertz, quite flatly say, "To be human is to be Javanese."[47]

And yet out of the midst of this attitude Caliban wins a momentary victory that is, quite simply, an assertion of inconsolable human pain and bitterness. And out of the midst of this attitude Prospero comes, at the end of the play, to say of Caliban, "this thing of darkness I / Acknowledge mine" (V. i. 275–76). Like Caliban's earlier reply, Prospero's words are ambiguous; they might be taken as a bare statement that the strange "demi-devil" is one of Prospero's party as opposed to Alonso's, or even that Caliban is Prospero's slave. But again the lines refuse to mean this: they acknowledge a deep, if entirely unsentimental, bond. By no means is Caliban accepted into the family of man; rather, he is claimed as Philoctetes might claim his own festering wound. Perhaps, too, the word "acknowledge" implies some moral responsibility, as when the Lord, in the King James translation of Jeremiah, exhorts men to "acknowledge thine iniquity, that thou hast transgressed against the Lord thy God" (3:13). Certainly the Caliban of Act V is in a very real sense Prospero's creature, and the bitter justness of his retort early in the play still casts a shadow at its close. With Prospero restored to his dukedom, the match of Ferdinand and Miranda blessed, Ariel freed to the elements, and even the wind and tides of the return voyage settled, Shakespeare leaves Caliban's fate naggingly unclear. Prospero has acknowledged a bond; that is all.

Arrogant, blindly obstinate, and destructive as was the belief that the Indians had no language at all, the opposite conviction—that there was no significant language barrier between Europeans and savages—may have had consequences as bad or worse. Superficially, this latter view is the more sympathetic and seductive, in that it never needs to be stated. It is hard, after all, to resist the story of the *caciques* of the Cenu Indians who are reported by the Spanish captain to have rebutted the official claim to their land thus:

> what I said about the Pope being the Lord of all the universe in the place of God, and that he had given the land of the Indies to the King of Castile, the Pope must have been drunk when he did it, for he gave what was not his; also . . . the King, who asked for, or received, this gift, must be some madman, for that he asked to have that given him which belonged to others.[48]

It is considerably less hard to resist the account of the *caciques* of new Granada who declared in a memorial sent to the pope in 1553 that "if by chance Your Holiness has been told that we are bestial, you are to understand that this is true inasmuch as we follow devilish rites and ceremonies."[49] The principle in both cases is the same: whatever the natives may have actually thought and said has been altered out of recognition by being cast in European diction and syntax.

Again and again in the early accounts, Europeans and Indians, after looking on each other's faces for the first time, converse without the slightest difficulty; indeed the Indians often speak with as great a facility in English or
Spanish as the Renaissance gentlemen themselves. There were interpreters, to be
sure, but these are frequently credited with linguistic feats that challenge belief.
Thus Las Casas indignantly objects to the pretense that complex negotiations
were conducted through the mediation of interpreters who, in actual fact,
"communicate with a few phrases like 'Gimme bread,' 'Gimme food,' 'Take
this, gimme that,' and otherwise carry on with gestures."[50] He argues that the
narratives are intentionally falsified, to make the *conquistadores'* actions appear
fairer and more deliberative than they actually were. There may have been such
willful falsification, but there also seems to have been a great deal of what we
may call "filling in the blanks." The Europeans and the interpreters themselves
translated such fragments as they understood or thought they understood into a
coherent story, and they came to believe quite easily that the story was what
they had actually heard. There could be, and apparently were, murderous
results.[51]

They savages in the early accounts of the New World may occasionally make
strange noises—"Oh ho" or "bow-wow"[52]—but, once credited with intelligible
speech, they employ our accents and are comfortable in our modes of thought.
Thus the amorous daughter of a cruel *cacique*, we learn in *The Florida of the
Inca*, saved the young Spanish captive with the following words:

> Lest you lose faith in me and despair of your life or doubt that I will do every-
> thing in my power to save you . . . I will assist you to escape and find refuge if
> you are a man and have he courage to flee. For tonight, if you will come at a cer-
> tain hour to a certain place, you will find an Indian in whom I shall entrust both
> your welfare and mine.[53]

It may be objected that this is narrative convention: as in adventure movies, the
natives look exotic but speak our language. But such conventions are almost never
mere technical conveniences. If it was immensely difficult in sixteenth-century
narratives to represent a language barrier, it is because embedded in the narrative
convention of the period was a powerful, unspoken belief in the isomorphic relationship between language and reality. The denial of Indian language or of the language barrier grew out of the same soil that, in the mid-seventeenth century,
would bring forth the search for a universal language. Many sixteenth-century
observers of the Indians seem to have assumed that language—their language—
represented the true, rational order of things in the world. Accordingly, Indians
were frequently either found defective in speech, and hence pushed toward the
zone of wild things, or granted essentially the same speech as the Europeans. Linguists in the seventeenth century brought the underlying assumption to the surface, not, of course, to claim that English, or Latin, or even Hebrew expressed the
shape of reality, but to advocate the discovery or fashioning of a universal language that would do so.

Behind this project, and behind the narrative convention that foreshadowed
it, lay the conviction that reality was one and universal, constituted identically
for all men at all times and in all places. The ultimate grounds for this faith were

theological and were many times explicitly voiced, as here by Ralegh in his *History of the World:*

> The same just God who liueth and gouerneth all thinges for euer, doeth in these our times giue victorie, courage, and discourage, raise, and throw downe Kinges, Estates, Cities, and Nations, for the same offenses which were committed of old, and are committed in the present.[54]

There is a single faith, a single text, a single reality.

This complex of convictions may illuminate that most startling document, the *Requerimiento,* which was drawn up in 1513 and put into effect the next year. The *Requerimiento* was to be read aloud to newly encountered peoples in the New World; it demands both obedience to the king and queen of Spain as rulers of the Indies by virtue of the donation of the pope, and permission for the religious fathers to preach the true faith. If these demands are promptly met, many benefits are promised, but if there should be refusal or malicious delay, the consequences are made perfectly clear:

> We shall take you and your wives and your children, and shall make slaves of them, and as such shall sell and dispose of them as their Highnesses may command; and we shall take away your goods, and shall do you all the mischief and damage that we can, as to vassals who do not obey, and refuse to receive their lord, and resist and contradict him; and we protest that the deaths and losses which shall accrue from this are your fault, and not that of their Highnesses, or ours, nor of these cavaliers who come with us. And that we have said this to you and made this Requisition, we request the notary here present to give us his testimony in writing, and we ask the rest who are present that they should be witnesses of this Requisition.[55]

Las Casas writes that he doesn't know "whether to laugh or cry at the absurdity" of the *Requerimiento,* an absurdity born out in the stories of its actual use.[56] In our times, Madariaga calls it "quaint and naive," but neither adjective seems to me appropriate for what is a diabolical and, in its way, sophisticated document.[57]

A strange blend of ritual, cynicism, legal fiction, and perverse idealism, the *Requerimiento* contains at its core the conviction that there is no serious language barrier between the Indians and the Europeans. To be sure, there are one or two hints of uneasiness, but they are not allowed to disrupt the illusion of scrupulous and meaningful communication established from the beginning:

> On the part of the King, Don Fernando, and of Doña Juana, his daughter, Queen of Castile and Leon, subduers of the barbarous nations, we their servants notify and make known to you, as best we can, that the Lord our God, Living and Eternal, created the Heaven and the Earth, and one man and one woman, of whom you and we, and all the men of the world, were and are descendants, and all those who come after us.[58]

The proclamation that all men are brothers may seem an odd way to begin a document that ends with threats of enslavement and a denial of responsibility for all ensuing deaths and losses, but it is precisely this opening that justifies the close. That all human beings are descended from "one man and one woman" proves that there is a single human essence, a single reality. As such, all problems of communication are merely accidental. Indeed, the *Requerimiento* conveniently passes over in silence the biblical account of the variety of languages and the scattering of mankind. In Genesis 11, we are told that "the whole earth was of one language, and of one speech," until men began to build the tower of Babel:

> And the Lord said, Behold, the people is one, and they have all one language; and this they begin to do: and now nothing will be restrained from them, which they have imagined to do. Go to, let us go down, and there confound their language, that they may not understand one another's speech. So the Lord scattered them abroad from thence upon the face of all the earth: and they left off to build the city. (Gen. 11:6–8)

In place of this, the *Requerimiento* offers a demographic account of the dispersion of the human race:

> on account of the multitude which has sprung from this man and woman in the five thousand years since the world was created, it was necessary that some men should go one way and some another, and that they should be divided into many kingdoms and provinces, for in one alone they could not be sustained.[59]

The Babel story has to be omitted, for to acknowledge it here would be to undermine the basic linguistic premise of the whole document.

The *Requerimiento,* then, forces us to confront the dangers inherent in what most of us would consider the central liberal tenet, namely the basic unity of mankind. The belief that a shared essence lies beneath our particular customs, stories, and language turns out to be the cornerstone of the document's self-righteousness and arrogance. It certainly did not cause the horrors of the Conquest, but it made those horrors easier for those at home to live with. After all, the Indians had been warned. The king and queen had promised "joyfully and benignantly" to receive them as vassals. The *Requerimiento* even offered to let them see the "certain writings" wherein the pope made his donation of the Indies. If, after all this, the Indians obstinately refused to comply, they themselves would have to bear responsibility for the inevitable consequences.

The two beliefs that I have discussed in this paper—that Indian language was deficient or non-existent and that there was no serious language barrier—are not, of course, the only sixteenth-century attitudes toward American speech. I have already mentioned some of the Europeans, missionaries, and laymen who took native tongues seriously. There are, moreover, numerous practical acknowledgments of the language problem which do not simply reduce the native speech to gibberish. Thus René de Laudonnière reports that the Indians "every houre made us a 1000 discourses, being merveilous sory that we could not understand them." Instead of simply throwing up his hands, he proceeds to ask the Indian names for various objects and comes gradually to understand a part of what they are saying.[60]

But the theoretical positions on Indian speech that we have considered press in from either side on the Old World's experience of the New. Though they seem to be opposite extremes, both positions reflect a fundamental inability to sustain the simultaneous perception of likeness and difference, the very special perception we give to metaphor. Instead they either push the Indians toward utter difference—and thus silence—or toward utter likeness—and thus the collapse of their own, unique identity. Shakespeare, in *The Tempest*, experiments with an extreme version of this problem, placing Caliban at the outer limits of difference only to insist upon a mysterious measure of resemblance. It is as if he were testing our capacity to sustain metaphor. And in this instance only, the audience achieves a fullness of understanding before Prospero does, an understanding that Prospero is only groping toward at the play's close. In the poisoned relationship between master and slave, Caliban can only curse; but we know that Caliban's consciousness is not simply a warped negation of Prospero's:

> I prithee, let me bring thee where crabs grow;
> And I with my long nails will dig thee pig-nuts;
> Show thee a jay's nest, and instruct thee how
> To snare the nimble mamoset; I'll bring thee
> To clustering filberts, and sometimes I'll get thee
> Young scamels from the rock.
>
> (II. ii. 167–72)

The rich, irreducible concreteness of the verse compels us to acknowledge the independence and integrity of Caliban's construction of reality. We do not sentimentalize this construction—indeed the play insists that we judge it and that we prefer another—but we cannot make it vanish into silence. Caliban's world has what we may call *opacity*, and the perfect emblem of that opacity is the fact that we do not to this day know the meaning of the word "scamel."

But it is not until Vico's *New Science* (1725) that we find a genuine theoretical breakthrough, a radical shift from the philosophical assumptions that helped to determine European response to alien languages and cultures. Vico refuses to accept the position by then widely held that "in the vulgar languages meanings were fixed by convention," that "articulate human words have arbitrary significations." On the contrary, he insists, "because of their natural origins, they must have had natural significations."[61] Up to this point, he seems simply to be reverting to the old search for a universal character. But then he makes a momentous leap:

> There remains, however, the very great difficulty: How is it that there are as many different vulgar tongues as there are peoples? To solve it, we must here establish this great truth; that, as the people have certainly by diversity of climates acquired different natures, from which have sprung as many different customs, so from their different natures and customs as many different languages have arisen. (p. 133)

For Vico, the key to the diversity of languages is not the arbitrary character of signs but the variety of human natures. Each language reflects and substantiates the specific character of the culture out of which it springs.

Vico, however, is far away from the first impact of the New World upon the Old, and, in truth, his insights have scarcely been fully explored in our own times. Europeans in the sixteenth century, like ourselves, find it difficult to credit another language with opacity. In other words, they render Indian language transparent, either by limiting or denying its existence or by dismissing its significance as an obstacle to communication between peoples. And as opacity is denied to native speech, so, by the same token, is it denied to native culture. For a specific language and a specific culture are not here, not are they ever, entirely separable. To divorce them is to turn from the messy, confusing welter of details that characterize a particular society at a particular time to the cool realm of abstract principles. It is precisely to validate such high-sounding principles— "Eloquence brought men from barbarism to civility" or "All men are descended from one man and one woman"—that the Indian languages are peeled away and discarded like rubbish by so many of the early writers. But as we are now beginning fully to understand, reality for each society is constructed to a significant degree out of the *specific* qualities of its language and symbols. Discard the particular words and you have discarded the particular men. And so most of the people of the New World will never speak to us. That communication, with all that we might have learned, is lost to us forever.

Notes

1. Samuel Daniel, *Poems and a Defence of Ryme,* ed. Arthur Colby Sprague (Cambridge 1930) 11, 957–962.
2. Peter Martyr, *The Decades of the Newe Worlde (De orbe novo),* trans. Richard Eden, Decade 3, Book 9, in *The First Three English Books on America,* ed. Edward Arber (Birmingham 1885) 177.
3. Antonio de Nebrija, *Gramática de la lengua castellana,* ed. Ig. González-Llubera (Oxford 1926) 3; Lewis Hanke, *Aristotle and the American Indians: A Study in Race Prejudice in the Modern World* (Chicago and London 1959) 8.
4. Martyr (n. 2 above) Decade 2, Book 1, p. 106.
5. Christopher Columbus, *Journals and Other Documents on the Life and Voyages of Christopher Columbus,* trans. and ed. Samuel Eliot Morison (New York 1963) 65. For the Spanish, see Cristoforo Colombo, *Diario de Colón, libro de la primera navegación y descubrimiento de la Indias,* ed. Carlos Sanz López [facsimile of the original transcript] (Madrid 1962) fol. 9b. There has been considerable debate about Columbus' journal, which survived only in Las Casas' transcription. But Las Casas indicates that he is quoting Columbus here, and the words are revealing, no matter who penned them.
6. Augustine, *Concerning The City of God against the Pagans,* trans. Henry Bettenson, ed. David Knowles (Harmondsworth 1972) Book 19, Ch. 7, p. 861. The whole passage, with its reference to Roman linguistic colonialism, is interesting in this context:

   . . . the diversity of languages separates man from man. For if two men meet, and are forced by some compelling reason not to pass on but to stay in company, then if neither knows the other's language, it is easier for dumb animals, even of different kinds, to associate together than these men, although both are human beings. For when men cannot communicate their thoughts to each other, simply because of difference of language, all the similarity of their common human nature is of no avail to unite them in fellowship. So true is this that a man would be more cheerful with his dog for company than with a foreigner. I shall be told that the Imperial City has been at pains to impose on conquered peoples not only her yoke but her language also, as a bond of peace and fellowship, so that there should be no lack of interpreters but even a profusion of them. True; but think of the cost of this achievement! Consider the scale of those wars, with all that slaughter of human beings, all the human blood that was shed!

For a variation of the theme of linguistic isolation, see Shakespeare, *Richard II,* ed. Peter Ure (Cambridge, Mass. 1956) I. iii. 159–173.

7. Robert Fabian, in Richard Hakluyt, *The Principal Navigations, Voyages, Traffiques, and Discoveries of the English Nation . . .* (12 vols. Glasgow 1903–05) 7. 155. Roy Harvey Pearce, "Primitivistic Ideas in the *Faerie Queene,*" *Journal of English and Germanic Philology* 44 (1945) 149.

8. In Hakluyt (n. 7 above) 7. 282.

9. See Lee Eldridge Huddleston, *Origins of the American Indians; European Concepts, 1492–1729,* Latin American Monographs 11 (Austin, Tex. 1967) 66.

10. Milton, *Prolusiones,* ed. Donald Leman Clark, trans. Bromley Smith, in *Works,* ed. Frank Allen Peterson (18 vols. New York 1931–38) 12. 277.

11. John H. Parry, *The Spanish Seaborne Empire* (London and New York 1966) 163. Cf. France V. Scholes and Ralph L. Roys: "Although some of the friars, notably Fray Luis de Villalpando and Fray Diego de Landa, learned to speak and write Maya and gave instruction to the others, it is doubtful whether more than half of the clergy became proficient in the language." Quoted in *Landa's relación de las cosas de Yucatán,* trans. Alfred M. Tozzer, *Papers of the Peabody Museum of American Archaeology and Ethnology* 18 (1941) 70 n. 313.

12. Martyr (n. 2 above) Decade 1, Book 1, p. 67. See, in the same volume, Sebastian Münster, p. 29, and Martyr, Decade 2, Book 1, p. 138. For examples of word lists, see Martyr, Decade 3, Book 1, p. 45; Francisco López de Gómara, *The Pleasant Historie of the Conquest of the Weast India, now called New Spayne,* trans. T. N. (London 1578) 370 ff.; John Davis, in Hakluyt (n. 7 above) 7. 398–399; Sir Robert Dudley, in Hakluyt, 10. 211–212; William Strachey, *The Historie of Travell into Virginia Britania (1612),* ed. Louis B. Wright and Virginia Freund, Hakluyt Society, Ser. 2, 103 (London 1953) 174–207; James Rosier, "Extracts of a Virginian Voyage made An. 1605. by Captaine George Waymouth," in Samuel Purchas, *Hakluytus Posthumus, or Purchas his Pilgrimes,* Hakluyt Society, Extra series (20 vols. Glasgow 1905–07; rpt. of 1625 ed.) 18. 359. The most delightful of the lists is Roger Williams, *A Key into the Language of America* (London 1643; rpt. Providence, R.I. 1936). There are also sample conversations in Indian languages; see Williams, *Key;* Jean de Léry, *Navigatio in Brasiliam Americae,* Ch. 19, in Theodor de Bry, *Americae tertia pars* (Frankfort 1592) 250 ff.; Martyr (n. 2 above) Decade 3, Book 8, p. 170.

13. Lescarbot, in Claude Duret, *Thresor de l'histoire des langues de cest univers* (Cologny 1613) 954–955. I am indebted for this reference and for many useful suggestions to Professor Natalie Zemon Davis.

14. Montaigne, *Selected Essays,* trans. John Florio, ed. Walter Kaiser (Boston 1964) 79. The possibility that Indian language has traces of Greek is explored by Sarmiento de Gamboa and Gregorio García (see Huddleston [n. 9 above] 30, 73), and by Thomas Morton, *New English Canaan,* in *Tracts and Other Papers Relating Principally to the Origin, Settlement, and Progress of the Colonies in North America,* comp. Peter Force (4 vols. Washington [c. 1836–47]; rpt. New York 1947 and Gloucester, Mass. 1963) 2. 15–18.

15. Raleigh, *The Discoverie of the large and bewtiful Empire of Guiana,* ed. V. T. Harlow (London 1928) 38.

16. Quoted in Gary B. Nash, "The Image of the Indian in the Southern Colonial Mind," in *The Wild Man Within: An Image in Western Thought from the Renaissance to Romanticism,* ed. Edward Dudley and Maximillian E. Novak (Pittsburgh 1972) 72. See, likewise, Cornelius J. Jaenen, "Amerindian Views of French Culture in the Seventeenth Century," *Canadian Historical Review* 55 (1974) 276–277.

17. Bartolomé de Las Casas, *A Selection of his Writings,* trans. and ed. George Sanderlin (New York 1971) 144. Thomas More makes the same point in the early sixteenth century to defend English: "For as for that our tong is called barbarous, is but a fantasye. For so is, as euery lerned man knoweth, euery strange language to other." *(Dialogue concerning Heresies,* quoted in J. L. Moore, *Tudor-Stuart Views on the Growth, Status, and Destiny of the English Language,* Studien zur Englischen Philologie 41 (Halle 1920) 19.)

18. Oviedo, quoted in Sir Arthur Helps, *The Spanish Conquest of America and its Relation to the History of Slavery and to the Government of Colonies,* ed. M. Oppenheim (4 vols. London 1900–04; rpt. New York 1966) 1. 269.

19. For a nineteenth-century variation, see Daniel Webster's remark in a letter to Ticknor, 1 March 1826: "I ought to say that I am a total unbeliever in the new doctrines about the Indian languages. I believe them to be the rudest forms of speech; and I believe there is as little in the languages of the tribes as in their laws, manners, and customs, worth studying or worth knowing. All this is heresy, I know, but so I think"; see George Ticknor Curtis, *Life of Daniel Webster* (2 vols. New York 1872) 1 . 260. By 1826, it should be noted, Webster is on the defensive. I owe this reference to Professor Larzer Ziff.

20. Cicero, *De oratore* I. viii. 33, in *On the Good Life,* trans. Michael Grant (Harmondsworth 1971) 247.

21. Andrea Ugo and Andrea Brenta, in Karl Müllner, *Reden und Briefe Italienischer Humanisten* (Vienna 1899) 110–111, 75–76. See, likewise in the same volume, the orations of Lapo de Castiglionchio, Andrea Giuliano of Venice, Francesco Filelfo, Antonio da Rho, Tiphernas (Gregorio da Città di Castello), and Giovanni Toscanella.

22. George(?) Puttenham, *The Arte of English Poesie* (London 1589; Scolar Press facs. ed. Menston 1968) 3–4. The myth that Orpheus tamed wild beasts by his music is intended to show, according to Puttenham, "how by his discreete and wholsome lessons vttered in harmonie and with melodious instruments, he brought the rude and sauage people to a more ciuill and orderly life, nothing, as it seemeth, more preuailing or fit to redresse and edifie the cruell and sturdie courage of man then it" (4). Without speech, according to Hobbes, "there had been amongst men, neither commonwealth, nor society, nor contract, nor peace, no more than amongst lions, bears, and wolves," *Leviathan,* ed. Michael Oakeshott (Oxford 1960) 18.

23. Puttenham (n. 22 above) 7. See also Sir Philip Sidney, *An Apologie for Poetrie,* in *English Literary Criticism: The Renaissance,* ed. O. B. Hardison, Jr. (New York 1963): "Euen among the most barbarous and simple Indians where no writing is, yet haue they their Poets, who make and sing songs, which they call *Areytos,* both of theyr Auncestors deedes and praises of theyr Gods: a sufficient probabilitie that if euer learning come among them, it must be by hauing theyr hard dull wits softned and sharpened with the sweete delights of Poetrie. For vntill they find a pleasure in the exercises of the minde, great promises of much knowledge will little perswade them that knowe not the fruites of knowledge" (102). On the Indian *Areytos,* see Martyr (n. 2 above) Decade 3, Book 7, pp. 166–167: likewise, Las Casas, *History of the Indies,* trans. and ed. Andrée Collard (New York 1971) 279–280. For a comparable phenomenon in the British Isles, see J. E. C. Hill. "Puritans and The Dark Corners of the Land,'" *Royal Historical Society Transactions,* Ser. 5, 13 (1963) 82: "On Sundays and holy days, we are told of North Wales about 1600, 'the multitude of all sorts of men, women and children' used to meet to hear 'their harpers and crowthers sing them songs of the doings of their ancestors.'"

24. *The Faerie Queene,* VI. iv. 11, in *The Works of Edmund Spenser. A Variorum Edition,* ed. Edwin Greenlaw *et al.* (9 vols. Baltimore 1932–49). On Spenser's Wild Man,

see Pearce (n. 7 above) and Donald Cheney, *Spenser's Image of Nature: Wild Man and Shepherd in "The Faerie Queene"* (New Haven 1966). On the figure of the Wild Man, see Dudley and Novak (n. 16 above); Richard Bernheimer, *Wild Men in the Middle Ages: A Study in Art, Sentiment, and Demonology* (Cambridge, Mass. 1952).

25. On the comparison of Indian and Old World words, see Huddleston (n. 9 above) esp. 23, 30, 37, 44, 91–92. The Indians were described by Cotton Mather as "the veriest *ruines of mankind,* which [were] to be found any where upon the face of the earth": quoted in Roy Harvey Pearce, *Savagism and Civilization: A Study of the Indian and the American Mind* (Baltimore 1965; rpt. 1967) 29.

26. Hayden White, "The Forms of Wildness: Archaeology of an Idea," in Dudley and Novak (n. 16 above) 21.

27. "Thei vse no lawful coniunction of mariage, but euery one hath as many women as him listeth, and leaueth them agayn at his pleasure," Sebastian Münster, *A Treatyse of the Newe 'India',* trans. Richard Eden, in Arber (n. 2 above) 37. See, likewise, Martyr (n. 2 above) Decade 3, Book 1, p. 138; Martyr, trans. Michael Lok, in *A Selection of Curious, Rare, and Early Voyages and Histories of Interesting Discoveries chiefly published by Hakluyt . . .* (London 1812) Decade 8, Ch. 8, p. 673; Laudonnière, in Hakluyt (n. 7 above) 8. 453; Henry Hawks, in Hakluyt (n. 7 above) 9. 386; Bernal Diaz del Castillo, *The Conquest of New Spain,* trans. J. M. Cohen (Baltimore 1963) 19, 122, 124. On one of Frobisher's voyages, a native man and woman, captured separately, are brought together before the silent and eagerly expectant sailors. The observers are astonished at the "shamefastnes and chastity of those Savage captives" (in Hakluyt [n. 7 above] 7. 306).

28. Martyr, trans. Lok (n. 27 above) Decade 7, Ch. 4, p. 627. "Wandering up and down" seems almost as much of an offense as idolatry. There is trace of this disapproval and anxiety in the description of Othello as an "erring barbarian," an "extravagant and wheeling stranger."

29. See for example, Martyr, trans. Lok (n. 27 above) Decade 4, Ch. 9, p. 539: "with such a countenance, as we use to paint hobgoblings or spirites which walke by night."

30. In Hakluyt (n. 7 above) 11.297. Note that Spenser uses the same metaphor for his Wild Man: "For he was swift as any bucke in chace" (*FQ,* VI. iv. 8).

31. In Hakluyt (n. 7 above) 8.201–202.

32. Martyr, ed. Arber (n. 2 above) Decade 3, Book 8, p. 173.

33. *Of the newe landes,* in Arber (n. 2 above) p. xxvii; cf. Wilberforce Eames, "Description of a Wood Engraving Illustrating the South American Indians (1505)," *Bulletin of the New York Public Library* 26 (1922) 755–760.

34. See Horst Woldemar Janson, *Apes and Ape Lore in the Middle Ages and the Renaissance* (London 1952).

35. Cicero, *De oratore* I. viii. 32, in *On the Good Life* (n. 20 above) 247.

36. Quoted in Lewis Hanke, "Pope Paul III and the American Indians," *Harvard Theological Review* 30 (1937) 84.

37. Quoted in Hanke (n. 36 above) 72; likewise in Hanke (n. 3 above) 19.

38. Quoted in Hanke (n. 36 above) 102. On his death-bed, Domingo de Betanzos recanted his denigration of the Indians.

39. Massée, in Duret (n. 13 above) 945.

40. For a more sympathetic grasp of the problem of translating religious concepts, see Las Casas (n. 23 above) 238–239; Marc Lescarbot, *History of New France,* trans. W. L. Grant (3 vols. Toronto 1907–14) 2. 179–180: José de Acosta, *The Natural and Moral History of the Indies,* trans. Edward Grimston [1604], ed. Clements R. Markham, Hakluyt Society 60–61 (2 vols. London 1880) 2. 301–302. Cornelius Jaenen (n. 16 above) suggests that the difficulty was more cultural than linguistic: "The

natives saw some danger in divulging their religious vocabulary to the evangelists of the new religion, therefore they refused to cooperate extensively in the linguistic task of compiling dictionaries and grammars, and of translating religious books" (277).

41. *The Tempest,* ed. Frank Kermode (Cambridge, Mass. 1954) III. ii. 90–93.

42. Duret (n. 13 above) 935; Chaumonot, quoted in Jaenen (n. 16 above) 275–276.

43. Terence Hawkes, *Shakespeare's Talking Animals* (London 1973) 211. For another appraisal of colonialism in *The Tempest,* see Dominique O. Mannoni, *Prospero and Caliban: The Psychology of Colonization,* trans. Pamela Powesland (New York 1956) 97–109.

44. "Raids on the inarticulate"—the quotation is from T. S. Eliot's *Four Quartets* and, as Hawkes uses it, eerily invokes the sixteenth-century fantasy that the Indians were without speech.

45. The lines are sometimes attributed, without any textual authority, to Prospero. "Which any print of goodness wilt not take," it might be noted, plays on the *tabula rasa* theme.

46. Shakespeare even appeals to early seventeenth-century class fears by having Caliban form an alliance with the lower-class Stephano and Trinculo to overthrow the noble Prospero. On class-consciousness in the period, see Christopher Hill, "The Many-Headed Monster in Late Tudor and Early Stuart Political Thinking," in *From the Renaissance to the Counter-Reformation. Essays in Honor of Garrett Mattingly,* ed. Charles H. Carter (New York 1965) 296–324.

47. Clifford Geertz, "The Impact of the Concept of Culture on the Concept of Man," in his selected essays, *The Interpretation of Cultures* (New York 1973) 52. I am indebted throughout to this suggestive essay.

48. Enciso, *Suma de geographia,* quoted in Helps (n. 18 above) 1. 279–280.

49. Quoted in Hanke (n. 36 above) 95. It is not impossible that the *caciques* said something vaguely similar; see Las Casas (n. 23 above) 82: "what could we expect from these gentle and unprotected Indians suffering such torments, servitude and decimation but immense pusillanimity, profound discouragement and annihilation of their inner selves, to the point of doubting whether they were men or mere cats?"

50. Las Casas (n. 23 above) 241.

51. *Ibid.,* 50–52, 130–131.

52. Both are in James Rosier (n. 12 above) 18. 342, 344.

53. Garcilaso de la Vega, *The Florida of the Inca,* trans. and ed. John Grier Varner and Jeannette Johnson Varner (Austin, Tex. 1951) 69–70; quoted by Howard Mumford Jones, *O Strange New World, American Culture: The Formative Years* (New York 1964; Viking paperback ed. 1967) 25–26.

54. Sir Walter Ralegh,. *The History of the World* (London 1614) II. xix. 3, pp. 508–509.

55. In Helps (n. 18 above) 1. 266–267.

56. Las Casas (n. 23 above) 196. "For the actual use of the *Requerimiento,* see Lewis Hanke, *The Spanish Struggle for Justice in the Conquest of America* (Philadelphia 1949; rpt. Boston 1965) 34.

57. Salvador de Madariaga, *The Rise of the Spanish American Empire* (New York 1947) 12.

58. In Helps (n. 18 above) 1. 264.

59. *Ibid.*

60. In Hakluyt (n. 7 above) 8. 466.

61. Giambattista Vico, *The New Science,* trans. Thomas G. Bergin and Max H. Fisch (Ithaca 1948) 132.

Donna Haraway (1944–)

Haraway is particularly well known for her scholarship in feminist theory, science studies, and cultural studies. Her interdisciplinary approach merges research in technology, anthropology, sociology, biology, and socialist feminist theory. She has undergraduate degrees in zoology and philosophy from Colorado College and received a Ph.D. in biology from Yale University in 1972. She is currently a professor in the History of Consciousness Program at the University of California at Santa Cruz. Previously, she had been a professor at the University of Hawaii and The John Hopkins University. Haraway's focus on new systems of power relations driven by technological advances highlights a paradigm shift in cultural domination. Given newer threats posed by consolidations of technologies by power blocs, Haraway has argued that people working for progressive changes of cultural and social systems will need new methods of resistance. The cyborg identity potentially offers political strategies conducive to challenging technoscientific domination. A cyborg is "a hybrid of machine and organism, a creature of social reality as well as a creature of fiction," according to Haraway in the upcoming selection, "A Cyborg Manifesto: Science, Technology, and Socialist-Feminism in the Late Twentieth Century." While "contemporary science fiction is full of cyborgs," as Haraway notes, are we ourselves cyborgs, or are we in cyborg-friendly environments? As Haraway demonstrates, such questions of identity and of our surroundings intersect with other questions about politics, information, work, and social relationships. This essay first appeared in the *Socialist Review* in 1985. Some of Haraway's other major texts include *Primate Visions: Gender, Race, and Nature in the World of Modern Science* (1989) and *Simians, Cyborgs, and Women: The Reinvention of Nature* (1991).

A Cyborg Manifesto: Science, Technology, and Socialist-Feminism in the Late Twentieth Century[1]

An Ironic Dream of a Common Language for Women in the Integrated Circuit

This chapter is an effort to build an ironic political myth faithful to feminism, socialism, and materialism. Perhaps more faithful as blasphemy is faithful, than as reverent worship and identification. Blasphemy has always seemed to require taking things very seriously. I know no better stance to adopt from within the secular-religious, evangelical traditions of United States politics, including the politics of socialist feminism. Blasphemy protects one from the moral majority within, while still insisting on the need for community. Blasphemy is not apostasy. Irony is about contradictions that do not resolve into larger wholes, even dialectically, about the tension of holding incompatible things together because both or all are necessary and true. Irony is about humour and serious play. It is also a rhetorical strategy and a political method, one I would like to see more honoured within socialist-feminism. At the centre of my ironic faith, my blasphemy, is the image of the cyborg.

A cyborg is a cybernetic organism, a hybrid of machine and organism, a creature of social reality as well as a creature of fiction. Social reality is lived social relations, our most important political construction, a world-changing fiction. The international women's movements have constructed "women's experience," as well as uncovered or discovered this crucial collective object. This experience is a fiction and fact of the most crucial, political kind. Liberation rests on the construction of the consciousness, the imaginative apprehension, of oppression, and so of possibility. The cyborg is a matter of fiction and lived experience that changes what counts as women's experience in the late twentieth century. This is a struggle over life and death, but the boundary between science fiction and social reality is an optical illusion.

Contemporary science fiction is full of cyborgs—creatures simultaneously animal and machine, who populate world ambiguously natural and crafted. Modern medicine is also full of cyborgs, of couplings between organism and machine, each conceived as coded devices, in an intimacy and with a power that was not generated in the history of sexuality. Cyborg "sex" restores some of the lovely replicative baroque of ferns and invertebrates (such nice organic prophylactics against heterosexism). Cyborg replication is uncoupled from organic reproduction. Modern production seems like a dream of cyborg colonization work, a dream that makes the nightmare of Taylorism seem idyllic. And modern war is a cyborg orgy, coded by C^3I, command-control-communication-intelligence, an $84 billion item in 1984's US defence budget. I am making an argument for the cyborg as a fiction mapping our social and bodily reality and as an imaginative resource suggesting some very fruitful couplings. Michel Foucault's biopolitics is a flaccid premonition of cyborg politics, a very open field.

By the late twentieth century, our time, a mythic time, we are all chimeras, theorized and fabricated hybrids of machine and organism; in short, we are cyborgs. The cyborg is our ontology; it gives us our politics. The cyborg is a condensed image of both imagination and material reality, the two joined centers structuring any possibility of historical transformation. In the traditions of "Western" science and politics—the tradition of racist, male-dominant capitalism; the tradition of progress; the tradition of the appropriation of nature as resource for the productions of culture; the tradition of reproduction of the self from the reflections of the other—the relation between organism and machine has been a border war. The stakes in the border war have been the territories of production, reproduction, and imagination. This chapter is an argument for *pleasure* in the confusion of boundaries and for *responsibility* in their construction. It is also an effort to contribute to socialist-feminist culture and theory in a postmodernist, non-naturalist mode and in the utopian tradition of imagining a world without gender, which is perhaps a world without genesis, but maybe also a world without end. The cyborg incarnation is outside salvation history. Nor does it mark time on an oedipal calendar, attempting to heal the terrible cleavages of gender in an oral symbiotic utopia or post-oedipal apocalypse. As Zoe Sofoulis argues in her unpublished manuscript on Jacques Lacan, Melanie Klein, and nuclear culture, *Lacklein*, the most terrible and perhaps the most promising monsters in cyborg worlds are embodied in non-oedipal narratives with a different logic of repression, which we need to understand for our survival.

The cyborg is a creature in a post-gender world; it has no truck with bisexuality, pre-oedipal symbiosis, unalienated labour, or other seductions to organic wholeness through a final appropriation of all the powers of the parts into a higher unity. In a sense, the cyborg has no origin story in the Western sense—a "final" irony since the cyborg is also the awful apocalyptic *telos* of the "West's" escalating dominations of abstract individuation, an ultimate self untied at last from all dependency, a man in space. An origin story in the "Western," humanist sense depends on the myth of original unity, fullness, bliss and terror, represented by the phallic mother from whom all humans must separate, the task of individual development and of history, the twin potent myths inscribed most powerfully for us in psychoanalysis and Marxism. Hillary Klein has argued that both Marxism and psychoanalysis, in their concepts of labour and of individuation and gender formation, depend on the plot of original unity out of which difference must be produced and enlisted in a drama of escalating domination of woman/nature. The cyborg skips the step of original unity, of identification with nature in the Western sense. This is its illegitimate promise that might lead to subversion of its teleology as star wars.

The cyborg is resolutely committed to partiality, irony, intimacy, and perversity. It is oppositional, utopian, and completely without innocence. No longer structured by the polarity of public and private, the cyborg defines a technological polis based partly on a revolution of social relations in the *oikos*, the household. Nature and culture are reworked; the one can no longer be the resource for appropriation or incorporation by the other. The relationships for forming wholes from parts, including those of polarity and hierarchical domination, are at issue in the cyborg world. Unlike the hopes of Frankenstein's monster, the cyborg does not expect its father to save it through a restoration of the garden; that is, through the fabrication of a heterosexual mate, through its completion in a finished whole, a city and cosmos. The cyborg does not dream of community on the model of the organic family, this time without the oedipal project. The cyborg would not recognize the Garden of Eden; it is not made of mud and cannot dream of returning to dust. Perhaps that is why I want to see if cyborgs can subvert the apocalypse of returning to nuclear dust in the manic compulsion to name the Enemy. Cyborgs are not reverent; they do not remember the cosmos. They are wary of holism, but needy for connection—they seem to have a natural feel for united front politics, but without the vanguard party. The main trouble with cyborgs, of course, is that they are illegitimate offspring of militarism and patriarchal capitalism, not to mention state socialism. But illegitimate offspring are often exceedingly unfaithful to their origins. Their fathers, after all, are inessential.

I will return to the science fiction of cyborgs at the end of this chapter, but now I want to signal three crucial boundary breakdowns that make the following political-fictional (political-scientific) analysis possible. By the late twentieth century in United States scientific culture, the boundary between human and animal is thoroughly breached. The last beachheads of uniqueness have been polluted if not turned into amusement parks—language, tool use, social behaviour, mental events, nothing really convincingly settles the separation of human and animal. And many people no longer feel the need for such a separation; indeed, many branches of feminist culture affirm the pleasure of connection of human and other living creatures. Movements for animal rights are not irrational denials of human uniqueness; they are a clear-sighted recognition of connection across the discredited breach of nature and culture. Biology and evolutionary theory over the last two centuries have simultaneously produced modern organisms as objects of knowledge and reduced the line between humans and animals to a faint trace re-etched in ideological struggle or professional disputes between life and social science. Within this framework, teaching modern Christian creationism should be fought as a form of child abuse.

Biological-determinist ideology is only one position opened up in scientific culture for arguing the meanings of human animality. There is much room for radical political people to contest the meanings of the breached boundary.[2] The cyborg appears in myth precisely where the boundary between human and animal is transgressed. Far from signalling a walling off of people from other living beings, cyborgs signal disturbingly and pleasurably tight coupling. Bestiality has a new status in this cycle of marriage exchange.

The second leaky distinction is between animal-human (organism) and machine. Pre-cybernetic machines could be haunted; there was always the spectre of the ghost in the machine. This dualism structured the dialogue between materialism and idealism that was settled by a dialectical progeny, called spirit or history, according to taste. But basically machines were not self-moving, self-designing, autonomous. They could not achieve man's dream, only mock it. They were not man, an author to himself, but only a caricature of that masculinist reproductive dream. To think they were otherwise was paranoid. Now we are not so sure. Late twentieth-century machines have made thoroughly ambiguous the difference between natural and artificial, mind and body, self-developing and externally designed, and many other distinctions that used to apply to organisms and machines. Our machines are disturbingly lively, and we ourselves frighteningly inert.

Technological determination is only one ideological space opened up by the reconceptions of machine and organism as coded texts through which we engage in the play of writing and reading the world.[3] "Textualization" of everything in poststructuralist, postmodernist theory has been damned by Marxists and socialist feminists for its utopian disregard for the lived relations of domination that ground the "play" of arbitrary reading.[4] It is certainly true that postmodernist strategies, like my cyborg myth, subvert myriad organic wholes (for example, the poem, the primitive culture, the biological organism). In short, the certainty of what counts as nature—a source of insight and promise of innocence—is undermined, probably fatally. The transcendent authorization of interpretation is lost, and with it the ontology grounding "Western" epistemology. But the alternative is not cynicism or faithlessness, that is, some version of abstract existence, like the accounts of technological determinism destroying "man" by the "machine" or "meaningful political action" by the "text." Who cyborgs will be is a radical question; the answers are a matter of survival. Both chimpanzees and artefacts have politics, so why shouldn't we (de Waal, 1982; Winner, 1980)?

The third distinction is a subset of the second: the boundary between physical and non-physical is very imprecise for us. Pop physics books on the consequences of quantum theory and the indeterminacy principle are a kind of popular scientific equivalent to Harlequin romances [The US equivalent of Mills & Boon] as a marker of radical change in American white heterosexuality: they get it wrong, but they are on the right subject. Modern machines are quintessentially microelectronic devices: they are everywhere and they are invisible. Modern machinery is an irreverent upstart god, mocking the Father's ubiquity and spirituality. The silicon chip is a surface for writing; it is etched in molecular scales disturbed only by atomic noise, the ultimate interference for nuclear scores. Writing, power, and technology are old partners in Western stories of the origin of civilization, but miniaturization has changed our experience of mechanism. Miniaturization has turned out to be about power; small is not so much beautiful as pre-eminently dangerous, as in cruise missiles. Contrast the TV sets of the 1950s or the news cameras of the 1970s with the TV wrist bands or hand-sized video cameras now advertised. Our best machines are made of sunshine; they are all light and clean because they are nothing but signals, electromagnetic waves, a section of a spectrum, and these machines are eminently portable, mobile—a matter of immense human pain in Detroit and Singapore. People are nowhere near so fluid, being both material and opaque. Cyborgs are ether, quintessence.

The ubiquity and invisibility of cyborgs is precisely why these sunshine-belt machines are so deadly. They are as hard to see politically as materially. They are about consciousness—or its simulation.[5] They are floating signifiers moving in pickup trucks across Europe, blocked more effectively by the witch-weavings of the displaced and so unnatural Greenham women, who read the cyborg webs of power so very well, than by the militant labour of older masculinist politics, whose natural constituency needs defence jobs. Ultimately the "hardest" science is about the realm of greatest boundary confusion, the realm of pure number, pure spirit, C[3]I, cryptography, and the preservation of potent secrets. The new machines are so clean and light. Their engineers are sun-worshippers mediating a new scientific revolution associated with the night dream of post-industrial society. The diseases evoked by these clean machines are "no more" than the minuscule coding changes of an antigen in the immune system, "no more" than the experience of stress. The nimble fingers of "Oriental" women, the old fascination of little Anglo-Saxon Victorian girls with doll's houses, women's enforced attention to the small take on quite new dimensions in this world. There might be a cyborg Alice taking account of these new dimensions. Ironically, it might be the unnatural cyborg women making chips in Asia and spiral dancing in Santa Rita jail [a practice at once both spiritual and political that linked guards and arrested anti-nuclear demonstrators in the Alameda Country jail in California in the early 1980s] whose constructed unities will guide effective oppositional strategies.

So my cyborg myth is about transgressed boundaries, potent fusions, and dangerous possibilities which progressive people might explore as one part of needed political work. One of my premises is that most American socialists and feminists see deepened dualisms of mind and body, animal and machine, idealism and materialism in the social practices, symbolic formulations, and physical artefacts associated with "high technology" and scientific culture. From *One-Dimensional Man* (Marcuse, 1964) to *The Death of Nature* (Merchant, 1980), the analytic resources developed by progressives have insisted on the necessary domination of technics and recalled us to an imagined organic body to integrate our resistance. Another of my premises is that the need for unity of people trying to resist world-wide intensification of domination has never been more acute. But a slightly perverse shift of perspective might better enable us to contest for meanings, as well as for other forms of power and pleasure in technologically mediated societies.

From one perspective, a cyborg world is about the final imposition of a grid of control on the planet, about the final abstraction embodied in a Star Wars apocalypse waged in the name of defence, about the final appropriation of women's bodies in a masculinist orgy of war (Sofia, 1984). From another perspective, a cyborg world might be about lived social and bodily realities in which people are not afraid of their joint kinship with animals and machines, not afraid of permanently partial identities and contradictory standpoints. The political struggle is to see from both perspectives at once because each reveals both dominations and possibilities unimaginable from the other vantage point. Single vision produces worse illusions than double vision or many-headed monsters. Cyborg unities are monstrous and illegitimate; in our present political circumstances, we could hardly hope for more potent myths for resistance and recoupling, I like to imagine LAG, the Livermore Action Group, as a kind of cyborg society, dedicated to realistically converting the laboratories that most fiercely embody and spew out the tools of technological apocalypse, and committed to building a political form that actually manages to hold together witches, engineers, elders, perverts, Christians, mothers, and Leninists long enough to disarm the state. Fission Impossible is the name of the affinity group in my town. (Affinity; related not by blood but by choice, the appeal of one chemical nuclear group for another, avidity.)[6]

Fractured Identities

It has become difficult to name one's feminism by a single adjective—or even to insist in every circumstance upon the noun. Consciousness of exclusion through naming is acute. Identities seem contradictory, partial, and strategic. With the hard-won recognition of their social and historical constitution, gender, race, and class cannot provide the basis for belief in "essential" unity. There is nothing about being "female" that naturally binds women. There is not even such a state as "being" female, itself a highly complex category constructed in contested sexual scientific discourses and other social practices. Gender, race, or class consciousness is an achievement forced on us by the terrible historical experience of the contradictory social realities of patriarchy, colonialism, and capitalism. And who counts as "us" in my own rhetoric? Which identities are available to ground such a potent political myth called "us," and what could motivate enlistment in this collectivity? Painful fragmentation among feminists (not to mention among women) along every possible fault line has made the concept of *woman* elusive, an excuse for the matrix of women's dominations of each other. For me—and for many who share a similar historical location in white, professional middle-class, female, radical, North American, mid-adult bodies—the sources of a crisis in political identity are legion. The recent history for much of the US left and US feminism has been a response to this kind of crisis by endless splitting and searches for a new essential unity. But there has also been a growing recognition of another response through coalition—affinity, not identity.[7]

Chela Sandoval (n.d., 1984), from a consideration of specific historical moments in the formation of the new political voice called women of colour, has theorized a hopeful model of political identity called "oppositional conscious- ness," born of the skills for reading webs of power by those refused stable mem- bership in the social categories of race, sex, or class. "Women of color," a name contested at its origins by those whom it would incorporate, as well as a histori- cal consciousness marking systematic breakdown of all the signs of Man in "Western" traditions, constructs a kind of postmodernist identity out of other- ness, difference, and specificity. This postmodernist identity is fully political, whatever might be said about other possible postmodernisms. Sandoval's opposi- tional consciousness is about contradictory locations and heterochronic calen- dars, not about relativisms and pluralisms.

Sandoval emphasizes the lack of any essential criterion for identifying who is a woman of colour. She notes that the definition of the group has been by con- scious appropriation of negation. For example, a Chicana or US black woman has not been able to speak as a woman or as a black person or as a Chicano. Thus, she was at the bottom of a cascade of negative identities, left out of even the privileged oppressed authorial categories called "woman and blacks," who claimed to make the important revolutions. The category "woman" negated all non-white women; "black" negated all non-black people, as well as all black women. But there was also no "she," no singularity, but a sea of differences among US women who have affirmed their historical identity as US women of colour. This identity marks out a self-consciously constructed space that cannot affirm the capacity to act on the basis of natural identification, but only on the basis of conscious coalition, of affinity, of political kinship.[8] Unlike the "woman" of some streams of the white women's movement in the United States, there is no naturalization of the matrix, or at least this is what Sandoval argues is uniquely available through the power of oppositional consciousness.

Sandoval's argument has to be seen as one potent formulation for feminists out of the world-wide development of anti-colonialist discourse; that is to say, discourse dissolving the "West" and its highest product—the one who is not ani- mal, barbarian, or woman; man, that is, the author of a cosmos called history. As orientalism is deconstructed politically and semiotically, the identities of the occi- dent destabilize, including those of feminists.[9] Sandoval argues that "women of colour" have a chance to build an effective unity that does not replicate the impe- rializing, totalizing revolutionary subjects of previous Marxisms and feminisms which had not faced the consequences of the disorderly polyphony emerging from decolonization.

Katie King has emphasized the limits of identification and the political/poetic mechanics of identification built into reading "the poem," that generative core of cultural feminism. King criticizes the persistent tendency among contemporary feminists from different "moments" or "conversations" in feminist practice to taxonomize the women's movement to make one's own political tendencies appear to be the *telos* of the whole. These taxonomies tend to remake feminist history so that it appears to be an ideological struggle among coherent types persisting over time, especially those typical units called radical, liberal, and socialist-feminism. Literally, all other feminisms are either incorporated or marginalized, usually by building an explicit ontology and epistemology.[10] Taxonomies of feminism produce epistemologies to police deviation from official women's experience. And of course, "women's culture," like women of colour, is consciously created by mechanisms inducing affinity. The rituals of poetry, music, and certain forms of academic practice have been pre-eminent. The politics of race and culture in the US women's movements are intimately interwoven. The common achievement of King and Sandoval is learning how to craft a poetic/political unity without relying on a logic of appropriation, incorporation, and taxonomic identification.

The theoretical and practical struggle against unity-through-domination or unity-through-incorporation ironically not only undermines the justifications for patriarchy, colonialism, humanism, positivism, essentialism, scientism, and other unlamented -isms, but *all* claims for an organic or natural standpoint I think that radical and socialist/Marxist-feminisms have also undermined their/our own epistemological strategies and that this is a crucially valuable step in imagining possible unities. It remains to be seen whether all "epistemologies" as Western political people have known them fail us in the task to build effective affinities.

It is important to note that the effort to construct revolutionary standpoints, epistemologies as achievements of people committed to changing the world, has been part of the process showing the limits of identification. The acid tools of postmodernist theory and the constructive tools of ontological discourse about revolutionary subjects might be seen as ironic allies in dissolving Western selves in the interests of survival. We are excruciatingly conscious of what it means to have a historically constituted body. But with the loss of innocence in our origin, there is no expulsion from the Garden either. Our politics lose the indulgence of guilt with the *naïveté* of innocence. But what would another political myth for socialist-feminism look like? What kind of politics could embrace partial, contradictory, permanently unclosed constructions of personal and collective selves and still be faithful, effective—and, ironically, socialist-feminist?

I do not know of any other time in history when there was greater need for political unity to confront effectively the dominations of "race," "gender," "sexuality," and "class." I also do not know of any other time when the kind of unity we might help build could have been possible. None of "us" have any longer the symbolic or material capability of dictating the shape of reality to any of "them." Or at least "we" cannot claim innocence from practising such dominations. White women, including socialist feminists, discovered (that is, were forced kicking and screaming to notice) the non-innocence of the category "woman." That consciousness changes the geography of all previous categories; it denatures them as heat denatures a fragile protein. Cyborg feminists have to argue that "we" do not want any more natural matrix of unity and that no construction is whole. Innocence, and the corollary insistence on victimhood as the only ground for insight, has done enough damage. But the constructed revolutionary subject must give late-twentieth-century people pause as well. In the fraying of identities and in the reflexive strategies for constructing them, the possibility opens up for weaving something other than a shroud for the day after the apocalypse that so prophetically ends salvation history.

Both Marxist/socialist-feminisms and radical feminisms have simultaneously naturalized and denatured the category "woman" and consciousness of the social lives of "women." Perhaps a schematic caricature can highlight both kinds of moves. Marxian socialism is rooted in an analysis of wage labour which reveals class structure. The consequence of the wage relationship is systematic alienation, as the worker is dissociated from his (sic) product. Abstraction and illusion rule in knowledge, domination rules in practice. Labour is the pre-eminently privileged category enabling the Marxist to overcome illusion and find that point of view which is necessary for changing the world. Labour is the humanizing activity that makes man; labour is an ontological category permitting the knowledge of a subject, and so the knowledge of subjugation and alienation.

In faithful filiation, socialist-feminism advanced by allying itself with the basic analytic strategies of Marxism. The main achievement of both Marxist feminists and socialist feminist was to expand the category of labour to accommodate what (some) women did, even when the wage relation was subordinated to a more comprehensive view of labour under capitalist patriarchy. In particular, women's labour in the household and women's activity as mothers generally (that is, reproduction in the socialist-feminist sense), entered theory on the authority of analogy to the Marxian concept of labour. The unity of women here rests on an epistemology based on the ontological structure of "labour." Marxist/socialist-feminism does not "naturalize" unity; it is a possible achievement based on a possible standpoint rooted in social relations. The essentializing move is in the ontological structure of labour or of its analogue, women's activity.[11] The inheritance of Marxian humanism, with its pre-eminently Western self, is the difficulty for me. The contribution from these formulations has been the emphasis on the daily responsibility of real women to build unities, rather than to naturalize them.

Catherine MacKinnon's (1982, 1987) version of radical feminism is itself a caricature of the appropriating, incorporating, totalizing tendencies of Western theories of identity grounding action.[12] It is factually and politically wrong to assimilate all of the diverse "moments" or "conversations" in recent women's politics named radical feminism to MacKinnon's version. But the teleological logic of her theory shows how an epistemology and ontology—including their negations—erase or police difference. Only one of the effects of MacKinnon's theory is the rewriting of the history of the polymorphous field called radical feminism. The major effect is the production of a theory of experience, of women's identity, that is a kind of apocalypse for all revolutionary standpoints. That is, the totalization built into this tale of radical feminism achieves its end—the unity of women—by enforcing the experience of and testimony to radical non-being.

As for the Marxist/socialist feminist, consciousness is an achievement, not a natural fact. And MacKinnon's theory eliminates some of the difficulties built into humanist revolutionary subjects, but at the cost of radical reductionism.

MacKinnon argues that feminism necessarily adopted a different analytical strategy from Marxism, looking first not at the structure of class, but at the structure of sex/gender and its generative relationship, men's constitution and appropriation of women sexually. Ironically, MacKinnon's "ontology" constructs a non-subject, a non-being. Another's desire, not the self's labour, is the origin of "woman." She therefore develops a theory of consciousness that enforces what can count as "women's experience—anything that names sexual violation, indeed, sex itself as far as "women" can be concerned. Feminist practice is the construction of this form of consciousness; that is, the self-knowledge of a self-who-is-not.

Perversely, sexual appropriation in this feminism still has the epistemological status of labour; that is to say, the point from which an analysis able to contribute to changing the world must flow. But sexual objectification, not alienation, is the consequence of the structure of sex/gender. In the realm of knowledge, the result of sexual objectification is illusion and abstraction. However, a women is not simply alienated from her product, but in a deep sense does not exist as a subject, or even potential subject, since she owes her existence as a woman to sexual appropriation. To be constituted by another's desire is not the same thing as to be alienated in the violent separation of the labourer from his product.

MacKinnon's radical theory of experience is totalizing in the extreme; it does not so much marginalize as obliterate the authority of any other women's political speech and action. It is a totalization producing what Western patriarchy itself never succeeded in doing—feminists' consciousness of the nonexistence of women, except as products of men's desire. I think MacKinnon correctly argues that no Marxian version of identity can firmly ground women's unity. But in solving the problem of the contradictions of any Western revolutionary subject for feminist purposes, she develops an even more authoritarian doctrine of experience. If my complaint about socialist/Marxian standpoints is their unintended erasure of polyvocal, unassimilable, radical difference made visible in anti-colonial discourse and practice, MacKinnon's intentional erasure of all difference through the device of the "essential" non-existence of women is not reassuring.

In my taxonomy, which like any other taxonomy is a re-inscription of history, radical feminism can accommodate all the activities of women named by socialist feminists as forms of labour only if the activity can somehow be sexualized. Reproduction had different tones of meanings for the two tendencies, one rooted in labour, one in sex, both calling the consequences of domination and ignorance of social and personal reality "false consciousness."

Beyond either the difficulties or the contributions in the argument of any one author, neither Marxist nor radical feminist points of view have tended to embrace the status of a partial explanation; both were regularly constituted as totalities. Western explanation has demanded as much; how else could the "Western" author incorporate its others? Each tried to annex other forms of domination by expanding its basic categories through analogy, simple listing, or addition. Embarrassed silence about race among white radical and socialist feminists was one major, devastating political consequence. History and polyvocality disappear into political taxonomies that try to establish genealogies. There was no structural room for race (or for much else) in theory claiming to reveal the construction of the category woman and social group women as a unified or totalizable whole. The structure of my caricature looks like this:

> socialist feminism—structure of
>   class//wage labour//alienation
> labour, by analogy reproduction, by
>   extension sex, by addition race
> radical feminism—structure of
>   gender//sexual
>   appropriation//objectification
> sex, by analogy labour, by extension
>   reproduction, by addition race

In another context, the French theorist, Julia Kristeva, claimed women appeared as a historical group after the Second World War, along with groups like youth. Her dates are doubtful; but we are now accustomed to remembering that as objects of knowledge and as historical actors, "race" did not always exist, "class" has a historical genesis, and "homosexuals" are quite junior. It is no accident that the symbolic system of the family of man—and so the essence of woman—breaks up at the same moment that networks of connection among people on the planet are unprecedentedly multiple, pregnant, and complex. "Advanced capitalism" is inadequate to convey the structure of this historical moment. In the "Western" sense, the end of man is at stake. It is no accident that woman disintegrates into women in our time. Perhaps socialist feminists were not substantially guilty of producing essentialist theory that suppressed women's particularity and contradictory interests. I think we have been, at least through unreflective participation in the logics, languages, and practices of white humanism and through searching for a single ground of domination to secure our revolutionary voice. Now we have less excuse. But in the consciousness of our failures, we risk lapsing into boundless difference and giving up on the confusing task of making partial, real connection. Some difference are playful; some are poles of world historical systems of domination. "Epistemology" is about knowing the difference.

The Informatics of Domination

In this attempt at an epistemological and political position, I would like to sketch a picture of possible unity, a picture indebted to socialist and feminist principles of design. The frame for my sketch is set by the extent and importance of rearrangements in world-wide social relations tied to science and technology. I argue for a politics rooted in claims about fundamental changes in the nature of class, race, and gender in an emerging system of world order analogous in its novelty and scope to that created by industrial capitalism; we are living through a movement from an organic, industrial society to a polymorphous, information system—from all work to all play, a deadly game. Simultaneously material and ideological, the dichotomies may be expressed in the following chart of transitions from the comfortable old hierarchical dominations to the scary new networks I have called the informatics of domination:

Representation	Simulation
Bourgeois novel, realism	Science fiction, postmodernism
Organism	Biotic component
Depth, integrity	Surface, boundary
Heat	Noise
Biology as clinical practice	Biology as inscription
Physiology	Communications engineering
Small group	Subsystem
Perfection	Optimization
Eugenics	Population Control
Decadence, *Magic Mountain*	Obsolescence, *Future Shock*
Hygiene	Stress Management
Microbiology, tuberculosis	Immunology, AIDS
Organic division of labour	Ergonomics/cybernetics of labour
Functional specialization	Modular construction
Reproduction	Replication
Organic sex role specialization	Optimal genetic strategies
Biological determinism	Evolutionary inertia, constraints
Community ecology	Ecosystem
Racial chain of being	Neo-imperialism, United Nations humanism
Scientific management in home/factory	Global factory/Electronic cottage
Family/Market/Factory	Women in the Integrated Circuit
Family wage	Comparable worth
Public/Private	Cyborg citizenship
Nature/Culture	Fields of difference
Co-operation	Communications enhancement

Freud	Lacan
Sex	Genetic engineering
Labour	Robotics
Mind	Artifical Intelligence
Second World War	Star Wars
White Capitalist	Informatics of
Patriarchy	Domination

This list suggests several interesting things.[13] First, the objects on the right-hand side cannot be coded as "natural," a realization that subverts naturalistic coding for the left-hand side as well. We cannot go back ideologically or materially. It's not just that "god" is dead; so is the "goddess." Or both are revivified in the worlds charged with microelectronic and biotechnological politics. In relation to objects like biotic components, one must think not in terms of essential properties, but in terms of design, boundary constraints, rates of flows, systems logics, costs of lowering constraints. Sexual reproduction is one kind of reproductive strategy among many, with costs and benefits as a function of the system environment. Ideologies of sexual reproduction can no longer reasonably call on notions of sex and sex role as organic aspects in natural object like organisms and families. Such reasoning will be unmasked as irrational, and ironically corporate executives reading *Playboy* and anti-porn radical feminists will make strange bedfellows in jointly unmasking the irrationalism.

Likewise for race, ideologies about human diversity have to be formulated in terms of frequencies of parameters, like blood groups or intelligence scores. It is "irrational" to invoke concepts like primitive and civilized. For liberals and radicals, the search for integrated social systems gives way to a new practice called "experimental ethnography" in which an organic object dissipates in attention to the play of writing. At the level of ideology, we see translations of racism and colonialism into languages of development and under-development, rates and constraints of modernization. Any objects or persons can be reasonably thought of in terms of disassembly and reassembly; no "natural" architectures constrain system design. The financial districts in all the world's cities, as well as the export-processing and free-trade zones, proclaim this elementary fact of "late capitalism." The entire universe of objects that can be known scientifically must be formulated as problems in communications engineering (for the managers) or theories of the text (for those who would resist). Both are cyborg semiologies.

One should expect control strategies to concentrate on boundary conditions and interfaces, on rates of flow across boundaries—and not on the integrity of natural objects. "Integrity" or "sincerity" of the Western self gives way to decision procedures and expert systems. For example, control strategies applied to women's capacities to give birth to new human beings will be developed in the languages of population control and maximization of goal achievement for individual decision-makers. Control strategies will be formulated in terms of rates, costs of constraints, degrees of freedom. Human beings, like any other component or subsystem, must be localized in a system architecture whose basic modes of operation are probabilistic, statistical. No objects, spaces, or bodies are sacred in themselves; any component can be interfaced with any other if the proper standard, the proper code, can be constructed for processing signals in a common language. Exchange in this world transcends the universal translation effected by capitalist markets that Marx analysed so well. The privileged pathology affecting all kinds of components in this universe is stress—communications breakdown (Hogness, 1983). The cyborg is not subject to Foucault's biopolitics; the cyborg simulates politics, a much more potent field of operations.

This kind of analysis of scientific and cultural objects of knowledge which have appeared historically since the Second World War prepares us to notice some important inadequacies in feminist analysis which has proceeded as if the organic, hierarchical dualisms ordering discourse in "the West" since Aristotle still ruled. They have been cannibalized, or as Zoe Sofia (Sofoulis) might put it, they have been "techno-digested." The dichotomies between mind and body, animal and human, organism and machine, public and private, nature and culture, men and women, primitive and civilized are all in question ideologically. The actual situation of women is their integration/exploitation into a world system of production/reproduction and communication called the informatics of domination. The home, workplace, market, public arena, the body itself—all can be dispersed and interfaced in nearly infinite, polymorphous ways, with large consequences for women and others—consequences that themselves are very different for different people and which make potent oppositional international movements difficult to imagine and essential for survival. One important route for reconstructing socialist-feminist politics is through theory and practice addressed to the social relations of science and technology, including crucially the systems of myth and meanings structuring our imaginations. The cyborg is a kind of disassembled and reassembled, postmodern collective and personal self. This is the self feminists must code.

Communications technologies and biotechnologies are the crucial tools recrafting our bodies. These tools embody and enforce new social relations for women world-wide. Technologies and scientific discourses can be partially understood as formalizations, i.e., as frozen moments, of the fluid social interactions constituting them, but they should also be viewed as instruments for enforcing meanings. The boundary between tool and myth, instrument and concept, historical systems of social relations and historical anatomies of possible bodies, including objects of knowledge. Indeed, myth and tool mutually constitute each other.

Furthermore, communications sciences and modern biologies are constructed by a common move—*the translation of the world into a problem of coding,* a search for a common language in which all resistance to instrumental control disappears and all heterogeneity can be submitted to disassembly, reassembly, investment, and exchange.

In communications sciences, the translation of the world into a problem in coding can be illustrated by looking at cybernetic (feedback-controlled) systems theories applied to telephone technology, computer design, weapons deployment, or data base construction and maintenance. In each case, solution to the key questions rests on a theory of language and control; the key operation is determining the rates, directions, and probabilities of flow of a quantity called information. The world is subdivided by boundaries differentially permeable to information. Information is just that kind of quantifiable element (unit, basis of unity) which allows universal translation, and so unhindered instrumental power (called effective communication). The biggest threat to such power is interruption of communication. Any system breakdown is a function of stress. The fundamentals of this technology can be condensed into the metaphor C^3I, command-control-communication-intelligence, the military's symbol for its operations theory.

In modern biologies, the translation of the world into a problem in coding can be illustrated by molecular genetics, ecology, sociobiological evolutionary theory, and immunobiology. The organism has been translated into problems of genetic coding and read-out. Biotechnology, a writing technology, informs research broadly.[14] In a sense, organisms have ceased to exist as objects of knowledge, giving way to biotic components, i.e., special kinds of information-processing devices. The analogous moves in ecology could be examined by probing the history and utility of the concept of the ecosystem. Immunobiology and associated medical practices are rich exemplars of the privilege of coding and recognition systems as objects of knowledge, as constructions of bodily reality for us. Biology here is a kind of cryptography. Research is necessarily a kind of intelligence activity. Ironies abound. A stressed system goes awry; its communication processes break down; it fails to recognize the difference between self and other. Human babies with baboon hearts evoke national ethical perplexity—for animal rights activists at least as much as for the guardians of human purity. In the US gay men and intravenous drug users are the "privileged" victims of an awful immune system disease that marks (inscribes on the body) confusion of boundaries and moral pollution (Treichler, 1987).

But these excursions into communications sciences and biology have been at a rarefied level; there is a mundane, largely economic reality to support my claim that these sciences and technologies indicate fundamental transformations in the structure of the world for us. Communications technologies depend on electronics. Modern states, multinational corporations, military power, welfare state apparatuses, satellite systems, political processes, fabrication of our imaginations, labour-control systems, medical constructions of our bodies, commercial pornography, the international division of labour, and religious evangelism depend intimately upon electronics. Microelectronics is the technical basis of simulacra; that is, of copies without originals.

Microelectronics mediates the translations of labour into robotics and word processing, sex into genetic engineering and reproductive technologies, and mind into artificial intelligence and decision procedures. The new biotechnologies concern more than human reproduction. Biology as a powerful engineering science for redesigning materials and processes has revolutionary implications for industry, perhaps most obvious today in areas of fermentation, agriculture, and energy. Communications sciences and biology are constructions of natural-technical objects of knowledge in which the difference between machine and organism is thoroughly blurred; mind, body, and tool are on very intimate terms. The "multinational" material organization of the production and reproduction of daily life and the symbolic organization of the production of culture and imagination seem equally implicated. The boundary-maintaining images of base and superstructure, public and private, or material and ideal never seemed more feeble.

I have used Rachel Grossman's (1980) image of women in the integrated circuit to name the situation of women in a world so intimately restructured through the social relations of science and technology.[15] I used the odd circumlocution, "the social relations of science and technology," to indicate that we are not dealing with a technological determinism, but with a historical system depending upon structured relations among people. But the phrase should also indicate that science and technology provide fresh sources of power, that we need fresh sources of analysis and political action (Latour, 1984). Some of the rearrangements of race, sex, and class rooted in high-tech-facilitated social relations can make socialist-feminism more relevant to effective progressive politics.

The "Homework Economy" Outside "The Home"

The "New Industrial Revolution" is producing a new world-wide working class, as well as new sexualities and ethnicities. The extreme mobility of capital and the emerging international division of labour are intertwined with the emergence of new collectivities, and the weakening of familiar groupings. These developments are neither gender- nor race-neutral. White men in advanced industrial societies have become newly vulnerable to permanent job loss, and women are not disappearing from the job rolls at the same rates as men. It is not simply that women in Third World countries are the preferred labour force for the science-based multinationals in the export-processing sectors, particularly in electronics. The picture is more systematic and involves reproduction, sexuality, culture, consumption, and production. In the prototypical Silicon Valley, many women's lives have been structured around employment in electronics-dependent jobs, and their intimate realities include serial heterosexual monogamy, negotiating childcare, distance from extended kin or most other forms of traditional community, a high likelihood of loneliness and extreme economic vulnerability as they age. The ethnic and racial diversity of women in Silicon Valley structures a microcosm of conflicting differences in culture, family, religion, education, and language.

Richard Gordon has called this new situation the "homework economy."[16] Although he includes the phenomenon of literal homework emerging in connection with electronics assembly, Gordon intends "homework economy" to name a restructuring of work that broadly has the characteristics formerly ascribed to female jobs, jobs literally done only by women. Work is being redefined as both literally female and feminized, whether performed by men or women. To be feminized means to be made extremely vulnerable; able to be disassembled, reassembled, exploited as a reserve labour force; seen less as workers than as servers; subjected to time arrangements on and off the paid job that make a mockery of a limited work day; leading an existence that always borders on being obscene, out of place, and reducible to sex. Deskilling is an old strategy newly applicable to formerly privileged workers. However, the homework economy does not refer only to large-scale deskilling, nor does it deny that new areas of high skill are emerging, even for women and men previously excluded from skilled employment. Rather, the concept indicates that factory, home, and market are integrated on a new scale and that the places of women are crucial—and need to be analysed for differences among women and for meanings for relations between men and women in various situations.

The homework economy as a world capitalist organizational structure is made possible by (not caused by) the new technologies. The success of the attack on relatively privileged, mostly white, men's unionized jobs is tied to the power of the new communications technologies to integrate and control labour despite extensive dispersion and decentralization. The consequences of the new technologies are felt by women both in the loss of the family (male) wage (if they ever had access to this white privilege) and in the character of their own jobs, which are becoming capital-intensive; for example, office work and nursing.

The new economic and technological arrangements are also related to the collapsing welfare state and the ensuing intensification of demands on women to sustain daily life for themselves as well as for men, children, and old people. The feminization of poverty—generated by dismantling the welfare state, by the homework economy where stable jobs become the exception, and sustained by the expectation that women's wages will not be matched by a male income for the support of children—has become an urgent focus. The causes of various women-headed households are a function of race, class, or sexuality; but their increasing generality is a ground for coalitions of women on many issues. That women regularly sustain daily life partly as a function of their enforced status as mothers is hardly new; the kind of integration with the overall capitalist and progressively war-based economy is new. The particular pressure, for example, on US black women, who have achieved an escape from (barely) paid domestic service and who now hold clerical and similar jobs in large numbers, has large implications for continued enforced black poverty *with* employment. Teenage women in industrializing areas of the Third World increasingly find themselves the sole or major source of a cash wage for their families, while access to land is ever more problematic. These developments must have major consequences in the psychodynamics and politics of gender and race.

Within the framework of three major stages of capitalism (commercial/early industrial, monopoly, multinational)—tied to nationalism, imperialism, and multinationalism, and related to Jameson's three dominant aesthetic periods of realism, modernism, and postmodernism—I would argue that specific forms of families dialectically relate to forms of capital and to its political and cultural concomitants. Although lived problematically and unequally, ideal forms of these families might be schematized as (1) the patriarchal nuclear family, structured by the dichotomy between public and private and accompanied by the white bourgeois ideology of separate spheres and nineteenth-century Anglo-American bourgeois feminism; (2) the modern family mediated (or enforced) by the welfare state and institutions like the family wage, with a flowering of a-feminist heterosexual ideologies, including their radical versions presented in Greenwich Village around the First World War, and (3) the "family" of the homework economy with its oxymoronic structure of women-headed households and its explosion of feminisms and the paradoxical intensification and erosion of gender itself. This is the context in which the projections for world-wide structural unemployment stemming from the new technologies are part of the picture of the homework economy. As robotics and related technologies put men out of work in "developed" countries and exacerbate failure to generate male jobs in Third World "development," and as the automated office becomes the rule even in labour-surplus countries, the feminization of work intensifies. Black women in the United States have long known what it looks like to face the structural underemployment ("feminization") of black men, as well as their own highly vulnerable position in the wage economy. It is no longer a secret that sexuality, reproduction, family, and community life are interwoven with this economic structure in myriad ways which have also differentiated the situations of white and black women. Many more women and men will contend with similar situations, which will make cross-gender and race alliances on issues of basic life support (with or without jobs) necessary, not just nice.

The new technologies also have a profound effect on hunger and on food production for subsistence world-wide. Rae Lessor Blumberg (1983) estimates that women produce about 50 per cent of the world's subsistence food.[17] Women are excluded generally from benefiting from the increased high-tech commodification of food and energy crops, their days are made more arduous because their responsibilities to provide food do not diminish, and their reproductive situations are made more complex. Green Revolution technologies interact with other high-tech industrial production to alter gender divisions of labour and differential gender migration patterns.

The new technologies seem deeply involved in the forms of "privitization" that Ros Petchesky (1981) has analysed, in which militarization, right-wing family ideologies and policies, and intensified definitions of corporate (and state) property as private synergistically interact.[18] The new communications technologies are fundamental to the eradication of "public life" for everyone. This facilitates the mushrooming of a permanent high-tech military establishment at the cultural and economic expense of most people, but especially of women. Technologies like video games and highly miniaturized televisions seem crucial to production of modern forms of "private life." The culture of video games is heavily orientated to individual competition and extraterrestrial warfare. High-tech, gendered imaginations are produced here, imaginations that can contemplate destruction of the planet and a sci-fi escape from its consequences. More than our imaginations is militarized; and the other realities of electronic and nuclear warfare are inescapable. These are the technologies that promise ultimate mobility and perfect exchange—and incidentally enable tourism, that perfect practice of mobility and exchange, to emerge as one of the world's largest single industries.

The new technologies affect the social relations of both sexuality and of reproduction, and not always in the same ways. The close ties of sexuality and instrumentality, of views of the body as a kind of private satisfaction- and utility-maximizing machine, are described nicely in sociobiological origin stories that stress a genetic calculus and explain the inevitable dialectic of domination of male and female gender roles.[19] These sociobiological stories depend on a high-tech view of the body as a biotic component or cybernetic communications system. Among the many transformations of reproductive situations is the medical one, where women's bodies have boundaries newly permeable to both "visualization" and "intervention." Of course, who controls the interpretation of bodily boundaries in medical hermeneutics is a major feminist issue. The speculum served as an icon of women's claiming their bodies in the 1970s; that handcraft tool is inadequate to express our needed body politics in the negotiation of reality in the practices of cyborg reproduction. Self-help is not enough. The technologies of visualization recall the important cultural practice of hunting with the camera and the deeply predatory nature of a photographic consciousness.[20] Sex, sexuality, and reproduction are central actors in high-tech myth systems structuring our imaginations of personal and social possibility.

Another critical aspect of the social relations of the new technologies is the reformulation of expectations, culture, work, and reproduction for the large scientific and technical work-force. A major social and political danger is the formation of a strongly bimodal social structure, with the masses of women and men of all ethnic groups, but especially people of colour, confined to a home work economy, illiteracy of several varieties, and general redundancy and impotence, controlled by high-tech repressive apparatuses ranging from entertainment to surveillance and disappearance. An adequate socialist-feminist politics should address women in the privileged occupational categories, and particularly in the production of science and technology that constructs scientific-technical discourses, processes, and objects.[21]

This issue is only one aspect of enquiry into the possibility of a feminist science, but it is important. What kind of constitutive role in the production of knowledge, imagination, and practice can new groups doing science have? How can these groups be allied with progressive social and political movements? What kind of political accountability can be constructed to tie women together across the scientific-technical hierarchies separating us? Might there be ways of developing feminist science/technology politics in alliance with anti-military science facility conversion action groups? Many scientific and technical workers in Silicon Valley, the high-tech cowboys included, do not want to work on military science.[22] Can these personal preferences and cultural tendencies be welded into progressive politics among this professional middle class in which women, including women of colour, are coming to be fairly numerous?

Women in the Integrated Circuit

Let me summarize the picture of women's historical locations in advanced industrial societies, as these positions have been restructured partly through the social relations of science and technology. If it was ever possible ideologically to characterize women's lives by the distinction of public and private domains—suggested by images of the division of working-class life into factory and home, of bourgeois life into market and home, and of gender existence into personal and political realms—it is now a totally misleading ideology, even to show how both terms of these dichotomies construct each other in practice and in theory. I prefer a network ideological image, suggesting the profusion of spaces and identities and the permeability of boundaries in the personal body and in the body politic. "Networking" is both a feminist practice and a multinational corporate strategy—weaving is for oppositional cyborgs.

So let me return to the earlier image of the informatics of domination and trace one vision of women's "place" in the integrated circuit, touching only a few idealized social locations seen primarily from the point of view of advanced capitalist societies: Home, Market, Paid Work Place, State, School, Clinic-Hospital, and Church. Each of these idealized spaces is logically and practically implied in every other locus, perhaps analogous to a holographic photograph. I want to suggest the impact of the social relations mediated and enforced by the new technologies in order to help formulate needed analysis and practical work. However, there is no "place" for women in these networks, only geometrics of difference and contradiction crucial to women's cyborg identities. If we learn how to read these webs of power and social life, we might learn new couplings, new coalitions. There is no way to read the following list from a standpoint of "identification," of a unitary self. The issue is dispersion. The task is to survive in the diaspora.

> *Home:* Women-headed households, serial monogamy, flight of men, old women alone, technology of domestic work, paid homework, reemergence of home sweat-shops, home-based businesses and telecommuting, electronic cottage, urban homelessness, migration, module architecture, reinforced (simulated) nuclear family, intense domestic violence.
>
> *Market:* Women's continuing consumption work, newly targeted to buy the profusion of new production from the new technologies (especially as the competitive race among industrialized and industrializing nations to avoid dangerous mass unemployment necessitates finding ever bigger new markets for ever less clearly needed commodities); bimodal buying power, coupled with advertising targeting of the numerous affluent groups and neglect of the previous mass markets; growing importance of informal markets in labour and commodities parallel to high-tech, affluent market structures; surveillance systems through electronic funds transfer; intensified market abstraction (commodification) of experience, resulting in ineffective utopian or equivalent cynical theories of community; extreme mobility (abstraction) of marketing/financing systems; interpenetration of sexual and labour markets; intensified sexualization of abstracted and alienated consumption.
>
> *Paid Work Place:* Continued intense sexual and racial division of labour, but considerable growth of membership in privileged occupational categories for many white women and people of colour; impact of new technologies on women's work in clerical, service, manufacturing (especially textiles), agriculture, electronics; international restructuring of the working classes; development of new time arrangements to facilitate the homework economy (flex time, part time, over time, no time); homework and out work; increased pressures for two-tiered wage structures; significant numbers of people in cash-dependent populations world-wide with no experience or no further hope of stable employment; most labour "marginal" or "feminized."

State: Continued erosion of the welfare state; decentralizations with increased surveillance and control; citizenship by telematics; imperialism and political power broadly in the form of information rich/information poor differentiation; increased high-tech militarization increasingly opposed by many social groups; reduction of civil service jobs as a result of the growing capital intensification of office work, with implications for occupational mobility for women of color; growing privatization of material and ideological life and culture; close integration of privatization and militarization, the high-tech forms of bourgeois capitalist personal and public life; invisibility of different social groups to each other, linked to psychological mechanisms of belief in abstract enemies.

School: Deepening coupling of high-tech capital needs and public education at all levels, differentiated by race, class, and gender; managerial classes involved in educational reform and refunding at the cost of remaining progressive educational democratic structures for children and teachers; education for mass ignorance and repression in technocratic and militarized culture; growing anti-science mystery cults in dissenting and radical political movements; continued relative scientific illiteracy among white women and people of colour; growing industrial direction of education (especially higher education) by science-based multinationals (particularly in electronics- and biotechnology-dependent companies); highly educated, numerous élites in a progressively bimodal society.

Clinic-hospital: Intensified machine-body relations; renegotiations of public metaphors which channel personal experience of the body, particularly in relation to reproduction, immune system functions, and "stress" phenomena; intensification of reproductive politics in response to world historical implications of women's unrealized, potential control of their relation to reproduction; emergence of new, historically specific diseases; struggles over meanings and means of health in environments pervaded by high technology products and processes; continuing feminization of health work; intensified struggle over state responsibility for health; continued ideological role of popular health movements as a major form of American politics.

Church: Electronic fundamentalist "super-saver" preachers solemnizing the union of electronic capital and automated fetish gods; intensified importance of churches in resisting the militarized state; central struggle over women's meanings and authority in religion; continued relevance of spirituality, intertwined with sex and health, in political struggle.

The only way to characterize the informatics of domination is as a massive intensification of insecurity and cultural impoverishment, with common failure of subsistence networks for the most vulnerable. Since much of this picture interweaves with the social relations of science and technology, the urgency of a socialist-feminist politics addressed to science and technology is plain. There is much now being done, and the grounds for political work are rich. For example, the efforts to develop forms of collective struggle for women in paid work, like SEIU's District 925, [Service Employees International Union's office worker's organization in the US] should be a high priority for all of us. These efforts are profoundly tied to technical restructuring of labour processes and reformations of working classes. These efforts also are providing understanding of a more comprehensive kind of labour organization, involving community, sexuality, and family issues never privileged in the largely white male industrial unions.

The structural rearrangements related to the social relations of science and technology evoke strong ambivalence. But it is not necessary to be ultimately depressed by the implications of late twentieth-century women's relation to all aspects of work, culture, production of knowledge, sexuality, and reproduction. For excellent reasons, most Marxisms see domination best and have trouble understanding what can only look like false consciousness and people's complicity in their own domination in late capitalism. It is crucial to remember that what is lost, perhaps especially from women's points of view, is often virulent forms of oppression, nostalgically naturalized in the face of current violation. Ambivalence towards the disrupted unities mediated by high-tech culture requires not sorting consciousness into categories of "clear-sighted critique grounding a solid political epistemology" versus "manipulated false consciousness," but subtle understanding of emerging pleasures, experiences, and powers with serious potential for changing the rules of the game.

There are grounds for hope in the emerging bases for new kinds of unity across race, gender, and class, as these elementary units of socialist-feminist analysis themselves suffer protean transformations. Intensifications of hardship experienced world-wide in connection with the social relations of science and technology are severe. But what people are experiencing is not transparently clear, and we lack sufficiently subtle connections for collectively building effective theories of experience. Present efforts—Marxist, psychoanalytic, feminist, anthropological—to clarify even "our" experience are rudimentary.

I am conscious of the odd perspective provided by my historical position—a PhD in biology for an Irish Catholic girl was made possible by Sputnik's impact on US national science-education policy. I have a body and mind as much constructed by the post-Second World War arms race and cold war as by the women's movements. There are more grounds for hope in focusing on the contradictory effects of politics designed to produce loyal American technocrats, which also produced large numbers of dissidents, than in focusing on the present defeats.

The permanent partiality of feminist points of view has consequences for our expectations of forms of political organization and participation. We do not need a totality in order to work well. The feminist dream of a common language, like all dreams for a perfectly true language, of perfectly faithful naming of experience, is a totalizing and imperialist one. In that sense, dialectics too is a dream language, longing to resolve contradiction. Perhaps, ironically, we can learn from our fusions with animals and machines how not to be Man, the embodiment of Western logos. From the point of view of pleasure in these potent and taboo fusions, made inevitable by the social relations of science and technology, there might indeed be a feminist science.

Cyborgs: A Myth of Political Identity

I want to conclude with a myth about identity and boundaries which might inform late twentieth-century political imaginations. I am indebted in this story to writers like Joanna Russ, Samuel R. Delany, John Varley, James Tiptree, Jr., Octavia Butler, Monique Wittig, and Vonda McIntyre.[23] These are our storytellers exploring what it means to be embodied in high-tech worlds. They are theorists for cyborgs. Exploring conceptions of bodily boundaries and social order, the anthropologist Mary Douglas (1966, 1970) should be credited with helping us to consciousness about how fundamental body imagery is to world view, and so to political language. French feminists like Luce Irigaray and Monique Wittig, for all their differences, know how to write the body; how to weave eroticism, cosmology, and politics from imagery of embodiment, and especially for Wittig, from imagery of fragmentation and reconstitution of bodies.[24]

American radical feminists like Susan Griffin, Audre Lorde, and Adrienne Rich have profoundly affected our political imaginations—and perhaps restricted too much what we allow as a friendly body and political language.[25] They insist on the organic, opposing it to the technological. But their symbolic systems and the related positions of ecofeminism and feminist paganism, replete with organicisms, can only be understood in Sandoval's terms as oppositional ideologies fitting the late twentieth century. They would simply bewilder anyone not preoccupied with the machines and consciousness of late capitalism. In that sense they are part of the cyborg world. But there are also great riches for feminists in explicitly embracing the possibilities inherent in the breakdown of clean distinctions between organism and machine and similar distinctions structuring the Western self. It is the simultaneity of breakdowns that cracks the matrices of domination and opens geometric possibilities. What might be learned from personal and political "technological" pollution? I look briefly at two overlapping groups of texts for their insight into the construction of a potentially helpful cyborg myth: constructions of women of colour and monstrous selves in feminist science fiction.

Earlier I suggested that "women of colour" might be understood as a cyborg identity, a potent subjectivity synthesized from fusions of outsider identities and in the complex political-historical layerings of her "biomythography," *Zami* (Lorde, 1982; King, 1987a, 1987b). There are material and cultural grids mapping this potential. Audre Lorde (1984) captures the tone in the title of her *Sister Outsider*. In my political myth, Sister Outsider is the offshore woman, whom US workers, female and feminized, are supposed to regard as the enemy preventing their solidarity, threatening their security. Onshore, inside the boundary of the United States, Sister Outsider is a potential amidst the races and ethnic identities of women manipulated for division, competition, and exploitation in the same industries. "Women of colour" are the preferred labour force for the science-based industries, the real women for whom the world-wide sexual market, labour market, and politics of reproduction kaleidoscope into daily life. Young Korean women hired in the sex industry and in electronics assembly are recruited from high schools, educated for the integrated circuit. Literacy, especially in English, distinguishes the "cheap" female labour so attractive to the multinationals.

Contrary to orientalist stereotypes of the "oral primitive" literacy is a special mark of women of colour, acquired by US black women as well as men through a history of risking death to learn and to teach reading and writing. Writing has a special significance for all colonized groups. Writing has been crucial to the Western myth of the distinction between oral and written cultures, primitive and civilized mentalities, and more recently to the erosion of that distinction in "postmodernist" theories attacking the phallogocentrism of the West, with its worship of the monotheistic, phallic, authoritative, and singular work, the unique and perfect name.[26] Contests for the meanings of writing are a major form of contemporary political struggle. Releasing the play of writing is deadly serious. The poetry and stories of US women of colour are repeatedly about writing; about access to the power to signify; but this time that power must be neither phallic nor innocent. Cyborg writing must not be about the Fall, the imagination of a once-upon-a-time wholeness before language, before writing, before Man. Cyborg writing is about the power to survive, not on the basis of original innocence, but on the basis of seizing the tools to mark the world that marked them as other.

The tools are often stories, retold stories, versions that reverse and displace the hierarchical dualisms of naturalized identities. In retelling origin stories, cyborg authors subvert the central myths of origin of Western culture. We have all been colonized by those origin myths, with their longing for fulfillment in apocalypse. The phallogecentric origin stories most crucial for feminist cyborgs are built into the literal technologies—technologies that write the world, biotechnology and microelectronics—that have recently textualized our bodies as code problems on the grid of C^3I. Feminist cyborg stories have the task of recording communication and intelligence to subvert command and control.

Figuratively and literally, language politics pervade the struggles of women of colour; and stories about language have a special power in the rich contemporary writing by US women of colour. For example, retellings of the story of the indigenous woman Malinche, mother of the mestizo "bastard" race of the new world, master of languages, and mistress of Cortés, carry special meaning for Chicana constructions of identity. Cherríe Moraga (1983) in *Loving in the War Years* explores the themes of identity when one never possessed the original language, never told the original story, never resided in the harmony of legitimate heterosexuality in the garden of culture, and so cannot base identity on a myth or a fall from innocence and right to natural names, mother's or father's.[27] Moraga's writing, her superb literacy, is presented in her poetry as the same kind of violation as Malinche's mastery of the conqueror's language—a violation, an illegitimate production, that allows survival. Moraga's language is not "whole"; it is self-consciously spliced, a chimera of English and Spanish, both conqueror's languages. But it is this chimeric monster, without claim to an original language before violation, that crafts the erotic, competent, potent identities of women of colour. Sister Outsider hints at the possibility of world survival not because of her innocence, but because of her ability to live on the boundaries, to write without the founding myth of original wholeness, with its inescapable apocalypse of final return to a deathly oneness that Man has imagined to be the innocent and all-powerful Mother, freed at the End from another spiral of appropriation by her son. Writing marks Moraga's body, affirms it as the body of a woman of colour, against the possibility of passing into the unmarked category of the Anglo father or into the orientalist myth of "original illiteracy" of a mother that never was. Malinche was mother here, not Eve before eating the forbidden fruit. Writing affirms Sister Outsider, not the Woman-before–the-Fall-into-Writing needed by the phallogocentric Family of Man.

Writing is pre-eminently the technology of cyborgs, etched surfaces of the late twentieth century. Cyborg politics is the struggle for language and the struggle against perfect communication, against the one code that translates all meaning perfectly, the central dogma of phallogocentrism. That is why cyborg politics insist on noise and advocate pollution, rejoicing in the illegitimate fusions of animal and machine. These are the couplings which make Man and Woman so problematic, subverting the structure of desire, the force imagined to generate language and gender, and so subverting the structure and modes of reproduction of "Western" identity, of nature and culture, of mirror and eye, slave and master, body and mind. "We" did not originally choose to be cyborgs, but choice grounds a liberal politics and epistemology that imagines the reproduction of individuals before the wider replication of "texts."

From the perspective of cyborgs, freed of the need to ground politics in "our" privileged position of the oppression that incorporates all other dominations, the innocence of the merely violated, the ground of those closer to nature, we can see powerful possibilities. Feminisms and Marxisms have run aground on Western epistemological imperatives to construct a revolutionary subject from the perspective of a hierarchy of oppressions and/or a latent position of moral superiority, innocence, and greater closeness to nature. With no available original dream of a common language or original symbiosis promising protection for hostile "masculine" separation, but written into the play of a text that has no finally privileged reading or salvation history, to recognize "oneself" as fully implicated in the world, frees us of the need to root politics in identification, vanguard parties, purity, and mothering. Stripped of identity, the bastard race teaches about the power of the margins and the importance of a mother like Malinche. Women of colour have transformed her from the evil mother of masculinist fear into the originally literate mother who teaches survival.

This is not just literary deconstruction, but liminal transformation. Every story that begins with original innocence and privileges the return to wholeness imagines the drama of life to be individuation, separation, the birth of the self, the tragedy of autonomy, the fall into writing, alienation; that is, war, tempered by imaginary respite in the bosom of the Other. These plots are ruled by a reproductive politics—rebirth without flaw, perfection, abstraction. In this plot women are imagined either better or worse off, but all agree they have less selfhood, weaker individuation, more fusion to the oral, to Mother, less at stake in masculine autonomy. But there is another route to having less at stake in masculine autonomy, a route that does not pass through Woman, Primitive, Zero, the Mirror Stage and its imaginary. It passes through women and other present tense, illegitimate cyborgs, not of Woman born, who refuse the ideological resources of victimization so as to have a real life. These cyborgs are the people who refuse to disappear on cue, no matter how many times a "Western" commentator remarks on the sad passing of another primitive, another organic group done in by "Western" technology, by writing.[28] These real-life cyborgs (for example, the Southeast Asian village women workers in Japanese and US electronic firms described by Aihwa Ong) are actively rewriting the texts of their bodies and societies. Survival is the stakes in this play of readings.

To recapitulate, certain dualisms have been persistent in Western traditions, they have all been systemic to the logics and practices of domination of women, people of colour, nature, workers, animals—in short, domination of all constituted as others, whose task is to mirror the self. Chief among these troubling dualisms are self/other, mind/body, culture/nature, male/female, civilized/primitive, reality/appearance, whole/part, agent/resource, maker/made, active/passive, right/wrong, truth/illusion, total/partial, God/man. The self is the One who is not dominated, who knows that by the service of the other, the other is the one who holds the future, who knows that by the experience of domination, which gives the lie to the autonomy of the self. To be One is to be autonomous, to be powerful, to be God; but to be One is to be an illusion, and so to be involved in a dialectic of apocalypse with the other. Yet to be other is to be multiple, without clear boundary, frayed, insubstantial. One is too few, but two are too many.

High-tech culture challenges these dualisms in intriguing ways. It is not clear who makes and who is made in the relation between human and machine. It is not clear what is mind and what body in machines that resolve into coding practices. In so far as we know ourselves in both formal discourse (for example, biology) and in daily practice (for example, the homework economy in the integrated circuit), we find ourselves to be cyborgs, hybrids, mosaics, chimeras. Biological organisms have become biotic systems, communications devices like others. There is no fundamental, ontological separation in our formal knowledge of machine and organism, of technical and organic. The replicant Rachel in the Ridley Scott film *Blade Runner* stands as the image of a cyborg culture's fear, love, and confusion.

One consequence is that our sense of connection to our tools is heightened. The trance state experienced by many computer users has become a staple of science-fiction film and cultural jokes. Perhaps paraplegics and other severely handicapped people can (and sometimes do) have the most intense experiences of complex hybridization with other communication devices.[29] Anne McCaffrey's pre-feminist *The Ship Who Sang* (1969) explored the consciousness of a cyborg, hybrid of girl's brain and complex machinery, formed after the birth of a severely handicapped child. Gender, sexuality, embodiment, skill: all were reconstituted in the story. Why should our bodies end at the skin, or include at best other beings encapsulated by skin? From the seventeenth century till now, machines could be animated—given ghostly souls to make them speak or move or to account for their orderly development and mental capacities. Or organisms could be mechanized—reduced to body understood as resource of mind. These machine/organism relationships are obsolete, unnecessary. For us, in imagination and in other practice, machines can be prosthetic devices, intimate components, friendly selves. We don't need organic holism to give impermeable wholeness, the total woman and her feminist variants (mutants?). Let me conclude this point by a very partial reading of the logic of the cyborg monsters of my second group of texts, feminist science fiction.

The cyborgs populating feminist science fiction make very problematic the statuses of man or woman, human, artefact, member of a race, individual entity, or body. Katie King clarifies how pleasure in reading these fictions is not largely based on identification. Students facing Joanna Russ for the first time, students who have learned to take modernist writers like James Joyce or Virginia Woolf without flinching, do not know what to make of *The Adventures of Alyx* or *The Female Man,* where characters refuse the reader's search for innocent wholeness while granting the wish for heroic quests, exuberant eroticism, and serious politics. *The Female Man* is the story of four versions of one genotype, all of whom meet, but even taken together do not make a whole, resolve the dilemmas of violent moral action, or remove the growing scandal of gender. The feminist science fiction of Samuel R. Delany, especially *Tales of Nevèrÿon,* mocks stories of origin by redoing the neolithic revolution, replaying the founding moves of Western civilization to subvert their plausibility. James Tiptree, Jr., an author whose fiction was regarded as particularly manly until her "true" gender was revealed, tells tales of reproduction based on non-mammalian technologies like alternation of generations of male brood pouches and male nurturing. John Varley constructs a supreme cyborg in his arch-feminist exploration of Gaea, a mad goddess-planet-trickster-old woman-technological device on whose surface an extraordinary array of post-cyborg symbioses are spawned. Octavia Butler writes of an African sorceress pitting her powers of transformation against the genetic manipulations of her rival (*Wild Seed*), of time warps that bring a modern US black woman into slavery where her actions in relation to her white master-ancestor determine the possibility of her own birth (*Kindred*), and of the illegitimate insights into identity and community of an adopted cross-species child who came to know the enemy as self (*Survivor*). In *Dawn* (1987), the first installment of a series called *Xenogenesis,* Butler tells the story of Lilith Iyapo, whose personal name recalls Adam's first and repudiated wife and whose family name marks her status as the widow of the son of Nigerian immigrants to the US. A black woman and a mother whose child is dead, Lilith mediates the transformation of humanity through genetic exchange with extra-terrestrial lovers/rescuers/destroyers/genetic engineers, who reform earth's habitats after the nuclear holocaust and coerce surviving humans into intimate fusion with them. It is a novel that interrogates reproductive, linguistic, and nuclear politics in a mythic field structured by late twentieth-century race and gender.

Because it is particularly rich in boundary transgressions, Vonda McIntyre's *Superluminal* can close this truncated catalogue of promising and dangerous monsters who help redefine the pleasures and politics of embodiment and feminist writing. In a fiction where no character is "simply" human, human status is highly problematic. Orca, a genetically altered diver, can speak with killer whales and survive deep ocean conditions, but she longs to explore space as a pilot, necessitating bionic implants jeopardizing her kinship with the divers and cetaceans. Transformations are effected by virus vectors carrying a new developmental code, by transplant surgery, by implants of microelectronic devices, by analogue doubles, and other means. Laenea becomes a pilot by accepting a heart implant and a host of other alterations allowing survival in transit at speeds exceeding that of light. Radu Dracul survives a virus-caused plague in his outer-world planet to find himself with a time sense that changes the boundaries of spatial perception for the whole species. All the characters explore the limits of language; the dream of communicating experience; and the necessity of limitation, partiality, and intimacy even in this world of protean transformation and connection. *Superluminal* stands also for the defining contradictions of a cyborg world in another sense; it embodies textually the intersection of feminist theory and colonial discourse in the science fiction I have alluded to in this chapter. This is a conjunction with a long history that many "First World" feminists have tried to repress, including myself in my readings of *Superluminal* before being called to account by Zoe Sofoulis, whose different location in the world system's informatics of domination made her acutely alert to the imperialist moment of all science fiction cultures, including women's science fiction. From an Australian feminist sensitivity, Sofoulis remembered more readily McIntyre's role as writer of the adventures of Captain Kirk and Spock in TV's *Star Trek* series than her rewriting the romance in *Superluminal*.

Monsters have always defined the limits of community in Western imaginations. The Centaurs and Amazons of ancient Greece established the limits of the centred polis of the Greek male human by their disruption of marriage and boundary pollutions of the warrior with animality and woman. Unseparated twins and hermaphrodites were the confused human material in early modern France who grounded discourse on the natural and supernatural, medical and legal, portents and diseases—all crucial to establishing modern identity.[30] The evolutionary and behavioural sciences of monkeys and apes have marked the multiple boundaries of late twentieth-century industrial identities. Cyborg monsters in feminist science fiction define quite different political possibilities and limits from those proposed by the mundane fiction of Man and Woman.

There are several consequences to taking seriously the imagery of cyborgs as other than our enemies. Our bodies, ourselves; bodies are maps of power and identity. Cyborgs are no exception. A cyborg body is not innocent; it was not born in a garden; it does not seek unitary identity and so generate antagonistic dualisms without end (or until the world ends); it takes irony for granted. One is too few, and two is only one possibility. Intense pleasure in skill, machine skill, ceases to be a sin, but an aspect of embodiment. The machine is not an *it* to be animated, worshipped, and dominated. The machine is us, our processes, an aspect of our embodiment. We can be responsible for machines; *they* do not dominate or threaten us. We are responsible for boundaries; we are they. Up till now (once upon a time), female embodiment seemed to be given, organic, necessary; and female embodiment seemed to mean skill in mothering and its metaphoric extensions. Only by being out of place could we take intense pleasure in machines, and then with excuses that this was organic activity after all, appropriate to females. Cyborgs might consider more seriously the partial, fluid, sometimes aspect of sex and sexual embodiment. Gender might not be global identity after all, even if it has profound historical breadth and depth.

The ideologically charged question of what counts as daily activity, as experience, can be approached by exploiting the cyborg image. Feminists have recently claimed that women are given to dailiness, that women more than men somehow sustain daily life, and so have a privileged epistemological position potentially. There is a compelling aspect to this claim, one that makes visible unvalued female activity and names it as the ground of life. But *the* ground of life? What about all the ignorance of women, all the exclusions and failures of knowledge and skill? What about men's access to daily competence, to knowing how to build things, to take them apart, to play? What about other embodiments? Cyborg gender is a local possibility taking a global vengeance. Race, gender, and capital require a cyborg theory of wholes and parts. There is no drive in cyborgs to produce total theory, but there is an intimate experience of boundaries, their construction and deconstruction. There is a myth system waiting to become a political language to ground one way of looking at science and technology and challenging the informatics of domination—in order to act potently.

One last image: organisms and organismic, holistic politics depend on metaphors of rebirth and invariably call on the resources of reproductive sex. I would suggest that cyborgs have more to do with regeneration and are suspicious of the reproductive matrix and of most birthing. For salamanders, regeneration after injury, such as the loss of a limb, involves regrowth of structure and restoration of function with the constant possibility of twinning or other odd topographical productions as the site of former injury. The regrown limb can be monstrous, duplicated, potent. We have all been injured, profoundly. We require regeneration, not rebirth, and the possibilities for our reconstitution include the utopian dream of the hope for a monstrous world without gender.

Cyborg imagery can help express two crucial arguments in the essay: first, the production of universal, totalizing theory is a major mistake that misses most of reality, probably always, but certainly now; and second, taking responsibility for the social relations of science and technology means refusing an antiscience metaphysics, a demonology of technology, and so means embracing the skilful task of reconstructing the boundaries of daily life, in partial connection with others, in communication with all of our parts. It is not just that science and technology are possible means of great human satisfaction, as well as a matrix of complex dominations. Cyborg imagery can suggest a way out of the maze of dualisms in which we have explained our bodies and our tools to ourselves. This is a dream not of a common language, but of a powerful infidel heteroglossia. It is an imagination of a feminist speaking in tongues to strike fear into the circuits of the supersavers of the new right. It means both building and destroying machines, identities, categories, relationships, space stories. Though both are bound in the spiral dance, I would rather be a cyborg than a goddess.

Notes

1. Research was funded by an Academic Senate Faculty Research Grant from the University of California, Santa Cruz. An earlier version of the paper on genetic engineering appeared as "Lieber Kyborg als Göttin: für eine sozialistisch-feministische Unterwanderung der Gentechnologie," in Bernd-Peter Lange and Anna Marie Stuby, eds., Berlin: Argument-Sonderband 105, 1984, pp 66–84. The cyborg manifesto grew from my "New machines, new bodies, new communities: political dilemmas of a cyborg feminist," "The Scholar and the Feminist X: The Question of Technology," Conference, Barnard College, April 1983.

The people associated with the History of Consciousness Board of UCSC have had an enormous influence on this paper, so that it feels collectively authored more than most, although those I cite may not recognize their ideas. In particular, members of graduate and undergraduate feminist theory, science, and politics, and theory and methods courses contributed to the cyborg manifesto. Particular debts here are due Hilary Klein (1989), Paul Edwards (1985), Lisa Lowe (1986), and James Clifford (1985).

Parts of the paper were my contribution to a collectively developed session, "Poetic Tools and Political Bodies: Feminist Approaches to High Technology Culture," 1984 California American Studies Association, with History of Consciousness graduate students Zoe Sofoulis, "Jupiter space"; Katie King, "The pleasures of repetition and the limits of identification in feminist science fiction: reimaginations of the body after the cyborg"; and Chela Sandoval, "The construction of subjectivity and oppositional consciousness in feminist film and video." Sandoval's (n.d) theory of oppositional consciousness was published as "Women respond to racism: A Report on the National Women's Studies Association Conference." For Sofoulis's semiotic-psychoanalytic readings of nuclear culture, see Sofia (1984). King's unpublished papers ("Questioning tradition: canon formation and the veiling of power"; "Gender and genre: reading the science fiction of Joanna Russ"; "Varley's *Titan* and *Wizard*: feminist parodies of nature, culture, and hardware") deeply informed the cyborg manifesto.

Barbara Epstein, Jeff Escoffier, Rusten Hogness, and Jaye Miler gave extensive discussion and editorial help. Members of the Silicon Valley Research Project of UCSC and participants in SVRP conferences and workshops were very important, especially Rick Gordon, Linda Kimball, Nancy Snyder, Langdon Winner, Judith Stacey, Linda Lim, Patricia Fernandez-Kelly, and Judith Gregory. Finally, I want to thank Nancy Hartsock for years of friendship and discussion on feminist theory and feminist science fiction. I also thank Elizabeth Bird for my favourite political button: "Cyborgs for Earthly Survival."

2. Useful references to left and/or feminist radical science movements and theory and to biological/biotechnical issues include: Bleier (1984, 1986), Harding (1986), Fausto-Sterling (1985), Gould (1981), Hubbard *et al.* (1982), Keller (1985), Lewontin *et al.* (1984), *Radical Science Journal* (became *Science as Culture* in 1987), 26 Freegrove Road, London N7 9RQ; *Science for the People*, 897 Main St, Cambridge, MA 02139.

3. Starting points for left and/or feminist approaches to technology and politics include: Cowan (1983), Rothschild (1983), Traweek (1988), Young and Levidow (1981, 1985), Weizenbaum (1976), Winner (1977, 1986), Zimmerman (1983), Athanasiou (1987), Cohn (1987a, 1987b), Winograd and Flores (1986), Edwards (1985); *Global Electronics Newsletter*, 867 West Dana St, #204, Mountain View, CA 94041; *Processed World*, 55 Sutter St, San Francisco, CA 94104; ISIS, Women's International Information and Communication Service, PO Box 50 (Cornavin), 1211 Geneva 2, Switzerland, and Via Santa Maria Dell'Anima 30, 00186 Rome, Italy. Fundamental approaches to modern social studies of science that do not continue the liberal mystification that it all started with Thomas Kuhn, include: Knorr-Cetina (1981), Knorr-Cetina and Mulkay (1983), Latour and Woolgar (1979), Young (1979). The 1984 Directory of the Network for the Ethnographic Study of Science, Technology, and Organizations lists a wide range of people and projects crucial to better radical analysis; available from NESSTO, PO Box 11442, Stanford, CA 94305.

4. A provocative, comprehensive argument about the politics and theories of "post-modernism" is made by Fredric Jameson (1984), who argues that postmodernism is not an option, a style among others, but a cultural dominant requiring radical rein-vention of left politics from within; there is no longer any place from without that gives meaning to the comforting fiction of critical distance. Jameson also makes clear why one cannot be for or against postmodernism, an essentially moralist move. My position is that feminists (and others) need continuous cultural reinvention, post-modernist critique, and historical materialism; only a cyborg would have a chance. The old dominations of white capitalist patriarchy seem nostalgically innocent now: they normalized heterogeneity, into man and woman, white and black, for example. "Advanced capitalism" and post-modernism release heterogeneity without a norm, and we are flattened, without subjectivity, which requires depth, even unfriendly and drowning depths. It is time to write *The Death of the Clinic*. The clinic's methods required bodies and works; we have texts and surfaces. Our dominations don't work by medicalization and normalization any more; they work by networking, communi-cations redesign, stress management. Normalization gives way to automation, utter redundancy. Michel Foucault's *Birth of the Clinic* (1963), *History of Sexuality* (1976), and *Discipline and Punish* (1975) name a form of power at its moment of implosion. The discourse of biopolitics gives way to technobabble, the language of the spliced substantive; no noun is left whole by the multinationals. These are their names, listed from one issue of *Science*: Tech-Knowledge, Genentech, Allergen, Hybritech, Compupro, Genen-cor, Syntex, Allelix, Agrigenetics Corp., Syntro, Codon, Repligen, MicroAngelo from Scion Corp., Percom Data, Inter Systems, Cyborg Corp., Statcom Corp., Intertec. If we are imprisoned by language, then escape from that prison-house requires language poets, a kind of cultural restriction enzyme to cut the code; cyborg heteroglossia is one form of radical cultural politics. For cyborg poetry, see Perloff (1984); Fraser (1984). For feminist modernist/post-modernist "cyborg" writing, see HOW(ever), 871 Corbet Ave, San Francisco, CA 94131.

5. Baudrillard (1983). Jameson (1984, p. 66) points out that Plato's definition of the simulacrum is the copy for which there is no original, i.e., the world of advanced capitalism, of pure exchange. See *Discourse* 9 (Spring/ Summer 1987) for a special issue on technology (cybernetics, ecology, and the postmodern imagination).

6. For ethnographic accounts and political evaluations, see Epstein (forthcoming), Stur-geon (1986). Without explicit irony, adopting the spaceship earth/whole earth logo of the planet photographed from space, set off by the slogan "Love your Mother," the May 1987 Mothers and Others Day action at the nuclear weapons testing facility in Nevada none the less took account of the tragic contradictions of views of the earth. Demonstrators applied for official permits to be on the land from officers of the Western Shoshone tribe, whose territory was invaded by the US government when it built the nuclear weapons test ground in the 1950s. Arrested for trespassing, the demonstrators argued that the police and weapons facility personnel, without authorization from the proper officials, were the trespassers. One affinity group at the women's action called themselves the Surrogate Others; and in solidarity with the creatures forced to tunnel in the same ground with the bomb, they enacted a cybor-gian emergence from the constructed body of a large, non-heterosexual desert worm.

7. Powerful developments of coalition politics emerge from "Third World" speakers, speaking from nowhere, the displaced center of the universe, earth: "We live on the third planet from the sun"—*Sun Poem* by Jamaican writer, Edward Kamau Braith-waite, review by Mackey (1984). Contributors to Smith (1983) ironically subvert

naturalized identities precisely while constructing a place from which to speak called home. See especially Reagon (in Smith, 1983, pp. 356–698). Trinh T. Minh-ha (1986–87).

8. Hooks (1981, 1094); Hull *et al.* (1982). Bambara (1981) wrote an extraordinary novel in which the women of colour theatre group. The Seven Sisters, explores a form of unity. See analysis by Butler-Evans (1987).

9. On orientalism in feminist works and elsewhere, see Lowe (1986); Said (1978); Mohanty (1984); *Many Voices, One Chant: Black Feminist Perspectives* (1984).

10. Katie King (1986, 1987a) developed a theoretically sensitive treatment of the working of feminist taxonomies as genealogies of power in feminist ideology and polemic. King examines Jaguar's (1983) problematic example of taxonomizing feminisms to make a little machine producing the desired final position. My caricature here of socialist and radical feminism is also an example.

11. The central role of object relations versions of psychoanalysis and related strong universalizing moves in discussing reproduction, caring work, and mothering in many approaches to epistemology underline their authors' resistance to what I am calling postmodernism. For me, both the universalizing moves and these versions of psychoanalysis make analysis of "women's place in the integrated circuit" difficult and lead to systematic difficulties in accounting for or even seeing major aspects of the construction of gender and gendered social life. The feminist standpoint argument has been developed by: Flax (1983), Harding (1986), Harding and Hintikka (1983), Hartsock (1983a, b), O'Brien (1982), Rose (1983), Smith (1974, 1979). For rethinking theories of feminist materialism and feminist standpoints in response to criticism, see Harding (1986, pp. 163–96), Hartsock (1987), and H. Rose (1986).

12. I make an argumentative category error in "modifying" MacKinnon's positions with the qualifier "radical," thereby generating my own reductive critique of extremely heterogeneous writing, which does explicitly use that label, by my taxonomically interested argument about writing which does not use the modifier and which brooks no limits and thereby adds to the various dreams of a common, in the sense of univocal, language for feminism. My category error was occasioned by an assignment to write from a particular taxonomic position which itself has a heterogeneous history, socialist-feminism, for *Socialist Review*. A critique indebted to MacKinnon, but without the reductionism and with an elegant feminist account of Foucault's paradoxical conservatism on sexual violence (rape), is de Lauretis (1985; see also 1986, pp. 1–19). A theoretically elegant feminist social-historical examination of family violence, that insists on women's, men's and children's complex agency without losing sight of the material structures of male domination, race, and class, is Gordon (1988).

13. This chart was published in 1985. My previous efforts to understand biology as a cybernetic command-control discourse and organisms as "natural-technical objects of knowledge" were Haraway (1979, 1983, 1984). The 1979 version of this dichotomous chart appears in this vol., ch 3; for a 1989 version, see ch. 10. The differences indicate shifts in argument.

14. For progressive analyses and action on the biotechnology debates: *GeneWatch, a Bulletin of the Committee for Responsible Genetics,* 5 Doane St, 4th Floor, Boston, MA 02109; Genetic Screening Study Group (formerly the Sociobiology Study Group of Science for the People), Cambridge, MA; Wright (1982, 1986); Yoxen (1983).

15. Starting references for "women in the integrated circuit": D'Onofrio-Flores and Pfafflin (1982), Fernandez-Kelly (1983), Fuentes and Ehrenreich (1983), Grossman

(1980), Nash and Fernandez-Kelly (1983), Ong (1987), Science Policy Research Unit (1982).

16. For the "homework economy outside the home" and related arguments: Gordon (1983); Gordon and Kimball (1985); Stacey (1987); Reskin and Hartmann (1986); *Women and Poverty* (1984); S. Rose (1986); Collins (1982); Burr (1982); Gregory and Nussbaum (1982); Piven and Coward (1982); Microelectronics Group (1980); Stallard *et al.* (1983) which includes a useful organization and resource list.

17. The conjunction of the Green Revolution's social relations with biotechnologies like plant genetic engineering makes the pressures on land in the Third World increasingly intense. AID's estimates (*New York Times,* 14 October 1984) used at the 1984 World Food Day are that in Africa, women produce about 90 per cent of rural food supplies, about 60–80 per cent in Asia, and provide 40 per cent of agricultural labour in the Near East and Latin America. Blumberg charges that world organizations' agricultural politics, as well as those of multinationals and national governments in the Third World, generally ignore fundamental issues in the sexual division of labour. The present tragedy of famine in Africa might owe as much to male supremacy as to capitalism, colonialism, and rain patterns. More accurately, capitalism and racism are usually structurally male dominant. See also Blumberg (1981); Hacker (1984); Hacker and Bovit (1981); Busch and Lacy (1983); Wilfred (1982); Sachs (1983); International Fund for Agricultural Development (1985); Bird (1984).

18. See also Enloe (1983a, b).

19. For a feminist version of this logic, see Hrdy (1981). For an analysis of scientific women's story-telling practices, especially in relation to sociobiology in evolutionary debates around child abuse and infanticide, see this vol., ch. 5.

20. For the moment of transition of hunting with guns to hunting with cameras in the construction of popular meanings of nature for an American urban immigrant public, see Haraway (1984–5, 1989b,) Nash (1979), Sontag (1977), Preston (1984).

21. For guidance for thinking about the political/cultural/racial implications of the history of women doing science in the United States see: Haas and Perucci (1984); Hacker (1981); Keller (1983); National Science Foundation (1988); Rossiter (1982); Schiebinger (1987); Haraway (1989b).

22. Markoff and Siegel (1983). High Technology Professionals for Peace and Computer Professionals for Social Responsibility are promising organizations.

23. King (1984). An abbreviated list of feminist science fiction underlying themes of this essay: Octavia Butler, *Wild Seed, Mind of My Mind, Kindred, Survivor;* Suzy McKee Charnas, *Motherliness;* Samuel R. Delany, the Nevèrÿon Series; Anne McCaffery, *The Ship Who Sang, Dinosaur Planet;* Vonda McIntyre, *Superluminal, Dreamsnake;* Joanna Russ, *Adventures of Alyx , The Female Man;* James Tiptree, Jr., *Star Songs of an Old Primate, Up the Walls of the World;* John Varley, *Titan, Wizard, Demon.*

24. French feminisms contribute to cyborg heteroglossia. Burke (1981); Irigaray (1977, 1979); Marks and de Courtivron (1980); *Signs* (Autumn 1981); Witting (1973); Duchen (1986). For English translation of some currents of francophone feminism see *Feminist Issues: A Journal of Feminist Social and Political Theory,* 1980.

25. But all these poets are very complex, not least in their treatment of themes of lying and erotic, decentred collective and personal identities. Griffin (1978), Lorde (1984), Rich (1978).

26. Derrida (1976, especially part II); Lévi-Strauss (1961, especially "The Writing Lesson"); Gates (1985); Kahn and Neumaier (1985); Ong (1982); Kramarae and Treichler (1985).

27. The sharp relation of women of color to writing as theme and politics can be approached through: Program for "The Black Woman and the Diaspora: Hidden Connections and Extended Acknowledgements," an International Literary Conference, Michigan State University, October 1985, Evans (1984); Christian (1985); Carby (1987); Fisher (1980); *Frontiers* (1980, 1983); Kingston (1977); Lerner (1973); Giddings (1985); Moraga and Anzaldúa (1981); Morgan (1984). Anglophone European and Euro-American women have also crafted special relations to their writing as a potent sign: Gilbert and Gubar (1979), Russ (1983).

28. The convention of ideologically taming militarized high technology by publicizing its applications to speech and motion problems of the disabled/differently abled takes on a special irony in monotheistic, patriarchal, and frequently anti-semitic culture when computer-generated speech allows a boy with no voice to chant the Haftorah at his bar mitzvah. See Sussman (1986). Making the always context-relative social definitions of "ableness" particularly clear, military high-tech has a way of making human beings disabled by definition, a perverse aspect of much automated battlefield and Star Wars R&D. See Welford (I July 1986).

29. James Clifford (1985, 1988) argues persuasively for recognition of continuous cultural reinvention, the stubborn non-disappearance of those "marked" by Western imperializing practices.

30. DuBois (1982), Daston and Park (n.d.), Park and Daston (1981). The noun *monster* shares its root with the verb *to demonstrate*.

Arlie Russell Hochschild (1940–)

Hochschild is a professor of sociology and director of the Center for Working Families at the University of California, Berkeley. Her scholarship examines how capitalism directs and shapes our everyday lives, and her books and articles have reached a wide readership both inside and outside of academia. Marxist, psychoanalytic, and sociological theories influence Hochschild's scholarship. She begins the next reading selection, "From the Frying Pan into the Fire," with a close reading of an oatmeal advertisement, which allows her to demonstrate how the once seemingly separate spaces of home and work intersect daily and influence our conceptions of home life in light of workplace norms. "From the Frying Pan into the Fire" appears in her 2003 book *The Commercialization of Intimate Life: Notes from Home and Work*. Hochschild has also written the following books: *The Managed Heart: The Commercialization of Human Feeling* (1983) and *The Time Bind: When Working Becomes Home and Home Becomes Work* (1997). She earned her B.A. degree in international relations from Swarthmore College, in Pennsylvania, in 1962; in 1965 she earned her M.A. in sociology and in 1969 her Ph.D. in sociology from the University of California, Berkeley. From 1969 to 1971, Hochschild taught sociology at the University of California at Santa Cruz and then joined the faculty at Berkeley in 1971.

From the Frying Pan into the Fire

An advertisement for Quaker Oats cereal in an issue of *Working Mother* magazine provides a small window on the interplay between consumption and the application of the idea of efficiency to private time in modern America.[1] In the ad, a mother, dressed in a business suit, affectionately hugs her smiling son. Beneath the image, we read: "Instant Quaker Oatmeal, for moms who have a lot of love but not a lot of time." The ad continues with a short story: "Nicky is a very picky eater. With Instant Quaker Oatmeal, I can give him a terrific hot breakfast in just 90 seconds. And I don't have to spend any time coaxing him to eat it!"

The ad then presents "facts" about mother and child: "Sherry Greenberg, with Nicky, age four and a half, Hometown: New York City, New York, Occupation: Music teacher, Favorite Flavor: Apples and Cinnamon." The designers of this ad, we could imagine, want us to feel we've been let in on an ordinary moment in a middle-class American morning. In this ordinary moment, Sherry Greenberg is living according to closely scheduled, rapidly paced "adult" time, while Nicky is living according to a more dawdling, slowly paced "child" time. So the mother faces a dilemma. To meet her work deadline, she must get Nicky on "adult" time. But to be a good mother it is desirable to give her child a hot breakfast—"hot" being associated with devotion and love. To cook the hot breakfast, though, Sherry needs *time*. The ad suggests that it is the cereal itself that solves the problem. It conveys love because it is hot, but it permits efficiency because it's quickly made. The cereal would seem to reconcile an image of American motherhood of the 1950s with the female work role of 2000 and beyond.

The cereal also allows Sherry to avoid the unpleasant task of struggling with her child over scarce time. In the ad, Nicky's slow pace is implicitly attributed to his character ("Nicky is a very picky eater") and not to the fact that he is being harnessed to an accelerating pace of adult work time or protesting an adult speed-up by staging a "slowdown." By permitting the mother to avoid a fight with her son over time, the ad brilliantly evokes a common problem and proposes a commodity as a solution.

Attached to the culture of time shown in the ad is a key but hidden social logic. This modern working mother is portrayed as resembling Frederick Taylor, the famed efficiency expert of modern industry. The principle of efficiency is not located, here, at work in the person of the owner, the foreman, or the worker. It is located in the worker-as-mother. We do not see a boss pressing the worker for more efficiency at the office. Instead, we see a mother pressing her son to eat more efficiently at home. This efficiency-seeking is transferred from man to woman, from workplace to home, and from adult to child. Nicky becomes his own task master, quickly gobbling his breakfast himself because it is so delicious. Frederick Taylor has leapt the fence from factory to home, adult to child, and jumped, it seems, into the cereal box itself. Frederick Taylor has become a commodity. *It* provides efficiency. Thus, the market reinforces the idea of efficiency twice—once at a locus of production, where the worker is pressed to work efficiently, and again, as a supplier of consumer goods, where it promises to deliver the very efficiency it also demands.

Quaker Oats cereal may be a paradigm for a growing variety of goods and services—frozen dinners, computer shopping services, cell phones,[2] and the like—that claim to save time for busy working parents. They often save time at home. But the ethic of "saving time" raises the question of what we want to save time for.[3] In the case above, the photo of the happy mother and child suggests that the mother is rushing her son through breakfast, not to race out to an all-absorbing job at a dot-com company, but to teach a few piano lessons. The picture doesn't challenge our idea of the primacy, even sacredness, of Nicky's home. So we don't much notice the sly insinuation of Frederick Taylor into the scene.

Conventional Versus Unconventional Wisdom

If, through modern Western eyes, the Greenbergs of this ad were a normal family, we could imagine them feeling that family life superseded all other aspects of life. That is, according to modern conventional wisdom, a happy family life is an end in itself. Earning and spending money are the means for achieving this end. Home and community are primary; workplace and mall are secondary. When we go out to work, it's to put bread on the table for the family. When we shop at the mall, it's often to buy a Christmas, birthday, or house present "for the family." Put in other terms, we often see the home and the community as sacred, and the workplace and the mall as profane. We are who we are at home and in our communities. We do what we do at work and buy what we buy at the mall.

To be sure, we make exceptions for the odd workaholic here or shopaholic there, but, as the terms imply, an overconcern with the profane realms of work and mall are, given this way of seeing things, off moral limits. Sherry Greenberg fits right in. She is in her kitchen feeding her son. She has what one imagines to be a manageable job. It's just that she's wanting to hurry things along a bit.

Implicit in this conventional view of family life is the idea that our use of time is like a language. We speak through it. By either what we say we want to spend time doing or what we actually spend time doing, we say what it is we hold sacred. Maybe we don't think of it just this way, but we assume that each "spending time" or each statement of feeling about time ("I wish I could spend time") is a bow from the waist to what we hold dear. It is a form of worship. Again, Sherry Greenberg is symbolizing the importance of family. It's just that she's slightly on the edge of that conventional picture because she's in a hurry to get out of it. The Quaker Oats ad both appeals to this family-comes-first picture of life and subtly challenges it, by taking sides with her desire to feed Nicky "efficiently."

The subtle challenge of the ad points, I believe, to a larger contradiction underlying stories like that of the Greenbergs. Reflecting on my research on the Fortune 500 company I call Amerco, I'll try to explore it. Increasingly, our belief that family comes first conflicts with the emotional draw of both workplace and mall. Indeed, I would argue that a constellation of pressures is pushing men and women further into the world of workplace and mall. And television—a pipeline, after all, to the mall—is keeping them there. Family and community life have meanwhile become less central as places to talk and relate, and less the object of collective rituals.

Many of us respond to these twin trends, however, not by turning away from family and community, but by actually elevating them in moral importance. Family and community are not a realm in decline, as David Popenoe argues about the family and Robert Putnam argues for the community. To many people, both have become even more important morally. We encapsulate the idea of the cherished family.[4] We separate ideal from practice. We separate the idea of "spending time with X" from the idea of "believing in the importance of X." We don't link what we think with what we do. Or as one Amerco employee put it, using company language," I don't walk the talk at home." This encapsulation of our family ideal allows us to accommodate to what is both a pragmatic necessity and a competing source of meaning—the religion of capitalism. I say pragmatic necessity, because most Americans, men and women alike, have to work for food and rent.

At the same time, a new cultural story is unfolding. It is not that capitalism is an unambiguous object of worship. After all, American capitalism is, in reality, a highly complex, internally diverse economic system for making, advertising, and selling things. But, without overstating case, it seems true that capitalism is a cultural as well as an economic system and that the symbols and rituals of this cultural system compete with, however much they seem to serve, the symbols and rituals of community and family. This means that working long hours and spending a lot of money—instead of spending time together—have increasingly become *how* we say "I love you" at home. As Juliet Schor argues in *The Overspent American,* over the last twenty years, Americans have raised the bar on what feels like enough money to get along. In 1975, according to a Roper poll, 10 percent of people mentioned a second color TV as part of "the good life," and 28 percent did in 1991. A 1995 Merck Family Fund poll showed that 27 percent of people who earned $100,000 or more agreed with the statement, "I cannot afford to buy everything I really need." At the same time, between 1975 and 1991, the role of family in people's idea of "the good life" declined while the importance of having money increased. The importance of having a happy marriage to "the good life" declined from 84 percent in 1975 to 77 percent in 1991. Meanwhile having "a lot of money" went from 38 percent in 1975 to 55 percent in 1991.[5]

How much of a stretch is it, I wonder, to go from the trends Schor points out to Harvey Cox's daring thesis: that capitalism has become a religion? As Cox puts it:

> Just as a truly global market has emerged for the first time in human history, that market is functioning without moral guideposts and restraints, and it has become the most powerful institution of our age. Even nation-states can often do little to restrain or regulate it. More and more, the idea of "the market" is construed, not as a creation of culture ("made by human hands," as the Bible says about idols), but as the "natural" way things happen. For this reason, the "religion" the market generates often escapes criticism and evaluation or even notice. It becomes as invisible to those who live by it as was the religion of the preliterate Australians whom Durkheim studied, who described it as just "the way things are."[6]

Capitalism has, Cox suggests, its myth of origin, its legends of the fall, its doctrine of sin and redemption, its notion of sacrifice (state belt-tightening), and its hope of salvation through the free market system. Indeed, if in the Middle Ages the church provided people with a basic orientation to life, the multinational corporation's workplace, with its "mission statements," its urgent deadlines, its demands for peak performance and total quality, does so today. Paradoxically, what would seem like the most secular of systems (capitalism), organized around the most profane of activities (making a living, shopping), provides a sense of the sacred. So what began as a *means* to an end—capitalism the means, a good living as the end—has become an *end* itself. It's a case of mission drift writ large. The cathedrals of capitalism dominate our cities. Its ideology dominates our airwaves. It calls for sacrifice, through long hours of work, and offers its blessings, through commodities. When the terrorists struck the twin towers on 9/11, they were, perhaps, aiming at what they conceived of as a more powerful rival temple, another religion. Heartless as they were, they were correct to see capitalism, and the twin towers as its symbol, as a serious rival religion.

Like older religions, capitalism partly creates the anxieties to which it poses itself as a necessary answer. Like the fire-and-brimstone sermon that begins with "Man, the lowly sinner," and ends with "Only this church can redeem you," so the market ethos defines the poor or unemployed as "unworthy slackers" and offers work and a higher standard of living as a form of salvation. Capitalism is not, then, simply a system in the *service* of family and community; it *competes* with the family. When we separate our fantasy of family life, our ideas of being a "good mother and father" from our daily expressions of parenthood, our ideals live timelessly on while we worship at the biggest altar in town, with ten-hour days and long trips to the mall.

A constellation of forces seems to be pressing in the direction of the religion of capitalism. And while no one wants to go back to the "frying pan" of patriarchy, we need to look sharp about the fire of market individualism under capitalism. It is in the spirit of looking at that fire that we can examine several conditions that exacerbate the tendency to apply the principle of efficiency to private life.

The first factor is the inevitable—and on the whole I think beneficial—movement of women into the paid workforce.[7] Exacerbating this squeeze on time is the overall absence of government or workplace policies that foster the use of parental leave or shorter, more flexible hours. Over the last twenty years, workers have also been squeezed by a lengthening workweek. According to a recent International Labor Organization report on working hours, Americans are putting in longer hours than workers of any other industrialized nation. We now work two weeks longer each year than our counterparts in Japan, the vaunted long-work-hour capital of the world.[8] American married couples and single-parent families are also putting in more hours in the day and more weeks in the year than they did thirty years ago. Counting overtime and commuting time, a 1992 national sample of men averaged 48.8 hours of work, and women, 41.7.[9] Work patterns vary by social class, ethnicity, race, and the number and ages of children, of course. But, overall, between 1969 and 1996 the increase in American mothers' paid work combined with a shift toward single-parent families has led to an average decrease of 22 hours a week of parental time available (outside of paid work) to spend with children.[10] And the emotional draw of a work culture is sometimes strong enough to outcompete a weaker family culture (see "Emotional Geography and the Flight Plan of Capitalism," chapter 15).

The Other Side of the Market Religion: Not Walking the Talk at Home

If capitalism began as a means but became an end in itself, then families and local communities must daily face a competing urgency system and a rival conception of time. Company deadlines compete with school plays. Holiday sales at the mall vie with hanging out at home. The company's schedule and rules have come, for workers, to define those of families. For the managers and production workers at Amerco, the company I studied for the *Time Bind,* the debut of a certain kind of product and its "product life cycle" came to prevail over personal anniversaries and school holidays. When family events did take precedence, they did so on company terms. As one woman explained, "My mother died and I went back to arrange for the funeral and all. I went for four days. The company gives us that for bereavement, and so that's the time I spent." In the early industrial period in Europe, whole workforces disappeared at festival time, or workers put an iron bar in the machinery, stopped the assembly line, and took a break. Company time did not always rule.

In response to the challenge of this competing urgency system, I've argued, many families separate their ideal of themselves as a "a close family" from a life that in reality is more hurried, fragmented, crowded, and individualized than they would like. They develop the idea of a hypothetical family, the family they would be if only they had time. And then they deal with life in a contrary fashion.

Many Amerco employees came home from a long workday to fit many necessary activities into a limited amount of time. Although there were important exceptions, many workers tried to go through domestic chores rapidly if for no other reason than to clear some space in which to go slowly. They used many strategies to save time—they planned, delegated, did several things simultaneously. They packed one activity close up against the next, eliminating the framing around each event, periods of looking forward to or back upon an event, which might have heightened its emotional impact. A 2:00 to 2:45 play date, 2:45 to 3:15 shopping trip, 3:15 to 4:45 visit to Grandma, and so on. As one mother, a sales manager, said with satisfaction, "What makes me a good employee at work is what makes me able to do all I do at home; I'm a multitasker, but [with a laugh] at work I get paid for it."

With all these activities, family time could be called "hurried" or "crowded." But in fact many working parents took a sporting "have fun" attitude toward their hurried lives: "Let's see how fast we can do this! Come on, kids, let's go!" They brought their image of the family closer to the reality of it by saying, in effect, "We like it this way." They saw hassle as challenge. In other families, parents seemed to encourage children to develop schedules parallel to and as hectic as their own. For example, the average annual vacation time both at Amerco—and in the United States as a whole—is twelve days, while schoolchildren typically have summer holidays of three months. So one Amerco mother placed her eight-year-old son in a nearby summer program and explained to him, in a you're-going-to-love-this way, "You have your job to go to, too." She talked about her schedule as she might have talked about a strenuous hike. She was having fun roughing it with multitasking and chopped-up time.

Another way of resolving the contradiction between ideal and reality was to critique the fun ethic and say, in effect, "Family life isn't supposed to be fun. It's supposed to be a hassle, but we're in the hassle together, and why isn't that okay?" This often carried families over long stretches of time, but it prevented family members from giving full attention to each other. Time was hurried (not enough time allotted for an activity—15-minute baths, 20-minute dinners, for example). Or time was crowded (one or more people were doing more than one thing at a time). Or it was uncoordinated. Only two out of four people could make it to dinner, the ball game, the reunion. If there was not some chronic avoidance of a deep tension, families usually also took another approach. They *deferred* having a good time. Instead of saying, "This hassle is fun," they said, in effect, "This hassle isn't fun. But we'll have fun *later*." They waited for the weekend, for their vacation, for "quality time."

But the more a family deferred the chance for relaxed communication, the more anxious they sometimes became about it. One man told me: "My wife and I hadn't had time together for a long time, so we decided to take some 'marital quality time' by going out to a restaurant to eat dinner together. We had a nice dinner and afterwards went for a walk. We passed a toy store and my wife wanted to shop for a toy for our child. But I told her, 'No, you have a different quality time with our child. This is *our* quality time.' So we spent the rest of the evening arguing about whose quality time it was we were spending."

Another long-hours Amerco executive seemed to take this strategy of deferral to an extreme. When I asked him whether he wished he'd spent more time with his three daughters when they were growing up, he answered, "Put it this way, I'm pleased with how they turned out." This father loved his daughters, but he loved them as results. Or rather, his feeling was "I want my wife to enjoy the process of raising them. I'll enjoy that vicariously. What I will enjoy directly is the result, the young adults." So he didn't think family life should or shouldn't be fun while the kids were small and adolescent. That was his wife's specialty. He was deferring his real enjoyment until his daughters had grown up. Even Amerco parents who spent far more time with their children occasionally justified this time in terms of future results. They were pleased at how "old for their age" their children were, how "ahead," given a limited expenditure of parental time. Perhaps, most parents held a double perspective on their children—they cared about the child as he or she was growing up and about the child as he or she emerged in adulthood. Most oriented toward the family as a source of intrinsic pleasure were women and workers in the middle or lower ranks of the company; least oriented in this way were upper management or professional men—the congregation and the priests.

From the top to the bottom of the Amerco workforce, workers were forced to answer the challenge of capitalism—not simply as a system that gave them jobs, money, and stuff, but as a system that offered them a sense of purpose and guidance in a confusing time. They had to deal with the religion of capitalism, its grip on honor and sense of worth, its subtraction from—or absorption of—family and community life. We've emerged from an era in which most women had little or no paid work to a era in which most do. Are women jumping from the frying pan of patriarchy into the fire of capitalism? Just as the early industrial workforces took off at festival time, because they were not yet "disciplined" to capitalism, maybe postindustrial ones will work out their own way of living a balanced life. There could be a balance not just between the role of piano teacher, say, and mother, but between the unpaid *world* of home and community and the money *world* of work and mall. That may be the deeper issue underlying the ad for Quaker Oats cereal. For, our cultural soil is surreptitiously prepared for ads, like that for Quaker Oats cereal, that make you spend time buying one more thing that promises to save time—which increasingly we spend earning and buying.

Notes

This essay, which has been substantially revised, takes as its starting point "Globalization, Time, and the Family," first published in German by the Institut für die Wissenschaften von Menchen, Vienna, 1998, and included in *Am Ende des Millenniums,* edited by Krzysztof Michalski (Stuttgart: Klett-Cotta, 2000), pp. 180–203.

1. See Hochschild 1997a.
2. Cell phones, home fax machines, car dictating machines, and similar gadgets are marketed, purchased, and used on the premise that these machines, like the cereal, will "save time"—so that the consumer can then enjoy more leisure. In practice, though, such technology often becomes a delivery system for pressure to do more paid work. Along with new technology come new norms. Electronic mail, for example, once hailed as a way of "saving time" has escalated expectations shortening the period of time one has before one is considered rude or inattentive not to reply.
3. Among affluent Americans, time-saving goods and services also force parents to define parenthood less in terms of production and more in terms of consumption. For example, a "good mother" in the American middle class is often seen as one who prepares her child's birthday, bakes the cake, blows up the balloons, invites her child's friends to a party. Increasingly, the busy working mother is tempted to buy the cake; in addition, new birthday services are available in American cities to help organize the party, send out the invitations, buy the gifts, blow up the balloons, and set up the food. The definition of a "good mother" moves from production to consumption. The "good mother" is now one who enjoys the party with the child. The gift is one of derationalized time.
4. See Gillis 1994; also Popenoe 1989 and Putnam 2000.
5. Schor 1998, pp. 16–17.
6. Cox 2001, p. 124.

7. Some commentators blame women's movement into paid work for the strains experienced at home—including the high divorce rate. But I would argue that it is not women's paid work per se, but work in the absence of the necessary social adjustments in the structure of care—male sharing of care at home, family-friendly workplace policies, and social honor associated with care—that makes the difference.

8. Doohan 1999. The 600-page ILO report compared hours of work in 240 countries. Useem (2000) cites 751 time-management titles listed on Amazon.com, including *Eating on the Run* and *Please Hold: 102 Things to Do While You Wait on the Phone.*

9. Galinsky, Bond, and Friedman 1993, p. 9.

10. "Families and Labor Market, 1969–1999: Analyzing the Time Crunch," May 1999, Report by the Council of Economic Advisors, Washington, D.C. Also a 2000 report found that 46 percent of workers work 41 hours or longer, 18 percent of them 51 hours or longer (see Center for Survey Research and Analysis, University of Connecticut, "2000 Report on U.S. Working Time"). Another recent study found that elementary school teachers—those in what is often thought to be a "woman's" job—reported working ten-hour days (see Drago et al. 1999). Less time away from work means less time for children. Nationwide, half of children wish they could see their fathers more, and a third wish they could see their mothers more (Coolsen, Seligson, and Garbino 1985; Hewlett 1991, p. 105). A growing number of commentators draw links, often carelessly, between this decline in family time and a host of problems, including school failure and alcohol and drug abuse (Hewlett 1991).

Questions to Consider

1. What are some of your definitions of progress? How do these beliefs affect the choices you make in your own life regarding career aspirations? educational plans? Is there such a thing as progress in literature, or are classics such as Shakespeare's plays simply the standard against which all other literary productions are measured?

2. What relations do you see between efficiency, technology, and education? How have such relations affected your own education? Is there, or should there be, a model for the efficient study of literature or theory? What would Burke and Haraway likely say about efficiency and writing?

3. Working from Kuhn's ideas of anomaly and paradigm shift, try to identify when and how you might have experienced a movement between different paradigms, or even what you might call a paradigm shift in your own education, perhaps as you moved from theory to theory, class to class, or school to school. Identify and examine the paradigms and shifts Greenblatt, Haraway, and Hochschild discuss.

4. In Shakespeare's play *The Tempest,* Caliban complains that his instruction in Prospero's language has taught him to curse. In other words, he criticizes the imposition of a new, or seemingly innovative, language. What has instruction in different theoretical discourses taught you? Hopefully, the instruction has taught you to do more than curse. What has the theoretical

instruction via the essays in this section taught you about technological claims and claims of progress?

5. Think about the term "cyborg." How does Haraway's discussion of the term help you think about some of the other key terms in essays in this section: "anomaly" and "paradigm shift," "equipment for living," the "savage" versus the "civilized," and "efficiency"? Are you part machine and human? Are there others who are more so than you?

6. Think about how the theorists in this section link attention to language with questions of technology and progress. How is language—something old— also a technology and also closely linked to ideas like progress? Given these connections, how is critical theory, like proverbs, also "equipment for living"? When, and in what ways, is it useful to you? How does such critical theorizing of your own experiences equip you to lead a better life?

Appendix A

ALTERNATE CONTENTS

Contents Arranged by Contemporary Methodologies

Anthropological

Cultural Studies

718

Deconstruction and Poststructuralism

Feminist Theory

Gay, Lesbian, and Queer Theory

Marxism

New Historicism

Phenomenology

Postcolonial

Psychoanalysis

Race and Ethnicity

Reader Response

Rhetoric

Structuralism and Semiotics

Contents Arranged by Theme

Aesthetics

Authorship

The Body

The Canon

Class

Gender and Sexuality

Ideology

Postmodern

Race

Subjectivity

Contents Arranged by Chronology

Appendix B

FOUNDATIONAL TEXTS

Plato (ca. 427–ca. 347 B.C.E.)

Although Plato may be best known as a philosopher, he is also credited, in the West, with the title of first literary theorist. What makes Plato's *Republic* a foundational text is its discussion of pedagogy and poetry in philosophical terms, a discussion that places poetry and philosophy in an adversarial relationship and that has spurred much literary debate down through the centuries. In Book X, Plato argues that because poetry is mimetic, imitative, or representational, it is not merely one step removed from Truth but two steps. For Plato, the Truth is only to be found in timeless universals, which he refers to as Forms or Ideas, and thus he argues that the poet who writes a poem about a bed is even farther removed from the Truth than the carpenter who builds a bed. Because Plato sees the work of poets as deceptive, he advocates the censorship of poets. If Plato's ideal republic had become a reality, the works of Homer and Hesiod would have been so heavily excised as to render them unrecognizable as the great literary masterpieces they have become.

From *Republic*, Book X

Of the many excellences which I perceive in the order of our State, there is none which upon reflection pleases me better than the rule about poetry.
To what do you refer?
To the rejection of imitative poetry, which certainly ought not to be received; as I see far more clearly now that the parts of the soul have been distinguished.

What do you mean?

Speaking in confidence, for I should not like to have my words repeated to the tragedians and the rest of the imitative tribe—but I do not mind saying to you, that all poetical imitations are ruinous to the understanding of the hearers, and that the knowledge of their true nature is the only antidote to them.

Explain the purport of your remark.

Well, I will tell you, although I have always from my earliest youth had an awe and love of Homer, which even now makes the words falter on my lips, for he is the great captain and teacher of the whole of that charming tragic company; but a man is not to be reverenced more than the truth, and therefore I will speak out.

Very good, he said.

Listen to me then, or rather, answer me.

Put your question.

Can you tell me what imitation is? for I really do not know.

A likely thing, then, that I should know.

Why not? for the duller eye may often see a thing sooner than the keener.

Very true, he said; but in your presence, even if I had any faint notion, I could not muster courage to utter it. Will you inquire yourself?

Well then, shall we begin the inquiry in our usual manner: Whenever a number of individuals have a common name, we assume them to have also a corresponding idea or form:—do you understand me?

I do.

Let us take any common instance; there are beds and tables in the world—plenty of them, are there not?

Yes.

But there are only two ideas or forms of them—one the idea of a bed, the other of a table.

True.

And the maker of either of them makes a bed or he makes a table for our use, in accordance with the idea—that is our way of speaking in this and similar instances—but no artificer makes the ideas themselves: how could he?

Impossible.

And there is another artist,—I should like to know what you would say of him.

Who is he?

One who is the maker of all the works of all other workmen.

What an extraordinary man!

Wait a little, and there will be more reason for your saying so. For this is he who is able to make not only vessels of every kind, but plants and animals, himself and all other things—the earth and heaven, and the things which are in heaven or under the earth; he makes the gods also.

He must be a wizard and no mistake.

Oh! you are incredulous, are you? Do you mean that there is no such maker or creator, or that in one sense there might be a maker of all these things but in another not? Do you see that there is a way in which you could make them all yourself?

What way?

An easy way enough; or rather, there are many ways in which the feat might be quickly and easily accomplished, none quicker than that of turning a mirror round and round—you would soon enough make the sun and the heavens, and the earth and yourself, and other animals and plants, and all the other things of which we were just now speaking, in the mirror.

Yes, he said; but they would be appearances only.

Very good, I said, you are coming to the point now. And the painter too is, as I conceive, just such another—a creator of appearances, is he not?

Of course.

But then I suppose you will say that what he creates is untrue. And yet there is a sense in which the painter also creates a bed?

Yes, he said, but not a real bed.

And what of the maker of the bed? were you not saying that he too makes, not the idea which, according to our view, is the essence of the bed, but only a particular bed?

Yes, I did.

Then if he does not make that which exists he can not make true existence, but only some semblance of existence; and if any one were to say that the work of the maker of the bed, or of any other workman, has real existence, he could hardly be supposed to be speaking the truth.

At any rate, he replied, philosophers would say that he was not speaking the truth.

No wonder, then, that his work too is an indistinct expression of truth.

No wonder.

Suppose now that by the light of the examples just offered we inquire who this imitator is?

If you please.

Well then, here are three beds: one existing in nature, which is made by God, as I think that we may say—for no one else can be the maker?

No.

There is another which is the work of the carpenter?

Yes.

And the work of the painter is a third?

Yes.

Beds, then, are of three kinds, and there are three artists who superintend them: God, the maker of the bed, and the painter?

Yes, there are three of them.

God, whether from choice or from necessity, made one bed in nature and one only; two or more such ideal beds neither ever have been nor ever will be made by God.

Why is that?

Because even if He had made but two, a third would still appear behind them which both of them would have for their idea, and that would be the ideal bed and not the two others.

Very true, he said.

God knew this, and He desired to be the real maker of a real bed, not a particular maker of a particular bed, and therefore He created a bed which is essentially and by nature one only.

So we believe.

Shall we, then, speak of Him as the natural author or maker of the bed?

Yes, he replied; inasmuch as by the natural process of creation He is the author of this and of all other things.

And what shall we say of the carpenter—is not he also the maker of the bed?

Yes.

But would you call the painter a creator and maker?

Certainly not.

Yet if he is not the maker, what is he in relation to the bed?

I think, he said, that we may fairly designate him as the imitator of that which the others make.

Good, I said; then you call him who is third in the descent from nature an imitator?

Certainly, he said.

And the tragic poet is an imitator, and therefore, like all other imitators, he is thrice removed from the king and from the truth?

That appears to be so.

Then about the imitator we are agreed. And what about the painter?—I would like to know whether he may be thought to imitate that which originally exists in nature, or only the creations of artists?

The latter.

As they are or as they appear? you have still to determine this.

What do you mean?

I mean, that you may look at a bed from different points of view, obliquely or directly or from any other point of view, and the bed will appear different, but there is no difference in reality. And the same of all things.

Yes, he said, the difference is only apparent.

Now let me ask you another question: Which is the art of painting designed to be—an imitation of things as they are, or as they appear—of appearance or of reality?

Of appearance.

Then the imitator, I said, is a long way off the truth, and can do all things because he lightly touches on a small part of them, and that part an image. For example: A painter will paint a cobbler, carpenter, or any other artist, though he knows nothing of their arts; and, if he is a good artist, he may deceive children or simple persons, when he shows them his picture of a carpenter from a distance, and they will fancy that they are looking at a real carpenter.

Certainly.

And whenever any one informs us that he has found a man who knows all the arts, and all things else that anybody knows, and every single thing with a higher degree of accuracy than any other man—whoever tells us this, I think that we can only imagine him to be a simple creature who is likely to have been deceived by some wizard or actor whom he met, and whom he thought all-knowing, because he himself was unable to analyze the nature of knowledge and ignorance and imitation.

Most true.

And so, when we hear persons saying that the tragedians, and Homer, who is at their head, know all the arts and all things human, virtue as well as vice, and divine things too, for that the good poet can not compose well unless he knows his subject, and that he who has not this knowledge can never be a poet, we ought to consider whether here also there may not be a similar illusion. Perhaps they may have come across imitators and been deceived by them; they may not have remembered when they saw their works that these were but imitations thrice removed from the truth, and could easily be made without any knowledge of the truth, because they are appearances only and not realities? Or, after all, they may be in the right, and poets do really know the things about which they seem to the many to speak so well?

The question, he said, should by all means be considered.

Now do you suppose that if a person were able to make the original as well as the image, he would seriously devote himself to the image-making branch? Would he allow imitation to be the ruling principle of his life, as if he had nothing higher in him?

I should say not.

The real artist, who knew what he was imitating, would be interested in realities and not in imitations; and would desire to leave as memorials of himself works many and fair; and, instead of being the author of encomiums, he would prefer to be the theme of them.

Yes, he said, that would be to him a source of much greater honor and profit.

Then, I said, we must put a question to Homer; not about medicine, or any of the arts to which his poems only incidentally refer: we are not going to ask him, or any other poet, whether he has cured patients like Asclepius, or left behind him a school of medicine such as the Asclepiads were, or whether he only talks about medicine and other arts at second-hand; but we have a right to know respecting military tactics, politics, education, which are the chiefest and noblest subjects of his poems, and we may fairly ask him about them. "Friend Homer," then we say to him, "if you are only in the second remove from truth in what you say of virtue, and not in the third—not an image maker or imitator—and if you are able to discern what pursuits make men better or worse in private or public life, tell us what State was ever better governed by your help? The good order of Lacedaemon is due to Lycurgus, and many other cities great and small have been similarly benefited by others; but who says that you have been a good legislator to them and have done them any good? Italy and Sicily boast of Charondas, and there is Solon who is renowned among us; but what city has anything to say about you?" Is there any city which he might name?

I think not, said Glaucon; not even the Homerids themselves pretend that he was a legislator.

Well, but is there any war on record which was carried on successfully by him, or aided by his counsels, when he was alive?

There is not.

Or is there any invention of his, applicable to the arts or to human life, such as Thales the Milesian or Anacharsis the Scythian, and other ingenious men have conceived, which is attributed to him?

There is absolutely nothing of the kind.

But, if Homer never did any public service, was he privately a guide or teacher of any? Had he in his lifetime friends who loved to associate with him, and who handed down to posterity an Homeric way of life, such as was established by Pythagoras who was so greatly beloved for his wisdom, and whose followers are to this day quite celebrated for the order which was named after him?

Nothing of the kind is recorded of him. For surely, Socrates, Creophylus, the companion of Homer, that child of flesh, whose name always makes us laugh, might be more justly ridiculed for his stupidity, if, as is said, Homer was greatly neglected by him and others in his own day when he was alive?

Yes, I replied, that is the tradition. But can you imagine, Glaucon, that if Homer had really been able to educate and improve mankind—if he had possessed knowledge and not been a mere imitator—can you imagine, I say, that he would not have had many followers, and been honored and loved by them? Protagoras of Abdera, and Prodicus of Ceos, and a host of others, have only to whisper to their contemporaries: "You will never be able to manage either your own house or your own State until you appoint us to be your ministers of education"—and this ingenious device of theirs has such an effect in making men love them that their companions all but carry them about on their shoulders. And is it conceivable that the contemporaries of Homer, or again of Hesiod, would have allowed either of them to go about as rhapsodists, if they had really been able to make mankind virtuous? Would they not have been as unwilling to part with them as with gold, and have compelled them to stay at home with them? Or, if the master would not stay, then the disciples would have followed him about everywhere, until they had got education enough?

Yes, Socrates, that, I think, is quite true.

Then must we not infer that all these poetical individuals, beginning with Homer, are only imitators; they copy images of virtue and the like, but the truth they never reach? The poet is like a painter who, as we have already observed, will make a likeness of a cobbler though he understands nothing of cobbling; and his picture is good enough for those who know no more than he does, and judge only by colors and figures.

Quite so.

In like manner the poet with his words and phrases may be said to lay on the colors of the several arts, himself understanding their nature only enough to imitate them; and other people, who are as ignorant as he is, and judge only from his words, imagine that if he speaks of cobbling, or of military tactics, or of anything else, in metre and harmony and rhythm, he speaks very well—such is the sweet influence which melody and rhythm by nature have. And I think that you must have observed again and again what a poor appearance the tales of poets make when stripped of the colors which music puts upon them, and recited in simple prose.

Yes, he said.

They are like faces which were never really beautiful, but only blooming; and now the bloom of youth has passed away from them?

Exactly.

Here is another point: The imitator or maker of the image knows nothing of true existence; he knows appearances only. Am I not right?

Yes.

Then let us have a clear understanding, and not be satisfied with half an explanation.

Proceed.

Of the painter we say that he will paint reins, and he will paint a bit?

Yes.

And the worker in leather and brass will make them?

Certainly.

But does the painter know the right form of the bit and reins? Nay, hardly even the workers in brass and leather who make them; only the horseman who knows how to use them—he knows their right form.

Most true.

And may we not say the same of all things?

What?

That there are three arts which are concerned with all things: one which uses, another which makes, a third which imitates them?

Yes.

And the excellence or beauty or truth of every structure, animate or inanimate, and of every action of man, is relative to the use for which nature or the artist has intended them.

True.

Then the user of them must have the greatest experience of them, and he must indicate to the maker the good or bad qualities which develop themselves in use; for example, the flute-player will tell the flute-maker which of his flutes is satisfactory to the performer; he will tell him how he ought to make them, and the other will attend to his instructions?

Of course.

The one knows and therefore speaks with authority about the goodness and badness of flutes, while the other, confiding in him, will do what he is told by him?

True.

The instrument is the same, but about the excellence or badness of it the maker will only attain to a correct belief; and this he will gain from him who knows, by talking to him and being compelled to hear what he has to say, whereas the user will have knowledge?

True.

But will the imitator have either? Will he know from use whether or no his drawing is correct or beautiful? or will he have right opinion from being compelled to associate with another who knows and gives him instructions about what he should draw?

Neither.

Then he will no more have true opinion than he will have knowledge about the goodness or badness of his imitations?

I suppose not.

The imitative artist will be in a brilliant state of intelligence about his own creations?

Nay, very much the reverse.

And still he will go on imitating without knowing what makes a thing good or bad, and may be expected therefore to imitate only that which appears to be good to the ignorant multitude?

Just so.

Thus far then we are pretty well agreed that the imitator has no knowledge worth mentioning of what he imitates. Imitation is only a kind of play or sport, and the tragic poets, whether they write in Iambic or in Heroic verse, are imitators in the highest degree?

Very true.

And now tell me, I conjure you, has not imitation been shown by us to be concerned with that which is thrice removed from the truth?

Certainly.

[. . .]

We may state the question thus:—Imitation imitates the actions of men, whether voluntary or involuntary, on which, as they imagine, a good or bad result has ensued, and they rejoice or sorrow accordingly. Is there anything more?

No, there is nothing else.

But in all this variety of circumstances is the man at unity with himself—or rather, as in the instance of sight there was confusion and opposition in his opinions about the same things, so here also is there not strife and inconsistency in his life? Though I need hardly raise the question again, for I remember that all this has been already admitted; and the soul has been acknowledged by us to be full of these and ten thousand similar oppositions occurring at the same moment?

And we were right, he said.

Yes, I said, thus far we were right; but there was an omission which must now be supplied.

What was the omission?

Were we not saying that a good man, who has the misfortune to lose his son or anything else which is most dear to him, will bear the loss with more equanimity than another?

Yes.

But will he have no sorrow, or shall we say that although he can not help sorrowing, he will moderate his sorrow?

The latter, he said, is the truer statement.

Tell me: will he be more likely to struggle and hold out against his sorrow when he is seen by his equals, or when he is alone?

It will make a great difference whether he is seen or not.

When he is by himself he will not mind saying or doing many things which he would be ashamed of any one hearing or seeing him do?

True.

There is a principle of law and reason in him which bids him resist, as well as a feeling of his misfortune which is forcing him to indulge his sorrow?

True.

But when a man is drawn in two opposite directions, to and from the same object, this, as we affirm, necessarily implies two distinct principles in him?

Certainly.

One of them is ready to follow the guidance of the law?

How do you mean?

The law would say that to be patient under suffering is best, and that we should not give way to impatience, as there is no knowing whether such things are good or evil; and nothing is gained by impatience; also, because no human thing is of serious importance, and grief stands in the way of that which at the moment is most required.

What is most required? he asked.

That we should take counsel about what has happened, and when the dice have been thrown order our affairs in the way which reason deems best; not, like children who have had a fall, keeping hold of the part struck and wasting time in setting up a howl, but always accustoming the soul forthwith to apply a remedy, raising up that which is sickly and fallen, banishing the cry of sorrow by the healing art.

Yes, he said, that is the true way of meeting the attacks of fortune.

Yes, I said; and the higher principle is ready to follow this suggestion of reason?

Clearly.

And the other principle, which inclines us to recollection of our troubles and to lamentation, and can never have enough of them, we may call irrational, useless, and cowardly?

Indeed, we may.

And does not the latter—I mean the rebellious principle—furnish a great variety of materials for imitation? Whereas the wise and calm temperament, being always nearly equable, is not easy to imitate or to appreciate when imitated, especially at a public festival when a promiscuous crowd is assembled in a theatre. For the feeling represented is one to which they are strangers.

Certainly.

Then the imitative poet who aims at being popular is not by nature made, nor is his art intended, to please or to affect the rational principle in the soul; but he will prefer the passionate and fitful temper, which is easily imitated?

Clearly.

And now we may fairly take him and place him by the side of the painter, for he is like him in two ways: first, inasmuch as his creations have an inferior degree of truth—in this, I say, he is like him; and he is also like him in being concerned with an inferior part of the soul; and therefore we shall be right in refusing to admit him into a well-ordered State, because he awakens and nourishes and strengthens the feelings and impairs the reason. As in a city when the evil are permitted to have authority and the good are put out of the way, so in the soul of man, as we maintain, the imitative poet implants an evil constitution, for he indulges the irrational nature which has no discernment of greater and less, but thinks the same thing at one time great and at another small—he is a manufacturer of images and is very far removed from the truth.

Exactly.

But we have not yet brought forward the heaviest count in our accusation:— the power which poetry has of harming even the good (and there are very few who are not harmed), is surely an awful thing?

Yes, certainly, if the effect is what you say.

Hear and judge: The best of us, as I conceive, when we listen to a passage of Homer, or one of the tragedians, in which he represents some pitiful hero who is drawling out his sorrows in a long oration, or weeping, and smiting his breast— the best of us, you know, delight in giving way to sympathy, and are in raptures at the excellence of the poet who stirs our feelings most.

Yes, of course I know.

But when any sorrow of our own happens to us, then you may observe that we pride ourselves on the opposite quality—we would fain be quiet and patient; this is the manly part, and the other which delighted us in the recitation is now deemed to be the part of a woman.

Very true, he said.

Now can we be right in praising and admiring another who is doing that which any one of us would abominate and be ashamed of in his own person?

No, he said, that is certainly not reasonable.

Nay, I said, quite reasonable from one point of view.

What point of view?

If you consider, I said, that when in misfortune we feel a natural hunger and desire to relieve our sorrow by weeping and lamentation, and that this feeling which is kept under control in our own calamities is satisfied and delighted by the poets;—the better nature in each of us, not having been sufficiently trained by reason or habit, allows the sympathetic element to break loose because the sorrow is another's; and the spectator fancies that there can be no disgrace to himself in praising and pitying any one who comes telling him what a good man he is, and making a fuss about his troubles; he thinks that the pleasure is a gain, and why should he be supercilious and lose this and the poem too? Few persons ever reflect, as I should imagine, that from the evil of other men something of evil is communicated to themselves. And so the feeling of sorrow which has gathered strength at the sight of the misfortunes of others is with difficulty repressed in our own.

How very true!

And does not the same hold also of the ridiculous? There are jests which you would be ashamed to make yourself, and yet on the comic stage, or indeed in private, when you hear them, you are greatly amused by them, and are not at all disgusted at their unseemliness;—the case of pity is repeated;—there is a principle in human nature which is disposed to raise a laugh, and this which you once restrained by reason, because you were afraid of being thought a buffoon, is now let out again; and having stimulated the risible faculty at the theatre, you are betrayed unconsciously to yourself into playing the comic poet at home.

Quite true, he said.

And the same may be said of lust and anger and all the other affections, of desire and pain and pleasure, which are held to be inseparable from every action—in all of them poetry feeds and waters the passions instead of drying them up; she lets them rule, although they ought to be controlled, if mankind are ever to increase in happiness and virtue.

I can not deny it.

Therefore, Glaucon, I said, whenever you meet with any of the eulogists of Homer declaring that he has been the educator of Hellas, and that he is profitable for education and for the ordering of human things, and that you should take him up again and again and get to know him and regulate your whole life according to him, we may love and honor those who say these things—they are excellent people, as far as their lights extend; and we are ready to acknowledge that Homer is the greatest of poets and first of tragedy writers; but we must remain firm in our conviction that hymns to the gods and praises of famous men are the only poetry which ought to be admitted into our State. For if you go beyond this and allow the honeyed muse to enter, either in epic or lyric verse, not law and the reason of mankind, which by common consent have ever been deemed best, but pleasure and pain will be the rulers in our State.

That is most true, he said.

And now since we have reverted to the subject of poetry, let this our defence serve to show the reasonableness of our former judgment in sending away out of our State an art having the tendencies which we have described; for reason constrained us. But that she may not impute to us any harshness or want of politeness, let us tell her that there is an ancient quarrel between philosophy and poetry; of which there are many proofs, such as the saying of "the yelping hound howling at her lord," or of one "mighty in the vain talk of fools," and "the mob of sages circumventing Zeus," and the "subtle thinkers who are beggars after all;" and there are innumerable other signs of ancient enmity between them. Notwithstanding this, let us assure our sweet friend and the sister arts of imitation, that if she will only prove her title to exist in a well-ordered State we shall be delighted to receive her—we are very conscious of her charms; but we may not on that account betray the truth. I dare say, Glaucon, that you are as much charmed by her as I am, especially when she appears in Homer?

Yes, indeed, I am greatly charmed.

Shall I propose, then, that she be allowed to return from exile, but upon this condition only—that she make a defence of herself in lyrical or some other metre?

Certainly.

And we may further grant to those of her defenders who are lovers of poetry and yet not poets the permission to speak in prose on her behalf: let them show not only that she is pleasant but also useful to States and to human life, and we will listen in a kindly spirit; for if this can be proved we shall surely be the gainers—I mean, if there is a use in poetry as well as a delight?

Certainly, he said, we shall be the gainers.

If her defence fails, then, my dear friend, like other persons who are enamored of something, but put a restraint upon themselves when they think their desires are opposed to their interests, so too must we after the manner of lovers give her up, though not without a struggle. We too are inspired by that love of poetry which the education of noble States has implanted in us, and therefore we would have her appear at her best and truest; but so long as she is unable to make good her defence, this argument of ours shall be a charm to us, which we will repeat to ourselves while we listen to her strains; that we may not fall away into the childish love of her which captivates the many. At all events we are well aware that poetry being such as we have described is not to be regarded seriously as attaining to the truth; and he who listens to her, fearing for the safety of the city which is within him, should be on his guard against her seductions and make our words his law.

Yes, he said, I quite agree with you.

Yes, I said, my dear Glaucon, for great is the issue at stake, greater than appears, whether a man is to be good or bad. And what will any one be profited if under the influence of honor or money or power, aye, or under the excitement of poetry, he neglect justice and virtue?

Yes, he said; I have been convinced by the argument, as I believe that any one else would have been.

William Wordsworth (1770–1850)

Wordsworth defined himself primarily as a poet rather than a critic. In fact, in 1830, he stated the following quite unequivocally: "I am not a critic and set little value upon the art." And yet his preface to *Lyrical Ballads* is considered one of the most important documents in English literary criticism because it both raises and confronts such fundamental questions as "What is a poet?" and "To whom does he address himself?" What makes the preface such an important document is its political as well as its literary agenda, its break from the authority of neo-classical rules and conventions. Inspired by the democratic sentiments of the French Revolution during the early 1790s, Wordsworth's preface advocates a poetry that uses the language of real people and that takes as its subject matter things that hitherto had not been deemed appropriate—the mad, the marginalized, the "low and rustic life."

From Preface to *Lyrical Ballads*

The first Volume of these Poems has already been submitted to general perusal. It was published as an experiment, which, I hoped, might be of some use to ascertain how far, by fitting to metrical arrangement a selection of the real language of men in a state of vivid sensation, that sort of pleasure and that quantity of pleasure may be imparted, which a Poet may rationally endeavour to impart.

[. . .]

Several of my Friends are anxious for the success of these Poems, from a belief that, if the views with which they were composed were indeed realised, a class of Poetry would be produced, well adapted to interest mankind permanently, and not unimportant in the quality and in the multiplicity of its moral relations: and on this account they have advised me to prefix a systematic defence of the theory upon which the Poems were written. But I was unwilling to undertake the task, knowing that on this occasion the Reader would look coldly upon my arguments, since I might be suspected of having been principally influenced by the selfish and foolish hope of *reasoning* him into an approbation of these particular Poems: and I was still more unwilling to undertake the task, because adequately to display the opinions, and fully to enforce the arguments, would require a space wholly disproportionate to a preface. For, to treat the subject with the clearness and coherence of which it is susceptible, it would be necessary to give a full account of the present state of the public taste in this country, and to determine how far this taste is healthy or depraved; which, again, could not be determined without pointing out in what manner language and the human mind act and re-act on each other, and without retracing the revolutions, not of literature alone, but likewise of society itself. I have therefore altogether declined to enter regularly upon this defence; yet I am sensible that there would be something like impropriety in abruptly obtruding upon the Public, without a few words of introduction, Poems so materially different from those upon which general approbation is at present bestowed.

It is supposed that by the act of writing in verse an Author makes a formal engagement that he will gratify certain known habits of association; that he not only thus apprises the Reader that certain classes of ideas and expressions will be found in his book, but that others will be carefully excluded. This exponent or symbol held forth by metrical language must in different eras of literature have excited very different expectations: for example, in the age of Catullus, Terence, and Lucretius, and that of Statius or Claudian; and in our own country, in the age of Shakespeare and Beaumont and Fletcher, and that of Donne and Cowley, or Dryden, or Pope. I will not take upon me to determine the exact import of the promise which, by the act of writing in verse, an Author in the present day makes to his reader; but it will undoubtedly appear to many persons that I have not fulfilled the terms of an engagement thus voluntarily contracted. They who have been accustomed to the gaudiness and inane phraseology of many modern writers, if they persist in reading this book to its conclusion, will, no doubt, frequently have to struggle with feelings of strangeness and awkwardness: they will look round for poetry, and will be induced to inquire by what species of courtesy these attempts can be permitted to assume that title. I hope, therefore, the reader will not censure me for attempting to state what I have proposed to myself to perform; and also (as far as the limits of a preface will permit) to explain some of the chief reasons which have determined me in the choice of my purpose: that at least he may be spared any unpleasant feeling of disappointment, and that I myself may be protected from one of the most dishonourable accusations which can be brought against an Author: namely, that of an indolence which prevents him from endeavouring to ascertain what is his duty, or, when his duty is ascertained, prevents him from performing it.

The principal object, then, proposed in these Poems, was to choose incidents and situations from common life, and to relate or describe them throughout, as far as was possible, in a selection of language really used by men, and, at the same time, to throw over them a certain colouring of imagination, whereby ordinary things should be presented to the mind in an unusual aspect; and further, and above all, to make these incidents and situations interesting by tracing in them, truly though not ostentatiously, the primary laws of our nature: chiefly, as far as regards the manner in which we associate ideas in a state of excitement. Humble and rustic life was generally chosen, because in that condition the essential passions of the heart find a better soil in which they can attain their maturity, are less under restraint, and speak a plainer and more emphatic language; because in that condition of life our elementary feelings co-exist in a state of greater simplicity, and, consequently, may be more accurately contemplated, and more forcibly communicated; because the manners of rural life germinate from those elementary feelings, and, from the necessary character of rural occupations, are more easily comprehended, and are more durable; and, lastly, because in that condition the passions of men are incorporated with the beautiful and permanent forms of nature. The language, too, of these men has been adopted (purified indeed from what appear to be its real defects, from all lasting and rational causes of dislike or disgust), because such men hourly communicate with the best objects from which the best part of language is originally derived; and because, from their rank in society and the sameness and narrow circle of their intercourse, being less under the influence of social vanity, they convey their feelings and notions in simple and unelaborated expressions. Accordingly, such a language, arising out of repeated experience and regular feelings, is a more permanent, and a far more philosophical language, than that which is frequently substituted for it by Poets, who think that they are conferring honour upon themselves and their art in proportion as they separate themselves from the sympathies of men, and indulge in arbitrary and capricious habits of expression, in order to furnish food for fickle tastes and fickle appetites of their own creation.[1]

I cannot, however, be insensible to the present outcry against the triviality and meanness, both of thought and language, which some of my contemporaries have occasionally introduced into their metrical compositions; and I acknowledge that this defect, where it exists, is more dishonourable to the Writer's own character than false refinement or arbitrary innovation, though I should contend at the same time that it is far less pernicious in the sum of its consequences. From such verses the Poems in these volumes will be found distinguished at least by one mark of difference, that each of them has a worthy *purpose*. Not that I always began to write with a distinct purpose formally conceived, but habits of meditation have, I trust, so prompted and regulated my feelings, that my descriptions of such objects as strongly excite those feelings will be found to carry along with them a *purpose*. If this opinion be erroneous, I can have little right to the name of a Poet. For all good poetry is the spontaneous overflow of powerful feelings: and though this be true, Poems to which any value can be attached were never produced on any variety of subjects but by a man who, being possessed of more than usual organic sensibility, had also thought long and deeply. For our continued influxes of feeling are modified and directed by our thoughts, which are indeed the representatives of all our past feelings; and as, by contemplating the relation of these general representatives to each other, we discover what is really important to men, so, by the repetition and continuance of this act, our feelings will be connected with important subjects, till at length, if we be originally possessed of much sensibility, such habits of mind will be produced that, by obeying blindly and mechanically the impulses of those habits, we shall describe objects, and utter sentiments, of such a nature, and in such connection with each other, that the understanding of the Reader must necessarily be in some degree enlightened, and his affection strengthened and purified.

It has been said that each of these Poems has a purpose. Another circumstance must be mentioned which distinguishes these Poems from the popular Poetry of the day; it is this, that the feeling therein developed gives importance to the action and situation, and not the action and situation to the feeling.

A sense of false modesty shall not prevent me from asserting that the Reader's attention is pointed to this mark of distinction, far less for the sake of these particular Poems than from the general importance of the subject. The subject is indeed important! For the human mind is capable of being excited without the application of gross and violent stimulants; and he must have a very faint perception of its beauty and dignity who does not know this, and who does not further know, that one being is elevated above another in proportion as he possesses this capability. It has therefore appeared to me, that to endeavour to produce or enlarge this capability is one of the best services in which, at any period, a Writer can be engaged; but this service, excellent at all times, is especially so at the present day. For a multitude of causes, unknown to former times, are now acting with a combined force to blunt the discriminating powers of the mind, and, unfitting it for all voluntary exertion, to reduce it to a state of almost savage torpor. The most effective of these causes are the great national events which are daily taking place, and the increasing accumulation of men in cities, where the uniformity of their occupations produces a craving for extraordinary incident which the rapid communication of intelligence hourly gratifies. To this tendency of life and manners the literature and theatrical exhibitions of the country have conformed themselves. The invaluable works of our elder writers, I had almost said the works of Shakespeare and Milton, are driven into neglect by frantic novels, sickly and stupid German Tragedies, and deluges of idle and extravagant stories in verse.

[. . .]

Having dwelt thus long on the subjects and aim of these Poems, I shall request the Reader's permission to apprise him of a few circumstances relating to their *style,* in order, among other reasons, that he may not censure me for not having performed what I never attempted. The Reader will find that personifications of abstract ideas rarely occur in these volumes, and are utterly rejected as an ordinary device to elevate the style and raise it above prose. My purpose was to imitate, and, as far as is possible, to adopt the very language of men; and assuredly such personifications do not make any natural or regular part of that language. They are, indeed, a figure of speech occasionally prompted by passion, and I have made use of them as such; but have endeavoured utterly to reject them as a mechanical device of style, or as a family language which Writers in metre seem to lay claim to by prescription. I have wished to keep the Reader in the company of flesh and blood, persuaded that by so doing I shall interest him. Others who pursue a different track will interest him likewise; I do not interfere with their claim, but wish to prefer a claim of my own. There will also be found in these volumes little of what is usually called poetic diction; as much pains has been taken to avoid it as is ordinarily taken to produce it; this has been done for the reason already alleged, to bring my language near to the language of men; and further, because the pleasure which I have proposed to myself to impart is of a kind very different from that which is supposed by many persons to be the proper object of poetry. Without being culpably particular, I do not know how to give my Reader a more exact notion of the style in which it was my wish and intention to write, than by informing him that I have at all times endeavoured to look steadily at my subject; consequently there is, I hope, in these Poems little falsehood of description, and my ideas are expressed in language fitted to their respective importance. Something must have been gained by this practice, as it is friendly to one property of all good poetry, namely, good sense: but it has necessarily cut me off from a large portion of phrases and figures of speech which from father to son have long been regarded as the common inheritance of Poets. I have also thought it expedient to restrict myself still further, having abstained from the use of many expressions, in themselves proper and beautiful, but which have been foolishly repeated by bad Poets, till such feelings of disgust are connected with them as it is scarcely possible by any art of association to overpower.

If in a poem there should be found a series of lines, or even a single line, in which the language, though naturally arranged, and according to the strict laws of metre, does not differ from that of prose, there is a numerous class of critics, who, when they stumble upon these prosaisms, as they call them, imagine that they have made a notable discovery, and exult over the Poet as over a man ignorant of his own profession. Now these men would establish a canon of criticism which the Reader will conclude he must utterly reject, if he wishes to be pleased with these volumes. And it would be a most easy task to prove to him that not only the language of a large portion of every good poem, even of the most elevated character, must necessarily, except with reference to the metre, in no respect differ from that of good prose, but likewise that some of the most interesting parts of the best poems will be found to be strictly the language of prose when prose is well written. The truth of this assertion might be demonstrated by innumerable passages from almost all the poetical writings, even of Milton himself. To illustrate the subject in a general manner, I will here adduce a short composition of Gray, who was at the head of those who, by their reasonings, have attempted to widen the space of separation betwixt Prose and Metrical composition, and was more than any other man curiously elaborate in the structure of his own poetic diction.

> "In vain to me the smiling mornings shine,
> And reddening Phoebus lifts his golden fire;
> The birds in vain their amorous descant join,
> Or cheerful fields resume their green attire.
> These ears, alas! for other notes repine;
> *A different object do these eyes require;*
> *My lonely anguish melts no heart but mine;*
> *And in my breast the imperfect joys expire;*
> Yet morning smiles the busy race to cheer,
> And new-born pleasure brings to happier men;
> The fields to all their wonted tribute bear;
> To warm their little loves the birds complain.
> *I fruitless mourn to him that cannot hear,*
> *And weep the more because I weep in vain.*"

It will easily be perceived, that the only part of this Sonnet which is of any value is the lines printed in Italics; it is equally obvious that, except in the rhyme and in the use of the single word "fruitless" for fruitlessly, which is so far a defect, the language of these lines does in no respect differ from that of prose.

By the foregoing quotation it has been shown that the language of Prose may yet be well adapted to Poetry; and it was previously asserted that a large portion of the language of every good poem can in no respect differ from that of good Prose. We will go further. It may be safely affirmed that there neither is, nor can be, any *essential* difference between the language of prose and metrical composition. We are fond of tracing the resemblance between Poetry and Painting, and, accordingly, we call them Sisters: but where shall we find bonds of connection sufficiently strict to typify the affinity betwixt metrical and prose composition? They both speak by and to the same organs; the bodies in which both of them are clothed may be said to be of the same substance, their affections are kindred, and almost identical, not necessarily differing even in degree; Poetry[2] sheds no tears "such as Angels weep," but natural and human tears; she can boast of no celestial ichor that distinguishes her vital juices from those of Prose; the same human blood circulates through the veins of them both.

If it be affirmed that rhyme and metrical arrangement of themselves constitute a distinction which overturns what has just been said on the strict affinity of metrical language with that of Prose, and paves the way for other artificial distinctions which the mind voluntarily admits, I answer that the language of such Poetry as is here recommended is, as far as is possible, a selection of the language really spoken by men; that this selection, wherever it is made with true taste and feeling, will of itself form a distinction far greater than would at first be imagined, and will entirely separate the composition from the vulgarity and meanness of ordinary life; and, if metre be superadded thereto, I believe that a dissimilitude will be produced altogether sufficient for the gratification of a rational mind. What other distinction would we have? Whence is it to come? And where is it to exist? Not, surely, where the Poet speaks through the mouths of his characters: it cannot be necessary here, either for elevation of style, or any of its supposed ornaments; for, if the Poet's subject be judiciously chosen, it will naturally, and upon fit occasion, lead him to passions, the language of which, if selected truly and judiciously, must necessarily be dignified and variegated, and alive with metaphors and figures. I forbear to speak of an incongruity which would shock the intelligent Reader, should the Poet interweave any foreign splendour of his own with that which the passion naturally suggests: it is sufficient to say that such addition is unnecessary. And, surely, it is more probable that those passages, which with propriety abound with metaphors and figures, will have their due effect if, upon other occasions where the passions are of a milder character, the style also be subdued and temperate.

But, as the pleasure which I hope to give by the Poems now presented to the Reader must depend entirely on just notions upon this subject, and as it is in itself of high importance to our taste and moral feelings, I cannot content myself with these detached remarks. And if, in what I am about to say, it shall appear to some that my labour is unnecessary, and that I am like a man fighting a battle without enemies, such persons may be reminded that, whatever be the language outwardly holden by men, a practical faith in the opinions which I am wishing to establish is almost unknown. If my conclusions are admitted, and carried as far as they must be carried if admitted at all, our judgments concerning the works of the greatest Poets, both ancient and modern, will be far different from what they are at present, both when we praise and when we censure: and our moral feelings influencing and influenced by these judgments will, I believe, be corrected and purified.

Taking up the subject, then, upon general grounds, let me ask, what is meant by the word Poet? What is a Poet? To whom does he address himself? And what language is to be expected from him?—He is a man speaking to men: a man, it is true, endowed with more lively sensibility, more enthusiasm and tenderness, who has a greater knowledge of human nature, and a more comprehensive soul, than are supposed to be common among mankind; a man pleased with his own passions and volitions, and who rejoices more than other men in the spirit of life that is in him; delighting to contemplate similar volitions and passions as manifested in the goings-on of the Universe, and habitually impelled to create them where he does not find them. To these qualities he has added a disposition to be affected more than any other men by absent things as if they were present; an ability of conjuring up in himself passions, which are indeed far from being the same as those produced by real events, yet (especially in those parts of the general sympathy which are pleasing and delightful) do more nearly resemble the passions produced by real events than anything which, from the motions of their own minds merely, other men are accustomed to feel in themselves:—whence, and from practice, he has acquired a greater readiness and power in expressing what he thinks and feels, and especially those thoughts and feelings which, by his own choice, or from the structure of his own mind, arise in him without immediate external excitement.

But whatever portion of this faculty we may suppose even the greatest Poet to possess, there cannot be a doubt that the language which it will suggest to him must often, in liveliness and truth, fall short of that which is uttered by men in real life under the actual pressure of those passions, certain shadows of which the Poet thus produces, or feels to be produced, in himself.

However exalted a notion we would wish to cherish of the character of a Poet, it is obvious that, while he describes and imitates passions, his employment is in some degree mechanical compared with the freedom and power of real and substantial action and suffering. So that it will be the wish of the Poet to bring his feelings near to those of the persons whose feelings he describes, nay, for short spaces of time, perhaps, to let himself slip into an entire delusion, and even confound and identify his own feelings with theirs; modifying only the language which is thus suggested to him by a consideration that he describes for a particular purpose, that of giving pleasure. Here, then, he will apply the principle of selection which has been already insisted upon. He will depend upon this for removing what would otherwise be painful or disgusting in the passion; he will feel that there is no necessity to trick out or to elevate nature: and the more industriously he applies this principle the deeper will be his faith that no words, which *his* fancy or imagination can suggest, will be to be compared with those which are the emanations of reality and truth.

But it may be said by those who do not object to the general spirit of these remarks, that, as it is impossible for the Poet to produce upon all occasions language as exquisitely fitted for the passion as that which the real passion itself suggests, it is proper that he should consider himself as in the situation of a translator, who does not scruple to substitute excellences of another kind for those which are unattainable by him; and endeavours occasionally to surpass his original, in order to make some amends for the general inferiority to which he feels he must submit. But this would be to encourage idleness and unmanly despair. Further, it is the language of men who speak of what they do not understand; who talk of Poetry, as of a matter of amusement and idle pleasure; who will converse with us as gravely about a *taste* for Poetry, as they express it, as if it were a thing as indifferent as a taste for rope-dancing, or Frontiniac or Sherry. Aristotle, I have been told, has said, that Poetry is the most philosophic of all writing: it is so: its object is truth, not individual and local, but general and operative; not standing upon external testimony, but carried alive into the heart by passion; truth which is its own testimony, which gives competence and confidence to the tribunal to which it appeals, and receives them from the same tribunal. Poetry is the image of man and nature. The obstacles which stand in the way of the fidelity of the Biographer and Historian, and of their consequent utility, are incalculably greater than those which are to be encountered by the Poet who comprehends the dignity of his art. The Poet writes under one restriction only, namely, the necessity of giving immediate pleasure to a human Being possessed of that information which may be expected from him, not as a lawyer, a physician, a mariner, an astronomer, or a natural philosopher, but as a Man. Except this one restriction, there is no object standing between the Poet and the image of things; between this, and the Biographer and Historian, there are a thousand.

[. . .]

To this knowledge which all men carry about with them, and to these sympathies in which, without any other discipline than that of our daily life, we are fitted to take delight, the Poet principally directs his attention. He considers man and nature as essentially adapted to each other, and the mind of man as naturally the mirror of the fairest and most interesting properties of nature. And thus the Poet, prompted by this feeling of pleasure, which accompanies him through the whole course of his studies, converses with general nature, with affections akin to those which, through labour and length of time, the Man of science has raised up in himself, by conversing with those particular parts of nature which are the objects of his studies. The knowledge both of the Poet and the Man of science is pleasure; but the knowledge of the one cleaves to us as a necessary part of our existence, our natural and unalienable inheritance; the other is a personal and individual acquisition, slow to come to us, and by no habitual and direct sympathy connecting us with our fellow-beings. The Man of science seeks truth as a remote and unknown benefactor; he cherishes and loves it in his solitude; the Poet, singing a song in which all human beings join with him, rejoices in the presence of truth as our visible friend and hourly companion. Poetry is the breath and finer spirit of all knowledge; it is the impassioned expression which is in the countenance of all Science. Emphatically may it be said of the Poet, as Shakespeare hath said of man, "that he looks before and after." He is the rock of defence for human nature; an upholder and preserver, carrying everywhere with him relationship and love. In spite of difference of soil and climate, of language and manners, of laws and customs: in spite of things silently gone out of mind, and things violently destroyed; the Poet binds together by passion and knowledge the vast empire of human society, as it is spread over the whole earth and over all time. The objects of the Poet's thoughts are everywhere; though the eyes and senses of man are, it is true, his favourite guides, yet he will follow wheresoever he can find an atmosphere of sensation in which to move his wings. Poetry is the first and last of all knowledge—it is as immortal as the heart of man. If the labours of Men of science should ever create any material revolution, direct or indirect, in our condition, and in the impressions which we habitually receive, the Poet will sleep then no more than at present; he will be ready to follow the steps of the Man of science, not only in those general indirect effects, but he will be at his side, carrying sensation into the midst of the objects of the science itself. The remotest discoveries of the Chemist, the Botanist, or Mineralogist, will be as proper objects of the Poet's art as any upon which it can be employed, if the time should ever come when these things shall be familiar to us, and the relations under which they are contemplated by the followers of these respective sciences shall be manifestly and palpably material to us as enjoying and suffering beings. If the time should ever come when what is now called science, thus familiarised to men, shall be ready to put on, as it were, a form of flesh and blood, the Poet will lend his divine spirit to aid the transfiguration, and will welcome the Being thus produced as a dear and genuine inmate of the household of man.—It is not, then, to be supposed that any one, who holds that sublime notion of Poetry which I have attempted to convey, will break in upon the sanctity and truth of his pictures by transitory and accidental ornaments, and endeavour to excite admiration of himself by arts, the necessity of which must manifestly depend upon the assumed meanness of his subject.

What has been thus far said applies to Poetry in general, but especially to those parts of compositions where the Poet speaks through the mouths of his characters; and upon this point it appears to authorise the conclusion that there are few persons of good sense who would not allow that the dramatic parts of composition are defective in proportion as they deviate from the real language of nature, and are coloured by a diction of the Poet's own, either peculiar to him as an individual Poet or belonging simply to Poets in general; to a body of men who, from the circumstance of their compositions being in metre, it is expected will employ a particular langauge.

It is not, then, in the dramatic parts of composition that we look for this distinction of language; but still it may be proper and necessary where the Poet speaks to us in his own person and character. To this I answer by referring the Reader to the description before given of a Poet. Among the qualities there enumerated as principally conducing to form a Poet, is implied nothing differing in kind from other men, but only in degree. The sum of what was said is, that the Poet is chiefly distinguished from other men by a greater promptness to think and feel without immediate external excitement, and a greater power in expressing such thoughts and feelings as are produced in him in that manner. But these passions and thoughts and feelings are the general passions and thoughts and feelings of men. And with what are they connected? Undoubtedly with our moral sentiments and animal sensations, and with the causes which excite these; with the operations of the elements, and the appearances of the visible universe; with storm and sunshine, with the revolutions of the seasons, with cold and heat, with loss of friends and kindred, with injuries and resentments, gratitude and hope, with fear and sorrow. These, and the like, are the sensations and objects which the Poet describes, as they are the sensations of other men and the objects which interest them. The Poet thinks and feels in the spirit of human passions. How, then, can his language differ in any material degree from that of all other men who feel vividly and see clearly? It might be *proved* that it is impossible. But supposing that this were not the case, the Poet might then be allowed to use a peculiar language when expressing his feelings for his own gratification, or that of men like himself. But Poets do not write for Poets alone, but for men. Unless, therefore, we are advocates for that admiration which subsists upon ignorance, and that pleasure which arises from hearing what we do not understand, the Poet must descend from this supposed height; and, in order to excite rational sympathy, he must express himself as other men express themselves. To this it may be added, that while he is only selecting from the real language of men, or, which amounts to the same thing, composing accurately in the spirit of such selection, he is treading upon safe ground, and we know what we are to expect from him. Our feelings are the same with respect to metre; for, as it may be proper to remind the Reader, the distinction of metre is regular and uniform, and not, like that which is produced by what is usually called POETIC DICTION, arbitrary, and subject to infinite caprices, upon which no calculation whatever can be made. In the one case, the Reader is utterly at the mercy of the Poet, respecting what imagery or diction he may choose to connect with the passion; whereas, in the other, the metre obeys certain laws, to which the Poet and Reader both willingly submit because they are certain, and because no interference is made by them with the passion but such as the concurring testimony of ages has shown to heighten and improve the pleasure which co-exists with it.

It will now be proper to answer an obvious question, namely, Why, professing these opinions, have I written in verse? To this, in addition to such answer as is included in what has been already said, I reply, in the first place, Because, however I may have restricted myself, there is still left open to me what confessedly constitutes the most valuable object of all writing, whether in prose or verse; the great and universal passions of men, the most general and interesting of their occupations, and the entire world of nature before me—to supply endless combinations of forms and imagery. Now, supposing for a moment that whatever is interesting in these objects may be as vividly described in prose, why should I be condemned for attempting to superadd to such description the charm which, by the consent of all nations, is acknowledged to exist in metrical language? To this, by such as are yet unconvinced, it may be answered that a very small part of the pleasure given by Poetry depends upon the metre, and that it is injudicious to write in metre, unless it be accompanied with the other artificial distinctions of style with which metre is usually accompanied, and that, by such deviation, more will be lost from the shock which will thereby be given to the Reader's associations than will be counterbalanced by any pleasure which he can derive from the general power of numbers. In answer to those who still contend for the necessity of accompanying metre with certain appropriate colours of style in order to the accomplishment of its appropriate end, and who also, in my opinion, greatly under-rate the power of metre in itself, it might, perhaps, as far as relates to these Volumes, have been almost sufficient to observe, that poems are extant, written upon more humble subjects, and in a still more naked and simple style, which have continued to give pleasure from generation to generation. Now, if nakedness and simplicity be a defect, the fact here mentioned affords a strong presumption that poems somewhat less naked and simple are capable of affording pleasure at the present day; and, what I wished *chiefly* to attempt, at present, was to justify myself for having written under the impression of this belief.

But various causes might be pointed out why, when the style is manly, and the subject of some importance, words metrically arranged will long continue to impart such a pleasure to mankind as he who proves the extent of that pleasure will be desirous to impart. The end of poetry is to produce excitement in co-existence with an overbalance of pleasure; but, by the supposition, excitement is an unusual and irregular state of the mind; ideas and feelings do not, in that state, succeed each other in accustomed order. If the words, however, by which this excitement is produced be in themselves powerful, or the images and feelings have an undue proportion of pain connected with them, there is some danger that the excitement may be carried beyond its proper bounds. Now the co-presence of something regular, something to which the mind has been accustomed in various moods and in a less excited state, cannot but have great efficacy in tempering and restraining the passion by an intertexture of ordinary feeling, and of feeling not strictly and necessarily connected with the passion. This is unquestionably true; and hence, though the opinion will at first appear paradoxical, from the tendency of metre to divest language, in a certain degree, of its reality, and thus to throw a sort of half-consciousness of unsubstantial existence over the whole composition, there can be little doubt but that more pathetic situations and sentiments, that is, those which have a greater proportion of pain connected with them, may be endured in metrical composition, especially in rhyme, than in prose. The metre of the old ballads is very artless, yet they contain many passages which would illustrate this opinion; and, I hope, if the following poems be attentively perused, similar instances will be found in them. This opinion may be further illustrated by appealing to the Reader's own experience of the reluctance with which he comes to the reperusal of the distressful parts of "Clarissa Harlowe," or the "Gamester"; while Shakespeare's writings, in the most pathetic scenes, never act upon us, as pathetic, beyond the bounds of pleasure—an effect which, in a much greater degree than might at first be imagined, is to be ascribed to small, but continual and regular impulses of pleasurable surprise from the metrical arrangement.— On the other hand (what it must be allowed will much more frequently happen), if the Poet's words should be incommensurate with the passion, and inadequate to raise the Reader to a height of desirable excitement, then (unless the Poet's choice of his metre has been grossly injudicious), in the feelings of pleasure which the Reader has been accustomed to connect with metre in general, and in the feeling, whether cheerful or melancholy, which he has been accustomed to connect with that particular movement of metre, there will be found something which will greatly contribute to impart passion to the words, and to effect the complex end which the Poet proposes to himself.

[. . .]

I have said that poetry is the spontaneous overflow of powerful feelings: it takes its origin from emotion recollected in tranquillity; the emotion is contemplated till, by a species of re-action, the tranquillity gradually disappears, and an emotion, kindred to that which was before the subject of contemplation, is gradually produced, and does itself actually exist in the mind. In this mood successful composition generally begins, and in a mood similar to this it is carried on; but the emotion, of whatever kind, and in whatever degree, from various causes, is qualified by various measures, so that in describing any passions whatsoever, which are voluntarily described, the mind will, upon the whole, be in a state of enjoyment. If Nature be thus cautious to preserve in a state of enjoyment a being so employed, the Poet ought to profit by the lesson held forth to him, and ought especially to take care that, whatever passions he communicates to his Reader, those passions, if his Reader's mind be sound and vigorous, should always be accompanied with an over-balance of pleasure. Now the music of harmonious metrical language, the sense of difficulty overcome, and the blind association of pleasure which has been previously received from works of rhyme or metre of the same or similar construction, an indistinct perception perpetually renewed of language closely resembling that of real life, and yet, in the circumstance of metre, differing from it so widely—all these imperceptibly make up a complex feeling of delight, which is of the most important use in tempering the painful feeling always found intermingled with powerful descriptions of the deeper passions. This effect is always produced in pathetic and impassioned poetry; while, in lighter compositions, the ease and gracefulness with which the Poet manages his numbers are themselves confessedly a principal source of the gratification of the Reader. All that it is *necessary* to say, however, upon this subject, may be effected by affirming, what few persons will deny, that of two descriptions, either of passions, manners, or characters, each of them equally well executed, the one in prose and the other in verse, the verse will be read a hundred times where the prose is read once.

    [. . .]

Notes

1. It is worth while here to observe that the affecting parts of Chaucer are almost always expressed in language pure and universally intelligible even to this day.
2. I here use the word "Poetry" (though against my own judgment) as opposed to the word Prose, and synonymous with metrical composition. But much confusion has been introduced into criticism by this contradistinction of Poetry and Prose, instead of the more philosophical one of Poetry and Matter of Fact, or Science. The only strict antithesis to Prose is Metre; nor is this, in truth, a *strict* antithesis, because lines and passages of metre so naturally occur in writing prose, that it would be scarcely possible to avoid them, even were it desirable.

Friedrich Nietzsche (1844–1900)

Nietzsche's "On Truth and Lies in a Nonmoral Sense" is a foundational text for poststructuralist theory, because Nietzsche goes after sacred cows of the Western philosophic tradition, particularly Plato's efforts to assert foundational arguments about eternal, unchanging truth. Nietzsche presents an antifoundationalist claim: what someone calls truth is based on a specific perspective and, therefore, is limited, as no one perspective can view and understand an issue, person, or event in comprehensive totality. Truth for Nietzsche might be understood as a pragmatic fiction.

From "On Truth and Lies in a Nonmoral Sense"*

I

Once upon a time, in some out of the way corner of that universe which is dispersed into numberless twinkling solar systems, there was a star upon which clever beasts invented knowing. That was the most arrogant and mendacious minute of "world history," but nevertheless, it was only a minute. After nature had drawn a few breaths, the star cooled and congealed, and the clever beasts had to die.—One might invent such a fable, and yet he still would not have adequately illustrated how miserable, how shadowy and transient, how aimless and arbitrary the human intellect looks within nature. There were eternities during which it did not exist. And when it is all over with the human intellect, nothing will have happened. For this intellect has no additional mission which would lead it beyond human life. Rather, it is human, and only its possessor and begetter takes it so solemnly—as though the world's axis turned within it. But if we could communicate with the gnat, we would learn that he likewise flies through the air with the same solemnity, that he feels the flying center of the universe within himself. There is nothing so reprehensible and unimportant in nature that it would not immediately swell up like a balloon at the slightest puff of this power of knowing. And just as every porter wants to have an admirer, so even the proudest of men, the philosopher, supposes that he sees on all sides the eyes of the universe telescopically focused upon his action and thought.

It is remarkable that this was brought about by the intellect, which was certainly allotted to these most unfortunate, delicate, and ephemeral beings merely as a device for detaining them a minute within existence. For without this addition they would have every reason to flee this existence as quickly as Lessing's son. The pride connected with knowing and sensing lies like a blinding fog over the eyes and senses of men, thus deceiving them concerning the value of existence. For this pride contains within itself the most flattering estimation of the value of knowing. Deception is the most general effect of such pride, but even its most particular effects contain within themselves something of the same deceitful character.

As a means for the preserving of the individual, the intellect unfolds its principles powers in dissimulation, which is the means by which weaker, less robust individuals preserve themselves—since they have been denied the chance to wage the battle for existence with horns or with the sharp teeth of beasts of prey. This art of dissimulation reaches its peak in man. Deception, flattering, lying, deluding, talking behind the back, putting up a false front, living in borrowed splendor, wearing a mask, hiding behind convention, playing a role for others and for

*Edited and translated by Daniel Breazeale.

oneself—in short, a continuous fluttering around the *solitary* flame of vanity—is so much the rule and the law among men that there is almost nothing which is less comprehensible than how an honest and pure drive for truth could have arisen among them. They are deeply immersed in illusions and in dream images; their eyes merely glide over the surface of things and see "forms." Their senses nowhere lead to truth; on the contrary, they are content to receive stimuli and, as it were, to engage in a groping game on the backs of things. Moreover, man permits himself to be deceived in his dreams every night of his life. His moral sentiment does not even make an attempt to prevent this, whereas there are supposed to be men who have stopped snoring through sheer will power. What does man actually know about himself? Is he, indeed, ever able to perceive himself completely, as if laid out in a lighted display case? Does nature not conceal most things from him—even concerning his own body—in order to confine and lock him within a proud, deceptive consciousness, aloof from the coils of the bowels, the rapid flow of the blood stream, and the intricate quivering of the fibers! She threw away the key. And woe to that fatal curiosity which might one day have the power to peer out and down through a crack in the chamber of consciousness and then suspect that man is sustained in the indifference of his ignorance by that which is pitiless, greedy, insatiable and murderous—as if hanging in dreams on the back of a tiger. Given this situation, where in the world could the drive for truth have come from?

Insofar as the individual wants to maintain himself against other individuals, he will under natural circumstances employ the intellect mainly for dissimulation. But at the same time, from boredom and necessity, man wishes to exist socially and with the herd; therefore, he needs to make peace and strives accordingly to banish from his world at least the most flagrant *bellum omni contra omnes*. This peace treaty brings in its wake something which appears to be the first step toward acquiring that puzzling truth drive: to wit, *that* which shall count as "truth" from now on is established. That is to say, uniformly valid and binding designation is invented for things, and this legislation of language likewise establishes the first laws of truth. For the contrast between truth and lie arises here for the first time. The liar is a person who uses the valid designations, the words, in order to make something which is unreal appear to be real. He says, for example, "I am rich," when the proper designation for his condition would be "poor." He misuses conventions by means of arbitrary substitutions or even reversals of names. If he does this in a selfish and moreover harmful manner, society will cease to trust him and will thereby exclude him. What men avoid by excluding the liar is not so much being defrauded as it is being harmed by means of fraud. Thus, even at this stage, what they hate is basically not deception itself, but rather the unpleasant, hated consequences of certain sorts of deception. It is in a similarly restricted sense that man now wants nothing but truth: he desires the pleasant, life-preserving consequences of truth. He is indifferent toward pure knowledge which has no consequences; toward those truths which are possibly harmful and destructive he is even hostilely inclined. And besides, what about these linguistic conventions themselves? Are they perhaps products of knowledge, that is, of the sense of truth? Are designations congruent with things? Is language the adequate expression of all realities?

It is only by means of forgetfulness that man can ever reach the point of fancying himself to possess a "truth" of the grade just indicated. If he will not be satisfied with truth in the form of tautology, that is to say, if he will not be content with empty husks, then he will always exchange truths for illusions. What is a word? It is the copy in sound of a nerve stimulus. But the further inference from the nerve stimulus to a cause outside of us is already the result of a false and unjustifiable application of the principle of sufficient reason. If truth alone had been the deciding factor in the genesis of language, and if the standpoint of certainly had been decisive for designations, then how could we still dare to say "the stone is hard," as if "hard" were something otherwise familiar to us, and not merely a totally subjective stimulation! We separate things according to gender, designating the tree as masculine and the plant as feminine. What arbitrary assignments! How far this oversteps the canons of certainty! We speak of a "snake": this designation touches only upon its ability to twist itself and could therefore also fit a worm. What arbitrary differentiations! What one-sided preferences, first for this, then for that property of a thing! The various languages placed side by side show that with words it is never a question of truth, never a question of adequate expression; otherwise, there would not be so many languages. The "thing in itself" (which is precisely what the pure truth, apart from any of its consequences, would be) is likewise something quite incomprehensible to the creator of language and something not in the least worth striving for. This creator only designates the relations of things to men, and for expressing these relations he lays hold of the boldest metaphors. To begin with, a nerve stimulus is transferred into an image: first metaphor. The image, in turn, is imitated in a sound: second metaphor. And each time there is a complete overleaping of one sphere, right into the middle of an entirely new and different one. One can imagine a man who is totally deaf and has never had a sensation of sound and music. Perhaps such a person will gaze with astonishment at Chladni's sound figures; perhaps he will discover their causes in the vibrations of the string and will now swear that he must know what men mean by "sound." It is this way with all of us concerning language: we believe that we know something about the things themselves when we speak of trees, colors, snow, and flowers; and yet we possess nothing but metaphors for things—metaphors which correspond in no way to the original entities. In the same way that the sound appears as a sand figure, so the mysterious X of the thing in itself first appears as a nerve stimulus, then as an image, and finally as a sound. Thus the genesis of language does not proceed logically in any case, and all the material within and with which the man of truth, the scientist, and the philosopher later work and build, if not derived from nevernever land, is at least not derived from the essence of things.

In particular, let us further consider the formation of concepts. Every word instantly becomes a concept precisely insofar as it is not supposed to serve as a reminder of the unique and entirely individual original experience to which it owes its origin; but rather, a word becomes a concept insofar as it simultaneously has to fit countless more or less similar cases—which means, purely and simply, cases which are never equal and thus altogether unequal. Every concept arises from the equation of unequal things. Just as it is certain that one leaf is never totally the same as another, so it is certain that the concept "leaf" is formed by arbitrarily discarding these individual differences and by forgetting the distinguishing aspects. This awakens the idea that, in addition to the leaves, there exists in nature the "leaf": the original model according to which all the leaves were perhaps woven, sketched, measured, colored, curled, and painted—but by incompetent hands, so that no specimen has turned out to be correct, trustworthy, and faithful likeness of the original model. We call a person "honest," and then we ask "why has he behaved so honestly today?" Our usual answer is, "on account of his honesty." Honesty! This in turn means that the leaf is the cause of the leaves. We know nothing whatsoever about an essential quality called "honesty"; but we do know of countless individualized and consequently unequal actions which we equate by omitting the aspects in which they are unequal and which we now designate as "honest" actions. Finally we formulate from them a *qualitas occulta* which has the name "honesty." We obtain the concept, as we do the form, by overlooking what is individual and actual; whereas nature is acquainted with no forms and no concepts, and likewise with no species, but only with an X which remains inaccessible and undefinable for us. For even our contrast between individual and species is something anthropomorphic and does not originate in the essence of things; although we should not presume to claim that this contrast does not correspond to the essence of things: that would of course be a dogmatic assertion and, as such, would be just as indemonstrable as its opposite.

What then is truth? A movable host of metaphors, metonymies, and anthropomorphisms: in short, a sum of human relations which have been poetically and rhetorically intensified, transferred, and embellished, and which, after long usage, seem to a people to be fixed, canonical, and binding. Truths are illusions which we have forgotten are illusions; they are metaphors that have become worn out and have been drained of sensuous force, coins which have lost their embossing and are now considered as metal and no longer as coins.

We still do not know where the drive for truth comes from. For so far we have heard only of the duty which society imposes in order to exist: to be truthful means to employ the usual metaphors. Thus, to express it morally, this is the duty to lie according to a fixed convention, to lie with the herd and in a manner binding upon everyone. Now man of course forgets that this is the way things stand for him. Thus he lies in the manner indicated, unconsciously and in accordance with habits which are centuries' old; and precisely *by means of this unconsciousness* and forgetfulness he arrives at his sense of truth. From the sense that one is obliged to designate one thing as "red," another as "cold," and a third as "mute," there arises a moral impulse in regard to truth. The venerability, reliability, and utility of truth is something which a person demonstrates for himself from the contrast with the liar, whom no one trusts and everyone excludes. As a "*rational*" being, he now places his behavior under the control of abstractions. He will no longer tolerate being carried away by sudden impressions, by intuitions. First he universalizes all these impressions into less colorful, cooler concepts, so that he can entrust the guidance of his life and conduct to them. Everything which distinguishes man from the animals depends upon this ability to volatilize perceptual metaphors in a schema, and thus to dissolve an image into a concept. For something is possible in the realm of these schemata which could never be achieved with the vivid first impressions: the construction of a pyramidal order according to castes and degrees, the creation of a new world of laws, privileges, subordinations, and clearly marked boundaries—a new world, one which now confronts that other vivid world of first impressions as more solid, more universal, better known, and more human than the immediately perceived world, and thus as the regulative and imperative world. Whereas each perceptual metaphor is individual and without equals and is therefore able to elude all classification, the great edifice of concepts displays the rigid regularity of Roman columbarium and exhales in logic that strength and coolness which is characteristic of mathematics. Anyone who has felt this cool breath [of logic] will hardly believe that even the concept—which is as bony, foursquare, and transposable as a die—is nevertheless merely the *residue of a metaphor,* and that the illusion which is involved in the artistic transference of a nerve stimulus into images is, if not the mother, then the grandmother of every single concept. But in this conceptual crap game "truth" means using every die in the designated manner, counting its spots accurately, fashioning the right categories, and never violating the order of caste and class rank. Just as the Romans and Etruscans cut up the heavens with rigid mathematical lines and confined a god within each of the spaces thereby delimited, as within a *templum,* so every people has a similarly mathematically divided conceptual heaven above themselves and henceforth thinks that truth demands that each conceptual god be sought only within *his own* sphere. Here one may certainly admire man as a mighty genius of construction, who succeeds in piling up an infinitely complicated dome of concepts upon an unstable foundation, and, as it were, on running water. Of course, in order to be supported by such a foundation, his construction must be like one constructed of spiders' webs: delicate enough to be carried along by the waves, strong enough not to be blown apart by every wind. As a genius of construction man raises himself far above the bee in the following way: whereas the bee builds with wax that he gathers from nature, man builds with the far more delicate conceptual material which he first has to manufacture from himself. In this he is greatly to be admired, but not on account of his drive for truth or for pure knowledge of things. When someone hides something behind a bush and looks for it again in the same place and finds it there as well, there is not much to praise in such seeking and finding. Yet this is how matters stand regarding seeking and finding "truth" within the realm of reason. If I make up the definition of a mammal, and then, after inspecting a camel, declare "look, a mammal," I have indeed brought a truth to light in this way, but it is a truth of limited value. That is to say, it is thoroughly anthropomorphic truth which contains not a single point which would be "true in itself" or really and universally valid apart from man. At bottom, what the investigator of such truths is seeking is only the metamorphosis of the world into man. He strives to understand the world as something analogous to man, and at best he achieves by his struggles the feeling of assimilation. Similar to the way in which astrologers considered the stars to be in man's service and connected with his happiness and sorrow, such an investigator considers the entire universe in connection with man: the entire universe as the infinitely fractured echo of one original sound—man; the entire universe as the infinitely multiplied copy of one original picture—man. His method is to treat man as the measure of all things, but in doing so he again proceeds from the error of believing that he has these things [which he intends to measure] immediately before him as mere objects. He forgets that the original perceptual metaphors are metaphors and takes them to be the things themselves.

Only by forgetting this primitive world of metaphor can one live with any repose, security, and consistency: only by means of the petrification and coagulation of a mass of images which originally streamed from the primal faculty of human imagination like a fiery liquid, only in the invincible faith that *this* sun, *this* window, *this* table is a truth in itself, in short, only by forgetting that he himself is an *artistically creating* subject, does man live with any repose, security, and consistency. If but for an instant he could escape from the prison walls of this faith, his "self consciousness" would be immediately destroyed. It is even a difficult thing for him to admit to himself that the insect or the bird perceives an entirely different world from the one that man does, and that the question of which of these perceptions of the world is the more correct one is quite meaningless, for this would have to have been decided previously in accordance with the criterion of the *correct perception,* which means, in accordance with a criterion which is *not available.* But in any case it seems to me that "the correct perception"—which would mean "the adequate expression of an object in the subject"—is a contradictory impossibility. For between two absolutely different spheres, as between subject and object, there is no causality, no correctness, and no expression; there is, at most, an *aesthetic* relation: I mean, a suggestive transference, a stammering translation into a completely foreign tongue—for which there is required, in any case, a freely inventive intermediate sphere and mediating force. "Appearance" is a word that contains many temptations, which is why I avoid it as much as possible. For it is not true that the essence of things "appears" in the empirical world. A painter without hands who wished to express in song the picture before his mind would, by means of this substitution of spheres, still reveal more about the essence of things than does the empirical world. Even the relationship of a nerve stimulus to the generated image is not a necessary one. But when the same image has been generated millions of times and has been handed down for many generations and finally appears on the same occasion every time for all mankind, then it acquires at last the same meaning for men it would have if it were the sole necessary image and if the relationship of the original nerve stimulus to the generated image were a strictly causal one. In the same manner, an eternally repeated dream would certainly be felt and judged to be reality. But the hardening and congealing of a metaphor guarantees absolutely nothing concerning its necessity and exclusive justification.

Every person who is familiar with such considerations has no doubt felt a deep mistrust of all idealism of this sort: just as often as he has quite clearly convinced himself of the eternal consistency, omnipresence, and infallibility of the laws of nature. He has concluded that so far as we can penetrate here—from the telescopic heights to the microscopic depths—everything is secure, complete, infinite, regular, and without any gaps. Science will be able to dig successfully in this shaft forever, and all the things that are discovered will harmonize with and not contradict each other. How little does this resemble a product of the imagination, for if it were such, there should be some place where the illusion and unreality can be divined. Against this, the following must be said: if each of us had a different kind of sense perception—if we could only perceive things now as a bird, now as a worm, now as a plant, or if one of us saw a stimulus as red, another as blue, while a third even heard the same stimulus as a sound—then no one would speak of such a regularity of nature, rather, nature would be grasped only as a creation which is subjective in the highest degree. After all, what is a law of nature as such for us? We are not acquainted with it in itself, but only with its effects, which means in its relation to other laws of nature—which, in turn, are known to us only as sums of relations. Therefore all these relations always refer again to others and are thoroughly incomprehensible to us in their essence. All that we actually know about these laws of nature is what we ourselves bring to them—time and space, and therefore relationships of succession and number. But everything marvelous about the laws of nature, everything that quite astonishes us therein and seems to demand our explanation, everything that might lead us to distrust idealism: all this is completely and solely contained within the mathematical strictness and inviolability of our representations of time and space. But we produce these representations in and from ourselves with the same necessity with which the spider spins. If we are forced to comprehend all things only under these forms, then it ceases to be amazing that in all things we actually comprehend nothing but these forms. For they must all bear within themselves the laws of number, and it is precisely number which is most astonishing in things. All that conformity to law, which impresses us so much in the movement of the stars and in chemical processes, coincides at bottom with those properties which we bring to things. Thus it is we who impress ourselves in this way. In conjunction with this, it of course follows that the artistic process of metaphor formation with which every sensation begins in us already presupposes these forms and thus occurs within them. The only way in which the possibility of subsequently constructing a new conceptual edifice from metaphors themselves can be explained is by the firm persistence of these original forms. That is to say, this conceptual edifice is an imitation of temporal, spatial, and numerical relationships in the domain of metaphor.

[. . .]

Sigmund Freud (1856–1939)

Freud towers over the twentieth century like a magnificent giant, his theories, while disturbing to many, having taken root in and permeated our culture to such a degree that our understanding of human subjectivity has changed forever. With his groundbreaking *The Interpretation of Dreams,* published in 1900, Freud moves beyond speaking of dreams in general symbolic terms to the creation of an everyday grammar and syntax of dreams. For the literary critic, Freud's work is of special importance because it makes use of literary texts not only to illustrate or confirm his theories about unconscious, contradictory, or ambivalent desires, but also to identify and understand these desires in the first place.

From *The Interpretation of Dreams*

In my experience, which is already extensive, the chief part in the mental lives of all children who later become psychoneurotics is played by their parents. Being in love with the one parent and hating the other are among the essential constituents of the stock of psychical impulses which is formed at that time and which is of such importance in determining the symptoms of the later neurosis. It is not my belief, however, that psychoneurotics differ sharply in this respect from other human beings who remain normal—that they are able, that is, to create something absolutely new and peculiar to themselves. It is far more probable—and this is confirmed by occasional observations on normal children—that they are only distinguished by exhibiting on a magnified scale feelings of love and hatred to their parents which occur less obviously and less intensely in the minds of most children.

This discovery is confirmed by a legend that has come down to us from classical antiquity: a legend whose profound and universal power to move can only be understood if the hypothesis I have put forward in regard to the psychology of children has an equally universal validity. What I have in mind is the legend of King Oedipus and Sophocles' drama which bears his name.

Oedipus, son of Laïus, King of Thebes, and of Jocasta, was exposed as an infant because an oracle had warned Laïus that the still unborn child would be his father's murderer. The child was rescued, and grew up as a prince in an alien court, until, in doubts as to his origin, he too questioned the oracle and was warned to avoid his home since he was destined to murder his father and take his mother in marriage. On the road leading away from what he believed was his home, he met King Laïus and slew him in a sudden quarrel. He came next to Thebes and solved the riddle set him by the Sphinx who barred his way. Out of gratitude the Thebans made him their king and gave him Jocasta's hand in marriage. He reigned long in peace and honour, and she who, unknown to him, was his mother bore him two sons and two daughters. Then at last a plague broke out and the Thebans made enquiry once more of the oracle. It is at this point that Sophocles' tragedy opens. The messengers bring back the reply that the plague will cease when the murderer of Laïus has been driven from the land.

> But he, where is he? Where shall now be read
> The fading record of this ancient guilt?[1]

The action of the play consists in nothing other than the process of revealing, with cunning delays and ever-mounting excitement—a process that can be likened to the work of a psycho-analysis—that Oedipus himself is the murderer of Laïus, but further that he is the son of the murdered man and of Jocasta. Appalled at the abomination which he has unwittingly perpetrated, Oedipus blinds himself and forsakes his home. The oracle has been fulfilled.

Oedipus Rex is what is known as a tragedy of destiny. Its tragic effect is said to lie in the contrast between the supreme will of the gods and the vain attempts of mankind to escape the evil that threatens them. The lesson which, it is said, the deeply moved spectator should learn from the tragedy is submission to the divine will and realization of his own impotence. Modern dramatists have accordingly tried to achieve a similar tragic effect by weaving the same contrast into a plot invented by themselves. But the spectators have looked on unmoved while a curse or an oracle was fulfilled in spite of all the efforts of some innocent man: later tragedies of destiny have failed in their effect.

If *Oedipus Rex* moves a modern audience no less than it did the contemporary Greek one, the explanation can only be that its effect does not lie in the contrast between destiny and human will, but is to be looked for in the particular nature of the material on which that contrast is exemplified. There must be something which makes a voice within us ready to recognize the compelling force of destiny in the *Oedipus,* while we can dismiss as merely arbitrary such dispositions as are laid down in [Grillparzer's] *Die Ahnfrau* or other modern tragedies of destiny. And a factor of this kind is in fact involved in the story of King Oedipus. His destiny moves us only because it might have been ours—because the oracle laid the same curse upon us before our birth as upon him. It is the fate of all of us, perhaps, to direct our first sexual impulse towards our mother and our first hatred and our first murderous wish against our father. Our dreams convince us that that is so. King Oedipus, who slew his father Laïus and married his mother Jocasta, merely shows us the fulfilment of our own childhood wishes. But, more fortunate than he, we have meanwhile succeeded, in so far as we have not become psychoneurotics, in detaching our sexual impulses from our mothers and in forgetting our jealousy of our fathers. Here is one in whom these primaeval wishes of our childhood have been fulfilled, and we shrink back from him with the whole force of the repression by which those wishes have since that time been held down within us. While the poet, as he unravels the past, brings to light the guilt of Oedipus, he is at the same time compelling us to recognize our own inner minds, in which those same impulses, though suppressed, are still to be found. The contrast with which the closing Chorus leaves us confronted—

> . . . Fix on Oedipus your eyes,
> Who resolved the dark enigma, noblest champion and most wise.
> Like a star his envied fortune mounted beaming far and wide:
> Now he sinks in seas of anguish, whelmed beneath a raging tide . . .[2]

—strikes as a warning at ourselves and our pride, at us who since our childhood have grown so wise and so mighty in our own eyes. Like Oedipus, we live in ignorance of these wishes, repugnant to mortality, which have been forced upon us by Nature, and after their revelation we may all of us well seek to close our eyes to the scenes of our childhood.[3]

There is an unmistakable indication in the text of Sophocles' tragedy itself that the legend of Oedipus sprang from some primaeval dream-material which had as its content the distressing disturbance of a child's relation to his parents owing to the first stirrings of sexuality. At a point when Oedipus, though he is not yet enlightened, has begun to feel troubled by his recollection of the oracle,

Jocasta consoles him by referring to a dream which many people dream, though, as she thinks, it has no meaning:

> Many a man ere now in dreams hath lain
> With her who bare him. He hath least annoy
> Who with such omens troubleth not his mind.[4]

To-day, just as then, many men dream of having sexual relations with their mothers, and speak of the fact with indignation and astonishment. It is clearly the key to the tragedy and the complement to the dream of the dreamer's father being dead. The story of Oedipus is the reaction of the imagination to these two typical dreams. And just as these dreams, when dreamt by adults, are accompanied by feelings of repulsion, so too the legend must include horror and self-punishment. Its further modification originates once again in a misconceived secondary revision of the material, which has sought to exploit it for theological purposes. (Cf. the dream-material in dreams of exhibiting, p. 341 f.) The attempt to harmonize divine omnipotence with human responsibility must naturally fail in connection with this subject-matter just as with any other.

Another of the great creations of tragic poetry, Shakespeare's *Hamlet,* has its roots in the same soil as *Oedipus Rex.* But the changed treatment of the same material reveals the whole difference in the mental life of these two widely separated epochs of civilization: the secular advance of repression in the emotional life of mankind. In *Oedipus* the child's wishful phantasy that underlies it is brought into the open and realized as it would be in a dream. In *Hamlet* it remains repressed; and—just as in the case of a neurosis—we only learn of its existence from its inhibiting consequences. Strangely enough, the overwhelming effect produced by the more modern tragedy has turned out to be compatible with the fact that people have remained completely in the dark as to the hero's character. The play is built up on Hamlet's hesitations over fulfilling the task of revenge that is assigned to him; but its text offers no reasons or motives for these hesitations and an immense variety of attempts at interpreting them have failed to produce a result. According to the view which was originated by Goethe and is still the prevailing one to-day, Hamlet represents the type of man whose power of direct action is paralysed by an excessive development of his intellect. (He is 'sicklied o'er with the pale cast of thought'.) According to another view, the dramatist has tried to portray a pathologically irresolute character which might be classed as neurasthenic. The plot of the drama shows us, however, that Hamlet is far from being represented as a person incapable of taking any action. We see him doing so on two occasions: first in a sudden outburst of temper, when he runs his sword through the eavesdropper behind the arras, and secondly in a premeditated and even crafty fashion, when, with all the callousness of a Renaissance prince, he sends the two courtiers to the death that had been planned for himself. What is it, then, that inhibits him in fulfilling the task set him by his father's ghost? The answer, once again, is that it is the peculiar nature of the task. Hamlet is able to do anything—except take vengeance on the man who did away with his father and took that father's place with his mother, the man who shows him the repressed wishes of his own childhood realized. Thus the loathing which should drive him on to revenge is replaced in him by self-reproaches, by scruples of conscience, which remind him that he himself is literally no better than the sinner whom he is to punish. Here I have translated into conscious terms what was bound to remain unconscious in Hamlet's mind; and if anyone is inclined to call him a hysteric, I can only accept the fact as one that is implied by my interpretation. The distaste for sexuality expressed by Hamlet in his conversation with Ophelia fits in very well with this: the same distaste which was destined to take possession of the poet's mind more and more during the years that followed, and which reached its extreme expression in *Timon of Athens*. For it can of course only be the poet's own mind which confronts us in Hamlet. I observe in a book on Shakespeare by Georg Brandes (1896) a statement that *Hamlet* was written immediately after the death of Shakespeare's father (in 1601), that is, under the immediate impact of his bereavement and, as we may well assume, while his childhood feelings about his father had been freshly revived. It is known, too, that Shakespeare's own son who died at an early age bore the name of 'Hamnet', which is identical with 'Hamlet'. Just as *Hamlet* deals with the relation of a son to his parents, so *Macbeth* (written at approximately the same period) is concerned with the subject of childlessness. But just as all neurotic symptoms, and, for that matter, dreams, are capable of being 'over-interpreted' and indeed need to be, if they are to be fully understood, so all genuinely creative writings are the product of more than a single motive and more than a single impulse in the poet's mind, and are open to more than a single interpretation. In what I have written I have only attempted to interpret the deepest layer of impulses in the mind of the creative writer.[5]

I cannot leave the subject of typical dreams of the death of loved relatives, without adding a few more words to throw light on their significance for the theory of dreams in general. In these dreams we find the highly unusual condition realized of a dream-thought formed by a repressed wish entirely eluding censorship and passing into the dream without modification. There must be special factors at work to make this event possible, and I believe that the occurrence of these dreams is facilitated by two such factors. Firstly, there is no wish that seems more remote from us than this one: 'we couldn't even *dream*'—so we believe—of wishing such a thing. For this reason the dream-censorship is not armed to meet such a monstrosity, just as Solon's penal code contained no punishment for parricide. Secondly, in this case the repressed and unsuspected wish is particularly often met half-way by a residue from the previous day in the form of a *worry* about the safety of the person concerned. This worry can only make its way into the dream by availing itself of the corresponding wish; while the wish can disguise itself behind the worry that has become active during the day. [Cf. p. 708 f.] We may feel inclined to think that things are simpler than this and that one merely carries on during the night and in dreams with what one has been turning over in one's mind during the day; but if so we shall be leaving dreams of the death of people of whom the dreamer is fond completely in the air and without any connection with our explanation of dreams in general, and we shall thus be clinging quite unnecessarily to a riddle which is perfectly capable of solution.

It is also instructive to consider the relation of these dreams to anxiety-dreams. In the dreams we have been discussing, a repressed wish has found a means of evading censorship—and the distortion which censorship involves. The invariable concomitant is that painful feelings are experienced in the dream. In just the same way anxiety-dreams only occur if the censorship has been wholly or partly overpowered; and, on the other hand, the overpowering of the censorship is facilitated if anxiety has already been produced as an immediate sensation arising from somatic sources. [Cf. above p. 332 ff.] We can thus plainly see the purpose for which the censorship exercises its office and brings about the distortion of dreams: it does so *in order to prevent the generation of anxiety or other forms of distressing affect.*

Notes

1. Lewis Campbell's translation (1883), line 108 f.
2. Lewis Campbell's translation, line 1524 ff.
3. *Footnote added* 1914:] None of the findings of psychoanalytic research has provoked such embittered denials, such fierce opposition—or such amusing contortions—on the part of critics as this indication of the childhood impulses towards incest which persist in the unconscious. An attempt has even been made recently to make out, in the face of all experience, that the incest should only be taken as 'symbolic'.— Ferenczi (1912) has proposed an ingenious 'over-interpretation' of the Oedipus myth, based on a passage in one of Schopenhauer's letters.—[*Added* 1919:] Later studies have shown that the 'Oedipus complex', which was touched upon for the first time in the above paragraphs in the *Interpretation of Dreams,* throws a light of undreamt-of importance on the history of the human race and the evolution of religion and morality. (See my *Totem and Taboo,* 1912–13 [Essay IV].)—[Actually the gist of this discussion of the Oedipus complex and of the *Oedipus Rex,* as well as of what follows on the subject of *Hamlet,* had already been put forward by Freud in a letter to Fliess as early as October 15th, 1897. (See Freud, 1950*a,* Letter 71.)
4. Lewis Campbell's translation, line 982 ff.
5. *Footnote added* 1919:] The above indications of a psycho-analytic explanation of *Hamlet* have since been amplified by Ernest Jones and defended against the alternative views put forward in the literature of the subject. (See Jones, 1910*a* [and, in a completer form, 1949].—[*Added* 1930:] Incidentally, I have in the meantime ceased to believe that the author of Shakespeare's works was the man from Stratford. [See Freud, 1930*e.*]—[*Added* 1919:] Further attempts at an analysis of *Macbeth* will be found in a paper of mine [Freud, 1916*d*] and in one by Jekels (1917).—[Freud further discussed *Hamlet* in a posthumously published sketch dealing with 'Psychopathic Characters on the Stage' (1942*a*), probably written in 1905 or 1906.

Ferdinand de Saussure (1857–1913)

De Saussure's *Course in General Linguistics* is a foundational text for structuralist and poststructuralist critical theory because it highlights the arbitrary nature of the linguistic sign. For example, speakers of English use the word "door," but

Spanish speakers use the word "puerta." The word "door" is no more appropriate or accurate a print or sound designation (sign) than the Spanish word, and neither of these words is more appropriate or accurate than the French word *"porte"* for designating a barrier that allows entrance to and exit from a room, house, or building. The point is that the words we use for things and ideas result from arbitrary conventions and not from a natural correspondence between the words and the things or ideas (the signified). Saussure's theories about language as a structured system of coded practices became the foundation of structuralist and semiotic approaches to language and literature.

From *Course in General Linguistics:* Nature of the Linguistic Sign

Translated by Wade Baskin

1. Sign, Signified, Signifier

Some people regard language, when reduced to its elements, as a naming-process only—a list of words, each corresponding to the thing that it names. For example:

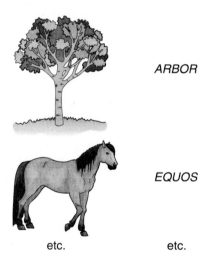

ARBOR

EQUOS

etc.   etc.

This conception is open to criticism at several points. It assumes that ready-made ideas exist before words; it does not tell us whether a name is vocal or psychological in nature (*arbor,* for instance, can be considered from either viewpoint); finally, it lets us assume that the linking of a name and a thing is a very simple operation—an assumption that is anything but true. But this rather naïve approach can bring us near the truth by showing us that the linguistic unit is a double entity, one formed by the associating of two terms.

We have seen in considering the speaking-circuit that both terms involved in the linguistic sign are psychological and are united in the brain by an associative bond. This point must be emphasized.

The linguistic sign unites, not a thing and a name, but a concept and a sound-image. The latter is not the material sound, a purely physical thing, but the psychological imprint of the sound, the impression that it makes on our senses. The sound-image is sensory, and if I happen to call it 'material', it is only in that sense, and by way of opposing it to the other term of the association, the concept, which is generally more abstract.

The psychological character of our sound-images becomes apparent when we observe our own speech. Without moving our lips or tongue, we can talk to ourselves or recite mentally a selection of verse. Because we regard the words of our language as sound-images, we must avoid speaking of the 'phonemes' that make up the words. This term, which suggests vocal activity, is applicable to the spoken word only, to the realization of the inner image in discourse. We can avoid that misunderstanding by speaking of the *sounds* and *syllables* of a word provided we remember that the names refer to the sound-image.

The linguistic sign is then a two-sided psychological entity that can be represented by the drawing:

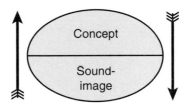

The two elements are intimately united, and each recalls the other. Whether we try to find the meaning of the Latin word *arbor* or the word that Latin uses to designate the concept 'tree', it is clear that only the associations sanctioned by that language appear to us to conform to reality, and we disregard whatever others might be imagined.

Our definition of the linguistic sign poses an important question of terminology. I call the combination of a concept and a sound-image a *sign,* but in current usage the term generally designates only a sound-image, a word, for example (*arbor,* etc.). One tends to forget that *arbor* is called a sign only because it carries the concept 'tree', with the result that the idea of the sensory part implies the idea of the whole.

Ambiguity would disappear if the three notions involved here were designated by three names, each suggesting and opposing the others. I propose to retain the word *sign (signe)* to designate the whole and to replace *concept* and *sound-image* respectively by *signified (signifié)* and *signifier (significant);* the last two terms have the advantage of indicating the opposition that separates them from each other and from the whole of which they are parts. As regards *sign,* if I

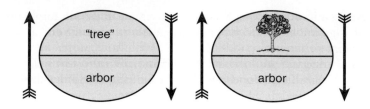

am satisfied with it, this is simply because I do not know of any word to replace it, the ordinary language suggesting no other.

The linguistic sign, as defined, has two primordial characteristics. In enunciating them I am also positing the basic principles of any study of this type.

2. Principle I: The Arbitrary Nature of the Sign

The bond between the signifier and the signified is arbitrary. Since I mean by sign the whole that results from the associating of the signifier with the signified, I can simply say: *the linguistic sign is arbitrary.*

The idea of 'sister' is not linked by any inner relationship to the succession of sounds *s-ö-r* which serves as its signifier in French; that it could be represented equally by just any other sequence is proved by differences among language and by the very existence of different language: the signified 'ox' has as its signifier *b-ö-f* on one side of the border and *o-k-s (Ochs)* on the other.

No one disputes the principle of the arbitrary nature of the sign, but it is often easier to discover a truth than to assign to it its proper place. Principle I dominates all the linguistics of language; its consequences are numberless. It is true that not all of them are equally obvious at first glance; only after many detours does one discover them, and with them the primordial importance of the principle.

One remark in passing: when semiology becomes organized as a science, the question will arise whether or not it properly includes modes of expression based on completely natural signs, such as pantomime. Supposing that the new science welcomes them, its main concern will still be the whole group of systems grounded on the arbitrariness of the sign. In fact, every means of expression used in society is based, in principle, on collective behaviour or—what amounts to the same thing—on convention. Polite formulas, for instance, though often imbued with a certain natural expressiveness (as in the case of a Chinese who greets his emperor by bowing down to the ground nine times), are none the less fixed by rule; it is this rule and not the intrinsic value of the gestures that obliges one to use them. Signs that are wholly arbitrary realize better than the others the ideal of the semiological process; that is why language, the most complex and universal of all systems of expression, is also the most characteristic; in this sense linguistics can become the master-pattern for all branches of semiology although language is only one particular semiological system.

The word *symbol* has been used to designate the linguistic sign, or, more specifically, what is here called the signifier. Principle I in particular weighs against the use of this term. One characteristic of the symbol is that it is never wholly arbitrary; it is not empty, for there is the rudiment of a natural bond between the signifier and the signified. The symbol of justice, a pair of scales, could not be replaced by just any other symbol, such as a chariot.

The word *arbitrary* also calls for comment. The term should not imply that the choice of the signifier is left entirely to the speaker; I mean that it is unmotivated, i.e. arbitrary in that it actually has no natural connection with the signified. . . .

3. Principle II: The Linear Nature of the Signifier

The signifier, being auditory, is unfolded solely in time from which it gets the following characteristics: (a) it represents a span, and (b) the span is measurable in a single dimension; it is a line.

While Principle II is obvious, apparently linguists have always neglected to state it, doubtless because they found it too simple; nevertheless, it is fundamental, and its consequences are incalculable. Its importance equals that of Principle I; the whole mechanism of language depends upon it. In contrast to visual signifiers (nautical signals, etc.) which can offer simultaneous groupings in several dimensions, auditory signifiers have at their command only the dimension of time. Their elements are presented in succession; they form a chain. This feature becomes readily apparent when they are represented in writing and the spatial line of graphic marks is substituted for succession in time.

Sometimes the linear nature of the signifier is not obvious. When I accent a syllable, for instance, it seems that I am concentrating more than one significant element on the same point. But this is an illusion; the syllable and its accent constitute only one phonational act. There is no duality within the act but only different oppositions to what precedes and what follows.

Immutability and Mutability of the Sign

1. Immutability

The signifier, though to all appearances freely chosen with respect to the idea that it represents, is fixed, not free, with respect to the linguistic community that uses it. The masses have no voice in the matter, and the signifier chosen by language could be replaced by no other. This fact, which seems to embody a contradiction, might be called colloquially 'the stacked deck'. We say to language: 'Choose!' but we add: 'It must be this sign and no other.' No individual, even if he willed it, could modify in any way at all the choice that has been made; and what is more, the community itself cannot control so much as a single word; it is bound to the existing language.

No longer can language be identified with a contract pure and simple, and it is precisely from this viewpoint that the linguistic sign is a particularly interesting object of study; for language furnishes the best proof that a law accepted by a community is a thing that is tolerated and not a rule to which all freely consent.

Let us first see why we cannot control the linguistic sign and then draw together the important consequences that issue from the phenomenon.

No matter what period we choose or how far back we go, language always appears as a heritage of the preceding period. We might conceive of an act by which, at a given moment, names were assigned to things and a contract was formed between concepts and sound-images; but such an act has never been recorded. The notion that things might have happened like that was prompted by our acute awareness of the arbitrary nature of the sign.

No society, in fact, knows or has ever known language other than as a product inherited from preceding generations, and one to be accepted as such. That is why the question of the origin of speech is not so important as it is generally assumed to be. The question is not even worth asking; the only real object of linguistics is the normal, regular life of an existing idiom. A particular language-state is always the product of historical forces, and these forces explain why the sign is unchangeable, i.e., why it resists any arbitrary substitution.

Nothing is explained by saying that language is something inherited and leaving it at that. Cannot existing and inherited laws be modified from one moment to the next?

To meet that objection, we must put language into its social setting and frame the question just as we would for any other social institution. How are other social institutions transmitted? This more general question includes the question of immutability. We must first determine the greater or lesser amounts of freedom that the other institutions enjoy; in each instance it will be seen that a different proportion exists between fixed tradition and the free action of society. The next step is to discover why, in a given category, the forces of the first type carry more weight or less weight than those of the second. Finally, coming back to language, we must ask why the historical factor of transmission dominates it entirely and prohibits any sudden widespread change.

There are many possible answers to the question. For example, one might point to the fact that succeeding generations are not superimposed on one another like the drawers of a piece of furniture, but fuse and interpenetrate, each generation embracing individuals of all ages—with the result that modifications of language are not tied to the succession of generations. One might also recall the sum of the efforts required for learning the mother language and conclude that a general change would be impossible. Again, it might be added that reflection does not enter into the active use of an idiom—speakers are largely unconscious of the laws of language; and if they are unaware of them, how can they modify them? Even if they were aware of these laws, we may be sure that their awareness would seldom lead to criticism, for people are generally satisfied with the language they have received.

The foregoing considerations are important but not topical. The following are more basic and direct, and all the others depend on them.

(i) *The arbitrary nature of the sign*   Above, we had to accept the theoretical possibility of change; further reflection suggests that the arbitrary nature of the sign is really what protects language from any attempt to modify it. Even if people were more conscious of language than they are, they would still not know how to discuss it. The reason is simply that any subject in order to he discussed must have a reasonable basis. It is possible, for instance, to discuss whether the monogamous form of marriage is more reasonable than the polygamous form and to advance arguments to support either side. One could also argue about a system of symbols, for the symbol has a rational relationship with the thing signified; but language is a system of arbitrary signs and lacks the necessary basis, the solid ground for discussion. There is no reason for preferring *sœur* to *sister, Ochs* to *bœuf,* etc.

(ii) *The multiplicity of signs necessary to form any language* Another important deterrent to linguistic change is the great number of signs that must go into the making of any language. A system of writing comprising twenty to forty letters can in case of need be replaced by another system. The same would be true of language if it contained a limited number of elements; but linguistic signs are numberless.

(iii) *The over-complexity of the system* A language constitutes a system. In this one respect language is not completely arbitrary but is ruled to some extent by logic; it is here also, however, that the inability of the masses to transform it becomes apparent. The system is a complex mechanism that can be grasped only through reflection; the very ones who use it daily are ignorant of it. We can conceive of a change only through the intervention of specialists, grammarians, logicians, etc.; but experience shows us that all such meddlings have failed.

(iv) *Collective inertia towards innovation* Languages—and this consideration surpasses all the others—is at every moment everybody's concern; spread throughout society and manipulated by it, language is something used daily by all. Here we are unable to set up any comparison between it and other institutions. The prescriptions of codes, religious rites, nautical signals, etc., involve only a certain number of individuals simultaneously and then only during a limited period of time; in language, on the contrary, everyone participates at all times, and that is why it is constantly being influenced by all. This capital fact suffices to show the impossibility of revolution. Of all social institutions, language is least amenable to initiative. It blends with the life of society, and the latter, inert by nature, is a prime conservative force.

But to say that language is a product of social forces does not suffice to show clearly that it is unfree; remembering that it is always the heritage of the preceding period, we must add that these social forces are linked with time. Language is checked not only by the weight of the collectivity but also by time. These two are inseparable. At every moment solidarity with the past checks freedom of choice. We say *man* and *dog.* This does not prevent the existence in the total phenomenon of a bond between the two antithetical forces—arbitrary convention, by virtue of which choice is free, and time, which causes choice to be fixed. Because the sign is arbitrary, it follows no law other than that of tradition, and because it is based on tradition, it is arbitrary.

2. Mutability

Time, which insures the continuity of language, wields another influence apparently contradictory to the first: the more or less rapid change of linguistic signs. In a certain sense, therefore, we can speak of both the immutability and the mutablility of the sign.

In the last analysis, the two facts are interdependent: the sign is exposed to alteration because it perpetuates itself. What predominates in all change is the persistence of the old substance; disregard for the past is only relative. That is why the principle of change is based on the principle of continuity.

Change in time takes many forms, on any one of which an important chapter in linguistics might be written. Without entering into detail, let us see what things need to be delineated.

First, let there be no mistake about the meaning that we attach to the word 'change'. One might think that it deals especially with phonetic changes under-gone by the signifier, or perhaps changes in meaning which affect the signified concept. That view would be inadequate. Regardless of what the forces of change are, whether in isolation or in combination, they always result in *a shift in the relationship between the signified and the signifier.*

Here are some examples. Latin *necāre* 'kill" became *noyer* 'drown' in French. Both the sound-image and the concept changed; but it is useless to sepa-rate the two parts of the phenomenon; it is sufficient to state with respect to the whole that the bond between the idea and the sign was loosened, and that there was a shift in their relationship. If, instead of comparing Classical Latin *necāre* with French *noyer,* we contrast the former term with *necare* of Vulgar Latin of the fourth or fifth century meaning 'drown', the case is a little different; but here again, although there is no appreciable change in the signifier, there is a shift in the relationship between the idea and the sign.

Old German *dritteil* 'one-third' became *Drittel* in Modern German. Here, although the concept remained the same, the relationship was changed in two ways; the signifier was changed not only in its material aspect but also in its grammatical form: the idea of *Teil* 'part' is no longer implied; *Drittel* is a simple word. In one way or another there is always a shift in the relationship.

In Anglo-Saxon the pre-literary form *fot* 'foot' remained while its plural ★*fōti* became *fēt* (Modern English *feet*). Regardless of the other changes that are implied, one thing is certain: there was a shift in their relationship; other corre-spondences between the phonetic substance and the idea emerged.

Language is radically powerless to defend itself against the forces which from one moment to the next are shifting the relationship between the signified and the signifier. This is one of the consequences of the arbitrary nature of the sign.

Unlike language, other human institutions—customs, laws, etc.—are all based in varying degrees on the natural relations of things; all have of necessity adapted the means employed to the ends pursued. Even fashion in dress is not entirely arbitrary; we can deviate only slightly from the conditions dictated by the human body. Language is limited by nothing in the choice of means, for apparently nothing would prevent the associating of any idea whatsoever with just any sequence of sounds.

To emphasize the fact that language is a genuine institution, Whitney quite justly insisted upon the arbitrary nature of signs; and, by so doing, he placed lin-guistics on its true axis. But he did not follow through and see that the arbitrari-ness of language radically separates it from all other institutions. This is apparent from the way in which language evolves. Nothing could be more com-

plex. As it is a product of both the social force and time, no one can change anything in it, and, on the other hand, the arbitrariness of its signs theoretically
entails the freedom of establishing just any relationship between phonetic substance and ideas. The result is that each of the two elements united in the sign
maintains its own life to a degree unknown elsewhere, and that language
changes, or rather evolves, under the influence of all the forces which can affect
either sounds or meanings. The evolution is inevitable; there is no example of a
single language that resists it. After a certain period of time, some obvious shifts
can be recorded.

Mutability is so inescapable that it even holds true for artificial languages:
Whoever creates a language controls it only so long as it is not in circulation;
from the moment when it fulfils its mission and becomes the property of everyone, control is lost. Take Esperanto as an example; if it succeeds, will it escape
the inexorable law? Once launched, it is quite likely that Esperanto will enter
upon a fully semiological life; it will be transmitted according to laws which
have nothing in common with those of its logical creation, and there will be no
turning back. A man proposing a fixed language that posterity would have to
accept for what it was would be like a hen hatching a duck's egg: the language
created by him would be borne along, willy-nilly, by the current that engulfs all
languages.

Signs are governed by a principle of general semiology: continuity in time is
coupled to change in time; this is confirmed by orthographic systems, the speech
of deaf-mutes, etc.

But what supports the necessity for change? I might be reproached for not
having been as explicit on this point as on the principle of immutability. This is
because I failed to distinguish between the different forces of change. We must
consider their great variety in order to understand the extent to which they are
necessary.

The causes of continuity are a priori within the scope of the observer, but the
causes of change in time are not. It is better not to attempt giving an exact
account at this point, but to restrict discussion to the shifting of relationships in
general. Time changes all things; there is no reason why language should escape
this universal law.

Let us review the main points of our discussion and relate them to the principles set up in the Introduction.

1. Avoiding sterile word definitions, within the total phenomenon represented
   by speech we first singled out two parts: 'langue' and 'parole'. Langue is
   speech less speaking. It is the whole set of linguistic habits which allow an
   individual to understand and to be understood.

2. But this definition still leaves language outside its social context; it makes
   language something artificial, since it includes only the individual part of
   reality; for the realization of languages, a community of speakers (*masse
   parlante)* is necessary. Contrary to all appearances, language never exists
   apart from the social fact, for it is a semiological phenomenon. Its social
   nature is one of its inner characteristics. Its complete definition confronts us
   with two inseparable entities. [See below.]

But under the conditions described language is not living—it has only potential life; we have considered only the social, not the historical, fact.

3. The linguistic sign is arbitrary; language, as defined, would therefore seem to be a system which, because it depends solely on a rational principle, is free and can be organized at will. Its social nature, considered independently, does not definitely rule out this viewpoint. Doubtless it is not on a purely logical basis that group psychology operates; one must consider everything that deflects reason in actual contacts between individuals. But the thing which keeps language from being a simple convention that can be modified at the whim of interested parties is not its social nature; it is rather the action of time combined with the social force. If time is left out, the linguistic facts are incomplete and no conclusion is possible.

If we considered language in time, without the community of speakers—imagine an isolated individual living for several centuries—we should probably notice no change; time would not influence language. Conversely, if we considered the community of the social forces that influence language. To represent the actual facts, we must then add to our first drawing a sign to indicate the passage of time:

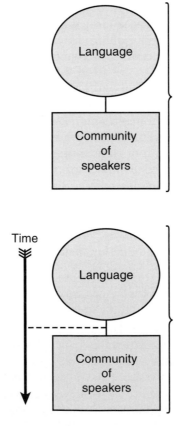

Language is no longer free, for time will allow the social forces at work on it to carry out their effects. This brings us back to the principle of continuity, which cancels freedom. But continuity necessarily implies change, varying degrees of shifts in the relationship between the signified and the signifier.

Virginia Woolf (1882–1941)

Woolf has been profoundly influential as both a modernist writer and a feminist. Not only did she experiment with form and style, radically rethinking how a novel can operate or what it can do, but also she set in motion the movement that we now call modern feminist criticism. *A Room of One's Own* is the result of two lectures Woolf was invited to present at Cambridge University's Newnham and Gerton Colleges in 1928. In this foundational text, located at the intersection of modernism and feminism, Woolf makes a distinction between women as objects of representation and women as authors of representation, suggesting that the absence of books by women is the direct result of inequities in the economic order. Her basic argument is that if women enjoyed the same rights to property that men do, their artistic output would be radically altered for the better.

From *A Room of One's Own*

Next day the light of the October morning was falling in dusty shafts through the uncurtained windows, and the hum of traffic rose from the street. London then was winding itself up again; the factory was astir; the machines were beginning. It was tempting, after all this reading, to look out of the window and see what London was doing on the morning of the twenty-sixth of October 1928. And what was London doing? Nobody, it seemed, was reading, *Antony and Cleopatra*. London was wholly indifferent, it appeared, to Shakespeare's plays. Nobody cared a straw—and I do not blame them—for the future of fiction, the death of poetry or the development by the average woman of a prose style completely expressive of her mind. If opinions upon any of these matters had been chalked on the pavement, nobody would have stooped to read them. The nonchalance of the hurrying feet would have rubbed them out in half an hour. Here came an errand-boy; here a woman with a dog on a lead. The fascination of the London street is that no two people are ever alike; each seems bound on some private affair of his own. There were the business-like, with their little bags, there were the drifters rattling sticks upon area railings; there were affable characters to whom the streets serve for clubroom, hailing men in carts and giving information without being asked for it. Also there were funerals to which men, thus suddenly reminded of the passing of their own bodies, lifted their hats.

And then a very distinguished gentleman came slowly down a doorstep and paused to avoid collision with a bustling lady who had, by some means or other, acquired a splendid fur coat and a bunch of Parma violets. They all seemed separate, self-absorbed, on business of their own.

At this moment, as so often happens in London, there was a complete lull and suspension of traffic. Nothing came down the street; nobody passed. A single leaf detached itself from the plane tree at the end of the street, and in that pause and suspension fell. Somehow it was like a signal falling, a signal pointing to a force in things which one had overlooked. It seemed to point to a river, which flowed past, invisibly, round the corner, down the street, and took people and eddied them along, as the stream at Oxbridge had taken the undergraduate in his boat and the dead leaves. Now it was bringing from one side of the street to the other diagonally a girl in patent leather boots, and then a young man in a maroon overcoat; it was also bringing a taxi-cab; and it brought all three together at a point directly beneath my window; where the taxi stopped; and the girl and the young man stopped; and they got into the taxi; and then the cab glided off as if it were swept on by the current elsewhere.

The sight was ordinary enough; what was strange was the rhythmical order with which my imagination had invested it; and the fact that the ordinary sight of two people getting into a cab had the power to communicate something of their own seeming satisfaction. The sight of two people coming down the street and meeting at the corner seems to ease the mind of some strain, I thought, watching the taxi turn and make off. Perhaps to think, as I had been thinking these two days, of one sex as distinct from the other is an effort. It interferes with the unity of the mind. Now that effort had ceased and that unity had been restored by seeing two people come together and get into a taxi-cab. The mind is certainly a very mysterious organ, I reflected, drawing my head in from the window, about which nothing whatever is known, though we depend upon it so completely. Why do I feel that there are severances and oppositions in the mind, as there are strains from obvious causes on the body? What does one mean by "the unity of the mind," I pondered, for clearly the mind has so great a power of concentrating at any point at any moment that it seems to have no single state of being. It can separate itself from the people in the street, for example, and think of itself as apart from them, at an upper window looking down on them. Or it can think with other people spontaneously, as, for instance, in a crowd waiting to hear some piece of news read out. It can think back through its fathers or through its mothers, as I have said that a women writing thinks back through her mothers. Again if one is a woman one is often surprised by a sudden splitting off of consciousness, say in walking down Whitehall, when from being the natural inheritor of that civilization, she becomes, on the contrary, outside of it, alien and critical. Clearly the mind is always altering its focus, and bringing the world into different perspectives. But some of these states of mind seem, even if adopted spontaneously, to be less comfortable than others. In order to keep oneself continuing in them one is unconsciously holding something back, and gradually the repression becomes an effort. But there may be some state of mind in which one could continue without effort because nothing is required to be held back. And this perhaps, I thought, coming in from the window, is one of them. For certainly when I saw the couple get into the taxi-cab the mind felt as if, after being divided, it had come together again in a natural fusion. The obvious reason would be that it is natural for the sexes to co-operate. One has a profound, if irrational, instinct in favour of the theory that the union of man and woman makes for the greatest satisfaction, the most complete happiness. But the sight of the two people getting into the taxi and the satisfaction it gave me made me also ask whether there are two sexes in the mind corresponding to the two sexes in the body, and whether they also require to be united in order to get complete satisfaction and happiness. And I went on amateurishly to sketch a plan of the soul so that in each of us two powers preside, one male, one female; and in the man's brain, the man predominates over the woman, and in the woman's brain, the woman predominates over the man. The normal and comfortable state of being is that when the two live in harmony together, spiritually cooperating. If one is a man, still the woman part of the brain must have effect; and a woman also must have intercourse with the man in her. Coleridge perhaps meant this when he said that a great mind is androgynous. It is when this fusion takes place that the mind is fully fertilised and uses all its faculties. Perhaps a mind that is purely masculine cannot create, any more than a mind that is purely feminine, I thought. But it would be well to test what one meant by man-womanly, and conversely by woman-manly, by pausing and looking at a book or two.

Coleridge certainly did not mean, when he said that a great mind is androgynous, that it is a mind that has any special sympathy with women; a mind that takes up their cause or devotes itself to their interpretation. Perhaps the androgynous mind is less apt to make these distinctions than the single-sexed mind. He meant, perhaps, that the androgynous mind is resonant and porous; that it transmits emotion without impediment; that it is naturally creative, incandescent and undivided. In fact one goes back to Shakespeare's mind as the type of the androgynous, of the man-womanly mind, though it would be impossible to say what Shakespeare thought of women. And if it be true that it is one of the tokens of the fully developed mind that it does not think specially or separately of sex, how much harder it is to attain that condition now than ever before. Here I came to the books by living writers, and there paused and wondered if this fact were not at the root of something that had long puzzled me. No age can ever have been as stridently sex-conscious as our own; those innumerable books by men about women in the British Museum are a proof of it. The Suffrage campaign was no doubt to blame. It must have roused in men an extraordinary desire for self-assertion; it must have made them lay an emphasis upon their own sex and its characteristics which they would not have troubled to think about had they not been challenged. And when one is challenged, even by a few women in black bonnets, one retaliates, if one has never been challenged before, rather excessively. That perhaps accounts for some of the characteristics that I remember to have found here, I thought, taking down a new novel by Mr. A, who is in the prime of life and very well thought of, apparently, by the reviewers. I opened it. Indeed, it was delightful to read a man's writing again. It was so direct, so straightforward after the writing of women. It indicated such freedom of mind, such liberty of person, such confidence in himself. One had a sense of physical well-being in the presence of this well-nourished, well-educated, free mind, which had never been thwarted or opposed, but had had full liberty from birth to stretch itself in whatever way it liked. All this was admirable. But after reading a chapter or two a shadow seemed to lie across the page. It was a straight dark bar, a shadow shaped something like the letter "I." One began dodging this way and that to catch a glimpse of the landscape behind it. Whether that was indeed a tree or a woman walking I was not quite sure. Back one was always hailed to the letter "I." One began to be tired of "I." Not but what this "I" was a most respectable "I"; honest and logical; as hard as a nut, and polished for centuries by good teaching and good feeding. I respect and admire that "I" from the bottom of my heart. But—here I turned a page or two, looking for something or other—the worst of it is that in the shadow of the letter "I" all is shapeless as mist. Is that a tree? No, it is a woman. But . . . she has not a bone in her body, I thought, watching Phoebe, for that was her name, coming across the beach. Then Alan got up and the shadow of Alan at once obliterated Phoebe. For Alan had views and Phoebe was quenched in the flood of his views. And then Alan, I thought, has passions; and here I turned page after page very fast, feeling that the crisis was approaching, and so it was. It took place on the beach under the sun. It was done very openly. It was done very vigorously. Nothing could have been more indecent. But . . . I had said "but" too often. One cannot go on saying "but." One must finish the sentence somehow, I rebuked myself. Shall I finish it, "But—I am bored!" But why was I bored? Partly because of the dominance of the letter "I" and the aridity, which, like the giant beech tree, it casts within its shade. Nothing will grow there. And partly for some more obscure reason. There seemed to be some obstacle, some impediment of Mr. A's mind which blocked the fountain of creative energy and shored it within narrow limits. And remembering the lunch party at Oxbridge, and the cigarette ash and the Manx cat and Tennyson and Christina Rossetti all in a bunch, it seemed possible that the impediment lay there. As he no longer hums under his breath, "There has fallen a splendid tear from the passion-flower at the gate," when Phoebe crosses the beach, and she no longer replies, "My heart is like a singing bird whose nest is in a water'd shoot," when Alan approaches what can he do? Being honest as the day and logical as the sun, there is only one thing he can do. And that he does, to do him justice, over and over (I said, turning the pages) and over again. And that, I added, aware of the awful nature of the confession, seems somehow dull. Shakespeare's indecency uproots a thousand other things in one's mind, and is far from being dull. But Shakespeare does it for pleasure; Mr. A, as the nurses say, does it on purpose. He does it in protest. He is protesting against the equality of the other sex by asserting his own superiority. He is therefore impeded and inhibited and self-conscious as Shakespeare might have been if he too had known Miss Clough and Miss Davies. Doubtless Elizabethan literature would have been very different from what it is if the woman's movement had begun in the sixteenth century and not in the nineteenth.

What, then, it amounts to, if this theory of the two sides of the mind holds good, is that virility has now become self-conscious—men, that is to say, are now writing only with the male side of their brains. It is a mistake for a woman to read them, for she will inevitably look for something that she will not find. It is the power of suggestion that one most misses, I thought, taking, Mr. B the critic in my hand and reading, very carefully and very dutifully, his remarks upon the art of poetry. Very able they were, acute and full of learning; but the trouble was, that his feelings no longer communicated; his mind seemed separated into different chambers; not a sound carried from one to the other. Thus, when one takes the sentence of Mr. B into the mind it falls plump to the ground—dead; but when one takes a sentences of Coleridge into the mind, it explodes and gives birth to all kinds of other ideas, and that is the only sort of writing of which one can say that it has the secret of perpetual life.

But whatever the reason may be, it is a fact that one must deplore. For it means—here I had come to rows of books by Mr. Galsworthy and Mr. Kipling— that some of the finest works of our greatest living writers fall upon deaf ears. Do what she will a woman cannot find in them that fountain of perpetual life which the critics assure her is there. It is not only that they celebrate male virtues, enforce male values and describe the world of men; it is that the emotion with which these books are permeated is to a woman incomprehensible. It is coming, it is gathering, it is about to burst on one's head, one begins saying long before the end. That picture will fall on old Jolyon's head; he will die of the shock; the old clerk will speak over him two or three obituary words; and all the swans on the Thames will simultaneously burst out singing. But one will rush away before that happens and hide in the gooseberry bushes, for the emotion which is so deep, so subtle, so symbolical to a man moves a woman to wonder. So with Mr. Kipling's officers who turn their backs; and his Sowers who sow the Seed; and his Men who are alone with their Work; and the Flag—one blushes at all these capital letters as if one had been caught eavesdropping at some purely masculine orgy. The fact is that neither Mr. Galsworthy nor Mr. Kipling has a spark of the woman in him. Thus all their qualities seem to a woman, if one may generalize, crude and immature. They lack suggestive power. And when a book lacks suggestive power, however hard it hits the surface of the mind it cannot penetrate within.

And in that restless mood in which one takes books out and puts them back again without looking at them I began to envisage an age to come of pure, of self-assertive virility, such as the letters of professors (take Sir Walter Raleigh's letters, for instance) seem to forebode, and the rulers of Italy have already brought into being. For one can hardly fail to be impressed in Rome by the sense of unmitigated masculinity; and whatever the value of unmitigated masculinity upon the state, one may question the effect of it upon the art of poetry. At any rate, according to the newspapers, there is a certain anxiety about fiction in Italy. There has been a meeting of academicians whose object it is "to develop the Italian novel." "Men famous by birth, or in finance, industry or the Fascist corporations" came together the other day and discussed the matter, and a telegram was sent to the Duce expressing the hope "that the Fascist era would soon give birth to a poet worthy of it." We may all join in that pious hope, but it is doubtful whether poetry can come out of an incubator. Poetry ought to have a mother as well as a father. The Fascist poem, one may fear, will be a horrid little abortion such as one sees in a glass jar in the museum of some county town. Such monsters never live long, it is said; one has never seen a prodigy of that sort cropping grass in a field. Two heads on one body do not make for length of life.

However, the blame for all this, if one is anxious to lay blame, rests no more upon one sex than upon the other. All seducers and reformers are responsible, Lady Bessborough when she lied to Lord Granville; Miss Davies when she told the truth to Mr. Greg. All who have brought about a state of sex-consciousness are to blame, and it is they who drive me, when I want to stretch my faculties on a book, to seek it in that happy age, before Miss Davies and Miss Clough were born, when the writer used both sides of his mind equally. One must turn back to Shakespeare then, for Shakespeare was androgynous; and so was Keats and Sterne and Cowper and Lamb and Coleridge. Shelley perhaps was sexless. Milton and Ben Jonson had a dash too much of the male in them. So had Wordsworth and Tolstoi. In our time Proust was wholly androgynous, if not perhaps a little too much of a woman. But that failing is too rare for one to complain of it, since without some mixture of the kind the intellect seems to predominate and the other faculties of the mind harden and become barren. However, I consoled myself with the reflection that this is perhaps a passing phase; much of what I have said in obedience to my promise to give you the course of my thoughts will seem out of date; much of what flames in my eyes will seem dubious to you who have not yet come of age.

Even so, the very first sentence that I would write here, I said, crossing over to the writing-table and taking up the page headed Women and Fiction, is that it is fatal for any one who writes to think of their sex. It is fatal to be a man or woman pure and simple; one must be woman-manly or man-womanly. It is fatal for a woman to lay the least stress on any grievance; to plead even with justice any cause; in any way to speak consciously as a woman. And fatal is no figure of speech; for anything written with that conscious bias is doomed to death. It ceases to be fertilized. Brilliant and effective, powerful and masterly, as it may appear for a day or two, it must wither at nightfall; it cannot grow in the minds of others. Some collaboration has to take place in the mind between the woman and the man before the act of creation can be accomplished. Some marriage of opposites has to be consummated. The whole of the mind must lie wide open if we are to get the sense that the writer is communicating his experience with perfect fullness. There must be freedom and there must be peace. Not a wheel must grate, not a light glimmer. The curtains must be close drawn. The writer, I thought, once his experience is over, must lie back and let his mind celebrate its nuptials in darkness. He must not look or question what is being done. Rather, he must pluck the petals from a rose or watch the swans float calmly down the river. And I saw again the current which took the boat and the undergraduate and the dead leaves; and the taxi took the man and the woman, I thought, seeing them come together across the street, and the current swept them away, I thought, hearing far off the roar of London's traffic, into that tremendous stream.

Here, then, Mary Beton ceases to speak. She has told you how she reached the conclusion—the prosaic conclusion—that it is necessary to have five hundred a year and a room with a lock on the door if you are to write fiction or poetry. She has tried to lay bare the thoughts and impressions that led her to think this. She has asked you to follow her flying into the arms of a Beadle, lunching here, dining there, drawing pictures in the British Museum, taking books from the shelf, looking out of the window. While she has been doing all these things, you no doubt have been observing her failings and foibles and deciding what effect they have had on her opinions. You have been contradicting her and making whatever additions and deductions seem good to you. That is all as it should be, for in a question like this truth is only to be had by laying together many varieties of error. And I will end now in my own person by anticipating two criticisms, so obvious that you can hardly fail to make them.

No opinion has been expressed, you may say, upon the comparative merits of the sexes even as writers. That was done purposely, because, even if the time had come for such a valuation—and it is far more important at the moment to know how much money women had and how many rooms than to theorise about their capacities—even if the time had come I do not believe that gifts, whether of mind or character, can be weighed like sugar and butter, not even in Cambridge, where they are so adept at putting people into classes and fixing caps on their heads and letters after their names. I do not believe that even the Table of Precedency which you will find in Whitaker's *Almanac* represents a final order of values, or that there is any sound reason to suppose that a Commander of the Bath will ultimately walk in to dinner behind a Master in Lunacy. All this pitting of sex against sex, of quality against quality; all this claiming of superiority and imputing of inferiority, belong to the private-school stage of human existence where there are "sides," and it is necessary for one side to beat another side, and of the utmost importance to walk up to a platform and receive from the hands of the Headmaster himself a highly ornamental pot. As people mature they cease to believe in sides or in Headmasters or in highly ornamental pots. At any rate, where books are concerned, it is notoriously difficult to fix labels of merit in such a way that they do not come off. Are not reviews of current literature a perpetual illustration of the difficulty of judgment? "This great book," "this worthless book," the same book is called by both names. Praise and blame alike mean nothing. No, delightful as the pastime of measuring may be, it is the most futile of all occupations, and to submit to the decrees of the measurers the most servile of attitudes. So long as you write what you wish to write, that is all that matters; and whether it matters for ages or only for hours, nobody can say. But to sacrifice a hair of the head of your vision, a shade of its colour, in deference to some Headmaster with a silver pot in his hand or to some professor with a measuring-rod up his sleeve, is the most abject treachery, and the sacrifice of wealth and chastity which used to be said to be the greatest of human disasters, a mere flea-bite in comparison.

Next I think that you may object that in all this I have made too much of the importance of material things. Even allowing a generous margin for symbolism, that five hundred a year stands for the power to contemplate, that a lock on the door means the power to think for oneself, still you may say that the mind should rise above such things; and that great poets have often been poor men. Let me then quote to you the words of your own Professor of Literature, who knows better than I do what goes to the making of a poet. Sir Arthur Quiller-Couch writes:[1]

"What are the great poetical names of the last hundred years or so? Coleridge, Wordsworth, Byron, Shelly, Landor, Keats, Tennyson, Browning, Arnold, Morris, Rossetti, Swinburne—we may stop there. Of these, all but Keats, Browning, Rossetti were University men; and of these three, Keats, who died young, cut off in his prime, was the only one not fairly well to do. It may seem a brutal thing to say, and it is a sad thing to say: but, as a matter of hard fact, the theory that poetical genius bloweth where it listeth, and equally in poor and rich, holds little truth. As a matter of hard fact, nine out of those twelve were University men: which means that somehow or other they procured the means to get the best education England can give. As a matter of hard fact, of the remaining three you know that Browning was well to do, and I challenge you that, if he had not been well to do, he would no more have attained to write *Saul* or *The Ring and the Book* than Ruskin would have attained to writing *Modern Painters* if his father had not dealt prosperously in business. Rossetti had a small private income; and, moreover, he painted. There remains but Keats; whom Atropos slew young, as she slew John Clare in a mad-house, and James Thomson by the laudanum he took to drug disappointment. These are dreadful facts, but let us face them. It is—however dishonouring to us as a nation—certain that, by some fault in our commonwealth, the poor poet has not in these days, nor has had for two hundred years, a dog's chance. Believe me—and I have spent a great part of ten years in watching some three hundred and twenty elementary schools—we may prate of democracy, but actually, a poor child in England has little more hope than had the son of an Athenian slave to be emancipated into that intellectual freedom of which great writings are born."

Nobody could put the point more plainly. "The poor poet has not in these days, nor has had for two hundred years, a dog's chance . . . a poor child in England has little more hope than had the son of an Athenian slave to be emancipated into that intellectual freedom of which great writings are born." That is it. Intellectual freedom depends upon material things. Poetry depends upon intellectual freedom. And women have always been poor, not for two hundred years merely, but from the beginning of time. Women have had less intellectual freedom than the sons of Athenian slaves. Women, then, have not had a dog's chance of writing poetry. That is why I have laid so much stress on money and a room of one's own. However, thanks to the toils of those obscure women in the past, of whom I wish we knew more, thanks, curiously enough, to two wars, the Crimean which let Florence Nightingale out of her drawing-room, and the European War which opened the doors to the average woman some sixty years later, these evils are in the way to be bettered. Otherwise you would not be here tonight, and your chance of earning five hundred pounds a year, precarious as I am afraid that it still is, would be minute in the extreme.

Still, you may object, why do you attach so much importance to this writing of books by women when, according to you, it requires so much effort, leads perhaps to the murder of one's aunts, will make one almost certainly late for luncheon, and may bring one into very grave disputes with certain very good fellows? My motives, let me admit, are partly selfish. Like most uneducated Englishwomen, I like reading—I like reading books in the bulk. Lately my diet has become a trifle monotonous; history is too much about wars; biography too much about great men; poetry has shown, I think, a tendency to sterility, and fiction—but I have sufficiently exposed my disabilities as a critic of modern fiction and will say no more about it. Therefore I would ask you to write all kinds of books, hesitating at no subject however trivial or however vast. By hook or by crook, I hope that you will possess yourselves of money enough to travel and to idle, to contemplate the future or the past of the world, to dream over books and loiter at street corners and let the line of thought dip deep into the stream. For I am by no means confining you to fiction. If you would please me—and there are thousands like me—you would write books of travel and adventure, and research and scholarship, and history and biography, and criticism and philosophy and science. By so doing you will certainly profit the art of fiction. For books have a way of influencing each other. Fiction will be much the better for standing cheek by jowl with poetry and philosophy. Moreover, if you consider any great figure of the past, like Sappho, like the Lady Murasaki, like Emily Brontë, you will find that she is an inheritor as well as an originator, and has come into existence because women have come to have the habit of writing naturally; so that even as a prelude to poetry such activity on your part would be invaluable.

But when I look back through these notes and criticise my own train of thought as I made them, I find that my motives were not altogether selfish. There runs through these comments and discursions the conviction—or is it the instinct?—that good books are desirable and that good writers, even if they show every variety of human depravity, are still good human beings. Thus when I ask you to write more books I am urging you to do what will be for your good and for the good of the world at large. How to justify this instinct or belief I do not know, for philosophic words, if one has not been educated at a university, are apt to play one false. What is meant by "reality"? It would seem to be something very erratic, very undependable—now to be found in a dusty road, now in a scrap of newspapers in the street, now in a daffodil in the sun. It lights up a group in a room and stamps some casual saying. It overwhelms one walking home beneath the stars and makes the silent world more real than the world of speech—and then there it is again in an omnibus in the uproar of Piccadilly. Sometimes, too, it seems to dwell in shapes too far away for us to discern what their nature is. But whatever it touches, it fixes and makes permanent. That is what remains over when the skin of the day has been cast into the hedge; that is what is left of past time and of our loves and hates. Now the writer, as I think, has the chance to live more than other people in the presence of this reality. It is his business to find it and collect it and communicate it to the rest of us. So at least I infer from reading *Lear* or *Emma* or *La Recherche du Temps Perdu*. For the reading of these books seems to perform a curious couching operation on the senses; one sees more intensely afterwards; the world seems bared of its covering and given an intenser life. Those are the enviable people who live at enmity with unreality; and those are the pitiable who are knocked on the head by the thing done without knowing or caring. So that when I ask you to earn money and have a room of your own, I am asking you to live in the presence of reality, an invigorating life, it would appear, whether one can impart it or not.

Here I would stop, but the pressure of convention decrees that every speech must end with a peroration. And a peroration addressed to women should have something, you will agree, particularly exalting and ennobling about it. I should implore you to remember your responsibilities, to be higher, more spiritual; I should remind you how much depends upon you, and what an influence you can exert upon the future. But those exhortations can safely, I think, be left to the other sex, who will put them, and indeed have put them, with far greater eloquence than I can compass. When I rummage in my own mind I find no noble sentiments about being companions and equals and influencing the world to higher ends. I find myself saying briefly and prosaically that it is much more important to be oneself than anything else. Do not dream of influencing other people, I would say, if I knew how to make it sound exalted. Think of things in themselves.

And again I am reminded by dipping into newspapers and novels and biographies that when a woman speaks to women she should have something very unpleasant up her sleeve. Women are hard on women. Women dislike women. Women—but are you not sick to death of the word? I can assure you that I am. Let us agree, then, that a paper read by a woman to women should end with something particularly disagreeable.

But how does it go? What can I think of? The truth is, I often like women. I like their unconventionality. I like their subtlety. I like their anonymity. I like—but I must not run on in this way. That cupboard there,—you say it holds clean table-napkins only; but what if Sir Archibald Bodkin were concealed among them? Let me then adopt a sterner tone. Have I, in the preceding words, conveyed to you sufficiently the warnings and reprobation of mankind? I have told you the very low opinion in which you were held by Mr. Oscar Browning. I have indicated what Napoleon once thought of you and what Mussolini thinks now. Then, in case any of you aspire to fiction, I have copied out for your benefit the advice of the critic about courageously acknowledging the limitations of your sex. I have referred to Professor X and given prominence to his statement that women are intellectually, morally and physically inferior to men. I have handed on all that has come my way without going in search of it, and here is a final warning—from Mr. John Langdon Davies.[2] Mr. John Langdon Davies warns women "that when children cease to be altogether desirable, women cease to be altogether necessary." I hope you will make a note of it.

How can I further encourage you to go about the business of life? Young women, I would say, and please attend, for the peroration is beginning, you are, in my opinion, disgracefully ignorant. You have never made a discovery of any sort of importance. You have never shaken an empire or led an army into battle.

The plays of Shakespeare are not by you, and you have never introduced barbarous race to the blessings of civilisation. What is your excuse? It is all very well for you to say, pointing to the streets and squares and forests of the globe swarming with black and white and coffee-coloured inhabitants, all busily engaged in traffic and enterprise and love-making, we have had other work on our hands. Without our doing, those seas would be unsailed and those fertile lands a desert. We have borne and bred and washed and taught, perhaps to the age of six or seven years, the one thousand six hundred and twenty-three million human beings who are, according to statistics, at present in existence, and that, allowing that some had help, takes time.

There is truth in what you say—I will not deny it. But at the same time may I remind you that there have been at least two colleges for women in existence in England since the year 1866; that after the year 1880 a married woman was allowed by law to possess her own property; and that in 1919—which is a whole nine years ago—she was given a vote? May I also remind you that the most of the professions have been open to you for close on ten years now? When you reflect upon these immense privileges and the length of time during which they have been enjoyed, and the fact that there must be at this moment some two thousand women capable of earning over five hundred a year in one way or another, you will agree that the excuse of lack of opportunity, training, encouragement, leisure and money no longer holds good. Moreover, the economists are telling us that Mrs. Seton has had too many children. You must, of course, go on bearing children, but, so they say, in twos and threes, not in tens and twelves.

Thus, with some time on your hands and with some book learning in your brains—you have had enough of the other kind, and are sent to college partly, I suspect, to be uneducated—surely you should embark upon another stage of your very long, very laborious and highly obscure career. A thousand pens are ready to suggest what you should do and what effect you will have. My own suggestion is a little fantastic, I admit; I prefer, therefore, to put it in the form of fiction.

I told you in the course of this paper that Shakespeare had a sister; but do not look for her in Sir Sidney Lee's life of the poet. She died young—alas, she never wrote a word. She lies buried where the omnibuses now stop, opposite the Elephant and Castle. Now my belief is that this poet who never wrote a word and was buried at the crossroads still lives. She lives in you and in me, and in many other women who are not here tonight, for they are washing up the dishes and putting the children to bed. But she lives; for great poets do not die; they are continuing presences; they need only opportunity to walk among us in the flesh. This opportunity, as I think, it is now coming within your power to give her. For my belief is that if we live another century or so—I am talking of the common life which is the real life and not of the little separate lives which we live as individuals—and have five hundred a year each of us and rooms of our own; if we have the habit of freedom and the courage to write exactly what we think; if we escape a little from the common sitting-room and see human beings not always in their relation to each other but in relation to reality; and the sky, too, and the trees or whatever it may be in themselves; if we look past Milton's bogey, for no human being should shut out the view; if we face the fact, for it is a fact, that there is no arm to cling to, but that we go alone and that our relation is to the world of reality and not only to the world of men and women, then the opportunity will come and the dead poet who was Shakespeare's sister will put on the body which she has so often laid down. Drawing her life from the lives of the unknown who were her forerunners, as her brother did before her, she will be born. As for her coming without that preparation, without that effort on our part, without that determination that when she is born again she shall find it possible to live and write her poetry, that we cannot expect, for that would be impossible. But I maintain that she would come if we worked for her, and that so to work, even in poverty and obscurity, is worth while.

Notes

1. *The Art of Writing*, by Sir Arthur Quiller-Couch.
2. *A Short History of Women*, by John Langdon Davies.

W. E. B. Du Bois (1868–1963)

Du Bois's "Criteria of Negro Art" is a foundational text for critical theories with orientations toward social justice. Art understood as an aesthetic object is seemingly at odds with so-called political art. Unlike New Critics, Du Bois understands art as being necessarily political; art is not a pristine, apolitical entity to be studied and praised for its organic unity and beauty. Because art is not secluded from economic, social, and historical forces, Du Bois encourages African-American writers and artists to incorporate into their pursuits of beauty the inequities of life in the United States.

Criteria of Negro Art

I do not doubt but there are some in this audience who are a little disturbed at the subject of this meeting, and particularly at the subject I have chosen. Such people are thinking something like this: "How is it that an organization like this, a group of radicals trying to bring new things into the world, a fighting organization which has come up out of the blood and dust of battle, struggling for the right of black men to be ordinary human beings—how is it that an organization of this kind can turn aside to talk about Art? After all, what have we who are slaves and black to do with Art?"

Or perhaps there are others who feel a certain relief and are saying, "After all it is rather satisfactory after all this talk about rights and fighting to sit and dream of something which leaves a nice taste in the mouth".

Let me tell you that neither of these groups is right. The thing we are talking about tonight is part of the great fight we are carrying on and it represents a forward and an upward look—a pushing onward. You and I have been breasting hills; we have been climbing upward; there has been progress and we can see it day by day looking back along blood-filled paths. But as you go through the valleys and over the foot-hills, so long as you are climbing, the direction,—north, south, east, or west,—is of less importance. But when gradually the vista widens and you begin to see the world at your feet and the far horizon, then it is time to know more precisely whither you are going and what you really want.

What do we want? What is the thing we are after? As it was phrased last night it had a certain truth: We want to be Americans, full-fledged Americans, with all the rights of other American citizens. But is that all? Do we want simply to be Americans? Once in a while through all of us there flashes some clairvoyance, some clear idea, of what America really is. We who are dark can see America in a way that white Americans can not. And seeing our country thus, are we satisfied with its present goals and ideals?

In the high school where I studied we learned most of Scott's "Lady of the Lake" by heart. In after life once it was my privilege to see the lake. It was Sunday. It was quiet. You could glimpse the deer wandering in unbroken forests; you could hear the soft ripple of romance on the waters. Around me fell the cadence of that poetry of my youth. I fell asleep full of the enchantment of the Scottish border. A new day broke and with it came a sudden rush of excursionists. They were mostly Americans and they were loud and strident. They poured upon the little pleasure boat,—men with their hats a little on one side and drooping cigars in the wet corners of their mouths; women who shared their conversation with the world. They all tried to get everywhere first. They pushed other people out of the way. They made all sorts of incoherent noises and gestures so that the quiet home folk and the visitors from other lands silently and half-wonderingly gave way before them. They struck a note not evil but wrong. They carried, perhaps, a sense of strength and accomplishment, but their hearts had no conception of the beauty which pervaded this holy place.

If you tonight suddenly should become full-fledged Americans; if your color faded, or the color line here in Chicago was miraculously forgotten; suppose, too, you became at the same time rich and powerful;—what is it that you would want? What would you immediately seek? Would you buy the most powerful of motor cars and outrace Cook County? Would you buy the most elaborate estate on the North Shore? Would you be a Rotarian or a Lion or a What-not of the very last degree? Would you wear the most striking clothes, give the richest dinners and buy the longest press notices?

Even as you visualize such ideals you know in your hearts that these are not the things you really want. You realize this sooner than the average white American because, pushed aside as we have been in America, there has come to us not only a certain distaste for the tawdry and flamboyant but a vision of what the world could be if it were really a beautiful world; if we had the true spirit; if we had the Seeing Eye, the Cunning Hand, the Feeling Heart; if we had, to be sure, not perfect happiness, but plenty of good hard work, the inevitable suffering that always comes with life; sacrifice and waiting, all that—but, nevertheless, lived in a world where men know, where men create, where they realize themselves and where they enjoy life. It is that sort of a world we want to create for ourselves and for all America.

After all, who shall describe Beauty? What is it? I remember tonight four beautiful things: The Cathedral at Cologne, a forest in stone, set in light and changing shadow, echoing with sunlight and solemn song; a village of the Veys in West Africa, a little thing of mauve and purple, quiet, lying content and shining in the sun; a black and velvet room where on a throne rests, in old and yellowing marble, the broken curves of the Venus of Milo; a single phrase of music in the Southern South—utter melody, haunting and appealing, suddenly arising out of night and eternity, beneath the moon.

Such is Beauty. Its variety is infinite, it possibility is endless. In normal life all may have it and have it yet again. The world is full of it; and yet today the mass of human beings are choked away from it, and their lives distorted and made ugly. This is not only wrong, it is silly. Who shall right this well-nigh universal failing? Who shall let this world be beautiful? Who shall restore to men the glory of sunsets and the peace of quiet sleep?

We black folk may help for we have within us as a race new stirrings; stirrings of the beginning of a new appreciation of joy, of a new desire to create, of a new will to be; as though in this morning of group life we had awakened from some sleep that at once dimly mourns the past and dreams a splendid future; and there has come the conviction that the Youth that is here today, the Negro Youth, is a different kind of Youth, because in some new way it bears this mighty prophecy on its breast, with a new realization of itself, with new determination for all mankind.

What has this Beauty to do with the world? What has Beauty to do with Truth and Goodness—with the facts of the world and the right actions of men? "Nothing", the artists rush to answer. They may be right. I am but an humble disciple of art and cannot presume to say. I am one who tells the truth and exposes evil and seeks with Beauty and for Beauty to set the world right. That somehow, somewhere eternal and perfect Beauty sits above Truth and Right I can conceive, but here and how and in the world in which I work they are for me unseparated and inseparable.

This is brought to us peculiarly when as artists we face our own past as a people. There has come to us—and it has come especially through the man we are going to honor tonight[1]—a realization of that past, of which for long years we have been ashamed, for which we have apologized. We thought nothing could come out of that past which we wanted to remember; which we wanted to hand down to our children. Suddenly, this same past is taking on form, color and reality, and in a half shamefaced way we are beginning to be proud of it. We are remembering that the romance of the world did not die and lie forgotten in the

Middle Age; that if you want romance to deal with you must have it here and now and in your own hands.

I once knew a man and woman. They had two children, a daughter who was white and a daughter who was brown; the daughter who was white married a white man; and when her wedding was preparing the daughter who was brown prepared to go and celebrate. But the mother said, "No!" and the brown daughter went into her room and turned on the gas and died. Do you want Greek tragedy swifter than that?

Or again, here is a little Southern town and you are in the public square. On one side of the square is the office of a colored lawyer and on all the other sides are men who do not like colored lawyers. A white woman goes into the black man's office and points to the white-filled square and says, "I want five hundred dollars now and if I do not get it I am going to scream."

Have you heard the story of the conquest of German East Africa? Listen to the untold tale: There were 40,000 black men and 4,000 white men who talked German. There were 20,000 black men and 12,000 white men who talked English. There were 10,000 black men and 400 white men who talked French. In Africa then where the Mountains of the Moon raised their white and snow-capped heads into the mouth of the tropic sun, where Nile and Congo rise and the Great Lakes swim, these men fought; they struggled on mountain, hill and valley, in river, lake and swamp, until in masses they sickened, crawled and died; until the 4,000 white Germans had become mostly bleached bones; until nearly all the 12,000 white Englishmen had returned to South Africa, and the 400 Frenchmen to Belgium and Heaven; all except a mere handful of the white men died; but thousands of black men from East, West and South Africa, from Nigeria and the Valley of the Nile, and from the West Indies still struggled, fought and died. For four years they fought and won and lost German East Africa; and all you hear about it is that England and Belgium conquered German Africa for the allies!

Such is the true and stirring stuff of which Romance is born and from this stuff come the stirrings of men who are beginning to remember that this kind of material is theirs; and this vital life of their own kind is beckoning them on.

The question comes next as to the interpretation of these new stirrings, of this new spirit: Of what is the colored artist capable? We have had on the part of both colored and white people singular unanimity of judgement in the past. Colored people have said: "This work must be inferior because it comes from colored people." White people have said: "It is inferior because it is done by colored people." But today there is coming to both the realization that the work of the black man is not always inferior. Interesting stories come to us. A professor in the University of Chicago read to a class that had studied literature a passage of poetry and asked them to guess the author. They guessed a goodly company from Shelley and Robert Browning down to Tennyson and Masefield. The author was Countée Cullen. Or again the English critic John Drinkwater went down to a Southern seminary, one of the sort which "finishes" young white women of the South. The students sat with their wooden faces while he tried to get some response out of them. Finally he said, "Name me some of your Southern poets". They hesitated. He said finally, "I'll start out with your best: Paul Laurence Dunbar"!

With the growing recognition of Negro artists in spite of the severe handicaps, one comforting thing is occurring to both white and black. They are whispering, "Here is a way out. Here is the real solution of the color problem. The recognition accorded Cullen, Hughes, Fauset, White and others shows there is no real color line. Keep quiet! Don't complain! Work! All will be well!"

I will not say that already this chorus amounts to a conspiracy. Perhaps I am naturally too suspicious. But I will say that there are today a surprising number of white people who are getting great satisfaction out of these younger Negro writers because they think it is going to stop agitation of the Negro question. They say, "What is the use of your fighting and complaining; do the great thing and the reward is there". And many colored people are all too eager to follow this advice; especially those who are weary of the eternal struggle along the color line, who are afraid to fight and to whom the money of philanthropists and the alluring publicity are subtle and deadly bribes. They say, "What is the use of fighting? Why not show simply what we deserve and let the reward come to us?"

And it is right here that the National Association for the Advancement of Colored People comes upon the field, comes with its great call to a new battle, a new fight and new things to fight before the old things are wholly won; and to say that the Beauty of Truth and Freedom which shall some day be our heritage and the heritage of all civilized men is not in our hands yet and that we ourselves must not fail to realize.

There is in New York tonight a black woman molding clay by herself in a little bare room, because there is not a single school of sculpture in New York where she is welcome. Surely there are doors she might burst through, but when God makes a sculptor He does not always make the pushing sort of person who beats his way through doors thrust in his face. This girl is working her hands off to get out of this country so that she can get some sort of training.

There was Richard Brown. If he had been white he would have been alive today instead of dead of neglect. Many helped him when he asked but he was not the kind of boy that always asks. He was simply one who made colors sing.

There is a colored woman in Chicago who is a great musician. She thought she would like to study at Fontainebleau this summer where Walter Damrosch and a score of leaders of Art have an American school of music. But the application blank of this school says: "I am a white American and I apply for admission to the school."

We can go on the stage; we can be just as funny as white Americans wish us to be; we can play all the sordid parts that America likes to assign to Negroes; but for any thing else there is still small place for us.

And so I might go on. But let me sum up with this: Suppose the only Negro who survived some centuries hence was the Negro painted by white Americans in the novels and essays they have written. What would people in a hundred years say of black Americans? Now turn it around. Suppose you were to write a story and put in it the kind of people you know and like and imagine. You might get it published and you might not. And the "might not" is still far bigger than the "might". The white publishers catering to white folk would say, "It is not interesting"—to white folk, naturally not. They want Uncle Toms, Topsies, good "darkies" and clowns. I have in my office a story with all the earmarks of truth. A young man says that he started out to write and had his stories accepted. Then he began to write about the things he knew best about, that is, about his own people. He submitted a story to a magazine which said, "We are sorry, but we cannot take it". "I sat down and revised my story, changing the color of the characters and the locale and sent it under an assumed name with a change of address and it was accepted by the same magazine that had refused it, the editor promising to take anything else I might send in providing it was good enough."

We have, to be sure, a few recognized and successful Negro artists; but they are not all those fit to survive or even a good minority. They are but the remnants of that ability and genius among us whom the accidents of education and opportunity have raised on the tidal waves of chance. We black folk are not altogether peculiar in this. After all, in the world at large, it is only the accident, the remnant, that gets the chance to make the most of itself; but if this is true of the white world it is infinitely more true of the colored world. It is not simply the great clear tenor of Roland Hayes that opened the ears of America. We have had many voices of all kinds as fine as his and America was and is as deaf as she was for years to him. Then a foreign land heard Hayes and put its imprint on him and immediately America with all its imitative snobbery woke up. We approved Hayes because London, Paris and Berlin approved him and not simply because he was a great singer.

Thus it is the bounden duty of black America to begin this great work of the creation of Beauty, of the preservation of Beauty, of the realization of Beauty, and we must use in this work all the methods that men have used before. And what have been the tools of the artist in times gone by? First of all, he has used the Truth—not for the sake of truth, not as a scientist seeking truth, but as one upon whom Truth eternally thrusts itself as the highest handmaid of imagination, as the one great vehicle of universal understanding. Again artists have used Goodness—goodness in all its aspects of justice, honor and right—not for sake of an ethical sanction but as the one true method of gaining sympathy and human interest.

The apostle of Beauty thus becomes the apostle of Truth and Right not by choice but by inner and outer compulsion. Free he is but his freedom is ever bounded by Truth and Justice; and slavery only dogs him when he is denied the right to tell the Truth or recognize an ideal of Justice.

Thus all Art is propaganda and ever must be, despite the wailing of the purists. I stand in utter shamelessness and say that whatever art I have for writing has been used always for propaganda for gaining the right of black folk to love and enjoy. I do of care a damn for any art that is not used for propaganda. But I do care when propaganda is confined to one side while the other is stripped and silent.

In New York we have two plays: "White Cargo" and "Congo". In "White Cargo" there is a fallen woman. She is black. In "Congo" the fallen woman is white. In "White Cargo" the black woman goes down further and further and in "Congo" the white woman begins with degradation but in the end is one of the angels of the Lord.

You know the current magazine story: A young white man goes down to Central America and the most beautiful colored woman there falls in love with him. She crawls across the whole isthmus to get to him. The white man says nobly, "No". He goes back to his white sweetheart in New York.

In such cases, it is not the positive propaganda of people who believe white blood divine, infallible and holy to which I object. It is the denial of a similar right of propaganda to those who believe black blood human, lovable and inspired with new ideals for the world. White artists themselves suffer from this narrowing of their field. They cry for freedom in dealing with Negroes because they have so little freedom in dealing with whites. DuBose Heywood writes "Porgy" and writes beautifully of the black Charleston underworld. But why does he do this? Because he cannot do a similar thing for the white people of Charleston, or they would drum him out of town. The only chance he had to tell the truth of pitiful human degradation was to tell it of colored people. I should not be surprised if Octavius Roy Cohen had approached the *Saturday Evening Post* and asked permission to write about a different kind of colored folk than the monstrosities he has created; but if he has, the *Post* has replied, "No. You are getting paid to write about the kind of colored people you are writing about."

In other words, the white public today demands from its artists, literary and pictorial, racial pre-judgment which deliberately distorts Truth and Justice, as far as colored races are concerned, and it will pay for no other.

On the other hand, the young and slowly growing black public still wants its prophets almost equally unfree. We are bound by all sorts of customs that have come down as second-hand soul clothes of white patrons. We are ashamed of sex and we lower our eyes when people will talk of it. Our religion holds us in superstition. Our worst side has been so shamelessly emphasized that we are denying we have or ever had a worst side. In all sorts of ways we are hemmed in and our new young artists have got to fight their way to freedom.

The ultimate judge has got to be you and you have got to build yourselves up into that wide judgment, that catholicity of temper which is going to enable the artist to have his widest chance for freedom. We can afford the Truth. White folk today cannot. As it is now we are handing everything over to a white jury. If a colored man wants to publish a book, he has got to get a white publisher and a white newspaper to say it is great; and then you and I say so. We must come to the place where the work of art when it appears is reviewed and acclaimed by our own free and unfettered judgment. And we are going to have a real and valuable and eternal judgment only as we make ourselves free of mind, proud of body and just of soul to all men.

And then do you know what will be said? It is already saying. Just as soon as true Art emerges; just as soon as the black artist appears, someone touches the race on the shoulder and says, "He did that because he was an American, not because he was a Negro; he was born here; he was trained here; he is not a Negro—what is a Negro anyhow? He is just human; it is the kind of thing you ought to expect".

I do not doubt that the ultimate art coming from black folk is going to be just as beautiful, and beautiful largely in the same ways, as the art that comes from white folk, or yellow, or red; but the point today is that until the art of the black folk compells recognition they will not be rated as human. And when through art they compell recognition then let the world discover if it will that their art is as new as it is old and as old as new.

I had a classmate once who did three beautiful things and died. One of them was a story of as folk who found fire and then went wandering in the gloom of night seeking again the stars they had once known and lost; suddenly out of blackness they looked up and there loomed the heavens; and what was it that they said? They raised a mighty cry: "It is the stars, it is the ancient stars, it is the young and everlasting stars!"

Note

1. Carter Godwin Woodson, 12th Spingarn Medallist.

John Crowe Ransom (1888–1974)

Ransom's "Criticism, Inc." is a foundational text for formalist approaches to literature, such as the New Criticism, a dominant twentieth-century methodology in the United States well into the 1970s and early 1980s. In their teaching of literature to students, Ransom and other New Critics emphasized close, careful scrutiny of how a text's language forms an aesthetic whole when the writing is well done. New Critics sought, in Ransom's words, to "enjoy the aesthetic or characteristic values of literature," and they sought to avoid critical methods that emphasized rhetorical and political effects of art, which suggested art's implication in social and historical networks and not its presumed autonomy from the New Critical perspective.

From "Criticism, Inc."

It is strange, but nobody seems to have told us what exactly is the proper business of criticism. There are many critics who might tell us, but for the most part they are amateurs. So have the critics nearly always been amateurs; including the best ones. They have not been trained to criticism so much as they have simply undertaken a job for which no specific qualifications were required. It is far too likely that what they call criticism when they produce it is not the real thing.

There are three sorts of trained performers who would appear to have some of the competence that the critic needs. The first is the artist himself. He should know good art when he sees it; but his understanding is intuitive rather than dialectical—he cannot very well explain his theory of the thing. It is true that literary artists, with their command of language, are better critics of their own art than are other artists; probably the best critics of poetry we can now have are the poets. But one can well imagine that any artist's commentary on the art-work is valuable in the degree that he sticks to its technical effects, which he knows minutely, and about which he can certainly talk if he will.

The second is the philosopher, who should know all about the function of the fine arts. But the philosopher is apt to see a lot of wood and no trees, for his theory is very general and his acquaintance with the particular works of art is not persistent and intimate, especially his acquaintance with their technical effects. Or at least I suppose so, for philosophers have not proved that they can write close criticism by writing it; and I have the feeling that even their handsome generalizations are open to suspicion as being grounded more on other generalizations, those which form their prior philosophical stock, than on acute study of particulars.

The third is the university teacher of literature, who is styled professor, and who should be the very professional we need to take charge of the critical activity. He is hardly inferior as critic to the philosopher, and perhaps not on the whole to the poet, but he is a greater disappointment because we have the right to expect more of him. Professors of literature are learned but not critical men. The professional morale of this part of the university staff is evidently low. It is as if, with conscious or unconscious cunning, they had appropriated every avenue of escape from their responsibility which was decent and official; so that it is easy for one of them without public reproach to spend a lifetime in compiling the data of literature and yet rarely or never commit himself to a literary judgment.

Nevertheless it is from the professors of literature, in this country the professors of English for the most part, that I should hope eventually for the erection of intelligent standards of criticism. It is their business.

Criticism must become more scientific, or precise and systematic, and this means that it must be developed by the collective and sustained effort of learned persons—which means that its proper seat is in the universities.

Scientific: but I do not think we need be afraid that criticism, trying to be a sort of science, will inevitably fail and give up in despair, or else fail without realizing it and enjoy some hollow and pretentious career. It will never be a very exact science, or even a nearly exact one. But neither will psychology, if that term continues to refer to psychic rather than physical phenomena; nor will sociology, as Pareto, quite contrary to his intention, appears to have furnished us with evidence for believing; nor even will economics. It does not matter whether we call them sciences or just systematic studies; the total effort of each to be effective must be consolidated and kept going. The studies which I have mentioned have immeasurably improved in understanding since they were taken over by the universities, and the same career looks possible for criticism.

Rather than occasional criticism by amateurs, I should think the whole enterprise might be seriously taken in hand by professionals. Perhaps I use a distasteful figure, but I have the idea that what we need is Criticism, Inc., or Criticism, Ltd.

The principal resistance to such an idea will come from the present incumbents of the professorial chairs. But its adoption must come from them too. The idea of course is not a private one of my own. If it should be adopted before long, the credit would probably belong to Professor Ronald S. Crane, of the University of Chicago, more than to any other man. He is the first of the great professors to have advocated it as a major policy for departments of English. It is possible that we will have made some important academic history.

2

[. . .]

It is not anybody who can do criticism. And for an example, the more eminent (as historical scholar) the professor of English, the less apt he is to be able to write decent criticism, unless it is about another professor's work of historical scholarship, in which case it is not literary criticism. The professor may not be without aesthetic judgments respecting an old work, especially if it is "in his period," since it must often have been judged by authorities whom he respects. Confronted with a new work, I am afraid it is very rare that he finds anything particular to say. Contemporary criticism is not at all in the hands of those who direct the English studies. Contemporary literature, which is almost obliged to receive critical study if it receives any at all, since it is hardly capable of the usual historical commentary, is barely officialized as a proper field for serious study.

Here is contemporary literature, waiting for its criticism; where are the professors of literature? They are watering their own gardens; elucidating the literary histories of their respective periods. So are their favorite pupils. The persons who save the occasion, and rescue contemporary literature from the humiliation of having to go without a criticism, are the men who had to leave the university before their time because they felt themselves being warped into mere historians; or those who finished the courses and took their punishment but were tough, and did not let it engross them and spoil them. They are home-made critics. Naturally they are not too wise, these amateurs who furnish our reviews and critical studies. But when they distinguish themselves, the universities which they attended can hardly claim more than a trifling share of the honor.

It is not so in economics, chemistry, sociology, theology, and architecture. In these branches it is taken for granted that criticism of the performance is the prerogative of the men who have had formal training it its theory and technique. The historical method is useful, and may be applied readily to any human performance whatever. But the exercise does not become an obsession with the university men working in the other branches; only the literary scholars wish to convert themselves into pure historians. This has gone far to nullify the usefulness of a departmental personnel larger, possibly, than any other, and of the lavish endowment behind it.

3

Presumably the departments of English exist in order to communicate the understanding of the literary art. That will include both criticism and also whatever may be meant by "appreciation." This latter term seems to stand for the kind of understanding that is had intuitively, without benefit of instruction, by merely being constrained to spend time in the presence of the literary product. It is true that some of the best work now being done in departments is by the men who do little more than read well aloud, enforcing a private act of appreciation upon the students. One remembers how good a service that may be, thinking perhaps of Professor Copeland of Harvard, or Dean Cross at Greeley Teachers College. And there are men who try to get at the same thing in another way, which they would claim is surer: by requiring a great deal of memory work, in order to enforce familiarity with fine poetry. These might defend their strategy by saying that at any rate the work they required was not as vain as the historical rigmarole which the scholars made their pupils recite, if the objective was really literary under-standing and not external information. But it would be a misuse of terms to employ the word instruction for the offices either of the professors who read aloud or of those who require the memory work. The professors so engaged are properly curators, and the museum of which they had the care is furnished with the cherished literary masterpieces, just as another museum might be filled with paintings. They conduct their squads from one work to another, making appro-priate pauses or reverent gestures, but their own obvious regard for the master-pieces is somewhat contagious, and contemplation is induced. Naturally they are grateful to the efficient staff of colleagues in the background who have framed the masterpieces, hung them in the proper schools and in the chronological order, and prepared the booklet of information about the artists and the occasions. The colleagues in their turn probably feel quite happy over this division of labor, thinking that they have done the really productive work, and that it is appropri-ate now if less able men should undertake a little salesmanship.

Behind appreciation, which is private, and criticism, which is public and negotiable, and represents the last stage of English studies, is historical scholar-ship. It is indispensable. But it is instrumental and cannot be the end itself. In this respect historical studies have the same standing as linguistic studies: language and history are aids.

On behalf of the historical studies. Without them what could we make of Chaucer, for instance? I cite the familiar locus of the "hard" scholarship, the cen-ter of any program of advanced studies in English which intends to initiate the student heroically, and once for all, into the historical discipline. Chaucer writes allegories for historians to decipher, he looks out upon institutions and customs unfamiliar to us. Behind him are many writers in various tongues from whom he borrows both forms and materials. His thought bears constant reference to clas-sical and mediaeval philosophies and sciences which have passed from our effec-tive knowledge. An immense labor of historical adaptation is necessary before our minds are ready to make the aesthetic approach to Chaucer.

Or to any author out of our own age. The mind with which we enter into an old work is not the mind with which we make our living, or enter into a contem-porary work. It is under sharp restraints, and it is quite differently furnished. Out of our actual contemporary mind we have to cancel a great deal that has come there under modern conditions but was not in the earlier mind at all. This is a technique on the negative side, a technique of suspension; difficult for practical persons, literal scientists, and aggressive moderns who take pride in the "truth" or the "progress" which enlightened man, so well represented in their own instance, has won. Then, on the positive side, we must supply the mind with the precise beliefs and ways of thought it had in that former age, with the specific content in which history instructs us; this is a technique of make-believe. The whole act of historical adaptation, through such techniques, is a marvelous feat of flexibility. Certainly it is a thing hard enough to justify university instruction. But it is not sufficient for an English program.

The achievement of modern historical scholarship in the field of English literature has been, in the aggregate, prodigious; it should be very proud. A good impression of the volume of historical learning now available for the students of English may be quickly had from inspecting a few chapters of the Cambridge History, with the bibliographies. Or, better, from inspecting one of a large number of works which have come in since the Cambridge History: the handbooks, which tell all about the authors, such as Chaucer, Shakespeare, Milton, and carry voluminous bibliographies; or the period books, which tell a good deal about whole periods of literature.

There is one sense in which it may be justly said that we can never have too much scholarship. We cannot have too much of it if the critical intelligence functions, and has the authority to direct it. There is hardly a critical problem which does not require some arduous exercises in fact-finding, but each problem is quite specific about the kind of facts it wants. Mountains of facts may have been found already, but often they have been found for no purpose at all except the purpose of piling up into a big exhibit, to offer intoxicating delights to the academic population.

To those who are aesthetically minded among students, the rewards of many a historical labor will have to be disproportionately slight. The official Chaucer course is probably over ninety-five per cent historical and linguistic, and less than five per cent aesthetic or critical. A thing of beauty is a joy forever. But it is not improved because the student has had to tie his tongue before it. It is an artistic object, with a heroic human labor behind it, and on these terms it calls for public discussion. The dialectical possibilities are limitless, and when we begin to realize them we are engaged in criticism.

4

What is criticism? Easier to ask, What is criticism not? It is an act now notoriously arbitrary and undefined. We feel certain that the critical act is not one of those which the professors of literature habitually perform, and cause their students to perform. And it is our melancholy impression that it is not often cleanly performed in those loose compositions, by writers of perfectly indeterminate qualifications, that appear in print as reviews of books.

Professor Crane excludes from criticism works of historical scholarship and of Neo-Humanism, but more exclusions are possible than that: I should wish to exclude:

1. Personal registrations, which are declarations of the effect of the artwork upon the critic as reader. The first law to be prescribed to criticism, if we may assume such authority, is that it shall be objective, shall cite the nature of the object rather than its effects upon the subject. Therefore it is hardly criticism to assert that the proper literary work is one that we can read twice; or one that causes in us some remarkable physiological effect, such as oblivion of the outer world, the flowing of tears, visceral or laryngeal sensations, and such like; or one that induces perfect illusion, or brings us into a spiritual ecstasy; or even one that produces a catharsis of our emotions. Aristotle concerned himself with this last in making up his definition of tragedy—though he did not fail to make some acute analyses of the objective features of the work also. I have read that some modern Broadway producers of comedy require a reliable person to seat himself in a trial audience and count the laughs; their method of testing is not so subtle as Aristotle's, but both are concerned with the effects. Such concern seems to reflect the view that art comes into being because the artist, or the employer behind him, has designs upon the public, whether high moral designs or box-office ones. It is an odious view in either case, because it denies the autonomy of the artist as one who interests himself in the artistic object in his own right, and likewise the autonomy of the work itself as existing for its own sake. (We may define a chemical as something which can effect a certain cure, but that is not its meaning to the chemist; and we may define toys, if we are weary parents, as things which keep our children quiet, but that is not what they are to engineers.) Furthermore, we must regard as uncritical the use of an extensive vocabulary which ascribes to the object properties really discovered in the subject, as: *moving, exciting, entertaining, pitiful; great,* if I am not mistaken, and *admirable,* on a slightly different ground; and, in strictness, *beautiful* itself.

2. Synopsis and paraphrase. The high-school classes and the women's clubs delight in these procedures, which are easiest of all the systematic exercises possible in the discussion of literary objects. I do not mean that the critic never uses them in his analysis of fiction and poetry, but he does not consider plot or story as identical with the real content. Plot is an abstract from content.

3. Historical studies. These have a very wide range, and include studies of the general literary background; author's biography, of course with special reference to autobiographical evidences in the work itself; bibliographical items; the citation of literary originals and analogues, and therefore what, in general, is called comparative literature. Nothing can be more stimulating to critical analysis than comparative literature. But it may be conducted only superficially, if the comparisons are perfunctory and mechanical, or if the scholar is content with merely making the parallel citations.

4. Linguistic studies. Under this head come those studies which define the meaning of unusual words and idioms, including the foreign and archaic ones, and identify the allusions. The total benefit of linguistics for criticism

would be the assurance that the latter was based on perfect logical under-standing of the content, or "interpretation." Acquaintance with all the lan-guages and literatures in the world would not necessarily produce a critic, though it might save one from damaging errors.

5. Moral studies. The moral standard applied is the one appropriate to the reviewer; it may be the Christian ethic, or the Aristotelian one, or the new proletarian gospel. But the moral content is not the whole content, which should never be relinquished.

6. Any other special studies which deal with some abstract or prose content taken out of the work. Nearly all departments of knowledge may conceiv-ably find their own materials in literature, and take them out. Studies have been made of Chaucer's command of mediaeval sciences, of Spenser's view of the Irish question, of Shakespeare's understanding of the law, of Milton's geography, of Hardy's place-names. The critic may well inform himself of these materials as possessed by the artist, but his business as critic is to dis-cuss the literary assimilation of them.

5

With or without such useful exercises as these, probably assuming that the intel-ligent reader has made them for himself, comes the critical act itself.

Mr. Austin Warren, whose writings I admire, is evidently devoted to the aca-demic development of the critical project. Yet he must be a fair representative of what a good deal of academic opinion would be when he sees no reason why crit-icism should set up its own house, and try to dissociate itself from historical and other scholarly studies; why not let all sorts of studies, including the critical ones, flourish together in the same act of sustained attention, or the same scheduled "course"? But so they are supposed to do at present; and I would only ask him whether he considers that criticism prospers under this arrangement. It has always had the chance to go ahead in the hands of the professors of literature, and it has not gone ahead. A change of policy suggests itself. Strategy requires now, I should think, that criticism receive its own charter of rights and function inde-pendently. If he fears for its foundations in scholarship, the scholars will always be on hand to reprove it when it tries to function on an unsound scholarship.

I do not suppose the reviewing of books can be reformed in the sense of being turned into pure criticism. The motives of the reviewers are as much mixed as the performance, and indeed they condition the mixed performance. The reviewer has a job of presentation and interpretation as well as criticism. The most we can ask of him is that he know when the criticism begins, and that he make it as clean and definitive as his business permits. To what authority may he turn?

I know of no authority. For the present each critic must be his own author-ity. But I know of one large class of studies which is certainly critical, and neces-sary, and I can suggest another sort of study for the critic's consideration if he is really ambitious.

Studies in the technique of the art belong to criticism certainly. They cannot belong anywhere else, because the technique is not peculiar to any prose materials discoverable in the work of art, nor to anything else but the unique form of that art. A very large volume of studies is indicated by this classification. They would be technical studies of poetry, for instance, the art I am specifically discussing, if they treated its metric; its inversions, solecisms, lapses from the prose norm of language, and from close prose logic; its tropes; its fictions, or inventions, by which it secures "aesthetic distance" and removes itself from history; or any other devices, on the general understanding that any systematic usage which does not hold good for prose is a poetic device.

A device with a purpose: the superior critic is not content with the compilation of the separate devices; they suggest to him a much more general question. The critic speculates on why poetry, through its devices, is at such pains to dissociate itself from prose at all, and what it is trying to represent that cannot be represented by prose.

I intrude here with an idea of my own, which may serve as a starting point of discussion. Poetry distinguishes itself from prose on the technical side by the devices which are, precisely, its means of escaping from prose. Something is continually being killed by prose which the poet wants to preserve. But this must be put philosophically. (Philosophy sounds hard, but it deals with natural and fundamental forms of experience.)

The critic should regard the poem as nothing short of a desperate ontological or metaphysical manoeuvre. The poet himself, in the agony of composition, has something like this sense of his labors. The poet perpetuates in his poem an order of existence which in actual life is constantly crumbling beneath his touch. His poem celebrates the object which is real, individual, and qualitatively infinite. He knows that his practical interests will reduce this living object to a mere utility, and that his sciences will disintegrate it for their convenience into their respective abstracts. The poet wishes to defend his object's existence against its enemies, and the critic wishes to know what he is doing, and how. The critic should find in the poem a total poetic or individual object which tends to be universalized, but is not permitted to suffer this fate. His identification of the poetic object is in terms of the universal or commonplace object to which it tends, and of the tissue, or totality of connotation, which holds it secure. How does he make out the universal object? It is the prose object, which any forthright prosy reader can discover to him by an immediate paraphrase; it is a kind of story, character, thing, scene, or moral principle. And where is the tissue that keeps it from coming out of the poetic object? That is, for the laws of the prose logic, its superfluity; and I think I would even say, its irrelevance.

A poet is said to be distinguishable in terms of his style. It is a comprehensive word, and probably means: the general character of his irrelevances, or tissues. All his technical devices contribute to it, elaborating or individualizing the universal, the core-object; likewise all his material detail. For each poem even, ideally, there is distinguishable a logical object or universal, but at the same time a tissue of irrelevance from which it does not really emerge. The critic has to take the poem apart, or analyze it, for the sake of uncovering these features. With all the finesse possible, it is rude and patchy business by comparison with the living integrity of the poem. But without it there could hardly be much understanding of the value of poetry, or of the natural history behind any adult poem.

The language I have used may sound too formidable, but I seem to find that a profound criticism generally works by some such considerations. However the critic may spell them, the two terms are in his mind: the prose core to which he can violently reduce the total object, and the differentia, residue, or tissue, which keeps the object poetical or entire. The character of the poem resides for the good critic in its way of exhibiting the residuary quality. The character of the poet is defined by the kind of prose object to which his interest evidently attaches, plus his way of involving it firmly in the residuary tissue. And doubtless, incidentally, the wise critic can often read behind the poet's public character his private history as a man with a weakness for lapsing into some special form of prosy or scientific bondage.

Similar considerations hold, I think, for the critique of fiction, or of the non-literary arts. I remark this for the benefit of philosophers who believe, with propriety, that the arts are fundamentally one. But I would prefer to leave the documentation to those who are better qualified.

GLOSSARY

Aesthetic: The word "aesthetic" typically refers to theories of art, particularly theories of the beautiful. The word comes from the Greek words *aisthetikos,* meaning "of sense perception," and *aisthanesthai,* meaning "to perceive." A branch of philosophy focuses on aesthetics, and the theories of the eighteenth-century German philosopher Immanuel Kant in his book *Critique of Judgment* were highly influential in shaping views about taste and about the aesthetic. Contemporary theorist Terry Eagleton offers a reassessment of the aesthetic in his 1990 book *The Ideology of the Aesthetic:* "The category of the aesthetic assumes the importance it does in modern Europe because in speaking of art it speaks of these other matters too, which are at the heart of the middle class's struggle for political hegemony. The construction of the modern notion of the aesthetic artefact is thus inseparable from the construction of the dominant ideological forms of modern class-society, and indeed from a whole new form of human subjectivity appropriate to that social order" (3). In his 1979 book *Distinction: A Social Critique of the Judgment of Taste,* the French sociologist Pierre Bourdieu also offers an influential revision of Kant's philosophy of taste and the aesthetic.

Alterity: This term is often used interchangeably with "otherness." Although theories of alterity are used in a number of different contexts, these theories generally explore the ambivalence manifested in relationships between subject and other, same and different. Homi Bhabha, for example, has used a theory of alterity taken from film theory and psychoanalysis to explain colonial and race relations as an oscillation, on the part of the colonial subject, between identification with and alienation from the colonized other. In postcolonial studies, this colonized other has come to be referred to as the "subaltern," a term that combines the Latin *sub* (meaning "under") with *alter* (meaning "other").

Antifoundationalist: This term describes people who reject the proposition that ideals such as "truth with a capital T" are definitive. Antifoundationalists argue that truth is contingent on one's perspective and that truths change over time. In other words, antifoundationalists recognize that what one person understands as the truth may not be accepted by someone else. Truth is not an either/or category: either person *X*'s view of the truth is the correct one or person *Y*'s view of the truth is the correct one. The antifoundationalist sees claims of truth as human constructions dependent on persuasion; what persuades one group or generation will not necessarily persuade another group or generation.

Binary Opposition: Although ancient peoples were able to think of concepts such as light and dark in completely positivistic terms, we moderns think of the two in differential terms. That is, we understand dark in relation to light; we understand dark as the absence of light. We might say, "Turn on the light," but we would rarely say, "Turn on the dark." Because of Saussure's emphasis on binary contrasts as the source of meaning, we cannot conceptualize light without conceptualizing its opposite, dark. A binary opposition, then, is the coupling of two terms understood to be opposed or opposite in composition: e.g., light/dark, man/woman, and culture/nature. The problem with binary oppositions is that one of the two terms is always privileged: one term is seen as lacking something the other term has.

Canon: In literary study, this term refers to the texts accorded special status by the discipline. Proponents of the traditional canon of Anglo-American literature, for instance, would presumably agree that Shakespeare is central to the canon, but would dispute the claim that Margaret Cavendish is a part of the canon. The canon, in this traditional sense, means the *best* texts. How one can possibly determine what makes one poem or novel one of the best and another poem or novel not one of the best, however, remains a hotly debated issue. That some texts have historically been viewed as noncanonical means, for many critics, that the texts should indeed be taught, because they offer perspectives that presumably do not reinforce the dominant power structure that canonical texts presumably do reinforce.

Cultural Capital: This term has been used by sociologist Pierre Bourdieu to describe valuable cultural knowledge that people acquire through education and that helps distinguish them socially and, in effect, helps justify their elevated status. Foregrounding cultural capital is one way for people to differentiate themselves from others in a competitive market economy. Familiarity with the traditional Western literary canon is one sign of cultural capital. Fashion tastes, food preferences, and one's pastimes also signal one's cultural capital.

Deconstruction: This term refers to a process of reading texts, literary and nonliterary. Typically, the methodology is associated with the French poststructuralist theorist Jacques Derrida. In a deconstructive reading of a poem or novel, the critic does not seek to demonstrate how parts of the text—its form and content—work harmoniously together to form a whole. Instead, the deconstructive critic carefully examines the text's rhetoric, its arrangement, its style, and its "logic" to show how the text's rhetoric masks or glosses over contradictions or gaps in logic in the text. Such an approach demonstrates that the notion of artistic wholeness is a fantasy. The close textual analysis of deconstruction does not destroy a text.

Rather, it shows how texts are multivocal; that is, language offers different, and often competing, meanings, not just one single, essential meaning.

Defamiliarization: The term "defamiliarization" is the English translation of *ostrenanie,* a term coined by Russian formalist Victor Shklovsky, who was one of the leading figures in the Society for the Study of Poetic Language, founded in 1916. Shklovsky used the term defamiliarization (or "making strange") alongside the term *zatrudnenie* (or "making difficult") to suggest a difference between practical and poetic language. In Shklovksy's view, practical language is oriented toward communication, while the function of poetic language is to shock us into awareness by short-circuiting automatic responses. Defamiliarization, later referred to by playwright Bertolt Brecht as the "alienation effect," is thus a literary technique used to make what is normally taken for granted appear strange. It shocks us out of our usual assumptions, allowing us to see things in a fresh light.

Diachronic: In critical theory, the term "diachronic" refers to the study of language over time. The diachronic sweep of time reveals how language is contingent or protean: it is changing shape, evolving over time. In his linguistic study of the arbitrary nature of the sign, Ferdinand de Saussure gave preference to the synchronic study of language, i.e., the study of language at a particular point or state in time.

Dialectical: One way to understand the term "dialectical" is through Hegel's notion of thesis, antithesis, and synthesis. The easiest way to understand what is meant by the word, however, is to define it as a process that involves reciprocal interaction. Let's say, for example, that you and a friend are having an argument. If you're really listening to each other instead of simply digging in your heels, you'll find yourselves engaging in a dialectical process whereby you say something that causes your friend to slightly modify her position. This, in turn, causes you to slightly modify yours. The end result of these gradual modifications is a reconciliation of viewpoints or some kind of synthesis, compromise, or conclusion that you and your friend can both accept.

Feminism: Although feminist criticism as a distinctive approach to literature was not formally instituted until the late 1960s, there were important precursors who fought for women's rights in social, legal, and cultural domains. Among the writers who have most profoundly influenced the modern feminist movement are Mary Wollstonecraft, Virginia Woolf, and Simone de Beauvoir. The term "feminism," now frequently used in the plural, suggests a wide range of theoretical approaches and political concerns. While the term may suggest many things to many people, those who practice feminism do share certain assumptions, despite contention or debate: (1) Western civilization is male centered and controlled; (2) while anatomy determines sex, cultural constructs permeated by patriarchal biases determine gender; (3) patriarchal ideology has determined what is considered great art, and this is why art created by women has not always gotten the attention it deserves; and (4) canon revision is needed so that women artists will be properly represented.

Formalist: In literary criticism, the term "formalist" refers to a critic or theorist who focuses on the form or shape of a text. For instance, a formalist is less concerned with the historical context of a work and more concerned with the arrangement of parts of the work with respect to the whole. A formalist examines a work's structure. In Kenneth Burke's helpful analogy, the formalist critic focuses on the container (form) as much as or more than on the thing contained (the content). A formalist demonstrates how stylistic features of art work together to produce an aesthetic object.

Foundationalist: This term describes a view or orientation that insists on recognizing a discernable and stable reality, a reality independent of contingency. People who hold a foundationalist view would not recognize their beliefs as simply one perspective among many; rather, they would insist, for example, that "truth with a capital *T*" exists and is eternally unchanging. That there is an unchanging "Truth" implies that humans similarly possess an irreducible self that can be known through objectivity and reason. Antifoundationalists oppose such views.

Gaze, the: In psychoanalytic theory, the term "gaze" is generally used as a noun, not a verb. We do not gaze upon objects; instead, we are subjected to the gaze. As Jacques Lacan says, "In the scopic field, the gaze is outside, I am looked at, that is to say, I am a picture." (*Four Fundamental* 106) For Lacan, we humans are not so much the representers as that which is represented. Lacan also refers to the gaze as an "object small *a*," an object that is not, properly speaking, an object, as it has no tangible content. According to Lacan, these (non)objects are what create desire in us. For example, we may think that we're attracted to someone because of certain qualities he or she possesses, such as good looks, intelligence, or sense of humor. But the real cause of our attraction might be the particular way he or she looks at us, a way of looking that mimics the look we received from our parents. This look, which we may not even be aware of, is what Lacan would call the gaze or one of the objects small *a*.

Hegemony: A basic dictionary definition of hegemony is leadership or predominant influence, especially when exercised by one state over another. While terms such as "leadership" or "influence" may not necessarily have negative connotations, the word "hegemony," when used in various theoretical discourses such as feminism and postcolonial studies, has taken on very negative connotations indeed. A feminist, for example, might refer to a patriarchal society as a hegemonic society in which things male are privileged over things female. Or in postcolonial studies, one might speak of a colonial power as exercising a hegemonic relation to a colonized people.

Hermeneutics: Frequently coupled with the term "hermeneutics" is the word "interpretation." In fact, the term "hermeneutics" was originally used to refer to principles of interpretation applied specifically to the Bible. These principles determined the validity of an interpretive reading as well as commentary on the application of the interpretation. It was not until the nineteenth century that the term came to designate the theory of interpretation in general. The first to use the term in its general sense was German theologian Friedrich Schleiermacher, who, in a series of lectures given in 1819, defined hermeneutics as the art of understanding texts of all kinds, whether they be literary, legal, historical, or biblical.

Identity Politics: In the 1960s, identity politics came into play during the women's movement and the civil rights movement. In both cases, groups of people banded together in order to effect change because they identified with one another, on the basis of either sex or race. The downside of identity politics concerns differences within a category such as sex or race. For example, two women may identify with each other on the basis of sex, but may have radically different experiences vis-à-vis economic status or racial oppression. In other words, a wealthy white woman might have radically different concerns from those of a poor black woman, just as a wealthy black woman might have radically different concerns from those of an Asian woman who has recently immigrated to the United States.

Ideology: Over time, this term has come to mean a network of ideas connecting and supporting economic and politic discourse. We see or make sense of our world through ideology. For Karl Marx and Friedrich Engles, ideology meant "false consciousness"; in other words, ideology signified illusion or false thought. But, in Marxist thought, ideology also meant the beliefs of a particular group or class. From this latter signification, we get notions like lower class or ruling-class ideology. In ordinary or popular speech, "ideology" is often used as a negative or pejorative term; for instance, pundits on television often dismiss their opponents' explanations of issues or events as simply "liberal ideology" or "conservative ideology," as if the views the pundits themselves hold dear are free of ideology. In other words, in this pejorative sense, one's views are sensible, fair, and balanced, whereas one's opponent's views are ideological or biased.

Imperialism: In postcolonial studies, imperialism is understood as the globalization of the capitalist mode of production. It can thus be distinguished from colonialism, defined as the conquest and direct control of other people's land, if we understand colonialism as a particular phase in the history of imperialism. Although the formal dissolution of colonial empires began in 1947, continuing Western influence in previously colonized countries has led Marxists to adopt the term neocolonialism to refer to the persistence of imperialist practices in the contemporary world, which can be located in flexible combinations of the economic, the political, the military, and the ideological.

Intertextuality: This term refers to citations, echoes, parodies, and quotations of a text or texts within the body of another text. A scene or episode in a novel may recall for readers a similar scene in another literary work. For example, the late-twentieth-century novel *A Thousand Acres,* by Jane Smiley, seems to many readers a contemporary reworking of Shakespeare's play *King Lear.* Focus on intertextuality developed from Ferdinand de Saussure's studies of linguistics, and some major theorists who have extended and revised the concept of intertextuality include Mikhail Bakhtin, Julia Kristeva, Roland Barthes, and Harold Bloom. Intertextuality is not a component of a formalist methodology, because formalist practices such as New Criticism bracket a work's historical and literary historical context, as well as its author's biography. One consequence of opening up a text by examining its reflection of other texts, i.e., its moments of intertextuality, is that readers are able to see how a text's meaning is not immanent, i.e., existing or operating within, but operates through networks of genre, style, myth, linguistics, and history.

Logocentricism: The Greek word *logos* can be translated most simply as "word" or "speech." To be logocentric is to presume the possibility of an unmediated access to truth or knowledge and to accord the word a central place in determining that truth or knowledge. Logocentricism refers to a tradition that assigns the origins of truth to the *logos*, to the word as transparent and self-evident meaning maker, and that assumes the existence of a stable foundation from which meaning is generated.

Marxist Criticism: The Marxist critical methodology is informed by Karl Marx's and Friedrich Engels's economic and political theories. There is no single, essential Marxist literary theory. While Marxist critics tend to look at power relations in texts, focusing particularly on class representations, the Marxist critic Georg Lukács promoted an aesthetic of realism, whereas the Marxist playwright Bertolt Brecht favored antirealistic estranging effects in art. Marxism as a philosophy is materialist, i.e., materiality or matter ranks above beliefs and slogans. For Marxists, literature must be understood as a social act and not as different from other material practices. The realities of class position direct or orient one's understanding of the world, and literature will convey or mirror the orientations of class. Attention to class orientation in the work of the British Marxist critic Raymond Williams has been influential in the development of cultural studies, one of the burgeoning fields of interdisciplinary practice and theory in the late twentieth and early twenty-first centuries. In addition to Williams, the Marxist critic Fredric Jameson has been influential in insisting on historical approaches to scholarly and theoretical practice.

Mediation: This term refers to theories that challenge the ideal of linguistic transparency. Language is a medium through which we access ideas and our sense of reality. The idea of mediation calls our attention to factors one must account for when examining communication, information, and signifying practices such as literature. Generic conventions and styles mediate or stand between the reader and the text; similarly, cultural codes and other ideologies mediate our experience of literary and social texts. Mediation cannot simply be transcended or overcome by a process of translation. The inquirer or critic must also account for her or his own status as mediator with respect to cultural codes, sign systems, and social status.

Metalanguage: In critical theory, metalanguage means language or discourse that refers to itself. For example, a poem can be understood to be about the art or act of poetry. Similarly, fiction can be metafictional; in other words, it can be fiction about fiction. Such reflexivity is also evident in critical theory that is about theory. Critics and theorists are interested in how metafiction and metatheory call attention to levels of linguistic complexity.

New Criticism: This term refers to a theory and practice that was popular in American literary criticism during the middle of the twentieth century. Although the term "New Criticism" comes from John Crowe Ransom's *The New Criticism,* published in 1941, the principles of New Criticism are derived largely from I. A. Richards's *Principles of Literary Criticism* (1924) and *Practical Criticism* (1929) and from the critical essays of T. S. Eliot. During its heyday, New Criticism differed from the usual practices of criticism in that it opposed the prevailing interest in the biographies of authors, the social and historical contexts of literature, and the affective responses of a reader. Instead, New Critics favored close reading, a detailed examination of the text as an independent entity isolated from its attendant circumstances and effects.

New Historicism: This term refers to a critical methodology that examines inter-relationships between literary texts and their cultural and historical contexts. A New Historicist sees a literary text as part of a larger web of discourses and forces. New Historicists often show how literary texts participate in political and social practices and reinforce political and social codes that are often implicit within the culture. Unlike formalist critics, who analyze a literary text without taking into account its contexts, and unlike some poststructuralist critics, whose method of deconstructing a text similarly pays little attention to history, while foregrounding textual *aporias* or gaps and linguistic double binds, New Historicists seek to articulate relationships between a text's inside and outside, its rhetoric and its society's rhetoric.

Phallocentric: It has been and continues to be argued that many Freudian concepts, such as penis envy and the castration complex, are phallocentric, since they seem to privilege the phallus (the Greek term for penis) as the symbol and source of power. In a phallocentric world, the penis is something to be envied if one is without it and something to desperately fear losing if one has it. While either sex can be guilty of phallocentrism, the term is a slightly more elegant, and certainly more academic, way of calling someone a male chauvinist.

Poetics: This term refers to a critical approach to texts (written, verbal, and visual) that emphasizes not meaning (or interpretation), but *how* texts mean something. In other words, through poetics one does not seek to interpret or figure out the true meaning of a text. Instead, through poetics, one examines the constituent parts of a text in order to better understand the relationships of parts to the whole, of form to content, and of rhetoric to logic in the text. For many theorists, poetics thus represents a science of literature—a theory that accounts for the explicit and implicit linguistic and rhetorical properties that presumably make some uses of language literary.

Postcolonial Studies: The text most often credited with establishing the theory and practice of postcolonial studies is Edward Said's *Orientalism,* published in 1978. Said's analysis of what he called "cultural imperialism" led him to conclude that this particular type of imperialism does not operate by force, but through a Eurocentric discourse that privileges everything "occidental" (i.e., Western or European) and views the "oriental" as an exotic and inferior other. Although the field of postcolonial studies is not unified in practice or methodology, several recurrent issues or concerns can be identified: (1) a rejection of the master narratives of Western imperialism in which the colonized subject is not only marginalized, but erased as a cultural being with agency; (2) a concern with how the colonized subject has been constructed and represented in Western discourse and how he or she can revise these constructions and representations; and (3) a concern with expanding the literary canon to include colonial and postcolonial writers such as Bessie Head, V.S. Naipaul, and Salmon Rushdie, to name only a few.

Postmodernism: Although the term "postmodernism" is frequently used interchangeably with the term "poststructuralism," it is useful to make a distinction between the two. If we were to place the two words in a sentence together, we might say the following: "The late twentieth century used poststructuralist practices and theories to produce postmodern art." In other words, we might reserve the word "postmodern" for recent developments in literature and other arts and use the word "poststructural" for recent theories of criticism and intellectual inquiry. Although postmodernism can be seen as a continuation of modernism's countertraditional experiments, it also diverges from modernism in its attempts to overthrow the elitism of modernist "high art" through its use of models of "mass culture" taken from film, television, cartoons, and popular music. Many of the works of postmodern literature resist classification within traditional literary rubrics because of their blending of genres, cultural and stylistic levels, and the serious and the playful. The theorists most often associated with the postmodern are Jean Baudrillard, Fredric Jameson, and François Lyotard.

Poststructuralism: This term is used to cover a broad array of critical perspectives and procedures that, in the 1970s, replaced structuralism as the prominent way of dealing with language and other signifying systems. The names most frequently associated with poststructuralism are Jacques Derrida, who attacked the systematic, quasiscientific approach of structuralism; Michel Foucault; Jacques Lacan; and (in his later years) Roland Barthes. Some of the central features of poststructuralism are (1) an opposition to inherited ways of thinking in all provinces of knowledge; (2) an attempt to challenge, destabilize, undermine, or subvert foundational assumptions, concepts, procedures, and findings in traditional modes of discourse; and (3) an opposition to the validity of the function or role assigned in Western thought to a uniquely individual author understood as the purposeful planner of a text and determiner of its meaning.

Pragmatism: This term refers to a philosophic doctrine that emphasizes practical actions and practical concerns rather than abstract principles and metaphysical absolutes. Pragmatism as a theory or orientation emphasizes contingency and relativism. In this sense, pragmatism can be understood as being antifoundation-alist. Pragmatism was particularly associated in the early twentieth century with American philosophers Charles Sanders Peirce, William James, and John Dewey and in the late twentieth century with literary critics such as Stanley Fish, Steven Knapp, and Walter Benn Michaels and with the philosopher Richard Rorty. Pragmatism has often been discussed as an American philosophy, an identifica-tion Rorty responds to in his 1994 essay "Truth Without Correspondence to Reality": "I think the most one can do by way of linking up pragmatism with America is to say that both the country and its most distinguished philosopher [John Dewey] suggest we can, in politics, substitute *hope* for the sort of knowl-edge which philosophers have usually tried to attain" (24; emphasis in original).

Rhetoric: This term has many meanings. Whereas Aristotle defined rhetoric as available means of persuasion, other people have defined rhetoric as eloquence or as fanciful use of language. Others understand rhetoric to mean the body of tropes and figures of speech catalogued by classical rhetoricians. Many other people use the term to mean the antithesis of reason and truth. Today, people often use the term pejoratively or negatively to dismiss someone else's ideas. For example, we have all heard politicians accuse their opponents of stooping to "mere rhetoric" to stir up people's emotions instead of sticking to the facts of the matter. In contemporary literary theory, rhetoric is often associated with antifoundationalist views and with the rise of theory in general, the so-called rhetorical turn, in the 1970s and 1980s.

Semiotics: This term refers to the study of sign systems. Typically, scholars link the genesis and early development of semiotics to Ferdinand de Saussure, a Swiss linguist, and Charles Sanders Peirce, a U.S. philosopher. As a theory, semiotics can help one determine how people make sense of a whole host of texts—how sign systems as varied as literary texts, commercials, advertisements, and sport-ing events are intelligible. In literary criticism, semiotics often addresses literary conventions and codes rather than meanings of literary texts.

Split Subject: What psychoanalyst Jacques Lacan refers to as the split subject is also known as the "subject in language" or the "speaking subject," both of which are meant to show the connection between identity, subjectivity, and lan-guage. In poststructuralist discourse, you will rarely find the individual person referred to as a "self," since this term implies a unified, whole being with agency, intentionality, and mastery of self. Poststructuralism sees this notion of the self as illusory. One way to think about why poststructuralism rejects the concept of a unified self is through the syntax of language. The "I" that we use to speak of ourselves is only ours during the moment in which we speak, after which it must be relinquished to our interlocutor. The "I," then, is always on loan. When we speak, we occupy the position of the subject. We are the "I" of the sentence. But when someone else speaks, we occupy the position of the object; we become the "you" of the sentence. Thus, we are always in oscillation, shuttling back and forth between the position of subject and object. "JE est un autre," or "I am another," aptly remarked the French poet Rimbaud, which means that we are never who we take ourselves to be. Like Rimbaud, Lacan says of the self that it is "an/other," hence his notion of the split subject.

Structuralism: Although structure has been an important aspect of literary theory since the time of Aristotle, what we refer to as structuralism or structuralist criticism has its beginnings in the work of Ferdinand de Saussure, whose linguistic model was applied to literature by Russian formalists such as Roman Jakobson. It is, however, Claude Lévi-Strauss who is credited with founding the structuralist movement when he applied Saussure's linguistic model to the field of anthropology. Perhaps the easiest way to define structuralism is as a theoretical grid through which behavior, institutions, and texts can be analyzed in relation to an underlying network of relationships. One of the most important features of structuralism is its emphasis on the underlying rules and conventions of language rather than on the way a particular speech exchange is configured at the surface level.

Synchronic: In critical theory, the term "synchronic" refers to the study of language at a particular point or state in time. In his linguistic study of the arbitrary nature of the sign, Ferdinand de Saussure gave preference to the synchronic study of language over the diachronic study of language, i.e., the study of language over time. In his 1986 book *Ferdinand de Saussure,* Jonathan Culler writes, "The fact that the sign is arbitrary or wholly contingent makes it subject to history but also means that signs require an ahistorical analysis. . . . Since the sign has no necessary core that must persist, it must be defined as a relational entity, in its relations to other signs. And the relevant relations are those which obtain at a particular time" (46).

Transhistorical: The Latin word *trans* means "across" or "over." At its most literal, then, the word "transhistorical" means something that stretches across or over history. The word "transhistorical" is frequently used to describe something that remains the same throughout history or something that is perceived to be essentially unchanging over the course of history.

Trope: This term can refer to figures of speech such as metaphor, synecdoche, metonymy, and irony. It comes from the Greek word meaning "to turn." In this sense, a trope turns or twists a word or a phrase's meaning. A writer may turn, or trope, a word or phrase for literary effect. The term "trope" is also used by some people to refer to a recurring image or topic, as in the Noble Savage trope or the trope of miscegenation, i.e., racial mixing. Critical theories that emphasize the study of tropes include New Criticism, deconstruction, New Historicism, and rhetorical approaches.

Unconscious, the: Although the concept of the unconscious has been around for centuries, it was Freud who gave the term its present theoretical currency, and thus it is to Freud, and his disciple Lacan, that we turn for a definition. One way to conceptualize the unconscious is as a simmering cauldron that contains everything the conscious speaking subject wants to keep a lid on (i.e., keep repressed), such as a desire to kill one's father and sleep with one's mother, two of the biggest taboos in our culture: patricide and incest, respectively. We have little access to the unconscious, except when the cauldron momentarily bubbles over and some of the repressed material escapes into the conscious world, through dreams and slips of the tongue and pen. Because the unconscious has been said to have a structure, just as language does, it is also possible to think of the conscious and the unconscious as twin chains of discourse that run simultaneously along parallel tracks, the unconscious occasionally jumping its track and disrupting the "proper" functioning of conscious discourse. The subject (or "self") is said to be split precisely because of these two chains of discourse that often function in opposition to each other.

WORKS CITED

Barthes, Roland. *The Pleasure of the Text*. Trans. Richard Miller. New York: Hill and Wang, 1975.

Bellah, Robert N. "Finding the Church: Post-Traditional Discipleship." *Christian Century Foundation*. Online. Internet. 22 July 2003. <http://www.religion-online.org>

Berlin, Isaiah. *The Hedgehog and the Fox*. 1953. Chicago: Elephant Books, 1993.

Berry, Wendell. *Standing By Words*. San Francisco: North Point Press, 1983.

Bloom, Harold, et al. *Deconstruction & Criticism*. New York: Seabury Press, 1979.

Bourdieu, Pierre. "The politics of protest." Interview with Kevin Ovenden. *Socialist Review*. June 2000. <http://pubs.socialistreviewindex.org.uk/sr242/ovenden.htm.>

Carroll, David. Introduction. *The States of "Theory": History, Art, and Critical Discourse*. Ed. David Carroll. Stanford: Stanford UP, 1990. 1–23.

Clavreul, Jean. "The Perverse Couple." *Returning to Freud: Clinical Psychoanalysis in the School of Lacan*. Ed. and trans. Stuart Schneiderman. New Haven: Yale UP, 1980. 215–233.

Culler, Jonathan. *Structuralist Poetics: Structuralism, Linguistics, and the Study of Literature*. 1975. Ithaca, New York: Cornell UP, 1976.

—. *Ferdinand de Saussure*. Rev. Ed. Ithaca, New York: Cornell U P, 1986.

cummings, e.e. "my father moved through dooms of love." *The Norton Anthology of American Literature*. Ed. Nina Baym, et al. Shorter fifth edition. New York: W. W. Norton, 1999.

Eagleton, Terry. *The Ideology of the Aesthetic*. Oxford: Blackwell, 1990.

Fink, Bruce. *The Lacanian Subject: Between Language and Jouissance*. Princeton: Princeton UP, 1995.

Fish, Stanley. *Is There a Text in This Class? The Authority of Interpretive Communities*. Cambridge: Harvard UP, 1980.

Freud, Sigmund. "The Uncanny." *Standard Edition of the Complete Psychological Works of Sigmund Freud*. Vol. XVII. Trans. James Strachey. London: Hogarth Press, 1955.

Gadamer, Hans-Georg. *Philosophical Hermeneutics*. Trans. and ed. David E. Linge. Berkeley: U of California P, 1976.

Garner, Dwight. "Sneak Peeks: Book review of Paul Fussell's *Doing Battle: The Making of a Skeptic*." *Salon* 1999. Online. Internet. 23 July 2003. <http://www.salon.com/sneaks/sneakpeeks960927.html>

Geertz, Clifford. "Thick Description: Toward an Interpretive Theory of Culture." *The Interpretation of Cultures*. New York: Basic Books, 1973. 3–30.

—. *Available Light: Anthropological Reflections on Philosophical Topics*. Princeton: Princeton UP, 2000.

Gonçalves, José Reginaldo. Interview with James Clifford. *AVATAR* 1 (March 2001): 124–136. Online. Internet. 19 July 2003.
<http://humwww.ucsc.edu/~james_clifford/pages/goncalves_interview.html>

Greenblatt, Stephen. "Towards a Poetics of Culture." *The New Historicism*. Ed. H. Aram Veeser. New York: Routledge, 1989. 1–14.

Heidegger, Martin. *Poetry, Language, Thought*. Trans. Albert Hofstadter. New York: Harper and Row, 1971.

Jabès, Edmond. "The Book or The Four Phases of a Birth." *Performance in Postmodern Culture*. Ed. Michel Benamou and Charles Caramello. Madison, Wisconsin: Coda Press, Inc., 1977. 123–136.

Kuhn, Thomas. *The Structure of Scientific Revolutions*. 1962. 2nd. Ed. Enlarged. Chicago: U of Chicago P, 1970.

Lacan, Jacques. *The Four Fundamental Concepts of Psycho-Analysis*. Ed. Jacques-Alain Miller. Trans. Alan Sheridan. New York: W. W. Norton, 1997.

—. *The Seminar of Jacques Lacan: Book VII, The Ethics of Psychoanalysis 1959–1960*. Ed. Jacques-Alain Miller. Trans. Dennis Porter. New York: W. W. Norton, 1992.

Mitchell, W. J. T. "Translator translated. (interview with cultural theorist Homi Bhabha)." *Artforum* 33.7 (March 1995): 80–84. Online. Internet. 22 July 2003.
<http://prelectur.stanford.edu/lecturers/bhabha/interview.html>

Percy, Walker. *The Message in The Bottle: How Queer Man Is, How Queer Language Is, and What One Has to Do with the Other*. New York: Farrar, Straus and Giroux, 1954.

Ponting, Clive. *The Twentieth Century: A World History*. New York: Henry Holt and Company, 1998.

Pratt, Mary Louise. *Imperial Eyes: Travel Writing and Transculturation*. London: Routledge, 1992.

Robbins, Derek. *The Work of Pierre Bourdieu*. Boulder, Colorado: Westview, 1991.

Rorty, Richard. "Truth Without Correspondence to Reality." *Philosophy and Social Hope*. London: Penguin Books, 1999. 23–46.

—. "Thomas Kuhn, Rocks and the Laws of Physics." *Philosophy and Social Hope*. London: Penguin Books, 1999. 175–189.

—. *Achieving Our Country: Leftist Thought in Twentieth-Century America*. 1998. Cambridge, Massachusetts: Harvard UP, 1999.

Roudinesco, Elisabeth. *Jacques Lacan*. Trans. Barbara Bray. New York: Columbia UP, 1997.

Rousseau, Jean-Jacques. *Confessions: From Book I*. 1781–1788. *The Norton Anthology of World Masterpieces*. Ed. Sarah Lawall and Maynard Mack, et al. Vol. II. Seventh edition. New York: W. W. Norton, 1999. 429–432.

Sartre, Jean-Paul. *Existentialism*. Trans. Bernard Frechtman. New York: Philosophical Library, 1947.

Scudder, Samuel. "Learning to See." *The Dolphin Reader*. Ed. Douglas Hunt and Carolyn Perry. Third edition. Boston: Houghton Mifflin Company, 1993. 661–664.

Sharlet, Jeff. "Noted Medievalist Seeks Out the Wolf Beneath the Skin." *The Chronicle of Higher Education* (22 June 2001). Online. Internet. 21 July 2003.
<http://chronicle.com/free/v47/i41/41a01401.htm>

Vernant, Jean-Pierre. Interview: E discussion presented by Michele Nouilhan. Online. Internet. 22 July 2003.
<http://www.ombres-blanches.fr/pages/bulletin/octnov 1998/mulitple.html>

CREDITS

INDEX

Boldfaced entries indicate reading selections and selection authors that appear in the text.